K A T A K A

ア	a	イ	i	ウ	u	エ			
カ	ka	キ	ki	ク	ku	ケ	ke	コ	ko
サ	sa	シ	shi	ス	su	セ	se	ソ	so
タ	ta	チ	chi	ツ	tsu	テ	te	ト	to
ナ	na	ニ	ni	ヌ	nu	ネ	ne	ノ	no
ハ	ha	ヒ	hi	フ	fu	ヘ	he	ホ	ho
マ	ma	ミ	mi	ム	mu	メ	me	モ	mo
ヤ	ya			ユ	yu			ヨ	yo
ラ	ra	リ	ri	ル	ru	レ	re	ロ	ro
ワ	wa							ヲ	o
ン	n								

キャ	kya	キュ	kyu	キョ	kyo
シャ	sha	シュ	shu	ショ	sho
チャ	cha	チュ	chu	チョ	cho
ニャ	nya	ニュ	nyu	ニョ	nyo
ヒャ	hya	ヒュ	hyu	ヒョ	hyo
ミャ	mya	ミュ	myu	ミョ	myo

リャ	rya	リュ	ryu	リョ	ryo

ガ	ga	ギ	gi	グ	gu	ゲ	ge	ゴ	go
ザ	za	ジ	ji	ズ	zu	ゼ	ze	ゾ	zo
ダ	da	ヂ	ji	ヅ	zu	デ	de	ド	do
バ	ba	ビ	bi	ブ	bu	ベ	be	ボ	bo
パ	pa	ピ	pi	プ	pu	ペ	pe	ポ	po

ギャ	gya	ギュ	gyu	ギョ	gyo
ジャ	ja	ジュ	ju	ジョ	jo

ビャ	bya	ビュ	byu	ビョ	byo
ピャ	pya	ピュ	pyu	ピョ	pyo

KODANSHA'S Communicative English-Japanese Dictionary

KODANSHA'S Communicative English-Japanese Dictionary

日本語学習 英和辞典

Peter Sharpe

EDITED BY
Michael Staley and Keiko Yoshida

KODANSHA INTERNATIONAL
Tokyo • New York • London

Distributed in the United States by Kodansha America, Inc., and in the United Kingdom and continental Europe by Kodansha Europe Ltd.

Published by Kodansha International Ltd., 17–14 Otowa 1-chome, Bunkyo-ku, Tokyo 112–8652, and Kodansha America, Inc.

First edition, 2006
15 14 13 12 11 10 09 08 07 06   10 9 8 7 6 5 4 3 2 1

Library of Congress Cataloging-in-Publication Data

Sharpe, Peter, 1947–
Kodansha's communicative English-Japanese dictionary / Peter Sharpe.— 1st ed.
p. cm.
ISBN-13: 978–4–7700–1808–3
ISBN-10: 4–7700–1808–8
1. English language—Conversation and phrase books—Japanese. 2. English language—Dictionaries—Japanese. I. Title.

PE1130.J3S43 2006
423'.956—dc22

2005054504

www.kodansha-intl.com

C O N T E N T S

Preface vii

How to Use This Dictionary ix

Abbreviations and Notations xx

A–zucchini 1–1147

Appendixes

- A Notes about Japanese Grammar 1149
- B Addressing Letters in Japan 1174
- C Common Japanese Surnames Ranked by Frequency 1175
- D Japanese Era Conversion 1176
- E National Holidays in Japan 1177
- F Japanese Government Ministries and Agencies 1178

EDITORIAL TEAM

Editorial Director
Mitsuru Tomita

Chief Editors
Michael Staley
Keiko Yoshida

Consultants
Kay Yokota
Yoko Kasai
Yoshiko Shimizu
Hisae Sakamoto
Tom Gally
Charles De Wolf
Jeff Garrison
Janet Ashby

Translators
Miho Sonehara
Miyuki Murayama
Masahiro Kaneda
Kay Yokota
Megumi Unno
Megumi Fujisaki
Kaoru Kikuchi
Yoshiko Moore
Reiko Matsuda

PRODUCTION TEAM

Designer
Kazuhiko Miki

Typesetter
Toyoko Kon

Illustrator
Miaki Aoto

PREFACE

This dictionary is intended for students of Japanese whose native or second language is English. It is designed to help them expand their vocabulary, especially of everyday spoken Japanese, so that they will be able to express themselves more naturally and fluently. The English headwords, as well as their meanings, have been chosen on the basis of frequency. There are over 22,000 entries and more than 19,000 example sentences. The various items of information that can be found in the entries are illustrated in the "How to Use This Dictionary" section (pp. ix–xix).

We have endeavored to make the translations of the example sentences as natural as possible and not to stilt them to match the English. Naturally, a number of problems arise when translating into a language so different from English. Japanese is context-sensitive and, consequently, it is very difficult to have a sentence that is neutral and which could be spoken by everyone—young and old, men and women, and both in- and out-group members. Japanese speech levels are also affected by place of utterance—at work, home, or on neutral ground. To offer just one example: personal pronouns, such as "I," "you," etc., are neither as frequent nor as neutral as they are in English. To avoid creating the false impression that spoken Japanese uses personal pronouns in the same way as English, names—usually typical Japanese surnames—and titles often appear in the English sentences.

Edward Gibbon, the author of *The History of the Decline and Fall of the Roman Empire,* listed the "humble, though indispensable, virtues of a compiler" as "method, choice, and fidelity." I have done my utmost to apply these virtues, but in any endeavor of this magnitude there are bound to be some oversights. I take full responsibility where they may exist.

I would like to acknowledge my gratitude to the following for their help and support in the compilation of this dictionary. In its initial research stages, The Great Britain Sasakawa Foundation, The Daiwa Anglo-Japanese Foundation and The Japan Foundation. To both Dr. R.R.K. Hartmann, who was Director of the Dictionary Research Centre (then Exeter University, now Birmingham), and Professor Stefan Kaiser of The Graduate School of Humanities and Social Sciences, Tsukuba University, Japan, for their encouragement and advice. In the compilation of the first manuscript, I thank my wife Shimako Tsuno for her hard work as well as her expert comments as a freelance writer and journalist. In the latter stages, when the original manuscript was greatly expanded, I owe a debt of gratitude to the expertise shown by the editors of Kodansha International—the late, and much missed, Paul Hulbert and his successors Michael Staley and Keiko Yoshida, who did the bulk of the work. And last but not least, to students and friends who have answered numerous queries, in particular, Mamiko Ando and Osamu Tagami.

Peter Sharpe

PETER SHARPE
Professor, Takushoku University, Tokyo

HOW TO USE THIS DICTIONARY

This dictionary has been designed for learners at all levels, but it is assumed that the user has at least learned, or is in the process of learning, the Japanese syllabaries—hiragana and katakana. Knowing these, one can read any of the Japanese words or phrases in this book, even if one has never studied kanji. That is because all of the words have been given hiragana or katakana readings in small print called *furigana*.

Japan *n.* 日本(にほん), 日本(にっぽん), (classical name) 大和(やまと)(の国(くに)), ((*in abbr.*)) 日(にち)
Japan–U.S. relations 日米関係(にちべいかんけい)

For hiragana and katakana charts, see the front endpaper.

HOW TO FIND THE WORD YOU'RE LOOKING FOR

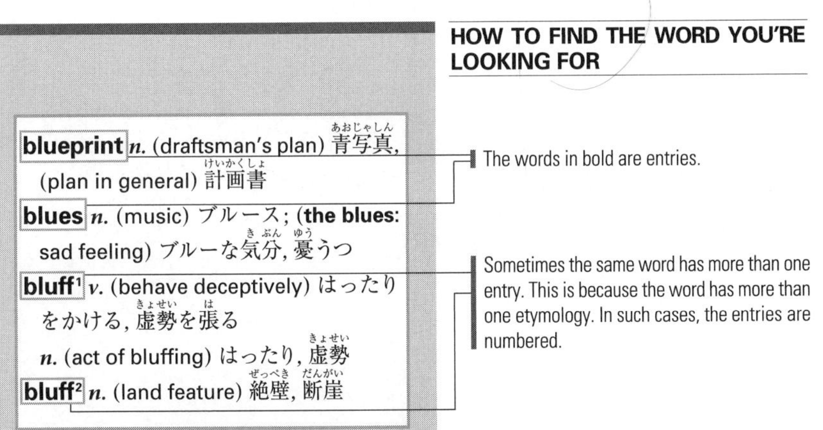

blueprint *n.* (draftsman's plan) 青写真(あおじゃしん), (plan in general) 計画書(けいかくしょ)
blues *n.* (music) ブルース; (**the blues:** sad feeling) ブルーな気分(きぶん), 憂(ゆう)うつ
bluff¹ *v.* (behave deceptively) はったりをかける, 虚勢(きょせい)を張(は)る
n. (act of bluffing) はったり, 虚勢(きょせい)
bluff² *n.* (land feature) 絶壁(ぜっぺき), 断崖(だんがい)
The words in bold are entries.
Sometimes the same word has more than one entry. This is because the word has more than one etymology. In such cases, the entries are numbered.

The spellings of the words are standard American spellings. Unless it is otherwise confusing, variant spellings are not listed. Nor are British spellings.

labor *n.* (hard work) 労働(ろうどう), (workers) 労働者(ろうどうしゃ); (stage of pregnancy) 陣痛(じんつう)
v. 働(はたら)く, 仕事(しごと)をする
physical/manual labor 肉体労働(にくたいろうどう)
labor and management 労使(ろうし)
go into labor 陣痛(じんつう)が始(はじ)まる
♦**laborer** *n.* 労働者(ろうどうしゃ)
labor of love *n.* 好(す)きでする仕事(しごと)
labor union *n.* 労働組合(ろうどうくみあい)
laboratory *n.* (for scientific experimentation) 実験室(じっけんしつ), (for research in general) 研究所(けんきゅうじょ), (at university) 研究室(けんきゅうしつ)

Because it helps to see related words grouped together, some words of low frequency are nestled underneath the main entry. The first of these is always marked with a ♦ so you can see at a glance where the list begins.

majority *n.* 大多数(だいたすう), 大部分(だいぶぶん), (of votes) 過半数(かはんすう)
The majority was in favor.
大多数(だいたすう)の人(ひと)は賛成(さんせい)した。
The bill passed by a narrow majority.
法案(ほうあん)は過半数(かはんすう)ぎりぎりで通過(つうか)した。
get/win a majority 過半数(かはんすう)を得(え)る
♦ **majority leader** *n.* 多数党(たすうとう)の院内総務(いんないそうむ)

Idioms and phrases also appear underneath the main entry. In cases where there are both idioms and related vocabulary (marked by ♦), the idioms are listed first.

pawnshop *n.* 質屋

pay *v.* (...にお金を) 払う, 支払う
n. (salary) 給料
We paid someone to repair the roof.
お金を払って屋根を修理してもらいました。

pay attention to → ATTENTION
pay back *v.* (return money to) ...にお金を返す, ...に返済する, (punish in retribution) ...に仕返しをする
pay for *v.* ...の代金を払う
pay off *v.* (debt) 借金をすべて返す, (person: bribe) ...にわいろを贈る; (be profitable) うまくいく, 利益をもたらす
Did your business plan pay off?
事業計画は、うまくいきましたか？

payable *adj.* (payable to...) (...に) 支払う

Sometimes a group of words is enclosed in brackets. This is when the words make up a family. Note that a family of words follows an alphabetical order independent of the rest of the dictionary, so that the word(s) that come before the closing bracket may or may not alphabetically precede the word(s) that come after it. Also, when a bracketed set of words carries on from a right-hand page to a left-hand page, the running head at the top of the right-hand page is always the first word within the family (**PAY**, for example).

Phrasal verbs are usually given as entries within word families.

trade *n.* (buying/selling of goods) 商売, 取引, 商業, (between countries) 貿易; (occupation) 職業
v. (exchange) 交換する, (trade A for B) (AをBと) 取り替える
a trade balance 貿易収支
♦**trade in** *v.* 下取りに出す
I traded in my old car for a new one.
古い車を下取りに出して新車を買った。
trader *n.* 商人, 貿易商

Occasionally, phrasal verbs appear as related vocabulary.

HOW TO FIND THE SENSE OF THE WORD YOU'RE LOOKING FOR

There are two types of entry arrangement. The first—the non-numbered one—is organized by part of speech: the most common or useful part of speech comes first. (For a list of abbreviations for parts of speech, see p. xx.) For simple words having this arrangement, you can find the sense you're looking for by identifying the part of speech.

bribe *n.* わいろ
v. (…に) わいろを使う, (…を) 買収する
offer a bribe わいろを贈る
The politician accepted a bribe.
その政治家はわいろを受け取った。
He tried to bribe me.
その男は私を買収しようとした。

Throughout this dictionary, glosses are given for words that have more than one meaning, to help you identify the sense of the word you're looking for. These take the form of hints or abbreviated definitions, or suggest the meaning by giving common collocations.

English *n.* (language) 英語, (**the English**: people) イギリス人, 英国人
adj. (of language) 英語の, (of England, British culture) イギリスの, 英国の
English grammar 英語の文法

formulate *v.* (idea, response etc.) 順序立てて述べる

However, when a word has one primary meaning that native-English speakers understand, no space is wasted in defining it.

helmet *n.* ヘルメット, (traditional Japanese helmet worn by samurai) かぶと

Sometimes a gloss appears in bold. This is when the word or group of words in bold differs from the entry word in some way—for example, it is a phrase or plural form. In such cases, the Japanese equivalent that follows is a translation of the element in bold, not of the main entry word itself.

implicate *v.* (**be implicated in**: crime) …に巻き込まれる, …に関係する
implication *n.* (meaning) 裏の意味, 含み, (**implications**: influences) 影響
have serious implications for …に大きな影響がある

lighten[1] *v.* (make/become brighter) 明るくする/なる

Lighten up! もっと気楽に, 落ち着いて, くよくよしないで

lighten[2] *v.* (make less heavy) 軽くする

This dictionary does not give separate part-of-speech listings for transitive and intransitive verbs. (See pp. 1161–63 for a discussion of transitive/intransitive verbs.) Instead, where necessary, it tells you whether the sense of the verb being defined is transitive or intransitive by the phrasing of the gloss.

water

NOTE: Japanese distinguishes "cold water" (お)水 from "hot water" お湯.

1 *n.* LIQUID: (お)水, (hot water) お湯, (drinking water) 飲み水, ((*formal*)) 飲料水

2 *v.* GIVE WATER TO: (plant) (...に) 水をやる, (**water the ground**) 地面に水をまく [NOTE: In Japan, people sometimes water the pavement in front of their homes or shops in order to clean it or keep it cool on hot summer days.]

3 *v.* SECRETE BODY FLUID: (of eyes) 涙が出る, (of mouth) よだれが出る

4 *n.* ZONE OF WATER: (**waters**) 水域

5 *n.* PUBLIC FACILITY: 水道

1 a glass of water コップ1杯の水
a bowl of hot water ボウル1杯のお湯

2 Has anyone watered the plants yet?
もう誰か植木に水をやった？

3 My eyes are watering.
涙が出てきた。

4 uncharted waters 海図にない水域
territorial waters 領海

5 water and electricity 水道と電気

The second type of entry arrangement is the numbered one. Highly frequent words, or words with a lot of different meanings, follow this pattern. Their senses are numbered and defined, and (where necessary) their parts of speech are also given. Scan the senses (indicated in **SMALL CAPITAL LETTERS**) until you find the right meaning. Then look at the glosses (the words in parentheses) to find the specific sense you're looking for.

Finally, skip down to the examples (numbered to correspond with the senses defined) to find out how the word is used in real Japanese.

Occasionally, despite the editor's best efforts, a word does not translate into Japanese, so no equivalents can be given. For such recalcitrants, we say, "See examples below." The example sentences show exactly how the word defies translation.

who

1 ***interrogative pron.*** 誰(だれ), ((*polite*)) どなた

2 ***interrogative pron.*** **INTRODUCING A WHO-CLAUSE:** 誰(だれ)...か, ((*polite*)) どなた...か

3 ***relative pron.*** See examples below [NOTE: No equivalent in Japanese.]

For certain words you look up, you'll find a cross-reference to another word or to an illustration. This means that more detailed information can be found at that entry.

zone *n.* 地帯(ちたい), 区域(くいき), 地区(ちく), -帯(たい) [→ AREA]

a military zone 武装地帯(ぶそうちたい)

a no-smoking zone 禁煙区域(きんえんくいき)

a no-fly zone 飛行禁止区域(ひこうきんしくいき)

a traffic-free zone 車両通行止め区間(しゃりょうつうこうどくかん)

the Temperate Zone 温帯(おんたい)

If the sense of the word you're looking for is a phrase or compound, chances are you'll find it at the end of the entry in a list of idioms or related vocabulary.

UNDERSTANDING THE JAPANESE

The Japanese equivalents in this dictionary have been painstakingly selected on the basis of how closely, in real speech, they match the English. Explanatory equivalents that the Japanese do not utter in real life, but which nonetheless are found in other dictionaries, have been dispensed with. In cases where an English word simply does not translate into Japanese, this dictionary makes no bones about it.

Many Japanese words have both plain and polite forms. The form listed in this dictionary is in most cases the plain form—which is to say, the form used in everyday conversation among friends and family. (For more on plain and polite forms, see pp. 1155–56.) The plain form is also the standard form listed in most dictionaries and the form from which it is possible to figure out, for example, a verb's patterns of conjugation.

about

1 ***prep.*** ON THE SUBJECT OF: ...について, ((*formal*)) ...に関して/関する

2 ***adv.*** APPROXIMATELY: (大体)...くらい/ぐらい, ...ほど, ((*formal*)) およそ, 約, (in reference to time) ...ころ/ごろ

3 ***adv.*** IN THE VICINITY: あたりに, 近くに

4 ***adv.*** IN CIRCLES: <-ます stem> + 回す/回る

Ellipsis points [...] indicate missing words. In this dictionary they show that the Japanese words coming before or after them are used in connection with other words.

Sometimes part of a Japanese word is given in parentheses. This means that the part in parentheses can be omitted, although sometimes not without a change in nuance.

Occasionally grammatical notations are used to show how words connect to each other. See p. xx for an explanation of these.

assign ***v.*** (assign A [homework] to B) (AをBに)出す, (assign A [person] to B [post, position]) (AをBに)任命する

In Japanese, particles are often used with verbs. This dictionary tries to show which particles go with which verbs by placing the particle in parentheses before the verb.

ban ***v.*** (forbid) 禁止する, 禁じる

n. 禁止

The government banned all demonstrations.
政府はあらゆるデモを禁止した。

The player was banned from playing for a month.
その選手は1ヵ月間、出場停止になった。

However, in many cases the particle is omitted. Suffice it to say that if the verb (or the sense of the verb) being defined is transitive (takes a direct object), and no particle is given in parentheses, the omitted particle is the object-marker を.

degenerate ***v.*** (retrogress) 退化する, (worsen) 悪化する

n. (person) 堕落した人

The meeting degenerated into a shouting match.
会議は、ののしり合いと化した。

The situation in the Middle East is degenerating rapidly.
中東の情勢は急速に悪化している。

Likewise, if the verb (or the sense of the verb) being defined is intransitive (does not take a direct object), and no particle is given, the missing particle is the subject-marker が (or the topic-marker は).

The other case in which a verb's particle is dropped is when the particle is the same as the one that went with the verb listed before it.

If the particle is part of the translation of the verb itself (rather than information supplied for the learner's convenience), it is not enclosed in parentheses.

を is normally omitted. But in cases like these, it is given in parentheses for clarity, so you do not assume that the particle is the same as the one that went with the previous verb.

follow *v.*

1 PURSUE: (…の後に) ついて来る, ついて行く, (…の後を) 追いかける, 追う, (tail, follow in secret) 尾行する

2 OCCUR AFTER: (as in sequence) …の後に続く, (of trouble) …の後に起きる

3 ADVICE/INSTRUCTIONS: (…に) 従う, (…を) 守る

4 EXAMPLE: (…に) ならう, (…を) まねる

5 UNDERSTAND: (…が) わかる, (…を) 理解する

6 TAKE A KEEN INTEREST IN: (news story) (…に) 注目する, (trend) 追う

7 BE NECESSARILY TRUE: …(という) ことになる

A slash [/] is often used with particles. The slash means that either particle can be used, although sometimes, depending on the context, one particle is preferable.

If more than one sense of a word is defined with a slash, a slash also appears between the corresponding pair of equivalents.

in

1 *prep., adv.* INDICATING LOCATION: …に/で, …には/では, (…の) 中に/へ, (present somewhere) いて, (= at home) 家にいて, 在宅して [→ INSIDE, INTO]

2 *prep.* INDICATING TIME: …に, …で, …には

3 *prep.* STATE/SITUATION: …に/で, …では, …においては

4 *prep.* USED WITH NUMBERS: See examples below

5 *prep.* USED WITH SHAPES: …をつくって, …になって

6 *prep.* IN REGARD TO: …では, (be strong/weak in) …に (強い/弱い)

inland ***adj., adv.*** 内陸の/へ, 奥地の/へ

A slash is also used between particles or other elements of a word when the equivalents for two parts of speech are given on the same line. Here the slash shows how the word can be changed to correspond to either part of speech. Parentheses are also used for this purpose.

ivory ***n., adj.*** 象牙(の), (color) 象牙色(の)

liven up ***v.*** (make/become more lively) 活気づける/活気づく, 面白くする/なる, 盛り上げる/盛り上がる

This should liven things up a bit.
これで少し活気づくはずです。

rattle ***v.*** (make a short sharp sound) ガタガタ/ガラガラ音を立てる, (cause to make a sharp sound) ガタガタ/ガラガラさせる

n. (sound) ガタガタ/ガラガラ(いう音); (child's toy) ガラガラ

A slash is also used with pairs of transitive and intransitive verbs, and with onomatopoeic words (see pp. 1166–67) to show variations of the word.

un- ***pref.*** (in-) 不-, (non-) 非-, (-less) 無-, (not yet) 未-

unpleasant 不愉快な
unofficial 非公式の

Hyphens in this dictionary are used with Japanese words that typically serve as prefixes or suffixes.

venomous ***adj.*** (of animal) 毒を出す, 毒-

a venomous snake 毒蛇

Hyphens are also used when a word is the first element of a kanji compound.

visitor ***n.*** 客, ((*polite*)) お客さん, ((*formal*)) 来客, (tourist) 観光客

Sometimes the Japanese translations are preceded by speech labels. These tell you how the word or sentence is used in Japanese. (For a list and description of speech labels, see p. xx.)

Brackets are sometimes used in the example sentences to present variations of the sentences or phrases. The English and Japanese words that appear in the brackets match each other.

wage *n.* 賃金(ちんぎん), 給料(きゅうりょう) [→ PAY, SALARY]
v. (war, campaign) する, 行(おこな)う
low [high] wages 低(てい)[高(こう)]賃金(ちんぎん)
Wages are low in the service sector.
サービス業(ぎょう)は賃金(ちんぎん)が低(ひく)い。
an hourly [a weekly, a monthly] wage
時給(じきゅう)[週給(しゅうきゅう), 月給(げっきゅう)]

Brackets are also used to indicate that the enclosed words or phrases can be used interchangeably with the underlined words or phrases that come before them.

year *n.* 年(とし), -年(ねん), (one-year period) 年間(ねんかん), (financial year) 年度(ねんど), (year in school) 学年(がくねん), (counting age: ...**years old**) 年(とし), -歳(さい)
this year 今年(ことし) [((*formal*)) 本年(ほんねん)]
the year 2020 ２０２０年(にせんにじゅうねん)
the year of the dragon (according to the Chinese calendar) 辰年(たつどし)
last year 去年(きょねん) [((*formal*)) 昨年(さくねん)]
next year 来年(らいねん)
the following year 翌年(よくとし) [次(つぎ)の年(とし)]
the year after next 再来年(さらいねん)

But when an entire sentence can be interchanged with another, the two sentences are separated by a slash, not by brackets.

Be a man!
((*masculine*)) 男(おとこ)らしくしろ/((*feminine*)) 男(おとこ)らしくしなさいよ!

LEARNING MORE

This dictionary has dozens of special entries and illustrations to help you expand your vocabulary.

Columns about Japanese usage give you tips on how to express yourself in Japanese.

EXPRESSING AGREEMENT

There are several ways to express agreement in Japanese, just as there are in English. そのとおりです or, for emphasis, 全(まった)くそのとおりです is used in ordinary polite speech to mean, "That's right" or "I agree with what you have just said." Its informal counterparts are そうだよ, そうだね, and the feminine そうよ.

"This responsibility is his." 「責任(せきにん)は彼(かれ)にあります」

"I agree." 「そのとおりです」

To express agreement when one's opinion/approval is sought of a plan/vote, use (私(わたし)は)賛成(さんせい)です or, for emphasis, (私(わたし)は)大賛成(だいさんせい)です, "I wholeheartedly agree."

KANJI BRIDGE

開 ON: かい
KUN: ひら(く/ける), あ(く/ける) **OPEN**

begin	開始(かいし)する
development	開発(かいはつ)
(*sign*) do not leave open	開放厳禁(かいほうげんきん)
open a meeting	開会(かいかい)する
open a new school	開校(かいこう)する
open a new store	開店(かいてん)する
opening and closing	開閉(かいへい)
opening ceremony	開会式(かいかいしき)
open to the public	公開(こうかい)する
reopen, resume	再開(さいかい)する

Strategically placed Kanji Bridges show you how a kanji related to an entry you are looking at combines with other kanji to form words.

The *on* readings (there are typically more than one) are the Chinese sounds of the character—or rather Japanese approximations of the sounds, as they were rendered long ago. Kanji are usually pronounced with *on* readings when they are combined with other kanji to form compounds.

The *kun* readings are the purely Japanese glosses given to the kanji, usually closely approximating the character's original meaning in Chinese. Kanji are typically pronounced with *kun* readings when they stand on their own (i.e., are not combined with other kanji) or are used with hiragana to form words. *Kun* readings are also more common in personal names than *on* readings.

The hiragana in parentheses are called *okurigana*. They are not part of the character's reading, but come after the character to form words.

ABBREVIATIONS AND NOTATIONS

PARTS OF SPEECH

The following abbreviations are used for parts of speech.

n.	noun	***pref.***	prefix
v.	verb	***suf.***	suffix
adj.	adjective	***interj.***	interjection
adv.	adverb	***aux.***	auxiliary verb
conj.	conjunction	***abbr.***	abbreviation
pron.	pronoun		

OTHER ABBREVIATIONS

sb	somebody
sth	something
lit.	literally
as opp. to	as opposed to

SPEECH LABELS

Speech labels that appear before Japanese words or sentences give you information about how the Japanese is used. This dictionary uses the following labels.

((*derogatory*)) The word belittles the person to which it is applied.

((*emphatic*)) The word is emphatic.

((*euphemistic*)) The word is used euphemistically.

((*feminine*)) The word or sentence is used mainly by women.

((*figurative*)) The word or sentence is used figuratively.

((*formal*)) The word or sentence is used mostly in formal speech.

((*honorific*)) The word or sentence expresses respect for the person or thing to which it is applied by elevating him, her, or it.

((*humble*)) The word or sentence deprecates the person or thing to which it is applied (often the speaker), thereby elevating the status of the other party.

((*informal*)) The word or sentence is used mostly in informal speech.

((*masculine*)) The word or sentence is used mainly by men.

((*offensive*)) The word or sentence is offensive, and you should be very cautious about using it.

((*old-fashioned*)) The word or sentence is going or has gone out of use.

((*poetic*)) The word or sentence has a poetic ring to it.

((*polite*)) The word or sentence is polite.

((*rude*)) The word or sentence is rude and you should avoid using it.

((*written*)) The word or sentence is used mainly in writing.

GRAMMATICAL NOTATIONS

Where necessary, this dictionary uses the following grammatical notations, either in place of Japanese equivalents or as part of them.

<adj. stem> The stem form of an adjective. See table 9 in Appendix A.

<causative form of verb> The form of the verb that expresses causation. See tables 3, 4, and 5 in Appendix A.

<-ます stem> The part of the verb that comes before -ます. See tables 3, 4, and 5 in Appendix A.

<potential form of verb> The form of the verb that expresses ability. See tables 3, 4, and 5 in Appendix A.

<-て form of adj.> The -て form of an adjective. See table 9 in Appendix A.

A, a

A, a[1] ***n.*** (letter) A, (first item in a series) 第1, 甲, (grade) A, 優

I'm not interested in what kind of car it is; I just want to get from A to B.
車の種類はどうでもいい、移動さえできればいいんだ。

grade-A beef 最高級牛肉

Hikaru got an A on the exam.
光は試験でAを取った。

a[2]**, an** *article*

NOTE: Usually not translated into Japanese.

1 ONE/ONE OF A SET: 一つの, (of person) 一人の [→ p. 1168 about "Counters"]

2 INDICATING PROFESSION: See examples below

3 INDICATING GENUS: See examples below

4 PER: ...に, ...当たり, ...につき

5 USED WITH PROPER NOUNS: (used with a person's name: **a Mr./Ms....**) ...という方, (used with an artist's name to indicate a work of art) ...の作品

1 It's a camera. カメラです。

He's a friend of mine.
彼は友達です。

Could you pass me a fork, please?
フォークを取っていただけませんか？

I'd like a coffee, please.
コーヒーをお願いします。

It was a Christmas I won't forget.
忘れられないクリスマスでした。

It was a spring day, I remember.
それは、ある春の日のことでした。

It's always on a Saturday.
いつも土曜日にあります。

a week or two ago 1、2週間前

half a million dollars 50万ドル

a third 3分の1

2 Mr. Sato is a teacher.
佐藤さんは(学校の)先生です。

She wants to be a writer.
彼女は作家になりたいんです。

3 A bird is an animal.
鳥は動物である。

A camel can go without water for weeks.
ラクダは何週間も水なしでいられる。

Is blowfish a fish you can eat?
フグは食べられる魚ですか？

I think it's a metal.
金属だと思います。

4 three times a week 週に3回

I go there once a year.
そこには年に1度行っている。

It costs ¥500 a kilo.
1キロ(当たり)500円です。

¥1,000 an hour 1時間1000円

5 A Mr. Hoshino called this morning.
けさ、星野さんという方からお電話がありました。

There was a Rembrandt on display.
レンブラントの作品が展示してあった。

abacus ***n.*** そろばん

abalone ***n.*** アワビ

abandon ***v.*** (desert) 捨てる, (leave in the lurch) 見捨てる, (relinquish: right) 放棄する, (quit) 中止する, やめる

The baby was found abandoned at a train station.
その赤ちゃんは駅に捨てられているのが見つかった。

A

He abandoned the right to enter the competition.
彼は大会の出場権を放棄した。

The project was abandoned for lack of funding.
企画は資金不足のため、中止になった。

abandon ship 船を離れる, 船から退避する

The situation became so dangerous that the crew decided to abandon ship.
あまりにも危険な事態になったので、船員は船から退避することにした。

abatement ***n.*** (of strength, power) 軽減, 減少, (of cost) 減額

abbreviate ***v.*** 短縮する, 省略する

abbreviation ***n.*** 短縮, 省略, (short form of a word) 略語

ABCs ***n.*** (the alphabet) アルファベット, (the basics) いろは, 基本

abdicate ***v.*** (renounce the throne) 王位を捨てる, 退位する; (relinquish: right, responsibility) 放棄する

abdicate responsibility 責任を放棄する

abdomen ***n.*** (part of the body) 腹, ((*formal*)) 腹部

abdominal ***adj.*** 腹の, 腹部の

abduct ***v.*** 拉致する, (kidnap) 誘拐する

abhor ***v.*** ひどく嫌う, 憎む, (…が) 大嫌いだ

abide ***v.*** (**abide by**) 守る

Let's abide by the rules.
規則を守ろう。

ability ***n.*** (capability, knack) 力, 能力, (gift, talent) 才能

the ability to see 視力

ability to remember 記憶力

He has the ability to do the work.
彼にはその仕事をこなす力がある。

They don't have the ability to govern.
彼らには国を治める能力がない。

The ability to make quick decisions is an important one for CEOs.
速やかに決断する能力は、社長にとって重要なものです。

students of mixed ability
いろいろな能力をもつ生徒たち

a person with an ability for music
音楽の才能がある人

do to the best of one's ability (…に) 最善を尽くす, 全力を尽くす

He did the job to the best of his ability.
彼はその仕事に最善を尽くした。

ablaze ***adj.*** (on fire) 燃え立っている

able ***adj.*** (**be able to do**) (…が)できる, …することができる, <potential form of verb> [→ CAN[1]]

She wasn't able to move her right arm after the operation.
彼女は手術の後、右腕を動かすことができなかった。

I won't be able to check my e-mail for a week.
1週間、eメールをチェックすることができません。

I didn't think I'd be able to get here today.
今日ここに来られるとは思わなかった。

-able ***suf.*** …できる

abnormal ***adj.*** 異常な, 普通ではない, (strange) おかしい, 変わった

abnormal conditions 異常な状態

abnormal weather 異常気象

My boss is a little abnormal.
私の上司はちょっと変わった人です。

aboard ***adv., prep.*** …に乗って

All aboard!
皆さん、お乗りください。

There were two hundred passengers aboard the plane.
飛行機には200人が搭乗していた。

life aboard a submarine 潜水艦暮らし

abode ***n.*** (home) 家

abolish ***v.*** 廃止する

These taxes should be abolished.
これらの税は廃止するべきだ。

abominable ***adj.*** ひどい

♦ **Abominable Snowman** ***n.*** 雪男

aborigine ***n.*** (native Australian) オーストラリア先住民, アボリジニ

abort ***v.*** (stop) 中止する

abortion ***n.*** (妊娠)中絶

have an abortion 中絶する, ((*informal*)) 子供をおろす

about

1 ***prep.*** ON THE SUBJECT OF: …について, ((*formal*)) …に関して/関する

2 ***adv.*** APPROXIMATELY: (大体)…くらい/ぐらい, …ほど, ((*formal*)) およそ, 約, (in reference to time) …ころ/ごろ

3 ***adv.*** IN THE VICINITY: あたりに, 近くに

4 ***adv.*** IN CIRCLES: <-ます stem> + 回す/回る

1 What should I talk about?
何について話しましょうか？

I'll have to think about that.
それに関してはちょっと考えさせてください。

It's a book about plants.
植物に関する本です。

Hayashi told everyone all about it.
林さんはみんなに全部言ってしまった。

You don't have to worry about it.
気にすることはないよ。

There's no doubt about it.
間違いない。

What I like about him is his smile.
彼の好きなところは笑顔です。

We couldn't do anything about it.
私たちには何もできなかった。

There's something odd about him.
あの人はなんか変だ。

2 "About how much was the car?"
"About ¥750,000."
「その車は大体いくらぐらいだったの？」
「７５万円ぐらい」

We got married about ten years ago.
私たちは10年ぐらい前に結婚しました。

We had to wait in line for about an hour.
1時間ほど並んで待たなければいけなかった。

It's about half a kilometer from here to the station.
ここから駅までは500メートルほどです。

It was about 3 o'clock, I think.
3時ごろだったと思います。

About what time did you get up this morning?
けさは何時ごろ起きたの？

3 There was nobody about.
あたりには誰もいなかった。

The dog must be somewhere about.
犬は、どこかこの辺にいるはずだ。

4 Please stop waving your arms about.

腕を振り回すのをやめてください。

be about to do …しようとする

I was just about to go home when she arrived.
ちょうど帰ろうとしていた時に、彼女が来たんです。

I was about to get in the bath when the phone rang.
おふろに入ろうとしていたところに、電話が鳴った。

be not about to do …するつもりはない

above

1 *prep.* AT A HIGHER LEVEL THAN: …の上に, (**above sea level**) 海抜

2 *adj., adv.* MENTIONED EARLIER IN A TEXT: 前の, 先の, 上記の

3 *prep.* MORE THAN: …より上, …以上, …ちょっと [→ OVER]

4 *prep.* HIGHER IN RANK THAN: …の上に/で

1 The painting above the clock is quite valuable.
時計の上に掛かっている絵は、かなり貴重なものです。

We were standing on a bridge above a railway line.
私たちは線路の上の橋に立っていました。

We're on the fifth floor, and there are several more floors above us.
ここは5階ですが、この上にも何階かあります。

People say there's a hermit who lives in the hills above the town.
町の向こうの丘に、世捨て人が住んでいるそうです。

2 in the above example 上記の例で

in Chapter 3 above 先の第3章で

3 It was just above freezing.
0度よりほんの少し上でした。

4 He's above me in rank.
あの人は私より地位が上だ。

above all 何よりも, とりわけ

Above all, don't forget to mention the meeting tonight.
何よりも、今晩の会議のことを忘れずに伝えてください。

above and beyond …に加えて, …のほかに

above and beyond the call of duty
義務に加えて

above average 平均以上

Tadashi is an above-average student.
正君は平均以上の生徒です。

aboveboard *adj.* (straightforward) 公明正大だ, (not deceitful) 隠しだてしない

abrasive *adj.* (of person) 不快な, しゃくにさわる; (of substance) 研磨-

abreast *adv.* (side by side) 並んで

walk two abreast 2人並んで歩く

abridge *v.* (book) 要約する

♦ **abridged edition** *n.* 簡約版

abroad *adv.* (to/in a foreign country) 海外へ/に, 外国へ/に [→ FOREIGN]

a trip abroad 海外旅行

go abroad 海外 [外国] へ行く

come back from abroad 帰国する

study abroad 留学する

spend some years abroad
海外で何年か過ごす

abrupt *adj.* (sudden) 突然の, 急な, (curt) ぶっきらぼうな

♦ **abruptly** *adv.* (suddenly) 突然, 急に,

(curtly) ぶっきらぼうに

abscess ***n.*** はれ物, 膿瘍

absence ***n.*** 不在, (from school) 欠席, (from work) 欠勤

absent ***adj.*** 不在の, (be absent from school/work) (...を) 欠席/欠勤する, 休む

Who is absent today?
今日は誰が欠席ですか？

Mr. Shimizu was absent from the office because of a cold.
清水さんはかぜで会社を休みました。

absentminded ***adj.*** 忘れっぽい

absolute ***adj.*** 絶対の, 絶対的な, (used emphatically: complete) 全くの, 完全な

It was an absolute failure.
全くの失敗だった。

absolutely ***adv.*** (without fail) 絶対に, (utterly) 全く; (expressing agreement) そのとおり, もちろん

Would I have done such a thing? Absolutely not!
私がそんなことすると思う？ 絶対しないよ！

Am I going? Absolutely. I wouldn't miss it for the world.
行くかって？ もちろん。絶対行くよ。

I absolutely agree.
全くそのとおりだと思います。

absorb ***v.*** (soak up) 吸収する, 吸い込む; (**be absorbed in**: task, activity) ...に没頭している, ...に夢中になっている

This cloth should absorb the moisture.
この布が水分を吸収するはずです。

He was absorbed in his study of butterflies.
彼はチョウの研究に没頭していた。

abstain ***v.*** (**abstain from doing**) ...しない, (=from voting) 棄権する

Mr. Ishida abstained from voting.
石田さんは投票を棄権した。

abstract ***adj.*** 抽象的な

n. (summary) 要約, 抜粋, (dissertation abstract) 序論

These ideas are very abstract. Can't you give me some concrete examples?
これらの考えは非常に抽象的です。具体的な例を挙げてくれませんか？

The magazine wants an abstract of your article.
雑誌側があなたの論文の要約を欲しがっています。

absurd ***adj.*** ばかげた, とんでもない

an absurd request ばかげた要求

♦ **absurdity** ***n.*** 不条理, 不合理

abundant ***adj.*** 豊富な

Iraq has abundant oil resources.
イラクは石油資源が豊富だ。

abuse ***v.*** (misuse) 乱用する, 悪用する; (maltreat) 虐待する, 暴行する, (**sexually abuse**) 性的虐待をする

n. (improper use) 乱用, 悪用; (cruelty) 虐待, (**verbal abuse**) 悪口, ののしり

drug abuse 薬物の乱用

an abuse of power 権力の乱用

child abuse 児童虐待

abysmal ***adj.*** (terrible) 最低の, 最悪の

abyss ***n.*** (deep hole) ((*also figurative*)) どん底, 深淵

an abyss of despair 絶望のどん底

academic ***adj.*** (scholarly) 学問的な, (scholastic) 大学の

n. (scholar) 学者
<ruby>学者<rt>がくしゃ</rt></ruby>

academic background <ruby>学歴<rt>がくれき</rt></ruby>

academy *n.* (technical/vocational school)
<ruby>専門学校<rt>せんもんがっこう</rt></ruby>, (in proper names) -<ruby>学院<rt>がくいん</rt></ruby>

accelerate *v.* (car) <ruby>加速<rt>かそく</rt></ruby>する

accelerator *n.* (gas pedal) アクセル [→
picture of CAR]

put one's foot down on the accelerator
アクセルを<ruby>踏<rt>ふ</rt></ruby>む

accent *n.* (way of speaking) なまり, -<ruby>弁<rt>べん</rt></ruby>,
(stress on part of a word) アクセント

You have an American accent, don't you?
あなたの<ruby>英語<rt>えいご</rt></ruby>はアメリカ<ruby>英語<rt>えいご</rt></ruby>ですね。

Mr. Ito has a Tohoku accent.
<ruby>伊藤<rt>いとう</rt></ruby>さんは<ruby>東北<rt>とうほく</rt></ruby>なまりがある。

The Kyoto accent is soft.
<ruby>京都弁<rt>きょうとべん</rt></ruby>はやわらかい。

an accent mark アクセント<ruby>符号<rt>ふごう</rt></ruby>

accept *v.* (take, receive) <ruby>受<rt>う</rt></ruby>け<ruby>取<rt>と</rt></ruby>る, もら
う, ((humble)) いただく, (invitation) ((for-
mal/written)) (...に) <ruby>応<rt>おう</rt></ruby>じる, (decision,
outcome, person) <ruby>受<rt>う</rt></ruby>け<ruby>入<rt>い</rt></ruby>れる, (proposal, candidate for a job) <ruby>採用<rt>さいよう</rt></ruby>する,
(responsibility) <ruby>負<rt>お</rt></ruby>う, (theory, attitude,
person) <ruby>認<rt>みと</rt></ruby>める; (difficult thing) (...に)
<ruby>耐<rt>た</rt></ruby>える [→ RECEIVE]

I accepted the present.
プレゼントを<ruby>受<rt>う</rt></ruby>け<ruby>取<rt>と</rt></ruby>った。

accept gratefully ありがたくいただく

She accepted the invitation.
<ruby>彼女<rt>かのじょ</rt></ruby>は<ruby>招待<rt>しょうたい</rt></ruby>に<ruby>応<rt>おう</rt></ruby>じた。

This machine won't accept bills.
この<ruby>機械<rt>きかい</rt></ruby>では<ruby>紙幣<rt>しへい</rt></ruby>が<ruby>使<rt>つか</rt></ruby>えない。

He probably won't accept the advice.
<ruby>彼<rt>かれ</rt></ruby>はたぶん<ruby>忠告<rt>ちゅうこく</rt></ruby>を<ruby>聞<rt>き</rt></ruby>かないでしょう。

She accepted it as fate.
<ruby>彼女<rt>かのじょ</rt></ruby>はそれを<ruby>運命<rt>うんめい</rt></ruby>として<ruby>受<rt>う</rt></ruby>け<ruby>入<rt>い</rt></ruby>れた。

The group gradually accepted her as a
member.
しだいにみんなは<ruby>彼女<rt>かのじょ</rt></ruby>をグループの<ruby>一<rt>いち</rt></ruby>
<ruby>員<rt>いん</rt></ruby>として<ruby>受<rt>う</rt></ruby>け<ruby>入<rt>い</rt></ruby>れるようになった。

The plan was accepted by the company.
その<ruby>企画<rt>きかく</rt></ruby>は<ruby>会社<rt>かいしゃ</rt></ruby>に<ruby>採用<rt>さいよう</rt></ruby>された。

I was accepted for the job.
<ruby>私<rt>わたし</rt></ruby>はその<ruby>仕事<rt>しごと</rt></ruby>に<ruby>採用<rt>さいよう</rt></ruby>されました。

The short story was accepted for publication.
<ruby>短編小説<rt>たんぺんしょうせつ</rt></ruby>は<ruby>出版<rt>しゅっぱん</rt></ruby>されることになった。

I just couldn't accept the responsibility.
どうしてもその<ruby>責任<rt>せきにん</rt></ruby>を<ruby>負<rt>お</rt></ruby>うことができ
なかった。

I accepted full responsibility for the
accident.
<ruby>私<rt>わたし</rt></ruby>は<ruby>事故<rt>じこ</rt></ruby>の<ruby>全責任<rt>ぜんせきにん</rt></ruby>を<ruby>認<rt>みと</rt></ruby>めた。

That theory is generally accepted.
その<ruby>理論<rt>りろん</rt></ruby>は<ruby>広<rt>ひろ</rt></ruby>く<ruby>認<rt>みと</rt></ruby>められている。

I accept it as true.
それを<ruby>事実<rt>じじつ</rt></ruby>と<ruby>認<rt>みと</rt></ruby>めます。

I just can't accept the situation any longer.
この<ruby>状況<rt>じょうきょう</rt></ruby>にもうこれ<ruby>以上<rt>いじょう</rt></ruby><ruby>耐<rt>た</rt></ruby>えられない。

acceptable *adj.* (agreeable) <ruby>受<rt>う</rt></ruby>け<ruby>入<rt>い</rt></ruby>れ
られる, (satisfactory) けっこうな, (pass-
able, tolerable) まあまあの

acceptable conditions
<ruby>受<rt>う</rt></ruby>け<ruby>入<rt>い</rt></ruby>れられる<ruby>条件<rt>じょうけん</rt></ruby>

an acceptable performance
まあまあの<ruby>演技<rt>えんぎ</rt></ruby>

acceptance *n.* <ruby>受<rt>う</rt></ruby>け<ruby>入<rt>い</rt></ruby>れること, (acknowl-
edgment that sth/sb is right, true etc.)
<ruby>承認<rt>しょうにん</rt></ruby>

accepted *adj.* <ruby>受<rt>う</rt></ruby>け<ruby>入<rt>い</rt></ruby>れられている, <ruby>一般<rt>いっぱん</rt></ruby>

に認められている

the accepted theory 定説

access ***n.*** (way of reaching a place) (…に) 行く方法, アクセス, (way in) 入口, (way in and out) 出入り, (**have access to sb/sth**) …に会える/…を使える

v. (…に) アクセスする

He has access to the president.
あの人は大統領に面会できる人です。

Will we have access to a phone?
電話の使える場所にいるでしょうか？

Can you access that kind of information on the Internet?
インターネットでそういう情報にアクセスできますか？

accessory ***n.*** (additional item) 付属品, (jewelry etc.) アクセサリー; (accessory to a crime) 従犯者

accident ***n.*** (serious mishap) 事故; (chance) 偶然

a car accident 交通事故

have a serious accident 大事故にあう

by accident 偶然, たまたま

We met by accident.
私たちは偶然出会ったんです。

Quite by accident they were on the same train.
たまたま彼らは同じ電車に乗り合わせた。

without accident 無事に

accidental ***adj.*** (happening by chance) 偶然の, (unintended) 思いがけない

accidentally ***adv.*** うっかり, 誤って

acclaim ***n.*** 賞賛

v. ほめたたえる, 賞賛する

receive international acclaim
国際的な賞賛を浴びる

♦ **acclaimed** ***adj.*** ほめたたえられた, 賞賛を浴びた

A

accommodate ***v.*** (have sufficient space for) 収容できる, (respond to: request) (…に) 対応する

The room accommodates 20 people.
その部屋は２０人収容できます。

accommodation ***n.*** 宿泊施設, 泊まる所

student accommodations 学生宿泊施設

This hotel provides accommodation for over 300 people.
このホテルは300人以上泊まれる。

accompaniment ***n.*** (musical) 伴奏

without accompaniment 伴奏なしで

accompany ***v.*** (go with) (…と) いっしょに行く, (…に) ついて行く, ((*formal*)) (…に) 同行する, (play music with) (…の) 伴奏をする

Mr. Shimada accompanied the VIPs.
島田氏は要人に同行した。

Will you accompany me on the piano?
ピアノで伴奏していただけますか？

accompanied by …を同伴して

Accompanied by three students, Professor Tanaka left for Paris.
学生３人を同伴して、田中教授はパリに出かけた。

accomplish ***v.*** (succeed in doing) 成し遂げる, 達成する [→ ACHIEVE]

Mr. Harada accomplished a great deal in his short life.
原田さんは短い生涯で多くのことを成し遂げた。

We've accomplished nothing!

私たちは何も成し遂げていないよ！

accordingly *adv.* (fittingly) それに応じて; (therefore) したがって, それゆえに

according to *prep.* …によると, …によれば, …では, (person's words) …の話では

According to the weather forecast, it's going to rain.
天気予報によると雨になるらしい。

According to this map, we should be arriving there soon.
この地図によれば、まもなくそこに着くはずです。

According to his instructions, we were to wait there.
彼の指示により、そこで待つことになっていた。

According to the old lady, there was a big earthquake.
おばあさんの話では、大地震があったそうです。

accordion *n.* アコーディオン

account *n.*

1 BANK ACCOUNT: 口座
2 RECORD OF MONEY USED: 会計簿, 帳簿
3 EXPLANATION: 説明, (testimony) 証言
4 E-MAIL: メールアカウント
5 BUSINESS CLIENT: 取引先

1 a bank account 銀行口座
a savings account 普通預金口座
a checking account 当座預金口座
(*at bank*) "I would like to open an account."
「口座を開きたいのですが」

2 Tanaka's wife keeps a daily account of their household expenses.
田中さんの奥さんは毎日家計簿をつけています。

3 He gave an account of what happened.
何が起こったかを彼は説明した。
an eyewitness account 目撃証言

4 set up an e-mail account
メールアカウントを設定する

on account of …のため, …により [→ BECAUSE OF]

accountable *adj.* 責任がある

You've got to be accountable for your actions.
自分の行動には責任をもたなくてはいけません。

♦ **accountability** *n.* 説明責任

a lack of accountability
説明責任の欠如

accountant *n.* (certified) 会計士, (in company) 会計係, 経理担当者

accounting *n.* 経理

accumulate *v.* (pile up) 積み重なる, (of dust) たまる; (collect) 集める

Dust has accumulated on the shelves.
ほこりが棚の上にたまっている。

I've accumulated a lot of junk over the years.
何年もかけてがらくたをたくさん集めてきた。

accumulate a fortune 財産を築く

accuracy *n.* 正確さ, 精密さ

accurate *adj.* (exact) 正確な, 精密な

accurate data 正確なデータ

How accurate are these measurements?
この数値はどのくらい正確ですか？

♦ **accurately** *adv.* 正確に

accusation *n.* 告訴, 告発

accuse *v.* 非難する, 責める, (say angrily)

怒る, (in court) 訴える, 告訴する

The boss accused the men of slacking.
上司は、部下たちがたるんでいると非難した。

They accused me of being lazy.
あの人たちは、私が怠けていると言って非難した。

Everyone accused Kentaro of stealing.
健太郎が盗んだに違いないとみんな彼を責めた。

My mother accused me of spending too much.
母は、私がお金を使いすぎると言って怒った。

The boss was accused (in court) of sexual harassment.
その上司はセクハラで訴えられた。

The bank employee was accused of embezzlement.
その銀行員は横領の罪で告訴された。

♦ **the accused** *n.* 被告(人)

accustom *v.* 慣らす, (**get/grow accustomed to**) …に慣れる [→ USED TO]

ace *n.* (in tennis) エース; (skilled person) 達人; (**aces**: suit of cards) エース

acetaminophen *n.* アセタミノフェン

acetate *n.* (salt of acetic acid) 酢酸塩, (fabric/plastic made from cellulose acetate) アセテート

acetic acid *n.* 酢酸

acetylene *n.* (gas used in welding) アセチレン(ガス)

ache *v.* (be sore) 痛い, 痛む, (of old injury or due to rheumatism) うずく

n. 痛み [→ PAIN]

My back aches and I feel awful.
背中が痛くてすごくつらい。

achieve *v.* 成し遂げる, 達成する, やり遂げる

We've achieved it at last!
ついにやった!

You'll achieve nothing by complaining all the time.
文句ばかり言っていても、何も成し遂げられないよ。

We have achieved our goals.
私たちは目標を達成した。

He achieved the highest grade in the class.
彼はクラスで一番の成績を取った。

achievement *n.* (accomplishment) 達成, (success) 成功, (scholarly/professional accomplishment) 業績, (brilliant feat) 快挙

a sense of achievement 達成感

That's quite an achievement.
それは大変な快挙ですね。

♦ **achievement test** *n.* アチーブメントテスト, 学力テスト

Achilles tendon *n.* アキレス腱

acid *n.* 酸

adj. (sour) すっぱい, (having the properties of acid) 酸性の

acid rain 酸性雨

an acid taste すっぱい味

♦ **acidity** *n.* 酸味

acknowledge *v.*

1 RECOGNIZE: 認める

2 THANK: 感謝する

3 REPLY TO: (**acknowledge receipt of**) (受け取ったことを)通知する, 知らせる

4 SAY HELLO TO: (…に) あいさつする

1 He acknowledged his part in the affair.
彼はその事件とのかかわりを認めた。

She acknowledged that she was wrong.
彼女は自分が悪いと認めた。

His theory has been acknowledged by the scientific community.
彼の理論は科学の学会で認められた。

2 Ms. Yamada was acknowledged in the book's preface.
その本の前書きで山田さんに感謝の言葉が書かれていた。

3 Was your letter acknowledged?
手紙を受け取ったと、知らせて来ましたか？

4 He didn't even acknowledge me.
あの人は私にあいさつさえしなかった。

acne *n.* (pimples) にきび, (disease) ざそう

acorn *n.* どんぐり

acoustic *adj.* (of instrument) アコースティックな, (of space) 音響の
n. (**acoustics**: in room) 音響効果
an acoustic guitar アコースティックギター

acquaintance *n.* 知り合い, 知人
He has a large number of acquaintances but very few friends.
あの人には知り合いは多いが、友人はとても少ない。

acquire *v.* 手に入れる, (land, wealth) 取得する, 獲得する, (skill) 身につける, 習得する

acquisition *n.* (of skill) 身につけること, 習得, (of thing) 入手, (thing purchased) 入手したもの

acre *n.* エーカー

acrobat *n.* 軽業師, 曲芸師

across

1 *prep., adv.* FROM ONE SIDE TO THE OTHER: …を [NOTE: Usually used with a verb that denotes crossing. → CROSS]

2 *prep., adv.* OVER THE SURFACE OF: …に

3 *prep., adv.* ON THE OTHER SIDE OF/FROM: (…の) 反対側の/に, 向こう側の/に

4 *prep.* SPANNING: …にかかって

5 *prep.* THROUGHOUT: -中に, (**across the country**) 全国に, (**across the world/globe**) 全世界に

6 *adv.* IN WIDTH/DIAMETER: (in width) 幅…, (in diameter) 直径…

1 I walked across the park.
公園を横切った。

She swam across the river.
彼女は川を泳いで渡った。

The road goes across the mountains.
道路は山を横切っている。

The part of the movie where all the refugees were running across the bridge to freedom was really exciting.
映画で、亡命者たちが自由へ向かって橋を走って渡る場面が本当によかった。

I just walked across to her and said, "Wanna dance?"
僕はまっすぐ彼女のところに歩いて行って「踊らない？」と言った。

2 That child has scribbled across my book.
あの子が私の本に落書きをした。

He leaned across to get the pepper.
彼は身を乗り出してこしょうを取った。

She put her coat across her knees.
彼女はコートをひざにかけた。

3 the playground across the street
道の向こう側の遊び場

The building across from us is so high it cuts out the sunlight.
向かいの建物が高くて、日差しがさえぎられています。

4 The bridge across the river is very old and shaky.
その川にかかっている橋は、すごく古くてグラグラしている。

5 The news was broadcast across the country.
そのニュースは全国に放送された。

6 There was a hole 15 meters across.
直径15メートルの穴があった。

acrylic *n.* (paint) アクリル(絵の具), (fiber) アクリル(繊維)

act

1 *n.* THING DONE: 行為, 行い

2 *v.* TAKE ACTION: ((*formal/written*)) 行動する

3 *v.* BEHAVE: 態度をとる, ふるまう, (pretend to be...) ...ふりをする

4 *v.* PLAY A PART: (act the role of) (...の)役をする, ((*formal/written*)) 演じる, (act in: appear in) (...に)出る, (act in order to deceive) (お)芝居をする

5 *n.* PERFORMANCE: (on/off stage) 演技

6 *n.* PART OF FILM/PLAY: 場面, シーン, (of play) 幕

7 *n.* LAW: (**Act**) 法令, -法

1 a terrorist act テロ行為
an act of treason 反逆行為

2 We have to act now.
今すぐ行動しなくてはいけない。

3 He acted as if he'd never met her before.
彼はまるで一度も彼女に会ったことがないかのような態度をとった。

Stop acting like a child.
子供みたいなことはやめなさい。
act sober 酔っていないふりをする
act cool かっこつける

4 Mifune acted Musashi Miyamoto.
三船は宮本武蔵(の役)を演じた。
Isn't that the man who acted in the play we saw last Friday?
あの人は、先週の金曜日に見たお芝居に出ていた人じゃない?

5 He's good at putting on an act.
あの人は演技がうまい。
He put on a good act to get out of that.
その場を逃れるために、彼は一芝居打った。

6 The last act was the best.
最後の幕が一番よかった。

7 the Education Act 教育法
the Traffic Act 交通法

get one's act together → TOGETHER

acting *adj.* (temporarily standing in for another) 代理の
n. (performance, playing of a role) 演技
the acting dean 学部長代理
good [bad] acting うまい [下手な] 演技
I wonder what led him into acting.
彼はなぜ演劇の世界に入ったんだろう。

action *n.* (deed, **actions**: behavior) 行動, (movement) 動作, (functioning) 作用
adj. (of movie) アクション-
His actions were suspicious.
その男の行動は怪しかった/その男は挙動不審だった。
an action movie アクション映画

take legal action (against) (...を相手

取って)訴訟を起こす

activate *v.* (cause to start) 動かす, (switch on: machine) 作動する

active *adj.* (energetic) 元気な, 行動的な, (lively) 活発な, (of military personnel) 現役の

Mr. Ito is over seventy but still active.
((*polite*)) 伊藤さんは70歳を越えていらっしゃいますが、今でもお元気です。

She's active in politics.
彼女は政治に積極的にかかわっています。

an active person 行動的な人

an active child 活発な子

♦**active ingredient** *n.* 有効成分

active volcano *n.* 活火山

actively *adv.* 積極的に, 活発に

He's actively involved in charity work.
彼はチャリティ活動を積極的にやっている。

activist *n.* 活動家, 運動家

activity *n.* 活動, 行動

actor/actress *n.* (performer) 俳優, 役者, (actor) 男優, (actress) 女優, (**child actor**) 子役, (**voice actor**) 声優

a kabuki actor 歌舞伎役者

become an actor 俳優になる

He's a good actor.
彼はいい役者だね。

actual *adj.* (real) 本当の, 実際の, (used emphatically: **the actual...**) 実際の, ...そのもの

the actual size/mass 実物大

the actual dimensions 原寸大

the actual person 本人

The preparations took weeks, but the actual wedding took only a couple of hours.
準備には何週間もかかったのに、結婚式そのものはほんの2、3時間で終わってしまった。

actually *adv.* (in fact) 本当に, 実際に, (used to draw attention to sth) 本当は, 実のところ, (on the contrary) 実は

Can you actually speak three languages?
本当に3ヵ国語話せるんですか？

No one actually saw it happen.
それが起きるのを実際に見た人はいませんでした。

Actually, he was a spy.
実のところ、彼はスパイだったんです。

I'm studying, actually.
実は、今勉強しているんだよ。

He said there was nothing unusual about it, but actually there was.
何も変わったことはないって彼は言ったけど、実はあったんです。

actuary *n.* 保険数理士

acupuncture *n.* はり, はり治療

acute *adj.* (of pain) 激しい, (of illness) 急性の, (of senses) 鋭い, 敏感な

The old woman has acute arthritis.
その老婦人は急性の関節炎にかかっている。

an acute observer 観察の鋭い人

♦**acute accent** *n.* 鋭アクセント

Coup d'état is spelled with an acute accent over the *e*.
「クーデター」のスペルにはeの上に鋭アクセントが付きます。

acute angle *n.* 鋭角

AD *abbr.* (anno Domini) 紀元..., 西暦...

in the third century AD (紀元)3世紀に

ad → ADVERTISEMENT

adage ***n.*** ことわざ, 格言

adamant ***adj.*** 譲らない

Adam's apple ***n.*** のどぼとけ

adapt ***v.*** (adapt to: adjust to: situation) (…に)慣れる, 適応する; (rewrite) 書き換える, (**adapt to film**) 映画化する

I just couldn't adapt to the customs of the country.
どうしてもあの国の慣習に慣れることができませんでした。

We'll have to adapt more quickly to new technology.
我々は、新しい科学技術にもっと迅速に適応していかなければならないだろう。

The story has been adapted for younger readers.
その小説は若い読者向けに書き換えられた。

♦ **adaptable** ***adj.*** (of person) 順応性のある, 融通のきく

adaptation ***n.*** (for TV, film) 脚色, 映画化; (to situation, environment) 適合

adapter ***n.*** アダプター

add ***v.*** (count) 足す, 加える; (say further) 付け加える

Four added to four makes eight.
4足す4は8。

If you add on consumer tax, it's more expensive.
消費税を入れるともっと高くなる。

And I'd like to add to that…
(それに) 付け加えますと…

♦ **add up** ***v.*** (total) 合計する, (**add up to**: come to) …になる; (make sense) 意味をなす

We added up everything we spent.
使ったお金を合計した。

It adds up to a grand total of $6,000.
合計で6000ドルになります。

When you think about it, what he says does not add up to much.
よく考えると、彼の言っていることは大して意味がない。

added ***adj.*** さらなる

There were added complications.
さらなる問題があった。

adder ***n.*** (snake) クサリヘビ

addict ***v.*** (**be addicted to**) (games) …に熱中する, …にはまる, (drugs) -中毒だ, -依存症だ

n. 常用者, 中毒者

He's addicted to alcohol.
彼はアルコール依存症だ。

That boy is a TV addict.
あの子はテレビっ子だ。

a drug addict 麻薬中毒者

♦ **addiction** ***n.*** 中毒

addition ***n.*** (process of adding) 足し算; (thing added) 追加したもの

Addition is the first math skill we learn.
足し算は最初に習う計算です。

in addition その上, さらに

In addition, we had to attend meetings every evening.
その上、毎晩会議に出なければならなかった。

additional ***adj.*** 追加の

an additional charge 追加料金

additive ***n.*** (in food) 添加物

address

1 *n.* POSTAL DETAILS: 住所, (on envelope) 宛名 [→ p. 1174]

2 *v.* INDICATE AN ADDRESS ON: …あてにする, (…に) 宛名を書く

3 *v.* MAKE A SPEECH TO: (…に) 演説する

4 *v.* RESPOND TO: (problem, concern) (…に) 対応する, 取り組む

5 *n.* FORMAL SPEECH: あいさつ, 演説, -辞

1 Write down your name and address here, please.
((*polite*)) ここにお名前とご住所をご記入ください。

2 Address the letter to me.
手紙は私あてにしてください。

It's addressed to Ms. Suzuki.
鈴木さんあてです。

3 The president addressed the nation.
大統領は国民に演説をした。

4 The problem has not been addressed yet.
その問題はまだ対応されていない。

5 a farewell address 送別のあいさつ

a weekly radio address 毎週のラジオ演説

♦ **address book** *n.* 住所録

addressee *n.* 受取人

adequate *adj.* 十分な

adhere *v.* (**adhere to**: stick to) …にくっつく, …に接着する, (abide by) 守る

adhere to the rules 規則を守る

♦ **adhesion** *n.* 接着, 粘着

adhesive *n.* (glue) 接着剤, のり

adj. 粘着性の

adhesive tape 粘着テープ

adjacent *adj.* (next to) 隣の, (adjoining) 隣接している

adjective *n.* 形容詞

adjourn *v.* (of court) 休廷する, (of meeting) 休会する [→ POSTPONE]

adjust *v.* (alter to fit) 合わせる, (tune) 調節する, 調整する; (adjust to: get used to) (…に) 慣れる

If you adjust the antenna, you'll get a better picture.
アンテナを調節すると、映りがよくなるよ。

adjust one's watch 時計を合わせる

adjust the lens focus
レンズの焦点を合わせる

adjust the volume 音量を調整する

It took me quite some time to adjust to the crowds in Tokyo.
東京の人込みに慣れるのに、ずいぶん時間がかかりました。

adjustable *adj.* 調節できる, 調整できる

an adjustable tool 調整できる道具

adjustment *n.* (of things) 調整, (of train fare) 精算; (to situation) 適応, 慣れ

ad-lib *n.* アドリブ, 即興

v. アドリブでやる, 即興でやる

adv. (**ad lib**) アドリブで, 即興で

administer *v.* (run, manage) 運営する

administration *n.* (management of things) 管理, 運営, (department) 総務, (government administration) 政権, 政府

Many people are involved in the administration of this program.
このプログラムの運営には多くの人がかかわっています。

business administration 企業経営

the Bush Administration ブッシュ政権

administrative *adj.* 管理の, 経営の

administrative problems 管理の問題

♦ **administrative staff** *n.* 職員

administrator *n.* 管理者(かんりしゃ)

admirable *adj.* (splendid) 立派(りっぱ)な, みごとな

admiral *n.* (in U.S. Navy) 大将(たいしょう)

admiration *n.* 賞賛(しょうさん), (for person) あこがれ

admire *v.* (deeds, sights) (…に) 感心(かんしん)する, (people) (…に) あこがれる

I admire her courage.
彼女(かのじょ)の勇気(ゆうき)には感心する。

admirer *n.* (in general) あこがれている人(ひと), (of entertainer) ファン, (of respected person) 崇拝者(すうはいしゃ), 賞賛者(しょうさんしゃ)

a secret admirer 隠れファン

admission *n.* 入場(にゅうじょう), (to school) 入学(にゅうがく)

Admission to that school is strict.
あの学校(がっこう)への入学(にゅうがく)は厳(きび)しい。

♦ **admission fee** *n.* (in general) 入場料(にゅうじょうりょう), (for school) 入学金(にゅうがくきん)

KANJI BRIDGE

入   ON: にゅう   KUN: い(る/れる), はい(る) | ADMISSION

admission	入場(にゅうじょう)
admission fee	入場料(にゅうじょうりょう)
admission ticket	入場券(にゅうじょうけん)
admission to a school	入学(にゅうがく)
admission to a society/club	入会(にゅうかい)
admission to a company	入社(にゅうしゃ)
admission to a hospital	入院(にゅういん)
introductory book/course	入門(にゅうもん)

---

admit *v.*

1 PERMIT TO ENTER: 入(い)れる [→ LET IN], (school) (…に) 入学(にゅうがく)を認(みと)める, (be admitted to the hospital) 入院(にゅういん)する

2 GRANT TO BE TRUE: 認(みと)める

3 HOLD: (…が) 入(い)れる, 入(はい)る, (accommodate) 収容(しゅうよう)できる

1 They were admitted because they had entrance passes.
入場許可証(にゅうじょうきょかしょう)を持(も)っていたので、彼(かれ)らは入(はい)ることができた。

2 He admitted it was his mistake.
彼(かれ)はそれが自分(じぶん)の間違(まちが)いだと認(みと)めた。

All right, I admit it. It's true—I was drunk.
((*masculine*)) わかった、認(みと)めるよ。確(たし)かに俺(おれ)は酔(よ)ってた。

The prime minister admitted taking bribes.
首相(しゅしょう)はわいろを受(う)け取(と)ったことを認(みと)めた。

3 The new public bath will admit 100 people.
新(あたら)しくできた銭湯(せんとう)は100人(ひゃくにん)が入(はい)れます。

That theater can admit 1,000 people.
あの劇場(げきじょう)は1000人(せんにん)を収容(しゅうよう)することができる。

I must admit... 正直言(しょうじきい)って

I must admit, I completely forgot about it.
正直言(しょうじきい)って、全(まった)く忘(わす)れていました。

adolescence *n.* (puberty) 思春期(ししゅんき), (youth) 青春(せいしゅん)

adopt *v.* (**adopt a child**) 養子(ようし)にする, 養子縁組(ようしえんぐみ)をする; (customs) 取(と)り入(い)れる, (method) 採用(さいよう)する

I was adopted by the Yamadas when I was eight years old.
私(わたし)は8歳(はっさい)の時(とき)、山田家(やまだけ)の養子(ようし)になった。

Actually, it's not easy to adopt children.
実際(じっさい)には、養子縁組(ようしえんぐみ)は簡単(かんたん)にはできない。

Western customs have been adopted in numerous countries.

西洋の習慣は多くの国々に取り入れられてきた。

We need to adopt these new methods.
この新しい方式を採用する必要がある。

♦ **adopted child** ***n.*** 養子, ((*informal*)) もらい子, (girl) 養女

adoption ***n.*** 養子縁組

put a baby up for adoption
赤ん坊を養子に出す

adore ***v.*** (like, love) (…が) 大好きだ, (worship) 敬愛する

I adore cats. 猫が大好きです。

adorn ***v.*** 飾る

adult ***n.*** おとな, ((*formal*)) 成人

an adult's idea おとなの考え

become an adult おとなになる

adults only (=minors not allowed)
未成年者お断り

adult education 成人教育

♦ **adulthood** ***n.*** 成年期

adultery ***n.*** 不倫, ((*formal*)) 不貞

commit adultery 不倫する

advance

1 ***v.*** **GO FORWARD:** (…に向かって) 進む, (of army) 前進する, (progress) 進む, 進歩する

2 ***n.*** **FORWARD PROGRESS:** 進歩, 向上

3 ***v.*** **PUT FORTH:** 出す, 提案する

4 ***n.*** **PREPAYMENT:** 前払い, 前金

1 Tamura has advanced to the next stage of the competition.
田村さんは大会で、次の段階に勝ち進みました。

The army advanced to meet the enemy.
軍隊は敵に向かって前進して行った。

Medical science has advanced a great deal.
医学は著しく進歩しました。

2 a medical advance 医学の進歩

a technological advance 技術的な向上

3 advance an opinion 意見を出す

advance a proposal 提案する

4 They said they wanted an advance.
先方は前金が欲しいと言った。

in advance 前もって

We booked our theater tickets in advance.
前もって劇場のチケットを取った。

in advance of …の前に, ((*formal*)) …に先立って

We need to prepare ourselves in advance of the meeting.
私たちは会議の前に準備をしておかなくてはいけない。

advanced ***adj.*** (of technology, method) 先進的な, (of student, course) 上級の

an advanced country 先進国

He's taking the advanced course.
彼は上級コースを取っています。

advantage ***n.*** (edge, upper hand) 有利, (benefit) 利点, (strength) 強み

Mayumi's got an advantage because she can speak English.
英語を話せるのは、真弓さんの強みです。

His weight gives him the advantage in this contest.
彼の体重が、この競技では有利になっている。

The Internet has many advantages over traditional, printed media.
インターネットは従来の活字メディアより多くの利点がある。

be to one's advantage …のためにな

る, …に有利になる

It might be to your advantage to learn Chinese.
中国語をやっておくと、ためになりますよ。

take advantage of 利用する

advantageous *adj.* 有利な

adventure *n.* (experience) 冒険, (unexpected experience) 意外な出来事, 珍しい経験

Going to the North Pole was a great adventure.
北極に行くのは大冒険でした。

What an adventure that was!
あれは珍しい経験だったよ。

adverb *n.* 副詞

adversary *n.* 敵, (in sport) 相手

adverse *adj.* (not good) 悪い, 良くない

adversity *n.* 逆境

advertise *v.* (publicize) 宣伝する, 広告する; (tell, spread) 言いふらす

That shampoo has been advertised on TV.
そのシャンプーはテレビで宣伝していた。

a poster advertising milk
牛乳を宣伝しているポスター

Every day there are jobs advertised in the papers.
毎日、新聞には求人広告が載っています。

You don't need to advertise the fact that you're single.
独身だということを言いふらすことないよ。

advertisement *n.* (printed or on Internet) 広告, 宣伝, (on TV, radio) コマーシャル, CM

I don't like that site. It has too many advertisements.
そのサイトは好きじゃないです。広告が多すぎます。

We had a fantastic response to our advertisement.
我々の広告にものすごい反響があった。

put an advertisement in the newspaper
新聞に広告を出す

think of a catch phrase for an advertisement
宣伝のためのキャッチフレーズを考える

advertising *n.* (business) 広告業, (promotion) 宣伝

work in advertising 広告業界で働く

That company spends a lot of money on advertising.
あの企業は宣伝にけっこうお金をかけている。

advice *n.* 忠告, アドバイス, ((*formal/written*)) 助言

a teacher's advice 先生の忠告

give advice (to) (…に)助言する

ask someone for advice 誰かに相談する

advise *v.* (…に) アドバイスする, 忠告する, 助言する, (recommend) 勧める

His doctor advised him to stop smoking.
医者は彼にたばこをやめるよう忠告した。

We were advised to leave early.
早く出発するよう勧められた。

adviser *n.* アドバイザー, 顧問, (academic adviser) 指導教官

adzuki bean *n.* 小豆

aerial *adj.* (from the air) 航空の, (in the air) 空中の

n. (antenna) アンテナ [→ picture of

HOUSE]
an aerial photograph 航空写真

aerobics ***n.*** エアロビクス

aerogram ***n.*** 航空書簡

aeroplane ***n.*** 飛行機

aerosol ***n.*** スプレー

aesthetic ***adj.*** 美的な, 審美的な

aesthetics ***n.*** 美学

afar ***adv.*** (**from afar**) 遠くから

affair ***n.***

1 CONCERN: 問題, 事, 事柄

2 SEXUAL RELATIONSHIP: 浮気, 不倫, ((*old-fashioned*)) 情事

3 EVENT: 事件

1 personal affairs 個人的な事 [私事]

international [political] affairs
国際 [政治] 問題

affairs of state 国事

That's not my affair.
それは私の知った事ではない。

2 have a love affair 浮気をする

I believe he's having an affair with his secretary.
彼は秘書と関係をもっていると思う。

3 The whole affair was blown out of proportion.
事件は、とんでもなくおおげさなことになった。

affect ***v.*** (influence) (…に) 影響を与える, (**be affected**) 影響を受ける, (harm) 悪くする, ((*written*)) 冒す, (…に) 害を与える

The shock began to affect his behavior.
その衝撃は彼の行動に影響を与え始めた。

How many people are going to be affected by this decision?
この決定によってどのくらいの人が影響を受けるんですか？

Smoking affects your lungs.
たばこは肺を冒す [悪くする]。

affected ***adj.*** (artificial) 気取った

affection ***n.*** (among family) 愛情, (liking) 好意, (fondness) 愛着

affectionate ***adj.*** (of words, behavior) 愛情のこもった, (of person) 愛情の深い

affidavit ***n.*** 宣誓供述書

affiliated ***adj.*** (with organization) (…と) 提携している

affinity ***n.*** (between things) 類似性, (between people) 相性 ; (points in common) 共通点

affirm ***v.*** (declare) 断言する, (state positively) 肯定する

affirmative ***adj.*** 肯定的な

an affirmative sentence 肯定文

affix ***n.*** (in grammar) 接辞

afflict ***v.*** (**be afflicted with**) …で苦しんでいる

affluence ***n.*** 豊かさ, 裕福

affluent ***adj.*** 豊かな, 裕福な

afford ***v.*** 余裕がある

But can you afford such an expensive car?
でもそんなに高価な車を買う余裕があるの？

It's a great opportunity and you can't afford to miss it.
すばらしいチャンスなんだから、見逃すわけにはいかないでしょう。

Afghanistan ***n.*** アフガニスタン

afloat ***adj.*** (floating) 浮かんでいる

afraid ***adj.*** (frightened) 怖い, (speaking

about sb else) 怖がる, (worried) 心配する

Are you afraid of the dark?
暗やみが怖い？

She's afraid of spiders.
彼女はクモを怖がる。

He looked afraid.
彼は怖がっているようでした。

The cat seems afraid to go out at night.
その猫は夜外に出るのが怖いみたいだ。

Don't be afraid to ask questions.
遠慮なく(何でも)聞いてください。

He's afraid he might get lost.
彼は迷わないか心配している。

I'm afraid... (unfortunately...) 残念ながら, あいにく

I'm afraid she said she can't come.
残念ながら彼女は来られないそうです。

"Can you ski?"
"I'm afraid not."
「スキーはできる？」
「残念ながらできないんです」

I'm afraid he's not in the office at the moment.
あいにくただいま外出しております。

afresh *adv.* 改めて, 新たに

We had to start afresh.
新たに出直さなければならなかった。

Africa *n.* アフリカ

African *adj.* (of continent, culture, language) アフリカの, (of person) アフリカ人の

n. アフリカ人

African-American *n.* (person) アフリカ系アメリカ人, (アメリカ)黒人

adj. (of culture, language) アフリカ系アメリカ人の, (アメリカ)黒人の

after

1 *prep., conj.* SUBSEQUENT TO: ...の後(で), (**after doing**) ...してから, ...した後(で), ...したら

2 *prep.* PAST THE HOUR: -過ぎ

3 *prep.* FOLLOWING: ...の次に, ...の下に, ...の後に

4 *prep.* INDICATING RANK/POSITION: ...に次ぐ, ...に次いで

5 *prep.* SEEKING: (chasing) ...を追って, ...を追いかけて, (angling for) ...をねらって, (looking for) ...を探して

1 I went to the library after class.
(私は)授業の後、図書館に行った。

Let's meet after the lunch break.
昼休みの後で会いましょう。

After the war Morita returned to Tokyo.
戦後、森田さんは東京に戻りました。

Let's go after eating dinner.
晩ご飯を食べてから行きましょう。

I'll play tennis after I've cleaned my room.
部屋の掃除をしてからテニスをします。

She came just after the meeting had started.
彼女は会議が始まった直後に来ました。

I'll be an elementary school teacher after graduating.
大学を卒業したら、小学校の先生になります。

After what you've just said, I don't think I want to go there.
それを聞いたら、行きたくなくなった。

2 There's no point in arriving after 7 o'clock.

7時過ぎに着いても意味がありません。

It's five after eight.
8時5分過ぎです。

3 If you would just write your name and address after his, please.
この方の<u>次</u>[下]にお名前とご住所をお書きください。

The hotel is just after the intersection on your left.
ホテルは交差点を渡ってすぐ左にあります。

4 Osaka is the largest city after Tokyo.
大阪は東京に次ぐ大都市です。

He's third in charge after Matsuoka.
彼は松岡氏に次いで3番目の責任者だ。

5 The police are after him.
警察はその男を追っている。

The cat ran after the mouse.
猫はネズミを追いかけた。

He's after my job.
((*masculine*)) あいつは俺の仕事をねらっている。

after all (finally) 結局, (as was to be expected) やはり, ((*informal*)) やっぱり

It's not worth going after all.
結局、行く価値はないよ。

after you (please go first) どうぞ(お先に)

call/shout (out) after …の後ろから呼びかける

I called out after him, but he didn't seem to hear me.
後ろから呼びかけたけど、聞こえなかったみたいだ。

clean up after ((*also figurative*)) …の後始末をする

I'm always cleaning up after you.
私はいつもあなたの後始末をしているんだよ。

aftereffects ***n.*** 後遺症

afterlife ***n.*** 来世, あの世

afternoon ***n.*** 午後

Classes will be held in the afternoon.
授業は午後、行われます。

I will be out all afternoon.
午後はずっと出かけています。

It's time for my afternoon walk.
午後の散歩の時間だ。

Sunday afternoon 日曜(日)の午後

aftershave ***n.*** アフターシェーブローション

aftershock ***n.*** (of earthquake) 余震, ((*figurative*)) 余波

aftertaste ***n.*** 後味, 後口

afterward(s) ***adv.*** あとで, そのあと

again ***adv.*** また, もう一度, ((*formal/written*)) 再び, (**never ... again**) 二度と…ない

See you again. (= Good-bye.)
またね/じゃ、また/((*formal*))またお目にかかりましょう。

What! Are you going there again?
えっ、またあそこに行くの?

You'll soon be well again.
またすぐにお元気になりますよ。

It was just like being a student again.
まるで、また学生に戻ったようでした。

Could you say that again, please?
もう一度おっしゃっていただけますか?

What was her name again?
((*informal*)) 彼女の名前は何でしたっけ?

Once again, I'd like to thank you for your kindness.

本当にご親切ありがとうございました。

I'll never do that again.
二度とそんなことはしません。

again and again 何度も, 繰り返し

I keep hearing that song again and again.
あの歌が繰り返し聞こえてくるんだ。

over again → OVER

then/there again しかしまた, また一方

Then again, why did he say such a thing?
しかしまた、どうして彼はそんなことを言ったのだろう?

against *prep.*

1 IN CONTRAST TO: …に対して, …と対照して, (**against the background of**) …を背景に

2 IN DISAGREEMENT WITH: (law, principle etc.) …に反対して, …に反して

3 IN COMPETITION WITH: …と, 対-

4 TO THE DISADVANTAGE OF: …に不利な, …に対する

5 IN COMPARISON WITH: (currency) …に換算して, …に対して

1 Yellow looks too bright against blue.
黄色は青に対して明るすぎます。

The tall building stood out against the blue sky.
その高いビルは、青空を背景にくっきりそびえていた。

The question should be considered against the background of social unrest.
この問題については、背景にある社会不安も考慮すべきです。

2 I am totally against the sale of weapons.
武器の販売には絶対に反対です。

Everyone's against him.
全員、彼に反対している。

Are you for or against it?
賛成ですか、それとも反対ですか?

It's against my principles.
それは私の主義に反します。

It was against my wishes, but I was forced to do it.
意志に反して、させられたんです。

It's against the law to litter.
道にごみを捨てるのは法律違反です。

3 Who are we competing against?
誰と競っているんだろう?

It's Brazil against Germany.
ブラジル対ドイツです。

4 racial discrimination against blacks
黒人に対する人種差別

All odds are against us.
私たちには勝ち目がない。

5 The dollar is at its lowest value against the yen in ten years.
ドルの円に対する為替レートは過去10年で最低です。

age

1 *n.* LENGTH OF LIFE: 年, ((*formal*)) 年齢

2 *n.* PERIOD: 時代

3 *n.* LONG TIME: (**ages**) 長い間, (**ages ago**) とっくに, ずっと前に

4 *v.* BECOME OLDER: 老ける, 年をとる

1 We are the same age.
私たちは同い年です。

According to her birth certificate, her age is seventy-two.
出生証明書によると、彼女の年齢は72です。

Mr. Takada won't let anyone know his age.

高田さんは誰にも自分の年を教えない。

When I was your age, I was working.
君の年ごろには、私は働いていたよ。

2 this age of new technology
新しい科学技術のこの時代

the Stone [Bronze, Iron] Age
石器 [青銅器, 鉄器] 時代

the Middle Ages 中世

3 They've known each other for ages.
彼らはお互い長い付き合いです。

I haven't eaten steak for ages.
もう長い間ステーキを食べていません。

"Have you done your homework yet?" "I did it ages ago."
「もう宿題はやったの？」
「とっくに済ませたよ」

4 He's aged since his wife died.
奥さんが亡くなってから、彼は老け込んだ。

♦ **age group** ***n.*** 同年代(の人々)

ageless ***adj.*** (of person) 年をとらない

aged ***adj.*** (old) 年をとった, (of wine, cheese) 熟成した

agency ***n.*** (business) 代理店, 取次店; (government) -庁, 官庁, 機関 [→ p. 1178]

a model agency モデルエイジェンシー

a travel agency 旅行代理店

agenda ***n.*** (plan) 予定, (list of points) 議題

What's on the agenda for this evening?
今夜の予定はどうなっていますか？

agent ***n.*** (person/company who acts on behalf of another) エイジェント, 代理人/代理店, (government agent) 役人, (spy) スパイ; (doer of an action) 行為者

aggravate ***v.*** (situation) 悪化させる, (person) いらいらさせる, (**be aggravated**) いらいらする, 頭にくる

aggression ***n.*** 攻撃, (military) 侵略

Aggression will not be tolerated.
不当な攻撃は許されないことだ。

aggressive ***adj.*** (of person) 強引な, 押しの強い, 挑戦的な, (ready to fight) ((*informal*)) けんか腰の, (of military) 好戦的な, 攻撃的な, (assertive) 積極的な

He's disliked because he's always aggressive.
あの人はいつも強引なので嫌われている。

an aggressive salesman
押しの強いセールスマン

I always get aggressive when I speak to him.
彼と話しているといつもけんか腰になってしまう。

aggressive military action
攻撃的な軍事行動

Be aggressive! 積極的にやりなさい。

agile ***adj.*** (nimble) すばしこい, 機敏な, (mentally) 頭の回転が速い

have an agile mind 頭の回転が速い

aging ***adj.*** 年をとった

n. (of wine) 熟成

agitate ***v.*** (upset) 動揺させる, (**agitate for**: industrial action etc.) 扇動する

agnostic ***n.*** 不可知論者

ago ***adv.*** …前(に)

I went to Russia for the first time 15 years ago.
15年前初めてロシアに行きました。

We should've arrived ten minutes ago.
10分前に着くはずだった。

How long ago was that?
それはどのくらい前のことですか？

"When did you speak with them?"
"Just a few moments ago."
「いつ彼らと話しましたか？」
「ほんのちょっと前です」

long ago 昔(は), (as written in fairy tales) 昔々, 今は昔

agony ***n.*** (pain) 激しい痛み, 激痛, 苦痛

She was in agony during childbirth.
彼女は出産の間、激痛に苦しんだ。

agree ***v.***

1 HAVE THE SAME OPINION: 同じ意見をもつ, 意見が合う, (reach a consensus) 意見が一致する, ((*formal*)) 合意する [→ DISAGREE], (**agree to / to do**) …に/…することに賛成する, ((*formal*)) …に/…することに同意する

2 CONSENT: ((*formal/written*)) 承諾する

3 SUIT/MATCH: (…に)合う

1 Do you agree with him?
彼と同じ意見ですか？

EXPRESSING AGREEMENT

There are several ways to express agreement in Japanese, just as there are in English. そのとおりです or, for emphasis, 全くそのとおりです is used in ordinary polite speech to mean, "That's right" or "I agree with what you have just said." Its informal counterparts are そうだよ, そうだね, and the feminine そうよ.

"This responsibility is his." 「責任は彼にあります」
"I agree." 「そのとおりです」

To express agreement when one's opinion/approval is sought of a plan/vote, use (私は)賛成です or, for emphasis, (私は)大賛成です, "I wholeheartedly agree."

"Let's try to negotiate with him." 「彼と交渉してみましょう」
"I'm for that." 「賛成です」

To say simply, "I think so, too," use 私もそう思います.

"I think it's a good idea." 「いい考えだと思います」
"I think so, too." 「私もそう思います」

Finally, to agree to do something that someone has asked of you—in other words, to express compliance with a request or an order—use はい, "OK."

"Could you copy this for me?" 「これをコピーしてくれますか」
"OK." 「はい」

Children find it hard to agree among themselves.
子供同士で意見をまとめるのは難しい。

Even doctors can't agree on the treatment.
医者の間でさえ、その治療について意見が合わない。

Finally, we agreed with the decision not to buy.
最終的に買わないということで意見が一致した。

The employers and employees agreed on a 2% salary increase.
雇用者側と従業員は2％の昇給に合意した。

2 The publishers agreed not to release photos of the juvenile delinquents.
出版社は未成年の犯罪者の写真を掲載しないことを承諾した。

3 The climate doesn't agree with me.
この気候は私に(は)合いません。

at the agreed time 決めた時間に

agreeable ***adj.*** (pleasant) 気持ちのいい, 愉快な

agreeable weather
気持ちのいい(お)天気

agreement ***n.*** (treaty) 協定, (contract) 契約, (promise) 約束; (consensus) 賛成, ((*formal/written*)) 同意, 合意, ((*formal*)) 一致

a trade agreement 貿易協定

Agreement was reached at the meeting.
会議で合意に達した。

agricultural ***adj.*** 農業の

agricultural products 農産物

agriculture ***n.*** 農業

ahead ***adv.***

1 IN FRONT OF/BEFORE: 前に, 先に
2 FORWARD: 前に進んで
3 ADVANCED: 進歩して, 発達して, 進んで
4 IN THE LEAD: リードして, 先行して
5 IN THE FUTURE: これから先

1 There were a lot of people ahead of me in line.
私の前に大勢の人が並んでいました。

It was so foggy I could only see a few meters ahead.
霧がとても濃くて、数メートル先しか見えなかった。

Please go ahead.
お先にどうぞ。

They've already gone on ahead of us.
彼らはもう先に行ってしまいました。

2 The car moved ahead slowly.
車はゆっくり前に進んだ。

The train went speeding ahead.
電車は速度を上げながら進んで行った。

3 She's well ahead of everyone else in the class.
彼女はクラスの誰よりも、勉強が先に進んでいます。

Medical science is much further ahead than it was 50 years ago.
医学は50年前と比べてずいぶん進歩している。

4 They're two goals ahead.
彼らは2点リードしている。

The ruling party is 5% ahead in the polls.
世論調査によると、与党の支持率のほうが5％上回っている。

5 Who knows what lies ahead?
これから先、何が起こるか誰にもわか

らないよ。

We should plan three years ahead.
3年先の計画を立てるべきです。

aid *n.* (assistance) 援助, (money) 支援金; (instrument that assists) 補助器具
v. 助ける, 援助する
economic aid 経済援助
overseas aid 海外援助
visual aids 視覚教材
a hearing aid 補聴器

AIDS *n.* エイズ

aikido *n.* 合気道

aim

1 *v.* POINT TOWARD: (aim A at/toward B) (AをBに)向ける, (take aim) ねらいを定める

2 *v.* INTEND: めざす

3 *n.* OBJECTIVE: 目的, 目標

1 He aimed a punch at me.
彼は僕を殴ろうとした。

I aimed at the target.
的にねらいを定めた。

2 What's he aiming at?
彼は何をめざしているのですか？

We aim to increase production by 30% next year.
来年は30%の増産をめざしています。

What time are you aiming to get there by?
何時までに向こうに着くつもりですか？

3 The aim is to help developing countries.
目的は開発途上国を援助することです。

What are your aims in life?
人生の目標は何ですか？

aimless *adj.* 目的のない, 当てのない

♦ **aimlessly** *adv.* 目的もなく, 当てもなく

air *n.* (atmosphere) 空気, 大気
v. (broadcast) 放映する, 放送する; (also **air out**: room) 風を通す, 換気する
air pollution 大気汚染

The ocean air was wonderful.
海辺の空気はすばらしかった。

I took a deep breath of air.
私は深呼吸した。

There was a peculiar smell in the air.
あたりに変なにおいが漂っていた。

The air stank of fried onions and hamburgers.
オニオンフライとハンバーガーのにおいがしていた。

The program was aired during prime time to catch the largest audience.
番組はできるだけ多くの視聴者を獲得しようと、ゴールデンタイムに放映された。

by air (by airplane) 飛行機で, (by airmail) 航空便で

on (the) air 放送中で, オンエアで

air-conditioned *adj.* (with air conditioner) エアコン付きの, (chilled by air conditioner) 冷房の効いた

air conditioner *n.* エアコン, 冷暖房機

air conditioning *n.* 冷暖房装置, 空調設備

Does the school have air conditioning?
学校には冷暖房装置がありますか？

aircraft *n.* 航空機, (airplane) 飛行機

♦ **aircraft carrier** *n.* 航空母艦, 空母

air force *n.* 空軍

airless *adj.* (stuffy) 息苦しい, むっとする, (poorly ventilated) 風通しの悪い

airletter *n.* 航空書簡

airline *n.* 航空会社

airmail *n.* エアメール, 航空便

airplane *n.* 飛行機

fly in an airplane 飛行機に乗る

fly an airplane 飛行機を操縦する

airport *n.* (large) 空港, (small) 飛行場, (in proper names) -空港

What's the fastest way of getting to the airport?
空港まで一番早い行き方は何ですか?

Kansai International Airport
関西国際空港

airship *n.* 飛行船

airtight *adj.* (sealed) 気密の, 密閉した

airy *adj.* (well ventilated) 風通しのいい

aisle *n.* 通路

an aisle seat 通路側の席

alarm *n.* (warning sound) 警報, (device) 警報器, 報知器; (fear) 恐怖, 不安; (clock) 目覚まし(時計)

a burglar alarm 盗難(防止)警報

The fire alarm went off by mistake.
間違って火災報知器が鳴った。

a feeling of alarm 不安感

I set the alarm for 6 o'clock.
目覚まし(時計)を6時にセットした。

The alarm didn't go off.
目覚まし(時計)が鳴らなかった。

♦**alarm clock** *n.* 目覚まし(時計)

alas *interj.* (sadly) ああ, 残念ながら

albatross *n.* (bird) アホウドリ

albeit *conj.* (even though) …ではあるが, (in spite of) …にもかかわらず

albino *n.* 白子

album *n.* アルバム

Their new album is excellent.
彼らの新しいアルバムはすばらしい。

alcohol *n.* (substance) アルコール, (alcoholic drinks) (お)酒

alcoholic *n.* アルコール依存症患者, ((*derogatory*)) アル中患者

alcoholism *n.* アルコール依存症, ((*derogatory*)) アルコール中毒, アル中

alcove *n.* (in Japanese home) 床の間 [→ picture of ROOM]

ale *n.* エール [→ BEER]

alert *adj.* (responsive to danger) 油断のない, (quick to respond) てきぱきした, 機敏な

n. 警戒, 警報

v. (warn) (…に) 警報を出す

Try to stay alert.
油断しないようにね。

algebra *n.* 代数

alias *n.* (different name) 別名, (false name) 偽名

alibi *n.* アリバイ

alien *n.* (foreigner) 外国人, 外人, (creature from space) 宇宙人, 異星人, エイリアン

adj. (foreign) 外国の, 外国人の; (be alien to) (…に)合わない, なじみがない

alight *v.* (from bus, train) (…から) 降りる, (from train) 下車する

align *v.* (make parallel) 一直線にそろえる, (wheels) 調整する; (**align oneself with**: ally with) …と提携する, …と手を結ぶ

alike *adj.* (similar) 似ている, (the same)

同じだ

adv. 同じように, 同様に

The brothers are very alike.
あの兄弟はよく似ています。

They're so alike in their ways.
彼らは、やり方がとても似ている。

alimony *n.* (after divorce) 離婚手当, (after separation) 別居手当

alive *adj.*

1 LIVING: 生きている, ((*formal*)) 生存している

2 LIVELY: 活気がある, にぎやかだ

3 SWARMING WITH: (be alive with) (…が) たくさんいる

1 Is this fish alive?
この魚は生きていますか？

I think his father is still alive.
((*polite*)) 彼のお父様はご健在のはずです。

According to the paper, five people are alive and ten are dead.
新聞には5人生存、10人死亡と出ていました。

2 Tokyo is really alive. There are so many exciting places.
東京はいつもにぎやかですよ。楽しめる所がたくさんあります。

3 The pond was alive with fish.
池には魚がたくさんいた。

come alive (of place) にぎやかになる, 活気づく

The fish market comes alive at 4 o'clock in the morning.
魚市場は朝4時から活気づく。

alkali *n.* アルカリ

all

1 *pron.* THE ENTIRETY: (of people) 皆, 全員, ((*informal*)) みんな, (of things) すべて, 全部

2 *adj.* THE ENTIRETY OF: すべての, 全部の, (**all the people**) 皆, ((*informal*)) みんな, (**all day**) 一日中, (**all one's life**) 生涯, (**all the time**) いつも

3 *pron., adv.* FOLLOWED BY A PREPOSITION: See examples below

4 *pron.* THE ONLY THING: …だけ, …ばかり

5 *adv.* COMPLETELY: 全く, 全部, すっかり, 完全に

1 They all live together in the same dorm.
彼らは皆いっしょに同じ寮に住んでいます。

All of us sat down and rested.
みんなで座って、休憩した。

I didn't understand it all.
全部はわかりませんでした。

All of which makes me think I'd rather not go.
そのどれをとっても行きたくないと思うんです。

2 She did it for all the people back home.
彼女は故郷のみんなのためにやったんです。

All the students in the class thought it was a great idea.
クラス全員がそれは名案だと思った。

He was a bachelor all his life.
彼は生涯独身だった。

3 The program was all about contraception.
その番組は避妊について詳しく取り上げていた。

There's pollution all along the coast.

沿岸全体が汚染されている。

He spilled beer all over the table.
彼はテーブル一面にビールをこぼした。

4 Is that all you have to say?
言いたいことはそれだけですか？

All you have to do is add honey.
はちみつを加えるだけです。

Give me a chance. That's all I want.
チャンスを下さい。私の願いはそれだけなんです。

All you do is complain.
あなたは文句ばかり言っているね。

5 We got wet all through.
すっかりぬれてしまった。

The movie would've been all over by the time we got there.
私たちが着くころには、映画は全部終わっていたでしょう。

all along (the entire while) ずっと, (from the beginning) 始めから

I knew all along that he was going to do that.
彼はそうするだろうと、始めからわかっていました。

all around (scattered about) あたり一面に, (in all respects) あらゆる点で

There were leaves all around.
あたり一面に葉っぱが落ちていた。

all at once → ONCE

all in all 大体, 全体的に, 全般的に見て

All in all, it's a good idea.
全般的に見て、それはいい考えです。

all or nothing 一か八か

It is all or nothing. There can be no quitting now.
一か八かです。今さらやめるわけにはいかない。

all right → ALL RIGHT

all together (みんな)いっしょに

All together now—one, two, three.
さあみんないっしょに、1、2、3。

all too あまりにも

I'm afraid that sort of attitude is all too common these days.
残念ながら、最近はそういう態度があまりにも多い。

not all すべて…とは限らない, 全部…わけではない

Not all dogs are friendly.
すべての犬が人なつっこいとは限らない。

Not all teachers are as strict as she is.
全部の教師が彼女ほど厳しいわけではない。

not at all → NOT

of all the (things, places, people) まさか, ((*used negatively*)) よりによって

Of all the places to meet! This is the last place I expected to see you.
まさかこんな所で会うなんて夢にも思わなかった。

Of all the members of the committee, they chose *him* as chair.
ほかにもたくさん委員はいるのに、彼らはよりによって彼を委員長に選んだ。

that's all それだけです

Well, that's all I wanted to say.
私が言いたかったのはそれだけです。

"Is there anything else you'd like to order?"
"No, that's all for the moment."
「ほかに何かご注文は？」
「いいえ、とりあえず、それだけです」

KANJI BRIDGE

全 ON: ぜん KUN: まった(く)	ALL
all over the world	全世界
all the members	全員
annihilation	全滅
complete works	全集
full responsibility	全責任
nationwide	全国的な
total amount	全額
total area	全域
total destruction	全壊
whole body	全身

Allah ***n.*** アラー

allegation ***n.*** 申し立て, 主張

allege ***v.*** 主張する

alleged ***adj.*** ...とされている

♦ **allegedly** ***adv.*** 申し立てによると, 伝えられるところ

allergy ***n.*** アレルギー, 異常過敏症

alleviate ***v.*** (pain) 緩和する, 軽減する, 楽にする, (situation) 改善する

The arrival of UN troops helped alleviate the situation.
国連軍の到着で事態は改善の方向に向かった。

alley ***n.*** (street) 路地, 裏通り, (between buildings) 通路

alliance ***n.*** (between countries/organizations) 同盟, (between companies) 提携

a business alliance 業務提携

in alliance with ...と同盟して, ...と提携して, ...と手を組んで

allied ***adj.*** 同盟した, 提携した

♦ **Allied Forces** ***n.*** 連合軍

alligator ***n.*** ワニ

allocate ***v.*** 割り当てる, 配分する

♦ **allocation** ***n.*** 割り当て, 配分

allow ***v.***

1 PERMIT: 許す, 許可する, (when asking/giving permission: **be allowed to do**) ...してもいい, (**be not allowed to do**) ...してはいけない, ...してはだめだ

2 INCLUDE IN PLANNING: (**allow for**) 見込む, 考えに入れる, 考慮する

1 Inmates are allowed to meet their parents for about ten minutes once a week.
受刑者たちは週に1度、10分ほど両親との面会を許されている。

"Are we allowed to go in?"
"No, only adults are."
「入ってもいいですか?」
「いいえ、おとなじゃないとだめです」

I was allowed to sit in on the meeting.
私は会議を傍聴させてもらった。

I'm not allowed to stay out after 10 o'clock.
10時以後は外出してはいけないんです。

You're not allowed to smoke in the office.
オフィスでたばこを吸ってはいけませんよ。

(*sign*) No Dogs Allowed 犬お断り

2 You have to allow enough time for changing trains.
電車の乗り換え時間も、十分見込んでおかなくてはいけませんよ。

We have to allow for human error.
人為的ミスも考慮しなければなりません。

allowance ***n.***

1 MONEY: (for special purpose) 手当,

(pocket money) (お)こづかい

2 INCLUSION: (in calculation) 控除額

1 an allowance for travel expenses
通勤手当

I still haven't received my travel allowance yet.
交通費をまだいただいていないのですが。

housing allowance 住宅手当

2 an allowance for tax deductions
税金控除額

make allowances for (view with exception/toleration) 大目に見る, (take into account) 考慮に入れる

alloy *n.* 合金

all right *adj.* (fine, OK) 大丈夫だ, (favorable, without problem) 順調だ; (indicating you have understood what sb has said) わかった, 了解した

interj. → OK

adv. (changing topic) じゃあ, それでは; (well) うまく, よく, ちゃんと, (safely) 無事に

"Are you all right?"
"Yes, I'm all right."
「大丈夫ですか？」
「はい、大丈夫です」

It was all right at first, but then it got worse.
最初のうちは順調でしたが、その後悪くなりました。

"How's it going?"
"All right, thanks."
「どうですか？」
「ええ、うまくいっています」

All right. I'm coming.
わかりました、すぐ行きます。

All right, let's get going now.
じゃあ、行きましょうか。

Is he doing all right in school?
あの子は学校でちゃんとやっている？

all-rounder *n.* 何でもできる人, 何でも上手な人, 器用な人, 万能選手

all-time *adj.* (record-breaking) 記録的な, (unprecedented) 空前の, かつてない

ally *n.* (country) 同盟国, (person) 味方, 同盟者

v. (ally with) (country) (…と)同盟する, (person) 結び付く

alma mater *n.* (school) 母校, 出身校

almost *adv.* ほとんど, ほぼ, …近く, (followed by a verb in the past tense) もう少しで, <-ますstem>+そうになった

You can buy almost anything in Hong Kong.
香港ではほとんど何でも買えます。

He's almost deaf.
彼はほとんど耳が聞こえません。

I spent almost a month in Hokkaido.
1ヵ月近くを北海道で過ごしました。

It cost almost a million yen.
100万円近くかかりました。

We almost reached the summit.
私たちはもう少しで頂上に到達できた。

I almost threw up.
吐きそうになった。

I was so tired I almost fell asleep.
あまりにも疲れていたので、眠ってしまうところだった。

alone *adj., adv.* (by oneself) 一人で, ((*formal*)) 単独で

Leave me alone.

一人にしておいて/ほっといて/((*feminine*)) 私にかまわないで。

He lives alone.
彼は一人で住んで[暮らしをして]いる。

let alone (to say nothing of) …は言うまでもなく, …どころか

You'll never be a music teacher, let alone a musician.
君はミュージシャンどころか、音楽教師にだってなれないよ。

along ***prep.*** …を, …に沿って, …沿いに

adv. (together) みんなで, いっしょに

walk along the street 通りを歩く

Go straight along this road and turn left at the end.
この道をまっすぐ行って、突き当たりを左に曲がってください。

There are trees along the river.
川沿いに木が並んでいます。

Well, let's go along and find out.
じゃあ、いっしょに行って見てみましょう。

He ran along beside me.
彼は私と並んで走りました。

all along → ALL

along with (together with) …といっしょに, (in the same way as) …と同じように

Along with her was her roommate.
彼女のルームメイトもいっしょだった。

alongside ***adv.*** 横に, 並んで, (near) 近くに

aloof ***adj.*** よそよそしい

Matsumoto is rather aloof.
松本さんは、どうもよそよそしい。

aloud ***adv.*** 声を/に出して

The teacher read the story aloud to the class.
先生はその物語を声に出して、生徒に読み聞かせました。

alphabet ***n.*** アルファベット

♦**alphabetical order** ***n.*** アルファベット順, (of kana syllabary) 50音順, あいうえお順

alphabetize ***v.*** アルファベット順にする

already ***adv.*** もう, すでに

I'm already behind in my work.
すでに仕事が遅れているんです。

Have you finished already?
もう終わったの？

I've already done my homework.
もう宿題を済ませた。

I've eaten already, thank you.
せっかくですが食事はもう済ませました。

Have you had lunch already?
もうお昼は食べた？

By the time I got to the theater, she was already there.
私が劇場に着いた時には、彼女はすでに来ていました。

It was early, but she had already set off.
まだ早かったが、彼女はすでに出発していた。

alright → ALL RIGHT

also ***adv.*** (additionally) …も, …もまた, そしてまた, それに

conj. その上, さらに

Hiroko also went.
弘子も行った。

She was also chosen.
彼女も選ばれました。

The trip was useful. It was also fun.

旅はためになったよ。それに楽しかった。

Not only is he rich, he's also handsome.
彼は金持ちで、その上ハンサムです。

alter ***v.*** (make different) 変える, 変更する, (garment) 仕立て直す, (become different) 変わる

We'll have to alter these plans.
この計画は変更しなくてはいけない。

Don't alter anything until I get back.
私が戻るまで何も変えないでください。

Have you altered the dress in some way?
ドレスをどこか仕立て直しましたか？

alteration ***n.*** (of plans) 変更, 修正, (to building) 改修, 改造, (to garment) (仕立て)直し

make an alteration 変更する

a slight [major] alteration to the plan
計画のわずかな [大幅な] 変更

alternate ***v.*** (alternate with) (…と) 交互にくる, 交替する, (alternate A with B) (AとBを) 交互にやる, (alternate between A and B) (AとBを) 行ったり来たりする

adj. (happening by turns) 交互の; (every other) 一つおきの; (alternative) 代わりの

alternative ***n.*** ほかの方法, 選択肢

adj. 代わりの, もう一つの, ほかの

We had no alternative but to go.
私たちは行くよりほかなかった。

Is there any alternative?
ほかに方法がありますか？

an alternative plan 代(替)案

♦ **alternatively** ***adv.*** (その)代わりに, あるいは

alternative medicine ***n.*** 代替医療

although ***conj.*** …けれど(も) [→ BUT, THOUGH]

Although he's rich, he's not happy.
彼は金持ちだけれど、幸せではない。

altitude ***n.*** (above sea level) 海抜, 標高, (of airplane) 高度

alto ***n.*** (voice) アルト

altogether ***adv.*** (in total) 全部で; (completely) 全く

Altogether, 20 students went to Canada.
全部で20名の学生がカナダに行った。

aluminum ***n.*** アルミニウム

always ***adv.*** (at all times) いつも, いつでも, しょっちゅう, (without fail) 必ず, (forever) いつまでも, 永遠に

He always gets to work on time.
彼はいつも時間どおりに出勤します。

I don't always get up this early. Today is an exception.
いつもはこんなに早く起きないんです。今日は特別です。

It's always raining when I come here.
ここに来る時はいつも雨が降っている。

They always talked about food and only food.
彼らはいつも食べ物のことばかり話していた。

You can always ask the teacher if you have any difficulties.
何かわからないことがあったらいつでも先生に聞けばいいんですよ。

There will always be poverty.
貧困はいつでも存在するでしょう。

My old man is always drinking.
うちのおやじは、しょっちゅう酒を飲んでいる。

Night always follows day.
夜は必ず昼の後に来る。

She'll always remember that experience.
彼女はいつまでもその経験を忘れないでしょう。

as always いつものとおり, いつものように, 相変わらず

not always いつも/必ずしも…とは限らない

First impressions aren't always right.
第一印象がいつも正しいとは限りません。

Expensive hotels aren't always comfortable.
高いホテルが必ずしも快適とは限らない。

Alzheimer's disease *n.* アルツハイマー病, (senile dementia) 老人性認知症

am → BE

A.M., a.m. *abbr.* (morning) 午前…

9:30 A.M. 午前9時半

amateur *n., adj.* アマチュア(の), 素人(の)

No, they're not professionals, they're amateurs.
いいえ、彼らはプロではなく、アマチュアです。

When it comes to acting, he's a real amateur.
演技となると、彼はずぶの素人です。

an amateur photographer
アマチュアのカメラマン

amaze *v.* びっくりさせる, 驚かせる

We were amazed at the friendliness of the locals.
私たちは地元の人々の親切さに驚いた。

amazement *n.* 驚き, 仰天

to my amazement 驚いたことに(は)

amazing *adj.* (surprising) 驚くべき, (marvelous) すばらしい

an amazing ability 驚くべき能力

It was an amazing (musical) performance.
とてもすばらしい演奏でした。

ambassador *n.* 大使

the Japanese ambassador to the United States 駐米日本大使

amber *n.* (substance) こはく, (color) こはく色

ambiguity *n.* あいまいさ, どっちつかず

ambiguous *adj.* はっきりしない, あいまいな, どっちつかずの

ambition *n.* 夢, 大望, 野心

He doesn't seem to have any ambition.
彼は全く野心をもっていないようだ。

ambitious *adj.* (of person) 大きな夢をもった, 野心のある, 出世欲のある, (of plan) 野心的な, 意欲的な

ambivalence *n.* アンビバレンス, 相反するもの

ambulance *n.* 救急車

call an ambulance 救急車を呼ぶ

amend *v.* (contract) 修正する, 改正する

amendment *n.* (to rule, law) 修正, 改正

amends *n.* 償い, 埋め合わせ

make amends 償う, 埋め合わせをする

amenity *n.* (**amenities**) (=facilities) 施設, 設備, (=comfortableness) 心地よさ, 快適さ

the basic amenities 基本的な施設

all the amenities of modern life
現代生活のあらゆる快適さ

America *n.* (United States) アメリカ, アメリカ合衆国, 米国, ((*in abbr.*)) 米

the Americas 南北アメリカ [アメリカ大陸]
North America 北米
Central America 中米
South America 南米

American *n.* (person) アメリカ人
adj. (of country, culture) アメリカの, 米国の, (of person) アメリカ人の
an American from Texas
テキサス州出身のアメリカ人
a Native American アメリカ先住民
a Japanese-American 日系アメリカ人
Are you Canadian or American?
(あなたは)カナダ人ですか、それともアメリカ人ですか？

amid *prep.* …の中に/で [→ AMONG]

amino acid *n.* アミノ酸

amiss *adj.* (wrong) 間違っている, おかしい

amoeba *n.* アメーバ

among *prep.* …の間で(は), …の中で, (surround by) …に囲まれて, …の中に
Rock music is very popular among teenagers.
ロックは、10代の若者の間でとても人気がある。
I found my umbrella among all the coats and hats.
コートや帽子の山の中から自分の傘を見つけた。
The children played happily among themselves.
子供たちは仲間同士で楽しそうに遊んでいました。
They divided the money among themselves.
彼らは自分たちでお金を分けた。
be among family
家族に囲まれている
Among the tall buildings, there was a small house built of wood.
高いビルに囲まれて、木造の小さな家があった。

amongst → AMONG

amount *n.* (quantity) 量, (of money) 金額, 総額, 額, (total) 合計, 総計
v. (**amount to**) …になる
the amount of rainfall 降雨量
I was amazed at the small amount of money she gets for her work.
彼女が仕事で得る収入の少なさに驚いた。
The bill amounted to a total of $300.
請求は合計 300ドルになった。
Whether you come or not, it amounts to the same thing.
来ても来なくても、同じことですよ。
Despite the hype, the film did not amount to very much.
大々的な宣伝にもかかわらず、その映画は大したことはなかった。

ampere *n.* アンペア

ample *adj.* (sufficient) 十分な
There was ample space in the car.
車の中には十分なスペースがあった。

amuse *v.* 楽しませる, 笑わせる [→ AMUSED], (**amuse oneself**) (=pass time) 時間を過ごす, (=kill time) 時間をつぶす
The boss did not seem amused by that comment.
上司はそのコメントを快く思っていないようだった。

amused *adj.* (be amused) 楽しむ ,

(speaking about sb else) 面白がる

They were all amused by his jokes.
みんな彼のジョークを面白がった。

amusement *n.* (fun) 楽しみ, (play) 遊び

♦ **amusement arcade** *n.* ゲームセンター

amusement park *n.* 遊園地

amusing *adj.* 面白い

an → A²

anal *adj.* (of anus) 肛門の; (of person) 極度に神経質な

analgesic *n.* 鎮痛薬

analog *n.* アナログ

analogy *n.* 類似(性)

analysis *n.* 分析

analyst *n.* アナリスト, (of news) 解説者

analytical *adj.* 分析的な

an analytical mind 分析的な考え方

analyze *v.* (scientifically) 分析する, (examine carefully) 検討する

Have you analyzed the results yet?
もう結果を分析しましたか？

anatomy *n.* (the body) 体; (study) 解剖学; (structure) 組織, 構造

ancestor *n.* 先祖, 祖先

anchor *n.* (for boat) いかり; (anchorperson) アンカー, ニュースキャスター, (in relay) アンカー

v. (make secure) しっかりと固定する

drop anchor いかりを下ろす

lie at anchor 停泊する

anchovy *n.* カタクチイワシ, (canned) アンチョビー

ancient *adj.* (belonging to ancient history) 古代の, (very old) 大昔の, 古来の, かなり古い, (old-style) 旧式の

ancient civilization(s) 古代文明

ancient ruins 古代遺跡

This wood-block print looks ancient.
この木版画はかなり古そうだ。

and *conj.*

1 CONNECTING INCLUSIVE PAIRS/SETS: …と…

2 NONINCLUSIVE: …や…, …と…

3 SIMULTANEOUS ACTION: …しながら

4 SEQUENTIAL ACTION: (and then) …してから, そして, それから

5 BUT: …けれど(も), …が

6 INTENSIVE REPETITION: …も…も

7 LINKING ADJECTIVES: <-てform of adj.>

8 ADDED TO: …足す…

9 LINKING NUMBERS: See examples below

10 LINKING ACTIONS: …したり…したりする

1 a knife and fork ナイフとフォーク
cats and dogs 犬と猫
ham and eggs ハムエッグ
men and women 男女
black and white 白黒

2 We took sandwiches, fruits, and drinks for the picnic.
ピクニックにサンドイッチや果物、飲み物を持って行きました。

We have a cat and a puppy, too.
私たちは猫とそれに子犬も飼っています。

3 She was reading the paper and eating a doughnut.
彼女は新聞を読みながらドーナツを食べていました。

4 He ate some cheese and then served himself something to drink.
彼はチーズを食べてから飲み物をいれた。

She stopped walking and turned toward

me.
彼女は立ち止まって、そして振り向いた。

I took a bath and then had a cup of coffee.
おふろに入って、それからコーヒーを飲んだ。

5 She promised to write to us and didn't.
彼女は手紙を書くと約束したけれど、くれませんでした。

He studied hard and still failed the exam.
彼は一生懸命勉強したが、それでも試験に落ちた。

6 time and time again 何度も何度も

ages and ages ago 何年も前 [ずっと昔]

more and more ますます

7 nice and warm 快適で暖かい

This is a quiet and peaceful village.
ここは静かで平和な村ですね。

He's cool and handsome.
彼はかっこよくてハンサムです。

8 Two and two make four.
2足す2は4。

9 My daughter is three and a half today.
娘は今日で3歳半です。

How old is he? Two and four months?
あの子はいくつ？ 2歳4ヵ月だったっけ？

10 I spent the vacation swimming, sunbathing, playing tennis, and so on.
休みは泳いだり、日光浴したり、テニスをしたりして過ごした。

anemia *n.* 貧血, 貧血症

angel *n.* 天使

anger *n.* 怒り

v. 怒らせる

in anger 怒って

angina *n.* 狭心症

angle *n.* 角, 角度; (standpoint) 見方, 観点, 立場, 視点

It's a right angle.
それは直角です。

a 45-degree angle 45度の角度

What's the author's angle?
著者の視点はどのようなものですか？

angry *adj.* 怒った, 腹を立てた, (**get angry**) 怒る, 腹を立てる, ((*informal*)) 頭にくる

Are you angry with me?
((*feminine*)) 私のこと怒ってる？

The teacher was angry with the class.
先生は生徒たちにカンカンに怒っていた。

She was angry at him for being stood up.
彼女は、彼にデートをすっぽかされて腹を立てていた。

I didn't mean to make you angry.
怒らせるつもりはなかった。

The comments in the newspaper made me angry.
新聞の論評に腹が立った。

The dog barking next door made her angry.
隣の(家の)犬がほえるので彼女は頭にきた。

angst *n.* (anxiety) 不安, (dread) 恐怖

animal *n.* 動物, (monster) 獣

adj. 動物的な

wild animals 野生動物

domestic animals 家畜

animal instinct(s) 動物的本能

♦ **animal rights** *n.* 動物の権利

animation *n.* アニメ(ーション)

anime *n.* (Japanese animation) アニメ

ankle ***n.*** 足首 [→ picture of BODY]

sprain one's ankle
足首をくじく[ねんざする]

annex ***n.*** (to building) 別館, 離れ

anniversary ***n.*** 記念日

Today is our fifteenth (wedding) anniversary.
今日は私たちの15 回目の結婚記念日です。

announce ***v.*** (declare) 発表する, (to public) 公表する

It was announced that the prime minister has been admitted to the hospital.
首相が入院したことが発表されました。

When are you going to announce your engagement to Pamela?
パメラさんとの婚約はいつ公表するんですか？

announcement ***n.*** (declaration) 発表, (public announcement) 公表, (bulletin) 告示, (notice) お知らせ, (over loudspeaker) 案内

announcer ***n.*** アナウンサー

annoy ***v.*** (irritate) いらいらさせる, (trouble) 悩ます, (cause to feel displeasure) いやがらせる, (be a nuisance to) 煩わせる, (**be annoyed**) いらいらする, ((*informal*)) むっとする

He really annoys me.
あの人にはほんとにいらいらする。

The manager only said it to annoy Ms. Maeda.
部長は前田さんに、いやがらせで言ったんですよ。

Is the noise of the fan annoying you?
換気扇の音がうるさいですか？

I was annoyed at missing my bus.
私はバスに乗り遅れてむっとした。

The boss was particularly annoyed at his not wearing a tie.
上司は彼がネクタイをしていないことが特に気に入らなかった。

annoying ***adj.*** 気にさわる, 迷惑な, うっとうしい, (noisy) うるさい

Cut it out! That is really annoying.
やめて！ ほんとにうるさいから。

annual ***adj.*** (every year) 毎年の, 年 1 回の, (of event) 恒例の, (of or for one year) 1 年間の, 1 年分の
n. (publication) 年報, 年鑑

an annual event 恒例の行事
an annual salary 年収
an annual bonus 年間賞与

anode ***n.*** 陽極

anonymous ***adj.*** 匿名の

an anonymous phone call 匿名の電話

anorexia ***n.*** 拒食症

another ***adj.*** (a second...) もう一つの, (a different...) 別の, ほかの, (an additional...) あと ..., もう ..., (of helping of food/drink) (...の) お代わり

another person 別の人

Oh, and there's another thing—don't forget to mail the letters.
そうそう、それともう一つ、手紙を出すのを忘れないで。

OK, he's not a liar. Let's put it another way—he's economical with the truth.
わかった、彼はうそつきじゃない。別の言い方をしよう——彼は事実を出し惜しみしてるんだ。

We need another four chairs.
椅子があと四つ必要です。

We had to wait another ten minutes.
もう10分待たなければならなかった。

I'd like another bowl of rice, please.
ご飯のお代わりを下さい。

one after another 次から次へと

He smokes one cigarette after another.
あの人は次から次へとたばこを吸う。

one another (お)互いに

They didn't want to talk to one another after that.
そのあと、二人は(互いに)口をききたがりませんでした。

answer

1 *v.* RESPOND TO: (question) (…に) 答える, (=on exam) (…に) 解答する, (letter) (…に)返事を出す, (phone)(…に)出る, (**be answered**: prayers) かなう

2 *n.* RESPONSE: 返事, 答え, 回答

3 *n.* SOLUTION: (to exam problem) 解答, (to social problem) 解決策

4 *v.* SOLVE: 解決する

1 I couldn't answer the question.
質問に答えられなかった。

I never answered her letter.
彼女の手紙に一度も返事を出さなかった。

He never answered my e-mail.
彼は一度もメールの返事をくれなかった。

Could you answer the phone, please?
電話に出ていただけませんか？

It's OK. I'll answer the door.
いいですよ。私が出ますから。

Did you answer the advertisement?
その募集(広告)に応募しましたか？

One day my prayers will be answered.
いつか私の願いがかなうでしょう。

2 We are waiting for an answer from him.
彼からの返事を待っているんです。

Her answer was ambiguous.
彼女の答えはあいまいだった。

That's not the answer I was hoping for.
それは望んでいた回答ではありません。

3 The correct answer is… 正解は…

Two answers out of five were correct.
5問中2問が正解でした。

There is no easy answer to the problems of crime and poverty.
犯罪や貧困という問題には、簡単な解決策はありません。

4 Does that answer your problem?
それで問題は解決しますか？

in answer to (question) …に答えると, (demand) …に応じて

In answer to your question, yes, we do offer discounts.
ご質問に答えますと、確かに割引を申し出ています。

♦ **answer back** *v.* 口答えする

answering machine *n.* 留守番電話

ant *n.* アリ, 蟻

Antarctic *n., adj.* 南極(の), 南極圏(の)

♦ **Antarctic Ocean** *n.* 南極海, 南氷洋

Antarctica *n.* 南極大陸

antenna *n.* (on TV, radio) アンテナ [→ picture of HOUSE]; (on insect) 触覚, 角

anthracite *n.* 無煙炭

anthrax *n.* 炭疽(病)

anti- *pref.* 反-, 対-, 抗-

antigovernment demonstrations

反政府デモ

antisocial behavior 反社会的行動

antiabortion 中絶反対

antibiotic *n.* 抗生物質

antibody *n.* 抗体

anticipate *v.* (foresee) (…があると) 思う, 予想する, (expect) 期待する, (look forward to) 楽しみに待つ

I don't anticipate any trouble at the meeting.
会議は特に問題なくいくと思う。

Inflation rose faster than anticipated.
予想以上に速くインフレが進んだ。

I had anticipated the question.
その質問を予想していた。

We anticipate good news.
いい知らせを期待しています。

anticipation *n.* (excitement) 期待

in anticipation of …を期待して, …を見越して

antique *n.* アンティーク, 骨董品

adj. 古風な, 時代物の, 古い

♦ **antique dealer** *n.* 古美術商

antique shop *n.* アンティークの店, 骨董品店, 骨董屋

antiseptic *adj.* 殺菌力のある

n. 消毒薬, 防腐剤

antonym *n.* 反意語

anus *n.* 肛門

anxiety *n.* 心配, 不安

anxious *adj.* (worried) 心配している, (**anxious to do**) …したい, (speaking about sb else) …したがる

He's anxious about his mother.
彼はお母さんのことを心配しているんだ。

The children are anxious to get home.
子供たちは帰りたがっている。

any

NOTE: Often not translated into Japanese.

1 *adj., pron.* IN QUESTIONS AND CONDITIONAL CLAUSES: (in reference to a thing) 何か, どれか, (in reference to a person) 誰か, (some, a little) 少し, いくらか

2 *adj., pron.* IN NEGATIVE SENTENCES: 全く, (in reference to a thing) 少しも, 何も, (in reference to a person) 誰も, 一人も

3 *adj., pron.* IN AFFIRMATIVE SENTENCES: (in reference to a thing) どんな…でも, どの…でも, どれでも, (in reference to a person) 誰でも, (in reference to a place) どこでも

4 *adv.* A LITTLE: 少しは, (in negative sentences) 少しも

1 "Do you have any change?"
"No, I don't have any."
「小銭はありますか？」
「いいえ、ありません」

Did any of you see that film?
誰かその映画を見た人はいますか？

If you hear any interesting news, please let me know.
何か面白いニュースを聞いたら、ぜひ教えてください。

"Have you done any work?"
"No, I haven't done any at all."
「少しは仕事をしましたか？」
「いいえ、全くしていません」

2 I don't have any change.
小銭は全く持っていない。

I couldn't find any of the books I was looking for at that bookstore.

あの書店では、探していた本は1冊も見つからなかった。

There aren't any good teachers at that university.
あの大学にはいい先生は一人もいない。

3 Any box will do.
どんな箱でもかまいません。

Any one of them could have been the culprit.
彼らの中の誰が犯人だったとしても、おかしくない。

You can buy them at any store.
どこの店でも買えるよ。

4 Do you feel any better?
少しはよくなりましたか？

Crying about it is not going to do any good.
泣いたって、何にもよくはならないよ。

I can't run any further.
もうこれ以上走れない。

anybody ***pron.***

1 IN QUESTIONS AND CONDITIONAL CLAUSES: 誰か

2 IN NEGATIVE SENTENCES: 誰も, 誰にも

3 IN AFFIRMATIVE SENTENCES: 誰でも, 誰だって

1 Is anybody there?
誰かいますか？

Is anybody else coming?
ほかに誰か来ますか？

If anybody asks, tell them I've gone out.
誰かが尋ねたら、私は出かけたと言ってください。

2 There wasn't anybody there.
そこには誰もいなかった。

I didn't see anybody I knew at the party.
パーティーでは、知っている人に誰にも出会わなかった。

3 Anybody can do that.
それは誰でもできるよ。

I would happily go with anybody.
誰とでも喜んで行きます。

Anybody can make a mistake.
誰だって間違いはおかします。

The noise was enough to wake anybody.
誰もが目を覚ますほど、すごい音だった。

You can bring anybody you like.
誰でも連れて来ていいですよ。

anyhow ***adv.*** (in any case) いずれにしても, とにかく, ((*informal*)) どっちみち, (changing subject) それはそうと, (even so) それでも

Anyhow, why don't you try asking her?
とにかく、彼女に聞いてみたらどう？

It's too late now, anyhow.
どっちみち、もう遅すぎます。

anymore ***adv.*** もう

I don't work there anymore.
もうそこでは働いていません。

He's not going out with her anymore.
彼は彼女とはもう付き合っていない。

anyone → ANYBODY

anything ***pron.***

1 IN QUESTIONS AND CONDITIONAL CLAUSES: 何か

2 IN NEGATIVE SENTENCES: 何も

3 IN AFFIRMATIVE SENTENCES: 何でも, どんな物/ことでも

1 Has anything happened?
何かあったのですか？

If you want anything, let me know.

何か欲しい物があったら言ってください。

Don't you have anything better than this?

これよりいい物はありませんか？

2 There isn't anything to be worried about.

何も心配することはない。

He doesn't understand anything.

彼は何もわかってない。

I couldn't find anything cheaper.

これ以上安い物は見つからなかった。

3 I'll eat anything.

私は何でも食べます。

He'd do anything for money.

彼はお金のためなら何でもするでしょう。

Anything is better than staying another night here.

どんなことも、ここでもう１泊するよりましだ。

anything but …以外は何でも

I'll do anything but that.

それ以外のことなら何でもします。

for anything どんなことがあっても, どうしても

I wouldn't do that for anything.

どんなことがあっても、そんなことをやろうとは思わないよ。

anytime *adv.* (whenever) いつでも, どんな時でも, (any time of day) 何時でも; (soon) そろそろ

Anytime will do.

いつでもかまいません。

Anytime before 10 o'clock is fine.

10時前でしたらいつでもけっこうです。

You can come anytime you like.

お好きな時にいつでもいらしてください。

He should arrive anytime now.

彼はもうそろそろ来るはずだ。

anyway *adv.* (in any case) いずれにしても, とにかく, ((*informal*)) どっちみち, (changing subject) それはそうと, (even so) それでも, (by whatever means) どうしても

anywhere *adv.*

1 IN QUESTIONS AND CONDITIONAL CLAUSES: どこかへ/に, ((*informal*)) どっかへ/に

2 IN NEGATIVE SENTENCES: どこへも, どこにも

3 IN AFFIRMATIVE SENTENCES: どこでも, どこへでも, どこにでも

1 Has he gone anywhere in particular?

彼は、どこか特定の所へ行ったのですか？

If he comes anywhere near me, he's in trouble.

私に近づいたら、彼は痛い目にあうよ。

2 I don't think he's gone anywhere.

彼はどこへも行っていないと思う。

I can't find my glasses anywhere.

めがねがどこにも見当たらない。

3 Oh, just put it down anywhere.

ああ、どこでもいいから置いておいてください。

Anywhere will do, as long as I'm a thousand miles away from him.

彼からできるだけ遠く離れられれば、どこでもかまわない。

apart *adv.* (at a distance) 離れて, (separately) 別々に, (into/to pieces) ばらばらに

Their homes are not far apart.

彼らの家はそんなに離れていない。

They are living apart.
彼らは別々に暮らしている。

Why don't you try cutting it apart?
切ってみたらどう？

All the pieces had fallen apart.
部品は全部ばらばらになっていた。

apart from (not counting, aside from) …は別として, …を除けば

Apart from the noise of the nearby traffic, it's a good apartment.
近くの道路がうるさいことを除けば、いいアパートです。

live apart (of separated married couple) 別居する

apartment *n.* アパート, マンション [→ picture below]

live in a luxury apartment
高級マンションに住む

an apartment for rent 貸室

♦ **apartment complex** *n.* 団地

ape *n.* サル, 類人猿

apologize *v.* 謝る, わびる [→ SORRY 1]

He apologized for his mistake.
彼は間違いを謝った [あやまちをわびた]。

Kenji apologized to his mother for breaking the dish.
賢治は母親にお皿を割ったことを謝った。

The conductor apologized for the delay.
車掌は電車の遅れをわびた。

Apologize to her!
((*masculine*)) 彼女に謝れよ！

I must apologize 申し訳ありません

apology *n.* (お)わび, 謝罪

a written apology わび状

apostrophe *n.* アポストロフィ

appalling *adj.* ひどい

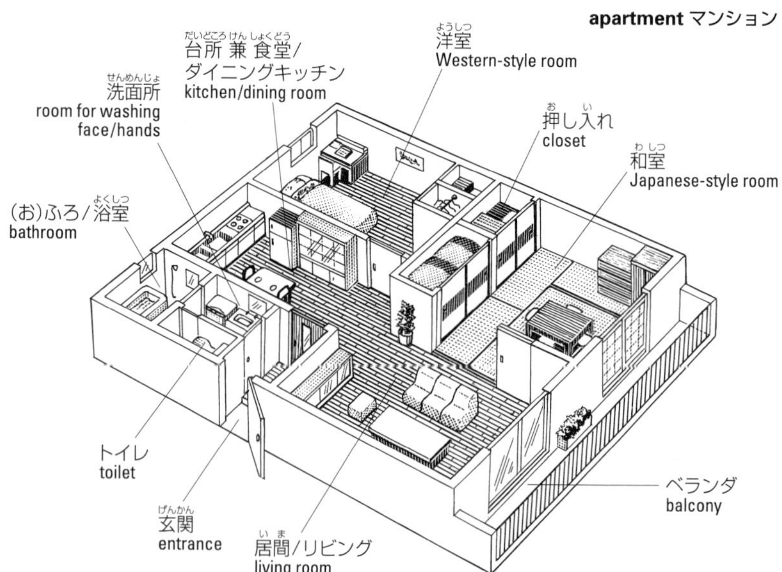

apparatus ***n.*** 器具, 装置

apparel ***n.*** 服, 服装, アパレル

apparent ***adj.*** (clear) 明らかな, 明白な, (seeming) …ような

It was apparent from what he said that he was not interested.
彼の発言からして、関心がないことは明らかだった。

He sighed with apparent disgust and left the room.
彼はうんざりしたようにため息をついて、部屋を出て行った。

apparently ***adv.*** (どうやら)…らしい, …よう, …みたい [→ LOOK 4, SEEM]

Apparently he is very pleased with the result.
どうやら彼はその結果を大変喜んでいるようです。

"I thought he was a Spaniard."
"Apparently not."
「彼はスペイン人だと思っていました」
「そうじゃないみたいですよ」

appeal

1 ***v.*** MAKE A REQUEST: 願う, 懇願する, (to public) 訴える, 呼びかける, アピールする

2 ***v.*** BE ATTRACTIVE: (appeal to) (=be attractive to) (…にとって) 魅力がある, (…は) 気に入る, (=be popular among) (…に) 人気がある, うける

3 ***v.*** FIGHT A COURT'S DECISION: 控訴する

4 ***n.*** ATTRACTIVENESS: 魅力

5 ***n.*** POPULARITY: 人気

6 ***n.*** REQUEST FOR A NEW TRIAL: 訴え

1 The parents appealed to the principal not to expel the boy.
両親は息子を退学させないよう、校長に懇願した。

2 His art work really appeals to me.
彼の作品は本当に気に入っています。

These comics appeal to adults as well as children.
これらの漫画は子供だけでなく、おとなにも人気がある。

This type of song appeals to teenagers.
こういう歌は10代の若者にうける。

3 They appealed the decision of the court.
彼らは裁判の判決を不服として控訴した。

4 What is the appeal in that?
その魅力は何ですか？

sex appeal セックスアピール

5 have appeal 人気がある

6 Their appeal was turned down.
彼らの訴えは却下された。

appealing ***adj.*** (of food) おいしそうな, (of idea) 興味のわく

appear ***v.***

1 COME INTO VIEW: 現れる, 姿を現す, 出る, 見えてくる, (of actor on stage, product on market) 登場する, (of name on list, in magazine/newspaper) 載る, (of person on TV, in film) 出る

2 SEEM: …ように見える, …らしい, …ようだ, …みたいだ

1 They appeared out of nowhere.
彼らはどこからともなく現れた。

At last the train appeared in the distance.
ようやく遠くに電車が見えてきた。

Computers began to appear in offices in the 1970s.

コンピューターがオフィスに登場し始めたのは70年代です。

His name doesn't appear on this list.
このリストに彼の名前は載っていません。

She has appeared on lots of TV shows.
彼女はたくさんのテレビ番組に出ている。

2 It appears that they are going to sell the house after all.
結局彼らは家を売るつもりらしい。

She appeared to be confident.
彼女は自信があるようだった。

KANJI BRIDGE

出 ON: しゅつ, すい KUN: で(る), だ(す) | APPEAR

appear	出現する
appear (at meeting)	出席する
appear (in court)	出廷する
appear (of book on market)	出版する
appear (on stage, TV)	出演する

appearance ***n.*** (of building, street) 外観, (of person) 外見, 見かけ; (arrival) 出現

I don't know why you worry so much about your appearance.
なぜそんなに見かけを気にするのかわからない。

put in an appearance (at party) 顔を出す, (at meeting) 出席する

I haven't been there for a long time, so I'd better put in an appearance.
長いこと行っていないから、顔を出したほうがよさそうだ。

appendicitis ***n.*** 盲腸(炎), 虫垂炎

appendix ***n.*** (to book) 付録, 追加; (organ) 盲腸, 虫垂

appetite ***n.*** 食欲, (desire) 欲求

have an appetite 食欲がある

Browsing through all these cookbooks has given me an appetite.
こういう料理本をパラパラめくっているうちに、食欲がわいてきた。

His appetite for adventure remains as strong as ever.
彼は相変わらず冒険心がとても強い。

applaud ***v.*** (…に) 拍手かっさいする

applause ***n.*** 拍手かっさい

apple ***n.*** リンゴ

♦**apple juice** ***n.*** リンゴジュース

apple pie ***n.*** アップルパイ

appliance ***n.*** 器具

applicable ***adj.*** 当てはまる, 適用できる

applicant ***n.*** (for school) 出願者, 志願者, (for job) 応募者

application ***n.*** (request) 申し込み, 申請, (letter of application) 申込書, 申請書, 願書; (of paint etc.) 塗ること; (medicine) 外用薬, (cosmetic) 化粧品; (software) アプリケーション

an application for a work permit
労働許可証の申請書

Did you mail your application in time?
期限内に願書を送りましたか?

♦**application form** ***n.*** 申込用紙, 申請書

applied ***adj.*** 応用の

applied linguistics 応用言語学

apply ***v.***

1 REQUEST IN WRITING: 申し込む, (turn in an application) 申込書/申請書/願書を出す, (for job) 応募する, (for school) 出願する

2 BE RELEVANT: 適用される, 当てはまる

3 PUT TO USE: 応用する, 当てはめる

4 PAINT/SPREAD ON: つける, 塗る, 当てる

1 Three scientists from my university applied for research grants this year.
今年、うちの大学からは3人の科学者が研究助成金を申し込みました。

A lot of people applied for the job.
たくさんの人がその仕事に応募した。

Are you going to apply for the job?
その職に応募するつもりですか？

How many schools have you applied to?
いくつの大学に出願したの？

apply for a patent 特許を申請する

2 The new law applies to all taxpayers.
新しい法律はすべての納税者に適用されます。

3 Charles Babbage's ideas were applied to modern computer technology.
チャールズ・バベッジの考えは現代のコンピューター技術に応用された。

4 You ought to apply a little antiseptic.
少し消毒液をつけたほうがいい。

appoint *v.* (assign) 指名する, (to public office) 任命する

Who are you going to appoint as the new captain of the team?
チームの新しいキャプテンに誰を指名するんですか？

Ikeda was appointed prime minister.
池田氏が首相に任命された。

♦ **appointed** *adj.* (of place, time) 約束の

the appointed time 約束の時間

appointment *n.* (commitment) 約束, (previous commitment) 先約, (business engagement) アポ(イント), (doctor's appointment) 診察予約; (to office) 任命

I have an appointment at 5 o'clock.
5時に約束があるんです。

I've canceled the appointment.
約束はキャンセルした。

What time's the appointment?
アポイントは何時ですか？

Could I make an appointment to meet you?
お会いする時間を取っていただけませんか？

The appointment with the doctor is for 6 o'clock.
診察予約時間は6時です。

make an appointment (make a reservation) 予約する, (make a business appointment) アポ(イント)を取る

appraisal *n.* 評価

appraise *v.* (assess) 評価する

appreciate *v.*

1 FEEL GRATEFUL FOR: (…に) 感謝する, (…を) ありがたく思う

2 UNDERSTAND: わかる, 理解する, (recognize the worth of) 評価する, 認める, (art) 鑑賞する

3 RISE IN VALUE: 上がる

1 I really appreciated your help today.
今日は手伝っていただいて、本当に<u>感謝しています</u> [ありがたかったです]。

We appreciate all you've done for us.
私たちのためにやっていただいたことすべてに感謝しています。

2 Can you appreciate how much work went into this?
これにどれだけの労力がつぎ込まれ

たか、わかっていますか？

He just does not appreciate how hard she works.
彼女がどんなによく働くか、彼は全くわかっていない。

It would be good if young people could be taught to appreciate art.
若い人に、芸術を鑑賞することを知ってもらえたらいいのですが。

3 The cost of housing will continue to appreciate.
住宅費は今後も上がり続けるでしょう。

appreciation *n.* (gratitude) 感謝, (understanding) 理解, (of art) 鑑賞; (rise in value) 上昇

apprentice *n.* 見習い, ((*old-fashioned*)) 徒弟

approach

1 *v.* GET CLOSER TO: (…に) 近づく, 接近する, (problem) (…に) 取り組む, (approach A about B) (AにBについて) 話をもちかける, アプローチする

2 *n.* METHOD: 接近法, アプローチ

3 *n.* DRAWING NEAR: 近づくこと, 接近, (of aircraft to runway) 進入

4 *n.* ACCESS ROAD: 入口

1 We approached the house from the front.
私たちは正面から家に近づいた。

The end of the term is approaching.
学期末が近づいて来ている。

Typhoon 12 is approaching.
台風 12 号が接近しています。

We need to approach this problem differently.
この問題には別の方法で取り組むべきだ。

I was approached by a headhunter who asked if I would prefer to work for another company.
別の会社で仕事をしたくはないかと、ヘッドハンターから話をもちかけられた。

2 What sort of approach should we adopt?
どのようなアプローチを取るべきだろうか？

3 I didn't notice his approach.
彼が近づいて来ていることに気づかなかった。

appropriate *adj.* 適当な, 適切な, (just right) ちょうどいい, (appropriate to/for: suitable to/for) …に合っている

I think it was an appropriate decision.
適切な決定だったと思う。

Is the text appropriate to the abilities of the students?
テキストは生徒の実力に合っていますか？

approval *n.* (authorization) 許し, 許可, 承認, (agreement) 賛成, ((*formal*)) 同意

Did you get your parents' approval?
ご両親の許しをもらいましたか？

You'll need to get approval first.
まずは許可を得る必要があります。

With your approval, we would like to proceed.
(あなたの)同意がいただけるようであれば、進めたいと思います。

♦ **approval rating** *n.* 支持率

approve *v.* (allow) 許可する, 承認する, (consent to) (…に) 賛成する, ((*formal*)) 同意する, (pass: bill) 可決する

The bill was approved by the Upper House.

法案は上院で可決された。

♦ **approved** ***adj.*** (of plan) 承認された

approximate ***adj.*** 大体の, おおよその

What's the approximate time of arrival?
到着時刻は大体何時ごろですか？

approximately ***adv.*** (大体)…くらい/ぐらい, ほぼ, ((*formal*)) およそ, 約

It was approximately midnight.
大体、夜中の12時くらいだった。

The newspaper has a daily circulation of approximately two million.
その新聞は、1日の発行部数が約200万部です。

apricot ***n.*** (fruit) アンズ, 杏, アプリコット, (tree) アンズの木

April ***n.*** 4月, 四月

♦ **April Fool's Day** ***n.*** エイプリルフール, 4月ばかの日

apron ***n.*** エプロン, 前掛け

apt ***adj.*** (**be apt to do**) …しそうだ; (fitting) ふさわしい, 適した

aquarium ***n.*** (tank for fish) 水槽, (building) 水族館

Aquarius ***n.*** (the Water Bearer) 水瓶座

Arab ***n.*** (person) アラブ人

adj. (of country, culture) アラブの, アラビアの, (of person) アラブ人の

Arabic ***n., adj.*** (language) アラビア語(の)

♦ **Arabic numeral** ***n.*** アラビア数字, 算用数字

arc ***n.*** (curving shape) 弧, 円弧

arcade ***n.*** (game center) ゲームセンター; (shopping arcade) 商店街

arch ***n.*** アーチ; (of foot) 足の甲

archaeologist ***n.*** 考古学者

archaeology ***n.*** 考古学

archbishop ***n.*** (Catholic) 大司教, (Protestant) 大主教

archery ***n.*** (Western-style) アーチェリー, (Japanese-style) 弓道, 弓術

archipelago ***n.*** 列島, 群島

architect ***n.*** 建築家, 建築技師

architecture ***n.*** 建築, (subject of study) 建築学, (architectural style) 建築様式

archive ***n.*** (**archives**) (= collection of documents) 公文書, 古い記録, (= building) 公文書館, 記録保管所

Arctic ***n., adj.*** 北極(の), 北極圏(の)

♦ **Arctic Circle** ***n.*** 北極圏

Arctic Ocean ***n.*** 北極海

are → BE

area ***n.*** (region) 地方, 地域, (of land, for living) 土地, (place) 場所, (district, precinct) 地区, エリア, (part of a particular place) 部分; (surface measure) 面積; (field of knowledge) 分野

the Kanto area 関東地方

This toy store is the biggest in the area.
このおもちゃ屋が、この辺では一番大きい。

This is a residential area.
ここは住宅街です。

This area is going to be developed into a shopping center.
この地区はショッピングセンターとして開発される予定です。

I'd like you to clear this area of the garden.
庭のこの部分をきれいにしてください。

The area was about thirty hectares.

A

面積は約30ヘクタールだった。

That is outside his area of expertise.
その分野は彼の専門外です。

♦ **area code** *n.* 市外局番

arena *n.* (for sports) アリーナ, 競技場

arguable *adj.* 議論の余地がある

arguably *adv.* 間違いなく, …と言える

argue *v.* (quarrel) 言い争う, 口げんかする, もめる, 口論する, (debate) 議論する

Will you please stop arguing?
けんかするのはやめてくれませんか?

They were arguing about whose turn it was to do the dishes.
彼らは皿を洗うのは誰の番かで、もめていた。

They're arguing the pros and cons of legalizing marijuana.
彼らはマリファナを合法化することの是非を議論している。

argument *n.* (quarrel) 口論, 口げんか, (debate) 議論, (reason) 論拠, (assertion) 主張

have an argument 口げんかをする

a strong [weak] argument
有力な [弱い] 論拠

argumentative *adj.* (quarrelsome) 理屈っぽい, けんか腰の

Aries *n.* (the Ram) 牡羊座

arise *v.* (come about) 生じる, 起こる

If any other problem should arise, let me know.
ほかに何か問題が起こったら、知らせてください。

aristocracy *n.* (**the aristocracy**: the nobility) 貴族, (system of government) 貴族政治, (country) 貴族政治の国

arithmetic *n.* 算数, 計算, (mental arithmetic) 暗算

arm¹ *n.* 腕, 手 [→ picture of BODY], (of chair) ひじ掛け, (of jacket) そで

Takeshi hurt his arm playing basketball.
武はバスケットをしていて腕を痛めた。

Her arms are long.
彼女の手は長いですね。

He took her in his arms and kissed her.
彼は彼女を抱いてキスした。

Is the alarm clock within arm's reach?
手の届くところに目覚まし時計を置いている?

He put his mug down on the arm of the chair.
彼は椅子のひじ掛けにマグカップを置いた。

There's a hole in the arm of your sweater.
セーターのそでに穴があいていますよ。

arm² *n.* (**arms**: weapons) 武器, 兵器 [→ WEAPON]

v. (provide with weapons) (…に) 武装させる, (**arm oneself**) 武装する

The sale of arms is big business.
武器の売買は一大産業だ。

armament *n.* (weapon) 武器, (**armaments**: military personnel/weapons/facilities) 軍備

armed *adj.* 武装した, 武器を持った

armor *n.* よろいかぶと, 甲冑

♦ **armored vehicle** *n.* 装甲車

armpit *n.* わきの下 [→ picture of BODY]

army *n.* (land forces) 陸軍, (military) 軍隊, (group) 団体, (host) 一団, 集団

the United States Army アメリカ軍

Which would you like to join: the Army, Navy, or Air Force?
陸軍、海軍、空軍、どこに入隊したいですか？

An army of children went exploring.
子供たちの一団が探検に出かけた。

around

1 *adv., prep.* IN A CIRCULAR OR CURVED MOTION ABOUT: (...を) 回って

2 *prep., adv.* IN A POSITION SURROUNDING: (...の) 周りに

3 *adv., prep.* FROM PLACE TO PLACE: (...の) あちこちに

4 *prep., adv.* NEARBY: (...の) あたりに, (...の) 近くに

5 *prep.* ON/TO THE FAR SIDE OF: ...の方に

6 *prep., adv.* APPROXIMATELY: (大体)...くらい/ぐらい, ((*formal*)) およそ, (in reference to time)...ころ/ごろ [→ ABOUT 2]

1 After walking around the pond, we sat down on a bench.
池を回ってからベンチに座った。

We seem to be going around in circles.
なんだか堂々巡りをしているようだ。

Would you pass these photos around, please?
この写真を順に回していただけますか？

He drove around the bend too quickly.
彼はカーブを曲がるのに、スピードを出しすぎていた。

Should we move the furniture around?
家具の向きを変えようか？

2 There's a fence around the parking lot.
駐車場の周りにさくがある。

He put a bandanna around his head.
彼はバンダナを頭に巻いた。

We all stood around looking at the experiment.
みんな取り囲むように立って、実験を見ていました。

3 Why does he go around causing trouble?
あの人は、どうしてあちこちで面倒を起こすんだろう？

He moved around talking to everyone.
彼は動き回って一人一人に話しかけた。

4 There are lots of restaurants around here.
このあたりには、レストランがたくさんあります。

I'll just check to see if anyone's still around.
まだ誰かいるかちょっと見てきます。

5 The trash bins are around the back.
ごみ箱は裏の方にあります。

There's a store around the corner.
角を曲がった所にお店がある。

6 You can get a pretty good dinner there for around ¥3,000.
そこは3000円くらいで、かなりおいしい食事が食べられます。

arouse *v.* (awaken) 起こす, (...の) 目を覚まさせる, (interest, curiosity) 引き起こす, (sexually excite) 興奮させる

arrange *v.*

1 PLAN/PREPARE: アレンジする, 手配する, (...の) 手はずを整える, (prepare) 用意する, 準備する, (hotel) 予約する, (decide on, fix, set) 決める

2 PUT IN ORDER: 配列する, (arrange in a line) 並べる, (flowers) 生ける

3 MUSIC: 編曲する

1 I've arranged to be there at 2 o'clock.
そこには2時に着くようにしました。

I'll arrange for a taxi to meet you.
出迎えのタクシーを手配します。

Could you arrange a meeting?
会議の手はずを整えてもらえますか？

We are arranging a big international conference in Kyoto.
京都で開催される大きな国際会議の準備をしています。

Have you arranged a time and date?
日程と時間を決めましたか？

2 Let's arrange the tables and chairs properly.
テーブルと椅子をきちんと並べよう。

She's very good at arranging flowers.
彼女は花を生けるのがとても上手です。

♦ **arranged marriage** *n.* (お)見合い結婚

arrangement *n.* (settlement) 取り決め, (preparation) 準備, 手配, 手はず

a temporary arrangement 仮の取り決め

make arrangements for …の手配をする

array *n.* (**an array of**) ずらりと並んだ

arrest *v.* (capture and take into custody) 逮捕する, 捕まえる, 捕らえる, 検挙する *n.* (capture) 逮捕, 検挙

The policeman made several arrests.
警官は何人かを逮捕した。

The police arrested the chairman of the company on suspicion of bribery.
警察は、その会社の会長を贈賄の容疑で逮捕した。

He was arrested by the police for stealing.
彼は盗みを働いて警察に捕まった。

I heard he was under arrest.
あの人は捕まったそうだ。

arrival *n.* (of train, flight) 到着, (**arrivals**: people) 到着した人; (**new arrival**: baby) 生まれた子

arrive *v.* (…に) 着く, 到着する; (be born) 生まれる; (of opportunity, season) 到来する

Since arriving they have done nothing but sleep.
着いてから彼らは寝てばかりいる。

What time do you think you will arrive?
何時ごろ着くと思いますか？

They arrived in Tokyo late last night.
彼らはゆうべ遅く東京に到着した。

arrogance *n.* 横柄さ, 傲慢さ

arrogant *adj.* (conceited) 横柄な, 傲慢な, (overbearing) いばっている

arrow *n.* (weapon) 矢, (sign to show direction) 矢印

a bow and arrow 弓矢

shoot an arrow 矢を射る

This arrow is a cross-reference sign.
この矢印は相互参照の印です。

arson *n.* (act of setting property on fire) 放火, (crime) 放火罪

art *n.*

1 FINE ARTS: アート, (performing arts) 芸術, (visual art) 美術, (work of art) 芸術品, 美術品

2 HUMANITIES: (**arts**) 人文科学

3 SKILL: 技術, -術

1 Do you know much about art?
美術に詳しいですか？

I intend to study Oriental art.
私は東洋美術を研究するつもりです。

an art collection 収集美術品

2 a degree in arts 人文科学の学位

The government spends a lot more on the sciences than it does on the arts.
政府は人文科学よりも自然科学に、ずっと多くの資金を支出している。

3 the art of self-defense 護身術

♦ **art gallery** ***n.*** (museum) 美術館, (small gallery) 画廊, ギャラリー

artery ***n.*** (blood vessel) 動脈

arthritis ***n.*** 関節炎

arthropod ***n.*** 節足動物

artichoke ***n.*** アーティチョーク, 朝鮮アザミ

article ***n.*** (piece of writing) 記事, (section of document) 条項; (thing, merchandise) 品物, 商品, -品; ("a," "the" etc.) 冠詞

an article in the newspaper 新聞の記事

Look at Article 7.
第７条をご覧ください。

an article of clothing 衣料品(１点)

Cosmetic articles are quite expensive at department stores.
化粧品はデパートではかなり高い。

artificial ***adj.*** (man-made) 人工の, 人造の [→ FALSE]

artificial flowers 造花

an artificial lake 人造湖

♦ **artificial insemination** ***n.*** 人工授精

artificial intelligence ***n.*** 人工知能, ＡＩ

artist ***n.*** (one who practices a fine art) 芸術家, アーティスト, (well-known painter) 画家, (very skilled person) 達人, 名人

This picture was painted by a famous artist.
この絵は有名な画家が描いたものです。

You can tell by the beautiful way in which she has decorated her home that she is quite an artist.
彼女の家のみごとな飾り方から、彼女がかなりのアーティストであることがわかる。

artistic ***adj.*** 芸術的な

as

1 ***conj.*** LIKE: …と同じように, …ように, …とおりに

2 ***prep.*** INDICATING A ROLE/FUNCTION: …として, …に

3 ***adv., conj.*** COMPARING ONE PERSON/THING TO ANOTHER: (**as…as**) …と同じくらい… [→ "MAKING COMPARISONS" on p. 189], (**as…as possible**) できるだけ…, (**as…as one likes**) 好きなだけ…

4 ***conj.*** BECAUSE: …ので

5 ***conj.*** WHEN/WHILE: (when) …時, …ころ, (while) …間に, (in proportion as) …につれて, …に応じて

6 ***conj.*** SHOWING PURPOSE: (**so as to…**) …よう(に), …ために, …には

7 ***prep.*** REGARDING: (**as for**) …は, …については

1 He's worked hard, as has everyone.
彼はがんばったし、みんなも同じようにがんばった。

I just did as everyone else did.
私はほかの人と同じようにしただけです。

We can't all do as we want.
誰もが、やりたいようにやるわけにはいかない。

As you said, it was crowded.
あなたの言ったとおり混んでいました。

As I've said before, the deadline is tomorrow.

前にも言いましたが、締め切りは明日です。

As I understand it, you want us to work twice as hard for half the pay?
つまり、半分の給料で倍働いてほしいということですか？

2 Let's use this as a table.
これをテーブルとして使おう。

She worked as a waitress.
彼女はウェートレスとして働いた。

He took it as a joke.
彼はそれを冗談として受け止めた。

I give you this as a token of my gratitude.
感謝の印に、これを差し上げます。

My father gave it to me as a present.
父がプレゼントにくれたんです。

3 She can run as fast as he can.
彼女は彼と同じくらい速く走れます。

I'd like it done as soon as possible.
できるだけ早くやっていただきたいのですが。

I'll be back to work as soon as I'm feeling better.
気分がよくなり次第、すぐ仕事に戻るつもりです。

Please take as many as you like.
好きなだけお取りください。

I've eaten as much as I can.
((*humble*)) もう十分いただきました。

It is twice as big as we thought.
私たちが思っていたよりも倍大きい。

4 I bought plenty, as it was cheap.
安かったのでたくさん買った。

His identity couldn't be revealed, as he was a minor.
彼は未成年だったので、身元は明かされなかった。

As he was undecided, she decided to marry someone else.
彼が決めかねていたので、彼女は別の男性と結婚することにした。

5 As I was listening to the radio, the children were playing upstairs.
私がラジオを聞いていた時、子供たちは2階で遊んでいた。

This is a photo of my father as a young man.
これは父が若いころの写真です。

As I was shopping at the corner store, the delivery man came.
角の店で買い物している間に、宅配便の配達の人が来た。

The air grew thinner as we climbed higher.
登って行くにつれて、空気は薄くなった。

As they retire, we will hire new recruits.
その人たちが定年退職するのに応じて、新入社員を採用します。

6 I picked it up with care so as not to break it.
壊さないよう、気をつけて手に取った。

You turn it this way so as to lock it.
かぎをかけるには、こういうふうに回すんです。

7 As for myself, I'm not worried.
私は心配していません。

As for your last point, do you think you could elaborate?
最後の点については、詳しく説明していただけませんか？

As for the cause, no one is sure.
原因については、誰にもよくわからない。

as if → IF

asbestos ***n.*** 石綿, アスベスト

ascend ***v.*** (mountain, ladder) (…に) 登る, (river) さかのぼる, (of road) 上り坂になる; (throne) (…に) 就く

ash ***n.*** 灰

ashamed ***adj.*** 恥ずかしい, 情けない, (be ashamed of) 恥ずかしく思う, 恥じる, (**be ashamed to do**) …して恥ずかしい

I'm ashamed of myself for being so stupid.
自分のばかさかげんが恥ずかしいよ。

Don't be ashamed to admit it.
正直に認めるのは恥ずかしいことじゃないよ。

That's nothing to be ashamed of.
それを恥ずかしく思うことはありません。

He looked ashamed of himself.
彼は自分を恥じているようだった。

Even his father was ashamed of him.
父親でさえ彼を情けなく思った。

ashore ***adv.*** 岸に/へ, 浜に/へ, 陸に/へ

go/come ashore 上陸する

ashtray ***n.*** 灰皿

Asia ***n.*** アジア

Southeast Asia 東南アジア

Asian ***n.*** (person) アジア人

adj. (of country, culture) アジアの, (of person) アジア人の

aside ***adv.*** わきへ/に, (**aside from**) …は別として

ask ***v.***

1 ASK A QUESTION: (…に) 質問をする, 聞く, 尋ねる, ((*humble*)) 伺う

2 MAKE A REQUEST TO: (…に) 頼む, お願いする, 求める, ((*formal*)) 要求する

3 INVITE: 誘う, 招く, 呼ぶ, 招待する

1 I asked the teacher a question.
先生に質問をしました。

Yamada started asking lots of questions.
山田さんは質問をたくさんし始めた。

She asked us what book we were reading in class.
彼女は私たちがクラスで何の本を読んでいるのか聞いた。

Would you ask her if it's all right for me to come, too?
私もいっしょに行ってもいいか、彼女に聞いてもらえませんか？

There's something I'd like to ask you.
((*humble*)) 伺いたいことがあるんですが。

2 I asked my teacher if he would speak more slowly.
先生にもう少しゆっくり話してくれるよう頼みました。

I asked the manager for permission to leave early.
早退させてほしいと、部長にお願いした。

Would you ask the hotel manager to call me, please?
私に電話をくれるようにと、ホテルの支配人に伝えてくださいますか？

Excuse me. I asked for a glass of beer. Where is it?
すみません。ビールを頼んだんですが、どうなってますか？

I asked for Mr. Kinoshita at the reception desk.
受付で木下さんに面会を求めた。

3 He asked us over again.
彼はまた私たちを誘ってくれた。

Let's ask them to come over this weekend.
今週末に彼らを招待しましょう。

asleep *adj.* (sleeping) 眠っている, 寝ている, (numb) しびれている

I fell asleep while waiting.
待っているうちに眠ってしまった。

The dog was fast asleep.
犬はぐっすり寝ていた。

My leg's fallen asleep.
足がしびれた。

asparagus *n.* アスパラ(ガス)

aspect *n.* (facet) 面, ところ

It's an aspect of his character that I don't like.
そこが彼の性格で好きじゃないところだ。

China has had a great influence on many aspects of Japan's society.
中国は、日本の社会のさまざまな面に大きな影響を与えてきました。

We need to look at all the different aspects of this case.
この件のありとあらゆる側面を見る必要がある。

asphalt *n.* アスファルト

aspiration *n.* (desire) 希望, 願望, 欲

aspire *v.* (**aspire to do/be**) …したい/…になりたいと切望する, (**aspire to sth**) 求める

aspirin *n.* (mild analgesic) アスピリン, (tablet) アスピリン錠

ass *n.* (animal) ロバ; (fool) ばか者

assassinate *v.* 暗殺する

assassination *n.* 暗殺

assault *n.* (by army) 攻撃, 襲撃, (on person) 暴行

assemble *v.* (bring together) 集める, (come together) 集まる, (of people) 集合する; (put together) 組み立てる

Would everybody assemble in the hall for a fire drill.
みなさん、防火訓練のため廊下に集まっていただけますか。

Do you have any idea how to assemble this bed?
このベッドをどうやって組み立てるか、わかりますか？

assembly *n.* (gathering) 集会, 集まり, (meeting) 会議; (act of putting together) 組み立て

♦ **assembly line** *n.* 流れ作業

assert *v.* 主張する

assertion *n.* 主張

assess *v.* (income, tax) 査定する, (situation) 評価する, 判断する

assessment *n.* (evaluation) 査定, 評価, (judgment) 判断

a tax assessment 税金の査定

What's your assessment of the situation?
この事態をどう判断しますか？

asset *n.* (also **assets**) 資産, 財産; (valuable thing/person) 大切な物/人

assign *v.* (assign A [homework] to B) (AをBに) 出す, (assign A [person] to B [post, position]) (AをBに) 任命する

assignment *n.* (homework) 宿題, (task) 仕事

assist *v.* 援助する, 手伝う [→ HELP]

He assisted us with grading the exams.
彼は試験の採点を手伝ってくれた。

assistance *n.* 援助

assistant *n.* (helper) 助手, アシスタント, (in titles: deputy) 助-, 副-

an assistant professor 助教授
an assistant manager 副支配人

associate

1 *v.* CONNECT IN ONE'S MIND: (associate A with B) (AからBを) 連想する, 思い出す, (AとBを) 結び付けて考える

2 *v.* BE OFTEN IN THE COMPANY OF: (associate with)(…と) 付き合う, 交際する

3 *n.* COLLEAGUE: 同僚

4 *adj.* IN TITLES: 準-

1 I associate cowboys with the United States.
カウボーイというとアメリカを連想する。

I associate snow with my childhood.
雪を見ると子供のころを思い出す。

Well, I never would have associated Ms. Hashimoto with horse racing.
いやあ、橋本さんと競馬なんて全く結び付かなかったよ。

2 If I were you, I wouldn't associate with the likes of him.
((*feminine*)) 私なら、彼のような人とは付き合わないわ。

He only associates with snobs.
彼は気取った人とばっかり付き合ってる。

3 "Who? Kurihara? Oh, he's an old associate of mine."
「誰? 栗原さん? ああ、彼は昔の同僚だよ」

4 an associate professor 準教授
an associate member 準会員

associated *adj.* 関連した, (be associated with) (…と) 関係がある, かかわりがある, (in proper names) …連合, …連盟

They're associated with a right-wing group.
彼らは右翼団体とかかわりがある。

♦ **Associated Press** *n.* ＡＰ通信社

association *n.* 協会, 会, 組合

the Association for Japanese-Language Teaching
国際日本語普及協会

assume *v.* (believe) (…と) 思う, 当然(…と) 考える, (imagine) (…と) 仮定する

I assumed that he was telling the truth.
彼は本当のことを言っていると私は思っていた。

Look, don't assume they're going to help you.
いいですか、彼らが当然手伝ってくれると思ってはいけません。

Let's assume he was at the golf course.
彼がゴルフ場にいたと仮定しましょう。

assuming (that)… (もし)…たら, …とすれば

Assuming you're helping us, we'll finish cleaning in a few hours.
手伝ってくれたら、掃除は2、3時間で終わりますよ。

♦ **assumed name** *n.* 偽名

assumption *n.* 仮定

assurance *n.* (promise) 保証, (confidence) 確信, 自信

assure *v.* (…に) 保証する, 請け合う

asterisk *n.* 星印, 米印, アステリスク

asteroid *n.* 小惑星

asthma *n.* ぜんそく

have asthma ぜんそくにかかっている

astonish *v.* 驚かす, びっくりさせる

We were astonished at the speed at which he drove.
彼が出した車のスピードに、私たちはびっくりした。

astonishing *adj.* 驚くべき, びっくりするような

astonishment *n.* 驚き

astrology *n.* 占星術, 星占い

astronaut *n.* 宇宙飛行士

astronomer *n.* 天文学者

astronomy *n.* 天文学

asylum *n.* (political) 亡命

seek asylum 亡命を求める

at *prep.*

1 INDICATING PLACE: (indicating a place where an action occurs) …で, (indicating a place where sb/sth is located) …に

2 INDICATING TIME/AGE: …に, …時, (age) …歳で, (indicating a starting point) …から

3 INDICATING DIRECTION OF AN ACTION: …を, …に(向けて)

4 GOOD/BAD AT: …が

5 INDICATING LEVEL/PRICE/DEGREE: …で

1 They met at a café.
彼らは喫茶店で会った。

I studied at home.
私は家で勉強した。

At work we have to wear a suit and tie.
職場ではスーツとネクタイをしなければなりません。

What happened at the meeting?
会議で何があったのですか？

I've only just arrived at the airport.
ちょうど空港に着いたところです。

Where are you working at now?
今どちらにお勤めですか？

He's living at a residential hotel.
彼はウイークリーマンションに住んでいる。

At the far end of town, there's a castle.
街のずっと外れに、お城があります。

2 I'll be home at 7 o'clock this evening.
今晩 7 時に帰るよ。

At what time will you know?
何時にわかりますか？

I got up at dawn.
明け方に起きました。

The phone rang at the same time.
同時に電話が鳴った。

At birth, the child seemed normal.
生まれた時は、子供には異常がないように見えた。

She first visited the United States at age 16.
彼女は 16 歳の時初めてアメリカを訪れた。

Mr. Mori died at 84.
森さんは 84 歳で亡くなった。

At 90 years old, she was still very active.
90 歳になってもまだとても元気でした。

Work starts every day at 9:30 A.M.
仕事は毎朝9時半に始まります。

The lecture began at 2 o'clock in the afternoon.
講義は午後 2 時から始まりました。

3 He kept staring at me.
彼は私をじっと見つめていた。

I waved at them.
彼らに手を振りました。

You'll need to work hard at it.
がんばってやらないといけないよ。

The policy aims at cutting pollution.
その政策は公害の削減をめざしている。

4 She's good at tennis.

彼女はテニスがうまい。

He's not bad at sports.
彼はスポーツがなかなかうまい。

He's not good at numbers.
彼は数字に弱い。

5 He was traveling at about ninety kilometers per hour.
彼は時速約90キロで走っていた。

At ¥5,000, you're going to have a hard time selling it.
5000円で売るのは難しいと思うよ。

At thirty degrees, it was hot.
30度で暑かった。

athlete *n.* スポーツ選手, スポーツマン

athletic *adj.* (skilled at sports) 運動の得意な, (of build) がっしりした

athletics *n.* 運動競技, スポーツ競技, アスレチック

♦**athletics meeting** *n.* 運動会

Atlantic Ocean *n.* 大西洋

atlas *n.* 地図帳

atmosphere *n.* (gases surrounding the earth) 大気, 大気圏, (air) 空気, (feeling) 雰囲気, ムード

Very few people have ever left the earth's atmosphere.
(地球の)大気圏から出たことのある人は、とても少ない。

We should all make a conscious effort not to pollute the atmosphere.
私たちは皆、空気を汚さないよう努めていかなくてはいけない。

The atmosphere at the meeting was friendly.
会議の雰囲気は和やかだった。

atmospheric *adj.* 大気の

♦**atmospheric pressure** *n.* 気圧

atoll *n.* 環状サンゴ礁, 環礁

atom *n.* 原子

atomic *adj.* 原子の

♦**atomic bomb** *n.* 原子爆弾

atomic energy *n.* 原子力

attach *v.* (label, tag) 付ける, (appliance) 取り付ける, (to bulletin board) 張り付ける, (file to e-mail) 添付する; (**be attached to**) (= have affection for) ...が好きだ, ...に愛着がある, (= be affiliated with) ...に付属している

They told us to attach these tags to our suitcases.
スーツケースに荷札を付けるよう言われた。

I soon became attached to the place.
すぐにその場所が好きになりました。

This hospital is attached to the university.
この病院は大学の付属病院です。

He is attached to the Foreign Ministry.
彼は外務省に所属している。

attaché *n.* (大使の) 随行員

attachment *n.* (to camera, machine) 付属品, (to e-mail) 添付ファイル; (fondness) 愛着

attack *v.* (assault) 攻撃する, 攻める, (raid, assail) 襲う, (criticize) 非難する, (of illness) 襲う, (grapple with: problem) (...に) 取り組む, 挑戦する
n. (assault) 攻撃, (criticism) 非難; (of asthma etc.) 発作

The city was attacked by warplanes.
街は戦闘機に爆撃された。

She was attacked by a swarm of bees.

彼女はハチの大群に襲われた。

The president was attacked by the press for his indecision.
大統領は優柔不断さをマスコミに非難された。

The whole team attacked the problem with enthusiasm.
チーム全体で、熱意をもってその問題に取り組みました。

A dawn attack was planned.
夜明けの攻撃が計画された。

It was a personal attack on his character.
彼の人格に対する個人攻撃だった。

He had a heart [an asthma] attack.
彼は<u>心臓</u> [ぜんそくの] 発作を起こした。

♦ **attacker** ***n.*** 攻撃する人, (in sport) アタッカー

attain *v.* (gain, achieve) やり遂げる, 達成する, (reach) (...に) 達する

attain one's goal 目標を達成する

attain enlightenment 悟りを開く

attempt *v.* 試みる, (**attempt to do**) ...しようとする, (plan) 企てる [→ TRY]

n. 試み

Nothing like this has ever before been attempted.
このようなことは、今まで一度も試みられたことがなかった。

The military attempted a coup d'état.
軍部はクーデターを企てた。

It was his third attempt to swim the English Channel.
彼がイギリス海峡を泳いで渡ろうとするのは、3度目の試みだった。

♦ **attempted** ***adj.*** 未遂の

attempted suicide 自殺未遂

attend *v.* (church, party, class) (...に) 出席する, 出る, (**attend to**) (= patient in hospital) ...に付き添う, 看護する, (= look after) ...の世話をする, ...の面倒を見る, (= take responsibility for) 担当する

Did you attend class yesterday?
昨日、授業に出た?

The nurse is attending to him now.
看護師さんが彼の世話をしているところです。

Who is going to attend to this matter?
この件は誰が担当しますか?

attendance ***n.*** (presence) 出席

take attendance 出席を取る

♦ **attendance book** ***n.*** 出席簿

attention ***n.*** 注意, (interest) 関心, (concentration) 集中; (affection) 思いやり, 心づかい

A child's attention is easily distracted.
子供はすぐに注意散漫になる。

His attention was focused on what was happening near the door.
彼は、ドアのそばで起きていることに気を取られていました。

This matter should have been brought to my attention earlier.
このことはもっと早く私に知らせるべきだった。

Hayashi always seems to be the center of attention.
林さんはいつも注目の的のようですね。

She complained that she doesn't get enough attention from her husband.
彼女は夫の思いやりが足りないと、ぐちをこぼした。

attract attention 注意を引く, 気を引く, 人目を引く

I tried to attract her attention, but she wouldn't look this way.
((*masculine*)) 彼女の注意を引こうとしたが、こっちを向いてくれなかった。

How can I attract his attention?
((*feminine*)) どうすれば彼の気を引くことができるかしら?

Stop it! You're attracting attention!
やめて! みんなが見てるよ。

pay attention to ...に注意を払う

You need to pay more attention to your work.
君はもっと仕事に注意を払うべきですね。

They (the class) paid no attention to what the teacher said.
生徒たちは先生の言うことを、まるで聞こうとしなかった。

♦ **attention-seeker** *n.* 目立ちたがり屋

attic *n.* (space above ceiling and beneath roof) 屋根裏, (room) 屋根裏部屋

attitude *n.* (way of behaving) 態度, (mind-set) 心構え, (way of thinking) 考え方, (opinion) 意見

I think he has an attitude problem.
あの人の態度には問題があると思います。

That's not the right attitude. Be positive!
そういう考え方はよくない。前向きになりなさい。

attorney *n.* (lawyer) 弁護士

♦ **Attorney General** *n.* 司法長官

attract *v.* (audience) 引き付ける, (attention) 引く [→ ATTENTION], (**be attracted to**: person) ...に魅力を感じる, (...が) 好きだ

Scandal always attracts a lot of media attention.
スキャンダルは、いつでも多くのマスコミを引き付ける。

The band attracted a small audience.
そのバンドに聴衆が少し集まった。

To be frank, I'm not really attracted to her.
正直なところ、彼女にはあまり魅力を感じないんだ。

attraction *n.* (charm) 魅力, (at show, fairground) アトラクション

attractive *adj.* (pretty) きれいな, (charming) 魅力的な, (of room, layout) 見栄えがする, (of idea) 興味をそそる

attribute *v.* (attribute A to B) (AをBの) 結果と考える, (**be attributed to**: of book/painting to writer/artist) ...の作品と考えられている

n. (feature) 属性, 特質

attributive *adj.* (in grammar) 限定的な

auburn *n., adj.* 赤褐色(の), 金褐色(の)

auction *n.* オークション, 競売

v. 競売にかける, せり売りする

an on-line auction オンラインオークション

audience *n.* (gathering) 観衆, (at concert, lecture) 聴衆, (at theater) 観客, (listeners) リスナー, 聴取者, (of TV program) 視聴者

The audience clapped loudly.
観客は盛大な拍手をした。

What kind of audience do you expect?
どんな観客を予想していますか?

audio *n., adj.* オーディオ(の), 音響(の)

audiovisual *adj.* 視聴覚の

A

n. (**audiovisuals**) 視聴覚設備

audit *n.* (examination of accounts) 会計監査

v. (examine the accounts of) (…の) 会計監査をする; (listen in on: lecture) 聴講する

audit a course/class 講義を聴講する

audition *n.* オーディション

v. (audition for) (…の) オーディションを受ける, (audition sb) (…の) オーディションをする

August *n.* 8月, 八月

aunt *n.* (one's own) おば, (sb else's) おばさん [NOTE: People, especially children, use おばさん of middle-aged women, too, in place of the person's name.]

Is Aunt (Jane) visiting us today?
今日(ジェーン)おばさんが来るの？

My aunt was a teacher.
おばは教師をしていました。

♦**auntie** *n.* おばちゃん

Australia *n.* オーストラリア, 豪州, ((*in abbr.*)) 豪

Australian *n.* (person) オーストラリア人

adj. (of country, culture) オーストラリアの, (of person) オーストラリア人の

Austria *n.* オーストリア

authentic *adj.* 本物の, 本当の, 真正の

author *n.* (person who writes for a living) 作家, (writer of a particular work) 著者, 作者 [→ WRITER]

authority *n.* (power/right to give orders) 権威, 権限, 権力, (**the authorities**) 当局; (expert) 専門家, 大家; (power to convince/persuade) 説得力

He has no authority over you.
彼には、あなたに指示する権限はないよ。

People show far less respect for authority than they used to.
人々は昔に比べ、権威を重んじなくなっている。

You can't argue with the authorities.
当局と言い争ってもどうにもならない。

She is an authority on ancient Japanese history.
彼女は日本の古代史の大家です。

He spoke with authority on the subject.
そのテーマについて、彼は説得力のある話をした。

authorize *v.* (important political matter) (…に) 権限を与える, (allow) 許可する, 公認する, 認可する

auto *n.* 車, 自動車 [→ picture of CAR]

the auto industry 自動車産業

autobiography *n.* 自伝, 自叙伝

autograph *n.* (signature) サイン

automatic *adj.* (self-acting) 自動の, (of reaction: natural) 自然な, (unconscious) 無意識の, (mechanical) 機械的な

n. (car) オートマチック車, ((*informal*)) オートマ

automatic doors 自動ドア

It was an automatic reaction.
それは自然な反応でした。

automatically *adv.* (by itself) 自動的に, (naturally) 自然に, おのずと

automobile *n.* 自動車, 車 [→ picture of CAR]

autonomous *adj.* (self-governing) 自主的な, 自治権のある

autonomy ***n.*** (independence) 自治

autopsy ***n.*** 検死

autumn ***n.*** 秋

early [late] autumn 初秋 [晩秋]

♦ **autumnal** ***adj.*** 秋の, 秋らしい

auxiliary ***adj.*** (assistant) 補助の

♦ **auxiliary verb** ***n.*** 助動詞

available ***adj.*** (on hand, obtainable) 手に入る, 入手できる, (gathered neatly together in one spot) そろっている, (for use, usable) 利用できる, (free, not busy) 手があいている, (of hotel room) あいている, (of person: not involved in a relationship) 付き合える

These books are readily available.
この本は手に入りやすい。

That information is available to anyone.
その情報は誰でも自由に入手できる。

Everything you need is available in the office.
必要な物はすべて、事務室にそろっています。

Are you available for the meeting tomorrow?
明日の会議に出席できますか？

I'm afraid Mr. Hori is not available at the moment.
あいにく、堀はただいま席を外しております。(lit., "Hori is not at his seat.")

If you're available, could you lend a hand?
((*informal*)) 手があいてたら、手伝ってくれる？

avalanche ***n.*** (of snow) なだれ

avant-garde ***adj.*** 前衛的な, アバンギャルドの

avarice ***n.*** 強欲, 貪欲 [→ GREED]

avenue ***n.*** 大通り, (in names of streets) -街

A

average ***n.*** (the arithmetical mean) 平均, 標準

adj. (mean) 平均の, (standard) 標準の, (ordinary) 普通の, 並の

v. (calculate the average of) 平均する

This figure is above [below] average.
この数字は標準以上 [以下] です。

What's the average monthly salary?
月給は平均いくらですか？

Even an average player could have done better.
普通の選手でも、もっとうまくできたはずだ。

on average 平均して

On average, there are several traffic accidents a day.
平均して1日に数件の交通事故がある。

aviation ***n.*** (flying) 飛行, 航空, (operation and production of aircraft) 航空機産業

avocado ***n.*** アボカド

avoid ***v.*** 避ける, よける, ((*formal*)) 回避する, (**avoid doing**) …しないようにする

We tried to avoid the rush hour.
ラッシュアワーを避けようとした。

We tried to avoid the puddles.
水たまりをよけながら歩いた。

Fortunately, the strike was avoided.
幸いにして、ストは回避された。

I try to avoid talking with him.
あの人とはしゃべらないようにしている。

You'll avoid making mistakes if you just read through what you've written.

書いたことを読み返すだけで、間違いは避けられますよ。

await *v.* (wait for) 待つ, (look forward to) 期待する

awake *adj.* 目が覚めている, 眠らずにいる [→ WAKE]

Are you still awake?
まだ起きてる?

I'm wide awake now.
すっかり目が覚めました。

I lay awake all night thinking.
一晩中、眠らずに考えていた。

The noise of the construction outside kept me awake.
外の工事の音がうるさくて眠れなかった。

award *n.* (prize) -賞, 賞品, (prize money) 賞金, (compensation) 賠償金

v. (...に) 賞を与える, (**award compensation to**) ...に賠償金を支払う

Tanabe received the highest award.
田辺さんは最優秀賞を受賞しました。

There was even an award for best effort.
努力賞までありました。

Who awarded the prizes?
誰が賞を渡したんですか? (lit., "Who handed over the prizes?")

They were awarded compensation.
彼らに賠償金が支払われた。

♦ **award winner** *n.* 受賞者

award-winning *adj.* 受賞した

aware *adj.* (be aware of) (...に) 気づいている, (...を) 知っている, 意識している

It was already too late by the time they became aware of the dangers of the situation.
事態の危険性に気づいた時には、すでに遅かった。

Are you aware that everyone is talking about you?
皆があなたのうわさをしているって知ってる?

I was not awarc of this bcforc I started the job.
この仕事を始めるまで、このことは知らなかった。

Are you aware of all the trouble you've caused?
自分がどれだけの問題を引き起こしたか、わかっていますか?

She's aware that she's attractive.
彼女は、自分が魅力的だということを意識している。

♦ **awareness** *n.* 認識

away

1 *adv.* SEPARATE OR AT A DISTANCE FROM: 離れて, 離れた所に, 遠くに

2 *adv.* CONTINUOUSLY: ずっと, 絶えず, せっせと

3 *adj.* ABSENT: 留守だ, 不在だ, (**be away on vacation**) 休暇を取っている

4 *adv.* IMMEDIATELY: (**right away**) すぐに, さっさと

5 *adj.* OF GAME: アウェーの, 敵地での

1 It's about ten kilometers away.
10キロほど離れた所にあります。

I was about four hours away from Tokyo.
私は東京から4時間くらい離れた所にいました。

Oh, it's miles away.
ああ、あそこはすごく遠いよ。

2 The whole day she just kept working away without stopping.

一日中、彼女は休まず働き続けていた。

3 My parents were away for a few days.
両親は数日(間)留守でした。

4 Do it right away!
今すぐやりなさい！

5 an away game アウェーゲーム [遠征試合]

awe ***n.*** 畏敬, 畏怖

awesome ***adj.*** (awe-inspiring) すさまじい, (great) すごくいい, 最高の

awful ***adj.*** (horrible) いやな, ひどい

He's such an awful man.
彼は本当にいやな人だ。

There was an awful accident here last year.
ここで去年、ひどい事故がありました。

His taste in clothes is awful.
彼は服の趣味がとても悪い。

awfully ***adv.*** (very) すごく, 本当に; (horribly) ひどく

I'm awfully sorry.
本当にすみません。

awkward ***adj.*** (of timing) 都合の悪い, (of atmosphere, silence) 気まずい, 気詰まりな; (badly designed, difficult to use) 使いにくい, 扱いにくい, (of things, people: troublesome) 難しい, 厄介な

There was an awkward silence.
気まずい沈黙があった。

I feel very awkward around him.
彼といるとすごく気詰まりなんです。

This is an awkward machine to use.
これは扱いにくい機械です。

He's an awkward customer.
彼は厄介なお客だ。

This is a very awkward situation.
とてもまずい状況ですね。

ax ***n.*** おの

axis ***n.*** 軸, (on graph) 軸線; (**the Axis**) 枢軸国

the X axis χ 軸

axle ***n.*** 軸, 車軸

azalea ***n.*** ツツジ

B

B, b

B, b ***n.*** (letter) Ｂ, (second item in a series) 第２, 乙; (grade) Ｂ, 良

BA ***abbr.*** (qualification) 文学士の学位

baboon ***n.*** ヒヒ

baby ***n.*** 赤ちゃん, ((*sometimes rude*)) 赤ん坊

What a cute baby you've got.
とってもかわいい赤ちゃんですね。

When was your baby born?
赤ちゃんは、いつ生まれたの？

Don't be such a baby! It didn't hurt.
赤ん坊みたいなまねはやめなさい。痛くなんかなかったでしょう。

♦**baby carriage** ***n.*** 乳母車

babyish ***adj.*** (like a baby) 子供のような, ((*used negatively*)) 子供じみた

baby tooth ***n.*** 乳歯

baby-sit ***v.*** (…の) 子守りをする

♦**baby-sitter** ***n.*** ベビーシッター

bachelor ***n.*** (unmarried man) 独身男性; (college graduate) 学士

Do you know if he's a bachelor or not?
彼が独身かどうか知ってる？

a bachelor's degree 学士号

back

1 ***adv.*** BACKWARD: 後ろに/へ, (**move/step back**) 後ろに下がる, (**lean back**) もたれる, (**fall back**: retreat) 退却する

2 ***n.*** OPPOSITE OF FRONT: (of building, piece of paper) 裏, (of car, train) 後ろ, (of room) 奥

3 ***adv.*** TO A FORMER STATE/PLACE: (**go/get back**) 戻る, (**put back**) 戻す

4 ***adv.*** IN RETURN: <-ます stem> + 返す

5 ***n.*** PART OF THE BODY: 背中 [→ picture of BODY], (of hand) 甲 [→ picture of HAND]

6 ***n.*** OF CHAIR: 背もたれ

1 She moved back to avoid the drunk.
彼女は酔っ払いをよけようとして、後ろへ下がった。

I stepped back to let him by.
１歩下がって、彼を通してあげた。

I leaned back in my chair and fell asleep.
椅子の背にもたれて眠ってしまった。

2 the back of the building ビルの裏

the back (=end pages) of the book
本の後ろ [末尾]

Three people can fit in the back of the car.
この車の後部座席には、３人座れる。

Let's sit near the back.
後ろの方に座ろう。

at the back of the shop 店の奥で

3 I went back to sleep.
また寝た。

Have they gone back to work?
彼らは仕事に戻りましたか？

I'll be back next week.
来週戻ります。

(*returning home*) "I'm back." "Hi."
「ただいま」「お帰り(なさい)」

Everything is back to normal now.
すべて通常の状態に戻っている。

Please put the book back in its place.
本は、元の場所に戻しておいてください。

You'll get nothing back without a receipt.
領収書がなければ、払い戻しは一切できないですよ。

He wants his money back.
彼はお金を返してもらいたいんだ。

4 He took it from me, so I took it back.
彼が取ったから、取り返した。

You've got to learn to fight back.
やり返すことを学ばなくてはいけないよ。

Could you write back again?
またお手紙くださいますか？

5 My back is aching.
背中が痛い。

the horse's back 馬の背(中)

He just lay there on his back, without a care in the world.
彼は何も気にせず、ただそこであお向きに寝転がっていた。

the back of the hand 手の甲

6 The back of the chair is wobbly.
椅子の背もたれがぐらぐらしている。

put one's back out (strain one's back) ぎっくり腰になる

turn one's back on (abandon) 見捨てる

♦**back door** *n.* 裏口

back issue *n.* バックナンバー

back road *n.* 裏道, 裏通り

back tooth *n.* 奥歯

back out *v.* (of driveway) (…から) 出る, (of plan) (…から) 手を引く

back up *v.*

1 SUPPORT: 支援する, 支持する

2 MOVE IN REVERSE: (step back) 後ろに下がる, 後退する, (in car) (車を) バックさせる

3 MAKE A COPY OF: (data) (…の) バックアップを取る

1 He backed me up all the way.
彼はずっと私を支援してくれた。

2 I had to back up a few meters.
2、3メートルバックさせなくてはいけなかった。

3 They say you should back up your hard drive every month.
毎月ハードディスクのバックアップを取ったほうがいいそうだ。

backache *n.* 背中の痛み, (lower back ache) 腰痛

I have a backache.
腰が痛いんです。

backbone *n.* (part of the body) 背骨; (main support) 主力, (courage) 勇気, (strength of character) 気骨, 根性

backdrop *n.* 背景

backgammon *n.* バックギャモン

background *n.* (of event, situation, condition) 背景 [→ AGAINST 1], (of picture) 背景, バック; (basic knowledge) 知識; (personal history/experience) 経歴

the social background 社会的背景

the economic background 経済的背景

the political background 政治的背景

the background of the photo 写真の背景

have a solid background in physics
しっかりした物理の知識がある

What's her background? I mean, is she the person for the job?
彼女はどういう経歴の人ですか？ つまり、この仕事に適した人ですか？

backhand *n.* (in tennis) バックハンド

backing *n.* (support) 支援

backlash *n.* (adverse reaction) 反動, 反発

backpack *n.* バックパック, リュックサック, (as worn by elementary school kids in Japan) ランドセル

v. (travel) (バックパックを背負って) 旅行する, (hike) ハイキングする

backstage *adv.* (behind/to room behind stage) 舞台裏で/に, 楽屋で/に

♦**backstage pass** *n.* 関係者パス, 通行証

backstroke *n.* 背泳, 背泳ぎ

do the backstroke 背泳ぎで泳ぐ

backup *n.* (support) 支援; (backup of data) バックアップ

adj. (spare) 予備の, 控えの

We need a backup plan in case things go wrong.
うまくいかなかったときのために、予備計画が必要です。

♦**backup disk** *n.* バックアップディスク

backup drive *n.* バックアップドライブ

backward

1 *adj.* DIRECTED TOWARD THE REAR: 後ろの方への

2 *adj.* UNDEVELOPED/PRIMITIVE: (of country, society) (発達の) 遅れた

3 *adv.* TO THE REAR: (also **backwards**) 後ろに/へ, (facing backward) 後ろ向きに

4 *adv.* IN REVERSE ORDER: (also **backwards**) 逆に, 反対に

1 a backward movement 後退

give a backward glance 振り向いて見る

2 He comes from a very backward part of the country.
彼は国の中でも非常に遅れた地域の出身です。

These people are not "backward" just because they don't have TVs.
テレビを持っていないからと言って、この人たちが「遅れている」というわけではないよ。

3 Are we going backwards or forwards?
後ろへ進んでいるんですか、それとも前へ進んでいるんですか？

Careful you don't fall backward!
後ろに倒れないように気をつけて！

4 Can you count backwards?
数を逆から数えられますか？

know backwards and forwards 知り尽くしている, 熟知している

I know my hiragana backwards and forwards.
平がなのことなら、知り尽くしています。

backyard *n.* 裏庭

bacon *n.* ベーコン

bacon and eggs ベーコンエッグ

bacteria *n.* バクテリア, 細菌

bad *adj.*

1 UNPLEASANT/DISTURBING: いやな, 悪い, 不愉快な

2 TERRIBLE/SEVERE: ひどい

3 UNSKILLED: 下手な

4 EVIL/NAUGHTY: 悪い, (of child) 行儀の悪い, いけない

5 UNHEALTHY: 体に悪い, 体によくない

6 INAPPROPRIATE/DISADVANTAGEOUS: まずい, 悪い

7 OF FOOD: (bad-tasting) まずい, (**go bad**: become rotten) 腐る

8 GUILTY: (**feel bad**) すまないと思う [→ GUILTY]

1 I had a bad day. いやな1日だった。

This is really bad news.
ほんとに悪いニュースです。

The bad weather is likely to continue.
この悪天候は続きそうです。

He's in a bad mood right now.
彼は今、機嫌が悪いんです。

It's bad manners to yawn with your mouth wide open.
大口をあけてあくびをするのは、行儀が悪いよ。

That was a really bad experience.
すごく不愉快な経験だった。

2 I've caught a bad cold.
ひどいかぜをひいてしまった。

His grade on the exam was very bad.
彼の試験の成績はとてもひどかった。

Rush hour traffic is bad.
ラッシュアワーの交通渋滞はひどいものだ。

3 bad Japanese 下手な日本語

He's bad at sports.
あの人はスポーツが下手だ。

What a bad actor!
なんて大根役者なんだ！

4 They're bad people and you should stay away from them.
やつらは悪だから、近づかないほうがいいよ。

He's a bad boy.
あの子はいけない子だよ。

5 Don't you know smoking is bad for your health?
たばこが体に悪いのを知らないの？

He's had a bad leg ever since the accident.
事故以来、彼は片足を悪くしています。

6 The timing was bad, that's all.
時機が悪かっただけです。

It would be bad if they found out.
ばれたらまずい。

7 This tastes bad.
これはまずい。

This peach has gone bad.
この桃は腐っている。

8 I feel bad about not being able to go to your party.
パーティーに行けなくて残念です。

that's too bad それは残念ですね

KANJI BRIDGE

悪 ON: あく, お KUN: わる(い) | BAD

abuse	悪用
bad/poor taste	悪趣味
bad reputation	悪評
bad smell	悪臭
bad weather	悪天候
devil	悪魔
good and evil	善悪, 善し悪し
ill-tempered	意地悪な
ill will	悪意
nightmare	悪夢
of poor quality	質の悪い
speak ill of	(…の) 悪口を言う
the worst	最悪
worsen	悪化する

badge *n.* バッジ, 記章
a school badge 校章

badger *n.* アナグマ, 穴熊
v. (**badger to do/into doing**) (…に) …するようしつこくせがむ

badly *adv.*
1 POORLY: 悪く, まずく, ひどく, (unskill-

fully) 下手に

2 SERIOUSLY/SEVERELY: ひどく

3 VERY MUCH: すごく, ものすごく

1 I don't think badly of them.
あの人たちのことを悪くは思っていない。

He treats his staff badly.
彼は部下に対してひどい扱いをする。

It went badly.
うまくいかなかった。

Let's face it—you did badly on the test.
認めようよ、テストはひどいもんだったでしょ。

a badly phrased sentence 下手な文

2 He was badly injured.
彼はひどいけがをした [重傷を負った]。

3 I am badly in need of a shower.
すごくシャワーを浴びたい。

badminton *n.* バドミントン

bad-tempered *adj.* 怒りっぽい

baffle *v.* 当惑させる, 困らせる

I was baffled by the question.
その質問には困った。

bag *n.* 袋, (handbag) (ハンド)バッグ, (satchel, briefcase) かばん, (paper bag) 紙袋, (trash bag) ゴミ袋

That's a very nice bag.
とてもすてきなバッグですね。

a shoulder bag ショルダーバッグ

a shopping bag 買い物袋

baggage *n.* (luggage) 手荷物, 荷物, (emotional baggage) 障害, 妨げ

baggy *adj.* (of clothes) だぶだぶの

baggy pants バギーパンツ

bagpipe(s) *n.* バグパイプ

bail[1] *n.* 保釈, (money) 保釈金

v. (**be bailed out** of jail) 保釈される

pay bail 保釈金を払う

be out on bail 保釈中である

skip/jump bail 保釈後出廷しない

bail[2] *v.* (**bail sb out**) (save) 救い出す; (**bail out**) (of airplane) (…から) 脱出する, (of unhappy situation) (…から) 逃げる

bait *n.* (fishing bait) えさ

bake *v.* 焼く, (**be baked**) 焼ける

Shall we bake a cake?
ケーキでも焼く?

Mmmm, smells good. Are you baking something?
ああ、いいにおい! オーブンで何か焼いているの?

Are the potatoes baked yet?
ジャガイモはもう焼けましたか?

baked *adj.* 焼いた, 焼き…

♦ **baked potatoes** *n.* ベークドポテト

baker(y) *n.* パン屋(さん)

baking dish *n.* オーブン用食器

baking powder *n.* ベーキングパウダー, ふくらし粉

balance

1 *v.* MAKE STEADY: (balance A with/and B) (AとBの) バランスをとる, つり合いをとる, (keep one's balance) バランスを保つ; (budget, account) 決算する

2 *n.* STEADINESS: バランス, つり合い, 均衡, (of color, shape, sound) 調和, (of mind) 平静

3 *n.* REMAINING MONEY: 残高

4 *n.* INSTRUMENT FOR WEIGHING: はかり, 天秤

1 balance on a tightrope
綱渡りのロープの上でバランスをとる

balance a ball on one's finger
バランスをとりながらボールを指の上にのせる

2 keep one's balance バランスを保つ
lose one's balance バランスを失う
be off balance バランスが崩れる

3 check one's (bank) balance
(口座の)残高を照会する

be in the balance どちらとも決まらない, どうなるかわからない
The outcome is still in the balance.
結果はまだ、どうなるかわからない。

♦**balance of payments** *n.* 国際収支

balanced *adj.* (of report) バランスがいい

balcony *n.* (of building) バルコニー, ベランダ [→ picture of APARTMENT, HOUSE], (in theater) 2階席, さじき

bald *adj.* (of head) はげた, 髪のない, (of carpet) すり切れた
He's as bald as a coot.
あの人は、つるつるにはげている。
The carpet's gone bald here.
カーペットはここがすり切れている。

go bald (of person) はげる

ball *n.* ボール, 玉, 球
a snow ball 雪玉
a rice ball おにぎり
Look at the kitten playing with that ball of wool.
見て、子猫が毛糸玉で遊んでいるよ。

play ball (play a ball game) ボール遊びをする, (play baseball) 野球をする; (cooperate) 協力する

ballad *n.* バラード

ballast *n.* バラスト, 底荷

ball bearing *n.* ボールベアリング

ballerina *n.* バレリーナ

ballet *n.* バレエ
Swan Lake is probably the best-known ballet.
『白鳥の湖』はおそらく最もよく知られているバレエです。

♦**ballet dancer** *n.* バレエダンサー

ball game *n.* (in general) 球技, (baseball game) 野球; (competition) 競争

balloon *n.* バルーン, (toy) 風船, (hot-air balloon) 熱気球; (space for words in a cartoon) 吹き出し

ballot *n.* (vote) 投票, (voting sheet) 投票用紙
v. (…に) 投票を求める, (**ballot for/against**) …に賛成/反対の投票をする
The union decided to ballot the members.
組合は会員に投票を求めることにした。

♦**ballot box** *n.* 投票箱

ballpoint pen *n.* ボールペン [→ picture of STATIONERY]

ballroom *n.* ダンスホール

♦**ballroom dancing** *n.* 社交ダンス

bamboo *n.* タケ, 竹
a bamboo grove 竹やぶ

♦**bamboo shoots** *n.* 竹の子, 筍

ban *v.* (forbid) 禁止する, 禁じる
n. 禁止
The government banned all demonstrations.
政府はあらゆるデモを禁止した。
The player was banned from playing for a month.
その選手は1ヵ月間、出場停止になった。

a ban on nuclear testing 核実験の禁止

banana *n.* バナナ

a bunch of bananas バナナ一房

go bananas 頭がおかしくなる

band[1] *n.* (group of people) 一団, 群れ, (group of musicians) バンド, 楽団

a band of youths 若者の一団

a rock band ロックバンド

band[2] *n.* (stringlike fastener) バンド, (headband) はち巻き

a hair band ヘアーバンド

a rubber band 輪ゴム

bandage *n.* 包帯 [→ picture of FIRST-AID KIT]

v. (…に) 包帯を巻く

put a bandage on/around the knee
ひざに包帯を巻く

bang[1] *n.* ドン(という音), ドスン, (explosion) ドカン, (slamming sound) バタン

v. (strike: head etc.) ガンとぶつける, (knock loudly) ドンドンとたたく

What was that bang?
あのバーンという音は何でしょう?

The door shut with a bang.
ドアがバタンと閉まった。

She banged her head against the shelf.
彼女は棚に頭をゴツンとぶつけた。

He was banging the wood into place.
彼は木材をたたいてはめ込んでいた。

He banged on the door.
男はドンドンとドアをたたいた。

bang[2] *n.* (**bangs**) 前髪

banish *v.* 追放する

♦**banishment** *n.* 追放

banister *n.* 手すり

banjo *n.* バンジョー

bank[1] *n.* (establishment for handling money) 銀行

v. (**bank on**) 当てにする, …に頼る

Ms. Kimura works at a bank.
木村さんは銀行で働いています。

open a bank account 銀行に口座を開く

♦**bank account** *n.* (銀行)預金口座

bank balance *n.* (銀行)預金残高

bankbook *n.* 預金通帳

banker *n.* 銀行家, 銀行役員

bank holiday *n.* 休日, 祭日 [→ HOLIDAY]

banking *n.* (business) 銀行業, 銀行業務, (depositing/withdrawing of funds) 預金の出し入れ, バンキング

bank statement *n.* (銀行の)取引明細書

bank[2] *n.* (**banks**) (=of river) 川岸, (=of earth) 土手, 堤

bankrupt *adj.* (of company) 倒産した, (of person) 破産した, (of bank) 破綻した

v. 倒産させる

go bankrupt 倒産する, つぶれる

Even banks can go bankrupt.
銀行だって破綻することはあります。

bankruptcy *n.* (of company) 倒産, (of person) 破産, (of bank) 破綻

banner *n.* (horizontal) 横断幕, (vertical) 垂れ幕

banquet *n.* 宴会

baptism *n.* 洗礼, (ceremony) 洗礼式

baptize *v.* (…に) 洗礼を施す, (**be baptized**) 洗礼を受ける

bar

1 *n.* DRINKING PLACE: バー, (bar counter) カウンター

2 *n.* METAL ROD: 棒, (**bars**) 格子

3 *n.* PIECE: (**a bar of...**) ...1個

4 *v.* OBSTRUCT: ふさぐ, (**bar from doing**) (...が)...するのを禁止する, (**be barred from school**) 停学になる

1 It's my favorite bar.
僕の行きつけのバーだよ。

He was sitting alone at the bar.
彼はカウンターに一人で座っていた。

2 an iron bar 鉄の棒

The prisoners sawed off the bars of their cells.
囚人は、監房の鉄格子をのこぎりで切り落とした。

3 a bar of soap せっけん1個

a chocolate bar 板チョコ

4 They barred our way by blocking the corridor.
彼らは廊下をふさいで、私たちが通れないようにした。

The man was barred from drinking at that pub.
男はそのパブで飲むことを禁止された。

She was barred from school last year.
彼女は去年停学になった。

bar none 例外なく

barbarian *n.* 野蛮人

barbaric *adj.* (savage) 野蛮な, (cruel) 残酷な

barbecue *n.* バーベキュー

barbed wire *n.* 有刺鉄線

barber *n.* 理容師

♦ **barbershop** *n.* 理髪店, 床屋(さん)

bar code *n.* バーコード

bare *adj.* (naked) 裸の, (exposed) むき出しの, (empty) 空の

We were bare from our waists up.
僕らは上半身裸だった。

I did it with my bare hands.
素手でやったんです。

The trees are bare during these cold months.
この寒い時季には、木々は落葉している。

the bare earth むき出しの地面

The floor was bare.
床には何もなかった。

The cupboards were completely bare.
戸棚はすっかり空だった。

the bare minimum 最低, 最低限

5% is the bare minimum we can expect.
最低5パーセントは期待できます。

barefoot *adj., adv.* はだしの/で

walk barefoot はだしで歩く

bare-handed *adj., adv.* 素手の/で

barely *adv.* (just) ぎりぎり, かろうじて, (hardly) ほとんど...ない

I barely made it on time.
ぎりぎり間に合った。

There's barely enough time.
ほとんど時間がない。

bargain *n.* (item bought cheaply) バーゲン品, 掘り出し物; (agreement) 契約, 取引

v. (negotiate) 交渉する, (negotiate a price) 値切る

This coat was a bargain.
このコートは掘り出し物だった。

He bargained till he got the price he wanted.
彼は希望の価格まで値切った。

reach/strike a bargain 取り決めをする,

手を打つ

They struck a bargain.
彼らは手を打った。

barge *n.* (ship) はしけ
v. (**barge in**: rudely enter) 押しかける, (**barge in on**: conversation) …に口を挟む

baritone *n.* バリトン

bark[1] *n.* (of dog) ほえる声, ワンワン
v. ほえる
That dog barks every time someone comes near.
あの犬は誰かが近寄るたびにほえる。

bark[2] *n.* (of tree) 木の皮, 樹皮

barley *n.* 大麦

barn *n.* 納屋

barometer *n.* (pressure gauge) 気圧計; (indicator of change) バロメーター, 指標

baron *n.* 男爵

baroness *n.* 男爵夫人

barrel *n.* (of alcohol) たる, (of oil) バレル; (of gun) 銃身

barricade *n.* バリケード
v. (build a barricade across) (…に) バリケードを築く, (**barricade oneself in**) …に立てこもる

barrier *n.* (obstruction) 障害, (wall) 壁, (fence, railing) さく

bartender *n.* バーテン

barter *v.* 物々交換する, (barter A for B) (AをBと) 交換する

base[1]
1 *n.* BOTTOM: 土台, 台
2 *n.* FOUNDATION: 土台, 基礎, 元
3 *n.* MILITARY BASE: 基地
4 *n.* IN BASEBALL: -塁, ベース
5 *n.* MAIN INGREDIENT: 主成分, ベース
6 *n.* SUBSTANCE: (in chemistry) 塩基
7 *v.* FOUND: (**be based on**) …に基づいている

1 the base of the tower 塔の土台
the base of the lamp スタンドの台
the base of the tree 木の根元

2 His life was the base for a famous movie.
彼の人生は、有名な映画の元になった。

3 a naval base 海軍基地
He lives on base.
彼は基地で生活している。

4 first base 一塁
home base ホームベース
The runner was off base.
走者はベースを離れていた。

5 a cocktail with a vodka base
ウォッカをベースにしたカクテル

6 Is it an acid or a base?
酸ですか、塩基ですか？

7 The report is based on a survey.
この報告書は調査に基づいている。
Are these stories based on fact?
この話は事実に基づいているんですか？

base[2] *adj.* (wicked) 卑しい, (having no morals) 卑劣な

baseball *n.* 野球
play baseball 野球をする
♦**baseball cap/hat** *n.* 野球帽
baseball player *n.* 野球選手

base camp *n.* ベースキャンプ

baseline *n.* (in sport) ベースライン

basement *n.* 地下, 地下室

bashful *adj.* 内気な, はにかんだ, (be

bashful about) 恥ずかしがる

basic *adj.* (fundamental) 基本的な, 基礎的な, 根本的な, (elementary) 基本の, ベーシックな

There are certain basic rules that need to be observed.
守らねばならない基本的な規則というものがある。

The facilities were very basic.
設備は非常に基本的なものだった。

He has a basic understanding of Urdu.
彼はウルドゥー語の基礎ができています。

basically *adv.* (essentially) 基本的に, (put simply) 要するに, 簡単に言えば

basics *n.* (**the basics**) 基本, 基礎, (the first steps) 始め, 初歩

basil *n.* (herb, leaf) バジル

basin *n.* (bowl for washing face) 洗面器 [→ picture of BATHROOM], (washtub) たらい; (land feature) 盆地

basis *n.* (foundation) 根拠, 基礎

What was the basis of his philosophy?
彼の人生観の根拠は何だったのですか？

on a temporary basis 臨時で

Mr. Yamada is only working here on a temporary basis.
山田さんはここで臨時で働いているだけです。

on the basis of …に基づいて

On the basis of this agreement, can we move forward?
この合意に基づいて、進めてよろしいですか？

basket *n.* かご, バスケット, (basketful) かご1杯, (in basketball) ゴールネット, (point scored) 得点, 1点

a shopping basket 買い物かご

basketball *n.* バスケットボール

bass[1] *n.* (sound) バス, 低音, (instrument) ベース

♦**bass guitar** *n.* ベース(ギター)

bass[2] *n.* (fish) バス

bassoon *n.* バスーン, ファゴット

bastard *n.* (illegitimate child) ((*offensive*)) 私生児; (jerk) 野郎

bat[1] *n.* (in baseball) バット

bat[2] *n.* (animal) コウモリ

batch *n.* 1回分, (of papers) 一束, (group) 1群

a batch of letters 手紙の束

bath *n.* (お)ふろ, 入浴 [→ picture of BATHROOM] [NOTE: an open-air bath 露天ぶろ]

Are you going to take a bath?
おふろに入る？

Who's going to get into the bath first?
誰が最初におふろに入る？

Is he out of the bath yet?
彼はもうおふろから上がった？

We'd like a room with a bath, please.
おふろ付きの部屋をお願いします。

♦**bath towel** *n.* バスタオル

bathe *v.* (wash) 水につける, 洗う, (put in a bath) (お)ふろに入れる, (take a bath) (お)ふろに入る, 入浴する

We bathed the dog.
犬をおふろに入れた。

bathing *n.* (in bath) 入浴

♦**bathing suit** *n.* 水着

bathrobe *n.* バスローブ

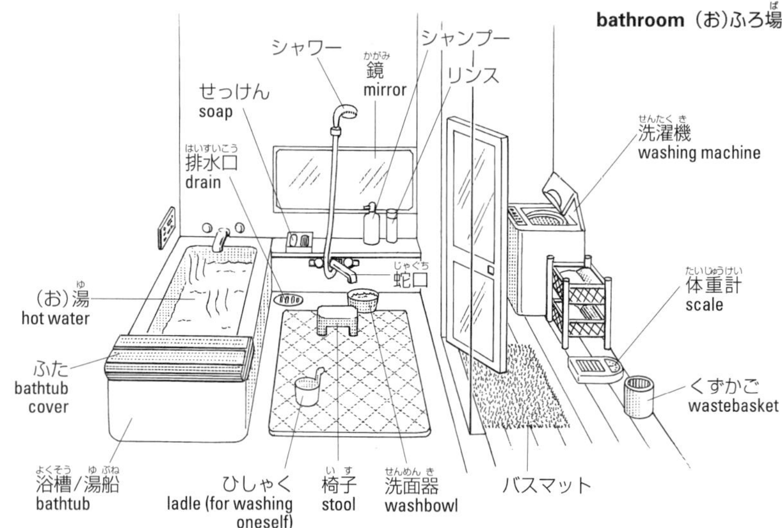

bathroom ***n.*** (room with a toilet) お手洗い, トイレ [→ picture of TOILET], (room with a bath) (お)ふろ場, 浴室 [→ picture above]

I have to go to the bathroom.
トイレに行かないと。

bathtub ***n.*** 浴槽, 湯船, バスタブ [→ picture above, PUBLIC BATH]

baton ***n.*** (conductor's) 指揮棒, タクト, (police officer's) 警棒, (runner's) バトン

batter[1] ***v.*** (beat) 殴る, 乱打する

a husband who batters his wife
妻を殴る夫

batter[2] ***n.*** (in baseball) 打者, バッター

batter[3] ***n.*** (cooking liquid) 衣の生地

tempura batter 天ぷらの衣の生地

battery ***n.*** (for electronic devices) 電池, (for car) バッテリー

These batteries need recharging.
この電池は充電が必要だ。

The battery is dead.
バッテリーが上がった。

battle ***n.*** 戦い, 戦闘, (struggle) 闘い, (competition) 闘争

v. (struggle) 闘う [→ FIGHT]

the Battle of Sekigahara 関ヶ原の合戦

The battle against poverty has only just begun.
貧困との闘いはまだ始まったばかりです。

♦**battlefield** ***n.*** 戦場

battleship ***n.*** 戦艦

bay ***n.*** 湾, (in proper names) ...湾

Tokyo Bay 東京湾

bay leaf ***n.*** ベイリーフ, 月桂樹の葉

bazaar ***n.*** (fund-raising sale) バザー; (Middle-Eastern market) バザール, 市場

BC ***abbr.*** (before Christ) 紀元前...

200 BC 紀元前200年

be

1 *v.* FOLLOWED BY A COMPLEMENT: (**is/was** ...) ...だ/だった, ((*polite*)) ...です/でした, ((*written*)) ...である/であった

2 *v.* EXIST: (of inanimate objects) ある, (of animate objects) いる

3 ***aux.*** CONTINUOUS TENSE: (**is/was doing**) ...している/していた, (**have been doing**) ずっと...している

4 ***aux.*** USED TO FORM THE PASSIVE VOICE: <passive form of verb>

5 ***aux.*** EXPRESSING INTENTION: (**is/am/are going to do** or **is/am/are doing**) ...するつもりだ, ...する

6 *v.* PERFECT TENSE: (**have been to**: a place) ...に行ったことがある

7 *v.* BECOME: (...に)なる

8 *v.* COST: (**is/was...**) ...だ/だった

9 ***aux.*** FOLLOWED BY "TO" AND AN INFINITIVE: (**is/am/are to do**) (expressing intention) ...する予定だ, ...することになっている

1 I am John, and this is Melanie.
僕はジョン、こちらはメラニーです。

He's Chinese, isn't he?
あの人は中国人でしょ?

Mr. Tanaka is a carpenter.
田中さんは大工さんです。

He's twenty-seven years old.
彼は 27 歳です。

It is May 4th today.
今日は5月4日です。

The room is new and spacious.
部屋は新しくて、広い。

Are you ready? 用意はいい?

Be careful! 気をつけて!

It isn't a very good idea.
あまりいい考えではないね。

This sweater isn't pure wool.
このセーターは純毛じゃない。

She was ill.
彼女は病気だったんです。

It was very hot. すごく暑かった。

She was an old friend of mine.
彼女は旧友でした。

Trouble is, it'll be too late then.
問題は、それじゃ遅すぎるってことです。

The funny thing is, nobody knew anything about it.
おかしなことに、そのことについては誰も何も知らなかったんです。

2 There are some good books there.
あそこにはいい本があります。

It's on the table.
(それは)テーブルの上にある。

She's upstairs.
彼女は2階にいます。

Are they in Kyoto?
彼らは京都にいるんですか?

"Where have you been?"
"I've been in the basement."
「どこにいたの?」
「地下室にいたんだよ」

3 It's always raining in this country.
この国ではしょっちゅう雨が降っている。

What I'm talking about is something different from that.
私が話しているのは、それとは違うことです。

He's cooking dinner.
彼は夕飯を作っているところです。

B

You're being very kind today.
今日はずいぶん優しいね。

She was reading.
彼女は本を読んでいた。

She's been waiting for hours.
彼女は何時間もずっと待っているんですよ。

By the time you get your medical degree, you will have been studying for 11 years.
医学の学位を取るころには、11 年も勉強したことになりますよ。

4 They'll be told off if they do that again.
もう一度同じことをやったら、彼らはしかられるでしょう。

She is very well known around here.
あの人は、このあたりではよく知られています。

He is disliked by everyone.
あの人はみんなに嫌われている。

5 I am going to the office tomorrow.
明日、事務所に行くつもりです。

What are you doing this evening?
今夜、何をするの？

I am leaving tomorrow.
明日たちます。

6 He's been to Greece.
あの人はギリシャに行ったことがある。

"Have you ever been to India?"
"Yes, I have."
「インドに行ったことはありますか？」
「ええ、あります」

7 She decided to be a teacher.
彼女は教師になろうと決めた。

8 "How much was it?"
"It was only ¥1,000."
「いくらだった？」
「たった1000円だったよ」

9 I'm to make the arrangements.
私が手配することになっています。

He's to be respected for it.
彼はそのことで尊敬されるべきです。

What is to be done about this?
これはどうすればいいのでしょう？

If this project is to be finished by October, we'd better get a move on.
この企画を10月までに終わらせるつもりなら、そろそろ始めたほうがいいですね。

beach *n.* 浜, 浜辺, 海辺, 海岸, ビーチ
go to the beach 海岸に行く

♦**beach hut** *n.* 浜辺の小屋, 海の家

bead *n.* (**beads**) (for making jewelry) ビーズ, (of Buddhist rosary) じゅず; (of sweat, water) 玉, しずく

beagle *n.* ビーグル犬

beak *n.* くちばし

beam *n.* (of light) 光線, (radio beam) ビーム; (wooden beam) けた, はり
v. (smile with joy) ほほえむ

bean *n.* 豆 [NOTE: Popular beans in Japan include soybeans 大豆, adzuki beans 小豆, kidney beans インゲン豆, string beans サヤインゲン, peas エンドウ豆/グリーンピース, broad beans 空豆, snow

beans and peas 豆

サヤインゲン
string/green beans

空豆
broad/fava/horse beans

エンドウ豆/グリーンピース
peas

絹さや
snow peas

peas 絹さや/サヤエンドウ, and young soybeans in the pod 枝豆.]

spill the beans うっかり秘密を漏らす

beanbag *n.* (toy) お手玉

bean curd *n.* 豆腐

bean sprouts *n.* もやし

bear¹ *v.*

1 TOLERATE: がまんする, (…に) 耐える, (bear up) 耐える, くじけずにがんばる

2 CARRY: 運ぶ, (weight) 支える, (responsibility) 負う, (cost) 払う

3 PRODUCE: (children) 産む, (**bear fruit**) 果物が実る, 実がなる

4 HEAD IN A PARTICULAR DIRECTION: (…に) 向かう, 進む

1 I can't bear it anymore. I must meet her.
もうがまんできない。彼女に会わなきゃ。

I just can't bear the noise anymore!
もうこれ以上あの騒音には耐えられない!

2 The chair couldn't bear his weight.
その椅子は彼の体重を支えられなかった。

Somebody is going to have to bear the responsibility for this blunder.
この失敗の責任は、誰かが負わなければならない。

3 She holds the national record for the number of children she has borne.
産んだ子供の数では、彼女はこの国の最高記録をもっている。

After the cold winds we had this spring, I doubt if the trees will bear much fruit.
この春あんな冷たい風が吹いた後では、果物はあまり実らないんじゃないかと思う。

4 Just keep bearing left and you'll find it.
左に進んで行けば見つかりますよ。

bear² *n.* (animal) クマ, 熊

Are there any bears left in Hokkaido?
北海道にはまだクマがいますか?

beard *n.* ひげ, あごひげ

grow a beard ひげを生やす

have a beard ひげを生やしている

♦**bearded** *adj.* (あご)ひげを生やした, ひげのある

bearing *n.* (**bearings**: sense of direction) 自分の位置; (influence) 影響, 関係; (**bearings**: metal devices) 軸受け, ベアリング [→ BALL BEARING]

take one's bearings
自分の位置を確かめる

have a bearing on …に関係がある

beast *n.* (animal) 獣, 野獣; (cruel person) 残酷な奴, けだもの

beat

1 *v.* OVERCOME: (…に) 勝つ, (**be beaten**) 負かされる, (**beat a record**) 記録を破る

2 *n.* RHYTHMIC MOVEMENT: (in music) ビート, 拍子, (of heart) 心拍, 鼓動

3 *v.* STRIKE: (person) 殴る, たたく, (**beat up**) さんざん殴る, (**beat against**: of rain) …に打ちつける, (**beat down on**: of sunlight) …にカンカン照りつける

4 *v.* MIX BY STIRRING RAPIDLY: (eggs etc.) かき混ぜる, 泡立てる

5 *v.* FLAP: (**beat wings**) 翼をパタパタ/バタバタさせる, 羽ばたく

6 *v.* OF HEART: 鼓動する, (with excitement/anxiety) ドキドキする

1 We beat them easily.
彼らに簡単に勝った [楽勝した]。

They were beaten.

彼らは(打ち)負かされた。

Let's try to beat the record.
記録を破るようがんばりましょう。

2 Try to keep to the beat.
ビートに合わせるようにして。

3 He beat me with a stick.
男は私を棒で殴った。

He was beaten up by some yakuza thugs.
彼は数人のやくざにさんざん殴られた。

The rain beat against the window.
雨が窓に打ちつけた。

4 First, you need to beat the eggs.
まず卵を泡立てます。

5 The bird beat its wings.
鳥が羽ばたいた。

6 The doctor said the patient's heart was beating unusually fast.
患者の脈拍が異常なほど速くなっていると、医者は言った。

beats me わからない

be dead beat 疲れ果てている, くたくただ

I'm off to bed. I'm dead beat.
寝るよ。くたくたなんだ。

beating ***n.*** (of heart) 鼓動; (pummeling) 殴ること

give someone a beating ぶん殴る

beautiful ***adj.*** 美しい, きれいな, (splendid) すばらしい, みごとな

a beautiful woman 美人

a beautiful sunset
美しい [きれいな] 夕焼け

a beautiful mind 美しい心

It's a beautiful photograph.
すばらしい写真です。

♦**beautifully** ***adv.*** 美しく, きれいに, (splendidly) すばらしく

beauty ***n.*** 美しさ, (beautiful woman) 美人

♦**beauty parlor** ***n.*** 美容院

beaver ***n.*** ビーバー

because ***conj.*** …ので, …から, (**just because**) …からといって

I can go because I'm free that day.
その日はあいているので、行けますよ。

"Why didn't you go?"
"Because I was sick."
「どうして行かなかったの？」
「病気だったんだ」

Just because you got a better grade than me doesn't mean you're smarter.
((*masculine*)) 僕よりいい点を取ったからといって、君のほうが賢いとは限らない。

because of (due to) …のため(に), …で, (implying blame) …のせいで, (expressing gratitude) ((*also ironic*)) …のおかげで

He didn't play because of an injury.
けがのため彼は試合に出なかった。

And because of this you quit?
それでやめたの？

I couldn't see Mt. Fuji because of the clouds.
雲のせいで、富士山は見えなかった。

The project succeeded because of you.
(あなたの)おかげで、このプロジェクトは成功しました。

It was only possible because of your hard work.
あなたのがんばりのおかげで、できたことです。

become ***v.*** (come to be) (…に) なる

Much to everyone's surprise, he became a pilot.
誰もが驚いたことには、彼はパイロットになった。

We gradually became good friends.
だんだんいい友達になっていった。

It became clear that it was a no-win situation.
勝ち目のない状況にあることが明らかになった。

She became more and more beautiful as time passed.
時がたつにつれて、彼女はますます美しくなっていきました。

I wonder what will become of him.
あの人はどうなるんだろう。

I wonder what became of that old car Mr. Ono had.
小野さんが持っていたあの古い車は、どうなったんだろう。

bed ***n.*** (piece of furniture) ベッド; (**bed of flowers**) 花壇

a single bed シングルベッド

a double bed ダブルベッド

I sat down on the bed.
ベッドに腰かけた。

Which do you prefer, a bed or a futon?
ベッドか布団か、どちらが好きですか？

Sorry, did I get you out of bed?
ごめんなさい。起こしてしまった？

I stayed in bed all day.
一日中、寝ていた。

go to bed 寝る

I went to bed early. 早く寝た。

make the bed ベッドを整える

Haven't you made the bed yet?
まだベッドを整えてないの？

put to bed 寝かしつける

I've already put the children to bed.
子供たちはもう寝かしつけました。

bed and breakfast ***n.*** (Japanese-style) (朝食付き) 民宿, (Western-style) B & B

bedclothes ***n.*** シーツと毛布, 寝具

bedcover ***n.*** ベッドカバー

bedding ***n.*** 寝具

bedridden ***adj.*** 寝たきりの

bedroom ***n.*** 寝室

bedsore ***n.*** 床ずれ

bedspread ***n.*** ベッドカバー

bedtime ***n.*** 寝る時間, 就寝時間

bee ***n.*** ミツバチ, 蜜蜂

beech ***n.*** (tree) ブナ, (wood) ブナ材

beef ***n.*** 牛肉, ビーフ

roast beef ローストビーフ

Kobe beef is famous throughout Japan.
神戸牛は全国的に有名です。

beefsteak ***n.*** ビーフステーキ

beehive ***n.*** ハチの巣

beep ***n.*** ビーッ/ピーッ(という音)

beeper ***n.*** ポケベル, ポケットベル

beer ***n.*** ビール, (bottled beer) びんビール, (draft beer) 生ビール, (microbrew) 地ビール

a bottle of beer ビール1本

I've had two glasses of beer.
ビールを2杯飲んだ。

beet ***n.*** ビート

♦**beetroot** ***n.*** ビートの根

beetle ***n.*** カブトムシ

before

1 ***prep.*** IN ADVANCE OF: …の前に, …より先に

2 *prep.* IN FRONT OF: …の前に

3 *conj.* SOONER THAN: (**before one does sth**) …する前に, (**before sth happens**) …しないうちに

4 *adv.* PREVIOUSLY: 今まで(に), 以前(に), 前に

1 the day before yesterday
おととい [((*formal*)) 一昨日]

It was just before the summer holidays.
ちょうど夏休みの前のことだった。

You have to sign here before going in.
((*polite*)) お入りになる前に、ここにご署名ください。

before 1930 １９３０ 年以前に

I got there before you.
私のほうが先に着いた。

2 He stood before the entrance.
彼は入口の前に立った。

The hotel is about two hundred meters before the bridge.
ホテルは橋の200メートルほど手前です。

She's got a bright future before her.
彼女の前途には明るい未来がある。

I've got a difficult few months before me.
これからの数ヵ月は大変です。

You've got your whole life before you.
人生は、まだこれからじゃないですか。

3 Can I speak to you before you leave?
((*polite*)) お帰りになる前にお話しできますか？

But before we do that, I'd like to eat.
でもそれをする前に食事がしたいんです。

We used to use typewriters before computers became commonplace.
コンピューターが普及する前は、タイプライターを使っていた。

We had a meeting before we decided to continue with the project.
その事業を続行すると決める前に会議を開いた。

Let's go back before it gets dark.
暗くならないうちに帰りましょう。

4 Have you been to Japan before?
今までに日本に行ったことがありますか？

I've heard that before.
それは前に聞いたよ。

a week before １週間前

half an hour before ３０ 分前

It had rained the night before.
前の晩に雨が降った。

We met the weekend before in Paris.
その前の週末にパリで出会った。

beforehand *adv.* あらかじめ, 前もって

If you can come, could you let us know beforehand?
もし来られるなら、前もって知らせてくれますか？

beg *v.* (**beg for**) 請う, …してくださいと頼む, 熱心に頼む, (only of beggar: scrounge change) 物乞いをする

I beg your pardon? → PARDON

♦**beggar** *n.* こじき, 物乞いする人

begin *v.* (initiate) 始める, 開始する, (**begin doing / to do**) …し始める, …しかける, …し出す, (start to happen) 始まる

Okay, let's begin.
じゃあ、始めましょう。

begin reading 読み始める

begin to understand わかりかける

It began to rain. 雨が降り出した。

We're beginning to like her.
私たちは彼女が好きになってきた。

What time did the program begin?
この番組は何時に始まったんですか？

The class didn't begin until 10:20.
授業は10時20分まで始まらなかった。

Hurry up! The game has already begun.
早く！ 試合はもう始まっているよ。

This is where the fun begins.
これからがお楽しみだ。

He began as a bellboy and rose to hotel manager.
彼はホテルのボーイから仕事を始め、支配人にまで出世した。

to begin with (in the beginning) 最初は, (first of all) まず第一に

beginner *n.* 初心者

beginning *n.* (start) 始め, 最初, (**beginnings**) (=person's background) 幼少期, (=origins) 起源, 源, 起こり

At the beginning, all was well.
最初はすべてうまくいっていた。

I liked the beginning of the film, but the end was sad.
映画の始まりはよかったけれど、終わりは悲しかった。

I read the book from beginning to end in one sitting.
その本は始めから終わりまで一気に読みました。

behalf *n.* (**on behalf of**) ...を代表して, ...に代わって

behave *v.* ふるまう, 態度をとる, (behave well) 行儀よくする

Just tell me why you're behaving so strangely.
どうしてそんなおかしな態度をとっているのか、教えてよ。

The children behaved very badly.
子供たちはひどく行儀が悪かった。

Behave yourself!
いいかげんにしなさい。

behavior *n.* (actions) 行動, (attitude) 態度, (demeanor) ふるまい

behind

1 *prep.* AT/TO/IN THE REAR OF: ...の後ろに/で, ...の後に/で, (behind a building) ...の裏に/で, (beyond) ...の向こうに/で, (behind and hidden from view) ...の陰に/で

2 *adv.* LATE/SLOW: 遅れて

3 *prep.* UNDERLYING: ...の背後に

4 *adv., prep.* MAKING SLOWER PROGRESS (THAN): (...より) 遅れて, 劣って

1 There were two people sitting behind me.
私の後ろには2人の人が座っていました。

Just behind the supermarket there's a small movie theater.
スーパーのすぐ裏に小さな映画館がある。

Shut the door behind you (as you come in), please.
入った後はドアを閉めてくださいね。

What's behind this wall?
この壁の向こうには何があるんですか？

The child hid behind his mother.
子供はお母さんの後ろに隠れた。

The sun has gone behind a cloud.
太陽が雲の陰に隠れた。

2 She is behind in her credit card payments.
彼女はクレジットカードの支払いが遅れている。

My watch is five minutes behind.
私の時計は5分遅れています。

3 Explain what's behind all these rumors.

このうわさの背後に何があるのか説明してください。

4 He's behind everyone in math.
彼は数学では皆より遅れている。

behind one's back 陰で, …のいないところで

He was going around behind my back saying I was a liar.
あの人は、陰で私のことをうそつきだと言いふらしていた。

behind the scenes 裏で, 背後で

God knows what goes on behind the scenes.
裏で一体何が起こっているのかは、誰にもわからない。

beige ***n., adj.*** ベージュ(の)

being ***n.*** (living entity) 生き物, 生命体, (state of existence) 存在

a being from another planet
別の惑星からの生命体

belch ***n.*** げっぷ

v. (burp) げっぷが出る, (belch smoke etc.) 噴出する

Belgium ***n.*** ベルギー

belief ***n.*** (opinion) 意見, (faith) 信仰, (conviction) 信念

believe ***v.*** (give credence to) 信じる, (think) (…と) 思う, 考える

I don't believe a word he says.
彼の言うことなんて、一言も信じない。

I don't believe in ghosts.
幽霊は信じていません。

I believe what she says even if you don't.
あなたが信じなくても、私は彼女の言うことを信じますよ。

I believe that's true.
それは本当だと思う。

I believe I know him.
その人のことは知っていると思う。

It is believed that four climbers are missing.
登山者が4名行方不明になったと思われます。

There are believed to be three culprits.
犯人は3人いると考えられている。

believe it or not 信じないかもしれないけど

Believe it or not, he wears a wig!
信じないかもしれないけど、あの人はかつらだよ。

believe (you) me 本当ですよ, いいですか

Believe me, the section chief is not going to like this.
いいですか、これは課長はきっと気に入らないよ。

believer ***n.*** (of religion) 信者

belittle ***v.*** けなす, 見くびる

bell ***n.*** (of church, temple) 鐘, (handheld bell) 鈴, ベル, (doorbell) 呼び鈴

ring a bell ベルを鳴らす

The (door)bell rang.
(玄関の) 呼び鈴が鳴った。

bellhop ***n.*** ボーイ

bellow ***v.*** (groan) うめく

bell pepper ***n.*** ピーマン

belly ***n.*** おなか, 腹, (lower) 下腹部, (upper) 胃 [→ picture of BODY]

a beer belly ビール腹

belly button ***n.*** (navel) (お)へそ [→ picture of BODY]

belong ***v.***

1 BE OWNED BY: (**belong to**) …のものだ

2 BE A MEMBER OF: (**belong to**) (club) …の会員だ, (organization) …に所属する

3 GO/COME WITH: (**belong with**) …に属する, …につく

4 FIT IN/BE SUITABLE: ふさわしい, 合う

1 That does not belong to you, so leave it where it is.
それはあなたのものじゃないんだから、元の場所に置いておきなさい。

Do you know who this land belongs to?
この土地は誰が所有しているか知っていますか？

2 Does he belong to this golf club?
彼はこのゴルフクラブの会員ですか？

We all belong to the same labor union.
全員同じ労働組合に所属しています。

3 I can't find the belt that belongs with these pants.
このズボンについているベルトが見つからない。

4 You don't belong here.
君はここでは場違いだ/君がいる所じゃない。

This page doesn't belong here. It should be at the beginning.
このページはここには合わない。冒頭にあるべきだ。

belonging *n.* (**sense of belonging**) 帰属意識; (**belongings**) 持ち物, 所持品

below

1 *prep., adv.* BENEATH: (…の) 下に/で, (…より) 低く

2 *adv.* IN WRITING: (indicating information that comes afterwards) 下記の/に, 以下の/に

3 *adv.* OF TEMPERATURE: 零下…

4 *prep.* OF RANK: …の下に/で

1 There is a parking lot below the building.
ビルの地下に駐車場があります。

I could see the traffic and crowds below me.
眼下に行き交う車や大勢の人が見えた。

Is there anything below this room?
この部屋の下には何かあるんですか？

They're having a party on the floor below.
下の階でパーティーをしている。

Down below we could see a river flowing in the valley.
下の方に谷を流れる川が見えた。

2 See below for further details.
詳細は下記のとおり。

The three points mentioned below…
以下に述べる三つの点は…

3 It was twenty below outside.
外は零下20度だった。

4 Mr. Hara has five people below him.
原さんには5人の部下がいる。

belt *n.* (item of clothing) ベルト

tighten [loosen] one's belt
ベルトを締める [ゆるめる]

fasten one's seat belt
シートベルトを締める

bench *n.* (outdoors) ベンチ, (indoors) 長椅子; (for doing work) 作業台

bend *v.* (force into a curve) 曲げる, (become curved) 曲がる, (be supple) しなる, (**bend over**: stoop) かがむ, 身をかがめる

n. (curve in road) カーブ; (**the bends**: decompression sickness) 潜水病

bend a wire [coat hanger]

ワイヤー [ハンガー] を曲げる

bend one's knees ひざを曲げる

Years of hard work in the rice fields had bent her back.

田んぼでの長年の重労働で、彼女の背中は曲がっていた。

The road bends sharply near the bridge.

道路は橋の近くで急カーブする。

The branch is bending.

枝が曲がっている。

Bamboo bends easily.

竹は、よくしなる。

She was bending over, pulling out weeds.

彼女はかがんで雑草を抜いていた。

Can you bend backwards?

体を後ろに反らせることができますか？

There's a nasty bend up ahead.

この先に危険なカーブがあります。

Steady as you go round this bend.

このカーブを曲がるときは気をつけて。

bend over backwards 懸命に努力する, できる限りのことをする

We bent over backwards to help them.

その人たちを助けるために、できる限りのことをした。

beneath *prep.* (…の) 下に/で [→ BELOW, UNDER, UNDERNEATH]

beneficial *adj.* 有益な, ためになる

benefit *n.* (advantage) 利益, (**benefits:** money) 手当, 給付金

v. (be beneficial for) (…の) ためになる, 利益になる, (get as a benefit) 利益を得る

Do the benefits outweigh the risks?

利益がリスクを上回っていますか？

For the benefit of those who missed last week's lecture…

先週の講義を聴き逃した人のために…

unemployment benefits 失業手当

The new tax plan will benefit small businesses.

新しい税制計画は中小企業に有利にはたらくだろう。

What do we stand to benefit from all this?

これによって、どういう利益があるんですか？

benign *adj.* (kind) 親切な, (of tumor) 良性の

bent *adj.* (not straight) 曲がった, (**be bent on doing**) …しようと決心している

The fork was bent in the middle.

フォークは真ん中で曲がっていた。

His head was bent forward over his books.

彼は本の上に顔をうつむけていました。

bento *n.* (box lunch) 弁当

bequeath *v.* (bequeath A to B) (AをBに) 遺言で贈る

bereaved *n.* (**the bereaved**) 遺族

bereavement *n.* 死別

beret *n.* ベレー(帽)

berry *n.* ベリー, 果実

beside *prep., adv.* …の横に/で, …のそばに/で, …の隣に/で

Just put it beside the sink.

流しの横に置いておいて。

We lived beside a lake.

私たちは湖のそばに住んでいました。

If you all stand together beside the wall,

I'll take a photograph.
壁際に並んで立ってくれたら、写真を撮ってあげるよ。

A fat man sat down beside me.
太った男が私の隣に座った。

be beside oneself with (anger) 怒り狂う, (joy) 狂喜する, 有頂天になる

He was beside himself with anger.
彼は怒り狂った。

The children were beside themselves with joy.
子供たちはうれしくて、すっかり有頂天になっていた。

beside the point 的はずれで, 無関係で

Whether he's foreign or not is beside the point.
その人が外国人かどうかは無関係です。

besides ***prep.*** (apart from) …以外に, …のほかに

adv. (used at the beginning of a sentence: in addition) それに, おまけに

What other sports can you play besides baseball and soccer?
野球とサッカーのほかに、どんなスポーツができる?

She's the only musician in the family besides her grandfather.
あの家族の中で音楽家は、おじいさん以外では彼女だけです。

Besides, it's fun.
おまけに、楽しい。

best ***adj.*** 最もよい, 一番いい

adv. 最もよく, 一番…

n. (**the best**) 最もよいもの, 最良, (best effort) 全力, 最善, 精いっぱい

It is the best movie I've ever seen.
今までに見た映画の中で一番いい。

This is the best room.
これが一番いい部屋です。

Is he your best friend?
彼が一番の親友なの?

I'm only trying to do what's best for you.
一番君のためになることをやろうとしているだけだよ。

I think the red and black outfit suits you best.
赤と黒の服が一番似合うと思うよ。

And, best of all, there was a happy ending.
それに何より、ハッピーエンドでした。

Who did the best on the exam?
試験で一番よくできたのは誰ですか?

It was the best they could manage.
それが彼らにできる精いっぱいのことだった。

all the best ご成功を, (used at the end of a letter) お元気で

I wish you all the best in your new career.
新しいお仕事でのご成功 [ご活躍] をお祈りします。

at best せいぜい

She speaks only a little Italian at best.
彼女はせいぜい少しイタリア語が話せる程度です。

(at) one's best 最高の状態で

I'm not at my best in the morning.
朝は最高の状態じゃないんです。

best of luck がんばって (lit.,"persevere")

"I have my driving test today."
"Best of luck."
「今日、運転免許の試験があるんです」

「がんばってね」

do one's best 全力を尽くす, ベストを尽くす, 最善を尽くす

Just do your best.
とにかく全力を尽くしなさい。

You can't blame them—they did their best.
彼らを責められないよ—最善を尽くしたんだから。

hope for the best うまくいくよう祈る, 幸運を願う

All we could do was hope for the best.
できることと言えば、幸運を願うことだけだった。

it's best if …したほうがいい

It's probably best if I go first.
たぶん、私が先に行ったほうがいい。

It's best if you leave the computer running.
コンピューターは、つけっぱなしにしておくほうがいいよ。

make the best of できるだけよくしようとする

The hotel was not good, but we made the best of it.
ホテルはよくなかったが、それなりに楽しもうとした。

second best (person/thing) 2位の人/もの, 2番目にいい人/もの

There's no shame in being second best.
2位だからといって恥じることはないよ。

best man *n.* 新郎の付添人

bestow *v.* 与える, ((*formal*)) 授ける

bestseller *n.* ベストセラー

bet *n.* (wager) 賭け

v. (**bet on**: wager money on) …に金を賭ける; (**I bet that…**) きっと…

I thought it was a sure bet.
確実だと思ったんです。

Did you bet a lot of money on the horse?
あの馬に大金を賭けたの？

Yamaguchi bet ¥10,000.
山口さんは1万円賭けた。

I bet she'll be there.
きっと彼女もいるよ。

betray *v.* (turn one's back on) 裏切る

betray somebody's trust
人の信頼を裏切る

♦**betrayal** *n.* 裏切り

better

1 *adj.* SUPERIOR: (…のほうが) いい, (preferable but not great) ましな, (**be better than…**) (…のほうが)…よりいい

2 *adj.* IMPROVED: (of conditions: **become/get better**) よくなる, 改善する, (**get better**: become healthier than before) よくなる, 回復する

3 *adv.* MORE SKILLFULLY: うまく, 上手に

4 *v.* MAKE BETTER: よりよくする, (**better oneself**) (=improve one's social position) 出世する, (=improve/cultivate one's character) 自分を磨く

1 Which book do you think is better?
どっちの本がいいと思う？

This car is better than that one.
この車は、あれよりもいい。

He's a lot better than you at golf.
ゴルフは彼のほうが君よりずっとうまい。

It would be better for him if he did not talk so much.
あの人、あんなにしゃべらないほうがい

いのにね。

2 Things have gotten a lot better since the new manager came.
新しい経営者が来てから、状況はずっとよくなった。

"How are you now?"
"Much better, thanks."
「気分はどうですか？」
「かなりよくなりました。ありがとう」

3 My husband cooks better than me.
夫は私より料理がうまい。

4 It's only natural for people to want to better themselves.
出世したいと思うのは、ごく自然なことです。

be better off (be living better) 以前より暮らし向きがいい, (**be better off doing**) …するほうがいい

They're much better off now than they used to be.
あの人たちは、今のほうが以前よりずっと暮らし向きがいい。

You'd be better off running your own business.
自分で事業をやるほうがいいよ。

be no better than… …も同然だ, …と変わらない

You're no better than the rest.
君だってほかの人と変わらない。

for the better part of …の大部分, …の大半

He's been in bed for the better part of the day.
彼は今日、大半をベッドの中で過ごしています。

get the better of 負かす, …に勝つ

The other team got the better of us.
我々は相手チームに負かされた。

had better do …するほうがいい, …したほうがいい

You'd better go wash up.
体を洗ってきたほうがいいよ。

I don't think you'd better say that to him.
彼にそれを言わないほうがいいと思う。

Better leave her alone.
そっとしておいたほうがいい。

Better not wake him.
彼を起こさないほうがいいよ。

the sooner the better 早ければ早いほどいい

The sooner he gets here the better.
あの人がここに着くのは、早ければ早いほどいい。

between ***prep.*** …の間に/の, …の中間に/の

Russia lies between Japan and Europe.
ロシアは日本とヨーロッパの間にある。

You have to be there between 3 and 4 P.M.
午後3時から4時の間は、そこにいなければなりません。

Commuting between my home and the office each day takes up a lot of my time.
自宅と会社の間を毎日往復するのに、ずいぶん時間を取られています。

I'd say he's between 35 and 40.
あの人は 35 歳から 40 歳の間だと思う。

Is there something between them?
二人の間には何かあるの？

There's very little communication between us these days.
最近、私たちの間にはほとんど会話が

B

ない。

Between them, they own practically the entire district.
あの二人だけで、地域のほとんどすべてを所有しています。

between ourselves/just between you and me ここだけの話だが

Between ourselves, she has no talent.
ここだけの話ですけど、彼女には才能はないですよ。

Just between you and me, I'd say he's being a little too optimistic.
ここだけの話、あの人はちょっと楽観的すぎると思う。

in between (…の)間に, 中間に

In between the holidays, I work very hard.
休暇と休暇の間は、一生懸命働きます。

beverage *n.* 飲み物, 飲料

beware *v.* (beware of) (…に) 気をつける, 用心する, 注意する

bewilder *v.* (**be bewildered by**) …にとまどう

beyond *prep.* (on/to the farther side of) …の向こうに/へ/の; (later than) …以降に; (**be beyond**: exceed) …を超えている

The village lies beyond the mountains.
村は山の向こうにある。

Any applications submitted beyond this date will not be accepted.
この期日以降に提出された出願書は、無効となります。

It was beyond our understanding.
私たちの理解を超えていた。

It is beyond anyone's power to control.
それは誰の手にも負えませんよ。

be beyond reach 手の届かない所にある

bias *n.* 先入観, 偏った見方

v. (**be biased**) 先入観をもつ, 偏った考えをもつ

biased *adj.* (of opinion, judgment) 偏った

bib *n.* (for baby) よだれ掛け, (for adult eating messy food) 胸当て

bible *n.* (**the Bible**) 聖書, バイブル, (definitive book on a particular subject) バイブル

bibliography *n.* (list of references) 参考文献

biceps *n.* 二頭筋, 腕の筋肉

bicker *v.* 言い争う, 口げんかする

bicycle *n.* 自転車

Mr. Fujita goes to work by bicycle.
藤田さんは自転車で通勤している。

♦**bicycle parking lot** *n.* 駐輪場

bid *n.* (offer) 付け値, 入札; (attempt) 試み

v. (offer as a price) 値をつける, 入札する, (**bid for**: compete for at an auction) 競り合う

How much did you bid for the painting?
あの絵をいくらで入札したんですか？

♦**bidder** *n.* 入札者

bidding *n.* 競り, 入札

bifocals *n.* 遠近両用メガネ, 二焦点メガネ

big *adj.*

1 LARGE: 大きい, 大きな, (of room: spacious) 広い

2 IMPORTANT: 大切な, 重要な, 重大な, (of person) 偉い, (of plan) 大規模な

3 OLDER: 年上の

1 a big dog 大きな犬

He's too big to wear this jacket.
あの人は大きいから、このジャケットは着られません。

The table isn't big enough.
このテーブルでは小さすぎるよ。(lit., "This table is too small.")

This dress is big on me.
このドレスは私には大きい。

How big is the house?
家はどれくらいの広さですか？

a big dance hall 広いダンスホール

2 a big problem 重大な問題

a big opportunity 大きなチャンス

a big deal 大したもの

a big actor 大物俳優

a big project 大事業

3 my big brother [sister] 私の兄 [姉]

♦**big talk** *n.* 自慢話, ほら

big toe *n.* 足の親指

bike *n.* (bicycle) 自転車, (motorcycle) オートバイ, バイク, (moped) バイク

bikini *n.* ビキニ

bilateral *adj.* (between two countries) 2国間の, 両国の

bilateral relations 両国の関係

bile *n.* 胆汁

bilingual *adj.* (of person) バイリンガルの, (of text) 2カ国語の

bill[1] *n.* (written request for money owed) 請求書, (at restaurant) (お)勘定, (お)会計; (paper money) 紙幣, (お)札; (proposal for a law) 法案

v. (send a request for money to) (…に) 請求書を送る

a gas [electricity, water] bill
ガス [電気, 水道] 代の請求書

a credit card bill
クレジットカードの請求書

Can we have the bill, please?
お勘定、お願いします。

Do you think the bill will become law?
その法案は法制化されると思いますか？

fit the bill (suit perfectly) ぴったり合う, (of person for job) 必要条件を満たす

foot the bill (勘定を) 払う

split the bill 割り勘にする

bill[2] *n.* (large beak) くちばし

billboard *n.* 広告板

billiards *n.* ビリヤード

billion *n.* 10億

billionaire *n.* 億万長者

bin *n.* (garbage bin) ごみ箱, ごみ入れ

binary *adj.* 二進法の

bind

1 *v.* TIE UP: 縛る, (bind A to B) (AをBに) 縛り付ける, (bind a wound) (…に) 包帯をする, 包帯を巻く

2 *v.* CAUSE TO UNITE: (people) 結び付ける

3 *v.* OBLIGATE: (**be bound by**: rule, contract etc.) …に縛られる, …に束縛される [→ BOUND[1] 2]

4 *v.* BOOK: 製本する, 装丁する

5 *n.* NO-WIN SITUATION: 苦しい立場

6 *n.* NUISANCE: 面倒なこと

1 Bind the package tightly with string.
その包みをひもでしっかり縛って。

She was bound and gagged.
彼女は縛られて口をふさがれた。

Bind the wound with a sterile bandage.
傷口に殺菌した包帯を巻きなさい。

2 Natural disasters such as earthquakes can bind communities together.
地震などの自然災害が、地域の結び付きを強めることもある。

Americans are bound together by their love of freedom.
アメリカ人は、自由を愛する心で共に結び付いている。

3 Your company is bound by contract to finish this job before June.
貴社は6月までにこの仕事を終える契約になっています。

4 The books will be printed and bound in January.
本は1月に印刷、製本されます。

5 I'm in a bind. Do you think you could lend me some money?
困ってるんです。いくらかお金を貸してもらえませんか？

6 Having to go to the meeting was a bind, but there was no way out of it.
会議に出るのは面倒だったけど、行くしかなかった。

♦**bind up** *v.* (bundle up) 束ねる, くくる

binding *adj.* (of contract) 拘束力のある *n.* (book cover) 装丁, (act of putting pages of a book together) 製本

binoculars *n.* 双眼鏡

biochemistry *n.* 生化学

biodegradable *adj.* 生分解性の

bioengineering *n.* 生物工学

biographer *n.* 伝記作家

biography *n.* 伝記

biological *adj.* 生物学の

♦**biological weapon** *n.* 生物兵器

biologist *n.* 生物学者

biology *n.* 生物学

biotechnology *n.* バイオテクノロジー, 生物工学

birch *n.* (tree) カバの木, (wood) カバ材

bird *n.* 鳥, (small bird) 小鳥

What sort of bird is that?
何という種類の鳥ですか？

a bird's nest 鳥の巣

♦**bird's-eye view** *n.* 鳥瞰図

bird-watching *n.* バードウォッチング, 野鳥観察

birth *n.* (being born) 誕生, 出生, (giving birth) 出産

It was a difficult birth.
難産だった。

by birth 生まれは

He's Iranian by birth.
彼の生まれはイランだ。

give birth to 産む, 出産する

She gave birth to twins.
彼女は双子を出産した。

birth certificate *n.* 出生証明書

birth control *n.* 産児制限, (contraception) 避妊

♦**birth-control pill** *n.* ピル, ((*formal*)) 経口避妊薬

birthday *n.* 誕生日, バースデー [→ HAPPY BIRTHDAY!]

When's your birthday?
お誕生日はいつですか？

My birthday is February 10th.
私の誕生日は2月10日です。

Are you going to have a birthday party?
誕生パーティーを開きますか？

birthmark *n.* あざ

birthplace *n.* 出生地

birthrate *n.* 出生率

biscuit *n.* (small bread roll) 小型パン, (cookielike food) ビスケット

a dog biscuit 犬用ビスケット

bisexual *adj.* (of sexual orientation) バイセクシュアルの

n. (person) バイセクシュアル

bishop *n.* (Catholic) 司教, (Protestant) 主教

bison *n.* バイソン, 野牛

bit[1] *n.*

1 A LITTLE: (**a bit**) 少し, ちょっと

2 SMALL PIECE: (slice, piece) 一切れ, (fragment, shard) かけら, 破片

3 PART/SECTION: 部分, ところ

1 Can I have a bit?
少しもらっていいですか？

Can you just wait a bit?
ちょっとだけ待ってくれる？

She's a bit deaf.
彼女は、少し耳が遠いんです。

You're a bit like me.
あなたは、ちょっと私に似たところがあるんです。

These pants are a bit too small for me.
このズボンは僕には少し小さすぎる。

You're a bit late, aren't you?
ちょっと遅いんじゃない？

Frankly, I think he's a bit of a nuisance.
正直言って、あの人はちょっと困ったもんだと思う。

2 Would you like a bit of cheese?
チーズを一切れ、いかがですか？

Have you got a bit of old cloth?
古い布の切れ端はありますか？

There were bits of glass all over the carpet.
カーペット中に、ガラスの破片が落ちていた。

3 The really delicious bit is at the center.
本当においしいところは芯なんだ。

I enjoyed the book, especially the sexy bits.
本は面白かった、特に色っぽい部分が。

a bit much あんまりな, ひどすぎる

It's all been a bit much for me.
私にとっては何もかもがあんまりだった。

bit by bit 少しずつ

bits and pieces こまごました物, がらくた

do one's bit 自分の本分を尽くす, 分担を果たす

not a bit (not at all) 少しも…ない, ちっとも…ない

He hasn't changed a bit.
彼は少しも変わっていない。

"Are you scared of him?"
"No, not a bit."
「彼のことが怖いの？」
「いや、ちっとも」

bit[2] *n.* (tool) 刃; (for horse) はみ

bitch *n.* (female dog) めす犬, (woman) いやな女

v. (gripe) ぶつぶつ不平を言う

bite *v.* かむ, (**bite into**) …にかじりつく, (**bite off**) かみ切る, (**be bitten**: by insect) (…に) 刺される

n. (mouthful) 一口, (insect bite) 虫刺され, (animal bite) かまれた傷

The dog looked like it was going to bite me.

犬は今にもかみついてきそうだった。

I was bitten by mosquitoes.
蚊に刺された。

Here, take a bite.
ほら、一口食べて。

bitter *adj.* (of taste, experience) 苦い, (of cold, struggle) 厳しい, (of enemy) 憎い, (of remark) しんらつな

n. (kind of beer) ビター

a bitter taste 苦味 [苦い味]

a bitter disappointment 深い失望

to the bitter end (to the very end) 最後の最後まで, あくまで(も)

♦**bitterly** *adv.* ひどく

bitterness *n.* (taste) 苦味; (pain) 苦しさ

bizarre *adj.* 変な, 奇妙な, とっぴな

black

1 *adj.* OF COLOR: 黒い, (of person of African descent) 黒人の

2 *n.* COLOR: 黒, 黒色

3 *n.* PERSON: 黒人

4 *adj.* OF COFFEE: ブラックの

1 a black cat 黒猫

She has long black hair.
彼女は長い黒髪です。

Abe has a black belt in judo.
阿部さんは柔道で黒帯です。

black musicians 黒人のミュージシャン

2 She always wears black.
あの人はいつも黒を着ている。

an old TV show in black and white
白黒 [モノクロ] の古いテレビ番組

3 the first black to become president
大統領になった初めての黒人

4 Do you want your coffee black?
コーヒーはブラックにしましょうか?

♦**black out** *v.* (lose consciousness) 意識を失う, 失神する

black-and-white *adj.* (of photo) 白黒の, モノクロの, (of perspective) 白黒のはっきりした

blackboard *n.* 黒板

blacken *v.* (make black) 黒くする; (ruin: reputation etc.) 汚す

black hole *n.* ブラックホール

black humor *n.* ブラックユーモア

blacklist *n.* ブラックリスト

v. ブラックリストに載せる

blackmail *n.* ゆすり, 恐喝

v. ゆする, 恐喝する

black market *n.* やみ市

blackout *n.* (power failure) 停電; (loss of consciousness) 意識がなくなること

black sheep *n.* 厄介者, 持て余し者

blacksmith *n.* かじ屋

bladder *n.* ぼうこう

blade *n.* (edge for cutting) 刃; (leaf) 葉

The blade is blunt.
刃の切れ味が悪い。

a blade of grass 草の葉っぱ

blame *v.* (blame A for B, blame B on A) (BをAの) せいにする, (criticize) 非難する, 責める

n. (responsibility for error) 責任, (condemnation) 非難

He blames the divorce on his wife.
彼は、離婚を奥さんのせいにしている。

Don't blame me if it goes wrong.
うまくいかなくても、私のせいにしないで。

You could hardly blame her for quit-

ting.
彼女が辞めることをとても責められやしない。

Kondo took the blame even though it wasn't his fault.
近藤さんは、自分に落ち度はないのに責任を取った。

Why do I get all the blame?
どうして私ばっかり非難されるの？

shift the blame 責任を転嫁する

Don't shift the blame onto others.
人に責任を転嫁するな。

blameless ***adj.*** 非難するところのない

blank ***adj.*** (of paper) 空白の, 白紙の; (of look) ぼんやりした, うつろな

n. (empty space) 空白, 空欄

a blank sheet of paper 白紙

a blank expression うつろな表情

fill in the blanks 空欄を埋める

draw a blank (fail to remember) 思い出せない, ((*informal*)) 度忘れする; (find nothing) むだになる, 見つからない

When asked to write the character on the board, I drew a complete blank.
ボードにその文字を書くよう言われた時、全く思い出せなかった。

The detective searched the study for clues, but drew a blank.
探偵は研究室で手がかりを探していたが、むだだった。

go blank (of mind) 空っぽになる, 真っ白になる

blanket ***n.*** (bedding) 毛布, (covering) 一面におおうもの

a blanket of snow [clouds]
一面の雪 [雲]

blast ***n.*** (explosion) 爆発, (of bomb) 爆風, (of wind) 突風

♦**blast off** ***v.*** (of rocket) 打ち上げられる, 発射される

blatant ***adj.*** (obvious) 明らかな, 見え透いた

a blatant lie 見え透いたうそ

blaze ***n.*** (fire) 火事, (flame) 炎

v. (burn) 燃える [→ BURN, FIRE]

It took a day to put out the blaze.
鎮火に 1 日かかった。

♦**blaze up** ***v.*** 燃え上がる

The campfire suddenly blazed up.
キャンプファイヤーがぱっと燃え上がった。

blazer ***n.*** ブレザー(コート)

bleach ***n.*** 漂白剤

v. 漂白する, (hair) 脱色する

♦**bleached** ***adj.*** 漂白した, (of hair) 脱色した

bleak ***adj.*** (of situation, outlook) 暗い, わびしい

bleed ***v.*** (lose blood) 出血する, 血が出る, 血が流れる

My nose is bleeding.
鼻血が出た。

How can we stop the cut from bleeding?
傷口を止血するにはどうしたらいい？

blend ***v.*** (blend A and B together) (AとBを) 混ぜ合わせる, (become blended) 混じり合う, (be in harmony) 調和する

n. (of coffee, tea) ブレンド

Blend the margarine and sugar together.
マーガリンと砂糖を混ぜ合わせます。

a blend of tea ブレンドティー

♦**blend in** ***v.*** (match, be in harmony) と

B

け込む, 調和する

try to blend in at a party

パーティーにとけ込もうとする

bless *v.* (give God's blessing to) 祝福する; (**be blessed with**) …に恵まれる

The priest blessed the congregation.

司祭は信徒たちを祝福しました。

He's blessed with good health.

彼は健康に恵まれている。

bless you (said when sb sneezes) お大事に

blessing *n.* (godsend) 天の恵み, 幸運; (prayer) (お)祈り; (approval) 承認

blind *adj.* 目の見えない, 目の不自由な, 盲目の; (of guess) 当てずっぽうの, (reckless) 行き当たりばったりの

v. (dazzle) (…の) 目をくらます

n. (**blinds**: window shades) ブラインド

a blind person 目の不自由な人

a blind guess 当て推量

blind faith 盲目的な信仰 [盲信]

be blinded by the brightness of the lights

照明がまぶしくて目がくらむ

open [close] the blinds

ブラインドを上げる [下ろす]

be blind drunk 泥酔する

be blind to (unwilling/unable to see) …を見る目がない, …に気づかない

turn a blind eye to …に目をつぶる, …を見て見ぬふりをする

♦**blindly** *adv.* (recklessly) 盲目的に, やみくもに

blind date *n.* ブラインドデート

blindfold *n.* 目隠し, 目隠し用の物

v. (…に) 目隠しをする

blink *v.* (of eyes) まばたきする, (of light) 点滅する

blister *n.* (on skin) 水ぶくれ, (caused by burn) 火ぶくれ, (caused by shoes) まめ, (of paint) 気泡

I've got a blister on my foot.

足にまめができている。

blizzard *n.* 猛吹雪, ブリザード

blob *n.* (of ink) しみ

block *n.* (of ice, wood) 一片, かたまり, (city block) ブロック, 区画; (mental block) 思考停止, 度忘れ

v. (obstruct) ふさぐ, さえぎる, 妨げる

a block of ice 氷のかたまり

two blocks away 2ブロック先

The road was blocked by a bunch of fallen trees.

何本もの倒木で道はふさがれていた。

The person in front of me was blocking my view.

前にいた人が視界をさえぎっていた。

He blocked the way.

彼は行く手を阻んだ。

My nose is blocked.

鼻が詰まっているんです。

blond(e) *adj.* ブロンドの, 金髪の

n. ブロンドの人, 金髪の人

blood *n.* (liquid) 血, 血液, (kinship) 血統, 血縁

give blood 献血する

What's your blood type?

あなたの血液型は何ですか?

They are related by blood.

あの人たちは血がつながっている。

in cold blood 冷酷に

KANJI BRIDGE

血 ON: けつ KUN: ち | BLOOD

anemia	貧血
blood bank	血液銀行
blood donor	献血者
blood pressure	血圧
blood relation	血族, 血縁者
bloodshed	流血
bloodshot	充血した
bloodstain	血痕
bloodstream	血流
blood test	血液検査
blood type	血液型
blood vessel	血管

bloody ***adj.*** 血まみれの, (of battle) 血みどろの

a bloody nose 鼻血

bloom ***n.*** (flower) 花

v. (of flowers) 咲く, 開花する

be in bloom (花が)咲いている

be in full bloom 満開だ

blossom ***n., v.*** 花(が咲く)

The cherry blossoms are out.
桜の花が咲いている。

blot ***n.*** (stain) しみ, 汚れ, (to character) 汚点, 損なうもの

v. (stain) (…に) しみをつける, (remove: stain) ぬぐい取る

a blot on the landscape
景観を損なうもの

blouse ***n.*** ブラウス

blow

1 *v.* OF WIND: 吹く, (**blow away**: cause to fly elsewhere) 吹き飛ばす, (**blow down**: cause to fall over) 吹き倒す

2 *v.* FROM MOUTH: (**blow up**: inflate) 膨らます, (**blow on**) …に息を吹きかける, (**blow off/away**: dust/crumbs from surface) 吹き飛ばす, 吹き払う

3 *v.* USE A WIND INSTRUMENT: (blow a horn/trumpet) 吹く, (blow a whistle) 鳴らす, (of whistle: be blown) 鳴る

4 *v.* OF FUSE: 飛ぶ

5 ***n.*** HIT/SHOCK: 打撃

1 The wind is blowing.
風が吹いている。

The wind has blown my hat away.
風で帽子が吹き飛ばされた。

The wind blew the door shut.
風でドアが閉まった。

The fence has been blown down.
風でフェンスがなぎ倒されました。

2 blow up a balloon 風船を膨らます

If you blow on it, it will dry faster.
息を吹きかけると、早く乾くよ。

I blew the dust off the book.
本のほこりを吹き払った。

I'd rather you didn't blow smoke over our food.
食べ物にたばこの煙がかからないようにしてもらえるといいんだけど。

3 blow on a horn ホルン [角笛] を吹く

blow a whistle ホイッスルを鳴らす

4 The fuses blew. ヒューズが飛んだ。

5 a blow to the head 頭への一撃

It was a terrible blow to his pride.
それは彼の自尊心に大きな打撃を与えた。

blow one's nose 鼻をかむ

blow out *v.* (extinguish) 吹き消す, (of candle: stop burning) 消える

Now make a wish and blow out the candles.
さあ、願い事をしてろうそくの火を消して。

blow up *v.* (explode) 爆発する, (cause to explode) 爆破する; (lose one's temper) かっとなる; (enlarge: photograph) 引き伸ばす

blow up a building ビルを爆破する

---

blowfish *n.* フグ, 河豚

blue *adj.* (of color) 青い, ブルーの; (of emotion) 憂うつな, ブルーの [→ BLUES]
n. 青, 青色

out of the blue だしぬけに, 思いがけず

blueberry *n.* ブルーベリー

blue-collar *adj.* 肉体労働の, ブルーカラーの

a blue-collar worker 肉体労働者

blueprint *n.* (draftsman's plan) 青写真, (plan in general) 計画書

blues *n.* (music) ブルース; (**the blues**: sad feeling) ブルーな気分, 憂うつ

bluff[1] *v.* (behave deceptively) はったりをかける, 虚勢を張る
n. (act of bluffing) はったり, 虚勢

bluff[2] *n.* (land feature) 絶壁, 断崖

blunder *n.* 大失敗, どじ, へま
v. 大失敗する, どじを踏む, へまをやる

blunt *adj.* (of blade) 切れない, 鈍い, (of pencil) 先が太い; (of speech, expression) ぶっきらぼうな, そっけない

to be blunt... 率直に言えば...

blur *v.* (**be blurred**: of vision) かすむ, ぼやける

blurred, blurry *adj.* ぼやけた, はっきりしない, (of photo) ピンぼけの

blush *v.* 赤面する, 顔を赤らめる
n. 赤面, (cosmetic) ほお紅

boar *n.* (wild boar) イノシシ, (male pig) おす豚

board

1 *n.* PIECE OF WOOD: 板

2 *n.* FOR BOARD GAME: -盤

3 *n.* COMMITTEE: 委員会

4 *n.* MEAL: 食事, 賄い

5 *v.* GO/GET ABOARD: (…に) 乗る

1 Nail the boards together.
板を釘で留めてください。

2 a chess board チェス盤

3 a board of directors 理事会

There's a board meeting next week.
来週委員会が開かれます。

4 room and board 部屋代と食事代

5 board a boat [plane, train]
船 [飛行機, 電車] に乗る

across the board (involving everyone) 一律に, (everywhere) 全域にわたって

be on board 乗っている

Is everyone on board?
全員乗りましたか？

board game *n.* 盤ゲーム, ボードゲーム

boarding house *n.* 賄い付き下宿

boarding pass *n.* 搭乗券, ボーディングパス

boarding school *n.* 寄宿学校, 全寮制の学校

boast *v.* (brag) 自慢する, 鼻にかける,

(about sth one is not good at or does not have) ほらを吹く

He's always boasting about how good he is at golf.
彼はいつも、いかにゴルフがうまいか自慢ばかりしている。

boat ***n.*** (small) ボート, (large) 船

a fishing boat 釣り船

row a boat ボートをこぐ

sail a boat 船を操縦する

bobsled ***n., v.*** ボブスレー(に乗る)

body ***n.***

1 OF HUMAN/ANIMAL: 体, ((*formal*)) 身体, (human corpse) 死体, ((*polite*)) 遺体

2 GROUP: 団体, かたまり

3 MAIN PART: 本体, (of essay) 主文, (of car) 車体, ボディー

4 OF WATER: -域

1 body and soul 心身

His body ached all over.
彼は全身に痛みを覚えた。

An elephant's body is enormous.
象の体は巨大だ。

There were three dead bodies at the scene of the accident.
事故現場には3人の遺体がありました。

2 The protesters moved as a body toward the factory gates.
抗議する人たちは一団となって工場の門へと押しかけた。

3 The main body of the thesis was good, but the introduction and conclusion were weak.
論文の主文はよく書けていたが、導入部と結論が弱かった。

The engine is all right, but the body is rusting.
エンジンは大丈夫ですが、ボディーがさびていますね。

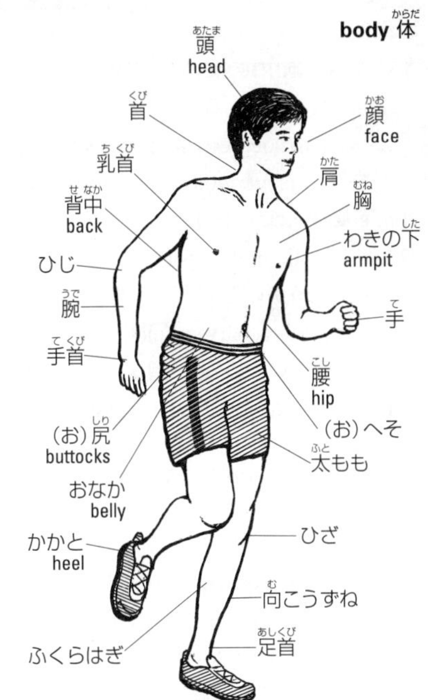

4 a body of water 水域

♦**bodily** ***adj.*** 体の, 肉体の

cause bodily harm (to) (…の)体に危害を加える

bodybuilding ***n.*** ボディービル

bodyguard ***n.*** ボディーガード, 護衛, ((*old-fashioned*)) 用心棒

body language ***n.*** ボディーランゲージ, 身振り言語

body odor ***n.*** わきが, 体臭

bog ***n.*** 沼地

get bogged down 動きが取れなくなる

bogus ***adj.*** (false) 偽の

boil[1]

1 *v.* BUBBLE WITH HEAT: 沸く, 沸騰する, (**boil over**) 吹きこぼれる

2 *v.* CAUSE TO BUBBLE WITH HEAT: (water) 沸かす, (eggs, vegetables, soba) ゆでる

3 *n.* BOILING STATE: 沸騰

1 Is the kettle boiling yet?
お湯はもう沸いた？

2 Are you going to fry or boil the cabbage?
キャベツはいためる？ それともゆでる？

How long do you like your eggs boiled for?
卵は、どのくらいの時間ゆでたのが好きですか？

3 keep at a boil 沸騰させる

boil down to (amount to) せんじつめると…になる, 要するに…ということだ

What it all boils down to is simple human error.
せんじつめると、単純な人為的なミスということになる。

boil[2] *n.* (sore) おでき, できもの

He has a large, nasty boil on his neck.
彼は首に大きなひどいできものがある。

boiler *n.* ボイラー

boiling *adj.* (in a boiling state) 沸騰している, (very hot) すごく暑い

♦**boiling point** *n.* 沸点

boisterous *adj.* (noisy) 騒々しい

bold *adj.* (daring) 大胆な, (courageous) 勇敢な, (impudent) ずうずうしい, 厚かましい; (of text: boldface) 太い, (of color: bright) 派手な, (of design) 際立った

It was a bold and imaginative plan.
大胆で想像力に富んだ計画でした。

It was in bold print.
太字で印字されていた。

Morita likes to wear bold colors.
森田さんは派手な色を着るのが好きです。

♦**boldly** *adv.* (bravely) 大胆に, (impudently) ずうずうしく

boldness *n.* (fearlessness) 大胆さ, (impudence) 厚かましさ

bolt *n.* (on door) かんぬき, (screw that fits into a nut) ボルト [→picture of TOOL]

v. (lock) (…に) かんぬきをかける

bomb *n.* 爆弾

v. 爆撃する, (drop bombs on) (…に) 爆弾を落とす

The news says terrorists have planted a bomb in the building.
テロリストがビルに爆弾を仕掛けたと、ニュースで伝えられている。

The bombs were dropped on the city during the night.
爆弾は夜間、町に落とされた。

The bridge was bombed during the war.
その橋は戦時中、爆撃されました。

♦**bomber** *n.* (aircraft) 爆撃機, (person) 爆破犯人

a suicide bomber 自爆テロ犯

bombing *n.* 爆撃

bombshell *n.* (shocking utterance) 爆弾発言

drop a bombshell 爆弾発言をする

bona fide *adj.* (real) 真実の, 真の

bond

1 *n.* PERSONAL TIE: きずな, 縁

2 *v.* HAVE A CLOSE RELATIONSHIP: きずなを結ぶ

3 *n.* CERTIFICATE OF DEBT: 債券, 証書

4 *n.* ROPE: **(bonds)** 縄, ひも

1 a bond of friendship [affection]
友情 [愛情] のきずな

2 The father and son are bonding.
その父親と息子はきずなを強めている。

3 a government bond 国債

4 At last he managed to free himself from his bonds.
やっとのことで、彼は縄をほどいて自由になることができた。

bondage *n.* (tying people up for sexual pleasure) ボンデージ, 縛り

bone *n.* 骨

v. (debone) (…の) 骨を取り除く

Wada broke a bone in his wrist.
和田さんは手首を骨折した。

Careful you don't eat the bones.
骨があるから気をつけて食べて。

I believe it's made of whalebone.
クジラのひげでできていると思うんです。

(as) dry as bone 干からびた, からからに乾いた

make no bones about (say clearly) はっきりと言う, (do without hesitation) 平気で…する

bonfire *n.* たき火

bonito *n.* (fish) カツオ, 鰹

dried bonito かつお節

bonnet *n.* (hood of car) ボンネット [→ picture of CAR]

bonsai
盆栽

bonsai *n.* 盆栽

bonus *n.* (payment) ボーナス, 賞与 [NOTE: In Japan, regular company employees generally receive a bonus on top of their salaries twice a year, in June and in December.]; (added benefit) おまけ

How much was your bonus this year?
今年のボーナスは、いくらだった？

The extra software is a bonus.
付いてきたソフトは、おまけです。

bony *adj.* (of figure) 骨ばった, (of fish) 骨が多い

boo *interj.* ブー, バァー

v. (jeer) ブーイングする, やじを飛ばす

♦**booing** *n.* ブーイング, やじ

book *n.* (bound text) 本, ((*formal*)) 書物, 書籍, (for accounting purposes) 帳簿; (packet: of stamps, coupons etc.) 一つづり, -帳

v. (reserve) 予約する

a hardcover [paperback] book
ハードカバー [ペーパーバック] の本

a small (paperback) book (in Japanese)
文庫本

one's favorite book 愛読書

You certainly have a lot of books on your shelves.
すごい数の本がありますね。

"How many books did you buy last week?" "Five."
「先週何冊本を買った？」「5冊」

a telephone book 電話帳

an account book 帳簿

a book of stamps 切手帳

Have you booked our train seats?
電車の予約はもうしてくれましたか？

I couldn't get tickets for the concert. It was all booked up.
コンサートのチケットは取れなかったよ。

B

もう全部売り切れてた。

bookcase *n.* 本箱

booking *n.* 予約

♦**booking office** *n.* 切符売り場, チケット予約センター

bookkeeping *n.* 簿記

booklet *n.* 小冊子, パンフレット

bookmark *n.* しおり

bookshelf *n.* 本棚

bookshop *n.* 本屋(さん), 書店

bookworm *n.* 本の虫

boom *n.* (sound) ブーン(という音); (economic boom) ブーム, にわか景気

v. (of business) 景気がよくなる

a building boom 建築ブーム

Business is booming. 景気がいい。

boomerang *n.* ブーメラン

boost *v.* (raise) 上げる, (sales) 伸ばす

n. (increase) 上昇

How can we boost sales?

どうすれば売り上げを伸ばせるだろう?

boot *n.* (high boot) ブーツ, 長靴, (rubber boot) ゴム靴, (for car wheel) クランプ, 車輪止め; (trunk of car) トランク [→ picture of CAR]

booth *n.* (small room) ボックス, (at fair, restaurant) ブース, (stall where goods are sold) 売店

a telephone booth 電話ボックス

a voting booth 投票用ブース

border *n.* (boundary) 境, 境界(線), (between countries) 国境; (of dress) 縁飾り; (in garden) 植え込み

v. (be adjacent to) (...に) 接する

the border between North and South Korea 北朝鮮と韓国との国境

We crossed the border into Afghanistan.

国境を越えてアフガニスタンに入った。

They live north of the border.

彼らは国境の北側に住んでいる。

The dress has a white border.

ドレスには白の縁飾りがしてある。

♦**border on** *v.* (verge on) ...に近い, ...と言っていい

This borders on the ridiculous.

これは、ばかげていると言っていい。

borderline *n.* ボーダーライン, 境界線, (of country) 国境線

bore[1] *v.* (make weary) 退屈させる, うんざりさせる

Grandpa always bores us with his war stories.

おじいちゃんの戦争の話には、いつも退屈させられる。

bore[2] *v.* (**bore a hole**) 穴をあける

bored *adj.* 退屈する, 飽きる

If you're bored, why don't you come play cards with us?

退屈なら、私たちといっしょにトランプをやりませんか?

He's already bored with that game.

彼はもうあのゲームに飽きてしまった。

I'm bored by all this stupid talk.

こんなくだらない話は、もうたくさんだ。

boredom *n.* 退屈

boring *adj.* つまらない, 退屈な

born *v.* (**be born**) 生まれる

adj. (being/having from birth) 生まれつきの, 生まれながらの, (**born to do/become**: destined) ...をする/...になる運命の; (**-born**) -生まれ

I was born in 1982.
１９８２年生まれです。

I was born and raised in this city.
私はこの町で生まれ育ちました。

Did you see the baby being born?
赤ちゃんが生まれるところを見た？

He's a born fool.
あいつは生まれつきのばかだ。

He was born to be president.
彼は大統領になる運命だった［なるべくしてなった］。

Tokyo-born 東京生まれ

♦**born-again** ***adj.*** (of Christian) 生まれ変わった

borrow ***v.*** 借りる [NOTE: To ask somebody if you may borrow something, use 借りてもいいですか or, more politely, 貸してくれませんか/貸してもらえませんか/貸していただけませんか.]

How many books did you borrow from the library?
図書館で何冊借りました？

He's always borrowing things and never returning them.
彼はしょっちゅう人から物を借りて、全然返さない。

Can I borrow your pen for a minute?
ちょっとペンを貸してもらえませんか？

♦**borrower** ***n.*** 借り手

boss ***n.*** ボス, 上役, 上司, -長, (person in charge) 責任者, (of tradesmen, wrestlers) 親方, (employer) 雇い主

Who's the boss here?
ここの責任者はどなたですか？

She's the boss of this section.
あの人がここの課長です。

His wife is the boss in his home.
彼は奥さんの尻に敷かれている/あそこの家は、かかあ天下だ。

BOSSES IN A JAPANESE COMPANY

boss (in general) 上司
company president 社長
division chief 部長
section chief 課長
senior staff member 主任
office manager 室長

♦**boss around** ***v.*** こき使う, いばりちらす

He was bossing his employees around.
彼は従業員をこき使っていた。

bossy ***adj.*** 親分風を吹かす, あごで人を使う

botanist ***n.*** 植物学者

botany ***n.*** 植物学

both

1 ***adj.*** 両方の, どちらの…も, ((*informal*)) どっちの…も

2 ***pron.*** 両方, どちらも, ((*informal*)) どっちも, (things) 二つとも, (people) 二人とも

3 ***adv.*** …も…も

1 Both places are wet.
どっちもぬれている。

Both her parents are dead.
彼女の両親はどちらも亡くなっています。

We're hoping to buy both houses.
２軒とも買いたいと思っています。

2 Both is too many. 両方だと多すぎる。

Both are too big. どっちも大きすぎる。

I was pleased with how both of them did.
二人ともよくやってくれました。

They have both agreed to sell.

どちらも売ることに同意しています。

They are both middle-aged.
二人とも中年です。

3 Both Tom and Bill are satisfied.
トムもビルも満足しています。

It's both hot and humid.
暑くてむしむしする。

bother *v.* (annoy) 煩わす, (trouble) (…に) 迷惑/面倒/手数をかける, (worry) 悩ます, (disturb) (…の) じゃまをする, (get on one's nerves) (…の) 気にさわる, 気になる, (**bother to do**: take the trouble to do) わざわざ…する

n. (trouble) 面倒, 手数, 厄介, じゃま

I wouldn't bother him about it now.
今は、そのことについて彼を煩わさないほうがいい。

Is that man bothering you?
あの人が煩わしいの？

I can tell it's bothering her.
彼女がそのことで悩んでいるのがわかる。

Don't bother me now. I'm busy.
今はじゃましないで。忙しいから。

Sorry to bother you, but could I just speak to you for a moment?
すみませんが、ちょっとお時間を頂いてもいいですか？

I can't study…the noise of the construction next door bothers me.
隣の工事の音が気になって勉強できない。

The heat is beginning to bother me.
そろそろ暑さが応えてきた。

Does the noise outside bother you?
外の音は耳ざわりですか？

Don't bother to come and see me off at the station.
わざわざ駅まで見送りに来なくていいよ。

It's such a bother having to clean up every day.
毎日掃除しなくちゃいけないなんて、本当に面倒です。

What a bother these pets are!
このペットたちはなんて厄介なんだ！

can't be bothered to do わざわざ…する気になれない, とても…できない

I couldn't be bothered to do it.
とてもやる気になれませんでした。

bothersome *adj.* 煩わしい, 面倒な, 厄介な

bottle *n.* (receptacle) びん, (wine bottle) ボトル, (baby bottle) 哺乳びん

v. (put in a bottle) びんに入れる, びんに詰める

empty beer bottles ビールの空きびん

We ordered a bottle of wine.
ワインを1本注文した。

There are two bottles here.
ここにびんが2本ある。

keep a bottle (at a bar) ボトルキープする [NOTE: At most bars in Japan, it is possible to purchase a full bottle of liquor for future visits.]

♦**bottle opener** *n.* 栓抜き [→ picture of COOKING UTENSILS]

bottleneck *n.* (narrow part of highway) 狭くなっている道路, (area of congested traffic) 渋滞する所

bottom *n.* (lowest part) 下, 一番下, 下のほう, (of hill) ふもと, (deepest part: of valley, ocean, box, cup) 底, (underside)

下側, (lowest rank in a company) 最下位, 末端, (buttocks) (お)尻

Can you see what that says at the bottom of the page?
ページの一番下に何と書いてあるか読めますか？

Somebody's waiting at the bottom of the stairs.
階段の下で誰かが待っています。

The bakery is at the bottom of the hill.
パン屋さんは丘のふもとにある。

at the bottom of the box 箱の底に

I found myself working at the bottom of a large organization.
気がつくと自分は大きな組織の末端で働いていた。

at bottom 本当は, 根は

At bottom, he's a good guy.
根は、いい人なんだ。

from the bottom of one's heart 心の底から, 本心から

I meant it from the bottom of my heart.
私の本心から出た言葉です。

get to the bottom of …の真相を究明する, …の真相を突き止める

Holmes was determined to get to the bottom of the mystery.
ホームズは事件の真相を突き止めようと心に決めていた。

bottomless ***adj.*** 底なしの, 際限のない

bough ***n.*** 大枝

bounce ***v.*** はずむ, バウンドする, (rebound) はね返る, (jump up and down) 跳びはねる, (cause to rebound) はね返す; (of check) 不渡りになる

The ball bounced into the road.
ボールはバウンドして道路へ飛び出した。

The car bounced off the curb.
車が縁石にはね返された。

Quit bouncing on the bed.
ベッドの上で跳びはねるのはやめなさい。

bound[1] ***adj.***

1 CERTAIN: (**be bound to do/happen**) きっと…する/なるだろう

2 OBLIGATED: (**be bound to do**) …する義務がある, (**be bound by**: rule, contract etc.) …に縛られる, …に束縛される

3 TIED UP: 縛られた

4 OF BOOK: 製本された

1 He's bound to turn up soon.
彼はきっともうすぐ来るよ。

It's bound to be crowded.
きっと混むでしょう。

It was bound to happen sooner or later.
いずれはそうなる運命だった。

2 I felt bound to tell the truth.
真実を話す義務があると感じました。

3 be bound and gagged
縛られて口をふさがれる

4 The books are bound.
本は製本されています。

bound[2] ***v.*** (jump) 跳び上がる, (bounce) はね返る

bound[3] ***n.*** (**bounds**: limits) 限界, 際限

v. (**be bounded by**: be surrounded by) …に囲まれる

know no bounds 際限がない

out of bounds (in sport) 場外で, (in golf) ＯＢ

bound[4] ***adj.*** (**bound for/-bound**: of train, bus) …行きの

This train is bound for Osaka.
この電車は大阪行きです。

boundary *n.* (border) 境界(線), 境 [→ BORDER]

There is not a clear boundary between the two properties.
二つの土地の間には、はっきりした境界がありません。

bouquet *n.* 花束, ブーケ

bourbon *n.* バーボン

boutique *n.* ブティック

bow[1] *v.* (incline body) おじぎする, (incline head) (頭を)下げる

n. (gesture) おじぎ

bow and scrape (to superiors) ぺこぺこする

He's always bowing and scraping to his bosses.
あの男はいつも上司にぺこぺこしている。

bow[2] *n.* (in archery, kyudo) 弓, (for instrument) 弓; (bowknot) ちょう結び

♦**bow tie** *n.* ちょうネクタイ, ボウタイ

bowl[1] *n.* (container) 入れ物, 容器, -入れ, (ceramic vessel for food) どんぶり, (metal/plastic bowl for mixing food) ボウル [→ picture of COOKING UTENSILS], (rice bowl) (お)茶わん, (soup bowl) おわん, (**a bowl of**) ボウル1杯の

Have you seen that bowl I keep my paper clips in?
いつもクリップを入れている入れ物を見かけなかった?

Do we have a sugar bowl?
砂糖入れはある?

"How many (rice) bowls do we need?"
"Seven."
「お茶わんはいくつ要る?」
「七つ」

He can eat as many as three or four bowls of rice.
彼は3、4杯ものご飯を食べられる。

bowl[2] *v.* (do bowling) ボウリングをする

Whose turn is it to bowl?
次は誰が投げる番?

♦**bowler** *n.* (in bowling) ボウラー, (in cricket) 投手

bowlegged *adj.* O脚の, がにまたの

bowling *n.* (game) ボウリング

♦**bowling alley** *n.* ボウリング場

bowls *n.* (game) ローンボウリング

box[1] *n.* (container) 箱

v. (put in a box) 箱に入れる, 箱に詰める

What a pretty box! きれいな箱!

I need a fairly big cardboard box to send all this stuff.
これを全部送るには、かなり大きな段ボール箱が要りますね。

box[2] *v.* (do boxing) ボクシングをする

♦**boxer** *n.* ボクサー, ボクシング選手

boxing *n.* ボクシング

♦**boxing ring** *n.* ボクシングのリング

box office *n.* 切符売り場

boy *n.* 男の子, 少年, (young man) 男性, (**boys**: drinking pals) 飲み仲間 [→ SON]

Who's that boy? あの男の子は誰?

He's only a boy of twelve.
まだ12歳の少年です。

There were five boys and two girls.
男子5人と、女子が2人いました。

Are you going out with the boys tonight?
今夜、仲間と出かけるの?

How are your boys?
坊ちゃんたちは、お元気ですか？

boycott ***n., v.*** ボイコット(する)

Why don't we boycott the meeting?
会議をボイコットしません？

boyfriend ***n.*** ボーイフレンド, 彼, 彼氏

boyish ***adj.*** 男の子らしい, 少年のような, (of woman) ボーイッシュな

bra ***n.*** ブラ(ジャー)

brace ***n.*** (**braces**: for teeth) (歯の)矯正装置, ブレース

v. (**brace oneself for**: be ready for) 覚悟する

bracelet ***n.*** ブレスレット

bracket ***n.*** (**brackets**: square parentheses) (角)かっこ, ブラケット; (L-shaped support for shelf) L字形金具

v. (put in brackets) (角)かっこに入れる

brag ***v.*** (boast) 自慢する, 鼻にかける

braid ***n.*** (rope) 組みひも, (**braids**) 三つ編み, お下げ, (French braid) 編み込み

braille ***n.*** 点字

brain ***n.*** (organ) 脳, 脳みそ, (**brains**: intelligence) 頭脳, 頭, (intelligent person) 頭のいい人, 秀才

♦**brainy** ***adj.*** 頭のいい

brainstorm ***v.*** ブレーンストーミングする

brainwash ***v.*** 洗脳する, 教え込む

brake ***n.*** (device for reducing speed) ブレーキ [→ picture of CAR]; (restriction) 歯止め

v. (...に)ブレーキをかける

Are the brakes working properly?
ブレーキはちゃんとかかりますか？

Don't slam on the brakes.
急ブレーキをかけないで。

All these rules are putting a brake on progress.
このような規則が、発展に歯止めをかけている。

Now start braking gradually.
さあ、徐々にブレーキを踏んで。

♦**brake light** ***n.*** ブレーキライト

bran ***n.*** (wheat bran) ふすま, (rice bran) ぬか

branch ***n.*** (of tree) 枝; (of store, bank) 支店, (of newspaper, broadcasting station) 支局, (branch office) 支部, 支社; (specialized field) 部門, 分野

The children have climbed onto the branch.
子供たちが枝に登ってしまった。

I've been sent to the Nagoya branch.
名古屋支社に転勤[異動]になりました。

Metaphysics? Isn't that a branch of philosophy?
形而上学？ 哲学の一部門じゃないんですか？

♦**branch family** ***n.*** 分家

branch line ***n.*** (of railway) 支線

branch off ***v.*** (of road) 分かれる, 分岐する

branch out ***v.*** 手を広げる, 拡張する

brand ***n.*** (trademark) ブランド, 商標, 銘柄; (type) (特有の)種類

v. (person) (...に)烙印を押す

be branded a liar
うそつきの烙印を押される

brand name ***n.*** (trade name) ブランド名, 商標名

adj. (**brand-name**) (有名)ブランドの

B

brand-new *adj.* 新品の

brandy *n.* ブランデー

brass *n.* (metal) 真ちゅう; (also **brasses**: musical instruments) 金管楽器

♦**brass band** *n.* ブラスバンド

brassiere *n.* ブラジャー

brave *adj.* (courageous) 勇敢な, 勇気のある, 勇ましい, (admirable) 立派な, (of weak/disadvantaged person's efforts) けなげな

v. (…に) 勇敢に立ち向かう

It takes a brave person to do that.
勇気のある人じゃないとできない。

It was brave of you to stand up to him.
彼に立ち向かったのは立派でした。

♦**bravely** *adv.* 勇敢に, 立派に

fight bravely 勇敢に戦う

bravery *n.* 勇気

Brazil *n.* ブラジル

Brazilian *n.* ブラジル人

breach *n.* (of law, contract) 違反; (in defenses) 突破口, (rift, break) 割れ目, (tear) 裂け目, (hole) 穴

v. (violate, break) 破る, 破棄する

It was a breach of contract.
契約違反だった。

The enemy was unable to breach our defenses.
敵は我々の守りを突破できなかった。

bread *n.* パン, (living) 生計

bake bread パンを焼く

butter the bread パンにバターを塗る

a slice of bread パン1枚

It's the only way he can earn his bread.
彼には、それしか生計を立てる方法がない。

♦**breadcrumbs** *n.* パンくず, (for cooking) パン粉

breadth *n.* (width) 幅, (range) 広さ [→ WIDTH]

have a breadth of knowledge
幅広い知識をもっている

breadwinner *n.* 大黒柱

---

break

1 *v.* MAKE/BECOME BROKEN: (glass) 割る/割れる, (bone) 折る/折れる, (destroy) 壊す, (come/fall apart) 壊れる

2 *v.* VIOLATE: (promise) 破る, (contract) 破棄する, (…に) 違反する, (law) 破る, 犯す

3 *v.* HURT: (spirit, resolve) くじく

4 *v.* CRACK: (code) 解く, 解読する

5 *v.* OUTDO: (record) 破る

6 *v.* REST: 休む, 休憩する

7 *v.* OF NEWS: 報道される, 報じられる, (**break headlines**) 大見出しになる

8 *v.* GIVE BAD NEWS TO: (break A to B) (AをBに) 知らせる, 打ち明ける

9 *n.* PERIOD OF REST/RELAXATION: (short break) 休み, 一休み, 休憩, (vacation) 休暇, -休み

10 *n.* OPENING: (crack, tear) 裂け目, (crack) ひび割れ, (in clouds) 切れ目

11 *n.* OPPORTUNITY: チャンス, 機会

1 Careful you don't break it. It's our best china.
割らないように気をつけてね。家で一番上等な陶器なんだから。

Oh my God, I've broken the window!

どうしよう、窓を割ってしまった!

He broke his leg skiing.
彼はスキーをしていて足を骨折した。

Have you ever broken a rib?
あばら骨を折ったことがある?

Don't bang on it! You'll break it.
たたいちゃだめ! 壊れるでしょ。

The damn thing broke as soon as I took it out of the box.
全く、これは箱から取り出したとたん壊れた。

2 She's not the sort to break a promise.
あの人は約束を破るような人ではない。

Let's hope they don't break the contract.
彼らが契約違反をしないことを願おう。

3 Despite all the setbacks, his spirit was not broken.
相次ぐ逆境にも、彼はくじけなかった。

4 The code was easily broken.
暗号は簡単に解けた。

5 She broke a world record.
彼女は世界記録を破った。

6 We broke for about an hour's rest.
私たちは1時間ほど休憩しました。

7 The story broke headlines in all major newspapers.
そのニュースはすべての大手新聞で大見出しになった。

8 One of these days you'll need to break it to her.
近いうちに、彼女にそのことを打ち明けないといけないよ。

I hate to break the news to you, but...
本当に言いにくいのですが...

9 Let's take a break.
一息いれましょう/休憩しましょう。

The lunch break is thirty minutes.
お昼休みは30分です。

We have to work eight hours without a break.
8時間、休憩なしで働かなくてはならない。

I'm going to take a two-week break from work.
2週間、休暇を取ります。

Any plans for the break?
休み中は、何か計画はある?

summer [winter] break 夏[冬]休み

10 Look, there's a break here in the lining.
ほら、裏地のここに裂け目がある。

11 Everybody in show business needs a lucky break.
ショービジネスの世界では、みんなビッグチャンスが必要です。

give me a break (you've got to be kidding) 冗談はやめて, 勘弁してよ

break down *v.* (of machine: become broken) 故障する, 壊れる; (of person: have a breakdown) がっくりする, (dissolve into tears) わっと泣き崩れる; (of negotiations, plans) 行き詰まる, 決裂する; (analyze) 分析する, 分解する

The car broke down.
車が<u>故障</u> [えんこ] した。

She broke down on hearing the terrible news.
彼女はそのむごい知らせを聞いて、わっと泣き崩れた。

The talks broke down because of fundamental differences.
根本的な食い違いで、会談は決裂した。

Let's break the figures down to make the facts clearer.

事実をはっきりさせるために、数字を分析してみましょう。

break in *v.* (enter by force) (…に)押し入る, 侵入する; (**break in on**: interrupt) …に口を差し挟む, …に口出しする; (**break one's shoes in**) はき慣らす

A thief broke in.
泥棒が入った。

Do you mind not breaking in on our conversation like that?
そんなふうに、私たちの会話に口出しするのはやめてくれませんか？

I broke these shoes in within a matter of days.
この靴は数日のうちにはき慣らした。

break into *v.* (enter by force) …に押し入る, …に侵入する; (begin doing: song, dance etc.) <-ますstem> + 出す

break into a building [computer]
ビル [コンピューター] に侵入する

break into a laugh/smile 笑い出す

break into a dance 踊り出す

break into a run 走り出す

break into a sweat 汗が噴き出す

break off *v.* (break and fall off) 外れる, 折れる, (piece of chocolate) 折る; (of negotiations) 中断する, (relationship) 断つ, (engagement) 解消する, 破棄する

She broke off the engagement.
彼女は婚約を破棄しました。

break out *v.* (**break out of**: escape from) …から逃げ出す, (**break out of jail**) 脱獄する; (of war) 勃発する, 起こる, (of fight) 始まる, 起こる; (**break out in pimples/rash**) 発疹が出る

According to the news, three prisoners have broken out of jail.
ニュースによれば、囚人が3人脱獄したらしい。

I don't expect war will break out.
戦争になるとは思わない。

A fight broke out. けんかが始まった。

break up *v.* (of couple: separate) 別れる; (separate into pieces) ばらばらにする, (crumble) ばらばらになる; (bring to an end) 終わりにする, (come to an end) 終わる; (of crowd: disperse) ちりぢりになる, 解散する

I had to break up with him.
彼と別れなくてはならなかった。

Their marriage broke up after only a few months.
二人の結婚はたった数ヵ月で破綻した。

The box was broken up and thrown away.
箱は、ばらばらにして捨てられました。

They tried to break up the fight.
彼らは、けんかをやめさせようとした。

The crowd eventually broke up and dispersed.
人々は、しだいにちりぢりになって解散した。

breakable *adj.* 壊れやすい
n. 壊れやすい物, 割れ物

breakdown *n.* (nervous breakdown) 神経衰弱, (mechanical failure) 故障; (analysis) 分析

He had a nervous breakdown.
彼は神経衰弱になった。

Give me the breakdown of the figures.

数値の分析結果を見せてください。

breakfast *n.* 朝ご飯, 朝食, ((*masculine/informal*)) 朝飯

What would you like for breakfast?
朝ご飯は何を食べたい?

breaking point *n.* 限界, 限度

breakthrough *n.* (big discovery) 大発見, (big advance) 躍進

The discovery of penicillin was a major breakthrough.
ペニシリンの発見は大きな躍進だった。

breakup *n.* (of organization) 解散; (separation) 別れ, (divorce) 離婚

It marked the breakup of their marriage.
そのことが離婚の原因となった。

breakwater *n.* 防波堤

breast *n.* (chest) 胸 [→ picture of BODY], (of woman) バスト, 乳房, ((*slang/also used by infants*)) おっぱい; (of meat) 胸肉

breast-feed *v.* (…に) 授乳する

breaststroke *n.* 平泳ぎ

breath *n.* 息, 呼吸

hold one's breath 息を止める
be out of breath 息が切れる
have bad breath 息が臭い
take a deep breath 深呼吸をする

catch one's breath (try to breathe normally) 息をつく, (rest) 一休みする

I had to stop several times to catch my breath.
息をつくために何度か立ち止まらなくてはならなかった。

draw (a) breath (rest) 休む

breathalyze *v.* (…に) 酒気検査をする

breathalyzer *n.* 酒気検査器

breathe *v.* 呼吸する, 息をする

breathe in [out] 息を吸う [吐く]

He had difficulty breathing.
彼は息が苦しくなった。

breathing *n.* 呼吸

breathless *adj.* 息切れする, 息を切らす

breathtaking *adj.* (of scene) 息をのむような

breed *v.* (raise) 飼う, 飼育する, (have babies) 子供を産む, (reproduce) 繁殖する

n. (of animal) 血統

be born and bred in …で生まれ育つ

She was born and bred in Glasgow.
彼女はグラスゴーで生まれ育った。

breeding *n.* (of animals) 繁殖; (of people: upbringing) 育ち

breeze *n.* 風, そよ風

a cool breeze 涼しい風
a sea breeze 海風

brew *v.* (beer) 醸造する

brewery *n.* 醸造所

bribe *n.* わいろ

v. (…に) わいろを使う, (…を) 買収する

offer a bribe わいろを贈る

The politician accepted a bribe.
その政治家はわいろを受け取った。

He tried to bribe me.
その男は私を買収しようとした。

bribery *n.* 贈収賄, (giving a bribe) 贈賄罪, (accepting a bribe) 収賄罪

brick *n.* れんが

a brick house れんが(造り)の家

bridal *adj.* (for/of bride) 花嫁の, (for/of wedding) 結婚の

B

a bridal party 結婚披露宴

bride *n.* 花嫁, 新婦

bride and groom 新郎新婦

bridegroom *n.* 花婿, 新郎

bridesmaid *n.* 新婦の付添人

bridge[1] *n.* 橋, (in proper names) -橋, (bridge over road/railway) 陸橋, (pedestrian bridge) 歩道橋, (railroad bridge) 鉄橋; (intermediary) 橋渡し; (for teeth) ブリッジ

v. (construct a bridge over) (…に) 橋をかける; (**bridge the gap between**) (…の) 橋渡しをする

There's a little bridge further downstream.
もう少し下流に小さな橋がある。

There are plans to build a bridge to the island.
島に橋をかける計画があります。

London Bridge ロンドン橋

We crossed the road by going over the bridge.
歩道橋を渡って道路を横断した。

act as a bridge between …の橋渡し役を務める

act as a bridge between Japan and China
日本と中国の橋渡し役を務める

bridge[2] *n.* (game) ブリッジ

brief *adj.* (short) 短い, 短期間の, (concise) 簡潔な, 簡単な

v. (inform) (…に) 概要を説明する, 簡単に説明する

a brief visit to New York
短期間のニューヨーク訪問

There was a brief discussion about who should do it.
誰がやるか短い話し合いがあった。

a brief description 簡単な説明

They briefed us on what to expect when we arrived.
到着したらどんなことがあるのか、簡単に説明してくれました。

in brief 手短に言えば, 要するに, 要約すると

In brief, then, what's your opinion?
要するに、じゃあ、あなたのご意見は？

♦**briefly** *adv.* 手短に, 簡単に

briefcase *n.* かばん, ブリーフケース

briefing *n.* 概要説明

give a briefing (to)
(…に) 概要説明をする

briefs *n.* (underwear) パンツ, ブリーフ, 下着 [→ PANTS]

brigadier general *n.* (in U.S. Army/Air Force/Marine Corps) 准将

bright *adj.*

1 GIVING OUT LOTS OF LIGHT: 明るい, (too bright to look at) まぶしい

2 OF COLOR: 明るい, (colorful) 華やかな, (vivid) 鮮やかな, (gaudy) 派手な

3 CHEERFUL: 元気な, 明るい

4 INTELLIGENT: 賢い, 利口な, 頭のいい

1 The room is not very bright.
部屋はあまり明るくない。

It was a lovely bright morning.
よく晴れた、明るい朝でした。

My eyes are sensitive to bright light.
私の目は明るい光に敏感なんです。

Could you turn off the light? It's too bright.
電気を消してもらえませんか？ ちょっとまぶしすぎるんです。

2 He has bright blue eyes.
彼の目は明るいブルーです。

The (Japanese Shinto) shrines are painted with such bright colors.
神社は、とても鮮やかな色に塗られていますね。

The tie was a little too bright.
ネクタイの色がちょっと派手すぎた。

3 He's usually so bright and cheerful.
あの人は、いつもはすごく明るくて、はつらつとしているのに。

a bright smile 晴れやかな笑顔

4 She's a bright child.
あの子は<u>賢い</u>[頭がいい]。

He's one of the brightest kids in the school.
彼は学校でも1、2を争うほど優秀です。

bright and early 朝早く, 朝一番に

look on the bright side (物事の)いい面を見る, 楽観的に考える

♦**brightly** *adv.* 明るく

brightness *n.* 明るさ

brighten *v.* (make brighter) 明るくする, (become sunnier) 晴れる, 天気がよくなる, (of mood) 明るくなる, (**brighten up**) 元気を出す

We need to brighten up this place.
ここをもっと明るい感じにしなくては。

Do you think it'll brighten up later in the day?
このあと、天気はよくなると思う?

Would you please stop moping about and just brighten up?
お願いだから暗い顔をするのはやめて、元気を出してくれない?

brilliant *adj.* (of idea) すばらしい, みごとな; (of light) 光り輝く, キラキラ光る

It was a brilliant plan.
すばらしい案でした。

a brilliant sunrise 光り輝く日の出

brim *n.* (of cup) 縁, (of hat) つば

brine *n.* 塩水

---

bring *v.*

1 TAKE SOMEWHERE: (thing) 持って来る, 持って行く, (person) 連れて来る, 連れて行く [NOTE: The difference between -て来る and -て行く depends on the direction of the action: if it is toward the speaker, use -て来る, and if it is away from him/her, use -て行く.]

2 CAUSE: もたらす, 招く, 引き起こす

3 PROVIDE/SPONSOR: 提供する

1 He brought loads of CDs.
彼はＣＤをたくさん持って来た。

Should we bring a dish of some kind?
何か食べ物を持って行ったほうがいい?

I'll bring it to you tomorrow.
明日持って行きます。

Could you bring me a hot cocoa, please?
ホットココアをいただけますか?

The festival brings people from all parts of the country.
そのお祭りに国中から人が集まって来る。

Can I bring a friend?
友達を連れて行ってもいい?

Buddhism was brought to Japan from China via Korea.
仏教は中国から韓国を経て日本に伝えられた。

Your question brings me to my next point.

その質問のおかげで、次に私が話したかったところに進めます。

2 The drought brought famine to the village.
干ばつはその村にききんをもたらした。

Does wealth bring happiness?
お金は幸せをもたらすだろうか？

That kind of behavior is bound to bring trouble.
そのような態度はトラブルを招きますよ。

What in the world could have brought you to do such a thing?
一体なんでそんな事を引き起こしてしまったの？

He brought shame on the whole family.
彼は、家族みんなに恥をかかせた [みんなの顔に泥を塗った (lit., "painted dirt on the faces of…")]。

3 This program was brought to you by ATN.
((*polite*)) この番組はＡＴＮの提供でお送りいたしました。

bring about *v.* (cause to happen) もたらす, 引き起こす, 起こす

bring about a change [cure, solution]
変化 [回復, 解決] をもたらす

We're all hoping that diplomacy will bring about a peaceful settlement.
外交によって平和的解決がもたらされることを誰もが望んでいます。

The accident was brought about by a bit of carelessness.
事故は、ちょっとした不注意によって引き起こされた。

What on earth could have brought about such a tragedy?
一体なぜそんな惨事が起こってしまったんだろう？

bring along *v.* (person) 連れて来る, (thing) 持って来る

Ms. Sato always brings her children along.
佐藤さんはいつも自分の子供たちを連れて来る。

Remember to bring along your glasses.
忘れずにコップを持って来てください。

bring around *v.* (help back to consciousness) (…の) 意識を回復させる; (persuade) 説得する

The doctor brought her around with oxygen.
医者が酸素を吸入して、彼女の意識は戻った。

Try as we might, we couldn't bring him around to our point of view.
どんなに説得しても、彼に私たちの言い分はわかってもらえなかった。

bring back *v.*

1 TAKE BACK: (gift from elsewhere/abroad) 持って帰る, (person) 連れて帰る, (return: borrowed item) 返す

2 CALL TO MIND: 思い出させる

3 RESTORE/REINSTATE: 復活させる, (fashion) 再びはやらせる

1 She brought back gifts for everyone.
彼女は皆におみやげを持って帰って来た。

Bring me back some chocolate, will you.
チョコレートを買って来てくれる？

I asked for it a month ago and he still hasn't brought it back to me.
1ヵ月前に返してほしいと言ったのに、彼はまだ返してくれていない。

2 Seeing her again brought back a lot of memories.
彼女と再会して、いろいろなことを思い出しました。

3 bring back an old custom
古いしきたりを復活させる

Let's bring back bell-bottoms.
ベルボトムをもう一度はやらせよう。

bring back to life 生き返らせる

bring down *v.* (lower) 下ろす, (price) 下げる, (topple) 倒す, (shoot down: aircraft) 撃墜する

Could you bring the books down from the attic?
屋根裏部屋から本を下ろしてくれない？

Competition is the friend of the consumer—it brings down prices.
競争は消費者の味方です、何しろ物の値段が下がりますから。

The wind brought the fence down.
風でさくが倒れた。

Riots alone failed to bring down the government.
暴動だけでは、政府を倒すことはできなかった。

The terrorists claim to have brought down a helicopter.
テロリストたちは、ヘリコプターを撃墜したと言っている。

bring in *v.* (take in from outside) 中に持ち込む, 取り入れる; (earn) 稼ぐ [→ INTRODUCE]

You'd better bring in the laundry. It looks like it's going to rain.
洗濯物を取り込んだほうがいいよ。雨が降って来そうだから。

This part-time work brings in about ¥30,000 a week.
パートの収入は週に3万円くらいです。

bring off *v.* (achieve) 成し遂げる

bring on *v.* (illness) 引き起こす, 招く

The stress of it all brought on a heart attack.
あまりのストレスが心臓発作を引き起こした。

bring out *v.*

1 TAKE OUT: 取り出す, (bring outside) 外に出す

2 PRODUCE: (album, book) 出す

3 DRAW OUT: (behavior, talent, quality) 引き出す

1 He opened the drawer and brought out a sealed envelope.
彼は引き出しをあけて、封をした封筒を取り出した。

Would you mind bringing out the trash on your way out the door?
出かける時に、ついでにごみを出してくれない？

2 They've just brought out a new album.
彼らはニューアルバムを出したばかりだ。

When is his new novel going to be brought out?
新しい小説はいつ出るんだろう？

3 Tragedy often brings out the best in people.
悲劇は、しばしば人間の一番いい部分を引き出す。

Competition seems to bring out the worst in him.
競争となると彼の一番悪いところが出てしまうようです。

bring up *v.*

1 REAR: (child) 育てる
2 SUBJECT: (raise) 持ち出す, (broach) 切り出す, (dredge up) 蒸し返す
3 VOMIT: 吐く, もどす

1 It's tough bringing up a child.
子供を育てることは大変なことだ。

You were born in New York, but were you brought up there, too?
生まれはニューヨークでしたね、育ったのもそこですか？

2 Yet again they brought up the subject of my resignation.
彼らはまた、私の退職の話を持ち出した。

3 The cat obviously didn't like what it ate, because it brought it up on the floor.
猫は食べた物が気に入らなかったみたいだ。床に吐いていたから。

---

brink *n.* (of war) 瀬戸際, 間際, (of cliff) 縁

America was on the brink of war.
アメリカは戦争をするかしないかの瀬戸際に立っていた。

bristle *n.* (stubble) ひげ, (of brush) 毛, (of animal) 剛毛

Britain *n.* イギリス, 英国

British *adj.* (of country, culture) イギリスの, 英国の, (of person) イギリス人の, 英国人の

n. (**the British**) イギリス人, 英国人

brittle *adj.* (easily broken) 壊れやすい, もろい, (of bones) 折れやすい

broach *v.* (subject) 切り出す

broad *adj.* (spacious) 広い, (wide-ranging) 幅が広い, (of subject) 大きな, (general) 大まかな; (of accent: strong) 強い

The jacket doesn't fit because the shoulders are too broad.
この上着は肩幅が広すぎて合わない。

Communication is a very broad subject.
コミュニケーションは非常に大きなテーマです。

She speaks with a broad rural accent.
彼女のなまりはとても強い。

in broad daylight 真っ昼間に, 白昼に

broad bean *n.* ソラマメ, 空豆 [→ picture of BEAN]

broadcast *v.* 放送する, (by TV only) 放映する; (spread the word) 言いふらす

broadcast across the nation
全国放送する

The program was broadcast by satellite.
その番組は衛星放送で放映されていた。

broaden *v.* (make broad) 広げる, 広くする, (knowledge, experience) 深める, (become broad) 広がる, 広くなる

The road needs to be broadened.
この道路は道幅を広げる必要がある。

He needs to broaden his interests.
あの人はもっと興味を広げたほうがいい。

They say travel broadens the mind.
旅は視野を広げてくれるという。

broadly *adv.* (generally) おおざっぱに, 大まかに, (widely) 広く

broadly speaking おおざっぱに言って, 一般的に言って

broadminded *adj.* おうような, 寛容な, 心の広い

broccoli *n.* ブロッコリー

brochure *n.* パンフレット, 案内書

broil *v.* 焼く

broiler *n.* (oven) オーブン

broke *adj.* (penniless) 一文なしだ
go broke 無一文になる, 破産する

broken *adj.* (damaged) 壊れた, (busted) 故障した, (destroyed) 崩壊した, (cracked) 割れた, (of bone) 折れた; (of speech) 片言の, 下手な; (of promise) 破られた
a broken vase 壊れた花びん
a broken vending machine
故障した自動販売機
The telephone's broken.
電話が故障している。
a broken home 崩壊した家庭
broken glass 割れたガラス
He had a broken arm.
彼は腕を骨折していた。
broken English 片言の英語
a broken promise 破られた約束

♦**broken heart** *n.* 失恋

broker *n.* (stockbroker) 株式仲買人, ブローカー

bronchitis *n.* 気管支炎

bronze *n., adj.* 青銅(の), ブロンズ(の)
a bronze statue 銅像

♦**Bronze Age** *n.* 青銅器時代

brooch *n.* ブローチ

broom *n.* ほうき
sweep with a broom ほうきではく

brother *n.* (one's own older brother) 兄, 兄貴, (sb else's) お兄さん, (one's own younger brother) 弟, (sb else's) 弟さん, (**brothers**) 男兄弟
"Are you the oldest or the youngest brother?"
"Neither, I'm in the middle."
「あなたが一番上ですか、それとも下ですか？」
「どちらでもなくて、真ん中です」
Those two are like brothers.
二人はまるで兄弟のようだ。

brother-in-law *n.* 義理の兄弟, (older) 義理の兄, (younger) 義理の弟

brow *n.* (forehead) 額 [→picture of FACE]

brown *n.* 茶色, 褐色
adj. (of color) 茶色の, 褐色の, (of suntanned skin) 小麦色に焼けた
v. (cook/fry until brown) きつね色に焼く/いためる
dark brown こげ茶色
a brown paper bag 茶色の紙袋
She has brown eyes and long brown hair.
彼女は茶色のひとみに、長い茶色の髪をしている。
Your legs are nice and brown, but your back's still white.
足はきれいな小麦色に焼けてるけど、背中はまだ白いよ。
Leave the chicken in the oven till it's roasted brown.
チキンは、きつね色になるまでオーブンで焼いてください。

♦**brown bread** *n.* 黒パン
brown rice *n.* 玄米
brown sugar *n.* 黒砂糖

browse *v.* (through items in a store) 商品を見て回る, (through book/magazine: scan with the eyes) (…に) ざっと目を通す, (through books/magazines: stand at a store and read) 立ち読みする, (on Internet) 見る, ネットサーフィンする; (of animals: feed on grass/leaves) 草/葉

を食べる

browser *n.* (for Internet) ブラウザ

bruise *n.* あざ, 打ち身, 打撲傷

v. (injure) ((*also figurative*)) 傷つける, (arm/leg) (腕/足に) あざをつくる

I got a nasty bruise on my elbow.
ひじにひどいあざができた。

She suffered nothing but a few cuts and bruises.
彼女は、数ヵ所の切り傷と打ち身程度で済んだ。

Have you bruised yourself badly?
ひどい打撲を負ったんですか？

You really bruised his ego.
彼の自尊心をほんとに傷つけたよ。

brunch *n.* ブランチ, (late breakfast) 遅い朝食

brunette *adj.* 茶色の髪の

n. ブルネットの人

brush *n.* (for hair) ブラシ, (artist's) 絵筆, (for calligraphy) 筆 [→ picture of CALLIGRAPHY]

v. (hair) ブラッシングする, (...に) ブラシをかける, (teeth) 磨く [→ POLISH]

♦ **brush against** *v.* (touch lightly) ...に触れる, かする

brush aside *v.* (criticism, question, complaint) 無視する, 軽くあしらう

brush off *v.* (ignore) 無視する, (reject) はねつける

brush up on *v.* (review) 復習する

brussels sprout *n.* 芽キャベツ

brutal *adj.* (cruel) 残虐な, (savage) 野蛮な, (brutish) 獣のような

brute *n.* けだもの, 人でなし

by/with brute force 暴力で, 腕力で

BSc *abbr.* (qualification) 理学士の学位

BSE *n.* (mad cow disease) 狂牛病

bubble *n.* 泡, (**bubbles**: foam, froth) あぶく; (speculative bubble) バブル; (speech bubble) 吹き出し

v. (form bubbles) 泡立つ, (boil) 沸騰する, 沸く, (emphasizing sound) ぶくぶくと音を立てる, (**bubble over**) あふれ出る

Look at the bubbles on the pond.
池の水面のあぶくを見て。

a bubble economy バブル経済

The champagne bubbled over.
シャンパンの泡があふれ出た。

She was bubbling with joy.
彼女は喜びにあふれていた。

bucket *n.* バケツ, (bucketful) バケツ1杯

The bucket is full.
バケツはいっぱいだ。

Would you empty the bucket?
バケツを空けてくれませんか？

buckle *n.* バックル, 留め金

v. (fasten) 留める, 締める; (become bent out of shape as by pressure/heat) 曲がる, ゆがむ

buckle one's belt [seat belt]
ベルト [シートベルト] を締める

bucktooth *n.* 出っ歯, 出歯

♦ **bucktoothed** *adj.* 出っ歯の

buckwheat *n.* (plant) ソバ, (grain) ソバの実, (flour) ソバ粉

♦ **buckwheat noodles** *n.* そば, 蕎麦

bud *n.* 芽, つぼみ

v. 芽を出す

All the trees are budding.

木々がみんな芽を出している。

come into bud 芽を吹く

These flowers come into bud early.
この花は芽を吹く時期が早い。

Buddha *n.* (person) 仏陀, お釈迦様, (statue) 仏像, (big statue) 大仏

Buddha 大仏

Buddhism *n.* 仏教

Buddhist *adj.* 仏教の

n. 仏教徒

a Buddhist country 仏教国

♦**Buddhist monk** *n.* お坊さん, 僧侶

buddy *n.* 仲間, 相棒

budge *v.* (**not budge**) 全く動かない

The cupboard is too heavy. It won't budge an inch.
食器棚は重すぎて、全く動かない。

budget *n.* (sum of money for a particular purpose) 予算, (plan) 予算案

v. (budget A for B) (BにAの)予算を組む, (budget for: take into consideration when making a budget) 予算に入れる

Is it in the budget?
それは予算に入っていますか？

They put ¥1.5 million in the budget for translation.
翻訳料に１５０万円の予算を組んだ。

budget one's time 時間をうまく使う

♦**budget deficit** *n.* 赤字予算, 財政赤字

buff *n.* (enthusiast) マニア, ファン, -通

v. (polish) 磨く

buffer *n.* ((*also figurative*)) 緩衝剤, (**buffers**: for train) 車止め, 緩衝器

buffet[1] *n.* (at restaurant) バイキング料理, (stand-and-eat type of meal/party) 立食; (piece of furniture) サイドボード

buffet[2] *v.* (**be buffeted**: by wind, waves, fate) もまれる, 打ちのめされる, ほんろうされる

The plane was buffeted by the wind.
飛行機は風にほんろうされた。

bug *n.* (insect) 虫; (anomaly in computer program) バグ; (microphone) 盗聴器

bugle *n.* らっぱ

blow a bugle らっぱを吹く

build

1 *v.* CONSTRUCT: (building) 建てる, 造る, 建築する, (sth small) 作る, (sth new) 創る, (sth abstract: relationship, reputation, trust) 築く, 確立する

2 *v.* INCREASE: (also **build up**: funds) 築く, 築き上げる, (**build confidence**) 自信がつく; (of traffic) 増える, (of tension, excitement) 高まる

3 *n.* PHYSIQUE: 体格

1 They built their own house.
彼らは自分たちの手で家を建てた。

Kids like building models.
子供は模型を作るのが大好きだ。

build a nest 巣を作る

Are there plans to build a new robot?
新しいロボットを作る計画はありますか？

Their relationship was built upon trust.
彼らの関係は信頼に基づいたものだった。

She built a name for herself as a writer of children's stories.
彼女は童話作家としての名声を築いた。

You should try building her trust up

more.
もっと彼女との信頼を築くべきです。

The organization was built up over generations.
その組織は何世代もかかって確立された。

2 Mr. Wada built up a fortune.
和田さんは一財産を築き上げた。

The traffic builds up around 5 o'clock.
5時ごろになると交通量が増えます。

3 He has the same build as me.
彼は僕と同じような体格だ。

♦**builder** ***n.*** 建築業者

building ***n.*** (structure for living/working in) 建物, ビル

a high-rise building 高層ビル

a renovated building 改装された建物

a modern building 近代的な建物

a derelict building 廃屋

the second building before the traffic signal 信号の二つ手前のビル

This building is going to be demolished.
このビルは取り壊される予定です。

built-in ***adj.*** (of furniture) 作り付けの, (of device in machine) 内蔵した

bulb ***n.*** (light bulb) 電球; (part of plant) 球根

The bulb has burned out.
電球が切れた。

bulge ***n.*** 膨らみ, 出っ張り

v. 膨らむ, 膨れる, 出っ張る

Your stomach is bulging out.
おなかが出ているよ。

bulimia ***n.*** 過食症

bulk ***n.*** (**the bulk of...**) ...の大半, ...の大部分; (size) 大きさ, (mass) かさ

The bulk of the work has been done.
仕事の大半は終わりました。

in bulk 大口で, まとめて, 大量に

purchase [sell] in bulk
まとめて買う[売る]

The grain is shipped to Russia in bulk.
穀物が大量にロシアに送られている。

bulky ***adj.*** かさばった, 大きい

a bulky sweater バルキーセーター

bull ***n.*** (animal) 雄牛; (lie) うそ

bulldog ***n.*** ブルドッグ

bulldozer ***n.*** ブルドーザー

bullet ***n.*** 弾丸, 銃弾, ((*informal*)) 弾

How many bullets were fired?
弾丸は何発発砲されたんですか？

♦**bulletproof** ***adj.*** 防弾の

a bulletproof vest 防弾チョッキ

bulletin ***n.*** (news bulletin) ニュース速報, (company newsletter) 社報, (university newsletter) 紀要

bulletin board ***n.*** 掲示板

bull's-eye ***n.*** 的の中心

hit the bull's-eye 的に的中する, ((*also figurative*)) 的を射る

bullshit ***n.*** でたらめ, うそ

v. でたらめを言う

bully ***n.*** いじめっ子

v. いじめる

♦**bullying** ***n.*** いじめ

bum ***n.*** (lazy person) 怠け者, (good-for-nothing) ろくでなし, (vagrant) 浮浪者, (homeless person) ホームレスの人, (enthusiast of a particular sport) -狂; (buttocks) (お)尻

He's nothing but a bum!

あいつは全くろくでなしだ!

a ski bum スキー狂

a beach bum 浜辺でぶらぶら過ごす人

a surfing bum サーフィン野郎

♦**bum around** *v.* うろつく, ぶらぶらする

bump *v.* (strike) ぶつける; (**bump along**: move in a shaky fashion) ガタガタ揺れて進む; (**bump into**: encounter by chance) …に偶然出会う, …にばったり出くわす

n. (injury) こぶ, (hole in the road) でこぼこ; (collision) 衝突

I bumped the back of my head against the wall.
後頭部を壁にぶつけた。

Careful you don't bump the car.
車をぶつけないよう気をつけてね。

The old bus bumped along.
古いバスはガタゴト走って行った。

We bumped into each other in the station.
駅でばったり[偶然]会ったんです。

I have a bump on my knee.
ひざにこぶがある。

bumper[1] *n.* (part of car) バンパー [→ picture of CAR]

bumper to bumper じゅずつなぎの, 渋滞している

The traffic was bumper to bumper.
車はじゅずつなぎになっていた/道路は渋滞していた。

bumper[2] *adj.* (very large) 大量の

a bumper crop 大豊作

bumpy *adj.* (of surface) でこぼこの

bun *n.* (hairstyle) おだんご, (traditional Japanese hairstyle) まげ; (bread for hamburger) パン

bunch *n.* (of things: batch) 束, 房, (of people: band, group) 一団, (crowd) 一群, (lot) 連中

a bunch of grapes 一房のぶどう

a bunch of keys かぎの束

a bunch of flowers 花束

a bunch of high-school students
高校生の一群

a bunch of idiots まぬけな連中

bundle *n.* (cluster, batch) 束, (parcel) 包み; (**a bundle of**: lots of) たくさんの

v. (**bundle up**) (=gather together) 束ねる, (=tie up) くくる, (=dress warmly) 暖かくする, 厚着する

a bundle of bills 札束

bundle up the newspapers
新聞を束ねる

It's cold outside, so you'd better bundle up.
外は寒いから暖かくしていきなさい。

bunraku *n.* (puppet theater) 文楽

buoy *n.* ブイ, 浮標

buoyancy *n.* 浮力

burden *n.* (responsibility) 負担, 重荷, (heavy load) 荷物

bear a heavy burden 重荷を背負う

burdock *n.* ゴボウ

bureau *n.* (piece of furniture) 整理だんす; (government department) 局

bureaucracy *n.* 官僚制

bureaucrat *n.* 官僚

bureaucratic *adj.* 官僚的な

burger *n.* ハンバーガー

burglar *n.* 泥棒, 空き巣

♦ **burglar alarm** *n.* 盗難警報器

burglary *n.* 泥棒, (crime) 住居侵入罪

burial *n.* (burying of a body) 埋葬, (ceremony) 埋葬式

burn

1 *v.* BE/SET ABLAZE: 燃える/燃やす, (be destroyed by fire) 焼ける, (destroy by fire) 焼く, (set fire to: house etc.) (…に) 放火する

2 *v.* FOOD: (cause to char) 焦がす, (become charred) 焦げる

3 *v.* BODY PART: やけどする, (**get burned**: get sunburned) 日焼けする

4 *v.* ITCH/STING: ひりひりする

5 *n.* INJURY: (by fire, steam) やけど, (by sun: sunburn) 日焼け

1 There was a fire burning in the hearth.
暖炉では火が燃えていた。

This burns easily. これは燃えやすい。

The protesters burned a flag.
抗議する人々は旗を燃やした。

Father's out back burning garbage.
お父さんは裏でごみを燃やしている。

The city burned to the ground.
町はすっかり焼けてしまった [焼け野原と化した]。

There was a fire next door, and the whole house burned down.
隣の家で火事があって、家は全焼した。

2 The fish was burned black.
魚が真っ黒に焦げてしまった。

Do you smell something burning?
何かが焦げるにおいがしない？/何か焦げくさくない？

3 Careful you don't burn yourself!
やけどしないように気をつけて！

His skin burns easily.
彼は日焼けしやすい。

4 The rash is burning.
発疹がひりひりする。

5 That's a terrible burn on your arm.
その腕のやけどはひどいですね。

be burned alive 焼け死ぬ, 焼死する

Some people could not escape and were burned alive.
中には逃げ遅れて焼死した人もいました。

burning *adj.* (of fire, coal) 燃えている, (of ambition) 熱烈な

n. (act of burning) 燃焼 [→ ARSON]

burp *n., v.* げっぷ(をする)

burst *v.* (of pipe) 破裂する, (of balloon) 割れる, (of bubble) はじける, (of bag) 破れる, (of dam) 決壊する, (of door: **burst open**) バーンとあく

A water main has burst.
水道管が破裂しました。

The bubble burst in 1989.
バブルは１９８９年にはじけた。

The bag burst and my shopping fell out onto the pavement.
袋が破れて、買った物が道路に散らばった。

The river may burst its banks.
川が決壊するかもしれません。

The door burst open and in came the teacher.
ドアがバーンとあいて先生が入って来た。

burst in on *v.* (barge in on) …に飛び込む, …に押しかける, (conversation) …の話に割り込む

burst into *v.* (**flames**) ぱっと燃え上がる, (**laughter**) どっと笑い出す, (**tears**) わっと泣き出す

The kerosene burst into flames.
灯油がぱっと燃え上がった。

Everyone burst into laughter.
みんながどっと笑い出した。

---

bury *v.* (put into the ground) 埋める, (body at funeral) 埋葬する, 葬る

I buried the garbage.
ごみを埋めた。

She will be cremated and buried in the cemetery.
彼女は火葬されて、墓地に埋葬されます。

bus *n.* バス

go by bus バスで行く

get on [off] a bus バスに乗る [を降りる]

take a bus バスに乗る

a bus driver バスの運転手

♦**bus fare** *n.* バス料金, ((*informal*)) バス代

bus stop *n.* バス停, 停留所

bush *n.* (shrub) 低木, かん木, (thicket) やぶ, (**the bush**: the wilderness) 奥地

beat around the bush 遠回しに言う

bushy *adj.* (of hair, fur) ふさふさした

business *n.*

1 LINE OF WORK: 仕事, ビジネス, (occupation) 職業, (industry) -業, -業界

2 BUYING AND SELLING: 商売, ビジネス, (business conditions) 景気

3 COMPANY: 会社

4 THINGS TO DO: 用事, 用件

5 CONCERN: See examples below

1 I'm here on business.
こちらには仕事で来ました。

What sort of business are you in?
どんなお仕事をなさっているんですか？

the advertising business 広告業

show business ショービジネス

2 Business is business.
商売は商売だ。

Why don't you go into business?
事業を興したらどう？

(*sign*) Open for Business 営業中

Business is good [bad].
景気がいい [悪い]。

3 He runs a consultancy business.
彼はコンサルタント会社を経営している。

a home business 在宅ビジネス

4 I'm sorry, I can't make it tomorrow. I've got some business to attend to.
申し訳ありませんが、明日はちょっと無理です。ほかに用事がありますので。

unfinished business
済ませていない用件

5 That's none of your business!
あなたには関係ない！

Mind your own business!
余計な干渉をするな/大きなお世話だ！

♦**business card** *n.* 名刺

business class *n.* ビジネスクラス

business deal *n.* 商取引

business district *n.* 商業地, オフィス街

business hours *n.* (of shop) 営業時間, (of library) 開館時間

business office *n.* 事務所

business school *n.* 経営学大学院, ビジネススクール

business trip *n.* 出張

KANJI BRIDGE

業 ON: ぎょう, ごう KUN: わざ | BUSINESS

business hours	営業時間
commerce	商業
family business	家業
main business	本業
occupation	職業
salesman	営業マン
side job	副業
trader	業者

businesslike *adj.* ビジネスライクな, 事務的な

businessman, -person, -woman *n.* 実業家, ビジネスマン [NOTE: ビジネスマン refers especially to male office workers.]

bust[1] *n.* (sculpture) 胸像, (upper body) 上半身, (chest) 胸 [→ picture of BODY], (of woman) バスト [→ BREAST]

It was a bust of a Greek god.
それはギリシャの神の胸像でした。

♦ **bust measurement** *n.* 胸囲, バスト

bust[2] *v.* (break) 壊す, (**be busted**: be arrested) ((*informal*)) 捕まる

go bust (of person) 破産する, (of company) つぶれる, 倒産する

busy *adj.*

1 OCCUPIED: 忙しい, (**too busy to do**) 忙しくて…する暇がない, (of phone line) 話し中だ

2 FULL OF ACTIVITY: 活気のある, (of streets) にぎやかな, (of restaurant: crowded) 人の多い, 混む, (of road) 交通量の多い

3 OF PATTERN: ごてごてした, うるさい

1 We were busy all day.
一日中ずっと忙しかった。

I'm not usually so busy in the mornings.
午前中はいつもはこんなに忙しくない。

I'm too busy to make dinner.
忙しくて晩ご飯を作る暇がない。

The line is busy. 話し中です。

2 This market is always busy.
この市場はいつも活気があります。

This place gets really busy around 8 o'clock.
ここは8時ごろが、すごく混んでいる。

3 That pattern's too busy for me.
その柄は、ごてごてしすぎている。

♦ **busily** *adv.* 忙しく

busy signal *n.* 話し中の音

but

1 *conj.* HOWEVER: …が, …けれど(も), ((*informal*)) …けど

2 *conj.* CONTRARY TO EXPECTATION: …のに, (used at the beginning of a sentence) でも, しかし, ところが

3 *prep.* EXCEPT: …ほかは, …以外に

4 *adv.* ONLY: ほんの, たった…だけ, (at least) (せめて)…さえ

1 I was going to refuse, but I changed my mind.
断るつもりだったんですが、気が変わりました。

Excuse me, but I believe you're mistaken.
恐縮ですが、間違っておられると思います。

He didn't say whether he would come, but he did say he would let us know soon.
彼は来るかどうか言わなかったけれど、近いうちに返事をすると言っていました。

I'll do anything, but don't ask me to do that.
何でもするけど、それだけは勘弁して。

I may not win, but I sure can try.
勝てないかもしれないけど、やるだけはやってみる。

You don't need to learn that, but you do need to learn this.
あれはいいとしても、これは覚えなくてはいけませんよ。

2 We thought the film would be good, but it wasn't.
いい映画だろうと思っていたのに、そうでもなかった。

It was cheap, but it works very well.
安かったのに、性能はすごくいい。

It was bad enough losing my job. But this is terrible news.
失業しただけでも十分困っているのに、この知らせは厳しいよ。

That's all very well. But he's not going to agree.
それはけっこうなことです。でも彼は賛成しないと思いますよ。

3 I couldn't do anything but lie in bed.
ベッドで寝ているほかなかった。

No one but Henry can do that.
ヘンリー以外の人にはできないでしょう。

Who but a madman would do such a crazy thing?
狂った人でなきゃ、誰にそんなばかげたことができる？

4 Come on, don't be angry. He's but a child.
((*feminine*)) まあまあ、怒らないで。相手はほんの子供じゃないの。

It's but four kilometers away.
たった4キロ離れているだけです。

Had I but known my client was waiting...
お客さんが待っていることを知ってさえいたら…

not A but B AではなくB

I'm not an artist but a craftsman.
私は芸術家じゃなくて職人なんです。

butcher ***n.*** (お)肉屋(さん)
v. (animal) 解体する, (person) 虐殺する

butt¹ ***v.*** (hit with one's head) 頭で押す, (…に) 頭突きする
n. 頭突き

♦**butt in** ***v.*** (interfere) 口出しする, 干渉する, (steal a place in line) 割り込む

butt² ***n.*** (of cigarette) 吸い殻; (buttocks) (お)尻 [→ picture of BODY]

butter ***n.*** バター
v. (…に) バターを塗る

♦**buttery** ***adj.*** (of food) バターたっぷりの, (of substance: butterlike) バターのような

butterfly ***n.*** (insect) チョウ, 蝶, ((*informal*)) ちょうちょ, (style of swimming) バタフライ

buttocks ***n.*** (お)尻 [→ picture of BODY]

button ***n.*** (fastening) ボタン
v. (…の) ボタンを留める, ボタンをかける

push/press sb's buttons (anger) 怒らせる, (sexually excite) その気にさせる

buy ***v.*** (purchase) 買う, ((*formal*)) 購入する, (get) 手に入れる

"What did you buy?"
"I bought a pair of shoes and a blouse."
「何を買ったの？」

B

「靴とブラウスを買ったの」

Please don't buy anything for me.
私には何も買わなくていいですよ。

I've been meaning to buy that book, but I still haven't gotten around to it.
その本を買おうと思いながら、いまだに買っていない。

I bought my daughter a Swiss watch for her twenty-first birthday.
娘の 21 歳の誕生日にスイス製の腕時計を買ってやりました。

Did you buy that at the supermarket?
あれはスーパーで買ったんですか？

Do you know where I can buy a bonsai tree?
盆栽はどこで手に入るか知ってる？

I wanted to buy that new computer, but I couldn't afford it.
あの新型コンピューターが欲しかったんですが、手が届きませんでした。

buyer *n.* 買い手, ((*formal*)) 購入者, (purchasing agent) バイヤー, 仕入れ係

buzz *n.* (of insect) ブンブン(いう音), (of machine) うなり

v. (of insect) ブンブンいう, (of machine) うなる

buzzer *n.* ブザー

buzzword *n.* はやりの専門語

by *prep., adv.*

1 NEAR: (…の)そばに, 近くに, (next to) (…の)隣に

2 BY MEANS OF: …で, (according to: rules etc.) …に従って, …どおり

3 CREATED BY: …の

4 UP TO AND BEYOND: (**go/pass by**) (…のそばを) 通る, 通り過ぎる, (of time: **go/fly by**) 過ぎ去る

5 NOT LATER THAN: …までに

6 DURING: …の間に

7 BY AMOUNT/INCREMENT OF: (by amount of) …単位で, (by increment of) …ずつ

8 GIVING DIMENSIONS: …かける

9 DIVIDED BY: See example below

1 I always keep a flashlight by my bed.
いつも、ベッドのそばに懐中電灯を置いています。

There's a small park by the gas station.
ガソリンスタンドの隣に小さな公園があります。

2 by air/airmail 航空便で

by land 陸路で

by mail 郵便 [郵送] で

by accident/chance 偶然, たまたま

by mistake 間違って

He was killed by a single bullet.
彼は1発の銃弾で殺された。

I knew by the way she looked at me that she was angry.
彼女の私を見る目つきで、怒っているのがわかった。

We'd better do it by the rules.
規則どおりやったほうがよさそうですね。

3 It was written by Shakespeare.
(それは) シェイクスピアの作品です。

It's a painting by Degas.
(それは)ドガの作です。

4 He passed by me without even saying hello.
彼はあいさつもしないで、私のそばを通り過ぎた。

Do you go by the supermarket on your way to work?

仕事に行く途中、スーパーのそばを通りますか？

The traffic flowed by endlessly.
交通はとだえることなく続いた。

Time flew by.
時が飛ぶように過ぎ去った。

Time goes by so quickly when you're having fun.
楽しいときには、時のたつのが早い。

5 We have to be there by 9 o'clock.
9時までには着いていないといけない。

The applications should be mailed by this Friday at the latest.
願書は、遅くとも今週の金曜日までに郵送しなくてはいけません。

6 The work must be carried out by night.
この仕事は夜の間にやらなくちゃいけない。

by day 昼間は

7 You can buy it by the kilo.
キロ単位で買えます。

You'll be paid by the hour.
給料は時間給で支払われます。

little by little 少しずつ

Step by step, he began to improve.
一歩一歩、彼は上達し始めた。

8 The size is three meters by two and a half.
サイズは3メートルかける2.5メートルです。

9 What is a hundred divided by seven?
100割る7はいくつですか？

bye *interj.* さよなら, じゃあ [→ GOOD-BYE]

bye-bye *interj.* バイバイ [→ GOOD-BYE]

bypass *n.* (detour) バイパス, う回路
v. う回する, 避けてバイパスを通る

by-product *n.* (industrial by-product) 副産物, (side effect) 副作用

bystander *n.* 傍観者, 見物人

byte *n.* バイト

C, c

C, c *n.* (letter) C, (third item in a series) 第3, 丙, (grade) C, 普通

cab *n.* (taxi) タクシー, (part of truck) 運転台

cabaret *n.* (nightclub) ナイトクラブ, (show) ショー

cabbage *n.* キャベツ, (Chinese cabbage) 白菜

cabin *n.* (of ship) キャビン, 船室, (of airplane) キャビン; (small house) 小屋

a log cabin 丸太小屋

cabinet *n.* キャビネット, (display case) 飾り棚, (cupboard) 戸棚, (filing cabinet) 書類整理棚; (group of government ministers) 内閣

cable *n.* (thick wire) ケーブル, (electric cable) ケーブル, -線; (cable TV) ケーブルテレビ

♦**cable car** *n.* ケーブルカー

cackle *v.* (laugh) キャッキャッと笑う, (of hen) コッコッと鳴く

cactus *n.* サボテン

cadaver *n.* (corpse) 死体

caddie *n.* キャディー

v. (caddie for) (…の) キャディーをする

caddy *n.* 茶筒, お茶の缶

caesarean → CESAREAN SECTION

café *n.* (coffee shop) 喫茶店, カフェ

cafeteria *n.* カフェテリア, 食堂

caffeine *n.* カフェイン

cage *n.* (for small animals) かご, (for midsize to large animals) おり

a bird cage 鳥かご

Have you put the hamster back in its cage?
ハムスターをかごに戻した？

I don't like seeing animals kept in cages.
おりに入れられた動物を見るのは好きじゃない。

cagey *adj.* (be cagey about) (…について) 話したがらない

cajole *v.* (**cajole into doing**) うまいこと言って(…に)…させる

cake *n.* ケーキ, 洋菓子

calamity *n.* 災難

calcium *n.* カルシウム

calculate *v.* (compute) 計算する, (forecast) 予測する, 予想する

♦**calculating** *adj.* 打算的な

calculated *adj.* (intended) 故意の, (planned) 計画的な

a calculated crime 計画的な犯罪

take a calculated risk 危険を承知でやる

calculation *n.* 計算

calculator *n.* 計算器, 電卓

calculus *n.* 微分積分学

calendar *n.* カレンダー, 暦 [→ YEAR]

the lunar calendar (太)陰暦

calf[1] *n.* (young cow) 子牛, (young of animal other than cow) …の子

calf[2] *n.* (part of the body) ふくらはぎ [→ picture of BODY]

caliber *n.* (quality of sb's ability) 手腕; (diameter of gun barrel) 口径, (diameter of bullet/tube) 直径

calibrate *v.* (adjust) (…の) 目盛りを調整する, (measure the caliber of: gun) (…の) 口径を測る

calisthenics *n.* (exercises) 美容体操

call

1 *v.* REFER TO AS: (…と) いう, 呼ぶ, (denounce) …呼ばわりする, (**be called…**: be named…) …という名前だ

2 *v.* SUMMON: (taxi, police) 呼ぶ, (meeting) 招集する

3 *v.* SHOUT: (in distress) 叫ぶ, (to get sb's attention) 大声で言う

4 *n., v.* TELEPHONE: (…に) 電話(する)

5 *n.* CRY OF AN ANIMAL: 鳴き声

1 That's what we call democracy.
それが民主主義というものです。

I don't call that fair.
それは公平じゃない。

Mori called him an idiot.
森さんは、その人をばか呼ばわりした。

"Oh, what's he called again?"
"We all call him DJ."
「えーと、彼は何という名前だったっけ?」
「みんなＤＪと呼んでいるよ」

a blues singer called Billie
ビリーという名のブルースシンガー

2 You'd better call the police.
警察を呼んだほうがいい。

Should we call an ambulance?
救急車を呼びましょうか?

A meeting has been called.
会議が招集されました。

3 They were calling for help.
彼らは助けを求めて叫んでいたんです。

We called out his name, but there was no answer.
大きな声で彼の名前を呼んだけど、返事はなかった。

4 I got a call from Ms. Uchida yesterday.
昨日、内田さんから電話がありました。

Do you want me to give you a call?
お電話を差し上げましょうか/((*informal*))電話しようか?

A telephone call doesn't cost much.
電話をかけるのは、大してかかりません。

a local [long-distance] call
市内 [長距離] 通話

I called, but there was no answer.
電話したけど、誰も出なかった。

5 the call of a dolphin イルカの鳴き声

be on call 待機している

We are on call twenty-four hours.
２４時間待機しています。

Dr. Sakamoto is on call tonight.
今晩の当直医は坂本先生です。

call back *v.* (return a phone call) 電話をかけ直す, 折り返し電話をする

Look, I'm busy right now. I'll call them back.
今ちょっと手が離せないんだ。こっちからかけ直すよ。

call by *v.* …に(立ち)寄る [→ CALL IN ON]

call for *v.* (go to meet) 迎えに行く/来る; (need) (…が) 必要だ

I'll call for you at 9 o'clock.
9時に迎えに行きます。

This calls for immediate action.
これには迅速な行動が必要だ。

call in on *v.* …に(立ち)寄る

I called in on Grandma on my way home.
帰る途中、おばあちゃんのところに寄った。

call off *v.* やめる, 取りやめる, 中止する

Let's just call the whole thing off.
それじゃ、すべて取りやめましょう。
The strike has been called off.
ストライキは中止された。

call on *v.* (visit) 訪ねる, ((*formal*)) 訪問する

call out *v.* (sb's name) 大声で呼ぶ
Did they call out your name?
お名前を呼ばれましたか？

call up *v.* (telephone) (…に)電話をかける; (for military service) 徴兵する, 召集する

caller *n.* (telephoner) 電話をかける人, ((*formal*)) 発信者, (guest, visitor) お客さん

♦**caller ID** *n.* 発信者番号通知サービス

calligraphy *n.* (brush writing) 書道, (instruction in brush writing) 習字, (writing with pen) カリグラフィー, (handwriting) 筆跡

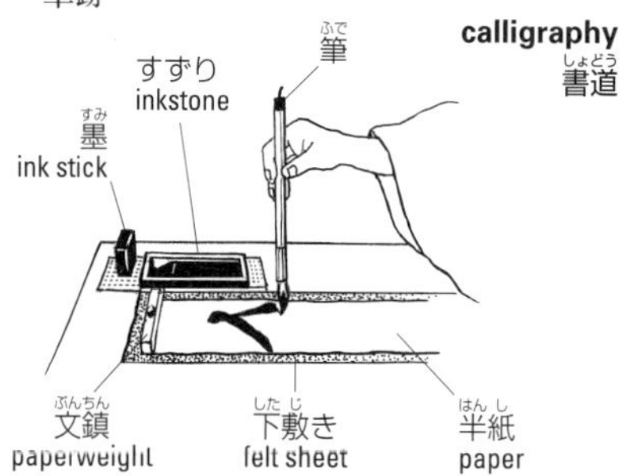

calling *n.* (vocation) 天職

calling card *n.* (phone card) テレホンカード

call-up *n.* (compulsory summons for military service) 徴兵, 召集

calm *adj.* (of sea) 穏やかな, のどかな, (of weather: windless) 風のない, (of person, voice) 落ち着いた
n. (stillness) 静けさ
v. (make calm) 落ち着かせる
a calm sea 穏やかな [のどかな] 海
a calm day 風のない日
We need someone who can keep calm.
物に動じない人物が必要だ。
the calm before the storm
嵐の前の静けさ
Is there no way to calm the child?
その子を落ち着かせる方法はないの？

♦**calmly** *adv.* 静かに, (coolly) 冷静に
calmness *n.* 静けさ

calm down *v.* (regain one's composure) 落ち着く, 気を静める
Would you calm down, please?
どうか、落ち着いてください。

calorie *n.* カロリー

calypso *n.* (music) カリプソ

cam *n.* (engine part) カム

camaraderie *n.* 友情

camcorder *n.* ビデオカメラ

camel *n.* ラクダ

camellia *n.* ツバキ, 椿

camera *n.* カメラ
load film into a camera
カメラにフィルムを入れる

cameraman, -woman *n.* カメラマン, 撮影技師

camouflage *n.* (clothing) 偽装, (pattern)

迷彩, (blending in with one's environment) カムフラージュ

v. (**camouflage oneself**) カムフラージュする, 偽装する

camp *n.* (campsite) キャンプ場, (for soldiers) 駐留地; (countryside educational program for children) キャンプ

v. キャンプする

a camp by the river 川辺でのキャンプ場

a base camp ベースキャンプ

make [break] camp

テントを張る [たたむ]

a refugee camp 難民キャンプ [収容所]

a prisoner-of-war camp 捕虜収容所

a summer camp サマーキャンプ

go camping キャンプに行く

Let's go camping this summer.

今年の夏はキャンプに行こうよ。

campaign *n.* (political) 運動, 活動, キャンペーン, (military) 軍事行動, (advertising/sales campaign) キャンペーン

v. (**campaign for/against**) …の運動をする/…に対して反対運動をする

an election campaign 選挙運動

The sales campaign begins today.

セールスキャンペーンは、今日からです。

We must campaign against injustice.

不正に対して反対運動を起こすべきだ。

campaign for reelection

再選のための選挙運動をする

camper *n.* (person) キャンプする人, キャンパー; (vehicle) キャンピングカー

camphor tree *n.* クスノキ, 楠

campus *n.* キャンパス, 大学構内

can[1] *aux.*

1 INDICATING ABILITY: (**can do**) (…が)できる, …することができる, <potential form of verb> [→ ABLE]

2 GIVING/ASKING PERMISSION: (**you can…**) …してもいい, (**can I…?**) …してもいいですか

3 FORBIDDING: (**you cannot…**) …してはいけない, …してはだめです

4 ASKING A FAVOR: (**can you…?**) …してくれますか, ((*polite*)) …してくださいますか

5 INDICATING POSSIBILITY: (**can be**) …ことがある, …場合もある, (**cannot be**) …はずがない

1 He says he can drive.

彼は車の運転ができると言っている。

"Can you swim?" "Yes, I can."

「泳げますか？」「はい、泳げます」

I can't speak German. Can you?

私はドイツ語は話せません。あなたは？

Do the best you can. 最善を尽くせ。

The kids are as happy as can be.

子供たちは有頂天になっている。

You can't do it in a day.

１日ではできないよ。

You can't buy a cell phone without an ID.

身分証明書がないと携帯電話は買えません。

2 You can leave anytime you like.

好きな時に帰っていいよ。

"Can I go now?"

"Yes, you can."

「もう帰ってもいいですか？」

「ええ、いいですよ」

3 You can't park here.

ここに駐車してはいけません。

You can't speak to people like that.
人にあんな口のきき方をするもんじゃありません。

4 Can you wait here for a moment?
ちょっとここで待っててくれる？

Can you hand me the salt, please?
塩を取って [回して] くださいますか？

5 He can be very serious at times.
彼は時々とても真剣になることがある。

It can be cold in the winter months.
冬場は、けっこう冷え込む時もある。

all one can do is …しかない

All one can do is wait.
待つしかない。

as…as one can できるだけ…

Get here as fast as you can.
できるだけ早くここに来て。

I'm working as hard as I can.
一生懸命がんばっています。

can but do …するよりほかかない, ただ…するだけだ

We can but hope.
祈るよりほかありません。

can't be too… いくら … <-て form of adj.> + もしすぎることはない

One can never be too cautious.
いくら用心しても、しすぎることはない。

can't but do …せずにはいられない, …せざるを得ない

I can't but think he's lying.
あの人がうそをついていると思わざるを得ない。

can[2] ***n.*** (container) 缶

an empty can 空き缶

open a can 缶をあける

cans of beer 缶ビール

an aluminum can アルミ缶

♦**canned *adj.*** 缶詰の

canned tuna ツナ缶 [マグロの缶詰]

Canada *n.* カナダ, ((*in abbr.*)) 加

Canadian *n.* (person) カナダ人

adj. (of country, culture) カナダの, (of person) カナダ人の

canal *n.* 運河

the Panama Canal パナマ運河

cancel *v.* (order, reservation) キャンセルする, 取り消す, (meeting) 中止する, 取りやめる, (flight) 欠航にする, (train, bus) 運休する

Have you canceled the appointment?
予約はキャンセルしましたか？

It's OK—the meeting's been canceled.
大丈夫。会議は中止になりました。

All flights to and from Sapporo have been canceled.
札幌発着の便はすべて欠航です。

cancellation *n.* (of order, reservation) キャンセル, 取り消し, (of flight) 欠航

Cancer *n.* (the Crab) かに座

cancer *n.* (illness) がん

breast cancer 乳がん

lung cancer 肺がん

candid *adj.* (frank) 率直な, 遠慮のない

candidate *n.* (nominee) 候補者, (applicant) 志願者

candle *n.* ろうそく, キャンドル

candlestick *n.* ろうそく立て, 燭台

candy *n.* (sweets) (お)菓子, (hard candy) あめ, キャンディ

♦**candy store *n.*** (お)菓子屋(さん)

cane ***n.*** (hard stem) 茎, (sugarcane) さとうきび; (walking stick) ステッキ, つえ, (stick used to punish) むち; (material for basket/furniture) トウ, 籐

v. (hit with a cane) むちで打つ

get the cane むちで打たれる

canine ***n.*** (dog) 犬; (tooth) 犬歯

canister ***n.*** キャニスター, (can) 缶

cannabis ***n.*** 大麻

cannibal ***n.*** 人食い人種

cannon ***n.*** 大砲

cannot → CAN[1]

canoe ***n.*** カヌー

can opener ***n.*** 缶切り [→ picture of COOKING UTENSILS]

cantaloupe ***n.*** カンタループ

cantankerous ***adj.*** 怒りっぽい, 気難しい

canteen ***n.*** (cafeteria) 食堂; (water flask) 水筒

canvas ***n.*** (for painting) カンバス, 画布, (material) キャンバス地, 帆布

canvas shoes ズック靴

canvass ***v.*** (**canvass for**: politician, party) …のために選挙運動をする

canyon ***n.*** 峡谷

the Grand Canyon グランドキャニオン

cap

1 ***n.*** **COVERING FOR THE HEAD:** 帽子, (baseball cap) 野球帽, (school cap) 学帽

2 ***n.*** **TOP/LID:** (bottle cap) ふた, キャップ, (stopper) 栓, (pen cap) キャップ

3 ***v.*** **PUT A TOP/LID ON:** (…に)ふた/栓をする

1 put on [take off] one's cap
帽子をかぶる [取る]

The man wore a cap.
その男は帽子をかぶっていました。

Do you remember the old school cap?
昔の学帽を覚えてる?

2 Does the bottle have a cap?
そのびんにはふたがありますか?

Please remember to put the cap back on once you've opened it.
一度あけたら、またふたをするのを忘れないでください。

3 Could you cap the whiskey, please?
ウイスキーにキャップをしてくれない?

capability ***n.*** 能力, 手腕, 力

be beyond one's capabilities
能力を超えている

capable ***adj.*** (able) 能力のある, (competent) 有能な, (**be capable of doing**) …する力がある [→ CAN[1]]

She's a very capable person.
彼女は非常に有能な人です。

He's capable of better work.
彼はもっといい仕事ができるのに。

Just show your boss what you are capable of.
上司にあなたの実力を見せなさい。

She's not capable of doing that.
彼女には、それをする力はない。

capacity ***n.*** (seating capacity) 収容力, 定員, (production capacity) 生産能力; (of ship: payload) 積載量; (ability) 能力, 才能; (role) 役割, 役職, 立場

The theater's seating capacity is about two thousand.
この劇場の定員はおよそ2000人です。

The theater was filled to capacity.
劇場は満席でした。

at full (production) capacity フル稼働

C

で, フル操業で

We're operating at full capacity.

フル稼働 [操業] しています。

cape[1] *n.* (garment) ケープ

cape[2] *n.* (land feature) 岬

capillary *n.* (blood vessel) 毛細血管

capital *n.* (capital city) 首都; (capital letter) 大文字; (funds) 資本金

adj. (uppercase) 大文字の

London is the capital of England.

ロンドンはイギリスの首都です。

River names are spelled with capital letters.

川の名前は大文字で始まる。

The company has a capital of ¥200 million.

その会社の資本金は2億円です。

capitalism *n.* 資本主義

capitalist *n.* 資本主義者

adj. (of country, economy) 資本主義の

capital punishment *n.* 死刑

Capitol *n.* (**the Capitol**) (=building in which the U.S. Congress meets) 連邦議会議事堂, (=building in which a state legislature meets) 州議会議事堂

caprice *n.* (whim) 気まぐれ

Capricorn *n.* (the Goat) 山羊座

capsize *v.* (become overturned) 転覆する, (cause to overturn) 転覆させる

The boat capsized within seconds.

ものの数秒で船は転覆した。

capsule *n.* (containing medicine) カプセル; (space capsule) 宇宙カプセル

♦ **capsule hotel** *n.* カプセルホテル

captain *n.* (of team) 主将, キャプテン, (of merchant ship) 船長, (of airplane) 機長, (in U.S. Army/Air Force/Marine Corps) 大尉, (in U.S. Navy) 大佐

caption *n.* (title) タイトル, 表題, (explanation) キャプション, 説明文

captive *n.* (prisoner) 捕虜

adj. 捕らわれた, 捕虜になった

take [hold] captive

捕虜にする [しておく]

captivity *n.* (of animal) 捕獲

in captivity 捕獲されて

captor *n.* 捕らえる人, 逮捕する人

capture *v.* (person, animal) 捕まえる, (city) 占領する, (in competition: get) 取る, (acquire, win) 獲得する, (heart) とらえる, (epitomize: essence, atmosphere) とらえる, (attract: attention) 引く

n. (of criminal) 逮捕, (of animal) 捕獲

The prisoner was captured shortly after his escape.

囚人は、脱走後まもなく捕まった。

The city was captured after a two-week bombardment.

町は2週間の爆撃の後、占領された。

capture a market 市場を獲得する

He captured her heart.

彼は彼女の心をとらえた。

The artist has captured the atmosphere of the place.

画家はその場の雰囲気をとらえている。

♦ **capture the flag** *n.* (game) 旗取りゲーム

car *n.* (automobile) 車, 自動車 [→ picture at right], (lightweight: 660 cc or less) 軽自動車; (segment of train) 車両, -号車

car 車(くるま)

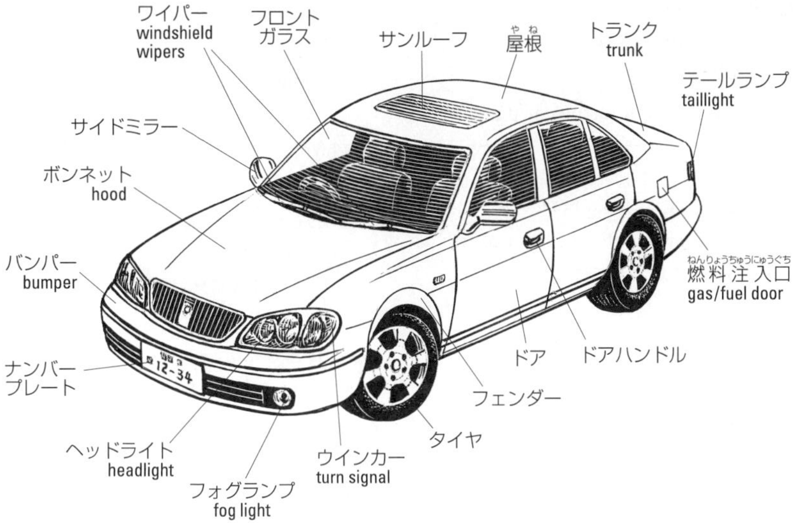

ワイパー windshield wipers
フロントガラス
サンルーフ
屋根(やね)
トランク trunk
テールランプ taillight
サイドミラー
ボンネット hood
バンパー bumper
燃料注入口(ねんりょうちゅうにゅうぐち) gas/fuel door
ナンバープレート
ドア
ドアハンドル
フェンダー
タイヤ
ヘッドライト headlight
ウインカー turn signal
フォグランプ fog light

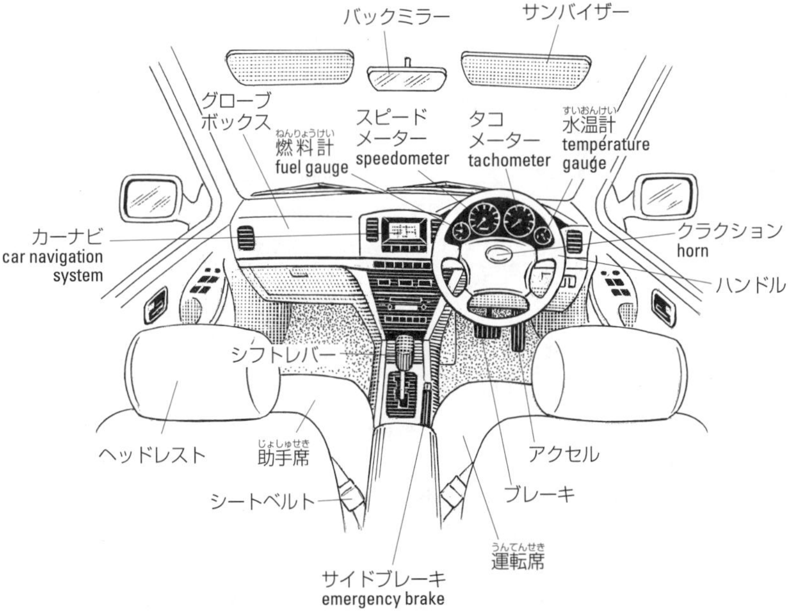

バックミラー
サンバイザー
グローブボックス
燃料計(ねんりょうけい) fuel gauge
スピードメーター speedometer
タコメーター tachometer
水温計(すいおんけい) temperature gauge
カーナビ car navigation system
クラクション horn
ハンドル
シフトレバー
ヘッドレスト
助手席(じょしゅせき)
アクセル
ブレーキ
シートベルト
運転席(うんてんせき)
サイドブレーキ emergency brake

C

It's quicker to go by car.
車で行くほうが速い。

Can you drive a car?
運転できますか？

When I got out of the car it started to rain.
車から降りたら雨が降り出した。

"Which car are you in?"
"I'm in car No. 8, for nonsmokers."
「何号車にお乗りですか？」
「禁煙車の8号車です」

♦ **car bomb** *n.* 自動車爆弾

car exhaust *n.* (車の)排気ガス

car navigation system *n.* カーナビ

car wash *n.* (place) 洗車場

rent-a-car, rental car *n.* レンタカー

carafe *n.* (for serving wine) カラフェ

caramel *n.* (candy) キャラメル, (burnt sugar) カラメル

carat *n.* カラット [→ KARAT]

caravan *n.* (group of people on a journey) キャラバン, (of camels) 隊商

carbohydrate *n.* 炭水化物

carbon *n.* (element) 炭素; (carbon paper) カーボン紙

carbonated *adj.* 炭酸入りの

carbonated drinks 炭酸飲料

carbon dioxide *n.* 二酸化炭素, 炭酸ガス

carbon monoxide *n.* 一酸化炭素

carcass *n.* (of animal) 死骸

carcinogen *n.* 発がん物質

card *n.* (playing card) カード, (**cards:** game) トランプ, (business card) 名刺, (greeting card) カード, -状

v. (ask to be shown ID) (…に) 身分証明書の提示を求める

a deck of cards トランプ一組

Let's play cards. トランプをしましょう。

deal [shuffle] the cards
トランプを配る [切る]

a birthday card バースデーカード

a New Year's card 年賀状

Does one get carded at liquor stores in Japan?
日本では酒屋で身分証明書を見せなくてはいけませんか？

cardboard *n.* ボール紙, 段ボール

a cardboard box 段ボール(箱)

cardiac *adj.* 心臓の

a cardiac arrest 心(臓)停止

cardigan *n.* カーディガン

cardinal *adj.* (of utmost importance) きわめて重要な

n. (cardinal number) 基数; (religious official) 枢機卿

a cardinal sin 重罪

care

1 *v.* MIND: 気にする, 気にかける, かまう, (**not care**) 気にしない, 何でもかまわない

2 *n.* SUPERVISION: 世話, (for the elderly) 介護

3 *n.* CAUTION: 注意, 用心

4 *n.* CONCERN: 心配事

5 *n.* UPKEEP: 手入れ, ケア

6 *v.* LIKE: (**care for**) (…が) 好きだ, (**would you care for…?**) …はいかがですか

1 I don't care what she says about me.
彼女が私のことを何て言っているかなんて、気にしません。

Don't you care about the environment?

環境のことは気にかけないの？

"What shall we do tonight?"
"I don't really care."
「今晩は何をしよう？」
「何でもかまわないよ」

2 These children need special care.
この子供たちには、特別な世話が必要だ。

care for the elderly
お年寄りの世話 [老人介護]

3 Do it with care.
注意してやってください。

4 I didn't have a care in the world back then.
あのころは、何の心配事もなかった。

5 skin care 肌の手入れ

hair care ヘアケア

6 I care for her, but she doesn't seem to care for me.
彼女のことが好きだけど、彼女は僕に気がないみたいだ。

Would you care for something to drink?
お飲み物はいかがですか？

care of (as abbr. "c/o" in address) …気付, (to sb's house) …方

could/couldn't care less 全く気にかけない

He couldn't care less whether he lost his job or not.
彼は職を失うかどうかなど、全く気にかけていない。

for all I care 平気だ, ちっともかまわない

They can badmouth me as much as they like for all I care.
あの人たちがどんなに悪口を言おうと、私は平気ですよ。

in the care of (in the hands of) …の手に

Her mother died when she was young, and she was left in the care of her aunt.
彼女は若くして母親を亡くして、おばの手に預けられた。

take care 気をつける, (good-bye) じゃあね

take care of (person) …の世話をする, …の面倒をみる, みておく, (patient) …の看病をする, (invalid) 介護する, (place) みておく

Take care of yourself.
(お体を)お大事に。

Our next-door neighbor is going to take care of the children while we're out.
留守の間、お隣が子供の面倒をみてくれるんです。

Would you take care of the office while I attend to this matter?
この件に取りかかっている間、オフィスをみておいてくれる？

take care that (you don't…) (…しない)よう気をつける

Take care that you don't hurt yourself.
けがをしないよう気をつけて。

career *n.* (lifelong job) 職業, 一生の仕事, (professional background) 経歴, キャリア

adj. 職業の, 専門の

find a career in Japan
日本で職を見つける

a career in medicine
医師としてのキャリア

Her career prospects are promising.
彼女の仕事の将来は明るい。

a career teacher 教員

forward one's career 早く出世する

C

He only thinks of forwarding his career.
彼は、早く出世することしか頭にない。

make a career of 一生の仕事にする, …で身を立てる

He's made a career of catering.
彼は仕出し屋で身を立てた。

carefree *adj.* のんびりとした, のんきな, 気楽な

live a carefree life 気楽な生活を送る

careful *adj.* (attentive) 注意深い, 慎重な, (cautious) 気をつける; (thorough, painstaking) 綿密な

a careful driver
注意深いドライバー [慎重に運転する人]

a careful worker 仕事の入念な人

Careful you don't slip.
滑らないよう気をつけて。

I was careful not to say anything out of place.
場違いなことを口にしないよう気をつけた。

a careful study of
…についての綿密な調査

carefully *adv.* 注意深く, 慎重に, じっくり

Set it down carefully.
注意して置いてください。

I read the letter very carefully.
手紙をとても注意深く読みました。

careless *adj.* (inattentive) 不注意な, (of mistake) うかつな, うっかりした, (rash, hasty) 軽率な, (heedless, unmindful) むとんちゃくな, (shoddy) いいかげんな

careless driving 不注意な運転

It was a careless mistake.
ケアレス [うっかり] ミスでした。

Don't be careless! ぼやぼやするな！

It was careless of me to tell him about that.
彼にそのことについて話したのは軽率だった。

He's careless about his appearance.
あの人は自分の外見にむとんちゃくだ。

do a careless job (on)
(…で) いいかげんな仕事をする

♦**carelessly** *adv.* (without paying due attention) 不注意に, (absentmindedly) うっかり(して), (rashly) 軽率に

carelessness *n.* (inattentiveness) 不注意

caretaker *n.* (janitor) 管理人

cargo *n.* 貨物, 積み荷

caribou *n.* カリブー

caricature *n.* (drawing) 風刺(漫)画, カリカチュア

caring *adj.* 愛情深い, 思いやりのある

She's a very caring person.
彼女はとても思いやりのある人です。

carnation *n.* カーネーション [NOTE: Japanese children give their mothers a red carnation on Mother's Day.]

carnival *n.* カーニバル

carnivore *n.* 肉食動物

♦**carnivorous** *adj.* 肉食(性)の

carol *n.* (Christmas carol) キャロル

carp *n.* (fish) コイ, 鯉

carpenter *n.* 大工(さん)

carpentry *n.* 大工仕事

carpet *n.* じゅうたん, カーペット

lay/put down a carpet
じゅうたんを敷く

carport *n.* カーポート

carriage *n.* (horse-drawn) 馬車, (for baby) ベビーカー, 乳母車, (segment of train) 車両, -号車

carrier *n.* (transport company) 運送会社; (harborer of disease) 保菌者, キャリア [→ AIRCRAFT CARRIER]

carrot *n.* ニンジン, 人参

---

carry *v.*

1 MOVE WHILE SUPPORTING: (in hands or on person) 持つ, ((*formal*)) 携帯する, 携行する, (in arms) 抱く, かかえる, (on shoulders) 担ぐ, (on back) 負う, 背負う, (baby on back) おんぶする, おぶう

2 TAKE/BRING: (take) 持って行く, (bring) 持って来る, (transport) 運ぶ

3 SUPPORT: (cargo, passengers) 乗せる, (weight) 支える, (responsibility, burden) 負う, 担う

4 INVOLVE/ENTAIL: 伴う

5 CONNOTE: (**carry meaning**) 意味をもつ, (**carry nuance**) ニュアンスがある

6 EXTEND: (idea) 推し進める

7 PUBLISH: (story/photo in newspaper etc.) 載せる, 掲載する

8 OF VOTE: (**be carried**) 可決される, 通過する

9 OF SOUND: 伝わる, 通る, 届く

1 Can I carry your suitcase for you?
スーツケースをお持ちしましょうか?

You're not allowed to carry drinks in the theater.
劇場では飲み物の持ち込みはできません。

At these festivals, the men carry shrines through the streets on their shoulders.
こうしたお祭りでは、男たちはおみこしを肩に担いで通りを練り歩きます。

She was carrying one baby on her back, another in her arms, and shopping bags.
彼女は赤ん坊を背中に一人おんぶし、前に一人抱っこした上、買い物袋をぶら下げていました。

2 Would you carry this package to the post office for me?
この小包を郵便局へ持って行ってくれませんか?

Next time, carry along a camera.
今度は、カメラを持って来て。

The seeds were carried by the wind.
種は風に運ばれた。

The current carried me downstream.
私は川下へと流された。

Flies carry germs.
ハエは病原菌を媒介する。

3 I don't know how the car will carry that many people.
あんなに大勢の人を、どうやって車に乗せて行くんだろう。

The bus can carry fifty-odd people.
バスには50人ちょっと乗れます。

I'm not sure these old timbers can carry the weight.
この古い木材が、その重さを支えきれるかなあ。

The burden of carrying so much responsibility has turned his hair gray.
重責を担う心労で、彼の髪は白くなった。

4 This investment carries a lot of risk.
この投資は多大なリスクを伴う。

Espionage carries the death penalty in

C

some countries.
国によっては、スパイ行為は死刑になる。

5 These ideas carry a good deal of significance even today.
こうした考え方は今日でも大きな意味をもっています。

That word carries a bad nuance.
その言葉には悪いニュアンスがある。

6 Let's carry this idea one step further.
この考えを、もう一歩推し進めてみましょう。

7 The paper carried an article about the prime minister's daughter.
新聞には総理の娘に関する記事が載っていた。

8 The motion was carried by a large majority.
動議は大差で可決されました。

9 Sound really carries in this room.
この部屋は、音がよく通るね。

carry around *v.* 持ち歩く

You carried that around with you the entire trip?
旅行中ずっとそれを持ち歩いていたの？

carry away *v.* (**get carried away**) (=forget oneself) 我を忘れる, (=become absorbed in) 夢中になる, (=become overly enthusiastic/excited) 興奮する

Don't get carried away and buy everything.
我を忘れて全部買ったりしないでよ。

I usually stay up all night when I get carried away with something.
何かに夢中になったときはよく徹夜する。

He got completely carried away and made an utter fool of himself.
彼はすっかり興奮して醜態をさらした。

carry off *v.* (haul off) 連れ去る, (by police) 連行する; (do successfully) うまくやってのける [→ WIN]

The man was carried off to prison.
男は刑務所に連行された。

I can't believe you carried it off.
君がうまくやってのけたなんて、信じられないよ。

carry on *v.* (continue) 続ける, (**carry on doing**) ...し続ける; (behave) ふるまう

Don't let me stop you. Please carry on with your work.
私のことはおかまいなく。どうぞお仕事を続けてください。

"Shall I stop?" "No, carry on."
「やめましょうか？」「いいえ、続けて」

He just carried on reading.
彼はただ読み続けた。

The way he carries on you'd think he owns the place.
あの男のふるまいときたら、まるで主人気取りだよ。

carry out *v.* (a plan) 実施する, 実行する

I don't think he will carry out his threat.
彼が脅しを実行に移すとは思わない。

carry-on luggage *n.* (機内持ち込み) 手荷物

cart *n.* (shopping cart) (ショッピング) カート, (for baggage) 荷車
v. (transport) 運ぶ

a golf cart ゴルフカート

cartel *n.* カルテル, 企業連合

cartilage *n.* 軟骨

carton *n.* (of milk, eggs) パック, (of cigarettes) カートン

cartoon ***n.*** (comic) 漫画, (anime) アニメ, 漫画映画

a political cartoon 風刺漫画

♦**cartoonist** ***n.*** 漫画家

cartridge ***n.*** (of film, ink) カートリッジ, (of ammunition) 弾薬筒

carve ***v.*** (slice) スライスする, 切り分ける, (sculpt) 彫刻する, 刻む, (engrave, cut out) 彫る

I carved my name in the tree.
木に名前を彫った。

carving ***n.*** (sculpture) 彫刻, 彫り物

carving knife ***n.*** (肉の) 切り分けナイフ, カービングナイフ

cascade ***n.*** (small waterfall) 小さな滝

case[1] ***n.***

1 **INSTANCE:** 場合, ケース, 例, (of illness) 症状

2 **COURT CASE:** 訴訟

3 **ARGUMENT:** (assertion) 主張, (reason) 論拠

4 **CRIME/ACCIDENT:** 事件

5 **PATIENT:** 患者

1 In this case, I'll make an exception.
この場合は例外としましょう。

It's a bit different in our case.
私たちの場合はちょっと違う。

This case is very unusual.
こういうケースは大変珍しい。

a case in point ぴったりの例

In nine cases out of ten, it survives.
十中八九、生き延びます。

It was just a case of the jitters, that's all.
ちょっと神経が参っただけで、何でもないよ。

a case of measles はしかの症状

2 a civil [criminal] case 民事 [刑事] 訴訟

Case dismissed. 却下します。

3 There's a strong case for eliminating capital punishment.
死刑の廃止を支持する説得力のある論拠があります。

4 a case of blackmail 恐喝事件

a case still under investigation
まだ捜査中の事件

5 a mental case 精神病患者

as is often the case よくあることだが

As is often the case, we realized our mistake too late.
よくあることだが、間違いに気づくのが遅すぎた。

as the case may be 場合によっては

case by case 1件ずつ, 個別に, ケースバイケースで

We consider our applicants case by case.
我々は応募者を個別に検討します。

in any case とにかく, いずれにしても

In any case, I will call you tomorrow.
いずれにしても、明日電話します。

in case ...ときのために

I brought a map in case we get lost.
迷ったときのために地図を持って来たよ。

You should be there in case we need you.
君の手が必要になったときのために、そこにいるほうがいい。

in case of ...の場合(に)は, ...に備えて

In case of a fire, use the stairs.
火災の場合は、階段をお使いください。

in either case どちらにしても, ((*infor-*

mal)) どっちにしても, どっちみち

In either case, we win.
どっちにしても、僕らの勝ちだ。

just in case 念のため(に), 万が一…場合のために

I took an umbrella just in case.
念のために傘を持って行った。

Just in case you need to call me, here's my number.
万が一電話が必要になった場合のために、これが私の番号です。

make a case for (正しいと)主張する

Can one really make a case for preemptive war?
本当に、先制攻撃の戦争を正しいと言えますか？

case[2] *n.* (container for storage/display) ケース, (box) 箱, (of 12 beverages) 一ケース

a glass case ガラスケース

a camcorder case ビデオカメラのケース

a pencil case 筆箱

Could you pick up a case of beer on your way home?
帰りにビールを一ケース買って来てくれない？

cash *n.* (money) お金, 現金, キャッシュ
v. (convert to bills) 現金にする, 換金する

Do you have any cash on you?
(手持ちの)お金はある？

We have to pay in cash, I'm told.
支払いは現金だけだって。

Do you know where I can cash some traveler's checks?
トラベラーズチェックをどこで換金できるかご存じですか？

♦ **cash in on** *v.* (make a profit from) 利用してもうける, (exploit) …につけ込む

cash machine *n.* ＡＴＭ, 現金自動預け払い機

cash register *n.* レジ

cashier *n.* (at supermarket) レジ係, (at bank) 出納係

cashmere *n.* カシミヤ

casino *n.* カジノ

cask *n.* たる

a cask of sake 酒だる

casket *n.* (coffin) ひつぎ, お棺; (small box) 小箱

casserole *n.* (dish) キャセロール, (food) なべ焼き料理

cassette *n.* (audio) カセット(テープ)

cast

1 *v.* THROW: (shadow) 落とす, (doubt) 投げかける, もつ, (eye, look) 向ける, (stone, dice) 投げる, (fishing line) 投げ入れる

2 *v.* IN ROLE: (cast A as B) (AにBの役を)振り当てる

3 *v.* IN MOLD: 鋳造する

4 *v.* SUBMIT: (vote) 投じる

5 *n.* GROUP OF ACTORS: 配役, キャスト, 出演者

6 *n.* COVERING FOR BROKEN ARM/LEG: ギブス

1 The building cast a long shadow across the street.
ビルが路上に長い影を落としていた。

She cast a glance my way.
彼女は私の方をちらっと見た。

2 He was cast as the villain.
彼は悪役を振り当てられた。

3 a human figure cast in gold
金で鋳造された人間の像

4 cast a vote/ballot 1票を投じる

5 The cast came on stage.
出演者が舞台に現れた。

6 be in a cast ギブスをする
remove a cast ギブスを取る

castanet *n.* カスタネット

castigate *v.* (harshly criticize) 厳しく非難する

cast iron *n.* 鋳鉄
adj. (**cast-iron**) 鋳鉄の

castle *n.* (お)城, (in proper names) -城
Osaka Castle 大阪城
a castle town 城下町

casual *adj.*

1 INFORMAL: (of dress) カジュアルな, (of person, attitude) 気楽な, のんきな

2 UNPLANNED: (of remark: offhand) 何気ない, (occurring by chance) 偶然の

3 NOT REGULAR/INTIMATE: (of acquaintance) ちょっとした, (of relationship) 軽い

4 OF WORK: (temporary) 臨時の

1 casual wear カジュアルウェア
Casual dress is OK, they said.
普段着でいいと言っていた。
He spoke in a casual manner.
彼は気楽な話し方をした。

2 Even a casual remark can hurt someone.
何気ない言葉が、人を傷つけることもあります。
a casual encounter 偶然の出会い

3 Oh, he's just a casual acquaintance.
ああ、あの人はただのちょっとした知り合いよ。
a casual relationship 軽い関係
casual sex 行きずりのセックス

4 casual labor 臨時雇い

♦ **casually** *adv.* (of manner, remark) 何気なく; (of dress) 普段着で, カジュアルに

casualty *n.* (of accident) 死傷者, 負傷者, (of war) 戦死者 [→ VICTIM]

cat *n.* 猫
a stray cat のら猫

♦ **cat litter** *n.* 猫砂

catalog(ue) *n.* (of products) カタログ, (in library) 目録, (of companies, university courses) 要覧

catalyst *n.* (substance) 触媒, (person/thing) 触発する人/物

catapult *n.* カタパルト

cataract *n.* (of eyes) 白内障

catarrh *n.* カタル

catastrophe *n.* 大惨事, (natural disaster) 大災害, (fiasco) 大失敗

catastrophic *adj.* (tragic) 悲劇的な, (disastrous) 壊滅的な

catch

1 *v.* CAPTURE: 捕まえる, 捕らえる, (fish) 捕る, (=with a fishing line) 釣る; (**catch sb's attention**) (…の) 注意を引く

2 *v.* TAKE INTO HANDS: (ball) 取る, キャッチする, (grab, take hold of) つかむ

3 *v.* HEAR: 聞き取る

4 *v.* SEE: (**catch sb doing**) (…が) …しているところを見る, (**catch a glimpse of**) ちらっと見る, (**catch sight of**) 見つける

5 *v.* BUS/TRAIN: (get on) (…に) 乗る, (be

C

on time for) (…に) 間に合う

6 *v.* **CATCH UP WITH:** (…に) 追い付く, (to be able to speak to) (…に) 接触する, (…を) 捕まえる

7 *v.* **ILLNESS:** (cold) ひく, (fever, disease) (…に) かかる

8 *v.* **GET STUCK/HOOKED (ON):** (…に) 引っ掛かる

9 *v.* **CAUSE TO BE SHUT/PINCHED IN:** (hand/finger in drawer/machine) 挟む

10 *n.* **HIDDEN DRAWBACK:** 落とし穴, 引っ掛け

11 *n.* **THING CAUGHT:** (animal, prize) 獲物, (quantity of fish) 捕獲量

12 *n.* **CATCHING OF A BALL:** 捕球

13 *n.* **GAME:** キャッチボール

14 *n.* **LOCK:** 留め金, 掛け金

1 The cat caught a mouse.
猫がネズミを捕まえた。

The police didn't catch the burglar immediately.
警察は、すぐには強盗を捕まえなかった。

Did you catch any fish?
何か(魚は)釣れましたか？

2 The goalkeeper jumped up and caught the ball.
ゴールキーパーは飛び上がってボールを取った。

3 "Did you catch what he just said?" "I didn't catch every word."
「彼が今言ったこと、聞き取れた？」「全部は聞き取れなかった」

I'm sorry I didn't catch that.
すみません、聞こえませんでした。

4 I caught her shoplifting.
彼女が万引きしているところを見た。

I expect we will catch him dozing in his chair.
きっと彼は椅子で居眠りしているでしょう。

5 What time do we catch the train tomorrow?
明日は何時の電車に乗るの？

From there I caught a bus to Chicago.
そこからシカゴ行きのバスに乗った。

Did you manage to catch your plane?
飛行機に間に合った？

6 If you hurry you may catch him before he leaves.
急げば、彼がたつ前に追い付くかもしれないよ。

You can usually catch him at his office.
彼は、たいていオフィスにいるよ。

Have I caught you at a bad time?
悪い時にお電話しました？

7 Careful you don't catch a cold.
かぜをひかないよう気をつけて。

I'd hate to catch hepatitis.
肝炎にかかるのはいやだ。

8 My sweater caught on my watch as I was taking it off.
セーターを脱いだ時、腕時計に引っ掛かった。

9 Apparently he caught his hand in a snowblower and lost three fingers.
どうやら、彼は除雪機に手を挟んで指を3本なくしたらしい。

10 Is there a catch?
裏[引っ掛け]があるの？

There's a catch in this contract somewhere.
この契約には、どこかに落とし穴がある。

11 They came back with a big catch of fish.

彼らは魚をたくさん捕って帰って来た。

12 Did you see that catch? What brilliant fielding!
あの捕球を見た？ みごとな守備だね！

13 Let's play catch.
キャッチボールをしよう。

14 Did you put the catch down?
掛け金をかけましたか？

be caught by surprise びっくりする

be caught off guard 不意打ちを食らう

catch fire 火がつく, 燃え出す

catch on *v.* (understand) 理解する; (become popular) はやる, 流行する

She's a bit slow to catch on.
彼女は少し理解が遅い。

This new dance is catching on like wildfire.
この新しいダンスは爆発的にはやっている。

catch up (with) *v.* (draw level with) (…に) 追い付く

We had to run to catch up with them.
彼らに追い付くには走らないといけませんでした。

You'll have to work hard if you want to catch up with the rest of the class.
クラスのみんなに追い付きたいのなら、一生懸命勉強しないとね。

catch up on *v.* (sleep) (睡眠不足を) 取り戻す, (gossip, fashion) (…に) 遅れないようついて行く

---

catchphrase *n.* キャッチフレーズ

catchy *adj.* (easy to remember) 覚えやすい

categorical *adj.* (unequivocal) 断定的な, 明確な

categorize *v.* 分類する

category *n.* カテゴリー, 範ちゅう, 種類

cater *v.* (prepare food) 食事を賄う, 仕出しをする; (**cater to**) (=to the needs of) (…の必要に) 応じる, (=to the demands/whims of) (…の要求/気まぐれを) 満たす, (=to the tastes of) (…の趣味を) 満足させる

They said they don't cater to our age group.
我々の年齢層向けのものではないと言われました。

This type of magazine caters to the worst possible taste.
この手の雑誌は、最も低俗な趣味を満足させるものだ。

♦**caterer** *n.* 仕出し屋(さん)

catering *n.* (providing of food) 仕出し, (business) 仕出し業

Have you arranged for a company to do the catering?
仕出し業者の手配は済んでいますか？

caterpillar *n.* 毛虫

catfish *n.* ナマズ

cathedral *n.* 大聖堂

Catholic *adj.* カトリック(教)の
n. カトリック教徒

catnap *n., v.* うたた寝(する)

cattle *n.* 牛

catty *adj.* (spiteful) 意地の悪い

Caucasian *n., adj.* 白人(の)

cauliflower *n.* カリフラワー

causative *adj.* (of verb) 使役形の

♦**causative form** *n.* (verb form) 使役形

causative-passive form *n.* (verb form)

使役受身形

cause

1 *v.* BRING ABOUT: 引き起こす, (…の) 原因となる, 元になる

2 *n.* THING THAT PRODUCES AN EFFECT: 原因, たね

3 *n.* PRINCIPLE: 主義, 主張

1 Who caused this disturbance?
この騒ぎを引き起こしたのは誰ですか？

Smoking causes cancer.
喫煙はがんの元です。

It caused me a lot of trouble.
そのせいでずいぶん迷惑をこうむった。

2 cause and effect 原因と結果 [因果]

a cause of death 死因

The cause of the explosion was a gas leak.
爆発の原因はガス漏れだった。

I have no cause to complain.
不満のたねはありません。

His wild behavior is giving his parents cause for concern.
彼の乱暴な行動が、ご両親の心配のたねになっている。

3 Does he support the cause?
彼はその主張を支持しているんですか？

caution *n.* (carefulness) 用心, (warning) 警告

v. 警告する

cautious *adj.* 用心深い, 注意深い, 慎重な

He's a very cautious person.
とても用心深い人です。

cave *n.* 洞窟, 洞穴

v. (**cave in**) 崩れる, 陥没する

caveman *n.* (cave dweller) 原始人, (brutal man) 荒っぽい人

caviar *n.* キャビア

cavity *n.* (in tooth) 虫歯

CD *n.* (compact disc) ＣＤ

CD player *n.* ＣＤプレーヤー

CD-ROM *n.* ＣＤ－ＲＯＭ

cease *v.* (come to an end) やむ, 終わる, (put an end to) やめる

ceasefire *n.* 停戦, 休戦

ceaseless *adj.* 絶え間のない

cedar *n.* (tree) スギ, 杉

ceiling *n.* (to room) 天井; (upper limit) 上限

hit the ceiling/roof 頭にくる, かっとなる

celebrate *v.* 祝う, (…の) お祝いをする

Where are we going to celebrate Christmas this year?
今年はどこでクリスマスを祝おう？

Aren't you going to have a house party to celebrate your move?
引っ越しを祝って新居でパーティーを開かないの？

celebrated *adj.* (famous) 有名な, (well-known) よく知られた

celebration *n.* お祝い, ((*formal*)) 祝賀, (party, event) 祝賀会, 祝典

celebrity *n.* 有名人, 芸能人

celery *n.* セロリ

celibacy *n.* 禁欲

practice celibacy 禁欲する

cell *n.* (prison cell) 独房, (part of the body) 細胞, (small group belonging to a larger organization/network) 小集団

a terrorist cell テロリストの小集団

cellar *n.* (basement) 地下室, (basement

storage room) 地下貯蔵室

cello *n.* チェロ

cellophane *n.* セロハン

cellular *adj.* (of cells) 細胞の

cellular phone *n.* 携帯(電話)

cellulose *n.* セルロース

Celsius *adj.* セ氏の [NOTE: Usually pronounced せっし], C

twenty degrees Celsius セ氏20度

cement *n.* (powder) セメント, (concrete) コンクリート

cemetery *n.* 墓地

censor *n.* 検閲官

v. 検閲する

censorship *n.* 検閲

census *n.* 国勢調査

cent *n.* セント, ¢

centennial *n.* 100周年記念, 100年祭

adj. 100年目の, 100年祭の

a centennial anniversary 100周年記念

center

1 *n.* MIDDLE: 真ん中, 中央, 中心

2 *n.* PLACE: (building where an activity takes place or services are offered) -センター, (central district) 中心地

3 *n.* FOCUS: 的, 中心

4 *v.* PUT IN CENTER: (…の) 真ん中/中心に置く

1 in the center of the circle 円の真ん中に

The table was in the center of the room.
テーブルは部屋の中央にあった。

This chocolate has a nut at the center.
このチョコレートは真ん中にナッツが入っている。

Organized crime was at the center of the scandal.
スキャンダルの中心に組織犯罪があった。

2 a shopping center ショッピングセンター

London is the financial center of Europe.
ロンドンはヨーロッパの金融の中心地だ。

3 She always likes to be the center of attention.
彼女はいつも注目の的になっていたいんです。

4 Could you center the vase?
花びんを真ん中に置いてくれますか？

♦**center of gravity** *n.* 重心

centigrade *adj.* セ氏の, C

centimeter *n.* センチ(メートル)

centipede *n.* ムカデ

central *adj.* 中央の, 中心の, 真ん中の, (important) 重要な, 中心的な, 大切な

the central government 中央政府

a central figure of the novel [play, story]
小説 [劇, 話] の中心人物

The central issue is that of public trust.
重要な課題は国民の信頼である。

Central to the argument were recent archaeological finds.
論議の中心は、最近発見された出土品だった。

♦**central heating** *n.* セントラルヒーティング, 集中暖房(装置)

central nervous system *n.* 中枢神経系

Central America *n.* 中央アメリカ, 中米

centralize *v.* (bring together under a central authority) 中央に集める, 中央に集中させる

century *n.* 世紀

the beginning of the nineteenth century
１９世紀の初め [初頭]

the end of the twentieth century
２０世紀の終わり[末]

ceramic *adj.* 陶磁器の, 陶製の
n. **(ceramics)** (=works) 陶磁器, (=art) 陶芸

cereal *n.* (wheat, oats etc.) 穀類, 穀物, (breakfast food) シリアル

cerebral *adj.* 脳の

♦ **cerebral palsy** *n.* 脳性小児麻痺

ceremony *n.* (ritual) 儀式, 式典, -式; (formal behavior) 儀礼

hold a wedding ceremony
結婚式を挙げる

We watched the opening ceremony on TV.
テレビで開会式を見ました。

The French president was welcomed with great ceremony.
フランスの大統領は盛大に迎えられた。

stand on ceremony 儀式ばる, 形式ばる

There's no need to stand on ceremony on this occasion.
今回は、形式ばる必要はありません。

without ceremony 形式ばらずに

certain *adj.*

1 PARTICULAR: ある, 例の
2 SURE: 確かな, 確実な, 間違いない
3 INEVITABLE: 避けられない, 必ず起こる

1 a certain amount [degree] of…
ある量[程度]の…

On a certain day in June…
６月のある日…

a certain amount of tolerance
いくらかの寛容

There's a certain story he tells at every dinner party.
夕食会のたびに、彼が決まってする話があるんです。

I cannot reveal my sources, but I heard it from a certain person.
情報源は明かせませんが、ある人から聞きました。

2 a certain fact 確かな事実

"How certain are you?"
"I am 99 percent certain."
「どれくらい確実ですか？」
「９９パーセント確実です」

Are you certain about the time?
時間については間違いないんでしょうね？

I'm certain she said she was coming.
彼女は来ると、確かに言っていた。

3 spell certain doom (for…)
必ず(…の)破滅の元となる

be almost certain to do/be きっと…する

The night sky is clear, so it's almost certain to be a fine day tomorrow.
夜空が晴れているから、明日はきっといい天気になりますよ。

If they're playing mahjong, he's almost certain to be there.
彼らが麻雀をしているのなら、彼はきっとそこにいるだろう。

for certain 確かに, 確実に

There is no way to know for certain.
確実に知る方法はない。

make certain 確かめる, 確認する

Would you make certain that the car's locked?
車がロックされていることを確かめてくれますか？

certainly *adv.* (by all means) もちろん; (surely) 確かに, (without fail) 必ず

"Would you care to join me?"
"Certainly."
「いっしょに行く?」
「もちろん」

"Would you say it was difficult?"
"Yes, certainly."
「難しかったと思います?」
「ええ、それはもう」

"Can I stop now?"
"Certainly not. You're nowhere near finished."
「もうやめてもいい?」
「とんでもない。まだ全然終わってないじゃない」

"Are you sure he heard you?"
"Well, I certainly said it loud enough."
「あなたの言ったこと、本当に彼に聞こえていたの?」
「まあ、十分聞こえる大きさで言ったよ」

Certainly it was a good experience.
確かにいい経験でした。

She will certainly be famous one day.
彼女はいつか必ず有名になりますよ。

certainty *n.* 必然性, 確実性, (thing that is sure to happen) 間違いないこと

certificate *n.* (document of proof) 証明書, (of completion) 修了証書

a birth [wedding] certificate
出生 [結婚] 証明書

♦ **certificate of alien registration** *n.* (government-issued ID required for all foreigners living in Japan) 外国人登録証明書

certify *v.* 証明する

cervix *n.* 子宮頸部

cesarean section *n.* 帝王切開

cesspool *n.* 汚水だめ, 汚水槽

CFC *n.* フロンガス

chain

1 *n.* METAL CORD: 鎖, (on bike, toilet, machine) チェーン

2 *n.* SEQUENCE: 連続, 連鎖

3 *n.* BUSINESS: チェーン

4 *v.* FASTEN BY MEANS OF A CHAIN: (chain A to B) (AをBに) 鎖でつなぐ

5 *v.* USED FIGURATIVELY: (**be chained to**) …に縛られる

1 Where's the dog's chain?
犬の鎖はどこ?

She wore a gold chain around her neck.
彼女は金の鎖のネックレスをしていた。

The chain is broken.
チェーンが切れている。

2 a chain of events 一連の出来事
a chain of islands 列島
the chain of command 指揮系統
the food chain 食物連鎖

3 Is this restaurant part of a chain?
このレストランはチェーン店ですか?

4 Better chain up the dog.
犬を鎖でつないだほうがいい。

5 I don't want to be chained to this job.
この仕事に縛られたくない。

♦ **chain reaction** *n.* 連鎖反応
chain store *n.* チェーン店, チェーンストア

chair

1 *n.* PIECE OF FURNITURE: 椅子, (without legs and on a tatami floor) 座椅子

2 *n.* POSITION: (chair of an academic department) 学部長 [→ CHAIRMAN]

3 *v.* BE IN CHARGE OF: (conference) (…の) 議長を務める, 司会をする, (committee) (…の) 委員長を務める

1 There don't seem to be enough chairs for everyone.
全員分の椅子はないようです。

These chairs aren't very comfortable.
この椅子はあまり座り心地がよくない。

Just pull up a chair and sit down, will you.
とにかく、おかけください。

2 Who is chair of this department?
ここの学部長は誰ですか？

3 Who will chair the conference?
会議の議長を務めるのは誰ですか？

chairlift *n.* (at ski slope) リフト

chairman, -person, -woman *n.* (of meeting) 議長, 司会者, (of committee) 委員長, (of company) 社長, (of organization) 会長

chalk *n.* チョーク, 白墨

chalkboard *n.* 黒板

challenge *n.* チャレンジ, 挑戦, (difficulty) 難題, 課題

v. (question the truth/validity of) 問題にする, (challenge A to B) (AにBを) 挑む, 挑戦する, 申し込む

He'd accept any challenge.
彼はどんな挑戦でも受けて立つでしょう。

We face a challenge.
我々は難題に直面している。

The idea has never been seriously challenged.
その考えは今までに一度も、まともに問題にされたことがない。

We were challenged to a game of croquet.
クロッケーの試合を申し込まれた。

♦**challenger** *n.* 挑戦者

challenging *adj.* (difficult) 難しい, (of job) やりがいのある

chamber *n.* (conference hall) 会館, 会議所, (room) -室

a decompression chamber 減圧室

♦**Chamber of Commerce** *n.* 商工会議所

chamber music *n.* 室内楽

chameleon *n.* (reptile) カメレオン

chamois *n.* シャモア

champ → CHAMPION

champagne *n.* シャンパン

champion *n.* 優勝者, チャンピオン, 覇者

championship *n.* (title) 選手権, (tournament) 選手権大会, (finals) 決勝戦

chance

1 *n.* OPPORTUNITY: 機会, きっかけ, チャンス

2 *n.* POSSIBILITY: 可能性, 見込み

3 *n.* LUCK: 運

4 *v.* RISK: (…に) 賭ける

1 an ideal chance 絶好の機会

the chance of a lifetime
一生に一度の [またとない] チャンス

blow [jump at] a chance
チャンスを逃す [に飛びつく]

All I want is a second chance.
もう一度チャンスが欲しいだけです。

You should see the museum, too, if you have the chance.
機会があったら、美術館も行くといいよ。

You have to take your chances in life.
人生には、勝負を賭けるべき時があるものだ。

2 Is there a chance that you threw the file away?

そのファイルを捨てたという可能性はありますか？

Do I have a chance?
私に見込みはありますか？

The chances are slim.
見込みはわずかです。

3 Let's just leave it to chance.
運に任せよう。

4 Are you going to chance it or not?
それに賭けてみますか/一か八かやってみますか？

by any chance ひょっとして

He wasn't by any chance a tall man, was he?
ひょっとして、その人は背の高い人じゃありませんでした？

Do you have the book with you by any chance ?
ひょっとして今、その本を持ってる？

by chance 偶然, たまたま

By chance, the person who sat next to me went to the same university as me.
偶然にも、隣に座ったのは同じ大学に行っていた人だった。

I took a different road than I usually do and, by chance, found a wonderful café.
いつもと違う道を通ったら、たまたますてきな喫茶店を見つけた。

not stand a chance of doing …する見込みがない

He doesn't stand a chance of winning.
彼には勝つ見込みがない。

on the chance that… もしかすると…かもしれないと思って

I went on the chance that I might meet her.
もしかすると彼女に会えるかもしれないと思って行った。

chancellor ***n.*** (prime minister) 首相, (of U.S. university) 学長, (of U.K. university) 名誉総長

chancy ***adj.*** (risky) 危なっかしい, (uncertain) 不確かな

chandelier ***n.*** シャンデリア

change

1 ***n.*** ALTERATION: 変化, 移り変わり, (of plans) 変更, (of places, turns) 交代, 交替

2 ***v.*** REPLACE/EXCHANGE: (replace) 変える, (取り)替える, (exchange) 交換する, (places, turns) 交代する, 交替する

3 ***v.*** MAKE/BECOME DIFFERENT: 変える/変わる, 変化する, (**change jobs**) 転職する

4 ***v.*** PUT ON DIFFERENT CLOTHES: 着替える

5 ***n.*** MONEY: (owed/returned as result of a transaction) おつり, (coins) 小銭, 細かいお金

6 ***v.*** BUSES/TRAINS: 乗り換える

7 ***v.*** MONEY: (for foreign currency or smaller bills) 両替する, (bill for coins) くずす

1 a change in the weather 天候の変化

a change of heart 心変わり

a change for the better 好転

There had been so many changes, I could scarcely recognize the place.
すっかり変わってしまっていて、どこなのか、わからないくらいだった。

We need to make changes in the way we work.
仕事の仕方に変更を加える必要がある。

a change of government/regime
政権交代

2 change the sheets シーツを替える

Time to change the baby's diaper.
赤ちゃんのおしめを取り替える時間だ。

Are you going to change the decor?
模様替えをするんですか？

Have you changed your oil lately?
最近、オイル交換をした？

Let's change places.
交代しましょう。

3 That experience changed my life.
その経験が私の人生を変えた。

She changed her mind again.
彼女はまた気が変わった。

change for the better [for the worse]
好転 [悪化] する

The weather has changed.
天気が変わった。

He hasn't changed a bit.
あの人はちっとも変わっていない。

4 I'd like to go home and change.
家に帰って着替えたいんです。

I'll go and change my pants.
ズボンをはき替えて来ます。

5 You'd better count your change.
おつりを数えたほうがいいよ。

Do you have any small change?
小銭をお持ちですか？

6 You need to change trains twice, first at Shinjuku and then at Ikebukuro.
2回乗り換えなければなりません、最初は新宿で、次は池袋で。

7 Do you know of a place where I can change dollars into yen?
((*polite*)) ドルを円に両替できる所を、どこかご存じですか？

for a change 気分転換に, たまには

Let's have pizza for a change.
たまにはピザを食べよう。

changed ***adj.*** 全く違う, すっかり変わる

He's a changed man now.
彼は今や人が変わったみたいだ。

channel ***n.*** (on TV, radio) チャンネル, (of river: water passage) 水路, (broad strait) 海峡, (route) 経路, ルート
v. (information) 流す, (**channel one's energies into**) …に打ち込む

choose a channel チャンネルを選ぶ
change the channel チャンネルを変える
the English Channel イギリス海峡

chant ***v.*** (intone) 唱える, 詠唱する
n. (of crowd) シュプレヒコール, (canticle etc.) 聖歌

chaos ***n.*** (disorder) 混沌, カオス, (confusion) 混乱, (bustle) 混雑

chaotic ***adj.*** 混乱した, めちゃくちゃな, 混沌とした

chapel ***n.*** 礼拝堂, チャペル

chaperon ***n.*** 付き添い

chaplain ***n.*** (of prison) 教戒師, (of hospital) 牧師

chapter ***n.*** (of book) 章

Chapter 5 第5章

"How many chapters are there?"
"Three chapters."
「何章ありますか？」
「3章です」

character ***n.***

1 PERSONALITY: 人格, 性格, 気質
2 UNIQUENESS: 特色, 特徴
3 IN FILM/PLAY: (person) (登場) 人物

4 MORAL STRENGTH: 品性, 高潔さ

5 CHINESE / JAPANESE IDEOGRAM: 漢字

1 a man of good [bad] character
性格のいい [悪い] 人

He has a weak character.
あの人は弱い性格だ。

the Irish character アイルランド人気質

2 The character of the village will be lost if they build that highway nearby.
近くに幹線道路が通ったら、村の特色がなくなるでしょう。

That bar has character.
そのバーは独特の雰囲気がある。

3 the main character 主人公

He portrayed an evil character.
彼は悪役を演じた。

4 He has character.
彼は品性がある [人格者だ]。

5 How many characters are there in Chinese?
中国語には漢字はいくつありますか？

characteristic *n.* 特徴, 特色
adj. 特有の, 独特の

What are its main characteristics?
主な特徴は何ですか？

It's a family characteristic.
一家の特質なんです。

a characteristic smell 独特のにおい

characterize *v.* (embody the essence of) (…の) 特徴を表す, (characterize A as B) (AをBと) 特徴づける

charcoal *n.* 炭

♦ **charcoal-broiled** *adj.* 炭焼きの

charge

1 *n.* PRICE FOR SERVICE: 料金, 代金, -代, -料 [→ FEE], チャージ, (seating charge) 席料, (for obligatory bar food) お通し代

2 *v.* REQUIRE TO PAY: 請求する, (charge A to B) (AをBに) つける

3 *v.* ACCUSE OF WRONGDOING: (blame) 責める, (criticize) 非難する, (charge with a crime) 告訴する, 告発する

4 *v.* PAY FOR BY CREDIT CARD: カードで払う

5 *v.* ENERGIZE: (battery) 充電する

6 *v.* RUSH AT: (…に) 突撃する

1 a hotel charge ホテル代

free of charge 無料

an admission charge 入場料

Is there an additional charge?
追加料金はありますか？

2 How much were you charged?
いくら請求されました？

I told them to charge it to my bill.
料金は私につけるよう伝えておきました。

3 The man was charged with assault.
その男は暴行で告訴された。

4 I charged the meal to my credit card.
食事代はクレジットカードで支払った。

5 How long does it take to charge the battery?
この電池は充電するのにどのくらいかかるんですか？

6 The army charged the palace.
軍隊は宮殿に突撃した。

be falsely charged ぬれぎぬを着せられる

He was falsely charged with murder.
彼は殺人のぬれぎぬを着せられた。

be in charge of 担当している, …の責任者だ

He's in charge of the personnel division.
彼は人事部の責任者です。

be put in charge of …の責任者に任命される

Mr. Kobayashi was put in charge of the accounts section.
小林さんは経理課の課長に任命された。

take charge of 担当する, 引き受ける

Thank goodness someone was there to take charge of the situation.
この件を引き受けてくれる人がいてよかった。

charisma *n.* カリスマ

charitable *adj.* 慈善の

charity *n.* チャリティ, 慈善

a charity organization 慈善団体

charlatan *n.* いかさま師

charm *n.* (amulet) お守り, 魔よけ; (attraction) 魅力

v. (attract) 魅惑する, うっとりさせる

Is that a lucky charm you're wearing?
その、身に着けていらっしゃるのは、お守りですか？

I can't see what charm this place is supposed to have.
この場所に一体どんな魅力があるとされているのか、私にはわからない。

He has hidden charms, according to Melissa.
メリッサによれば、彼には隠れた魅力があるのだそうだ。

charming *adj.* (attractive) 魅力的な, (of person: pleasant) チャーミングな

chart *n.* (graph, table etc.) 図, 図表, (nautical) 海図

charter *v.* (rent: airplane, bus) チャーターする, 借り切る; (approve) 認可する

n. (deed) 特許状

a chartered bus 貸し切りバス

chase *v.* 追いかける, 追跡する, (**chase away**) 追う, 追い払う, (**chase out**) 追い出す

n. (pursuit) 追跡, (**the chase**: going after what one wants) 追求

Quick! You'd better chase after him and give him his umbrella.
早く！ 追いかけて行って傘を渡してあげなさい。

The children are chasing one another in the garden.
子供たちは庭で追いかけっこをしている。

That must be the umpteenth time I've chased away that cat.
もう何度あの猫を追い払ったか、わかりゃしない。

a high-speed chase 猛スピードの追跡

chasm *n.* (gorge) 小峡谷, 深い割れ目; (difference) 溝, 隔たり

chassis *n.* (part of car) シャーシー, 車台

chastise *v.* (rebuke) 責める

chat *v.* しゃべる, おしゃべりする, (on Internet) チャットする

n. (お)話, 雑談, (on Internet) チャット

They're always chatting about something.
あの連中は、いつもぺちゃくちゃしゃべっている。

I think we need to have a chat about this, don't you?
このことで、ちょっとお話をしたほうがいいと思うんですが、どうですか？

♦ **chat room** *n.* チャットルーム

chatter ***v.*** (talk quickly/noisily) ぺちゃくちゃしゃべる; (of teeth) ガタガタ鳴る ***n.*** (idle talk) おしゃべり, (of birds) さえずり, (of other animals) 鳴き声

chatterbox ***n.*** おしゃべり

chauffeur ***n.*** おかかえ運転手

chauvinism ***n.*** 熱狂的愛国主義, (male chauvinism) 男性優越主義

♦ **chauvinist** ***n.*** 熱狂的愛国主義者, (male chauvinist) 男性優越主義者

cheap ***adj.*** (inexpensive) 安い, (of or appearing to be of poor quality) 安っぽい, (vulgar) 下劣な, 下品な

adv. (inexpensively) 安く

Was it cheap? 安かった？

You call that cheap! You could've gotten it at half the price here.
安かったって？ ここなら半額で買えたのに。

It may have cost a lot, but it looks cheap.
高かったのだろうけど、安っぽく見える。

He's a cheap trickster.
あいつは、下劣なペテン師だ。

If you buy cheap, you buy twice.
安物買いの銭失いだよ。

♦ **cheaply** ***adv.*** 安く

cheapskate ***n.*** けち, けちん坊, しみったれ

cheat ***v.*** (on exam) カンニングする, (in game) いかさまをする, ((*informal*)) ずるをする; (in relationship) 浮気する; (cheat A out of B) (AからBを) だまし取る

n. ずるい奴, 詐欺師

It looked like he was cheating.
彼はいかさまをしているように見えた。

I was cheated out of $30.
私は３０ドルをだまし取られた。

♦ **cheat on** ***v.*** …を裏切って浮気をする

C

check

1 ***v.*** EXAMINE TO VERIFY: 調べる, 確認する

2 ***v.*** FOR MISTAKES: 点検する, チェックする, 検査する, (check an exam) 採点する

3 ***v.*** RESTRAIN: 抑える, 抑制する

4 ***v.*** MARK WITH "✓": チェックする,「✓」をつける

5 ***v.*** LUGGAGE: (also **check in**) 預ける

6 ***n.*** PATTERN: 格子模様, チェック

7 ***n.*** PAYMENT NOTE: 小切手

8 ***n.*** BILL: (at restaurant) (お)勘定, (お)会計

9 ***n.*** MARK: チェック(の印),「✓」

10 ***n., interj.*** IN CHESS: チェック, 王手

1 He says he's going to check the prices.
価格を調べると言っています。

Did you check the oil level?
オイルの量を確認した？

"I checked everywhere. I couldn't find it."
"Have you checked your pockets?"
「至る所を調べたけど、見つからなかった」
「ポケットも確認した？」

2 We'd better check this.
これは点検しておいたほうがいいね。

It has been checked once already. Do you want us to check it again?
すでに１度検査済みですが、もう１度確認しますか？

The exams haven't been checked yet.
試験はまだ採点されていない。

C

3 I was about to tell him the truth, but I checked myself.
本当のことを彼に言いそうになったが、自分を抑えた。

4 Check either "yes" or "no."
「はい」か「いいえ」のどちらかにチェックをつけてください。

5 Have you checked your luggage in yet?
荷物はもう預けた？

6 What dreadful taste! He was wearing a check shirt with a striped tie.
ひどい趣味だね。チェックのシャツにストライプのネクタイをしていたんだよ。

7 traveler's checks トラベラーズチェック
Can we pay by check?
小切手で払ってもいいですか？

8 Check, please.
お勘定、お願いします。

check in *v.* (register) チェックインする, (arrive) 到着する
What time do you expect to check in at your hotel?
ホテルには何時にチェックインする予定ですか？

check out *v.* (leave) チェックアウトする, 出る
You pay when you check out.
お支払いはチェックアウトの時です。

check up on *v.* (obtain information about) 調べる, 検討する, (person, to see whether they are all right) 調べる

checkbook *n.* 小切手帳

checkers *n.* (game) チェッカー

check-in *n.* チェックイン

checking account *n.* 当座預金

checklist *n.* チェックリスト

check mark *n.* チェックの印

checkmate *n., interj.* チェックメート
v. チェックメートする, 王手詰みにする

checkout *n.* チェックアウト

checkpoint *n.* 検問所, チェックポイント

checkup *n.* (medical) 健康診断, (general) 検査, 点検
How often do you have a medical checkup?
健康診断はどのくらいの間隔で受けていますか？

cheddar *n.* チェダーチーズ

cheek *n.* (part of the face) ほお, ほほ, ((*informal*)) ほっぺた [→ picture of FACE], (of buttocks) (お)尻; (impudence) 厚かましさ, ずうずうしさ
Her cheeks had a healthy glow.
彼女のほおは健康的で血色がよかった。
What cheek! なんて厚かましい！

♦ **cheekbone** *n.* ほお骨

cheeky *adj.* 厚かましい, 生意気な

cheer *v.* (comfort and encourage) 励ます, (make cheerful) 元気づける, (applaud) 応援する
n. (shout of encouragement) 声援
He looks so depressed. What can we do to cheer him up?
彼はひどく落ち込んでいるように見えるよ。どうしたら元気づけてあげられるだろう？
We cheered and cheered, but the Giants still lost.
みんなで声を限りに応援したのに、それでもジャイアンツは負けてしまった。

♦ **cheer on** *v.* 応援する
cheer up *v.* (become cheerful) 元気が

出る, (make cheerful) 元気づける

Seeing you cheered me up.

あなたにお会いしたら元気が出ました。

cheerful *adj.* 明るい, 朗らかな, 機嫌のいい, 陽気な

♦ **cheerfully** *adv.* 明るく, 機嫌よく, 陽気に

cheers *interj.* (said before drinking) 乾杯

cheese *n.* チーズ

cheetah *n.* チータ

chef *n.* コック長, 料理長, シェフ, (of Japanese restaurant) 板長

chemical *n.* (substance) 化学物質

adj. 化学の, 化学的な

a chemical reaction 化学反応

chemical weapons 化学兵器

♦ **chemical engineering** *n.* 化学工学

chemist *n.* (expert in chemistry) 化学者 [→ PHARMACIST, PHARMACY]

chemistry *n.* 化学, (as distinguished from 科学, "science") ((*informal*)) 化け学

chemotherapy *n.* 化学療法

cherish *v.* (hold dear) 大事にする, (in memory) 心にいだく

cherry *n.* (tree) サクラ, 桜(の木), (fruit) サクランボ, 桜桃, チェリー

cherry blossom *n.* 桜(の花)

We went to see the cherry blossoms at Ueno Park.

上野公園の桜を見に行きました。

cherry blossom viewing (お)花見

chess *n.* チェス

play chess チェスをする

♦ **chessboard** *n.* チェス盤

chest *n.* (part of the body) 胸, 胸部 [→ picture of BODY]; (piece of furniture) たんす, 整理だんす, (box) 箱

a treasure chest 宝物箱

chestnut *n.* (tree) クリ, 栗(の木), (nut) 栗

chew *v.* かむ

chewing gum *n.* チューインガム

chic *adj.* (elegant) シックな, いきな, 上品な

chicanery *n.* (trickery) ごまかし

chick *n.* (of chicken) ひよこ

chicken *n.* (bird) 鶏, (meat) とり肉, チキン; (coward) 弱虫, 臆病者

♦ **chicken out** *v.* 手を引く, (**chicken out of**) おじけづいて…から手を引く

chickenhearted *adj.* 気の小さい, 臆病な

chickenpox *n.* 水ぼうそう, 水痘

chicory *n.* チコリ

chief *n.* (boss) -長, チーフ, かしら, (head of tribe) 酋長

adj. (main) 主要な, 最も重要な, 第一の; (in titles) 主任-

the chief of police 警察署長

a section chief 課長

a division chief 部長

His father was a Native American chief.

彼の父親はアメリカ先住民の酋長だった。

Our chief concern is safety.

我々の第一の関心は安全性です。

He's the chief engineer.

彼は主任技術者です。

♦ **chief justice** *n.* 裁判長

chiefly *adv.* (mainly) 主に, (especially) 特に

chiffon *n.* (fabric) シフォン

chilblain *n.* しもやけ

child *n.* 子, 子供, (speaking about sb

else's) お子さん; (of era) 申し子

He's not a child anymore.
彼はもう子供ではない。

a mother and her two teenage children
母親と２人の１０代の子供

The child behaved himself very well.
その子はとてもお行儀よくしていた。

Stop behaving like a child!
子供じみたふるまいはやめなさい！

And how are your children?
で、お子さんたちはお元気ですか？

She's a child of the sixties.
彼女は６０年代の申し子だ。

♦ **childless** *adj.* 子供のいない

childbirth *n.* お産, 出産

childhood *n.* 子供のころ, 子供時代

childish *adj.* (typical of a child) 子供っぽい, (immature) 幼稚な, おとなげない

childlike *adj.* 子供らしい

chili *n.* (hot spice) チリ(トウガラシ) [→ PEPPER]

chill *n.* (in air) 冷気, 冷え, (sensation of coldness) 寒け, (dread) 恐怖, ぞっとすること

v. (cool) 冷やす

I felt a chill of fear. 私はぞっとした。

Should we chill the wine?
ワインを冷やそうか？

♦ **chilly** *adj.* (of weather) ひんやりした, うすら寒い

chime *n.* (of clock) チャイム, (of bell) 鐘(の音)

v. チャイムを鳴らす

chimney *n.* 煙突

chimpanzee *n.* チンパンジー

chin *n.* あご, 下あご [→ picture of FACE]

China *n.* 中国, ((*in abbr.*)) 中

china *n.* (porcelain) 磁器, (chinaware) 瀬戸物

chinchilla *n.* (rodent) チンチラ

Chinese *n.* (person) 中国人, (language) 中国語

adj. (of country, culture) 中国の, (of person) 中国人の, (of language) 中国語の

♦ **Chinese food** *n.* 中国料理, 中華料理

chip

1 *n.* SMALL FRAGMENT: かけら, 破片

2 *n.* PLACE WHERE STH HAS BROKEN OFF: 欠けた所, 欠け, 傷

3 *n.* TINY ELECTRONIC DEVICE: チップ

4 *n.* POTATO CHIP: (**chips**) ポテトチップ, (= French fries) フライドポテト

5 *v.* BREAK: 割る, (become broken) 割れる, (become cracked) 欠ける

1 chips of ice 氷のかけら

wood chips 木くず

Careful—there are chips of glass on the floor.
気をつけて——床にガラスの破片が落ちてるから。

2 There are chips in the paint here.
ここにペンキのはげた所がある。

The glass had a chip on the rim.
グラスの縁が欠けていた。

3 The invention of the silicon chip has affected everyone's life.
シリコンチップの発明は、あらゆる人々の生活に影響を及ぼした。

One chip can hold the contents of a dictionary.
１枚のチップに、辞書１冊分の内容を収

めることができます。

4 Eating a whole bag of chips at once isn't good for your health.
一度にポテトチップを一袋食べるのは健康によくないよ。

fish and chips フィッシュアンドチップス

5 Be careful you don't chip it.
割らないように気をつけて。

The bowl was chipped.
お茶わんは欠けていた。

♦**chip in** *v.* (contribute money) お金を出し合う; (interrupt) 口を出す

chipmunk *n.* シマリス

chiropody *n.* (foot treatment) 足治療

chiropractor *n.* 脊柱指圧師

♦**chiropractic** *n.* カイロプラクティック, 脊柱指圧療法

chirp *n.* (of bird) 小鳥の鳴き声, さえずり, (of insect) 虫の鳴き声

v. さえずる, チュッチュッ/チーチーと鳴く

chisel *n.* のみ [→ picture of TOOL]

v. のみで彫る, のみで削る

chit *n.* (bill) 勘定書, 請求書, (memo) メモ

chitchat *n., v.* 世間話(をする)

chives *n.* エゾネギ, チャイブ

chloride *n.* 塩化物

chlorine *n.* 塩素, (in tap water) カルキ

chloroform *n.* クロロホルム

chlorophyll *n.* 葉緑素, クロロフィル

chocolate *n., adj.* (food) チョコレート(の), (color) チョコレート色(の)

hot chocolate ココア

choice *n.* (act of choosing) 選ぶこと, 選択, (right to choose) 選ぶ権利, (freedom to choose) 選択の余地, (thing chosen) 選んだこと/もの, (range of choice) 選択の範囲

I made a choice and it was the wrong one.
私が選んだことだが、それは誤った選択だった。

My choice wouldn't have been the same as yours.
私なら、あなたと同じ選択はしなかったでしょう。

Did you have a choice?
選択の余地はあったの？

There's a wide choice of colors.
たくさんの色の中から選ぶことができる。

there is no choice (but to...) (...するよりほかに) 仕方がない, ...せざるを得ない

There was no choice but to fire her.
彼女を首にするほか仕方なかった。

There's no choice. We simply have to go.
仕方がない。行かざるを得ないよ。

choir *n.* (singing group) 合唱団, (church choir) 聖歌隊

choke *v.* (become unable to breathe properly) のどが詰まる, 息が詰まる, (**choke on**) ...でのどを詰まらせる, (strangle) 窒息させる, (**be choked with**: smoke, dust etc.) ...でむせる

choker *n.* (necklace) チョーカー

cholera *n.* コレラ

cholesterol *n.* コレステロール

choose *v.* (select from alternatives) 選ぶ, 選択する, (**choose to do**) ...しようと決める, ...することにする

Mr. Suzuki was chosen as the team leader.
鈴木さんがチームリーダーに選ばれた。

They are very difficult to choose between.
(この中から)選ぶのは非常に難しい。

People chose to ignore the warnings.
人々は警告を無視することにした。

choosy ***adj.*** (fussy) 気難しい, (be choosy about) (…に)こだわる

chop ***v.*** (cut up with a heavy knife) たたき切る, ぶった切る, (mince) 細かく刻む, みじん切りにする, (wood) 割る
n. (thick slice of meat) 厚切り肉; (karate chop) 空手チョップ

Don't chop the carrots too thinly.
ニンジンを薄く切りすぎないでね。

We need to chop the wood before we can make a fire.
火をおこす前に、まきを割らないといけない。

Do you like pork chops?
ポークチョップはお好きですか?

chopper ***n.*** (helicopter) ヘリコプター; (large meat knife) 肉切り包丁

chopsticks ***n.*** (for eating) (お)はし, (for serving) 取りばし

a pair of chopsticks おはし1ぜん
disposable chopsticks 割りばし

chord ***n.*** (in music) 和音, コード

strike a chord (with) (resound with meaning) (…の)心の琴線に触れる, 胸を打つ

chore ***n.*** (routine) 日課, (**chores**) (=minor tasks) 雑用, (=household chores) 家事

chorus ***n.*** (choir) 合唱団, (part of song) 折り返し(句), (piece of music) 合唱曲

♦**choral** ***adj.*** 合唱の

chosen ***adj.*** 選ばれた, (after difficulty, struggle) 選び抜かれた

chowder ***n.*** チャウダー

clam chowder クラムチャウダー

Christ ***n.*** キリスト, イエス・キリスト

christen ***v.*** (baptize) (…に)洗礼を施す, (give a name to as part of baptism) (…に) 洗礼名を授ける

Christian ***n.*** クリスチャン, キリスト教徒
adj. キリスト教の

♦**Christian name** ***n.*** (name given at baptism) 洗礼名, (first name) 名前

Christianity ***n.*** キリスト教

Christmas ***n.*** クリスマス

Merry Christmas to you!
クリスマスおめでとう/メリークリスマス!

♦**Christmas card** ***n.*** クリスマスカード
Christmas Day ***n.*** クリスマスの日
Christmas Eve ***n.*** クリスマスイブ
Christmas tree ***n.*** クリスマスツリー

chrome ***n.*** クロム

chrome plating クロムめっき

chromosome ***n.*** 染色体

chronic ***adj.*** 慢性の

chronicle ***n.*** (account, record) 記録, (annals) 年代記
v. (record) 記録に残す

chronology ***n.*** (time line) 年代記, (table) 年表, (ordering) 年代順配列

chrysalis ***n.*** さなぎ

chrysanthemum ***n.*** キク, 菊

chubby ***adj.*** (of person, figure) ぽちゃぽちゃした

chubby cheeks

ぽちゃぽちゃしたほっぺた

chuck *v.* (cast away) 投げる, (throw away: garbage) 捨てる

Some kids were chucking stones into the pond.
池に石を投げている子供たちがいた。

If it's trash, just chuck it!
ごみなら、捨てちゃいなさい！

chuckle *v.* くすくす笑う

chunk *n.* (thick mass) かたまり, (large amount) かなりの量

That was a big chunk of meat you gave the dog.
大きな肉のかたまりを犬にやったんだね。

A big chunk of plaster fell from the ceiling.
天井から、大きなしっくいのかたまりが落ちた。

church *n.* (building) 教会, (service) 礼拝

Did you go to church last Sunday?
この前の日曜日、教会へ行きましたか？

chutney *n.* チャツネ

CIA *n.* ＣＩＡ, 中央情報局

cicada *n.* セミ

cider *n.* リンゴジュース, (containing alcohol) リンゴ酒 [NOTE: The Japanese word サイダー refers to a carbonated beverage.]

cigar *n.* 葉巻, シガー

cigarette *n.* たばこ, 煙草

a cigarette butt 吸い殻

light [put out] a cigarette
たばこに火をつける [の火を消す]

offer [take] a cigarette
たばこを勧める [もらう]

♦ **cigarette case** *n.* たばこケース

cigarette lighter *n.* ライター

cinch *n.* (easy thing) 簡単なこと, ((*informal*)) 朝飯前, 楽勝

Today's exam was a cinch.
今日の試験は簡単だった。

cinema *n.* (building) 映画館, (film industry) 映画産業

cinnamon *n.* シナモン

cipher *n.* (code) 暗号

circa *prep.* (around) およそ… [→ ABOUT 2]

circle

1 *n.* SHAPE: 輪, 丸, 円

2 *v.* MOVE IN A CIRCLE: (overhead) 旋回する, (around) (…の) 周りを回る

3 *n.* GROUP: (of friends) 仲間, (of people with a mutual interest) -界, サークル

4 *v.* DRAW A CIRCLE AROUND: 丸で囲む

5 *v.* SURROUND: 取り囲む, 包囲する

1 They formed a circle.
みんなで輪になった。

I've put a circle around your spelling mistakes.
スペルミスを丸で囲んでおいたよ。

The children ran around in circles.
子供たちは、ぐるぐると駆け回った。

2 The plane circled overhead.
上空で飛行機が旋回した。

How many moons circle Jupiter?
木星の周りを回る衛星はいくつありますか？

3 He has a wide circle of friends.
彼は付き合い [顔] が広い。

The journal is well known in academic circles.
その雑誌は学界ではよく知られている。

She belongs to our reading circle.

彼女は私たちの読書会のメンバーです。

4 Circle the correct answer.
正しい答えを丸で囲みなさい。

5 The police circled the building.
警察は建物を取り囲んだ [包囲した]。

circuit *n.* (path for electric current) 回路, (lap, journey around sth) 1 周

♦**circuitry** *n.* 電気回路

circular *adj.* (of shape) 丸い, 円形の, 環状の, (of route) 循環する, (of tour) 周遊の, (of argument) 遠回しの

circulate *v.* (of traffic) 流れる, (of air, blood) 循環する, (of rumor, news) 広まる, (distribute: report etc.) 回す, (**be circulated**: of newspaper etc.) 出回る, 配布される

circulation *n.* (of blood) (血液の) 循環, (of newspaper: number of copies printed/distributed) 発行部数, (of money) 流通

circumcise *v.* (for religious purposes) (…に) 割礼を行う, (**be circumcised**) 包茎手術を受ける

circumference *n.* (of circle) 円周, (of irregular shape/area) 周辺, 周囲

circumstance *n.* (**circumstances**) 状況, 事情, (of one's life) 身の上, 境遇

the actual circumstances 実情

the present circumstances 現状

In these circumstances, it's usually wiser to say nothing.
こういう状況では、普通何も言わないほうが賢明です。

I don't know. It just depends on the circumstances.
さあどうでしょう、状況によりますから。

under the circumstances こういう/そういう事情では, この/その状況では

Under the circumstances, I have to decline.
こういう事情では、私は辞退させていただくしかない。

circumstantial *adj.* 状況の

circumstantial evidence 状況証拠

circus *n.* サーカス

cirrhosis *n.* 肝硬変

cistern *n.* (for toilet) 貯水タンク, (for rainwater) 貯水池

cite *v.* (quote) 引用する

citizen *n.* (of country) 国民, (of city) 市民, 住民

citizenship *n.* 市民権, 公民権, 国籍

apply for citizenship 市民権を申請する

citron *n.* (fruit) シトロン

citrus *adj.* かんきつ類の

citrus fruits かんきつ類

city *n.* 都市, 都会, (in proper names) -市

the capital city 首都

It's the second largest city in the world.
世界第2の大都市です。

She grew up in a big city.
彼女は大都市で育った。

Were you born in a city or the country?
お生まれは都会ですか、田舎ですか？

city hall *n.* 市役所, 市庁舎

civil *adj.* (public) 市民の, 公民の, (opposite of military) 民間人の; (courteous) 礼儀正しい, (polite) 丁寧な, (polite but not very friendly) 丁重な

We're civil with one another.
私たちはお互いに礼儀正しく接している。

a civil reply 丁重な返事

civil disobedience *n.* 市民的不服従

civil engineer *n.* 土木技師

♦**civil engineering** *n.* 土木工学

civilian *n.* 民間人, 一般市民

adj. 民間の, 民間人の

civilian casualties 民間人の犠牲者

civilization *n.* 文明

ancient civilizations 古代文明

The Romans brought civilization to what is now Great Britain.

ローマ人は今のグレートブリテン島に文明をもたらした。

Civilization itself is under threat.

文明そのものが脅威にさらされている。

civilize *v.* 文明化する

civilized *adj.* (of society) 文明化した, (of person) (=cultured) 上品な, (=polite) 礼儀正しい

civilized society 文明社会

civil law *n.* 民法

civil liberty *n.* 市民の自由

civil rights *n.* 公民権

civil servant *n.* 公務員

civil service *n.* 行政機関, 官庁, (people) 公務員

civil war *n.* 内戦, (in U.S. history: **the Civil War**) 南北戦争

claim *v.* (demand) 要求する, 請求する, (claim as one's own) 主張する, (assert) 主張する

n. (demand) 要求, 請求, (assertion) 主張

claim a tax deduction

税金の控除を要求する

Are you going to claim expenses?

費用を請求しますか？

You have rights and you should claim them.

権利があるのですから、それを主張すべきですよ。

He'll probably try to claim credit.

おそらく自分の功績を主張しようとするだろう。

Has anyone claimed the umbrella?

傘の持ち主は現れた？

She claims she was not responsible for the accident.

自分には事故の責任はなかったと、彼女は主張している。

They've put in a claim for higher wages.

彼らは賃上げを要求した。

He filed a claim against the doctor.

彼は医師に対して賠償請求を起こした。

♦**claimant** *n.* 主張者, 要求者, (in court) 原告

clairvoyant *adj.* 透視力のある, 千里眼の

n. 千里眼の人, (medium) 霊能者

♦**clairvoyance** *n.* 透視力, 千里眼

clam *n.* ハマグリ

clamp *n.* (tool) 留め金, かすがい, (for car wheel) クランプ, 車輪止め

v. (clamp A to B) (AをBに) 留める, くっつける, (clamp together) ぎゅっと締まる

clan *n.* (group of related families) 一族, (group of people in general) 仲間

clandestine *adj.* 内々の, 秘密の

clap *v.* (applaud) 拍手する, 手をたたく, (strike hands together in time with music) 手拍子をする

clarify *v.* (explain) 説明する, (make clearer: explanation) はっきりさせる

clarinet *n.* クラリネット

clarity *n.* (of argument) 明瞭さ, 明快さ

clash

1 *v.* MAKE A LOUD NOISE: ガチャンと音がする

2 *v.* NOT MATCH: 合わない, 調和しない, (of personalities: conflict) 合わない, ぶつかる

3 *v.* COME INTO VIOLENT CONTACT: 衝突する, ぶつかる

4 *n.* LOUD NOISE: ガチャン(という音)

5 *n.* CONFLICT: (of interests, opinions) 衝突, 食い違い

1 The two armies' shields clashed.
両軍の盾が音を立ててぶつかった。

2 That color clashes with your pink tie.
その色はピンクのネクタイと合わない。

Their personalities clash.
二人の性格がぶつかる。

3 The antiwar protesters clashed with police outside the embassy.
反戦を訴える人々が大使館の前で警官隊と衝突した。

4 a clash of swords
剣と剣がカチンとぶつかる音

5 a clash of interests 利害の衝突

a clash of cultures 文化の衝突

clasp *n.* (latch, brooch) 留め金, 締め具, (buckle) バックル

v. (grasp) 握る, 握りしめる

a brass clasp 真ちゅうの留め金

He clasped both my hands in gratitude.
彼は感謝の気持ちから私の両手を握りしめた。

class *n.*

1 GROUP OF STUDENTS: クラス, 組, 学級, (alumni) 卒業生

2 LESSON: 授業

3 KIND: 種類

4 SOCIAL STRATUM: 階級

5 ELEGANCE: 気品

6 TAXONOMIC CATEGORY: 綱

1 We're not in the same class.
私たちは同じクラスじゃありません。

the class of 2006 2006年卒業生

a class reunion 同窓会 [クラス会]

2 Did you go to class today?
今日は授業に出た?

What classes are you taking this term?
今学期はどの授業を取るの?

He decided to take a class in history.
彼は歴史の授業を受けることにした。

3 There are various classes of painkillers.
痛み止めには､いろいろな種類がある。

4 the working [middle, upper] classes
労働者 [中流, 上流] 階級

It's a class-conscious society.
階級意識の強い社会です。

5 She's got class. 彼女には気品がある。

classic *adj.* (of example) 典型的な; (of film, work of literature etc.) 傑作の

n. (work of literature, film) 傑作, 名作; (**classics**: study of languages / literatures of the ancient world) 古典(文学)

It was a classic example of mismanagement.
それは管理ミスの典型的な例だった。

a classic opera オペラの傑作

classical *adj.* (of music) クラシックの, (of the ancient world) 古典の

classical Chinese 漢文

classical Japanese literature 日本の古典文学

♦ **classical music** ***n.*** クラシック

classification ***n.*** (act of classifying) 分類, (category) 範ちゅう, 部類

classified ***adj.*** (of document) 機密の, 極秘の

n. (**the classifieds**: classified ads) 案内広告

classify ***v.*** (arrange by class) 分類する

How has it been classified?
どういうふうに分類されていますか？

classmate ***n.*** クラスメート, 同級生

classroom ***n.*** 教室

clatter ***v.*** (of dishes) カタカタ/ガチャガチャ音を立てる

n. カタカタ/ガチャガチャ(いう音)

clause ***n.*** (in contract) 条項, (part of sentence) 文節, 節

claustrophobia ***n.*** 閉所恐怖症

clavichord ***n.*** クラビコード

clavicle ***n.*** (collarbone) 鎖骨

claw ***n.*** 爪, (of crab) はさみ

v. ひっかく

clay ***n.*** (mud) 粘土, (used by potters) 陶土

clean

1 ***adj.*** **NOT DIRTY:** きれいな, (neat and clean) 清潔な, (of clothes: freshly washed) 洗いたての, (of page: blank) 白紙の, (of copy: not written on) 清書した

2 ***adj.*** **OF PERSON:** (guiltless) 潔白な, (drug/alcohol-free) 麻薬/(お)酒をやっていない

3 ***v.*** **MAKE TIDY:** きれいにする, 掃除する, (put in order) 片付ける

4 ***v.*** **WASH:** 洗う, (clothes) 洗濯する

1 Do you think this water's clean?
この水はきれいだと思います？

The air was clean and fresh.
空気はきれいで、さわやかだった。

Always use a clean towel.
必ず清潔なタオルをご使用ください。

You'd better put on a clean shirt.
洗いたてのシャツを着たほうがいいよ。

Don't you have a clean copy?
清書した [きれいな] のはないの？

2 He says he's been clean (=off alcohol) for six months.
彼は6ヵ月間(お酒を)飲んでいないと言っています。

3 Have you cleaned the sink?
流しをきれいにした？

4 I had my shirt cleaned.
ワイシャツを洗濯してもらった。

come clean 真実を話す, 白状する

clean out ***v.*** (…の)中をきれいに掃除する

Let's clean out the cupboards.
食器棚の中をきれいに掃除しよう。

clean up ***v.*** (put in order) 片付ける

He has to clean up his room before his father gets back.
父親が戻る前に、彼は部屋を片付けないといけない。

cleaner ***n.*** (person) 掃除する人, 清掃員, (product for washing) 洗剤

cleaning ***n.*** (act of cleaning up) 掃除

do the cleaning 掃除する

cleanliness ***n.*** (state) 清潔さ, (habit) き

れい好き

That hotel has a reputation for cleanliness.

そのホテルは清潔で評判だ。

cleanly *adj.* (of person) きれい好きな

adv. きれいに

cleanser *n.* クレンザー

clear

1 ***adj.*** **EASILY UNDERSTOOD:** わかりやすい, はっきりした

2 ***adj.*** **OBVIOUS:** 明らかな, 明白な

3 ***adj.*** **TRANSPARENT:** (of liquid, glass) 透明な, (of water, sky) 澄んだ

4 ***adj.*** **CLOUDLESS:** 晴れた

5 ***adj.*** **UNOBSTRUCTED:** (of road) すいた, (of view) 妨げるもののない

6 ***adj.*** **OF SKIN:** きれいな, 色つやのいい

7 ***adj.*** **OF COLOR:** (vivid) 鮮やかな

8 ***v.*** **TIDY UP:** 片付ける, きれいにする

9 ***v.*** **OF WEATHER:** 晴れる

10 ***v.*** **GO OVER:** (hurdle) 飛び越える, クリアする

11 ***v.*** **AUTHORIZE:** 認可する, 認める

12 ***v.*** **ACQUIT:** (of charge) (嫌疑を)晴らす

13 ***adv.*** **OUT OF THE WAY:** 離れて

1 Is that clear? わかったかな？

His answer wasn't very clear, was it?
あの人の答えは、あまりはっきりしてなかったですよね。

I made myself perfectly clear.
自分の考えをはっきりさせました。

2 It was a clear case of racial discrimination.
人種差別の明らかな事例だった。

It's not clear what the president meant.
大統領が何を意味したのか明らかでない。

It is clear that we don't have enough time.
十分な時間がないことは明白だ。

3 The water was so clear you could see all the way down to the bottom.
水はすごく澄んでいて、底までずっと見通せた。

The skies are so clear today.
今日は空が澄み渡っている。

4 It's going to be a clear day today.
今日は晴れるでしょう。

It was a clear night and you could see the stars.
晴れ渡った夜で、星が見えた。

5 The road is clear up ahead.
この先は道がすいています。

We have a clear view of the sea from our window.
窓から海が見渡せる。

6 She has a clear complexion.
彼女は色つやのいい顔色をしている。

7 The walls are a clear blue.
壁は鮮やかなブルーだ。

8 Come on, it's time to clear the table.
さあ、食卓を片付けよう。

The room had been cleared of furniture.
部屋からは、家具が運び出されていた。

9 The fog is supposed to clear later this morning.
霧は午前中には晴れるとのことです。

10 The runner cleared the bar.
走者はバーをクリアした。

11 The plane was not cleared for takeoff.
飛行機は離陸を認められなかった。

12 He was cleared of the charge.
彼の嫌疑は晴れた。

13 Stand clear, please.
離れていてください。

be clear about/on …は確かだ, はっきり知っている

Are you quite clear about this?
このことは、確かですか？

clear a path 道をあける

Let's clear a path so people can get in and out.
人が出入りできるように、道をあけましょう。

clear one's name 汚名をそそぐ

clear one's throat せき払いをする

He cleared his throat and then began to speak.
彼はせき払いをしてから話し始めた。

make clear (mystery, situation) 解明する, はっきりさせる

clear away *v.* (dishes) (食器を)片付ける, 下げる

clear out *v.* (closet etc.) (…の)中を片付ける, (empty) 空にする

clear up *v.* (tidy up) 片付ける; (solve: problem) 解く, 解決する; (of weather) 晴れる

Do you want some help clearing up the dishes?
食器の後片付けに、手は要る？

You know, I won't rest until this whole matter is cleared up.
この件がすべて解決するまでは、休まないよ。

It might clear up later this afternoon.
午後遅くなって晴れるかもしれない。

The skies cleared up and the stars came out.
空が晴れてきて、星が出た。

---

clear-cut *adj.* 明白な, はっきりした

clearly *adv.* (obviously) 明らかに, (so as to be understood) はっきり(と)

cleaver *n.* (meat knife) 肉切り包丁

clef *n.* 音部記号

clergy *n.* (in general) 聖職者

♦**clergyman** *n.* (Catholic) 神父, (Protestant) 牧師

clerical *adj.* (of work) 事務員の, 書記の, (of clergy) 牧師の, 聖職者の

clerk *n.* (shop assistant) 店員

clever *adj.* (smart) 頭のいい, 利口な, 賢い

He's a clever kid all right.
なるほどあの子は頭のいい子だね。

Hachiko was a clever dog.
ハチ公は賢い犬だった。

They were clever not to get involved in that scheme.
その計画にかかわらなくて、彼らは賢明でした。

♦**cleverly** *adv.* (wisely) 賢く, (skillfully) 巧みに, うまく, 上手に

cleverness *n.* できのよさ, 利口さ

cliché *n.* 陳腐な決まり文句

click

1 *n.* SOUND: (of lock) カチッ(という音), (of switch) パチッ(という音), (of camera shutters) パチパチ(いう音), (of mouse) クリック

2 *v.* MAKE A CLICKING SOUND: カチッと音がする, (**click one's tongue**) 舌打ちする

3 *v.* **USE A MOUSE:** クリックする

4 *v.* **COME TO MIND:** ピンとくる

5 *v.* **GET ALONG FROM THE START:** 意気投合する, うまが合う

1 With the click of a button, you can access the entire database.
ボタンをクリックすると、データベース全体にアクセスできます。

2 Did the latch click?
掛け金はカチッと音がした？

3 Click here to clear the window.
画面を消すには、ここをクリックしてください。

4 It just didn't click at the time.
その時はピンとこなかった。

client *n.* クライアント, (of lawyer) 依頼人, (customer) 客, ((*polite*)) お客さん, ((*formal*)) 顧客

cliff *n.* がけ, 絶壁

climate *n.* (meteorological conditions) 気候, (mood, atmosphere) 雰囲気, (situation) 情勢

a tropical climate 熱帯性気候

Japan has a comparatively temperate climate.
日本は比較的、気候が温暖です。

the political climate 政治情勢 [政局]

climax *n.* (peak) 頂点, 絶頂, (of film) クライマックス, 山場; (orgasm) オルガスムス

climb *v.* (…に) 登る, (do mountain climbing) 山登りする, 登山する, (rise in rank) 昇進する, (move upward) 上がる, 上昇する, (of plant) 伸びる, はいのぼる, (of sun, moon) 昇る

n. (act of climbing) 登り, 登ること

They climbed Mt. Everest.
彼らはエベレストに登頂した [登った]。

Want to go climbing next weekend?
次の週末、山登りに行く？

As the plane climbed we waved at it.
しだいに上昇する [高度を上げる] 飛行機に手を振りました。

Over the years he climbed to the top of the organization.
何年もかけて、彼は組織のトップにまで昇りつめた。

Prices will climb if inflation is not stopped.
インフレが止まらない限り、物価は上昇します。

The ivy has climbed right up the wall.
ツタが壁の上の方まで、はいのぼっている。

♦**climb in through** *v.* …からもぐり込む

Can you climb in through the window?
窓から中にもぐり込めますか？

climb into *v.* (car, taxi) …に乗り込む

climb over *v.* 乗り越える

The children climbed over the wall.
子供たちは塀をよじ登って乗り越えた。

climb up onto *v.* …に登る, …によじ登る

The toddler climbed up onto the chair.
幼児が椅子によじ登った。

climber *n.* (mountain climber) 登山者, (professional) 登山家, (rock climber) ロッククライマー

climbing *n.* (of mountains) 山登り, (of rock) クライミング

cling *v.* (to mother) (…に) くっつく, まとわりつく, (to idea, belief) (…に) 固執する; (of clothes) くっつく

cling film *n.* ラップ

clinic *n.* (medical facility) 診療所

clinical *adj.* (of testing, treatment, diagnosis) 臨床の; (of approach: objective) 客観的な, (cold, impersonal) 冷淡な

clink *v.* (of glass object) チリン/カチンと鳴る

n. チリン/カチン(と鳴る音)

clip

1 *v.* CUT: (with scissors) (はさみで) 切る, (hair, hedge) 刈る, (clip A out of B) (AをBから) 切り抜く

2 *v.* FASTEN: (with clip) (クリップで) 留める, (be fastened) 留まる

3 *n.* FASTENER: (paper clip) クリップ [➡ picture of STATIONERY], (hair clip) 髪留め

4 *n.* OF FILM: 1カット

1 I clipped this advertisement out of the paper.
新聞から、この広告を切り抜きました。

It looks as though the hedge has been clipped.
生け垣は刈り込まれたようです。

2 We'd better clip them together so we don't lose one.
なくさないように、クリップで留めておいたほうがいい。

How does this clip on?
これは、どうやったら留まるんですか?

clipboard *n.* クリップボード

clipping *n.* (from newspaper) 切り抜き

clique *n.* 仲間

clitoris *n.* クリトリス, 陰核

cloak *n.* マント

clock *n.* 時計, (alarm clock) 目覚まし時計, (grandfather clock) 柱時計

Have you set the clock?
時計を合わせた?

The clock's fast [slow].
時計が進んで [遅れて] いる。

♦ **clock in** *v.* (show up for work) 出勤する, (punch in) タイムカードを押す

clock out *v.* (leave work) 退社する, (punch out) タイムカードを押す

clockwise *adv.* 時計回りに, 右回りに

clone *n.* クローン

v. (…の) クローンを作る

a human clone クローン人間

close[1] *v.*

1 SHUT: (door, shop) 閉める, (eyes, book) 閉じる, (become shut) 閉まる, (of shop) 閉店する

2 END: 終わる, (bring to an end: discussion) 終える, 終わりにする

3 DRAW NEAR: (**close in on**) …に近づく

1 Close the door on your way out.
出て行く時はドアを閉めて。

Close your books and listen up.
本を閉じて、聞いてください。

Excuse me, what time do you close?
すみません、ここは何時までですか [何時に閉店しますか] ?

You don't close on Sundays, do you?
日曜日は休業じゃないですよね?

2 The ceremony closed with everyone singing "The Star-Spangled Banner."
式は、全員でアメリカ国歌を歌って終わった。

Let's close this discussion.
この話し合いは終わりにしましょう。

3 They're closing in on us.

彼らはだんだん近づいている。

close a deal 取引を終える, 契約をまとめる

in closing (used in speech) 最後になりましたが

> **KANJI BRIDGE**
>
> **閉** ON: へい KUN: し(める/まる), と(じる/ざす) | CLOSE
>
> adjournment .... 閉会
> claustrophobia .... 閉所恐怖症
> closing/closure (of factory, road) .. 閉鎖
> closing (of shop) .... 閉店
> closing ceremony .... 閉会式
> opening and closing .... 開閉

close[2] *adj.*

1 NEAR: 近い, 近くの

2 OF RELATIONSHIP: (friendly) 親しい, 仲のいい, (closely related) 近い, (of contact) 密接な, 密な

3 OF CONTEST/GAME: (almost a draw) 接戦の, 五分五分の

4 CAREFUL: (of attention) 細心の

5 SIMILAR: よく似た, 近い

1 Are we close to the beach yet?
もう海辺は近い？

The company is close to where I live.
会社は家の近くです。

Stand back. You're too close to the edge.
下がって。端に近づきすぎているよ。

2 We're close friends.
私たちは親友です。

She's a close relative.
彼女は近い親戚です。

Do you stay in close contact with each other?
お互いに密に連絡を取り合ってるんですか？

3 a close finish きわどいフィニッシュ

It's a close game.
接戦だね/五分五分だね。

4 Now, pay close attention. I'm only going to say this once...
さあ、よく注意して聞くんですよ。1回しか言いませんから。

5 That's not what I wanted, but it's close enough.
欲しかった物ぴったりじゃないけど、すごく近いよ。

close by すぐ近くに, そばに

There's a bicycle parking lot close by.
すぐ近くに駐輪場があるんです。

close shave (near miss) 間一髪

It was a close shave. I nearly got hit by the bus.
間一髪だった。もう少しでバスにはねられるところだった。

come close to doing もう少しで…しそうになる

I came very close to losing my temper.
もう少しで、切れそうになった。

closed *adj.* (shut) 閉まった, 閉じた, (of road, factory) 閉鎖された, (for business) 閉まっている, 休業している

The banks are closed on Sundays.
銀行は日曜日は閉まっている。

The road was closed because of an accident.
事故のため、道路が閉鎖されていた。

closely *adv.* (carefully) 念入りに, 注意深く

closet *n.* 押し入れ, クローゼット [→ picture of APARTMENT, FUTON]

close-up *n.* クローズアップ, 大写し

take a close-up of …のクローズアップを撮る, 大写しにする

clot *n.* (blood clot) 血のかたまり

cloth *n.* (fabric) 布, 生地, (piece of cloth) きれ, (rag for cleaning) ぞうきん, (for wiping table/dishes) ふきん

clothe *v.* (…に) 着せる

clothes *n.* 服, 洋服, 衣類

fold one's clothes 服をたたむ

put on [take off] one's clothes
服を着る [脱ぐ]

hang the clothes out 洗濯物を干す

♦ **clothes/laundry basket** *n.* 洗濯かご

clothesline *n.* 物干し [洗濯] ロープ

clothespin *n.* 洗濯ばさみ

clothing *n.* 服, 衣類

traditional Japanese clothing
着物

cloud *n.* (airborne water vapor) 雲; (swarm) 大群

v. (cloud over: become foggy) 曇る, (dim, blur) 曇らせる, (make dull: judgment) 鈍らせる

I like the shape of that cloud.
あの雲の形、好きだなあ。

Where's that cloud of smoke coming from?
あのもうもうと立ちのぼる煙は、どこから出ているんですか？

It's clouded over again.
また曇っている。

Sleep clouded his mind.
眠気で彼の頭が鈍った。

cloudy *adj.* (of sky) 曇った, (of liquid) 濁った

cloudy weather 曇り

clout *n.* (influence) 影響力

have a lot of clout
強い影響力をもっている

clove *n.* クローブ, 丁字

clover *n.* クローバー, シロツメクサ

clown *n.* (circus clown) ピエロ, 道化師; (fool) ばか

♦ **clown around** *v.* ふざける, おどける

club

1 *n.* SOCIETY: クラブ, サークル, 同好会, (in names of clubs) -部, -会

2 *n.* CLUBHOUSE: (building) クラブハウス, (room at university for club activities) 部室

3 *n.* STICK: 棒, こん棒

4 *n.* SUIT OF CARDS: (**clubs**) クラブ

5 *n.* NIGHTCLUB: ナイトクラブ

6 *v.* **BEAT WITH A STICK:** こん棒で殴る

1 It's a members-only club.

そこは会員制のクラブです。

Naoko's a member of the volleyball club.

直子はバレーボール部の一員です。

C

2 I'll meet you back at the club.

あとで部室で会おう。

3 I feel like I've been hit over the head with a club.

棒で頭を殴られたような感じです。

4 the king of clubs クラブのキング

cluck *v.* (of hens) コッコッと鳴く

clue *n.* (thing that leads to a solution) 糸口, (hint) ヒント, (to riddle, investigation) 手がかり

Could you give me a clue?

ヒントをくれますか？

The police have found one or two clues.

警察は、一つ二つ手がかりをつかんだ。

not have a clue 見当がつかない, さっぱりわからない

I don't have a clue where he is.

彼がどこにいるのか、見当がつかない。

clump *n.* (piece of sth) かたまり; (sound) ドスン/ドシン(という音)

v. (walk noisily) ドシンドシンと歩く; (**clump together**) (gather together) 集まる, (harden) 固まる

clumsy *adj.* (awkward, inept) 不器用な, ぎこちない, (coarse) 雑な, 粗雑な, (hard to use) 扱いにくい

He's clumsy. あの人は不器用だ。

What a clumsy piece of writing this is.

なんて粗雑な文章なんだ。

By modern standards, it's a clumsy machine.

今の基準からすると使いにくい機械です。

cluster *n.* (bunch) 房, 一団

a cluster of grapes 一房のブドウ

a cluster of stars 星団

clutch *n.* (in car) クラッチ

v. (hold tightly) 握る, しっかりとつかむ

clutter *n.* (of things) 散乱

be in a clutter (物が)散らかっている

co- *pref.* 共同-, 共-

KANJI BRIDGE

共 ON: きょう KUN: とも | CO-, BOTH

coauthor	共著者
coed	(男女)共学の
coeditor	共編者
coeducational school	共学校
coexist	共存する
collaborate	共同して働く
costar	共演者

coach *n.* コーチ, 指導員

v. (direct: team, player) コーチする, 指導する, (teach) 教える

coal *n.* 石炭

♦**coalfield** *n.* 炭田

coal mine *n.* 炭鉱

coalition *n.* (alliance) 連合, 合同, (of political parties) 連立

form a coalition 連合 [連立] をつくる

coarse *adj.* (poor in quality) 粗末な, (of texture: rough) きめの粗い, ざらざらした, (of person) 下品な, 粗野な, (of speech) 荒っぽい

This is coarse material.

この生地は、きめが粗い。

He's a coarse fellow.

あいつは、粗野な男だ。

coast ***n.*** 海岸, 沿岸

There are lots of secluded beaches along the coast.

海沿いには、人目につかない浜辺がたくさんある。

♦ **coastal** ***adj.*** 海岸沿いの, 沿岸の, 海辺の

a coastal town 海辺の町

coaster ***n.*** (for drink) コースター

coast guard ***n.*** (armed service) 沿岸警備隊, (coastguardsman) 沿岸警備隊員

coastline ***n.*** 海岸線

coat ***n.*** (garment) コート, 上着, (fur layering) 毛; (of paint) 上塗り, 塗装

v. (cover: with coating of paint etc.) 塗る, (food) (…に) かける

Are you going to wear a coat?

コートを着て行きますか?

This dog certainly has a thick coat.

確かにこの犬は毛がふさふさしているね。

I think it needs another coat of paint, don't you?

もう一度ペンキで上塗りする必要があると思いませんか?

The pancakes were coated in syrup.

パンケーキにシロップがかかっていた。

coat hanger ***n.*** ハンガー

coating ***n.*** (of paint) 上塗り, (on food) 衣

coatroom ***n.*** クローク

coax ***v.*** (persuade) 説得する

cobalt ***n.*** コバルト

cobbler ***n.*** (shoe repairer) 靴の修理屋

cobra ***n.*** コブラ

cobweb ***n.*** クモの巣

cocaine ***n.*** コカイン

cock ***n.*** (adult male chicken) おんどり; (faucet) 栓, コック

cockatoo ***n.*** オウム

cockpit ***n.*** (of airplane) 操縦室, コックピット, (of racecar) 運転席

cockroach ***n.*** ゴキブリ

cocktail ***n.*** カクテル

make a cocktail カクテルを作る

cocky ***adj.*** (cheeky) 生意気な

cocoa ***n.*** ココア

coconut ***n.*** (fruit) ココナツ, ヤシの実, (tree) ココヤシの木

♦ **coconut milk** ***n.*** ココナツミルク

coconut oil ***n.*** ココナツオイル, ヤシの実油

cocoon ***n.*** まゆ

cod ***n.*** タラ

♦ **cod roe** ***n.*** たらこ

code ***n.*** (number) 記号, 番号, (in computer programming) コード, (cipher) 暗号, (system of rules) 規定, 規約

a postal code 郵便番号

an area code 市外局番

break/crack a code 暗号を解く

♦ **code name** ***n.*** コード名

codicil ***n.*** 遺言補足書

coed ***adj.*** (of school, dorm) 男女共学の

coeducation ***n.*** (男女)共学

coefficient ***n.*** 係数

coerce ***v.*** (**coerce into doing**) (…に) 無理に…させる

coercive ***adj.*** 強制的な

coffee ***n.*** (drink) コーヒー

C

I'd like a cup of coffee, please.
コーヒーを(1杯)お願いします。

♦**coffee bean** *n.* コーヒー豆

coffee break *n.* お茶の時間, 休憩時間

coffee grinder *n.* コーヒーミル, 豆ひき

coffee grounds *n.* (コーヒーの)かす

coffeehouse *n.* 喫茶店, コーヒーショップ

coffeemaker *n.* コーヒーメーカー

coffee pot *n.* コーヒーポット

coffin *n.* お棺, 棺桶, ((*polite*)) ひつぎ

cog *n.* (tooth of cogwheel) (歯車の) 歯, (cogwheel) 歯車

cognac *n.* コニャック

cohabit *v.* (live together with) (…と) 同棲する

♦**cohabitation** *n.* 同棲

coherent *adj.* (of words, argument) 筋の通った

coil *n.* (of rope) 一巻き, (of hair) 巻き毛, (of electrical wire) コイル; (contraceptive) 避妊リング

v. (make into a coil) ぐるぐる巻く, (coil A around B) (AをBに) 巻き付ける, (**coil around**: become wrapped around) …に巻き付く, (of snake: **coil itself up**) とぐろを巻く [→ TWIST 4]

Some coils of barbed wire had been left behind.
有刺鉄線が、何巻きか置きっぱなしになっていた。

Ivy had coiled its way up the tree.
ツタが木に巻き付いて伸びていた。

The snake had coiled itself up.
蛇はとぐろを巻いていた。

coin *n.* (metal money) 硬貨, コイン

Do you have a one-hundred yen coin?
百円玉を持ってる?

These coins are quite rare.
この硬貨はすごく珍しい。

coincide *v.* (happen simultaneously) 同時に起こる, (be consistent) 一致する

coincidence *n.* 偶然, 偶然の一致

What a coincidence meeting you here!
ここでお会いするとは、なんという偶然でしょう!

cola *n.* コーラ

colander *n.* 水切りボウル, ざる [→ picture of COOKING UTENSILS]

cold

1 *adj.* NOT HOT: (of weather) 寒い, (of thing) 冷たい, (chilled) 冷えた, (of food: no longer warm) 冷めた

2 *n.* ILLNESS: かぜ

3 *n.* COLDNESS: (of air temperature) 寒さ, (of water, food) 冷たさ

4 *adj.* OF PERSON: 冷たい, 冷淡な

1 It's cold today, isn't it?
今日は寒いですね。

The winters are cold and the summers hot.
冬は寒く、夏は暑い。

The room was very cold.
部屋は冷え冷えとしていた。

My hands are cold.
手が冷たい。

The engine's cold and won't start.
エンジンが冷えていて、かからない。

Your food is getting cold. Hurry up and eat it.
食事が冷めてしまいますよ。早くお上がりなさい。

2 I think I've caught a cold.
どうやら、かぜをひいたらしい。

3 The cold of the water woke me up.
水の冷たさで目が覚めた。

4 He's a cold fish, that one.
あいつは冷たい奴だ。

be out cold (be unconscious) 気を失っている, 失神している

go cold (of food) 冷める

KANJI BRIDGE

冷 ON: れい KUN: つめ(たい), ひ(える/やす), さ(める/ます) | COLD

air-conditioning	冷房
cold-blooded, cruel	冷酷な
cold front	寒冷前線
cold shoulder	冷淡な態度
cold war	冷戦
cold water	冷水
frigidity (of climate)	寒冷
refrigeration	冷蔵
refrigerator	冷蔵庫

cold-blooded ***adj.*** (of reptile) 冷血の; (cruel) 冷酷な

cold cream ***n.*** コールドクリーム

coldly ***adv.*** (of manner) 冷たく, 冷淡に

coleslaw ***n.*** コールスロー

collaborate ***v.*** 共同する, 協力する

collaboration ***n.*** 共同, 協力, コラボレーション

in collaboration with …と共同で

collapse ***v.*** (cave in) ((*also figurative*)) つぶれる, 崩れる, 崩壊する, (fall over, faint) 倒れる [→ FALL]

The whole building has collapsed.
建物は全壊した。

It looks as if the government will collapse.
政権が崩壊しそうな雲行きです。

She collapsed from exhaustion.
疲労こんぱいして、彼女は倒れた。

collar ***n.*** (part of garment) えり, カラー; (for animal) 首輪

collarbone ***n.*** 鎖骨

collateral ***n.*** (property used as guarantee) 担保(物件)

colleague ***n.*** 同僚, 仕事仲間

collect ***v.*** (gather) 集める, (mail, garbage) 回収する, (stamps) 収集する, (salary, pension) 受け取る, (taxes, rent, payments) 徴収する, 集金する, (contributions) 募金する; (**collect oneself**) 気持ちを落ち着かせる; (of dust) たまる, 積もる

Mail is collected twice a day.
郵便物は毎日2回集められます。

A small truck comes around to collect old newspapers and magazines.
小さなトラックが巡回して、古新聞、古雑誌を回収します。

He collects old coins.
あの人は古銭を収集している。

He collects his pension every month from the post office.
その人は毎月、郵便局で年金を受け取っています。

Go and collect your refund.
払戻金を取りに行っておいでよ。

We're collecting for Save the Children.

私たちはセーブ・ザ・チルドレンの募金活動をしております。

Look at all the dust that has collected on these books.
本の上に積もったこのほこりを見て。

C

♦ **collect call** *n.* コレクトコール

make a collect call
コレクトコールする

collected works *n.* (of writer) 全集

collection *n.* (group of objects) コレクション, 収集, (act of collecting: mail, waste, debts) 回収, (collecting of tax) 徴収

a fine collection of Byzantine art
ビザンチン美術のみごとなコレクション

When's the next mail collection?
郵便物の次の回収はいつですか？

collective *adj.* (cooperative) 共同の

collectively *adv.* (as a whole) 全体として

collector *n.* (of art) 収集家, コレクター

college *n.* 大学, カレッジ [→ UNIVERSITY]

Where did you go to college?
どこの大学に行ったんですか？

a junior college 短期大学

collegiate *adj.* 大学の, (of dictionary) 大学生用の

collide *v.* 衝突する [→ CRASH 2]

collie *n.* コリー

collision *n.* 衝突

colloquial *adj.* 口語の, 日常会話の

♦ **colloquial expression** *n.* 話し言葉, 口語表現

cologne *n.* (オーデ)コロン

colon[1] *n.* (punctuation mark) コロン

colon[2] *n.* (part of the body) 結腸

colonel *n.* (in U.S. Army/Air Force/Marine Corps) 大佐

colonial *adj.* (of colony) 植民地の

colonial days 植民地時代

colonial architecture コロニアル風建築

colonialism *n.* 植民地主義

colonize *v.* 植民地にする

♦ **colonization** *n.* 植民地化

colony *n.* (territory) 植民地, (group of emigrants) 移民団; (of animals) 群れ, (of plants) 群生

Hong Kong is no longer a British colony.
香港はもうイギリスの植民地ではない。

a colony of apes 猿の群れ

color *n.* 色, カラー, 色彩

v. (apply color to) (...に) 色をつける, (paint) (...に) 色を塗る

What color is this?
これは何色ですか？

I could see all the colors of the rainbow.
にじの色が全部見えました。

The color has faded.
色があせてしまった。

You shouldn't wash it in hot water. The color will run.
熱いお湯で洗わないほうがいい。色がにじむから。

a color photograph カラー写真

It is going to be shown in color.
カラーで見られますよ。

How are you going to color it?
どんな色に塗るの？

♦ **color-blind** *adj.* 色盲の, 色覚異常の

color-code *v.* 色分けする

color film *n.* カラーフィルム

colorless *adj.* 無色の

colored *adj.* 色のついた, カラーの

colorful *adj.* (full of color) カラフルな, 色鮮やかな, 華やかな

coloring *n.* (tinting) 着色, (complexion) 顔色, 血色, (in food) 着色料

♦**coloring book** *n.* 塗り絵帳

colt *n.* (young male horse) 若い雄の馬

column *n.* (of building) 柱, 円柱, (of page) 欄, コラム

columnist *n.* コラムニスト

coma *n.* 昏睡状態

be in a coma 昏睡状態にある

comb *n.* くし

v. (**comb one's hair**) 髪をとかす; (search thoroughly) くまなく捜索する

Here, you can use my comb.
どうぞ、私のくしを使って。

Wait! You haven't combed your hair.
待ちなさい! 髪をとかしてないでしょ。

The police combed the woods.
警察は森をくまなく捜索した。

combat *n.* 戦闘

v. (…と) 戦う [→ FIGHT]

combination *n.* (to lock) 組み合わせ数字; (arrangement) 組み合わせ

an interesting combination
面白い組み合わせ

in combination with …と組んで, …といっしょに

combine *v.* (mix) 混ぜ合わせる, (band together) 団結する, (of organizations) 合併する, (of elements) 結合する

Combine the flour and the milk, and stir well.
小麦粉と牛乳を混ぜ合わせて、よくかき混ぜてください。

If all the small political parties combined, they would have much more clout.
小さな政党が全部団結すれば、もっとずっと大きな影響力をもてるはずだ。

Hydrogen combines with oxygen to form water.
水素は酸素と結合して水になる。

combined *adj.* (joint) 共同の, 合同の

come *v.*

1 MOVE: 来る, ((*honorific*)) いらっしゃる, おいでになる, (toward listener) 行く, ((*humble*)) 参ります

2 ARRIVE: 着く, 到着する, (**come home**) 帰って来る, (**come back**) 戻って来る; (**come to**: conclusion) …に至る

3 COME FOR/TO DO: …しに来る

4 IN ORDER: (**come before/after/next**) (…の) 前/後/次に来る, (**come in first/second place**) 1/2着に入る

5 OF TIME/EVENT: 来る, (subjunctive usage, used at the beginning of a sentence: **Come…**) (…が) 来ると, (…に) なったら

6 BECOME: (**come to…**) …になる, (**come true**) 実現する

7 COME TO MIND: (心/頭に) 浮かぶ, ピンとくる, (**come as a shock/surprise**) ショック/驚きだ

8 APPEAR: 現れる, 出る

9 BE AVAILABLE: ある

10 HAVE AN ORGASM: いく

1 Come here, please.

ここへ来てください。

She said she'd come this evening.
今晩来ると言っていました。

I'm going to go use the bathroom before the train comes.
電車が来る前に、ちょっとお手洗いに行って来ます。

Here comes the mailman.
郵便屋さんが来てるよ。

Can I come to your party?
パーティーに行ってもいいですか？

2 They've come. 来ました/着きました。

What time will you come?
何時にいらっしゃいますか？

The bus came at 9:15.
バスは９時１５分に到着した。

He hasn't come home yet?
まだ帰って来てないの？

He came back from Thailand yesterday.
彼は昨日タイから帰国しました。

3 He said he'd come for his books later.
あとで本を取りに来ると言っていた。

Some friends are coming for dinner tonight.
今夜は友人たちが夕飯を食べに来ます。

The waiter came to take our order.
ウェイターが注文を聞きに来た。

They've come to paint the house.
彼らは家にペンキを塗りに来た。

4 A comes before B, and B before C.
ＡはＢの前に来て、ＢはＣの前に来る。

"What comes next?" "Apple pie."

COMING AND GOING

The Direction of the Action

In Japanese, "come" 来る is an action directed toward the speaker, and "go" 行く an action away from him or her. This may appear to correspond with our thinking in English, but the difference lies in not imagining oneself to be where the other person is as we often do in English. Thus, if someone phones from the station to say they have arrived, an English speaker might respond by saying, "I'm coming," imagining that he or she is already at the station. In Japanese, however, the reply is 迎えに行く "I'm going (there) to meet you."

Auxiliary Verb Usage

Unlike "come" and "go," the Japanese verbs 来る and 行く can be used as auxiliary verbs. That is, they attach to the -て forms of various verbs to express special meanings. Their chief usages as auxiliaries are as follows.

1. To indicate the direction of an action. [→ BRING, TAKE]
   a) He came into the room.
   その人は部屋に入って来た。(lit., "He [has] entered the room.")

「次は何が出るの？」「アップルパイ」

You come next. 次はあなたです。

My horse came in third.
私の馬は3着に入った。

5 The time has come to make amends.
償いをする時が来た。

I hope the day never comes.
その日が来ないことを祈る。

Come the election, we're going to be busy.
選挙の時期になったら、忙しくなる。

6 Over the years, I've come to like this country.
年月がたつにつれ、この国が好きになった。

How did things ever come to this?
一体どうしてこんなことになったんだ？

I doubt if my dream will come true.
果たして夢は実現するのだろうか。

7 The idea came to me while I was taking a bath.
おふろに入っていた時、そのアイデアが浮かんだ。

This news of their divorce will no doubt come as a shock to her parents.
二人の離婚の知らせは、奥さんのご両親にとってはきっとショックだろう。

8 An error message came on the screen.
エラーメッセージが画面に出ました。

9 The wallpaper comes in three colors.
壁紙の色は3色あります。

come alive → ALIVE

come and go 行ったり来たりする, 出

b) He went into the room.
その人は部屋に入って行った。(lit., "He [has] entered the room.")

NOTE: In (*a*) the speaker is in the room, and in (*b*) he or she is not.

2 To indicate continuation or progression of an action. -てくる indicates an action that started in the past and has continued "up till now," and -ていく an action that, whether it started in the past or present, will continue "from now."

a) I've learned it this way up to now.
今までそう習ってきました。

b) The population of this town will probably carry on increasing.
この町の人口は、ますます増えていくだろう。

3 -てくる can mean "begin" or "start" when used with certain intransitive verbs that describe a process that takes time to complete.

a) It started to rain.
雨が降ってきた。

b) The nights are getting [starting to get] longer.
夜が長くなってきている。

入りする

come clean → CLEAN

come to think of it 考えてみると

Come to think of it, that's not a bad idea.
考えてみると、それも悪くないね。

for some time to come ここしばらく(は)

Abortion will remain controversial for some time to come.
ここしばらくはまだ、妊娠中絶は議論を呼ぶことだろう。

how come なぜ, どうして

How come you left her?
なぜ彼女のもとを去ったんですか？

How come you didn't call me last night?
どうしてゆうべ電話をくれなかったの？

what's…coming to …はどうなっているのか

What's this country coming to! So many people without work!
この国はどうなっているんだ！ こんなにたくさん失業者がいるなんて！

when it comes to …のことになると

She may not know much about history, but when it comes to music, she's a wiz.
彼女は、歴史についてはあまり知らないが、音楽のこととなるとすごいよ。

come about *v.* (happen) 起こる, ((*formal*)) 生じる

It came about by accident.
たまたま起きたことだった。

A political solution came about through peaceful negotiation.
平和的な話し合いによって政治的解決がもたらされた。(lit., "was brought about")

come across *v.*

1 ENCOUNTER BY CHANCE: (find) 偶然見つける, (meet) …に偶然出会う, ((*informal*)) …にばったり会う

2 BE COMMUNICATED: 理解される, 伝わる, (**come across as**: give the impression of being…) …という印象を与える, …という感じがする

1 I came across an old photo of her while cleaning out the drawers.
引き出しを掃除していたら、彼女の昔の写真を偶然見つけた。

Guess who I came across while shopping?
買い物の途中で、誰にばったり会ったと思う？

2 Her point did not come across.
彼女の言いたいことは伝わらなかった。

He comes across as a very sincere person.
彼はとても真面目な人という感じがする。

come after *v.* (pursue) …の後を追う, 追って来る; (follow in sequence) …の後に来る

Run! They're coming after us.
逃げろ！ 彼らが追いかけて来てる。

New Year's comes after Christmas.
お正月はクリスマスの後に来ます。

What comes after C?
Cの次は何ですか？

come along *v.* (come along with) (…と)いっしょに来る; (appear) 現れる; (progress) 進む

Would you like to come along with us?
いっしょにいらっしゃいませんか？

She just came along for the ride.
彼女はただ楽しみでいっしょに乗って来た。

An athlete of his caliber doesn't come along every year.
彼ほどの優秀なスポーツ選手は、そう毎年現れるわけではない。

When the opportunity comes along, take it!
チャンスが来たら、つかみなさい。

"How's dinner coming along?" "Great."
「食事の準備はどうなってる？」「大丈夫だよ」

come along (now) (hurry) さあ早く

Come along now. Tidy up this mess.
さあ早く、この散らかってるものを片付けなさい。

come apart *v.* (break into pieces) ばらばらになる

I'm sorry. It just came apart in my hands.
すみません。手に取ったら、ばらばらになってしまったんです。

It comes apart for storage.
ばらばらにして、しまっておけます。

come apart at the seams (of plan) だめになる, (of person: break down) 参る, ガタガタになる

come around *v.* (come by) やって来る, 立ち寄る, (of event: return, recur) 巡って来る, やって来る; (regain consciousness) 意識を取り戻す

My uncle usually comes around every Monday.
おじは、たいてい月曜日にやって来る。

The next election will come around in two years.
次の選挙は2年後に巡って来る。

Fortunately, the patient came around after a few minutes.
幸い、患者は数分後に意識を取り戻した。

come away *v.* (come away from: step back from) (…から) 離れる, (peel off) はがれる

Come away from the (cliff's) edge.
(がけの) 縁から離れなさい。

The plaster's coming away from the wall.
壁のしっくいが、はがれてきている。

come back *v.*

1 RETURN: (home) 帰って来る, (to previous location) 戻って来る, (to subject of conversation) 戻る

2 BECOME FASHIONABLE AGAIN: 復活する, 再びはやる

3 OF THOUGHT/MEMORY: 思い出される

4 IN GAME: (make a comeback) 巻き返す

1 What time are you coming back?
何時に帰って [戻って] 来るの？

I'll come back to that point later.
あとでまたその話に戻ります。

It all comes back to what I said earlier.
つまり、私が前に言ったことです。

2 Do you think stonewashed jeans will ever come back?
ストーンウォッシュのジーンズが、またはやると思いますか？

3 It's all coming back to me now.
今すっかり思い出した。

4 The home team came back in the second half.
試合の後半で、地元チームが巻き返した。

come before *v.* (court) …で審議される, (of issue before committee) …に提出される; (in order) …の前に来る, (take precedence over) …より優先する

come by *v.*

1 VISIT: やって来る, 立ち寄る

2 ACQUIRE: (get hold of) 手に入れる, (find) 見つける

1 Takuya came by at his usual time.
拓也は、いつもの時間にやって来た。

He said he'd come by later tonight.
今夜あとで立ち寄ると言っていた。

2 How on earth did you come by that picture?
一体どうやって、その写真を手に入れたの？

Good jobs are hard to come by.
いい仕事を見つけるのは難しい。

come down *v.* (be reduced) 下がる, (in price) 値下がりする, (of person from high place) 下りる, (of person in world) 落ちぶれる, (of rain, snow) 降る, (of leaves) 落ちる, (of fence, tree) 倒れる

Computer prices have come down.
コンピューターが値下がりした。

He came down from the stage.
ステージから下りた。

Come down off the roof.
屋根から下りていらっしゃい。

She has really come down in the world since she started taking drugs.
麻薬に手を出すようになってから、あの人はすっかり落ちぶれてしまった。

The rain's really coming down now.
すっかり本降りになっているね。

Looks like the fence came down in the storm.
嵐で塀が倒れたようです。

when it comes down to it 結局…, つまるところ…

When it comes down to it, he's no different from us despite his fine education.
どんなに学歴があろうと、結局彼も私たちと何も変わらない。

come down with *v.* (become ill with) …にかかる

Mom has come down with the flu.
お母さんがインフルエンザにかかった。

come for *v.* (come to get) 取りに来る [→ COME 3]

come forward *v.* (volunteer one's services) 買って出る, (**come forward to do**) 進んで…する, (step forward) 進み出る; (**come forward with**: idea, suggestion) 出す, 提出する

People are reluctant to come forward to help the police.
人々は、進んで警察に協力しようとはしません。

He came forward to receive his prize.
賞品を受け取るため、彼は前に進み出た。

Let's wait until she comes forward with a better plan.
もっといいプランを出してくるまで待ちましょう。

come from *v.* (originate from) …から来る, …に由来する, (be made from) …から作られる, (of person: be from) …の出身だ; (of sound) …から聞こえて来る, (of smell) …から漂って来る

This vase comes from China.
このつぼは、中国から来た品です。

Steel comes from iron ore.

スチールは鉄鉱石から作られる。

"Where do you come from?"
"Brazil."
「どちらのご出身ですか/お国はどちらですか？」
「ブラジルです」

There was music coming from upstairs.
上の階から音楽が聞こえて来た。

There's a smell of curry coming from the kitchen.
台所からカレーのにおいが漂って来る。

come in *v.* (enter) 入る, 入って来る, (**come in on**: join) …に入る, …に参加する, …に加わる; (of tide) 満ちてくる

"May I come in?"
"Yes."
「入ってもよろしいですか？」
「どうぞ」

He tripped as he came in.
中に入ろうとしたところ、つまずいた。

The robber came in through the window.
泥棒は窓から侵入した。

A report has just come in about an earthquake.
地震に関する情報が、たった今入ってきました。

Can we come in on this plan?
この計画に、私たちも加わっていいかな？

The tide is coming in.
潮が満ちてきている。

come in handy 役に立つ

come into *v.* [→ COME IN]; (inherit) 相続する; (begin to exist in a state) <-ます stem> + 始める, <-ます stem> + 出す

He came into a fortune.
彼は財産を相続した。

The cherry trees have come into blossom.
桜が咲き始めました。

Bell-bottoms came into fashion in 1966.
ベルボトムは1966年にはやり出した[流行し始めた]。

come into being/existence 生まれる

When did the notion of Sun Gods come into existence?
太陽神という概念は、いつ生まれたんでしょう？

come of *v.* (be the result of) …の結果だ

I'm not surprised you failed the exam. That's what comes of partying so much.
君が試験に落ちたのも当然だよ。遊びほうけていた結果だ。

come off *v.*

1 DETACH: 外れる, 取れる, (peel off) はがれる, (fall off) 落ちる

2 BE SUCCESSFUL: うまくいく, 成功する

3 STOP USING: (drug, alcohol) やめる

1 The top came off when it fell.
落ちた時に、上の部分が外れてしまった。

The wallpaper is coming off.
壁紙が、はがれてきている。

The jockey came off his mount at the second jump.
騎手は二つ目のジャンプで落馬した。

2 It didn't come off as planned.
計画どおりには、うまくいかなかった。

3 She has come off drugs completely.
彼女は麻薬を完全にやめた。

Come off it! でたらめを言うのはやめろ！

Come off it! You're talking nonsense.
やめろ！ でたらめを言うのは。

come on *v.*

1 SPOKEN USAGES: (**Come on!**) (=You can

C

do it!) さあ！, がんばれ, (=Hurry up!) 急げ, (=Don't be ridiculous!) いいかげんにして！, ((*masculine*)) よせよ, (trying to start a fight) かかって来い

2 TURN ON: (of machine, lights) つく

3 OF ILLNESS: See examples below

4 START: (of TV program) 始まる

1 Come on! You can do it!
さあ！ 君ならできるよ！

Come on, or you'll miss the bus.
急いで！ バスに乗り遅れるよ。

Come on! That was years ago.
((*masculine*)) よせよ！ 何年も前のことじゃないか。

2 The lights suddenly came on.
電気が突然ついた。

3 I think I have a cold coming on.
どうやらかぜをひいたようだ。

I can feel a migraine coming on.
偏頭痛がし出した。

4 The show comes on at 9 o'clock.
その番組は9時から始まる。

come out *v.*

1 EMERGE: 出る, 出て来る, (appear) 現れる, (in photograph) 写っている, (of flowers: bloom) 咲く, (of photograph: be taken) 撮れている

2 OF PRODUCT ON THE MARKET: 出る

3 OF FACT/TRUTH: 明らかになる

4 FADE/DISAPPEAR: (of color) なくなる, 落ちる, (of stain) 取れる

5 MAKE KNOWN THAT ONE IS GAY: ゲイであることを公言する, カミングアウトする

1 He came out of the office and turned down the corridor.
彼はオフィスを出て、廊下を曲がって行った。

The sun hardly ever came out.
太陽はほとんど顔を出さなかった。

The stars are coming out.
星が出ている。

She came out well in the photo.
彼女は、よく写っていました。

Did your photos come out OK?
写真はうまく撮れていましたか？

2 His new book comes out in March.
彼の新しい本は3月に出ます。

When is the article supposed to come out?
その記事はいつ出ることになっていますか？

3 The truth finally came out.
ついに真相が明らかになった。

When it came out that he had accepted bribes, he was forced to resign.
わいろを受け取っていたことが明らかになり、彼は辞任せざるを得なかった。

4 All the colors came out.
色が全部、落ちてしまった。

Do you think this stain will come out?
このしみ、取れると思う？

come over *v.*

1 OF FEELING: 急に…を感じる

2 VISIT: 来る, 遊びに来る

3 GIVE IMPRESSION: (**come over as**) …という感じがする, …という印象だ

1 A feeling of terror came over the witness as she took the stand.
証言台に立った時、証人は急に恐怖を感じた。

I really don't know what came over me.

どうしちゃったのか、自分でもさっぱりわからない。

2 Friends are coming over tonight.
今夜、友達が遊びに来る。

3 He comes over as intelligent and witty.
彼は知的でユーモアのある感じがする。

come through *v.* (difficulties) 切り抜ける, 乗り切る

Most of the passengers came through unharmed.
乗客の大半は、けがもなく切り抜けた。

come to *v.* (amount to) …になる; (arrive at) …に着く; (regain consciousness) 意識を取り戻す; (come to mind) (心に) 浮かぶ [→ COME 7]

The total cost came to $1,000.
総費用は1000ドルになった。

come under *v.* (be categorized under) …に分類される

I think this rock comes under the metamorphic category.
この石は変成岩に分類されると思います。

come under criticism 非難を受ける

Mr. Mori came under a lot of criticism for that remark.
その発言で森氏は多くの非難を受けた。

come under the authority of …の管轄に入る

That office comes under the authority of the Ministry of Foreign Affairs.
その局は外務省の管轄です。

come up *v.*

1 TO SPEAKER/LOCATION: 近寄って来る
2 ARISE: 出てくる, 出る, 起こる, ((*formal*)) 生じる
3 REACH: (come up to: of water: reach the level of) (…に) 達する, (…まで) 届く, (**come up to one's expectations**) (…の) 期待に添う
4 IN CONVERSATION: (of topic) 話題にのぼる, (of name) (話の中に) 出てくる
5 THINK UP: (**come up with**) 考え出す
6 OF EVENT: (**be coming up**: be near at hand) もうすぐだ, 控えている
7 OF PLANTS: 芽を出す
8 IN WORLD/SOCIETY: 出世する

1 He came up to me and shook my hand.
彼は近寄って来て、私の手を握った。

She came up to the bar and sat down next to me.
彼女はバーにやって来て、隣に座った。

2 A number of problems came up that we were unable to solve.
我々には解決できない問題が、いくつか出てきた。

That idea has come up before.
その考えは以前、出ました。

Look, I'm sorry. Something's come up. I can't meet you tonight.
すみませんが、急に用ができて今夜は会えなくなったんです。

Did the question come up on the exam?
その問題は試験に出た?

3 The water came up to my knees.
水はひざまで達した。

The vacation didn't come up to our expectations.
休暇は期待外れに終わった。

4 Their divorce came up in the conversation.
二人の離婚が話題にのぼった。

Your name came up.

あなたの名前が話に出たよ。

5 It would be helpful if someone could come up with a couple of good ideas.
どなたか、いいアイデアを2、3出していただけるとありがたいのですが。

C

6 The festival is coming up soon.
お祭りはもうすぐだ。

7 I don't think the chrysanthemums I planted are going to come up.
私が植えた菊は芽を出しそうにない。

8 She's really come up in the world.
あの人は本当に出世しましたね。

come up against *v.* (difficulties) …に直面する, …にぶつかる

We came up against deep-rooted prejudices.
私たちは根深い偏見にぶつかった。

---

comeback *n.* (in game) カムバック, 復帰, (coming back into fashion) 復活, 再流行; (retort) 返す言葉, 反論

comedian *n.* コメディアン, 喜劇役者

comedy *n.* コメディ, 喜劇

comet *n.* すい星

comfort

1 *n.* FEELING: (contentment) ほっとする気持ち, (physical comfort) 快適さ, (solace in grief/pain) 慰め

2 *v.* GIVE SOLACE TO: 慰める, 元気づける

3 *v.* RELIEVE PAIN IN/OF: 和らげる, 楽にする

4 *n.* MATERIAL POSSESSIONS: (**comforts**) 生活を快適にする物, 便利な物

1 What a comfort it is to get home, put your feet up and have a cup of tea.
わが家に帰って足を投げ出し、1杯のお茶を飲むと、本当にほっとする。

Everyone wants to live in comfort.
誰もが、快適に暮らすことを望んでいる。

It's a comfort for her just to have someone visit her bedside (at the hospital).
誰かがお見舞いに来てくれるだけで、彼女には慰めになるんです。

2 No words could comfort the grieving parents.
悲しみにくれるご両親を慰める言葉などありませんでした。

I tried to comfort her, but I didn't know what to say.
元気づけようとしたけれど、何と言っていいかわからなかった。

3 The green tea comforted his stomach.
緑茶を飲んだら、彼は胃が楽になった。

4 Happiness can't be measured by how many material comforts you have.
便利で快適な物をいくつ持っているかで幸せを計ることはできない。

comfortable *adj.* 楽な, 快適な, 気持ちいい, (in/of clothing) 着心地のいい, (in/of chair) 座り心地のいい, (in/of bed) 寝心地のいい, (in/of car) 乗り心地のいい, (in social setting) 居心地のいい; (of income) 十分な

It was a comfortable journey.
快適な旅行でした。

Please make yourself comfortable.
どうぞ楽になさってください。

I found the chair so comfortable I was loath to get up.
あまりに座り心地のいい椅子なので、立ち上がるのがいやになった。

It's certainly a comfortable car.
確かに乗り心地のいい車です。

They have a comfortable income and

can afford long vacations.
あの人<ruby>達<rt></rt></ruby>たちは十分な<ruby>収入<rt>しゅうにゅう</rt></ruby>があるから、<ruby>長<rt>なが</rt></ruby>い<ruby>休暇<rt>きゅうか</rt></ruby>が<ruby>楽<rt>たの</rt></ruby>しめる。

comfortably *adv.* (easily) <ruby>気楽<rt>きらく</rt></ruby>に, (suitably) <ruby>十分<rt>じゅうぶん</rt></ruby>, (not wanting for anything) <ruby>何不自由<rt>なにふじゆう</rt></ruby>なく

be comfortably off
<ruby>何不自由<rt>なにふじゆう</rt></ruby>なく<ruby>暮<rt>く</rt></ruby>らしている

comforter *n.* (bedcover) ベッドカバー, (for futon) <ruby>羽毛布団<rt>うもうぶとん</rt></ruby>, <ruby>掛<rt>か</rt></ruby>け<ruby>布団<rt>ぶとん</rt></ruby> [→ picture of FUTON]

comic *n.* (comic book) <ruby>漫画<rt>まんが</rt></ruby>, コミック, (**comics**: comic strips) <ruby>連続<rt>れんぞく</rt></ruby><ruby>漫画<rt>まんが</rt></ruby>; (comedian) コメディアン, <ruby>喜劇役者<rt>きげきやくしゃ</rt></ruby>
adj. (funny) <ruby>面白<rt>おもしろ</rt></ruby>い, おかしな

comical *adj.* <ruby>面白<rt>おもしろ</rt></ruby>い, おかしな, こっけいな

coming *adj.* (next) <ruby>次<rt>つぎ</rt></ruby>の, <ruby>今度<rt>こんど</rt></ruby>の, <ruby>来<rt>き</rt></ruby>たるべき
n. (**the coming of**) …の<ruby>到来<rt>とうらい</rt></ruby>

comings and goings <ruby>行<rt>い</rt></ruby>き<ruby>来<rt>き</rt></ruby>, <ruby>出入<rt>でい</rt></ruby>り, <ruby>往来<rt>おうらい</rt></ruby>

♦**Coming-of-age ceremony** *n.* <ruby>成人式<rt>せいじんしき</rt></ruby>
Coming-of-Age Day *n.* <ruby>成人<rt>せいじん</rt></ruby>の<ruby>日<rt>ひ</rt></ruby>

comma *n.* コンマ

command *n.* (order) <ruby>命令<rt>めいれい</rt></ruby>, (control) <ruby>指揮<rt>しき</rt></ruby>, <ruby>支配権<rt>しはいけん</rt></ruby>, (in computing) コマンド, <ruby>命令<rt>めいれい</rt></ruby>
v. (order) <ruby>命令<rt>めいれい</rt></ruby>する, (control) <ruby>指揮<rt>しき</rt></ruby>する; (**command respect**) <ruby>尊敬<rt>そんけい</rt></ruby>を<ruby>集<rt>あつ</rt></ruby>める, <ruby>尊敬<rt>そんけい</rt></ruby>に<ruby>値<rt>あたい</rt></ruby>する

Who gave the command?
<ruby>誰<rt>だれ</rt></ruby>がその<ruby>命令<rt>めいれい</rt></ruby>を<ruby>下<rt>くだ</rt></ruby>したのですか?

He's in command of NATO forces.
その<ruby>人<rt>ひと</rt></ruby>はNATO<ruby>軍<rt>ぐん</rt></ruby>を<ruby>指揮<rt>しき</rt></ruby>している。

He no longer commands the army.
<ruby>彼<rt>かれ</rt></ruby>はもはや<ruby>軍隊<rt>ぐんたい</rt></ruby>の<ruby>支配権<rt>しはいけん</rt></ruby>を<ruby>握<rt>にぎ</rt></ruby>っていない。

have a command of (language etc.) <ruby>駆使<rt>くし</rt></ruby>できる

commander *n.* (officer in charge) <ruby>指揮官<rt>しきかん</rt></ruby>, <ruby>部隊長<rt>ぶたいちょう</rt></ruby>, (in U.S. Navy) <ruby>中佐<rt>ちゅうさ</rt></ruby>

♦**commander in chief** *n.* <ruby>司令長官<rt>しれいちょうかん</rt></ruby>

commandment *n.* おきて, <ruby>戒律<rt>かいりつ</rt></ruby>

the Ten Commandments
(モーゼの)<ruby>十戒<rt>じっかい</rt></ruby>

commando *n.* <ruby>特殊部隊<rt>とくしゅぶたい</rt></ruby>の<ruby>隊員<rt>たいいん</rt></ruby>

commemorate *v.* <ruby>記念<rt>きねん</rt></ruby>する

commemoration *n.* <ruby>記念<rt>きねん</rt></ruby>

in commemoration of …を<ruby>記念<rt>きねん</rt></ruby>して

In commemoration of the 100th anniversary... 100<ruby>周年<rt>しゅうねん</rt></ruby>を<ruby>記念<rt>きねん</rt></ruby>して...

commemorative *adj.* <ruby>記念<rt>きねん</rt></ruby>の

commence *v.* (begin) <ruby>開始<rt>かいし</rt></ruby>する, ((formal)) <ruby>着手<rt>ちゃくしゅ</rt></ruby>する

commend *v.* (praise) ほめる

commendable *adj.* <ruby>立派<rt>りっぱ</rt></ruby>な, <ruby>感心<rt>かんしん</rt></ruby>な

comment *n.* コメント, <ruby>解説<rt>かいせつ</rt></ruby>, <ruby>批評<rt>ひひょう</rt></ruby>
v. <ruby>言<rt>い</rt></ruby>う, ((formal)) <ruby>批評<rt>ひひょう</rt></ruby>する

Did he make a comment?
<ruby>彼<rt>かれ</rt></ruby>はコメントしましたか?

He commented on your sharp appearance.
あなたのことをおしゃれだって<ruby>言<rt>い</rt></ruby>ってたよ。

no comment ノーコメント

The president said, "No comment."
<ruby>大統領<rt>だいとうりょう</rt></ruby>は「ノーコメント」と<ruby>言<rt>い</rt></ruby>った。

commentary *n.* <ruby>解説<rt>かいせつ</rt></ruby>

commentator *n.* <ruby>解説者<rt>かいせつしゃ</rt></ruby>, コメンテーター

commerce *n.* <ruby>商業<rt>しょうぎょう</rt></ruby>, <ruby>貿易<rt>ぼうえき</rt></ruby>

the Department of Commerce <ruby>商務省<rt>しょうむしょう</rt></ruby>

commercial *adj.* (pertaining to trade, business) 商業の, 商業上の, (of product, art) 営利的な, (of TV, radio) 民放の *n.* (advertisement) コマーシャル, ＣＭ

Sadly for individuals, commercial interests often override basic human rights.
個々の人間にとっては悲しいことですが、商業上の利益が、基本的人権よりも優先されることが、しばしばあります。

commercialism *n.* 商業主義, もうけ主義

commercialized *adj.* 商業化された

commiserate *v.* (commiserate with) (…に) 同情する

commission *n.* (fee) 手数料, 歩合, コミッション; (committee) 委員会 *v.* (**commission to do**) (…に) …するよう依頼する

commit *v.* (crime) 犯す; (**commit oneself to doing**: pledge to do) …することを約束する, (**commit oneself to**: devote oneself to) …に専念する

Ninety-five percent of all violent crimes are committed by men.
暴力犯罪の ９５ パーセントは男性が犯している [加害者だ]。

It's rumored that he committed suicide.
彼は自殺したと、うわさされている。

I am totally committed to this job.
私はこの仕事に専念しています [かかりっきりです]。

They've been going out for a long time, but she's been hesitant to commit herself to the idea of getting married.
二人は長い間交際しているが、いざ結婚となると、彼女は決心がつかずにいる。

commitment *n.* (obligation) 義務, (responsibility) 責任, (promise) 約束

I'm sorry. I have a prior commitment.
ごめんなさい。先約がありますので。

committee *n.* 委員会

commodity *n.* (article) 商品, 品物

common *adj.* (often found or experienced) よくある, よく見られる, ありふれた, (ordinary) 並の, 一般の, (shared by all) 共通の, 共同の

That kind of flower is very common in these parts.
あの花は、このあたりではよく見られる。

the common people 一般大衆

a common language 共通の言語

This dormitory has a common bathroom.
この寮には共同のトイレがある。

have in common with …と共通点がある

What do we have in common with them?
彼らとどんな共通点があるのだろう？

commonly *adv.* (often) よく, (usually, generally) 一般に

commonplace *adj.* ありふれた, 平凡な

common sense *n.* 常識, 良識

What one may think is common knowledge or common sense varies from one country to another.
人が共通の知識や常識と思っている事柄も、国によって異なります。

communal *adj.* 共同の

commune *n.* コミューン

communicate *v.* (talk) 話をする, (convey) 伝える, ((*formal*)) 伝達する, (keep in touch) 連絡を取り合っている

Do you communicate at all these days?

最近、話をしてる？

I can't communicate what I'm trying to say.

言いたいことをうまく伝えられません。

Ants have a unique way of communicating.

アリには、特有の伝達手段がある。

We tried to communicate, but neither of us could understand each other's language.

コミュニケーションを図ろうとしたけれど、互いに相手の言語がわからなかった。

They communicate by e-mail.

彼らはメールで連絡を取り合っています。

communication ***n.*** (exchange of ideas, information etc.) コミュニケーション, 伝達, 通信, (**communications**: media such as telephone etc.) 通信機関

There has been a revolution in communications in the last decade.

この10年で、通信機関に大変革が起きた。

be in communication with …と連絡を取り合っている

communicative ***adj.*** (of person) 話し好きの, (of communication) コミュニケーションの

communion ***n.*** 聖さん, (**Communion**: religious ceremony) 聖さん式

communiqué ***n.*** コミュニケ, 公式声明

communism ***n.*** (doctrine) 共産主義, (system) 共産主義体制

communist ***n.*** 共産主義者

adj. 共産主義の

♦**Communist Party** ***n.*** 共産党

community ***n.*** (people living in one place) 共同体, 共同社会, (district) 地域(社会), (town, village) 市町村, (society) 社会

Urban centers often lack the community feeling of smaller rural villages and towns.

都心には、地方の小さな村や町に見られる共同体らしさが欠けていることが多い。

What a friendly community this is.

ここは、なんて友好的な地域なんだろう。

♦**community center** ***n.*** コミュニティーセンター

community college ***n.*** コミュニティーカレッジ, 地域短期大学

community service ***n.*** 地域奉仕, 社会奉仕

commute ***v.*** (go) 通う, 行く, (to work) 通勤する, (to school) 通学する

How long does it take you to commute to work?

通勤時間はどれくらいですか？

I seem to spend a good part of the day commuting rather than working.

1日のうち、かなりの時間を、仕事ではなく通勤に費やしているような気がします。

♦**commuting** ***n.*** (to work) 通勤, (to school) 通学

commuter ***n.*** 通勤者

♦**commuter ticket** ***n.*** 定期券

compact ***adj.*** (of car, camera) 小型の, (of house) こぢんまりした

n. (cosmetic case) コンパクト

compact disc ***n.*** ＣＤ

companion ***n.*** 仲間, 連れ

companionship ***n.*** (お)付き合い, 交際

C

company *n.*

1 BUSINESS: 会社, 企業, (stock company) 株式会社, (limited company) 有限会社; (theater company) 劇団

2 COMPANIONSHIP: いっしょにいること, (お)付き合い, 交際, (guests, visitors) 客, ((*polite*)) お客さん, (companions) 仲間

1 What sort of company is it?
どういった会社ですか？

Is the company listed on the stock market?
その会社は(株式取引所に)上場していますか？

Did you say he works for a multinational company?
彼は多国籍企業に勤務していると、おっしゃいましたか？

2 I'm expecting company today.
今日はお客さんが来るんです。

keep sb company …のお付き合いをする, …に同行する

I'll keep you company.
お付き合いしましょう。

part company with (leave) …と別れる, (disagree) …と意見が違う

♦**company car** *n.* 会社の車, ((*formal*)) 社用車

company housing *n.* 社宅

comparable *adj.* (can be compared) (…と) 比較できる, (**be comparable to**: be equivalent to) (…に) 匹敵する, (…と) 同等だ

comparative *adj.* (relative) 比較による, 比較の

n. (in grammar: "-er," "more") 比較級

[NOTE: There is no comparative form in Japanese. → next page]

comparatively *adv.* (relatively) わりあい, 比較的, ((*informal*)) わりと

compare *v.* 比べる, 比較する, (bear comparison) 比べられる, (**not compare**: not rival) 比べものにならない

It's interesting to compare the two countries.
両国を比べてみると面白い。

He doesn't begin to compare with the great musicians.
彼は、偉大な音楽家にはとても及ばない [とは比べものにならない]。

compared to/with …と/に比べれば, …と/に比較すると, (in proportion to) …のわりに

Compared to him, I'm hopeless at golf.
彼と比べれば、僕のゴルフなんて話にならないですよ。

It's cheap compared with most shops.
ほかの店と比較すると、安い。

Her legs are long compared with the rest of her body.
あの人は体のわりに足が長い。

comparison *n.* 比較, 比べること

Just for the sake of comparison, look at this suitcase.
ちょっと比較のために、このスーツケースを見てよ。

in comparison with …と比べると

In comparison with Masao, Akira's a genius!
正男と比べると、明は天才だ！

there is no comparison (between…) (…は) 比較にならない, 比べものにな

MAKING COMPARISONS

There is no comparative form for adjectives in Japanese. "A is more ... than B" can be expressed with either AのほうがBより followed by an adjective, or B よりAのほうが followed by an adjective.

Russia is bigger than the United States.
ロシアのほうがアメリカより広い/アメリカよりロシアのほうが広い。

To ask the question, "Which/What is more..., A or B?" use the pattern AとBと どちら(のほう)が followed by an adjective and ですか.

a) Which is more expensive, this TV or that one?
このテレビとそのテレビと、どちら(のほう)が高いですか？

b) Which is quicker, going by bus or going by train?
バスで行くのと電車で行くのと、どちら(のほう)が速いですか？

NOTE: The particle の after the verb 行く in (*b*) turns the verb into a noun analogous to "going."

There is no superlative form for Japanese adjectives, either. "The most ..." can be expressed in a variety of ways but usually by the adverb 一番 (or, more formally, 最も) followed by an adjective.

a) This is the smallest. これが一番小さい。

b) Aiko is the most skilled among them. みんなの中で愛子さんが一番上手です。

c) Who is fastest? 一番速いのは誰ですか？

NOTE: The particle の in (*c*) turns the adjective 速い into a noun.

To say, "A is as ... as B," use AはBと同じくらい followed by an adjective. [→ AS 3].

He's as smart as his brother. 彼はお兄さんと同じくらい頭がいい。

Finally, to state that "A is not as ... as B," use the form AはBほど followed by an adjective in the negative form.

a) I'm not as tall as he is. 私は彼ほど背が高くない。

b) It's not that bad. それほど悪くないですよ。

NOTE: The topic marked by は can be omitted, as in (*b*), when it is understood from context.

らない

There's no comparison between the two teams.

両チームは比べものになりません。

compartment *n.* (storage space) 区画, 仕切った部分, (in plane: overhead compartment) 荷物入れ; (room in train) コンパートメント

compass *n.* (magnetic) 羅針盤, コンパス, (for drawing circles) コンパス

compassion *n.* 哀れみ, 情け

compatible *adj.* (of people) 気が合う, (of ideas) 両立できる, (of computers, hardware) 互換性がある

Their marriage ended in divorce because they weren't compatible.

二人は結局、気が合わずに離婚した。

compel *v.* (**compel to do**) (…に) 強制的に…させる, (**be compelled to do**) …せざるを得ない, (**feel compelled to do**) …せずにはいられない

compensate *v.* (victim) (…に) 補償する, 弁償する, (compensate for: emotional loss) (…に) 償う, 埋め合わせをする, (shortcoming) 補う

The victims had to wait a long time before they were compensated for the loss of their livelihood and health.

犠牲者は奪われた生計と健康への補償を受けるのに、長い間待たされた。

Nothing could compensate for the loss of her child.

子供を失った悲しみを彼女は、どんなことでも埋め合わせることができなかった。

His hard work more than compensated for his lack of talent.

猛烈な働きぶりは、彼の才能のなさを補って余りあった。

compensation *n.* (money) 賠償金, 補償金, 慰謝料, (consolation) 埋め合わせ, 償い, 慰め

compete *v.* 競争する, 競い合う, ((*formal*)) 競合する, (compete with/against: have as an opponent) (…と) 対戦する, (compete in: athletic event) (…に) 出場する

Our company is competing in domestic and international markets.

当社は、国内市場でも国際市場でも競い合っています。

They are going to compete in the Olympics.

彼らはオリンピックに出場します。

competence *n.* (ability) 能力, 適性

competent *adj.* 有能な, (**be competent to do**) …する能力がある

competition *n.* (rivalry) 競争, (match) 試合, (contest) 競技会, (golf competition) コンペ, (art/music contest) コンクール; (competitor) 競争相手

The competition is intense.

競争が激しい。

You can win a car in this competition.

この競技会に勝てば、車がもらえます。

There's no competition. It'll be easy.

競争相手がいないから、楽勝ですよ。

competitive *adj.* 競争の, (of person) 競争心の強い, 勝ち気な, (of situation) 競争の激しい

a competitive edge/advantage

競争での優位

Admission into that university is competitive.

その大学への入学は競争が激しい。

competitor ***n.*** (person, company) 競争相手, ライバル; (participant) 参加者

compile ***v.*** (data) まとめる, (book) 編集する, (dictionary) 編さんする

compiler ***n.*** (of book) 編集者, (of dictionary) 編さん者; (computer program) コンパイラー

complacency ***n.*** 自己満足, 独りよがり

complacent ***adj.*** 自己満足の, 独りよがりの

You can't afford to be complacent about safety at nuclear power stations.
原子力発電所の安全性については、自己満足している場合じゃない。

complain ***v.*** 不平を言う, (ぐちを)こぼす, (grumble) ぶつぶつ文句を言う, (protest, petition, sue) 訴える, 苦情を言う

If we hadn't complained, nothing would have been done about the problem.
私たちが不平を言わなかったら、その問題は野放しになっていたでしょうね。

Quit complaining!
ぶつぶつ文句を言うのはやめなさい!

It's no good complaining. They never do anything.
苦情を言ってもむだだ。彼らは何一つやらないんだから。

We complained to the police about the noise.
我々はその騒音について警察に訴えた。

complaint ***n.*** (dissatisfaction) 不平, 不満, 文句, 苦情, (criticism) 非難, (protest) 訴え, 告発, 抗議

My only complaint is that...
唯一の不満は...です。

We filed a complaint with the police.
私たちは警察に訴えました。

There were complaints from the neighbors.
近所の人から抗議があった。

complement ***n.*** (thing that completes another) 補うもの, (in grammar) 補語 ***v.*** 補う, 補足する, (go with) (...と) 合う

complete

1 ***adj.*** **UTTER:** 全くの, 完全な, 徹底した

2 ***adj.*** **FINISHED:** 完成した, 完了した, 終わった

3 ***adj.*** **ENTIRE:** 全部の, 全部そろった, (**a complete set of...**) ...一式, ...一そろえ

4 ***v.*** **FINISH:** 終える, 仕上げる, 完成する, 完成させる

5 ***v.*** **COMPLETE A SET/COLLECTION:** 完成する, 完成させる, 全部そろえる

6 ***v.*** **FILL IN:** (...に) 記入する, 書き込む

1 It's complete nonsense.
全くの、たわごとですよ。

He made a complete fool of himself.
彼は全くばかなこと[ドジ]をしでかした。

It was a complete success.
文句なしの大成功だった。

2 Is this sculpture complete?
この彫刻は完成していますか?

You can watch TV when your homework is complete.
宿題が終わったらテレビを見ていいよ。

3 You can buy the complete works of Shakespeare for a small amount.
シェークスピア全集なら安く買えるよ。

4 I completed the jigsaw puzzle.
ジグソーパズルを完成させた。

Have you completed the course yet?

もう講座は修了されたのですか？

5 I've just completed my collection of stamps.
ちょうど切手のコレクションが完成したところです。

6 Please complete this form, then hand it in at that window on the far left.
この用紙に記入して、左奥の窓口に提出してください。

completely *adv.* 完全に, 全く, すっかり
The building is completely ruined.
建物は完全に破壊されている。

completion *n.* 完成, 完了
bring to completion 完成させる

complex *adj.* (complicated) 複雑な, 難しい
n. (psychological) コンプレックス; (industrial) コンビナート
a complex equation 複雑な方程式
He has a complex about his height.
彼は身長のことでコンプレックスをもっています。
a petrochemical complex
石油化学コンビナート

complexion *n.* 顔色

complexity *n.* 複雑さ

compliance *n.* 従うこと, 服従

compliant *adj.* 従順な

complicate *v.* 複雑にする, 難しくする

complicated *adj.* 複雑な, 込み入った

complication *n.* (problem) 問題, (condition) 複雑な状態, 紛糾

compliment *n.* ほめ言葉
v. ほめる
One has to be able to distinguish between compliment and flattery.
ほめ言葉とお世辞の違いが見分けられるようでなければならない。
He complimented me on how I handled the situation.
彼は事態への私の対応をほめてくれた。

complimentary *adj.* (free) 無料の
a complimentary ticket 無料招待券

comply *v.* (comply with) (…に) 従う

component *n.* (part) 部品, 構成部分, (constituent element) 要素
Look at these tiny electrical components.
このちっちゃな電子部品を見てごらんよ。

compose *v.* (**be composed of**) …からできている, …で構成されている, …から成り立っている; (write) 書く, 作る, (music) 作曲する; (**compose oneself**) 気を落ち着ける
What kind of elements is this substance composed of?
この物質は、どんな元素からできているんですか？
The committee is composed of a team of economic experts.
委員会は、経済の専門家たちで構成されています。
a piece composed by Bach バッハの作品

KANJI BRIDGE

作 ON: さく, さ KUN: つく(る) | MAKE, COMPOSE

act of composing (music)	作曲
composer	作曲家
composition, essay	作文
crops	作物
lyricist	作詞家
work (of art)	作品
writer	作家

composer *n.* 作曲家

composition *n.* (general makeup) 構成; (essay) 作文, (musical composition) 曲, (work of art/literature) 作品, (chemical composition) 構成成分

compost *n.* 堆肥

composure *n.* 落ち着き, 平静

keep [lose] one's composure
落ち着きを保つ [失う]

compound *n.* (chemical) 合成物, 化合物

compound interest *n.* 複利

comprehend *v.* 理解する, わかる

I can't comprehend these equations.
この方程式が理解できない。

comprehension *n.* (ability to understand) 理解力, (of particular subject) 理解, (knowledge) 知識

comprehensive *adj.* (broad in scope) 広範囲の

compress *v.* (air, data) 圧縮する

compressor *n.* コンプレッサー, 圧縮機

comprise *v.* (consist of) (…から) 成る, (include) 含む

compromise *n.* 妥協, 歩み寄り

v. (settle differences) 妥協する, 歩み寄る, (budge) 譲歩する

a compromise plan 妥協案

A compromise seems the only answer.
妥協するしか手がなさそうです。

Can't we compromise over this?
この点は歩み寄れないでしょうか？

compulsive *adj.* (of liar, thief) 病的な

compulsory *adj.* (obligatory) 義務的な, (required by law) 強制的な

Education is compulsory up to 15.
15歳までは義務教育です。

compute *v.* (calculate) 計算する

computer *n.* コンピューター, (PC) ((*informal*)) パソコン

Computers have had an enormous effect upon our work.
コンピューターは、私たちの仕事に非常に大きな影響を及ぼしている。

♦ **computer graphics** *n.* コンピューター・グラフィックス, ＣＧ

computer programmer *n.* コンピューター・プログラマー

computer programming *n.* コンピューター・プログラミング

comrade *n.* (friend) 仲間, (like-minded person) 同志

con[1] *n.* (argument against) 反対論 [→ PRO[1]]

con[2] *v.* (cheat, deceive) だます, (**con into doing**) だまして…させる, (con A out of B) (Aを)だまして(Bを)巻き上げる

concave *adj.* 凹形の, くぼんだ

a concave lens 凹レンズ

conceal *v.* 隠す [→ HIDE[1]]

concede *v.* 認める [→ ADMIT 2]

concede defeat 敗北を認める

conceit *n.* うぬぼれ

conceited *adj.* (arrogant) うぬぼれた, うぬぼれの強い

She's very conceited about her looks.
あの人は自分の容姿がいいと、うぬぼれている。

conceivable *adj.* (possible) ありうる, (thinkable) 考えられる

C

conceive *v.* (think up) 考えつく, (imagine) 想像する; (**conceive a child**) 子を宿す, (become pregnant) 妊娠する

concentrate *v.* (focus) 集中する, (on problem) (…に) 専念する, (**be concentrated**: in location) (…に) 集中している, 密集している

If you want to get it right, you're going to have to concentrate.
当てたかったら、まずは気持ちを集中させなきゃ。

Do you mind keeping your voices down? I'm trying to concentrate.
声を落としていただけませんか? 集中しようとしているので。

I think it would be wise for you to concentrate your energies on the task before you.
目の前の仕事に専念するほうが賢明だと思いますよ。

Most of the industry is concentrated near the coast.
産業は、ほとんど沿岸に集中しています。

concentrated *adj.* (of juice) 濃縮した

concentration *n.* (focusing of thought/attention) 集中, 専念, (ability to focus) 集中力; (of substance) 濃度

lose one's concentration
集中力を失う

concept *n.* (idea) 概念, コンセプト, (thought) 考え

conception *n.* (birth) 妊娠; (idea) 概念

concern

1 *v.* HAVE TO DO WITH: (…に) 関係がある, 関係する, かかわる

2 *n.* INTEREST: 関心, (worry) 心配, 不安, ((*formal*)) 懸念

3 *v.* WORRY: 心配させる

4 *v.* TAKE AN INTEREST IN: (**concern oneself with/about**) …に関係している, …に関心をもつ

5 *n.* RESPONSIBILITY: 責任

1 I don't think this concerns you.
これはあなたに関係のないことだと思います。

It's a problem that concerns all of us.
私たち全員にかかわる問題だ。

2 There's a great deal of concern among the public regarding food safety.
食物の安全性については、世間の関心は非常に高い。

Our main concern is just getting there on time.
一番心配なのは、時間どおりに到着できるかどうかです。

The official statement said there was no cause for concern.
公式声明は、懸念する理由は何もないとしていた。

3 The problem really concerns me.
その問題はとても心配しています。

It concerns me that you have no appetite.
(あなたに)食欲がないのが心配です。

4 Young people ought to concern themselves with the current political debate.
若い人たちは、今行われている政治論争に関心をもつべきです。

5 That's the local education board's concern, not ours.
それは私たちではなく、地元の教育委員会が対処すべき問題です。

to whom it may concern 関係者の方へ

concerned *adj.* (worried) 心配する, 気にかける, (involved) かかわる, 関係する

She didn't seem to be the least bit concerned that her children were playing so near to a busy street.
車の多い通りのすぐそばで子供たちが遊んでいるのに、母親は全く気にかけていないようだった。

all those concerned 関係者全員

as far as ... is concerned ...に関する限り

It never happened, as far as we're concerned.
私たちに関する限り、それは起こらなかった。

concerning *prep.* (regarding) ...について, ...に関して, (used at the beginning of a sentence in formal writing) ...については, ...の件ですが

concert *n.* コンサート, 音楽会, 演奏会

It was a marvelous concert.
すばらしいコンサートでした。

♦ **concert hall** *n.* 音楽堂, コンサートホール

concerted *adj.* 共同の

a concerted effort 協力

concerto *n.* 協奏曲, コンチェルト

concession *n.* (compromise) 譲歩, (admission) 許容; (discount) 割引

concise *adj.* 簡潔な

conclude *v.* (deduce) (...という) 結論に達する, (...と) 判断する; (bring to an end) 終える, (wrap up) 締めくくる, (end) 終わる, 終了する [→ END 3, FINISH 1]

After calling several times and receiving no answer, I concluded he was out.
何回か電話をして出なかったので、留守だと判断した。

How do you think we ought to conclude this evening's entertainment?
どういうふうに、今晩の接待を締めくくるべきだと思いますか？

The conference concluded without a hitch.
会議は滞りなく終わりました。

conclusion *n.* 結論, (decision) 決定; (end of story) 結末

reach a conclusion
結論に達する

conclusive *adj.* 決定的な

conclusive evidence 決定的な証拠

concoct *v.* (make) 作る, (story, excuse) でっち上げる

concoct an excuse 口実をでっち上げる

concrete *n.* (material) コンクリート

adj. (definite) 具体的な, 実際の

It's made of concrete and steel.
コンクリートと鋼鉄でできています。

There is no concrete evidence to support that claim.
あの主張を裏付ける具体的な証拠はありません。

Could you offer some concrete examples?
具体的な例を出していただけませんか？

concussion *n.* 脳しんとう

have a concussion
脳しんとうを起こす

condemn *v.* (criticize) 非難する; (in court: condemn A for B) (Bの罪でAに) 有罪の判決を下す

condensation *n.* (formation of water droplets on windows) 結露, (water droplets) 水滴; (changing of gas to liquid)

液化, 凝縮

condense *v.* (shorten: text) 簡約する, 要約する; (convert to liquid) 液化する, (of gas) 凝縮する

In this experiment, the gas condenses into a liquid.
この実験では、気体が凝縮して液体になります。

condescend *v.* 見下す

condition *n.*

1 STATE: (of health) 具合, 調子, 状態, (athlete's) コンディション, (of patient) 容体, (of building) 状態

2 STIPULATION: 条件, 状況

1 be in good [bad] condition
調子がいい [悪い]

The doctor says you're in no condition to go to work.
君は到底、仕事に出られるような状態じゃないと医者が言ってるんだよ。

"Tell me, Doctor, how would you describe his condition?"
"I would say he's in stable condition."
「先生、正直なところ、彼の容体はどうなんでしょう?」
「安定していると思いますよ」

What's the condition of the building?
建物の状態はどうですか？

The car was in good condition when we rented it.
借りた時は、車の状態は良好でした。

2 There's no such condition in the contract.
契約にそんな条件はありません。

under no condition (**should one do**)
どんなことがあっても(...してはいけない)

Remember, under no condition should you get in a stranger's car.
いいこと、どんなときでも絶対、知らない人の車に乗ってはいけないよ。

conditional *adj.* (having a condition attached) 条件付きの

n. (conditional clause) 条件節, (conditional word) 仮定語句

♦ **conditional form** *n.* (in Japanese grammar: "ba form") ば形, 仮定形

conditioner *n.* (hair conditioner) リンス, ヘアコンディショナー

condolence *n.* お悔やみ

a letter of condolence お悔やみ状

Please accept my condolences.
ご愁傷さまでした。

condom *n.* コンドーム

condominium *n.* 分譲マンション

condone *v.* (deem acceptable) 容赦する, 許す, (tolerate) 大目に見る

condor *n.* コンドル

conduct

1 *v.* CARRY OUT: 行う

2 *v.* BEHAVE: (**conduct oneself**) ふるまう

3 *n.* BEHAVIOR: (actions) 行動, 行為, 行い, ふるまい

4 *n.* MANAGEMENT: 管理, 運営, (carrying out) 実施

5 *v.* ORCHESTRA: 指揮する

6 *v.* HEAT/ELECTRICITY: 伝える, 伝導する

1 The government is conducting a number of surveys on education.
政府は、教育に関するいくつかの調査を行っている。

conduct business 事業を行う

2 He conducted himself as a gentleman would.
彼は、紳士らしくふるまった。

3 His conduct at school and at home is terrible.
あの子の行動は学校でも家でもひどい。

4 There's going to be an independent investigation into the conduct of this campaign.
このキャンペーンの実施については、独自の調査が行われます。

5 Who was conducting the orchestra?
(オーケストラの) 指揮者は誰でした？

6 Copper conducts heat.
銅は熱を伝える。

conductor ***n.*** (of orchestra) 指揮者, (of train) 車掌; (of electricity) 伝導体

cone ***n.*** (shape) 円錐形, (edible, for ice cream) コーン

confectionery ***n.*** (sweets) 菓子類

confederation ***n.*** (alliance) 同盟, (federation of states) 連邦

confer ***v.*** (confer with) (…と) 相談する, 打ち合わせる; (give) 授与する

conference ***n.*** (meeting, convention) 会議, (**news conference**) 記者会見

in conference 会議中で

confess ***v.*** (admit) 認める, (secret) 打ち明ける, 告白する, (bad deed) 白状する, (criminal guilt) 自白する

The boy confessed to having played truant.
少年は学校をずる休みしたと白状した。

The suspect has confessed to the crime.
容疑者は犯行を自白した。

I must confess 実を言うと, 正直なところ

Well, I must confess: I have a soft spot for chocolates.
実を言うと、チョコレートが大好きです。

confession ***n.*** (admission of guilt) 白状, (religious) 告白, (criminal) 自白

confetti ***n.*** 紙吹雪

confide ***v.*** (confide in/to) (…に) 打ち明ける

confidence ***n.*** (in oneself) 自信, (in sb else: trust) 信頼

Do you have the confidence to get up on stage and do this?
舞台に上がって、これをやる自信がありますか？

You shouldn't have betrayed her confidence.
彼女の信頼を裏切るべきじゃなかったんだよ。

in confidence 内々で/に, ((*informal*)) 内緒で

That was told to you in confidence.
あれは内々で君に伝えられたことだ。

confident ***adj.*** (assured) 自信のある, しっかりした, 自信をもっている

She's a very confident young lady.
とてもしっかりしたお嬢さんですよ。

Are you confident of winning the match?
試合に勝つ自信はありますか？

confidential ***adj.*** 極秘の, 内々の

confine ***v.*** (**confine oneself to doing**) …するにとどめる, …するだけにする, (confine to a room) (…に) 閉じ込める, (**confine oneself** to a room) (…に) 閉じこもる

confined ***adj.*** (of space: narrow) 狭い

confinement ***n.*** (imprisonment) 監禁

solitary confinement 独房監禁

confirm *v.* (reservation) 確認する, 確かめる, (suspicion, belief) 裏付ける

I'd like to confirm my reservation.
予約を確認したいんですが。

Unfortunately, my doubts were confirmed—the man is not to be trusted.
残念ながら、その男を信用してはいけないという私の疑いは裏付けられた。

confirmation *n.* (ascertainment) 確認; (religious ceremony) 堅信礼

confiscate *v.* (goods) 没収する, (as police evidence) 押収する

conflagration *n.* 大火事

conflict *n.* (battle) 争い, 戦い, 紛争, (of interests, opinions) 衝突, 対立, 食い違い, (of smaller group against established order) 闘争

v. (be at odds) 対立する, 矛盾する

an ethnic conflict 民族紛争

He appears to thrive on conflict.
彼は争いを生きがいにしているようだ。

We had a conflict of views, so we talked it over.
意見の食い違いがあったので、それについて話し合った。

♦**conflicting** *adj.* (contradictory) 矛盾する, (of interests) 対立する

conform *v.* (to rules) (…に) 従う

conformity *n.* (obedience) 服従, (sameness) 同一, 一致

confront *v.* (face: situation) (…に) 立ち向かう, 直面する, (confront sb) (…と) 対決する, (confront A with B) (AにBを) 突き付ける, (confront A about B) (AにBのことを) 問い詰める

Did you confront him about it?
そのことを彼に問い詰めたんですか？

confrontation *n.* (confronting) 直面, (being at odds) 対決, (arguing) 争い

He doesn't like confrontation.
彼は、人と争うのが好きじゃないんだ。

Confucianism *n.* 儒教

Confucius *n.* 孔子

confuse *v.* (cause to be confused) 混乱させる, (complicate) ややこしくする, (mistake) 混同する, 間違える

Don't confuse him.
彼を混乱させないで。

Don't confuse the issue by talking about what's already past.
もう済んだことの話をして、問題をややこしくしないで。

I'm sorry, I think you must be confusing me with someone else.
失礼ですが、どなたかと混同なさっているようです。

confused *adj.* 混乱している, 頭がこんがらがっている

Could you explain that again? I'm confused.
もう一度説明していただけますか？ 頭がこんがらがってしまいました。

Don't be confused by what you see.
見た目に惑わされてはいけない。

confusing *adj.* わかりにくい, 紛らわしい

confusion *n.* 混乱, 混同

In the confusion, I forgot my camera.
混乱の中で、カメラを忘れた。

be thrown into confusion 混乱に陥る

congested *adj.* (of roads) 混んでいる,

(of nose) 詰まった

congestion ***n.*** (of roads) 混雑; (of nose) 鼻詰まり

conglomerate ***n.*** (business) 複合企業, コングロマリット

congratulate ***v.*** 祝う, (...に) お祝いを言う

My friends threw a party to congratulate me on my engagement.
婚約を祝って、友達がパーティーを開いてくれた。

Mr. Ikeda congratulated Tom with a slap on the back.
池田さんは、よくやったねとトムの背中をポンとたたいた。

congratulations ***interj.*** おめでとう(ございます)

n. (congratulatory words) お祝いの言葉

Congratulations on passing the exam.
合格おめでとう。

congregate ***v.*** 集合する

congregation ***n.*** (religious) 集会

congress ***n.*** (**Congress**: law-making body in the U.S.) 議会

♦**congressperson** ***n.*** (国会)議員

conifer ***n.*** (needle pine) 針葉樹

conjugate ***v.*** (cause to inflect) 活用させる, (of verb) 活用する

♦**conjugation** ***n.*** 活用, 変化

conjunction ***n.*** (conjoining) 結合; (part of speech) 接続詞

in conjunction with ...と合わせて, ...と共同して

These rules should be read in conjunction with the brochure.
これらの規則は、パンフレットと合わせて読んでください。

con man ***n.*** ぺてん師, 詐欺師

connect ***v.*** つなぐ, 結び付ける, (machine to machine, computer to Internet) 接続する, (associate) 連想する, (**be connected with**: be associated with) ...と関係がある

The new bridge connected the main land with the island.
新しい橋が本土と島をつないだ。

After a long wait, my call was finally connected.
長い間待たされて、ようやく電話はつながった。

Are they connected with this project in any way?
彼らは、このプロジェクトと何か関係があるんですか?

connected ***adj.*** (linked) 関連した, (socially connected) コネのある, 人脈をもっている, (of machine) 接続している

Are these two events connected?
この二つの出来事は関連しているのですか?

Mr. Suzuki is well connected.
鈴木さんは強力な人脈をもっている。

connection ***n.*** (relationship) 関係, つながり, (correlation) 関連, (**connections**: personal contacts) コネ, 人脈, (electrical contact) 接触, (linkage to Internet) 接続, (to airplane) 乗り換え

Does his disappearance have any connection with that religious sect?
彼の失踪は、例の宗派と関係があるんですか?

There's absolutely no connection between these two issues.

この二つの問題には、全く何の関連もありません。

He has a number of connections in high places.
あの人は地位の高い人にたくさんのコネがある。

It's not working because of a loose connection in the plug.
動かないのは、プラグの接触不良のせいです。

I missed my connection to New York.
ニューヨーク行きに乗り換えそこなった。

in connection with …に関して, …をめぐって, …とのからみで

The police would like to interview her in connection with the accident.
警察は、その事故とのからみで、彼女から事情を聴取したがっている。

connoisseur ***n.*** 鑑定家, 目利き, ((*informal*)) 通

be a connoisseur of …に目が利く, …通だ

conquer ***v.*** (enemy) 征服する, (fear, doubts) 克服する, (…に) 打ち勝つ

♦**conqueror** ***n.*** 征服者, 勝利者

conquest ***n.*** (of country) 征服

conscience ***n.*** 良心, 分別, 誠意

have a guilty [clear] conscience
心にやましいところがある [ない]

conscientious ***adj.*** (sincere) 誠実な, (serious-minded) 真面目な, (hardworking) 勤勉な

conscious ***adj.*** 意識がある, (after concussion) 意識を取り戻している, (aware) 気づいている, 意識している

The patient is now fully conscious.
患者は、完全に意識を取り戻しています。

I was conscious of his presence in the room.
彼が部屋にいることに気づいていました。

consciously ***adv.*** (with awareness) 意識して, (deliberately) わざと

consciousness ***n.*** 意識

lose [regain] consciousness
意識を失う [取り戻す]

conscript ***n.*** 徴集兵

v. 徴兵する

conscription ***n.*** 徴兵

consecutive ***adj.*** -連続

three consecutive days 3日連続

He made his fourth consecutive win.
彼は4連勝を達成した。

consensus ***n.*** (of opinion) (意見の) 一致, 合意, コンセンサス

reach a consensus 合意に達する

build a consensus
コンセンサスを得る

consent ***v.*** (**consent to / to do**) …に/…することに賛成する, ((*formal/written*)) 同意する

n. (approval) 同意, 承諾

with sb's consent (…の) 同意を得て

consequence ***n.*** (result) 結果; (importance) 重要性

You know the consequences.
結果は [どういうことになるか] わかってるでしょ。

a person of consequence 重要人物

in consequence of …の結果として

consequent ***adj.*** (…の) 結果として起こる

consequently ***adv.*** したがって, その結果

conservation ***n.*** (of environment, cultural asset) 保護, (of artifact) 保存

energy conservation 省エネ

Because of their natural beauty, these woods have become a conservation area.
この森は、その自然の美しさから保護地区になりました。

conservationist ***n.*** 自然保護論者

conservative ***adj.*** (cautious, moderate) 保守的な; (be conservative about: amount etc.) 控える, (of guess) 控えめな, (of fashion) 地味な, スタンダードな; (of Conservative Party) 保守党の ***n.*** (person with conservative views) 保守的な人, (**Conservative**: member of political party) 保守党員

Ichiro's taste in clothes is very conservative.
一郎は、服の趣味がとても地味だね。

♦ **Conservative Party** ***n.*** 保守党

conservatory ***n.*** (greenhouse) 温室; (music school) 音楽学校

conserve ***v.*** (environment) 守る, 保護する, (energy) 節約する

consider ***v.*** (regard) 考える, (think) (…と) 思う, (think carefully about) 考慮する, (judge) 判断する

Which do you consider to be the best option?
どの選択肢がベストだとお考えですか?

I didn't consider it rude to tell him so.
彼にそう伝えることが失礼になるとは、思いませんでした。

considerable ***adj.*** かなりの, 相当な [→ GREAT, LARGE]

have a considerable advantage (over) (…より) かなり優位に立っている

♦ **considerably** ***adv.*** かなり, ずいぶん

considerate ***adj.*** (thoughtful) 思いやりのある, (be considerate) 気が利く

consideration ***n.*** (careful thought) 考慮, (deliberation) 検討; (thoughtfulness toward others) 思いやり, 気配り, 配慮

The whole matter is presently under consideration.
すべての事柄を現在、検討中です。

She shows a great deal of consideration to others.
彼女は人に対して、とても思いやりがある。

in consideration of …を考慮して, ((*formal*)) …にかんがみて

In consideration of your years of good service, the company would like to present this gold watch to you.
((*formal*)) 長年の功労にかんがみて、社より、この金時計を贈呈いたします。

considering ***prep.*** …のわりには, …を考えれば

Considering he's only recently arrived in Japan, his Japanese is pretty good.
日本に来てから日が浅いわりには、あの人はなかなか日本語が上手ですね。

consist ***v.*** (consist of) (…から) 成る

The course consists of both practical and theoretical units.
この講座は、理論の時間と実践の時間の両方から成っています。

consistency ***n.*** (uniformity) 統一, 一貫性, (of liquid) 濃度, 粘り

consistent ***adj.*** (uniform) 統一した, 一

貫した, 首尾一貫した, (not contradictory) 矛盾のない

Good theories are consistent. This one isn't.

すぐれた理論というのは首尾一貫しているものだ。これはそうじゃない。

Sakurai has been a consistent opponent of reform.

桜井さんは一貫して改革に反対してきた人です。

You're not being consistent.

あなたの言っていることは矛盾しています。

♦ **consistently** *adv.* (uniformly) 一貫して, (always) 絶えず

consolation *n.* 慰め

be a consolation to ...の慰めとなる

♦ **consolation prize** *n.* 残念賞

console[1] *v.* (comfort) 慰める

I tried to console her, but it was to no avail.

彼女を慰めようとしましたが、全くむだでした。

console[2] *n.* (piece of furniture) コンソール, 操作台, (game console) ゲーム機

consolidate *v.* (one's position) 固める, 強化する, (companies) 統合する, (of companies: merge) 合併する

consommé *n.* コンソメ(スープ)

consonant *n.* 子音

conspicuous *adj.* 目立つ, 人目につきやすい

His bright red hair and beard make him very conspicuous.

その人は真っ赤な髪とひげで、とても目立ちます。

conspiracy *n.* 陰謀

♦ **conspiracy theory** *n.* 陰謀説

conspire *v.* 陰謀を企てる, たくらむ, (conspire with) (...と) 共謀する

constant *adj.* (unchanging) 一定の, いつもの, (incessant) 絶え間ない

The world is in a constant process of change.

世界は常に [いつも] 変化し続けている。

The temperature must remain constant.

温度は一定に保たないといけません。

She's been a constant friend over the years.

彼女とは、ずっと変わらず友達付き合いをしてきました。

The constant noise from the construction is a distraction.

工事の騒音が絶え間なくするので、気が散る。

constantly *adv.* 常に, 絶えず

constellation *n.* 星座, (in names of constellations) -座

constipated *adj.* 便秘している

constipation *n.* 便秘

constituency *n.* (area for which sb is elected) 選挙区

constitute *v.* (be) ...である, ...となる, (comprise) 構成する

constitution *n.* (**the Constitution**) 憲法; (of the body) 体質, (of things) 構成

constitutional *adj.* 憲法の, (allowed by the Constitution) 憲法で認められた

a constitutional right

憲法で認められた権利

constrain *v.* (repress) 抑える, 制限する, (**feel constrained to do**) ...せざるを得

ない

As foreigners, our movements were constrained by strict rules.
外国人である私たちは、厳しい規則で行動を制限された。

I felt constrained to tell the truth.
本当のことを言わざるを得なかった。

constraint ***n.*** (restriction) 制限

Muslim law places many constraints on behavior.
イスラム法は多くの行動を制限している。

construct ***v.*** (make) 造る, (build: building) 建設する, (put together) 組み立てる [→ BUILD 1]

construction ***n.*** (act of building) 建設, 建造, (construction work) 工事

Construction of this building begins tomorrow.
このビルの建設は、明日始まります。

The road is under construction, and this is causing traffic delays.
道路が工事中のため、渋滞が起きている。

constructive ***adj.*** (of comment) 建設的な

constructive criticism 建設的な批評

consul ***n.*** 領事

consulate ***n.*** 領事館

consult ***v.*** (speak with) (...に) 相談する, (seek advice from) (...に) 助言を求める, (doctor) (...に) 診察してもらう, 診てもらう, (dictionary) 引く, (book) 調べる

You'd better consult a doctor.
医者に診てもらったほうがいいよ。

consultant ***n.*** コンサルタント, 相談員

a financial consultant 財務コンサルタント

consultation ***n.*** 相談, 協議

seek consultation
相談に乗ってもらう

consume ***v.*** 消費する, 使い果たす, (food) 食べ尽くす, 平らげる

It's the industrialized nations that consume most of the world's resources.
世界の資源の大半を消費しているのは工業先進国です。

It looks as if you've consumed the entire cake.
ケーキを全部平らげてしまったようだね。

consumer ***n.*** 消費者

consumerism ***n.*** (activity) 消費(活動), (belief) 消費至上主義

consumption ***n.*** 消費

♦**consumption tax** ***n.*** 消費税

contact ***v.*** (get in touch with) (...に) 連絡する, (...と) 連絡を取る

n. (**contacts**: personal connections) コネ, つて, 縁故; (interaction) 付き合い, 交際, (physical/electrical contact) 接触

How can I contact Mr. Kikuchi?
どうしたら菊池さんに連絡が取れますか?

a useful contact 役に立つコネ

He has many contacts in the government.
彼は官庁につてがたくさんある。

be in contact with ...と連絡を取っている

They are in contact with each other.
二人は互いに連絡を取り合っています。

lose contact with ...と接触がなくなる, 付き合いがなくなる

We lost contact with them several years

ago.
もう何年か前に、あの人たちとは付き合いがなくなりました。

contact lens ***n.*** コンタクトレンズ

contagious ***adj.*** (of disease, laughter) 移りやすい, (of disease) 伝染性の, (of person with disease) 伝染病にかかっている

a contagious disease 伝染病

contain ***v.***

1 INCLUDE: 含む, (…が) 入っている

2 RESTRAIN: (emotion) 抑える, こらえる, (**contain oneself**) 自制する, 落ち着く

3 KEEP UNDER CONTROL: (disease, fire) (…の) 広がりを抑える

1 These sweets contain a lot of additives.
このお菓子は多くの添加物を含んでいる。

What does the box contain?
その箱には何が入っているんですか？

That book contains wonderful pictures of the Himalayas.
その本には、ヒマラヤ山脈のすばらしい写真が載っています。

2 I could not contain my laughter.
笑いをこらえることができなかった。

If you could just contain yourself for a minute, I'll explain what's happened.
少しの間落ち着いてくれたら、何があったのか話すよ。

3 The disease could not be contained.
その病気の広がりは抑えられなかった。

container ***n.*** (holder) 入れ物, 容器, (large box for transporting goods) コンテナ

The container broke and the goods were damaged.
コンテナが壊れて、品物が損傷した。

♦**container ship** ***n.*** コンテナ船

contaminate ***v.*** (pollute) 汚染する

contemplate ***v.*** じっくり(と)考える, 熟慮する, (**contemplate doing**) …しようと思う

contemporary ***adj.*** 現代の [→ MODERN]
n. (person of the same generation) 同世代の人, 同時代の人間

a contemporary author 現代作家

contemporary architecture 現代建築

Marlowe was a contemporary of Shakespeare.
マーローは、シェークスピアと同時代の人間だ。

contempt ***n.*** (scorn, disdain) 軽蔑, (**contempt of court**) 法廷侮辱罪

I can only feel contempt for these ignorant racists.
こういう無知な人種差別主義者には、軽蔑しか感じない。

contemptible ***adj.*** (hateful) 卑劣な

contemptuous ***adj.*** (of attitude) 軽蔑的な, (of gesture) ばかにしたような

contend ***v.*** (maintain) 強く言う, 主張する [→ COMPETE, FIGHT]

contender ***n.*** (in competition) 選手

content[1] ***adj.*** (satisfied) 満足している, (**be content to do**) 喜んで…する

They seem very content together.
二人はお互いにとても満足しているように見えます。

He is not content unless he's working.
彼は仕事をしていないと気がすまない。

It's all right. I'm quite content to stay at home.
大丈夫。喜んで留守番するよ。

♦ **contented** ***adj.*** 満足した, 満足そうな

contentment ***n.*** 満足

content[2] ***n.*** (of book, packet) 内容, 中身, (of speech, book: purport) 趣旨, (**contents**: table of contents) 目次

the bottle's contents びんの中身

The report had no content whatsoever.
その報告書は、全く内容がなかった。

contest ***n.*** (match) 試合, (speech, fashion) コンテスト, (art, music) コンクール; (social struggle) 争い

v. (object to) (…に) 異議を唱える

This is a contest of wills.
これはがまん比べですね。

The contest is about who can answer the questions fastest.
これは解答の速さを競うコンテストです。

Who won the contest?
コンテストで、誰が勝ちましたか？

contestant ***n.*** 出場者

context ***n.*** (of text) 文脈, 前後関係, (background setting) 背景, 状況

Let's look at the context and see if we can figure out what it means.
文脈を見て、意味がわかるかみてみよう。

The prime minister's remark was quoted out of context.
首相の発言は、前後の文脈を無視して引用された。

I think we should try to understand these problems in context.
これらの問題は、背景も含めて理解すべきだと思います。

continent ***n.*** (land mass) 大陸, (**the Continent**: Europe) ヨーロッパ大陸

continental ***adj.*** (of continent) 大陸の, (of Europe) ヨーロッパ大陸の

continual ***adj.*** (repetitive) 繰り返しの, (nonstop) 連続的な, (incessant) 絶え間ない

continually ***adv.*** (without a break) 絶え間なく, (frequently) 頻繁に, (always) 絶えず

continuation ***n.*** 継続

continue ***v.*** (of person: **continue to do**) …し続ける, (of event, process, situation, thing) 続く, 継続する

I'd like you to continue to work here.
あなたには、ここで引き続き働いていただきたい。

The fine weather is likely to continue over the next week.
この好天は来週いっぱい、続きそうです。

Until when is this work due to continue?
この仕事は、いつまで継続する予定ですか？

continued ***adj.*** 続いている, 連続的な

to be continued つづく

continuity ***n.*** 連続性

continuous ***adj.*** (incessant) 絶え間ない, (uninterrupted) 途切れのない, (of process) 連続的な

contort ***v.*** (body) ゆがめる, ねじ曲げる

contour ***n.*** (outline) 輪郭; (line on map) 等高線

contraband ***n.*** 禁制品, 密輸品

contraception ***n.*** 避妊

contraceptive ***adj.*** 避妊の

n. (device) 避妊用具

♦ **contraceptive pill** ***n.*** 避妊薬, ピル

contract

C

1 *n.* **BINDING AGREEMENT:** 契約, (document) 契約書

2 *v.* **BECOME SMALLER:** 縮まる, 収縮する

3 *v.* **AGREE UPON FORMALLY:** (contract with) (…と) 契約する, (**be contracted to do**) 請け負う

4 *v.* **CATCH:** (disease) (病気に) かかる, (virus) (ウイルスに) 感染する

5 *v.* **SHORTEN:** (word) 短縮する, 縮める

1 My contract expires in June.
契約は6月に切れます。

I've signed a contract stating that I'll work for them for a minimum of two years.
最低2年間は働くという契約書に署名した。

2 The metal has contracted.
その金属は収縮した。

3 We're contracted to do the plumbing work, not the construction.
うちが請け負ったのは配管工事であって、建築工事ではありません。

4 He contracted the virus in Hong Kong.
彼は香港でウイルスに感染した。

5 *Apartment* is contracted to *apāto* in Japanese.
"Apartment"は、日本語では「アパート」と短縮される。

contraction *n.* (of word) 短縮

contractor *n.* (building contractor) 建築業者, 請負人

contradict *v.* (deny) 否定する, (be inconsistent) (…と) 矛盾する

contradiction *n.* 否定, 矛盾

That's a contradiction.
それは矛盾している。

contralto *n.* (voice) コントラルト, アルト, (singer) アルト歌手

contrary *adj.* (opposite, opposing) 反対の, 逆の

n. (**the contrary**) 逆

Mrs. Nakano alone expressed a contrary view.
中野さんだけは、皆と逆の意見を述べた。

To our surprise, the contrary proved true.
驚いたことに、逆だったんだ。

contrary to …に反して, …と逆に

Contrary to popular belief, Japanese is not such a difficult language.
一般に考えられているのとは逆に、日本語はそんなに難しい言語ではない。

on the contrary それどころか, とんでもない

"You won't enjoy it."
"On the contrary, I think we will."
「あなたたちには面白くないでしょう」
「とんでもない。楽しめると思います」

contrast *n.* (comparison) 対照, (person/thing) 対照的な人/もの, (difference) 違い, 相違, (of picture, TV screen) コントラスト

v. 対照する, 比べる

What a contrast to his older brother!
お兄さんと、なんて対照的なんだろう!

Put the two together so we can contrast them.
二つを並べて、比べてみよう。

in contrast to …とは大違いで, …と対照的に

Well, it's true the weather's not perfect, but in contrast to last week's storms, it's an improvement.

まあ確かにすばらしい天気じゃありませんが、先週の雨風とは大違いで、まだましですよ。

contribute *v.* (donate) 寄付する, (offer) 提供する, (to cause) 貢献する, (article to journal/newspaper) 投稿する, 寄稿する, (to discussion) 参加する; (be a contributing factor) 一因となる

All of these companies contribute to local charities.
これらの会社はすべて、地元の慈善団体に寄付しています。

If everyone could contribute something—not just money, but time or ideas—it would help a great deal.
みなさん一人一人が何か——お金だけじゃなく、時間やアイデアを——ご提供いただければ、大いに助かります。

She contributes articles to an arts magazine.
彼女は芸術雑誌に寄稿している。

Carelessness contributed to the accident.
不注意が事故の一因となった。

contribution *n.* (of money) 寄付金, (to campaign, cause) 貢献

contrive *v.* (devise) 工夫する, (scheme) たくらむ, 企てる, (**contrive to do**) どうにか…する

control

1 *n.* POWER: 支配, 管理, (ability to direct) 支配力, (authority to direct) 支配権, (authority to manage) 経営権 [→ COMMAND]

2 *v.* KEEP IN CHECK: 支配する, 管理する, (emotion) 抑制する, 抑える, コントロールする, (**control oneself**) 自分を抑える, 自制する; (disease, fire: control the spread of) (…の) 広がりを防ぐ

3 *n.* LIMITATION/REGULATION: (also **controls**) 制限, (by government) 統制, (of traffic) 規制, (of emotion) 抑制

4 *v.* MANIPULATE: (machine) 操作する, 制御する

5 *n.* MANIPULATION: (of machine) 制御, 操作

6 *n.* CONTROL PANEL/SYSTEM: (**controls**) 制御装置, (=seat) 操縦席

7 *n.* BUTTON ON A KEYBOARD: コントロールキー

8 *n.* IN EXPERIMENT: 対照

1 Who's in control here?
ここを管理しているのは誰ですか？

Their control is growing weaker.
彼らの支配力は弱まりつつある。

The army has seized control of the country.
軍隊が国の支配権を掌握した。

The brothers bought control of the company.
その兄弟が、会社の経営権を買いました。

The enemy has gained control of a vital highway.
敵は、主要幹線道路を手中に収めた。

2 The police had a lot of trouble controlling the crowd.
警察は群衆を抑えるのに手を焼いた。

He managed to control his anger.
彼はどうにか怒りを抑えた。

Some people are more used to showing their feelings. Others control them in public.
自分の感情をすんなり出せる人もいれば、人前では感情を抑える人もいます。

Eventually the medical team was able to control the disease.
しばらくして、医療班はその病気の広がりを防ぐことに成功した。

3 birth control 産児制限

The citizens were under wartime control at the time.
当時、国民は戦時統制下にあった。

We need some controls in place to check the flow of traffic.
交通の流れを制限するために、何らかの規制措置が必要だ。

4 Who's supposed to control this machine?
この機械は誰が操作することになっているのですか？

5 He quickly regained control of the car once it started to skid.
車がスリップしかけたが、彼は素早く車を制御した。

remote control 遠隔操作

6 No one was at the controls.
誰も操縦席にいなかった。

be out of control 制御しきれない, 手に負えない

His parents don't know what to do with him. He's out of control.
ご両親は息子さんをどうしていいかわからないんだ。手に負えなくなっている。

be under control (be progressing well) うまくいっている, (be under one's control) (...の) 管理下にある

It's OK. Everything's under control.
大丈夫。万事うまくいっています。

Look, none of this is under my control. I can't do anything about it.
だから、これは僕が管理していることじゃないんだ。どうしようもできないよ。

controller *n.* (of accounts) 会計検査官, 監査役

controversial *adj.* 論議を呼ぶ, 物議をかもす

a controversial new book
物議をかもす新刊本

controversy *n.* 論争, 議論

The decision to cut bonus payments created quite a controversy.
賞与の支給額を引き下げる決定は、大論争を引き起こした。

convalesce *v.* (recuperate) (健康を) 回復する, 快方に向かう

convalescence *n.* (recuperation) (健康) 回復, (period) (健康) 回復期

convene *v.* (assemble) 招集する

convenience *n.* (convenient thing) 便利な物, (convenient time) 都合のいい時

at your earliest convenience
ご都合がつき次第

♦ **convenience store** *n.* コンビニ

convenient *adj.* (suitable) 便利な, 都合のいい, 適当な

When would be a convenient time to meet?
お会いするのは、いつがご都合よろしいですか？

It's a convenient spot. It's close to the stores.
便利な場所なんです。商店街は近いし。

conveniently *adv.* 便利に, 都合よく

convention *n.* (custom) 習慣, 慣例, しきたり, (accepted practice) 約束事; (conference) 大会, 会議

conventional *adj.* (of opinion) 型にはまった, 月並みな, (of method, machine)

従来の, 伝統的な, (of weapon) 通常の

converge *v.* (...に) 集まる, 集中する

conversation *n.* 会話, 雑談, 談話

They were in the middle of a conversation, so I didn't interrupt.
彼らは話をしていたので、じゃまするのはやめた。

conversely *adv.* 逆に言えば

conversion *n.* (of religion) 改宗 ; (of money) 両替

convert *v.* (change) 変える, (room etc. for a different use) 改造する; (convert to: accept as a new faith) (...に) 改宗する
n. (person) 改宗者

Can you convert Celsius to Fahrenheit?
摂氏を華氏に換算できますか？

convertible *n.* (car) コンバーチブル, オープンカー
adj. (changeable) 変えられる

a convertible bed ソファーベッド

convex *adj.* 凸の

a convex lens 凸レンズ

convey *v.* (communicate) 伝える, (deliver) 運ぶ

Please convey my condolences to the family.
お悔やみ申し上げますと、どうぞご遺族にお伝えください。

conveyor belt *n.* ベルトコンベヤー

convict *v.* (declare guilty) (...に) 有罪の判決を下す, 有罪を宣告する
n. (guilty person) 罪人, (person serving time) 受刑者, 服役囚

He was convicted of first degree murder.
彼は第一級殺人で有罪を宣告された。

conviction *n.* (for crime) 有罪判決; (belief) 信念

convince *v.* 納得させる, 確信させる, (**be convinced that...**) ...と確信している

You have to convince them that our product is better.
うちの製品のほうがいいということを、彼らに納得させるんだよ。

What do I have to do to convince you that I didn't do it?
どうしたら、やっていないということをわかってもらえますか？

convincing *adj.* 納得のいく, 説得力のある

a convincing argument
説得力のある議論

convoy *n.* (of ships) 護送船団

cook *v.* (cook food) 料理する, (cook a meal) (料理を)作る, (**cook for oneself**) 自炊する, (boil) 煮込む, (rice) 炊く
n. (person who cooks) 料理する人, (at restaurant) コック(さん), 料理人, (at Japanese restaurant) 板前(さん), (licenced cook) 調理師

Who's going to cook dinner tonight?
今日は、夕食は誰が作るの？

It's not much fun cooking for yourself.
自炊するのは味気ないでしょう。

Let it cook for at least twenty minutes.
２０分以上煮込んでください。

Try cooking it on low heat.
弱火でコトコト煮込んでみたら？

He wants to be a cook.
彼は料理人になりたいんです。

She's a fantastic cook.
彼女は料理がすごくうまい。

EXPRESSIONS USED IN COOKING

bake a cake ケーキを焼く

barbecue a steak ステーキを焼く

boil an egg 卵をゆでる

broil 焼く, あぶる

cook rice ご飯を炊く

deep-fry 油で揚げる

grill/broil a fish 魚を焼く

steam dumplings 団子を蒸す

stir-fry vegetables 野菜をいためる

cookbook ***n.*** 料理の本

cooker ***n.*** (gas burner) ガス台

cookery ***n.*** 料理法

cookie ***n.*** クッキー

cooking ***n.*** 料理

cooking utensils ***n.*** 調理器具 [→ picture below]

cool

1 ***adj.*** **NEARER COLD THAN HOT:** (of weather, clothes) 涼しい, (of drink) 冷たい

2 ***adj.*** **OF PERSON/ATTITUDE:** (unfriendly) 冷たい, 無愛想な, そっけない, (calm) 落ち着いた, (cool-headed) 冷静な

3 ***v.*** **BECOME COLDER:** (also **cool down**) (of weather) 涼しくなる, (of water) 冷たくなる, (of beverage in refrigerator) 冷える, (of cooked meal) 冷める

4 ***v.*** **CHILL:** (beverage) 冷やす, (cooked food) 冷ます

5 ***adj.*** **COOL-LOOKING:** かっこいい

1 It's much cooler today than it was yesterday.
今日は昨日よりずっと涼しい。

It's going to be hot, so you'd better wear something cool.
暑くなるから、涼しい格好をしたほうがいいよ。

a fresh, cool orange juice
絞りたての冷たいオレンジジュース

2 It was not a warm welcome. In fact, it

was a cool reception we got.
私たちが受けたのはあたたかい歓迎ではなく、むしろ、そっけないものだった。

Stay cool. Things will work out.
落ち着いて。何とかなるよ。

3 According to the papers, it's going to cool down in the next few days.
新聞によると、あと何日かで涼しくなるようだ。

4 Cool the beer in ice water.
氷水につけて、ビールを冷やしなさい。

5 Those are cool sunglasses.
かっこいいサングラスですね。

keep one's cool 冷静さを保つ

play it cool 冷静にふるまう

cool down *v.* (of hot thing: food etc.) 冷める, (calm down) 落ち着く, (after exercise) クールダウンする

---

co-op *n.* (profit-sharing retailer) 生協, (housing co-op) 住宅協同組合

cooperate *v.* 協力する, 協同する

If they would only cooperate, there would be no need for all this bother.
彼らが協力さえしてくれれば、こういう面倒なことはしないですむのに。

cooperation *n.* 協力

get somebody's cooperation
(...の) 協力を得る

cooperative *adj.* 協力的な

n. → CO-OP

a cooperative effort 協力

coordinate *v.* (organize) コーディネートする, 調整する, (cause to work in harmony) 協調させる, (clothes: coordinate A with B) (AをBと) 組み合わせる, コーディネートする

n. (**coordinates**) (on map) 位置, (on graph) 座標

Our job was to plan and coordinate the exhibition.
展示会の企画を練り、コーディネートするのが、我々の仕事だった。

I'd like you to coordinate closely with Ms. Katayama on this project.
このプロジェクトに関しては、片山さんと緊密に連携を取っていただきたい。

After the accident, he couldn't coordinate his hand and eye movements.
事故にあってから、彼は手と目をうまく協調させることができなかった。

coordination *n.* (management) コーディネート, 調整, (of muscles) 協調

coordinator *n.* コーディネーター, まとめ役

cop *n.* (police officer) おまわり, 警官

cope *v.* (manage) うまくこなす, 処理する, (cope with: endure) (...に) 対処する

He couldn't cope by himself.
彼は一人では処理できなかった。

Do you think you can cope with all this work?
こんなに大量の仕事をすべてこなせると思いますか?

She just couldn't cope with the stress.
彼女はそのストレスにどうにも対処できなかった。

copilot *n.* 副操縦士

copper *n.* (metal) 銅

copula *n.* (linking verb) 連結動詞, (in Japanese grammar) 断定の助動詞

copy

1 *n.* DUPLICATE: コピー, 写し, 複写

2 ***n.*** **SINGLE ISSUE:** (of book, magazine) -冊, -部, (of newspaper) -部

3 ***v.*** **REPRODUCE:** (by hand) 書き写す, (by photocopier, computer) コピーする, (counterfeit) 偽造する

4 ***v.*** **IMITATE:** (…の) まねをする, ((*formal*)) 模倣する

5 ***n.*** **COUNTERFEIT/IMITATION:** 偽物, (of picture, painting) 複製, 模写

6 ***n.*** **SOURCE FOR A STORY:** ネタ, 新聞種

7 ***n.*** **TEXT FOR AN ADVERTISEMENT:** コピー

1 Could I have a copy of the letter?
手紙の写しをいただけますか？

You ought to keep copies of important documents.
大事な書類はコピーを取っておくほうがいいよ。

2 Do you have a copy of Soseki's *Botchan*?
漱石の『坊っちゃん』をお持ちですか？

That book has sold over a million copies.
その本は100万部以上売れている。

3 Would you copy this into the notebook?
これをノートに書き写してくれる？

It's a criminal act to copy money.
貨幣を偽造するのは犯罪行為です。

4 Quit copying me!
僕のまねをするのはやめろ！

5 It was a copy, not the real thing.
偽物で、本物ではなかった。

copyright ***n.*** 著作権, 版権

copywriter ***n.*** コピーライター

coral ***n.*** サンゴ

♦**coral reef** ***n.*** サンゴ礁

cord ***n.*** (rope) ひも, 綱, (electrical cord) コード

♦**cordless** ***adj.*** (of electrical appliance) コードレスの

cordon ***v.*** (**cordon off**: streets) (…に)非常線を張る, (…を)封鎖する

corduroy ***n.*** (fabric) コーデュロイ, コール天, (**corduroys**) コーデュロイのズボン

core ***n.*** (of fruit) しん; (of organization) 中枢, (of problem) 核心

coriander ***n.*** コリアンダー

cork ***n.*** (for bottle) コルクの栓, (material) コルク

corkscrew ***n.*** コルク抜き [→ picture of COOKING UTENSILS]

cormorant ***n.*** ウ, 鵜

corn[1] ***n.*** (food)トウモロコシ, (crop) 穀物

♦**corn on the cob** ***n.*** 軸付きトウモロコシ

corn[2] ***n.*** (on foot) たこ, 魚の目

cornea ***n.*** 角膜

corner ***n.*** (of object, street) 角, (inside room/box) 隅

v. (trap) 追い詰める

cornerstone ***n.*** (of success) 土台, 基礎, (of building) 隅石, 礎石

cornet ***n.*** (musical instrument) コルネット

cornflakes ***n.*** コーンフレーク

corny ***adj.*** ありきたりの, くだらない

coronation ***n.*** (ceremony) 戴冠式

coroner ***n.*** 検死官

corporal ***n.*** (in U.S. Army/Marine Corps) 伍長

corporal punishment ***n.*** 体罰

corporate ***adj.*** (of corporation) 法人の, 企業の

corporation ***n.*** (stock company) 株式会社, (limited company) 有限会社

corpse ***n.*** 死体

corpuscle ***n.*** (blood cell) 血球

corral ***n.*** (cattle corral) さく, 囲い

correct ***adj.*** 正しい, (accurate) 正確な
v. (mark errors in) 直す, 訂正する, 修正する, (exam) 採点する

That's not the correct answer.
それは正解ではありません。

"The train arrives at 7:30?"
"That's correct."
「電車は7時30分に到着するんですね?」
「そうです」

If I'm correct, he's pretty high up in the company.
私の記憶が正しければ、あの人は会社の幹部のはずです。

Would you correct my mistakes?
私の間違いを直していただけますか？

It's going to take hours to correct all these exams.
これだけの答案を採点するには何時間もかかります。

correct me if I'm wrong, but... 間違っていたら直していただきたいんですが...

correction ***n.*** 訂正, 修正

correctly ***adv.*** ちゃんと, 正確に, 正しく

Did you answer all the questions correctly?
すべての質問に正確に答えましたか？

correspond ***v.*** (exchange letters) 手紙のやり取りをする, 文通する; (correspond to: match) (...と) 合う, 一致する, (...に) 相当する

They've been corresponding with each other for over twenty years.
二人は、かれこれ20年以上も文通しています。

The findings don't correspond.
調査結果が一致しません。

correspondence ***n.*** (communication by letter etc.) 文通, (letters) 手紙, 書簡; (equivalence) 一致

correspondent ***n.*** (journalist) 記者, 特派員; (letter writer) 手紙を書く人

a lazy correspondent 筆無精な人

corresponding ***adj.*** (...に) 対応する, 相当する, (same) (...と) 同じ

What was the figure for the corresponding month last year?
昨年同月の数値はどうだった？

corridor ***n.*** 廊下, (in train, airplane) 通路

corrode ***v.*** (of metal) 腐食する, (cause to corrode) 腐食させる

corrupt ***adj.*** (dishonest) 不正な, 腐敗した, (easily bribed) わいろのきく

a corrupt government official
汚職公務員

corruption ***n.*** 腐敗, (illegal activity) 汚職, (bribery) 贈収賄

corset ***n.*** コルセット

cosmetic ***n.*** (**cosmetics**) 化粧品
adj. 化粧の

♦ **cosmetic surgery** ***n.*** 美容整形

cosmic ***adj.*** 宇宙の

cosmopolitan ***adj.*** (of city) 国際的な, (of person) 国際感覚のある

cosmos ***n.*** (**the cosmos**: the universe) 宇宙; (flower) コスモス

cost ***n.*** (price) 値段, 価格, (expense) 費用, 経費, -費, コスト

C

v. (require: money, time, effort) (…が)かかる, (cause to lose) 失わせる

The cost of a loaf of bread has gone up.
パン1斤の値段が上がった。

What was the total cost?
費用は全部でどのくらいでした？

We need to cut costs.
経費を削減する必要がある。

the cost of living 生活費

"How much did it cost?"
"Not much."
「いくらでした/いくらかかりました？」
「大した額ではありませんでした」

It cost a lot of time and effort to build that boat.
あのボートを造るには、たくさんの時間と労力がかかりました。

That house must have cost them a fortune.
あの家は相当お金がかかったに違いない。

That stupid remark cost him his job.
あんなばかなことを言ったばかりに、彼は職を失った。

The strain of their relationship cost him many sleepless nights.
二人の関係に伴う心労から、彼は何日も眠れない夜を過ごした。

at all costs どんなことがあっても

A nuclear war needs to be avoided at all costs.
核戦争は、どんなことがあっても回避しなくてはなりません。

costar *n.* 共演スター

v. (costar with) (…と) 共演する

costly *adj.* (expensive) お金のかかる, 高価な, (involving big sacrifice) 犠牲の大きい, 手痛い

a costly mistake
手痛い間違い

costume *n.* 服装, 衣装, コスチューム

cottage *n.* コテージ

cottage cheese *n.* カテージチーズ

cotton *n.* (material) 木綿, コットン, (thread) 木綿糸

♦**cotton candy** *n.* 綿菓子, 綿あめ

cotton swab *n.* 綿棒 [→ picture of FIRST-AID KIT]

cotton wool *n.* (raw cotton) 原綿, (absorbent cotton) 脱脂綿 [→ picture of FIRST-AID KIT]

couch *n.* ソファー, カウチ

cougar *n.* クーガ, アメリカライオン

cough *n.* せき, (to attract sb's attention) せき払い

v. (こんこん)せきをする, (to attract sb's attention) せき払いをする

That's a nasty cough you've got.
たちの悪いせきですね。

Is your cough better?
せきは、よくなりましたか？

You're not coughing as badly as you were yesterday.
昨日ほど、ひどくせきは出ませんね。

could *aux.*

1 PAST TENSE OF "CAN": …ことができた, <potential form of verb, past> [→ CAN[1]]

2 ASKING A FAVOR: (**could you…?**) …してくださいませんか, お + <-ますstem> + いただけませんか

3 ASKING FOR STH/ASKING PERMISSION: (**could**

I have…?) いただけますか, (**could I…?**) …して(も)いいでしょうか, …して(も)かまいませんか

4 MIGHT: …かもしれない [→ MAY, MIGHT[1]]

1 I couldn't get there on time.
時間どおりに着くことができなかった。

He could speak Chinese when he was a child, but he can't anymore.
彼は子供のころは中国語が話せたが、今は話せない。

I could climb Mt. Fuji a few years ago, but not now.
数年前なら富士山に登れましたが、今はもう無理です。

2 Could you open the window, please?
窓をあけてくださいませんか？

Could you wait here for a moment, please?
ここでしばらくお待ちいただけますか？

3 Could I have a glass of water?
水を１杯いただけますか？

Could I use your bathroom?
お手洗いをお借りしていいでしょうか？

4 He could be in Russia for all I know.
ひょっとすると、彼はロシアにいるかもしれないよ。

You could have left your glasses in the car.
めがねは、車の中に忘れたのかもしれませんね。

"Why isn't Naoki here?"
"Could be that he's not well."
「どうして直樹は来てないの？」
「調子がよくないのかも」

council *n.* (assembly) 協議会, (meeting) 会議, (council members) 議員

a city [town, county] council
市 [町, 郡] 議会

councilor *n.* 議員

counsel *n.* (advice) 助言, 忠告, (lawyer) (法廷) 弁護士, (team of lawyers) 弁護団

counseling *n.* カウンセリング

counselor *n.* (psychotherapist) カウンセラー, (camp counselor) キャンプの指導員

C

count[1]

1 *v.* **ADD UP:** 数える

2 *n.* **TOTAL NUMBER:** 数, 総数

3 *v.* **BE IMPORTANT:** 大切だ, 重要だ

4 *v.* **QUALIFY:** (count as) (…と) みなされる, (count for) (…に) 値する

5 *v.* **INCLUDE:** 数に入れる, 勘定に入れる

6 *v.* **CONSIDER:** (…と) みなす, 思う

7 *n.* **ACT OF COUNTING:** 数えること

8 *n.* **IN BOXING:** カウント

1 Let's count how many chairs we need.
椅子が何脚要るか、数えてみよう。

The child can already count up to a hundred.
あの子はもう、100まで数えられるよ。

When are you going to count the money?
そのお金はいつ数えるんですか？

2 The official count of unemployed has at last gone down.
公式発表の失業者数が、やっと減少した。

a high cholesterol count
高いコレステロール値

3 Every minute counts.
１秒１秒が大切です。

What really counts here is commitment.
ここで重要なのは、全力で取り組む姿勢です。

4 No, that doesn't count as a point.
いいえ、今のは得点とみなされません。

Attendance will count for 5% of your final grade.
出席は最終成績の5 ％ に値する。

5 Count me in!
私も入れて！

You can count me out!
私を勘定に入れなくていいよ。

6 Naturally, he counted himself as one of the elite.
もちろん、彼は自分をエリートだと思っていた。

7 (do) a head count 人数(を数える)

keep count (of) (...の)数を覚えている

It's difficult to keep count of all the comings and goings here.
ここを出入りした人の数を、すべて覚えているのは大変なことだ。

lose count (of) 数えきれなくなる

I've lost count of how many times I've told you not to leave the door open.
ドアをあけっぱなしにしないでと、もう何度言ったか、数えきれないよ。

count on *v.* (rely on) 当てにする [→ RELY ON]

I was counting on you, but you didn't come.
当てにしてたのに、来てくれなかったね。

You can count on me being there.
必ず行くから大丈夫よ。

count out *v.* (cash) 数え上げる; (**count out loud**) 声に出して数える [→ COUNT[1] 5, LEAVE OUT]

The cashier counted out the change.
レジ係がおつりを数え上げた。

---

count[2] *n.* (nobleman) 伯爵

Count Dracula ドラキュラ伯爵

countdown *n.* 秒読み, カウントダウン

counter[1] *v.* (oppose) (...に) 対抗する, 逆らう

adj., adv. 反対の/に

The hike in interest rates was intended to counter inflation.
利率の引き上げは、インフレへの対抗措置だった。

counter[2] *n.* (long narrow table at bar/café) カウンター

counter[3] *n.* (machine) 計算器, カウンター; (in Japanese grammar) 助数詞 [→ p. 1168]

counter- *pref.* 反対-, 反-, 逆-

a counterexample 反例

counteract *v.* (weaken the influence/effect of) (...の)影響/効果を弱める, (of medicine) 中和する, 消す

counterattack *n.* 反撃, 切り返し

counterclockwise *adv.* 左回りに

counterfeit *n.* 偽物

adj. 偽の, 偽りの

v. 偽造する

countermeasure *n.* 対抗策, 対策

counterpart *n.* (equivalent person/thing) (...に) 対応する人/物

counterproductive *adj.* 逆効果を招く, 逆効果の

countess *n.* (noblewoman) 伯爵夫人

countless *adj.* 数えきれない, 無数の

country *n.* (nation) 国, 国家, (=motherland) 母国, (=fatherland) 祖国, (countryside) 田舎, 地方 [→ COUNTRY MUSIC]

This country needs a strong leader.
この国には強い指導者が必要です。

Which do you prefer, the country or the city?
田舎と都会と、どちらが好きですか？

This is prime country for skiing.
ここはスキーには最適の地方です。

country music *n.* カントリーミュージック

countryside *n.* 田舎, 地方

county *n.* (in U.S.) -郡, (in U.K.) -州

coup *n.* (coup d'état) クーデター, (great success) 大成功

couple *n.* (two) 二つ, (two people) 二人, (married couple) 夫婦, (boyfriend and girlfriend) カップル; (a few: two or three) 2、3

I need a couple more nails.
釘がもう2本、要るな。

What a nice couple!
なんてすてきなご夫婦でしょう!

Are they a couple?
あの二人はカップルなの [付き合ってるの]？

We had a couple of drinks and then left.
2、3杯飲んでから出ました。

They left a couple of hours ago.
彼らは2、3時間前に帰りましたよ。

coupon *n.* (voucher) クーポン, 割引券

a coupon book
クーポンの冊子

a free-drink coupon
飲み物の無料サービス券

courage *n.* 勇気, 度胸 [→ BRAVE]

It took a lot of courage to do that.
やるのに、かなり勇気が要りました。

I would never have had the courage to do that.
私には、とてもそんなことをする度胸はなかったでしょうね。

courageous *adj.* 勇敢な, 勇気のある

a courageous deed
勇気ある行動

courier *n.* (messenger) 特使, (mail) 速達

course *n.*

1 ROUTE: 進路, コース, 方向, (of ship) 針路, (of river) 水路, 道筋, (running track) コース, 走路

2 OF EVENTS: (way in which things develop) 流れ, 成り行き

3 OF STUDY: 課程, コース

4 OF MEAL: 料理

5 OF TREATMENT: クール

6 COURSE OF ACTION: 行動方針, やり方, 対策

1 We've gone off course.
コース [進路] をそれてしまった。

The ship took a course due north.
船は北に針路を取った。

2 It's arguable that he changed the course of history.
彼が歴史の流れを変えたという意見には、議論の余地がある。

3 Eri is enrolling in a doctoral course this spring.
絵里さんはこの春、博士課程に進みます。

4 What's the next course?
次の料理は何ですか？

5 A course of antibiotics was prescribed.
1クール分の抗生物質が処方された。

6 I personally wouldn't advise such a course.
私個人としては、そんなやり方はお勧めできません。

a matter of course 当然のこと

She accepted the outcome as a matter of course.
その結果を、彼女は当然のこととして受け入れた。

in the course of time 時がたつうちに, やがて

In the course of time, they got used to life in Japan.
時がたつうちに、彼らは日本での生活に慣れた。

of course もちろん, 当然, (agreeing to a request) どうぞ

There is, of course, another possibility.
もちろん、ほかにも可能性はあります。

Now I know I was wrong. But that, of course, is the wisdom of hindsight.
今になってみると、間違っていたことがわかるけど、もちろん後知恵だからね。

He said he'd never been there. We didn't believe him, of course.
そこへは行ったことがないと彼は言い張っていたけど、もちろん、私たちは信じなかったよ。

"Are you going to the party?"
"Of course."
「パーティーへは行くの？」
「もちろん」

"Are there occasions when you feel homesick?"
"Yes, of course."
「ホームシックにかかることがありますか？」
「ええ、それはもちろん」

"May I sit down?"
"Of course."
「座ってもいいですか？」
「どうぞ(どうぞ)」

"Am I disturbing you?"
"No, of course not."
「おじゃまでしょうか？」
「いいえ、とんでもない」

court ***n.*** (court of law) 裁判所, 法廷, (palace) 宮殿, 宮廷, (tennis/basketball court) コート

As they couldn't settle out of court, she decided to take him to court.
彼と示談にできなかったので、彼女は裁判ざたにした。

♦**court('s) decision** ***n.*** 判決

court of appeal ***n.*** 控訴裁判所

courteous ***adj.*** 丁寧な, 礼儀正しい

courtesy ***n.*** (politeness) 礼儀, (polite behavior) 礼儀正しいふるまい, (polite remark) 丁寧な言葉

adj. (free) 無料の

He didn't even have the common courtesy to call and let us know he wasn't coming.
彼は、来ないことを電話で知らせるという基本的な礼儀さえもなかった。

a courtesy telephone 無料電話

court-martial ***n.*** 軍法会議

v. 軍法会議にかける

courtyard ***n.*** 中庭

couscous ***n.*** クスクス

cousin ***n.*** (first cousin) いとこ, (second cousin) はとこ, またいとこ

cover

1 *v.* TO PROTECT/CONCEAL: (cover A with B) (AをBで) おおう, (AにBを) かける, (conceal) 隠す, (put a lid on) (…に) ふたをする

2 *v.* TREAT: (topic) 取り扱う, (…に) 及ぶ, 触れる, (of the press) 報道する

3 *n.* LID: ふた

4 *n.* THING THAT PROTECTS: カバー, (**covers**: blankets) 毛布

5 *n.* OF BOOK/MAGAZINE: 表紙

6 *v.* PAY FOR: 賄う, 支払うのに足りる

7 *v.* TRAVEL: 旅する, 行く

8 *v.* WORK: (cover for: do sb else's work) (…の) 代わりをする, 代理をする

9 *n., v.* SONG: カバー(する)

10 *v.* OF INSURANCE: 補償する, (**be covered**) 保険に入っている

1 She covered her face and started to cry.
彼女は顔をおおい、泣き出した。

The fields were covered with snow.
田畑は雪でおおわれていた。

Most of the earth's surface is covered by water.
地球の表面は、大部分が水でおおわれている。

The police covered the body with a blanket.
警察は遺体に毛布をかけた。

Cover the dish so flies don't get on the food.
ハエがたからないように、料理におおいをかけなさい。

Better cover it so they can't see it.
見られないように、隠したほうがいい。

Cover and simmer for 15 minutes.
ふたをして15分間コトコト煮ます。

2 This book covers a wide range of subjects.
この本は幅広いテーマを取り扱っている。

The article covered the singer's childhood.
記事は、その歌手の子供時代の話にも及んでいた。

I don't think we've covered that topic yet.
その話題には、まだ触れていないと思う。

3 Shouldn't we put a cover over it?
ふたをしなくてもいいの？

4 The covers have slipped off the baby.
赤ちゃんの毛布が、ずれてしまった。

5 The front cover looked good, so I decided to buy the book.
表紙がよかったので、その本を買うことにした。

6 Does the $50 cover shipping?
５０ドルで運送費を賄えますか？

7 How many kilometers have we covered so far?
これまで何キロ旅をしてきたことになる？

8 Ms. Matsuda covered for me while I was on vacation.
私が休んでいる間、松田さんが私の代わりをしてくれました。

9 That has got to be the worst cover of all time.
それは今までで最悪のカバーだ。

10 Some life insurance policies cover critical illness, too.
生命保険の中には、重い病気も補償するものがあります。

be covered in/with (be sullied with) -だらけ, (mud, blood etc.) -まみれ

C

He was covered in bruises from head to toe.
頭のてっぺんから足の先まで、体中青あざだらけだった。

take cover 隠れる, 身を守る

We took cover to get out of the line of fire.
砲撃から逃れるため物陰に隠れた。

cover up *v.* (conceal) 隠す, (**cover up for**: hide the wrongdoing of) かばう

He tried to cover up for his friends, but they all got into trouble in the end.
彼は友人たちをかばおうとしたが、結局、全員捕まってしまった。

coverage *n.* (of news) 報道, 取材; (of insurance) 補償範囲

covering *n.* (thing that conceals/protects) おおい, (lid) ふた

covert *adj.* ひそかな, 隠された

coverup *n.* (of crime) もみ消し

cow *n.* ウシ, 牛, 乳牛

coward *n.* 臆病者, 弱虫

cowardice *n.* 臆病

cowardly *adj.* 臆病な, ひきょうな

cowboy *n.* カウボーイ

cowgirl *n.* カウガール

coyote *n.* コヨーテ

cozy *adj.* 気持ちのいい, 居心地のいい

crab *n.* カニ

♦**crabmeat** *n.* カニ(の身)

crack

1 *n.* FISSURE: 割れ目, 亀裂, (in china, glass) ひび, ひび割れ

2 *v.* BREAK: 割る, (become cracked) 割れる, ひびが入る, (**crack open**: egg, nut) 割る; (code) 解く, 解読する

3 *n.* SOUND: (of branch) ポキン(という音), (of lightning) バリバリ, (of rifle fire) ズドン, (of whip) パシッ, ピシッ

4 *v.* MAKE A SNAPPING SOUND: (with whip) パシッ/ピシッと鳴らす; (hit) ピシャリとたたく

5 *v.* CRACK A JOKE: (冗談を)とばす, 言う

6 *v.* OF VOICE: かすれる, (of boy's voice during puberty) 声変わりする

7 *n.* SMALL OPENING: すき間

8 *v.* HAVE A BREAKDOWN: くじける, 参る

1 There is a crack in the wall.
壁に亀裂が入っている。

Look here. There's a fine crack running through the vase.
ここを見て。この花びん、細いひびが入ってる。

Don't drink from that glass. There's a crack in it.
そのコップで飲まないで。ひびが入っているから。

2 Careful with that pot. It's old and may crack.
そのつぼは扱いに気をつけて。古いから割れるかもしれない。

Can you crack two eggs at once into the pan?
生卵を二ついっぺんに割って、フライパンに落とせる?

I think we've cracked the code.
暗号が解けたようです。

3 The donkey brayed at the crack of the whip.
むちのピシッという音に、ロバがいなな

いた。

4 crack a whip むちをピシッと鳴らす

crack somebody's butt
(...の)お尻をピシャリとたたく

5 He's always cracking jokes.
あの人はいつも冗談を言ってるんです。

6 He's at the age where his voice cracks.
彼は声変わりする年齢だよ。

7 Could you leave the door open just a crack?
ドアを、少しすき間をあけたままにしておいてくれますか？

8 He's lost his job, his family, everything. I'm amazed he hasn't cracked.
彼は職も家族もすべてを失ったのに、よく参ってしまわないものだと感心するよ。

at the crack of dawn 夜明けに

He was up at the crack of dawn.
彼は夜明けに起きていた。

take a crack at 試してみる, やってみる

Can I take a crack at it?
試してみてもいい？

crack down on *v.* (crime) 厳しく取り締まる

crack open *v.* (egg, nut) 割る, (drink) (ポンと) あける

Time to crack open the wine.
そろそろワインをあけよう。

crack up *v.* (laugh) 笑い転げる, ゲラゲラ笑い出す

She cracked up when I told her the joke.
冗談を言ったら、彼女は笑い転げた。

crackdown *n.* 厳しい取り締まり

cracked *adj.* (of china, bone) ひびの入った, (of earth) ひび割れた, (of voice) かすれた, (of lips) 荒れた

We got rid of the cracked dishes.
ひびの入ったお皿は処分しました。

The ground was cracked due to the drought.
日照りで地面がひび割れていた。

cracker *n.* クラッカー

crackle *v.* (of wood burning) パチパチ音を立てる

n. パチパチ(という音)

crackpot *n.* 変な人, 変わり者

cradle *n.* (for baby) 揺りかご

v. (lull) あやす

craft *n.* (craftwork) クラフト, 工芸, (skill) 技術; (trade) 職業

craftsman, -person, -woman *n.* 職人

crafty *adj.* ずるい

cram *v.* (cram A with B/B into A) (AにBを) 詰め込む; (study hard) 一生懸命勉強する

The thief crammed his bag with jewels.
泥棒は袋に宝石を詰め込んだ。

The subway train was crammed with people.
地下鉄の車内はすし詰めだった。

Taro crammed for his exams.
太郎は試験に向けて一生懸命勉強した。

cramp *n.* (muscle cramp) けいれん, こむら返り, (**cramps**: menstrual) 生理痛

get a cramp in one's leg
脚がつる

have cramps 生理痛がある

cramped *adj.* (crowded) 狭苦しい

cram school *n.* (for elementary and

middle school students) 塾, (college preparatory school) 予備校

cranberry *n.* クランベリー

cranberry sauce クランベリーソース

crane *n.* (bird) ツル, 鶴; (machine) クレーン

cranium *n.* 頭蓋骨

crank *n.* (machine part) クランク; (grouch) 気難し屋

v. (turn) 回す

crash

1 *n.* ACCIDENT: (plane crash) 墜落事故, (car crash) 交通事故, (collision) 衝突

2 *v.* HIT: (crash into: collide with) (…に) 衝突する, ぶつかる, (**crash one's car**) 車をぶつける

3 *v.* MAKE A NOISE: See examples below

4 *n.* FAILING: (of business) 倒産, (of stock market/prices) 暴落

5 *v.* FAIL: (of business) つぶれる, 倒産する, (of stock market) 暴落する

6 *n.* NOISE: (of door) バタン(という音), (of dishes) ガチャン, (of building) ガラガラ, (of heavy object) ドシン

7 *v.* SLEEP: (fall asleep quickly) 寝入る, (**crash at sb's house**) (…の)家に泊まる

8 *n., v.* OF COMPUTER: クラッシュ(する)

1 It was a terrible plane crash.
ひどい(飛行機の)墜落事故だった。

Did you see the crash?
車の衝突事故を見たの?

The crash caused the car to burst into flames.
衝突によって車は炎上した。

2 The bus crashed into a wall.
バスは塀に衝突した。

"Dad…I crashed the car."
「お父さん…車をぶつけてしまったんだ」

3 The lamp went crashing to the floor.
ランプが床にガシャンと落ちた。

The whole building came crashing down.
建物がまるごとガラガラと崩壊した。

4 a stock market crash
株式相場の暴落

5 Hundreds of companies crashed during the recession.
不景気の中、何百という企業が倒産した。

6 a crash of thunder 雷鳴

The dishes fell to the floor with a loud crash.
お皿がガチャンと大きな音を立てて床に落ちた。

7 I crashed as soon as I got home.
家に帰ったとたん、寝入ってしまった。

Can I crash at your place tonight?
今夜、あなたの家に泊めてくれない?

8 The computer crashed again.
コンピューターがまたクラッシュした。

♦**crash helmet** *n.* (安全)ヘルメット

crash landing *n.* 不時着, 胴体着陸

crash course *n.* 速成コース, 集中講座

a crash course in Japanese
日本語の集中講座

crass *adj.* 愚かな, ひどい

crate *n.* 木枠, かご

crater *n.* (of volcano) 噴火口, (lunar crater) 穴, クレーター

crave *v.* (…が) 欲しい

crawl *v.* (move on all fours) はう, (of baby) はいはいする, (of traffic: move slowly) のろのろと進む, (of insects: swarm) たかる

n. (swimming stroke) クロール

We had to crawl in under the fence.
フェンスの下から、はうようにして入らなければならなかった。

Look! The baby's beginning to crawl.
見て。赤ちゃんがはいはいを始めた。

We crawled along in the traffic jam for hours.
私たちは、何時間も渋滞の中をのろのろと進んだ。

Flies were crawling all over the food.
食べ物に一面にハエがたかっていた。

Can you do the crawl?
クロールはできますか?

be crawling with (insects/rats) (虫/ねずみが)がうようよしている

crayfish ***n.*** ザリガニ

crayon ***n.*** クレヨン

crazy ***adj.*** (stupid) ばかな, ばかげた, まともではない, (insane) 正気ではない

n. 頭のおかしい人

Most people thought my ideas were crazy, but look how successful they've been.
おおかたの人間は私の考えはばかげていると思ったようだけれど、結局、大成功だったじゃないですか。

It's crazy going out in this weather.
この天気の中を出かけるなんて、<u>正気じゃないよ</u> [どうかしてるよ]。

The man was crazy and had to be looked after.
その人は正気ではなかったので、監護する必要があった。

be crazy about/over/for (...が) 大好きだ, ...に夢中だ

He's crazy about soccer.
彼はサッカーが大好きだ。

drive sb crazy (irritate) いらいらさせる, (**drives me crazy**) 頭にくる, いらつく

His mother drives him crazy.
彼は母親には頭にきている。

like crazy めちゃくちゃ(に), 狂ったように

The book is selling like crazy.
その本はめちゃくちゃ売れている。

creak ***v.*** (of door/floorboard) キーキー/ミシミシ音を立てる

n. キーキー/ミシミシ(という音)

cream ***n.*** (fat from milk) クリーム, (color) クリーム色, (cosmetic cream) (化粧) クリーム

cream cheese ***n.*** クリームチーズ

creamy ***adj.*** (of dish) クリーミーな, (of substance) クリームを多く含んだ

crease ***n.*** (fold line) 折り目, (pleat) ひだ, (wrinkle) しわ

v. (make a fold line in) (...に) 折り目をつける, (become wrinkled) しわになる

create ***v.*** (cause) 引き起こす, もたらす, (make) 作る, 生み出す

We don't want to create a panic.
パニックを引き起こしたくないんです。

Her work in medicine has created a great deal of interest.
医学分野における彼女の仕事は、大きな関心を呼び起こした。

I want you to create a large, colorful mural.
大きくてカラフルな壁画を描いてもらいたい。

C

creation *n.* 創作, 創造, (**Creation**) (as performed by God) 天地創造, (everything in the universe) 万物

creative *adj.* 独創的な, 創造力のある, クリエイティブな

creativity *n.* 独創性, 創造力

creator *n.* 作る人, 創作者, クリエーター, (**the Creator**) 創造主

creature *n.* (animal) 動物, (living thing) 生き物

credentials *n.* (qualifications) 資格, (certification of official status) 信任状

credibility *n.* 信用, 信用性

lose credibility 信用を失う

credible *adj.* (convincing) 信用できる

credit *n.* (loan) 信用貸し, (method of payment) クレジット, (sale on credit) 掛け売り, ((*informal*)) つけ, (credit rating) 信用度, クレジット; (recognition for achievement) 評判, 名声, (in film, book) クレジット, (for university course) 単位

v. (**credit sb's bank account**) …の口座に振り込む; (credit A with B) (AにBの)功績があると考える

We bought the car on credit.
クレジットで車を買った。

She was refused credit.
彼女は、掛け売りを断られた。

I did it, but he took all the credit.
私がやったのに、彼は名声 [手柄] を独り占めした。

We'll credit your account each month with this amount.
口座に、毎月この金額を振り込みます。

Newton is often credited with discovering gravity.
ニュートンが引力を発見したと、しばしば思われている。

be a credit to …の誇りだ

Shoichi is a credit to his family.
正一さんは、ご家族の誇りです。

credit card *n.* クレジットカード

creditor *n.* 債権者, 貸し主

creek *n.* 小川

creep *n.* (person) いやな奴, ((*figurative*)) うじ虫

v. (crawl) はう, (**creep up on**) …に忍び寄る, (move slowly) のろのろ進む

give sb the creeps ぞっとさせる

He gives me the creeps.
あの人を見ると、ぞっとする。

creepy *adj.* (frightening) 気味の悪い, ぞっとする, 怖い

cremate *v.* 火葬にする

crematorium *n.* 火葬場

crépe *n.* (fabric) クレープ, ちりめん, (pancake) クレープ

crescent *adj.* (of shape) 三日月形の

n. (crescent moon) 三日月

crest *n.* (of hill) 頂, (of wave) 波頭, (of bird) とさか; (coat of arms) 紋章

crew *n.* (of ship) 乗組員, (of airplane) 乗務員

crewcut *n.* 角刈り

crewneck *n.* (sweater) 丸首のセーター

cricket[1] *n.* (insect) コオロギ

cricket[2] *n.* (sport) クリケット

crime *n.* (offense) 犯罪, 罪

the crime rate 犯罪発生率

organized crime 組織犯罪

She committed a crime.
彼女は罪を犯した。

It was a crime against humanity.
人道に対する犯罪だった。

He's wanted for the crime of murder.
男は殺人容疑で指名手配されている。

criminal ***n.*** 犯人, 犯罪者
adj. (of behavior) 犯罪の, 違法の, (of case, charge) 刑事-, (wrong) 最悪の

crimson ***n.*** 真紅, 真っ赤

crisis ***n.*** 危機, 最悪の状態
a midlife crisis 中年の危機
face a crisis 危機に直面する

crisp ***adj.*** (of food) パリパリした, カリカリした, (of weather) 寒くてからっとした
n. (**crisps**: potato chips) ポテトチップ

criterion ***n.*** 基準, 標準

critic ***n.*** 批判者, (literary critic) 評論家, 批評家

critical ***adj.*** (crucial) 重大な, 決定的な, (judgmental) 批判的な, (harsh) 手厳しい; (of illness: serious) 危険な, 危篤の; (discerning) 鑑識眼のある

critically ***adv.*** (seriously) 危篤で, 重体で; (with discernment) じっくり, (disapprovingly) 批判的に
be critically ill 危篤だ

criticism ***n.*** (condemnation) 非難, (evaluation) 批評, 評論

criticize ***v.*** (express disapproval toward) 非難する, 批判する
He was criticized for not getting things done more quickly.
やるのが遅いと、彼は非難された。

critique ***n., v.*** 批評(する)

croak ***n.*** (of frog) ゲロゲロ鳴く声
v. ゲロゲロ鳴く

crochet ***n.*** クローシェ編み, かぎ針編み

crockery ***n.*** 陶器

crocodile ***n.*** ワニ, (crocodile skin) ワニ革

crocus ***n.*** (herb) クロッカス

croissant ***n.*** クロワッサン

crook ***n.*** (dishonest person) 詐欺師

crop ***n.*** (plant) 作物, (yearly produce from soil) 収穫高
v. (hair) 刈り込む, (photograph) トリミングする, (…の)不要な部分を切り取る
a bumper crop 豊作
The crops have failed. 不作だった。

♦ **crop up** ***v.*** (come up) 持ち上がる, 突然現れる
His name cropped up before.
以前、その人の名前が突然挙がった。

croquet ***n.*** クローケー, (Japanese version) ゲートボール

croquette ***n.*** コロッケ

---

cross

1 ***v.*** TRAVERSE: (road, river) 渡る, 横切る, (road, continent) 横断する, (border) 越える [→ ACROSS 1]

2 ***n.*** RELIGIOUS SYMBOL: 十字架

3 ***n.*** MARK: ×印, ばってん

4 ***v.*** INTERSECT: 交差する, 交わる

5 ***v.*** FOLD: 組む

6 ***n.*** MIXTURE: (**a cross between**) …の入り交じったもの

7 ***v.*** BREED: 交配する, 掛け合わす

8 ***n.*** BURDEN: 苦難, 試練

1 Better to cross at the crosswalk.

あの横断歩道を渡ったほうがいいよ。

The river was so wide it took us half an hour to cross it.
川が大きくて、渡るのに３０分もかかった。

By nightfall we had crossed the state line.
夕暮れまでに州の境界線を越えていた。

2 Jesus died on the cross.
イエスは十字架にかけられて死にました。

She wore a tiny cross around her neck.
彼女は小さな十字架を首にかけていた。

On the tombstones you could see Celtic crosses.
墓石にはケルト十字が刻まれているのが見えた。

3 Put a cross where you think I've made mistakes.
私が間違えていると思われるところに、×印をつけてください。

4 Where the freeway crosses over the main road, you'll see a bank.
大通りの上を高速道路が交差しているあたりに、銀行があります。

5 She sat with her legs crossed.
彼女は脚を組んで座っていた。

6 I felt a cross between sad and angry.
悲しみと怒りが入り交じっていた。

7 A hinny is what you get when you cross a stallion with a donkey.
ケッティは種馬と(めすの)ロバを掛け合わせてできます。

cross one's mind 思いつく, ふと心に浮かぶ

sit cross-legged あぐらをかく

sit with legs crossed 脚を組んで座る

cross off/out *v.* 消す

crossbow *n.* 石弓

cross-country *adj.* クロスカントリー-

cross-dress *v.* (of man) 女装する, (of woman) 男装する

cross-examine *v.* (in court) (…に) 反対尋問する

cross-eyed *adj.* 斜視の, 寄り目の

crossfire *n.* 集中攻撃

crossing *n.* (pedestrian crossing) 横断歩道, (intersection) 交差点, (railroad crossing) 踏切

cross-reference *n.* 相互参照

crossroad(s) *n.* (intersection) 十字路, 交差点, (turning point) 岐路

the crossroads of life 人生の岐路

cross-section *n.* 断面

crosswalk *n.* 横断歩道

crosswind *n.* 横風

crossword (puzzle) *n.* クロスワードパズル

crouch *v.* (get close to the ground) かがむ, しゃがむ, うずくまる, (bend body) 身をかがめる

crouton *n.* クルトン

crow *n.* カラス, 烏

crowd *n.* (of people) 大勢の人, 群衆, 人込み

v. (…に) つめかける, 押しかける, (**crowd around**) …の周りに群がる, (**crowd into**) …につめかける

A crowd of people gathered to watch.
一目見ようと、大勢の野次馬が集まった。

Wherever you go there are crowds.
どこへ行っても、人で混み合っている。

I lost him in the crowd.

人込みで彼を見失った。

Crowds of people cheered.

群衆がかっさいした。

Everyone crowded around to see the present.

贈り物を見ようと、みんなが周りに群がって来た。

We crowded into the room to hear the news on TV.

テレビのニュースを聞こうと、部屋につめかけた。

crowded *adj.* 混んでいる, (of train) 満員の

a crowded train 満員電車

crown *n.* (royal headdress) 王冠, (throne, kingship) 王位

♦ **crown prince** *n.* 皇太子

crown princess *n.* 皇太子妃

crucial *adj.* 重大な, 決定的な

crucifix *n.* 十字架

crucifixion *n.* はりつけ

crucify *v.* はりつけにする

crude *adj.* (of language) 露骨な, (lacking taste) 下品な, (lacking tact) 粗野な, 無礼な, (of method) 雑な, 粗末な

That's a crude expression.

ずいぶん露骨な言い方ですね。

Such crude methods are unlikely to fool people.

そんな粗末なやり方で、人がだまされるはずがない。

♦ **crude oil** *n.* 原油

cruel *adj.* 残酷な, ひどい, むごい

Don't be so cruel! Pulling the dog's tail like that.

むごいことはやめなさい! 犬のしっぽをそんなふうに引っ張るなんて。

The judge told him he was a cruel and dangerous man.

判事は本人に向かって、残酷で危険な人間だと言った。

cruelty *n.* 残酷, (cruel treatment) 虐待

cruelty to animals 動物虐待

cruise *n.* (holiday cruise) 遊覧, 船旅

v. (in car) ぶらつく

cruiser *n.* (cabin cruiser) 行楽用モーターボート, (warship) 巡洋艦

crumb *n.* (of bread) パンくず

crumble *v.* (of bread) 粉々になる, (of plaster) はがれる, 崩れる

crumple *v.* (paper) くしゃくしゃにする

crunch *v.* (chew) カリカリ/パリパリかむ

n. (sound) カリカリ/パリパリ(いう音)

crunchy *adj.* カリカリ/パリパリの

crush *v.* (compress and break) 押しつぶす, (in hand) 握りつぶす, (flatten) ぺちゃんこにする; (subdue) 鎮圧する

First you crush the garlic, then you put it in the pan.

まずニンニクをつぶして、それからフライパンに入れます。

He crushed the lemon in his hand to a pulp.

彼は手にしたレモンを、ぐしゃぐしゃに握りつぶした。

We were all crushed together in the elevator.

エレベーターの中で、私たちは押しつぶされそうだった。

The army still thinks it can crush the rebels with the crude use of force.

軍隊は、荒っぽい武力行使で反乱者た

ちを鎮圧できるといまだに考えている。

crust ***n.*** (of bread) パンの耳

crustacean ***n.*** 甲殻類

crutch ***n.*** 松葉づえ

cry ***v.*** (shed tears) 涙を流す, 泣く, (shout) 大声で言う, 叫ぶ, (call out) 呼ぶ ***n.*** (shout) 叫び声, (of animal) 鳴き声

The old woman started to cry.
おばあさんは涙を流し始めた。

Come on now, don't cry.
ほらほら、もう泣くのはやめなさい。

The poor boy cried himself to sleep.
かわいそうにその子は、泣きながら眠りについた。

We cried for help but no one came.
大声で助けを呼んだが、誰も来てくれなかった。

Under the rubble, the rescuers could hear cries for help.
救助隊員たちには、がれきの下から助けを求める叫び声が聞こえた。

That bird has the most unusual cry.
あの鳥は、実に変わった鳴き声をしていますね。

♦ **crybaby** ***n.*** 泣き虫

crystal ***n.*** (mineral) 水晶, (glass) クリスタルガラス, (snow crystal) 結晶

cub ***n.*** (of animal) …の子

cube ***n.*** (shape) 立方体; (in math) 3乗 ***v.*** (raise to the third power) 3乗する

cubic ***adj.*** (of shape) 立方体の, (of measurement) 立方-

three cubic meters 3立方メートル

cubicle ***n.*** 小部屋

cuckoo ***n.*** カッコウ

cucumber ***n.*** キュウリ

cuddle ***v.*** (hug) 抱きしめる, ((*informal*)) 抱っこする, (cuddle together) 抱き合う

cue ***n.*** キュー, (hint) ヒント

cuff ***n.*** (of shirt) そで

cuisine ***n.*** クイジーン, 料理

cul-de-sac ***n.*** (dead end) 行き止まり, 袋小路

culinary ***adj.*** (of cooking) 料理の

culprit ***n.*** 犯人, 犯罪者

cult ***n.*** (religious) 新興宗教, カルト

♦ **cult film** ***n.*** カルト映画

cultivate ***v.*** (land) 耕す, (crops) 栽培する, 育てる; (nurture) 養う

cultivation ***n.*** (of land) 耕作, (of crops) 栽培; (culture) 教養

cultural ***adj.*** 文化的な

♦ **culturally** ***adv.*** 文化的に

culture ***n.*** 文化, (education and taste) 教養

the history of Greek culture
ギリシャの文化の歴史

There's not much culture in this town.
この町には、文化と呼べるようなものがあまりない。

Mr. Yasuda is a man of culture.
安田さんは教養人だ。

cultured ***adj.*** (educated) 教養のある

cumbersome ***adj.*** (difficult to use) 扱いにくい, (bulky) かさばった; (troublesome) 煩わしい

cumulative ***adj.*** 累積する

a cumulative deficit 累積赤字

cunning ***adj.*** ずるい, 悪賢い

cup ***n.*** カップ, コップ, (for Japanese tea) (お)茶わん, (お)湯飲み, (cupful) -杯,

-カップ; (prize) 優勝杯, カップ

a measuring cup 計量カップ

"What did you say was in the cup?" "Tadpoles."
「カップの中に何が入ってたって？」「オタマジャクシ」

I can't stand drinking from paper cups.
紙コップで飲むのはいやだ。

How many cups do we need?
お茶わんはいくつ要りますか？

Here, have a cup of tea.
さあ、お茶を一杯どうぞ。

three cups of sugar 砂糖３カップ

He received a cup for winning the race.
彼はレースに勝って優勝杯を手にした。

cups

(お)湯飲み
teacup
(Japanese-style)

ティーカップ
teacup
(Western-style)

マグカップ
mug

紙コップ
paper cup

cupboard ***n.*** (for dishes) 食器棚 [→ CABINET, CLOSET]

curator ***n.*** 管理者, 館長

curb ***n.*** (at side of road) 縁石, へり; (restraint) 抑制

v. (control) 抑える, (limit) 制限する

The tire scraped against the curb.
タイヤが歩道の縁石をすった。

Most governments are trying to curb public spending.
ほとんどの政府が公共支出を抑えようとしています。

cure ***v.*** (heal) 治療する, (病気を)治す, **(be cured)** 病気が治る

n. (means of healing) 治療法, (medicine) 薬, (remedy) 特効薬, 決め手

The medicine cured the illness.
その薬で病気が治った。

It was used to cure typhoid fever.
(それは) 腸チフスの治療に使われた。

How do you cure the hiccups?
しゃっくりは、どうすれば治る？

The cure remains to be discovered.
治療法はまだ解明されていない。

There isn't any cure for AIDS.
エイズを治す薬はない。

The best cure for you would be to find a girlfriend.
あなたにとっての特効薬は、恋人を見つけることでしょう。

♦**cured** ***adj.*** (recovered) 快復した

He's cured and back to normal.
彼は快復し、元の生活に戻りました。

curfew ***n.*** (time by which one must be home) 門限, (rule) 夜間外出禁止令

curiosity ***n.*** 好奇心

out of curiosity 好奇心から

curious ***adj.*** 好奇心の強い, (speaking about sb else) 知りたがる; (fascinating) 面白い, 興味深い, (odd) 奇妙な

There are many curious children in this class.
このクラスには、好奇心の強い子がたくさんいますね。

He was curious to know whether it was she who had written the letter.
その手紙を書いたのは彼女なのかどうか、彼はとても知りたがった。

That's a curious necklace you're wearing.
面白いネックレスをしていますね。

curl *v.* (hair) カールする, (become round/curved) 丸くなる, (curl A around B) (AをBの周りに) 巻き付ける
n. (of hair) 巻毛, カール

She's going to curl her hair.
彼女は髪をカールするつもりです。

The cat curled up on the sofa and went to sleep.
猫は、ソファーの上に丸くなって眠りについた。

♦ **curly hair** *n.* (hair with lots of curls) カーリーヘア, (frizzy hair) 縮れ毛, ちりちりの髪の毛

currency *n.* (system) 通貨, (money) 貨幣

Into what currency?
何の通貨に(替えますか)?

current *n.* (flow) 流れ, (electric current) 電流
adj. (being/happening now) 現在の, 今の, (new) 最新の; (accepted) 通用している

the direction of the current
流れの方向

a current of air 気流

a strong electrical current
強い電流

the current political climate
現在の政治情勢

That's not my current address.
それは現住所ではありません。

That theory is no longer current.
その説は、もはや通用しません。

♦ **current events/affairs** *n.* 時事問題

currently *adv.* 現在, 今, 今のところ

curriculum *n.* カリキュラム, 教科課程

curriculum vitae *n.* 履歴書

curry *n.* カレー

curse *v.* (put a curse on) のろう, (…に) のろいをかける, (swear) ののしる
n. (evil spell) のろい

Curse the day he was born!
あんな奴、生まれて来なけりゃよかったんだ!

He was cursing his luck.
彼は自分の不運をのろっていた。

Yuji cursed the man who had bumped into him.
雄二は、ぶつかって来た男をののしった。

The witch put a curse on the young prince.
魔法使いは、若い王子にのろいをかけました。

cursed *adj.* のろわれた, (of person: be cursed with) (…に) 苦しんでいる

cursor *n.* カーソル

curtain *n.* (in house) カーテン, (at theater) 幕

It's dark. Let's open the curtains.
暗いね。カーテンをあけましょう。

the final curtain 終幕

curve *n.* (in road) カーブ, (in line) 曲線, (curveball) カーブ
v. (bend) 曲がる, カーブする

There's a steep curve up ahead, so be careful.

この先に急カーブがあるから、気をつけてください。

First, she painted a curve on the canvas.
彼女はキャンバスに、まず曲線を描いた。

The road curves around the lake.
道は湖に沿ってカーブしている。

curved ***adj.*** (of shape) 曲がった, 湾曲した

cushion ***n.*** (Japanese-style) 座布団 [→ picture of ROOM], (Western-style) クッション

Do you want a cushion to sit on?
座布団は要りますか？

Here's a cushion for your head.
ほら、このクッションを枕にすればいい。

custard ***n.*** カスタード

♦ **custard pudding** ***n.*** プリン

custody ***n.*** (guardianship of a child) 保護監督, (police custody) 拘留, 拘置; (keeping) 保管

be held in custody (of suspect) 拘留されている

have custody of (child) 保護している, (suspect) 拘留している; (weapon) 保管している

Who has custody of the children?
誰が子供たちを保護しているんですか？

custom ***n.*** 習慣, (practice) しきたり, (regional custom) 風習, (code, convention) 慣例, (tradition) 伝統

It's a custom in Japan to take your shoes off when entering the house.
日本では、家に上がる前に靴を脱ぐのが習慣です。

customary ***adj.*** (usual) いつもの, 相変わらずの

customer ***n.*** 客, ((*polite*)) お客さん, お客様, ((*formal*)) 顧客, (special client) 得意先, ((*polite*)) お得意さん, お得意様

The customer complained to the store manager.
その客は店長に苦情を言った。

She's a difficult customer.
あの方は、気難しいお客さんです。

♦ **customer service** ***n.*** 顧客サービス

customize ***v.*** 特別注文で作る

custom-made ***adj.*** (of suit) オーダーメードの, あつらえた

customs ***n.*** (agency, procedure) 税関, (customs duty) 関税

go through customs
税関を通る

cut

1 ***n.*** **ON SKIN:** 傷, 切り傷

2 ***v.*** **SEVER:** 切る, (grass, hedge) 刈る, (communication lines) 切断する, (of knife: be capable of cutting) 切れる

3 ***v.*** **REDUCE:** 削減する, (**cut down on**) 省く, (**cut back on**) 減らす, (shorten) 短くする, (salary) 減給する, カットする

4 ***n.*** **REDUCTION:** 削減, (in price) 値引き, 値下げ, (of salary, film) カット

5 ***v.*** **DELETE:** カットする, 削除する, 取る, (**cut and paste**) カットアンドペーストする, 切り貼りする

6 ***v.*** **SKIP:** (school, work) サボる

7 ***n.*** **SHARE:** 分け前, 取り分

1 That's a nasty cut you've got on your hand.

その、手の傷は痛そうですね。

2 cut one's hair 髪を切る

Do you have some nail clippers? I need to cut my nails.
爪切りを持ってない？ 爪を切りたいんだけど。

Careful you don't cut yourself.
けがをしないよう気をつけて。

He was badly cut by falling glass.
落ちてきたガラスで、彼はひどい切り傷を負った。

It'd been cut up into small pieces.
小さく切り刻んであった。

This knife cuts well.
このナイフはよく切れる。

3 We need to cut production costs.
生産コストを削減する必要があります。

I'm going to cut back on smoking and drinking.
たばことお酒の量を減らすつもりです。

4 government cuts
政府の支出削減

tax cuts 減税

a price cut 値下げ

The censors made several cuts to the film.
検閲で、映画の数ヵ所がカットされた。

5 You can cut this part here.
この部分はカットしていいよ。

6 He cut class again today.
彼は今日また授業をサボった。

7 Where's my cut?
私の取り分は？

cut across *v.* (take a shortcut across) 横切って近道をする

cut in *v.* (interrupt) 口を挟む, 割り込む [→ INTERRUPT]

cut off *v.* (stop: supply of sth) 断つ, 止める, (chop off) 切り取る, 切り落とす

cut off food supplies
食料の供給を断つ

cut off aid
援助を打ち切る

Our electrical supply was cut off for several hours.
何時間か、電気の供給が止まった。

I cut off the wires I didn't need and threw them away.
必要ないワイヤーを切り取り、処分した。

I'm going to cut off this rotten wood.
この腐った木材は、切り落とそう。

cut out *v.* (omit) 取る, 削除する, (cut A out of B) (AをBから) 切り抜く, 取り除く

I think it'd be better if you cut out the part about how I fell in the ditch.
僕がどぶに落ちた話は、取ったほうがいいと思うよ。

I think I'll cut the article out and save it.
その記事は切り抜いて取っておこうと思います。

Cut it out! ((*masculine*)) やめろよ, ((*feminine*)) やめてよ

cut through *v.* (…の中を) 通り抜ける

We had to cut through the brambles to get to the shed.
納屋に行くには、イバラの中を通り抜けなければならなかった。

Let's cut through all the pleasantries and get straight down to business.
社交辞令は抜きにして本題に入りましょう。

cutback ***n.*** (reduction) 削減

cute ***adj.*** かわいい, キュートな

cutlery ***n.*** (tools for cutting) 刃物類 [→ SILVERWARE]

cutlet ***n.*** (thin slice of meat) 薄い切り身, (meat dipped in batter and fried) カツ

cutting board ***n.*** (for cooking) まな板 [→ picture of COOKING UTENSILS]

cuttlefish ***n.*** イカ

CV ***n.*** 履歴書

cyanide ***n.*** (poison) シアン化物, (potassium cyanide) 青酸カリ

cybercafé ***n.*** インターネットカフェ

cyberspace ***n.*** サイバースペース

cycle ***v.*** (go by bicycle) 自転車で行く, (do cycling) サイクリングする

n. (sequence) 周期, サイクル, (of Chinese zodiac: one cycle) 一回り

I like to cycle to work.
自転車で通勤するのが好きです。

The moon goes around the earth on roughly a 27-day cycle.
月は 27 日周期で地球を1周する。

It was a cycle of events that no one could have prevented.
それは誰にも防ぎようのない一連の出来事でした。

cyclist ***n.*** 自転車に乗る人, サイクリスト

cylinder ***n.*** (shape) 円柱, 円筒, (gas cylinder) ボンベ, (engine cylinder) シリンダー, -気筒

cylindrical ***adj.*** 円柱の, 円筒形の

cymbal ***n.*** シンバル

cynic ***n.*** 皮肉屋

cynical ***adj.*** 皮肉な, シニカルな

cypress ***n.*** イトスギ, 糸杉

D, d

D, d *n.* (letter) Ｄ, (fourth item in a series) 第４, (grade) Ｄ, 可

dab *v.* (paint) ペタペタ塗る, (ointment) 軽く塗る

dachshund *n.* ダックスフント

dad *n.* (one's own) 父, (addressing one's own) お父さん, (sb else's) お父さん

daddy *n.* パパ, お父さん

daffodil *n.* ラッパズイセン

daft *adj.* ばかな [→ STUPID]

dagger *n.* 短剣, 短刀

look daggers at にらみつける

dahlia *n.* ダリア

daily *adj.* (everyday) 毎日の, 日常の, (once a day) １日１回の, (published daily) 日刊の

adv. 毎日, 日ごとに

n. (daily paper) 日刊紙, 日刊新聞

daily life 日常生活

dairy *n.* (farm) 酪農場

adj. 乳製品の

dairy products 乳製品

daisy *n.* デージー, ヒナギク

dale *n.* 谷

dalmatian *n.* ダルメシアン

dam *n.* ダム

v. (dam a river) (川を)ダムでせき止める

A dam was built to provide a reservoir.
貯水池を設けるためにダムが建設された。

damage *n.* (harm) 被害, 害, 損害, (dent, scratch etc.) 損傷, (**damages**: compensation) 損害賠償(金)

v. 損なう, 傷つける, (goods, crops) (…に) 損害/被害を与える

The earthquake caused a lot of damage.
地震はかなりの被害をもたらした。

The damage to the car wasn't bad.
車の損傷は大したことはなかった。

They're claiming damages.
彼らは損害賠償金を要求しています。

Careful not to damage it.
傷つけないよう、気をつけてね。

Part of the building was damaged by the fire.
火事でビルの一部が焼けました。

Were the crops badly damaged by the floods?
洪水で農作物は大きな被害を受けましたか？

♦ **damaging** *adj.* (destructive) 損害を与える, (to health) (…に) 有害な, 悪い, (to reputation) (…を) 傷つける

damask *n.* (fabric) ダマスク織

damn *interj.* ちくしょう!, くそっ!, しまった!

v. (curse) ののしる

adj. 全くの, ものすごい

adv. とても, すごく

Damn! I've forgotten my wallet.
しまった！ 財布を忘れてきた！

Damn them all to hell!
ちくしょう！ いまいましい連中だ！

Oh, him! He's a damn fool.
あいつか！ あいつはとんでもないばかだ。

She's a damn good singer.
彼女はすごく歌がうまい。

not give a damn ちっとも気にしない, 知ったことじゃない

Frankly, I don't give a damn what he says.
正直言って、あの人が何を言おうと知ったことじゃないよ。

damp *adj.* (moist) 湿った, (humid) 湿っぽい, じめじめした
n. (moistness) 湿り気, 湿気

This towel is damp.
このタオルは湿っている。

This room is damp.
この部屋は湿気が多い。

♦ **dampness** *n.* 湿り気, 湿気

dampen *v.* (make damp) 湿らす, (put a damper on) (…に) 水を差す, (deaden: sb's resolve) (…の決意を) 鈍らせる, (weaken: sb's enthusiasm) (…の熱意を) そぐ

damper *n.* ダンパー
put a damper on …に水を差す, …の興をそぐ

dance *v.* (move to music) 踊る, ダンスをする, (**dance around**) 飛び回る
n. (act of dancing) 踊ること, (style of dance as art) ダンス, 舞踊, (social gathering) ダンスパーティー, 舞踏会

"Would you like to dance?"
"I can't dance."
((*masculine*))「踊りませんか？」
((*feminine*))「私、踊れないの」

The children were dancing around excitedly.
子供たちは大騒ぎで飛び回っていた。

Dance is a form of art.
ダンスは芸術の一つだ。

Traditional Japanese dance dates back many centuries.
日本舞踊は何世紀も前から続いている。

Are you going to the dance tonight?
今夜のダンスパーティーには行くの？

♦ **dance floor** *n.* ダンスフロア
dance hall *n.* ダンスホール
dance song *n.* ダンス曲

dancer *n.* ダンサー, 舞踊家

dancing *n.* 踊り, ダンス

dandelion *n.* タンポポ

dandruff *n.* ふけ

dandy *n.* (chic man) ダンディーな人, いきな男

danger *n.* 危険, おそれ

Are we out of danger yet?
危険はもう脱しましたか？

That man is a danger to society and himself.
その男は社会にとっても、彼自身にとっても危険だ。

dangerous *adj.* 危ない, 危険な

It's dangerous to go surfing today.
今日、サーフィンに行くのは危険だ。

A dangerous criminal has escaped from prison.
凶悪犯が刑務所から脱走した。

dangle *v.* (hang) ぶら下がる, (dangle A from B) (AをBから) ぶら下げる

A monkey was dangling from the tree.
猿が木にぶら下がっていた。

dapper *adj.* (stylish) いきな, (neat) きちんとした

dare *v.* (**dare to do**) 思い切って…する, あえて…する, …する勇気がある, (**I dare you to…**) …できるものなら…してみろ
n. (challenge) 挑戦

He was so furious, I didn't dare argue with him.
彼が怒り狂っていたので、彼と言い争う勇気がなかった。

how dare you よくも…できるもんだ, なんてことをするんだ

How dare you speak to your father like that!
父親に向かって、なんという口のきき方をするんだ!

daredevil *n.* 無謀な人, 命知らず
adj. (reckless) 向こう見ずな, 命知らずの

daresay *v.* (**I daresay...**) (=I think it is likely that...) おそらく/たぶん…だろう, (=I would venture to say that...) あえて…と言う

I daresay they've arrived by now.
おそらく、もう着いたでしょう。

daring *adj.* (bold) 大胆な, (brave) 勇気のある

a daring escape 大胆な逃走

dark

1 *adj.* OF COLOR: (deep) 濃い, (of hair color) 黒い, 黒っぽい, (of complexion) 浅黒い, 色黒の

2 *adj.* LACKING LIGHT: 暗い, 薄暗い

3 *adj.* EVIL: 腹黒い, 邪悪な

4 *n.* NIGHTTIME: (**the dark**) やみ, 暗やみ, 暗がり

5 *n.* LAUNDRY: (**darks**) 黒っぽい服, 黒い物

1 dark blue 紺色 [濃い青色]

Her hair is long and dark.
彼女の髪は長くて黒い。

That person has a dark complexion.
あの人は色黒だ。

2 a dark cave 暗い洞窟

This room is dark.
この部屋は薄暗いですね。

Let's go home before it gets dark.
暗くなる前に家に帰りましょう。

3 dark deeds 邪悪な行為

the dark underbelly of society
社会の暗黒部

4 Jun is afraid of the dark.
淳は暗やみを怖がる。

It got cold after dark.
日が暮れてから寒くなった。

♦ **dark age** *n.* (also **the Dark Ages**) 暗黒時代

darken *v.* (make dark) 暗くする, (=shade in) 黒くする, (become dark) 暗くなる

The sky darkened.
空が暗くなりました。

darkness *n.* やみ, 暗やみ, 暗黒

darkroom *n.* 暗室

darling *n.* (beloved) 最愛の人, (addressing husband/boyfriend) あなた
adj. (dear) 最愛の, いとしい, (favorite) お気に入りの

darn[1] *v.* (mend) つくろう, (…の穴を) かがる

darn[2] → DAMN

I'll be darned. 驚いたね。

dart *n.* (pointed projectile) 投げ矢, (**darts**: game) ダーツ
v. (rush) 突進する, 急いで走る

I hear that Mr. Hasegawa likes darts.
長谷川さんはダーツが好きらしい。

The children darted past me.
子供たちは、すごい勢いで私の前を通

り過ぎて行った。

dash *v.* (hurry) 急いで行く, (rush) 駆け付ける, (**dash out**) 駆け出す

n. (race) 競走; (small amount) 少し; (punctuation mark) ダッシュ

Don't dash across the road like that.
そんなに急いで道路を渡らないで。

He dashed out of the house.
彼は家から駆け出した。

the 100-meter dash 100メートル(競)走

Add a dash of salt.
お塩を少し入れてください。

dashboard *n.* (in car) ダッシュボード

data *n.* (information) 資料, 情報, データ

database *n.* データベース

date[1]

1 *n.* TIME: (day) 日にち, (year, month and day) 年月日, (day of event) 日取り, 日付

2 *v.* MARK WITH A DATE: (…に) 日付を書く, 日付をつける

3 *v.* ESTIMATE THE DATE OF: (fossil, artifact etc.) (…の) 年代を推定する

4 *n.* ROMANTIC OUTING: デート

5 *v.* HAVE A ROMANTIC RELATIONSHIP (WITH): (…と) 付き合う

1 date of birth 生年月日

date and time 日時

What's the date of the meeting?
会議の日にちはいつですか？

"What's today's date?"
"Monday, the 19th."
「今日は何日？」
「19日の月曜日」

What date is best for you?
どの日が一番都合がいい？

2 That's odd. The letter's not dated.
おかしいなあ。手紙に日付が書いてない。

3 How are they able to date these fossils?
この化石の年代をどうやって推定できるのですか？

4 a first date 初デート

I've got a date tonight.
今夜はデートがあります。

They're going on a date this Friday.
二人はこの金曜日にデートするんだって。

5 Are they dating?
あの二人は付き合ってるの？

be out of date 時代遅れの, 古くさい

That book is out of date.
その本は時代遅れだよ。

Those sunglasses are a little out of date, don't you think?
あのサングラスは、ちょっと古くさいと思わない？

date back to …にさかのぼる

This sculpture dates back to the seventh century.
この彫刻の製作年は7世紀にさかのぼる。

to date (until now) 今まで(に/の), これまで

This book has sold more than a million copies to date.
この本は今までに100万部以上売れている。

date[2] *n.* (fruit) ナツメヤシの実

dated *adj.* (marked with a date) 日付のある; (outdated) 時代遅れの

The contract is signed and dated.
契約書にはサインと日付が入っている。

daughter *n.* (one's own) 娘, (sb else's)

お嬢さん, 娘さん

one's first-born daughter 長女

one's second-born daughter 次女 [二女]

This is our youngest daughter, Keiko.
これは末娘の恵子です。

What university does your daughter attend?
お嬢さんは、どこの大学に行ってらっしゃるの?

They have three daughters and one son.
あの夫婦には女の子が3人と男の子が1人いる。

♦ **daughter-in-law** *n.* (one's own) 嫁, 義理の娘, (sb else's) お嫁さん

daunting *adj.* 手ごわい, 困難な

dawn *n.* ((*also figurative*)) 夜明け, ((*poetic*)) あけぼの, (beginning) 始まり

v. (grow light) 夜が明ける

before dawn 夜明け前 [((*formal*)) 未明]

They say that the hour before dawn is the coldest.
夜明け前の一時が一番寒いそうだ。

We worked from dawn to dusk.
私たちは夜明けから日暮れまで働いた。

♦ **dawn on** *v.* (become clear to) わかり始める, 気がつく

The seriousness of the situation gradually dawned on me.
状況の深刻さがしだいにわかり始めた。

It suddenly dawned on me that I had left the map at home.
突然、家に地図を置いてきてしまったことに気がついた。

day *n.* (24-hour period) 日, 1日, (day of the week) -曜日, (period of daylight) 昼, 昼間; (**days**: of one's life) (...の) 時代, ころ

He's only sleeping four hours a day.
あの人は1日4時間しか寝ていない。

I work six days a week.
週6日働いています。

What day is it today? 今日は何曜日?

The days were short and the nights long.
昼は短く、夜は長かった。

In my student days we had a lot of free time.
学生のころは自由な時間がたくさんあった。

Ah! Those were the days!
ああ、昔はよかったなあ!

all day (long) 一日中

I studied all day long.
一日中勉強した。

by day 昼間は

He's a student by day, a waiter by night.
彼は昼間は学生、夜はウェーターをしている。

day after day 毎日毎日

He kept calling me day after day.
毎日毎日彼は電話をしてきた。

day and night 昼夜の別なく, 昼も夜も

We worked day and night.
私たちは昼も夜もずっと働き続けました。

day by day 日ごとに, 日増しに, 日に日に

Day by day, I grew to understand him a little better.
日ごとに、あの人を少しずつ理解できるようになった。

every day 毎日

It snowed every day.
毎日雪が降った。

every other day 1日おきに, 隔日に

We met every other day.
私たちは1日おきに会っていました。

for days 何日(間)も, 数日

It hasn't rained for days.
何日間も雨が降っていません。

in a day or two 1日(か)2日で, 明日かあさってに, ((*formal*)) 一両日中に

You'll probably get the letter in a day or two.
明日かあさってに手紙は届くでしょう。

in those days そのころ(は), 当時(は)

In those days, ordinary people could not afford a television set.
そのころは、一般の人はテレビを買うことができなかったんだ。

one day ある日, (someday) いつか

Then one day he just turned up out of the blue.
そしてある日のこと、彼は突然現れた。

One day I'll be rich.
いつか大金持ちになるぞ。

one of these days 近いうちに, そのうち(に)

One of these days the situation will change.
近いうちに状況は変わるだろう。

One of these days I'll tell him what I really think of him.
そのうち彼に私の本心を言ってやる。

some days …日もある

Some days I'm lucky, some days I'm not.
運のいい日もあれば悪い日もあるさ。

the other day 先日, この間, この前

these days このごろ, 最近, 今どき

These days, there aren't many people who use cassette tapes.
今どき、カセットテープを使っている人はあまりいない。

daybreak ***n.*** 夜明け

daycare ***n., adj.*** (for infants) 保育(の), (for the elderly) 介護(の), デイケア(…)

a daycare center (for children) 保育所

D

daydream ***n.*** 空想, 白昼夢

v. (fantasize) 空想/白昼夢にふける, (space out) ぼうっとする

daylight ***n.*** (light of day) 昼の光, (sunlight) 日光

day shift ***n.*** 日勤

daytime ***n.*** 日中, 昼間

day-to-day ***adj.*** 日常の, 日ごろの

day trip ***n.*** 日帰り旅行

dazed ***adj.*** 頭がぼうっとする, (blinded) 目がくらむ, (mentally lost) 気が遠くなる

dazzle ***v.*** (blind) (…の) 目をくらます, (mesmerize) 魅惑する

dazzling ***adj.*** (bright) 目もくらむほどの, まぶしい, (marvelous) すばらしい

deacon ***n.*** (Catholic) 助祭, (Anglican, Presbyterian) 執事

dead

1 ***adj.*** NOT LIVING: (of human, animal) 死んだ, (of plant) 枯れた

2 ***adj.*** NOT ACTIVE: (of streets, town) 活気がない, (of machine) 切れた, (of phone line) 通じない

3 ***adj.*** OBSOLETE: すたれた, 死-

4 ***adj.*** NUMB: (**go dead**) しびれる, 感覚がなくなる

5 ***n.*** THE DECEASED: (**the dead**) 死者, 死亡者, 故人

1 Is the cat dead?

その猫、死んでるの？

That old man isn't dead yet.
あのおじいさんならまだ元気です。

a dead body 死体 [((*polite*)) 遺体]

All the plants are dead.
植物が全部枯れてしまった。

2 This town is dead in the winter months.
この街は冬の間は活気がない。

dead batteries 切れた電池

The line seems to be dead.
電話が通じていないようだ。

3 Socialist ideas are far from dead.
社会主義の思想は少しもすたれていない。

a dead language 死語

4 My legs have gone dead from sitting for so long.
長い間座っていたので、足がしびれてしまいました。

5 The dead could not be counted.
死亡者の数は数えられないほどだった。

dead end *n.* 行き止まり

dead heat *n.* 同着

deadline *n.* 締め切り

When is the deadline?
締め切りはいつですか？

make/meet a deadline
締め切りに間に合う

deadlock *n.* 行き詰まり, こう着状態

deadly *adj.* (life-threatening) 致命的な, (of storm) 激しい

a deadly weapon 凶器

The snake's venom is deadly.
そのヘビの毒は猛毒だ。

deadpan *adj.* (of expression) 無表情な, ポーカーフェースの

deadpan humor 真面目くさって言う冗談

deadwood *n.* (dead wood) 枯れ木; (useless thing/person) 役に立たない物/人

deaf *adj.* (unable to hear) 耳の聞こえない, 耳の不自由な, (hard of hearing) 耳が遠い, (**go deaf**) 耳が遠くなる

n. (**the deaf**) 耳の聞こえない人, 耳の不自由な人, ろう者

Mr. Kobayashi is going deaf.
小林さんは耳が遠くなっている。

deafen *v.* (make deaf) (…の) 耳をつんざく

♦ **deafening** *adj.* (loud) 耳をつんざくような

---

deal *n.* (transaction) 取引, (contract) 契約, (promise) 約束

v. (distribute) 配る, 分配する

It was a good deal for both companies.
両社にとって有利な取引だった。

deal (out) cards カードを配る

deal out punishment 罰を与える

a great deal (of) たくさん(の)

A great deal of money was spent on the project.
このプロジェクトには、たくさんのお金がつぎ込まれた。

make a (big) deal of おおげさに騒ぎ立てる

deal out → DEAL

deal with *v.* (treat, handle) 扱う, 取り扱う, (manage) 処理する, (…に) 対処する

The book deals with the issue of racial discrimination.
その本は人種差別の問題を取り扱っています。

You shouldn't deal with customers like that.
お客様にあんな態度をとってはいけません。

The problem was dealt with promptly.
その問題は迅速に処理された。

What's the best way of dealing with this?
これには、どう対処するのが一番いいですか？

---

dealer ***n.*** (seller) 業者, ディーラー; (distributor of cards) ディーラー

dealings ***n.*** (business) 取引, (buying and selling) 売買; (interaction, relationship) 付き合い, 関係

dean ***n.*** (of university) 学部長, (of cathedral) 主席司祭

dear

1 ***adj.*** IN LETTER: (**Dear...**) 拝啓 [NOTE: 拝啓 and 敬具 correspond respectively to "Dear Sir/Madam" and "Yours sincerely/faithfully." Both are formal terms used in letter writing. Less formal are 前略 and 草々. There is no English equivalent for 前略, which literally means "dispensing with preliminaries," but it does for our "Dear Mr./Mrs./Ms."]

2 ***interj.*** EXPRESSING DISAPPOINTMENT: (**Oh dear!**) おや, ((*feminine*)) あら, まあ

3 ***adj.*** PRECIOUS: いとしい, 親愛なる, 大切な

4 ***n.*** TERM OF ADDRESS: あなた

1 Dear Sir/Madam 拝啓
Dear Mr. Tanaka 田中様

2 Oh dear! What have you done?
((*feminine*)) あらまあ！何をしたの？

Dear, dear, dear! What a mess you've made.
おやおや！ なんてひどい散らかし方でしょう。

3 He is dear to me.
彼は私にとって大切な人です。

A dear friend of ours is coming to visit us tomorrow.
私たちの親友が明日訪ねて来ます。

4 You shouldn't say that, Dear.
あなた、そんなこと言っちゃだめだよ。

death ***n.*** 死, ((*formal*)) 死亡

His death was painless.
彼は苦しまずに死んだ。

Death comes to us all.
人は皆必ず死ぬ。

a sudden death 急死

the deaths of thousands 何千人もの死

put to death (execute) 処刑する

death penalty ***n.*** 死刑

death toll ***n.*** 死者の数, 死亡者数

debatable ***adj.*** (doubtful) 疑わしい, (arguable) 議論の余地がある

debate ***v.*** 議論する, ディベートする
n. 議論, ディベート

debit ***n.*** (opposite of credit) 借方, (direct debit) 引き落とし
v. (from bank account) (…から) 引き落とす

I will pay by direct debit.
口座引き落としで支払います。

Has the bank debited your account?
銀行は口座から引き落としましたか？

♦ **debit card** ***n.*** デビットカード

debris *n.* がれき

debt *n.* (money owed) 借金, 借り, (obligation) 恩義

He's up to his neck in debts.
彼には首が回らないほどの借金がある。

I owe a debt of thanks to Professor Tani.
谷先生には恩義があります。

debtor *n.* 債務者, 借り主

debut *n., v.* デビュー(する)

decade *n.* 10年間

decadence *n.* (moral decay) 退廃, 堕落, (in art) デカダンス

decadent *adj.* (of behavior) 退廃的な, (of art) デカダンの

decaffeinated *adj.* カフェイン抜きの

decanter *n.* デカンタ

decay *v.* (rot) 腐る, 腐敗する, (decline) 衰える

n. (decomposition) 腐敗, (decline) 衰え, 衰退

Candy causes tooth decay.
お菓子は虫歯の元になる。

deceased *adj.* 死んだ, ((*polite*)) 亡くなった, ((*formal*)) 死亡した

n. (**the deceased**) 亡くなった人, 故人

deceit *n.* 詐欺, ぺてん

an act of deceit 詐欺行為

deceitful *adj.* (of person) 人をだます, うそをつく, (of words, act) 人を惑わす

deceive *v.* だます

I've been deceived!
だまされた!

December *n.* 12月, 十二月

decency *n.* 礼儀正しさ

not have the decency to do …する礼儀もない

He didn't even have the decency to apologize.
あの人は謝る(だけの)礼儀さえなかった。

decent *adj.* (well-mannered) 礼儀正しい, きちんとした, (honest and sincere) まともな, (suitable) けっこうな, (adequate) 適当な, (good) 相当な, (kind, gentle) 親切な, (ordinary, respectable) 世間並みの, 人並みの

He seems to be a decent person.
彼はきちんとした人に見える。

No decent person would do such a thing.
まともな人なら、あんなことはしない。

He ought to do the decent thing and marry her.
彼は潔く彼女と結婚すべきです。

It was a decent dinner at a decent price.
値段も適当でまずまずの食事でした。

We're not even paid decent wages.
世間並みの給料さえもらっていません。

decentralize *v.* 地方分権にする

♦ **decentralization** *n.* 地方分権

deception *n.* ごまかし

decibel *n.* デシベル

decide *v.* (**decide to do**) …することを決心する, …することにする, (reach a decision) 決める, 決定する, (**decide on**: select) 選ぶ

I decided to take up Japanese.
日本語を習おうと決心しました。

She hasn't decided yet.
彼女はまだ決めてないんです。

They were unable to decide whether or not to accept the proposal.
先方はその提案を受け入れるかどうか、

決められませんでした。

He lets his parents decide everything for him.
彼はすべてを両親に決めてもらっている。

It's no good complaining. It's already been decided.
ぶつぶつ言ってもむだです。もう決まったことですから。

I had a hard time deciding on a present.
プレゼントを選ぶのに苦労しました。

deciduous ***adj.*** 落葉性の

decimal ***n.*** 小数

♦ **decimal point** ***n.*** 小数点 [→ POINT 10]

the decimal system ***n.*** 十進法

decipher ***v.*** (code) 解読する, (handwriting) 読み解く

decision ***n.*** (resolution) 決心, 決意, 決断, (choice) 決めたこと, (judgment) 判決

He took a long time to make a decision.
彼は、決意するまでたっぷり時間をかけた。

It's a difficult decision to make.
決断するのは難しい/決めにくいね。

So, what's your decision?
それで、あなたが決心したことは?

It's her decision, so leave her alone.
彼女の決めることだから、そっとしておいてあげて。

The judge's decision is final.
裁判官の判決は最終的なものである。

♦ **decision making** ***n.*** 意志決定

decisive ***adj.*** (of moment, fact) 決定的な, (of person: able to make decisions) 決断力のある

deck ***n.*** (of ship) デッキ, 甲板; (of cards) 一組

declaration ***n.*** (statement) 断言, (announcement) 発表, ((*formal*)) 宣言; (document) 申告書

the Declaration of Independence
(アメリカの) 独立宣言

declare ***v.*** (say emphatically) 強く言う, 断言する, (announce) 発表する, ((*formal*)) 声明する, 宣言する; (at customs) 申告する

decline ***v.*** (decrease) 減る, ((*formal*)) 減少する, (of health) 衰える, 弱る, (of business) 傾く; (refuse) 断る, 拒否する

n. (languishing) 衰え, 衰退

The birth rate is declining.
出生率が減少しつつある。

His health is declining.
彼の健康は衰えつつある。

The minister declined to comment.
大臣はコメントを断った。

The Decline and Fall of the Roman Empire 『ローマ帝国衰亡史』

The economy is on the decline.
経済は衰退している。

decode ***v.*** 解読する

decompose ***v.*** (break down) 分解する, (rot) 腐敗する

decongestant ***n.*** 充血緩和剤

decor ***n.*** 室内装飾, 内装

decorate ***v.*** 飾る, (furnish) 内装する [→ REDECORATE], (**be decorated**: with honors) (勲章を) 授けられる

decorate a Christmas tree
クリスマスツリーに飾り付けをする

We haven't had time to decorate the house yet.

これまで家の内装をする時間がなかった。

decoration ***n.*** (ornament) 飾り, (medal, award) 勲章

decorative ***adj.*** 装飾用の, 装飾的な

decoy ***n.*** おとり, デコイ

decrease ***v.*** (become less) 減る, ((*formal*)) 減少する, 低下する, (make less) 減らす, 低下させる

n. 減少, 低下

The birth rate is decreasing while the senior citizen population is increasing.
出生率が<u>減少</u> [低下] する一方、高齢者の人口は増加している。

The number of applicants had decreased.
出願者が減っていた。

dedicate ***v.*** ささげる, (**dedicate oneself to**: research, activity) …に専念する

Mother Teresa dedicated her life to the poor.
マザーテレサは貧しい人のために一生をささげた。

He dedicated his first novel to his mother.
彼は最初の小説を母にささげた。

The statue is dedicated to those who died in World War I.
彫像は第一次世界大戦の戦死者のためにささげられている。

She dedicates herself to archeological research.
彼女は考古学研究に専念しています。

dedicated ***adj.*** (of worker) ひたむきな, 熱心な

dedication ***n.*** (devotion) 献身; (in book) 献呈の辞

deduce ***v.*** (infer) 推論する

deduct ***v.*** (subtract) 控除する, 差し引く

deduction ***n.*** (subtraction) 控除, 差し引き; (inference) 推論

deed ***n.*** (act) 行為, 行動; (certificate of ownership) 権利証

Deeds speak louder than words.
行動は言葉よりも物を言う。

deem ***v.*** (…と) 思う

deep

1 ***adj.*** **OF HOLE/SEA/SLEEP:** 深い

2 ***adv.*** **FAR DOWN/BACK/BELOW:** 深く

3 ***adj.*** **GIVING MEASUREMENT:** (top to bottom) 深さ…, (front to back) 奥行き…

4 ***adj.*** **DARK:** 濃い

5 ***adj.*** **LOW:** 低い

6 ***adj.*** **PROFOUND:** 深い, 深遠な

7 ***adj.*** **SERIOUS:** 重大な, 深刻な, 大変な

1 a deep valley 深い谷

a deep river 深い川

I fell into a deep sleep.
深い眠りに落ちた。

The ocean gets very deep beyond the continental shelf.
海は大陸棚を越えると、非常に深くなっている。

The cupboards are very deep.
食器棚は奥行きが<u>深い</u> [ある]。

2 They went deep into the cave.
彼らは洞窟の奥深くに入って行った。

The wreckage lies deep beneath the sea.
船の残骸は海の底深くに横たわっている。

You should have dug it deeper.
もっと深く掘るべきだったよ。

3 The hole was about two meters deep and one meter wide.
その穴は深さ2メートル、幅1メートルほどだった。

4 a deep color 濃い色
deep blue 紺色 [濃紺]

5 He has a rather deep voice.
彼の声はどちらかと言うと低いね。

6 a deep understanding 深い理解

7 He's in deep trouble.
彼は大変な状況になっている。

deepen *v.* (of emotion, knowledge) 深まる, (of voice) 低くなる, (make deeper: knowledge) 深める

My knowledge of politics has deepened.
政治の知識が深まりました。

The tone of his voice deepened.
彼の声の調子が低くなった。

deep-fried *adj.* 唐揚げの, (dipped in batter and deep-fried) 天ぷらの, (covered in breadcrumbs and deep-fried) フライの

deep-fried chicken とりの唐揚げ
a deep-fried shrimp えびの天ぷら
a deep-fried oyster カキフライ

deep-fry *v.* 揚げる

deeply *adv.* (of feeling, thought) 深く, (of sleep) ぐっすりと; (emphasizing degree) ものすごく

be deeply in love (with)
(…に) ぞっこんほれ込んでいる

deep-seated *adj.* 根深い

deer *n.* シカ, 鹿

default *n.* (default setting) 初期設定, デフォルト

defeat *v.* (beat) 破る, 負かす, (**be defeated**) 敗れる, 負ける
n. 敗北, 負け

The ruling party was defeated by a narrow vote.
与党はわずかの票差で [僅差で] 敗れた。

Defeat was close at hand.
敗北は目前だった。

He would never admit defeat.
彼は自分の負けを絶対認めないだろう。

The team suffered a terrible defeat.
チームは惨敗した。

KANJI BRIDGE

敗 ON: はい KUN: やぶ(れる) | DEFEAT

crushing defeat	惨敗, 全敗
decay, decomposition	腐敗
defeat	敗北
defeated army	敗軍
failure	失敗
lost battle	敗戦
one defeat	一敗
successive defeats	連敗
victory or defeat	勝敗

defect *n.* (flaw) 欠陥, 欠点
v. (change sides) 転向する, (betray) 寝返る, (leave a political party) 離党する, (flee to another country) 亡命する

defective *adj.* (of product) 欠陥のある, 欠点のある

defend *v.* (protect, guard) 守る, 防衛する, (in court) 弁護する, (in argument) 擁護する, 弁護する

The first duty of the government is to defend the nation.
政府の第一の義務は、国民を守ることである。

He thinks he can defend himself just because he's taken karate.
彼は空手をやっていたというだけで、

D

身を守れると思っている。

The goalie wasn't defending the goal properly.

ゴールキーパーはゴールをきちんと守っていなかった。

The minister successfully defended his policy in the Diet.

大臣は自分の政策を国会でうまく擁護した。

Who is going to defend you in court?

法廷では誰が君を弁護するのかね？

♦ **defender** *n.* (in sport) ディフェンダー, 守備側の選手

defendant *n.* 被告, 被告人

defense *n.* 防衛, 防御, (in court: **the defense**) 被告側, (justification) 弁明; (in sport) 守備, ディフェンス

the defense of the city 街の防衛

national defense 国防

♦ **defenseless** *adj.* 無防備の

defensive *adj.* (of measure, weapon) 防御の, 自衛の, (of person) 身構えた, (in sport) 守備の, 守りの

get defensive (of person) 身構える

go on the defensive 守りに入る

defer *v.* (postpone) 延ばす, 延期する; (defer to: yield to) (…に) 従う

If possible, I'd prefer to defer payment till next month.

できれば、来月まで支払いを延期したいのですが。

defiance *n.* 反抗

defiant *adj.* 反抗的な

deficiency *n.* 不足, 欠乏

vitamin deficiency ビタミン不足

deficient *adj.* 不足している, 不十分な

deficit *n.* 赤字

reduce the budget deficit

財政赤字を削減する

define *v.* (give definition of) 定義する

Meaning is a difficult word to define.

「意味」という言葉は定義するのが難しい。

definite *adj.* (clear) 明らかな, はっきりした, (certain) 確かな, 確実な

We want a definite answer by tomorrow.

明日までに、はっきりとした答えをいただきたい。

Tall people have a definite advantage in games like basketball.

背の高い人は、バスケット(ボール)などのスポーツで明らかに有利だ。

There was no definite evidence, but…

確実な証拠は何もなかったが…

Is it definite? 確かなことですか？

definitely *adv.* (certainly) 確かに, (clearly) はっきりと, (without a doubt) 絶対, 間違いなく

That was definitely the best movie I've seen this year.

あれは今年見た中で、間違いなく一番の映画だ。

I definitely would not do that if I were you.

私があなたなら、そんなことは絶対しない。

definition *n.* (of word) 定義; (of photo) 鮮明度

definitive *adj.* 決定的な

deflate *v.* (release air from) (…の) 空気を抜く

deflation *n.* (economic) デフレ

deflect *v.* (light, bullet) そらす

deforestation *n.* (cutting down of woods) 森林伐採

deformed *adj.* 奇形の, (ugly) 不格好な

defraud *v.* (defraud A of B) (AからBを)だまし取る

defrost *v.* (cause to thaw) 解凍する, (freezer, windshield) (…の) 霜を取る

deft *adj.* 器用な

defuse *v.* (situation) 和らげる, 緩和する, (bomb) (…から) 信管を取り除く

defy *v.* (oppose) (…に) 逆らう, 反抗する, (**defy to do**: challenge to do) (…に) …できるものなら…してみろと言う

He defied his boss.
彼は上司に逆らった。

degenerate *v.* (retrogress) 退化する, (worsen) 悪化する

n. (person) 堕落した人

The meeting degenerated into a shouting match.
会議は、ののしり合いと化した。

The situation in the Middle East is degenerating rapidly.
中東の情勢は急速に悪化している。

♦ **degeneration** *n.* (retrogression) 退化, (worsening) 悪化

degradation *n.* (worsening) 低下, 悪化, (of morals) 堕落; (of substance) 分解

The degradation of the environment by pollution continues.
公害による環境の悪化は続いている。

degrade *v.* (lower the position/status of) (…の地位/身分を) 下げる, 格下げする, (insult) 侮辱する, (**degrade oneself**) 品位を落とす, 身を落とす, 堕落する; (of substance) 分解する

Don't degrade yourself by working for that pimp.
あんなひものために働いて、身を落としてはいけないよ。

degree *n.* (of angle, heat) -度, (extent) 程度; (academic qualification) 学位

It was twenty-nine degrees (Fahrenheit) below zero outside.
外の気温は(カ氏)零下２９度だった。

An angle of ninety degrees is called a right angle.
９０度の角度を直角という。

I reckon we are at least fifteen degrees off course.
我々は、コースから少なくとも15度は外れていると思う。

To what degree are you prepared to support us?
どの程度我々を支援していただけるのですか？

Mr. Hattori has a degree in physics.
服部さんは物理学の学位をもっています。

by degrees 少しずつ, 徐々に

dehumidifier *n.* 除湿器

dehydrate *v.* (become dehydrated) 水分がなくなる, 脱水状態になる

If you don't drink some water, you'll soon dehydrate.
水を飲まないと、そのうち脱水状態になってしまいますよ。

dehydrated *adj.* (of person) 脱水状態の, (of food) 乾燥の

delay *v.* (**be delayed**) 遅れる, (cause to be late) 遅らせる, (postpone) 延期する

n. (being late) 遅れ, (postponement) 延期

Sorry, I was delayed by traffic.
すみません。渋滞して遅れてしまいました。

The train's been delayed by a signal failure.
電車は信号機の故障で遅れています。

The Opposition is trying to delay the introduction of the bill.
野党は議案の提出を遅らせせようとしている。

If you delay any longer, the opportunity will be lost.
これ以上延期[先延ばし]したら機会を逃してしまうよ。

There was one delay after another.
次々と遅れが出た。

The film's release was subject to several delays.
映画の公開は何度か延期された。

without delay 早速, すぐ(に), ただちに

If you hear anything about it, let me know without delay.
それについて何か聞いたら、すぐに知らせてください。

delegate ***n.*** (representative) 代表

v. (entrust with: power, authority etc.) (...に) 委任する, (appoint as a representative) 代表に任命する

delegation ***n.*** (group) 代表団

delete ***v.*** 消す, 削除する

n. (button on keyboard) デリート(キー)

I deleted the file by mistake.
ファイルを間違って削除してしまいました。

deliberate ***adj.*** (intentional) 故意の, 意図的な, (careful) 慎重な, よく考えた

v. (ponder) (...について) よく考える, 熟考する

It was not deliberate.
意図的なものではありませんでした。

deliberately ***adv.*** (intentionally) わざと, 故意に, (carefully) 慎重に

She deliberately ignored me.
彼女は私をわざと無視した。

Did you do that deliberately?
故意にやったんですか/((*informal*)) わざとやったの?

delicacy ***n.*** (rare dish) 珍味; (tact) 心づかい, 思いやり, 機転

with delicacy (with tact) 思いやりをもって, 機転を利かせて

delicate ***adj.*** (finely made) 繊細な, 精巧な, (beautiful) 優美な, (fragile) 壊れやすい, きゃしゃな, (frail) 弱い, 虚弱な, (sensitive) 敏感な, デリケートな; (of smell) ほのかな, かすかな; (requiring tact) 微妙な, デリケートな, (difficult) 難しい

a delicate fringe of lace
繊細なレースの縁取り

a delicate flower 優美な花

a delicate wine glass
繊細な[壊れやすい]ワイングラス

a delicate child 体の弱い子供

a delicate task 気をつかう仕事

a delicate perfume ほのかな香りの香水

a delicate flavor 繊細な味

a delicate position 微妙な[難しい]立場

a delicate issue デリケートな問題

delicatessen ***n.*** (shop) デリ(カテッセン), (お)総菜屋(さん)

delicious ***adj.*** おいしい, ((*informal*)) うまい

delight ***n.*** 喜び, うれしさ, 楽しみ

v. (**delight in**) 喜ぶ, 楽しむ, (...が)うれしい

It was a delight to see you again.
またお目にかかれてうれしかったです。

The old man delights in showing people photos of his grandchildren.
あのおじいさんは、孫の写真を人に見せるのがうれしいんです。

take delight in 喜ぶ

delighted ***adj.*** うれしい

I'm delighted to make your acquaintance.
お知り合いになれて、うれしいです。

I'm delighted to hear you passed your entrance exams.
入学試験に合格したと聞いてうれしいわ。

He was delighted with the gift.
彼は贈り物を喜んでいた。

delightful ***adj.*** 楽しい, 愉快な

delinquency ***n.*** 非行

delinquent ***adj.*** 不良の, 非行の
n. (juvenile delinquent) 不良, 非行少年

become delinquent 非行に走る

delirious ***adj.*** (due to fever) 精神が錯乱した, (speaks incoherently) うわごとを言う

delirium ***n.*** 精神錯乱

deliver ***v.***

1 CONVEY: (mail) 届ける, 配達する, (message) 伝える

2 BABY: (give birth to) 生む, 出産する, 分娩する

3 HAND OVER: 引き渡す, 手渡す

4 GIVE: (**deliver a speech**) 演説をする, スピーチをする

1 They're going to deliver the TV free of charge.
テレビの配達は無料でしてくれる。

Could you deliver the message to him?
彼にこのメッセージを伝えていただけますか？

2 She delivered a baby girl.
彼女は女の子を出産しました。

The baby was delivered at home.
赤ちゃんは自宅で生まれました。

3 I want the money delivered in person.
現金は直接、手渡しにしていただきたいんです。

4 The president will deliver his State of the Union Address tonight.
大統領は今夜、一般教書演説をします。

delivery ***n.*** (of mail) 配達, 引き渡し; (of baby) 出産, 分娩

a delivery charge 配達料

delta ***n.*** (geologic) デルタ, 三角州

delude ***v.*** (**delude into doing**) だまして…させる [→ DECEIVE], (**delude oneself**) 勘違いする, 思い込む

He deluded himself into thinking that he could win easily.
たやすく勝てると彼は思い込んでいた。

delusion ***n.*** (false belief) 思い違い, 勘違い

be under the delusion that …と勘違いをしている

He's under the delusion that every woman finds him attractive.
あいつは、どの女性も自分に魅力を感じると勘違いをしている。

have delusions of grandeur 誇大妄想をいだく

deluxe ***adj.*** 豪華な, デラックスな

a deluxe edition (of a book) 豪華版

D

deluxe accommodation
デラックスな宿泊設備(しゅくはくせつび)

demand *v.* (ask for) 強(つよ)く求(もと)める, 要求(ようきゅう)する, (claim as one's due) 主張(しゅちょう)する, (require) 必要(ひつよう)とする, 要(よう)する
n. (claim) 要求(ようきゅう), 請求(せいきゅう); (public need) 需要(じゅよう)

She demanded to see the manager.
彼女(かのじょ)はマネージャーに会(あ)わせるよう強(つよ)く求(もと)めた。

The workers demanded their rights.
労働者(ろうどうしゃ)は自分(じぶん)たちの権利(けんり)を主張(しゅちょう)した。

He demanded a refund.
彼(かれ)は払(はら)い戻(もど)しを要求(ようきゅう)した。

I demand an apology!
謝罪(しゃざい)を要求(ようきゅう)します！

We can't accept these demands.
これらの要求(ようきゅう)を受(う)け入(い)れることは(わ)できません。

supply and demand 需要(じゅよう)と供給(きょうきゅう)

There's a great demand for cell phones.
携帯電話(けいたいでんわ)には大(おお)きな需要(じゅよう)がある。

demanding *adj.* (of person) 難(むずか)しい, 厳(きび)しい, (of job) 難(むずか)しい, きつい, 骨(ほね)の折(お)れる

Firefighting is a demanding job.
消防士(しょうぼうし)はきつい仕事(しごと)だ。

demerit *n.* 欠点(けってん), 短所(たんしょ), デメリット

demilitarize *v.* 非武装化(ひぶそうか)する

♦ **demilitarization** *n.* 非武装化(ひぶそうか)

demilitarized zone *n.* 非武装地帯(ひぶそうちたい)

democracy *n.* (system of government) 民主主義(みんしゅしゅぎ), (country) 民主主義国家(みんしゅしゅぎこっか)

Democracy is the freedom to vote.
民主主義(みんしゅしゅぎ)とは自由(じゆう)に投票(とうひょう)できることです。

democrat *n.* (believer in democracy) 民主主義者(みんしゅしゅぎしゃ), (**Democrat**: Democratic Party member) 民主党員(みんしゅとういん)

democratic *adj.* (of process) 民主的(みんしゅてき)な, (of country) 民主主義(みんしゅしゅぎ)の

♦ **Democratic Party** *n.* 民主党(みんしゅとう)

demolish *v.* (destroy: building) 破壊(はかい)する, 取(と)り壊(こわ)す, (theory) くつがえす

That coffee shop we used to go to has been demolished.
私(わたし)たちがよく通(かよ)ったあの喫茶店(きっさてん)が、取(と)り壊(こわ)されてしまった。

demon *n.* 鬼(おに), 悪魔(あくま)

♦ **demonize** *v.* 悪魔(あくま)のように言(い)う

demonstrate *v.* (show) 見(み)せる, 実演(じつえん)する, (prove) 証明(しょうめい)する, (theory) 立証(りっしょう)する; (participate in a protest) デモをする

The ski instructor demonstrated how to fall safely.
スキーのインストラクターは安全(あんぜん)な転(ころ)び方(かた)を見(み)せてくれた。

KANJI BRIDGE

証 ON: しょう KUN: — | PROOF, EVIDENCE, CERTIFICATE

certificate	証明書(しょうめいしょ)
evidence	証拠(しょうこ), 証明(しょうめい)
guarantee	保証(ほしょう)
license	免許証(めんきょしょう)
receipt	領収証(りょうしゅうしょう)
securities	証券(しょうけん)
testimony	証言(しょうげん)
witness	証人(しょうにん)

demonstration *n.* (protest) デモ; (proof) 証明(しょうめい), (of theory) 立証(りっしょう); (showing) 実演(じつえん), デモンストレーション

demonstrator *n.* (protester) デモ参加者(さんかしゃ)

demote *v.* 降格させる

demotion *n.* 降格

den *n.* (animal's) ねぐら, (cave) ほら穴, (child's) 隠れ家

denial *n.* (refusal to admit) 否定, (refusal to grant) 拒否

denim *n.* デニム

Denmark *n.* デンマーク

denounce *v.* (publicly condemn) 非難する, ((*formal*)) 弾劾する

dense *adj.* (of fog) 深い, 濃い, (of forest) うっそうとした, (of undergrowth) 茂った, 密生した, (of population) 密度の高い, (of substance) 高密度の; (of person: stupid) ばかな, 頭が悪い

a dense forest うっそうとした森 [密林]

We struggled through the dense undergrowth.
密生した茂みの中を進むのに苦労した。

A dense cloud loomed overhead.
厚い雲におおわれていた。

density *n.* (of population) 密度, (of liquid, gas) 濃度

a high [low] density 高[低]密度

dent *n.* くぼみ, へこみ

v. (put a dent in) くぼませる, へこませる

dental *adj.* (of/for teeth) 歯の, (of/for dental surgery) 歯科の

dentist *n.* 歯医者(さん), ((*formal*)) 歯科医

dentistry *n.* 歯学, 歯科

dentures *n.* 入れ歯

wear dentures 入れ歯をしている

deny *v.* (negate) 否定する, (refuse) 断る, 拒否する

He denied any involvement in the matter.
彼は、その件との関与を全面的に否定した。

You did it! Don't deny it!
((*masculine*)) 君がやったんだ! やってないなんて言うなよ!

The public should not be denied the truth.
国民は真実を知らされるべきだ。

We were denied entrance to the restaurant because of our clothes.
服装のせいで、レストランへの入店を断られた。

deodorant *n.* デオドラント, 防臭剤

depart *v.* 出発する, (of train) 発車する [→ LEAVE 1]

department *n.* (of school) 学部, 学科, (of civil service) -署, (of company) -課, -部, (of store) 売り場, コーナー, (of U.S. government) -省

Professor Iwata is the head of the Japanese Department.
岩田先生は日本語学部の学部長です。

the police [fire] department
警察 [消防] 署

Mita works in the Sales Department.
三田さんは営業部に勤務している。

♦ **departmental** *adj.* 部署ごとの, 部門別の

department store *n.* デパート, 百貨店

departure *n.* (setting out) 出発, (of train) 発車; (resignation) 辞任, 辞職; (deviation) 逸脱

We were all packed and ready for departure.
荷物はまとまって、出発の準備は整った。

His sudden departure was suspicious.
あの人の突然の辞職はどうも怪しい。

It was a departure from conventional

thinking.
それは、従来の考え方から逸脱するものだった。

Minister, does this statement amount to a departure from previous policy?
大臣、今の発言は方針の転換を意味するのでしょうか？

♦ **departure lounge** *n.* 出発ロビー
departure time *n.* 出発時刻

depend (on) *v.*
1 BE CONTINGENT (ON): …による, …次第だ, …にかかっている
2 RELY ON: 当てにする, …に頼る, …に依存する, (trust in) 信頼する, 信用する

1 "How do you react when people say that to you?"
"Well, it all depends."
「そう言われたときはどうしますか？」
「それは時と場合によります」

Whether we go or not depends on the weather.
行くかどうかは、お天気次第だ。

It depends on whether she turns up or not.
それは彼女が来るかどうかにかかっている。

2 We can't depend on them too much.
彼らをあまり当てにはできない。

Can we depend on them to help us?
あの人たちの助けを当てにしてもいいのですか？

We depend too heavily on fossil fuels for energy.
我々はエネルギーをあまりにも化石燃料に依存しすぎている。

I knew I could depend on you.
あなたは頼りになるとわかっていました。

♦ **dependable** *adj.* 頼りになる, 信頼できる
a dependable person 頼りになる人

dependence *n.* (reliance) 依存, (trust) 信頼, 信用

dependent *adj.* (**be dependent on**) (= be contingent on) …による, …次第だ, …にかかっている, (= be reliant on) …に頼っている, …に依存している
n. (family member) 扶養家族

depict *v.* 描く, 描写する
The movie depicted him as a villain.
映画はその人を悪人として描いていた。

♦ **depiction** *n.* 描写

depletion *n.* (of resources) 枯渇, (of energy, power) 消耗

deploy *v.* (troops) 配置する, 展開する

deport *v.* 国外追放にする

♦ **deportation** *n.* 国外追放

depose *v.* (remove from office) 退位させる, 退陣させる
The president was deposed by a military coup d'état.
軍のクーデターで大統領は退陣させられた。

deposit *v.* (into bank) 預ける, 預金する
n. (bank deposit) 預金; (down payment) 頭金, (security deposit) 保証金, (for rented accommodations) 敷金

depreciate *v.* (become less valuable) 価値が下がる

♦ **depreciation** *n.* 価値の下落
depreciation of the yen
円の下落 [円安]

depress *v.* (make sad) 憂うつにさせる, 落ち込ませる, (cause to fall: prices) 下落

させる; (press with hand/finger) 押す, (press with foot) 踏む

Don't let it depress you.
落ち込まないで。

The minister's statement further depressed stock prices.
大臣の発言は株価をさらに下落させた。

depressed ***adj.*** (of person) 落ち込んでいる, 気がめいっている, (of market) 不景気な

"What's wrong?"
"I'm depressed."
「どうしたの？」
「落ち込んでるんだ」

depressing ***adj.*** 暗い, 陰気な, うっとうしい

That's a depressing story.
暗い話ですね。

a depressing song 陰気な歌

depressing weather うっとうしい天気

depression ***n.*** (unhappiness) 憂うつ, 意気消沈, (illness) うつ病, (economic) 不景気; (geologic) くぼ地

the Great Depression 世界大恐慌

deprive ***v.*** (deprive A of B) (AからBを) 奪う, 奪い取る, (of rights/freedom) (…から権利/自由を) 剥奪する

depth ***n.*** (from top to bottom) 深さ, (from front to back) 奥行き, (of tone) 低さ

deputy ***n.*** (representative) 代理, (in titles) 副-

He will be the university's next deputy chancellor.
あの方が次期大学副総長です。

derail ***v.*** 脱線させる, (become derailed) 脱線する

♦**derailment** ***n.*** 脱線

deregulate ***v.*** 規制を緩和する, 自由化する

♦**deregulation** ***n.*** 規制緩和, 自由化

derivation ***n.*** (origin) 起源, 由来

derive ***v.*** (derive from: originate from) (…から) 来ている, (…に) 由来する, 起源をもつ; (get) 得る

The word *marathon* is derived from Greek.
「マラソン」という言葉はギリシャ語から来ている。

He derives satisfaction from his job.
彼は仕事から満足感を得ている。

dermatology ***n.*** 皮膚科学

descend ***v.*** (come down from) 降りる, 下る, (**descend to doing**) …するまでに落ちぶれる

They descended the ski slope.
彼らはスキー場の斜面を下った。

He descended to stealing.
彼は盗みをするまでに落ちぶれた。

be descended from …の系統をひく, …の子孫だ

He claims he is descended from Russian nobility.
彼は自分がロシア貴族の子孫だと言い張っている。

descendant ***n.*** 子孫, 末裔

descent ***n.*** (downward path/motion) 降下, 下り, (from mountain) 下山

describe ***v.*** (express) 言い表す, (state the characteristics of) (…の) 特徴を言う, (depict) 描く, 描写する, (explain) 説明する

I can't describe how I felt when I saw the ocean for the first time.
初めて海を見た時の気持ちを言い表すことができない。

Try describing the man to me.
その男性の特徴を言ってみてください。

The novel describes life in the eighteenth century.
その小説は18 世紀当時の生活を描いています。

The scene was impossible to describe.
その光景を説明することはできなかった。

description ***n.*** (explanation) 説明, 解説, (depiction) 描写

desert[1] ***n.*** (sterile land) 砂漠

desert[2] ***v.*** (abandon) 捨てる [→ ABANDON]

deserted ***adj.*** (of streets) 人けのない, 寂しい, (of house) 人の住んでいない, (of village) さびれた

deserve ***v.*** (merit) (…に) 値する, (**deserve to be ——ed**) …されて当然だ

He deserves respect.
彼は尊敬に値する人だ。

I don't think she deserves the prize at all.
彼女は賞を受けるに値しないと思います。

He deserves to be thrown out of school.
あの人は退学処分になって当然だ。

He got what he deserved!
当然の報いだよ / ((*informal*)) あの人は、ばちが当たったんだ!

design ***n.*** (pattern) 柄, デザイン, 模様, 図案, (of building) 設計, (subject of study) デザイン, (plan, purpose) 計画, 目的, (plot) 陰謀
v. デザインする, (building, machine etc.) 設計する

I like this curtain design.
このカーテンの柄が好きです。

draw up a design 図案をかく

The design for the harbor was not approved.
港の設計は承認されなかった。

Who designed this?
これをデザインしたのは誰ですか?

designate ***v.*** (signify, indicate) 示す, 明示する, (appoint) 指名する, 任命する

designer ***n.*** デザイナー

desirable ***adj.*** 望ましい, 好ましい

desire ***n.*** 欲望, 欲求, (sexual) 性欲
v. 望む, 願う

desk ***n.*** (piece of furniture) 机, (front desk: reception counter) 受付, フロント

That desk is too big for my room.
その机は私の部屋には大きすぎる。

He is away from his desk at the moment.
((*polite*)) ただいま席を外しております。

desktop ***n.*** (top of desk) 机の上, (part of computer OS) デスクトップ, (desktop computer) デスクトップ(コンピューター)

desolate ***adj.*** (lonely) 寂しい, 孤独な, (uninhabited) 人けのない, (rundown) 荒れ果てた

despair ***n.*** (hopelessness) 絶望, 失望
v. (lose hope) 絶望する, 失望する, あきらめる

desperate ***adj.*** (ready to do anything) 死にもの狂いの, 必死の, (reckless) やけくその, (hopeless) 絶望的な, (bitter, severe) 厳しい

They're desperate criminals.
彼らはやけくその凶悪犯だ。

It was a last, desperate attempt to win the title.
タイトル獲得のための最後のあがきだった。

It's a desperate situation. We must act now.
厳しい状況なので今すぐ行動しなければならない。

be desperate for 必死で求める, (…が)欲しくてたまらない

She's desperate for attention.
彼女は注目されたくてたまらないんだ。

They are desperate for food and shelter.
彼らは食べ物と住居を今すぐ必要としている。

be desperate to do …したくてたまらない

desperately *adv.* 必死に

despise *v.* 嫌う, 軽蔑する

despite *prep.* …にもかかわらず

Despite his poor health, he still perseveres.
彼は体の衰えにもかかわらず、まだがんばっている。

dessert *n.* デザート

destabilize *v.* (region, country) 不安定にする, (…に) 揺さぶりをかける

destination *n.* 行き先, 目的地

What's your destination, please?
行き先はどちらですか？

destiny *n.* 運命, 宿命 [→ FATE]

Napoleon was the master of his own destiny.
ナポレオンは自らの運命を切り開いていった。

destroy *v.* (demolish) 破壊する, 壊す, 滅ぼす, (mess up) 乱す

The city was destroyed by air strikes.
街は空襲で破壊された。

Some would say Japanese is being destroyed by loanwords.
日本語は外来語によって乱されていると思っている人もいる。

destroyer *n.* (warship) 駆逐艦

destruction *n.* 破壊, 破滅

destructive *adj.* 破壊的な

detach *v.* 取り外す, 引き離す

detached *adj.* (aloof) 無関心な

detail *n.* ディテール, 細かいこと, 詳しいこと, ((*formal*)) 細部, 詳細

She's amazing. She can remember every single detail.
彼女はすごいね。細かいことまでよく覚えている。

Attention to detail is the key to success.
細部にまで注意を払うことが、成功の秘訣です。

We don't have to go into detail at this stage.
今の段階では、詳しく説明しなくてもいい。

detailed *adj.* 細かい, 詳細な

a detailed explanation 詳細な説明

detain *v.* (keep back) 引き止める, (keep in custody) 拘留する, 留置する

detect *v.* (notice) (…に) 気がつく, (discover) 発見する

detective *n.* 刑事, (private detective) 探偵

a detective agency 興信所 [探偵社]

detector *n.* 探知器

a smoke detector 煙探知器

detention *n.* (at school) 居残り, (at police station) 留置

deter *v.* (discourage) 思いとどまらせる, やめさせる

Such laws are meant to deter people from drinking and driving.
このような法律は飲酒運転をやめさせるのが目的である。

detergent *n.* 洗剤 [→ picture of KITCHEN]

deteriorate *v.* 悪くなる, 悪化する

determination *n.* (resolve) 決意, 決心

determine *v.* (decide) 決定する, 左右する, (**be determined by**) …によって決まる; (figure out) 突き止める

Do you think the position of the planets determines our fate?
惑星の位置が私たちの運命を左右するのだと思う?

Meaning is determined by context.
意味は文脈によって決まるものだ。

First we need to determine how the accident happened.
まず、事故がどうやって発生したかを突き止める必要がある。

determined *adj.* (resolved) 決心した, 断固とした, (**be determined to do**) どうしても/絶対…しようとする, …しようと決心する

She was determined to get her way.
彼女は自分の思いどおりにやろうと決心した。

deterrent *n.* 防止するもの, (nuclear weapon) 核兵器

detonate *v.* (explode) 爆発する, (cause to explode) 爆発させる

detour *n.* 回り道

devalue *v.* (currency) (…の) 平価を切り下げる

devastate *v.* (destroy) 破壊する, (lay waste to) 荒らす

devastating *adj.* (destructive) 壊滅的な, (shocking) 衝撃的な

develop *v.*

1 BECOME/MAKE MORE ADVANCED: 発展する/させる, 発達する/させる, (skill) 伸びる/伸ばす, (of body, mind) 成長する, (land, resources, technology) 開発する

2 OF SITUATION: (…に) なる, 発生する, 現れる

3 ACQUIRE: (hobby, interest) もつ, (sense, strength) 身につける, 養う

4 FILM: 現像する

1 This country has developed very rapidly.
この国は急速に発展した。

What started as a misunderstanding has developed into a full-blown argument.
ちょっとした誤解が大論争へと発展してしまった。

Her skating skills have developed remarkably in the past year.
彼女のスケート技術は、この1年でめざましく伸びた。

The caterpillar develops first into a chrysalis and then into a butterfly.
いも虫は最初さなぎになって、それからちょうに成長します。

They are developing the area to attract more tourists.
観光客を増やすためにあの地域を開発している。

New technologies are being developed all the time.
新しい技術が常に開発されている。

Our company plans to develop a new machine each year.
当社は新機種を毎年1台開発する計画です。

2 How is the situation developing?
進行状況はどうなっていますか？

3 It would be good if he developed more interests.
彼がもっといろいろなことに興味をもつといいんだけど。

4 It will take an hour to develop the film.
現像するのに1時間かかります。

♦**developed country** *n.* 先進国

developing country *n.* 発展途上国

development *n.* (of sth new) 開発, (of existing resources) 発展, 発達

device *n.* 装置, (tool) 道具

devil *n.* (demon) 鬼, 悪魔, (**the Devil**: Satan) サタン

Speak of the devil! うわさをすれば影。

devise *v.* (plan, design) 考案する, 工夫する

devote *v.* (money, effort) ささげる, (time) あてる, (**devote oneself to/be devoted to**: hobby, job) …に身をささげる, …に熱中する, …に専念する

Mr. Ota devotes his free time to charity work.
太田さんは空き時間をボランティア活動にあてています。

devoted *adj.* (of teacher, spouse) 献身的な [→ DEVOTE]

devotion *n.* (dedication) 献身, (love) 愛情, (to religion) 帰依, 信心

dew *n.* 露, しずく

dextrose *n.* ブドウ糖

diabetes *n.* 糖尿病

diabetic *n.* 糖尿病患者

diagnose *v.* (diagnose A as/with B) (AをBと) 診断する

diagnosis *n.* 診断

diagonal *adj.* 斜めの
n. (line) 対角線, 斜線

diagram *n.* 図, 図表

dial *n.* (on telephone) ダイヤル, (on instrument) 文字盤
v. ダイヤルする, ダイヤルを回す, 番号を押す, (use telephone) 電話をかける

♦**dial tone** *n.* 発信音

dialect *n.* 方言

dialogue *n.* 対話, 会談

diameter *n.* (of circle) 直径, (of lens) -倍

diamond *n.* (jewel) ダイヤ (モンド), (shape) ひし形, (**diamonds**: suit of cards) ダイヤ

diaper *n.* おむつ, おしめ

Better change the baby's diaper.
赤ちゃんのおむつを替えたほうがいいね。

diaphragm *n.* (part of the body) 横隔膜; (of telephone, microphone) 振動板, (of lens) 絞り; (form of contraception) ペッサリー

diarrhea *n.* 下痢

have diarrhea 下痢をする

diary *n.* (daily record) 日記, (book) 日記帳

Do you keep a diary?
日記をつけていますか？

dice *n.* (for game) さいころ, ダイス
v. (chop up) さいの目に切る

throw dice さいころを振る

dictate *v.* (speak and have one's words

recorded) 書き取らせる, 口述する; (give orders) 命令する

dictation ***n.*** ディクテーション, 書き取り

dictator ***n.*** 独裁者

dictatorship ***n.*** (rule) 独裁, (system of government) 独裁政治

dictionary ***n.*** 辞書, 辞典, 字引き

Look it up in a dictionary.
辞書を引いてみて。

a kanji dictionary 漢字辞典

a Japanese-English dictionary 和英辞典

a learner's dictionary 学習辞典

a walking dictionary (i.e., person with encyclopedic knowledge) 生き字引き

♦ **dictionary form** ***n.*** (Japanese verb form) 辞書形

die ***v.*** 死ぬ, ((*polite*)) 亡くなる, ((*formal*)) 死亡する, (of plant) 枯れる

She died of leukemia.
あの人は白血病で亡くなった。

What did he die of?
死因は何だったんですか/((*polite*)) 何で亡くなられたんですか？

I wonder how many people have died of AIDS.
どのくらいの人がエイズで死んでいるのでしょう。

All the plants have died because you forgot to water them.
君が水をやるのを忘れたから、植物が全部枯れてしまったよ。

be dying for (…が) 欲しくてたまらない

I'm dying for a cigarette.
たばこを吸いたくてたまらない。

I'm dying for something to drink.
何か飲みたくてたまらない/のどが、からからだ。(lit., "My throat is dry.")

be dying to do …したくてたまらない, ものすごく…したい

I'm dying to see her again.
もう一度彼女に会いたくてたまらない。

die down ***v.*** (of fire) 消えそうになる, (of excitement) 静まる, (of wind) 弱くなる, おさまる, 静まる

die out ***v.*** (of animals) 絶滅する, (of fire) 消える

It's sad that so many animals are dying out.
こんなに多くの動物が絶滅しつつあるのは悲しいことだ。

diesel ***n.*** (engine) ディーゼル(エンジン), (car) ディーゼル車, (oil) ディーゼル油

diet[1] ***n.*** (weight-loss program) ダイエット, (food eaten) 食物

v. ダイエットする, 食事制限する

Are you on a diet?
ダイエット中なの？

a healthy diet of fruit and vegetables
フルーツと野菜の健康的な食事

diet[2] ***n.*** (**the Diet**: legislative assembly in Japan) 国会, 議会

dietetics ***n.*** 栄養学

differ ***v.*** (be unlike) 違う, 異なる, (have different opinions) 意見が違う

Our opinions clearly differ.
私たちの考えは明らかに違う。

They differ in their attitude toward work.
彼らは仕事に対する姿勢が異なる。

I beg to differ 私の考えは違うんです [→ "EXPRESSING DISAGREEMENT" on p.263]

difference *n.* 違い, 相違, 相違点, (degree of difference) 差, (difference in cost) 差額, (**differences**: disputes) 食い違い

There isn't a big difference between these cars.
これらの車には大した違いはない。

The difference is obvious.
相違点は明らかだ。

temperature difference
(of liquids, solids) 温度差, (of air) 気温差

The age difference is three years.
年の差は3歳です。

We paid the difference.
私たちは差額を支払った。

settle one's differences
食い違いを解消する

make all the difference 大違いだ

Your being there for me made all the difference.
あなたがそこにいるかいないかで、私にとっては大違いでした。

not make a difference if / whether ... (or ...) ...でも(...でも)違わない, どっちでもいい

It doesn't make a difference whether you go by bus or by train; it will take the same amount of time.
バスで行っても電車で行っても違わないよ。かかる時間は同じだから。

It doesn't make any difference if you write it by hand or type it out.
手書きでもタイプで打ってもどっちでもいい。

It doesn't make any difference!
((*informal*)) どうでもいいよ/大して変わらないよ!

different *adj.* (different from) (...と) 違う, 別の, 異なる, (unique) 独特の, (strange) 変わった; (other) 別の, ほかの; (various) いろいろな

"What did you think of it?"
"Well, it was different from what I had hoped for."
「どう思った?」
「うん、期待してたのとは違っていたね」

It's different from any film I've seen before.
これまで見たどの映画とも違います。

Let's go somewhere different for a change.
気分転換に違う所へ行ってみましょう。

I think I'll order something different this time.
今回は違うものを注文してみよう。

We need a different angle on this article.
この記事については別の見方が必要ですね。

Let's try a different approach.
別の方法を試してみよう。

There were all sorts of different birds there.
そこにはいろいろな種類の鳥がいた。

difficult *adj.* 難しい, (**difficult to do**) ...しにくい, ...しづらい, (of person: difficult to manage) 扱いにくい, (difficult to please) 気難しい, (of times: trying) 苦しい, つらい

Is it difficult? 難しいですか?

That is a very difficult question.
それは非常に難しい質問ですね。

It was difficult for us to understand what he was saying.
私たちには、彼の言っていることがわかりにくかった。

It's very difficult to concentrate when there's so much noise.
騒音がひどくて、とても集中しにくい。

That's easy to say but difficult to do.
言うは易く、行うは難し。

It's difficult to help someone like that.
ああいう人は、手の差し伸べようがない。

It's a difficult thing to tell him.
言いづらいことです。

He's a difficult customer.
(彼は)扱いにくい人だ。

Those were difficult times for our parents.
両親にとって、そのころは苦しい時代でした。

difficulty *n.* (problem) 困難, (degree of difficulty: of problem, language) 難しさ

dig *v.* 掘る, (look for) 探し出す, (probe, investigate) 掘り下げる, 探求する

The dog dug a hole to hide its bone.
犬は骨を隠す穴を掘った。

♦ **dig up/out** *v.* ((*also figurative*)) 掘り出す

digest *v.* (food) 消化する, (idea, information) 理解する

n. (book) 要約, ダイジェスト

That steak was difficult to digest.
あのステーキは消化しにくかった。

♦ **digestion** *n.* 消化

digit *n.* けた

a four-digit number 4けたの数字

digital *adj.* デジタルの

digital broadcasting デジタル放送

♦ **digital camera** *n.* デジタルカメラ, ((*informal*)) デジカメ

dignified *adj.* 堂々とした, 品位のある

dignity *n.* (self-respect) 威厳, (inherent worth) 尊厳, (decency) 品位

lose one's dignity 威厳を失う

digress *v.* 脱線する, 余談をする

dilemma *n.* ジレンマ, 板挟み

be in a dilemma 板挟みになる

diligence *n.* 勤勉

diligent *adj.* 勤勉な, まめな

dill *n.* ディル

dilute *v.* (liquid) 薄める, (argument, explanation) (…の) 効果を弱める

dim *adj.* (of light) 薄暗い, (of outline) ぼんやりした, はっきりしない, (of memory) かすかな, (of person: stupid) 頭の鈍い, ばかな, (of color) くすんだ

v. (make darker) 暗くする

dime *n.* (coin) 10セント硬貨

dimension *n.* (largeness) 大きさ, (**dimensions**: measurements) 寸法; (mathematical concept) 次元 ; (important factor) 要素

There's a political dimension to this problem.
この問題には政治的な要素がある。

diminish *v.* (become less) 減る, (of power: become weaker) 弱まる

dimple *n.* えくぼ

have dimples えくぼがある

dine *v.* 食事をする

♦ **dine out** *v.* 外食する

dining car *n.* 食堂車

dining/dinner table *n.* 食卓

dining room *n.* 食堂, ダイニング(ルーム) [→ picture of APARTMENT]

dinner *n.* 食事, ディナー, (evening meal) 晩ご飯, 夕食, (banquet) ディナーパーティー, 晩餐会

What time is dinner tonight?
晩ご飯は何時？

What did you have for dinner?
夕食に何を食べたの？

Let's go out for dinner tonight.
今夜は外で食事をしましょう。

dinosaur *n.* (prehistoric reptile) 恐竜; (sth big and obsolete) 大きくて時代遅れの物, 無用の長物

dioxin *n.* ダイオキシン

dip *v.* (immerse in liquid) 浸す; (of road) 下がる, (of sun) 沈む, (headlights) 下向きにする

n. (brief swim) 一泳ぎ; (slight hollow) くぼみ; (thick sauce) ディップ

Dip the cloth in the dye several times.
布を染料に何度か浸してください。

I think I'll go for a dip in the pool.
プールに、一泳ぎしに行ってくる。

diphtheria *n.* ジフテリア

diphthong *n.* 二重母音

diploma *n.* 卒業証書, 修了証書

diplomacy *n.* (political) 外交, (social) 駆け引き

diplomat *n.* 外交官

diplomatic *adj.* 外交上の, 外交的な, (of behavior) そつのない

diplomatic relations (between countries)
外交関係

direct

1 ***adj.*** IN A STRAIGHT LINE: (of route) 直行の, (of family line) 直系の, (of sunlight) 直射…, (of contact) 直接の

2 *v.* GUIDE AND CONTROL: (a project) 指揮する, (business operations) 管理する, (film) 監督する, (play) 演出する, (orchestra) 指揮する, (group) 指導する

3 *v.* SHOW THE WAY: 導く, (道を)教える

4 *v.* POINT/AIM: (attention, remark) 向ける, (energies) 注ぐ

5 ***adj.*** FORTHRIGHT: (of person, behavior) 率直な, (of question) 単刀直入な

6 ***adv.*** OF FLIGHT/TRAIN: 直行で, 直通で

7 *v.* ORDER: (**direct to do**) (…に)…するよう命令する

1 I flew the direct route.
直行ルートで飛びました。

Are there any direct flights to Atlanta?
アトランタまでの直行便はありますか？

She says she's a direct descendant of the Hapsburgs.
彼女は自分がハプスブルク家の直系だと言っている。

Keep it in a dry, cool place out of direct sunlight.
直射日光の当たらない、乾燥した涼しい場所に置いてください。

Her parents have no direct knowledge of what she's up to.
両親は彼女が何をしているか直接は知らない。

2 Who's going to direct the project?
そのプロジェクトは誰が指揮するのですか？

Who directed the movie?
その映画の監督は誰ですか？

3 Could you direct me to the nearest station?
最寄りの駅はどこか教えてもらえますか？

4 His remarks were directed at me.
その人の発言は私に向けられていた。

The country directed all its efforts to rebuilding the city after the earthquake.
国は地震後の街の再建に、全力をあげた。

5 His manner is very direct.
彼の態度はとても率直です。

That's a very direct question.
とても単刀直入な質問ですね。

6 You can't go direct. You have to change at Shinjuku Station.
直通では行けません。新宿駅で乗り換えなくてはなりません。

♦**direct current** *n.* 直流

direct mail *n.* ダイレクトメール, DM

direct object *n.* 直接目的語

direction *n.* (course) 方向, (cardinal point) 方角; (**directions**) (=instructions) 説明, 指示, (=to a place) 行き方, 道

I think we're going in the wrong direction.
私たち、間違った方向に進んでいる気がする。

I saw them head off in that direction.
あっちの方に向かって行くのを見ました。

I have no sense of direction, so I get lost all the time.
方向音痴なので、しょっちゅう道に迷う。

Just follow the directions on the bottle.
びんに書いてある指示に従えばいい。

In the end I had to ask someone for directions.
結局、人に道を聞かなければならなかった。

directly *adv.* (straight) まっすぐ, 直接(に), (immediately) すぐ, ただちに, (not through an intermediary) 直接(に), じかに

The sun was shining directly into my eyes.
日差しが直接、目に差し込んでいた。

Please send your invoice to me directly.
請求書は直接、私に送ってください。

I didn't speak with him directly, however.
その人と、じかには話さなかったけれど。

director *n.* (of company) 取締役, 重役, (of civil service) 局長, 署長, (of institute) 所長, (of project) 責任者, 指導者, (of film) 監督, (of TV program) ディレクター

an art director 美術監督

directory *n.* 人名簿, 住所録

a telephone directory 電話帳

a business directory 商工人名録

dirt *n.* (stain) 汚れ, (dust) ほこり, (grime) あか, (mud) 泥, (earth) 土

dirty *adj.* (soiled) 汚い, 汚れた, (unhygienic) 不潔な, (dirty-minded) エッチな, みだらな, (of joke) 下品な, わいせつな
v. (make dirty) 汚す

The floor is dirty.
床が汚れている。

Your clothes are dirty and your hands are filthy.
服は汚れているし、手も汚い。

This is a dirty job.
これは汚い仕事だ。

a dirty magazine エッチな雑誌

a dirty old man ((*offensive*)) スケベおやじ

He seems to enjoy telling dirty jokes.
彼は下品な冗談を言うのが好きらしい。

You've dirtied the carpet with your muddy shoes.
泥だらけの靴でカーペットを汚したでしょう。

Don't dirty it! I've only just cleaned it.
汚さないで！ たった今掃除したばかりなんだから。

give a dirty look にらむ

play a dirty trick on 卑劣な手でだます

dis- *pref.* (in-) 不-, (non-) 非-, (-less) 無-

disability *n.* 身体障害, ハンディキャップ

disable *v.* (alarm etc.) 作動させない

disabled *adj.* (of person) 身体に障害のある, 体の不自由な

n. (**the disabled**) 身体障害者

disadvantage *n.* 不利, (thing that puts one at a disadvantage) 不利となるもの, (unfavorable position/condition) 不利な立場/条件

It put us at a disadvantage.
そのことで我々は不利な立場に立たされた。

♦ **disadvantaged** *adj.* 恵まれない, 不利な

disagree *v.* (have different opinions) 意見が違う, 意見が合わない [→ AGREE], (be incongruent/inconsistent) 一致しない, 食い違う, (not suit) 合わない

I disagree. I think the company has made a mistake.
そうは思いません。会社は間違いをおかしたと思います。

He and I disagree on this matter.
この件については彼と私は意見が合わない。

D

EXPRESSING DISAGREEMENT

Direct disagreement can sound rude in Japanese. To gently disagree with someone, use どうでしょう, "I wonder," as in the following examples.

"Students these days—they don't read." 「今の大学生は本を読まない」
"Hmmm. I wonder about that." 「ううん…、どうでしょう」

(*in business*) "Their opinion is ridiculous. You can ignore it."
"Well, I don't know about that."
「先方の意見はばかげている。無視していいよ」
「それはどうでしょう」

そうですか, spoken with rising intonation on the last syllable, can also be used to express non-confrontational disagreement.

"It's a great movie." 「あの映画はいいね」
"Is it?" 「そうですか？」

NOTE: The less formal そうかなあ or the feminine そうかしら can be used in place of そうですか, but they are spoken with falling intonation.

Another strategy for disagreeing—also used in English—is to admit that what the other person has said might be true, before expressing doubt.

"His plan is unrealistic."
"That may well be the case, but somehow I don't think so."
「彼の計画は非現実的だ」
「それはそうかもしれませんが、どうも私はそう思いませんが」

If you cannot agree to a request or suggestion but it is difficult to say so outright, consider using 考えておきます, "I'll think about it" or また様子を見てから, "I'll have to gauge the situation." These words can imply "no."

Your account disagrees with what Ken says.
あなたの説明はケンの言っていることと一致しませんね。

I'm afraid garlic disagrees with me.
私、ニンニクはだめなんです。

agree to disagree 見解の相違を認める

This is a question about which we will have to agree to disagree.
この問題については、お互いの見解の相違を認めるしかありません。

disagreeable ***adj.*** (of thing) 不愉快な, (of person) 不機嫌な, 気難しい

disagreement ***n.*** (difference of opinion) 意見の不一致, (argument) けんか

disappear ***v.*** 消える, 消えていく, (from sight) 見えなくなる, 姿を消す, (of pen etc.: become lost) なくなる, (become extinct) 消滅する, 絶滅する

She can't have just disappeared!
彼女が今姿を消すはずはないのに!

The ship disappeared over the horizon.
船は水平線のかなたに見えなくなった。

How long ago was it that the dinosaurs disappeared?
恐竜が絶滅したのは、どのくらい前だったのですか?

♦ **disappearance** ***n.*** (of person) 失踪, 行方不明, (vanishing) 消滅

disappoint ***v.*** がっかりさせる, 失望させる

I'm sorry to disappoint you.
がっかりさせて申し訳ない。

I wouldn't be disappointed if I were you.
私だったら、がっかりしないけれど。

Frankly, I was disappointed with his reply.
正直言って、彼の返事に失望した。

disappointing ***adj.*** 期待外れの, がっかりさせられる

The result was very disappointing.
結果は期待外れだった。

disappointment ***n.*** (state of being disappointed) 失望, (thing that disappoints)

期待外れ, 失望のたね

disapproval *n.* (disfavor) 不賛成, (criticism) 非難

disapprove *v.* (disapprove of) よくないと思う, (…に) 賛成しない

She disapproves of his smoking.
彼女は彼の喫煙をよくないと思っている。

disarm *v.* (remove weapons from) (…の)武装を解除する

♦ **disarmament** *n.* 武装解除

nuclear disarmament 核武装の解除

disaster *n.* 災害, 災難, (natural) 天災, (man-made) 人災; (big mistake) 大失敗, さんたんたるもの

She was in Kobe when the (earthquake) disaster happened.
震災が起きた時、彼女は神戸にいました。

Chernobyl was a disaster waiting to happen.
チェルノブイリは起きて当然の [起こるべくして起きた] 災害だった。

The experiment was a disaster.
実験は大失敗だった。

My first day at the office was a disaster.
私の勤務初日はさんたんたるものだった。

disastrous *adj.* (calamitous) 災害を引き起こす, 破滅を招く, 壊滅的な, (tragic) 悲惨な [→ TERRIBLE]

disc *n.* → DISK, CD, DVD

discern *v.* (see) (…が) 見える, (tell apart) 見分ける, (understand) 理解する, (…が) わかる

I can't discern any difference between the original Picasso and the fake.
私には本物のピカソの絵と偽物の違いがわからない。

discharge *v.* (waste) 排出する, (electricity) 放電する, (water) 排水する; (**be discharged**) (=from hospital) 退院する, (=from military) 除隊する, (=be judged not guilty) 釈放される

n. (of waste) 排出, (of electricity) 放電, (of water) 排水; (from hospital) 退院, (from military) 除隊

This factory is discharging toxic waste into the atmosphere.
この工場は、有毒な廃棄物を大気中に排出しています。

disciple *n.* (follower) 弟子, (apostle) 使徒

the Disciples of Christ キリスト十二使徒

discipline *n.* (standards of conduct) 規律, (good behavior, the exaction of) しつけ, (training in habits of obedience) 訓練, (self-discipline) 自制心; (field of specialization/expertise) 学問, 専門分野

v. (punish) 罰する; (**discipline oneself**) 自制する

There is very little discipline in this school.
この学校には規律がほとんどありません。

The boy needs discipline.
その子にはしつけが必要だ。

His discipline is theology.
彼の専門分野は神学です。

The prisoner was severely disciplined for breaking the rules.
囚人は規律違反をしたために、厳しく罰せられた。

You've got to discipline yourself.
自制しなくてはいけませんよ。

disc jockey *n.* ディスクジョッキー, ＤＪ

disclose *v.* (make known) 明らかにす

る, 明かす, (announce) 発表する

The press could not disclose the boy's name because he was under twenty.
２０歳未満だったため、報道機関は少年の名前を明かすことができなかった。

The results will be disclosed tomorrow.
結果は明日発表されます。

♦ **disclosure** ***n.*** (revealing) 暴露, (making public) 公開, 開示

disco ***n.*** ディスコ

disconnect ***v.*** (telephone) 切る, (plug) 抜く

Have you disconnected the plug?
プラグを抜いた？

discontent ***n.*** 不満

♦ **discontented** ***adj.*** 不満な

discontinue ***v.*** (product) 製造中止にする, (talks) やめる

discotheque → DISCO

discount ***n.*** (reduction of price) 割引, 値引き, ディスカウント, (discount rate) 割引率

v. (lower the price of) 割り引く, 割り引きする, ((*informal*)) まける; (disregard) 無視する

Can you offer a discount?
まけて [安くして] もらえますか？

You'll get no discount at that store.
あの店は少しも値引きしてくれないよ。

discourage ***v.*** (**discourage from doing**) (…に) …するのを思いとどまらせる, (disappoint) がっかりさせる, (cause to lose confidence) (…の) 自信を失わせる, (**be discouraged**: be disappointed) がっかりする, 失望する, 落胆する, くじける

The difficulty of the entrance exams discouraged me from applying to that school.
その学校は入学試験が難しいので、出願するのをあきらめた。

His negative comments discouraged me.
彼の否定的な意見に失望した。

Don't be discouraged. You'll do better next time.
くじけないで。次はきっともっとうまくできるよ。

♦ **discouraging** ***adj.*** (of news) がっかりする, 思わしくない

discourse ***n.*** (speech) 講演, (writing) 論文, (formal discussion) 議論

discover ***v.*** 発見する, (understand) (…と) わかる, (notice) (…に) 気づく

Faraday discovered electricity.
ファラデーが電気を発見した。

Who was it that discovered the ruins?
その遺跡を発見したのは誰ですか？

It took me a long time to discover his real intentions.
彼の本当の意図がわかるまでには、かなりの時間がかかった。

discovery ***n.*** (act of discovering) 発見, (thing discovered) 発見されたもの

DNA was probably the most important discovery of the twentieth century.
ＤＮＡは２０世紀の最も重要な発見だろう。

discredit ***v.*** (cause people to lose trust in) 信頼させない, (damage the reputation of) (…の) 信用を傷つける

n. (distrust) 不信, (doubt) 疑惑, (damage to reputation) 不名誉

discreet *adj.* (cautious so as not to embarrass) 慎重な, 分別のある, (reserved) 目立たない, 控え目な

He was very discreet about his comings and goings.
彼は目立たないよう、ひっそり出入りしていた。

♦ **discreetly** *adv.* ひっそり(と)

discretion *n.* (caution) 慎重さ; (freedom to do as one sees fit) 自由裁量

discriminate *v.* (discriminate between A and B) (AとBを) 見分ける, 区別する; (**discriminate against**) 差別する

discriminating *adj.* (of person) 目の利く, 通の, (about food) 舌の肥えた

discrimination *n.* (unfair treatment) 差別; (ability to discern) 識別力

racial discrimination 人種差別
sexual discrimination 性差別

discus *n.* (object) 円盤, (sport) 円盤投げ

discuss *v.* (talk about) 話し合う, (when seeking another's advice/opinion) 相談する, (debate) 論じる, 討論する, 議論する

Let's discuss that when we meet.
その件については、お会いした時に話し合いましょう。

I think you'd better discuss that with your teacher.
それは先生に相談したほうがいいと思うよ。

discussion *n.* (talk) 話し合い, (conference) 相談, (formal debate) 議論, 討論

disease *n.* 病気, (in names of diseases) -病

Parkinson's disease パーキンソン病
a sexually transmitted disease 性病

disembark *v.* (...から) 降りる

disgrace *n.* (dishonor) 恥, 不名誉, (person/act that brings about shame) 恥さらし

v. (...の) 名を汚す, (**disgrace oneself**) 恥をかく, 面目を失う

She's a disgrace to the school.
彼女は学校の恥だ。

It's a disgrace. He should resign.
恥さらしな。あの人は辞職すべきだ。

He disgraced himself in front of everyone.
彼は皆の前で恥をかいた。

disgraceful *adj.* 恥ずかしい, 不名誉な, みっともない

disguise *v.* (...に) 見せかける, (**disguise oneself as**) ...に変装する, (conceal: emotion, intention etc.) 隠す

n. (costume) 変装; (pretense) まやかし, ごまかし

They disguised themselves as nuns.
彼らは修道女に変装した。

I saw through his disguise at once.
すぐに彼のまやかしを見抜いた。

disgust *n.* (dislike) 嫌け, 嫌悪, (feeling of revulsion) むかつき, 吐き気

v. (...に) 吐き気を催させる, (**be disgusted by**: be repulsed by) ...にぞっとする, (**be disgusted with**: be fed up with) ...にうんざりする

I left the meeting in disgust.
私は嫌けがさして会議室を後にした。

The smell disgusted me.
そのにおいに吐き気がした。

I was disgusted by his drunken behavior.
彼の酔っ払い方にはうんざりした。

disgusting *adj.* いやな, 気持ちが悪い

dish *n.* (crockery) (お)皿, 食器 [→ picture of KITCHEN], (small dish) 小皿, 取り皿, (large dish) 大皿, 盛り皿 [→ BOWL¹]; (plate of food) 料理

Do you have any smaller dishes?
もっと小さなお皿はありますか？

We need four more dishes.
お皿がもう4枚必要です。

do the dishes (お)皿洗いをする, 食器を洗う

Who's going to do the dishes?
食器は誰が洗うの？

dishcloth *n.* ふきん

dishonest *adj.* 不正直な, (cunning) ずるい, (of act, behavior) 不正な

dishonesty *n.* 不正直

dishwasher *n.* (appliance) 食器洗い機, (restaurant employee) (お)皿洗い

disillusioned *adj.* (disillusioned by/with) (…に) 幻滅する

disinfect *v.* 消毒する

disinfectant *n.* 消毒剤

disk *n.* 円盤, (disklike object) 円盤状の物; (between bones) 椎間板; (for computer) ディスク

slip a disk 椎間板ヘルニアになる

disk drive *n.* ディスクドライブ

dislike *v.* 嫌う, いやがる

n. 嫌い, 嫌け, 嫌悪

I don't dislike him—I hate him.
彼のことは、嫌いどころか大嫌いだ。

He's disliked by his classmates.
あの人はクラスメートに嫌われている。

take a dislike to (…が) 嫌いになる, …に嫌けがさす

I took an immediate dislike to her.
すぐに彼女が嫌いになった。

dislocate *v.* (shoulder etc.) 脱臼させる, (…の) 骨を外す

dismiss *v.* (from job) 解雇する, (from classroom) 退出させる; (disregard) 捨てる, (court case) 却下する

dismissal *n.* (from job) 解雇, (from public post) 解任; (disregarding) 放棄, (of case by court) 却下

disobedience *n.* 不服従, 反抗, (to law) 違反

disobey *v.* (not follow) (…に) 従わない, (not do as one is told) (…の) 言うことをきかない

The soldiers disobeyed their officer's orders.
兵士たちは上官の命令に従わなかった。

disorder *n.* (confusion) 混乱

disorganized *adj.* (of room) めちゃくちゃな, 混乱した, (of person) でたらめな

This room is completely disorganized.
この部屋は全くめちゃくちゃだ。

a disorganized person
きちんとしていない [でたらめな] 人

disoriented *adj.* (befuddled) 頭がぼうっとした, (has lost one's sense of direction) 方向感覚を失った

disown *v.* (son, daughter) 勘当する

disparity *n.* 相違, 格差, 差

dispatch *v.* (person) 派遣する

dispel *v.* (doubts) 晴らす, (worries) 振

り払う, 一掃する

dispense *v.* (**dispense with**: do without) 省く, …なしで済ます; (distribute without cost) 施す

Let's dispense with formalities and get straight to the point.
堅苦しいあいさつは省いて、本題に入りましょう。

dispenser *n.* (machine) ディスペンサー, (for cups) 取り出し器

a cash dispenser
現金自動支払機 [キャッシュディスペンサー]

disperse *v.* (of crowd) 散らばる, ちりぢりになる

display *n.* (of art) 展示, (of merchandise) ディスプレイ, (public performance) 演技; (computer screen) ディスプレイ
v. (show) 見せる, (exhibit: art) 展示する, (emotion) 表す, (skill) 披露する

It was a magnificent display of gymnastics.
すばらしい体操の演技だった。

a fireworks display 花火大会

be on display 展示されている

A number of exhibits were on display.
多数の作品が展示されていた。

disposable *adj.* 使い捨ての

disposal *n.* (throwing away) 処分

be at one's disposal (…の)自由に使える, 自由になる

dispose *v.* (**dispose of**: throw away) 処分する, 捨てる

dispute *n.* 論争, (labor dispute) 争議
v. 論争する, 議論する

disqualify *v.* (from serving, attending etc.) (…の) 資格を奪う, (in competition) 失格させる, (**be disqualified**) 資格を失う, 失格になる

disrespect *n.* 失礼, 無礼

♦ **disrespectful** *adj.* 失礼な, 無礼な

disrupt *v.* (interrupt: event, speech) 中断させる, 混乱させる, (**be disrupted**: of rail services) 不通になる

disruption *n.* 中断, 混乱, (to rail services) 不通

cause a disruption (in class)
混乱を起こす

dissatisfaction *n.* 不満, 不平

There was a lot of dissatisfaction among the workers.
労働者の間に、かなりの不満があった。

dissatisfied *adj.* 不満な

dissect *v.* (cut open) 解剖する, (analyze) 分析する

dissent *n.* 反対, 異議

dissertation *n.* (thesis) (学術)論文

dissident *n.* 反体制の人

dissolve *v.* (of substance: dissolve in a liquid) 溶ける, (cause to dissolve) 溶かす; (of meeting) 解散する

First let the salt dissolve, then add the other ingredients.
まず塩を溶かしてから、ほかの材料を加えてください。

dissuade *v.* (**dissuade from doing**) (…に)…するのを思いとどまらせる

distance *n.* 距離, (short distance) 間隔

Do you know the distance?
距離はわかりますか？

The distance from here to Morioka is about three hundred kilometers.
ここから盛岡までの距離は、約300キロです。

It's only a short distance. You could walk it.
ほんのわずかの距離です。歩いて行けますよ。

Have you measured the distance between the shelves?
棚の間隔を測りましたか？

the distance between the cars 車間距離

at a distance 少し離れて

from a distance 遠くから

I only saw it from a distance.
遠くから見ただけです。

in the distance 遠くに, はるか向こうに

Mt. Fuji could be seen miles away in the distance.
富士山が、はるか遠くに見えました。

distant ***adj.*** 遠い, 遠くの, (be distant from) (...から) 離れている

a distant star 遠くの星

distill ***v.*** 蒸留する

♦**distilled** ***adj.*** 蒸留...

distillery ***n.*** 蒸留酒製造所

distinct ***adj.*** (easily perceived: definite) はっきりした, 紛れもない, (unique) 独特の, (different from others) 別の, 異なる, 違う

There was a distinct smell of curry in the air.
カレーの独特の香りが漂っていた。

Oh no, socialist policies are quite distinct from communist ones.
いや、社会主義と共産主義の政策は全く異なるものだよ。

distinction ***n.*** (point of difference) 区別, 相違; (honor) 名誉, (excellence) 優秀

It's difficult to make a distinction between arts and crafts.
美術と工芸の区別をするのは難しい。

Tom graduated with distinction.
トムは優秀な成績で卒業しました。

distinctive ***adj.*** 独特の, 特徴のある

distinguish ***v.*** (distinguish A from B/between A and B) (AをBと/AとBを) 区別する, (tell apart) 見分ける, (sounds) 聞き分ける, (colors) 識別する

It's difficult to distinguish one twin from the other.
双子を見分けるのは難しい。

distinguished ***adj.*** (renowned) 有名な, 名高い, (illustrious) 輝かしい, (outstanding) 際立った, 顕著な

He had a distinguished career as a diplomat.
その人には外交官としての際立った経歴があった。

distort ***v.*** (fact, truth, situation) ゆがめる, (argument, meaning) 曲げる, 曲解する

Politicians regularly distort the truth.
政治家は真実をゆがめがちだ。

The tabloids are distorting the facts.
タブロイド紙は事実を歪曲している。

Don't distort my words.
私の言うことを曲解しないで。

distortion ***n.*** 歪曲, ゆがみ, (of sound, image) ひずみ

distract ***v.*** (...の) 注意をそらす, 気を散らす

Don't distract me while I'm trying to study.
勉強中は気の散るようなことをしないでね。

I was distracted by the noise.
騒音で気が散ってしまった。

distracting ***adj.*** 注意をそらす, 気を散らす, うるさい

distraction ***n.*** 気が散ること/もの

distress ***n.*** (suffering) 苦痛, 悩み, (sorrow) 悲しみ, 悲嘆; (being in danger) 遭難

v. (cause to suffer) 苦しめる, (worry) 悩ませる, (**be distressed**) 心が痛む

a distress signal 遭難信号

You can't imagine how much this divorce is distressing the children.
この離婚がどれほど子供たちを苦しめているか、想像もつかないだろう。

I was very distressed to hear the news.
そのニュースを聞いて心が痛んだ。

distressing ***adj.*** 痛ましい

distribute ***v.*** (deal out) 配る, 配布する, (ration out) 分配する, (goods to a shop) 卸す

He distributed the pamphlets.
彼はパンフレットを配った [配布した]。

distribution ***n.*** (dealing out) 配分, (supplying of goods) 流通, (by government) 配給; (geographical) 分布

He's the one in charge of distribution.
彼が流通の責任者です。

The distribution of food and medical supplies is the first priority.
食料と医療物資の配給が最優先だ。

distributor ***n.*** 卸売業者

district ***n.*** (of city) 地域, (administrative district) 地区, 区域, -区

This is a residential district.
ここは住宅地です。

the Osaka District Court
大阪地方裁判所

district attorney ***n.*** 州検察官

distrust ***n.*** (lack of trust) 不信, (doubt) 疑惑

v. (not trust) 信用しない, (doubt) 疑う

I can't imagine why you distrust him.
なぜ彼を信用できないのか、私には理解できない。

disturb ***v.*** (interrupt) じゃまする, (ruin the tranquility of) 乱す

Please don't disturb me. I've got work to do.
じゃましないで。仕事中なんだから。

I'm sorry, am I disturbing you?
すみません、おじゃまでしょうか？

The noise of jets passing overhead disturbs us in our sleep.
上空を通過するジェット機の騒音で、いつも眠りを妨げられる。

disturbance ***n.*** (interruption) じゃま; (commotion) 騒ぎ, 騒動

disturbed ***adj.*** (worried) 心配している, 不安な, (psychologically troubled/abnormal) 精神異常の

disturbing ***adj.*** (worrisome) 不安にさせる, (alarming) 気がかりな, (of news) 不穏な

The news was very disturbing.
とても不穏なニュースだった。

ditch ***n.*** どぶ, 溝

v. (person) 捨てる, (school, work) サボる

diuretic ***n.*** 利尿剤

dive ***v.*** (into water) 飛び込む, (beneath water) 潜る, 潜水する, (scuba dive) ダ

イビングする, (from up in the sky) 急降下する, (into room, train) 駆け込む

I dived into the pool.
プールに飛び込んだ。

The hawk dived down to the ground.
タカは地面に向かって急降下した。

We dived into the nearest doorway.
一番近くの戸口に駆け込んだ。

diver ***n.*** (scuba diver) ダイバー

diverse ***adj.*** (多種)多様な, 種々の

diversify ***v.*** (interests) 多様化する, (business) 多角化する

♦ **diversification** ***n.*** 多角化

diversion ***n.*** (sth entertaining) 気晴らし; (tactic) けん制, 陽動作戦

as a diversion (for a change of mood) 気分転換に, 気晴らしに

diversity ***n.*** 多様性

divert ***v.*** (traffic) 迂回させる, (attention) そらす, (funds) 流用する

Traffic has been diverted because of roadwork.
道路工事のため、車は迂回させられている。

The government is trying to divert the public's attention.
政府は大衆の注意をそらそうとしている。

divest ***v.*** (of position/right) (…から地位/権利を) 剥奪する

divide ***v.*** (separate into parts/shares) 分ける, 分割する, (area) 区切る, (land) 分断する; (classify) 分類する; (number) 割る

n. (mountain) 分水嶺

The money will be divided between the two of you.
お金はお二人で分けることになります。

He divided his wealth among his children.
彼は子供たちに財産を分与した。

The large house was divided into seven apartments.
その大きな家は七つの貸部屋に区切られていた。

The city was divided north and south by a river.
街は川で南北に分断されていた。

Animals are divided into vertebrates and invertebrates.
動物は脊椎動物と無脊椎動物に分類される。

What's 68 divided by 9?
６８ 割る９は、いくつでしょう?

a continental divide 大陸分水嶺

divided ***adj.*** 分かれた, 分裂した

Opinion is divided on the question of abortion.
妊娠中絶の問題については意見が分かれている。

dividend ***n.*** (share of profits) 配当金

pay a dividend 配当金を払う

divine ***adj.*** (sacred) 神聖な, (of God) 神の, (godlike) 神のような

v. (foretell) 占う, 予言する

division ***n.*** (in math) 割り算; (of company) 部門, -部, -局, -課; (of opinion) 不一致, 分裂; (taxonomic category) 門

do division 割り算をする

Ms. Nakajima works in the personnel division.
中島さんは人事部に勤務しています。

divorce ***n.*** 離婚

v. (…と) 離婚する [→ SEPARATE 3]

She wants a divorce.

彼女は離婚したがっている。

He has been divorced twice.

彼は２度離婚している。

♦**divorcé** *n.* 離婚した男性, ((*informal*)) (person who has been divorced once) バツイチ

divorcée *n.* 離婚した女性, ((*informal*)) (person who has been divorced once) バツイチ

divulge *v.* (secret) 漏らす, 暴く, 暴露する

dizzy *adj.* (be dizzy) めまいがする, 目が回る, ふらふら/くらくらする

DJ *n.* ＤＪ, ディスクジョッキー

DNA *n.* ＤＮＡ, デオキシリボ核酸

DNA fingerprinting ＤＮＡ指紋法

do *v.*

1 AUXILIARY: See examples below

2 CARRY OUT: (action) する, ((*formal*)) 行う, ((*informal*)) やる, ((*honorific*)) なさる, ((*humble*)) いたします

3 JOB/TASK: する, ((*informal*)) やる, (**have done**: have completed) 終わらせた, 済ませた, 仕上げた

4 SUFFICE: (**will do**) 間に合う, 足りる

5 DO FOR A LIVING: (…の仕事を) する

6 SPEED: (…の) スピードで走る, スピードを出す

7 COOKED: (**done**) (=grilled) 焼けた, (=boiled) 煮えた [→ DONE]

8 ONE'S HAIR: (髪を) 整える, セットする

1 "Does he want it?"
"I don't think so."
「彼はそれを欲しいのかな？」
「そうは思わないけれど」

You like him, don't you?

彼のこと好きでしょう？

She did go, didn't she?

彼女はもう行ったんですよね？

Didn't I tell you that?

そう言いませんでした？

Do be quiet! I'm trying to study.

静かにしてくれないか！ 勉強するんだから。

Don't do that! (=Cut it out!)

やめなさい！

2 What are you doing now?

今、何をしていますか？

There's nothing for me to do here.

ここではやることがない。

Shall I do it for you?

私がやりましょうか？

I don't know what to do with all these old books.

このたくさんの古本をどうしたらいいかわからない。

There's nothing I can do about it.

私にできることは何もありません。

The government said they were going to do something about that problem.

政府は、その問題に何らかの対処をすると述べた。

3 do one's homework 宿題をする

do one's room 部屋を片付ける

do the cooking 料理をする

You did it very well.

とても上手にできました。

do work 仕事をする

I've done my work.

仕事は終わらせました。

Haven't you done the dishes yet?
お皿洗いはまだ済ませてないの？

4 This umbrella will have to do.
この傘で間に合わせるしかない。

Will this do? Or would you like some more?
これで足りますか？ それとも、もう少し要りますか？

This outfit will do quite nicely for the party, wouldn't you say?
この服、パーティーに十分いけるでしょう？

5 What do you do?
お仕事は何ですか？

What are you going to do when you graduate?
卒業したらどうするつもりですか？

6 This car can do zero to sixty (kph) in five seconds.
この車なら５秒で時速 60 キロまで出せる。

7 How do you like your eggs done?
卵はどういう焼き方がいい？

8 How long does it take you to do your hair in the morning?
朝、髪をセットするのにどのくらい時間がかかりますか？

have nothing to do with …と/に(は)関係がない

It has nothing to do with you.
あなたには全く関係のないことです。

have to do with …と/に関係がある

Global warming has everything to do with the burning of fossil fuels.
地球温暖化は化石燃料の燃焼に大いに関係がある。

that does it (expressing anger) もうたくさんだ, もうがまんできない

do away with *v.* (get rid of) なくす, 廃止する, (kill) 殺す

We need to do away with all this red tape.
こんな厄介な手続きは全部廃止すべきだ。

do for *v.* (contribute) …のためにする; (substitute) …の代わりになる

He has done a lot for the homeless.
ホームレスの人のために彼はさまざまな活動をしてきた。

This box will do for a table.
この箱はテーブルの代わりになります。

do in *v.* (defeat, cheat) やっつける, (kill) 殺す, 殺してやる

do up *v.* (shoelaces) 結ぶ, (buttons) かける, はめる, (zipper) 締める, (hair) 結い上げる

Do your coat up.
コートのボタンをかけなさい。

do with *v.* (**could do with**: desire) (…が)欲しい

God, I could do with a smoke.
ああ、たばこが吸いたい。

do without *v.* (…が)なくてもいい, (…が)なくてもいける, …なしで済ます

I can do without her help.
彼女の助けがなくてもいい。

Surely you can do without sweets for a day.
１日くらい、甘い物がなくてもやっていけるでしょう。

Can't you do without alcohol for a night?
一晩、お酒なしではいられませんか？

dock ***n.*** (for repairing boats) ドック, (for mooring boats) 波止場, 埠頭
v. (enter a dock) ドックに入る, (direct into a dock) ドックに入れる; (of spacecraft) ドッキングする

dockworker ***n.*** 港湾労働者

doctor ***n.*** (of medicine) 医者, 医師, ((*polite*)) お医者さん, (of philosophy) 博士
You'd better call a doctor.
医者を呼んだほうがいい。
Why don't you go and see your doctor for a checkup?
かかりつけのお医者さんに健康診断に行ったら？

doctorate ***n.*** (qualification) 博士号(の学位)

doctrine ***n.*** (religious) 教義, 教え, (principle, belief) 信条, (-ism) 主義

document ***n.*** 書類, 文書
v. (record) 記録する

documentary ***n.*** ドキュメンタリー

dodge ***v.*** (ball) よける, (punch) かわす, (draft) 忌避する

dodo ***n.*** (extinct bird) ドードー

doe ***n.*** (female deer) めすジカ, (female rabbit) めすウサギ

dog ***n.*** 犬, -犬
Who would like to take the dog for a walk?
犬の散歩に行きたい人は誰ですか？
It's time to feed the dog.
犬にえさをやる時間だ。
"What kind of dog is it?"
"It's an Akita."
「どんな種類の犬ですか？」
「秋田犬です」

doghouse ***n.*** 犬小屋

dogma ***n.*** ドグマ, (religious) 教義

dogmatic ***adj.*** (of opinion) 独断的な

dogwood ***n.*** ハナミズキ

do-it-yourself ***adj.*** 日曜大工の

dojo ***n.*** 道場

doll ***n.*** 人形
v. (**doll oneself up**) おしゃれをする

dollar ***n.*** (currency) ドル, $, (a dollar bill) 1ドル紙幣
They would like us to pay in dollars.
ドルで支払ってほしいそうだ。

dolphin ***n.*** イルカ

domain ***n.*** (land) 領地, (sphere of concern) 分野; (on Internet) ドメイン

dome ***n.*** (roof) 丸屋根, (ceiling) 丸天井, (building) ドーム

domestic ***adj.*** (of the home) 家庭の, (of person) 家庭的な, (of internal affairs of a country) 国内の, 自国の, (of animal) 飼いならされた
Don't let your domestic problems affect your work.
家庭での問題を仕事に持ち込まないように。
Put your feet up, read the paper, light a pipe—domestic bliss!
足を伸ばして、新聞を読んで、パイプに火をつける——やっぱり家が一番！
domestic policy 国内の政策
♦ **domestic animal** ***n.*** 家畜
domestic violence ***n.*** 家庭内暴力

domesticate ***v.*** 飼いならす

dominant ***adj.*** (governing, controlling) 支配的な, (leading) 優勢な, (most influential) 最も有力な

dominate *v.* (control) 支配する, 左右する, (overpower) 威圧する; (of issue) 大きく占める

England no longer dominates the world as it used to.
イギリスはもはや、昔のように世界を支配してはいない。

His mother dominates him.
あの人は母親の言いなりだ。

Population growth will likely be the issue that dominates the twenty-first century.
人口の増加が、21 世紀を大きく占める課題となるだろう。

domination *n.* (control) 支配

domino *n.* ドミノ

♦ **domino effect** *n.* ドミノ効果

donate *v.* 寄付する, 寄贈する

donation *n.* (offering of money) 寄付金, (to shrine, temple) (お)さい銭, (gift) 寄贈品

done *adj.* (finished) 済んだ, 終わった; (boiled) 煮えた, (grilled, broiled) 焼けた

I'm done (with it).
もう済んだ。

Are the potatoes done?
ジャガイモはもう<u>煮えた</u> [焼けた] ?

all done 終わった

be done for やられる, だめになる

I'm done for.
僕はもうだめだ。

be done with (sever relations with) …と手を切る

donkey *n.* ロバ

donor *n.* (blood donor) 献血者, (of money, gift) 寄贈者

don't → NOT 2

doom *n.* (undesirable fate) 宿命, 運命

doomed *adj.* (**be doomed to do**) …する運命にある

door *n.* ドア, 戸, ((*also figurative*)) 扉, 入口, (doorway) 出入口, 戸口, (front door) 玄関, (back door) 裏口, 勝手口, (sliding partition in Japanese house) 障子, (sliding paper door) ふすま [→ picture of ROOM]; (house) -軒

Shall we open the door?
ドアをあけましょうか？

Could you close the door, please?
ドアを閉めてくれませんか？

Is there a back door?
裏口はありますか？

They live a few doors away.
彼らは2、3 軒先に住んでいる。

doorstep *n.* 戸口の踏み段

doorway *n.* 出入口, 戸口

dopamine *n.* ドーパミン

dormitory *n.* 寮

dormouse *n.* ヤマネ

dose *n.* (of medicine) 服用量, (one dose) 1 回分, (pill) 1 錠

Three doses, three times a day, it says.
1 日 3 回 3 錠ずつ服用すること、と書いてある。

dot *n.* (small mark) 点, (stain) しみ
v. (…に) 点を打つ

You've forgotten to dot the *i*.
'i' に点を打つのを忘れていますよ。

on the dot きっかりに, 時間どおりに

He showed up at 6 o'clock on the dot.

彼は6時きっかりに現れた。

dot-com ***n.*** ドットコム

dotted ***adj.*** 点々の, 点のついている, (be dotted with) (…が) 点在する

a dotted line 点線

a landscape dotted with farmhouses
農家が点在する風景

double

1 ***adj.*** TWICE AS MUCH: 倍の, 2倍の, ダブルの, (of blanket, chin) 二重の, (of petals) 八重の

2 ***n.*** TWICE AS MUCH: 倍, 2倍

3 ***v.*** MAKE / BECOME TWICE AS MUCH: 倍にする/なる, 2倍にする/なる, 倍増する

4 ***adj.*** FOR TWO PEOPLE: 二人用の, ダブルの

5 ***n.*** EXACT LIKENESS: そっくりな人, 生き写し, (of leader) 影武者

6 ***n.*** IN FILM: (stunt double) スタントマン

7 ***n.*** IN SPORT: (**doubles**) ダブルス

8 ***n.*** ROOM / BED / BEVERAGE: ダブル

1 It's double the size I expected.
思っていたサイズの2倍ある。

I'll have a double whiskey.
ウイスキーをダブルで下さい。

2 I'll pay you double what you get there.
そこでの収入の2倍お支払いしますよ。

They'll charge double if they think you're tourists.
観光客だと思われたら、2倍の値段を請求してくるよ。

3 The budget for this project needs to be doubled.
このプロジェクトの予算は2倍にする必要がある。

The population has doubled in a short time.
人口は短期間で倍増した。

4 There are two rooms with double beds.
ダブルベッドの部屋は二つあります。

5 He's your double.
彼はあなたにそっくりね。

6 It wasn't the actual actor; it was a stunt double.
本物の俳優ではなく､スタントマンだった。

7 Let's play doubles.
ダブルスをやろう。

double agent ***n.*** 二重スパイ

double bass ***n.*** コントラバス, ダブルベース

double-check ***v.*** 再点検する, ダブルチェックする

double-cross ***v.*** 裏切る

double life ***n.*** 二重生活

They say he leads a double life.
彼は二重生活をしているそうです。

double standard ***n.*** 二重基準, ダブルスタンダード

doubt ***n.*** (uncertainty) 疑い, 疑問, ((*formal*)) 疑惑

v. (be uncertain about) 疑う, (…に) 疑問を感じる, 疑いをいだく, (mistrust) 信用しない, 信じない

I still have doubts about this.
この件に関してはまだ疑問がある。

I have no doubt who is going to win.
誰が勝つか確信しています。

There's no doubt it won't be easy.
確かに簡単なことではない。

Our jobs are in doubt.
私たちの仕事は不確かだ。

I doubt if they will come here again.

彼らはもう、ここに来ないと思う。

I seriously began to doubt the point of the war.
その戦争の意義に本気で疑問を感じ始めた。

Why should I doubt his word?
どうして彼の言葉を信じちゃいけないの？

beyond (a) doubt 疑う余地もない, 確かに, 間違いなく

His innocence is beyond doubt.
あの人の無実は疑う余地もない。

doubt one's ears/eyes 耳/目を疑う

without (a) doubt 疑いなく, 間違いなく, 確かに

This is, without a doubt, the best steak I've ever had.
これは今まで食べた中で、間違いなく一番おいしいステーキです。

doubtful ***adj.*** (feeling doubt) 疑わしい, (not certain) 確かではない; (questionable) 怪しげな, うさんくさい

I am doubtful of the results.
結果は疑わしい。

a person of doubtful character
怪しげな人物

doubtless ***adv.*** 疑いなく, 間違いなく

dough ***n.*** パン生地, 練り粉

doughnut ***n.*** ドーナツ

dove ***n.*** ハト, 鳩

dowager ***n.*** (widow of nobleman) 貴族の未亡人

the empress dowager 皇太后

dowdy ***adj.*** (dull) 地味な

down

1 ***adv.*** TO/IN A LOWER POSITION: 下へ/に, 下の方へ/に

2 ***adv.*** TO/IN A RECUMBENT POSITION: See examples below

3 ***prep.*** INDICATING DIRECTION OF MOVEMENT: …に, …を

4 ***prep.*** INDICATING LOCATION: (along road, hallway, river etc.) …を

5 ***adv.*** INDICATING DEPLETION: (**be down to**) …しか残っていない

6 ***adj.*** OF PRICE: (**be down**) 下がっている

7 ***adj.*** DEPRESSED: (**be down**) 落ち込んでいる, 気がめいっている

8 ***adj.*** NOT WORKING: (of machine) 故障している, (of phone lines) 不通になっている, (of electricity) 停電している

9 ***v.*** DRINK: 飲み干す, 一気に飲む

1 Let's go down to the bottom.
下まで下りましょう。

Just put the box down over there.
その箱はあっちに置いてください。

Can I help you lift it down?
下ろすのを手伝いましょうか？

My pen's fallen down behind the desk.
机の後ろにペンが落ちてしまった。

We could see the river down below in the valley.
谷底に川が見えた。

2 You can sit down now.
もう座っていいですよ。

They knocked down the wall.
(彼らは)壁を取り壊した。

3 I ran my eyes down the list.
表にざっと目を通した。

I saw a rat go down the drain.
ネズミが排水溝に入って行くのを見た。

We climbed down the mountain in less than two hours.
2時間足らずで山を下りた[下山した]。

He walked down the road.
彼は道を歩いて行った。

4 It's down this passage and on the left.
この通路を行って左にありますよ。

There's a gas station down the road a little ways.
その道をちょっと行くとガソリンスタンドがあります。

5 I was down to my last drop of water, and extremely thirsty.
水が1滴しか残っていなくて、ひどくのどが渇いていた。

6 Better buy it while the prices are down.
値段が下がっているうちに買うほうがいい。

7 I'm feeling down today.
今日は気がめいってます。

8 The phone lines are down.
電話が不通になっている。

9 He downed his whiskey in one gulp.
彼はウイスキーを一気に飲み干した。

up and down → UP

ups and downs → UP

downfall *n.* (loss of rank, reputation etc.) 失墜, (of empire) 没落; (of snow/rain) 大降り, 豪雪/豪雨

downhill *adv.* 下って, 下り坂に
adj. 下りの, (of road) 下り坂の
go downhill (worsen) 落ち目になる

♦ **downhill skiing** *n.* 滑降スキー

download *v.* ダウンロードする

down payment *n.* 頭金

downscale *adj.* 大衆向けの, 安い

downsize *v.* (car) 小型化する, (staff) 削減する, (company) 縮小する

downstairs *adv.* 下の階に/へ, 階下に
adj. 階下の, 下の
n. 下の階

Let's go downstairs.
下(の階)に行きましょう。

She ran downstairs.
彼女は下の階に駆け下りて行った。

downstream *adv., adj.* 川下に/の, 下流に/の

Down syndrome *n.* ダウン症

downtown *n.* (central part of town) 中心街, 都心, (business district) 商業地区

downward *adv.* 下へ/に, 下の方へ/に, (downward facing) 下向きに
adj. 下方への

downwind *adv., adj.* 風下に/の

doze *v.* うたた寝する, うとうとする, 居眠りする
n. うたた寝, 居眠り

I dozed on the train.
電車で居眠りしてしまった。

have an afternoon doze
(お)昼寝する

dozen *n.* ダース, (twelve) 12個

two dozen doughnuts
24個のドーナツ

dozens of 何十 + <counter> + も [→ p.1168 about "Counters"], (lots of) たくさんの

Dr. *abbr.* -先生, -博士

draft *n.* (rough draft) 草稿, 下書き, (sketch) 下絵, 草案, (plan, design) 設計図; (current of air) すき間風; (compul-

sory summons for military service) 徴兵
v. (make a draft of) (…の) 草稿を書く, (bill) 起草する, (contract) (…の) 原案を立てる, (**be drafted** for military service) 徴兵される

There's a terrible draft from that window.
あの窓からひどいすき間風が入って来る。

♦ **draft beer** *n.* 生ビール

---

drag¹ *v.* 引きずる, 引っ張る, (riverbed) (川底を) さらう; (of tedious event) 長引く

The security guards dragged the man out of the building.
警備員たちは男を建物から引きずり出した。

Don't drag the chair! Lift it.
椅子を引きずらないで！ 持ち上げてください。

I dragged myself out of bed and made coffee.
ベッドからのろのろと起きて、コーヒーをいれた。

The divers dragged the river looking for clues.
ダイバーたちは手がかりを求めて川底をさらった。

The meeting dragged on and on.
会議はだらだら長引いた。

drag into *v.* (situation) …に引きずり込む

I was dragged into this situation against my will.
私は自分の意思に反して、この状況に引きずり込まれたんです。

drag up *v.* (unpleasant memory) 蒸し返す, 引っ張り出す

Why do you want to drag up that old argument again?
どうしてそんな古い話を、また蒸し返そうとするの？

---

drag² *n.* (women's attire) 女装, (men's attire) 男装

a man in drag 女装の男

dragnet *n.* (of police) 捜査網

dragon *n.* 竜, ドラゴン

dragonfly *n.* トンボ

drain *v.* (bathtub) (…の) 水を抜く, (sink) (…の) 水を流す, (food) (…の) 水気を切る, (saké cup) (杯を)飲み干す
n. (in sink, bathroom) 排水口 [→ picture of BATHROOM], (drainpipe) 排水管; (on resources) 消耗, 負担

Drain the bath, will you.
おふろの水を抜いてくれる？

My earring went down the drain.
イヤリングが排水口に落ちた。

The drain is blocked with leaves.
排水管が葉っぱで詰まっている。

drainage *n.* 排水

draining *adj.* (exhausting) 疲れる, 消耗する

drainpipe *n.* (gutter) 雨どい [→ picture of HOUSE], (pipe for waste water) 排水管

drama *n.* (sth exciting) ドラマ, (play) 劇, 芝居, (subject of study) 演劇

dramatic *adj.* (striking, exciting) 劇的な, ドラマチックな, (pertaining to theater) 劇の; (of attention-seeker: melodramatic) おおげさな

Don't you think she's being a little dramatic?

彼女って、ちょっとおおげさだと思わない？

dramatist ***n.*** 劇作家, 脚本家

dramatize ***v.*** (make into a play) 劇化する, (exaggerate) おおげさに表現する

drastic ***adj.*** 抜本的な, 思い切った

a drastic measure 抜本策

This country's civil service system is in need of drastic reform.

この国の公務員制度は、抜本的な改革を必要としている。

The author made drastic revisions to the manuscript.

著者は、原稿に思い切った修正を入れた。

draughts ***n.*** チェッカー

draw

1 ***v.*** **SKETCH:** (picture) (絵を) 描く, かく, (line) (線を) 引く

2 ***v.*** **PULL:** (cart) 引く, 引っ張る, (card) 取る, 引く, (curtains) 引く, (**be drawn**: of theater curtains) 下りる

3 ***v.*** **PULL OUT:** 引き抜く, (water) くむ, (lottery ticket) (くじを) 引く, (weapon) 抜く

4 ***v.*** **MOVE:** (**draw near**) 近づく, (**draw back**) 後ずさりする

5 ***n.*** **EQUAL OUTCOME:** (in game) 引き分け, ドロー, 同点

6 ***v.*** **END IN A TIE:** 引き分けになる

7 ***v.*** **ATTRACT:** (attention) 引く, 引き付ける, (audience) 動員する

8 ***v.*** **CONCLUSION/LESSON:** (結論/教訓を) 引き出す, 得る

9 ***v.*** **CRITICISM/PRAISE:** (非難/賞賛を) 浴びる

10 ***v.*** **SUCK IN:** (breath) (息を) 吸い込む

11 ***n.*** **LOT DRAWING:** くじ引き, 抽選

1 How about getting the kids to draw something?

子供たちに何か、描かせてみてはどうですか？

I don't know who drew this.

誰がこれをかいたのか知りません。

I can't draw. 絵はかけません。

First, draw two horizontal lines.

まず、横線を2本引いてください。

2 The festival floats were drawn by horses.

お祭りの山車は馬に引かれていた。

She drew the ace of spades.

彼女はスペードのエースを引いた。

I could see that the curtains were drawn.

カーテンが引かれているのが見えた。

3 The old man still draws water from the spring.

おじいさんは今でもその泉から水をくんでいます。

The lucky numbers will be drawn next week.

当選番号は来週、抽選で決まります。

4 The bus drew to a halt in front of us.

バスが近づいて来て、私たちの前で止まった。

As soon as everyone realized she had the flu, they drew back a step.

彼女がインフルエンザにかかっているとわかったとたん、みんな1歩後ずさりした。

5 The match ended in a draw.

試合は引き分けに終わった。

6 The teams drew nil nil.

0対0で両チームは引き分けになった。

Spain drew against England.

スペインはイングランドに引き分けた。

7 What drew my attention was his sus-

picious behavior.
目を引いたのは彼の不審な行動だった。

What drew her into prostitution in the first place?
彼女が売春に走ったきっかけは、何だったんですか？

8 What other conclusion is there to draw?
ほかにどんな結論が引き出せると言うのですか？

9 The prime minister's remarks on the issue have drawn criticism.
その問題についての首相の発言は、非難を浴びた。

10 Close your eyes and draw a deep breath.
目を閉じて､息を深く吸い込んでください。

11 The draw for the quarterfinals is tomorrow.
準々決勝の抽選は明日行われます。

draw a blank → BLANK

draw in *v.* (of car) 道路わきに寄る, 端に寄る, (of train) 到着する; (of days/nights: become shorter) 短くなる

The cab drew in and stopped.
タクシーは道路わきに寄って止まった。

The days are drawing in.
日が短くなってきている。

draw out *v.*

1 EXTRACT: (money) おろす, 引き出す, (secret, information) 聞き出す

2 PROLONG: (meeting) 長引かせる

3 CAUSE TO TALK: (…に) しゃべらせる, (…から) 話を引き出す

1 I need to draw out some money.
お金をおろさなきゃ。

2 The chairman deliberately drew the meeting out.
議長はわざと会議を長引かせた。

3 They're shy, so you'll have to try to draw them out a bit.
彼らは恥ずかしがり屋だから、打ち解けさせて話を引き出さなくてはいけませんね。

draw up *v.* (of car) (近づいて来て) 止まる, (pull up: chair) 引き寄せる; (document) 作成する, (plan, policy) 立てる

A big black car drew up.
大きな黒い車が近づいて来て止まった。

Draw up a chair. Let's have a chat.
まあ、ちょっと座って話をしようよ。

The company ought to draw up a policy.
会社は方針を立てるべきです。

---

drawback *n.* (demerit) 欠点

drawer *n.* 引き出し

I put all the papers in the drawer and locked it.
書類はすべて引き出しに入れて、かぎをかけました。

drawing *n.* (picture) 絵, 図画, (drawing pictures) 絵を描くこと

Can I see your drawings?
絵を見せてもらえますか？

I've never seen such a fine still-life drawing.
こんなにすばらしい静物画は見たことがない。

go back to the drawing board 白紙に戻る, 振り出しに戻る

dread *v.* (fear) 恐れる, (be anxious about) ひどく心配する

n. 恐怖

I'm dreading the exams.
試験のことを考えると気が重い。

dreadful *adj.* (frightening) 恐（おそ）ろしい, (terrible) ひどい

a dreadful mistake ひどい間違（まちが）い

dream *n.* ((*also figurative*)) 夢（ゆめ）, (ideal) 理想（りそう）
v. 夢（ゆめ）を見る, (**dream of doing / becoming**) …するのを/…になるのを夢（ゆめ）(に)見（み）る

I can never remember my dreams.
私（わたし）は, 夢（ゆめ）を全然（ぜんぜん）思（おも）い出（だ）せないんです。

I had an awful dream last night.
ゆうべ恐（おそ）ろしい夢（ゆめ）を見（み）た。

I never thought I'd win in my wildest dreams.
勝（か）てるとは夢（ゆめ）にも思（おも）っていなかった。

She's always dreaming of becoming a star.
彼女（かのじょ）はスターになるのをいつも夢見（ゆめみ）ている。

dreamland, dreamworld *n.* おとぎの国（くに）

dreamlike *adj.* 夢（ゆめ）のような, 夢（ゆめ）みたいな

dreamy *adj.* 夢見心地（ゆめみごこち）の, (fuzzy) ぼんやりした

dregs *n.* (of coffee, wine) かす, おり; (of society) くず, かす

drench *v.* ずぶぬれにする, (**be drenched**) びっしょりぬれる

be drenched with sweat
汗（あせ）でびっしょりだ

dress *v.* (clothe) (…に)服（ふく）を着（き）せる, (**dress oneself**) 服（ふく）を着（き）る, (put on clothes) 服（ふく）を着（き）る; (put a bandage on: wound) (…に)包帯（ほうたい）をする
n. (clothing) 服（ふく）, 洋服（ようふく）, 服装（ふくそう）, (article of clothing worn by women) ドレス, ワンピース, (formal attire) 正装（せいそう）

I dressed the child in a pink sweater.
子供（こども）にピンクのセーターを着（き）せた。

He's old enough now to dress himself.
あの子（こ）はもう一人（ひとり）で服（ふく）を着（き）られる年齢（ねんれい）です。

Everyone was dressed formally.
皆（みな）、正装（せいそう）していました。

Come on, get dressed.
早（はや）く服（ふく）を着（き）なさい。

He usually dresses casually.
彼（かれ）はたいていカジュアルな服（ふく）を着（き）ている。

That's a lovely dress you're wearing.
(それは)すてきなドレスですね。

♦ **dressmaking** *n.* 洋裁（ようさい）

dress up *v.* (in costume) 仮装（かそう）する, (in one's best clothes) 着飾（きかざ）る, 正装（せいそう）する

dressing *n.* (bandage) 包帯（ほうたい）; (salad dressing) ドレッシング

dressing room *n.* (in theater) 楽屋（がくや）, (in clothing store) 試着室（しちゃくしつ）

dribble *v.* (of liquid) したたる, (at mouth) よだれを垂（た）らす; (ball) ドリブルする

dried *adj.* 乾燥（かんそう）した, 干（ほ）した, 干（ほ）し-
dried goods 乾物（かんぶつ）
dried mushrooms 干（ほ）ししいたけ
dried bonito かつお節（ぶし）

drift *v.* (on water) 漂（ただよ）う, 漂流（ひょうりゅう）する, (on air) 漂（ただよ）う, (of person: move about without a purpose/goal) ぶらぶらする, (from job to job) (仕事（しごと）を)転々（てんてん）とする [→ WANDER]
n. (snowdrift) 雪（ゆき）の吹（ふ）きだまり

The smell of curry drifted from the kitchen.
カレーの香（かお）りが台所（だいどころ）から漂（ただよ）って来（き）た。

He just drifts through life.

あの人は、ぶらぶらして過ごしている。

♦ **drifter** *n.* (person) 流れ者

driftwood *n.* 流木

drill *n.* (tool) きり, ドリル [→ picture of TOOL]; (exercise) 練習, ドリル, (military exercise) 訓練

v. (**drill a hole in**) …に穴をあける, (drill for oil etc.) ボーリングをする; (drill A in/on B: teach by forcing to repeat) (AにBを) 繰り返し教え込む, たたき込む, (**drill oneself**) 練習する

a pneumatic drill 空気ドリル

There is a fire drill every three months.
3ヵ月ごとに火災訓練があります。

A number of companies have already started to drill for oil in the South China Sea.
南シナ海ではすでに数社が、石油を求めてボーリングを始めている。

I wonder what the instructor is going to drill us on today.
先生は、今日は私たちに何をたたき込むつもりだろう。

drink *v.* 飲む, (**drink down**) 飲み干す, (alcohol) (お)酒を飲む, (**drink to sb/sth**) …に乾杯する

n. (beverage) 飲み物, 飲料, (alcoholic beverage) (お)酒, (one glass of alcohol) 一杯, (a sip of a drink) 一口

We were just sitting there drinking coffee and chatting.
私たちはそこに座って、コーヒーを飲みながらしゃべっていただけです。

He drank it down in one gulp.
彼は一気に飲み干した。

He doesn't smoke or drink.
彼は、たばこも吸わないし、お酒も飲まない / ((*informal*)) 彼は、たばこもお酒もやらない。

I'll drink to that.
それに乾杯しよう。

There was plenty of food and drink.
食べ物も飲み物もたくさんあった。

I'd like a hot drink, please.
温かい飲み物を下さい。

Would you like a drink?
お飲み物はいかがですか？

Let me buy you a drink.
一杯おごらせて。

How about going out for a drink tonight?
今夜飲みに行かない？

drink sb under the table 飲み負かす, 酔いつぶれさせる

I could drink him under the table any day.
あいつならいつでも飲み負かせるよ。

drinker *n.* (of alcohol) (お)酒を飲む人 [→ HEAVY DRINKER]

drinking *n.* 飲酒

♦ **drinking and driving** *n.* 飲酒運転, 酔っ払い運転

drinking fountain *n.* 水飲み場

drinking problem *n.* アルコール依存症

That man has a drinking problem.
あの人はアルコール依存症です。

drinking water *n.* 飲み水, 飲料水

drip *v.* (of water, sweat) 垂れる, (continuously) したたる, ポタポタと落ちる, (produce drops) しずくを垂らす

n. (dripping) したたり, (drop) しずく, 水滴, (sound) しずくの音, ポタポタした

たる音; (IV) 点滴

Water is dripping from the tap.
水が蛇口からポタポタ垂れている。

Sweat was dripping from his chin.
あごから汗がポタポタとしたたっていた。

You are dripping all over the place!
そこらじゅうに、しずくを垂らしているよ!

He's in the hospital. It's not serious, but he's on a drip.
彼は病院にいます。大したことはありませんが、点滴を受けています。

drive

1 *v.* OPERATE A CAR: (車を)運転する, 車を走らせる

2 *v.* JOURNEY BY CAR: ドライブする, 車で行く

3 *v.* TRANSPORT BY CAR: 車で送る

4 *v.* POWER: (machine etc.) 動かす

5 *n.* JOURNEY IN A CAR: ドライブ, (referring to distance traveled) 距離, 道のり

6 *n.* ROAD: (in names of streets) -通り, -街道

1 Would you mind driving?
運転してもらえますか?

I didn't learn to drive until I was thirty.
３０歳になるまで運転は習いませんでした。

He drove off in a temper.
彼は怒って車で走り去った。

2 We drove all around Shikoku.
四国を車で一周しました。

We often drive out to the mountains on weekends.
私たちはよく週末に、山の方へドライブします。

3 I drove her to the station.
彼女を駅まで車で送った。

I'll ask him to drive me to the airport.
空港まで車で送ってくれるよう頼んでみます。

4 Steam is used to drive this machine.
この機械を動かすのに蒸気が使われている/この機械は蒸気で動いている。

5 Let's go for a drive.
ドライブに行こう。

It's a long drive from here.
ここからは長い道のりだ。

a two-hour drive
車で2時間の距離

♦ **drive away** *v.* (repel) 追い払う, (drive off in a car) (車で) 走り去る, 立ち去る

The police drove away the demonstrators.
警察はデモ隊を追い払った。

She drove away quickly.
彼女はすぐに車で立ち去った。

driver *n.* 運転する人, ドライバー, (of bus, taxi) 運転手(さん)

♦ **driver's license** *n.* 運転免許証

driver's seat *n.* 運転席 [→ picture of CAR]

driveway *n.* 車寄せ, 私道

driving *n.* 運転

♦ **driving instructor** *n.* 自動車教習所の教官

driving lesson *n.* 運転の教習, 車の教習

driving school *n.* 自動車教習所

driving test *n.* 運転免許試験

drizzle *v.* (rain) 霧雨がしとしと降る
n. (light rain) 霧雨

dromedary *n.* ヒトコブラクダ

drone *n.* (male bee) 雄バチ, (worker bee) 働きバチ

drop

1 *v.* **FALL:** 落ちる, ((*formal*)) 落下する, (from standing position) 倒れる, (of price, temperature) 下がる, (of road) 下る, 下り坂になる, (in altitude) 降下する

2 *v.* **ALLOW TO FALL:** (object, speed) 落とす, (price) 下げる, (bomb) 投下する

3 *v.* **MAKE/BECOME WEAKER:** (voice) 落とす/低くなる, (of wind) 弱まる, おさまる

4 *n.* **FALL:** (of temperature) 低下, (of price) 下落; (vertical drop) 落下距離

5 *n.* **GLOBULE:** (of rain) しずく, (of liquid) 1滴

6 *n.* **SMALL AMOUNT:** 少量, 微量

1 An apple dropped from the tree.
リンゴが木から落ちた。

The coin dropped to the bottom of the well.
井戸の底にコインが落ちた。

The lid dropped with a bang.
ふたはバタンと音を立てて落ちた。

The team has dropped to seventh place.
チームは7位まで後退してしまった。

Stock prices dropped on news of higher interest rates.
金利引き上げのニュースで株価が下落した。

The temperature drops once the sun goes down.
日が沈むと、気温は下がる。

The road drops suddenly further ahead.
道路はこの先で、急に下り坂になります。

2 I must have dropped my keys somewhere around here.
このあたりに、かぎを落としたはずなんだけど。

Careful you don't drop it!
落とさないように気をつけて!

You'd better drop your speed. This is a fifty-kilometer-per-hour zone.
スピードを落としたほうがいいよ。ここは時速50キロ区域だから。

3 He dropped his voice a notch.
彼は一段、声を落とした。

These strong winds are forecast to drop by tomorrow.
予報によると強風は、明日にはおさまるそうだ。

4 a drop in temperature of ten degrees
10度の気温の低下

It's a sheer drop of two hundred meters to the bottom.
底までは垂直距離で200メートルもある。

5 a drop of olive oil オリーブオイル1滴

He didn't spill a drop.
彼は1滴もこぼさなかった。

6 Could you put a drop of milk in, please?
少しだけミルクを入れてもらえますか?

drop a hint ほのめかす

drop the subject 話題を打ち切る

drop behind *v.* (in work, studies) 遅れる

He's dropped behind in all his classes.
彼はすべての授業で、勉強が遅れた。

drop by *v.* (visit) …に立ち寄る

drop off *v.*

1 **DECREASE:** 減る, 少なくなる

2 **ALLOW TO ALIGHT FROM A VEHICLE:** 降ろす

3 **DOZE OFF:** 居眠りする, うとうとする, うたた寝する

1 Demand has dropped off recently.
需要は最近減っています。

Public interest in this story seems to have dropped off.
この件への一般の関心は低くなったようだ。

2 Can you drop me off at the station?
駅で降ろしてもらえますか？

I'll drop you off at school on my way to work.
出勤のついでに学校まで送って行ってあげよう。

3 I must have dropped off while watching TV.
テレビを見ているうちに、うとうとしてしまったようだ。

drop out *v.* (of school) 中退する, 落ちこぼれる, (of society) 脱落する, (of game) 途中でおりる

Our son dropped out of the game because of an injury.
息子はけがのため、試合を途中退場しました。

---

drop-off *n.* (decrease) 減少; (in ocean) 断崖

dropout *n.* (from school) 中退者, 落ちこぼれ, (from society) 脱落者

droppings *n.* (of animal) ふん

drought *n.* 干ばつ, 日照り

drown *v.* (die by drowning) おぼれ死ぬ, 溺死する, (kill by drowning) おぼれ死にさせる

The crew drowned at sea.
船員は海で溺死した。

drug *n.* (medication) 薬, 薬剤, 薬品, (illegal drug) 麻薬, ドラッグ, 薬物
v. (sedate) 薬で眠らせる

do drugs 麻薬をやる

hard [soft] drugs
中毒性の強い [弱い] 麻薬

He's on drugs.
その人は麻薬をやっている。

drug addiction 麻薬 [薬物] 中毒

The racehorse had been drugged and stolen.
競走馬が薬で眠らされて盗まれた。

♦ **drug addict** *n.* 麻薬常習者, 麻薬中毒者

drugstore *n.* ドラッグストア, 薬局, 薬屋

drum *n.* (musical instrument) ドラム, (taiko) 太鼓; (cylindrical container) ドラム缶
v. (beat a drum) ドラムをたたく, (**drum on**: strike repeatedly) トントン/コツコツたたく, 打つ

I play the drums.
ドラムをやっています。

You can see the oil drums from here.
油のドラム缶がここから見えるでしょう。

drum into sb's head (…の) 頭にたたき込む

Try to drum some sense into his head, OK?
あの人の頭に、常識というものをたたき込んでくれないか？

drummer *n.* ドラマー

drumstick *n.* ドラムスティック, (for taiko) (太鼓の) ばち

drunk *adj.* 酔った, 酔っ払った
n. (drunk person) 酔っ払い, (person who gets drunk often) 飲んだくれ, 飲んべえ

get drunk 酔う [酔っ払う]

There are a lot of drunks around the station late at night.
夜遅くなると駅の周辺には酔っ払いが大勢いる。

be drunk as a skunk/lord/fish 泥酔している

D

♦ **drunkard** *n.* 飲んだくれ

drunk driving *n.* 飲酒運転, 酔っ払い運転

dry

1 *adj.* LACKING MOISTURE: (of cloth etc.) 乾いた, 乾燥した, (of river, well etc.) 水のかれた, 干上がった, (of climate, weather) 乾燥した, からっとした, (having little/no rainfall) 雨の降らない

2 *v.* BECOME/MAKE DRY: (become dry) 乾く, (of lake, well etc.) 干上がる, (make dry) 乾かす, (under the sun or by exposing to wind) 干す, (wipe dry: spill, dishes, tears) ふく

3 *adj.* OF WINE: 辛口の, ドライの

4 *adj.* LACKING NATURAL OILS: 乾燥した, (of skin) カサカサの, (of hair) パサパサの

5 *adj.* UNINTERESTING: つまらない, (of book) 無味乾燥な, (of lecture) 退屈な

6 *adj.* OF HUMOR: さりげない

7 *adj.* THIRSTY: のどが渇いた

1 Is the paint dry yet?
ペンキはもう乾いた？

This towel is damp. Do we have a dry one?
このタオルは湿ってる。乾いたのはある？

The ground is so dry the earth is beginning to crack.
地面が乾ききって、ひびが入り始めている。

The river is almost dry.
川の水がほとんどかれている。

The weather has been very dry lately.
このところ乾燥した天気が続いているね。

California is very dry.
カリフォルニアはからっとしている。

2 Has the laundry dried yet?
洗濯物はもう乾きましたか？

The plums have to be dried first.
まず始めに梅を干さなければなりません。

Let's dry the dishes.
お皿をふきましょう。

3 Is it a dry wine?
辛口のワインですか？

4 Your hair is really dry.
髪の毛がとても乾燥してるね。

5 It was a very dry presentation.
すごくつまらない発表だった。

6 He has a dry sense of humor.
彼には、さりげないユーモアのセンスがある。

7 I'm dry./My throat is dry.
のどが渇いた。

♦ **dryness** *n.* 乾燥

dry-clean *v.* (ドライ)クリーニングする

dry cleaner's *n.* (ドライ)クリーニング店

dryer *n.* (hair dryer) (ヘア)ドライヤー, (for laundry) 乾燥機

dry goods *n.* (textiles) 生地, 織物

dry ice *n.* ドライアイス

dual *adj.* 2重の

♦ **dual citizenship** *n.* 二重国籍

dub[1] *v.* (nickname) (…に) あだ名をつける

dub[2] *v.* (copy: CD, tape etc.) ダビングする, 複製する, (into another language) (…に) 吹き替える

The film had been dubbed into English.
その映画は英語に吹き替えられた。

dubious *adj.* (of character: questionable) 怪しげな, うさんくさい

duchess *n.* 公爵夫人

duchy *n.* 公爵領, 公国

duck¹ *n.* (domestic) アヒル, (wild) カモ, 鴨

duck² *v.* (lower head) 頭をひょいと下げる, ひょいとかがむ, (take cover) 身をかわす, 隠れる

The foreigner ducked as he got onto the train.
その外国人は電車に乗る時、頭をひょいと下げた。

duct *n.* (air duct) 通気管, ダクト

duct tape *n.* ダクトテープ

due

1 *adj.* EXPECTED: (**due to begin**) 始まる予定だ, (**due out**) 出る予定だ, (**due in**) 着く予定だ, (due to be paid) 支払われる予定だ, (of baby) 生まれる予定だ, (of homework) 提出期限だ

2 *adj.* OWED: (of money) 支払われるべき, (of respect) 与えられるべき, 払われるべき

3 *adj.* PROPER/ADEQUATE: 正当な, 十分な

4 *n.* MEMBERSHIP FEES: (**dues**) 会費

1 What time is the meeting due to begin?
会議は何時に始まる予定ですか？

The next issue is due out next month.
次号は来月出る [発行の] 予定です。

The train was due in at 1:00 P.M.
電車は(午後) 1 時に着くはずだった。

When's this money due to be paid?
お金は、いつ支払われる予定ですか？

On what day is the rent due?
家賃の支払い期限はいつですか？

I have three papers due tomorrow.
三つのレポートは、明日が提出期限だ。

2 You should claim any compensation that is due to you.
あなたに支払われるべき賠償金は、きちんと請求したほうがいい。

Some did not feel that they got the respect due to them.
中には、十分な敬意を払われていないと感じる人もいた。

Give credit where credit is due!
認めてしかるべきものを認めよ。

3 the due process (of law)
正当な(法の)手続き

Has due attention been given to the issue?
その問題には十分な配慮がなされましたか？

4 pay one's dues 会費を払う

due to (owing to) …によって, …のため(に), …に起因して, (implying blame) …のせいで

His illness is partly due to lack of rest.
彼の病気は、一つには休養が足りなかったせいだ。

give sb his/her due 正当に評価する, 公平に扱う

Give him his due. He did his best.
それなりに評価してあげよう。彼はベストを尽くしたんだから。

in due course (when the time is right) 適当な時期に, 時が来れば, (before long) やがて, そのうちに

We will consider the matter in due

course.
その件については、そのうち検討させていただきます。

with all due respect 失礼ですが

With all due respect, I think your figures may be wrong.
失礼ですが、数字が間違っているのではないでしょうか。

due date *n.* 締め切り

duel *n.* 決闘

duet *n.* (musical composition) デュエット, (instrumental) 二重奏, (vocal) 二重唱, (duet performers) デュエットする人

duffel bag *n.* ダッフルバッグ

duke *n.* 公爵, -公

dull *adj.*

1 BORING: つまらない, さえない, (tedious) 退屈な

2 OF COLOR/SOUND: 鈍い

3 OF BLADE: 切れない, 切れ味の悪い, なまっている

4 OF PAIN: 鈍い, 激しくない

5 OF SKY/WEATHER: 曇った, どんよりとした

1 What a dull story!
なんてつまらない話だ!

The novel was dull.
その小説はつまらなかった。

There's never a dull moment when Taro's around.
太郎がいると、退屈しないね。

I haven't heard such a dull lecture in a long time.
こんなに退屈な講義は久しぶりだ。

2 The ring had a dull shine.
指輪は鈍い輝きを放っていた。

It hit the floor with a dull thud.
鈍い音を立てて床に落ちた。

3 This knife is dull.
このナイフは、よく切れない。

4 I feel a dull pain in my right arm.
右腕に鈍い痛みがあります。

5 The sky was a dull gray.
空はどんより曇っていた。

dumb *adj.* (stupid) ばかな

dumbbell *n.* ダンベル

dump *v.* (unload) どさっと下ろす, (throw away) 投げ捨てる, (industrial waste) 投棄する, 処分する; (merchandise) 投げ売りする, ダンピングする; (person) 振る

n. (place for garbage) ごみ捨て場, (pile of garbage) ごみの山

The truck dumped its load.
トラックは荷をどさっと下ろした。

She dumped him for another guy.
別の人ができて、彼女は彼を振った。

This place looks like a garbage dump.
ここはまるで、ごみ捨て場みたいだ。

I hate the place; it's a dump.
その場所は嫌いだ、汚いから。

dump truck *n.* ダンプカー

dune *n.* 砂丘

dung *n.* ふん

dungeon *n.* 地下牢

duodenum *n.* 十二指腸

duplicate *n.* (reproduction) 複製, (photocopy) 複写, コピー, 写し

v. (replicate) 複製する, (photocopy) 複写する, コピーする, (...の) 写しを取る

adj. 複製の, (of document) 控えの

Not a single person noticed that the pic-

ture was a duplicate.
その絵が複製であることに、誰一人気づかなかった。

durable *adj.* (strong, sturdy) 丈夫な, (long-lasting) 長持ちする, 耐久性のある
durable goods 耐久消費材

duration *n.* 期間

durian *n.* ドリアン

during *prep.* …の間(に), -中
During the past year…
ここ1年の間に [は]…
The road is closed during the winter.
冬の間、その道路は閉鎖されます。
I worked in a hotel during summer break.
夏休み中、ホテルで働いていた。
During that time, she wrote to me every month.
そのころ彼女は毎月手紙をくれた。
And what do you intend to do during that week?
その週は何をするつもりですか？

dusk *n.* 日暮れ, 夕暮れ, ((*poetic*)) たそがれ

dust *n.* (dry/fine dirt) ほこり, ちり, (particles) 粉, -くず
v. (brush dust from) (…の) ほこりを払う
The room was covered in dust.
部屋はほこりだらけだった。
The wind blew the dust everywhere.
風がほこりをそこらじゅうに吹き散らした。
It's been dry, so there's a lot of dust in the air.
このところ乾燥しているので、ちりがたくさん空気中に漂っている。
gold dust 金粉
Let's start by dusting the furniture.
まず家具のほこりを払いましょう。

dustbin *n.* ごみ箱

duster *n.* (cloth) ぞうきん, (brush) はたき; (article of clothing) ダスターコート

dustman *n.* ごみ収集員

dustpan *n.* ちり取り
a dustpan and broom ちり取りとほうき

dusty *adj.* (covered in dust) ほこりだらけの, (of road, room) ほこりっぽい

Dutch *adj.* (of the Netherlands or its culture) オランダの, (of person) オランダ人の, (of language) オランダ語の
n. (language) オランダ語, (**the Dutch**: the people of the Netherlands) オランダ人

duty *n.* (moral obligation) 義務, (job, task) 職務, 任務, 務め, (official duty) 公務, (military duty) 軍務; (import tax) 関税, -税
a sense of duty 義務感
do one's duty 義務を果たす
It's every citizen's duty to help prevent crime.
犯罪防止を手助けするのは、市民の務めだ。
I reported for duty at 6 o'clock sharp.
6時ちょうどに仕事に就きました。
You'll have to pay customs duties.
関税を支払うことになりますよ。
The government is going to impose duties on alcohol and tobacco again.
政府は、アルコール類とたばこに再課税するつもりだ。
off duty 勤務時間外で, 非番で
She's off duty between twelve and one.
彼女は12時から1時まで休憩です。
on duty 勤務中で, 当番で

Are you on duty tomorrow?
明日はお仕事ですか？

duty-free ***adj., adv.*** 免税の/で
duty-free goods 免税品

♦ **duty-free shop** ***n.*** 免税品店

duvet ***n.*** (comforter) 羽毛布団

DVD ***n.*** ＤＶＤ

dwarf ***n.*** 小人

dwell ***v.*** 住む

♦ **dwell on** ***v.*** (keep talking about) くどくど話す, (keep thinking about) くよくよ考える

dwelling ***n.*** 居所, 住所

dye ***n.*** (substance) 染料
v. 染める
She dyed her hair brown.
彼女は髪を茶色に染めた。

dying ***adj.*** (last) 最後の, (of words, wish) 臨終の; (in throes of death) 死にかけている, 瀕死の

dynamic ***adj.*** 力強い, ダイナミックな, 活動的な, 精力的な, (lively, brisk) 活発な

dynamite ***n.*** ダイナマイト

dynamo ***n.*** (generator) 発電機, ダイナモ

dynasty ***n.*** 王朝, 王家
the Ming dynasty 明(王)朝

dysentery ***n.*** 赤痢

dyslexia ***n.*** 失読症

dyslexic ***adj.*** 失読症の

dyspepsia ***n.*** 消化不良

dystrophy ***n.*** ジストロフィー
muscular dystrophy 筋ジストロフィー

E, e

each ***pron.*** (each one) それぞれ, 各自
adj. それぞれの, めいめいの, 各-
adv. (to/for each thing) 1個につき, (to/for each person) 1人につき
To each his own. 人それぞれだ。
Each one of us must do our best.
各自全力を尽くしましょう。
There were two sheets for each person.
1人、2枚ずつありました。
They cost $5 each. 一つ、5ドルです。
She gave them a balloon each.
1人1個ずつ風船を渡した。
each other お互いに
They won't speak to each other.
二人ともお互いに口を利こうとしません。
each time …たびに, 毎回
Each time I call, I get an answering machine.
電話をするたびに、留守番電話だ。
Each time, it's different. 毎回、違う。

eager ***adj.*** 熱心な, 張り切っている, (be eager for) 熱望している, (**be eager to do**) ものすごく…したがる
Now, there's an eager student.
ほら、ああいう人を勉強熱心というのよ。
He was eager to join the army.
その人はとても軍隊に入りたがっていた。
The children are eager to get down to the beach.
子供たちが浜辺に行きたがっている。
♦**eagerly** ***adv.*** 熱心に, しきりに, ひたすら
eagerness ***n.*** 熱心

eagle ***n.*** ワシ, 鷲

ear ***n.*** 耳 [→ picture of FACE], (sense of hearing) 聴覚, (sense for music) 音感; (of cereal plant) 穂
have a good ear for music 音感がいい
by ear 楽譜なしで
keep one's ears open 耳をすましておく
lend an ear to …に耳を貸す
turn a deaf ear to …に全く耳を貸さない

earache ***n.*** 耳の痛み
have an earache 耳が痛い

eardrum ***n.*** 鼓膜

earl ***n.*** (nobleman) 伯爵

earlobe ***n.*** 耳たぶ [→ picture of FACE]

early
1 ***adj.*** BEFORE EXPECTED: 早い, 早めの, (early in the morning) 早朝の
2 ***adv.*** SOON: 早く, (ahead of time, sooner rather than later) 早めに
3 ***adj.*** OF OLD: 昔の, (ancient) 古代の, (of machine: first-generation) 初期の
4 ***adj.*** OF AGE: …の初め, -初期, (**at an early age**) 幼いころに, 若い時に
5 ***adv.*** BEFORE: (**earlier**) 先に, さっき, ((*formal*)) 先程
6 ***adj.*** OF CROP: 早生の

1 You're early! 早いね！
I don't know—it's too early to tell.
さあどうかな──話すには早すぎるんです。
"What's the earliest you can come?" "Six o'clock at the earliest."
「一番早くて、何時ごろ来られますか？」「早くて6時ですね」
He's an early riser.
あの人は早起きです。

an early train [flight]
早朝の電車 [便]

an early snowfall 早朝の雪

2 He gets up very early in the morning.
あの人はとても早起きです。

We got here as early as we could.
みんな、できるだけ早くここへ来た。

He came earlier than expected.
彼は、思ったより早く来ました。

If we leave early, we'll be on time.
早めに出れば間に合う。

I'll call again early next week.
来週初めに、またお電話します。

3 early civilizations 古代文明

The earliest TVs were black and white.
初期のテレビは白黒だった。

4 the early 1960s １９６０年代初期

The teacher is in his early fifties.
先生は５０代初めです。

5 The sun was shining earlier on.
さっきまで日が差していた。

As I said earlier, there will be no decision today.
先程も言いましたように、今日中には決まりません。

6 early corn 早生のトウモロコシ

earn *v.* (money) 稼ぐ, (living) 立てる, (respect) 得る, (interest) 生む

She earns her living by teaching.
彼女は教師をして生計を立てている。

She earned the respect of her friends.
彼女は友達の尊敬を得た。

The capital will earn interest.
その元金は利子を生む。

earnest *adj.* 真面目な, 真剣な

in earnest 真面目に, 本気で

say in earnest 本気で言う

earnings *n.* (of person) 所得, 収入, 稼ぎ, (of company) 収益, もうけ

earphone *n.* イヤホン, ヘッドホン

earplug *n.* 耳栓

earring *n.* イヤリング

earth *n.* (also **Earth**) 地球, (the world) 世界, (soil) 土, (opposite of sea) 陸地, (opposite of sky) 地, (ground) 地面; (of electrical device) アース

Earth is much smaller than Jupiter.
地球は木星よりずっと小さい。

The earth here is soft and good for growing.
ここの土は柔らかくて、栽培に適している。

come down to earth (be realistic) 地に足をつける, 現実的になる

what/why on earth 一体何/なぜ

earthquake *n.* 地震

A strong earthquake shook the building.
強い地震でビルが揺れた。

the Great Hanshin [Kanto] Earthquake
阪神 [関東] 大震災

earthworm *n.* ミミズ

earwax *n.* 耳あか

ease

n. (state of comfort) 気楽, 楽; (easiness) 容易さ, たやすさ

v. (of tension) ほぐれる, ゆるむ, (of pain) 弱くなる, 和らぐ, (reduce: tension) ほぐす, (alleviate: pain) 和らげる

He lives a life of ease.

あの人は気楽に暮らしている。

The tension of the last few days has eased a little.
ここ数日の緊張感が少しほぐれた。

The pain has eased somewhat.
痛みが少し和らいだ。

feel at ease 落ち着く, 安心する, くつろぐ

I feel at ease with him.
彼といると落ち着く。

put at ease 安心させる, ほっとさせる

ease off *v.* (become weaker) 弱まる, 弱くなる; (reduce the tension/pressure in/on) ゆるめる

The wind eased off. 風が弱まった。

Ease off the gas, will you.
速度をゆるめて/スピードを落として。

---

easel *n.* イーゼル, 画架

easily *adv.* 簡単に, 楽に, 容易に, (smoothly, fluently) すらすら(と); (without a doubt) 間違いなく, 断然

We found the place easily.
場所は簡単にわかった。

She is easily offended.
あの人は、すぐ怒る。

I want to be able to read manga easily.
漫画をすらすら読めるようになりたい。

This car is easily the best.
この車が間違いなく一番だね。

east *n.* 東, 東方, (eastern part) 東部; (**the East**: East Asia) 東洋
adj. 東の, (east-facing) 東向きの
adv. 東に/へ

The wind is blowing from the east.
風は東から吹いている。

The sun rises in the east and sets in the west.
日は東から昇り、西に沈む。

East Asia *n.* 東アジア

Easter *n.* イースター, 復活祭

easterly *adj.* (of wind) 東からの

eastern *adj.* (in the east) 東の, (east-facing) 東向きの; (**Eastern**: East Asian) 東洋の

eastward *adv.* 東の方へ, 東に向かって
adj. 東(へ)の

easy *adj.* (simple) 簡単な, たやすい, やさしい, 容易な, (**easy to do**) …しやすい, (easygoing) 楽な

It's easy. 簡単ですよ。

It was an easy test.
やさしいテストだった。

It was far from easy.
全然簡単ではなかった。

Can you make it easier?
もっと簡単にしてくれますか?

That's easier said than done.
口で言うのは、たやすいけどね。

These words are easy to remember.
これは覚えやすい言葉です。

He's got a very easy job.
あの人の仕事はとても楽です。

go easy on (treat kindly) 大目に見る, 寛大に扱う

I'd go easy on him if I were you. He's only a kid.
((*feminine*)) 私だったら、大目に見てあげるわ。まだ子供なんだから。

take it easy (relax) のんびり構える, 気楽にする, くつろぐ, (**Take it easy!**) (=

E

Calm down) 落ち着いて, (=Don't get angry) かりかりしないで, (=Pull yourself together!) しっかりしろよ

Take it easy. You don't have to get so angry.
落ち着いて。そんなに怒ることないでしょ。

easygoing ***adj.*** (of person) のんびりした, のんきな, (not fussy) こだわらない, (flexible) 適応性のある; (of job) 楽な

eat ***v.*** 食べる, ((*honorific*)) 召し上がる, ((*humble*)) いただく, ((*masculine/informal*)) 食う, (have meal) 食事を取る, 食事をする

Which is more fun, eating or cooking?
食べるのと料理するのと、どっちが楽しい?

I'm sorry—I can't eat spinach.
すみません、ほうれん草は食べられないんです。

What would you like to eat for dinner?
夕食は何を召し上がりますか?

Let's go and eat now, shall we?
それじゃあ、食事に行きましょうか?

Have you eaten already?
もう食事をした?

♦ **eat out** ***v.*** (dine out) 外食する, 外で食事をする

eaves ***n.*** (of house) 軒, ひさし [→ picture of HOUSE]

eavesdrop ***v.*** 盗み聞きする, 立ち聞きする [→ OVERHEAR]

ebb ***n.*** (tide) 引き潮; (decline) 衰退
v. (of tide) 引く; (decline) 衰える

ebony ***adj.*** (black) 真っ黒の, 漆黒の
n. コクタン, 黒檀

eccentric ***adj.*** (of person) 変な, 奇妙な, エキセントリックな
n. (oddball) 変人, 奇人

echo ***n.*** (sound) こだま, 反響
v. 響く, 反響する, こだまする

éclair ***n.*** エクレア

eclipse ***n.*** 食, (lunar) 月食, (solar) 日食, (partial) 部分食, (total) 皆既食

ecological ***adj.*** 生態学的な, (of policy, product: gentle to the environment) 環境に優しい

ecology ***n.*** 生態学, エコロジー

economic ***adj.*** 経済の, 経済上の, 経済的な

economic reform 経済改革
economic growth 経済成長
an economic advantage 経済上の利点
economic dependence 経済的な依存
an economic incentive 経済的な誘因
an economic policy 経済政策
economic sanctions 経済制裁

economical ***adj.*** (costing little) 経済的な; (thrifty) むだ使いをしない, 倹約する

♦ **economically** ***adv.*** 経済的に, むだなく, 節約して

economics ***n.*** 経済学

economist ***n.*** 経済学者

economize ***v.*** 節約する, 倹約する

economy ***n.*** 経済, (economic/business conditions) 景気; (thriftiness) 節約, 倹約

The economy is in bad shape.
経済は悪い状態です。

♦ **economy class** ***n.*** エコノミークラス

ecosystem ***n.*** 生態系, エコシステム

ecstasy ***n.*** 有頂天, (drug) エクスタシー

be in ecstasy / go into ecstasies 有頂天になる, うっとりする

ecstatic ***adj.*** 夢中の

eczema ***n.*** 湿疹

edge ***n.*** (of cliff) 縁, (of blade) 刃, (of chair, carpet, page) 端, (**water's edge**) 水際, (of town, forest) 外れ, (brink) 寸前; (advantage) 強み

v. (advance slowly) じりじり進む; (**be edged with**) …で縁取られている

The paper was torn at the edges.
紙の縁が破れていた。

They're standing too near the edge of the platform (alongside the train tracks).
あの人たちはホームの端に近寄りすぎだ。

We walked to the water's edge.
水際まで歩いて行った。

The factory is on the edge of town.
工場は町外れにあります。

The country is on the edge of economic collapse.
その国は経済が崩壊寸前だ。

The children edged closer to see.
もっとよく見ようと、子供たちはじりじりと近づいて行った。

The garden is edged with azaleas.
庭はツツジで縁取られています。

be on edge (be nervous) 神経が高ぶっている, (be tense) ぴりぴりしている, (be irritable) いらいらしている

edible ***adj.*** 食べられる, 食用の

n. (**edibles**) 食用品

Is it edible? 食べられる物ですか？

edit ***v.*** 編集する

edition ***n.*** -版

the first edition 初版

a revised edition 改訂版

The new edition will be out next year.
新版は来年出ます。

a Japanese edition 日本語版

editor ***n.*** 編集者, エディター

editorial ***n.*** (newspaper column) 社説, 論説

adj. 編集の, (of/for editor) 編集者の

editorial staff 編集部員

educate ***v.*** 教育する, (teach) (…に) 教える

She was educated abroad at a private school.
彼女は、外国の私立学校で教育を受けた。

It's not easy trying to educate people about the dangers of smoking.
喫煙の危険性を教えるのは、容易ではありません。

educated ***adj.*** (well schooled) いい教育を受けた, (cultured) 教養のある

♦ **educated guess** ***n.*** 経験に基づく推測

education ***n.*** 教育, (subject) 教育学

receive a good education
いい教育を受ける

Ms. Ishikawa majored in education.
石川さんは教育学を専攻した。

educational ***adj.*** (of experience) 教育的な, ためになる, (of policy) 教育の

an educational experience
ためになる経験

educational background 学歴

educational reform 教育改革

educator ***n.*** (teacher) 教育者, 教師

eel ***n.*** (freshwater eel) ウナギ, 鰻, (sea

E

eel) アナゴ, 穴子

effect *n.* 効果, (result) 結果, (influence) 影響, (impression) 印象, 感じ

the Doppler effect ドップラー効果

cause and effect 原因と結果

the effects of global warming
地球温暖化の影響

come into effect 実施される

And when do these new rules come into effect?
で、この新しい規則はいつ実施されるのですか？

for effect わざと, 効果をねらって

The teacher raised his voice for effect.
先生はわざと声を張り上げた。

have no effect on …に影響はない, …に効果はない

The decision will have no effect on us.
その決定は私たちには何の影響もない。

The comedian's jokes had no effect on the audience.
そのコメディアンのジョークは観客に全く受けなかった。

in effect 実際には, 事実上

put into effect 実施する, 実行する

take effect 効く, 効果が出る

The drug should start to take effect immediately.
薬はすぐに効き始めるはずです。

effective *adj.* 効果的な, 効果のある, 有効な, (of drug, warning) 効き目のある

The measures were effective and resulted in fewer traffic accidents.
対策は効果的で、その結果交通事故が減った。

Is there any really effective treatment for cancer?
がんに本当に効き目のある治療法はあるのですか？

effectively *adv.* (in effect) 実際には, (to good effect) 効果的に

efficiency *n.* 能率, 効率

Our company needs to improve efficiency.
わが社は、能率を上げる必要があります。

How can we measure efficiency?
効率はどうやって測ればいいのだろう？

efficient *adj.* (of machine) 効率のいい, 能率的な, 効率的な, (of person) 有能な

an efficient use of time
時間の効率的な使い方

♦**efficiently** *adv.* 効率よく, 能率的に

effluent *n.* (from factory) (工場)廃液, (from sewer) 下水, 汚水

effort *n.* (exertion) 努力, 骨折り, (attempt) 試み, 企て

Your efforts will be rewarded.
あなたの努力は報われますよ。

You can't succeed without effort.
努力なしに成功できません。

It was a good effort.
よくがんばったね。

egg *n.* 卵

a raw egg 生卵

a fried egg 目玉焼き

a poached egg 落とし卵 [ポーチドエッグ]

a scrambled egg
いり卵 [スクランブルエッグ]

a boiled egg ゆで卵

a hard-boiled [soft-boiled] egg
固ゆで [半熟] 卵

put all one's egg in one basket 一つのことにすべてを賭ける

eggnog ***n.*** エッグノッグ

eggplant ***n.*** ナス, 茄子

egg roll ***n.*** 春巻

eggshell ***n.*** 卵の殻

ego ***n.*** (the self) 自我, エゴ, (pride) 自尊心, (conceit) うぬぼれ

egotist ***n.*** 自己中心の人, エゴイスト

egotistical ***adj.*** 自己中心の

Egypt ***n.*** エジプト

eight ***n.*** 8, 八

adj.,pron. 8の, (people) 8人(の), (things) 8個(の), 八つ(の)

"How many people have you invited?" "Eight."
「何人招待したの?」
「8人」

I've heard that joke eight times already.
その冗談はもう8回も聞いたよ。

eighteen ***n.*** 18, 十八

adj., pron. 18の, (people) 18人(の), (things) 18個(の)

eighteenth ***n.*** 第18, 18番目, (date) 18日

adj. 第18の, 18番目の

eighth ***n.*** 第8, 8番目, (date) 8日, (one-eighth) 8分の1

adj. 第8の, 8番目の

eighty ***n.*** 80, 八十, **(the eighties)** 80年代, **(one's eighties)** 80代

adj., pron. 80の, (people) 80人(の), (things) 80個(の)

Eighty guests came.
80人ものお客さんが来ました。

Grandma is in her eighties.
おばあちゃんは、80代です。

either

1 ***conj.*** See examples below

2 ***adj.*** (one of the two) どちらかの, ((*informal*)) どっちかの, (both) どちらの…も, ((*informal*)) どっちの…も

3 ***pron.*** (one of two) どちらか, ((*informal*)) どっちか, (both) どちらも, ((*informal*)) どっちも

4 ***adv.*** (also) …も

1 He must be either American or Canadian.
彼はアメリカ人かカナダ人に違いない。

He's either a genius or a madman.
あの人は天才か、でなければ狂人だ。

2 You can have either one. They're both the same.
どっちを取ってもいいよ。両方とも同じだから。

I didn't like either book.
どちらの本も好きじゃなかった。

3 Either of them should be able to do it.
二人ともできるでしょう。

Either will do. どっちでもいける。

I didn't know either of them.
私はどっちも知りませんでした。

4 "I don't like that movie."
"I don't either."
「あの映画は好きじゃない」
「私も」

either way どっちみち

ejaculate ***v.*** (semen) 射精する

♦**ejaculation** ***n.*** (of semen) 射精

eject ***v.*** 外に出す, (CD etc.) 取り出す; (of pilot from aircraft) 緊急脱出する

elaborate *adj.* (of explanation, plan) 詳しい, 入念な, (of design) 凝った, (of workmanship) 精巧な

elapse *v.* たつ, 経過する

elastic *adj.* (stretchy) 弾力性のある, 伸び縮みする

n. (fabric) ゴム, (rubber band) 輪ゴム

elbow *n.* ひじ [→ picture of BODY]

elder *adj.* 年上の, 年長の

n. 年上の人, 年長者

be (...years) sb's elder ...より(...歳)年上だ

elderly *adj.* 年配の, (**the elderly**) 年配の人たち, お年寄り

eldest *adj.* 一番(年)上の

n. (**the eldest**) 一番(年)上

elect *v.* 選ぶ, 選挙する, 選出する, (**elect to do**: choose to do) ...することにする

election *n.* 選挙

a general [local] election 総[地方]選挙

I wonder which party will win the election.
どの党が選挙に勝つだろう。

electoral *adj.* 選挙の

electoral college 選挙人団

electoral vote 選挙人投票

electorate *n.* 選挙民

electric *adj.* 電気の

an electric carpet 電気カーペット

an electric blanket 電気毛布

an electric heater 電気ストーブ

an electric car 電気自動車

♦ **electric chair** *n.* 電気椅子

electric guitar *n.* エレキ(ギター)

electrical *adj.* 電気の, 電気関係の

electrical appliances 電気製品

electrician *n.* 電気技師, 電気屋(さん)

electricity *n.* 電気, (electric power) 電力

The electricity went out.
電気が消えた。

♦ **electricity bill** *n.* 電気料金請求書

electrocardiogram *n.* 心電図

electrocardiograph *n.* 心電計

electrocute *v.* (**be electrocuted**) 感電死する, (= be executed) 電気椅子で死刑になる

♦ **electrocution** *n.* (death by electric shock) 感電死, (form of execution) 電気死刑

electrode *n.* 電極

electrolysis *n.* 電気分解, 電解

electrolyte *n.* (liquid) 電解液

electron *n.* 電子, エレクトロン

electronic *adj.* 電子の

electronics *n.* (subject of study) 電子工学, エレクトロニクス; (electronic goods) 電気製品

elegant *adj.* (of manner) 上品な, エレガントな, 品のいい, 優雅な

♦ **elegance** *n.* 優雅さ, 上品さ

element *n.* (factor) 要素, (group of people) 分子, 集団, (chemical element) 元素; (**the elements**: harsh weather) 悪天候

There is an element of truth in his story.
あの人の話には真実味がある。

Appearance is just one element of what attracts us to people.
外見は、私たちが人にひかれる要素の一つにすぎない。

The criminal elements of society will probably always be there.

社会の犯罪分子は、おそらく常に存在するだろう。

Oxygen is one element of water.
酸素は水の元素の一つです。

elementary *adj.* (basic) 基本の, 初歩的な, (of education) 初等の

elementary school *n.* 小学校

elephant *n.* ゾウ, 象

elevate *v.* (**be elevated to**: be promoted to) …に昇進する

elevator *n.* エレベーター

You can take the elevator to the fourth floor.
4階には、エレベーターで行けます。

eleven *n.* 11, 十一
adj., pron. 11の, (people) 11人(の), (things) 11個(の)

eleventh *n.* 第11, 11番目, (date) 11日
adj. 第11の, 11番目の

elf *n.* 小妖精

elicit *v.* (information) 引き出す, 聞き出す, (reaction) 誘い出す, 導き出す

Were you able to elicit an answer from them?
彼らから返事を聞き出せましたか？

eligible *adj.* (be eligible for: be qualified for)(…の)資格がある, (suitable for marriage) 結婚相手としてふさわしい

be eligible for a loan
ローンを組む資格がある

Are we eligible to take this course?
私たちは、この講座を受講する資格がありますか？

eliminate *v.* なくす, 除く, (from contest) ふるい落とす; (kill) 殺す

elite *adj.* エリートの
n. (**the elite**) エリート

elk *n.* ヘラジカ

elm *n.* (tree) ニレ, (wood) ニレ材

eloquent *adj.* (of person) 雄弁な, (of speech, essay: persuasive) 説得力のある, 表現力のある

else

1 *adj.* IN ADDITION: (**something else**) ほかに何か, ほかに…こと/物, (**somebody else**) ほかに誰か, ほかに…人, (**somewhere else**) ほかにどこか, ほかに…場所

2 *adj.* DIFFERENT: 別の, 違う

3 *adv.* OTHERWISE: ほかに

1 Is there anything else we need to buy?
ほかに買わないといけない物はある？

Is there something else you would like to say?
ほかにおっしゃりたいことはありますか？

No one else seemed at all interested.
興味のありそうな人は、ほかに誰もいなかった。

Nobody else applied for the position.
応募した者は、ほかに誰もいなかった。

Who else did you invite?
ほかに誰を招待したの？

She has nowhere else to go.
彼女は、ほかにどこも行く所がない。

Everywhere else was packed.
ほかはどこも満員だった。

2 It wasn't there. It has to be somewhere else.
そこにはなかったから、別の場所にあるはずだ。

I thought it was her, but it turned out

to be somebody else.
彼女かと思ったら、別の [違う] 人だった。

3 How else can I do it?
ほかに、どうやれっていうの？

or else (そう)でなければ, あるいは, (making a threat: **or else!**) さもないと (ひどい目にあうぞ)

We could go out and eat, or else we could just stay at home.
食べに出てもいいし、あるいは家でのんびりしてもいいよ。

elsewhere *adv.* (どこか) ほかの所に/で, よそに/で

e-mail *n.* eメール, メール
v. メールで送る

♦**e-mail address** *n.* メールアドレス

emancipate *v.* (**be emancipated**: be liberated) 解放される

♦**emancipation** *n.* 解放

embargo *n.* 通商停止
v. (...の) 貿易を禁止する

embark *v.* (on ship/plane) (...に) 乗船/搭乗する; (on quest) (...に) 乗り出す

♦**embarkation card** *n.* 出国カード

embarrass *v.* 恥ずかしがらせる, 困らせる, (...に) 恥をかかせる

Please don't embarrass me any further with that story.
あんな話をして、これ以上恥をかかせないでよ。

The long silence embarrassed all of us.
長い沈黙に、みんなばつが悪かった。

embarrassed *adj.* 恥ずかしい, 戸惑う, ばつが悪い

I was too embarrassed to tell him his fly was open.
ズボンのチャックがあいているなんて、恥ずかしくてとても言えなかった。

embarrassing *adj.* 恥ずかしい, ばつの悪い

I made an embarrassing mistake in front of everyone.
みんなの前で恥ずかしい間違いをしてしまった。

It was an embarrassing situation.
ばつの悪い状況だった。

embarrassment *n.* (person) 厄介者, 困り者, (situation) ばつの悪い状況

embassy *n.* 大使館

emblem *n.* (symbol) 象徴, (representative design) 紋章, 記章, (school emblem) 校章, (family emblem) 家紋

embody *v.* (give concrete form to) 具体化する

embrace *v.* 抱きしめる, ((*written*)) 抱擁する

They embraced one another.
お互いに抱き合った。

embroider *v.* (embroider A with B / B on A) (AにBを) 刺しゅうする, 縫い込む

embroidery *n.* 刺しゅう

embryo *n.* 胎児

emcee *n.* 司会者
v. (...の) 司会をする

emerald *n.* (gem) エメラルド, (color) エメラルド色
adj. エメラルド色の

emerge *v.* (come out) 出て来る, 現れる, (become clear) 明らかになる, わかってくる

♦**emergence** *n.* 出現

emergency ***n.*** 緊急事態, 緊急の場合, 非常時
adj. 緊急の, (for use in an emergency) 非常用の
in case of an emergency 非常の際は
It was an emergency.
緊急事態だった。
an emergency exit 非常口

♦**emergency brake** ***n.*** (in car) サイドブレーキ [➞ picture of CAR]
emergency hospital ***n.*** 救急病院
emergency room ***n.*** 救急処置室

emigrant ***n.*** 移住者

emigrate ***v.*** 移住する

♦**emigration** ***n.*** 移住

eminent ***adj.*** 有名な, 著名な

emission ***n.*** 排出, (of gas) 排気, (substance emitted) 排出物

emotion ***n.*** 感情

emotional ***adj.*** 感情的な, (easily moved to tears) 涙もろい, (of appeal) 感情に訴える
an emotional experience
感情を動かされる体験
an emotional person 感情的な人
The bride got all emotional at the wedding.
花嫁は結婚式でとても涙もろくなった。

empathy ***n.*** 感情移入, 共感

emperor ***n.*** 皇帝, 帝, (Japanese emperor) 天皇

emphasis ***n.*** (stress) 強調, (attaching of importance) 重要視
put emphasis on …に重点を置く, 強調する

emphasize ***v.*** (stress) 強調する, 力説する, (treat with importance) 重視する
Our boss emphasized the importance of maintaining good customer relations.
上司は、客とよい関係を保つことの重要性を強調した。

empire ***n.*** 帝国
the British Empire 大英帝国

empirical ***adj.*** (of knowledge) 経験的な, (of evidence) 実証的な

employ ***v.*** (give work to) 雇う, 雇用する, (select for a job) 採用する; (use) 利用する
That company employs more than a thousand workers.
あの会社は1000人以上の従業員を雇っている。
I was employed by ABC Inc.
ＡＢＣ株式会社に勤めていました。
Ms. Noguchi was employed as an assistant manager.
野口さんは、係長として採用された。

employee ***n.*** 従業員, (company employee) 社員
a government employee 公務員

employer ***n.*** 雇い主, 雇用者

employment ***n.*** (act of employing) 雇用, 人事採用, (occupation) 職業, 職
I'm searching for employment.
今、求職中です/仕事を探しています。

♦**employment agency** ***n.*** (run by government) ハローワーク, 職業安定所, ((*in abbr.*)) 職安, (private) 人材派遣会社

empress ***n.*** 女帝, (Japanese empress) 皇后

empty ***adj.*** (of box, pocket, refrigerator) 何も入っていない, 空の, 空っぽの, (of room: containing no people) 誰もいない, (unoccupied) あいている, (of theater, train: not crowded) がらがらの, すいている, (of stomach) すいている

v. (rid of contents) 空にする, 空ける

an empty glass 空のコップ

The fridge is empty.
冷蔵庫は空っぽだ。

Don't throw away your empty cans. They can be recycled.
空き缶は捨てないでください。リサイクルできます。

The house seemed empty.
その家は誰もいないようだった。

There were plenty of empty seats.
空席がたくさん残っていた。

"Was it crowded on the airplane?"
"No, it was empty."
「飛行機は混んでましたか？」
「いいえ、がらがらでした」

"Was there a lot of traffic?"
"No, the roads were almost empty."
「道は混んでました？」
「いいえ、すいていました」

My stomach was empty and crying out for food.
空腹で [おなかがすいて]、何か食べたくてたまらなかった。

Let's empty the ashtrays.
灰皿を空にしましょう。

I emptied my pockets trying to find my ticket.
切符を捜すためにポケットを空にした。

empty-handed *adj.* (with no present) 手ぶらで

emu *n.* エミュー

enable *v.* (**enable to do**) ...できるようにする, (make possible) 可能にする

Winning the lottery enabled him to live the life of a king.
宝くじに当選したおかげで、あの人は王様のような生活ができた。

The tunnel enabled villagers to get to the other side of the mountain in an hour.
トンネルができて、村民は山の反対側まで1時間で行くことができるようになった。

enamel *n.* (kind of paint) エナメル, ほうろう; (on teeth) ほうろう質, エナメル質

encephalitis *n.* 脳炎

enchant *v.* (**be enchanted by**) ...に魅了される

encircle *v.* (surround) 取り囲む, (**be encircled by**) ...に囲まれている, (move in a circle around) 1周する

enclose *v.* (in envelope) 同封する

Some money was enclosed in the envelope.
封筒の中にお金が同封してあった。

encore *n.* アンコール曲

interj. アンコール！

encounter *v.* 出会う, 遭遇する

encourage *v.* (cheer on) 励ます, 元気づける, (**be encouraged by:** gain strength/confidence from) ...に力/自信を得る, (**encourage to do**) (...に) ...することを勧める, (promote: activity, interest) 奨励する, (spur on) 促す, 促進する

The good news encouraged me to work harder.
いいニュースに元気づけられて、もっとがんばろうと思った。

Don't encourage him! He smokes enough as it is.

彼にたばこを勧めないで！ 今でも吸い過ぎなんだから。

Sports are encouraged at that school.
その学校ではスポーツが奨励されています。

The cuts in interest rates encouraged economic growth.
金利の引き下げが経済成長を促した。

encouragement ***n.*** 激励, 励まし, 奨励

He needs encouragement to get the job done.
仕事をやり遂げるよう励ますことが必要です。

encouraging ***adj.*** 勇気づける, 励ましの, 激励の, (favorable) 好意的な

encouraging words 励ましの言葉

The news was encouraging.
そのニュースに勇気づけられた。

encyclopedia ***n.*** 百科事典

encyclopedic ***adj.*** 百科事典の, (of knowledge) 幅広い

end

1 ***n.*** LAST PART: 終わり, (of period) 終わり, -末, (of event) 最後, (of story) 結末, (of letter, contract) ((*written*)) 末尾

2 ***n.*** FURTHEST POINT: (of stick) 端, 先, (of street, corridor) 突き当たり, (of town) 外れ, (of journey) 果て

3 ***v.*** COME/BRING TO AN END: 終わる / 終わらせる, (of road) 行き止まる, (of day, year) 暮れる

4 ***n.*** OF TELEPHONE LINE: (**the other end**) 向こう側, 相手側

5 ***n.*** DEATH: 死, 最期

6 ***n.*** SMALL REMAINING PIECE: 残り物, 切れ端

1 the end of the twentieth century
２０世紀の終わり

the end of the week [month, year]
週末 [月末, 年末]

Oh, leave it till the end.
ああ、それは最後まで残しておいて。

At the end of my stay, I was sorry to leave.
滞在を終えるころには、帰りたくなくなっていた。(lit.,"I did not want to go home.")

The end of the film was disappointing.
映画の結末は期待外れだった。

2 the end of the table [sofa]
テーブル [ソファ] の端

Now, find the ends of the rope and give them to me.
ロープの先を探して渡してちょうだい。

At the end of this street, turn right.
この道の突き当たりで右に曲がってください。

a pub at the end of town
町外れの居酒屋

I'll wait for you at the other end.
向こうで待ってるよ。

3 It didn't end properly.
きちんと終わらなかった。

I can't go home till the course ends.
コースが終了するまで、家には帰れない。

There was no knowing when the speech would end.
スピーチがいつ終わるのか、まるで見当がつかなかった。

And that ended the discussion.
それで議論にピリオドが打たれた。

The woods ended and a plain lay before us.

E

森が終わり、目の前には平野が広がっていた。

The road ended about a kilometer past the fork.
道路は分岐点から1キロの所で行き止まりだった。

4 When I picked up the phone and said hello, no one was on the other end.
受話器を取って「もしもし」と言ったけど、向こうは誰も出なかった。

5 a peaceful, painless end
安らかな、痛みのない死

6 cigarette ends たばこの吸い殻

come to an end 終わる

The play finally came to an end at 10 o'clock.
芝居は10時にようやく終わった[幕になった]。

end to end 端と端をくっつけて, 縦1列に

Let's put the tables end to end.
テーブルの端と端をくっつけよう。

from beginning to end 最初から最後まで, 始めから終わりまで

It was fun from beginning to end.
最初から最後まで楽しかった。

in the end 最後に(は), 結局

In the end, she doesn't marry him.
結局、彼女は彼とは結婚しないんだ。

put an end to 終わらせる, やめさせる

The two sides agreed to put an end to the fighting.
両者は、戦いを終わらせることで合意した。

there's no end to …に終わりはない, …はきりがない

There's no end to this kind of work.
こういう仕事は、きりがない。

end up *v.* 結局…になる, 最後に(は)…になる

We got lost and ended up in the suburbs.
道に迷い、結局郊外に出てしまった。

I ended up crashing at my friend's house.
結局友達の家に泊まった。

We ended up walking home.
最後には、歩いて家に帰ることになった。

end with *v.* …で終わる, (of day, year) …で暮れる

KANJI BRIDGE

末 ON: まつ KUN: すえ | END, LAST

end of a semester	学期末
end of the month	月末
end of the year	年末, 歳末
final exam	期末試験
last years (of period)	末期
last day (of month)	末日
youngest child	末っ子

endanger *v.* 危険にさらす

endangered *adj.* (of animal) 危機に瀕した

an endangered species 絶滅危惧種

endeavor *v.* (**endeavor to do**) …しようと努力する, …しようと努める
n. 努力

ending *n.* 終わり, 最後, 結末

a happy ending ハッピーエンド

a sad ending 悲しい結末

endive *n.* エンダイブ, キクヂシャ

endless ***adj.*** (limitless) 無限の, 果てしない, きりのない, (of sea) ずっと続く; (ceaseless) 絶え間ない

endorse ***v.*** (approve) 承認する, (support) 支持する; (sign the back of: check) (…に) 裏書きする

endow ***v.*** (**be endowed with**) …に恵まれている; (give money to) (…に) 寄付する

endurance ***n.*** (patience) 忍耐力, がまん強さ, (stamina) 耐久力, 持久力

endure ***v.*** (put up with: pain etc.) がまんする, (…に) 耐える, (…を) 耐え忍ぶ; (last) 持ちこたえる, 持続する, (of friendship) 長続きする

It was more than I could endure.
がまんの限界だった。

I can't endure this noise any longer.
このうるささは、もうがまんできない。

No one could endure such pain.
誰だって、そんな痛みには耐えられない。

enema ***n.*** 浣腸

enemy ***n., adj.*** 敵(の)

He had lots of enemies.
あの人には敵がたくさんいた。

make an enemy of 敵にまわす

energetic ***adj.*** (of person) 精力的な, 元気いっぱいの, エネルギッシュな

energy ***n.*** (vigor) 元気, 活気, 精力, エネルギー, (power) エネルギー, 力

The children are full of energy.
子供たちは元気いっぱいだ。

I just don't have the energy to walk any further.
もうこれ以上、歩く力がない。

nuclear energy 原子力

enforce ***v.*** 実施する, ((*formal*)) 施行する

enforcement ***n.*** 実施, ((*formal*)) 施行

engage ***v.*** (**engage in / with**: be involved in / with) …に/とかかわる, (**engage in**: do) …に従事する, …をする

engage sb in a conversation / debate 会話/議論に引き込む

engaged ***adj.*** (have agreed to marry) 婚約している; (**be engaged in**: be involved in) (…に) 従事している, (…を) している

Are they engaged?
二人は婚約しているの?

They were engaged in heated debate.
二人は激しい議論をしていた。

engagement ***n.*** (marriage pledge) 婚約, (appointment) 約束

♦**engagement ring** ***n.*** エンゲージリング, 婚約指輪

engine ***n.*** (machine) エンジン

engineer ***n.*** エンジニア, 技師

engineering ***n.*** 工学

civil engineering 土木工学

England ***n.*** (United Kingdom) イギリス, 英国, ((*in abbr.*)) 英, (England) イングランド

English ***n.*** (language) 英語, (**the English**: people) イギリス人, 英国人
adj. (of language) 英語の, (of England, British culture) イギリスの, 英国の

English grammar 英語の文法

engrave ***v.*** 彫る, 刻み込む

♦**engraver** ***n.*** 彫刻家

engrossed ***adj.*** (be engrossed in) (…

に) 没頭する, 夢中になる

enhance *v.* 高める

enigma *n.* (mysterious person/thing) 不可解な人/こと, (riddle) なぞ

enjoy *v.* (derive pleasure from) 楽しむ, 面白く思う, (be blessed with: success, health etc.) (…に) 恵まれる

I thoroughly enjoyed the film.
その映画はとても面白かった。

Did you enjoy yourselves?
楽しめましたか？

enjoyable *adj.* (fun) 楽しい, (interesting) 面白い, (pleasurable) 愉快な

an enjoyable dinner 楽しい食事

enjoyment *n.* 楽しみ, 喜び

enlarge *v.* 大きくする, 拡大する, (photo) 引き伸ばす

enlargement *n.* 拡大, (enlarged photo) 引き伸ばし

enlightenment *n.* (act of enlightening) 啓蒙, (in Buddhism) 悟り; (**the Enlightenment**) 啓蒙運動

attain enlightenment 悟りを開く

enlist *v.* (join the military) 入隊する; (**enlist the support of**) …の支持を求める

en masse *adv.* 全部いっしょに, 一まとめに

enormous *adj.* (of object) 巨大な, ((*informal*)) でかい, でっかい, (of room) 広大な, (of amount) 莫大な

enough *adj.* (sufficient) 十分な, 足りる, (only just enough) 間に合う

adv., pron. 十分, たくさん

interj. もうたくさん

There was enough food.
食べ物は十分あった。

Is there enough room back there?
後ろの方には、ゆとりは十分ありますか？

Do you have enough change?
小銭は足りる？

I'm not getting enough sleep.
睡眠不足なんです。

Is this box large enough?
この大きさの箱で間に合いますか？

This is just not good enough.
これじゃ、とても十分とは言えない。

Eighteen is old enough to vote.
１８歳は投票するのに十分な年齢です。

It's bad enough having rain, but now gales.
雨だけでもいやなのに、強い風も出てきた。

I've got enough to do without having to do yours.
自分のことで精一杯なのに、人の分までかまっていられない。(lit.,"I can't concern myself with [the work of] others.")

Thank you, but I've had more than enough (food).
ありがとう、でも十分すぎるくらいいただきました。

Enough of your complaints!
ぐちはもうたくさんだ！

can't do enough いくら…しても足りない

I can't thank you enough.
お礼の申し上げようもありません。

enough is enough もうたくさんだ

OK, please stop now. Enough is enough.
さあ、もうやめなさい。たくさんだよ。

sure enough 案の定, やっぱり

We went to the bar, and sure enough,

he was there.
あのバーに行ったら案の定、彼がいた。

enquire → INQUIRE

enquiry → INQUIRY

enrich *v.* 豊かにする, 向上させる, (nuclear fuel) 濃縮する

♦**enriched** *adj.* (of nuclear fuel) 濃縮した
enriched uranium 濃縮ウラン

enroll *v.* (at school/university) (...に) 入学する, (in course) (...に) 登録する

enrollment *n.* (number of students) 在籍者数, (process of enrolling at school/university) 入学

en route *adv.* 途中で

ensemble *n.* アンサンブル, (of musicians) 合奏団, (of singers) 合唱団

ensign *n.* (in U.S. Navy) 少尉

ensure *v.* 保証する

enter

1 *v.* GO/COME INTO: (go into) (...に) 入る, (come into) (...に) 入って来る

2 *v.* BECOME A MEMBER OF: (company) (...に) 入社する, (school) (...に) 入学する [→ JOIN 1]

3 *v.* PARTICIPATE IN: (...に) 参加する

4 *v.* INPUT: (write in) 記入する, 記録する, (type in) 入力する

5 *n.* BUTTON ON KEYBOARD: エンター(キー)

1 Once you enter the building, take the elevator to the eighth floor.
建物に入ったら、エレベーターで8階まで上がってください。

The teacher entered the classroom.
先生が教室に入って来た。

2 Tanaka entered the company when he was young.
田中さんは若い時に入社しました。

You need good grades to enter that university.
あの大学に入るには、いい成績でないといけないよ。

3 Can we enter the competition?
私たちはコンクールに参加できますか？

4 The data was entered into a spreadsheet.
データがスプレッドシートに入力されていた。

5 press enter エンターを押す

KANJI BRIDGE

入 ON: にゅう KUN: い(る/れる), はい(る) | ENTER

enter a bid	入札する
enter a company	入社する
enter a country	入国する
enter a courtroom	入廷する
enter a hospital	入院する
enter a kindergarten/garden	入園する
enter a place (theater etc.)	入場する
enter a school	入学する

enterprise *n.* (business) 事業, (plan, project) 企て, (事業)計画; (company) 企業, 会社

entertain *v.* (treat with hospitality) もてなす, (amuse) 楽しませる

Mr. Ishida entertained the guests with French wine.
石田さんは、フランス産のワインで客をもてなした。

The performance was meant to entertain.
そのパフォーマンスは観客を楽しませ

るはずだった。

entertainer *n.* 芸能人, エンターテイナー, (non-professional) もてなす人

entertaining *adj.* (interesting) 面白い, (fun, amusing) 楽しい

entertainment *n.* (hospitality) もてなし, 歓待, (amusement) 楽しみ, (theatrical entertainment) 演芸, 余興, エンターテインメント

enthusiasm *n.* 熱心さ, 熱意

There was no matching his enthusiasm.
あの人の熱意には、かなわなかった。

enthusiast *n.* -ファン, -狂, -マニア

an art enthusiast 美術ファン

a wine enthusiast 大のワイン好き

enthusiastic *adj.* 熱狂的な, 熱心な, 乗り気だ

She wasn't very enthusiastic about the idea.
彼女は、その考えにあまり乗り気ではなかった。

entire *adj.* 全体の, 全部の, …全体

The entire building collapsed.
建物全体が崩れた。

The entire family got together at Christmas.
クリスマスには家族全員が集まった。

entirely *adv.* 全く, 完全に, (wholly) もっぱら

I entirely agree.
全く同感です/全くそのとおりです。

The ending to the book wasn't entirely convincing.
本の結末は完全に納得のいくものではなかった。

entitle *v.* (give a title to: book etc.) (…に) …という題をつける, **(entitle to do)** (…に) …する権利を与える, **(be entitled to do)** …する権利がある

entomology *n.* 昆虫学

entrails *n.* 内臓, はらわた

entrance *n.* (entryway) 入口, (to home) 玄関, (gate) 門 [→ picture of APARTMENT, HOUSE]; (act of entering: theater etc.) 入場, (coming onto stage) 登場

♦ **entrance examination** *n.* 入学試験, ((*in abbr.*)) 入試

entrance fee *n.* 入場料

entrepreneur *n.* 企業家, 起業家

entry *n.* (act of entering) 入ること, (into theater etc.) 入場, (into school) 入学, (into country) 入国, (into competition) 参加, (participant) 参加者; (listing in book) 記入事項, (listing in dictionary) 見出し語

(*sign*) No Entry 立入禁止

Entry is free for members.
会員の入場は無料です。

There were over a thousand entries for the competition.
競技会の参加者は1000人を超えました。

This dictionary has over twenty thousand entries.
この辞書には、2万語以上の見出しが収録されている。

♦ **entry visa** *n.* 入国ビザ

envelope *n.* 封筒

seal an envelope 封筒に封をする

envious *adj.* うらやましい

I'm envious of his salary.
彼の給料がうらやましい。

environment *n.* 環境, (natural environment) 自然環境

It's everyone's responsibility to take care of the environment.
自然環境を守るのは、みんなの義務です。

environmental *adj.* 環境の

an environmental disaster 環境災害
an environmental issue 環境問題
environmental protection 環境保護

environmentalist *n.* 環境保護論者

environmentally *adv.* 環境的に

environmentally conscious
環境のことを考える
environmentally friendly 環境に優しい

envoy *n.* (diplomat) 公使, (messenger) 使節

envy *n.* うらやましさ, 羨望, (object of envy) 羨望の的

v. うらやむ, うらやましく思う

I envy you. あなたがうらやましい。

enzyme *n.* 酵素

ephemeral *adj.* はかない, つかのまの, 短命な

epic *n.* (poem) 叙事詩, (literary work) 長編作品

epidemic *n.* 流行

adj. (of disease) 流行性の, 伝染性の

the SARS epidemic
新型肺炎 [SARS] の流行

epilepsy *n.* てんかん

epileptic *adj.* てんかんの

n. (person with epilepsy) てんかん患者

epilogue *n.* エピローグ, 結び

episode *n.* (of one's life) エピソード, 出来事, (of TV series) 1回分の話

in the first [second, last] episode
第1話 [第2話, 最終回] で

epitomize *v.* 典型的に示す, (…の) 典型だ

epoch *n.* (period) 時代, (geologic) -世; (event) 新時代を開く出来事

epoch-making *adj.* 画期的な

equal

1 *adj.* SAME: 同じ, 等しい, 同等な, (of rights) 平等の, (of opportunities) 均等な

2 *v.* BE EQUAL TO: (in value) (…に) 等しい, (in quality) (…に) 匹敵する, 劣らない

3 *n.* ONE'S MATCH: (one's equal) 同等の人, 匹敵する人

4 *adj.* BE ABLE TO DO: (**be equal to**) (…が) できる

1 Let's divide it up into equal portions.
同じ大きさに分けよう。

The density of an object is equal to its mass divided by its volume.
物体の密度は、その質量を体積で割ったものに等しい。

All people are created equal.
人間は皆平等に創られている。

There should be equal opportunities for people of all races.
どんな人種の人にも、均等な機会が与えられるべきだ。

2 Four plus three equals seven.
4足す3は7である。

Her excellent violin skills equal those of her sister.
彼女は姉に劣らない、すばらしいバイオリンの腕前をもっている。

3 No one is her equal.

E

あの人に匹敵するような人は誰もいない。

That horse is without equal on the racetrack.
競馬に出たら、あの馬にかなう馬はいない。

4 Is he equal to the task?
あの人に、この仕事ができるかな？

♦ **equal opportunity** *n.* 機会均等

equal sign *n.* 等号

equality *n.* (of rights) 平等, (of number, degree, size etc.) 均等

equality of opportunity 機会均等

equalize *v.* 平等にする, 等しくする, (in sport) 同点に追いつく

equally *adv.* (similarly) 同じくらいに, 同様に, (evenly) 等しく, 均等に

equation *n.* 等式, 方程式

equator *n.* 赤道

equestrian *adj.* 馬術の

equilateral *adj.* 等辺の

an equilateral triangle 正三角形

equilibrium *n.* (balance) つり合い, 均衡, バランス, (of mind) 平静

equinox *n.* (spring) 春分, (autumn) 秋分 [→ SOLSTICE]

equip *v.* (equip A with B) (AにBを) 備える, 用意する, 装備する, (equip with knowledge/skill) (…に知識/技術を) 身につけさせる, (**equip oneself with**) 身につける

The soldiers were equipped with the latest high-tech weaponry.
兵士たちは最新のハイテク兵器を装備していた。

We need to equip our young people with the skills they need for the future.
将来に必要な技術を、若い人たちに身につけさせる必要がある。

equipment *n.* (apparatus) 設備, 装置, 装備, (gear) 用具, 備品

stereo equipment ステレオ装置

equity *n.* (fairness) 公平, 公正; (value of property) 財産物件の純価, (net assets) 純資産, (**equities**: common stock) 普通株

equivalent *adj.* (equal) (…と) 同じ, 等しい, (corresponding) (…に) 相当する, 対応する

n. (equivalent thing) 同等のもの, (equivalent word) 相当語, 相当する言葉

There is no equivalent in English for the *itadakimasu*.
英語には、日本語の「いただきます」に相当する言葉はありません。

ER *n.* 救急処置室

era *n.* 時代 [→ p. 1176], (geologic) -代

the Meiji Era 明治時代

erase *v.* 消す, (delete) 削除する

eraser *n.* 消しゴム [→ picture of STATIONERY], (for blackboard) 黒板ふき, (for whiteboard) 白板ふき

erect *adj.* (of posture) 直立した, (of penis) 勃起した

v. (make upright) 立てる, (building) 建築する, (tent) 張る

stand erect 直立する

♦ **erection** *n.* (of penis) 勃起

erode *v.* 浸食する

♦ **erosion** *n.* 浸食, (wind erosion) 風食

erotic *adj.* エロチックな

errand *n.* お使い, 用事

Children enjoy going on errands.
子供はお使いに行くのが好きなんです。

I've got some errands to run.
ちょっと用事があるんです。

erratic ***adj.*** (not stable) 不安定な, (of behavior) とっぴな, (of person) 気まぐれな

error ***n.*** 間違い, 誤り, エラー [→ MISTAKE]

Please correct any errors.
間違いがあれば直してください。

He made an error of judgment.
あの人は、判断を誤った。

erupt ***v.*** (of volcano) 噴火する, 爆発する, (of violence) 起こる, (**erupt with anger**) 怒りを爆発させる

escalate ***v.*** (become/make greater) エスカレートする/させる, (tensions) 高まる/高める, (war) 拡大する/させる

escalator ***n.*** エスカレーター

go up [down] an escalator
エスカレーターで上がる [下りる]

escape ***v.*** 逃げる, 逃れる, (from danger) 免れる, (from prison) 脱走する, 逃亡する; (avoid) 避ける, 回避する; (leak) 漏れる

n. (from dangerous/unpleasant situation) 脱出, (from reality/society) 逃避, (from confinement) 脱走, 逃亡, (from prison) 脱獄; (**esc**: button on keyboard) エスケープ(キー)

The elephant escaped from its cage.
象が、おりから逃げた。

How many prisoners have escaped?
何人の囚人が脱走したのですか？

Sometimes we just need to escape from the hustle and bustle of the city to the peace and tranquility of the countryside.
時には、都会の喧騒から離れて、平和で静かな田舎へ行くことも必要です。

He's trying to escape from his responsibilities again.
あの人はまた、責任逃れをしようとしている。

Nothing escaped her notice.
彼女は、何一つ見逃さなかった。

Water seems to be escaping from the tank.
タンクから水が漏れているようだ。

He had a lucky escape and was unharmed.
彼は運よく脱出して、けがはなかった。

an escape from reality
現実(からの)逃避

escort ***v.*** (accompany) (…に) 付き添う, (as courtesy) エスコートする, (to protect) 護衛する

n. エスコート役, 付き添う人

I'll escort you to the door.
ドアまでご案内しましょう。

ESL ***n.*** 第二言語としての英語

esophagus ***n.*** 食道

ESP ***n.*** (extrasensory perception) 超感覚的知覚, ((*informal*)) 超能力

especially ***adv.*** (particularly) 特に, 特別(に), とりわけ, (purposely) わざわざ

It's especially hot this summer.
今年の夏は、特に暑い。

"Are you busy tonight?"
"No, not especially."
「今夜は忙しい？」
「いや、別に(忙しくない)」

No one was on time. And I had gone

especially early.
時間どおりに来た人はいなかった。私は特別 [わざわざ] 早く行ったのに。

Esperanto *n.* エスペラント語

espionage *n.* スパイ活動

espresso *n.* エスプレッソ

♦ **espresso machine** *n.* エスプレッソマシーン

essay *n.* (at school) 作文, (literary composition) 随筆, エッセー

essence *n.* 本質, 根本, (gist, core) 核心; (extract) エキス, エッセンス

capture the essence of
…の本質を捕らえる

the essence of the argument 議論の核心

essential *adj.* (necessary) 絶対必要な, 必須の, (fundamental) 基本的な, (indispensable) 欠かせない, 不可欠な

n. (**essentials**) (=daily essentials) (生活)必需品, (=basics) 基本

It's essential to learn the basics before you actually try doing it.
実際にやってみる前に基本を覚えることは、絶対必要です。

Qualifications aren't essential, but work experience is.
資格は必ずしも必要ではありませんが、実務経験は必須です。

Water is essential to life.
水は命に欠かせない。

essentially *adv.* (in essence) 根本的に, 本質的に, (basically) 基本的に

establish *v.* (business) 設立する, 創立する, (facts) 確認する, 証明する, (reputation) 築き上げる, 確立する

This company was established in 1894.
この会社は 1 8 9 4 年に設立されました。

First of all, let's establish what really happened.
まず最初に、実際に何が起きたのかを確認しよう。

She has established an international reputation.
彼女は国際的名声を築き上げた。

established *adj.* (fixed) 確立した, 定まった, (accepted) 認められた, (celebrated) 著名な

establishment *n.* (restaurant) 店; (**the Establishment**: those in power) 支配層, 体制

estate *n.* (land) 土地, 地所, (assets) 財産, (housing estate) 団地

♦ **(real) estate agent** *n.* 不動産屋(さん)

esteem *v.* (view with respect) 尊敬する, 尊重する

n. (respect) 尊敬, 敬意

esthetic → AESTHETIC

estimate *v.* (calculate roughly) 見積もる, ((*formal*)) 概算する

n. (rough calculation) ((*formal*)) 概算, (of cost) 見積もり, (statement of projected cost) 見積書

We estimated that it would take ten days to get there.
そこへ行くには、10日かかると見積もった。

Could you give me an estimate of the cost of repair?
修繕費の見積もりをお願いします。

estimation *n.* (evaluation) 評価

in my estimation 私の見たところ

estrogen ***n.*** エストロゲン

estuary ***n.*** 河口

et cetera ...その他, ...など, ((*informal*)) ...とか

etch ***v.*** **(be etched in)** ...に刻み込まれる

be etched in one's memory 記憶に深く刻み込まれる

be etched in stone (be decided) 決まっている

Nothing is etched in stone yet.
まだ何も決まっていない。

etching ***n.*** (work of art) エッチング, 銅版画

eternal ***adj.*** 永遠の

eternally ***adv.*** 永遠に, いつまでも, (always) いつも

be eternally grateful (to)
(...に) いつも感謝している

eternity ***n.*** 永遠, (after death) 来世, あの世

for all of eternity 永遠に

ethical ***adj.*** 倫理的な, 道徳的な

ethics ***n.*** (subject of study) 倫理学, (morals) 道徳, 倫理

ethnic ***adj.*** (racial, tribal) 民族の, (of food) エスニックの

ethnic tensions [violence]
民族間の緊張 [抗争]

ethnology ***n.*** 民族学

etiquette ***n.*** 礼儀, エチケット

etymology ***n.*** 語源, (subject of study) 語源学

eucalyptus ***n.*** ユーカリ

eunuch ***n.*** 宦官

euphemism ***n.*** 婉曲な表現, 婉曲な言い回し

euro ***n.*** ユーロ, €

Europe ***n.*** ヨーロッパ, 欧州

European ***adj.*** (of continent, culture, language) ヨーロッパの, (of person) ヨーロッパ人の

n. (person) ヨーロッパ人

European Union ***n.*** EU, ヨーロッパ連合, 欧州連合

euthanasia ***n.*** 安楽死

evacuate ***n.*** (place) (...から) 避難する, (people) 避難させる

evade ***v.*** (avoid) 回避する, 避ける, (capture, question, blow) かわす

evade taxes 脱税する

♦**evasion** ***n.*** 回避

evaluate ***v.*** (assess) 評価する, 査定する, (judge) 判断する

We need to evaluate the situation.
状況を判断する必要がある。

♦**evaluation** ***n.*** 評価, 査定

evangelical ***adj.*** 福音主義の

evangelist ***n.*** 伝道者, 宣教師

evaporate ***v.*** 蒸発する

♦**evaporation** ***n.*** 蒸発

evasive ***adj.*** (of action) 回避的な, (of answer: vague) あいまいな, (of person) 言い逃れをする

The airplane took evasive action.
飛行機は回避行動をとった。

eve ***n.*** (night before) -前夜, イブ

Christmas Eve クリスマスイブ

New Year's Eve 大みそか

even[1] ***adv.*** ...も/でも, ((*informal*)) ...だって, ((*emphatic*)) ...さえ, ((*formal*)) ...すら

There was even a swimming pool.
プールもあった。

I'm not going to tell anyone, even you.
誰にも言うつもりはありません、たとえあなたにでも。

Even I know that.
そのくらい私だって知っている。

We can still play rugby even if it's raining.
雨が降っていても、ラグビーはできるよ。

She didn't even look at it.
彼女は、目もくれなかった。

He had nothing, not even a single dollar.
彼は何一つ、たった1ドルすら持っていなかった。

No one dared even to ask a question.
あえて質問する人すら、いなかった。

even as ちょうど…時に

Even as the teacher spoke, people began to leave the room.
先生が話している時に、人々は部屋を出て行き始めた。

even if (たとえ)…ても/でも

Even if you do tell her, it won't make any difference.
たとえあの人に言っても、何も変わらないよ。

I'll go even if it rains.
<u>雨でも</u>[雨が降っても]行きます。

even now 今でも, いまだに

I can remember her even now.
今でも彼女のことを思い出せます。

even so それでも

Even so, I still think we ought to go.
それでも、行ったほうがいいと思う。

even then (even so) それでも, (even at that time) その時でも

I apologized, and even then he still wouldn't listen.
謝ったのに、それでもまだ話を聞こうとしてくれなかった。

even though …のに

They still love one another even though they've been married for 40-odd years.
結婚して四十数年にもなるのに、二人はまだ愛し合っている。

even[2] ***adj.*** (flat, level) 平らな, 平坦な, (smooth) 滑らかな, (of temperature, speed: fixed) 一定の, (orderly) 規則的な, (of teeth) きれいにそろった; (equal) 同じ, 等しい; (**even number**) 偶数

an even surface 平らな表面

The road is not even.
道路は平坦じゃない。

an even rhythm 規則的なリズム

even teeth きれいな歯並び

Use even amounts of soy sauce and mirin.
しょうゆとみりんを同量使います。

Now we're even.
これでおあいこだ。

break even 損得なしになる, ((*informal*)) トントンになる

get even with …に仕返しをする

♦**even out** ***v.*** (become flat/level) 平らになる, (become stable) 安定する

Housing prices in big cities have evened out recently.
大都市の家の値段は、最近安定してきた。

evening ***n.*** (early evening) 夕方, 夕暮れ, (after dusk) 晩, (late evening) 夜

this evening <u>今晩</u> [今夜]

every evening 毎晩

yesterday evening
ゆうべ [((*formal*)) 昨夜]

tomorrow evening
明日の夜 [((*formal*)) 明晩]

What are you doing this evening?
今晩、何をする予定?/今夜の予定は?

Did you do anything yesterday evening?
ゆうべは何かしましたか?

I'll be going out tomorrow evening.
明日の夜、出かけます。

The evenings are getting colder now.
最近は、夜冷えてきました。

Will you be back later this evening?
今夜は戻って来ますか?

♦ **evening paper** ***n.*** 夕刊

evenly ***adv.*** (so as to cover uniformly) 均一に, むらなく, (with equal parts/amounts going to each person) 均等に

Spread the frosting evenly over the cake.
ケーキに均一に糖衣を振りかけます。

The money will be split evenly.
お金は均等に分けられる。

event ***n.*** 出来事, 事件, (ceremony) 行事, (festival, convention) イベント, (competition) 試合, 種目

the events that led to the fall of the government
政府を崩壊に導いた一連の出来事

That was one of the most important events in my life.
それは、私の人生で最も重要な出来事の一つだった。

The event was widely reported by the media.
その事件は、マスコミに広く報道された。

an annual event 毎年(恒例)の行事

the main event メインイベント

in any event とにかく, いずれにしても

In any event, it didn't happen.
とにかく、そんなことは起きなかった。

In any event, this must be kept a secret.
いずれにしても、これは秘密にしておかなければいけない。

in either event いずれにしても, ((*informal*)) どっちみち

In either event, we need to be prepared.
いずれにしても、準備は必要だ。

in the event of …の場合(には), …の際は

In the event of a fire, sound the alarm.
火災の場合には、非常ベルを鳴らしてください。

eventual ***adj.*** (ultimate) 最後の, (resultant) 結果として起こる

eventually ***adv.*** (in the end) ついに, やっと, ようやく, (before long) そのうち(に), (someday) いつか, ゆくゆくは

She eventually turned up.
ようやく彼女が姿を見せた。

I'll get around to it eventually.
そのうちやるよ。

Try hard enough and eventually you will succeed.
がんばれば、いつか成功するよ。

Eventually he will go to medical school and hopefully become a doctor.
ゆくゆくは彼は医学部に入って、医者になるだろう。

ever ***adv.***

1 **AT ANY TIME:** (in the past) かつて, (until now) 今まで(に), (**have you ever done/**

been...?) ...したことがありますか, (in the future) いつか, (periodically: **do you ever...?**) ...することがありますか

2 AT ALL TIMES: いつも, 常に, (**ever after**) その後ずっと, それからいつまでも, (as long as possible) 末長く

3 TO GIVE EMPHASIS TO A QUESTION: 一体, そもそも

1 Nothing like it has ever been seen before.
こんなことは、かつて一度もなかった。

It's one of the best films ever made.
その映画は映画史上、最高傑作の一つだ。

She's looking more beautiful than ever.
あの人は前にもまして、きれいですね。

The exams are getting harder than ever.
試験は、ますます難しくなっている。

Have you ever been to India?
インドに行ったことがありますか？

Have you ever seen such rain?
こんなひどい雨、見たことある？

I don't think I'll ever be as sick as that again.
あんなにひどい病気になることは、もうないと思う。

It is very unlikely that she will ever meet him again.
彼女がまた彼に会うことは、もうないでしょう。

Do you cvcr wondcr why?
どうしてなのか、考えることがありますか？

2 Ever the optimist, I predicted good weather.
私はいつも楽観的だから、いい天気になると予想した。

All he ever does is complain.
あの人は、いつもぐちばかり言っている。

And they lived happily ever after.
それからいつまでも幸せに暮らしました。

3 Who ever could it be?
一体誰だろう？

What ever do you mean?
一体どういう意味？

Why ever did you go?
そもそもどうして行ったんだ？

as ever いつものように, 相変わらず

She's as cheerful as ever.
彼女は相変わらず明るいね。

ever since ...からずっと, ...以来(ずっと)

I've been fine ever since the operation.
手術してからはずっと元気です。

hardly ever めったに...ない

It hardly ever snows here.
ここでは、めったに雪は降りません。

evergreen *adj.* 常緑の
n. (tree) 常緑樹

everlasting *adj.* (eternal) 永遠の, 不朽の, (unending) きりのない

every *adj.* (each and every) すべての, あらゆる, どの...も; (of interval) 毎-, ...ごとに, (**every day**) 毎日

Every person is different.
人は皆、それぞれ違う。

I don't know every detail of the matter.
そのことについて、細かいことまですべて知っているわけじゃないよ。

Every single piece needs to be cleaned.
部品を一つ残らず、きれいにしなくてはいけない。

Every country has its own customs.
どの国にも、その国独特の風習がある。

I'm studying every night for the exams.
毎晩、試験勉強をしています。

There are traffic signals at every intersection.
交差点ごとに信号がある。

every now and again / then 時々

Every now and then I feel a pain in my shoulder.
時々、肩に痛みを感じる。

Every now and then I get the urge to stuff myself with something sweet.
時々、甘いものをおなかいっぱい食べたくなる。

every one どれも, 全部

Every one of the diamonds was a fake.
ダイヤはどれも偽物だった。

every other 一つおきの

every other day [week]
1日 [1週] おきに/隔日 [隔週] に

I usually visit them every other week.
大体、1週間おきに会いに行っている。

every so often 時々, 時折

We visit our grandparents every so often.
時々、祖父母に会いに行きます。

every time 毎回, ...たびに

I win every time.
毎回勝つんだ。

Every time I go there, it rains.
あそこへ行くたびに雨が降る。

everybody *pron.* 皆, 全員, すべての人, 誰でも, (addressing an audience) 皆さん; (in negative sentences: **not everybody** ...) 誰もが皆...(という)わけじゃない

Everybody was out.
みんな出かけていた。

Would everybody please sit down?
皆さん、お座りください。

I didn't get to talk with everybody at the party.
パーティーに来ていたすべての人とは、話せなかった。

Not everybody wants to be a lawyer.
誰もがみんな、弁護士になりたいわけじゃない。

everybody and their brother / hamster
猫も杓子も (lit., "even cats and ladles")

everyday *adj.* (daily) 毎日の, 日々の, 日常の, (ordinary) ふだんの, 平凡な

It was not an everyday occurrence.
それは、日常茶飯事のことではなかった。

Jogging is just a part of my everyday routine.
ジョギングは日課の一つです。

I'm going to wear my everyday clothes.
私は普段着を着て行きます。

everyone → EVERYBODY

everything *pron.* 全部, すべて, 何でも, 何もかも

I'll arrange everything.
全部手配します。

Everything is ready.
準備は、すべてできています。

It was impossible to understand everything.
すべてを理解するなんて無理だった。

Sports are everything to him.
スポーツは彼にとってすべてだ。

Everything I do seems to get on her nerves.
私のすることは何もかも、彼女の気にさわるようなんです。

"Is everything all right?"

“No, everything is not all right.”
「大丈夫ですか？」
「いや、大丈夫じゃないんです」

everywhere *adv.* どこでも，どこにも，どこにでも，どこも，どこへも，((*emphatic*)) どこもかしこも，至る所に/で

Everywhere you go, there is heavy traffic.
どこへ行っても、道路は混んでいる。

Oh, he’s been everywhere.
ああ、あの人はいろんな所に行ったことがあるんだ。

I’ve looked everywhere for it, but I can’t find it.
どこもかしこも捜したのに、ないんです。

Where have you been? I’ve been looking everywhere for you.
どこに行っていたの？ あちこち捜していたのよ。

evict *v.* (from premises) 立ち退かせる，(**be evicted**) 立ち退くよう言われる

♦ **eviction** *n.* 立ち退き

evidence *n.* (reason for believing sth) 証拠，(testimony) 証言，(traces) 形跡，印

The gun was presented as evidence.
証拠物件として、銃が提示された。

There was not enough evidence to convict him.
その人を有罪とするのに十分な証拠はなかった。

give evidence in court 法廷で証言する

His team found evidence of an early civilization.
彼のチームは古代文明の形跡を発見した。

evident *adj.* 明らかな，明白な，確かな

It was evident that the meeting had failed.
会議がうまくいかなかったのは、明らかだった。

evidently *adv.* (obviously) 明らかに，確かに

evil *adj.* 邪悪な，横しまな

n. 悪

good and evil 善悪

evocative *adj.* 何かを喚起する，(be evocative of) 思い出させる，呼び起こさせる

evoke *v.* (laughter) 誘う，(memory) 呼び起こす

evolution *n.* (process of life) 進化，(theory) 進化論，(development) 発展，発達

♦ **evolutionary** *adj.* 進化の

evolve *v.* (of living things) 進化する，(of plan, idea) (徐々に) 発展する

Once life finds a suitable niche within an environment, it stops evolving.
生物はひとたび自然環境の中に適した場所を見つけると、進化しなくなる。

Over the years, a simple idea evolved into an elaborate theory.
年月を経て、単純な発想が複雑な理論に発展した。

ewe *n.* 雌羊

ex *n.* (ex-wife) 先妻，(ex-husband) 前夫，(ex-girlfriend) 元の彼女，(ex-boyfriend) 元の彼

ex- *pref.* (former) 前-，元-

exact *adj.* (of numbers, meaning) 正確な，的確な，はっきりとした，(of likeness, fit) ぴったりの

Could you give me the exact date?
正確な日にちを教えていただけますか？

It’s an exact fit.
ぴったり合います。

to be exact 厳密に言えば

exactly *adv.* (precisely) ちょうど, 正確に, (sharp, on the dot) きっかり(に), (snugly) ぴったり; (agreeing with sb) 全く, そのとおり [→ "EXPRESSING AGREEMENT" on p. 23]

What exactly do you mean?
つまりどういうことですか？

Let me explain exactly what I mean.
私の言っている意味をきちんと説明します。

She came here at exactly 2 o'clock.
彼女は2時きっかりに来た。

It fits you exactly.
あなたにぴったりですね。

Exactly, I absolutely agree.
そのとおり、全く同感です。

exaggerate *v.* おおげさに言う, 誇張する

exaggeration *n.* 誇張, (exaggerated expression/story) おおげさな表現/話

exam, examination *n.* (test) 試験, (medical checkup) 診察, 健康診断, (physical) 身体検査

Were the exams difficult?
試験は難しかった？

What were your exam scores like?
試験の結果はどうでした？

pass [fail] an exam
試験に受かる [落ちる]

take an exam 試験を受ける

study for an exam 試験勉強をする

a university entrance exam
大学入学試験 [((*in abbr.*)) 入試]

have a medical examination
診察を受ける

♦ **examination hell** *n.* 受験地獄

examine *v.* (check) 調べる, 検査する, (medically) 診察する

♦ **examiner** *n.* (at school) 試験官

example *n.* (illustration of a rule) 例, 実例; (model) (お)手本, 模範

I'll give you an example.
例を挙げましょう。

Can you think of a typical example?
典型的な例を思いつきますか？

There are several good examples.
いい実例がいくつかあります。

for example 例えば

make an example of みせしめにする

We need to make an example of him so that others don't copy him.
ほかの者がまねをしないように、彼をみせしめにしないといけない。

set an example (for) (…に) 手本/模範を示す

He sets a good example for the rest of the class by working hard.
あの生徒はよく勉強するので、クラスのみんなにいいお手本となっている。

excavate *v.* (site) 発掘する, (bones) 掘り起こす

♦ **excavation** *n.* 発掘

exceed *v.* (number, amount, speed, limit) 超える, 超過する, オーバーする, (powers, expectations) 上回る, (…に) 勝る

Sales exceeded our expectations.
売り上げは予想を上回った [以上だった]。

exceedingly *adv.* きわめて, ものすごく, 非常に

excel *v.* (excel in/at) (…に) 秀でている,

(...が) 得意だ

He excels in math.
彼は数学が得意だ [できる]。

excellence ***n.*** 優秀さ

excellent ***adj.*** (of work) 優秀な, すぐれた, (wonderful) すばらしい, (expressing delight/approval) いいですね, けっこうですよ

He's an excellent translator.
あの人は優秀な翻訳家です。

"I'll be there at 3 o'clock sharp."
"Excellent!"
「3時きっかりに待っています」
「いいですね」

except ***prep.*** (other than) ...以外(は), ...のほか(は), ...は別として, ...を除いて

We all went except for Chris.
クリス以外はみんな行きました。

I can eat anything except cabbage.
キャベツ以外なら何でも食べられます。

I can't remember much about it now, except that the weather was very hot.
とても暑かったということ以外、今となってはあまりよく覚えていない。

I knew nothing about him except that he was a successful real-estate agent.
不動産屋として成功しているというほかは、あの人について何も知らなかった。

Except for my older brother, I have no blood relations.
兄のほかに、血縁はいません。

There was nothing I could do except write to her.
あの人に手紙を書くことしか、できることはなかった。

I work every day except Sundays.
日曜日を除いて、毎日働いています。

exception ***n.*** 例外

make an exception for 例外とする

with the exception of ...を除いて

exceptional ***adj.*** 例外的な, (rare) まれな; (excellent) 非常にすぐれた

excerpt ***n.*** 抜粋, 引用句

excess ***adj.*** 超過した, 余分の, -以上の

You'll pay a lot for any excess baggage.
超過手荷物は、高くつくよ。

excessive ***adj.*** (extreme) 極端な, 過度の

Don't you think some of his remarks were excessive?
あの人の発言の一部は、極端だと思いませんか?

exchange ***v.*** (exchange A for B) (AをBと) 取り替える, 交換する, (money) 両替する; (greetings) 交わす [→ CHANGE]
n. 交換, やりとり, (conversation) 会話; (currency exchange) 両替, 為替

(*at store*) Excuse me, I would like to exchange this.
すみません、これを取り替えてほしいんですが。

We exchanged our dollars for yen.
ドルを円に両替した。

We exchanged greetings.
私たちはあいさつを交わしました。

an exchange of information 情報の交換

an exchange of ideas 意見の交換

a meaningless exchange (of words)
意味のない(言葉の)やりとり

in exchange for ...と交換に, ...の代わりに

He gave me money in exchange for my tickets.

私のチケットと交換に、お金をくれた。

♦**exchange program** ***n.*** (for students) 交換留学のプログラム

exchange student ***n.*** 交換留学生

exchange rate ***n.*** 為替レート, 換算率

What is the dollar-to-yen exchange rate at the moment?

ドルから円への為替レートは、今いくらですか？

excite ***v.*** 興奮させる, わくわくさせる

Does the thought of going abroad excite you?

海外に行くことを考えると、わくわくする？

Stop exciting the dog, will you.

犬を興奮させるのはやめてくれない？

excited ***adj.*** 興奮した, わくわくした

Don't get so excited.

そんなに興奮しないでください。

excitement ***n.*** 興奮, (stimulation) 刺激

She says she needs more excitement in her life.

生活にもっと刺激が欲しいと、彼女は言っている。

exciting ***adj.*** (very interesting) すごく面白い, (thrilling) わくわくする, (stimulating) 刺激的な

The film was very exciting.

すごく面白い映画だった。

I don't know what people find so exciting about soccer.

どうしてみんなが、サッカーにそれほど熱中するのかわからない。

exclaim ***v.*** 叫ぶ

exclamation point/mark ***n.*** 感嘆符

exclude ***v.*** 締め出す, 除外する

excluding ***prep.*** …を除いて

exclusion ***n.*** 除外, 排除

exclusive ***adj.*** (of property) 独占的な, (**exclusive to**: for exclusive use by) …専用の; (of restaurant) 高級な, 一流の

n. (news) スクープ, (newspaper report) 独占記事

exclusive rights 独占権

an exclusive restaurant 高級レストラン

exclusively ***adv.*** (solely) もっぱら, …だけ

excrement ***n.*** 排泄物

excruciating ***adj.*** (very painful) ひどく痛い

excursion ***n.*** 小旅行, 遠足, 遠出, (day trip) 日帰り旅行

go on an excursion to the mountains 山へ遠足に行く

excuse ***n.*** (reason) 言い訳, 口実, 弁解, (opportunity) きっかけ

v. (pardon) 許す, (exempt) 免除する, (**be excused**: be allowed to leave) 失礼する, 中座する

Is he making excuses again?

あの人は、また言い訳してるの？

The boss is not going to believe that excuse about your mother falling ill again.

お母さんがまた病気になったなんていう例の口実を、上司はもう信じないよ。

The wet weather gave me a good excuse to stay at home.

雨で、家にいるいいきっかけができた。

That's no excuse.

それは理由にはならない。

I excused him this time.

今回は、許してあげた。

I asked to be excused from gym class because of a cold.
かぜをひいているので、体育の授業を免除してもらうよう頼んだ。

excuse me (trying to get sb's attention) すみませんが, 失礼ですが, (apologizing) 失礼しました, ごめんなさい, (excusing oneself from a place/situation) ちょっと失礼します

Excuse me, could you tell me where the nearest post office is?
すみませんが、一番近い郵便局はどこかご存じですか?

Excuse me for disturbing you.
おじゃまして、すみませんでした [ごめんなさい]。

(*at sb's house*) Excuse me, but it's time I was leaving.
すみませんが、そろそろおいとまします。

Excuse me for a moment.
ちょっと失礼します。

execute *v.* (kill) 死刑にする; (carry out) 実行する

The man was executed by lethal injection.
その男は、薬物注射により死刑が執行された。

execution *n.* (killing) 死刑執行, 処刑; (carrying out) 実行

♦ **executioner** *n.* 死刑執行人

executive *n.* (of company) 重役, 役員, 幹部, (of government) 行政官

a senior executive 重役

the executive branch of government
行政機関

exempt *v.* 免除する

exemption *n.* 免除, (from taxation) 非課税

exercise *n.* (physical exercise) 運動, (training) 訓練, (drill) 演習, (practice) 練習, (**exercises**: in textbook) 練習問題
v. (work out) 運動する, (do calisthenics) 体操する

You need more exercise.
もっと運動したほうがいいよ。

A military exercise is to be held next week.
来週、軍事演習が行われます。

I exercise every morning.
私は、毎朝運動しています。

All the workers at that factory exercise before they begin work.
あの工場では、仕事を始める前に [就業前に] 従業員は全員、体操をする。

♦ **exercise bike** *n.* エクササイズバイク, エアロバイク

exercise book *n.* 練習帳, ノート

exert *v.* (pressure) 与える, (influence) 及ぼす, 与える, (authority) ふるう; (**exert oneself**) 努力する, 力を尽くす, 骨を折る

exertion *n.* (effort) 努力, 尽力, 骨折り, (intense physical exercise) 激しい運動

exhale *v.* (breathe out) 息を吐く, (blow out: smoke etc.) 吐き出す

exhaust *n.* (gas) 排気ガス
v. (use up) 使い果たす, 使い尽くす, (topic) 論じ尽くす

car exhaust 車の排気ガス

an exhaust pipe 排気管

The country's resources were exhausted

by the long war.
長い戦争で、国の資源が使い尽くされてしまった。

Haven't we exhausted this topic?
この話題は論じ尽くさなかった？

exhausted ***adj.*** ひどく疲れた, 疲れ切った

We were exhausted after the climb.
登り終わったら、みんな疲れ切っていた。

exhibit ***v.*** (put on display) 展示する
n. (work of art on display) 展示品, (exhibition) 展覧会

exhibition ***n.*** (of art) 展覧会, 展示会, ショー, -展, (exhibiting) 展覧, 展示

be on exhibition 展示中だ

exhibitionist ***n.*** 自己顕示欲の強い人

exile ***n.*** (expulsion) (国外)追放, (defection) 亡命; (fugitive, asylum seeker etc.) 亡命者
v. 追放する

exist ***v.*** (of animate object) いる, 生きている, 生存する, (of inanimate object) ある, 存在する, 現存する

Do you think vampires really exist?
吸血鬼は本当にいると思う？

How camels can exist on so little water, I don't know.
どうしてラクダは、あんな少ない水で生きられるのだろう。

The manuscript no longer exists.
その写本はもう現存していません。

♦**existing** ***adj.*** 現在の, 現存する

existence ***n.*** (of animate object) 生存, (of inanimate object) 存在; (daily life) 生活, 暮らし

exit ***n.*** 出口

an emergency exit 非常口

exotic ***adj.*** (foreign) エキゾチックな, 異国風の, (of plants, animals) 外来の

expand ***v.*** (of metal, gas etc.) 膨張する, (increase) 増える, 増加する, (of business) 拡張する, 拡大する, (broaden the parameters of) 広げる

Metal expands with heat.
金属は、熱で膨張する。

The city's population has expanded in the last few years.
街の人口は、ここ数年で増加しました。

The company must expand or die.
会社は、拡張しない限り生き残れない。

The company has decided to expand the scope of the project.
会社は、そのプロジェクトの規模を拡大することにした。

expanse ***n.*** 広がり

expansion ***n.*** (enlargement) 拡大, 拡張, (increase) 増加

expatriate ***n.*** 国外居住者, 外国人
v. (leave one's country) 母国を離れる

expect ***v.*** (believe) (…と) 思う, (predict) 予想する, (look forward to) 期待する; (require) 要求する

I expect the prime minister will resign.
総理大臣はおそらく辞任すると思うよ。

I expect they'll arrive soon.
みんな、もうすぐ来ると思う。

I expect an apology from her.
彼女に謝ってほしい。

I expect he will explain what happened.
何が起きたのか、彼が説明してくれるだろう。

as expected 予想どおり, やはり, ((*infor-*

mal)) やっぱり

The bill passed, as expected.
予想どおり、法案は通過した。

As expected, the test was a breeze.
やっぱりテストは簡単だった。

be expecting (a baby) 妊娠中だ

She's expecting a baby.
彼女は妊娠中です。

when least expected 思いがけない時に

expectation *n.* 期待, 予想

have low [high] expectations
あまり期待していない [とても期待している]

expedition *n.* (journey) 探検, 遠征, (group) 遠征隊, 探検隊

go on an expedition
探検に行く[遠征する]

expel *v.* (from school) 退学させる, (**be expelled**) 退学になる

expenditure → EXPENSE

expense *n.* (cost) 費用, (**expenses**: of company) 経費, (outlay) 支出, 出費

wedding expenses 結婚費用

an expense of ¥1,000 a week
1週間で1000円の支出 [出費]

at one's own expense (using one's own money) 自費で

at the expense of (by sacrificing) …を犠牲にして

KANJI BRIDGE

費 ON: ひ KUN: つい(やす) | EXPENSE

accommodation expenses .... 宿泊費
annual expenses .... 歳費
consumption .... 消費
living expenses .... 生活費
medical expenses .... 医療費
membership fees .... 会費
school expenses .... 学費
transportation expenses .... 交通費
travel expenses .... 旅費

expensive *adj.* 高い, お金がかかる

That looks like an expensive tie.
そのネクタイは高そうね。

I wanted to buy it, but it was far too expensive.
買いたかったけれど、あまりにも高すぎました。

A trip to Las Vegas is very expensive.
ラスベガスへの旅行は、とてもお金がかかる。

experience *n.* 経験, 体験

v. 経験する, 体験する, (face) (…に) 直面する, (meet with) (…な) 目にあう, (taste) 味わう

in my experience 私の経験では

I've had no experience teaching.
教師の経験はありません。

It was the experience of a lifetime.
一生に一度の経験だった。

It was an interesting experience.
面白い体験でした。

None of us had experienced anything quite like it before.
誰もそんなことを経験したことがなかった。

We are experiencing great difficulties.
大変な困難に直面しています。

I've experienced similar (emotional) pain.
同じようなつらさを味わったことがある。

experienced *adj.* 経験豊かな, ベテラ

ンの

an experienced writer 経験豊富な作者

experiment *n.* 実験

v. 実験をする, (**experiment on**) 実験に使う

It's a shame, but I hear they use monkeys to experiment on.
ひどい話だけど、聞くところによると、そこはサルを実験に使うらしい。

experimental *adj.* 実験の, (based on experiment) 実験に基づいた, (intended as a test) 試しの, 試験的な

experimental music 実験音楽

expert *n.* 専門家, エキスパート, 達人, 名人, -通

adj. (of advice, opinion) 専門家の, (of person: skilled) 熟練した, 上手な

Ms. Hirano is an expert on the subject.
平野さんは、その道の専門家だ。

He's an expert on China.
あの人は、中国通です。

expertise *n.* (knowledge) 専門知識, (skills) 専門技術

expire *v.* 期限が切れる

explain *v.* (make clear) 説明する, (serve as a just explanation for) うなずける

Could you explain the problem to me?
問題を説明してくれますか？

I couldn't explain it in detail.
詳しくは説明できなかった。

Let me explain. 説明しましょう。

Could you explain why you left the door open?
なぜドアをあけたままにしておいたの？

I couldn't explain myself very well.
自分の考えをあまりうまく言えなかった。

If the window was left open, that explains how the burglar got in.
窓があいたままだったのなら、強盗がどうやって侵入したのか、うなずける。

explanation *n.* 説明, 解説, (excuse) 弁解

a plausible explanation
もっともらしい説明

His explanation was not very clear.
彼の説明は、あまり明確でなかった。

explanatory *adj.* 説明的な

explicit *adj.* (clear) 明白な, (clearly spoken) はっきりと口に出した; (obscene) 露骨な

explode *v.* (of bomb) 爆発する, (of person with anger) ものすごく怒る, かっとなる, (**explode with laughter**) 爆笑する

The bomb will explode in two minutes.
爆弾は2分後に爆発する。

He exploded when he heard that.
それを聞いて彼はかっとなった [彼の怒りは爆発した]。

They all exploded with laughter.
みんな、爆笑した [どっと笑った]。

exploit *v.* (resources) 開発する, (use: opportunity) 利用する, (take advantage of: weakness, situation) (…に) つけこむ, (workers) 搾取する, 食い物にする

exploitation *n.* 搾取

exploration *n.* 探検

space exploration 宇宙探検

explore *v.* (new territory) 探検する, (possibilities) 検討する, 探る

Wasn't Livingstone the first European to explore the African continent?

アフリカ大陸を探検した最初のヨーロッパ人は、リビングストンじゃなかったかな？

We need to explore this idea.
この案を検討する必要がある。

explorer *n.* 探検家

explosion *n.* 爆発

explosive *adj.* (of growth) 爆発的な, (of device, substance) 爆発しやすい
n. (device) 爆発物

exponent *n.* (supporter) 支持者; (number) 指数

exponential *adj.* (of growth) 急激な

export *n.* (**exports**) 輸出品
v. 輸出する

Exports are up. 輸出が伸びている。

A strong yen is not good for exports.
円高は輸出によくない。

How many cars did we export last year?
昨年は、車を何台輸出したのですか？

♦**exportation** *n.* 輸出

exporter *n.* (business) 輸出業者, (country) 輸出国

expose *v.* (to danger, sunlight) さらす, (secret, scandal) 暴く, 暴露する, (film) 感光させる

The workers have been needlessly exposed to radiation.
作業員たちは、不必要に放射能にさらされてしまった。

The politicians involved in the scandal have been exposed by the press.
そのスキャンダルにかかわっていた政治家が、マスコミに暴露された。

Careful you don't expose the film.
フィルムを感光させないよう、気をつけてください。

exposition *n.* (of products, cultural artifacts) 博覧会, (of art) 展示会; (explanation) 説明

exposure *n.*

1 TO ELEMENTS/DANGER: さらされること

2 REVEALING: (of secret, scandal etc.) 暴露, (of crime) 摘発

3 FOR PERSON: (experience) 経験, (publicity) 宣伝

4 IN PHOTOGRAPHY: (exposing of film to light) 露光, 露出, (single piece of film) 一コマ

1 Exposure to radiation is one of the dangers of space flight.
放射能にさらされることは、宇宙飛行の危険性の一つです。

2 The exposure of the scandal ruined his career.
スキャンダルを暴露されて、彼のキャリアは台なしになった。

3 It will be good exposure for us.
我々にとっていい宣伝になるでしょう。

express

1 *v.* CONVEY: (verbally) 言い表す, (verbally or in writing) ((*formal*)) 述べる, (verbally or by art) 表す, 表現する

2 *n.* TRAIN: 急行, (**semiexpress**) 準急, (**limited express**) 特急

3 *adj.* EXPLICIT: 明白な, はっきりとした

1 Could you express yourself more clearly?
思っていることを、もっとはっきり言ってくれませんか？

The president expressed his views on education.
大統領は、教育に関して意見を述べた。

I find it difficult to express my feeling

in Japanese.
日本語で自分の感情を表現するのは難しい。

2 Could you tell me from which platform the express is leaving?
(すみませんが、) 急行はどのホーム [何番線] から発車するのですか？

3 with the express purpose of…
…というはっきりとした目的で

♦ **express lane** *n.* 急行車線
express mail *n.* 速達

expression *n.* 表現, (way of saying sth) 言い方, 言い回し, (word) 言葉; (facial expression) 表情, 顔つき

You call that artistic expression!
それが、芸術的表現だっていうの！

Is that an American expression?
それはアメリカの言い方ですか？

I'm tired of hearing that expression.
その言葉はうんざりだよ。

You should've seen the expression on his face.
彼の顔つきを見せたかったよ。

♦ **expressionless** *adj.* 無表情の

expressive *adj.* (of performance) 表現力に富んだ, (of face) 表情豊かな

expressly *adv.* (purposely) わざわざ, (explicitly) はっきりと

expressway *n.* 高速道路

expulsion *n.* (from school) 放校, 除籍

exquisite *adj.* (of workmanship) 精巧な, (of meal etc.) 最高の, (of particular item) 極上の, (of performance) みごとな, (beautiful) 非常に美しい

extend *v.* (lengthen) 延ばす, 延長する, (building) 増築する

The employees aren't budging. They've extended the strike by a week.
従業員は譲らず、ストライキを1週間延長した。

They plan to extend the building.
ビルを増築する予定だ。

extend one's thanks / gratitude to …に感謝の意を表する, …にお礼を言う

I would like to extend our thanks to everyone who helped.
お世話になった皆様に、お礼を申し上げたいと思います。

extension *n.* (of time) 延長, (of building) 増築; (telephone) 内線

an extension number 内線番号

extensive *adj.* (of area) 広い, 広大な, (of coverage) 広範囲の, (of amount, degree, volume) 膨大な, 大量の

♦ **extensively** *adv.* 広く, 大々的に, 広範囲に(わたって)

extent *n.* (breadth) 広さ, (of problem) 大きさ, (degree) 程度, 範囲

The extent of the problem was greater than we had imagined.
問題の大きさは、想像していた以上だった。

No one knows yet the full extent of the damage.
被害の全貌は、まだ誰にもわかりません。

To what extent are you prepared to go to achieve this goal?
その目標を成し遂げる覚悟は、どこまでできていますか？

She worried to such an extent that she fell ill.

彼女は、病気になってしまうほど悩んだのです。

Well, to some extent, I agree.
まあ、ある程度は私も賛成です。

To a certain extent, I think Tanaka was right to resign.
ある意味では、田中さんが辞職したのは正しかったと思う。

exterior ***n.*** 外, 外部, 外側, (appearance) 外見
adj. 外の, 外部の, 外側の

The exterior of the building is badly damaged.
建物の外側がひどく傷んでいる。

He has a brash exterior, but inwardly he's kind.
あの人は外見は生意気そうだけど、心は優しいんですよ。

exterminate ***v.*** 根絶する, 絶滅させる, (murder) 皆殺しにする

external ***adj.*** 外の, 外部の, 外側の, (of appearance) うわべの, 表面的な

extinct ***adj.*** (of animal) 絶滅した

The dinosaurs became extinct long ago.
恐竜は、大昔に絶滅しました。

Dodoes are extinct.
ドードーは絶滅している。

an extinct volcano 死火山

♦ **extinction** ***n.*** 絶滅

extinguish ***v.*** (fire) 消す, (hopes) 失わせる

extra ***adj.*** (more than needed) 余分の, (additional) 追加の, (of charge) 割増しの, 別の; (spare) 予備の; (special) 特別の
adv. (especially) 特に, (extremely) きわめて, (additionally) 余分に
n. (actor) エキストラ; (newspaper) 号外

Do we have any extra eggs?
余分な卵はあるかな？

You'd better take an extra sweater.
セーターを余分に持って行ったほうがいいよ。

We need an extra $100 a month.
月に100ドルが、別に必要です。

extract ***v.*** (tooth, nail) 抜く, (a promise) 取り付ける, (information) 引き出す [→ TAKE OUT 1]
n. (excerpt) 抜粋

extradition ***n.*** 本国送還

extramarital ***adj.*** 婚姻外の

an extramarital affair 不倫

extraordinarily ***adv.*** (unusually) 並外れて, (extremely) 非常に

extraordinary ***adj.*** (beyond the ordinary) 並外れた, (amazing) 驚くべき, (superb) すばらしい, (of talent, life) 非凡な

It was an extraordinary experience.
驚くべき体験だった。

She was an extraordinary woman.
彼女は、非凡な女性でした。

extrasensory ***adj.*** 超感覚的な

extraterrestrial ***adj.*** 地球外の
n. 宇宙人, ((*formal*)) 地球外生物

extravagance ***n.*** (luxury) ぜいたく, (wasteful expenditure) 浪費, むだづかい, (glitz) 派手

extravagant ***adj.*** (wasteful) 浪費する, ぜいたくな; (of ideas) 途方もない, (wild) とっぴな

extreme *adj.* (of degree) 極端(きょくたん)な, 極度(きょくど)の, ((*informal*)) ものすごい, (of opinion: radical) 過激(かげき)な

n. 極端(きょくたん)

an extreme act [measure]
極端(きょくたん)な行為(こうい) [手段(しゅだん)]

the extreme cold of the Arctic
北極(ほっきょく)の極度(きょくど)の寒(さむ)さ

It was an extreme case of cruelty to animals.
動物虐待(どうぶつぎゃくたい)の極端(きょくたん)なケースだった。

Even in so-called developed countries, many people live in extreme poverty.
いわゆる先進国(せんしんこく)と呼(よ)ばれるような国(くに)でも、たくさんの人(ひと)が極貧生活(ごくひんせいかつ)をしています。

His views are considered extreme.
あの人(ひと)の考(かんが)え方(かた)は過激(かげき)と見(み)られている。

There is no need to go to that extreme.
そんなに極端(きょくたん)な行動(こうどう)に走(はし)る必要(ひつよう)はないよ。

in the extreme 極端(きょくたん)に

the opposite extreme 全(まった)く正反対(せいはんたい)

extremely *adv.* 非常(ひじょう)に, 極端(きょくたん)に, ((*informal*)) ものすごく

extremist *n.* 過激論者(かげきろんじゃ), 極端論者(きょくたんろんじゃ), (group) 過激派(かげきは)

extrovert *n.* 外向的(がいこうてき)な人(ひと)

extroverted *adj.* 外向性(がいこうせい)の

eye *n.* 目(め) [→ picture of FACE], (eyesight) 視力(しりょく), (gaze) 視線(しせん), 目(め)つき, ((*polite*)) まなざし

open [close] one's eyes
目(め)をあける [閉(と)じる]

He has blue eyes but dark hair.
あの人(ひと)は目(め)は青(あお)いのに、髪(かみ)の毛(け)は黒(くろ)い。

You've got good eyes. You don't need glasses.
君(きみ)は目(め) [視力(しりょく)] がいい。めがねは要(い)らないよ。

You can't see these microscopic life forms with the naked eye.
これらの微生物(びせいぶつ)は、肉眼(にくがん)では見(み)えません。

I could feel his eye on me.
あの人(ひと)の視線(しせん)を感(かん)じた。

She gave me the evil eye.
あの人(ひと)は私(わたし)に怖(こわ)い目(め)つきをした。

an eye for an eye 目(め)には目(め)を

An eye for an eye, a tooth for a tooth.
目(め)には目(め)を、歯(は)には歯(は)を。

be in the public eye 世間(せけん)で注目(ちゅうもく)されている

Now that you're on TV, you're very much in the public eye.
テレビに出(で)るようになったから、みんなの注目(ちゅうもく)の的(まと)だよ。

catch one's eye (…の) 目(め)にとまる, 目(め)を引(ひ)く

This dress just caught my eye, so I bought it.
このドレスが目(め)にとまったから買(か)ったの。

have a good eye for 見(み)る目(め)がある, …に目(め)が利(き)く

He has a good eye for antiques.
あの人(ひと)は骨董品(こっとうひん)に目(め)が利(き)く。

keep an eye on じっと見守(みまも)る, …から目(め)を離(はな)さないでいる

Keep an eye on my bag, will you.
かばんから目(め)を離(はな)さないでね。

He's very naughty, so you'd better keep an eye on him.
あの子(こ)はとってもいたずらだから、目(め)を離(はな)さないほうがいいよ。

open one's eyes to 気づかせる, 悟らせる

Seeing that movie opened my eyes to the need for gun control in America.
その映画を見て、アメリカの銃規制の必要性に気づかされた。

take one's eyes off …から目を離す, …から視線をそらす

He couldn't take his eyes off her.
彼は、彼女から目を離せなかった/彼の目は彼女に釘付けになった。

eyeball *n.* 眼球, 目玉

eyebrow *n.* 眉毛 [→ picture of FACE]

raise eyebrows (surprise) 人々を驚かす

eye-catching *adj.* 目立つ, 人目を引く

eyelash *n.* まつげ [→ picture of FACE]

eye level *n.* 目の高さ

adj. (**eye-level**) 目の高さの

eyelid *n.* まぶた [→ picture of FACE]

eyeliner *n.* アイライナー

eye shadow *n.* アイシャドー

eyesight *n.* 視力

eyesore *n.* 目ざわり

eyetooth *n.* 犬歯, 糸切り歯

eyewash *n.* (eye cleanser) 目薬

eyewitness *n.* 目撃者, 証人

an eyewitness account
目撃者の話 [証言]

F, f

F, f *n.* (letter) F, f, (grade) F, 不可

fable *n.* (moral story) 寓話 [→ LEGEND, MYTH]

fabric *n.* (material) 生地 [→ STRUCTURE]

fabricate *v.* (story, excuse) でっち上げる, 作り上げる

fabulous *adj.* (wonderful) すばらしい

facade *n.* (of building) 正面; (pretense) 見せかけ

face

1 *n.* PART OF THE BODY: 顔, (expression) 表情

2 *n.* SURFACE: (of cliff) 表面, (of bill, coin) 表, (of building) 正面, (of clock) 文字盤

3 *v.* LOOK TOWARD: (…の方に) 向く, 顔を向ける, (of building: be directed toward) (…に) 面する

4 *v.* CONFRONT: (also **face up to**: problem, facts) (…に) 直面する, 立ち向かう

5 *n.* HONOR: メンツ, 面目

1 I washed my face with cold water.
冷たい水で顔を洗った。

He stared into her face.
彼は、彼女の顔をまじまじと見た。

Stop making silly faces.
おどけた顔をするんじゃありません。

2 a cliff face がけの表面

the north face of Everest
エベレストの北側の斜面 [北壁]

the face of the clock 時計の文字盤

3 face the sun 太陽の方に向く

Face me. 私の方に向いてください。

The window faces north [the ocean].
窓は北向きです [海に面しています]。

4 We have to face up to these problems.
我々は、こうした問題に立ち向かわなくてはならない。

5 lose [save] face 面目を失う [保つ]

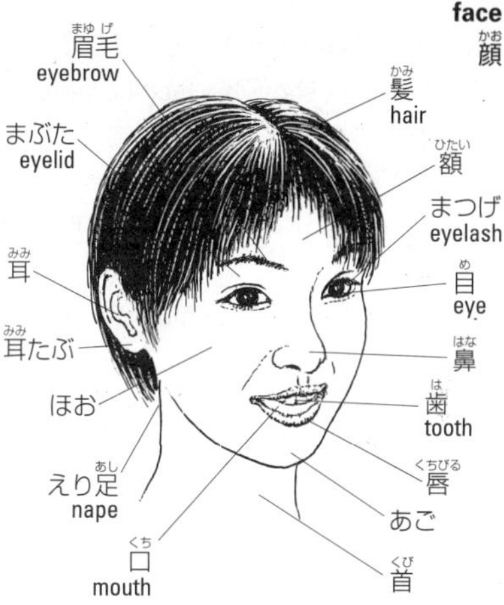

accept / take at face value (words) 額面どおり受け取る, 真に受ける

You shouldn't take what he says at face value.
彼が言うことを真に受けちゃだめだよ。

face to face 向き合って, 面と向かって

At last, they met face to face.
ようやく、二人は顔を合わせた。

Did you actually speak face to face with her?
実際に面と向かって、彼女に話したの?

in the face of …に直面して, (in spite of) …をものともせず

He was awarded a medal of honor for bravery in the face of danger.
彼は危険をものともしない勇敢な行為をたたえられて、勲章をもらった。

F

on the face of it 一見したところ, 表面上は

On the face of it, it seemed a simple enough problem to solve.
一見したところ、簡単に片付けられそうな問題だったが。

show one's face 顔を出す, 姿を見せる

He couldn't show his face because of embarrassment.
彼はバツが悪くて顔を出せなかった。

to one's face (…の)前で, (…に)面と向かって

If you really don't love him, you should tell him to his face.
彼のことを本気で愛していないのなら、面と向かって言うべきよ。

face-lift *n.* (operation) 顔の美容整形; (revamping of a building) 改装

facial *adj.* 顔の

n. (treatment) 顔のマッサージ, 美顔術

facilitate *v.* 楽にする, 容易にする

facility *n.* (building) 設備, 施設

facing *n.* (fabric stitched inside cuffs) へり取り; (of stone) 表面仕上げ

facsimile *n.* ファクシミリ, ファックス

send a facsimile
ファックスを送る [((*formal*)) 送信する]

fact *n.* (reality) 事実, 本当のこと, (circumstance, situation: **the fact that…**) …こと

a fact of life 紛れもない事実

You lied. That's a fact.
君はうそをついた。それは事実だ。

The facts speak for themselves.
事実を見れば明らかだ。

The fact is, he should not have been there.
実のところ、彼がそこにいたのは、まずかった。

No one knows what the facts of the matter are.
事の真相は誰にもわからない。

The fact that you speak Japanese is a big plus.
あなたが日本語を話せることは、大きな利点です。

as a matter of fact 実は, 実を言うと

As a matter of fact, I haven't had breakfast yet.
実を言うと、朝食をまだ済ませていません。

in fact 実際は

It sounds simple, but in fact it's very difficult.
簡単なように聞こえますが、実際は非常に難しいんです。

faction *n.* (political) 派閥, 党派

factor *n.* (element) 要因, 要素; (number) 因数

factory *n.* 工場 [→ WORKSHOP]

factual *adj.* 事実の, (based on fact) 事実に基づく

a factual account 事実に基づく説明

a factual error 事実誤認

faculty *n.* (group of related departments at a university) 学部, (teaching staff) 教授陣; (ability) 才能

fad *n.* ブーム, 一時的流行

fade *v.* (of color) あせる, 薄れる, (from washing) 落ちる, (from sight/earshot) 消えていく, (of memory, feeling) 薄れる, (weaken) 弱くなる, 弱まる, 衰える

The color has faded from this shirt.
このシャツは、色があせてしまった。

This suntan should fade by autumn.
この日焼けも、秋には消えるだろう。

The boat got smaller and then faded from view.
船はだんだん小さくなって、見えなくなった。

He's old, and those memories have faded now.
彼は年老いて、その時の記憶は薄れてきている。

The team's strength faded in the last thirty minutes.
終盤の３０分、チームの勢いが衰えた。

Fahrenheit *adj.* カ氏の, F

fail *v.*

1 BE UNSUCCESSFUL: 失敗する, (in one's duty) (義務を) 怠る, (**fail to do**) (=not do) ...しない, (=miss one's chance to do) ...しそびれる, ...しそこなう

2 FLUNK: (exam, course) (...に) 落ちる, (student) 落とす, 落第させる

3 DISAPPOINT: がっかりさせる, 失望させる

4 STOP FUNCTIONING: (of machine: break down) 故障する, (of brakes, treatment, medicine) きかなくなる

5 OF HEALTH/POWER: 衰える, 弱くなる

6 OF BUSINESS: つぶれる, 倒産する

7 OF CROPS: 不作になる

1 He failed in business.
あの人は事業に失敗した。

She failed to report the matter.
彼女はその件の報告を怠った。

I failed to see the mistake.
間違いを見落としてしまいました。

2 He failed the exam.
彼は試験に落ちた。

The examiners failed him.
試験官たちは彼を落とした [落第させた]。

3 Do not fail me.
失望させないで。

I've failed my family and friends.
私は家族と友人をがっかりさせた。

4 The machine failed.
機械が故障した。

The brakes failed, I hear.
ブレーキが、利かなくなったそうだ。

5 His eyesight is failing.
彼は視力が衰えている。

The boss's health failed.
上司が体調を崩しました。

6 According to the news, a number of banks have failed.
ニュースによると、いくつかの銀行が倒産したそうです。

7 The crops failed because of a drought.
干ばつのため不作でした。

if all/everything else fails 万策尽きたら

If all else fails, we'll just have to sell the house.
万策尽きたら、家を売るまでだ。

without fail 必ず

You're to report at 7 A.M. without fail.
必ず朝７時に出勤すること。

The pigeons come here every morning without fail.
毎朝必ず、ハトがここへやって来る。

failing *n.* (shortcoming) 弱点, 欠点

failure *n.* 失敗, (neglect) 怠慢, (of machine: breaking down) 故障; (loser) 落伍者, (dropout) 落ちこぼれ

Despite our efforts, the project ended in failure.
みんなの努力にもかかわらず、プロジェクトは失敗に終わった。

Failure to attend the meeting will not go unnoticed.
会議の出席を怠れば、気づかれずにはすまない。

engine failure エンジン故障

faint ***adj.*** (of light, color, sound, smell) かすかな, (of possibility) わずかな; (weak and dizzy) 気が遠くなる, めまいがする ***v.*** (lose consciousness) 失神する, 気絶する, 気を失う

A faint sound came from the room.
その部屋から、かすかな物音がした。

There was a faint smell of gas.
かすかにガスのにおいがした。

I'm feeling faint. I'd better sit down.
めまいがする。腰を下ろしたほうがよさそうだ。

Is it true the bride fainted at the wedding?
結婚式で花嫁が気絶したっていうのは本当？

fair[1] ***adj.***

1 JUST: 公正な, 正しい, 公平な, フェアな, 正々堂々とした

2 OF NUMBER/AMOUNT: かなりの, 相当の

3 OF WEATHER: 晴れた

4 OF COLOR: (of hair) ブロンドの, 金髪の, (of complexion) 色白の, (of skin) 白い

1 I think it was a fair decision.
公正な決定だったと思う。

The court's ruling was fair.
裁判所の評決は公正だった。

2 There were a fair number of people at the exhibition.
展示会は、かなりの人出だった。

3 The fair weather continued till the end of the week.
好天 [いい天気] が週末まで続いた。

4 He had fair hair and blue eyes.
その人は金髪で青い目をしていた。

fair enough (so be it) まあいいでしょう, それでいい, (understood) わかりました

"I'll do the shopping if you pick up the children, OK?"
"Fair enough."
「子供たちを迎えに行ってくれたら、買い物は私がしておくけど、どう？」
「それでいいよ」

fair[2] ***n.*** (exhibition, festival) 品評会, フェア, (exposition) 見本市, 展示会, (carnival) 移動遊園地, (festival) (お)祭り, 縁日

He said he bought the pig at a fair.
その豚は、品評会で買ったと言っていた。

fairly ***adv.*** (justly) 公正に, 公平に; (rather) かなり, 相当, なかなか

fairness ***n.*** (justness) 公正, (honesty) 正直; (whiteness) 白さ

fair play ***n.*** フェアプレー

fairway ***n.*** (in golf) フェアウェー

fairy ***n.*** 妖精

fairyland ***n.*** おとぎの国, 妖精の国

fairy tale ***n.*** 童話, おとぎ話, メルヘン

faith ***n.*** (in person) 信頼, 信用, (belief) 信念, 確信, (religious belief) 信仰, (the ...faith) -教

I have little faith in his judgment.
彼の判断力は、あまり信頼していない。

She seems to have lost faith in people.

彼女は人を信じられなくなったようだ。

It's her faith in God that keeps her going.
彼女を突き動かしているのは、(神への)信仰だ。

a leap of faith 盲信

in bad faith 悪意で, 裏切って

in good faith 誠意をもって, 誠実に

faithful *adj.* (loyal) 忠実な, (reliable) 誠実な; (accurate) 正確な

be faithful to one's wife/husband
浮気をしない (lit., "not cheat")

a faithful translation 正確な翻訳

faithfully *adv.* (loyally) 忠実に, (in good faith) 誠実に; (accurately) 正確に

fake *adj.* 偽の, まやかしの

n. (article) 偽物, (person) 偽者

v. (feign) (…の) ふりをする, (…のように) 見せかける, (forge) 偽造する, ねつ造する [→ PRETEND]

He faked illness to get out of school.
彼は学校から抜け出すために病気のふりをした [仮病をつかった]。

falcon *n.* タカ, ハヤブサ

fall

1 *v.* FALL DOWN: (from high place) 落ちる, ((*formal*)) 落下する, (from standing position) 倒れる, (lose one's balance and fall) 転ぶ

2 *v.* COME/GO DOWN: (of rain, snow) 降る, (of curtains) 下りる, (of hair) 垂れる, かかる, (of sun, moon) 沈む

3 *v.* DECREASE: 減る, 少なくなる, (of temperature, price) 下がる, (of sales, grades) 落ちる, (of standards) 低下する

4 *v.* BE DEFEATED: (of city) 陥落する, (of government) 倒れる, (of empire) 滅びる

5 *v.* TAKE PLACE: (**fall on a…**) (…に) 当たる, なる

6 *n.* ACT OF FALLING: 落下, 落ちること

7 *n.* SEASON: 秋

8 *n.* DECREASE: 減少, (of temperature) 低下, (of prices) 下落

9 *n.* COLLAPSE: (of building) 倒壊, 崩壊, (of government) 崩壊, (of empire) 滅亡

1 The pen fell off the table.
ペンがテーブルから落ちた。

The nest fell from the tree.
木から巣が落ちた。

The roof fell in.
屋根が落ちた [陥没した]。

The boy fell on some glass.
その子はガラスの上に倒れた。

She fell while going down some steps.
彼女は階段を下りていて転んだ。

2 The rain began to fall.
雨が降り出した。

As the curtain fell, the audience applauded.
幕が下りると、観客は拍手かっさいした。

Her hair fell to her shoulders.
彼女の髪は肩にかかっていた。

The sun fell below the horizon.
太陽が地平線に沈んだ。

3 Enrollment in universities is falling.
大学の在籍者数は減っている。

The temperature suddenly fell to almost freezing.
温度が急に氷点下近くまで下がった。

Land prices fell considerably.

F

土地の価格は、かなり下がった。

Are educational standards falling?
教育水準が低下しているのですか？

4 The city will not fall easily.
その街は簡単には陥落しないだろう。

5 This year Christmas falls on a Tuesday.
今年のクリスマスは火曜日に当たる。

6 The child was hurt in a fall from the roof.
その子は屋根から落ちてけがをした。

7 My favorite season is fall.
一番好きな季節は秋です。

8 a fall in the number of unemployed
失業者数の減少

9 the rise and fall of governments
政権の興亡

fall asleep 眠り込む, 眠りにつく

Eventually, we fell asleep.
ようやく、私たちは眠りについた。

fall ill 病気になる

fall in love 恋に落ちる

They fell in love the first time they saw each other.
(互いに)一目見て、二人は恋に落ちた。

fall apart *v.* (break up into pieces) ばらばらになる, (collapse) 崩れる, (of relationship) 破綻する, (end in failure) 失敗に終わる

This house is falling apart!
この家はぼろぼろだ！

Their marriage fell apart after their child died.
お子さんが亡くなってから、結婚生活が破綻したんです。

The whole plan was doomed from the beginning to fall apart.
計画自体が最初から、失敗に終わる運命だったんだ。

fall behind *v.* 遅れる

Because of his frequent absences, he fell behind in his schoolwork.
彼は欠席が多かったので、勉強が遅れた。

fall for *v.* (person) …にほれこむ

fall into *v.* (a certain category) …に属する, …に分類される

These butterflies fall into three categories.
これらのチョウは、3種類に分類される。

fall off *v.* (decrease) 減る, 減少する

fall out *v.* (of hair, teeth) 抜ける

fall through *v.* (not materialize) 実現しない, (come to nothing) だめになる

The plan fell through because of a lack of funds.
計画は、資金不足で実現しなかった。

---

fallen *adj.* (lying on the ground) 落ちた, (knocked over) 倒れた; (**the fallen**) 戦死者

a fallen leaf 落ち葉

falling-out *n.* (argument) けんか

have a falling-out with A over B
BのことでAとけんかする

fallout *n.* (nuclear fallout) 死の灰

false *adj.* (incorrect) 間違った, 正しくない, (not true) うその, (of charge) えん罪の; (artificial) 人造の, 偽の, 義-

It was false information.
誤報だった。

The story turned out to be false.
その話はうそだとわかった。

The box had a false bottom.
箱は上げ底になっていた。

false teeth 入れ歯

be falsely charged えん罪を被る

♦**false alarm** *n.* 間違い警報; (unnecessary trouble/panic) 取り越し苦労

false start *n.* (in race) フライング, (bad start) 出だしの失敗

falsehood *n.* (lie) うそ, ((*written*)) 偽り

falsetto *n.* ファルセット, 裏声

fame *n.* 有名, 名声

familiar *adj.* (well-known) よく知られている, (お)なじみの, (of voice) 聞き慣れた, (common) ありふれた; (friendly) 親しい, (**too familiar**) なれなれしい

He's a familiar face/visitor around here.
このあたりでは彼は顔なじみですよ。

It's a familiar sight in the parks around here.
このあたりの公園では、よく見かける光景です。

They're on familiar terms now.
今では、あの二人は親しい間柄です。

I think he's too familiar with her.
あの男は彼女に、なれなれしいと思うよ。

be familiar with (know well) よく知っている, …に詳しい

Are you familiar with the subject?
そのことに詳しいですか?

familiarity *n.* (with person) 親しさ, (with subject/field) 広い知識, 精通

family *n.* (one's own) 家族, 一家, 家庭, (including relatives) 一族; (taxonomic category) 科

His family is well known around here.
彼の家族は、この辺ではよく知られています。

Is your whole family going to emigrate?
ご一家で移住されるんですか?

Send my regards to your family.
ご家族によろしくお伝えください。

There have been three scientists in her family.
彼女の一家には3人の科学者がいます。

Are there any artistic people in your family?
ご家族に、芸術家肌の方はいらっしゃいますか?

family life 家庭生活

the cat family ネコ科

run in the family 遺伝する

start a family 子供をつくる

family name *n.* 名字, ((*formal*)) 姓

family register *n.* (official document in which family data is recorded) 戸籍

family tree *n.* 家系図

famine *n.* ききん

famous *adj.* 有名な

Paris is famous for its splendid buildings.
パリはみごとな建築物で有名だ。

a famous actor 有名な俳優

♦**famously** *adv.* (as everybody knows) よく知られているように, (well) うまく

fan[1] *n.* (handheld folding fan) 扇子, 扇, (handheld nonfolding fan) うちわ, (electric fan) 扇風機, (ventilation fan) 換気扇 [→ picture of KITCHEN]

v. (one's face) あおぐ, (a fire, dispute) あおる

fan[2] *n.* (supporter, enthusiast) ファン

fanatic *n.* 狂信者, -狂

fancier *n.* (of art, fishing) 愛好家, (of animals) 愛好家, (of plants) 栽培家

fancy

1 *adj.* EXPENSIVE / FASHIONABLE: 高級な, (stylish) しゃれた, (flashy) 派手な

2 *adj.* ELABORATE: 凝った

3 *v.* LIKE: (…が) 気に入る, 好きだ, (…を) 好む

4 *v.* IMAGINE: 想像する

5 *n.* IMAGINATION: 空想

1 Let's stay at a really fancy hotel.
超高級ホテルに泊まりましょうよ。

That's a fancy necktie you're wearing.
しゃれたネクタイですね。

a fancy hat 派手な帽子

2 a fancy design 凝ったデザイン

a fancy cake デコレーションケーキ

3 I don't fancy him as a teacher.
教師としての彼は、好きではありません。

A lot of girls fancy him.
彼は女の子にもてる。

4 Fancy her doing such a stupid thing.
彼女が、そんなばかなことをするとはね。

Well, fancy that! I never thought they would get engaged.
全く驚いたね！ あの二人が婚約するなんて、思ってもみなかった。

5 flights of fancy 空想の飛躍

take one's fancy (…の) 気に入る

It just took my fancy, so I bought it.
気に入ってしまって、買いました。

fandango *n.* (dance) ファンダンゴ

fanfare *n.* (of trumpets etc.) ファンファーレ; (commotion) 大騒ぎ

fang *n.* きば, (venomous) 毒牙

fanny pack *n.* ウエストポーチ

fantasize *v.* 空想する, (about sex) 想像する

fantastic *adj.* (marvelous) すばらしい, すてきな, (wild, strange) 奇妙な, (of fantasy) 幻想的な, (unrealistic) 現実離れした, とっぴな

What a fantastic party (it was)!
すばらしいパーティーだった！

That's a fantastic dress.
すてきなドレスですね。

It was a fantastic tale of dwarves and fairies.
小人や妖精の出て来る幻想的な物語だった。

It was a fantastic idea and totally impractical.
それは現実離れしたアイデアで、全く実現できそうになかった。

fantasy *n.* ファンタジー, (fairy land) メルヘンの世界, (idle dreaming) 空想

far *adv.*

1 DISTANT: 遠い, 遠くに, 離れて, はるか…

2 MUCH: ずっと, はるかに, ずいぶん, ((*informal*)) ものすごく

3 SPEAKING ABOUT PROGRESS: (**this / that far**) この/そのくらい; (**get far**) 進む

4 SPEAKING ABOUT TIME: (**far away in the future**) ずっと先, (**far gone**: of days past) はるか昔, (**far past**: time) とっくに過ぎた

1 Is it far?
遠いの？

How far is it from here?
ここからどのくらいありますか？

It isn't far. You could walk it.
遠くありません。歩いても行けます。

It was farther than we had thought.
思っていたより遠かった。

Far in the distance you could see a ship's sail.
はるかかなたに、船の帆が見えた。

Further down the river, there are lots of fish.
もっと川下には、魚がたくさんいます。

Kaoru sat the furthest away from the blackboard.
薫は黒板から一番遠い席に座った。

2 She is far better than me at tennis.
彼女は私より、テニスがはるかにうまい。

That's going a bit too far.
それはちょっと言い過ぎだよ。

3 I've only read this far.
これくらいしか読んでない。

4 It's far past your bedtime.
寝る時間をとっくに過ぎている。

as far as ... is/are concerned ...に関する限りでは, (as for one's own thoughts/opinion) ...(の考え)としては

As far as we're concerned, the whole matter should be forgotten.
我々としては、この件は一切水に流そう。

by far はるかに, 断然

It's by far the best.
断然いいね。

far and wide 広く, 至る所を

They've traveled far and wide.
彼らは広く各地を旅した。

far away はるかかなたに, ずっと遠くに

Far away in the distance, I could see a range of mountains.
はるかかなたに連山が見えた。

far from ...には程遠い, ...どころか

The problem is far from solved.
問題は解決には程遠い。

What he said was far from the truth.
彼が言ったことは真実からは程遠かった。

The case is far from over. In fact, the investigation has only just begun.
事件は落着するどころか、実際は調査が始まったばかりだ。

far off (of answer) 大きく外れて

It wasn't the right answer. But he wasn't far off.
彼の答えは正解ではないが、そう外れてもいなかった。

far out はるかかなたに

The islands lie far out in the Pacific.
その島々は、はるか太平洋のかなたにある。

go so far as to say ...とまで言う

He went so far as to say that I should leave town.
私が町を出るべきだとまで、彼は言った。

so far これまでは, 今(まで)のところ

So far, everything has gone smoothly.
これまでは、すべて順調にいってます。

So far so good. But we've only been lucky up to now.
今までのところ順調です。でも、ここまでは運がよかっただけです。

faraway *adj*. 遠い, 遠くの

fare *n*. 運賃, 料金, ((*informal*)) -代 [→ COST, FEE]

bus fare バス料金 [バス代]
train fare 電車の運賃 [電車代]
airfare 航空運賃 [飛行機代]

How much is the taxi fare?
タクシー代はいくらですか？

Far East *n.* 極東

farewell *interj.* さよ(う)なら [→ GOODBYE]

n. (parting) 別れ

a farewell party 送別会

far-fetched *adj.* 信じがたい, ありそうもない, (of excuse) こじつけの

farm *n.* 農場, 農園, (dairy farm) 酪農場

v. (be a farmer) 農業をやる, (cultivate: field) 耕作する

He says he'd like to work on a farm.
彼は農場で働きたいと言っている。

Their family has farmed for decades.
あの家は、何十年も農業をやっている。

farmer *n.* 農家, 農家の人, 農民

farmhouse *n.* 農家

farming *n.* 農業

farmland *n.* (with crops) 農地, 畑, (with animals) 牧場

farmyard *n.* 農家の庭

far-off → DISTANT

farsighted *adj.* (of vision) 遠視の; (having foresight) 先見の明のある

fart *n.* おなら, ((*masculine*)) へ

v. おならをする, ((*masculine*)) へをこく

farther *adv.* もっと先に, さらに遠くに [→ FAR 1, FURTHER 3]

farthest *adv.* 一番遠い, 最も遠くに [→ FAR 1]

fascinate *v.* (…の)興味をそそる, (charm) 魅惑する, 魅了する

I was fascinated by the cat's behavior.
その猫の行動に興味をそそられた。

fascinating *adj.* (interesting) とても面白い, 興味深い

fascination *n.* (captivation) 魅惑, (attraction) 魅力

fascism *n.* ファシズム

fascist *n.* ファシスト

adj. ファシストの, 極右の

fashion *n.* (public taste) はやり, 流行, (apparel) ファッション [→ POPULAR, WAY 5]

come into [go out of] fashion
はやり出す [すたれる]

be in [out] of fashion
はやって [すたれて] いる

follow [set] a fashion
流行を追いかける [つくり出す]

fashionable *adj.* (popular) はやりの, (stylish) しゃれた, おしゃれな

fast[1] *adj.* (quick) 速い, 素早い, (of clock: ahead of time) 進んでいる

adv. (quickly) 速く, 素早く [→ TIGHT]

What is the fastest animal?
一番足の速い動物は何ですか？

Now that's a fast car.
ああいうのを速い車と言うんだよ。

I'll take the fast train.
私は急行で行きます。

He's a fast one with women.
あいつは女に手が早い。

This clock is fast.
この時計は進んでいる。

I ran as fast as I could.
全速力で走った。

Please don't drive so fast.
そんなにスピードを出さないでください。

be fast asleep ぐっすり眠っている

hold fast to しっかり(と)つかむ

pull a fast one on だます

She tried to pull a fast one on me.
あの人は私をだまそうとした。

fast[2] *v.* (eat no food) 断食する

fasten *v.* (belt) 締める, (fasten A to B) (AをBに) 取り付ける, 留める, 固定する

Fasten your seat belts, please.
シートベルトをお締めください。

fastener *n.* 留め具, (zipper) ファスナー, チャック

fast food *n.* ファーストフード

fast-forward *n.* (button/function) 早送り
v. 早送りする

fastidious *adj.* (about details) 細かい, うるさい, (about cleanliness) 潔癖な

fat *adj.* (of person) 太った, 肥えた, (of thing: thick) 厚い; (of profit, salary) たっぷりの, 多い
n. (oil used in cooking) 油, (in meat, fish) 脂, (on body) 脂肪

That cat is really fat.
あの猫は本当に太っているね。

You've gotten fat.
太ったね。

You're fatter than you were last time I saw you.
この前会った時より、太ったね。

This was cooked in fat.
これは油で調理されていた。

There's a lot of fat on that beef.
その牛肉はたっぷり脂がのっている。

Look at the fat around your waist!
そのウエストの脂肪を見ろよ！

fatal *adj.* 致命的な, 命取りの, (grave, critical) 重大な

a fatal illness
命取りの [命にかかわる] 病気

a fatal injury 致命傷

a fatal error 致命的な [重大な] 誤り

fate *n.* 運命, (speaking about an encounter) 縁

It was fate that brought us together.
私たちを引き合わせてくれたのは運命です/私たちが出会ったのは縁があったからです。

fated *adj.* 運命の

father *n.* (one's own) 父, 父親, ((*masculine/informal*)) 親父, (addressing one's own) お父さん, (sb else's) お父さん, ((*polite*)) お父様; (religious title) 神父(さん)

Is Father coming with us?
お父さんも、いっしょに行くって？

How old is your father?
お父様はおいくつですか？

Her father was born in Scotland.
彼女の父親はスコットランド生まれだ。

Hugo Grotius is considered the father of international law.
フーゴ・グロティウスは国際法の父とされている。

♦**fatherland** *n.* 祖国

fatherly *adj.* 父親のような, 父親らしい

Father's Day *n.* 父の日

father-in-law *n.* しゅうと, 義理の父, 義父

fathom *n.* (measure of depth) 尋, ファゾム
v. (comprehend) わかる, 理解する, 見抜く

fatigue *n.* 疲れ, 疲労

fattening *adj.* (of food) 太る, 太らせる

fatty *adj.* (of food) 油っこい

n. (person) でぶ

faucet *n.* 蛇口 [→ TAP 2, picture of BATHROOM, KITCHEN]

fault

1 *n.* RESPONSIBILITY: (in general) 責任, (implying blame: sb's fault) (…の) せい

2 *n.* FLAW: 欠点, 欠陥

3 *v.* BLAME: 責める, 非難する

4 *n.* IN EARTH'S CRUST: 断層

5 *n.* IN TENNIS: フォールト

1 Whose fault is it?
誰の責任ですか？

It's not my fault, so don't blame me.
私のせいじゃないんだから、責めないでよ。

2 Despite his faults, he's a likeable guy.
欠点はあるけど、いい奴だよ。

The printer has developed a fault.
プリンターに欠陥が生じた。

3 You can't fault her for trying.
彼女がやろうとしていることを責められないよ。

4 the San Andreas Fault
サンアンドレアス断層

5 a double fault ダブルフォールト

find fault with …のあら探しをする, …にけちをつける

Try not to find fault with people.
人の欠点には目をつぶるようにしよう/人のあら探しはしないことだ。

faultless *adj.* 欠点のない, (perfect) 完璧な

fauna *n.* 動物相

favor *n.* (request) お願い, 頼み, (kindness) 好意, 親切, (support) 支持

v. (treat with partiality) (えこ)ひいきする, かわいがる, 優遇する

I have a small favor to ask.
ちょっとお願いがあるんですが。

He asked his boss to do him a favor and give him a few days off.
彼は上司に、2、3日、休みをもらえないかと頼んだ。

Could you do me a favor and pass me that ruler?
すみませんが、その定規を取ってくれますか？

ask a favor of …にお願いをする, …に頼み事をする

be in favor of …に賛成する

Are you in favor of capital punishment?
死刑に賛成ですか？

Are you in favor of going or staying?
行くか行かないか、どっちがいい？

curry favor with …に取り入る, …の機嫌を取る

fall out of favor with …の支持を失う, …に人気がなくなる

The prime minister seems to have fallen out of favor with the public.
首相は国民の支持を失ったようだ。

owe a favor to …に借りがある, …に恩がある

return a/the favor お返しをする

favorable *adj.* (amicable) 好意的な, (desirable) 好ましい

a favorable opinion
好意的な意見

favorably *adv.* 好意的に

look favorably on 好意的に見る

favorite *n.* (most preferred) お気に入り, 好み(のもの); (in contest: competitor/team likely to win) 優勝候補, (in horse race) 本命

adj. 一番好きな

She is obviously the teacher's favorite.
どう見ても彼女は、先生のお気に入りだ。

Which horse is the favorite?
どの馬が本命なの？

What's your favorite color?
一番好きな色は何ですか？

She's one of my favorite singers.
彼女は、一番好きな歌手の一人なんだ。

fawn[1] *n.* (young deer) 子ジカ

fawn[2] *v.* (**fawn over/on**: flatter, seek attention from) …にこびへつらう

fax → FACSIMILE

FBI *n.* ＦＢＩ, 連邦捜査局

FCC *n.* 連邦通信委員会

fear *n.* (terror) 恐れ, 恐怖, (uneasiness) 不安, (worry) 心配, (thing one is afraid of) 心配していること, 恐れていること

v. (be afraid of) 怖がる, 恐れる, (be worried that…) …と心配する [→ WORRY]

He has an irrational fear of spiders.
彼は、異常なほどクモを怖がる。

Do you have a fear of dying?
死ぬことに恐怖を覚えますか/死ぬのは怖いですか？

My worst fears were realized.
最も恐れて [心配して] いたことが、現実になってしまった。

She fears rejection.
彼女は拒絶されるのを恐れている。

for fear that… …(すること)を恐れて, …しないよう(に)

We didn't say anything for fear that we might make matters worse.
まずいことにならないよう、何も言いませんでした。

in fear 恐れて, おびえて, びくびくして

She shouted in fear, "Come back!"
彼女は「戻って！」とおびえて叫んだ。

No one should have to live in fear.
びくびくしながら暮らすもんじゃないよ。

fearful *adj.* (worried) 心配する, 恐れる, (terrible) 恐ろしい

fearless *adj.* (brave) 勇敢な

feasible *adj.* 実現可能な

feast *n.* (splendid meal) ごちそう, 祝宴, (religious festival) 祝祭

v. (eat a lot) いっぱい食べる, ごちそうになる

feat *n.* 手柄, 偉業

feather *n.* 羽, 羽毛

feature *n.* (characteristic part) 特徴, 特色, (**features**: of face) 顔立ち, 容貌; (article in newspaper) 特集記事

v. (of newspaper/magazine: treat as a news/story) 大きく取り上げる, 特集する, (of film: have as an actor/actress) 主演させる, 出演させる, (of product) 目玉にしている

She has unusual features.
彼女は、とても個性的な顔立ちをしている。

Does the car have any safety features?
その車には、安全装置がありますか？

There's a feature on drug smuggling.
麻薬の密輸に関する特集記事が載っている。

♦**feature in** *v.* (star in) …に主演する, …に出演する

February *n.* 2月, 二月

feces *n.* 大便, (of animal) ふん

federal *adj.* 連邦の

the federal government 連邦政府

a federal court 連邦裁判所

a federal agency
連邦政府の(関係)機関

federation *n.* 連邦, 連盟

fed up *adj.* うんざりする, 飽き飽きする, (**get fed up**) いやになる

fee *n.* (charge, payment) 料金, 代金, (service/processing fee) 手数料

a monthly fee 月謝

an entrance/admission fee 入場料

Is there a fee to join?
入会費はありますか？

Fortunately, they didn't charge a fee.
ありがたいことに、料金は取られなかった。

a registration fee 登録料

KANJI BRIDGE

料	ON: りょう KUN: —	FEE, CHARGE, FARE
代	ON: だい, たい KUN: か(わる/える), よ, しろ	

dentist's fees	歯医者代
drink expenses	酒代, 飲み代
entrance/admission fee	入場料
exam fee	受験料
fee for entering a public bath	(お)ふろ代, 入浴料
handling fee/charge	(取扱)手数料
insurance premium	保険料
medicine expenses	(お)薬代
taxi fare	タクシー代
tuition (fee)	授業料

feeble *adj.* (weak) 弱い, 弱々しい, (of person: ineffectual) 低能の, (of excuse: unconvincing) 説得力に乏しい

a feeble voice か細い声

a feeble excuse
説得力に乏しい弁解

feed *v.* (give food to) (…に) 食べ物を与える, (animal) (…に) えさをやる, (information to person/press) 流す, (paper into printer/shredder) 入れる

n. (meal) えさ

They were so poor they could hardly feed themselves.
彼らはあまりにも貧乏で、食べる物にも困っていた。

His income alone isn't enough to feed the family.
彼の収入だけでは一家を養えない。

Scraps of food were fed to the dog.
残飯は犬にやった。

Will someone please feed the cat?
誰か猫にえさをやってくれない？

Now feed some paper into the printer.
じゃあ、プリンターに用紙を入れてください。

cattle feed 牛のえさ

feedback *n.* フィードバック, (response) 反応, (ご)意見; (noise) ハウリング

feel

1 *v.* EMOTION/SENSATION: 感じる

2 *v.* THINK: 思う, (…のような) 気がする

3 *v.* EXPLORE BY TOUCHING: 触れる, 触ってみる, (**feel around for**) 手探りで捜す

4 *n.* SENSATION: 感覚, 感じ, (physical sensation) 感触, (of fabric) 手触り, (of clothes against body) 肌触り, (of food in mouth) 舌触り, 歯触り

5 *v.* NOTICE: 感じる

1 I felt happy.
幸せを感じた。

I was feeling tired, but I decided to go on.
疲れを感じていたけど、先へ進むことにした。

It felt heavy.
重く感じた/ずしりと重かった。

Are you feeling OK?
大丈夫ですか？

It felt good to be home.
家に帰ってほっとした。

It felt like summer.
まるで夏のようだった。

I felt like shouting at the top of my lungs.
大声で叫びたい気分だった。

2 She knew how I felt about him.
彼女は、私が彼のことをどう思っているか知っていました。

Don't you feel we ought to speak to him about it?
そのことについて、彼に話すべきだと思わない？

I felt I had to at least show my face at the meeting.
会合に、せめて顔だけでも出すべきだと思った。

I felt he was making a terrible mistake.
彼がとんでもない誤りをおかしているような気がした。

3 I felt the material.
素材を触ってみた。

I felt around in the darkness for a candle.
暗やみのなか、手探りでろうそくを捜した。

4 the feel of the breeze
そよ風の感触

I didn't like the feel of the blouse.
そのブラウスの肌触りが好きではなかった。

5 I felt him watching me.
彼が見ているの [彼の視線] を感じた。

The effects of Chernobyl will be felt for many years to come.
チェルノブイリの影響は今後、何年も消えることはない。

feel like/up to doing …したい(気がする/気分だ)

I feel like having a nap.
お昼寝したい気分だ。

I don't feel like studying right now.
今は勉強したくない。

feeling *n.* 感じ, 気分, (sensation) 感覚, (impression) 印象, 感想, 感じ, フィーリング, (**feelings**: emotions) 感情, 気持ち

I've got a bad feeling about this.
このことについては、いやな予感がするんだ。

What was your feeling about the meeting?
会議のご感想は？

I got the feeling that they weren't pleased to see us.
彼らは私たちに会うのを喜んでいないように感じた。

I've hurt his feelings.
彼の気持ちを傷つけてしまった。

KANJI BRIDGE

感 ON: かん KUN: —, | FEELING, SENSE

feeling of apprehension .... 不安感
feeling of hunger .... 空腹感
sense of duty .... 義務感
sense of justice .... 正義感
sense of mortality .... 無常感
sense of responsibility .... 責任感
sense of solidarity .... 連帯感

feet → FOOT

feign *v.* (pretend) 装う, (...の) ふりをする

feign illness
病気を装う [仮病をつかう]

fell *v.* (cut down) 切り倒す, 伐採する, (kill) 打ち倒す, 殺す

fellow *n.* (person) 人, ((*informal*)) 奴, (man) 男, (colleague) 同僚, 仲間

fellowship *n.* (association) 協会, (group) 団体; (scholarship) 奨学金, (research grant) 研究助成金

felon *n.* 重罪犯人

felony *n.* 重罪

felt *n.* フェルト

a felt-tip pen フェルトペン

female *n.* 女, 女性, 女の人, (girl) 女子, (animal) めす

adj. 女の, 女性の, (of animal) めすの

feminine *adj.* 女らしい, 女性的な, 女っぽい

feminine speech 女言葉

♦**femininity** *n.* 女らしさ

feminism *n.* フェミニズム

feminist *n.* フェミニスト

femur *n.* 大腿骨

fence *n.* 囲い, さく, 塀, (made of bamboo or clipped shrubbery) 垣根, (wire fence) フェンス

I can't see over the fence.
塀の向こうは見えません。

We need to put up a fence here to keep the dog in.
犬が逃げないように、ここにさくを作らなくちゃ。

There's a wire fence around the building.
建物の周りにフェンスが張り巡らされている。

fencing *n.* (sport) フェンシング [→ KENDO]

fend *v.* (**fend for oneself**) 自活する, 一人でやっていく

fennel *n.* ウイキョウ, フェンネル

ferment *v.* 発酵させる

♦**fermentation** *n.* 発酵

fern *n.* シダ

ferocious *adj.* (of animal) 凶暴な

ferret *n.* フェレット

ferry *n.* フェリー, 連絡船, (car ferry) カーフェリー

fertile *adj.* (of soil) 肥えた, 肥沃な, (of woman) 多産の, (of egg) 受精した

fertility *n.* (of soil) 肥沃, (of woman) 多産

fertilize *v.* (soil) (...に) 肥料をまく, (egg) 受精させる

fertilizer *n.* 肥料

festival *n.* (お)祭り, 祭典, (celebrating arts) フェスティバル, -祭

hold a festival (お)祭りをする
a film festival 映画祭

festive *adj.* (of atmosphere) お祭り気

分の

festivities *n.* (お)祝いの行事

feta *n.* フェタチーズ

fetch *v.* (thing) 持って来る, 取って来る, (person) 連れて来る

Would you fetch me my umbrella?
私の傘を取って来ていただけますか？

He went to fetch the documents.
彼は書類を取りに行った。

fetish *n.* (sexual) -フェチ

a foot fetish 足フェチ

fetus *n.* 胎児

feud *n.* 反目, 争い, 確執

v. 反目する, 争う

feudal *adj.* 封建的な

a feudal society 封建社会

♦**feudalism** *n.* 封建制度

fever *n.* 熱, (great interest) 興奮, 熱狂, フィーバー

She has a fever.
彼女は熱がある。

a high [slight] fever 高[微]熱

a resurgence of "disco fever"
「ディスコ熱」の再燃

♦**feverish** *adj.* 熱っぽい

few *adj.* (small number of) 少し, 多少の, 少数の, (some) いくつか, 何+<counter>+かの [→ p. 1168 about "Counters"], (practically none) ほとんどない/いない, 少ししか…ない/いない

pron. (few things) 少し, 少数, (few people) 少人数

a few days later
2、3日後

Just a few blocks away, there is a station.
数ブロック行った所に駅があります。

Only a few beers left, I'm afraid.
ビールはあと数本しか残ってないね。

The fewer the better.
少なければ少ないほどいい。

Only a few people came.
少ししか人が来なかった。

Few people manage to pass this exam.
この試験に受かる者はほとんどいない。

Very few of them succeeded.
成功した者は、ごくわずかだった。

as few as わずか…

As few as five people attended the meeting.
会合の出席者は、わずか5人だった。

quite a few かなりたくさん(の), かなり多く(の)

Quite a few people did not attend.
かなりたくさんの人が欠席した。

fiancé, fiancée *n.* 婚約者, フィアンセ

fiasco *n.* 大失敗

fiber *n.* 繊維

synthetic fibers 合成繊維

optical fiber 光ファイバー

fiberglass *n.* ファイバーグラス

fickle *adj.* 気まぐれの, 変わりやすい

fiction *n.* (genre) フィクション, (made-up story) 作り話, 作り事, 虚構

fiction and nonfiction
フィクションとノンフィクション

science fiction
サイエンスフィクション [ＳＦ]

Is that fact or fiction?
それは事実ですか、それとも作り話ですか？

F

fictional *adj.* 架空の

a fictional character 架空の人物

fiddle *n.* (musical instrument) バイオリン

v. (**fiddle with**) いじる, もてあそぶ

♦**fiddle around** *v.* (tinker with) いじくり回す; (waste time) のらくらして時間をつぶす

fidget *v.* (restlessly) もじもじする, (nervously) そわそわする

field *n.* (open area of land) 野原, (for growing) 畑, (for grazing) 牧草地, (rice paddy) 水田, (playing field) 競技場, フィールド; (field of study) 分野

an oil field 油田

♦**field event** *n.* フィールド競技

fierce *adj.* (of animal) どう猛な, (of storm, wind) 激しい

fife *n.* 横笛

fifteen *n.* 15, 十五

adj., pron. 15の, (people) 15人(の), (things) 15個(の)

fifteenth *n.* 第15, 15番目, (date) 15日

adj. 第15の, 15番目の

fifth *n.* 第5, 5番目, (date) 5日, (one fifth) 5分の1

adj. 第5の, 5番目の

fifty *n.* 50, 五十, (**the fifties**) 50年代, (**one's fifties**) 50代

adj., pron. 50の, (people) 50人(の), (things) 50個(の)

fifty-fifty *adj., adv.* 五分五分の/に, 半々の/に, 半分ずつ

go fifty-fifty (on restaurant bill) 割り勘にする

fig *n.* (fruit) イチジク

fight

1 *v.* COMBAT/STRUGGLE: (…と) 戦う, (take a stand against) (…と) 闘う

2 *v.* QUARREL: 争う, けんかする

3 *n.* FISTFIGHT: けんか, 殴り合い, (boxing match) 試合, 戦い

4 *n.* STRUGGLE: 戦い, 争い, ((*formal*)) 闘争

5 *n.* QUARREL: けんか, 口げんか, 口論

1 They fought bravely.
彼らは果敢に戦った。

He fought against the Germans in World War II.
第2次世界大戦で、彼はドイツ軍と戦った。

fight to the finish 最後まで戦い抜く

fight for one's life 命がけで戦う

fight for freedom 自由のために闘う

fight terrorism テロと闘う

2 fight over/about …をめぐって争う

They will fight among themselves.
彼らは仲間うちで、けんかするだろう。

3 get into a fight けんかになる

pick [start] a fight
けんかを売る [始める]

A fight broke out in the bar last night.
ゆうべ、飲み屋でけんかが起きた。

a dirty [clean] fight
卑劣な [正々堂々とした] 戦い

4 put up a fight 抵抗する

5 a bitter fight between husband and wife
激しい夫婦げんか

fight back *v.* (emotion) 抑える, (tears) こらえる; (strike back) 反撃する

She fought back the tears.

彼女は涙をこらえた。

Without spinach, Popeye couldn't fight back.

ホウレンソウがなかったら、ポパイは反撃できない。

The Tigers fought back to win the game.

タイガースは逆転勝利した。

fighter *n.* 戦う人, (boxer) ボクサー; (fighter jet) 戦闘機

fighting *n.* (battling) 戦い, (quarreling) けんか

adj. 戦う

♦**fighting chance** *n.* 努力次第の見込み, チャンス

figurative *adj.* (of expression) 比喩的な

figure *n.*

1 SHAPE OF BODY/THING: (of person) 姿, 容姿, スタイル, (of thing) 形

2 NUMBER: 数字

3 PERSON IN SOCIAL SETTING: 人, ((*formal*)) 人物, (famous figure) 名士, 大物

4 DIAGRAM: 図, 図形, 図案

5 REPRESENTATION OF PERSON: (statue) 彫像, (person in painting) 肖像

1 She has a fine figure.

彼女はスタイルがいい。

There was a dark figure in the shadows.

暗がりに黒い人影があった。

2 What do all these figures mean?

この数字はみんな、何を表しているんですか？

Are these figures correct?

この数字は間違いないですか？

3 Rev. Martin Luther King is an important figure in American history.

キング牧師はアメリカ史における重要な人物です。

a literary figure of the Meiji period

明治の文豪

4 Fig. 1 represents growth.

図1は、伸びを示しています。

5 a figure of the Amida 阿弥陀如来像

figure skating *n.* フィギュアスケート

file[1] *n.* ファイル, (folder) とじ込み帳, 書類差し, (dossier) 書類

v. (put away) ファイルする, ファイルに入れる, 整理する

open [close] a file

ファイルを開く[閉じる]

It's in the red file.

赤い書類差しの中に入っています。

keep a file on someone

…に関するファイルを保管する

The records are kept on file.

記録はファイルに保存されている。

copy [create, delete, edit, print] a file

ファイルをコピー[作成, 削除, 編集, 印刷]する

Have you filed those documents away?

あの書類はファイルしましたか？

♦**filing cabinet** *n.* ファイリングキャビネット, 書類整理棚

file[2] *n.* (tool) やすり [→ picture of TOOL]

v. (…に) やすりをかける

a nail file 爪やすり

File it down.

やすりをかけてください。

filial *adj.* 子としての

filial affection 子としての情愛

filial devotion/piety 親孝行（おやこうこう）

fill *v.* (make/become full) いっぱいにする/いっぱいになる, 満たす/満ちる, (vacancy) 補充（ほじゅう）する, 補（おぎな）う, (space) 詰（つ）める, (hole, crack) 埋（う）める, ふさぐ [→ FULL]

The air was filled with the lights and sounds of the festival.
あたりは、お祭（まつ）りの明（あ）かりと音（おと）で満（み）ちていた。

His head is filled with nonsense.
あの人（ひと）の頭（あたま）の中（なか）は、くだらないことでいっぱいだ/あの人（ひと）は、くだらないことばかり考（かんが）えている。

Please fill each of these bags with a cup of rice.
これらの袋（ふくろ）にお米（こめ）を1カップずつ入（い）れてください。

You'd better fill your stomach before we set off.
出（で）かける前（まえ）に腹（はら）ごしらえをしておいたほうがいい。

I prefer to fill my free time with enjoyable activities.
自分（じぶん）の自由（じゆう）になる時間（じかん）は、楽（たの）しいことをして過（す）ごしたい。

How should we fill these holes?
この穴（あな）をどうやってふさごうか？

fill in *v.* (blank, hole) 埋（う）める, (blank) 記入（きにゅう）する, 書（か）き込（こ）む; (**fill in for**: substitute for) …の代（か）わりをする; (fill A in on B: tell/explain details [= B] to A) (BについてAに) 教（おし）える/説明（せつめい）する
fill in the blanks 空欄（くうらん）に記入（きにゅう）する

The pool is going to be filled in.
プールは埋（う）め立（た）てられることになっている。

I need someone to fill in for me this Saturday.
今週（こんしゅう）の土曜日（どようび）、誰（だれ）か代（か）わってほしい。
Fill me in. 詳（くわ）しく聞（き）かせて。

fill out *v.* (write information in) (…に) 記入（きにゅう）する, 書（か）き込（こ）む; (become fat) 太（ふと）る

Please fill out this form.
この用紙（ようし）にご記入（きにゅう）ください。

She's really filled out since last year.
彼女（かのじょ）、去年（きょねん）からだいぶ太（ふと）ってきたね。

fill up *v.* (make/become full) いっぱいにする/いっぱいになる, (car with gasoline) 満（まん）タンにする

Let's fill up our water bottles.
水筒（すいとう）をいっぱいにしましょう。

Ramen noodles really fill you up.
ラーメンは、ほんとにおなかが膨（ふく）れる [いっぱいになる] ね。

Don't fill up before dinner.
夕飯（ゆうはん）の前（まえ）におなかをいっぱいにしないで。

The theater filled up pretty quickly.
劇場（げきじょう）はあっという間（ま）にいっぱいになった。

Fill 'er up, please.
満（まん）タンにしてください。

fillet *n.* (of meat) ヒレ肉（にく）, (of fish) 切（き）り身（み）
v. 切（き）り身（み）にする

filling *n.* (contents) 中身（なかみ）; (thing used to fill a space) 詰（つ）め物（もの）
adj. (of meal) おなかがいっぱいになる

This tooth needs filling.
この歯（は）は詰（つ）め物（もの）をしなくてはいけない。

film

1 *n.* MOVIE: 映画（えいが）

2 *n.* MATERIAL USED IN PHOTOGRAPHY: フィルム

3 *v.* **RECORD:** 撮影する, ((*informal*)) 撮る

1 There's a good film showing this week.
今週はいい映画をやっています。

Have you ever been in a film?
映画に出たことはありますか？

produce [direct] a film
映画を制作 [監督] する

show a film 映画を上映する

ban [censor, release, review] a film
映画を禁止 [検閲, 公開, 批評] する

2 a roll of film フィルム１本

develop film フィルムを現像する

black-and-white [color] film
白黒 [カラー] フィルム

load [take out] a roll of film
フィルムを入れる [取り出す]

3 Her most recent documentary was filmed in New York.
彼女の最新のドキュメンタリー作品は、ニューヨークで撮影された。

filmmaker *n.* 映画監督

filter *n.* (for liquid) ろ過器, 水こし, フィルター, (on lens, cigarette) フィルター
v. (pass through a filter) ろ過する, こす

♦**filter paper** *n.* (for coffee) フィルターペーパー, (in cooking) こし紙, (in chemistry) ろ過紙

filth *n.* (foul matter) 汚れ, 汚いもの, (grime) あか, (foul language) 汚い言葉, (lewd pictures) ひわいな写真

filthy *adj.* 汚い, 汚れた, 不潔な, (lewd) わいせつな, ((*informal*)) エッチな, (of language) 下品な

fin *n.* ひれ

final *adj.* (last in a series) 最後の, 最終の, (decisive) 最終的な, 決定的な
n. (exam) 期末試験; (**finals**: last round in a competition) 決勝戦

a final chance 最後のチャンス

a final episode 最終回

a final decision 最終決定

a final say 最終的な決定権

a final attempt on the summit
登頂への最後の試み [アタック]

♦**finalist** *n.* 決勝戦出場者

finalize *v.* 完結させる

finale *n.* フィナーレ

finally *adv.* (in the end) 最後に, 結局, (at last) とうとう, ついに, やっと, (last of all) 最後に

When did the train finally arrive?
結局、電車はいつ来たの？

After hours of being made to wait, she finally got fed up and left.
何時間も待たされて、彼女はとうとういやになって、立ち去った。

Finally, I would like to thank everyone for their support.
最後になりましたが、皆様のご支援に感謝いたします。

finance *n.* 財政, (subject of study) 財政学, (business) 金融, (**finances**) 財政状態, (**family finances**) 家計
v. (fund) (…に) 融資する

the Ministry of Finance 財務省

a finance company 金融会社

He works in finance.
彼は金融関係の仕事をしている。

financial *adj.* 財政上の, 財務の

a financial adviser 財務顧問

a financial risk 財政危機

♦**financial aid** *n.* 財政援助

financier *n.* 投資家

find

1 *v.* LOCATE: 見つける, (look for) 捜し出す, (**be able to find/be found**) (…が) 見つかる

2 *v.* DISCOVER: 見つける, 発見する

3 *v.* HAVE AS AN OPINION: See examples below

4 *v.* REALIZE: (…に) 気がつく, (…が) わかる

5 *v.* MAKE/HAVE AVAILABLE: (find the time/money) (時間/お金を) つくる

6 *n.* DISCOVERY: 発見

1 Could you help me find my car keys?
車のキーを捜す [見つける] のを手伝っていただけませんか？

I can't find my umbrella. Ah! Here it is.
傘が見つからないんだ。ああ、ここにあった。

Did you find the pen you lost?
なくしたペンは見つかりましたか？

I eventually found my glasses on the kitchen table.
結局、めがねは台所のテーブルの上にありました。

2 I found a nice little café in my neighborhood.
近所に、すてきな小さな喫茶店を見つけました。

Let's try to find a solution to this problem.
この問題の解決法を見つけましょう。

We found ourselves outside the station.
気がつくと駅の外にいました。

I found myself laughing my head off.
思わず大笑いしていました。

3 I found it hard to get up so early in the morning.
そんなに朝早く起きるのは、一苦労でした。

How did you find it, living in Beijing?
北京に住んでいて、どうだった？

4 I found that I was mistaken.
自分が間違っていたことに気がついた。

5 How do you find time to do all these things?
これだけのことを全部楽しむ時間を、どうやってつくるんですか？

Where am I going to find the money for that?
それを買うお金をどこでつくる [工面する] っていうの？

6 What a great find!
すばらしい発見だね！

finding *n.* (discovery) 発見, (**findings**: conclusion) 結論

fine[1]

1 *adj.* EXCELLENT: (splendid) すばらしい, みごとな, (admirable, magnificent) 立派な, (beautiful) 美しい, (outstanding) すぐれた, 優秀な

2 *adj.* OF FEELING: See examples below

3 *adj.* ADEQUATE: 大丈夫だ, けっこうだ

4 *adj.* OF QUALITY: (thin) 細い, (minute) 細かい, (high-quality) 上質の, 上等の

5 *adj.* OF WEATHER: いい, 晴れた

6 *adj.* SUBTLE: 微妙な

7 *adv.* WELL: うまく, よく

1 a fine view すばらしい眺め

It was a fine performance.
みごとな演技だった。

We had a fine time.

すばらしい時を過ごしました。

a fine writer すぐれた作家

2 “How are you?”
“I’m fine, thanks.”
「お元気ですか？」
「はい、おかげさまで」

“Are you OK?”
“Yes, I’m fine.”
「大丈夫ですか？」
「はい、大丈夫です」

3 The conclusion to the dissertation was fine.
論文の結論はけっこうだね。

“Am I dressed OK?”
“You look fine.”
「私の格好、大丈夫？」
「大丈夫だよ」

4 a fine thread 細い糸

a fine rain 霧雨

a fine mist 細かい霧

fine sand 細かい砂

fine silk 上質の絹

fine wine 上等のワイン

5 Fine weather, isn’t it?
いいお天気ですね。

6 a fine difference 微妙な差

7 Don’t worry. You’ll do fine.
心配しないで。うまくいくよ。

fine[2] ***n.*** (penalty) 罰金

v. (…に) 罰金を科する

pay a fine 罰金を払う

a fine for illegal parking
駐車違反の罰金

He was fined $50 by the police.
彼は警察から50ドルの罰金を科された。

fine arts ***n.*** 美術

finely ***adv.*** (into tiny pieces) 細かく, みじんに

Chop the garlic finely.
にんにくをみじん切りにします。

finger ***n.*** 指 [→ picture of HAND]

the index finger 人差し指

the middle finger 中指

the ring finger 薬指

the little finger 小指

point a finger at someone
人を指さす

put one’s finger on ずばり指摘する, はっきり示す

There’s something wrong with it, but I can’t put my finger on it.
どこかおかしいんだけれど、それがどこなのか、ずばり指摘できない。

fingernail ***n.*** (指の)爪 [→ picture of HAND]

fingerprint ***n.*** 指紋

take someone’s fingerprints
(…の) 指紋を採る

♦**fingerprinting** ***n.*** 指紋押捺

fingertip ***n.*** 指先

finish

1 ***v.*** COMPLETE: 終える, 仕上げる, 完成する, 完成させる, (**finish doing**) …し終える, …し終わる, 済ます, (a course) 修了する

2 ***v.*** END: 終わる, (of runner in race: finish in a particular state/rank) (…で) ゴールインする

3 ***n.*** LAST PART: 終わり, 最後, フィニッシュ, (final stage) 最終段階, (of race) ゴー

ルイン

4 *n.* **OF FURNITURE:** 表面の仕上げ

1 I finished the book.
本を読み終えた。

Have you finished the dishes?
お皿洗いは終わったの？

I'll call you back once I've finished eating.
食事を済ませたら折り返し電話します。

Did you finish on time?
締め切りに間に合いましたか？

2 The movie finishes at 11:15.
映画は11時15分に終わる。

I finished fifth.
5位でゴールインしました。

3 the finish of the race レースの最後

the finish line ゴール

4 a glossy finish 光沢仕上げ

finish off *v.* (drink) 空ける

I finished off the bottle.
ボトルを空けました。

finish up *v.* (food) 平らげる

finish with *v.* 終える, 済ます, (person: break up with) (...と) 別れる

Once you're finished with that, hand it to me.
終わったら私に渡してください。

Have you really finished with him?
本当に、彼とは別れた [終わった] の？

finished *adj.* 完成した

Is this painting finished?
この絵は完成していますか？

finite *adj.* 限定されている, 有限の

Finland *n.* フィンランド

fir *n.* (tree) モミの木, (wood) モミ材

fire

1 *n.* **ELEMENT:** 火, (campfire) たき火, (accidental fire) 火事, ((*formal*)) 火災

2 *v.* **SHOOT:** 撃つ, 発砲する

3 *v.* **DISMISS FROM A JOB:** 首にする, 解雇する

4 *n.* **HEATER:** ストーブ, ヒーター [→ HEATER]

1 fire and water 火と水

Let's light a fire.
火をつけよう。

start/make a fire 火をおこす

The dry grass caught fire.
枯草に火がついた。

Someone set fire to the building.
何者かがその建物に火をつけた。

It took more than an hour to put out the fire.
消火するのに1時間以上かかった。

The house was on fire.
家が燃えていた。

2 fire a gun 銃を撃つ

fire on the enemy 敵に発砲する

3 Mr. Harada was fired after just one week on the job.
原田さんは仕事に就いてわずか1週間で首になった。

fire alarm *n.* (sound) 火災警報, (device) 火災報知器

firearm *n.* (gun) (小)火器, 銃

firebomb *n.* 焼夷弾

v. (a city) 焼夷弾で攻撃する

firebreak *n.* 防火線

firecracker *n.* 爆竹, (cherry bomb) かんしゃく玉

fire department *n.* (brigade) 消防隊, (station) 消防署

fire drill ***n.*** (火災)避難訓練

fire engine ***n.*** 消防車

fire exit ***n.*** 非常出口

fire extinguisher ***n.*** 消火器

firefighter ***n.*** 消防士

firefly ***n.*** ホタル, 蛍

fire hydrant ***n.*** 消火栓

fireplace ***n.*** 暖炉

fireproof ***adj.*** 耐火性の, 防火-

fireside ***n.*** 炉端

fire station ***n.*** 消防署

firetrap ***n.*** (building) 燃えやすい建物

firewood ***n.*** まき, たきぎ

fireworks ***n.*** 花火

a fireworks display 花火大会

firm ***adj.*** かたい, (of body) 引き締まった, (of step, voice) しっかり(と)した

adv. かたく, しっかりと

The ground is firm. 地面が固い。

This mattress is firm and better for your back.
このぐらい硬いマットレスのほうが、腰にはいいんですよ。

be firm with …に厳しい

I was very firm with him and told him he had to do his homework.
宿題をやらなくてはいけないと、厳しく言っておいたよ。

♦**firmly** ***adv.*** かたく, しっかりと

He shook my hand very firmly.
彼は私とかたく握手を交わした。

first

1 ***adj.*** **BEING BEFORE ALL OTHERS:** 最初の, 初めの, (of experience, event) 初めての, (in order) 1番目の, 第1の

2 ***adv.*** **BEFORE ALL OTHERS:** 最初に, 初めに, (for the first time) 初めて, (first of all) まず(は)

3 ***n.*** **THE FIRST:** (in series) 第1, 1番目, (day of month) 1日, (in line of monarchs) 1世

1 the first Olympics 最初のオリンピック

My first guess was wrong.
初めの考えは間違っていた。

Were the Wright brothers the first to fly?
最初に空を飛んだのは、ライト兄弟ですか？

Is this your first time here?
ここは、初めてですか？

The first half of the game was better than the second.
試合は、前半のほうが後半よりもよかった。

2 The comet was first seen last week.
すい星が先週、最初に目撃された。

Well, who came in first?
それで、誰が1位だったの？

First, let's do the shopping, then let's visit Grandma.
まず買い物をして、それからおばあちゃんのうちへ行きましょう。

3 How about we meet on the first?
1日に会うっていうのはいかがですか？

January 1　1月1日

George I　ジョージ1世

at first 最初は, 初めは

At first, I didn't like him.
最初は、彼のことが好きではありませんでした。

first of all まず第一に, まず(は)

First of all, let's hear the hard facts.
まずは、具体的な事実から話してもらい

ましょう。

for the first time 初めて

For the first time in my life I realized the importance of good health.
生まれて初めて、健康の大切さを思い知りました。

in the first place まず第一に, そもそも

In the first place, you were late. In the second, you didn't call.
そもそも君は遅刻をした。おまけに電話もしてこなかった。

♦**first base** *n.* (in baseball) 一塁, ファースト

first-born *adj.* 最初に生まれた, 第一子の

one's first-born son [daughter]
長男 [長女]

first language *n.* 母語, 母国語

first person *n.* 一人称

first aid *n.* 応急手当

give first aid (to) (…に)応急手当をする

first-aid kit *n.* 救急用品, 救急箱 [→ picture below]

first class *n.* (quality) 一流, (accommodation) 1等, ファーストクラス

adj. (**first-class**) 一流の

firsthand *adj.* 直接の, じかの

firsthand knowledge
経験からじかに得た知識

first lady *n.* ファーストレディー, 大統領夫人

first lieutenant *n.* (in U.S. Army / Air Force / Marine Corps) 中尉

first name *n.* 名前, ((*honorific*)) お名前, ファーストネーム, ((*written*)) 名

fiscal *adj.* 会計の

♦**fiscal year** *n.* 会計年度

fish *n.* 魚, ((*formal*)) 魚類

v. 魚を釣る, 魚を捕る

What kind of fish is this?
これは、何という魚ですか？

fishbowl *n.* 金魚鉢

fisherman *n.* (professional) 漁師, (amateur) 釣り人

fishing *n.* (recreational) (魚)釣り, (commercial) 漁, 漁業

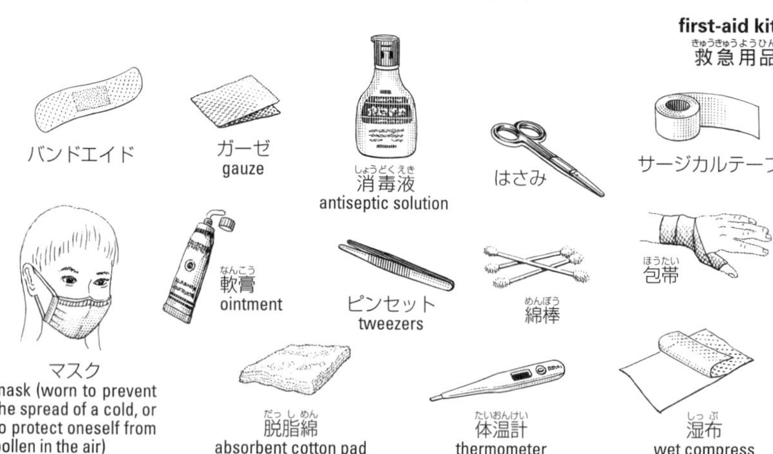

Let's go fishing.
釣りに行こう。

♦**fishing boat** *n.* (large) 漁船, (small) 釣り船

fishing pole *n.* 釣りざお

fishmonger *n.* 魚屋(さん)

fishy *adj.* (of smell) 生臭い; (suspicious) 怪しい

fission *n.* 分裂

fissure *n.* (crack) 割れ目, 裂け目 [→ CRACK]

fist *n.* (握り)こぶし, げんこつ

fistfight *n.* 殴り合い

fit

1 *v.* SUIT: (…に) 合う, ぴったり合う

2 *v.* BE THE APPROPRIATE SIZE/SHAPE: 合う, (**fit in/inside**) …に入る

3 *v.* PUT IN PLACE: (household appliance) 取り付ける, 備える

4 *adj.* PROPER/SUITABLE: ぴったりの, 適した, ふさわしい, 向いている

5 *n.* OF CLOTHING: 着心地

6 *adj.* IN GOOD HEALTH: 体調のいい, 体調の整った, (**get fit**) 体づくりをする

7 *n.* PHYSICAL REACTION: 発作

1 Do these pants fit me?
このズボンは、私に合ってますか？

These shoes don't fit me.
この靴は、私の足に合わない。

This music fits my mood perfectly.
この音楽は、今の気分にぴったりだ。

2 This piece doesn't fit.
これは合わない。

Can we all fit in (the car)?
みんな乗れる？

I don't think that table is going to fit through the door.
あのテーブルはドアを通れないと思う。

This plug doesn't fit.
このプラグは差し込めない。

3 We're going to have new carpets fitted.
新しいじゅうたんを敷いてもらうことになっています。

I would suggest you have locks fitted.
かぎを取り付けてもらったほうが、いいと思いますよ。

4 It was a fit conclusion to the story.
その物語にふさわしい結末だった。

I don't think you're fit for the job.
あなたはこの仕事に向いてないと思います。

5 These shoes are a tight fit.
この靴はきつい [窮屈だ]。

This jacket is a good fit.
この上着は、(体に)ぴったり合う。

6 Are you fit for the match next week?
来週の試合に向けて、体調はいいですか？

I'm going to start getting fit this summer.
この夏から、体づくりを始めるつもりです。

7 a fit of coughing せきの発作

a sneezing fit くしゃみの発作

throw a fit (get angry) かっとなる

He threw a fit when he found out.
彼はそれを知って、かっとなった。

fitness *n.* フィットネス

♦**fitness club** *n.* フィットネスクラブ

fitting *adj.* 適切な, ぴったりの, ふさわしい
n. (trying on of clothes) 試着

five *n.* 5, 五
adj., pron. 5の, (people) 5人(の),

F

(things) 5個(の), 五つ(の)

fix

1 *v.* **MAKE FIRM/FAST:** 取り付ける, 固定する

2 *v.* **REPAIR:** 直す, 修理する

3 *v.* **DECIDE:** (time, date etc.) 決める

4 *v.* **PREPARE:** (meal, drink) 作る, 用意する

5 *v.* **PREARRANGE:** (race) (…で) 八百長をしくむ, (jury) 買収する

6 *v.* **ONE'S HAIR:** 整える

7 *n.* **PREDICAMENT:** 苦しい羽目

1 I would like the shelves to be fixed to the walls.
棚は壁に固定していただきたいんです。

The wood is fixed together with nails.
材木は釘で留めてあります。

2 I was told the car will be fixed by Saturday.
車は、土曜日までに直ると言われた。

3 Have you fixed the details of tomorrow's meeting?
明日の会議の詳細は、決めましたか？

4 Would you like me to fix you a lunch?
お弁当を作ろうか？

5 The race was fixed.
レースはしくまれていた[八百長だった]。

6 I need a minute to fix my hair.
髪を整えるから、ちょっと待って。

7 We're in a real fix now, aren't we?
にっちもさっちもいかないね。

fixed *adj.* (of price) 一定の, (invariable) 固定した; (rigged) 八百長の

fixed ideas 固定観念

of no fixed address 住所不定の

a fixed game 八百長試合

♦**fixedly** *adv.* (of look) じっと

gaze fixedly at …をじっと見る

fizzy *adj.* 泡の出る

flag *n.* 旗

a flag flying in the breeze
風にひるがえる旗

raise [lower] a flag
旗を揚げる [下ろす]

flair *n.* (talent) 才能

Hanako has a flair for dancing.
花子にはダンスの才能がある。

flake *n.* かけら, (of snow) (雪の) 一片; (person) うっかり者

v. (of paint) はがれる

flamboyant *adj.* けばけばしい, 派手な

flame *n.* (of fire) 炎

a candle flame ろうそくの火 [炎]

burst into flames ぱっと燃え上がる

flamingo *n.* フラミンゴ

flammable *adj.* 燃えやすい, 火のつきやすい, 可燃性の

a flammable material/substance
可燃物

flannel *n.* (material) フランネル, フラノ, ネル

flannel goods フランネル製品

flap *n.* (of envelope) 折り返し, 垂れぶた, (of skin) 組織片, (of book jacket) 折り返し; (noise) バタバタ/パタパタする音

v. (of wings) バタバタ/パタパタする, (of flag) はためく

flare *v.* (of fire: flame up) 燃え上がる; (of clothing) 末広がりになる, フレアになる

n. (flame) ゆらめく炎, (device used for signaling) 閃光装置

♦**flared** *adj.* (of clothing) フレア-

flash

1 *n.* SUDDEN BURST OF LIGHT: 閃光(せんこう), (of lightning) 稲光(いなびかり), 稲妻(いなづま), (from camera) フラッシュ

2 *v.* GIVE OUT A SUDDEN BRIGHT LIGHT: 光(ひか)る, (using flashlight/headlights) ぱっと照(て)らす

3 *v.* COME SUDDENLY TO MIND: (**flash into/across one's mind**) ぱっと浮(う)かぶ, ひらめく

4 *v.* PASS SUDDENLY: さっと通(とお)り過(す)ぎる

5 *n.* PIECE OF NEWS: 速報(そくほう)

6 *n.* LIGHT FOR CAMERA: フラッシュ

7 *n.* OF INSPIRATION: ひらめき

1 a flash of light 閃光(せんこう)

There was a sudden flash of lightning.
不意(ふい)に、稲妻(いなづま)が走(はし)った。

As soon as I stepped on stage, I was blinded by the flash of cameras.
舞台(ぶたい)に上(あ)がったとたん、カメラのフラッシュで目(め)がくらんだ。

2 Lightning flashed even as the storm faded.
風雨(ふうう)はおさまりつつあったが、まだ稲光(いなびかり)は続(つづ)いていた。

Cameras flashed throughout the press conference.
記者会見(きしゃかいけん)の間中(あいだじゅう)、カメラのフラッシュがパチパチたかれていた。

3 An excellent idea flashed into my mind.
すばらしい考(かんが)えがひらめいた。

4 The cars flashed by.
車(くるま)が次々(つぎつぎ)に通(とお)り過(す)ぎた。

5 The news flash about the earthquake streamed across TV screens nationwide.
全国(ぜんこく)のテレビ画面(がめん)に、地震速報(じしんそくほう)が流(なが)れた。

6 The flash didn't work.
フラッシュが作動(さどう)しなかった。

7 a flash of inspiration
霊感(れいかん)のひらめき

in a flash すぐに, あっという間(ま)に

I'll be back in a flash.
すぐ戻(もど)って来(き)ます。

flashback *n.* フラッシュバック

flashlight *n.* 懐中電灯(かいちゅうでんとう)

flashy *adj.* 派手(はで)な, けばけばしい

flask *n.* (for liquor) ポケットびん, (used in laboratory) フラスコ, (Thermos) 魔法(まほう)びん

flat[1]

1 *adj.* SMOOTH AND LEVEL: (of surface) 平(たい)らな, (of shape) 平(ひら)たい, (of land, road) 平坦(へいたん)な

2 *adv.* LYING AT FULL LENGTH: (looking up) あお向(む)けに, (looking down) うつ伏(ぶ)せに, (against a vertical surface) ぴったり(と)

3 *adj.* OF TIRE: パンクした, ぺちゃんこになった

4 *adj.* OF BEVERAGE: 気(き)が抜(ぬ)けた

5 *adj.* OF MUSICAL NOTE: -フラット, 変(へん)-

6 *adj.* DULL: 退屈(たいくつ)な, つまらない

7 *adj.* OF PRICE/RATE: 均一(きんいつ)の, 一律(いちりつ)の

8 *adj.* UNEQUIVOCAL/BLUNT: きっぱりとした

9 *adj.* OF BATTERIES: 切(き)れた, 充電(じゅうでん)していない

10 *n.* LAND: (**flats**) 平地(へいち)

11 *n.* SHOES: (**flats**) かかとの低(ひく)い靴(くつ)

1 The house has a flat roof.
その家(いえ)は屋根(やね)が平(たい)らです。

The ground needs to be flat, not bumpy.
地面(じめん)が、でこぼこじゃなくて平(たい)らでなくてはだめなんだ。

It's flat enough here to play.
ここなら平坦だから、遊べるよ。

2 He was lying flat on the floor (on his back).
彼は床の上にあお向けに横たわっていた。

Let's push it flat against the wall.
ぴったり壁につけましょう。

3 The tires are flat.
タイヤがぺちゃんこだ。

4 This beer is flat.
このビールは気が抜けている。

5 I think the movement was played in B flat.
演奏はBフラット [変ロ] だったと思うな。

6 It's a flat film with flat characters.
つまらない登場人物の、退屈な映画だ。

7 a flat tax rate
均一税率

8 a flat denial
きっぱりとした否定

9 The batteries are flat.
電池が切れてる/バッテリーが上がった。

10 salt flats 塩田

flat[2] ***n.*** (apartment) (in low building) アパート, (in high or medium-height building) マンション [→ picture of APARTMENT]

I'm looking for a flat.
アパートを探しています。

a furnished [unfurnished] flat
家具付き [無し] のマンション

flatfish ***n.*** ヒラメ, カレイ

flatly ***adv.*** (unequivocally) きっぱり(と)

He flatly refused.
彼はきっぱり断った。

flatten ***v.*** (make level) 平らにする, (squash flat) ぺちゃんこにする, (destroy) 倒す, つぶす

The tornado flattened the town.
竜巻は町をぺちゃんこにした。

flatter ***v.*** (…に) お世辞を言う, おべっかを言う, ごまをする, (**flatter oneself**) 得意がる, うぬぼれる

You flatter me.
お世辞をおっしゃって。

I'm very flattered, but…
気持ちはうれしいけど…。

She's easily flattered.
あの人はすぐにおだてに乗る。

I'd be flattered.
((*formal*)) 光栄です。(lit.,"It'd be an honor")

♦**flatterer** ***n.*** ごますり, おべっか使い

flattery ***n.*** お世辞, おだて, おべっか

flaunt ***v.*** 見せびらかす, 誇示する, (**flaunt oneself**) わが物顔にふるまう

flavor ***n.*** (taste) 味, 味わい, (including smell) 風味

v. (give flavor to) (…に) 風味を添える, 味を付ける

It'll improve the flavor if you add some salt.
塩を足すと味がよくなりますよ。

flavoring ***n.*** 調味料

flaw ***n.*** (in product) 欠陥, (character flaw) 欠点

flawless ***adj.*** (of person) 欠点のない, (of performance) 完璧な

♦**flawlessly** ***adv.*** 完璧に

flea ***n.*** ノミ

flea market ***n.*** のみの市

flee *v.* 逃げる [→ ESCAPE]

fleece *n.* (coat of sheep's wool) 羊毛, (material) フリース

fleet *n.* (of warships) 艦隊, (of merchant ships) 船団

fleet admiral *n.* (in U.S. Navy) 元帥

fleeting *adj.* つかのまの

flesh *n.* 肉, (opposite of spirit) 肉体

flexible *adj.* (of stick) 曲げやすい, (of person: able to bend limbs easily) 柔らかい, しなやかな, (able to adapt) 順応性のある, (of plan) 柔軟な, 融通のきく

♦ **flexibility** *n.* 柔軟性

flick *v.* (with finger) はじく, (a switch on/off) パチッとつける/消す

n. (film) 映画

flicker *v.* (of flame) 揺らめく, (of light) 明滅する, チカチカする

flier *n.* (pamphlet) ちらし, びら

flight[1] *n.* (journey by airplane) 空の旅, (airplane) 便, フライト, (act of flying) 飛行; (flight of stairs) 一続きの階段

Did you enjoy your flight?
空の旅を楽しまれましたか？

The flight took six hours.
飛行時間は 6 時間だった。

the 8:30 flight to Nagoya
8時 3 0 分(発)の名古屋行きの便

a nonstop flight 直行便

flight[2] *n.* (escape) 逃避

flight attendant *n.* 客室乗務員

flimsy *adj.* (easily broken) 壊れやすい, もろい

fling *v.* (throw) 投げつける [→ THROW]

flipper *n.* (swimming aid) フィン, 足ひれ, (on animal) ひれ足

flirt *v.* いちゃつく

n. 浮気者

He's always flirting with the girls.
あいつは、いつも女の子といちゃついている。

float *v.* (be suspended on water/in air) 浮かぶ, (not sink) 浮く, (drift) 漂う, (float along on a current) 流れる

n. (in parade) 山車; (device used in fishing) 浮き

Wood floats, ducks swim, and metal sinks.
木は水に浮き、アヒルは泳ぎ、金属は沈む。

The leaves floated down the river.
木の葉が川面を流れて行った。

A strong smell of curry floated through the air.
濃厚なカレーのにおいが、あたりに漂っていた。

floating stock *n.* 浮動株

flock *n.* 群れ [→ CROWD]

v. 群がる, 集まる

flood *n.* (great quantity of water) 洪水, 氾濫; (surge) 殺到

v. (of river) 氾濫する

There was a flood here some years ago.
数年前、ここで洪水があった。

There was a flood of inquiries about the job offer.
その求人に、問い合わせが殺到した。

The river flooded all the low-lying neighborhoods.
川が氾濫して、付近の低地一帯が水浸しになった。

flooded ***adj.*** (of area) 浸水した, 水浸しになった, (be flooded with: be overflowing with) (…で) あふれる

The basement was flooded.
地下室が浸水していた。

The place was flooded with tourists.
そこは旅行客であふれていた。

floodlight ***n.*** 投光照明, フラッドライト

floor ***n.*** (of room) 床, (of sea) 底; (level/story of building) -階

Is that your jacket on the floor?
床に落ちているのは、あなたの上着？

Try not to drop things on the floor, please.
床に物を落とさないようにしてくださいね。

This building has five floors.
この建物は5階建てです。

floorboard ***n.*** 床板

flop ***n.*** (failure) 失敗 [→ FALL]

floppy ***adj.*** (of ears) だらりとした, 垂れた

flora ***n.*** 植物相

floral ***adj.*** 花の, (of design/pattern) 花柄の

florist ***n.*** (お)花屋(さん)

floss ***n.*** (dental) 糸ようじ, (デンタル)フロス

flotation ***n.*** 浮揚, (new issue of shares) (証券の)募集

flounder[1] ***v.*** (in sand, mud, marsh) もがく; (not know what to do) まごつく

The wrestlers floundered about in the mud.
レスラーたちが、ぬかるみの中でもがいていた。

flounder[2] ***n.*** (flatfish) ヒラメ, カレイ

flour ***n.*** 小麦粉

flourish ***v.*** (of culture) 栄える, 繁栄する, (of business) 繁盛する

flow ***v.*** 流れる, (of words) 滑らかに出る
n. 流れ

The traffic flowed into the city.
車の列が街に流れ込んでいた。

The river flowed through the village.
その川は村の中を流れていました。

the flow of the river 川の流れ

♦ **flow in** ***v.*** (of tide) 満ちる

flow out ***v.*** (of tide) 引く

flowchart ***n.*** フローチャート, 流れ図

flower ***n.*** (plant) (お)花, 草花
v. 花が咲く

artificial/fake flowers 造花

The flowers bloomed early.
開花が早かった。

Once the azalea flowers, it will brighten up this side of the house.
ツツジの花が咲くと、家のこちら側はいっぺんに華やぐ。

♦ **flower pot** ***n.*** 植木鉢

flower shop ***n.*** (お)花屋(さん)

flower arrangement ***n.*** 生け花

flower arrangement
生け花

flowery ***adj.*** (of smell) 花のような, (of prose) 飾り立てた

flu ***n.*** インフルエンザ, 流感

fluctuate ***v.*** 変動する, (of price) 上下する

fluent ***adj.*** 流ちょうな

♦**fluency** ***n.*** 流ちょうさ

fluently ***adv.*** ぺらぺら, 流ちょうに

fluid ***n.*** 流動体, 流体 [→ LIQUID]

fluff ***n.*** (ball of wool) 毛玉

fluffy ***adj.*** (of pillow) ふわふわした

flunk ***v.*** (exam, class) (...に)落ちる, 不合格になる, (student) 落とす, 落第させる

♦**flunk out** ***v.*** (of school) 退学する

fluorescent ***adj.*** 蛍光性の

a fluorescent light 蛍光灯

fluoride ***n.*** フッ化物

fluorine ***n.*** フッ素

flush ***v.*** (toilet) (...の) 水を流す, (flush down a toilet) (トイレに) 流してしまう; (turn red) 赤くなる

Don't forget to flush the toilet.
トイレの水を流すのを忘れないでね。

flute ***n.*** フルート

play the flute フルートを吹く

fly[1]

1 ***v.*** TRAVEL THROUGH AIR: 飛ぶ, (by airplane) 飛行機で行く, 飛行機に乗る/乗って行く

2 ***v.*** CONTROL AN AIRCRAFT: 操縦する

3 ***v.*** RAISE INTO THE SKY: (kite) 揚げる, (flag) 掲げる

4 ***v.*** TRANSPORT BY AIRPLANE: (cargo) 空輸する, (person) 運ぶ

5 ***v.*** GO QUICKLY: (**fly down**: street, corridor) 飛んで行く, 走って行く, (**fly out of**) ...から飛び出す, (**fly off**: of hat) 飛ぶ

6 ***n.*** OPENING IN FRONT OF PANTS: チャック, ((*euphemistic*)) 社会の窓

1 The jets flew across the city.
ジェット機が街の上空を飛んで行った。

A wasp flew into the classroom.
スズメバチが教室に飛び込んで来た。

We flew to Mumbai and then on to Delhi.
飛行機でまずムンバイへ行って、それからデリーへと飛びました。

2 Can you fly an airplane?
飛行機の操縦ができますか？

3 Let's go fly a kite. 凧揚げに行こう。

The flag flew at half-mast.
半旗が掲げられていた。

4 The diamonds will be flown to London tomorrow.
ダイヤモンドは、明日ロンドンに飛行機で運ばれます [空輸されます]。

5 He flew out of the room.
彼は部屋を飛び出した。

My hat just flew off.
帽子が、パッと飛んで行ったんです。

6 Your fly is open.
チャックがあいていますよ。

fly[2] ***n.*** (insect) ハエ

Can't you keep these damn flies off the food?
このうるさいハエが、食べ物にたからないようにできない？

fly-fishing ***n.*** フライフィッシング, 毛ばり釣り

flying ***adj.*** 飛ぶ

n. (traveling by air) 飛行機に乗ること, 飛行

♦**flying saucer** *n.* UFO

foal *n.* 馬の子

foam *n.* (bubbles) 泡, (foam rubber) 気泡ゴム

v. 泡立つ

be foaming at the mouth (be angry) 激怒している, かんかんに怒っている

focal point *n.* (of camera) 焦点, (of interest) 中心

focus *n.* (focal point) 焦点, (of attention) 中心, 的; (on camera) ピント

v. (put in focus: camera, image) (…の) 焦点を合わせる, ピントを合わせる, (**focus on**: direct attention toward) (…に) 注目する, 焦点を当てる

The picture was out of focus.
その写真はピントが外れていた [ピンぼけだった]。

There, now it's in focus.
よし、ピントが合った。

The new English teacher was the focus of attention for most of the evening.
その晩は新しい英語教師が、注目の的だった。

Let's focus on one problem at a time.
一つずつ、問題に焦点を当てていこう。

The government focused on tax reform.
政府は税制改革に的を絞った。

foe *n.* 敵, ((*old fashioned*)) かたき

fog *n.* 霧, もや

♦**foghorn** *n.* 霧笛

foggy *adj.* 霧のかかった, (of memory) ぼんやりした

The roads were foggy.
道路には霧がかかっていた。

foie gras *n.* フォアグラ

foil[1] *n.* (for wrapping up food) ホイル

foil[2] *v.* (thwart) 阻止する, じゃまする

fold *v.* (clothes) たたむ, (paper) 折る, (arms) 組む

n. (in paper, clothes) 折り目

Fold your clothes and put them in a drawer.
服をたたんで引き出しにしまいなさい。

Don't fold the map like that.
そんなふうに地図を折りたたまないで。

I'll have to iron it to get rid of the folds.
((*feminine*)) アイロンをかけて、折りじわを取らなくちゃ。

♦**fold up** *v.* (paper, furniture) 折りたたむ, (wrap up: in paper) 包む

Let's fold it up in some paper.
紙に包もう。

folder *n.* (file) フォルダー, 書類挟み

folk *n.* (**folks**) (people) 人々, (addressing people) みなさん; (folk music) フォーク, (Japanese folk music) 民謡 [→ FAMILY]

♦**folk song** *n.* フォークソング, (Japanese) 民謡

folk tale *n.* 民話

folklore *n.* 民間伝承

follow *v.*

1 PURSUE: (…の後に) ついて来る, ついて行く, (…の後を) 追いかける, 追う, (tail, follow in secret) 尾行する

2 OCCUR AFTER: (as in sequence) …の後に続く, (of trouble) …の後に起きる

3 ADVICE/INSTRUCTIONS: (…に) 従う, (…を) 守る

4 EXAMPLE: (…に)ならう, (…を)まねる

5 UNDERSTAND: (…が)わかる, (…を)理解する

6 TAKE A KEEN INTEREST IN: (news story) (…に)注目する, (trend) 追う

7 BE NECESSARILY TRUE: …(という)ことになる

1 Follow me! ついて来て！

They followed him.
一行は、彼について行った。

I'll follow in half an hour.
３０分ほどしたら、後を追いかけます。

Let's follow the car and see where it goes.
その車を追って、どこへ行くのか見てみよう。

I was being followed by a man.
男に尾行されていた。

Just follow the road for a kilometer or so.
１キロくらい、道なりに行ってください。

2 The meeting was followed by dinner.
会議の後に夕食が続きました。

In the days that followed, she was very ill.
その後何日間も、彼女はとても具合が悪かった。

A tidal wave followed the earthquake.
地震の後に津波が起きた。

3 I doubt if they will follow your advice.
彼らはあなたの助言に従わないと思う。

If you don't follow the rules, they might kick you out.
規則を守らないと、追い出されるかもしれないよ。

4 We did it first and then they followed our example.
私たちがまずやって、それから彼らがそれにならった。

5 I couldn't follow what the teacher was saying.
先生の言っていることが、よくわからなかった。

6 Do you follow baseball?
野球ファンですか？

7 It follows from what she said that she doesn't know anything about our plan.
彼女の言葉からすると、我々の計画を全く知らないことになる。

as follows 次のとおり, ((*written*)) 以下のとおり

not necessarily follow 必ずしも…とは限らない

It doesn't necessarily follow that your system will work.
必ずしも、あなたの方法がうまくいくとは限りませんよ。

follower *n.* (disciple) 弟子, (supporter) 支持者, (fan) ファン, (believer) 信奉者

following *adj.* 次の, ((*formal*)) 以下の, (of day, week, month, year) 翌-

n. (group of supporters) 支持者, (group of fans) ファン, (group of believers) 信奉者

the following morning [week, year]
翌朝 [週, 年]

The following day there was an earthquake.
翌日、地震があった。

The team has a large following.
そのチームにはファンが大勢いる。

follow-up *n.* (sequel) 続き, (further investigation) 追跡

folly *n.* (foolishness) 愚かな行為

fond *adj.* (of look) 優しい, 愛情のこもっ

た, (of memory) 懐かしい

a fond look 優しいまなざし

be fond of (…が) 好きだ

They seem to be fond of going for walks.
あの二人は散歩が好きみたいです。

She is very fond of her cousins.
彼女は、いとこたちがとても好きです。

grow fond of 好きになる, (thing, place) (…に) 愛着を覚える

He hasn't had time to grow fond of the place yet.
彼はまだ、愛着を覚えるほど、そこに長く暮らしていない。

♦**fondness** *n.* (for person) 愛情, (for thing, place) 愛着, (liking) 好み

fondle *v.* (caress) なでる, (molest) (…に) いたずらをする

font *n.* (style of print) フォント

food *n.* 食べ物, 食物, 食料, (foodstuff) 食品, (cuisine) 料理

Food, clothing, and shelter are essentials.
衣食住は不可欠なものです。

Japanese food 和食 [日本食]

Western food 洋食 [西洋料理]

Chinese food 中華料理

French food フランス料理

♦**food chain** *n.* 食物連鎖

food poisoning *n.* 食中毒, 食あたり

food processor *n.* フードプロセッサー

foodstuff *n.* 食品, 食料品

fool *n.* (person without much sense) ばか, ばか者, 愚か者

adj. (foolish) ばかな, 愚かな

v. (deceive) だます

He's a downright fool.
あいつは紛れもないばかだ。

A fool and his money are soon parted.
愚か者は、すぐにお金を使ってしまう。

I feel like a fool.
ばかを見た気分だ/ばかみたい。

He made me look like a fool.
あの人に恥をかかされた。

He was fool enough to try to do it.
彼は愚かにもそれに手を出した。

You don't fool me.
(君には)だまされないよ。

make a fool of ばかにする

play the fool おどける, ふざける

He's always playing the fool.
あいつはいつもおどけている。

fool around *v.* (goof off) ふざける, (play around) 遊ぶ; (**fool around with:** tinker with) いじる, いじくり回す

Quit fooling around!
ふざけるのは、やめなさい!

They just fool around all the time.
あの人たちは、遊んでばかりいる。

foolish *adj.* ばかな, 愚かな, (of behavior, idea) ばかげた, おかしい

foot *n.* (part of the body) 足, (of page) 下部, 下の部分, (of mountain) ふもと; (measure of length) フィート [30.48 cm]

My feet are killing me.
足が痛くてたまらない。

There's a note at the foot of the page.
ページの下の方に注釈があります。

The table measures six feet by four.

テーブルの寸法は6フィートかける4フィート[長さ6フィート、幅4フィート]です。

on foot 歩いて

put one's foot down (refuse to tolerate) きっぱりした態度をとる

put one's foot in it/one's mouth へまをする, どじを踏む

footage *n.* (film) 場面, 映像

football *n.* アメフト [short for アメリカンフットボール, "American football"], (soccer) サッカー; (ball) アメフトのボール

footbridge *n.* 歩道橋

foothills *n.* ふもとの丘

foothold *n.* 足掛かり, 足場

footing *n.* (area around the feet) 足元, (foothold) 足場

lose one's footing 足を滑らせる

footnote *n.* 脚注

footpath *n.* 歩道

footprint *n.* 足跡

footstep *n.* 足音

follow in the footsteps of …の跡を継ぐ

footstool *n.* 足のせ台, 足台

footwear *n.* はき物

footwork *n.* (in sport) フットワーク

for *prep.*

1 IN THE DIRECTION OF: …へ/に, …に向かって, (of bus, train: bound for) …行きの

2 FOR THE POSSESSION/BENEFIT OF: …のために, …に

3 FOR THE PURPOSE OF: …のに, …のために

4 FOR A PERIOD/DISTANCE OF: …の間, …にわたって

5 INDICATING CORRELATION: …に, …ごとに

6 IN PLACE OF: …の代わりに

7 WITH REGARD/RESPECT TO: …には

8 SUITABLE FOR: …向きの, …に適した

9 DATE: …に

10 PRICE: …で

11 IN SUPPORT OF: …に賛成して

12 OWING TO: …から, …ので

13 CONSIDERING THAT IT IS: (expressing surprise) …にしては, …のわりには

1 I left the office for the station at 6 o'clock.
6時に事務所を出て駅へ向かった。

The group set out for home.
一行は家路についた。

Hundreds of thousands of refugees left for Canada and Australia.
何十万人もの難民が、カナダやオーストラリアに向かった。

The economy is headed for disaster.
経済は非常に悪い方向に向かっている。

a train for Kyoto 京都行きの電車

2 I've got a present for you.
あなたにプレゼントがあるんです。

These are for you. これをどうぞ。

There don't seem to be enough for five people.
5人分は、ないみたいだね。

There's a letter for the teacher.
先生あての手紙があります。

3 This box will be useful for storing things.
この箱は、物をしまっておくのによさそうだ。

What will I need for the trip?
旅行には何を持って行けばいいですか?

What for?
何のため?/((*informal*)) なんで?

What did you say this thing was for?

F

これは何のためだと言ってましたっけ？

4 We'll be away for the whole summer.
夏の間ずっと留守にします。

I'll be here for a couple of days.
2、3日、ここにいます。

The guy talked nonstop for an hour.
その男は1時間にわたって、休みなく話し続けた。

We walked for about two kilometers.
私たちは2キロほど歩きました。

5 a household with one car for every member
1人に1台、車のある家庭

For every answer I got right on the test, there were two or three I got wrong.
試験で、1問の正解に対して、2、3問、間違えてしまった。

6 Here, use this for a blanket.
どうぞ、これを毛布の代わりに使ってください。

In the abbreviations *A.M.* and *P.M.*, the *m* is for *meridian*.
略語のA.M.とP.M.のMは、meridianつまり子午線を表します。

7 This is too difficult for me.
これは、私には難しすぎる。

She has a good ear for music.
彼女は音楽がよくわかる。

He's hard up for money.
彼は金に困っている。

8 This book is for children.
この本は子供向きです。

9 Put me down for Friday.
私は、金曜日にして。

10 I bought two for ¥1,000.
1000円で2個、買いました。

11 Are you for going or not?
行くのに賛成ですか、それとも反対ですか？

12 I bet you feel better for the long rest you've had.
((*polite*)) ゆっくりお休みになったから、ご気分がよくなったのではないですか？

13 For you, it's a very good grade.
君にしては、とてもいい成績だ。

It's quite warm for January.
1月にしては、ずいぶん暖かい。

She's tall for her age.
彼女は年のわりに背が高い。

as for …は, …については

As for me, I need some sleep.
私は少し眠りたい。

As for tomorrow's schedule, you'd better ask Mrs. Yamanaka.
明日の予定については、山中さんに聞いたほうがいいですよ。

forbid *v.* 禁止する, 禁じる

We were forbidden to speak to the press.
報道機関に話すことは禁じられていた。

forbidden *adj.* (of place) 立ち入り禁止の; (not allowed) 禁じられた

force

1 *n.* POWER: 力, 威力, (strength) 強さ, (vigor) 勢い, (violence) 暴力, (military might) 武力

2 *v.* COMPEL: (**force to do**) (…に) 無理やり…させる, 強制的に…させる, (**force oneself to do**) 無理に/無理して…する

3 *v.* PUSH/BREAK: (a lock) こじあける, (**force one's way into**) …に押し入る, (**force one's way through**: crowd) 押

し分けて進む

4 ***n.*** **BODY OF PEOPLE:** -隊, 一団, (**forces**: soldiers) 軍隊

1 the forces of nature 自然の力

Are they a force for good or evil?
それは世のためになる力か、それとも災いをもたらす力？

I've taken it back by force.
力ずくで取り戻して来たよ。

The force of the explosion was felt ten kilometers away.
爆発の威力は10キロ離れた所でも感じられた。

The use of force must be a last resort.
武力行使は、最後の手段とすべきだ。

2 I was forced into joining the army.
僕は無理やり軍隊に入隊させられた。

I can't force him to do it.
無理やりやらせることはできない。

I didn't want to do it. I was forced to do it.
やりたくなかったけど、強制的にやらされたんだ。

If you're already full, don't force yourself to eat it.
もうおなかがいっぱいなら、無理して食べなくていいですよ。

3 If the door doesn't open, don't force it.
ドアがあかなくても､こじあけないでね。

The man forced his way into the house.
男は、その家に押し入った。

4 the police force 警察

America has withdrawn its forces.
アメリカは軍隊を撤退させた。

come into force (come into effect) 有効になる, (of law) 施行される

The new tax laws come into force next month.
新しい税法は来月から施行されます。

forced ***adj.*** (compulsory) 強制的な, (affected) 不自然な, 無理につくった

a forced laugh/smile
作り笑い

forceful ***adj.*** (strong) 力強い, (convincing) 説得力のある

forceps ***n.*** (doctor's instrument) 鉗子

forearm ***n.*** 前腕

forecast ***v.*** (the weather) 予報する, (speculate) 予測する, 予想する [→ FORETELL]

n. (weather forecast) 天気予報

It's forecast to rain.
雨の予報が出ている。

The government is forecasting a downturn in the economy.
政府は、景気の悪化を予測している。

forefathers ***n.*** 祖先

forefinger ***n.*** 人差し指 [→ FINGER]

forego → FORGO

foreground ***n.*** (of painting) 前景

forehead ***n.*** 額 [→ picture of FACE]

foreign ***adj.*** 外国(から)の

This country received a lot of foreign visitors last year.
昨年、この国には外国から多くの旅行者が訪れた。

It's so much easier to visit foreign countries now than it used to be.
昔に比べれば、今は外国へ行くのはずっと簡単です。

a foreign language 外国語

a foreign worker 外国人労働者

♦**foreign minister** *n.* 外務大臣

foreigner *n.* 外国人, ((*informal*)) 外人

foreign exchange *n.* 外国為替

♦**foreign exchange rate** *n.* 為替レート, 換算率

foreman *n.* (of manual laborers) 親方, -長 [→ BOSS]

foremost *adj.* (in position) 一番の, (most important) 最も重要な

the foremost authority 第一人者

forensics *n.* 犯罪科学

forerunner *n.* (person) 先駆者, (thing) 先駆け, 前触れ

foresee *v.* 予想する, 予測する

foresight *n.* 先見の明

forest *n.* 森, ((*formal*)) 森林, 山林

forestry *n.* 林業

foretell *v.* (future) 予言する

forever *adv.* (for good) 永遠に, 永久に, いつまでも, (always) いつも, 常に, (continually) 絶えず

Nothing lasts forever.
永遠に変わらないものはない。

They're forever talking about fashion.
あの人たちは、いつもファッションの話ばかりしている。

forfeit *v.* (lose as punishment) 失う, (freedom, right) 剥奪される

forge *v.* (work metal) 鍛えて造る, 鍛造する, (counterfeit) 偽造する

forgery *n.* (counterfeit) 偽造, (crime) 偽造罪

forget *v.* 忘れる, (can't remember) 思い出せない, (umbrella etc.) 置き忘れる

Did you forget to mail the letter?
手紙を出すのを忘れたの？

I'd better not forget to tell him that.
忘れずに、彼にそのことを言わなくちゃ。

I bet he'll forget to call.
あの人きっと、電話するのを忘れるよ。

I almost forgot to lock the back door.
もう少しで裏口のかぎをかけ忘れるところだった。

I'll never forget that experience.
あの体験は、絶対に忘れません。

I've forgotten where I met her.
どこで彼女に会ったのか思い出せない。

Oh, just a minute. I've forgotten my keys.
あ、ちょっと待って。かぎを置いて来てしまった。

♦**forgetful** *adj.* 忘れっぽい

a forgetful person 忘れっぽい人

forgive *v.* 許す

Do you forgive me? 許してくれる？

I don't know how you could forgive him.
どうして彼を許せるのか、わからない。

I will never forgive you for this.
このことは絶対許さない。

I'll forgive you just this once.
今回だけは大目に見ましょう。

forgiveness *n.* 許し, 容赦

ask someone's forgiveness
(...の)許しを請う

forgiving *adj.* 寛大な

forgo *v.* (do without) ...なしで済ます, (pay raise) 見合わせる, (opportunity) 見送る

fork *n.* (for eating) フォーク, (for gardening) くまで; (in road) 分かれ道, 分岐点

forklift *n.* フォークリフト

F

form

1 *n.* PAPER: (printed paper to be filled in) 用紙, (application form) 申込用紙, (document) 書類

2 *v.* ESTABLISH: (group) 組織する, (organization, association) つくる, 結成する

3 *v.* GIVE SHAPE TO: 作る, …の形を作る

4 *n.* TYPE: (**a form of…**) …の一種, (=of art) …の一つの形式

5 *n.* SHAPE: 形, 型

6 *v.* DEVELOP: (idea, opinion) まとめる, (habit) (身に) つける, (relationship) つくる

7 *v.* CONSTITUTE: …である, …となる, 構成する

8 *n.* OF WORD: 語形, -形

1 Fill in this form and wait until your number is called.
この用紙に記入して、番号が呼ばれるまでお待ちください。

That's not the right form.
その書類じゃない。

2 They formed a pressure group to get the city council to clean up the environment.
市議会を環境浄化に取り組ませようと、彼らは圧力団体を組織した。

The association was formed some one hundred years ago.
その協会は、およそ百年前につくられました。

3 I formed a human figure out of the plaster.
その石膏で人の形を作った。

Let's form a circle. 輪になりましょう。

4 It's a form of punishment.
処罰の一種です。

This is a form of modern art.
これは現代美術の一つの形式です。

5 What form will the model take?
その模型はどんな形になるんですか？

6 He formed those ideas while he was in the Navy.
彼は海軍にいた時に、そうした考え方をするようになった。

form a bad habit 悪い習慣を身につける

7 The theory of relativity, along with quantum mechanics, forms the basis of modern physics.
相対性理論は、量子力学と並んで現代物理学の基礎を構成している。

8 a plural form 複数形

formal *adj.* (of ceremony) 正式な, フォーマルな, (official) 公式の, (in form only; lacking substance) 形式的な, (of language) 硬い, 改まった, 堅苦しい

The formal ceremony comes first.
まず正式な式典が行われます。

Is it going to be a formal dinner?
それは正式の晩さん会ですか？

I don't think formal dress is required.
正装する必要はないと思います。

A formal announcement will be made later.
後ほど、公式発表があります。

I've only exchanged formal greetings with him.
その人とは、形式的なあいさつを交わしたことしかない。

formality *n.* 形式的なこと, 形だけのこと, (of behavior) 堅苦しさ

The test is just a formality.
この試験は形だけのことだ。

formalize *v.* 正式なものとする

formally ***adv.*** 正式に, (officially) 公式に, (courteously) 礼儀正しく

The (company) president formally resigned yesterday.
社長は昨日、正式に辞任しました。

format ***n.*** (of computer document) フォーマット, 書式, (of book: size) 判型
v. (disk) 初期化する, フォーマットする

formation ***n.*** 形成, (of aircraft, army) 編隊

former ***adj.*** (previous) 前の, かつての, 以前の, 元-, 前-
n. (**the former**) 前者, ((*informal*)) 前のほう

a former colleague かつての同僚

Former prime ministers can still be influential.
元首相が、依然として影響力をもっている場合もある。

formerly ***adv.*** 以前(は), かつて(は)

formidable ***adj.*** (of opponent, task) 手ごわい, 手に負えそうにない, 大変な

formula ***n.*** (in math) 公式, (in chemistry) 化学式 [→ METHOD]

formulate ***v.*** (idea, response etc.) 順序立てて述べる

fornication ***n.*** 婚外の性交

fort ***n.*** とりで, 要塞

forth ***adv.*** (forward) 前へ, (out) 外へ, (**go forth**) 出る, 出て行く

From this day forth... 今日以降...

back and forth 行ったり来たり

forthcoming ***adj.*** (coming) 今度の, 来たるべき; (of person) 率直な, 協力的な

forthright ***adj.*** 率直な

forthwith ***adv.*** ただちに

fortify ***v.*** (strengthen) 強化する, 強くする

fortnight ***n.*** 2週間

fortress ***n.*** 要塞

fortunate ***adj.*** 運のよい, 幸運な, 幸いな

It was fortunate that you didn't arrive a few minutes earlier.
((*polite*)) お見えになったのが数分あとで、幸いでした。

fortunately ***adv.*** 運よく, 幸い(なことに)

Fortunately, the cost was well within our budget.
運よく、費用は十分予算内におさまった。

The damage was not too bad, fortunately.
幸い、被害は大きくなかった。

fortune ***n.*** (luck) 運, 運勢; (large amount of money) 大金

Fortune smiled on us.
私たちに運が向いてきた/幸運の女神が私たちにほほえんだ。

They spent a small fortune on their vacation.
あの二人は休暇に大金をつぎ込んだ。

That dress must have cost a fortune.
あのドレスは相当高かったに違いない。

tell sb's fortune (...の)運勢を占う

fortune-teller ***n.*** 占い師, 易者

♦**fortune-telling** ***n.*** 占い

forty ***n.*** 40, 四十, (**the forties**) 40年代, (**one's forties**) 40代
adj., pron. 40の, (people) 40人(の), (things) 40個(の)

forum ***n.*** フォーラム, (place for debate) 討論の場

forward

1 ***adv.*** TOWARD THE FRONT: (also **forwards**)

前に/へ, 前の方に/へ

2 *v.* **REDIRECT:** (letter, e-mail) 転送する

3 ***adj.*** **PUSHY:** 厚かましい, でしゃばりの

4 ***adj.*** **DIRECTED TOWARD THE FRONT:** 前の方への

1 Could you all move forward a bit?
みなさん、少し前の方へお詰め願えますか？

Let's face the seats forward (=in the direction the train/bus moves).
席を進行方向に向けよう。

Could you pull your chairs forward a bit?
椅子を、少し前に引き寄せてもらえますか？

Lean forward. 前かがみになって。

2 I suppose we have to forward all this mail to their new address.
この郵便物はみんな、あの人たちの転居先へ転送しないといけないんでしょうね。

3 I would describe him as a very forward person.
((*polite*)) あの方は、非常に厚かましいと申しましょうか。

4 a forward movement 前進
forward progress 進歩

look forward to → LOOK

fossil ***n.*** 化石

♦**fossil fuel** ***n.*** 化石燃料

foster *v.* (a child) 養育する; (encourage) 促進する

♦**foster parents** ***n.*** 里親

foul ***adj.*** (of smell) 臭い, (of language) 汚い

n. (in sport) 反則, ファウル

v. 反則する, (in baseball) ファウルを打つ

♦**foul up** ***v.*** (screw up) しくじる, (ruin) 台なしにする

found *v.* (institution) 創立する, (city) 建設する, (**be founded on**: of design, principle etc.) …に基づく

Aikido was founded by Morihei Ueshiba.
合気道は植芝盛平によって創始された。

Western law is founded on Christian principles.
西洋の法はキリスト教の原理に基づいている。

foundation ***n.*** (of building, idea) 基礎, 土台, (institution) 財団, (endowment) 基金; (cosmetic) ファンデーション

This foundation was formed to help women in developing countries.
この財団は、開発途上国の女性を支援するために設立されました。

the Japan Foundation 国際交流基金

founder ***n.*** 創立者

foundry ***n.*** 鋳造所, 鋳物工場

fountain ***n.*** 噴水

fountain pen ***n.*** 万年筆 [→ picture of STATIONERY]

four ***n.*** ４, 四 [also read し]

adj., pron. ４の, (people) ４人(の), (things) ４個(の), 四つ(の)

fourteen ***n.*** １４, 十四

adj., pron. １４の, (people) １４人(の), (things) １４個(の)

fourteenth ***n.*** 第１４, １４番目, (date) １４日

adj. 第１４の, １４番目の

fourth ***n.*** 第４, ４番目, (date) ４日, (a quarter) ４分の１

adj. 第４の, ４番目の

four-wheel drive *n.* 4WD

fowl *n.* 鶏, (meat) 鶏肉, 鳥肉

fox *n.* キツネ, 狐

♦**foxhunting** *n.* キツネ狩り

foyer *n.* ロビー

fraction *n.* 分数, (a little bit) 少し

fracture *n.* (break in bone) 骨折, (crack in bone) ひび

v. (break: bone) 折る, (crack: bone) (…に) ひびが入る

fragile *adj.* (easily broken) 壊れやすい, もろい; (of person) きゃしゃな, か弱い, ひ弱な

a fragile vase 壊れやすい花びん

Fragile. (Handle with care.)
割れ物注意

fragment *n.* 破片, 断片, かけら, (part of larger thing) 一部分

fragrance *n.* 香り

fragrant *adj.* 香りのよい

frail *adj.* (weak) 弱い, 虚弱な

The refugees looked so frail.
難民はとても弱っているように見えた。

frame

1 *n.* STRUCTURE: (window frame) 枠, (picture frame) 額縁, (of bed, machine) 骨組み, (**frames**: for glasses) 縁, フレーム

2 *v.* PUT IN A FRAME: (picture) 額に入れる

3 *v.* EXPRESS: (thought, question) 言い表す

4 *v.* CAUSE TO BE A SUSPECT OF A CRIME: (…に) ぬれぎぬを着せる, ((*informal*)) はめる

5 *n.* BODY: (of person) 体格, 骨格

6 *n.* OF FILM: こま

1 We have to assemble the frame first.
まず、骨組みを組み立てないと。

Those are stylish frames.
それは流行のフレームです。

2 You ought to frame it.
額に入れなくちゃいけないね。

3 I'm not sure how to frame the question.
その問題をどう言い表せばいいのかわからない。

4 He says he's been framed.
彼はぬれぎぬを着せられたと言っている。

framework *n.* 骨組み, 枠組み

France *n.* フランス, ((*in abbr.*)) 仏

franchise *n.* (business) フランチャイズ

frank *adj.* (of person) 率直な, 遠慮のない, (of expression) はっきりとした

We had a frank discussion.
私たちは率直に話し合った。

frankly *adv.* 率直に, 遠慮なく, はっきり(と), (used at the beginning of a sentence) はっきり言うと, 正直なところ

frantic *adj.* 熱狂した

fraternal *adj.* (brotherly) 兄弟の

fraternity *n.* (society of male university students) 男子学生社交クラブ, (group of friends) 仲間

fraud *n.* (deceit) 詐欺

freak *n.* (strange person) 変人, 変わった人, (enthusiast) フリーク, マニア, -狂

♦**freak accident** *n.* 異常な事故

freckle *n.* そばかす

free

1 *adj., adv.* AT LIBERTY: 自由な/に

2 *adj., adv.* AVAILABLE WITHOUT PAYMENT: 無料の/で, ((*informal*)) ただの/で

3 *adj.* LIBERATED: (**be free of/from**) …の

ない, …から逃れた

4 ***adj.*** **NOT BUSY:** あいている, 暇な

5 ***v.*** **SET FREE:** 自由にする, 解放する, (prisoner) 釈放する

6 ***adj., adv.*** **NOT FIXED:** 自由な/に, 固定していない/固定せずに

7 ***adj.*** **OF FOOD/DRINK:** (**-free**) …抜きの

1 A free society does not mean people can do as they please.
自由な社会といっても、やりたいようにやれるというわけではない。

We weren't free to talk about the matter.
その件について自由に発言することは、禁じられていた。

You are free to play now.
もう遊びに行ってもいいよ。

Feel free to stay here for a couple of days.
どうぞ、ご遠慮なく2、3日ゆっくりしていってください。

Let the bird go free.
鳥を逃がしてやりなさい。

2 I got a free ticket.
無料のチケットを手に入れた。

Today's screening will be free and open to the public.
本日の上映は無料で、どなたでもご覧になれます。

The drink was free.
飲み物はただ [サービス] だった。

3 a world free from oppression
迫害のない世界

be free from interference
干渉を受けない

be free from blame 何の罪もない

(*speaking of ex-husband*) I'm glad I'm finally free of him.
やっとあの人から逃れられてうれしい。

4 Are you free this Saturday?
今度の土曜日、あいてますか？

What do you do in your free time?
暇な時は何をしていますか？

I'm afraid he's not free at the moment.
あいにく、彼は今、手がふさがっています。(lit., "his hands are occupied")

5 Most of the political prisoners were freed.
政治犯の大半は釈放された。

6 The sliding door has come free of its groove.
押し入れの戸が外れてしまった。

7 caffeine-free coffee
カフェイン抜きのコーヒー

♦**free enterprise** ***n.*** 自由企業

free trade ***n.*** 自由貿易

freedom ***n.*** 自由

freelance ***adj.*** フリーの
n. フリーランサー

freely ***adv.*** 自由に, (without reserve) 遠慮なく

freestyle ***n.*** (type of competition) フリースタイル, (in swimming) 自由形, (=the crawl) クロール

freeway ***n.*** 高速道路

free will ***n.*** 自由意思

of one's own free will
自由意思で [自発的に]

freeze ***v.*** (become ice) 凍る, 凍結する, (become numb with cold) 凍える, (preserve by freezing) 冷凍する; (stop with fear) 凍りつく

Look! The lake has frozen.

ほら！湖が凍ってる。

I froze when I heard a knock at the door.
ドアをコツコツたたく音を聞いて、凍りついた。

freeze to death 凍え死ぬ

freeze-dried *v.* 凍結乾燥した, フリーズドライの

freezer *n.* 冷凍庫, フリーザー

freezing *adj.* (cold) 凍えるほど寒い, 凍るような

I'm freezing. Let's go in.
寒くて凍えそうだ。中に入りましょう。

It's freezing cold tonight.
今夜は凍えるほど寒い。

freight *n.* (transportation of cargo) 貨物運送, (cargo) 貨物, (freight train) 貨物列車, (charge) 運送料, 運賃

French *n.* (person) フランス人, (language) フランス語

adj. (of country, culture) フランスの, (of person) フランス人の, (of language) フランス語の

french fry *n.* フライドポテト

French horn *n.* フレンチホルン

frequency *n.* (number of times) 回数, (measure of occurrence: of word etc.) 頻度; (of radio) 周波数

frequent *adj.* たびたびの, しばしばの, 頻繁に…する

v. (visit) (…に) よく行く

He's a frequent visitor. 彼は常連だ。

frequently *adv.* よく, しばしば, しょっちゅう, 頻繁に

fresh *adj.*

1 OF FOOD: 新鮮な, 新しい, (of fish, vegetables) とれたての, (only of fish) 生きのいい, (of things just out of the oven: freshly baked) 焼きたての

2 NEW/RECENT: 新しい, 新たな, (of memory: vivid) 鮮やかな, (of paint etc. that has just been applied) 塗りたての

3 OF AIR/WEATHER: すがすがしい, さわやかな, (only of air) 新鮮な

4 OF MIND/FEELING: さわやかな, すっきりした

5 IMPUDENT: 生意気な

1 I bought some fresh fruit.
新鮮な果物を買って来たよ。

The fish they serve at that restaurant are always fresh.
そのレストランで出る魚は、いつでも新鮮だ。

The bakery across the street sells fresh bread every morning.
向かいのパン屋は毎朝、焼きたてのパンを売っている。

2 Well, this is certainly a fresh development.
なるほど、これは確かに新しい展開だ。

What we need most of all is a fresh approach to the problem.
何より必要なのは、この問題に対する新たな取り組み方です。

The smell of fresh paint in the hallway is overwhelming.
廊下は、塗りたてのペンキのにおいが強烈だ。

3 The air is wonderfully fresh.
空気が、とってもすがすがしい。

It's smoky in here. Let's open the window and let in some fresh air.

ここは煙いな。窓をあけて、新鮮な空気を入れましょう。

4 I'll write it tomorrow morning, when my mind is fresh.
明日の朝、すっきりした気分になってから書こう。

5 Don't be fresh with me, young man!
君、生意気な態度はよしなさい！

freshly ***adv.*** 新たに, 新しく

♦**freshly-squeezed** ***adj.*** (of juice) 絞りたての

freshman ***n.*** 1年生, 新入生

freshwater ***adj.*** 淡水(性)の
freshwater fish 淡水魚
a freshwater lake 淡水湖

friar ***n.*** 修道士

friction ***n.*** 摩擦

Friday ***n.*** 金曜日

fridge ***n.*** (refrigerator) 冷蔵庫

fried ***adj.*** (cooked using frying pan) 焼いた, いためた, (deep-fried) 揚げた
fried eggs (sunny-side up) 目玉焼き

friend ***n.*** 友達, 友人, ((*formal*)) 友, (helper, ally, support) 味方, 支持者, (buddy, mate) 仲間, 相棒
Is Matthew your friend?
マシューとはお友達ですか？
They've been good friends for many years.
彼らは古くからの親友だ。
It's not easy to make friends when you are shy.
人見知りをする人は、友達をつくるのも簡単ではない。
Dog is man's best friend.
犬は人間の最良の友です。
Do you want to be friends with him again?
彼と仲直りしたいの？

friendly ***adj.*** 親しみやすい, フレンドリーな, (kind) 親切な, 好意的な, (amiable) 愛想のいい, (of government) 友好的な

friendship ***n.*** 友情

frigate ***n.*** フリゲート艦

fright ***n.*** (fear) 恐怖

frighten ***v.*** 怖がらせる, (surprise) びっくりさせる, (threaten) 脅かす
Do rats frighten you?
ネズミは怖いですか？
You frightened the bejesus out of me.
びっくりさせないでよ。(lit., "Don't startle me.")

frightened ***adj.*** 怖い, おびえる, (speaking about sb else) 怖がる
Frightened? Who me? Are you kidding?
怖いかって？ 僕が？ まさか。
He's frightened by the look of your dog.
彼は、君の犬の形相におびえているよ。
She looked frightened.
彼女は怖がっているように見えた。

frightening ***adj.*** 怖い, 恐ろしい

frigid ***adj.*** (extremely cold) 極寒の; (of woman) 不感症の

Frigid Zone ***n.*** 寒帯

frill ***n.*** フリル
no frills (余分な)サービスなし

fringe ***n.*** (of hair: bangs) 前髪, (on material) 房飾り; (of place: outermost edge) 外れ, 周辺

♦**fringe benefit** ***n.*** 付加給付

Frisbee ***n.*** フリスビー

frisk *v.* (search) ボディーチェックする

frisky *adj.* 元気にはね回る

frivolous *adj.* (of words, activity) 不真面目な, 浅はかな

frog *n.* カエル, 蛙

♦**frog spawn** *n.* 蛙の卵

frogman *n.* 潜水夫

from *prep.*

1 POINT OF DEPARTURE: …から

2 STARTING TIME: …から

3 INDICATING ORIGIN/SOURCE: …から, (of person) …出身の, (of product) …産の

4 INDICATING COMPOSITION: …で, …から

5 KEEP/PREVENT FROM: …を

6 PLACE OF BELONGING: …から, …を

7 DIFFERENT FROM: …と(違って)

8 INDICATING CAUSE: …で/に, …のために

1 We took a taxi from the station.
駅からタクシーに乗りました。

We drove down from Chicago.
シカゴから車で来たんです。

Where did this train start from?
この電車は、どこ始発ですか/この電車の始発駅はどこですか？

Where is that light coming from?
この光はどこから差し込んでいるんだろう？

The children got down from the roof.
子供たちが屋根から下りて来た。

How far is it from here to your home?
ここからご自宅まで、どのくらいありますか？

You can't see the sea from here.
ここからは海は見えません。

Someone was shouting from a distance.
遠くで、誰かが大声を出していました。

2 From start to finish it took an hour and a half.
開始から終了まで、1時間半かかった。

I read the book from beginning to end in two hours.
その本を、始めから終わりまで2時間で読みました。

It rained on and off from 9 o'clock in the morning till 8 o'clock at night.
朝9時から夜8時にかけて、雨が降ったりやんだりした。

From October, our schedule is expected to change.
10月から、スケジュールが変わることになっています。

I've still got work to do from last night.
ゆうべからやっている仕事が、まだ残っているんだ。

3 He's the man from the insurance company.
保険会社から来た人です。

We got a letter from Jane yesterday.
昨日、ジェーンから手紙が届いた。

He said he'd heard about it from you.
彼は、あなたから聞いたと言っていたよ。

Ms. Sugiyama is from Sapporo.
杉山さんは札幌の人[出身]です。

Are these bananas from the Philippines?
このバナナはフィリピン産ですか？

4 Butter is made from milk.
バターは牛乳から作られます。

What's spaghetti made from?
スパゲティーの原料は何ですか/スパゲティーは何で作られますか？

5 He was wearing gloves to keep his hands from getting cold.

手を冷やさないように、彼は手袋をはめていた。

This medicine will prevent you from getting seasick.
この薬は船酔いを止めてくれるよ。

6 They escape from the big city every weekend.
週末になると、彼らは都会から脱出する。

She graduated from Harvard last year.
彼女は去年、ハーバードを卒業しました。

He retired from the company at sixty.
彼は６０歳で会社を退職した。

7 It was very different from what I had expected.
私の予想と、ずいぶん違いました。

Sometimes children of the same parents can be very different from one another.
同じ両親から生まれた子供でも、性格は一人一人全く違うことがある。

8 He suffers from migraine headaches.
彼は偏頭痛に悩んでいる [持ちだ]。

front

1 ***adj.*** **LOCATED AT THE FRONT:** 前の, 一番前の, (of building) 正面の, 表の, (of train) 先頭の

2 ***n.*** **FOREMOST SIDE/PART:** (**the front**) 前の方, 前方, 前面, (of building) 正面, 表, (of book) 表紙

3 ***n.*** **IN WAR:** (**the front**) 最前線

4 ***n.*** **WEATHER:** 前線

1 He has lost a front tooth.
彼は前歯を1本なくした。

The front entrance was locked.
正面玄関は、かぎがかかっていた。

If you get in the front car of the train, I'll know where to wait for you on the platform.
電車の先頭車両に乗ってくれたら、ホームのどこで待てばいいかわかるよ。

2 Come to the front, please.
前の方へ、いらしてください。

The front of the building is beautiful, but the back is dreadful.
建物の正面はきれいだけど、裏側は汚いです。

3 He fought at the front.
彼は最前線で戦った。

4 a cold [warm] front 寒冷 [温暖] 前線

in front of …の前に/で

He used to sit in front of me when we were in elementary school.
小学校の時、彼は私の前の席でした。

There's an enormous statue in front of the station.
駅前に、巨大な像が建っています。

She'd never say such a thing in front of her parents.
彼女が両親の前で、そんなことを言うはずがない。

♦**front desk** ***n.*** (of hotel) フロント

front door ***n.*** 正面玄関, 玄関口

front page ***n.*** (of book) 扉, (of newspaper) 第一面

front tooth ***n.*** 前歯

frontier ***n.*** (between countries) 国境; (of knowledge) 最前線, 最先端

frost ***n.*** 霜

frostbite ***n.*** 凍傷

frosting ***n.*** (for cake) アイシング, 砂糖衣

frown ***v.*** いやな顔をする, (grimace) 顔をしかめる, (**frown on**) 好まない, ((*formal*)) …に難色を示す

n. しかめっ面

frozen *adj.* 凍った, 凍結した, (of food) 冷凍の

The road is frozen.
道路が凍結している。

Most of the fish were frozen.
大半は冷凍の魚だった。

frugal *adj.* つましい, 節約する

fruit *n.* 果物, 果実

fruitful *adj.* 実り多い, 有意義な

fruitless *adj.* むなしい, むだな

frustrate *v.* (annoy) いらいらさせる, (hinder) じゃまする

frustrated *adj.* (annoyed) いらいらする, (dissatisfied) 欲求不満の

frustrating *adj.* (disappointing) 悔しい, (irritating) いらいらする, いらだたしい

frustration *n.* (dissatisfaction) 欲求不満, (vexation) フラストレーション

fry *v.* (with butter/oil in a pan) 焼く, (stir-fry) いためる, (deep-fry) 揚げる

♦**frying pan** *n.* フライパン

FTC *n.* 連邦取引委員会

fuck *v.* (have sex) (…と) やる

n. (act of having sex) セックス, (sex partner) (セックスの) 相手

interj. (expressing annoyance) ちくしょう, くそ

Fuck it! ちくしょう, くたばれ

Fuck off! うせろ, 消えろ

Fuck you! くたばれ, ばかやろう

I don't give a fuck 知ったことか, くそくらえだ

♦**fuck around** *v.* (fool around) ふざける, (sleep around) 誰とでも寝る

fucking *adv.* (used emphatically) すごく

fuck up *v.* (screw up) へまをやる, どじを踏む, (ruin) 台なしにする

fuck with *v.* (make a fool of) ばかにする; (tinker with) いじくり回す

fuel *n.* 燃料

v. (…に) 燃料を供給する

fudge *n.* (chocolate) ファッジ

v. (avoid) 避ける, はぐらかす

Stop fudging the issue and face the facts.
問題を避けて通るのはやめて、事実と向き合いなさい。

fugitive *n.* (person on the run) 逃亡者, (wanted person) 指名手配人

fulfill *v.* (function) 果たす, (condition, request, ambition) 満たす, かなえる, 実現する, (order) 実行する

You can't fulfill your ambitions if you don't make the effort.
努力しなければ、夢はかなえられないよ。

fulfilling *adj.* 充実感のある, 満ち足りた

fulfillment *n.* (satisfaction) 満足感, 充実感, (realization: of dream) 実現

full *adj.*

1 COMPLETELY FILLED: いっぱいの, (of seating) 満席の, (of train) 満員の

2 HAVING/CONTAINING A LOT: (be full of) (…で) いっぱいだ, あふれている

3 MAXIMUM: 最大限の

4 EMPHASIZING AMOUNT: まる-, 満-

1 The bucket was full.
バケツは、いっぱいだった。

I'm full and couldn't possibly eat anymore.
おなかがいっぱいで、これ以上食べら

れません。

The bar was full and there was nowhere to sit.
飲み屋はいっぱいで、座る所がなかった。

That flight is already full.
その便はもう満席です。

a full train 満員電車

2 The room was full of flowers.
部屋は花であふれていた。

He was full of news about his new project.
彼は、新しいプロジェクトの話ばかりした。

The train was full of people, and I just couldn't get on.
電車は満員で、乗れなかった。

These socks are full of holes.
この靴下は穴だらけだ。

3 Let's try to make full use of our time.
時間を最大限に活用しよう。

4 It's a full two-day journey on foot.
徒歩で、まる2日の行程です。

be full of oneself うぬぼれている

KANJI BRIDGE

満 ON: まん KUN: み(ちる/たす) | **FULL**

full	満杯
full bloom	満開
full moon	満月
full (of people)	満員
full (of seating)	満席
full (of stomach)	満腹
high tide	満潮
perfect score	満点
satisfaction	満足

full-fledged *adj.* (of lawyer etc.) 一人前の, (of company) 独立した

full-scale *adj.* (of model) 実物大の, (of operation) 全面的な
a full-scale war 全面戦争

full-size *adj.* 普通サイズの, 標準サイズの

full time *n.* フルタイム, 常勤

full-time *adj.* フルタイムの, 常勤の, (of teacher) 専任の
adv. フルタイムで, 常勤で
a full-time (company) employee 正社員

♦**full-time job** *n.* 常勤の仕事, (job that takes up all of one's time) かかりきりになる仕事

fully *adv.* (completely) 完全に, (sufficiently) 十分に; (emphasizing amount) 少なくとも, 優に

fumes *n.* (smoke) 煙, (gas) ガス
car exhaust fumes 車の排気ガス

fun *n.* 楽しみ, 面白さ
adj. 楽しい, 面白い
It was great fun. とても楽しかった。
Where's the fun in that?
それのどこが楽しいの?
You call that fun? Well, you really are weird.
あれが面白いだって? 君は、ほんとに変わり者だね。
It'll be a fun occasion where everybody can get to know one another.
みんなが仲良くなれるような、楽しい催しになりますよ。

for fun (for kicks) 面白半分に, (as a joke) 冗談で
They said they did it for fun.
面白半分にやったと言っていた。

have fun 楽しむ

We had a lot of fun at Junko's party.
淳子のパーティーは、とっても楽しかった。

make fun of (make a laughingstock of) 笑い者にする, (tease) からかう

You shouldn't make fun of people just because they're different from you.
自分と違うからといって、人を笑い者にすべきではない。

function *n.* (of machine) 機能, 働き; (role, purpose) 役目, 役割 [→ CEREMONY]

What exactly is his function in this organization?
この組織でのその人の役割は、具体的にはどういったものですか?

functional *adj.* 機能的な, (practical) 実用的な

fund *n.* 基金, 資金

v. (...に) 資金を出す

fundamental *adj.* 基本的な, 根本的な, (basic) 基礎の, (essential) 必須の, 欠かせない [→ BASIC]

the fundamental principles of physics
物理の基本原理

There are fundamental differences between the two sides.
両者には、根本的な違いがあります。

These methods are fundamental to good research.
これらの方法は、すぐれた研究には欠かせないものです。

fundamentalism *n.* 原理主義

fundamentalist *n.* 原理主義者

fundamentally *adv.* (basically) 基本的に, 根本的に

funding *n.* (money) 資金, (act of supplying money) 出資

fund-raising *n.* 募金

funeral *n.* (お)葬式, 葬儀, 告別式

hold a funeral 葬儀を行う

funeral money contribution (お)香典

♦**funeral director** *n.* 葬儀屋

funeral home *n.* 葬儀場

fungus *n.* (plant) キノコ, (mold) カビ

funk *n.* (music) ファンク

funky *adj.* ファンキーな

funnel *n.* (for pouring liquid) じょうご, (funnel-shaped object) じょうご形の物; (chimney) 煙突

v. (money) つぎ込む, (liquid) 注ぐ

funny *adj.* 面白い, おかしい, (laughable) 笑える, (comical) こっけいな, ひょうきんな, (odd) おかしい, 変な

It was a really funny movie.
すごくおかしい映画だった。

He's a funny guy.
彼はひょうきんな奴だよ。

That's funny. I thought I left my camera in the back of the car.
変だな。車の後部座席にカメラを置いて来たと思ったのに。

fur *n.* 毛, (of garment) 毛皮

furious *adj.* 激怒した, ものすごく怒った

furnace *n.* (boiler) ボイラー, (for melting metal etc.) 炉

furnish *v.* (install furniture in) (...に) 家具を備え付ける

furnished *adj.* 家具付きの

a furnished apartment 家具付きアパート

furniture *n.* 家具

furry *adj.* (of animal) 毛でおおわれた

further

1 *adv.* MORE: もっと, さらに, それ/これ以上

2 *adj.* ADDITIONAL: それ/これ以上の, ((*formal*)) さらなる

3 *adv.* FARTHER: もっと先に, さらに遠くに [→ FAR 1]

1 He fell further into debt.
彼は、さらに借金を重ねた。

I don't want to say anything further at this stage.
今の段階では、これ以上お話ししたくありません。

2 A further round of talks was arranged.
さらに、会談が行われることになった。

A further $100 is needed.
さらに100ドル必要です。

For further information, please see our website.
詳細はホームページをご覧ください。

3 If you go further down the road, you'll see it.
このまま道なりに行けば、見えてきますよ。

The further you go, the better it gets.
先へ行けば行くほど、よくなります。

Should we go further? Or should we turn back?
もっと先に進む？ それとも引き返す？

furthermore *adv.* さらに, その上, それに

furthest *adv.* 一番遠い, 最も遠くに [→ FAR 1]

fury *n.* (anger) 激怒, 怒り

fuse *n.* (part of electric circuit) ヒューズ

v. (join together) 融合する

blow a fuse ヒューズを飛ばす

fuselage *n.* 胴体, 機体

fusion *n.* (nuclear) 核融合, (of metals) 融解; (music) フュージョン, (food) フュージョン料理, 多国籍料理

fuss *n.* 空騒ぎ, 大騒ぎ

v. (about trivial matter) (…について) 騒ぎ立てる, (complain) うるさく言う, ぶつぶつ文句を言う [→ COMPLAIN, TROUBLE]

Will you stop making such a fuss!
そんなに騒ぎ立てるのは、やめてくれないか！

Would you please stop fussing about the state of my room?
私の部屋のことをうるさく言うのは、やめてくれない？

I'm sick of your fussing.
君のぐちには、もううんざりだ。

fussy *adj.* (irritatingly particular) うるさい, 小うるさい; (too elaborate) ごてごてした

futile *adj.* むだな, 無益な

futility *n.* 無益

an exercise in futility 徒労

futon *n.* 布団

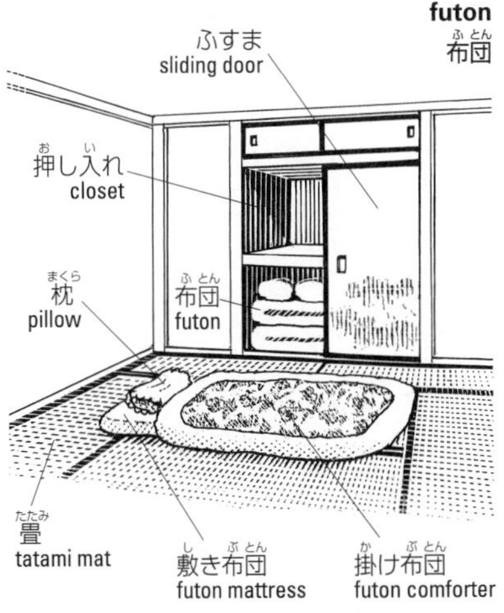

F

future

1 *n.* TIME/EVENTS TO COME: 将来, (distant future) 未来, (events yet to happen) 将来起こること, 今後のこと

2 *adj.* TO COME: これからの, 今後の, 将来の, (of the distant future) 未来の

3 *n.* GRAMMATICAL TENSE: 未来時制

1 She believes her future lies in politics.
彼女は将来、政治の道に進もうと思っている。

In the future, I'd rather you did not use this room.
今後は、この部屋の使用を控えてもらいたい。

I wonder what the computers of the future will be like.
未来のコンピューターは、どんなふうになるんだろう。

The future seems very uncertain right now.
現時点では、今後の成り行きは全くわからない。

in the not-too-distant future
それほど遠くない将来(に)

in the near future
近い将来(に)

in the foreseeable future
当面 [当分]

2 Keep it for future reference.
今後の参考に取っておいて。

We must protect the environment for future generations.
未来の世代のために環境を保護しなければならない。

fuzz *n.* (on person) うぶ毛, (on peach) 綿毛

fuzzy *adj.* (of picture) ぼやけた, (of memory, thoughts) ぼんやりした, はっきりしない, (vague) あいまいな, (of material) けば立った

fuzzy logic あいまい理論

G, g

gabardine *n.* ギャバジン

gadget *n.* 装置, 仕掛け

gag *n.* (for mouth) さるぐつわ; (comical remark) ギャグ

v. (…に) さるぐつわをかませる; (almost regurgitate) 吐き気を催す

The hostages were bound and gagged.
人質たちは縛られて、さるぐつわをかまされた。

gain

1 *v.* OBTAIN: 得る, (experience) 積む, (confidence) (…が) つく, (**gain an/the advantage**) 優位に立つ

2 *v.* INCREASE: 増やす, 増す, (**gain weight**) 太る

3 *v.* GO FAST: (of clock) 進む

4 *v.* BENEFIT: 得をする, 利益を得る

5 *v.* OF RUNNER: (**gain on**: close in on) …に追いつく, …に近づく

6 *n.* PROFIT: 得, 利益

1 Have we gained anything by doing this?
これをやることで、何か得るものはあったのか？

He's gained her trust.
彼は彼女の信頼を得た。

Flying to Japan, do you gain a day or lose one?
飛行機で日本に行くと、1日得することになるの、それとも損することになるの？

Some of his ideas are gaining ground.
彼のいくつかの学説は支持され始めた。

We've gained experience.
私たちは経験を積みました。

This seminar will help you gain confidence.
このセミナーで自信がつきますよ。

We can gain the advantage by marketing our product first.
我々の製品を一番先に市場に出せば、優位に立てます。

2 I've gained three kilos.
体重が3キロ増えた / 3キロ太った。

3 My watch has gained five minutes.
私の時計は5分進んでいる。

4 We only stand to gain by making the effort.
がんばった分だけ得をすることになる。

5 They're gaining on us!
彼らが追いついて来ている！

6 What gain could possibly come from this?
これから何が得られるというのですか？

galaxy *n.* 銀河

gale *n.* 強風, 強い風

gall *n.* (effrontery) 厚かましさ, ずうずうしさ

have the gall to do 厚かましく…する

gallbladder *n.* 胆のう

gallery *n.* (art museum) 美術館, (private art gallery) 画廊, ギャラリー; (in theater) 天井さじき

galley *n.* (ship) ガレー船; (galley proof) ゲラ

gallon *n.* ガロン [U.S. 3.785 *l*, U.K. 4.546 *l*]

gallop *v.* (of horse) ギャロップ / 全速力で駆ける

n. ギャロップ

break into a gallop 全速力で駆け出す

gallstone *n.* 胆石

G

galosh *n.* (**galoshes**) オーバーシューズ

gamble *v.* (money) 賭ける, (**gamble away**) 賭け事で失う, (do gambling) ギャンブルをする, ばくちを打つ, (take a risk) 賭ける

n. 賭け事, ギャンブル, ばくち

He gambled the family's wealth away.
あの人は賭け事で家の財産を失った。

You're gambling with your life.
命を賭けているんですね。

It's a gamble but let's do it.
一か八か、賭けてみよう。

gambler *n.* ギャンブラー, ばくち打ち

gambling *n.* ギャンブル, ばくち

game *n.*

1 FORM OF PLAY: 遊び, ゲーム, (competition) 試合, 競技, (a single game) 1戦, (of tennis: a single round) ゲーム, (**Games**: in names of tournaments) 大会, 競技会

2 STRATEGY: (ulterior motive) 魂胆, 下心, (political strategy) 策略, たくらみ

3 HUNTED WILD ANIMALS: 獲物, (meat) 肉

1 It's a children's game.
子供のお遊びだよ。

a board game ボードゲーム

a video game テレビゲーム

a game of skill 実力本位のゲーム

a ball game 球技

a game of tennis テニスの試合

win [lose] a game 試合に勝つ [負ける]

It's not winning or losing that matters—it's enjoying the game.
勝ち負けは問題じゃない。試合を楽しむことが大切なんだ。

How about a game of shogi?
将棋をやろうか？

He won four games in the first set.
彼は第1セットで4ゲーム取った。

the Olympic Games オリンピック

2 What's his game, I wonder.
あの人の魂胆は一体何だろう。

3 Is there game on the menu?
メニューに肉料理はありますか？

♦**game console** *n.* ゲーム機

gamekeeper *n.* 狩猟場の番人

game show *n.* ゲーム番組, クイズ番組

gang *n.* 一団, グループ, (of criminals) ギャング, 暴力団, (of friends) 仲間, 連中

a gang of kids 子供の一団

join a gang ギャングの一味に加わる

He's a member of a drug gang.
あいつは麻薬組織の一員だ。

gangrene *n.* 壊疽

gangster *n.* 暴力団員, ギャング

gap *n.* (opening) すき間, (between mountains) 峡谷; (disparity) 相違, ギャップ, 隔たり, (deficiency) 欠落, (missing part) 抜けた部分, (interval) 合間 [→ PAUSE]

There's a draft blowing in from the gap under the door.
ドアの下のすき間から、風が吹き込んで来る。

There's a gap in the fence.
フェンスに裂け目がある。

a generation gap
世代の断絶 [ジェネレーション・ギャップ]

There's a gap in the print.
文字が一部欠けています。

garage *n.* (building for parking car) 車

庫, ガレージ [→ picture of HOUSE], (for car repairs) 自動車修理工場

garbage *n.* ごみ, (raw garbage from kitchen) 生ごみ

take out the garbage ごみを出す

Where do we put the garbage?
ごみはどこへ捨てるの？

When will they come to collect the garbage?
ごみの収集日はいつですか？

burnable garbage 燃えるごみ

unburnable garbage 燃えないごみ

bulky garbage (= furniture etc.)
粗大ごみ

recyclable garbage 資源ごみ

garbage collection point/place
ごみ収集場所

garbage collector *n.* ごみ収集員

garbage truck *n.* ごみ収集車

garden *n.* (flower garden) 花畑, 花園, (vegetable garden) 野菜畑, 菜園, (rock garden) 石庭, (yard) 庭, 庭園,

water a garden 庭に水をまく

weed a garden 庭の草むしりをする

gardener *n.* (professional) 植木屋(さん), 庭師, (non-professional) 庭いじりする人

gardenia *n.* クチナシ

gardening *n.* 園芸, (as hobby) ガーデニング, 庭いじり, (as work) 造園, 庭仕事

gargantuan *adj.* 巨大な, ものすごく大きい, ((*informal*)) で(っ)かい

gargle *v.* うがいをする

garish *adj.* 派手な, けばけばしい

garland *n.* 花輪

garlic *n.* ニンニク, ガーリック

garment *n.* 服, (**garments**) 衣類 [→ CLOTHES]

garnet *n.* (mineral) ガーネット, ザクロ石

garnish *v.* (garnish A with B: food) (AにBを) 添える

garter *n.* 靴下留め, ガーター

gas *n.* (for heating and lighting) ガス, (substance) 気体, (gasoline) ガソリン, 石油

turn on [turn off] the gas
ガスの火をつける [消す]

natural gas 天然ガス

lethal gas 致死性ガス

CFC gas フロンガス

Hydrogen is a gas.
水素は気体である。

♦ **gas bill** *n.* ガス料金請求書

gas cooker/stove *n.* ガスレンジ, ガスこんろ

gas heater *n.* (for room) ガスストーブ

gas mask *n.* ガスマスク

gas meter *n.* ガスメーター

gasket *n.* ガスケット

gasoline *n.* ガソリン

gasp *v.* はっと息をのむ

gas station *n.* ガソリンスタンド

Could you pull in at the next gas station?
次のガソリンスタンドで車を止めてもらえますか？

gastric *adj.* 胃の

gastronomy *n.* 美食学

gate *n.* (entrance) 門, 入口 [→ picture of HOUSE], (at airport) ゲート

Go through the gate and up the path to the door.
門を通り抜けて、通路をそのままドアのところまで行ってください。

Let's meet at the main gate.
正門で待ち合わせよう。

gather *v.* (come together) 集まる, 集合する, (bring together) 集める, (flowers) 摘む; (surmise: **I gather...**) わかる, 察する, 思う, ...だろう

Everyone gathered around to listen.
みんなは周りに集まって、耳を傾けた。

I gathered all my things together and put them in a bag.
荷物をすべてかき集めて、バッグの中に入れた。

We gathered strawberries to make jam.
ジャムを作るために、イチゴを摘んだ。

I gather from what you've said that you don't like the guy.
その口ぶりからすると、あの人のことが好きじゃないんだね。

gathering *n.* 集まり, 集い, (party) 懇親会

gaudy *adj.* 派手な, けばけばしい, ちゃらちゃらした

gauge *n.* 計器, ゲージ

v. (measure) 測定する, (assess, judge) 評価する

gauze *n.* (surgical dressing) ガーゼ [→ picture of FIRST-AID KIT]

gay *adj.* (homosexual) ゲイの, 同性愛の

n. (homosexual man) ゲイ [→ LESBIAN]

gaze *v.* じっと見つめる, 凝視する

n. 視線, まなざし

I could feel him gazing at me.
彼が私を見つめているのを感じた。

She gazed blankly across the room.
彼女はぼんやりと部屋を見渡した。

His gaze was tinged with sadness.
彼のまなざしは悲しげでした。

gazelle *n.* ガゼル

gazette *n.* (newspaper) 新聞

gear *n.* (in car) ギア; (equipment) 用具, (machinery) 装置

Before starting, always check to see if the car is in or out of gear.
発車する前に、必ずギアが入っているかどうか確かめてください。

put (a car) into gear (車の)ギアを入れる

in low [high] gear 低速 [高速] ギアで

change gear ギアを変える

camping gear キャンプ用具

fishing gear 釣り用具

gearshift *n.* 変速レバー

geisha *n.* 芸者

gel *n.* (for styling hair) ジェル

gelatin *n.* (used in cooking) ゼラチン

gem *n.* 宝石

Gemini *n.* (the Twins) 双子座

gender *n.* 性, ジェンダー

gene *n.* 遺伝子

genealogy *n.* (of family) 家系図, (of language) 系統

general *adj.* (applying to most cases; not concerned with specifics/exceptions) 一般の, 一般的な, (applying to most people) 世間一般の, (overall) 全体的な, (rough) おおざっぱな

n. (in U.S. Army/Air Force/Marine Corps) 大将

the general public 一般大衆

It's a subject of general interest.
それは一般の人が関心をもっている話題です。

There's a general feeling that there are no honest politicians.
正直な政治家なんていないと、世間の人は思っている。

a general trend 全体的な傾向

It's only meant to be a general outline.
それは概要にすぎません。

He rose through the ranks to become a general.
さまざまな地位を経て、あの人は大将の地位に昇りつめた。

in general (usually) 一般に, 普通, たいてい, (for the most part) おおむね

I agree with you in general.
おおむね賛成です。

♦ **general of the Air Force/Army** *n.* 元帥

generalize *v.* 一般的に言う, 一般化する

Generalizing leads to stereotypes.
何事についても一般的に言ってしまうと、固定観念を生み出してしまう。

You can't generalize about a country from its food.
食べ物から、その国のことを一般化して言うことはできないよ。

You can't generalize about alcohol being bad for everyone.
お酒がすべての人に害を及ぼすとは、一概に言えない。

generally *adv.* 一般的に, 普通, たいてい, ((*formal*)) 概して

Generally speaking...
一般的に言うと...

generate *v.* (power, profit) 生み出す, (electricity) 発生させる, (panic, reaction) 起こす, 引き起こす

generation *n.* (of people) 世代, -代

These people have been coming here for generations.
こうした人々は何代にもわたって、この地を訪れています。

My family has run this business for five generations.
私の家は5代にわたってこの店を経営しています。

They are third-generation Americans.
あの人たちは三世のアメリカ人です。

from generation to generation 代々

generator *n.* (machine) 発電機

generic *adj.* 一般的な

generosity *n.* (willingness to give) 気前のよさ, (tolerance) 寛大さ

generous *adj.* (giving) 気前のいい, (tolerant) 寛大な, 心の広い; (of helping) 大きい, 十分な, たっぷりの

It was generous of him to treat everyone to dinner.
全員に夕食をごちそうしてくれるなんて、気前のいい人ですね。

He's a generous person.
あの人は心の広い人です。

a generous helping of rice ご飯の大盛り

That was a generous portion of cake you got.
君のケーキは一人分にしては大きかったね。

genetic *adj.* (of genetics) 遺伝の, (of gene) 遺伝子の

genetically modified food *n.* 遺伝子組み替え食品

genetics *n.* 遺伝学

genitals *n.* 生殖器, 外陰部

genius *n.* (person) 天才, (creative power) 才能, 天分

genocide *n.* 大量虐殺

genre *n.* (artistic) ジャンル, 分野

gentle *adj.* (of person, manner) 優しい, 穏やかな, (quiet) おとなしい, 静かな; (of slope) なだらかな, ゆるやかな

Ms. Tanabe is very gentle.
田辺さんはとても穏やかな人です。

He has a gentle voice.
その人、優しい声してるね。

gentleman *n.* (well-mannered man) 紳士, ジェントルマン, (man) 男の方, 男の人

There's a gentleman who says he knows you.
((*polite*)) あなたをご存じだという男の方がいらっしゃいます。

ladies and gentlemen みなさん

gently *adv.* (quietly) 静かに, (tranquilly) 穏やかに, (carefully, so as not to hurt/damage) そっと

genuine *adj.* (authentic) 本物の, 正真正銘の; (of person) 誠実な, (of feeling) 心からの, 純粋な

The painting is genuine.
その絵は本物です。

genuinely *adv.* (sincerely) 心から, (truly) 本当に

genus *n.* (taxonomic category) 属

geographical *adj.* 地理的な

geography *n.* 地理, (subject of study) 地理学, (topography) 地形, 地勢

geological *adj.* (of geology) 地質学の, (of quality of earth) 地質の

geology *n.* (subject of study) 地質学, (condition/quality of earth) 地質

geometry *n.* (subject of study) 幾何学

geothermal *adj.* 地熱の

geranium *n.* ゼラニウム, テンジクアオイ

gerbil *n.* アレチネズミ

geriatric *adj.* 老人病の

a geriatric disease 老人病

♦**geriatrics** *n.* 老年医学

germ *n.* ばい菌, 細菌

German *n.* (person) ドイツ人, (language) ドイツ語

adj. (of country, culture) ドイツの, (of person) ドイツ人の, (of language) ドイツ語の

germanium *n.* ゲルマニウム

German measles *n.* 風疹

Germany *n.* ドイツ, ((*in abbr.*)) 独

gerund *n.* 動名詞

gestation *n.* 妊娠, (period of) 妊娠期間

gesture *n.* (movement) 身振り, 手まね, しぐさ, ジェスチャー, (expression of feelings/intent) 意思表示

v. 身振りをする, (**gesture to do**) ...するよう身振りで示す

---

get *v.*

1 BECOME: See examples below

2 CAUSE TO DO/BE: (**get sb to do**) (...に)...させる, (=for you) (...に)...してもらう, (**get sth done**/adjective) ...してもらう, ...させる

3 POSSESS: (**have got**) (...が) ある, (...を)

持っている [→ HAVE 2]

4 ARRIVE: 着く, 到着する, (**get home**) 家に着く, 帰る [→ GET BACK]

5 BRING/FETCH: 取って来る, 持って来る, (person) 連れて来る, (doctor) 呼ぶ

6 OBTAIN: 得る, (also **get hold of**) 手に入れる, (…が) 手に入る, (buy) 買う, (gain: points in a game) 取る

7 RECEIVE: くれる, もらう, (impression) (…という印象を) 受ける, (**get to do**: be allowed to do) …させてもらうことになる

8 CATCH: (disease) (…に) かかる, なる; (criminal) 捕まえる, 捕らえる [→ CATCH 5]

9 UNDERSTAND: (…が) わかる

10 MUST: (**have got to do**) …しなければならない, …する必要がある, (**have got to be**) …じゃないとだめだ [→ MUST, NEED]

11 IN PASSIVE SENTENCES: (get ——ed) <passive form of verb>

1 They got wet. 彼らはぬれてしまった。

Tom gets bored easily.
トムはすぐに飽きてしまう [飽きっぽい]。

He's getting old.
あの人も年をとったね。

There's no point in getting angry.
怒っても仕方がないよ。

Did you get drunk? 酔っ払ったの？

They got married last year.
二人は去年結婚した。

If things get any worse, we'll be out of a job.
これ以上状況が悪くなったら、失業してしまう。

Suppose somebody gets hurt.
誰かが、けがをしたらどうする。

2 You must get Miki to do it.
美紀にやらせなきゃだめだ。

We must get them to face up to the facts.
みんなに事実を直視させなければ。

I've been trying to get him to do that for weeks.
彼にはもう何週間も、やるように言っている。

We managed to get him to talk about it.
なんとか彼にそのことを話してもらった。

get one's hair cut 髪を切ってもらう

I have to get the job done today.
今日中に仕事を終わらせないといけない。

Don't get your clothes dirty.
服を汚さないで。

I can't get the car going.
車がどうやっても動かない。

3 We've got plenty of DVDs.
ＤＶＤはたくさんあります。

Here, I've got some change.
小銭なら少し持ってるよ。

4 What time did you get there?
何時にそこに着いたんですか？

I got to work an hour late.
１時間遅れて、仕事場に着いた。

The plane got to Kennedy Airport thirty minutes late.
飛行機は３０分遅れで、ケネディ空港に到着した。

He didn't get back to the office till after 4 o'clock.
４時過ぎまで、彼はオフィスに戻らなかった。

I'll get home by about noon.
１２時までには家に着くよ。

5 I'll get it for you.
取って来てあげます。

Could you get the paper for me?
新聞を取って来てくれる？

Can I get (=bring) you a drink?
飲み物を持って来ましょうか？

I'm going to go get the mail.
郵便を取って来るよ。

Could you get this package to Mrs. Kato by this evening?
この包みを夕方までに加藤さんに届けてもらえますか？

She looks ill. We'd better get a doctor.
彼女、具合が悪そうだ。医者を呼んだほうがよさそうだよ。

6 Where did you get that?
それ、どこで手に入れたの？

Did you get hold of that book you were looking for?
お探しの本は手に入りましたか？

Why don't you get a car?
車を持てば [買えば]？

He's trying to get an apartment.
彼はアパートを借りようとしている。

I hope she gets a job when she finishes school.
卒業して、彼女に仕事があるといいんだけどね。

You can get advice easily enough.
気軽にアドバイスしてもらえるよ。

Where on earth did you get that idea from?
一体どこから、そんな考えを思いついたんですか？

get some rest 休憩を取る

get good grades いい成績を取る

get a visa ビザを取得する

7 Kenji got that watch for his birthday.
健治は誕生日にその時計をもらった。

I get a letter from her every week.
彼女から毎週手紙が来る。

We got a call from Mr. Tanaka.
田中さんから電話がありました。

How much did you get for your car?
車はいくらで買ってもらえましたか？

get a present プレゼントをもらう

get a prize 賞をもらう

get a pension 年金をもらう

get a grant 補助金 [助成金] をもらう

I got the impression he was interested.
彼は興味がありそうな印象を受けました。

8 She got herpes last year.
彼女は去年ヘルペスにかかった。

Did they get the bastard (=the wanted criminal)?
犯人は捕まった？

9 Do you get what I mean?
私の言いたいことがわかりますか？

I don't think he got the joke.
彼にその冗談は通じなかったと思う。

I got it! Now I know who that strange fellow must have been.
そうか！ あのおかしな人が誰かやっとわかったよ。

10 At some point, this situation has got to change.
いつか、こうした状況は変わらなければいけない。

We've got to go now.
もう行かなくてはいけません。

11 I got punched in the face.
顔を殴られた。

I did not get paid last month.
先月分の給料をもらっていません。

get going (leave) (そろそろ) 出かける, (continue moving at once) さっさと行く
I'd better get going.
私、そろそろ出ないと。

get to know 知り合う, 知り合いになる
I'd like to get to know her.
彼女と知り合いになりたいんです。

get across *v.* (cross) 渡る, 横断する; (communicate) 伝える, わからせる, (…が) 通じる
It's amazing that that old woman got across the street without help.
あのおばあさんが、助けを借りずに通りを渡ったなんて信じられない。
We got our point across.
私たちの意図はわかってもらった。

get along *v.* (of people) 仲よくやっていく, うまくやっていく
They (=those two) seem to get along fine.
あの二人はうまくやってるようですね。

get around *v.*
1 TRAVEL: (walk about) 歩き回る, 出歩く, (get to the other side of: fence, building) 回り道をする, 迂回する, (visit lots of places) あちこち飛び回る
2 CIRCUMVENT: (law) (法の網を)くぐる, (problem) 回避する, 切り抜ける
3 OF STORY/RUMOR: 広まる

1 He's old and can't get around much now.
あの方はもうお年だから、あまり出歩けないんです。
How do we get around this fence?
どうやって、この塀をよけて迂回しよう?
Singapore one week, Hong Kong the next. He really gets around.
ある週はシンガポール、次の週は香港。あの人、あちこち飛び回ってますね。

2 Is there a way to get around the law?
法の網をくぐる方法はある?
There's a lot of red tape, but I think we can get around it.
面倒な手続きはたくさんあるけど、なんとかできると思う。
It was a difficult problem, but she managed to get around it.
厄介な問題だったが、彼女はなんとか切り抜けた。

3 If this news gets around, we're in big trouble.
この話が広まったら、我々は窮地に立たされる。

get around to *v.* (**get around to doing**) …まで手が回る, (find the time/opportunity to do) …する時間/余裕ができる
I haven't got around to doing the dishes.
お皿洗いまで手が回らない。

get at *v.* (reach) 届く, (ascertain) 確かめる, 突き止める; (**getting at**: trying to say) 言おうとしている
I couldn't get at the window to clean it.
窓をふこうとしたけど、届かなかった。
To get at the truth—that's the task of real journalism.
真実を突き止めること——それが真のジャーナリズムの使命だ。
What are you getting at?
((*rude*)) 何を言おうとしているんですか/何が言いたいんですか?

get away *v.* (escape) 逃げる, 逃れる,

抜け出す, (leave) 離れる, 出る, (take a vacation) 休む, 休暇を取る

The thieves got away.
泥棒たちは逃げた。

Those kids got away without paying.
あの子たちは代金を払わずに逃げてしまった。

Sometimes I need to get away from the city.
私には、時々都会を離れることが必要なんだ。

I wanted to get away from the office earlier, but I couldn't.
もっと早く会社を出たかったんだけど、できなかった。

Let's get away for a few weeks—go on a cruise or something.
2、3 週間休暇を取って、船旅にでも出かけよう。

get away with *v.* (steal and flee with) 持ち逃げする, (go unpunished for) …の罰を逃れる, まんまとやってのける

The thieves got away with all the jewelry.
泥棒たちは宝石を全部持って逃げきった。

He's trying to get our customers, but I'm not going to let him get away with it.
あの人は我々の顧客を奪おうとしているけど、思いどおりにはさせない。

You won't get away with it next time.
次はただでは済みませんよ。

If you can get away with that, you can get away with anything.
それをやってのけられるのなら、何でもできるよ。

get back *v.*

1 RETURN: (home) 帰る, 帰って来る, (to starting point, topic, activity) 戻る

2 RECOVER POSSESSION OF: 取り戻す

3 BRING BACK: (book, DVD) 返す, 返却する

4 STEP BACK: (後ろへ) 下がる

5 GET REVENGE: (**get back at**) …に仕返しをする

6 GET IN CONTACT: (**get back to**) …に折り返し連絡する, …にあとで連絡する

1 What time do you think you'll get back?
帰りは何時ごろになる？

I don't know exactly what time I'll get back to the office, but it will be late.
何時に帰社できるか正確にはわかりませんが、遅くなりそうです。

Once the phone rang, I couldn't get back to sleep.
一度電話で起こされてから、もう寝付けなかった。

Can we just try and get back to the point?
本題に戻ってよろしいですか？

Let's get back to work again.
さあ、仕事に戻ろう。

2 I'll have to get that money back.
そのお金は取り戻さなければいけない。

Did you get your book back?
本を返してもらった？

3 You have to get those DVDs back to the store by Friday.
金曜日までにそのＤＶＤを店に返さなきゃならないよ。

4 Get back from the curb, please.
縁石から下がってください。

5 He's just trying to get back at you.
彼は君に仕返ししようとしているだけだよ。

6 I'll get back to you sometime next week.
来週、こちらからご連絡します。

get by *v.* (pass) 通る, 通り抜ける; (just barely survive) なんとかやっていく

Could you move, please, so we can get by?
通れるように、どちらかに寄ってくださいますか？

They manage to get by on very little money.
彼らは、わずかなお金でなんとかやっている。

get by without …なしで済ませる, (**get by without doing**) …せずに済ませる

I can get by without eating lunch.
お昼を食べずに済ませられるよ。

get down *v.*

1 DESCEND: 下りる

2 DEPRESS: (get sb down) 落ち込ませる, (…の) 気をめいらせる

3 WRITE DOWN: 書き留める

4 BEGIN: (**get down to**) …に(やっと)取りかかる

1 Get down from the attic.
屋根裏から下りて来なさい。

The cat won't get down from the tree.
猫が木から下りようとしない。

2 Don't let it get you down.
そんなことで落ち込まないで。

3 This part's important, so get it down.
ここは重要なところだから、書き留めておきなさい。

4 We finally got down to work.
ようやく仕事に取りかかった。

get in / into *v.*

1 ENTER: (car) (…に) 乗り込む, (building: of burglar) (…に) 侵入する

2 PUT/FIT INTO: …に入れる, (key into lock) …に差し込む

3 BRING INSIDE: (**get in**) 中に入れる

4 BECOME INVOLVED IN: (**get into**) …に巻き込まれる

5 WIN AN ELECTION: (**get in**) (選挙に)勝つ

6 UNIVERSITY: (**get into**) …に入る, …に入学する

7 HOBBY: (**get into**) (=become interested in) …に興味をもつ, (=begin) 始める

8 ARRIVE: (**get in**) 着く, (=arrive home) 帰宅する, (家に)帰る

1 We couldn't all get into the car.
全員が車に乗るのは無理だった。

How did the burglar get in?
泥棒はどうやって侵入したんだろう？

2 Can you get it in the closet?
それを押し入れに入れられる？

It was dark, and I had trouble getting the key into the door.
暗かったので、かぎをドアにうまく差し込めなかった。

3 Let's get the tools in out of the rain.
雨にぬれないように、道具を中に入れよう。

4 We got into a traffic jam.
渋滞に巻き込まれてしまった。

I don't want to get you into trouble.
君をトラブルに巻き込みたくない。

They're always getting into arguments.
あの二人はいつも口論になる。

5 Do you think the Democrats will get in?
民主党が勝つと思いますか？

6 He got into a prestigious university.
彼は名門大学に入学しました。

7 When did you get into scuba diving?

いつスキューバダイビングを始めたの？

8 What time did the train get in?
電車が着いたのは何時ですか？

I got in very late last night.
昨日はすごく遅く帰った。

get off *v.*

1 ALIGHT FROM: 降りる, (train) ((*formal*)) 下車する

2 REMOVE: (stain) 取る, 落とす, (clothes) 脱ぐ

3 ESCAPE: (punishment etc.) 逃れる, (**get off with**) ...で済む

4 SEND: (letter) 送る

1 He got off the train [his bike].
彼は電車 [自転車] を降りた。

We get off at the next (bus) stop.
次の停留所で降りますよ。

2 Let's try and get this stain off.
このしみが取れるか試してみよう。

You'd better get those wet clothes off.
ぬれた服を脱いだほうがいい。

3 The criminal got off lightly.
犯人は軽い刑で済んだ。

You're lucky you got off with just a scratch.
かすり傷で済んで、よかったね。

4 I'd better get this letter off.
この手紙を送らなくちゃ。

get on *v.* (make progress) 進む; (put on: clothes) 着る; (board) ...に乗る

How are you getting on with the project?
プロジェクトの進み具合はどうですか？

You'd better get your coat on.
コートを着たほうがいい。

I got on the train at 7 o'clock this morning.
けさ7時に電車に乗った。

get out (of) *v.*

1 LEAVE: (...から/を)出る, 出て行く, (escape)(...から/を)逃げ出す, 抜け出す

2 REMOVE: (stain) 取る, 抜く, (clothes) 脱ぐ

3 BATH/BED: (おふろ/ベッド) から上がる/から出る

4 THE/SB'S WAY: どける

5 OF NEWS: 漏れる

6 DERIVE: ...から引き出す

1 We'd better get out of here quick.
今すぐここを出たほうがいい。

I was glad to get out of that town.
あの町から抜け出せてほっとした。

How do we get out of this situation?
この状況からどうしたら抜けられるだろう？

2 There must be some way of getting these stains out.
このしみを抜く方法があるはずだ。

Get out of those wet clothes before you catch a cold.
((*feminine*)) 早くぬれた服を脱がないと、かぜをひくわよ。

3 I started to feel dizzy by the time I got out of the bath.
おふろから上がるころには、頭がふらふらし始めていた。

I didn't get out of bed till 10 o'clock this morning.
けさは10時までベッドから出なかった。

4 Get out of my way! どいてくれ！

5 If the content of this report gets out, the company is going to be in real trouble.
この報告書の内容が漏れたら、会社は

かなり困るだろう。

6 How do you get five out of this calculation?
この計算から、どうやって5という答えを引き出せるんですか？

get over *v.*

1 OVERCOME: 乗り越える, 克服する, (illness) (…が) よくなる, 治る, (shock) …から立ち直る; (forget) 忘れる

2 CROSS: 渡る

3 MAKE CLEAR TO: (…に) 理解させる, わからせる

1 Have you gotten over that nasty flu?
ひどいインフルエンザは治りましたか？

He eventually got over the shock.
ついに彼はそのショックから立ち直った。

Haven't you gotten over her yet?
彼女のことが、まだ忘れられないの？

2 How do we get over to the other platform?
向こうのホームにはどうやって行くんですか？

3 But how do we get it over to the public?
でもどうやって、それを世間にわからせるんだ？

get round → GET AROUND

get through *v.*

1 PASS/GO THROUGH: 通る, 通り抜ける

2 SURVIVE: 生き抜く, 切り抜ける

3 REACH BY TELEPHONE: (**get through to**) …と連絡がつく, …と電話がつながる

4 OF BILL/LAW: 通過する, 通る

5 WORK/EXAM: 終える, 済ます

6 CAUSE TO UNDERSTAND: (**get through to**) …にわからせる, …に理解させる

1 We got through the tunnel in ten minutes.
10分でトンネルを抜けた。

It's too crowded; we can't get through this way.
ものすごく混んでるね。この道は通り抜けられないね。

2 He got through two wars unscathed.
彼は無傷で2度の戦争を生き抜いた。

I hope he'll get through the operation.
無事に手術を乗り切ってくれることを祈っています。

3 I finally got through to the office.
やっとオフィスと電話がつながった。

4 This plan won't get through the next meeting.
この企画が、次の会議で通ることはないだろう。

5 I didn't have enough time to get through all of the questions.
時間が足りなくて、全部の問題を解けなかった。

6 It's impossible to get through to people like that.
そんなふうに人にわからせるのは難しい。

get through one's head (understand) (…が) わかる, (…を) 理解する

Can't you get it through your head that he's gone?
あの人はもういないんだってことが、まだわからないんですか？

get to *v.* (bother) いらいらさせる, 困らせる [→ GET 4, ARRIVE]

This rain is really beginning to get to me.
この雨は本当に困るなあ。

get together *v.* (come together) 集まる, (bring together) 集める

G

We're all going to get together next week and play golf.
来週みんなで集まってゴルフをする予定です。

get under *v.* ...の下に入る

Let's get under the blankets.
毛布の下に潜り込もう。

You'd better get under here if you don't want to get wet.
ぬれたくなかったら、この下に入ったほうがいい。

get up *v.* (stand up) 立ち上がる, 立つ, (on stage) (...に) 上がる, (get out of bed) 起きる, (climb) 登る

He got up onto the stage and sang a song.
彼はステージに上がって、歌を歌った。

About fifty people got up from their seats and left the conference in protest.
会議中、約50名が席を立ち、抗議して出て行きました。

I usually get up about 7 in the morning.
たいてい7時ごろに起きます。

It took us six hours to get up Mt. Fuji.
富士山に登るのに6時間かかりました。

get-together *n.* 集まり, 懇親会

geyser *n.* 間欠泉

ghetto *n.* ゲットー

ghost *n.* 幽霊, お化け

ghostwriter *n.* ゴーストライター

GI *n.* 米軍兵士, 米兵

giant *adj.* 巨大な, 大型の, ((*informal*)) で(っ)かい

n. (man of great height) 巨人, 大男

a giant corporation 大企業

gibbon *n.* テナガザル, 手長猿

gibe *v.* (taunt) あざける

n. あざけり

giblets *n.* (鶏の) 臓物

gift *n.* プレゼント, 贈り物, (souvenir) おみやげ; (talent) 才能

Here's a gift for Yoko.
陽子さんへのプレゼントです。

It's only a small gift.
心ばかりの物ですが。

He brought back lots of gifts from abroad.
彼は海外から、おみやげをたくさん持って帰って来た。

She seems to have a gift for languages.
彼女には語学の才能があるようです。

♦ **gift certificate/voucher** *n.* ギフト券, 商品券

gifted *adj.* 才能のある

a gifted child 天才児 [才能のある子供]

gig *n.* (booking for band) 出演, 演奏

gigabyte *n.* ギガバイト

gigahertz *n.* ギガヘルツ

gigantic *adj.* 巨大な, ものすごく大きい, ((*informal*)) で(っ)かい

giggle *v.* くすくす笑う

gill *n.* (of fish) (魚の)えら

gimmick *n.* (trick) 仕掛け, (stratagem) 戦略, (designed to cheat sb) 策略, 作戦, (new scheme) 新機軸

gin *n.* ジン

gin and tonic ジントニック

ginger *n.* ショウガ, 生姜, (served with sushi) がり

gingivitis *n.* 歯肉炎

ginkgo *n.* イチョウ

♦ **ginkgo nut** *n.* ぎんなん

ginseng ***n.*** (plant) チョウセンニンジン, 朝鮮人参, (root) 朝鮮人参の根

giraffe ***n.*** キリン

girdle ***n.*** (piece of underwear) ガードル

girl ***n.*** 女の子, 少女, (young woman) 女性

Do you know that girl over there?
向こうにいる女の子を知ってる?

The Wizard of Oz is the story of a girl named Dorothy.
『オズの魔法使い』はドロシーという名の少女の物語です。

She's the girl who works at the bakery.
彼女がパン屋さんで働いている子だよ。

She's the most attractive girl I've ever met.
彼女ほど魅力的な女性に会ったことがない。

That girl who just walked by was wearing the strangest dress.
今歩いて行った人、すごく変なワンピースを着てたね。

girlfriend ***n.*** ガールフレンド, 彼女

girlish ***adj.*** 女の子らしい, 少女のような

gist ***n.*** 要点, 要旨

---

give ***v.***

1 PRESENT TO: あげる, ((*humble*)) 差し上げる, (to oneself/the speaker) くれる, ((*humble*)) 下さる, (**be given**) もらう, ((*humble*)) いただく [→ "GIVING AND RECEIVING" on p. 402]

2 DO (AS A FAVOR) FOR: ...する, ...してあげる

3 HAND OVER: 渡す, (to oneself/the speaker) よこす, (entrust to) 預ける

4 PROVIDE: (advice, opportunity) 与える, (example) 挙げる [→ "COMMON EXPRESSIONS WITH GIVE" on p. 403]

5 DONATE: 寄付する

6 CONVEY: (regards) 伝える, (name, address, details) 教える

7 FEELING/IMPRESSION: (...という感じ/印象を) 与える

8 CAUSE: See examples below

9 YIELD UNDER PRESSURE: (break) 壊れる, (snap) 切れる, (collapse) 落ちる, (crumble) 崩れる; (yield) 屈する

1 I gave him a CD for his birthday.
彼の誕生日にCDをあげた [贈った]。

I would like to buy this book to give to my teacher.
この本を買って、先生に差し上げたい。

Who gave you that?
誰からもらったの/誰がくれたの?

My teacher gave me this pen.
先生がこのペンを下さった。

2 He gave his seat to an old lady.
彼はおばあさんに席を譲った。

I gave him a ride home.
彼を家まで車で送った [送ってあげた]。

3 Have you given Mr. Hara the package?
原さんに包みを渡してくれましたか?

Would you give me the salt, please?
塩を取っていただけませんか?

Just give me the money.
金をよこせばいいんだ。

I gave my bags to the agent at the check-in counter.
チェックインカウンターで、係員に荷物を預けた。

4 They gave me the chance to study abroad.
留学するチャンスを与えてもらった。

GIVING AND RECEIVING

There are several verbs for describing the actions of "giving" and "receiving" in Japanese, and the choice of word depends on the relationship of the giver and recipient. The most basic word for "give," when the recipient is someone other the speaker or a member of his or her in-group, is あげる.

I gave a watch to my friend.
私は友達に時計をあげました。

Mr. Yamada gave a necktie to his younger brother.
山田さんは弟にネクタイをあげました。

The polite 差し上げる is used in the same way as あげる but is reserved for cases when the recipient is of higher social status than the giver.

I gave a pen to my teacher.
私は先生にペンを差し上げました。

The verb used to describe the action of giving to a child, an animal, or a plant—a person or thing of lower social status than the speaker—is やる.

Give the plant some water.
植木に水をやってください。

To say that someone will give something to you, use くれる if the giver's social status is equal to or lower than your own status, or 下さる if it is higher.

(My friend) Watanabe gave me a handkerchief.
渡辺さんは私にハンカチをくれた。

My professor gave me a valuable book.
先生は私に貴重な本を下さいました。

To say that you will be given something—in other words, that you will "receive" something—use もらう, or いただく if the giver is of higher social status than you.

I was given a sweater by a colleague.
私は同僚からセーターをもらった。

I received a telephone call from my teacher's wife.
私は先生の奥様からお電話をいただきました。

To command someone to give you something, use the imperative form ちょうだい or the more polite 下さい (from 下さる). The form くれ (from くれる) is mainly used by men and is considered rude, so it's use should be avoided.

Give me one.
一つちょうだい。

Please give me a reply at your earliest convenience.
ご都合のいい時に、お返事を下さい。

She wasn't given a large enough room.
彼女は、十分な広さの部屋をあてがってもらえなかった。

He was given a raise. 彼は昇給した。

She began giving piano lessons when she graduated from music school.
音楽学校を卒業すると、彼女はピアノの指導を始めた。

5 I would like to give a part of my salary to a charity.
給料の一部をチャリティーに寄付したいと思います。

6 Give my regards to Mr. Sato.
佐藤さんによろしくお伝えください。

I gave him my name and address.
彼に名前と住所を教えた。

7 It gave me quite a shock.
かなりショックを受けました。

He tried to give the impression that he was rich.
彼は金持ちであることを印象づけようとした。

What gave you that idea?
そんな考えをどこから思いついた？

8 I thought I'd give you a surprise.
びっくりさせようと思ったんだ。

The exercise has given me an appetite.
運動をしたら、食欲が出てきました。

9 The chair gave under his weight.
彼の体重で椅子が壊れた。

The government gave in under pressure.
政府は圧力に屈した。

COMMON EXPRESSIONS WITH "GIVE"

give a cold to ...にかぜをうつす
give a cry 叫ぶ
give a lecture 講義をする
give an answer 返事をする
give an example 例を挙げる
give a nod うなずく
give a push 押す
give a shrug 肩をすくめる
give a sigh ため息をつく
give a smile ほほえむ, にっこりする
give attention to ...に注意を払う
give homework to ...に宿題を出す
give one's life for ...に命をささげる
give one's seat to ...に席を譲る
give tea to ...にお茶を出す
give thought to 考える

give away *v.* (secret) 明らかにする, 漏らす, ((*slang*)) ばらす; (as a gift) あげる [→ GIVE 1]

G

Did she give away your secret?
彼女は秘密をばらしたの？

Don't give away the ending!
結末を言わないで！

He gave his car away.
彼は自分の車を人にあげてしまった。

give back *v.* (return) 返す

Give that back to me. それを返してよ。

Did you give the essays back to the students?
生徒に作文を返しましたか？

I didn't give the engagement ring back to him.
婚約指輪はあの人に返しませんでした。

give in (to) *v.* (yield) (…に) 降参する, 屈する, 応じる [→ HAND IN]

I give in! I can't argue with you.
降参だよ。君と言い争ってもかなわない。

The government has no intention of giving in to the workers' demands.
政府は労働者の要求に応じるつもりはないようです。

give out *v.* (distribute) 配る, (phone number) 教える; (break down) 動かなくなる, 故障する

There's always someone standing at the exit giving out leaflets.
必ず出口のところで、ちらしを配っている人がいる。

Don't give out your phone number.
電話番号は教えないほうがいいよ。

The car finally gave out.
車がとうとう故障した。

give up *v.* (quit) やめる, (belief, hope) 捨てる, (idea, plan) 断念する, あきらめる; (**give oneself up**: turn oneself in) 自首する

He's tried to give up smoking many times before.
あの人は、これまで何度もたばこをやめようとしてきた。

I give up. You win.
降参だ。あなたの勝ちだ。

Don't give up hope. He may live.
望みを捨てないで。彼は命をとりとめるかもしれない。

You'd better give up the idea.
そんな考えはあきらめたほうがいいよ。

He gave himself up to the police.
その男は警察に自首した。

give up on (person: lose faith in) 見放す, …に愛想を尽かす, (idea, plan) 断念する, あきらめる

Don't give up on me, Dad.
お父さん、見放さないで。

---

give-and-take *n.* (cooperation) 持ちつ持たれつ, ギブアンドテイク, (compromise) 妥協; (exchange of ideas) 意見交換

given *adj.* (fixed, recognized) 定められた, 一定の

conj. (**given that…**) (…ということを) 考えれば, 考慮すると

n. (thing taken for granted) 当然のこと, (basic assumption) 前提

Contestants must finish within the given time.
競技者は、制限時間内に終了しなければならない。

Given that we're all rookies, I think we did well.

私たちみんなが新米だということを考えれば、よくやったと思うよ。

given name *n.* 名, 名前

glacier *n.* 氷河

glad *adj.* うれしい, 喜ぶ

I was glad to hear you passed your driving test.
運転免許の試験に合格したと聞いて、うれしかった。

Boy, am I glad to see you.
会えてほんとにうれしいよ。

Are you glad that you went?
行ってよかったですか？

gladiolus *n.* (plant) グラジオラス

glance *n.* 一見, ちらりと見ること, 一目
v. (look quickly) ちらっと見る, (read quickly) ざっと見る, ざっと目を通す

I took one glance and left.
ちらっと見て、その場を離れました。

"Have you read the report?"
"I've glanced at it."
「報告書を読みましたか？」
「ざっと目を通しました」

at first glance 一目見て, 一見して

throw sb a glance (…に)視線を投げかける

gland *n.* 腺

glare *v.* (shine) ぎらぎら光る; (glower) にらみつける
n. (light) まぶしい光; (glower) にらみ

glaring *adj.* (of light) まぶしい, (of mistake) 明白な

glass *n.* (substance) ガラス, (drinking glass) グラス, コップ, (one glass) 1杯

a sheet of glass ガラス板

I'd like a glass of orange juice, please.
オレンジジュースを下さい。

raise one's glass to (make a toast to) …に乾杯する

glasses *n.* めがね

wear glasses めがねをかけている

Put on your glasses.
めがねをかけてください。

glassware *n.* ガラス食器

glaucoma *n.* 緑内障

glaze *n.* (coating for pottery) うわ薬
v. (window) (…に) ガラスをはめる; (cake) (…に) 照りをつける

gleam *v.* (shine) かすかに光る
n. (light) かすかな光, (in eyes) 輝き

glen *n.* 峡谷, 谷間

glide *v.* 滑る, (on ground) 滑走する, (in the air) 滑空する

glider *n.* (aircraft) グライダー

glimmer *v.* ちらちら光る
n. (light) ちらちらする光

glimpse *n.* ひと目, ちらっと見る/見えること
v. ちらっと見る, (…が) ちらっと見える

catch a glimpse of ちらっと見る

I caught a glimpse of a deer in the woods.
森の中で鹿をちらっと見た。

glitter *v.* きらきら光る
n. (shiny flakes) きらきら光る物, (in eyes) 輝き, (on water) きらめき

global *adj.* (of the earth) 地球の, (for/concerning the whole world) 世界的な, (of the whole world) グローバルな; (of the whole) 全体的な

global warming *n.* 地球温暖化

globe *n.* (the earth) 地球, (model of the earth) 地球儀
across the globe 全世界に

globefish *n.* フグ, 河豚

glockenspiel *n.* グロッケンシュピール, 鉄琴

gloom *n.* (feeling) 憂うつ, (darkness) 暗やみ

gloomy *adj.* (dark) 薄暗い, (of mood) 陰気な, (of weather) うっとうしい, (pessimistic) 悲観的な

glorious *adj.* (wonderful) すばらしい, (splendid) みごとな, (full of glory) 華々しい, 栄光ある
a glorious day すばらしい日
a glorious victory 華々しい勝利

glory *n.* 栄光, 栄誉

gloss[1] *n.* (luster) つや, 光沢

gloss[2] *n.* (meaning gloss) 注釈

glossary *n.* (list of terminology) 用語集, (small dictionary) 小辞典

glossy *adj.* つやつやした, 光沢のある

glove *n.* 手袋, (baseball glove) グローブ, (boxing glove) グラブ
wear gloves 手袋をはめる
a pair of gloves (一組の)手袋

glow *v.* (give off light) 光る, (brightly, beautifully) 輝く, (of coals) 赤く燃える
n. 光, 輝き

♦**glow-in-the-dark** *adj.* 暗やみで光る

glucose *n.* グルコース, ブドウ糖

glue *n.* 接着剤, (paste) のり [→ picture of STATIONERY]
v. 接着剤でくっつける

glutton *n.* (person who eats a lot) 大食漢, 食いしん坊

gluttonous *adj.* 大食いの, 食いしん坊の

gluttony *n.* 大食い, 暴飲暴食

gnat *n.* ブヨ

gnaw *v.* (chew on) かじる, (a bone) しゃぶる

gnome *n.* 小人

---

go[1] *v.*

1 MOVE/TRAVEL: 行く, ((*honorific*)) いらっしゃる, ((*humble*)) 参ります, (commute) 通う, 通勤する, (**go home**) 帰る [→ "COMING AND GOING" on p.176]

2 BE PLACED: 置く

3 FIT INSIDE: 入る

4 WORK: (of moving parts) 動く

5 SUIT: (**go with**) ...に合う

6 BECOME: See examples below

7 OF TIME: たつ, 過ぎる

8 SELL FOR: (**go for**) ...で売れる

9 PROGRESS: うまくいく

10 WILL: (**be going to...**) (expressing intention) ...する, ...するつもりだ, (of imminent event) ...しようとしている, ...しそうだ

11 BE GOTTEN RID OF: 捨てられる

12 OF SONG: See examples below

13 FAIL: 衰える

14 DIE: 死ぬ

1 He went down a side street.
彼はわき道を歩いて行った。
Shall we go to France this year?
今年フランスに行こうか？
We didn't go to the movies. We just stayed at home.
映画には行かずに、家にいたんです。

Are you planning to go to Osaka this weekend?
今週末、大阪にいらっしゃる予定ですか?

I'm going home. 帰ります。

Well, it's time I was going.
そろそろ失礼します。

2 Where do the books go?
本はどこに置きますか?

It goes in the bottom drawer.
一番下の引き出しの中に入れます。

3 This box won't go into the closet.
この箱は押し入れには入りそうもない。

It's too big to go in the trunk of the car.
大きすぎて車のトランクに入りません。

4 I've been trying for over an hour, but I can't get it to go.
１時間以上も試してるんだけど、動かすことができない。

This toy train won't go.
このおもちゃの電車は動かないんだよ。

5 That tie doesn't go with your shirt.
そのネクタイはワイシャツに合わないよ。

Do these shoes go with my outfit?
この靴は洋服に合う?

6 She went pale.
彼女は顔色が悪くなった。

The apples have gone bad.
リンゴが腐ってしまった。

7 The time has gone so fast!
あっという間に時間がたってしまった。

Time goes by quickly when you're having fun.
楽しい時は時間がたつのが早い。

8 "How much did the car go for?"
"It went for next to nothing."
「車はいくらで売れたんですか?」
「ただ同然でした」

9 The meeting went very well.
会議は、うまくいきました。

How is work going?
お仕事は順調ですか?

10 We're going to complain.
苦情を言うつもりです。

I wasn't going to call her, but I changed my mind.
彼女に電話しないつもりだったけど、気が変わった。

Are you going to come visit us tomorrow?
明日、遊びに来てくれるの?

11 This chair has got to go.
この椅子はもう捨てよう。

12 How does the song go?
その歌はどんなメロディー?

No, the tune doesn't go like that.
いや、そういうメロディーじゃないよ。

13 His vision is beginning to go.
彼の視力は衰え始めている。

My hearing is going.
だんだん耳が遠くなってね。

14 He's gone. 彼は死んだ。

be on the go 忙しく動き回る

go dancing/swimming/fishing ダンスに/泳ぎに/釣りに行く

go missing 行方不明になる

go moldy かびが生える

Ready... Go! 用意、ドン!

go across *v.* (road, river) 渡る, 横切る, 横断する

We went across by boat.
僕らはボートで渡った。

Let's go across the park. It's quicker that way.
公園を横切ろう。そのほうが速い。

I'm going across the street to the supermarket to get some food.
食べ物を買いに、向かいのスーパーまで行くところです。

go after *v.* (pursue) ...の後を追う, 追いかける, (seek) 探す, 求める

I'm going to go after them until I find them.
彼らを見つけるまで、追いかけます。

go against *v.* (oppose) ...に反対する, ...に反する, ...に逆らう

It's no good going against their wishes. They are too powerful.
彼らの意思に逆らってもむだだよ。とにかく力のある人たちだから。

The tide has gone against us.
形勢は私たちに不利になった。

go ahead *v.* 先に行く, (with a plan) 進める; (please continue) どうぞ続けてください, (after you) お先にどうぞ

go along with *v.* (accompany) ...といっしょに行く; (agree with) ...に賛成する, ...に同調する

I went along with him to the post office.
郵便局まで彼といっしょに行きました。

She didn't want to go by herself, so we went along with her.
一人で行くのはいやだというので、いっしょに行ってあげた。

I went along with the general opinion at the meeting.
会議では、みんなの意見に賛成しました。

go around *v.*

1 MOVE: (move in a circle about) 回る, 回って行く, (take a detour) 回り道をする, (**go around doing**) ...して回る

2 FIT AROUND: 一回りする

3 CIRCULATE: (of rumor) 広まる, (of cold) はやる

1 The capsule went around the Earth twenty times.
カプセルは、地球の周りを２０回回った。

You can't go this way. You have to go around.
こっちには行けません。回り道をしてください。

I'd appreciate it if you wouldn't go around talking trash about me behind my back!
陰で私の悪口を言って回らないでね。

2 The string isn't long enough to go around.
ひもは、一回りするだけの長さがない。

Which wire goes around which part?
どのワイヤを、どこに巻き付ければいいんですか？

3 There's a nasty cold going around, I hear.
ひどいかぜが、はやっているそうです。

enough to go around 全員に行き渡る

Are there enough sandwiches to go around?
全員に行き渡るだけのサンドイッチはある？

go around and around ぐるぐる回る

go away *v.* (leave) 出て行く, (leave home) 出かける; (of pain) 消える, 治る

Go away! This is private property.
出て行け！ ここは私有地だぞ。

We're going away for the weekend.
週末は出かける予定です。

Has your headache gone away?
頭痛は治りましたか？

go back *v.* 戻る, (**go back home**) 帰る, (to one's home country) 帰国する; (date back) さかのぼる

We'd better go back now. Otherwise we'll be late.
そろそろ帰ろう。でないと遅れるよ。

Want to go back home instead?
それより、家に帰ろうか？

He went back to the Philippines last year.
昨年、彼はフィリピンに帰った [帰国した]。

The records of his family go back to the seventeenth century.
彼の家系は１７世紀までさかのぼれる。

go back on *v.* (promise) 破る

Now, don't go back on this promise, OK?
この約束は破らないでね。

go by *v.* (pass by) 通り過ぎる, (of time) たつ, 過ぎる, (of opportunity) 見逃す

"Where on earth is the restaurant?" "You've just gone by it."
「レストランは一体どこにあるんだろう？」「たった今通り過ぎたよ」

Time goes by so quickly, doesn't it?
時がたつのは、とても早いですね。

let an opportunity go by 機会を逃す, チャンスを見逃す

I don't know how you could let such a good opportunity go by like that.
せっかくのチャンスを、そんなふうに見逃すなんて…。

go down *v.*

1 DESCEND: (go down stairs etc.) 下りる, 下りて行く, (of road) 下る, 下りになる

2 BE RECEIVED: 受け入れられる, 気に入られる

3 SINK: 沈む

4 LOSE: 負ける, 敗れる

5 OF STANDARDS/TEMPERATURE/PRICE: 下がる, 低下する

6 OF AIRPLANE: (crash) 墜落する

7 OF POPULARITY: 落ちる, 下がる

1 We went down the stairs to the reception area.
階段を下りて、受付に行った。

We climbed to the top of the mountain and went down the other side.
山の頂上に登って、反対側に下りた。

The road goes down to the lake.
その道は湖まで下りになっています。

2 The party went down well.
パーティーはとても好評だった。

His remarks did not go down well.
彼の発言はあまり受け入れられなかった。

3 The sun went down below the horizon.
太陽が地平線の下に沈んだ。

They aren't sure why the ship went down.
船がなぜ沈没したのか、よくわかっていない。

4 They went down three goals to two.
彼らは2対3で負けた。

5 Educational standards are going down.
教育水準は低下しています。

6 The pilot did his utmost, but the plane went down in the middle of the Pacific.
パイロットは全力を尽くしたが、飛行機は太平洋の真ん中に墜落した。

7 His popularity is starting to go down.
彼の人気は落ち始めている。

go down in history (as...) (…として)

歴史に残る

go down on one's knees ひざまずく, ひざをつく

go down with → COME DOWN WITH

go for *v.*

1 GO TO GET: 取りに行く, (go out to buy) 買いに行く

2 CHOOSE: 選ぶ, …にする

3 TAKE A LIKING TO: (…が) 気に入る

4 ATTACK: 攻撃する, 襲う, (make as if to punch) …に手を出す

5 APPLY TO: …に当てはまる

1 I'm just going for some rice.
お米を買いに行くところです。

Let's go for a beer somewhere.
どこかに飲みに行こう。

2 I think I'll go for the shrimp curry.
エビカレーにしようかな。

3 Personally, I don't go for modern art.
個人的には、モダンアートは好きじゃありません。

She won't go for someone like him.
彼女は彼のような人は好きにならない。

4 I saw the whole thing. That guy on the right went for him first.
一部始終を見ていました。あの右側の男が先に手を出したんです。

5 Hurry up and get ready. And that goes for you, too!
急いで用意して。ほら、君も!

go for a swim/walk 泳ぎに/散歩に行く

go for it 一か八かやってみる

Go for it! It's a great opportunity.
またとないチャンスだよ。一か八かやってみなさいよ。

go in *v.* (go inside) 中に入る

Shall we go in? 中に入りましょうか?

He's already gone in.
彼はもう中にいます。

go into *v.*

1 DESCRIBE (IN DETAIL): (詳しく) 説明する

2 TAKE UP: …に入る

3 BE SPENT/WASTED: …に費やされる, …に投入される

4 ENTER/FIT INTO: …に入る

5 CRASH: …にぶつかる

1 I wouldn't go into a whole lot of detail.
あまり詳しく説明しないほうがいいよ。

2 Ever thought of going into law?
法曹界に入ろうと考えたことはある?

3 Three years went into this project.
この計画に3年も費やされた。

4 She went into her room.
彼女は自分の部屋に入って行った。

It won't go into this box.
この箱には入らない。

5 The car went into the side of the house.
車は家の横にぶつかって突っ込んだ。

go off *v.*

1 LEAVE: 出かける

2 STOP OPERATING: (of light) 消える, (of heater) 止まる, 切れる

3 EXPLODE: (of bomb) 爆発する, (of gun: fire) 発射する

4 SOUND: (of alarm) 鳴り出す

1 He's gone off to work.
彼は仕事に出かけた。

2 The light has gone off.
明かりが消えた。

3 The bomb went off early in the morning.

爆弾は早朝に爆発した。

4 The alarm went off.
警報器が鳴り出した。

go on *v.*

1 **CONTINUE:** (speaking) (話を)続ける, (of situation: persist) 続く, (move on) 進む, (**go on to**) (=head in the direction of) …に行く, …に向かう, (=to become) …になる

2 **HAPPEN:** ある, 起こる

3 **TURN ON:** (of lights) つく, (of heater) 入る

4 **PASS:** (of time) たつ, 過ぎる

1 He went on talking.
彼はしゃべり続けた。

Sounds bad. Go on.
それはひどいね。話を続けて。

Don't go on about it. Just forget it.
その話はやめよう。もう、いいよ。

If things go on like this, I'm going to quit.
こんなことが続くのなら、私は辞めます。

You can't go on. There's been an accident.
先へは進めません。事故がありましたので。

We went on to the hotel.
私たちはホテルに向かった。

She went on to become a doctor.
あの人はその後、医者になりました。

2 What's going on here?
一体ここで何があったんだ？

Do you have anything going on tonight?
今夜、何か予定がありますか？

A lot of talking goes on, but there's not much action.
みんな口先ばかりで、ちっとも行動が伴わない。

3 The lights have gone on.
電気がつきました。

The heating goes on automatically at a set time.
決まった時間になると、自動的に暖房が入ります。

4 As time goes on, you'll forget about it.
時がたつにつれて、忘れるよ。

go out *v.*

1 **DATE REGULARLY:** 付き合う

2 **SET OUT:** 出かける, 出る, (for entertainment, to nightclub etc.) 遊びに行く

3 **OF FIRE/LIGHTS:** 消える

4 **EBB:** (of tide) 引く, (of enjoyment) なくなる

1 They're going out.
あの二人は付き合っているよ。

I heard they've been going out since last year.
二人は去年から付き合っているそうだ。

2 They went out at about 7 o'clock.
彼らは7時ごろ出かけました。

Do you go out much in the evenings?
夜、遊びに出かけることは多いですか？

3 The fire went out. 火が消えた。

4 The tide has gone out. 潮が引いた。

All the fun has gone out of professional baseball.
プロ野球がつまらなくなった。

go over *v.*

1 **MOVE:** (…に)行く, (across ocean to another continent) 渡って行く

2 **REVIEW:** 復習する

3 **CHECK:** チェックする

1 Could you go over there, please?
向こうに行ってもらえませんか？

I went over to speak to her.
彼女に話しに行った。

2 We'll need to go over this lesson again.
このレッスンをもう一度復習する必要があります。

3 I'll go over what you've written later.
君が書いたものをあとでチェックしておくよ。

go round → GO[1] AROUND

go through *v.*

1 **PASS:** 通る, 通り抜ける, 通過する

2 **UNDERGO:** 経験する, (hardship) 切り抜ける, …に耐える

3 **SEARCH:** (baggage) 検査する, 調べる

1 We went through a tunnel.
トンネルを抜けた。

The train went through the station without stopping.
電車はその駅を通過した。

Did the proposal go through?
その企画は通りましたか？

2 He has gone through a lot.
彼は多くのつらいことを経験してきた。

I don't want to go through all that hassle again.
あんな面倒なことは、二度と経験したくない。

3 They went through my bags at customs.
税関で荷物を検査された［調べられた］。

go through with (carry out) やり遂げる, やり抜く

I just couldn't go through with it.
やり抜くことができなかった。

go together → GO[1] WITH 3

go under *v.* (go bankrupt) つぶれる, 倒産する; (sink) 沈む, 沈没する

That company has gone under.
あの会社は倒産した。

The ship went under after it hit the rocks.
船は暗礁にぶつかって沈没した。

go up *v.*

1 **RISE:** (of temperature, tax, price) 上がる, (of food prices, fares) 値上がりする

2 **BE BUILT:** 建てられる, 建つ

3 **CLIMB:** 登る

1 Taxes have gone up yet again.
また税金が上がった。

The cost of housing is going up.
家の値段が上がっている。

2 A lot of new buildings have gone up here in the last year.
ここ1年で、このあたりにはたくさんのビルが建ちました。

3 Have you gone up to the top of Mt. Fuji?
富士山の頂上に登ったことはある?

go with *v.*

1 **ACCOMPANY:** …といっしょに行く

2 **BE PART OF:** …に伴う, …に付いている

3 **SUIT:** …に合う [→ GO[1] 5]

1 I'll go with you. いっしょに行くよ。

You shouldn't go alone. Somebody should go with you.
一人で行っちゃだめだよ。誰かがいっしょに行かなきゃ。

2 The car went with the job.
その仕事に就いたから車も使えた。

3 That tie goes well with your jacket.
そのネクタイは上着によく合うよ。

go without *v.* (endure without) …なし

でがまんする, (manage without) …なしで済ませる

He can't go without a cigarette for more than ten minutes.
彼はたばこなしでは、10分以上がまんできないんです。

They went without food or sleep for three days.
彼らは3日間、食料も睡眠も取らずにいた。

If you don't like the food, you can go without.
嫌いなら、食べなくていい。

---

go[2] ***n.*** (board game) 囲碁, 碁
a go board 碁盤
a go stone 碁石
play go 碁を打つ

go-ahead ***n.*** (permission) 許可, ((*informal*)) ゴーサイン
We'll begin as soon as we get the go-ahead.
許可がおりたらすぐに始めます。

goal ***n.*** (aim, purpose) 目標, 目的; (point scored in a game) ゴール, 得点
He has no goals in life.
彼には人生の目標というものがない。
He scored two goals.
彼は2得点を挙げた。

♦ **goal kick** ***n.*** ゴールキック
goalpost ***n.*** ゴールポスト

goalkeeper ***n.*** ゴールキーパー

goat ***n.*** ヤギ, 山羊

goatee ***n.*** ヤギひげ

go-between ***n.*** (middleman) 仲介者, (matchmaker) (お)仲人(さん)

god ***n.*** (also **God**) 神(様)
pray to God 神に祈る
believe in God/gods 神様を信じる
for God's sake (pleading) お願いだから, (expressing irritation) いいかげんにして, 全くもう
oh my God (expressing distress) 困ったなぁ, 参ったなぁ, (expressing shock) なんてことだ, 大変だ, (expressing surprise) えっ, おやまあ

goddess ***n.*** 女神

gold ***n.*** (precious metal) 金, 黄金
adj. (of color) 金の, 金色の
♦ **gold dust** ***n.*** 金粉
goldsmith ***n.*** 金細工師

golden ***adj.*** 金色の
♦ **golden age** ***n.*** 黄金時代

goldfish ***n.*** 金魚

golf ***n., v.*** ゴルフ(をする)
♦ **golf ball** ***n.*** ゴルフボール
golf club ***n.*** ゴルフクラブ

golf course ***n.*** ゴルフ場

golfer ***n.*** ゴルファー

gong ***n.*** ゴング, (traditional Japanese gong) どら

gonorrhea ***n.*** 淋病

good
1 ***adj.*** DESIRABLE/FAVORABLE/SENSIBLE: いい, ((*formal*)) 良き, (expressing satisfaction/approval) いいですね, いいですよ
2 ***adj.*** SUITABLE: (fitting) (…に) 合う, ちょうどいい, (convenient) 都合のいい
3 ***adj.*** SKILLFUL: 上手な, うまい, 得意な
4 ***adj.*** ENJOYABLE: (fun) 楽しい, (interesting) 面白い
5 ***adj.*** OF PERSON/CHARACTER: (kind) 親切な,

(righteous) 立派な, 正しい, (of child: well behaved) 行儀のいい

6 ***adj.*** **DELICIOUS:** おいしい, ((*informal*)) うまい

7 ***adj.*** **QUALITY:** 質のいい, (of hotel) 高級な, (of work of literature) みごとな, すぐれた

8 ***adj.*** **HEALTHY:** 元気な, (feeling good) 気分がいい, (good for the body) 体にいい, (strong) 丈夫な

9 ***adj.*** **USEFUL:** いい, ためになる

10 ***adj.*** **OF TIME/DISTANCE:** (**a good...**) たっぷり..., (only of time) まる...

11 ***n.*** **OPPOSITE OF EVIL:** 善

1 the good old days 古き良き時代

That's a good idea.
それはいい考えだ。

He's a good guy. 彼はいい奴だよ。

She's a good friend.
彼女はいい友達 [親友] です。

She's got a good complexion.
彼女は顔色がいい。

It's a good thing we left early.
早めに出てよかった。

It would be a good idea to bring along your umbrella.
傘を持って行ったほうがいいよ。

Good! He's gone.
よかった! あいつがいなくなった。

2 That sweater looks good on you.
そのセーター、似合いますね。

When would be a good time to call?
お電話を差し上げるのは、いつがよろしいですか?

Thursday isn't good for me. How about Friday?
木曜日は都合が悪いので、金曜日はどうですか?

3 He's good at chess.
あの人はチェスがうまい。

She's no good at skiing.
彼女はスキーが下手だ。

Are you any good at math?
数学は得意ですか?

4 We had a good time last night.
ゆうべはとても楽しかった。

Seen any good movies lately?
最近、何か面白い映画見た?

5 He's very good to her.
あの人は彼女にとても親切だ。

6 That beer was good.
あのビールはおいしかった [うまかった]。

7 It's a very good hotel.
とても高級なホテルですよ。

8 Exercise is good for you.
運動は体にいい。

9 This will be a good experience for you.
あなたにとって、いい経験になりますよ。

10 The hotel is a good three hours from the airport.
ホテルは、空港からたっぷり3時間かかる。

11 Good will prevail over evil.
善は悪に勝つ。

good and evil 善悪

as good as (the same as) ...も同様

It's as good as new. 新品同様です。

for good 永遠に, 二度と(...ない)

We won't see him again. He's gone for good.
もう彼に会うことはないんだね。二度

と戻(もど)らないのだから。

for the good of …のために

He should resign for the good of the company.
彼(かれ)は会社(かいしゃ)のために辞(や)めるべきだ。

good for (beneficial to) …にいい, (valid for) …の間有効(あいだゆうこう)な

They say carrots are good for your eyes.
ニンジンは目(め)にいいらしいよ。

This warranty is good for one year.
この保証書(ほしょうしょ)は1年間有効(いちねんかんゆうこう)です。

no good (useless) 役(やく)に立(た)たない, (in vain) むだだ

This pen is no good.
このペンは役(やく)に立(た)たない。

It's no good trying to discuss it with them.
そのことについて向(む)こうと話(はな)し合(あ)おうとしてもむだだ。

good afternoon *interj.* こんにちは

good-bye *interj.* さよ(う)なら [→ BYE-BYE, SEE YOU!], (leaving home) 行(い)ってきます, (speaking to sb leaving home) 行(い)ってらっしゃい, (leaving workplace for the day) お先(さき)に(失礼(しつれい)します), (speaking to sb leaving workplace for the day) お疲(つか)れさま(でした), (said by boss to employee leaving after a day's work) ご苦労(くろう)さま(でした)

Good-bye for now. では後(のち)ほど。

good evening *interj.* こんばんは

good-looking *adj.* (of man) ハンサムな, (of woman) きれいな

good morning *interj.* おはよう, ((*polite*)) おはようございます

goodness *n.* (of person) 善良(ぜんりょう)さ

the goodness of human nature
人間(にんげん)の善良(ぜんりょう)さ

for goodness sake → FOR GOD'S SAKE

good night *interj.* ((*informal*)) おやすみ, ((*polite*)) おやすみなさい

goods *n.* (merchandise) 商品(しょうひん), 品物(しなもの), 製品(せいひん), (possessions) 所有物(しょゆうぶつ) [→ FREIGHT]

electronic goods 電気製品(でんきせいひん)

goodwill *n.* 善意(ぜんい), 好意(こうい), (between nations) 親善(しんぜん)

goose *n.* ガチョウ

gooseberry *n.* グーズベリー, スグリ

goose bumps *n.* 鳥肌(とりはだ)

get goose bumps 鳥肌(とりはだ)が立(た)つ

gopher *n.* ホリネズミ

gorge *n.* 峡谷(きょうこく)

gorgeous *adj.* (of person) 魅力的(みりょくてき)な, きれいな, (of clothes: colorful) 華(はな)やかな, (of weather, view) すばらしい, すごくいい, (of party, hotel) 豪華(ごうか)な

gorilla *n.* ゴリラ

gospel *n.* (**the Gospel**) 福音書(ふくいんしょ), (gospel music) ゴスペル

gossamer *n.* (spiderweb) 小(こ)グモの糸(いと)

gossip *n.* うわさ話(ばなし), (in magazine) ゴシップ, (person) ゴシップ好(ず)きな人(ひと)
v. うわさ話(ばなし)をする, (gossip with) (…と) 雑談(ざつだん)する

gourd *n.* ヒョウタン

gourmet *n.* 食通(しょくつう), グルメ

gout *n.* 痛風(つうふう)

govern *v.* (country) 治(おさ)める, (institution) 管理(かんり)する [→ CONTROL]

They are not fit to govern the country.

彼らには国を治める能力がない。

government *n.* 政府, (governing of a country) 政治, (ruling party) 与党, (cabinet) 内閣

the federal government 連邦政府
a state government 州政府
a prefectural government 県庁
a central government 中央政府
a local government 地方自治体
government agencies 省庁 [政府機関]
a democratic [totalitarian] government 民主 [全体主義] 政治
form a government 組閣する
overthrow a government 政権を倒す

governor *n.* (of U.S. state) 州知事, (of Japanese prefecture) 知事

gown *n.* ガウン, (surgeon's) 手術着

grab *v.* (take hold of) つかむ, (snatch away) ひったくる

The thief grabbed her purse.
泥棒は彼女のバッグをひったくった。

grace *n.* (of movement) 優雅さ, (of manner) 上品さ; (God's grace) (神の) 恵み

say grace (before a meal)
(食事の前に) お祈りをする

♦ **grace period** *n.* (for making a payment) 支払い猶予期間

graceful *adj.* 優雅な, 上品な

grade

1 *v.* EVALUATE: (assign a grade to) (...に) 成績をつける, (check) 採点する

2 *v.* EVALUATE AND ARRANGE IN GROUPS: 格付けする, 等級に分ける

3 *n.* QUALITY: (of goods) 品質, 質

4 *n.* SCORE ON HOMEWORK/EXAM: 成績

5 *n.* LEVEL/YEAR IN SCHOOL: 学年

6 *n.* SLOPE: 坂道

1 Are we going to grade the students?
生徒に成績をつけるのですか？
Who graded these papers?
このレポートを採点したのは誰ですか？

2 Hotels are graded from one to five stars.
ホテルは一つ星から五つ星までに格付けされている。

3 It's a low-grade product.
質の悪い製品だ。

4 What was your grade on the exam?
テストの成績はどうだった？

5 "What grade are you in?"
"I'm in sixth grade."
「(君は) 何年生ですか？」
「6年生です」

6 a steep grade 急な坂道 [傾斜]

♦ **grader** *n.* -年生

a fifth grader 5年生

grade point average *n.* 成績平均点

grade school *n.* 小学校

gradient *n.* (degree of inclination) 勾配, 傾斜度

gradual *adj.* 段階的な, 徐々の

There has been a gradual increase in gasoline prices.
ガソリンの価格が徐々に上昇している。

gradually *adv.* だんだん, しだいに, 徐々に, 少しずつ

You'll gradually get used to things here.
だんだん、ここに慣れていくよ。
We gradually caught up with them.
私たちは徐々に彼らに追いついて行った。

graduate *v.* 卒業する

n. 卒業生(そつぎょうせい)

adj. (postgraduate) 大学院(だいがくいん)の

She graduated from Harvard.
彼女(かのじょ)はハーバード大学(だいがく)を卒業(そつぎょう)した。

He's a Cambridge graduate.
彼(かれ)はケンブリッジ大学卒(だいがくそつ)です。

♦ **graduate school** n. 大学院(だいがくいん)

graduate student n. 大学院生(だいがくいんせい)

graduation n. 卒業(そつぎょう)

graffiti n. 落書(らくが)き

write graffiti 落書(らくが)きする

grain n. (food plant) 穀物(こくもつ), (a single grain) 一粒(ひとつぶ); (of wood) 木目(もくめ)

a husk of grain もみ

go against the grain (of) (...の) 性分(しょうぶん)に合(あ)わない

gram n. グラム

grammar n. 文法(ぶんぽう)

grammatical adj. 文法的(ぶんぽうてき)な, (grammatically correct) 文法的(ぶんぽうてき)に正(ただ)しい

a grammatical mistake 文法的(ぶんぽうてき)な間違(まちが)い

grand adj. (large) 大(おお)きい/大(おお)きな, (magnificent) 立派(りっぱ)な

grandchild n. (one's own) 孫(まご), (sb else's) お孫(まご)さん

granddaughter n. (女(おんな)の) 孫(まご), 孫娘(まごむすめ)

grandfather n. (one's own) 祖父(そふ), (addressing one's own) おじいちゃん, (sb else's) おじいさん

grandmother n. (one's own) 祖母(そぼ), (addressing one's own) おばあちゃん, (sb else's) おばあさん

grandparents n. 祖父母(そふぼ)

grandson n. (男(おとこ)の) 孫(まご), 孫息子(まごむすこ)

granite n. 花(か)こう岩(がん)

grant

1 v. GIVE: (permission, right) 与(あた)える, 認(みと)める, (status) ((formal)) 授(さず)ける

2 v. ALLOW TO COME TRUE: (wish, request) かなえる, 認(みと)める

3 n. MONEY: (scholarship) 奨学金(しょうがくきん), (research grant) 研究助成金(けんきゅうじょせいきん)

1 Permission was granted a few weeks ago.
数週間前(すうしゅうかんまえ)に許可(きょか)がおりた。

He was granted political asylum.
彼(かれ)は政治亡命者(せいじぼうめいしゃ)と認(みと)められた。

2 I'm afraid I cannot grant that wish.
残念(ざんねん)だけど、その願(ねが)いはかなえてあげられない。

Our request was granted.
私(わたし)たちの要求(ようきゅう)は認(みと)められた。

3 a university grant 大学(だいがく)の奨学金(しょうがくきん)

take for granted 当然(とうぜん)だと思(おも)う, 当(あ)たり前(まえ)のことと思(おも)う

grape n. ブドウ

grapefruit n. グレープフルーツ

graph n. グラフ, 図表(ずひょう)

draw/make a graph of ...のグラフをかく

graphic adj. (of sth unpleasant) 生々(なまなま)しい, (visual) 目(め)の当(あ)たりに見(み)るような

n. (graphics) グラフィックアート

graphic designer n. グラフィック・デザイナー

graphite n. 黒鉛(こくえん), グラファイト

grapple v. (with person) (...と) 格闘(かくとう)する, (with problem) (...に) 取(と)り組(く)む

grasp v. つかむ, 握(にぎ)りしめる, (understand) 把握(はあく)する, 理解(りかい)する

grass n. 草(くさ), (the grass) (= lawn) 芝生(しばふ), (= pasture) 牧草地(ぼくそうち)

cut the grass 芝生を刈る

The sheep were grazing on the grass.
羊は牧草を食べていた。

♦ **grasslands** ***n.*** 草原

grasshopper ***n.*** キリギリス

grass roots ***n.*** (**the grass roots**: the ordinary people) 一般大衆

grate[1] ***v.*** (food) おろす, (cheese) すりおろす

grate on sb's nerves (…の) 神経にさわる, (…を)いらいらさせる

grate[2] ***n.*** (metal lattice covering) 格子ぶた, (for fireplace) (暖炉の) 火床

grateful ***adj.*** (be grateful to A for B) (AにBを) 感謝する, ありがたく思う

I'm very grateful to you for your help.
ご協力、とても感謝しています/ご協力いただき、とてもありがたく思います。

♦ **gratefully** ***adv.*** ありがたく, 喜んで

gratitude ***n.*** 感謝

a debt of gratitude 義理

grave[1] ***n.*** (burial plot) (お)墓

visit a grave お墓参りをする

♦ **graveyard** ***n.*** 墓地

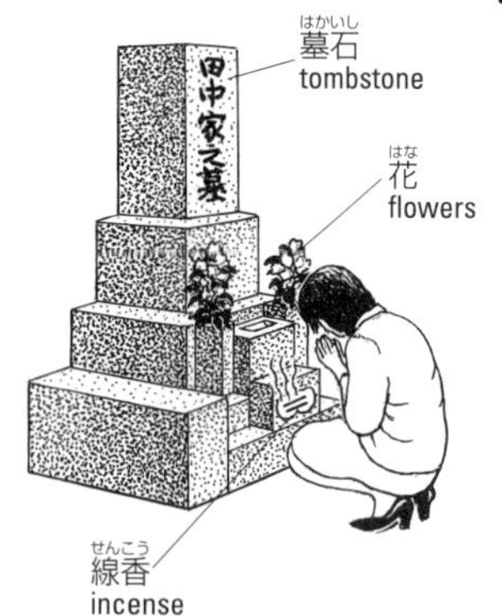

grave
墓

grave[2] ***adj.*** (serious) 重大な

gravel ***n.*** 砂利

gravity ***n.*** 重力, 引力; (of situation: seriousness) 重大さ

gravy ***n.*** グレービー, 肉汁

gray ***adj.*** 灰色の, ねずみ色の, (of sky) 曇った, どんよりした

gray hair
しらが [白髪]

graze ***v.*** 草を食べる, 草をはむ

grease ***n.*** (lubricant) グリース, 油, (melted animal fat) 獣脂, 脂

v. (add grease to) (…に) 油をさす, (frying pan) (…に) 油をひく

greasy ***adj.*** (of food) 脂っこい

great ***adj.*** [→ WELL[1] 1]

1 MASSIVE: 大きい, 大きな, 巨大な, ((*informal*)) で(っ)かい

2 OF AMOUNT: たくさんの, 多数の

3 MAGNIFICENT: 偉大な, 立派な, すばらしい, 偉い

4 ENJOYABLE: (fun) 楽しい, (interesting) 面白い

5 OF EVENT: 重大な, 大-

6 OF RELATIVE: (**great-**) 大-

1 a great rock 大きな岩

a great ship 巨大な船

2 A great number of people showed up.
たくさんの人がやって来た。

3 a great poet 偉大な詩人

a great achievement
みごとな業績

4 I had a great time!
すごく楽しかった。

a great TV program

面白いテレビ番組

5 It was one of the great events of our time.
我々の時代の大事件の一つだった。

6 one's great-aunt 大おば(さん)

a great deal of たくさんの, かなりの, 大変な
A great deal of time was spent making the movie.
その映画を作るのに、かなりの時間が費やされた。

greatly *adv.* 大いに, 非常に
This will greatly improve our chances of success.
これで、成功するチャンスは大いに向上するよ。

greatness *n.* 偉大さ

Greece *n.* ギリシャ

greed *n.* 貪欲, 欲張り

♦ **greedily** *adv.* (eat) がつがつ, 貪欲に
eat greedily がつがつ食べる

greedy *adj.* 欲張りな/の, 貪欲な

green *adj.* 緑色の, (of traffic light) 青い
n. (color) 緑, 緑色, グリーン, (**greens**: vegetables) 野菜, 青物
The traffic light has turned green.
信号が青に変わったよ。
Is this fabric green or blue?
この布は緑ですか、それとも青ですか?
It has green foliage and red flowers.
緑の葉をつけ、赤い花を咲かせます。
Eat plenty of greens.
野菜をたくさん食べなさい。

greengrocer *n.* 八百屋(さん)

greenhorn *n.* 青二才

greenhouse *n.* 温室

greenhouse effect *n.* 温室効果

green light *n.* (traffic signal) 青信号; (permission) 許可, ((*informal*)) ゴーサイン

green pepper *n.* ピーマン

green tea *n.* 緑茶

greet *v.* (…に) あいさつする, (give a warm welcome to) 歓迎する
They were greeted on their arrival.
到着すると、彼らは歓迎を受けた。

greeting *n.* あいさつ(の言葉)
exchange greetings
あいさつを交わす

gregarious *adj.* (social) 社交的な

gremlin *n.* グレムリン

grenade *n.* 手りゅう弾

grey → GRAY

greyhound *n.* グレーハウンド

grid *n.* (iron/wooden grid) 格子, (set of lines on a map/graph) 方眼

griddle *n.* 鉄板

grief *n.* 悲しみ, 悲嘆

grievance *n.* 苦情, 不平

grieve *v.* 悲しむ

grill *n.* (gridiron) (焼き)網
v. (cook) 網焼きにする, 焼く
a charcoal grill バーベキューコンロ
grilled meat 焼き肉

grille *n.* (metal grating) 格子, (on window) 格子窓

grim *adj.* 暗い, 厳しい, (pessimistic) 悲観的な

♦ **grim reaper** *n.* 死神

grime *n.* (dirt) 汚れ, あか

grin *v.* (grin at) (…に) にっこりほほえむ
n. にこやかな笑み

grind *v.* (food) ひく, (ax, blade) 研ぐ,

(**grind one's teeth**) 歯ぎしりする

Shall I grind the coffee beans for you?
豆をおひきしましょうか？

grip *v.* (ぎゅっと) 握る, つかむ
n. 握ること, (understanding) 把握, 理解
get a grip on oneself しっかりする, 自制する

grit *n.* (sand) 砂

groan *v.* (moan with pain) うめく [→ COMPLAIN]
n. うめき声, (expression of discontent) 不満の声

grocer *n.* 食料雑貨商, 食料雑貨店主

groceries *n.* 食料雑貨

grocery store *n.* 食料品店

groggy *adj.* ふらふらする

groin *n.* 股間

groom *n.* (bridegroom) 花婿, 新郎; (horse keeper) 馬丁
v. (brush: animal) (…の) 手入れをする, (**groom oneself**) 身支度をする

be well [badly] groomed
身だしなみがよい [悪い]

groove *n.* (dip, channel) 溝
get into a groove 型にはまる

grope *v.* (grope around) 手探りする, (grope for) 手探りで探す; (fondle roughly) (…の) 体をまさぐる

gross *adj.* (total) 総計の, 全体の; (vulgar) 下品な, (awful) ひどい
n. (grand total) 総計

♦**grossly** *adv.* ひどく, はなはだしく

grotesque *adj.* 異様な, グロテスクな

ground

1 *n.* SURFACE OF THE EARTH: 地面, (soil, earth) 土, (plot of land) 土地, (**grounds**: of building) 敷地

2 *n.* BASIS: (**grounds**) 根拠, 理由

3 *adj.* ON THE GROUND: 地上の

4 *v.* DETAIN: (**be grounded**) (of person) 外出禁止になる, (of aircraft) 離陸できない

5 *v.* BE BASED ON: (**be grounded in/on**) …に基づいている

6 *v.* KNOW THE BASICS OF: (**be grounded in**) …の基礎がわかっている

1 The ground is very hard here.
ここの地面はとても固い。

They're going to build an apartment building on this ground.
この土地に、マンションが建設される予定です。

What is this ground used for?
この土地は何に使われているのですか？

above [below] ground
地上 [地下] に

2 On what grounds was he fired?
どういう理由で、彼は解雇されたんですか？

3 the ground floor 1 階
ground troops 地上部隊

4 The boy was grounded for a week.
男の子は1 週間、外出禁止になった。

5 Her opinion is grounded on experience.
彼女の意見は経験に基づいている。

6 She is well grounded in French.
彼女はフランス語の基礎がよくわかっている。

break (new) ground 新天地を開拓する, 新天地を切り開く

give ground 譲歩する, 後退する

on one's own ground 自分の土俵で

on the grounds that... ...という理由で, ...が原因で

stand/hold one's ground 自分の立場を守る, 一歩も引かない

groundbreaking ***adj.*** 画期的な

grounding ***n.*** (basic knowledge) 基礎知識

have a grounding in physics
物理の基礎知識がある

groundwork ***n.*** 基礎, 土台

lay the groundwork 基礎 [土台] を築く

group ***n.*** グループ, 集まり, 集団, 班, (particular group) 一行, 一団, (organization) 団体, (faction) 派閥, -派, (of companies/musicians) グループ

v. (group people/things together) いっしょにする, グループにする, (**group together**: form a group) 集まる, (of animals) 群れをなす

A group of surfers always comes here in the summer.
毎年夏になると、サーファーの一団がここにやって来る。

a group leader 班長

They formed an animal rights group.
彼らは動物保護団体を組織した。

group into three sets
三つのグループに分ける

The birds group together in the evening.
鳥は夕方になると群れをなします。

♦**grouping** ***n.*** グループ分け

grouse ***n.*** ライチョウ, 雷鳥

grove ***n.*** 木立, やぶ

a bamboo grove 竹やぶ

grovel ***v.*** (behave humbly) ぺこぺこする

grow ***v.***

1 DEVELOP: (of person, plant) 成長する, (of person: grow taller) 背が伸びる, 大きくなる, (of hair, nails) 伸びる; (of business, economy) 発展する

2 INCREASE: 増える, ((*formal*)) 増加する

3 BECOME: See examples below

4 ALLOW TO GROW: (plant) 栽培する, 育てる, (beard) 生やす, (hair) 伸ばす

1 My, how you've grown!
まあ、ずいぶん大きくなったね。

This plant is growing well.
この植物は順調に生長しています。

Your hair grows quickly.
髪が伸びるのが早いですね。

Industry in this area is growing.
この地区の産業は発展しています。

2 The amount of traffic on this road has grown tremendously in the last couple of years.
ここ数年で、この道路の交通量は急激に増えました。

3 It grew cold.
寒くなった。

He's grown old.
彼も年をとりましたね。

4 He grows vegetables.
あの人は野菜を栽培しています。

You should grow a beard.
ひげを生やしたほうがいいよ。

grow into ***v.*** (type of person) (成長して) ...になる, (clothes) (...が) ぴったり合うようになる

These shoes are a bit big, but you'll grow into them.

この靴は、今はちょっと大きいけど、そのうちぴったりになるよ。

grow on *v.* …の気に入るようになる, …が好きになる

I didn't like the game at first, but it sort of grows on you.
私も始めは、そのゲームが好きじゃなかったけど、だんだん好きになるよ。

grow out of *v.* (clothes) (…が) 着られなくなる, (habit) しなくなる, ((*figurative*)) 卒業する; (of idea: develop from) …から生まれる

What! Have you grown out of those shoes already?
えっ！ あの靴がもうきつくなったの？

I wish he'd grow out of this habit of behaving like a gangster.
もうそろそろ、不良みたいなまねは卒業してくれたらいいのに。

The United Nations grew out of the League of Nations.
国連は国際連盟から生まれました。

grow up *v.* (be raised) 育つ, (become an adult) おとなになる

He grew up in a small town.
彼は小さな町で育ちました。

For God's sake! Will you just grow up?
いいかげんにして！ もっとおとなになってよ。

---

growl *v.* (of dog) うなる

n. うなり声

grown-up *n.* おとな, 成人

adj. おとなの, 成人した

growth *n.* (of business, economy) 発展, 発達, (of population) 増加, (of crops, the body) 成長, 発育; (lump in the body) 腫瘍

In the last three to four years, economic growth has slowed.
ここ3、4年で、経済成長は減速した。

The doctors say it's a malignant growth.
医者たちは、悪性の腫瘍だと言っている。

grubby *adj.* 汚い, 汚れた

grudge *n.* 恨み

bear a grudge 恨みをいだく

grueling *adj.* (of work) へとへとに疲れる

gruesome *adj.* ぞっとする(ような), 身の毛のよだつ

a gruesome murder
ぞっとするような殺人事件

grumble *v.* (complain) ぶつぶつ言う, 文句を言う

n. (complaint) 文句, 不平

♦**grumbler** *n.* ぐちっぽい人

grump *n.* 不機嫌な人

grumpy *adj.* 気難しい, 不機嫌な

grungy *adj.* (dirty) 汚い, 不潔な

grunt *v.* (of person) うなる, (of pig) ブーブー鳴く

n. うなり声, (of pig) ブーブー鳴く声; (low-ranking soldier) 兵卒, (low-paid worker) 下っ端

♦**grunt work** *n.* 下働き

guarantee *n.* 保証

v. (provide insurance/assurance) 保証する, (firmly promise) 約束する, (**be guaranteed to do/happen**) 絶対…する/起こる

a seven-year guarantee
7年(間)保証

I guarantee you will get your money back.
お金は絶対に戻ります。

This insurance guarantees your home for fire and theft.
この保険は、自宅の火災や盗難に対して補償します。

guarantor *n.* 保証人

guard *v.* (protect) 守る, (keep an eye on) 見張る, 警戒する, (**guard oneself against**) (...に) 用心する
n. (security guard) 警備員, ガードマン, (bodyguard) 護衛, (at school gate/door) 守衛, (prison guard) 看守

A high wall guarded the house.
高い塀が家を守っていました。

He was guarded for his safety.
彼は身の安全のために護衛された。

Be sure to guard yourself against pick-pockets.
すりには用心してね。

There was a security guard at the front gate.
正門には警備員がいました。

The president had an armed guard.
大統領には武装した護衛がついていた。

off guard 油断して

be thrown off guard
油断する

be caught off guard
不意を突かれる

♦**guard dog** *n.* 番犬

guardian *n.* 保護者

guava *n.* グアバ, バンジロウ

gubernatorial *adj.* 知事の

a gubernatorial election 知事選(挙)

guerrilla *n.* ゲリラ兵

guerrilla warfare ゲリラ戦

guess *v.* 推測する, 推量する, (take a guess at) 言い当てる, 当てる, (imagine) 想像する, (reckon) (...と) 思う
n. 推測, 推量, 推察

Guess who's coming over for dinner?
夕食に誰が来ると思う?

Guess why he did it?
どうして彼はそんなことをしたんだと思う?

I want you to guess the number.
その数を当ててごらん。

Don't guess at the answer. Think!
当てずっぽうで答えてはだめだ。ちゃんと考えて!

Don't tell them. Let's keep them guessing.
教えちゃだめだよ。考えさせておこう。

I guess that means we won't be going skiing.
スキーには行かないということね。

That was a lucky guess.
あれは、まぐれ(当たり)だった。

guess what ちょっと聞いて

Guess what! I got the job!
ちょっと聞いて! その仕事に採用されたんだ。

take a wild guess 当てずっぽうで言う

guesswork *n.* 当てずっぽう

guest *n.* 客, ((*polite*)) お客さん, お客様, (on TV, radio) ゲスト

have guests over for dinner
来客と夕食を共にする

The guests on that program are always

G

a little bit eccentric.
あの番組のゲストは、いつもちょっと変わっている。

♦**guest house** *n.* ゲストハウス

guest of honor *n.* 来賓

guest room *n.* 来客用の寝室

guest speaker *n.* 来賓演説者

guidance *n.* 指導, (for future) ガイダンス

♦**guidance counselor** *n.* 進路指導の先生

guide *n.* (person) ガイド, 案内人, (book/pamphlet) 案内書
v. (lead) 案内する, (direct, influence) 導く, (explain, supervise) 指導する

a tour guide
観光ガイド [旅行添乗員]

He guided us around the city.
彼は町をあちこち案内してくれた。

I guided his hand toward the door.
彼の手をドアまで導いてあげた。

It's hoped that his influence will help to guide young people away from crime.
若者の犯罪防止に、彼の影響力が役立つと期待されている。

You must try to guide people by example.
自ら模範を示して人を導くべきです。

guidebook *n.* 旅行案内書, ガイドブック

guidelines *n.* 指針, ガイドライン

guild *n.* 同業者組合

guillotine *n.* ギロチン, (paper cutter) 裁断機

guilt *n.* (feeling of guilt) 罪悪感

guilty *adj.* (has committed a crime) 罪を犯した, (in court: opposite of innocent) 有罪の, (of look) 身に覚えのある, (of conscience) やましい

The jury found him guilty.
陪審員は被告を有罪とみなした。

a guilty conscience
やましい心 [良心の呵責]

feel guilty 罪悪感を覚える, 申し訳なく思う, すまないと思う

I feel guilty about letting them go on their own.
彼らだけで行かせて、申し訳なく思っている。

guinea pig *n.* テンジクネズミ, ((*also figurative*)) モルモット, 実験台

guitar *n.* ギター

play the guitar
ギターを弾く

♦**guitarist** *n.* ギタリスト

gulf *n.* (part of sea) 湾, (in proper names) …湾; (gap) 隔たり, (格)差

the Persian Gulf
ペルシア湾

the gulf between rich and poor
貧富の差

gull *n.* カモメ

gullible *adj.* だまされやすい

gulp *v.* ごくごく/がぶがぶ飲む, (**gulp down**) 飲み込む
n. (a single gulp) 一口

in one gulp 一口で, 一気に

gum[1] *n.* (substance from trees) ゴム; (chewing gum) (チューイン)ガム

gum[2] *n.* (where teeth are) 歯茎

gun *n.* 銃, 拳銃, ピストル

fire a gun
銃を撃つ

♦**gun control** *n.* 銃規制

gun down *v.* 射殺する, 撃ち殺す

gunboat *n.* 砲艦

gunfire *n.* 発砲, 砲撃

gunman *n.* ガンマン

gunner *n.* 砲手, 射撃手

♦ **gunnery** *n.* 砲術, 射撃法

gunpowder *n.* 火薬

guppy *n.* グッピー

gush *v.* どっと噴き出す

He was gushing blood.
彼は血が噴き出していた。

The water gushed from the drain.
排水溝から水があふれ出した。

gut *n.* (intestinal organ) 腸, 内臓, はらわた; (**guts**: courage) 勇気, 根性, ガッツ *v.* (a fish) (...の) はらわたを抜く

He's got guts to do that.
それをやるなんて、彼には勇気があるね。

spill one's guts 洗いざらい話す

gutsy *adj.* 根性のある

gutter *n.* (in street and leading to sewer) 排水溝, (drainage pipe on house/building) とい, 雨どい [→ picture of HOUSE]

guy *n.* 男, 人, ((*informal*)) 奴

gym *n.* (sports/fitness club) スポーツ/フィットネスクラブ; (gym class) 体育 [→ GYMNASIUM]

gymnasium *n.* 体育館, ジム

gymnast *n.* 体操選手

gymnastics *n.* 体操

gynecologist *n.* 婦人科医

gynecology *n.* 婦人科医学

gypsy *n.* ジプシー

gyroscope *n.* ジャイロスコープ

H, h

ha *interj.* (expressing satisfaction) はあ, ほう, (**ha-ha**) あはは

haberdasher *n.* (retailer of men's clothing/accessories) 紳士雑貨商

habit *n.* 習慣, (bad habit) 癖

He's in the habit of getting up early.
彼には早起きの習慣がある。

It's difficult to break a habit of years.
長年の習慣を直すのは難しい。

She has a habit of biting her nails.
彼女には爪をかむ癖がある。

I'm trying to get out of the habit of smoking.
タバコをやめようと努力しています。

make a habit of doing …することにしている

habitable *adj.* 住める

habitat *n.* (of animal) 生息地, (of plant) 自生地

habitation *n.* (act of living somewhere) 居住, (residence) 住居

habitual *adj.* (usual) いつもの, (unable to stop because of habit) 常習的な

a habitual offender 常習犯

hack *v.* (with ax) たたき切る, (hack to pieces) ずたずたに切る

♦**hack into** *v.* (computer) …に(不法)侵入する

hack off *v.* 切り落とす

hack through *v.* (jungle) …の中を切り開く

hacker *n.* (computer hacker) ハッカー

hackneyed *adj.* 陳腐な, 使い古した

hacksaw *n.* 弓のこ

haddock *n.* ハドック, タラ

haggle *v.* 値切る

haiku *n.* (5-7-5 syllable poem) 俳句

a haiku poet 俳人

hail[1] *n.* (frozen rain) ひょう, あられ

v. ひょうが降る, あられが降る

hail[2] *v.* (**be hailed as**) …と賞賛される, …としてもてはやされる

hair *n.* (on the head) 髪, 髪の毛, (on the body) 毛, (a single hair) 1本の毛

She has long hair.
彼女は長い髪をしている。

comb one's hair 髪をとかす

You'd better hurry up and do your hair.
早く髪をまとめたほうがいいよ。

Jerry is beginning to lose his hair.
ジェリーは髪が薄くなってきた。

leg [arm] hair 足の [腕の] 毛

chest hair 胸毛

pubic hair 陰毛

hairbrush *n.* ヘアブラシ

haircut *n.* カット, (for men, children) 散髪

get a haircut 髪を切る [カットする]

I'm going to go get a haircut tomorrow.
明日髪を切りに行きます。

I'd like a haircut, please.
カットをお願いします。

hairdo *n.* 髪型, ヘアスタイル

hairdresser *n.* (hairstylist) 美容師, (**the hairdresser's**) 美容院

hairdryer *n.* ドライヤー

hairline *n.* 髪の生え際

a receding hairline 後退する生え際

hairpin *n.* ヘアピン

hairspray ***n.*** ヘアスプレー

hairstyle ***n.*** 髪型, ヘアスタイル

hairstylist ***n.*** 美容師

hairy ***adj.*** 毛深い

half

1 ***adj.*** **ONE HALF:** 半分の, 2分の1の

2 ***adv.*** **TO THE EXTENT OF A HALF:** 半分, 半ば, (partly) いくぶん, いくらか

3 ***n.*** **PART OF A WHOLE:** 半分, (**first half**) 前半, (**latter/second half**) 後半

1 half a kilo 0.5キロ

two and a half years 2年半

Everything was half price.
何でも半額だった。

2 The theater was half empty.
劇場は半分空席だった。

The work is only half done.
仕事が半分しか片付いていない。

This meat is only half cooked.
このお肉はまだ火が通っていない。

You look as if you're half asleep.
寝ぼけているみたいよ。

She's half Japanese and half American.
彼女は、両親が日本人とアメリカ人です。

3 Here, have half of my apple.
はい、リンゴを半分どうぞ。

The first half of the group came forward to be photographed while the second half waited.
半分の人が前に出て写真を撮っている間、残り半分は待っていた。

The first half of the match was boring, but the second half was good.
試合の前半は退屈だったけど、後半は面白かった。

by halves 中途半端に, いいかげんに

He doesn't do anything by halves.
彼は何をするにも中途半端なことはしない。

go halves/go half and half (on restaurant bill) 割り勘にする

not half as A as B Bほど全然Aでない

The film wasn't half as good as you said.
あの映画はあなたが言うほどは、全然よくなかったよ。

half-baked ***adj.*** (ill-conceived) 不十分な, 中途半端な

half brother/sister ***n.*** (by father) 異母きょうだい, (by mother) 異父きょうだい

half-cooked ***adj.*** 半生の, (of stew) 生煮えの, (of fish, meat) 生焼けの

half day ***n.*** 半日

halfhearted ***adj.*** いいかげんな

half-hour ***adj.*** 30分の, 半時間の

half-mast ***n.*** 半旗

The flag was at half-mast.
半旗が掲げられていた。

half-moon ***n.*** 半月

half-price ***adj., adv.*** 半額の/で

halftime ***n.*** ハーフタイム

halfway ***adj.*** 中間の, (incomplete) 中途半端な

adv. (midway) 中間で, 途中で

I fell asleep halfway through the movie.
映画の途中で眠ってしまった。

meet sb halfway (compromise with) …に譲歩する, …に折り合う

halibut ***n.*** オヒョウ

halitosis ***n.*** 口臭

hall ***n.*** (corridor) 廊下, (entrance hall) 玄

関, 玄関の広間, (assembly hall) 会館, ホール

a lecture hall 講堂

a dining hall 食堂

a conference hall 会議場

a banquet hall 宴会場

a concert hall コンサートホール

city hall 市役所

hallmark *n.* (characteristic) 特徴

Halloween *n.* ハロウィーン

hallucinate *v.* 幻覚を見る

hallucination *n.* 幻覚

hallucinogen *n.* 幻覚剤

hallway *n.* (entrance hall) 玄関, (corridor) 廊下

halogen *n.* ハロゲン

a halogen lamp ハロゲンランプ

halt *v.* (come to a halt) 止まる, (of train, bus) 停止する, (stop walking) 立ち止まる, (cause to stop) 中止する, (activity, process) 中断する

n. (stop) 停止

Halt! 止まれ!

The man suddenly halted when he saw the police officer approaching.
その男は警官が近づいて来るのを見て、いきなり立ち止まった。

The train came to a halt.
電車が停止した。

halve *v.* (divide into two equal parts) 半分に切る, 半分に分ける, (lessen by half) 半分に減らす

ham *n.* (hog meat) ハム; (bad actor) 大根役者

ham and eggs ハムエッグ

hamburger *n.* ハンバーガー

hammer *n.* (tool) 金づち, ハンマー [→ picture of TOOL]

v. (pound) 打ち込む, (**hammer on**: knock loudly on) ガンガンたたく, (hammer an idea/some sense into sb's head) (…の頭に思想/常識を) たたき込む

hammock *n.* ハンモック

hamster *n.* ハムスター

hamstring *n.* ひかがみの腱, ひざの後ろの腱

pull a hamstring 足がつる

hand *n.* (part of the body) 手, (round of applause) 拍手; (pointer on a clock) 針

v. (pass) 渡す, 手渡す, 取る

I hurt my hand. 手にけがをした。

The mailman had a letter in his hand.
郵便屋さんは手に手紙を持っていた。

Let's give him a big hand!
盛大な拍手を送りましょう!

the hour [minute, second] hand
時計の短針 [長針, 秒針]

Hand me the chisel, will you.
彫刻刀を取ってくれる?

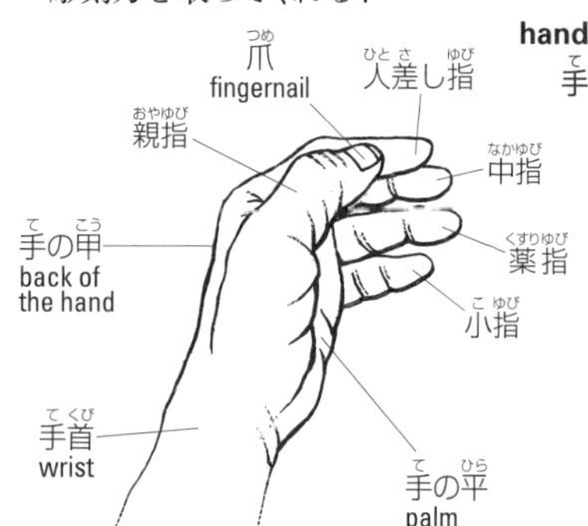

(close) at hand (imminent) まもなく, 間近に, (nearby) 手近に, すぐ手の届くところに

The moment of birth is at hand.
誕生の瞬間は間近です。

I always keep this dictionary close at hand.
この辞書はいつも手近に置いている。

be out of one's hands …の手を離れている

As far as I'm concerned, the whole matter is out of our hands now.
私としては、この件はもう私たちの手を離れています。

by hand 手で, (by handing over in person) 手渡しで, (in handwriting) 手書きで

For reasons of confidentiality, I delivered the document by hand.
機密保持のため、文書は手渡しした。

You'll make a better impression if you write the letter by hand.
手紙は手書きにしたほうが印象がいいですよ。

change hands 所有者が替わる

The company has changed hands many times in the past ten years.
会社はここ10年間で、何度も所有者が替わった。

get one's hands on (acquire) 手に入れる, (capture) 捕まえる

I read everything I can get my hands on.
手に入る物は何でも読みます。

Wait till I get my hands on that rascal.
この手であの悪党を捕まえてやる。

give/lend a hand 手を貸す, 手伝う

Could you give us a hand?
手を貸してもらえませんか？

Hands off! 手を触れるな, 触るな

Hands off! That's mine.
((*masculine*)) 触るな！ それは僕の物だ。

hold hands 手を取り合う, 手をつなぐ

I saw them walking through the park holding hands.
二人が手をつないで公園を歩いているのを見たんだ。

on the one hand 一方では

on the other hand 他方では, その反面

raise one's hand 手を挙げる

She raised her hand to ask a question.
彼女は質問しようと手を挙げた。

shake hands 握手する

They shook hands and then exchanged business cards.
彼らは握手をして、名刺を交換した。

try one's hand at やってみる

He'll try his hand at any sport.
彼はスポーツなら何でもやってみる。

hand back *v.* (return) 返す

The books have to be handed back by next Friday.
この本は、来週の金曜日までに返さなくてはいけない。

hand down *v.* (tradition) 伝える, 受け継ぐ, (clothes) お下がりにする

These customs have been handed down for hundreds of years.
これらの慣習は何百年も受け継がれている。

My older brother's clothes used to be handed down to me.
僕はいつも兄のお下がりをもらっていた。

hand in *v.* 出す, 提出する

Hand in your exam papers, please.
解答用紙を出してください。

He's handed in his resignation and it's been accepted.
彼は辞表を提出し、受け入れられた。

When is the deadline for handing in our application?
申し込み期限はいつですか？

hand on *v.* (pass on) 回す

Take one sheet and hand the rest on.
１枚ずつ取って、残りを回してください。

The job was handed on to me.
その仕事は、私に回って来た。

hand out *v.* (distribute) 配る, (hand over) 渡す, 手渡す

There was somebody handing out leaflets at the exit.
出口でビラを配っている人がいた。

Who is going to hand out the awards?
誰が賞を手渡すのですか？

hand over *v.* 渡す, 手渡す, (arms, hostage) 引き渡す

Both sides handed over their arms to UN peacekeepers.
両軍は、国連平和維持軍に武器を引き渡した。

handbag *n.* (ハンド)バッグ

handball *n.* (game) ハンドボール; (foul in soccer) ハンド

handbill *n.* ちらし, ビラ

handbook *n.* 手引書, ハンドブック

hand brake *n.* (emergency brake) サイドブレーキ [→ picture of CAR]

handclap *n.* (applause) 拍手, (rhythmic clap) 手拍子

hand cream *n.* ハンドクリーム

handcuffs *n.* 手錠, 手かせ

v. (…に) 手錠をかける

be handcuffed 手錠をかけられる

handful *n.* 一握り, 手いっぱい, (small number) 少数, (small amount) 少量; (recalcitrant child) 手に負えない子

a handful of candy 一握りのお菓子

He's only seven, but he's a handful.
あの子はたった７歳だけれど、手に負えない。

handicap *n.* 障害, ハンディキャップ, (disadvantage) 不利な条件, (in sport) ハンディキャップ

v. (put at a disadvantage) 不利な立場にする, (in sport: assign a handicap to) (…に) ハンディキャップをつける

handicapped *adj.* (physically) 身体に障害のある, (mentally) 精神に障害のある

n. (**the handicapped**) 障害者

handicraft *n.* (work of art) 手工芸品

handiwork *n.* 手仕事

handkerchief *n.* ハンカチ

He blew his nose with a handkerchief.
彼はハンカチで鼻をかんだ。

handle *n.* (on door, drawer, pot) 取っ手, (on broom, knife) 柄, (on cup) つまみ, (for turning/winding) ハンドル

v. (deal with) 扱う, 取り扱う, (…に) 対処する

Damn! The handle's come off the pot.
くそっ！ なべの取っ手が取れた。

The faucet handle is so tight, it won't budge.

蛇口のハンドルがかたくて動かない。

How are we going to handle this difficult customer?
そのうるさい客に、どう対処しようか？

handlebars ***n.*** ハンドル

handler ***n.*** (animal trainer) 調教師

handmade ***adj.*** 手作りの

hand-me-down ***n.*** (clothes) お下がり, お古

handout ***n.*** (paper distributed in class) プリント, 配布資料

handrail ***n.*** 手すり

handshake ***n.*** 握手

handsome ***adj.*** (of man) ハンサムな; (of salary) 相当の

a handsome man
ハンサムな男性 [美男子]

hands-on ***adj.*** (of experience, training) 実地-

handstand ***n.*** 逆立ち

handwriting ***n.*** (手書きの) 字

The more rushed I am, the sloppier my handwriting becomes.
急げば急ぐほど、字が汚くなる。

You have good handwriting.
字がきれいですね/達筆ですね。

♦ **handwriting analysis** ***n.*** 筆跡鑑定

handwritten ***adj.*** 手書きの

handy ***adj.*** (convenient) 便利な

come in handy 役に立つ, 重宝する

This small stapler really comes in handy.
この小さなホッチキスは本当に重宝する。

handyman ***n.*** 便利屋(さん)

hang ***v.*** (put up: picture etc.) 掛ける, (hang from the ceiling) つるす, (of hair, garment, rope) 垂れ下がる; (execute by hanging) 絞首刑にする

Which wall should we hang this picture on?
この絵をどの壁に掛けましょうか？

Her hair hung down to her waist.
彼女の髪は腰まであった。

They used to hang criminals in Britain.
英国では昔、犯罪者を絞首刑にしていた。

get the hang of …のこつをつかむ

hang in (there) (persevere) がんばる

hang around ***v.*** (spend time idly) ぶらぶらする, ぶらつく, (wait) 待つ

Look, there's no point in hanging around any longer. Let's go home.
ねえ、これ以上待ってもしようがないよ。帰ろう。

hang around with …といっしょに行動する, …とよくいっしょにいる

Do you hang around with Suzuki much?
鈴木さんとよくいっしょにいますか？

hang on ***v.***

1 WAIT: 待つ

2 HOLD ON TO: (**hang on to**) (=grip firmly) しっかりつかむ, (rope) …にしがみつく, (=keep) 取っておく

3 PERSEVERE: がんばる

1 Could you hang on a minute?
ちょっと待ってくれる？

2 He was hanging on to the rope for dear life.
彼は必死でロープにしがみついていた。

I'd hang on to that medal. It might appreciate in value.
私だったらそのメダルは取っておくよ。

価値が上がるかもしれないからね。

3 You've got to hang on until the bitter end.
最後の最後までがんばるんだよ。

hang out *v.*

1 LAUNDRY: 干す, 外に出す

2 SPEND TIME IDLY: ぶらぶらする, (of group of people: loiter) たむろする

3 LEAN OUT: (of window) (窓から) 身を乗り出す

4 OF TONGUE: 出る, 垂れる

1 Have you hung out the laundry yet?
洗濯物はもう干した？

2 They used to hang out at the park.
彼らは昔、よく公園にたむろしていた。

Let's hang out tonight.
今夜遊ぼう。

3 Don't hang out the window.
窓から身を乗り出さないで。

4 The dog's tongue was hanging out.
犬は舌を垂らしていた。

hang out with …とよくいっしょにいる

hang over *v.* (be overhead) …の上をおおう, (of cloud) …の上に垂れ込める, (hang over one's head: of problem) 気になってしようがない

A cloud hung over the hill.
雲が丘に垂れ込めていた。

be hung over 二日酔いだ

hang up *v.* (telephone) 電話を切る, (one's coat) 掛ける

He hung up on me.
彼に電話を切られた。

Where can we hang up our coats?
コートはどこに掛ければいいですか？

hangar *n.* (for aircraft) 格納庫

hanger *n.* (for clothes) ハンガー

hanger-on *n.* 取り巻き

hang gliding *n.* ハンググライディング

hanging *n.* (form of execution) 絞首刑

hangover *n.* 二日酔い

I have a hangover. 二日酔いなんだ。

hang-up *n.* コンプレックス, 悩み

hanky-panky *n.* (sexual fun) エッチ

haphazard *adj.* (disorganized) めちゃくちゃな

happen *v.*

1 TAKE PLACE: 起こる, 起きる, 生じる

2 BY CHANCE: (**happen to do**) たまたま…する, 偶然(に)…する

3 MEET / FIND BY CHANCE: (**happen on/upon**) (person) 偶然出くわす, (thing) たまたま見つける

1 When and where did it happen?
いつ、どこで起こったの？

She's always worrying that something will happen, but nothing ever does.
彼女はいつも何か起きるんじゃないかと気をもんでいるが、何も起きていない。

What would happen if he lost his job?
失業したら、彼はどうなるだろう？

If anything happens to the bike, you pay for it, OK?
この自転車に何かあったら、弁償してくださいね？

What happened to you? You're an hour late.
どうしたの？ 1時間も遅刻して。

2 There happened to be roadwork and a huge traffic jam that day.
その日はたまたま道路工事をしていて、

ひどい交通渋滞があった。

If you happen to see Mariko, tell her I'll call her tonight.
もし真理子に会ったら、今夜電話すると伝えておいてください。

Do you happen to know anyone by this name?
ひょっとして、この名前に心当たりはありませんか？

as it happens たまたま, (unfortunately) あいにく, (fortunately) 折よく

it just so happens 偶然にも

It just so happens a good friend of mine works in the same building.
偶然にも、同じビルで友達が働いているんです。

happening ***n.*** (event) 出来事

happily ***adv.*** (willingly) 喜んで, (fortunately) 幸いにも

I happily accepted the offer.
喜んで申し出を受け入れた。

happiness ***n.*** 幸せ, 幸福

find happiness 幸せを見つける

happy ***adj.*** うれしい, 幸せな, 幸福な, (be happy: be full of joy) 喜ぶ

The children were so happy to see their grandmother again.
子供たちはおばあさんにまた会えて、とても喜んでいた。

Did Yoko have a happy childhood?
陽子さんは幸せな子供時代を過ごしたのですか？

We spent many happy days together.
私たちは長い間、共に幸せな日々を送った。

It was the happiest day of my life.
人生で最良の日だった。

be happy to do 喜んで…する

I'll be happy to help you.
((*polite*)) 喜んでお手伝いいたします/お役に立てればうれしいです。

be happy with/about …に満足する

Were you happy with the outcome?
その結果に満足しましたか？

Happy birthday! お誕生日おめでとう(ございます)!

Happy New Year! (said after Jan. 1) (新年)明けましておめでとう(ございます), (said before Jan. 1) よいお年を(お迎えください)

harakiri ***n.*** (ritual disembowelment) 切腹

harass ***v.*** (…に) いやがらせをする

harassment ***n.*** いやがらせ

sexual harassment ((*informal*)) セクハラ

harbor ***n.*** 港

hard

1 ***adj.*** SOLID/FIRM: かたい

2 ***adj.*** DIFFICULT: 難しい, 大変な, (**hard to do**) …しにくい, …しがたい

3 ***adv.*** WITH GREAT EFFORT: 一生懸命, (desperately) 必死で

4 ***adj.*** DILIGENT: 勤勉な, 熱心な, がんばる

5 ***adj.*** FORCEFUL: (of push, rain) 強烈な, 強い, 激しい

6 ***adj.*** OF LIFE/TIMES: つらい, 苦しい, きつい

7 ***adj.*** OF WINTER: 厳しい

8 ***adj.*** OF WATER: 硬質の

9 ***adj.*** OF EVIDENCE: 確かな, 確実な

10 ***adv.*** FORCEFULLY: 強く, 激しく

1 This ground is hard.
ここの地面は固い。

a hard metal such as steel
鋼鉄のような硬い金属

2 This homework is hard.
この宿題は難しい。

It's hard to help people like him.
彼みたいな人を助けるのは大変だ。

Kato is a hard man to negotiate with.
加藤さんは交渉しにくい人だ。

It's hard to imagine her in a skirt.
彼女のスカート姿は想像しにくい。

It's hard to reply. 答えにくいです。

3 That girl studies hard.
その女性は一生懸命勉強する。

I thought hard about it but couldn't come up with a good solution.
必死で考えたけれど、いい解決策は浮かばなかった。

4 He's a hard worker.
彼は働き者[がんばり屋, 努力家]です。

5 Give the thing a hard push.
強く押してみて。

6 a hard life つらい人生

come upon hard times
苦しい時期を迎える

7 It's going to be a hard winter.
厳しい冬になりそうです。

8 The water is hard in this region.
この地域の水は硬水だ。

9 We need hard evidence.
確かな証拠が必要です。

10 It's raining harder now.
雨が激しくなってきた。

be hard at (work) …に精を出している

He's hard at work, as usual.
彼はいつものように、仕事に精を出している。

be hard of hearing 耳が遠い

He's hard of hearing, so speak up when you meet him.
彼は耳が遠いので、会った時は大きな声で話してあげてください。

be hard up for …に困っている

I'm hard up for money at the moment. Could you lend me some?
((*masculine*)) 今、金に困ってるんだ。いくらか貸してもらえないか?

give sb a hard time 困らせる [→ HARASS]

Don't give him a hard time.
彼を困らせないで。

have a hard time ひどい目にあう, 大変な思いをする, 苦労する

He had a hard time in the United States.
彼はアメリカでひどい目にあった。

I had a hard time learning to drive.
(車の) 運転を覚えるのに苦労した。

hardback ***adj., n.*** (book) ハードカバーの(本)

hard-boiled ***adj.*** (of writing style) ハードボイルドの; (of egg) 固ゆでの

hardcore ***adj.*** (of pornography) ハードコアの

hard disk ***n.*** ハードディスク

hard drive ***n.*** ハードドライブ

harden ***v.*** (make/become hard) 固める/固まる

hard-hearted ***adj.*** 無情な, 冷酷な

hard-line ***adj.*** (of policy) 強硬な

♦ **hard-liner** ***n.*** 強硬派

hardly ***adv.***

1 BARELY: ほとんど…ない, (**can hardly do**:

cannot very well do) とても…できない, …するわけにはいかない

2 ONLY JUST: (…した)ばかり, (**had hardly done … when**) …したとたん(に)

1 He has hardly done any work at all today.
彼は今日、ほとんど仕事をしていない。

There was hardly anybody there.
(そこには)ほとんど誰もいなかった。

We hardly ever go there these days.
このごろ、あまりあそこへは行きません。

The man was so drunk he could hardly stand up.
男はほとんど立ち上がれないほど、酔っ払っていた。

I hardly know her.
彼女のことは、ほとんど知りません。

Hardly a day passes without you complaining.
君が不平を言わない日はほとんどないね。

I can hardly skip going to work just because of a cold.
かぜくらいで仕事を休むわけにいかない。

I could hardly believe my ears.
自分の耳を疑った。

I got paid hardly anything for the work.
その仕事の報酬はほんのわずかだった。

2 We've hardly started.
今、始めたばかりです。

I'd hardly gotten out of the bath when the phone rang.
ちょうどおふろから出たとたんに、電話が鳴った。

hardness *n.* かたさ

hard-nosed *adj.* (stubborn) がんこな

hardship *n.* (difficulty) 困難, (suffering) 苦難

hardware *n.* (for computer) ハード(ウエア)

hardware store *n.* 金物屋(さん)

hardwood *n.* 硬材, 堅木

a hardwood floor 硬材の床

hard-working *adj.* 勤勉な, よく働く, (of student) よく勉強する

hare *n.* 野ウサギ

harm *n.* (damage, injury) 害, (by disaster, crime) 被害, (bodily harm) 危害
v. (cause injury to) 害する, 損傷する, (…に)危害を加える, 害を与える, (reputation) 傷つける

Smoking does harm to your health.
喫煙は体に有害です。

The harm has already been done.
すでに被害が出ている。

The oil spill harmed the environment.
石油の流出が環境に被害を及ぼした。

There is a danger that the hostages will be harmed.
人質に危害が加えられる恐れがある。

come to no harm 被害を受けない

I hope the climber comes to no harm.
登山者が無事であればいいですね。

do more harm than good ためになるどころか害になる

Your honesty has done more harm than good.
あなたの正直さは、ためになるどころか迷惑になってきた。

mean no harm 傷つけるつもりはない, 悪気はない

I'm sorry, I didn't mean any harm to anyone.

ごめんなさい。誰も傷つけるつもりはなかったんです。

where's the harm in...? ...しても何も悪いことじゃないだろう

harmful *adj.* 有害な

harmful ultraviolet rays 有害な紫外線

harmless *adj.* 無害な, (of joke) たわいのない

harmonica *n.* ハーモニカ

harmonize *v.* 調和する, (sing in harmony) ((*informal*)) ハモる

H

harmony *n.* (in general) 調和, (in music) ハーモニー

They live in harmony with nature.
彼らは自然と調和した暮らしをしている。

The three vocalists sang in beautiful harmony.
3人の歌手は美しいハーモニーで歌った。

harness *n.* (horse's) 馬具, (for climbing, parachuting etc.) 安全ベルト

v. (energy) 利用する

harp *n.* ハープ

harpsichord *n.* ハープシコード

harsh *adj.* (strict, severe) 厳しい, (cruel) 残酷な, (of sound) 耳障りな

the harsh climate of the Arctic
北極の厳しい気候

harvest *n.* (gathering of crops) 収穫, (time to gather crops) 収穫期, (gathered crops) 収穫物

v. 収穫する, 取り入れる, (rice, barley) 刈り入れる

hash browns *n.* ハッシュドポテト

hashish *n.* ハシシ

hassle *n.* (bother) 面倒, (nuisance) 厄介, 煩わしいこと

v. (bother) (...に) 面倒をかける

"Why don't you want to go?"
"It's a hassle."
「どうして行きたくないの？」
「面倒だから」

haste *n.* 急ぐこと, あわてること [→ HURRY, RUSH]

Haste makes waste.
せいては事を仕損じる。

hasty *adj.* (of departure) 急な, あわただしい, (of decision) 早まった, (of person) せっかちな, (**be hasty in doing**) 急いで...する

Don't make a hasty decision you'll regret later.
早まった決断をすると、あとで後悔しますよ。

♦**hastily** *adv.* 急いで, あわてて

hat *n.* 帽子

wear a hat 帽子をかぶる

take off one's hat 帽子を<u>取る</u> [脱ぐ]

tip one's hat to ...に脱帽する

♦**hatter** *n.* 帽子屋(さん)

hatch[1] *v.* (come out of egg) かえる; (devise in secret) たくらむ

hatch a plot 陰謀をたくらむ

hatch[2] *n.* (door) ハッチ

♦**hatchback** *n.* (car) ハッチバック

hatchet *n.* 手おの

hate *v.* (dislike) (...が) 嫌いだ, いやだ, (detest) 憎む, (...が) 大嫌いだ

I hate opera. 私はオペラが嫌いだ。

Don't you just hate having to cook every day?
毎日料理をしなきゃいけないなんて、

いやじゃないの？

hateful ***adj.*** 憎らしい, (unpleasant) いやな

a hateful person いやな奴

hatred ***n.*** 憎しみ, ((*written*)) 憎悪

have a hatred for ...に憎しみをいだく

haughty ***adj.*** 傲慢な, 横柄な, いばる

haul ***v.*** (drag) 引きずる, (with rope) 引っ張る, (transport) 運搬する

haunted ***adj.*** (of house: haunted by ghosts) 幽霊の出る

have ***v.***

1 AUXILIARY USAGES: (**have done**) ...した, (**have been doing**) ずっと...している, (**have been to**: a place) ...に行ったことがある, (**have done before**) ...したことがある, (**had done**) ...していた, (**had sb/sth done**) ...していたら, ...していれば, (**will have done/been**) ...してしまっている, ...したことになる

2 POSSESS: 持つ, 持っている, (...が)ある, ((*formal*)) 所有する/している

3 MUST: (**have to do**) ...しなければならない, ...する必要がある, (**have to be**) (expressing preference) ...じゃないとだめだ, (expressing conviction) ...に違いない

4 PARTAKE OF: (food) 食べる, (drink) 飲む, (cigarette) 吸う

5 CAUSE TO DO/BE: (**have sb do sth**) (...に)...させる, (=for you) (...に)...してもらう, (**have sth done**/adjective) ...してもらう, ...させる [→ GET 2]

6 UNDERGO: (operation) 受ける

7 SUFFER: (illness) (...に) かかっている, なっている

8 RECEIVE: もらう, ((*humble*)) いただく

9 NOT ALLOW: (**not have...**) ...してはいけない, 許さない

1

RECENT PAST

"Have you finished?"
"Yes, I have. [No, I haven't.]"
「終わった？」
「<u>うん、終わった</u> [いや、まだ]」

"Have they arrived yet?"
"No, not yet."
「彼らはもう着いた？」
「いいえ、まだです」

I haven't told her yet.
まだ彼女に話してない。

He has talked to her about it, hasn't he?
そのことについて彼は彼女に話したんでしょう？

I've already made the beds.
もうベッドメーキングしました。

They've bought a new house.
彼らは新しい家を買ったんだよ。

We've only just gotten back.
たった今帰って来たところです。

They've gone shopping for the afternoon.
彼らは午後は、買い物に出かけています。

"You've forgotten to lock the door."
"Oh, so I have."
「ドアのかぎを閉め忘れてるよ」
「ああ、本当だ」

I seem to have lost my glasses.
どうもめがねが見当たらない。

CONTINUOUS PAST

We've been cleaning up the house all

week.
今週はずっと家の片付けをしています。

Sachiko's been studying piano since she was a child.
幸子は子供のころからずっとピアノを習っている。

How long have you been living here?
ここに住んでどのくらいになりますか？

The Nakata brothers have been members for five years.
中田兄弟が会員になって5年たちます。

PAST WITH "EVER," "ONCE," "NEVER," "BEFORE"

Have you ever been to China?
中国に行ったことがありますか？

I've only been abroad once.
1度しか海外へ行ったことがない。

I've never skied in my life.
今まで一度もスキーをしたことがない。

She said she'd stayed at the hotel once before.
彼女は前に一度、そのホテルに泊まったことがあるんだって。

PAST PERFECT

By the time the police got there, the thieves had escaped.
警察が到着した時には、泥棒は逃げてしまっていた。

I had just turned the corner when the accident occurred.
ちょうど角を曲がったところで、事故が起きた。

If he had come, it would have been fun.
あの人が来ていたら、楽しかったのに。

Had he arrived on time, this would not have happened.
彼が時間どおりに着いていれば、こんなことにはならなかった。

FUTURE PERFECT

I will have finished this work by November of next year.
来年の11月までには、この仕事を終えることになっています。

By this time next month I will have known her for three years.
あと1ヵ月で、彼女と知り合って3年になります。

If they finish by the end of this week, the work will have been done in record time.
彼らが今週中に仕事を終えれば、最短記録になる。

2 The neighbors have three cars.
隣の家の人は車を3台持っている。

He has a farm in the country.
その人は田舎に農場を所有しています。

Do you have your books?
本は持っていますか？

Here, have an umbrella.
どうぞ、この傘を持って行って。

I don't have enough money for that.
それを買うだけのお金がない。

Do you have any brothers or sisters?
((*polite*)) ごきょうだいは、いらっしゃいますか？

He has brown hair.
彼の髪の毛は茶色い。

I'll have the book by next week, I'm sure.
来週にはきっと本が手に入るよ。

The apartment has two large rooms and one small one.
そのマンションには大きな部屋が二つと、小さな部屋が一つある。

I don't have the time for that.
その時間がないんです。

3 Do you have to attend the meeting?
その会議に出席しなければならないんですか？

We were told that all students have to register by the end of the week.
学生は全員、今週中に、登録手続きをしなければならないそうだ。

You don't have to wear a tie, you know.
ネクタイをする必要はないんですよ。

He has to be French.
あの人はフランス人に違いない。

4 Would you like to have a drink?
飲み物はいかがですか？

Here, have some food.
どうぞ、食べて [((*polite*)) 召し上がって]。

What did you have for lunch?
お昼は何を食べたの？

I usually have toast for breakfast.
朝食は、たいていトーストです。

5 I'll have him type it up by tomorrow.
明日までに彼に入力してもらおう。

Why don't you have them bring the food over?
食べ物を持って来てもらったらどう？

I'm going to have the car washed.
車を洗ってもらうつもりです。

6 She'll have an operation next week.
彼女は来週、手術を受けます。

7 I have a cold. かぜをひいています。

My father has cancer.
父が、がんなんです。

8 I'll take the red one.
赤いのをいただきます。

May I have your name and address, please?
お名前とご住所を教えていただけますか？

9 I won't have this noise in the house!
家の中でこんなに騒いではいけません！

We can't have her marrying him!
彼女は、あの人とは結婚させません！

COMMON EXPRESSIONS WITH "HAVE"

have a baby 子供を産む
have a bath おふろに入る
have a cold かぜをひく
have a look (at) 見てみる
have a meal 食事をする
have an operation 手術を受ける
have a rest 休む
have children 子供がいる/子供を持つ
have time 時間がある

had better do → BETTER

have (something) against …に反感をもつ, 嫌う

I don't know what he has against her.
彼がどうして彼女を嫌っているのかわからない。

have all to oneself 独占する

I have the house all to myself during August.
8月中は、私だけが家にいます。

have to do with …と関係がある, …とかかわる

I wouldn't have anything to do with that man.
あんな人とは絶対にかかわらない。

That has nothing to do with it.
それは全く関係ないよ。

Since I've retired, I've had little to do with the company.

退職以来、会社とはほとんどかかわりがなくなった。

Her business has something to do with importing.
彼女は輸入関係の仕事をしている。

you have (got) me there 知らない, わからない

You've got me there. I have no idea.
わからないなあ、全然。

have back *v.* (have returned) 返してもらう

Can I have my pen back, please?
ペンを返してもらえますか？

have off *v.* (time) 休む

Can I have tomorrow off?
明日、休んでもいいですか？

have on [→ WEAR 1]

have to [→ HAVE 3]

haven *n.* (resting place) 安息の地, (refuge) 避難所

havoc *n.* (destruction) 大破壊, (damage) 大損害, (chaos) 大混乱

wreak havoc on めちゃくちゃにする, (…に) 大惨事をもたらす

hawk *n.* タカ, 鷹

hawknose *n.* ワシ鼻, かぎ鼻

hawthorn *n.* サンザシ

hay *n.* 干し草

hay fever *n.* 花粉症 [→ POLLEN]

Do you get hay fever in the spring?
春になると花粉症になりますか？

hazard *n.* 危険 [→ DANGER]

a fire hazard 火災の原因

hazardous *adj.* 危険な, (of material) 有害な

Smoking is hazardous to your health.
喫煙は健康に有害です。

haze *n.* かすみ

hazel *n.* ハシバミ, (hazelnut) ハシバミの実, ヘーゼルナッツ; (color) 薄茶色

hazy *adj.* (of sky) かすんだ, (of memory) ぼんやりした

he *pron.* 彼は/が, あの人は/が [NOTE: Avoid using 彼 in reference to social superiors. Use the person's name, followed by さん, or job title instead.]

Is he coming? 彼は来ますか？

he and his wife and children
彼と奥さんと子供たち

He was known to everyone around here.
このあたりでは誰でも彼を知っていた。

He (= the company president) is going to make an important announcement today.
社長は今日、重要な発表を行います。

head

1 *n.* PART OF THE BODY: 頭 [→ picture of BODY]

2 *n.* INTELLIGENCE: 頭, 頭脳

3 *n.* LEADER: (of company) 社長, (of division/department of company) 部長, (of corporation) 理事長, (of institution) 所長, (of committee) 委員長, (of household) 世帯主

4 *n.* OF LINE: 先頭

5 *n.* TOP: (of nail, pin) 頭, (of page) 上, (**heads**: of coin) 表

6 *n.* OF BEER: 泡

7 *v.* GO: (head for/to) (…に) 向かう

8 *v.* LEAD: (be at the head of) 率いる, (…

の) 先頭に立つ, (be in charge of) 引率する, (direct) 案内する, 導く

9 *v.* **IN SOCCER:** ヘディングする

1 He has an unusually large head.
あの人の頭は特別、大きい。

The dog put its head on my lap.
犬が私のひざに頭をのせた。

Can you do this sum in your head?
これを暗算でできますか？

2 Use your head. 頭を使いなさい。

She has a good head on her shoulders.
彼女は頭がいい [頭脳明晰だ]。

3 Who is the head of the department?
部長は誰ですか？

Mr. Oda is the head of the organization.
小田さんはその組織のトップです。

4 We stood at the head of the line.
私たちは列の先頭に立っていた。

5 Put it at the head of the page.
ページの上に入れてください。

6 There's no head to this beer.
このビールは泡が立っていない。

7 Where are you heading to?
どこへ向かってるんですか？

8 Who is heading the procession?
行列の先頭は誰ですか？

be head over heels (in love) ぞっこんほれ込む

from head to foot 頭のてっぺんから足の先まで, 全身

The kids were covered in mud from head to foot.
子供たちは全身、泥だらけだった。

get it into one's head (that...) (…と) 思い込む

She's gotten it into her head that I'm some kind of artist.
私が何かの芸術家だと、彼女は思い込んでいる。

go to one's head 思い上がる, うぬぼれる

Success seems to have gone to his head.
彼は成功して思い上がっているようだ。

keep one's head 冷静でいる, 落ち着いている

She kept her head and didn't panic.
彼女は落ち着いていて、取り乱したりしなかった。

lose one's head 取り乱す, うろたえる, 動転する

He lost his head, panicked, and ran for the door.
彼は動転してパニックに陥り、ドアへ駆けて行った。

turn (a few) heads (人の) 目を引く

That short skirt certainly turned a few heads.
確かに、あの丈の短いスカートは人の目を引いた。

headache *n.* 頭痛 [→ ACHE], (annoying problem) 悩みのたね, 厄介なもの

I've got a bad headache.
ひどい頭痛がする。

The exams turned out to be a real headache for me.
試験は本当に厄介なものになった。

headband *n.* ヘアバンド, (Japanese-style) はち巻き

wear a headband
ヘアバンドをつける [はち巻きを締める]

header *n.* (in soccer) ヘディング; (in document) ヘッダー

headfirst *adv.* 頭から

go in headfirst 頭から入る

fall headfirst 真っ逆さまに落ちる

headhunt *v.* (**be headhunted**) 引き抜かれる

♦ **headhunting** *n.* ヘッドハンティング, 引き抜き

headhunter *n.* ヘッドハンター, 人材スカウト

heading *n.* (of chapter etc.) 表題; (direction of travel) 方向, 向き

headlight *n.* ヘッドライト [→ picture of CAR]

turn on [off] one's headlights

ヘッドライトをつける [消す]

headline *n.* (in newspaper) 見出し, (**headlines**: pieces of news on news program) 主な項目

v. (feature as main act) (…の) 主役をする

headlong *adj.* (of rush) まっしぐらの, (of fall) 真っ逆さまの

adv. (headfirst) 頭から, 真っ逆さまに, (recklessly) 無謀に

headmaster *n.* 校長

head-on *adj.* (真)正面の

adv. (真)正面から

It was a head-on collision.

正面衝突だった。

headphones *n.* ヘッドホン

headquarters *n.* 本部, (of company) 本社, (military headquarters) 司令部

head start *n.* (in race) 早いスタート, (advantage) 有利な出だし, (in game) ハンディをつけたスタート

headstone *n.* (of grave) 墓石 [→ picture of GRAVE]

headstrong *adj.* がんこな, 強情な

headwind *n.* 向かい風

heal *v.* (cause to heal) 治す, (recover) 治る

The cut has healed. 傷が治った。

health *n.* 健康, (condition) (体の)調子

be good [bad] for one's health

体にいい [悪い]

Oh, don't worry. He's in good health.

心配しないで。彼は健康だよ。

♦ **health care** *n.* 健康管理, (medical treatment) 医療

health checkup *n.* 健康診断, 健診

health food *n.* 健康食品

health insurance *n.* 健康保険

healthy *adj.* (having good health) 健康な, (good for health) 健康にいい, (healthy-looking) 元気な, (wholesome) 健全な

healthy parents 健康な両親

a healthy diet 健康にいい食事

Kato was looking healthy.

加藤さんは元気そうだった。

He has a healthy appetite.

彼は食欲旺盛だ。

healthy reading 健全な読み物

heap *n.* (pile) 山, (lots) たくさん

v. (pile up) 積み重ねる, 積み上げる

a heap of books 本の山

There's a heap of work to do.

仕事が山ほど [たくさん] ある。

He was seen heaping his plate with food at the banquet.

あの人は宴会で、取り皿に料理を山盛りにしていた。

hear *v.*

1 PERCEIVE SOUND: (hear the sound of) (…が) 聞こえる

2 LISTEN TO: 聞く

3 BE TOLD: (…と) 聞く, (rumor) 耳にする, (…が) 耳に入る, (**I hear that…/ I've heard that…**) …そうだ, …らしい

4 RECEIVE CORRESPONDENCE: (hear from) (…から) 連絡がある

1 I heard someone shouting.
誰かが叫んでいるのが聞こえた。

Can you hear the cars go by?
車の通る音が聞こえますか?

2 Let's hear what he has to say.
彼の言い分を聞きましょう。

I really don't like to hear you talk like that.
あなたからそんな言葉は聞きたくない。

3 Have you heard about this new wonder drug?
このすごい新薬のことを聞いた?

If you hear anything strange, call the police.
変わったことを耳にしたら、警察に通報してください。

I'm glad to hear that you found a job.
仕事が見つかってよかったですね。

I've heard Hayashi's going to quit the company.
林さんは会社を辞めるらしい。

I hear that you're getting married.
((*polite*)) 結婚なさるそうですね。

4 I haven't heard from Miyuki in a long time.
長いこと、美幸から連絡がない。

hear enough of 聞き飽きる, 耳にたこができるほど聞く

I've heard enough of your griping!
君のぐちは聞き飽きたよ!

make oneself heard 聞こえるように話す, 声が届く

It's difficult to make oneself heard with all the noise in there.
あんなうるさい所では話ができない。

hearing *n.* (power of hearing) 聴力, (one of the five senses) 聴覚

a hearing test 聴力検査

be hard of hearing 耳が遠い [→ HARD]

♦**hearing aid** *n.* 補聴器

hearsay *n.* うわさ

according to hearsay うわさによると

hearse *n.* 霊柩車

heart *n.*

1 PART OF THE BODY: 心臓, (chest) 胸

2 SHAPE: ハート形

3 CENTER OF THE EMOTIONS: 心, 胸

4 CENTRAL PART: 真ん中, 中心

5 OF MATTER / PROBLEM: 核心

6 SUIT OF CARDS: (**hearts**) ハート

1 I can hear my heart beating.
自分の心臓の鼓動が聞こえる。

2 heart-shaped candy ハート形のお菓子

The shirt has hearts printed on it.
シャツにはハートがプリントされている。

3 You have a warm heart.
君は心のあたたかい人だね。

When you're in trouble, listen to your heart.
困った時は、自分の心に聞きなさい。

I love her with all my heart.
彼女を心から愛している。

I hope with all my heart that things go well for you on your expedition.

探検がうまくいくよう、心から祈りしています。

My heart aches when I think of her lying in the hospital.
病院で寝ている彼女のことを思うと、胸が痛む。

My heart goes out to the victims and their families.
被害者とそのご家族に心から同情いたします。

4 a fancy hotel in the heart of New York ニューヨークの中心にある高級ホテル

5 the heart of the matter 問題の核心

6 the queen of hearts ハートのクイーン

at heart 本当は, ((*informal*)) 根は

He's a good guy at heart.
根は、いい奴なんだ。

break sb's heart (lover's heart) 傷つける, (...に) つらい思いをさせる, (**have one's heart broken**) 胸が張り裂ける思いをする, 悲嘆に暮れる

The sudden news of his mother's death nearly broke his heart.
母親の突然の訃報に、彼の胸は張り裂けそうだった。

by heart そらで

recite by heart そらで言う [暗唱する]

She had learned the passage by heart.
彼女は、そのくだりを暗記していた。

get to the heart of ...の核心をつかむ

It took some time, but we did eventually get to the heart of the matter.
多少時間はかかったが、ついに問題の核心をつかんだ。

have a change of heart 気が変わる

It seems he's had a change of heart.
彼は気が変わったようだ。

have the heart to do ...する勇気がある

I didn't have the heart to tell her.
彼女に言う勇気はなかった。

set one's heart on 欲しいと思う, (speaking about sb else) 欲しがる, (**set one's heart on doing**) ...しようと心に決める

It's no good setting your heart on something you know we can't afford.
買えないとわかっている物を欲しがっても、しようがないでしょ。

take to heart 真剣に受け止める

He took my words to heart and became very upset.
彼は私の言葉を真剣に受け止めて、うろたえた。

heartache *n.* 心痛

heart attack *n.* 心臓発作, 心臓麻痺

heartbeat *n.* 鼓動, 心拍

heartbreak *n.* (emotional shock) 失恋, (misery) 悲嘆

heartbreaking *adj.* (very sad) とてもつらい, 悲痛な

It was heartbreaking to see the grief on the faces of survivors who had lost loved ones.
身内を亡くした遺族の悲しい顔を見るのは、とてもつらかった。

heartbroken *adj.* とても傷ついた, ((*written*)) 悲嘆に暮れた

She was heartbroken when he dumped her.
彼女は彼に捨てられて、ひどく傷ついた。

heartburn *n.* 胸焼け

heart disease *n.* 心臓病

heart failure *n.* 心臓麻痺, 心不全

heartland *n.* 中心地, 心臓地帯

heartless *adj.* (pitiless) 薄情な, (cruel) 冷酷な

heartthrob *n.* (idol) アイドル

heart transplant *n.* 心臓移植

hearty *adj.* (of welcome, applause) あたたかい, 心からの, (of person) 元気な, (of appetite) (食欲)旺盛な, (of meal) たっぷりの, おなかいっぱいの

heat

1 *n.* HOTNESS: (of climate) 暑さ, (of water) 熱さ, (of sun) 熱; (temperature) 温度

2 *v.* MAKE HOT: (room) 暖かくする, 暖める, (food) 温める, (water) (湯を)沸かす, (metal, oil) 熱する

3 *n.* SOURCE OF HEAT: (in building) 暖房, (in cooking) 火

4 *n.* PART OF A COMPETITION: (**heats**) -戦

1 The heat is unbearable!
この暑さには耐えられない!

The sun's heat was incredible.
日差しの暑さはすごかった。

body heat 体温

2 The room is difficult to heat.
この部屋は暖まりにくい。

Heat it up in the microwave.
レンジで温めて。

3 Don't forget to turn off the heat.
暖房を切るのを忘れないで。

Cook it on a low [high] heat.
弱火 [強火] で調理します。

4 Our team didn't even get through the first heats.
我々のチームは初戦も突破できなかった。

in/on heat (of animal) 発情して

heated *adj.* (made warm/hot) 温めた; (of debate) 激しい, 白熱した

heated water お湯

a heated swimming pool 温水プール

The discussion became heated.
議論は白熱した。

heater *n.* 暖房, (stove used to heat a room) ストーブ, (in car) ヒーター

The heater isn't working.
暖房が利かない。

a gas [electric] heater
ガス [電気] ストーブ

heather *n.* (plant) ヘザー, (heath) ヒース

heating *n.* 暖房

heat rash *n.* あせも

heatstroke *n.* 熱射病

heat wave *n.* 熱波

heave *v.* (lift) 引き上げる, (toss) 投げる, (pull) 引っ張る; (vomit) 吐く, (gag) 吐き気を催す

heave a sigh ため息をつく

heaven *n.* ((*also figurative*)) 天国, (**the heavens:** the skies) 天, 空, ((*poetic*)) 天空

Grandma has gone to heaven.
おばあちゃんは天国に行ったんだよ。

It's heaven not having to go to work.
仕事に行かなくていいなんて天国だよ。

for heaven's sake (pleading) お願いだから, (expressing irritation) 全くもう, 冗談じゃない

heavily *adv.* 重く, どっしりと, (to a great extent) 大いに, (in large amounts) 多量に

heavy *adj.*

1 NOT LIGHT: 重い, ((*informal*)) 重たい, (of

person) がっしりした

2 EXCESSIVE: (of rain, snow) 激しい, 豪-, (of wind) 強い, (of traffic) 激しい, (of breathing) 荒い, (of smoker) ヘビー-; (of workload) 厳しい, ぎっしり詰まった

3 OF MEAL/FOOD: 重い, (difficult to digest) 胃にもたれる

4 HARD/STRICT: (**be heavy on**) …に厳しい

5 DIFFICULT TO UNDERSTAND: 難しい, 難解な

1 This bag is really heavy.
このかばんは本当に重い。
He has a heavy build.
彼はがっしりしている。

2 a heavy snowfall [rain] 豪雪[雨]
Are you a heavy smoker?
たばこは、かなり吸いますか？
She said she has a heavy schedule this week.
彼女は今週、予定がぎっしり詰まっていると言った。
The workload is heavy, but the pay is quite good.
仕事量は多いが、給料はかなりいい。

3 Let's not serve a heavy dessert since the meal itself will be plenty.
食事だけでたっぷりあるから、重いデザートを出すのはやめよう。

4 I think the teacher is being rather heavy on him, don't you?
先生はなんだか彼に厳しいと思わない？

5 It's a good book, but a heavy read.
いい本だけど、難解だね。

♦ **heavy drinker** *n.* 酒飲み, 酒豪, ((*informal*)) 飲んべえ, (person with a high tolerance for alcohol) ((*informal*)) ざる

heavy industry *n.* 重工業

heavy-duty *adj.* とても丈夫な, 頑丈な

heavy-handed *adj.* (rough) 乱暴な, (clumsy) 不器用な

heavy metal *n.* (music) ヘビーメタル

heck *interj.* まあ, いいか

what the heck → WHAT THE HELL

heckle *v.* やじる

hectare *n.* ヘクタール

hectic *adj.* (very busy) とても忙しい, ((*informal*)) てんてこ舞いの

hedge *n.* (bush forming barrier) 垣根, 生け垣

v. (not answer a question) はぐらかす
The hedge needs trimming.
生け垣には手入れが必要だ。

hedgehog *n.* ハリネズミ

hedonism *n.* 快楽主義

hedonist *n.* 快楽主義者

heed *v.* (…に) 注意を払う

heel *n.* (part of foot/shoe) かかと [→ picture of BODY]

heifer *n.* 若い雌牛

height *n.* (vertical measurement) 高さ, 丈, (of person) 身長, 背, (of mountain: height above sea level) 海抜, (of airplane: altitude) 高度; (zenith) 絶頂
What's the height of the ceiling?
天井の高さはどのくらいありますか？
What's your height?
身長はどのくらいですか？
What height was the plane flying at?
飛行機はどのくらいの高度で飛んでいたのですか？
the height of summer 真夏
the height of one's popularity 人気絶頂

heighten *v.* (raise) 高める, (rise) 高まる
heightened security 厳重警備

heir(ess) *n.* (to property) 相続人, (to throne, right, tradition) 継承者

heirloom *n.* 家宝

helical *adj.* らせんの

helicopter *n.* ヘリコプター

helium *n.* ヘリウム

helix *n.* らせん

hell *n.* 地獄, (place like hell) 地獄のような場所, (living hell) 生き地獄
interj. ちぇっ, まあ
I went through hell getting a divorce.
離婚で地獄を経験した。
Vietnam was a living hell.
ベトナムは生き地獄だった。
Hell, I could use a break.
まあ、休むとするか。
all hell breaks loose 大混乱が起こる, 大騒ぎになる
All hell is about to break loose.
大混乱が起ころうとしている。
Go to hell! くたばれ, 地獄へ落ちろ
Hell no! とんでもない, 冗談じゃない
just for the hell of it 面白半分に
He did it just for the hell of it.
彼はただ面白半分にやった。
what the hell (expressing surprise) 一体, 一体全体, (expressing indifference) まあいいよ
What the hell do you think you're doing?
一体どういうつもりなの？

hello *interj.* こんにちは, (answering telephone) もしもし
Hello Mr. Tanaka. Thank you for the other day.
こんにちは、田中さん。先日はどうもありがとうございました。
"Hello."
"Hello, who's speaking please?"
「もしもし」
「もしもし、どちら様ですか？」

helmet *n.* ヘルメット, (traditional Japanese helmet worn by samurai) かぶと

help
1 *n.* ASSISTANCE: 手伝い, (from danger) 助け, (financial assistance) 援助
2 *v.* ASSIST: 手伝う, (…に) 手を貸す, (be of use to) (…の) 役に立つ, 力になる, (help sb out of danger) 助ける, 救う
3 *n.* STH/SB THAT HELPS: 役立つ物/人
4 *v.* OF MEDICINE: 効く

1 They gave us some help.
彼らが手伝ってくれた。
Thanks for your help.
手伝ってくれてありがとう。
That's not a lot of help, is it?
あれではあまり助けにならないでしょう?
There was no help at hand.
助けてくれる人は近くにはいなかった。
Were the hints I gave you of any help?
私のヒントは役に立ちましたか？
I shouted for help.
大声で助けを呼んだ。

2 Can you help the others once you've finished?
自分の分が終わったら、ほかの人を手伝ってもらえますか？
His brother helped him out.
彼のお兄さんが手助けしていた。
Could you help me here?

ちょっと手を貸していただけませんか?

There was nothing we could do to help.
力になれることは何もなかった。

3 He is a great help to me.
彼のおかげで、とても助かっています。

4 This cough medicine should help.
このせき止めは効くはずですよ。

cannot help doing/but do …しないで(は)いられない, …せずに(は)いられない, …せざるを得ない

I couldn't help laughing.
笑わずにはいられなかった。

I couldn't help overhearing their conversation.
彼らの会話を盗み聞きしてしまった。

I couldn't help falling asleep during the lecture.
受講中に思わず居眠りしてしまった。

help oneself (to food/drink) 自由に取って食べる/飲む

I helped myself to some more rice.
自分でご飯をお代わりした。

Please help yourself.
ご自由に召し上がってください。

it can't be helped どうしようもない

I'm sorry to have to reschedule our appointment, but it really can't be helped.
約束の日時を変更して申し訳ない。でも本当にどうしようもないんだ。

helper *n.* 手伝う人, ヘルパー

helpful *adj.* 役に立つ

helping *n.* (of food: a single portion) -人前, (bowl) -ぜん, -杯, (plate) -皿

a second helping お代わり

helpless *adj.* (unable to do anything) 何もできない, (incompetent) 無力な

helter-skelter *adv.* (in a rushed manner) あわてて

adj. (hurried) あわてた

hem *n.* (on clothing) すそ

take the hem up すそ上げする

hematology *n.* 血液学

hemisphere *n.* 半球

the northern [southern] hemisphere
北[南]半球

hemlock *n.* (plant) ドクニンジン, 毒人参

hemoglobin *n.* ヘモグロビン

hemophilia *n.* 血友病

hemorrhage *n.* (多量の)出血

v. 多量に出血する

hemorrhoid(s) *n.* 痔

hemp *n.* (plant) 麻, (material) 麻の繊維

hen *n.* (female chicken) めんどり, (chicken) ニワトリ, 鶏

hence *adv.* (therefore) したがって

henceforth, henceforward *adv.* 今後は

henpeck *v.* (husband) (夫を)尻に敷く

hepatitis *n.* 肝炎

♦ **hepatitis A/B** *n.* A型/B型肝炎

her *adj.* 彼女の, あの人の

pron. 彼女, あの人, (as direct object) 彼女を, (as indirect object) 彼女に

Her coat is here.
彼女のコートはここにあります。

Jun is one of her best friends.
純君は彼女の親友の一人です。

Do you know her? 彼女を知ってる?

Would you give this to her, please?
これを彼女に渡してもらえますか?

herald *v.* (signal) (…の)兆しとなる, 到

来を告げる

n. (messenger) 使者

heraldry *n.* 紋章学

herb *n.* ハーブ, 香草, (used in medicine) 薬草

herb tea ハーブティー

herbicide *n.* 除草剤

herbivore *n.* 草食動物

♦**herbivorous** *adj.* 草食性の

herd *n.* 群れ

here *adv.* ここに/で, ((*polite*)) こちらに/で, ((*informal*)) こっちに/で, (at this point in time) ここで, 今, (referring to a point in a discussion) この点に/で

n. ここ

Now, where did I put my pen? Ah, here it is.
ええと、どこにペンを置いたっけ？ あっ、ここだ。

We're here on the map.
地図でいうと、私たちはここにいます。

Come over here, will you.
こっちに来てくれない？

Here comes Mother. お母さんが来た。

How far is it from here?
ここからどのくらいありますか？

around here このあたりに/で

It's around here somewhere.
どこかこのあたりです。

here and now 今ここで, 今すぐに, (the here and now) 現在

here and there あちこちに

Here and there you could see the remains of dead seabirds.
あちこちに海鳥の死骸があった。

here goes さあやるぞ

here we go again ああまたか

Here we go again—the same old story.
ああまたか——いつもの話が始まったよ。

neither here nor there 重要でない, 問題外で, 無関係で

Whether you succeed or not is neither here nor there.
成功するかしないかは、重要なことではない。

hereafter *adv.* 今後は, これからは

n. (the hereafter) 死後の世界, あの世

hereby *adv.* これによって, これにより

hereditary *adj.* 遺伝の, (of title, position) 世襲の

a hereditary disease/disorder 遺伝病

herein *adv.* この中に, ここに

hereof *adv.* (of this) これの, (about this) これに関して

hereon → HEREUPON

heresy *n.* (religious) 異端, (in general) 反論

hereto *adv.* これに, ここに

heretofore *adv.* 従来, これまで

hereunder *adv.* 以下に, 下記に

hereupon *adv.* (concerning) これに関して, (on this matter) ここに, ここにおいて

herewith *adv.* (in this envelope) 同封して, (with this e-mail) 添付して

heritage *n.* (cultural heritage) 文化遺産, (tradition) 伝統

hermaphrodite *n.* 両性具有者

hermit *n.* 世捨て人

hernia *n.* ヘルニア

have a hernia ヘルニアになる

hero *n.* 英雄, ヒーロー, (chief character in a story) 主人公

heroic *adj.* 英雄的な

heroin *n.* ヘロイン

heroine *n.* ヒロイン, (chief character in a story) 主人公

heroism *n.* (bravery) 勇敢さ

herpes *n.* ヘルペス, 疱疹

herring *n.* ニシン

hers *pron.* 彼女の(もの), あの人の(もの)

This is mine and that's hers.
これは私の(もの)、あれは彼女の(もの)です。

herself *pron.* 自分, (used emphatically after a name/title) …自身, (**she herself**) 彼女自身

by herself 一人で [→ ONESELF]

hertz *n.* ヘルツ, Hz

hesitant *adj.* ためらう, ちゅうちょする

hesitate *v.* ためらう, ちゅうちょする, (for reasons of modesty: be reserved) 遠慮する

If there's anything you don't understand, don't hesitate to ask.
わからないことがあったら、遠慮せずに聞いてください。

hesitation *n.* ためらい, ちゅうちょ

heterogeneous *adj.* (consisting of many different people/things) いろいろな人々/物から成る

a heterogeneous society
いろいろな民族から成る社会

heterosexual *adj.* 異性愛の
n. (person) 異性愛者

hexagon *n.* 六角形

hey *interj.* (trying to get sb's attention) ちょっと, すみません, もしもし, ((*masculine/rude*)) おい

heyday *n.* 盛り, 最盛期

hi *interj.* こんにちは, ((*masculine*)) やあ [→ HELLO]

hiatus *n.* (pause) 中断

hibachi *n.* (for cooking food) バーベキューこんろ [NOTE: In Japanese, a 火鉢 is a charcoal brazier.]

hibernate *v.* 冬眠する

hiccup *n., v.* しゃっくり(する)

hickory *n.* (tree) ヒッコリー

hidden *adj.* 隠れた, (deliberately hidden) 隠された, (secret) 秘密の

a hidden meaning 隠(さ)れた意味

hide[1] *v.* (keep oneself out of sight) 隠れる, (conceal) 隠す

There was nowhere to hide.
隠れる所はどこにもなかった。

Let's hide behind the curtains.
カーテンの後ろに隠れよう。

She tried to hide her feelings.
彼女は自分の気持ちを隠そうとした。

The photos were hidden in a drawer.
写真は引き出しの中に隠してあった。

It seems to me that they may have hidden everything away.
彼らは、全部隠したんじゃないかという気がする。

hide[2] *n.* (animal skin) 皮

hide-and-seek *n.* 隠れんぼ

hideous *adj.* (frightening) 恐ろしい, ぞっとする; (ugly) ひどく醜い

Seeing the hounds tearing at the flesh of

the fox was a hideous sight.
猟犬がキツネの肉をかみちぎっている光景には、ぞっとした。

hierarchy ***n.*** 階層制度, ヒエラルキー

hi-fi ***n.*** ハイファイ

high ***adj.*** 高い, (giving measurement) 高さ..., (of heat) 強い, (of speed) 速い, (of quality) 高い; (on drugs) ハイになっている

It's a very high building.
とても高いビルです。

How high is the ceiling?
天井の高さはどのくらいありますか？

The fence is two meters high.
フェンスは高さが2メートルあります。

Which mountain is higher?
どっちの山が高いですか？

I got the highest grade on the test.
テストで最高点を取った。

They were traveling at a high speed.
彼らはスピードを出していた。

He's high up in the company.
彼は会社で高い地位に就いている。

Her work is of the highest quality.
彼女は非常に質の高い仕事をします。

He was high on drugs.
彼は麻薬でハイになっていた。

high blood pressure ***n.*** 高血圧

highbrow ***adj.*** (for intellectuals) インテリ向きの

high-class ***adj.*** 高級な

higher education ***n.*** 高等教育

high-fat ***adj.*** 高脂肪の

high five ***n.*** ハイファイブ

give someone a high five
(...と) ハイファイブをする

high-grade ***adj.*** 質のいい, 高級な

high heels ***n.*** ハイヒール

high jump ***n.*** 走り高跳び

high-level ***adj.*** 高レベルの, ハイレベルの, (of talks) 高官(レベル)の

highlight ***v.*** (emphasize) 強調する, (of press/media: make a big issue/story of) 大きく取り上げる

n. ハイライト, (of event, show) 見せ場, 呼び物

highlighter ***n.*** 蛍光ペン, マーカー [→ picture of STATIONERY]

highly ***adv.*** (extremely) 非常に

think highly of (highly value) 高く評価する, (respect) 尊敬する

♦ **highly paid** ***adj.*** 高給の

high-pitched ***adj.*** 甲高い

high-powered ***adj.*** (of machine) 高性能の, (of person) 有能な

high-profile ***adj.*** (of person) 注目を集めている, 話題の

high-rise ***adj.*** 高層の

n. (building) 高層ビル

high school ***n.*** 高校, ((*formal*)) 高等学校

high society ***n.*** 上流社会

high-tech ***adj.*** ハイテク-

highway ***n.*** 幹線道路

hijack ***v.*** ハイジャックする, 乗っ取る

hijacker ***n.*** ハイジャック犯人, 乗っ取り犯人

hike ***v.*** ハイキングをする

n. ハイク, (rise) 引き上げ

hiker ***n.*** ハイカー

hiking ***n.*** ハイキング

H

hilarious *adj.* すごくおかしい

hill *n.* (small mountain) 丘, 小山, (slope) 坂, (grade) 傾斜

a steep hill 急な坂

hillbilly *n.* 田舎者

hillside *n.* 丘の中腹, 丘の斜面

hilly *adj.* 丘の多い, 丘陵の

him *pron.* 彼, あの人, (as direct object) 彼を, (as indirect object) 彼に

I love him. あの人を愛している。

The boss wants you to call him.
所長が電話してほしいとのことです。

I gave him a present.
彼に贈り物をしました。

I was with him all the time.
彼とずっといっしょだった。

Did you speak to him?
彼に話しましたか？

There's no need for him to worry.
彼が心配することはない。

himself *pron.* 自分, (used emphatically after a name/title) …自身, (**he himself**) 彼自身

by himself 一人で [→ ONESELF]

hind *adj.* (back) 後ろの

hind legs 後脚 [後ろ足]

hinder *v.* じゃまする, (movement, progress) 妨げる, 阻む

Snowstorms are hindering the rescue effort.
吹雪が救援活動を阻んでいる。

hindrance *n.* じゃま, (obstacle) 妨害物

hindsight *n.* 後知恵

in hindsight 後から考えてみると

Hindu *n.* ヒンズー教徒

adj. ヒンズー教の

hinge *n.* ちょうつがい

v. (**hinge on**: be contingent on) …にかかっている

hint *n.* (clue) ヒント, ほのめかし, (trace) 気配, (flavor) 風味

v. (suggest) ほのめかす

Please give me a hint.
ヒントを下さい。

He gave me a hint as to where she might be.
彼女の居場所をほのめかしてくれた。

There was a hint of spring in the air.
空気に春の気配があった。

There's a hint of blackberry to this wine.
このワインには、ブラックベリーの風味が感じられる。

He didn't come out and say so, but he hinted it.
彼はそうはっきり言ったわけではないが、ほのめかした。

hip[1] *n.* (part of the body) 腰 [→ picture of BODY]

hip[2] *adj.* (cool) かっこいい, いきな, (fashionable) ファッショナブルな, はやりの

hip-hop *n.* ヒップホップ

hippie *n.* ヒッピー

hippopotamus *n.* カバ

hire *v.* (employ) 雇う [→ RENT]

He has hired a lawyer.
彼は弁護士を雇った。

To hire a chauffeur for the day, you'll need about $100.
運転手を1日雇うと、100ドルぐらいかかります。

♦**hire out** *v.* 貸す

his ***adj.*** 彼の, あの人の

pron. 彼の(もの), あの人の(もの)

That's his signature.
それは彼の署名です。

His briefcase was beside the desk.
彼のブリーフケースは机のわきにあった。

That's his fault.
あれは彼のせいだよ。

She said his name was Bill.
あの人の名前はビルだと言っていた。

This is my car and that's his.
これは私の車で、あれは彼のです。

Hispanic ***n.*** (person) ヒスパニック

adj. (of country, culture) ラテンアメリカ(系)の

hiss ***n.*** シューという音

v. シューという音を出す, (of cat) シューとうなる

historian ***n.*** 歴史家, 歴史学者

historic ***adj.*** 歴史的な, 歴史上重要な

a historic event 歴史的な出来事

historical ***adj.*** 歴史の, 歴史的な, 歴史上の

a historical character 歴史上の人物

historically ***adv.*** 歴史的に, 歴史上

history ***n.*** 歴史, (subject of study) 歴史学; (record: of violence etc.) 前歴

the history of Russia ロシアの歴史

social history 社会史

ancient [medieval, modern] history
古代 [中世, 現代] 史

the history of film 映画史

one's medical history 病歴

The man has a history of violence.
その男には暴行の前歴がある。

hit

1 ***v.*** STRIKE: (punch) 殴る, (slap) たたく, (ball/nail with bat/hammer) 打つ, (bump) ぶつける, (collide with) (…に)ぶつかる, 衝突する, (aim for and hit: target) (…に) 当たる, 命中する, (of storm) 襲う

2 ***v.*** REACH: (…に) 達する

3 ***v.*** COME TO MIND: 思い浮かぶ, ひらめく

4 ***v.*** DAMAGE: (…に) 打撃/損害を与える

5 ***n.*** IN BASEBALL: ヒット, 安打

6 ***n.*** SUCCESS: 大成功, ヒット, 大当たり

7 ***n.*** FINDING ON THE INTERNET: ヒット

1 He hit me in the face.
((*masculine*)) あいつは俺の顔を殴った。

Ichiro hit a home run.
イチローはホームランを打った。

I accidentally hit my head on the door.
うっかりドアに頭をぶつけてしまった。

The car hit the wall.
車が壁にぶつかった。

The car was hit by a motorcycle.
車がオートバイにぶつけられた。

One of the reporters was hit by a bullet.
記者の一人が銃弾に当たった。

Did you hit the target?
的に命中した?

Typhoons usually hit Japan in autumn.
台風はたいてい秋に日本を襲う。

2 The temperature hit forty degrees.
温度が40度に達した。

3 The answer suddenly hit me.
答えが突然ひらめいた。

4 As usual, it's the poor who will be hit the worst.

いつも損をするのは貧乏人だ。

5 He got to third base off that hit.
彼は三塁打を打った。(lit., "He hit a triple.")

6 The song was an immediate hit.
その歌はたちまちヒットした。

7 When I put in a search for that word, I got over a million hits.
その言葉を検索したら、100万件以上ヒットした。

hit it off (with) (...と) うまが合う, 気が合う
We hit it off right from the start.
私たちは初めからうまが合った。

♦**hit on** *v.* (come up with) 思いつく; (person) ナンパする, (...に) 声をかける
He hit on a good business idea.
彼はうまいビジネスを思いついた。
I always get hit on when I go to that bar.
あのバーに行くといつも声をかけられる。

hit-and-run *adj.* (in baseball) ヒットエンドランの
n. (accident) ひき逃げ事故

hitchhike *v.* ヒッチハイクする

hitchhiker *n.* ヒッチハイカー

hither *adv.* ここへ, こちらへ
hither and thither/yon あちらこちらに, あちこちに

hitherto *adv.* 今まで, 従来

HIV *n.* エイズウイルス
HIV positive [negative]
ＨＩＶ陽性 [陰性]
contract HIV　ＨＩＶに感染する

hive *n.* 巣箱

hoard *n.* (of money) 蓄え, (of food) 買いだめ
v. ため込む
They can't throw anything away, even when it's old and useless, so they just hoard all their junk.
古くて使えない物も捨てられなくて、彼らはがらくたをため込んでいる。

hoax *n.* でっち上げ
The photograph of the UFO was a hoax.
ＵＦＯの写真はでっち上げだった。
play a hoax on ...にいたずらする, かつぐ

hobby *n.* 趣味

hockey *n.* (field hockey) ホッケー, (ice hockey) アイスホッケー

hoe *n.* くわ
v. くわで耕す

hog *n.* ブタ, 豚

hold

1 *v.* HAVE IN HANDS/ARMS: (have in hands) 持つ, 握る, (have in arms: hug, embrace) 抱く, (grip) つかむ

2 *v.* MAINTAIN: (pose) 保つ, (attention) 引き付ける

3 *v.* CONTINUE: 続く

4 *v.* HAVE: 持つ

5 *v.* CARRY OUT: (meeting) 開く, (event, ceremony) 行う, 開催する

6 *v.* BE CAPABLE OF CONTAINING: 入る, 入れる, (of stadium, hall) 収容できる, (of car) 乗れる

7 *v.* RESTRAIN: 押さえる, 取り押さえる, 制止する

8 *v.* SUPPORT THE WEIGHT OF: 支える

9 *v.* KEEP IN CUSTODY: 拘留する, 留置する

10 *v.* **CONTROL:** 支配する

11 *v.* **DEFEND:** 守る

12 *n.* **HANDLE/GRIP ON STH:** つかむこと, 握ること

1 Please hold this for me.
これを持っていて。

He was holding a bag in one hand and an umbrella in the other.
その人は片手にかばんを持ち、もう一方の手に傘を持っていた。

He held his elderly mother's hand.
彼は年をとった母親の手を握った。

She held the cat in her arms.
彼女は猫を抱いていた。

He held me by the arm.
彼は私の腕をつかんだ。

2 Just hold still a moment, will you.
ちょっとじっとしていてくれないか。

Hold that pose while I adjust the focus.
焦点を合わせるまで、そのままのポーズでいて。

How do we hold their attention for more than an hour?
1時間以上も、どうやって注意を引き付けていればいいのだろう?

3 The fine weather held throughout our trip.
旅行中ずっと、いい天気が続いた。

If these conditions hold, we may just arrive on time.
このまま順調にいけば、時間どおりに着けるかもしれない。

4 He holds a large number of shares in that company.
彼はその会社の株を相当持っている。

I hold strong views on that subject.
私は、そのことについては確固たる意見をもっています。

5 We'd better hold a meeting to decide the issue.
問題に決着をつけるために、会議を開くべきだ。

When is the festival to be held?
お祭りは、いつ行われるのですか?

6 This bottle holds one liter.
このびんには1リットル入る。

The movie theater holds only a hundred people.
その映画館は100人しか収容できない。

The car holds four comfortably.
車は4人でゆったり乗れる。

7 Hold him! あの男を押さえておけ!

They held him so that he couldn't move.
男が動けないよう取り押さえた。

8 That shelf won't hold those heavy books.
その棚はあんな重い本を支えきれない。

9 She is being held as a suspect by the police.
女は容疑者として警察に拘留されている。

10 How long do you think the guerrillas can hold the territory?
どのくらいの間、ゲリラはその地域を支配できると思いますか?

11 The government was not able to hold its majority.
政府は過半数を守りきれなかった。

12 Do you have a good hold on it?
しっかりつかまっている?

get a hold of 手に入れる

Is there any way I can get a hold of the first edition of this book?
この本の初版は、どうすれば手に入れられますか?

H

hold the line (on telephone) (そのまま) お待ちください

Please hold the line for a moment while I connect you.
しばらくお待ちください。電話をおつなぎします。

on hold 保留にして, (delayed) 延期して

hold back *v.*

1 KEEP FROM ADVANCING: (crowd) 押しとどめる, (keep from spreading: flood, fire) 食い止める

2 INFORMATION: 隠す, 伏せておく

3 EMOTION: 抑える, こらえる

4 HAMPER: じゃまする, 止める

1 The police did their best to hold back the crowd.
警察は群集を押しとどめようと全力を尽くした。

It was difficult to hold back the fans.
ファンを押しとどめておくのは難しかった。

2 The government is holding back important information.
政府は重要な情報を隠している。

3 She couldn't hold back her tears.
彼女は涙を抑えることができなかった。

4 Go ahead! No one is holding you back.
どうぞご自由に! 誰も止めていないよ。

hold down *v.* (restrain: person) 抑圧する, (limit: prices) 抑制する; (hold down a job) (仕事を) きちんと続ける

hold on *v.* (wait) 待つ, (do not hang up phone) そのまま待つ; (keep strong) がんばる; (**hold on to**) (=hold in hands) …につかまる, …にしがみつく, (=cherish) 手放さない

He held on to the branch for as long as he could.
彼はできるだけ長く枝にしがみついていた。

hold out *v.* (stick out: hand) 差し出す; (endure) 持ちこたえる, 耐える

I held out my hand for a free ticket.
無料券をもらおうと、手を差し出した。

I don't know if I'll be able to hold out much longer.
もうこれ以上持ちこたえられないかもしれない。

hold up *v.*

1 EXTEND: (hand) (手を) 挙げる

2 DELAY: 遅らせる

3 ROB: (…に) 強盗に入る, (…を) 襲う

1 All those who are in favor, please hold up your hand.
賛成の人は手を挙げてください /((*formal*)) 賛成の方は挙手を願います。

2 My client has just called to say he's held up in traffic.
お客様から、渋滞に巻き込まれて遅れると、たった今電話があった。

3 The gang held up a convenience store.
一味はコンビニに強盗に入った。

---

holder *n.* (case) 入れ物, ケース

hole *n.* 穴, (in road) くぼみ, へこみ, (for golf ball) ホール

There's a hole in my sock.
靴下に穴があいている。

dig [fill in] a hole 穴を掘る [ふさぐ]

a rabbit hole ウサギの巣穴

a hole in the road 道路のくぼみ

holiday *n.* (national holiday) 祭日, 祝日 [→ p.1177], (day off) 休日, (break) 休

暇, 休み

New Year's Day is a national holiday. 元日は祝日です。

a holiday resort 行楽地

holistic ***adj.*** (of approach) 全体的な, 全般的な

hollow ***adj.*** (of space) 空っぽの, 空洞の, (of sound) こもった, (superficial) うわべだけの; (of eyes: sunken) くぼんだ

n. くぼみ, へこみ

a hollow tube 中が空洞の管

a hollow sound こもった音

hollow eyes and sunken cheeks くぼんだ目とこけたほお

♦**hollow out** ***v.*** くり抜く

holly ***n.*** (tree) セイヨウヒイラギ, 西洋 柊

hollyhock ***n.*** タチアオイ

holocaust ***n.*** (disaster) 大破壊, (**the Holocaust**) ユダヤ人大虐殺, ホロコースト

holy ***adj.*** 神聖な, ((*formal*)) 聖なる

a holy man 聖者

a holy war 聖戦

This is a holy place for Muslims. ここはイスラム教徒にとっては聖なる場所です。

homage ***n.*** 敬意

pay homage to ...に敬意を払う

home

1 ***n.*** RESIDENCE: うち, 家, ((*formal*)) 住居, (one's own) 自宅, (sb else's) お住まい, お宅, (for the elderly etc.) 施設, ホーム

2 ***n.*** PLACE OF ORIGIN: (parent's house) 実家, (home country) 国, (hometown) ふるさと, 故郷, (place where sth comes from) 本場, 発祥(の)地

3 ***n.*** FAMILY: 家庭

4 ***n.*** HABITAT: (of animal) 生息地, (of plant) 自生地

5 ***adj.*** DONE AT HOME: 家庭-

1 build a home 家を建てる

Home is best. うちが一番だ。

Where's your home? ((*polite*)) お住まいはどちらですか?

We are going to make a new home here in Canada. ここカナダに新居を構えるつもりです。

They run a home for battered wives. 夫から暴力を受けた女性のための、施設を運営している。

2 Are you going home for the holidays? 休日は実家に帰りますか?

I have to go home (=to my home country) for a while. しばらく国に帰らなくてはいけない。

New Orleans is the home of jazz. ニューオーリンズはジャズ発祥の地だ。

3 a happy home 幸せな家庭

She comes from a good home. 彼女は良家のお嬢さんだ。

4 The Arctic is home for the polar bear. 北極はシロクマの生息地です。

5 home cooking 家庭料理

be at home 家にいる, ((*formal*)) 在宅している, (also **feel at home**) くつろぐ, 気楽にする

Will you be at home on Friday? 金曜日は家にいますか [ご在宅ですか]?

come/go home (家に)帰る, 帰宅する

What time are you coming home? 何時に帰るの/帰りは何時?

It's late. Let's go home.
もう遅いから、帰ろう。

make oneself at home くつろぐ

Just relax and make yourself at home.
どうぞごゆっくり、くつろいでください。

♦**home (base/plate)** *n.* ホーム, 本塁

home delivery *n.* 宅配

home run *n.* ホームラン, 本塁打

homegrown *adj.* (of plant) 自家製の, (of product) 地元産の

homeless *adj.* 家のない, ホームレスの

homemade *adj.* 手作りの, 自家製の

home page *n.* (website) ホームページ, (top page) トップページ

homesick *adj.* ホームシックの

get homesick ホームシックになる

homestay *n.* ホームステイ

hometown *n.* ふるさと, 故郷

homework *n.* 宿題

do homework 宿題をする

homicide *n.* (crime) 殺人

homogeneous *adj.* (of the same nature) 同質の, (of the same kind) 同種の

a homogeneous society 同質社会

homonym *n.* 同音異義語

homophone *n.* 同音異義語

homosexual *adj.* 同性愛の

n. (man) ホモ, ゲイ, (woman) レズビアン

honest *adj.* 正直な, (frank) 率直な

an honest person 正直な人 [正直者]

She was honest enough to take the wallet to the lost and found.
彼女は正直にも、拾った財布を遺失物係へ届け出た。

honestly *adv.* (the truth is) 本当に/は, (honestly speaking) 正直なところ, 正直に言うと

honesty *n.* 正直

Honesty is the best policy.
正直は最良の策。

in all honesty 正直なところ

honey *n.* はちみつ, ハニー

honeycomb *n.* ミツバチの巣, ハチの巣

honeymoon *n.* 新婚旅行, ハネムーン

go on a honeymoon 新婚旅行に行く

honeysuckle *n.* スイカズラ

honor *n.* (distinction) 名誉, (privilege) 光栄, (respect) 尊敬, 敬意, (military/cultural medal) 勲章; (**honors**: academic excellence) 優等; (addressing a judge: **Your Honor**) 裁判長

v. (pay tribute to) たたえる, (show respect for) (…に) 敬意を表する, (a promise/contract) 守る

It was an honor to be present at the ceremony.
式に出席させていただき、とても光栄でした。

She graduated with honors.
彼女は優等で卒業した。

They honored the dead.
死者をたたえた。

in honor of …に敬意を表して, …をたたえて

A banquet was held in honor of his outstanding career.
彼のすばらしい功績をたたえて、祝賀会が開かれた。

honorable *adj.* (deserving respect) 尊敬に値する, (of deed) 名誉ある, 名誉の,

(of person) 立派（りっぱ）な

honorary *adj.* 名誉（めいよ）の

honorific speech *n.* 敬語（けいご）

hood¹ *n.* (of car) ボンネット [→ picture of CAR], (of garment) フード

hood², hoodlum *n.* (gangster) やくざ, (violent punk) ちんぴら

hoof *n.* (of horse) ひづめ

hook *n.* (for clothes) 洋服（ようふく）掛（か）け, フック, (on dress) ホック, (fishing hook) 釣（つ）り針（ばり）
v. (…の) ホックを留（と）める

   get hooked on …に病（や）みつきになる, (drugs) …におぼれる

   let off the hook 窮地（きゅうち）から救（すく）う

♦ **hook up** *v.* (computer) 接続（せつぞく）する, つなぐ; (of couple) 付（つ）き合（あ）うようになる

hooligan *n.* (young punk) ごろつき, (soccer hooligan) フーリガン

hoop *n.* (large ring) 輪（わ）, (in basketball) リング

hooray → HURRAH

hop *v.* ひょいと跳（と）ぶ, (of frog, rabbit etc.) ピョンピョン跳（と）ぶ
n. (short, quick jump) ひょいと跳（と）ぶこと, ホップ

   The frog hopped into the pond.
   カエルが池（いけ）に跳（と）び込（こ）んだ。

hope

1 *v.* **EXPECT AND DESIRE:** 願（ねが）う, 望（のぞ）む, (expect) 期待（きたい）する, …といい（と思（おも）う）, (sb will do sth/sth will happen) …すれば/なればいい（と思（おも）う）

2 *v.* **ASSUME:** (I hope … not) …しなければいい（と思（おも）う）, …しないでほしい

3 *n.* **WISH / DESIRE:** 希望（きぼう）, 望（のぞ）み, (expectation) 期待（きたい）, (dream) 夢（ゆめ）

1 We're hoping for the best.
うまくいくよう願（ねが）っています。

All we can do is hope that everything turns out well.
すべてがうまくいくよう願（ねが）うしかない。

"I think it's going to be fine."
"Oh, I hope so."
「きっとうまくいくよ」
「そうだといいけど」

I hope the movie is good.
面白（おもしろ）い映画（えいが）だといいな。

I hope she won't be disappointed.
彼女（かのじょ）ががっかりしなければいいけど。

"It looks like it's going to rain."
"Oh, I hope not."
「雨（あめ）になりそうだね」
「えー、降（ふ）らないでほしいな」

"You don't look too well. Are you coming down with a cold?"
"I hope not."
「具合（ぐあい）が悪（わる）そうだね。かぜなんじゃない?」
「そうじゃないといいけれど」

2 I hope you're not thinking of leaving the company.
会社（かいしゃ）を辞（や）めようなんて考（かんが）えてないだろうね。

I hope you don't mind me saying this, but…
こんなことを言（い）って悪（わる）く思（おも）わないでほしいんだけど…

I hope I am not disturbing you.
おじゃましてすみませんが。

I hope you haven't forgotten the address.
住所（じゅうしょ）は忘（わす）れていないでしょうね。

3 There's not much hope of meeting him again.
もう一度（いちど）彼（かれ）に会（あ）える望（のぞ）みはあまりない。

He was our last hope.
その人が最後の頼みの綱だった。

I have hopes of one day traveling through Europe.
いつかヨーロッパ中を旅行したいという夢がある。

hopeful *adj.* (optimistic) 楽観的な, (promising) 有望な, 見込みのある

hopefully *adv.* うまくいけば

Hopefully everyone will arrive on time.
うまくいけば、全員時間どおりに到着できるだろう。

hopeless *adj.* (incompetent) どうしようもない, (bleak) 絶望的な, 望みのない

You're hopeless!
どうしようもない人だね!

The situation seems hopeless.
絶望的な状況に思える。

horizon *n.* 地平線; (**horizons:** range of knowledge/interests) 視野

expand one's horizons 視野を広げる

horizontal *adj.* 水平な, 横の
n. (line) 水平線, (plane) 水平面

hormone *n.* ホルモン

horn *n.* (on animal) 角; (in car) クラクション [→ picture of CAR], (in train) 警笛, (musical instrument) ホルン

hornet *n.* スズメバチ

horny *adj.* (wanting sex) エッチしたがっている

horoscope *n.* 星占い

read one's horoscope 星占いをする

horrible *adj.* (awful) ひどい, いやな, (terrifying) 恐ろしい

We had a horrible time.
ひどい目にあった。

horrific *adj.* 恐ろしい

horrify *v.* (scare) ぞっとさせる, 怖がらせる, (shock) (…に) ショックを与える

I was horrified to see her working in that kind of club.
彼女があんなクラブで働いているのを見て、ショックを受けた。

horrifying *adj.* 恐ろしい, ぞっとするような

It was a horrifying experience.
恐ろしい経験だった。

horror *n.* 恐怖, (genre) ホラー

♦ **horror movie** *n.* ホラー映画

hors d'oeuvre *n.* オードブル, 前菜

horse *n.* ウマ, 馬

ride a horse 馬に乗る

get on [off] a horse
馬に乗る [から下りる]

♦ **horsemeat** *n.* 馬肉, (raw horsemeat eaten as sashimi) 馬刺し

horse show *n.* ホースショー

horseback riding *n.* 乗馬

horsefly *n.* (ウシ)アブ,ウマバエ

horsepower *n.* 馬力

horse racing *n.* 競馬

♦ **horse-racing track** *n.* 競馬場

horseradish *n.* 西洋ワサビ, ホースラディッシュ

horticulture *n.* 園芸学

hose *n.* ホース

hospice *n.* ホスピス

hospitable *adj.* (be hospitable to) 手厚くもてなす, 歓待する

hospital *n.* 病院

go to a hospital 病院へ行く

be in the hospital 入院している

be discharged from a hospital 退院する

visit someone in the hospital

お見舞いに行く

hospitality ***n.*** (お)もてなし

Thank you for your hospitality.

おもてなし、ありがとうございます。

hospitalize ***v.*** (**be hospitalized**) 入院する

host ***n.*** (at party) ホスト, 主催者, (at small inn) 主人, (of TV/radio program) 司会者; (host computer) ホストコンピューター ***v.*** (host an event) 主催する

hostage ***n.*** 人質

be taken hostage 人質に取られる

hostel ***n.*** (youth hostel) ユースホステル

hostess ***n.*** (at nightclub) ホステス, (at small inn) 女主人, おかみ, (of TV/radio program) 司会者, (of home party) 主催者

host family ***n.*** ホストファミリー

hostile ***adj.*** (enemy) 敵の, (having ill will) 敵意のある, (be hostile to/toward) (=be against) (…に)反対だ, (=be unfriendly to) (…に)冷淡だ

hostility ***n.*** 敵意

hot ***adj.*** (of weather) 暑い, (hot and humid) 蒸し暑い, (of surface, liquid) 熱い, (of food: warm) 温かい, (spicy) 辛い, (of temper) 短気な

It was a very hot day today.

今日はとても暑かった。

The room was hot and stuffy.

部屋は蒸し暑かった。

I'm all hot and sweaty.

体が熱くて汗だくだ。

a hot bath 熱いおふろ

The handle is too hot to touch.

取っ手が熱くて触れない。

Be careful—the soup is very hot.

気をつけて――スープがすごく熱いから。

a hot curry 辛口カレー

He has a hot temper, so be careful.

彼は短気だから、気をつけなさい。

♦ **hot spring** ***n.*** 温泉

hot water ***n.*** (お)湯 [→ picture of BATHROOM, PUBLIC BATH]

scalding hot water 熱湯

hotbed ***n.*** 温床

hotel ***n.*** ホテル, (Japanese inn) 旅館

a deluxe hotel 豪華なホテル

a first-class hotel 一流ホテル

check into [out of] a hotel

ホテルにチェックインする [をチェックアウトする]

book a room at a hotel

ホテルの部屋を予約する

stay at a hotel ホテルに泊まる

hot pepper ***n.*** コショウ [→ PEPPER]

hound ***n.*** (hunting dog) 猟犬, (dog) 犬 ***v.*** しつこく悩ます

hour ***n.***

1 SIXTY MINUTES: 1時間

2 FIXED PERIOD OF TIME: -時間

3 FIXED POINT IN TIME: 時刻, 時

4 LONG TIME: (**hours**) 長時間, 何時間も

1 It lasted two hours and fifteen minutes.

2時間15分続いた。

We have an hour before boarding time.

搭乗時間まであと1時間ある。

H

After a couple of hours, I'll call again.
2、3時間後に、また電話します。

We worked for hours without a break.
何時間も休みなしに働いた。

They ought to be here in an hour.
1時間で着くはずだ。

be paid by the hour 時給で支払われる

50 kilometers per hour 時速50キロ

2 working hours 勤務時間

business hours 営業時間

visiting hours 面会時間

rush hour ラッシュアワー

3 the hour of death 死亡時刻

at an early hour <u>早くに</u> [早朝に]

4 I've been here for hours.
何時間もここにいたよ。

♦ **hourly** ***adj.*** 1時間ごとの

hourly wages 時給

house

1 ***n.*** **RESIDENCE:** 家, 住宅 [→ HOME 1, picture below]

2 ***v.*** **PROVIDE SHELTER FOR:** 収容する

3 ***n.*** **PARLIAMENT:** (**House**) 議会, 議院

1 an empty house 空き家

a house for rent 貸家

2 The evacuees were housed in the church.
避難した人は教会に収容された。

3 the House of Councilors 参議院

the House of Representatives 衆議院

the Upper [Lower] House 上[下]院

house arrest ***n.*** 自宅監禁, 軟禁

household ***n.*** (family) 家族, 一家, 世帯

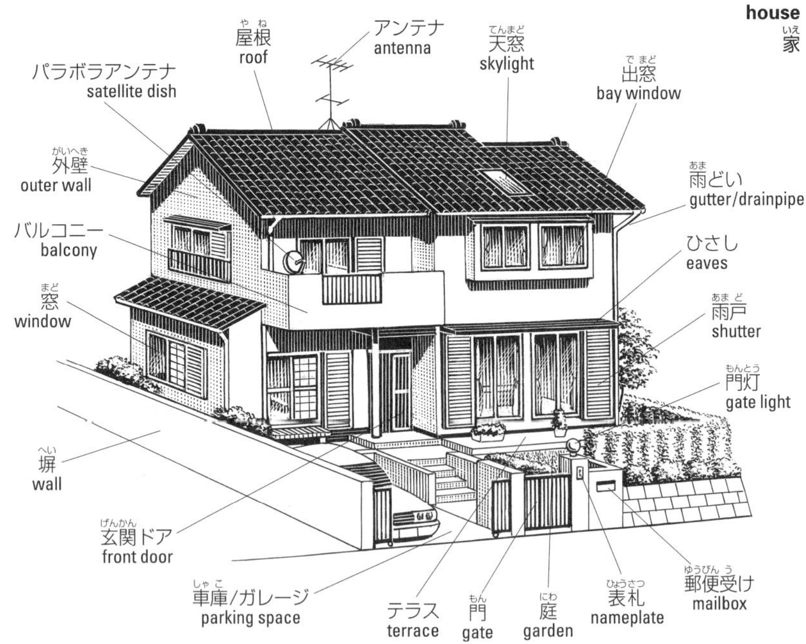

the head of the household 世帯主

housekeeper *n.* (maid) 家政婦

housekeeping *n.* 家事

housewife *n.* 主婦

housework *n.* 家事

housing *n.* 住宅, 住居

hover *v.* 舞う

hovercraft *n.* ホバークラフト

how

1 *adv., conj.* IN DIRECT / INDIRECT QUESTION: (in what way) どう, どうやって, どのように, どういうふうに, ((*formal*)) いかに

2 *adv.* TO WHAT EXTENT: どのくらい, どれくらい, どれほど

3 *adv.* USED EMPHATICALLY: なんと, なんて, なんという

1 How do you do this? どうやるの？

Could you please explain how to get there?

どうやって行けばいいか、説明していただけますか？

I don't know how to do this.

これをどうやるのかわからない。

I don't care how you do it, just do it!

やり方はどうでもいいから、とにかくやりなさい。

2 How much does it cost?

いくらですか？

How long will it take to get there?

そこまで行くのにどのくらい(時間が)かかりますか？

How tall are you?

身長はどのくらいありますか？

I don't care how crowded it is.

どんなに混んでいてもかまわない。

3 How marvelous! すばらしいね！

How incredibly stupid!

なんてばかばかしい / もう最悪！

how about ...(するの) はいかがですか, ...はどうでしょう

How about ordering a pizza?

ピザを注文するのはどう？

How about going to see a movie tonight?

今晩、映画を見に行かない？

how are you (doing)? お元気ですか, (asking about sb's physical condition) 調子はどうですか

How are you today? お元気ですか？

how come どうして [→ COME]

how do you do (greeting) 初めまして

how long どのくらい

How long has it been since we've seen each other?

この前会って [((*polite*)) お会いして] からどのくらいたつんでしょう？

how many いくつ [→ MANY]

how much いくら, どのくらい [→ MUCH]

how old いくつ, 何歳 [→ OLD]

how's that それはどういうわけですか

however *adv.* (no matter how...) どんなに...しても, どれほど...しても, どうやっても; (although) けれども, しかし, それにもかかわらず

conj. どんなやり方でも, どんなふうにでも

However much it rains, we are going.

どんなに雨が降っても、行きます。

However hard I tried, I couldn't remember.

どれだけ思い出そうとしても、思い出せなかった。

However important it may seem at the

moment, you must try to adopt a long-term perspective.
その時はとても重要に見えることでも、長期的な視点で考えなくてはだめだ。

That's one reason. However, there are others.
それも一つの理由だ。しかし、ほかにもある。

Most people like baseball. I don't, however.
ほとんどの人は野球が好きだ。でも私は好きじゃない。

You can do it however you like.
どんなふうにでも好きにやっていい。

howl *v.* (of wolf) 遠ぼえする, (of wind) ヒューヒューうなる; (laugh loudly) 大笑いする

hub *n.* (center of wheel) ハブ, (center) 中心

huff *v.* (say angrily) 怒って言う
n. 立腹
huff and puff (breathe) ハーハー息を切らす; (express annoyance) 騒ぎ立てる
in a huff プンプン怒って

hug *v.* 抱きしめる

huge *adj.* 巨大な, ものすごく大きい, ((*informal*)) で(っ)かい, (of profits, debts) 莫大な

hum *v.* (of machine, insect) ブンブン音を立てる, (of person) 鼻歌を歌う, ハミングする

human *n.* 人間, 人
adj. (of mankind) 人間の, 人の, (characteristic of mankind) 人間的な, 人間らしい
the human body
人間の体 [((*formal*)) 人体]
The cause of the accident was human error.
事故は人為的なミスによるものだった。
Humans are very different from animals.
人間は動物とは全く違う。
♦ **human being** *n.* 人, 人間
human nature *n.* 人間性
human race *n.* 人類
human rights *n.* 人権

humane *adj.* (of treatment) 人間味のある, 思いやりのある

humanitarian *adj.* 人道主義の, 人道的な
n. (person) 人道主義者

humanity *n.* (quality of being human) 人間性, 人間らしさ, (humans) 人間; (**the humanities**) 人文科学

humble *adj.* (poor) 貧しい, (of house, meal) 粗末な; (unassuming) 謙虚な

humble speech *n.* (modest language) 謙譲語

humid *adj.* 湿気の多い, じめじめした, (hot and humid) 蒸し暑い

humidity *n.* 湿気, 蒸し暑さ, (degree of humidity) 湿度

humiliate *v.* (shame) (…に) 恥をかかせる, (**be humiliated**) 恥をかく

humility *n.* 謙遜, 謙虚(さ)

humming bird *n.* ハチドリ

hummus *n.* ホムス

humor *n.* ユーモア, (mood) 気分, 機嫌
v. (humor sb) (…の) 機嫌をとる
He has a good sense of humor.
彼はユーモアのセンスがある。
He's not in a good humor today.

彼は今日は機嫌が悪い。

Humor me, will you.

((*feminine*)) お願いだから、ねっ?/((*masculine*)) 頼むよ。

humorous ***adj.*** ユーモアのある, 面白い

hump ***n.*** こぶ

hunch ***n.*** (feeling about the future) 予感

hunchback ***n.*** せむしの人

♦**hunchbacked** ***adj.*** せむしの

hundred ***n.*** 100, 百, (**hundreds**) 何百, 多数, たくさん

adj. 100の, (people) 100人の, (things) 100個の; (many) たくさんの

hundreds of thousands of people

数十万人

hunger ***n.*** 空腹, 飢え

die of hunger 飢え死にする [餓死する]

♦**hunger strike** ***n.*** ハンガーストライキ, ((*informal*)) ハンスト

hungry ***adj.*** おなかがすいた, 空腹の, ((*masculine/informal*)) 腹が減った, (very hungry) おなかがペコペコの, (genuinely starving) 飢えた

Are you hungry?

おなかはすいてますか/((*informal*)) おなかすいた?

I'm hungry!

おなかがすいた/((*masculine*)) 腹減った!

The refugees were very hungry.

難民たちはとても飢えていた。

hunt ***v.*** (animal) 狩る, ...狩りをする, 狩猟する, (do hunting) 狩りをする; (search for) 探す

n. 狩り, 狩猟, (for criminal) 捜索

The men go out hunting every day.

男たちは毎日狩りに出る。

The hunt for the escaped prisoner continued into the night.

夜になっても脱獄囚の捜索は続けられた。

hunter ***n.*** 狩人, ハンター

hunting ***n.*** 狩猟, 狩り

hurdle ***n.*** ハードル, (obstacle) 障害物, (problem) 障害, 問題, (**hurdles**: track event) ハードル競走

clear a hurdle 障害を乗り越える

hurl ***v.*** 投げつける, (**hurl oneself**) 飛びかかる

hurrah ***interj.*** フレー, 万歳

hurricane ***n.*** ハリケーン, 暴風雨

hurriedly ***adv.*** 急いで, あわてて

hurry ***v.*** 急ぐ, (hurry sb) 急がせる, せかす

n. 急ぎ, 急いでいること

You'd better hurry. It's late.

急いだほうがいい。もう遅いから。

Can't you hurry up and finish it?

急いで終わらせてくれない?

Hurry up! 急いで!

We all hurried down to the station.

全員、駅へ急いだ。

I hurried to the scene of the accident.

事故現場に急行した。

Don't hurry me so much!

そんなにせかさないでよ!

What's the hurry?

なぜそんなに急ぐの?

in a hurry 急いで, あわてて

I'm not in any great hurry.

別に急いではいませんよ。

hurt ***v.*** (suffer injury to) 痛める, (...に) けがをする, (feel painful) 痛む, (cause injury to) (…に) けがをさせる; (feelings) 傷つける, (…の) 気を悪くさせる

He hurt his hand.
彼は手を痛めた [手にけがをした]。

How did you hurt your foot?
どうやって足をけがしたんですか？

Ouch! That hurts! あっ、痛い！

Sorry, did I hurt you?
すみません、おけがはありませんか？

He was badly hurt by the fall.
彼は転落して大けがをした。

She was hurt by their remarks.
彼らの言葉に彼女は傷ついた。

it won't hurt to do …してもいいだろう

It won't hurt to have another chocolate.
もう一つチョコレートを食べてもいいでしょう。

husband *n.* (one's own) 夫, 主人, ((*informal*)) だんな, 亭主, (sb else's) ご主人, だんなさん

This is my husband. うちの主人です。

Is that your husband?
あちらがご主人ですか？

Whose husband did you say he was?
あの人は誰のだんなさんだって言った？

hush *v.* 静かにする

n. 静けさ

Hush! 静かに！/シッ！

hut *n.* 小屋

hyacinth *n.* ヒヤシンス

hybrid *n.* (plant, animal) 交配種, 雑種

adj. 雑種の

hydrant *n.* 消火栓

hydraulic *adj.* 水力の

a hydraulic plant 水力発電所

hydraulic pressure 水圧

hydraulic brakes 油圧ブレーキ

hydrogen *n.* 水素

hyena *n.* ハイエナ

hygiene *n.* 衛生, (subject of study) 衛生学

hype *n.* (media hype) 誇大広告

hyper- *pref.* 超-, (excessively) 極度に

hyperactive *adj.* (of child) 極度に活動的な

hypertext *n.* ハイパーテキスト

hyphen *n.* ハイフン

hypnosis *n.* 催眠

hypnotize *v.* (…に) 催眠術をかける

hypochondria *n.* 心気症, (excessive worry) 心配性

hypocrisy *n.* 偽善, 見せかけ

hypocrite *n.* 偽善者

hypocritical *adj.* 偽善的な, 見せかけの

hypodermic *adj.* 皮下の

n. (syringe) 皮下注射器, (needle) 皮下注射針

hypotenuse *n.* 斜辺

hypothesis *n.* 仮説

hypothetical *adj.* 仮説に基づく, 仮定の

a hypothetical question
仮説に基づく質問

a hypothetical situation 仮定の状況

hysterectomy *n.* 子宮摘出(手術)

hysteria *n.* ヒステリー

mass hysteria 集団ヒステリー

hysterical *adj.* ヒステリックな

become hysterical ヒステリックになる

I, i

I *pron.* 私は/が, ((*formal*)) 私は/が, ((*masculine*)) 僕は/が, ((*masculine/informal*)) 俺は/が, ((*feminine/informal*)) あたしは/が [NOTE: Once it is clear that "I," 私, is the grammatical subject of the sentence, it can be omitted.]

I used to play tennis, but I don't much anymore.
(私は)昔はよくテニスをしましたが、今はあまりやりません。

I'm not as good as she is at math.
私は彼女ほど数学が得意ではない。

My husband and I were invited to the party.
パーティーに主人と私が招待されました。

I thought you and I were on the same team.
(あなたと)同じチームだと思ったのに。

(*to receptionist*) "I'm here to see Mr. Tamura."
「田村さんにお会いしたいのですが」

ibis *n.* (bird) トキ

ice *n.* (frozen water) 氷

v. (**be iced over**) 氷が張る, (**be iced up**) 凍る, 凍結する

The ice melted. 氷が解けた。

crushed ice かち割り(氷)

scotch on ice スコッチのオンザロック

I slipped on the ice and fell down.
氷の上で滑って転んでしまった。

The pond is iced over.
池に氷が張っている。

The windshield is all iced up.
フロントガラスが凍結している。

♦**ice age** *n.* 氷河時代

ice pack *n.* 氷のう

ice water *n.* (for drinking) 冷たい水

iceberg *n.* 氷山

icebreaker *n.* (ship) 砕氷船

ice cream *n.* アイスクリーム

ice cube *n.* 角氷, 氷

ice hockey *n.* アイスホッケー

Iceland *n.* アイスランド

ice skate *n.* (**ice skates**) (アイス)スケート靴

v. (**ice-skate**) (アイス)スケートをする

♦**ice skater** *n.* (competitive) スケート選手

ice skating *n.* (アイス)スケート

icicle *n.* つらら

icing *n.* (for cake) アイシング, 糖衣

icon *n.* (cultural, popular) 偶像, (religious) イコン, 聖画像; (for computer software) アイコン

icy *adj.* (of street) 凍った, 凍結した, (of wind) 凍りつくような, (of attitude) 冷淡な, 冷たい

ID card *n.* 身分証明書

idea *n.*

1 THOUGHT: 考え, アイデア, (good idea that springs to mind, passing thought) 思いつき, (plan) 案, (proposal) 提案

2 UNDERSTANDING: (**have an idea**) わかる, (**I have no idea...**) 見当がつかない, 全くわからない, (**he/she has no idea...**) 全然わかってない

3 OPINION: (**ideas**) 考え, 意見

4 CONCEPT: 観念, 概念

1 Now that's a good idea.
それはいい考え [アイデア] だね。

Do you have any ideas?
何か<u>アイデア</u> [案] はありませんか？

I just had an idea!
いい考えがある/いいこと思いついた！

He stole my idea.
あの人は私のアイデアをとった。

The idea was dropped.
その提案は却下されました。

2 I've got a rough idea of what you mean.
おっしゃってることは大体わかりました。

Do you have any idea how long this is going to take?
どのくらいの時間がかかるか、見当はつきますか？

I had no idea you'd be here.
あなたがここにいるとは思いも寄らなかった。

3 What are your ideas about religion?
宗教について、どんなお考えをおもちですか？

4 the idea of relativity 相対性理論の概念

give the idea that …と思わせる, …という気にさせる

I don't want to give them the idea that it is going to be easy.
簡単なことだと思わせたくない。

What gave you the idea that you could use the car?
どうして車を使っていいと思ったの？

put ideas in sb's head (…に)考えを吹き込む

Stop putting silly ideas into your sister's head.
妹にそんなばかな考えを吹き込まないでください。

ideal *n.* 理想

adj. 理想的な, (just right) ちょうどいい, まさにぴったりの, (**ideal for**: perfect for) …に絶好の

That's an ideal and, unfortunately, impractical.
それは理想であって、残念ながら現実的じゃないね。

It's ideal weather for a swim.
一泳ぎするのに絶好の天気だ。

idealism *n.* 理想主義

idealist *n.* 理想主義者

idealize *v.* 理想化する

ideally *adv.* (used at the beginning of a sentence) 理想的には, 理想を言えば

identical *adj.* そっくりな, 同一の

The two photos are identical.
2枚の写真はそっくりだ。

♦ **identical twins** *n.* 一卵性双生児

identification *n.* 身元確認, 身分証明 [→ ID CARD]

identify *v.* (recognize) わかる, (distinguish between) 見分ける, (verify) 確認する

Birds can identify their young by their call.
鳥は鳴き声で自分の子がわかる。

Do you think you'll be able to identify the car?
その車を見分けられると思いますか？

He was identified as the criminal.
その男が犯人であることが確認された。

identity *n.* (of person) 身元, (=individuality) アイデンティティ

ideological *adj.* イデオロギーの

ideology *n.* イデオロギー, 観念形態

idiom *n.* 慣用句, イディオム

idiomatic ***adj.*** (of phrase) 慣用的な
an idiomatic expression 慣用表現
speak idiomatic Japanese
日本語らしい日本語を話す

idiot ***n.*** ばか
You idiot! You forgot to lock the door!
((*masculine*)) ばか！ドアのかぎを閉め忘れてたぞ。

idiotic ***adj.*** ばかばかしい, ばかげた

idle ***adj.*** (not in use) 使われていない, (lazy) 怠けている, 怠惰な
v. (of engine) アイドリングする; (**idle away**: time) ぶらぶら過ごす
That student is bone idle.
あの生徒はどうしようもない怠け者だ。
We idled away the time listening to music.
私たちは、のんびりと音楽を聞いて過ごしました。

idol ***n.*** (pop star) アイドル, (person whom one admires) あこがれの人; (religious idol) 偶像

idyllic ***adj.*** (of scene) のどかな

if ***conj.*** (もし)…(の)なら, (もし)…たら, …ば, …と
If Taro is going, I won't be.
もし太郎が行く(の)なら、私は行かない。
If you like Yumiko, why don't you tell her?
由美子が好きなら、告白したら？
If you've decided to go, you'd better book your flight right away.
行くと決めた(の)なら、すぐに飛行機を予約したほうがいいよ。
If you wanted to go, you should have told me so.
行きたかった(の)なら、そう言ってくれればよかったのに。
If Suzuki comes, please let me know.
鈴木さんが来たら、知らせてください。
Come to my room if you need help.
困ったことがあったら、私の部屋へ来てください。
I think I'll manage, if they help.
もし彼らが助けてくれたら [くれるのなら]、なんとかなると思う。
If it's a cat, I don't mind.
猫だったら [なら]、かまいませんよ。
If I had gotten that job, I would never have met Mr. Fujita.
あの仕事に就いていたら [いれば]、藤田さんとは出会えなかったはずです。
If she had not been so poor, I doubt she would have become a thief.
あんなに貧しくなかったら [なければ]、彼女は泥棒にはならなかったと思う。
If I had known then what I know now, I would not have done what I did.
あの時わかっていたら [いれば]、あんなことはしなかったのに。
If you go by car, you can get there in ten minutes.
車で行けば [なら] 10分で着きますよ。
I'll buy it if it's not so expensive.
そんなに高くなければ [なかったら]、買うよ。
If there's time, I'd like to visit the museum as well.
時間があれば [あったら]、美術館にも寄りたい。
I would have bought it if it had been of a higher quality.
もっと質がよければ、買ったんだけど。
If you take a look, you'll see what I mean.

I

ちょっと見ると、すぐわかるだろうと思う。

If you don't try, you'll never know.
やってみないと、わからないよ。

If I start to read that book, I'll quickly get sleepy.
その本を読み始めると、すぐに眠くなる。

as if まるで…かのように

He was talking as if he knew everything about the subject.
彼はまるで、そのことは何でも知っているかのように話していた。

even if → EVEN

if and when …ことになったら, …時が来たら

I'll speak to him if and when it's necessary.
必要になったら、彼に話します。

if any …としても

Few, if any, buyers will be found.
買い手は見つかったとしても、わずかだろう。

if it were not for / had not been for (もし)…がなかったら, (もし)…がなければ

If it weren't for you, I'd never have gotten this job.
あなたがいなければ、絶対この仕事に就けませんでした。

If it had not been for your quick thinking, I wouldn't be here alive today.
あなたの機転がなければ、私は今日ここに生きていられなかっただろう。

if not もしそうでないなら

The bus should be here by 5 o'clock. If not, phone the bus company.
バスはここに5時までには着くはずです。来なければ、バス会社に電話してみてください。

if only (expressing desire that sb do sth for you) …してくれたらなあ, …さえしてくれれば, (expressing regret: **if only one had done**) …さえしたら, (**if only one could**) …さえできたら

If only you had told me this yesterday.
せめて昨日、このことを話してくれていたらなあ。

If only he would realize that our relationship is over.
私たちの仲はもう終わりだってことに、あの人が気づいてさえくれればねえ。

If only I hadn't taken the wrong bus, I wouldn't have been late.
間違ったバスに乗りさえしなかったら、遅れずに済んだのに。

if so もしそうなら, そうしたら

They might try contacting you. If so, let me know, would you?
あなたに連絡してくるかもしれない。そうしたら、知らせてくれませんか？

what if → WHAT

igloo *n.* イグルー

ignite *v.* (set fire to) (…に) 火をつける, 点火する, (catch fire) 火がつく, 発火する [→ CAUSE]

ignition *n.* (in car) 点火装置

ignorance *n.* (lack of knowledge) 無知, (unawareness) 何も知らないこと

Ignorance is bliss. 知らぬが仏。

feign ignorance とぼける, 知らないふりをする

ignorant *adj.* うとい, 何も知らない

When it comes to mechanics, David is completely ignorant.

機械のことになると、デヴィッドは何も知らない。

ignore *v.* (disregard) 無視する, (not speak or listen to) 相手にしない, (pretend not to notice) (...に) 知らん顔をする

We can't ignore this problem any longer.
もうこれ以上、この問題を無視することはできません。

The man carried on talking, ignoring everyone's questions.
男はみんなの質問を無視して、話し続けた。

It's best to ignore him.
あの人は相手にしないのが一番だ。

iguana *n.* イグアナ

ill *adj.* (seriously ill) 病気の, (not feeling well) 具合が悪い, 調子が悪い; (of effects: bad) 悪い

become/fall/get ill 病気になる

be ill with food poisoning
食あたりで具合が悪い

There's a lot of ill feeling at the company about the new section chief.
新しい課長に対する社内の反感は強い。

be/feel ill at ease 落ち着かない, 気詰まりだ

I always feel ill at ease in her company.
彼女といっしょにいると、いつも落ち着けない [気詰まりだ]。

speak ill of ...のことを悪く言う

illegal *adj.* 法律に反した, 違法の, 不法な

It's illegal to park here.
ここに駐車するのは違法です。

He got sent to prison for illegal possession of a gun.
その人は、銃の不法所持で刑務所に送られた。

♦ **illegal alien/immigrant** *n.* 不法入国者

illegible *adj.* 読みにくい, 読みづらい

illegitimate *adj.* (of child) 非嫡出の, (illegal) 違法の

illiterate *adj.* (unable to read and write) 読み書きができない, (in a particular subject: not knowledgeable) 無知だ, うとい

illness *n.* 病気, -病

a serious illness 重病

a fatal [slight] illness
命にかかわる [軽い] 病気

recover from an illness 病気が治る

mental illness 精神病

illogical *adj.* 論理的ではない, 不合理な

ill-treat *v.* (abuse) 虐待する

illuminate *v.* (shine light on and brighten) 照らす, 明るくする, (decorate with lights) 照明で飾る, (tree) イルミネーションで飾る; (make clear) 明らかにする

illumination *n.* (decorative) イルミネーション, (light) 照明

illusion *n.* (false perception) 錯覚, (mistaken belief) 勘違い, (optical illusion) (目の) 錯覚

be under the illusion that ...と錯覚している, ...と勘違いしている

He's under the illusion that he has healing powers.
彼は自分に人をいやす力があると、錯覚している。

have no illusions about ...に幻想をいだいていない

illustrate *v.* (draw illustrations for) (...の) イラストをかく, 絵をかく, (explain) 説明

する, (explain by example) 例を挙げて説明する

The book was beautifully illustrated.
その本には美しい挿絵が入っていた。

Allow me to illustrate my point...
要点を説明させていただきますと...

illustration ***n.*** (drawing) 挿絵, イラスト, (example) 実例, 例

illustrator ***n.*** イラストレーター, 挿絵画家

im- → IN-

image ***n.*** (mental picture, outward/public appearance) イメージ, (picture on screen) 画像, (figure, reflection in mirror) 姿, (portrait) 肖像, (sculpture) 像

the company's image 会社のイメージ

project an image onto a screen
スクリーンに画像を映写する

be the image of ...そっくりだ, ...の生き写しだ

He's the image of his mother.
彼は母親そっくりだ。

imagery ***n.*** 像, (in mind) イメージ

imaginary ***adj.*** 想像上の, (fictional) 架空の

imagination ***n.*** (process of imagining) 想像, (ability to imagine) 想像力

imaginative ***adj.*** (creative) 想像力に富んだ

imagine ***v.*** (visualize) 想像する, (suppose, think) (...と) 思う, (misconceive) 思い違いをする, 思い込む

Can you imagine me being an actress?
女優になった私を想像できる?

I imagined the place as it must have been long ago.
その場所のずっと昔の姿を思い浮かべた。

It's difficult to imagine her doing such a cruel thing.
彼女が、そんなひどいことをするとは考えにくい。

I imagine your mother will be pleased to hear from you.
連絡があったら、お母さんはきっとお喜びでしょう。

You must be imagining things.
気のせい [考えすぎ] ですよ。

♦ **imaginable** ***adj.*** (conceivable) 考えられる限りの

imbalance ***n.*** アンバランス

imbecile ***n.*** ばか [→ FOOL, IDIOT]

imitate ***v.*** (mimic) まねる, (...の) まねをする

Children learn by imitating others.
子供は人のまねをして学ぶ。

imitation ***n.*** (a fake) 偽物 [→ IMPERSONATION]

immaculate ***adj.*** (very clean) きれいな; (perfect) 完璧な, 申し分(の)ない

immaterial ***adj.*** (unimportant) 重要ではない, (irrelevant) 関係ない

immature ***adj.*** 未熟な, (childish) おとなげない, 子供っぽい

immediate ***adj.*** (instant) 即座の, (direct) 直接の, (of problem) 当面の

an immediate reply 即答

There was an immediate response to our advertisement.
広告を出すとすぐに反響があった。

The immediate problem is a cash shortage.
当面の課題は現金不足です。

immediately *adv.* すぐに, 即座に, ((*formal*)) ただちに

I have to go immediately.
すぐに行かないといけない。

Call me immediately if you hear any news.
何か新しい情報を聞いたら、すぐに電話してください。

immense *adj.* (huge) 巨大な, (of benefits, amount) 莫大な

immerse *v.* 浸す, (**be immersed in**: study, work) …に没頭する

♦**immersion program** *n.* (for language-learning) 没入プログラム

immigrant *n.* 移民, 移住者

an immigrant from Brazil
ブラジルからの移民

immigration *n.* (entering a foreign country) 入国, (place at airport) 入国管理所, (moving to another country) 移住

the Immigration Office 入国管理局

imminent *adj.* 今にも…そうな, (of danger) 差し迫った

an imminent storm 今にも来そうな嵐

immobile *adj.* (unable to move) 動けない, (still) じっとしている

immoral *adj.* (wrong) 悪い, モラルに反する, (of sexual behavior) ふしだらな

immorality *n.* 不道徳

immortal *adj.* 不死の, 死なない, (remembered forever) 不滅の, 不朽の

n. (famous and remembered person) 不滅の人

immortality *n.* (never dying) 不死, (perpetuity) 不滅, 不朽

immovable *adj.* (unable to be moved) 動かせない

immune *adj.* 免疫のある

He was immune to the virus.
彼はそのウイルスに免疫があった。

♦**immune system** *n.* 免疫系

immunity *n.* (resistance to illness) 免疫; (exemption from law) 免除

immunize *v.* 免疫にする

♦**immunization shot** *n.* 予防注射

imp *n.* (little devil) 小悪魔, (mischievous child) いたずらっ子

impact *n.* (collision) 衝撃, 衝突, (influence) 影響

British pop music had a big impact abroad in the 1960s.
６０年代、イギリスのポップスは世界に大きな影響を与えた。

impair *v.* (make worse) 悪くする, (weaken) 弱める, (damage) 害する

impaired hearing 難聴

impala *n.* インパラ

impart *v.* (knowledge, information) 伝える, (flavor, atmosphere) 与える

impartial *adj.* (unbiased) 偏見のない, (fair) 公平な

♦**impartiality** *n.* 不偏, 公平

impasse *n.* 行き詰まり

impatient *adj.* (irritable) いらいらする, (short-tempered) 短気な, (hasty) せっかちな, (**be impatient**: be worked up) あせる, やきもきする, (**be impatient for**: be anxious for) 待ちこがれる, (…が) 待ち遠しい

I'm afraid I was impatient with her.
彼女にいらいらしてしまったんです。

an impatient old man
短気な [せっかちな] 老人

The kids are getting impatient.
子供たちが、じっとしていられなくなってきた。

Let's not be impatient, please.
やきもきするのはやめましょう。

I was impatient for something to happen.
何かが起こるのを待ちこがれていた。

impeach *v.* (president) 弾劾する

♦**impeachment** *n.* 弾劾

impeccable *adj.* (perfect) 完璧な, 申し分(の)ない

Mori's taste in wines is impeccable.
森さんのワインの趣味は申し分ない。

impede *v.* (hinder) じゃまする, (delay) 遅らせる

impediment *n.* 障害

a speech impediment 言語障害

impending *adj.* (of danger) 差し迫った

the impending crisis 差し迫った危機

imperative *adj.* (vital) 非常に大切だ, 重要だ, どうしても…なければならない
n. (imperative mood) 命令法

It is imperative that we complete this work today.
どうしても今日中に、この仕事を片付けなければならない。

♦**imperative form** *n.* (verb form) 命令形

imperfect *adj.* (incomplete) 不完全な, 不十分な, (having flaws) 欠点のある

♦**imperfection** *n.* (flaw) 欠点

imperial *adj.* (of country) 帝国の, (of emperor/empress) 皇帝の, (of Japanese emperor) 天皇の

Imperial Rome ローマ帝国

His [Her] Imperial Majesty
天皇 [皇后] 陛下

the imperial family 皇室

♦**Imperial Palace** *n.* (in Japan) 皇居

imperialism *n.* 帝国主義

imperialist *adj.* 帝国主義の
n. (person) 帝国主義者

impersonal *adj.* (cold) 非人間的な, 人間味のない, (of letter, service: businesslike) 事務的な

impersonate *v.* (mimic) (…の) まねをする, (act the part of) (…の) 役を演じる, (…に) 扮する, (so as to deceive) (… の) ふりをする

impersonation *n.* まね, 物まね

implant *v.* (put into the body) 埋め込む
n. 埋め込まれた物

implausible *adj.* (hard to believe) 信じがたい

implement *n.* (tool) 道具
v. (put into effect) 実行する, 実施する

What kind of implement is this?
これはどういう道具ですか？

implementation *n.* 実行, 実施

implicate *v.* (**be implicated in**: crime) …に巻き込まれる, …に関係する

implication *n.* (meaning) 裏の意味, 含み, (**implications**: influences) 影響

have serious implications for …に大きな影響がある

implicit *adj.* (total) 完全な, 全くの; (unspoken) 暗黙の

Taro had implicit faith in whatever his father did.

太郎は、父親がすることは何でも完全に信頼していた。

There was an implicit understanding between them.
彼らの間には暗黙の了解があった。

imply *v.* ほのめかす, (of fact, words) (…の) 意味を含む, (…を) 暗に意味する

The article implies that the media was to blame.
その記事は、メディアのほうに責任があったとほのめかしている。

I don't mean to imply that you're a liar.
あなたがうそつきだと言ってるわけじゃありません。

impolite *adj.* 失礼な [→ RUDE]

import *v.* (goods) 輸入する, (data) 取り込む

n. (meaning) 意味; (**imports**) 輸入品

Japan imports oil from the Middle East.
日本は中東から石油を輸入している。

Japan's imports are fewer than its exports.
日本は、輸入のほうが輸出より少ない。

♦ **importation** *n.* 輸入

importer *n.* (business) 輸入業者, (country) 輸入国,

importance *n.* 重要性, 大切さ, (meaningfulness) 意義

the importance of free medical care to the poor
貧しい人々への無料医療の重要性

important *adj.* 大切な, 重要な, 大事な, (essential) 肝心な, (influential) 有力な

It's important to brush your teeth both in the morning and before going to bed.
朝と寝る前の2回、歯を磨くことが大切です。

It may not be important to you, but it certainly is to me.
あなたにとっては重要なことではないかもしれませんが、私にはとても大事なことなんです。

It's important for him to understand this.
彼がこのことを理解することが肝心だ。

a very important person 有力者

♦ **importantly** *adv.* もったいぶって, (used at the beginning of a sentence) 重要なことには

impose *v.* (tax, duty) 課す, (conditions, opinions) 押し付ける, 無理強いする; (disturb, be a nuisance to) じゃまする

New duties have been imposed on wine and spirits.
ワインと蒸留酒に新たな税が課せられた。

I hope I'm not imposing.
じゃまするつもりはないけど。

impossible *adj.* 不可能な, 無理な, (looks like it can't be done) できそうもない, (inconceivable) あり得ない, (of person, circumstances: difficult, troublesome) どうしようもない

It's almost impossible to get a job these days.
近ごろは、仕事を見つけるのはほとんど不可能だ。

That's impossible! そんなの無理だよ!

It's impossible for me to be there.
そこにはいられそうもない。

It will be impossible to finish by June.
6月までに終えるなんてできそうもない。

It's impossible to know what the outcome will be.

結果がどうなるかは知りようがない。

He is impossible!

あの人はどうしようもない/あの人にはがまんならない! (lit.,"I can't stand him!")

an impossible situation

どうしようもない状況

impotence *n.* (inability to have sex) 性的不能, インポテンツ; (powerlessness) 無力

impotent *adj.* (powerless) 無力な; (unable to have sex) 性的不能の, インポの

impractical *adj.* (of plan) 実際的ではない, 現実的ではない, 非現実的な, (of person) 実務能力のない

The plan is impractical.

その計画は現実的ではない。

It's impractical to try to do so many things at once.

一度にそんなにたくさんのことをしようとするのは、非現実的だ。

impress *v.* (…に) 感動を与える, (**be impressed by/with**) …に感動する, …に感心する; (impress A upon B) (AをBに) 印象づける

I was impressed that so many people came.

あんなに大勢の人が来てくれて感動しました。

I was impressed by her good manners.

彼女の行儀のよさに感心した。

The vice-chancellor impressed me as being an eloquent speaker.

副学長は雄弁だという印象を受けました。

I tried to impress upon them the importance of appearance.

彼らに、外見の大切さを印象づけようとしました。

impression *n.* (emotional effect) 印象; (idea) 思い, 感じ; (impersonation) 物まね, まね

create an impression 印象づける

make an impression on

…に印象を与える

give the impression that…

…という印象を与える

a lasting impression 忘れられない印象

a first impression 第一印象

I got the impression that they didn't care.

彼らには関心がないという印象を受けました。

I was under the impression that we didn't have to go.

私たちは行く必要がないのかと思っていました。

The comedian did a good impression of the president.

そのコメディアンは大統領の物まねが、うまかった。

impressive *adj.* (striking) 印象的な, (moving) 感動的な

imprint *n.* (remaining mark) 跡, (impression) 印象

v. (**be imprinted on/in**: memory/mind) …に刻み込まれる, …に焼き付く

imprison *v.* 刑務所に入れる, 刑務所に収容する

improbable *adj.* ありそうもない

impromptu *adj.* 即座の, 即席の, (of performance) 即興の

an impromptu speech 即興のスピーチ

improper *adj.* (not fitting/appropriate) ふさわしくない, 不適当な, (incorrect) 正

しくない, 誤った

improve *v.* (make/become better) よくする/よくなる, 改良する, 改善する, (skill, understanding) (…が) 上達する, 向上する, (take a turn for the better) 好転する

His attitude has improved enormously.
彼の態度は格段によくなった。

Her condition has improved considerably.
彼女の調子はだいぶ改善した。

I need to improve my Japanese.
日本語がうまくならないといけない。

♦ **improved** *adj.* よくなった, 改良した, 改善した

improvement *n.* 改良, 改善, 向上, (advancement of skill/knowledge) 進歩, 上達, (change for the better) 改良点, 改善点

improvisation *n.* 即興, アドリブ

improvise *v.* 即興でやる, アドリブで…する; (using available materials) 間に合わせに作る

impulse *n.* 衝動, (electric impulse) インパルス

an impulse purchase 衝動買い

on impulse 衝動的に, 思わず

I bought it on impulse.
衝動買いをしてしまった。

impulsive *adj.* (of action) 衝動的な, 衝動に駆られた, (of person) 直情的な

impure *adj.* (not clean) 不潔な, 汚い, (of substance) 不純な

♦ **impurity** *n.* (substance) 不純物

in

1 *prep., adv.* INDICATING LOCATION: …に/で, …には/では, (…の) 中に/へ, (present somewhere) いて, (=at home) 家にいて, 在宅して [→ INSIDE, INTO]

2 *prep.* INDICATING TIME: …に, …で, …には

3 *prep.* STATE/SITUATION: …に/で, …では, …においては

4 *prep.* USED WITH NUMBERS: See examples below

5 *prep.* USED WITH SHAPES: …をつくって, …になって

6 *prep.* IN REGARD TO: …では, (be strong/weak in) …に(強い/弱い)

7 *prep.* BY MEANS OF: …で

8 *prep.* PUBLISHED IN: (**be in**) …に載る

9 *prep.* MOVIE: (**be in**) …に出る

10 *adj.* FASHIONABLE: (**be in**) はやっている

11 *adv.* TO ARRIVE: 到着して, 来て

1 It's in the box. 箱(の中)にある。

Put it in a bag. バッグ(の中)に入れて。

Here, sit in this chair.
ほら、この椅子に座りなさい。

I found it in the house.
家の中で見つけた。

"Where are my keys?"
"They're in your pocket, aren't they?"
「かぎはどこだろ？」
「ポケットの中じゃないの？」

I saw it in a shop window.
ショーウインドーで見た。

He was standing in the middle of the room.
彼は部屋の真ん中に立っていた。

We live in the city.
私たちは市内に住んでいます。

He was in the army at that time.

その時は、彼は陸軍に所属していた。

High in the sky I could see an eagle. 空高くに、ワシが見えた。

They were playing in the rain. 彼らは雨の中で遊んでいた。

There are three hospitals in this town. この町には病院が三つある。

Could you bring the laundry in? 洗濯物を中に取り入れてくれる?

(*on phone*) I'm sorry, she's not in right now. Can I take a message? 申し訳ありませんが、ただ今外出しております。ご伝言を 承 りましょうか?

2 in November 11月に

in 1963 1963年に

In the morning I like to have coffee. 朝にコーヒーを飲むのが好きです。

In the summer I play tennis. 夏はテニスをします。

I'll be back in five minutes. 5分で戻ります。

In the spring she (=our daughter) will enter elementary school. 娘は、春に小学校に入学します。

3 I found myself in an awkward situation. 気まずい状況に陥ってしまった。

You can see it in the light but not in the dark. 明るい所では見えるけど、暗がりでは見えないだろう。

In such circumstances, it's best to say nothing. そのような状況では、何も言わないのが一番だ。

In the excitement I forgot about the cake in the oven. みんなで騒いでいて、オーブンにケーキが入っているのを忘れていた。

In war, people sometimes lose control of themselves. 戦争状態においては、人は時に理性を失う。

Are you in debt? 借金があるの?

The cherry trees are in full bloom. 桜が満開です。

Could you put it in writing, please? それを文書にしていただけますか?

The book is still in print, isn't it? その本はまだ出版されていますね?

4 People arrived in the thousands. 数千人の人々が到着した。

He must be in his seventies. 彼は70代に違いない。

She's still in her teens. 彼女はまだ10代だ。

There's a one-in-three chance of success. 成功の確率は3分の1です。

5 stand in a row 1列に並ぶ

stand in a line 整列する

fly in a circle 輪になって飛ぶ

6 In my opinion, it was a mistake. 私の考えでは、あれは間違いだったと思う。

He's weak in math. 彼は数学に弱い。

7 He spoke in French. 彼はフランス語で話した。

8 Will it be in the newspapers? 新聞に載るでしょうか?

9 He was in *The Last Samurai*. あの人は『ラストサムライ』に出ていた。

10 Stone-washed jeans are not in.

ストーンウォッシュのジーンズは、はやってない。

11 What time is his flight due in?
彼の飛行機は何時に到着するんですか？

be in for (bad experience) (ひどい目)にあいそうだ

be in for it 厄介なことになりそうだ

be in on (plan) …に関係している, …にかかわっている, (secret) 知っている

in a minute/moment すぐに
I'll be there in a minute.
すぐに行きます。

in and out 出たり入ったりして
He was in and out in five minutes.
5分の間に、彼は出たり入ったりした/彼は5分で用事が済んだ。

in as much as → INASMUCH AS

in so far as → INSOFAR AS

the ins and outs 詳細, 一部始終
Mr. Ogawa knows all the ins and outs of the contract.
小川さんはその契約の詳細を知っている。

in- *pref.* 不-, (-less) 無-

inability *n.* 無力, 無能, できないこと

inaccessible *adj.* (of place) 行きにくい, (of person) 近寄りがたい

inaccurate *adj.* 不正確な, ずさんな

inactive *adj.* 活動的ではない, 活発ではない, (of life) 動かない, 運動不足の
an inactive club member
あまり活動しない会員
an inactive lifestyle 運動不足の生活

♦**inactive volcano** *n.* 休火山

inadequate *adj.* 不十分な
feel inadequate 不十分な気がする

inappropriate *adj.* ふさわしくない, 不適切な

inasmuch as *conj.* (being that) …から, …ので, …以上 [→ INSOFAR AS]
He was to blame inasmuch as he failed to report the accident.
事故の報告をしなかったのだから [以上]、彼には責任があった。

inattention *n.* 不注意

inattentive *adj.* 不注意な, (be inattentive to) (…に) 気を配らない
an inattentive driver 不注意な運転手

inaudible *adj.* 聞こえない, 聞き取れない

inaugurate *v.* (start, open) 開く; (**be inaugurated**: as president etc.) (…に) 就任する

inauguration *n.* 就任, (ceremony) 就任式

inbox *n.* (for e-mail) 受信トレイ, 受信ボックス

incapable *adj.* (not able) (…が) できない, (incompetent) 無能な

incarcerate *v.* 投獄する

incarnation *n.* 肉体化, (personification) 化身, (of evil) 権化

incendiary *adj.* 焼夷性の, (of speech) 扇動的な
an incendiary bomb 焼夷弾

incense *n.* (お)香, (incense stick) (お)線香 [→ picture of GRAVE[1]]
burn incense お香をたく
offer incense at a temple
お寺でお焼香する

incentive *n.* (encouragement) 刺激, 励み, (motive) 動機

He had no incentive to work.
彼には働く励みがなかった。

incessant *adj.* 絶え間のない

♦**incessantly** *adv.* 絶え間なく

incest *n.* 近親相姦

inch *n.* (measure of length) インチ [2.54 cm]; (very small distance) (ほんの) 少し
v. 少しずつ進む

One inch is about two and a half centimeters, isn't it?
1インチは約2.5センチですね？

every inch (thoroughly) 徹底的に, (completely) 完全に

I searched every inch (=in every corner) of the room and still I couldn't find it.
部屋の隅々まで捜したけれど、見つからなかった。

Our troops fought every inch of the way.
わが軍は徹底的に戦い抜いた。

inch by inch 少しずつ, じりじりと

We worked inch by inch toward our sales target.
売上目標に少しずつ近づいていった。

within an inch of doing …するまであと一息で, …する一歩手前で

We were within an inch of winning the contract.
契約の獲得まで、あと一息だった。

incident *n.* (event) 事件, 出来事

The number of incidents of violent, sex-related crimes is on the increase.
凶悪な性犯罪の件数が増加している。

incidentally *adv.* (by the way) ところで

incinerate *v.* 焼却する

♦**incineration** *n.* 焼却

incinerator *n.* 焼却炉

incite *v.* (a riot) 扇動する, あおる

inclination *n.* (to do sth) (…する) 気

Tanaka showed no inclination to leave.
田中さんは帰る気がなさそうだった。

incline *v.* (lean) 傾く, 傾斜する, (cause to lean) 傾ける, 傾斜させる
n. (slope) 坂, 斜面

inclined *adj.* (**be inclined to do**: be tempted to do) …したいと思う, …したい気がする

I'm inclined to agree with Professor Suzuki.
鈴木先生に賛成したいと思います。

include *v.* 含む, 含める, 入れる, (of room: include as a feature) (…も) 付く

The price includes breakfast.
料金は朝食代を含んでいます。

Does the price include tax?
税込みの値段ですか？

We're not going to include you. You're a sore loser.
君は入れないよ。負け惜しみが強いから。

The apartment includes a spacious balcony.
アパートには広いベランダも付いている。

including *prep.* …を含めて, …を入れて

Including shipping, it comes to ¥2,600.
送料込みで２６００円になります。

inclusion *n.* 含むこと, 含有

incoherent *adj.* 筋の通らない

income *n.* 収入, 所得

an annual income 年収 [年俸]

earn an income 収入を得る

live within [beyond] one's income
収入の範囲内で暮らす [以上の暮らしをする]

What's the average income for English teachers?
英語教師の平均所得は、どのくらいですか？

♦ **income tax** *n.* 所得税

incoming *adj.* 入って来る, (of flying object) 飛んで来る, (of phone call) かかって来る

incomparable *adj.* 比べものにならない, 比較にならない

incompatible *adj.* (of people) 気が合わない, 性格が合わない; (of software with computer) 互換性のない

incompetent *adj.* 能力のない, 無能な, (…する) 力がない

incomplete *adj.* (of work) 不完全な, 不備な

incomprehensible *adj.* 理解できない, 訳のわからない

inconceivable *adj.* (beyond the imagination's grasp) 想像もつかない, (hard to believe) 信じられない

incongruous *adj.* (not fitting) 合わない, (not harmonizing) 調和しない

inconsiderate *adj.* 思いやりのない, 気の利かない

inconsistent *adj.* 不統一な, 一貫性のない, (of argument) 矛盾した

inconspicuous *adj.* 目立たない

incontinent *adj.* (of adult) 失禁する, (of child) お漏らしする

inconvenience *n.* 不便, 面倒
v. (…に) 迷惑をかける

It was a terrible inconvenience.
ひどく不便だった。

the inconvenience of commuting long distances 遠距離通勤の面倒くささ

inconvenient *adj.* (of location) 不便な, (troublesome) 面倒くさい, (of arrangements) 都合の悪い

Thursday would be inconvenient for me.
木曜日は、ちょっと都合が悪いんです。

incorporate *v.* (include) 組み入れる

incorrect *adj.* 不正確な, 間違った, 誤った

incorrigible *adj.* どうしようもない, 救いがたい

increase *v.* (become greater) 増える, ((*formal*)) 増加する, 増す, (make greater) 増やす
n. 増加, 増大

Profits have increased by 10%.
利益が10　%　増えた [増加した]。

Class sizes will increase from thirty-five to forty students.
一クラスの生徒数が　35 人から 40 人に増えます。

a sudden/rapid increase 急増

a large increase 大幅な増加

a steady increase 着実な伸び

a salary increase 昇給

Spending is on the increase.
支出が増えている。

There's been an increase in unemployment.
失業者が増加している。

♦ **increased** *adj.* 増加した

increased crime 犯罪の増加

increasing *adj.* ますます増える

An increasing number of people are going abroad for their vacations.
休みに海外へ出かける人の数は、ます

ます増加している。

increasingly *adv.* ますます, どんどん

It is increasingly difficult to find a job these days.
最近、仕事を見つけることがますます難しくなっている。

incredible *adj.* 信じられないような, 驚くべき

incredibly *adv.* (very) とても, 非常に; (used at the beginning of a sentence) 信じられないことに

incriminate *v.* (cause to look guilty) 有罪にする, わなにはめる

incubate *v.* ふ化する

♦**incubation** *n.* ふ化

incubator *n.* ふ卵器

incur *v.* (debt) 負う, 受ける, (wrath) (怒りを)かう

incurable *adj.* (of illness) 治らない, 不治の, (of disposition) 根っからの

She is an incurable optimist.
あの人は根っからの楽天家だ。

indebted *adj.* (be indebted to) (…に) 非常に感謝している, 恩義がある

indecent *adj.* (lewd) みだらな, (vulgar) 下品な

indecision *n.* 優柔不断

indecisive *adj.* (of person) 決断力のない, 優柔不断の

indecorous *adj.* 無作法な

indeed *adv.* 確かに, 本当に, 実に, 全く, (used at the beginning of a sentence) 確かに, なるほど

It was indeed a great success.
本当に大成功だった。

indefinite *adj.* (of time) 不定の, 無期限の, (undecided) 決まっていない

indefinitely *adv.* (of time) 不定に, 無期限に

The meeting was postponed indefinitely.
会議は無期延期された。

independence *n.* (of country, institution) 独立, (of person: self-reliance) 自立, (of mind) 独立心

He says he wants his independence.
彼は自立したいと言っている。

Independence Day *n.* 独立記念日

independent *adj.* 独立した, (of action, perspective) 独自の, (of person, organization) 自立した, (unreliant on others) 人に頼らない, (**Independent**: of politician: unaffiliated) 無所属の

n. (**Independent**) (= politician) 無所属の政治家, (= voter) 無党派の人

The country became independent in 1972.
その国は１９７２年に独立した。

an independent thinker
独自の考えをもつ人

There's going to be an independent inquiry into the matter, I hear.
独自の調査が行われるという話だ。

independently *adv.* 独立して, 自主的に, (by oneself) 一人で, (without connection to) (…に) 関係なく, (freely) 自由に

Young people need the ability to act independently.
若者には、自主的に行動する力が必要です。

index *n.* (in book) 索引, インデックス

a price index 物価指数

index finger ***n.*** 人差し指 [➞ picture of HAND]

India ***n.*** インド, ((*in abbr.*)) 印

Indian ***n.*** (person of India) インド人, (Native American) アメリカ先住民, ネイティブアメリカン

adj. (of India) インドの, (of person of India) インド人の [➞ NATIVE AMERICAN]

Indian Ocean ***n.*** インド洋

Indian summer ***n.*** 小春日和

indicate ***v.*** (point to) 指す, 指さす, (signify) 示す, (express) 表す [➞ POINT 2, SHOW 2]

indication ***n.*** (direction) 指示, (sign) しるし, 徴候

Is there any indication that would lead you to believe that?
信じるに値する徴候があるのですか？

indicative ***adj.*** (be indicative of) 示す, 表す

n. (indicative mood) 直説法

indicator ***n.*** (sign) 指標, (device) 指示器, (pointer) 針, 指針, (turn signal) ウインカー [➞ picture of CAR]

the economic indicator 経済指標

indict ***v.*** 起訴する

♦**indictment** ***n.*** 起訴

indifference ***n.*** 無関心

indifferent ***adj.*** 無関心な, 平気な, 気にしない

indigenous ***adj.*** (of plants, animals) 原産の, (of people) 土着の, 現地の

indigestible ***adj.*** 消化しにくい, 胃にもたれる

indigestion ***n.*** 消化不良

indigo ***n., adj.*** 藍色(の), インディゴブルー(の)

indirect ***adj.*** (of effect) 間接的な, 二次的な, (of comment) 遠回しの, (of route) 遠回りの

An indirect result of the war was that women got the right to vote.
戦争の副産物は、女性が選挙権を獲得したことだった。

an indirect road 遠回りの道

♦**indirect object** ***n.*** 間接目的語

indirectly ***adv.*** 遠回しに, 間接的に

indiscreet ***adj.*** 無分別な, 軽率な

indiscretion ***n.*** 無分別, 軽率

indiscriminate ***adj.*** 無差別の

an indiscriminate killing 無差別殺人

indispensable ***adj.*** 絶対必要な, 不可欠な

indisputable ***adj.*** 疑う余地のない, 明白な

These facts are indisputable.
これらの事実は明白である。

indistinct ***adj.*** はっきりしない

individual ***n.*** (person) 個人

adj. (of/for one person) 個人の, (of/for one person/thing) 個々の, (distinct) 個性的な, 独自の

individuality ***n.*** 個性

individually ***adv.*** (separately) 個別に, (one-on-one) 一人一人

I don't have the time to speak to each of you individually.
みなさん一人一人と話す時間がありません。

indoctrinate ***v.*** (...に) 教え込む, (brainwash) 洗脳する

♦**indoctrination** ***n.*** 教え込むこと, 洗脳

Indonesia ***n.*** インドネシア

indoor ***adj.*** 室内の

indoor games 室内ゲーム

indoors ***adv.*** 室内に/で, 屋内に/で, 家の中に/で

We'd better go indoors.
家の中に入ったほうがいい。

stay indoors all day 一日中室内にいる

induce ***v.*** (**induce to do**) (…に) …する気にさせる, (bring about) もたらす

indulge ***v.*** (child) 甘やかす, (appetite, desire) 満足させる, (**indulge in**) …にふける, …に浸る, (eat/drink to one's heart's content) 存分に食べる/飲む

Most grandparents indulge their grandchildren too much.
たいていの祖父母は孫に甘すぎる。

indulgence ***n.*** (indulging in sth) ふけること, (thing done for pleasure) 道楽

indulgent ***adj.*** 甘い

industrial ***adj.*** 産業の, 工業の

♦ **industrial arts** ***n.*** (in school) 工芸, 工作

industrial revolution ***n.*** 産業革命

industrial waste ***n.*** 産業廃棄物

industrialize ***v.*** 工業化する

♦ **industrialization** ***n.*** 工業化

industrious ***adj.*** 勤勉な

industry ***n.*** 産業, (producing of goods in factories) 工業, -業

the steel industry 鉄鋼(産)業

a high-tech industry ハイテク産業

heavy industry 重工業

inedible ***adj.*** 食べられない

ineffective ***adj.*** 効果のない, むだな, (of worker) 役に立たない, 無能な

inefficient ***adj.*** (of machine, method) 効率の悪い, 非能率的な, (of worker) 役に立たない, 不手際な

ineligible ***adj.*** 資格のない, 不適格な

inept ***adj.*** (foolish) ばかげた, 不適当な, (clumsy) 不器用な, (incompetent) 無能な, (unskilled) 下手な

inequality ***n.*** 不平等, 不均等

sexual inequality 男女の不平等

inert ***adj.*** (not moving) 動いていない, (of person) 鈍い; (of gas) 不活性の

inertia ***n.*** 慣性

inevitable ***adj.*** (unavoidable) 避けられない, やむを得ない, (natural) 当然の, 当たり前の

n. (**the inevitable**) 避けられないもの/こと

It was inevitable that an accident would happen.
事故(が起きること)は避けられなかった。

A certain degree of sacrifice is inevitable.
ある程度の犠牲は、やむを得ない。

inevitably ***adv.*** 必然的に, 必ず

inexact ***adj.*** 不正確な, 厳密ではない

inexorable ***adj.*** 止められない

inexpensive ***adj.*** 高くない, 安い

inexperienced ***adj.*** 経験のない, 未経験の, 未熟な

inexplicable ***adj.*** 説明のつかない, 不可解な

inexpressibly ***adv.*** 何とも言えないほど

infamous ***adj.*** (of criminal) 悪名高い, (of act: despicable) 忌まわしい

infancy ***n.*** (time of infancy) 赤ん坊の時, 乳児期; (of thing) 初期

infant ***n.*** 赤ん坊, ((*formal*)) 乳児

infantry ***n.*** (soldiers) 歩兵, (infantry division) 歩兵隊

infatuated ***adj.*** (obsessed) (…に) 夢中になる

♦**infatuation** ***n.*** 夢中になること

infect ***v.*** (of disease) (…に) 感染する, (infect A with B) (AにBを) 感染させる, (**be infected with**) …に感染する, …にかかる

infected ***adj.*** (of cut) ばい菌の入った

The cut became infected.
切り傷に、ばい菌が入った。

infection ***n.*** 伝染, 感染, (disease) 感染症

infectious ***adj.*** 伝染性の, うつりやすい

an infectious disease 感染症

infer ***v.*** 推測する

inference ***n.*** 推測

inferior ***adj.*** (of rank, position) 下の, 低い, (of quality) 粗悪な, 劣った

She was dissatisfied with her inferior status in the company.
会社での低い地位に彼女は不満だった。

No culture is superior or inferior to another.
文化に優劣はない。

These goods are plainly inferior.
この品々は明らかに質が悪い。

I think he feels inferior to his brother.
彼は兄に劣等感をもっているようだ。

♦**inferiority complex** ***n.*** 劣等感, ひけめ

infertile ***adj.*** (of land) 不毛の; (of woman) 子供のできない

infidelity ***n.*** (being unfaithful to spouse) 不倫, ((*formal*)) 不貞

infield ***n.*** (in baseball) 内野

♦**infielder** ***n.*** 内野手

infiltrate ***v.*** (…に) 潜入する

infinite ***adj.*** (limitless) 無限の, 限りない, (immeasurable) 計りしれない, (innumerable) 数え切れない

n. (**the infinite**) 無限のもの

infinitely ***adv.*** (much more) はるかに

infinitive ***n.*** 不定詞

infinity ***n.*** 無限

inflammable ***adj.*** 燃えやすい, 可燃性の, 火のつきやすい

inflammation ***n.*** 炎症

inflate ***v.*** (cause to expand with air/gas) 膨らませる, 膨張させる, (put air into: tire) (…に) 空気を入れる

♦**inflatable** ***adj.*** 膨張性の

inflated ***adj.*** (filled with air/gas) 膨らんだ; (exaggerated) おおげさな; (of prices) 暴騰した, 高騰した

an inflated balloon 膨らんだ風船
inflated prices 高騰した<u>値段</u> [物価]

inflation ***n.*** (of prices) インフレ

inflect ***v.*** (of word) 語形変化する, (of verb) 活用する

♦**inflection** ***n.*** (of word) 語形変化, (of verb) 活用

inflexible ***adj.*** (of material) 曲がらない, (impossible to bend) 曲げられない, (stiff) 堅い, (of system, rule) 融通のきかない, (of person) がんこな, 頭の固い

inflict ***v.*** (inflict A on B) (BにAを) もたらす

influence ***n.*** 影響, (power to influence) 影響力

v. (…に) 影響を与える, 影響を及ぼす, (sway) 左右する

I

I don't think Yumiko's friends are a good influence on her.
友達が由美子にいい影響を及ぼしているとは思えない。

Under the influence of a good teacher, his grades improved.
いい先生の影響を受けて、彼の成績は上がった。

I don't have any influence over him.
私は彼に何の影響力ももっていない。

a person of influence 権力者

cultural influences 文化的な影響

This book is about ways to influence people.
この本は、人に影響を与える方法について書かれています。

TV coverage influenced the election.
テレビ報道が選挙に影響を及ぼした。

Humans are easily influenced by their surroundings.
人間は環境に左右されやすい。

influential ***adj.*** 有力な, 影響力のある

an influential person 有力者

an influential theory 有力な説

influenza ***n.*** インフルエンザ, 流感

influx ***n.*** (of people) 殺到, (of money) 流入

inform ***v.*** (…に) 知らせる, 教える, ((*formal*)) 通知する [→ TELL]

Please inform him of the time and date.
彼に日時を知らせてください。

I think you ought to inform the police.
警察に通報するべきだと思う。

informal ***adj.*** (of ceremony) 形式ばらない, くだけた, (unofficial) 非公式の, 正式ではない, (of atmosphere) うちとけた, (of language, attitude) くだけた

It's an informal gathering, so there's no need to get dressed up.
くだけた集まりなので、正装する必要はありません。

informal dress 普段着

informally ***adv.*** (without ceremony) 形式ばらずに, (casually) 気軽に, (unofficially) 非公式に

informant ***n.*** (on matters of language/customs) インフォーマント, 資料提供者; (person who gives away secret information) 密告者

information ***n.*** 情報, インフォメーション, (data) 資料, (guidance) 案内

We need to collect more information.
もっと情報収集しなくてはいけない。

Is it reliable information?
それは信頼できる情報ですか？

Do you have any information on the course?
その講座について何か資料はありますか？

♦ **information center** ***n.*** 案内所, インフォメーションセンター

information technology ***n.*** 情報工学, ＩＴ

informative ***adj.*** ためになる, 有益な

informed ***adj.*** 詳しい

infrared ***adj.*** 赤外線の

infrastructure ***n.*** (of system) 下部構造, 構造基盤, (of society) インフラ

infrequent ***adj.*** たまの, まれな, めったにない

♦ **infrequently** ***adv.*** たまに, まれに

infringe ***v.*** (violate) 破る, (…に) 違反す

る, (on a right) 侵害する

infringe a copyright 著作権を侵害する

♦**infringement** ***n.*** 違反, 侵害

infuriate ***v.*** 激怒させる

infuriating ***adj.*** 腹が立つ, 頭にくる

ingenious ***adj.*** (of person) 利口な, (of thing) よくできている, (of idea) 独創的な

ingot ***n.*** インゴット

ingrained ***adj.*** (deep-rooted) 根深い

ingrained prejudices 根深い偏見

be deeply ingrained in one's mind
心の中に深く根付いている

ingratitude ***n.*** 恩知らず

ingredient ***n.*** (of recipe) 材料, (of product) 成分, 原料, (of abstract thing) 要素

Perseverance is one ingredient of success.
不屈の努力は成功の一要素だ。

inhabit ***v.*** (of person: reside in) (…に) 住む, (of animal) (…に) 生息する

inhabitant ***n.*** (person) 住民

inhale ***v.*** 吸い込む, 吸う

inherent ***adj.*** (intrinsic) (…に) 固有の, 本来備わっている, 付き物の, (inborn) 持ち前の, 生まれつきの

Making mistakes is an inherent part of the language-learning process.
間違えることは、語学学習の過程に付き物です。

an inherent talent 生まれつきの才能

an inherent right
生まれながらもっている権利

♦**inherently** ***adv.*** 本質的に, 本来

Learning a musical instrument is inherently difficult.
楽器を学ぶことは本来、難しいものです。

inherit ***v.*** 受け継ぐ, (legally) 相続する, ((*informal*)) もらう

Will he inherit the land from his father?
彼は父親から土地を相続するんですか?

inheritance ***n.*** 遺産

receive an inheritance
遺産を受け取る

♦**inheritance rights** ***n.*** 相続権

inheritance tax ***n.*** 相続税

inhibit ***v.*** (**inhibit from doing**) …することを抑える, (production) 妨げる

inhibition ***n.*** 抑制

inhuman ***adj.*** (cruel) 残酷な, 冷酷な

inhumane ***adj.*** (cruel) 残酷な, 非人道的な

initial ***adj.*** (at the beginning) 最初の, 初めの

n. (**initials**) 頭文字, イニシャル

v. (…に頭文字を) 署名する [→ SIGN 4]

Whose initials are these?
これらは誰のイニシャルですか?

If you would just initial here, please.
ここに頭文字を署名してください。

initially ***adv.*** (at first) 最初は

initiate ***v.*** (start) 始める, (…の) 口火を切る; (**be initiated into**: group, organization) …に入る

Who initiated the conversation?
会話の口火を切ったのはどちらですか?

initiation ***n.*** 入会

an initiation ceremony 入会式

initiative ***n.*** (leadership) 主導権, イニシアチブ, (enterprise) 独創力, 進取の気性, (volition) 自発性

Makiko shows initiative.
真紀子は独創力を発揮している。

on one's own initiative 自ら進んで, 自発的に

He began studying on his own initiative.
彼は自発的に勉強を始めた。

take the initiative 率先してやる, 主導権を取る

inject *v.* (medicine) 注射する, 注入する; (introduce) 入れる, (funds) 投入する

injection *n.* (of medicine) 注射; (of funds) 投入

have an injection 注射をしてもらう

injunction *n.* (court order) 命令

take out an injunction 命令を下す

injure *v.* (suffer injury to) (…に) けがをする, (cause injury to) 傷つける, (…に) けがをさせる, (**be injured**) けがをする, 負傷する [→ HURT]

Careful you don't injure yourself.
けがをしないように気をつけて。

He was injured playing rugby.
彼はラグビーをしていて、けがをした。

injured *adj.* けがをした, 傷ついた

n. (**the injured**) 負傷者

injured pride 傷ついた自尊心

injury *n.* けが, 負傷

a serious injury 重傷

Were there any injuries?
けがはありませんでしたか?

♦ **injury time** *n.* ロスタイム

injustice *n.* 不当, (unfairness) 不公平

do sb an injustice 不当に扱う

ink *n.* インク, (for calligraphy) 墨 [→ picture of CALLIGRAPHY]

invisible ink あぶり出しインク

inland *adj., adv.* 内陸の/へ, 奥地の/へ

in-law *n.* 姻戚

a father-in-law 義理の父

inlet *n.* (body of water) 入江, (opening) 注入口, 吸入口

inmate *n.* (in prison) 収容者, (in hospital) 入院患者

in memoriam *prep.* (in memory of) …を記念として

inn *n.* (小さな)旅館, 宿屋

stay at an inn 宿屋に泊まる

innards *n.* (guts) 内臓, (of machine) 内部

innate *adj.* 生まれつきの, 生まれながらの

inner *adj.* 内側の, 内部の, (the heart/depths of) 奥の, (of the mind) 内面の

the inner ear 内耳

He never revealed his inner feelings.
彼は内に秘めた感情を、一度も見せることはなかった。

inner city *n.* (slum) スラム街

inning *n.* (in baseball) 回, イニング, (in cricket) 打ち番

innkeeper *n.* 宿の主人

innocence *n.* (guiltlessness) 無罪, 無実, (naivety) 無邪気

innocent *adj.* (of crime) 無罪の, 無実の, 潔白な, (harmless) 無害な, 悪気のない, (of victim: guiltless) 罪のない, (naive) 無邪気な, (inexperienced) 世間知らずの

Is he innocent of this crime?
彼は無罪なのですか?

an innocent bystander
関係のない第三者

innovation *n.* 革新, 刷新, (new method)

新しい手法, (new thing) 新しいもの, (introduction of new machine/system) 導入

innovative *adj.* 革新的な, 刷新的な

innovator *n.* (leader) イノベーター

innuendo *n.* ほのめかし, (negative comment) 当てこすり

innumerable *adj.* 数え切れない, 無数の

inoffensive *adj.* 当たり障りのない, 悪気のない

inorganic *adj.* 非有機的な

♦ **inorganic chemistry** *n.* 無機化学

input *n.* (ideas, opinions) 意見; (of data into computer) 入力, インプット

v. (into computer) 入力する, インプットする

inquest *n.* 査問, 審問, (into cause of death) 検死, (general investigation) 調査

inquire *v.* 尋ねる, 聞く, ((*formal*)) 問う [→ ASK]

I inquired after her health.
彼女の体調を尋ねた。

inquiry *n.* (question) 質問, 問い合わせ, (formal investigation) 捜査, 調査

make inquiries 問い合わせる

inquisitive *adj.* (curious) 好奇心が強い, (nosy) せんさく好きな

insane *adj.* 狂気の, 正気ではない, (absurd) ばかげた, 非常識な [→ MAD]

insanity *n.* (illness) 精神異常, (outright stupidity) 狂気

be insanity to do …するなんて狂気のさただ

inscrutable *adj.* 不可解な

inseam *n.* 内側の縫い目

insect *n.* 虫, (genus) 昆虫

insecticide *n.* 殺虫剤

insecure *adj.* (lacking self-confidence) 自信のない, (unstable) 不安定な

He seems a very insecure type.
彼はとても自信のないタイプに見える。

The future of the company is very insecure.
会社の行く末は、非常に不安定です。

insecurity *n.* (lack of confidence) 自信のなさ, (uncertainty, instability) 不安定, (danger) 危険, (anxiety) 不安感

insensitive *adj.* (uncaring) 思いやりのない, 無神経な, (unresponsive) 鈍感な

inseparable *adj.* 分けられない, 別れられない, (indivisible) 不可分の

Those two are inseparable!
あの二人は別れられないよ。

insert *v.* (put/include in) 入れる, (stick in) 差し込む, (into text) 挿入する

n. (in newspaper/magazine) 折り込み広告

inside

1 *adv.* 中へ/に/で

2 *prep.* …の中へ/に/で

3 *adj.* 中の, 内側の, 内部の

4 *n.* INTERIOR: (**the inside**) 中, 内側, 内部

1 Let's go inside. 中へ入りましょう。

I left my umbrella inside.
中に傘を置き忘れてきた。

Does it have pips inside?
種は入ってるの？

2 What's inside the box?
箱の中に何が入っているんですか？

She's not inside the house.
彼女は家にいない。

3 Have a look in your inside pocket.

内ポケットの中を見てみたら？

Sounds like inside information to me.
内部情報のように思える。

4 The inside was damp.
中は湿っていた。

Is the door locked from the inside?
ドアは内側から、かぎがかかっているのですか？

KANJI BRIDGE

内 ON: ない, だい KUN: うち | **INSIDE, WITHIN**

bashful	内気な
cabinet (of politicians)	内閣
contents	内容
heart, mind	内心
indoors	室内
inland	内陸
inside a car	車内に
inside an airplane	機内に
inside and outside (domestic and foreign)	内外に
inside the body	体内に
interior, inside, internal	内部
internal medicine	内科
internal organs	内臓
in the company	社内に
itemization	内訳
within	-以内に

inside out *adv.* 裏返しに, ひっくり返して

Your sweater is inside out.
セーターが裏返しだよ。

insider *n.* (of organization) 内部の人, (person trading/dealing illicitly) インサイダー

♦ **insider trading** *n.* インサイダー取引

insides *n.* (of body: guts) 内臓, (of machine) 中, 内部

insight *n.* 洞察, (ability) 洞察力

gain insight into 理解する

insignificant *adj.* (unimportant) 取るに足らない, (meaningless) 無意味な, (of amount) わずかな, 微々たる

The company's debt was insignificant.
会社の負債は微々たるものだった。

insincere *adj.* 不真面目な, 不誠実な, 誠意のない

insincere flattery お世辞

insist *v.* (say strongly) 強く言う, 主張する, 言い張る, (demand) 要求する

She insisted her decision had been correct.
自分の決断は正しかったと言い張った。

Mr. Tanaka insisted on my going.
田中さんは私に行けとしつこく言った。

I just don't think it's fair to insist that everyone do overtime.
全員に残業するよう要求するのは、公正じゃないと思う。

if you insist どうしてもと言うのなら

If you insist, I'll speak to him.
どうしてもと言うのなら、私が彼に話しましょう。

insistent *adj.* (of demands) しつこい, (be insistent on) 主張する, (...と) 言ってきかない

insofar as *conj.* ...する限り(では), ...する範囲で

Insofar as circumstances permit, you may use this land.
事情の許す限り、この土地を利用してもいいです。

I agree insofar as the house is concerned, but not as to its contents.
家に関しては了承しますが、中の家財についてては納得できません。

insolvent ***adj.*** (unable to pay) 破産した [→ BANKRUPT]

insomnia ***n.*** 眠れないこと, 不眠症

insomniac ***n.*** 不眠症の人

inspect ***v.*** 念入りに調べる, (accounts, luggage) 検査する, (machine) 点検する

The factory is to be inspected next week.
工場は来週、点検を受ける予定です。

inspection ***n.*** (general investigation) 検査, (of machine) 点検

inspector ***n.*** (in general) 調査官, (police inspector) 警視正

inspiration ***n.*** インスピレーション, ひらめき

provide inspiration for
...のひらめきを与える

be an inspiration to (of person) 励ます

inspire ***v.*** (stimulate) 刺激する, (**be inspired by**: be moved by) ...に感動する, (inspire A in B) (BにAを) 呼び起こす, いだかせる

Their music inspired me to learn to play an instrument.
彼らの音楽に刺激されて、楽器を習い始めた。

Who could fail to be inspired by the beauty of Venice?
ベニスの美しさに感動しない者がいるだろうか？

He inspires confidence in his staff.
彼はスタッフに自信をもたせる。

in spite of ***prep.*** ...のに, ...けど, ...にもかかわらず

We went in spite of the rain.
雨なのに行った。

I bought it in spite of the high price.
(値段は) 高かったけど買ってしまった。

Mr. Yamada came in spite of his poor health.
山田さんは体調が悪いにもかかわらず、来た。

instability ***n.*** 不安定

install ***v.*** (small thing) 取り付ける, (large thing) 設置する, (software) インストールする

We're going to have a Jacuzzi installed.
ジャクジーを設置するんです。

installation ***n.*** (of small thing) 取り付け, (of large thing) 設置, (of software) インストール, 設定

installment ***n.*** (one installment) 1回分, (monthly installment) 月賦

You didn't pay June's installment.
6月分が未納です。

♦**installment plan** ***n.*** 分割払い

instance ***n.*** (case) 場合, (example) 実例, 例 [→ EXAMPLE]

Most instances of the illness are not serious.
その病気はほとんどの場合、症状が重くない。

for instance 例えば, 例を挙げると

instant ***n.*** 瞬間

adj. (at once) すぐの, 即時の

I'll be there in an instant.
すぐに行きます。

It's just one instant in your life.
人生においては、ほんの一瞬にすぎないよ。

an instant decision 即断 [即決]

an instant reply 即答

♦**instant food** *n.* インスタント食品

instant messaging *n.* インスタントメッセージ

instant ramen *n.* インスタントラーメン, 即席ラーメン

instantaneous *adj.* すぐの, 即時の

♦**instantaneously** *adv.* すぐ(に), 即座に

instantly *adv.* すぐ(に), ただちに

He instantly accepted the job.
彼はその仕事をすぐに引き受けた。

instead *adv.* (その)代わりに

Let's use sesame oil instead.
代わりにゴマ油を使おう。

I planned to go by train but went by bus instead.
電車で行くつもりだったけど、代わりにバスで行ってしまった。

instead of …の代わりに, …ではなくて, (**instead of doing**) …しないで, …する代わりに

Instead of butter, let's use margarine.
バターの代わりに、マーガリンを使おう。

We ended up going to see a play instead of a movie.
結局、映画の代わりに芝居を見に行った。

Let's do something instead of just talking all the time.
しゃべってばかりいないで、何かしようよ。

instep *n.* 足の甲

instigate *v.* (cause to happen) 引き起こす, (start) 開始する

instinct *n.* 本能, (hunch, intuition) 直観

maternal instinct 母性本能

Follow your instincts.
直観に従いなさい。

instinctive *adj.* 本能的な, 本能の

an instinctive reaction 本能的な反応

♦**instinctively** *adv.* (know sth) 直観的に, (do sth: without thinking) 思わず

institute *n.* (society) 会, (academic society) 学会, (association) 協会, (research institute) 研究所

v. (start) 始める, (carry out) 行う, 実施する, (establish: law) 制定する

institution *n.* (organization) 機関, (facility) 施設, (mental institution) 精神病院; (custom) 慣習

a financial institution 金融機関

an educational institution 教育機関

♦**institutional** *adj.* 制度上の

institutionalized *adj.* 制度化された

instruct *v.* (teach) 教える, (tell) 指示する

He was instructed in the martial arts.
彼は武道を教わった。

♦**instructive** *adj.* 勉強になる

instructions *n.* (explanation) 説明, (instruction manual) 取扱説明書, 使用説明書, (orders) 命令, 指図

instructor *n.* インストラクター, 指導員

instrument *n.* (musical instrument) 楽器, (tool) 道具

instrumental *adj.* (helpful) 助けになる, 役立つ

n. (music) 器楽曲

insufficient *adj.* 不十分な, 不足している

insular *adj.* (narrow-minded) 視野が狭い, 狭量な

insulin *n.* インシュリン

insult ***n.*** 侮辱, 無礼

v. 侮辱する, ばかにする

Don't insult me. 侮辱しないで。

You insult her intelligence by telling her that.
彼女にそんなことを言うのは、知性を侮辱することですよ。

insurance ***n.*** 保険, (payment) 保険料

car [fire, health] insurance
自動車 [火災, 健康] 保険

♦**insurance policy** ***n.*** 保険証書

insure ***v.*** (car etc.) (…に) 保険をかける; (guarantee) 保証する

Is your luggage insured?
荷物に保険はかかっていますか？

intact ***adj.*** (unharmed) 無傷の, (unbroken) 壊れていない

intake ***n.*** (number of people accepted) 受け入れ人数, (in company) 採用人数; (of alcohol) 摂取量

intangible ***adj.*** 実体のない

integer ***n.*** 整数

integral ***adj.*** 欠かせない, (必要)不可欠な

n. (in math) 積分

be an integral part of …に欠かせないものだ

integrate ***v.*** (people) 融合する, とけ込む, (things) 統合する, (end racial discrimination) 差別をなくす; (in math) 積分する

integrated ***adj.*** (of school: having people of all races) 差別のない; (of system) 統合された

integrity ***n.*** (adherence to morals) 誠実

intellect ***n.*** 知性, 知力

intellectual ***n.*** (person) インテリ, 知識人

adj. 知的な, 理知的な, インテリの

♦**intellectual property** ***n.*** 知的財産

intellectual property rights 知的所有権

intelligence ***n.*** (mental) 知能, 知恵, 思考力; (military) 軍情報

He has a below-average intelligence.
あの人の知能は平均以下だ。

intelligent ***adj.*** 頭のいい, 賢い, 聡明な, 知的な, (of child) 利口な

an intelligent answer 頭のいい答え

intelligent life 知的生命体

She's a very intelligent child.
あの子はとても利口な子だ。

intelligible ***adj.*** 理解できる

intend ***v.*** (**intend to do**) …しようと思う, …するつもりだ, …する気だ, …する予定だ; (**be intended for**) …向けだ

Well, I intended to go, but I changed my mind because I didn't feel well.
行くつもりだったんだけど、気分が悪いからやめたんだ。

What do you intend to do about it?
どう対処するつもりですか？

Do you think she intends to sue?
彼女は訴える気だと思いますか？

That dictionary is intended for beginners.
その辞書は初心者向けです。

intense ***adj.*** (strong) 強い, 猛烈な, (of light, pain) 強烈な, 激しい, (of competition) し烈な, 激しい, (of person) 気性の激しい

the intense summer heat
夏の猛暑 [厳しい暑さ]

intense pain 激しい痛み [激痛]

He's a very intense person.
あの人はとても気性が激しい。

intensify *v.* 強める, 激しくする

intensity *n.* 強さ, 激しさ

intensive *adj.* (of course of study) 集中的な; (thorough) 徹底的な

♦ **intensive care** *n.* 集中治療, (unit of hospital) 集中治療室

intent *n.* 意図, 意志, (thought) 考え, (aim) 目的

adj. 熱心な, (be intent on) (…に) 没頭している

with intent to kill 殺す目的で

for/to all intents and purposes 事実上

intention *n.* 意図, つもり, (thought) 考え, (aim) 目的, (motive) 動機

intentional *adj.* 意図的な, 故意の, わざと…する

I don't think it was intentional.
わざと[意図的]だったとは思わない。

♦ **intentionally** *adv.* わざと, 故意に

inter- *pref.* …の間, -間, 相互-

interact *v.* (of people) 触れ合う, 交流する, (of things) 相互に作用する

interaction *n.* (of people) 人との触れ合い, 交流, (of things) 相互作用

interactive *adj.* (of game etc.) インタラクティブな, 双方向の, 対話型-

intercept *v.* (message) 横取りする, (missile) 迎撃する, (ball) インターセプトする

interchange *n.* (of opinions) 交換, やり取り, (of things) 入れ替え; (on highway) インターチェンジ

v. (interchange A with B) (AをBと) 入れ替える

I

interchangeable *adj.* 交換できる, 入れ替えられる

intercity *adj.* (of bus) 大都市間の, 都市間-

intercollegiate *adj.* (of game) 大学対抗の

intercom *n.* インターホン

intercontinental *adj.* 大陸間の

an intercontinental ballistic missile
大陸間弾道ミサイル

intercourse *n.* (sexual) セックス, 性交, (social) 社交, (contact) 交際

intercultural *adj.* 異文化間の

interdepartmental *adj.* (between academic departments) 各学部間の

interest

1 *n.* KNOWING OR WANTING TO LEARN: 興味, 関心

2 *n.* HOBBY: 趣味

3 *v.* KINDLE THE INTEREST OF: (…に) 興味/関心をもたせる [→ INTERESTED]

4 *n.* MONEY CHARGED ON A LOAN: 利息, 利子

5 *n.* ADVANTAGE: 利益, (**in one's interest**) (…の)ために

1 He has an interest in model railways.
彼は鉄道の模型に興味がある。

I just wish she'd take an interest in something other than pop music.
彼女がポップス以外にも何か興味をもってくれたらいいのに。

Can't you get the children to show an interest in their study?
子供の関心を勉強に向けられませんか?

2 Masashi's main interest is computers.
正志の主な趣味はコンピューターです。

3 The comment seemed to interest him.

そのコメントが、彼に興味をもたせたようだ。

4 There was a 5% interest on the loan.
ローンの金利は５％だった。

What's the rate of interest?
利率はどれくらい？

5 a conflict of interests 利害の衝突

But is it really in your interest to accept the offer?
その申し出を受けることが、本当に(あなたの)ためになるのですか？

♦ **interest group** ***n.*** 利益団体

interest rate ***n.*** 金利, 利率

interested ***adj.*** (be interested in) (…に) 興味/関心がある, (**be interested in doing**) …したい, …する気がある

Etsuko's interested in horseback riding.
悦子は乗馬に興味がある。

The students are more interested in sports than studying.
生徒たちは勉強よりスポーツに関心がある。

Are they interested in joining us?
彼らは私たちに加わる気はあるの？

John seemed interested in visiting Kyoto.
ジョンは京都に行きたいようだった。

Shimizu said he would be interested in coming along to have a look.
清水さんはぜひ見に来たいと言っていた。

♦ **interested party** ***n.*** 当事者, 関係者

interesting ***adj.*** 面白い, 興味深い, 興味のある

She's a very interesting person.
彼女はとても面白い人です。

There was an interesting program on TV the other night.
この間の夜、テレビで面白い番組をやっていた。

It was interesting to watch her reaction.
彼女の反応を見るのは面白かった。

Would it have been interesting for old people, too?
年配の人々も興味がもてただろうか？

It's interesting that he said nothing.
彼が何も言わなかったとは、興味深い。

interface ***n.*** (in computing) インターフェース, (point of contact/connection) 接点

interfere ***v.*** (meddle) (…に) 干渉する, 口出しする, (interrupt) じゃまする, (cut into conversation) さえぎる, (…に) 割り込む

Please don't interfere. This is a private matter.
口出ししないでください。これは個人的な問題ですから。

interference ***n.*** (meddling) 干渉, 口出し; (unwanted radio signals) 混信; (in sport) インターフェア, 妨害

interim ***n.*** 合間

in the interim その間に/は

interior ***adj.*** 内部の, 中の
n. 中, 内部, (of building) インテリア, (of continent) 奥地

♦ **interior decoration** ***n.*** 室内装飾, インテリア(デザイン)

interior designer ***n.*** インテリアデザイナー

interjection ***n.*** (word) 間投詞, 感嘆詞, (sudden utterance) 不意の言葉

interlude ***n.*** (period of time) 合間, (piece of music) 間奏曲

intermediary ***n.*** 仲介者, (matchmaker) (お)仲人(さん), (broker) 仲買人

adj. 仲介の

intermediate *adj.* 中級の

intermediate-level Japanese
中級の日本語

interminable *adj.* 果てしない

intermission *n.* (short break) 休憩, (during play) 幕間

The intermission lasted thirty minutes.
休憩は30分だった。

intermittent *adj.* 断続的な

intern *n.* (trainee doctor) インターン, 医学研修生, (in general) 研修生

v. (confine during war) 抑留する

internal *adj.* 内部の, 中の, (domestic, not foreign) 国内の, 内- [→ INSIDE]

♦**internal clock** *n.* 体内時計

internal medicine *n.* 内科

Internal Revenue Service *n.* 国税庁, 内国歳入庁

international *adj.* 国際的な, インターナショナルな

an international telephone call 国際電話

an international trade agreement
国際貿易協定

the international date line
(国際)日付変更線

the international community 国際社会

internationalize *v.* 国際化する

internationally *adv.* 国際的に

be known internationally
国際的に知られている

Internet *n.* インターネット

connect to the Internet
インターネットに接続する

♦**Internet café** *n.* (インター) ネットカフェ

interpret *v.* (translate) 通訳する, (construe) 解釈する

interpretation *n.* (of language) 通訳, (of meaning) 解釈, (explanation) 説明

interpreter *n.* 通訳者

interrogate *v.* 尋問する, 取り調べる

interrogation *n.* 尋問, 取り調べ

be under interrogation 取り調べを受けている

interrogative *adj.* 疑問の

n. 疑問詞, (interrogative sentence) 疑問文

interrupt *v.* じゃまする, (cut into conversation) さえぎる, (break off: conversation, game, TV program) 中断する

Please don't interrupt me.
じゃまし [さえぎら] ないでください。

The program was interrupted with news of an earthquake.
地震のニュースで、番組が中断された。

interruption *n.* (bother, obstruction) じゃま, (breaking off) 中断

intersect *v.* (of roads: cross each other) 交差する, (of line: connect to) (…と) 交わる [→ CROSS 4]

intersection *n.* (of roads) 交差点, (of lines) 交差

interstate *adj.* 州間-

n. (highway) 高速道路

interstellar *adj.* 星間-

interval *n.* 間, 間隔, (of time) 合間, (of space) 隔たり [→ INTERMISSION]

at regular five-minute intervals
きちんと5分間隔で

The posts were spaced at ten-meter in-

tervals.
柱は10メートル間隔で立っていた。

intervene *v.* (get involved) (…に) 介入する, (interfere) じゃまする, (in conversation) (…に) 割り込む

The police intervened when the protest turned violent.
抗議行動が激しくなり、警察が介入した。

intervention *n.* 介入

military intervention 軍事介入

interview *n.* インタビュー, (for job) 面接
v. インタビューする, (of journalist) 取材する, (interview for a job) 面接する

give an interview インタビューに応じる

have an interview with
…にインタビューする

be interviewed (for a job)
(会社の)面接を受ける

♦**interviewee** *n.* 面接を受ける人

interviewer *n.* (for job) 面接官

intestate *n.* 遺言状のない死亡者

intestine *n.* (gut) 腸

large [small] intestines 大 [小] 腸

♦**intestinal** *adj.* 腸の

intimacy *n.* (closeness) 親しさ, (sexual relationship) 性的関係

intimate *adj.* (of friendship) 親しい, 親密な, (be intimate with: be sexually involved with) (…と) 性的関係のある; (of place, atmosphere: cozy) くつろげる; (of details: pertaining to personal/private matter) 個人的な, 私的な

have an intimate knowledge of 熟知している

intimidate *v.* 怖がらせる, おびえさせる, びくびくさせる

Don't be intimidated by him.
((*masculine*)) 奴にびくびくしなくていい。

into *prep.* …に, …の中に/へ

put a handkerchief into one's pocket
ハンカチをポケットにしまう

pour milk into a glass
コップにミルクを注ぐ

bite into a pear 洋ナシにかぶりつく

The teacher came into the room.
先生は部屋に入って来た。

They drive into town (where I live) every Saturday.
彼らは毎週土曜日に、車で街に来る。

I jumped into the pool.
プールに飛び込みました。

Dirt got into the water.
泥が水に流れ込んだ。

intolerable *adj.* がまんできない, 耐えられない

intolerance *n.* 不寛容, がまんできないこと

intolerant *adj.* 寛容ではない, 偏狭な, (be intolerant of) 許せない, (…に) がまんできない, (= be unaccepting of) 認めない

intonation *n.* イントネーション, 抑揚

intoxication *n.* (being drunk) 酔い, (being excited) 陶酔

intransitive *adj.* (**intransitive verb**) 自動詞

intravenous *adj.* 静脈内の, 静脈-

an intravenous injection 静脈注射

♦**intravenous drip** *n.* 点滴

intricate *adj.* (of pattern) 入り組んだ, (complicated) 複雑な

I

intrigue ***n.*** (plot) 陰謀, 策略

intriguing ***adj.*** とても面白い, 興味をそそる

intrinsic ***adj.*** 本質的な, 固有の, 本来の

intrinsic value/worth 本来の価値

introduce ***v.*** 紹介する, (**introduce oneself**) 自己紹介する, (introduce A [person] to B [skill/pleasure]) (AにBを) 初めて教える, (AにBの) 手ほどきをする; (new product) 発表する, (new method/system) 導入する, (topic) 持ち込む

Hashimoto introduced me to his wife.
橋本さんは奥さんに私を紹介した。

"Oh, Mr. Smith. Let me introduce you. This is Mr. Tanaka."
"I'm Tanaka. How do you do?" (*bowing*)
"I'm Smith. How do you do?" (*bowing*)
「あぁ、スミスさん、ご紹介します。こちらは田中さんです」
「田中です。初めまして、どうぞよろしく(お願いします)」
「スミスです。こちらこそどうぞよろしく(お願いします)」

Please introduce yourselves.
自己紹介してください。

It was Mr. Aoyama who introduced me to golf.
私にゴルフを初めて教えて [の手ほどきをして] くれたのは、青山さんでした。

I'll introduce fractions in the next lesson.
次の授業では分数をやります。

introduction ***n.*** 紹介, (part of book) 前書き, 序論; (textbook) 入門書

a self-introduction 自己紹介

introductory ***adj.*** (of paragraph) 冒頭の, 前置きの; (of course) 入門の

an introductory book 入門書

introvert ***n.*** 内向的な人

introverted ***adj.*** 内向的な, 内向性の

an introverted person 内向的な人

intrude ***v.*** (on privacy) (…に) 立ち入る, 侵害する, (on conversation) (…に) 割り込む, (on property) 侵入する

intruder ***n.*** 侵入者, 乱入者

intrusion ***n.*** 侵入

intuition ***n.*** 直観, 勘

by/on intuition 勘で

intuitively ***adv.*** 直観的に, 勘で

invade ***v.*** (country) 侵略する, 侵攻する, (building) (…に) 侵入する, (privacy) 侵害する, 侵す, (of fans: invade a place) (…に) どっと押し寄せる

That country has been invaded many times.
その国は何度も侵略されてきた。

The place was invaded by teenage fans.
10代のファンがどっと押し寄せた。

invalid ***adj.*** (of comment) 根拠のない, (of document) 無効の

n. (disabled person) 体の不自由な人, (ill person) 病人, 病弱な人

invaluable ***adj.*** 非常に貴重な, ((*formal*)) とても有益な

invariably ***adv.*** いつも, きまって, 必ず [→ ALWAYS]

He's invariably late.
彼はきまって遅れて来る。

Whenever they meet, they invariably bicker.
二人は顔を合わせれば、必ず口論になる。

invasion ***n.*** (military invasion) 侵略, 襲来, (encroachment: of privacy) 侵害

an invasion of privacy
プライバシーの侵害

invent ***v.*** 発明する, (make up: excuse) でっち上げる

Who was it that invented the television?
テレビを発明したのは誰だったっけ？

invention ***n.*** (thing invented) 発明, (made-up story) でっち上げ, 作り話

inventor ***n.*** 発明家

inventory ***n.*** (stock) 在庫, (list) 目録, (taking of inventory) 棚卸し

v. (...の)目録を作る

invertebrate ***n.*** 無脊椎動物

adj. 脊椎のない

invest ***v.*** (in stock market) 投資する, (time/energy in some activity) (...に) つぎ込む, 費やす

Mr. Kobayashi only invests in large companies.
小林さんは大企業にしか投資しない。

♦ **invest in** ***v.*** (purchase) 買う

You ought to invest in a new car.
新しい車を買ったほうがいいと思います。

investigate ***v.*** 調べる, 調査する, (crime) 取り調べる, 捜査する, (probe) 掘り下げる

investigation ***n.*** (criminal) 捜査

investigator ***n.*** 捜査官, 調査員

investiture ***n.*** (ceremony) 授与式

investment ***n.*** (act of investing) 投資, (money invested) 投資金, 出資金, (thing) 投資物件, 買い物

The new computer is a good investment.
新しいコンピューターは、いい買い物だ。

investor ***n.*** 投資家, 投資者

invigorate ***v.*** 元気づける

invincible ***adj.*** (unbeatable) 無敵の, (of theory) 打ち負かせない

invisible ***adj.*** (目に)見えない

♦ **invisibly** ***adv.*** 見えないように

invitation ***n.*** (ご)招待, (お)誘い, (お)招き, (letter of invitation) 招待状

an invitation to a retirement party
引退パーティーへの招待

Are you going to turn down the invitation?
お誘い [招待] を断るつもり？

Thank you for the invitation.
((*polite*)) お招き [ご招待] いただき、ありがとうございます。

It's time to send out invitations.
招待状を発送する時期だ。

invitation cards 招待状

invite ***v.*** 誘う, 呼ぶ, (to party) 招く, 招待する; (discussion) 促す, 求める, (call on) (...に) 依頼する; (attention, criticism) 引き起こす, 招く

He was not invited.
彼は誘われなかった。

Let's invite the Koizumi family to dinner.
小泉さん一家を夕食に招待しよう。

They were invited to the party.
彼らはパーティーに招かれた。

It was kind of you to invite me.
ご招待してくださってありがとう。(lit., "Thank you for inviting me.")

The teacher stopped speaking and invited discussion.
先生は話をやめて、討論を促した。

Murata was invited to give a talk on par-

enting.
村田さんは育児についての講演を依頼された。

Such behavior invites criticism.
そういう行動は批判を招く。

inviting *adj.* 魅力的な

invoice *n.* (bill for services) 請求書
v. (...に) 請求書を送る

involuntary *adj.* (unintentional) 不本意な, (unconscious) 無意識の

♦**involuntarily** *adv.* (unconsciously) 思わず, 無意識に

involve *v.* (entail) 伴う, (require) 必要とする; (concern) (...に) 関係する, (**involve oneself in**) ...にかかわる, ...に巻き込まれる [→ INVOLVED]

The project involves a certain amount of risk.
その企画は、ある程度のリスクを伴う。

A lot of time and money is involved in making a movie.
映画製作には、多くの時間とお金が必要となる。

This does not involve you.
これはあなたに関係ありません。

I wish I had never involved myself in this.
この件に全くかかわらなければよかった。

involved *adj.* (**be involved in**) (task) ...に打ち込んでいる, (book) ...に熱中している, (=be mixed up in) ...に巻き込まれている, ...にかかわっている; (complex) 複雑な

He's totally involved in his work.
彼は仕事にすごく打ち込んでいる。

I don't want to get involved in the argument.
けんかに巻き込まれたくない。

He's involved in crime.
彼は犯罪にかかわっている。

involvement *n.* (taking part in: connection) 参加, 関与

inward *adj.* (inner) 内側の, (toward the inside) 内側への; (of feeling) 心の中の, 内心の
adv. 内側に/へ

♦**inwardly** *adv.* (in one's heart) 心の中で, ひそかに

ion *n.* イオン

positive [negative] ions 陽 [陰] イオン

ionosphere *n.* 電離層

IQ *n.* 知能指数, ＩＱ

ir- → IN-

Iran *n.* イラン

Iraq *n.* イラク

irate *adj.* 激怒した

Ireland *n.* アイルランド

iris *n.* (plant) アイリス, アヤメ, カキツバタ; (part of the eye) 虹彩

iron *n.* (metal) 鉄; (tool for ironing) アイロン
v. (press: clothes) (...に) アイロンをかける

an iron pipe 鉄パイプ

♦**Iron Age** *n.* 鉄器時代

ironic(al) *adj.* 皮肉な

That's really ironic, isn't it.
本当に皮肉なことですね。

ironically *adv.* 皮肉にも, 皮肉なことに

ironing *n.* アイロンがけ

do the ironing アイロンがけをする

♦**ironing board** *n.* アイロン台

irony *n.* 皮肉, 嫌み

irrational *adj.* (not reasonable) 不合理な, (of person, behavior) 理性のない

irregular *adj.* 不規則な, (of behavior) だらしない

an irregular verb 不規則動詞

irregularity *n.* 不規則, (**irregularities**: disorder in a system) 異常; (in surface) でこぼこ

irrelevant *adj.* (unrelated) 関係のない, (beside the point) 見当違いの, 的外れの

irreplaceable *adj.* (precious) かけがえのない

irresistible *adj.* 抵抗できない, (of desire: irrepressible) 抑えられない

irrespective of *prep.* …と/に関係なく

irresponsible *adj.* 無責任な, 責任を負わない

That was highly irresponsible of you.
それはかなり無責任ですよ。

irrigate *v.* (…に) 水を引く, (…を) かんがいする

irrigation *n.* かんがい

irritable *adj.* 怒りっぽい

irritant *n.* 刺激物

irritate *v.* (try the patience of) いら立たせる, いらいらさせる, (anger) 怒らせる, (**become irritated**) いらいらする, 腹を立てる

The noise irritated me.
騒音が私をいら立たせた。

I was irritated by the smoky atmosphere.
煙たい空気にいらいらしていた。

irritating *adj.* うるさい

irritation *n.* (being annoyed, irritable feeling) いら立ち; (painful reaction by the body) 炎症

IRS *n.* 国税庁

is → BE

-ish *suf.* (having the bad nature of) …っぽい, …じみた; (somewhat) …がかった [→ -LIKE]

childish 子供<u>っぽい</u> [じみた]
blackish 黒みがかった

Islam *n.* イスラム教, 回教

♦**Islamic** *adj.* イスラム教の

island *n.* 島, -島

the Japanese islands 日本列島

♦**islander** *n.* 島の人

isolate *v.* (cut off) 離す, 孤立させる, (quarantine) 隔離する [→ SEPARATE]; (discover) 発見する, 見つけ出す

Have you isolated the problem?
問題を発見しましたか？

isolated *adj.* (alienated) 孤立した, (distant) 山奥の, (far from civilization) 人里離れた; (singular) たった一つの

feel isolated from the rest of the world
ほかの世界から孤立していると感じる

It was an isolated incident.
たった一つの事件だった。

isolation *n.* (being away from others) 孤立

♦**isolation ward** *n.* 隔離病棟

isosceles *adj.* 二等辺の

an isosceles triangle 二等辺三角形

isotope *n.* アイソトープ, 同位体

Israel *n.* イスラエル

issei *n.* (first-generation immigrant from Japan) 一世

issue *n.* (important question) 問題, (point of discussion) 争点; (magazine number) -号, (printing of book) -版
v. 出す, (banknotes, licenses) 発行する

It's a very controversial issue.
非常に論議を呼ぶ問題だ。

I wouldn't make an issue of it.
私なら問題にしないでしょう。

a special issue 特別号

a spring issue 春号

The government issued a statement.
政府が声明を出した。

isthmus *n.* (land feature) 地峡

IT *n.* (information technology) 情報工学, ＩＴ

it *pron.* (subject) それは/が, (object) それを/に [NOTE: Often not translated into Japanese.]

"What is it?" "It's a lizard."
「(それは) 何ですか？」「トカゲです」

"Is it difficult?" "No, it's easy."
「(それは) 難しい?」「いいえ、簡単です」

"Where is it?" "It's in the drawer."
「どこにあるの？」「引き出しの中よ」

"Who is it?" "It's me!"
「誰？」「私よ」

I can't do it.
(それは)できません。

Can you read it?
(それを) 読めますか？

Let me have it, please.
それを下さい。

Did you give it to her?
(それを) 彼女にあげたの？

Could you pass it to me?
こちらに(それを)渡してもらえませんか？

Did you speak to him about it?
彼にそのことを話した？

It's snowing. 雪が降っている。

It's windy today.
今日は風が強いですね。

It's the fourteenth tomorrow.
明日は１４日です。

It's about half an hour by train.
電車で３０分ほどです。

It's about thirty kilometers from here.
ここから大体３０キロです。

Italian *n.* (person) イタリア人, (language) イタリア語
adj. (of country, culture) イタリアの, (of person) イタリア人の, (of language) イタリア語の

italic *adj.* イタリック体の, 斜字体の
n. (**italics**) イタリック体, 斜字体

Italy *n.* イタリア, ((*in abbr.*)) 伊

itch *n.* かゆみ, むずがゆさ
v. (…が) かゆい

itchy *adj.* かゆい, むずがゆい

item *n.* (thing) 品目, (thing on a list) 項目

itinerant *adj.* 巡回する

itinerary *n.* 旅行計画, 旅行の日程

its *adj.* その, それの

itself *pron.* それ自体, それ自身, そのもの
by itself (alone) それだけで, 単独で, (automatically) ひとりでに, 自然に

IVF *n.* (in vitro fertilization) 体外受精

ivory *n., adj.* 象牙(の), (color) 象牙色(の)

ivy *n.* ツタ

Ivy League *n.* アイビーリーグ

J, j

jab *v.* (stab) 突く, 突き刺す, (punch) (…に) ジャブを出す

n. (stab) 突き, (punch) ジャブ

jack *n.* (tool) ジャッキ; (socket) 差し込み口; (playing card) ジャック

♦**jack up** *v.* (car) ジャッキで持ち上げる, (price) つり上げる

jackal *n.* ジャッカル

jacket *n.* (garment) 上着, ジャケット; (of book) カバー, (of record) ジャケット

jackhammer *n.* 空気ドリル

jackknife *n.* ジャックナイフ

jack-o'-lantern *n.* カボチャちょうちん

jackpot *n.* (prize money) 積立賞金, (in poker) 積立賭け金, (in lottery, casino game) 大当たり, 大成功

hit the jackpot 大当たりを取る, 大もうけをする

jackrabbit *n.* 野ウサギ

Jacuzzi *n.* ジャクジー, 泡ぶろ

jade *n.* (mineral) ひすい, (color) ひすい色

jagged *adj.* ぎざぎざの, (sawlike) のこぎりの歯のような, (of rocks) とがった

a jagged line ぎざぎざの線

jaguar *n.* ジャガー

jail *n.* (police cell) 留置場

v. 留置する [→ IMPRISON]

jam[1] *v.* (into suitcase, closet) 押し込む, 詰め込む, (finger etc. in door) 挟む, (jam A against B) (AをBに) 押し付ける, (**be jammed with**: people) …で混み合う, (of people: jam into a train) (…に) 乗り込む; (of printer) 詰まる

n. (traffic jam) 渋滞, (paper jam) 紙詰まり; (predicament) 窮地, 苦境

I jammed my suitcase full of clothes.
スーツケースいっぱいに服を詰め込んだ。

My coat got jammed in the door.
コートがドアに挟まった。

The train was jammed with commuters.
電車は、通勤する人でとても混み合っていた。

The photocopier is jammed again.
コピー機がまた、紙詰まりを起こした。

We were stuck in a traffic jam for three hours.
渋滞に巻き込まれて、3時間動けなかった。

♦**jam on** *v.* (brakes, gas pedal) ぐいと踏む

jam[2] *n.* (jelly) ジャム

strawberry jam イチゴジャム

jam-packed *adj.* すし詰めの, ぎゅうぎゅう詰めの

janitor *n.* 管理人, 用務員

January *n.* 1月, 一月

Japan *n.* 日本, 日本, (classical name) 大和(の国), ((*in abbr.*)) 日

Japan–U.S. relations 日米関係

Japanese *n.* (person) 日本人, (language) 日本語

adj. (of country, culture) 日本の, 和-, (of person) 日本人の, (of language) 日本語の

Japanese customs 日本の習慣

Japanese literature 日本文学

Japanese food 和食

a Japanese–English dictionary 和英辞典

"What's your nationality?"
"I'm Japanese."
「国籍はどこですか？」

「日本です」

Japanese grammar 日本語の文法

jar[1] *n.* (glass) (広口の) びん, (earthenware) つぼ, (wide-necked, earthenware) かめ

jar[2] *v.* (jar with: not suit) (…と) 合わない

jargon *n.* (technical language) 専門用語, -用語

jarring *adj.* (of sound) 耳障りな

jasmine *n.* (plant) ジャスミン

jasmine tea ジャスミン茶

jasper *n.* 碧玉

jaundice *n.* 黄疸

jaundiced *adj.* (prejudiced) 偏った, 偏見のある

javelin *n.* (spear) やり, (**the javelin**: spear-throwing competition) やり投げ

jaw *n.* あご [→ picture of FACE]

♦**jawbone** *n.* 下あごの骨

jay *n.* (bird) カケス

jazz *n.* ジャズ

jazzy *adj.* (of music) ジャズっぽい; (of clothing: colorful) 派手な

jealous *adj.* しっと深い, しっとする, (of sb's success etc.) ねたんでいる

a jealous husband しっと深い夫

He's jealous of her success.
彼は彼女の成功をねたんでいる。

jealousy *n.* しっと, ジェラシー, 焼きもち, (envy) ねたみ, うらやましい気持ち

jeans *n.* ジーンズ, ジーパン

jeep *n.* ジープ

jeer *v.* (shout at) あざける, (boo) やじる

jelly *n.* (jam) ジャム, (gelatin dessert) ゼリー

jellyfish *n.* クラゲ

jeopardize *v.* 危険にさらす, 危うくする

jeopardize relations
関係を危うくする

jeopardy *n.* 危険, 危機

put in jeopardy 危機にさらす

jerk *v.* (move suddenly and quickly) ぐいと動く, (pull) ぐいと引っ張る

n. (obnoxious person) むかつく奴

jersey *n.* (fabric) ジャージー, メリヤス生地, (sweater) セーター

Jesus (Christ) *n.* イエス・キリスト

interj. (also **jesus**) あっ, ちぇっ

jet[1] *n.* (airplane) ジェット機; (surge) 噴出

a jumbo jet ジャンボジェット機

a jet of water 水の噴出

jet[2] *adj.* (color) 真っ黒な

jet lag *n.* 時差ぼけ

jetty *n.* (for protection against high waves) 突堤, 防波堤, (wharf) 波止場

Jew *n.* ユダヤ人

jewel *n.* (precious stone) 宝石

a jewel of a… 大切な…, 大事な…

jewelry *n.* 宝石, ジュエリー

wear jewelry 宝石を身につける

Jewish *adj.* (of person) ユダヤ人の, (of religion) ユダヤ教の

jibe → GIBE

jiggle *v.* 細かく揺する

jigsaw *n.* (puzzle) ジグソーパズル

jingle *v.* チリンチリン鳴る

n. チリンチリン(鳴る音)

jinx *n.* ジンクス, 不運, 悪運

put a jinx on …に不運をもたらす

be jinxed ついてない

jitters *n.* 神経質, 不安な状態

get the jitters 不安になる

jittery ***adj.*** (nervous) ぴりぴりする, どきどきする, (uneasy) そわそわする

job ***n.*** (occupation) 仕事, 職, 勤め口, 職業, (task, chore) 仕事, (duty) 役目, 役割

What's your job?
お仕事 [ご職業] は何ですか?

It's a good job. I like it.
いい仕事です。気に入っています。

Do you have a job?
仕事をしていますか?

She lost her job.
彼女は職を失った。

He's looking for a job.
彼は勤め口を探している。

It's getting harder for students to find jobs.
学生が就職することが、難しくなってきている。

As a parent, one of your jobs is to bring your children up well.
親としての役目の一つは、子供を立派に育てることだ。

Good job! 上出来だ, よくできた, よくやった

KANJI BRIDGE

職 ON: しょく KUN: — | **EMPLOYMENT, JOB**

craftsman/apprentice	職人
duty/function	職務
job hunting	就職活動
occupation/profession	職業
specialist job	専門職
staff	職員
type of occupation	職種
workplace	職場

jobless ***adj.*** (unemployed) 仕事のない, 失業中の

jockey ***n.*** 騎手, ジョッキー

jocular ***adj.*** (cheerful) 陽気な, (humorous) こっけいな, ひょうきんな

jodhpurs ***n.*** 乗馬ズボン, ジョッパーズ

jog ***v.*** ジョギングする

jogging ***n.*** ジョギング

join ***v.***

1 BECOME A MEMBER OF: (…に) 入る, (club) (…に) 入会する, 加入する, 加わる, (company) (…の) 社員になる, ((*formal*)) (…に) 入社する, (army, navy) (…に) 入隊する

2 ENTER THE COMPANY OF: (join sb) (…と) いっしょになる, ((*polite*)) ごいっしょする

3 CONNECT: つなぐ, (two ends) 合わせる, (one end to the other) 結ぶ, 結び付ける

4 MERGE WITH: (road/river) (…と/に) つながる/合流する [→ MERGE]

1 She decided to join the judo club.
彼女は柔道部に入ることにした。

You should join a fitness club.
フィットネスクラブに入ったほうがいい。

A new player has joined the team.
新しい選手がチームに加わった。

I joined the company at eighteen.
18歳で入社しました。

Have you ever considered joining the Army?
入隊しようかと考えたことはありますか?

2 May I join you?
ごいっしょしてもいいですか?

3 It's actually two houses joined into one.

実は、二つの家がつながって1軒になっている。

Join the edges (of the paper) together.
端と端を合わせてください。

4 This road joins the main road in about two kilometers.
この道路は約2キロ先で、幹線道路とつながっている。

join in *v.* …に参加する

Would you like to join in?
参加しませんか？

join up *v.* (enlist) 入隊する; (**join up with**: enter the company of) …といっしょになる, …に加わる

I'll join up with you later.
あとから加わります/((*informal*)) あとで合流するよ。

joint *n.* (in pipe) 継ぎ目, (of the body) 関節, (in bamboo) 節

adj. (shared) 共通の, 共同の

the shoulder joint 肩の関節

a bamboo joint 竹の節

a joint account 共同預金口座

joint management 共同経営

a joint concert ジョイントコンサート

a joint venture 合弁事業

be out of joint (of body part) (…の) 関節が外れている, (…を) 脱臼している

My elbow is out of joint.
ひじの関節が外れている。

joke *n.* 冗談, ジョーク, (practical joke) いたずら, (witticism) しゃれ

v. (tell a joke) 冗談を言う, (**joke around**) ふざける

He can't take a joke.
あの人は冗談が通じない。

It was only a joke!
ただの冗談だよ。

It's no joke!
冗談じゃないよ!

It's nothing to joke about.
笑い事じゃない。

I'm half-joking.
半分冗談です。

play a joke on …にいたずらをする

joker *n.* (playing card) ジョーカー, ばば

jolly *adj.* (cheerful) 陽気な; (fun) 楽しい

We had a jolly time in Europe.
ヨーロッパでは楽しい時を過ごしました。

jolt *v.* (cause to jerk) 激しく揺する, (of car) ガタンと揺れる

n. (shock) ショック, 衝撃

be jolted from one's sleep
(眠りから)急に起こされる

a jolt of electricity 電気ショック

Jordan *n.* ヨルダン

jostle *v.* (push and shove) 押し合いへし合いする, 押し合う

jot *v.* (also **jot down**) 書き留める, メモする

journal *n.* (magazine) 雑誌, -ジャーナル, (newspaper) -新聞; (diary) 日記

journalism *n.* ジャーナリズム

go into journalism
ジャーナリズムの道に進む

journalist *n.* ジャーナリスト, 記者

journey *n.* 旅, 旅行, (distance to be traveled) 道のり, (course, road) ((*also figurative*)) 旅路

v. 旅をする

a journey around the world 世界一周旅行

go on a journey 旅に出る

a long journey 長い旅 [道のり]

life's journey 人生の旅路

joy *n.* 喜び [→ HAPPY]

We all jumped for joy when we heard the news.
知らせを聞いて、みんな大喜びした。

Jr. *adj.* 息子のほうの, -ジュニア, -二世

The letter is addressed to John Smith Jr.
手紙はジョン・スミス、ジュニアあてです。

jubilee *n.* 記念祭, 祝祭

judge *v.* 評価する, 判断する, (serve as a judge for: contest) (…の) 審査をする

n. (in court) 裁判官, 判事, (of contest) 審査員, (of athletic competition) 審判, ジャッジ

The sanitary conditions are not very good when judged by Western standards.
欧米の基準で評価すると、衛生状態はあまりよくない。

You shouldn't judge people by their appearance.
外見で人を判断してはいけない。

It's hard to judge the distance.
距離を判断するのは難しい。

The contest will be judged by the mayor.
このコンテストは市長が審査します。

The judge found her innocent.
裁判官は彼女に無罪の判決を下した。

judgment *n.* (court ruling) 判決, (decision) 判定, 判断, (ability to judge) 判断力, (estimation) 意見, 見解, 考え

have good judgment 判断力 [分別] がある

a snap judgment 速断

In my judgment, it's a good (artistic) work.
私の考えでは、いい作品だと思います。

pass judgment on (criticize) 批判する

judicial *adj.* 裁判の, 司法の

the judicial branch of government 司法機関

judiciary *n.* (**the judiciary**) (= branch of government) 司法機関, (= the courts) 裁判官

the power/right of the judiciary 司法権

judo *n.* 柔道

♦**judoka** *n.* 柔道家

jug *n.* 水差し

juggle *v.* ジャグリングをする

♦**juggler** *n.* ジャグラー

juggling *n.* ジャグリング

juice *n.* (from fruits/vegetables) -ジュース, (from fruits) 果汁, (from meat) -汁

apple [orange, vegetable] juice
リンゴ [オレンジ, 野菜] ジュース

freshly squeezed juice 新鮮な絞り汁

♦**juicer** *n.* ジューサー

juicy *adj.* ジューシーな, (of fruit) 水分の多い, 汁の多い; (of gossip) 興味をそそる

jujitsu *n.* 柔術

jukebox *n.* ジュークボックス

July *n.* 7月, 七月

jumble *v.* (mix together) ごちゃ混ぜにする, ごちゃごちゃにする

n. ごちゃ混ぜ, 寄せ集め

jumbo *adj.* 特大の

n. (jumbo jet) ジャンボジェット機

jump

1 *v.* MOVE UPWARD/DOWNWARD: (**jump up onto/from**) …に/…から跳び上がる, (jump up and down) 跳びはねる, (**jump over**) 飛び越える, (**jump out of**) …から飛び出す, (**jump** down **from**) …から飛び降りる, (**jump into**: jump aboard) …に飛び乗る

2 *v.* INCREASE: 急増する, 激増する, 急上昇する

3 *v.* BE SURPRISED: びっくりする, (jump at: sound etc.) (…に)どきっ/びくっとする

4 *n.* UPWARD MOVEMENT: 跳び上がること, ジャンプ, (in sport) 跳躍

5 *n.* SUDDEN INCREASE: 急上昇, 急騰

1 The cat jumped onto the table.
猫はテーブルの上に跳び乗った。

The sound of the phone made me jump from my seat.
電話の音に、椅子から跳び上がった。

Stop jumping on the bed!
ベッドの上で跳びはねるのはやめなさい!

I bet you can't jump over that fence.
あのさくを飛び越えるなんて、できっこないよ。

They say he jumped from the tenth floor.
その人は10階から飛び降りたらしい。

I jumped into a taxi.
タクシーに飛び乗った。

2 The number of foreigners residing in Japan has jumped dramatically.
日本に住んでいる外国人の数は激増した。

3 God, you made me jump!
ああ、驚いた/もう、びっくりさせないでよ!

4 a long jump 長いジャンプ

the high [long] jump
走り高 [幅] 跳び

5 The jump in land prices was not unexpected.
地価の急騰は、予想外のことではありませんでした。

jump at the chance/opportunity チャンスに飛びつく

jumper *n.* (dress) ジャンパースカート, (sweater) セーター

jump rope *n.* 縄跳びの縄

jumpy *adj.* (nervous) 神経質な, びくびくする

junction *n.* (intersection) 交差点

June *n.* 6月, 六月

jungle *n.* ジャングル, 密林

the law of the jungle ジャングルのおきて

junior

1 *adj.* LOW-RANKING: 地位が下の, 下級の

2 *n.* YOUNGER PERSON: 年少者, (one's junior) 年下, (at company, school) 後輩

3 *n.* THIRD-YEAR STUDENT: 3年生, (11th grader in Japan's 3-year high school system) 高校2年生

4 → JR.

1 a junior appointment 下級職

a junior officer (in the army) 下級将校

a junior accountant 会計士補

2 He's three years my junior.
彼は3歳年下だ。

3 a junior in college 大学3年生

♦ **junior college** *n.* 短期大学

junior high (school) *n.* 中学校

juniper *n.* ネズ, 杜松

junk *n.* くず, がらくた

This junk! Why don't you throw it away?
こんながらくた！ どうして捨てないの？

♦**junk bond** *n.* ジャンクボンド, リスクの高い債券

junk food *n.* ジャンクフード

junk mail *n.* ダイレクトメール

junta *n.* (military regime) 軍事政府

Jupiter *n.* 木星

jurisdiction *n.* (of court) 裁判権, 司法権

jurisprudence *n.* (science of law) 法学

jurist *n.* (law expert) 法律専門家

juror *n.* 陪審員

jury *n.* 陪審

just

1 *adv.* EXACTLY: ちょうど, 全く, まさに, (of time) ちょうど, (of fitting) ぴったり

2 *adv.* RECENTLY: たった今, 今さっき, ついさっき, ちょうど…ばかり [→ NOW]

3 *adv.* MERELY: ただの, ほんの(…にすぎない), (**just doing**) ただ…しているだけ

4 *adv.* EMPHASIZING SMALLNESS OF AMOUNT: ほんの, わずか, たった

5 *adv.* EMPHASIZING QUESTION: 一体

6 *adj.* FAIR: 公正な, 公平な, 正当な

1 just right ちょうどいい

It's just past 7 o'clock.
ちょうど7時を過ぎたばかりだ。

It's just as you said.
全く、あなたの言ったとおりです。

She spoke just as I was about to.
話そうとしたら、彼女がしゃべり出した。

These pants fit just right.
このズボンはぴったりだ。

2 I just saw a shooting star!
たった今、流れ星を見たよ！

He's just gotten his driver's license.
彼は運転免許を取ったばかりだ。

3 It's just a story.
ただの作り話だ。

If only I could meet her…just once.
一度だけでも、彼女に会えたらなあ。

"What are you doing?"
"Oh, I'm just making some tea."
「何をしているの？」
「紅茶を入れているだけよ」

4 These are just a few of his paintings.
これらは、その人の絵のほんの一部にすぎません。

The post office is just twenty meters down the road.
郵便局はほんの20メートルほど先です。

5 Just what do you mean?
一体何が言いたいんですか？

6 It was a just verdict.
公正な判決だった。

a just cause 正当な理由 [大義]

it's just as well that (…して)よかった

It's just as well that you came.
来てくれてよかった。

It's just as well that it's raining.
雨が降っていて(かえって)よかった。

just about to do (ちょうど)…しようとする

I was just about to leave when the phone rang.
出かけようとしていたら、電話が鳴った。

I was just about to send it when I noticed I had misspelled her name.
ちょうど送信しようとした時、彼女の名前のつづりを間違えていたことに気づいた。

just a minute/moment ちょっと待って

Wait just a minute.
ちょっと待ってください。

Just one moment, please.
((*polite*)) 少々お待ちください。

just like... 全く...のよう, まるで...のよう

It's just like it used to be.
昔と全く同じようだ。

He's just like someone fresh out of college.
あの人はまるで、大学を卒業したばかりのようだ。

just like that (in an instant) あっという間に

She disappeared—just like that.
彼女は姿を消したんだ——あっという間にね。

just now (now) 今は, (a moment ago) たった今, ついさっき [→ NOW]

Don't ask any questions just now.
今は何も聞かないでください。

He was here just now.
ついさっきまで彼はここにいました。

only just → ONLY

justice ***n.*** (concept of) 正義, 公正, (correctness, fairness) 正しさ, 正当性, (system of) 司法; (judge) 裁判官, 判事

Where's the justice in that?
それのどこに正義があるの？

justifiable ***adj.*** 正当と認められる, もっともな

a justifiable defense 正当防衛

justification ***n.*** (good reason) 正当な理由

in justification of 正当化して, 弁護して

justified ***adj.*** 正しい, 公正な

The decision was justified.
その決定は正しかった。

justify ***v.*** 正当化する

You can't justify the use of violence.
暴力をふるうことは正当化できない。

He's always trying to justify his behavior.
あの人はいつも、自分の行いを正当化しようとする。

jut ***v.*** (**jut out**) 出っ張る, 突き出る

jute ***n.*** 黄麻, ジュート

juvenile ***n.*** (young person) 青少年, 少年少女, (teenage boy) 少年

adj. (of children) 児童の, (for children) 子供向きの; (of behavior: childish) 子供じみた, 子供っぽい

books for juveniles 児童書
juvenile behavior 子供じみた行動

♦**juvenile delinquent** ***n.*** (boy) 非行少年, (girl) 非行少女

juxtapose ***v.*** 並列する, 並べて置く

K, k

kabuki *n.* 歌舞伎

kale *n.* ケール, チリメンキャベツ

kaleidoscope *n.* 万華鏡

kangaroo *n.* カンガルー

kanji *n.* 漢字

♦**kanji for general use** *n.* 常用漢字

kaolin *n.* (clay) 陶土

karaoke *n.* カラオケ

sing with karaoke カラオケで歌う

karat *n.* -金

an 18-karat gold necklace
１８金のネックレス

karate *n.* 空手

karma *n.* (religious concept) 業, カルマ, (fate) 運命, 宿命

katydid *n.* キリギリス

kayak *n.* カヤック

kazoo *n.* カズー

keel *n.* (of ship) キール, 竜骨

♦**keel over** *v.* (of person: collapse) 倒れる, (=die) 死ぬ; (of boat) 転覆する

keen *adj.*

1 SHARP: (of senses, intellect) 鋭い, (of blade) 鋭い, よく切れる [→ SHARP 1]

2 INTENSE: (of competition) 激しい, (of interest, feeling) 強い

3 VERY INTERESTED/ENTHUSIASTIC: (**be keen on**) (...が)好きだ, (**be keen on doing/to do**) ...したい [→ WANT 1]

1 a keen sense of smell 鋭い嗅覚

Saito has keen eyes for spotting typos.
斉藤さんは誤植を見つける鋭い目をもっている。

the keen blade of a sword
刀の鋭い刃

2 a keen competition 激しい競争

He has a keen interest in sports.
あの人はスポーツに強い関心がある。

She has a keen sense of justice.
彼女は強い正義感をもっている。

3 She's not too keen on rap music.
彼女はラップがあまり好きじゃない。

I'm not too keen on going.
あまり行きたくない。

♦**keenly** *adv.* (intensely) 激しく, 強く; (eagerly) 熱心に

K

keep *v.*

1 CAUSE TO REMAIN IN A CONDITION: ずっと...しておく, ...ままにしておく

2 DETAIN: 引き止める

3 RETAIN: 持っておく, 取っておく, 置いておく, ((*informal*)) キープする

4 CONTINUE: (**keep doing**) ...し続ける, ずっと...している, ...しっぱなしだ

5 MAINTAIN: (family) 支える, 養う; (diary, accounts) つける, (records) 取る

6 STORE: 置いている, しまう, ((*formal*)) 保管する, 貯蔵する

7 PROMISE/SECRET: 守る

8 OWN: (pet) 飼う, (...の)世話をする

9 OF FOOD: もつ

1 Keep your hands up.
両手は挙げたままで。

Please keep still.
動かないでください。

The noise kept me awake all night.
騒音で一晩中眠れなかった。

Sorry to have kept you waiting.
お待たせして、すみません。

I was kept standing from morning till night.
朝から晩まで立ちっぱなしだった。

Please keep this document safe.
この書類を保管しておいてください。

2 No one is keeping you from going.
誰もあなたを引き止めていないよ。

The boy was kept after school.
その子は放課後、引き止められた。

keep someone in custody
拘留する

3 I'll keep them for you.
取っておいてあげますよ。

I always keep a spare umbrella.
いつも予備の傘を置いている。

She never keeps a job for very long.
彼女は仕事が長続きしたためしがない。

4 I keep thinking about it.
ずっと(そのことを)考えているんだ。

The phone kept ringing.
電話が鳴りっぱなしだった。

I keep making the same mistake.
同じ間違いを何度もやってしまう。

5 How does he expect to keep a family on such earnings?
彼は、そんな収入でどうやって家族を養えると思っているんだろう?

I keep a diary.
日記をつけています。

Are you keeping notes?
メモを取っていますか?

6 Where do you keep the spoons?
スプーンはいつもどこにしまっているの?

The wine is kept in the cellar.
ワインは地下室に貯蔵されている。

7 He kept his promise.
あの人は約束を守った。

Can you keep a secret?
秘密を守れる?

I can't keep the appointment.
約束の時間に行けなくなった。

8 Keeping a hamster is easy.
ハムスターを飼うのは簡単だよ。

9 This milk won't keep till tomorrow.
この牛乳は明日までもたない。

in keeping with (typical of) ...らしい; (in harmony with) ...と調和して

It was not in keeping with his character.
それはあの人らしくないね。

The new building was in keeping with its surroundings.
新しいビルは、周囲と調和していた。

keep an eye on → EYE

keep one's head → HEAD

keep trying/at it がんばる

Keep trying! You're almost there!
がんばれ! もう少しだ!

keep watch 見張る, 張り込む

The police kept a close watch on the house.
警察は、その家を厳重に見張っていた。

keep away *v.* (**keep away from**) (=not approach) 近づかない, 近寄らない, (=avoid) 避ける, (keep A away from B) (AをBから) 遠ざける

You'd better keep away from that place.
あの場所には近づかないほうがいいよ。

Keep away from the fire.

火に近寄らないこと。

I try to keep as far away from him as I can.
私はできるだけ彼を避けるようにしている。

Keep the chocolate away from the dog.
チョコレートを犬から遠ざけておいてね。

keep back *v.* (keep A back from B) (AをBに) 近寄らせない, (information) 隠しておく, (tears, emotion) 抑える

The guards kept the fans back from the stage.
警備員が、ファンをステージに近寄らせないようにしていた。

The company was clearly keeping back information.
会社側は、明らかに情報を隠していた。

keep back tears 涙を抑える

keep off *v.* (premises) (…に) 立ち入らない, (**keep one's hands off**) (…に) 触らない; (sweets, alcohol) 控える, 慎む

(*sign*) Keep Off the Grass
芝生立入禁止

Keep your hands off me!
私に触らないで!

You'd better keep off sweets.
甘いものは控えたほうがいいよ。

The doctor told me to keep off alcohol.
医者から酒を控えるよう言われた。

keep on *v.*

1 CONTINUE: (**keep on doing**) …し続ける, ずっと…している [→ KEEP 4]

2 RETAIN IN EMPLOYMENT: 雇い続ける, 雇っておく

3 CONTINUE TO WEAR: (coat) 着たままでいる, (shoes) はいたままでいる

1 She kept on sniffling.
彼女はずっと鼻をすすっていた。

He keeps on staring at me.
あの人がじっと私を見ている。

It kept on snowing.
雪は降り続いた。

2 He was kept on for another month.
彼はさらに1ヵ月雇われることになった。

3 May we keep our shoes on?
靴をはいたままでいいですか?

keep out *v.* (prevent from entering) 入らないようにする

Please keep the journalists out of the building for another ten minutes.
あと10分、記者たちがこの建物の中に入らないようにしてください。

I shut the window to keep out the mosquitoes.
蚊が入らないように、窓を閉めた。

keep out of sb's way/business …と/にかかわらない

It'd be best if you kept out of his way.
彼とはかかわらないのが一番だ。

Keep out of my affairs.
余計なお世話だ。(lit.,"[That's] excessive caring.")

keep up *v.* (maintain) 保つ; (progress at the same rate) (…に) ついて行く

keep up appearances 体面を保つ

Keep up the good work!
その調子でがんばれ!

He was so fast I couldn't keep up with him.
彼はとても速くて、ついて行けなかった。

There's so much to do, it's hard to keep up!
することが多すぎて、このペースでやっていけない!

keeper *n.* (of things) 所有者, (of animals) 飼い主

keepsake *n.* (inherited memento) 形見, (souvenir) 記念の品

kelp *n.* (in ocean) 海藻, (for eating) 昆布

kendo *n.* 剣道

kennel *n.* 犬小屋

kernel *n.* (of nut) 仁, (of grain) 穀粒,

kerosene *n.* 灯油

a kerosene heater 石油ストーブ

ketchup *n.* ケチャップ

kettle *n.* (teakettle) やかん, ケトル

kettledrum *n.* ティンパニ

key *n.* (to lock/door) かぎ, (on piano, keyboard) キー, (on map) 記号表, (in music) 調; (secret) 秘訣, かぎ

adj. (crucial) 重要な

I'll get these keys cut.

このかぎの合いかぎを作って来るよ。

in the key of C major ハ長調で

a key to success

成功の秘訣 [かぎ]

a key factor 重要な要因

♦ **key in** *v.* (data) 入力する

key money *n.* (obligatory one-time payment made to landlord in Japan) 礼金 [→ DEPOSIT]

keyboard *n.* キーボード

play a keyboard キーボードを演奏する

keyhole *n.* かぎ穴

khaki *n.* (color) カーキ色, (fabric) カーキ色の布

kick *v.* ける, (forcefully) けっ飛ばす, (in sport: kick a ball) キックする

n. キック, けり; (**kicks**: thrill) スリル

I kicked the ball.

ボールをけった。

Stop kicking my chair, will you.

僕の椅子をけるのはやめてくれないか?

a goal kick ゴールキック

for kicks スリルを楽しむために, 面白半分で

I just did it for kicks.

面白半分でやっただけだ。

kickoff *n.* キックオフ

kid *n.* (child) 子供, (young goat) 子ヤギ

v. (tease) からかう, 冗談を言う; (**kid around**) ふざける

I'm only kidding.

冗談ですよ。

I'm not kidding!

うそじゃないよ/本当だよ!

no kidding 冗談でしょう, 本当?

you're kidding 冗談でしょう, うそ!, まさか

kidnap *v.* 誘拐する

♦ **kidnapper** *n.* 誘拐犯

kidney *n.* 腎臓

kidney bean *n.* インゲン豆

kill *v.* 殺す, 死亡させる, (idea, project) つぶす, だめにする, (crops) 枯らす

Who killed him?

誰がその人を殺したの?

She was killed in a car accident.

彼女は交通事故で亡くなった。

The company decided to kill the project.

会社はその企画をつぶすことにした。

The crops were killed by the drought.

干ばつで作物が枯れてしまった。

kill oneself 自殺する

kill time 時間をつぶす

killer *n.* 殺人犯, (professional) 殺し屋

killer whale *n.* シャチ

kiln *n.* 窯

kilo *n.* キロ

kilobyte *n.* キロバイト

kilocalorie *n.* キロカロリー

kilogram *n.* キログラム, キロ

kilohertz *n.* キロヘルツ

kilometer *n.* キロメートル, キロ

several kilometers 数キロ

kilovolt *n.* キロボルト

kilowatt *n.* キロワット

kilt *n.* キルト

kimono *n.* 着物 [→ picture of CLOTHING]

kind[1] *adj.* (gentle) 親切な, 優しい

She's a kind person.
彼女は親切な人だ。

He's been kind to me.
彼は私に優しくしてくれる。

It was kind of you to make that donation (to our organization).
寄付をしていただき、どうもありがとうございました。

be kind enough to do (for oneself) (親切にも) ...してくれる

He was kind enough to help me carry my luggage.
彼は親切にも荷物を運ぶのを手伝ってくれた。

Would you be kind enough not to smoke here, please?
すみませんが、ここでの喫煙はご遠慮いただけないでしょうか？

kind[2] *n.* (type) 種類

It's a kind of vegetable, isn't it?
野菜の一種ですよね。

What kind of motorcycle is that?
それはどんなバイクですか?

all kinds of いろいろな, さまざまな

There are all kinds of people in this world.
世の中には、いろいろな人がいる。

kind of (a little) 多少, ちょっと

kindergarten *n.* 幼稚園

kindhearted *adj.* 親切な, 心の優しい

kindly *adv.* 親切に

kindness *n.* 親切, 優しさ

kindred *n.* (relatives) 親族

adj. (of the same type) 同族の, 同種の

kindred spirits 気の合う者同士

king *n.* (monarch) 王, 国王, ((*polite*)) 王様; (playing card) キング

kingdom *n.* 王国; (taxonomic category) 界

kingfisher *n.* カワセミ

kiosk *n.* 売店, キオスク

kipper *n.* 薫製のニシン

kiss *n., v.* (...に) キス(する), 口づけ(する)

a tender kiss 優しいキス

They kissed each other.
二人はキスをした。

Did you kiss him?
彼にキスしたの？

kit *n.* (set) 一式, セット, (of tools) 道具一式, (of gear) 用具一式, (assembly kit) キット

a first-aid kit
救急箱 [→ picture of FIRST-AID KIT]

a carpenter's kit
大工道具一そろい [→ picture of TOOL]

a camping kit キャンプ用具一式

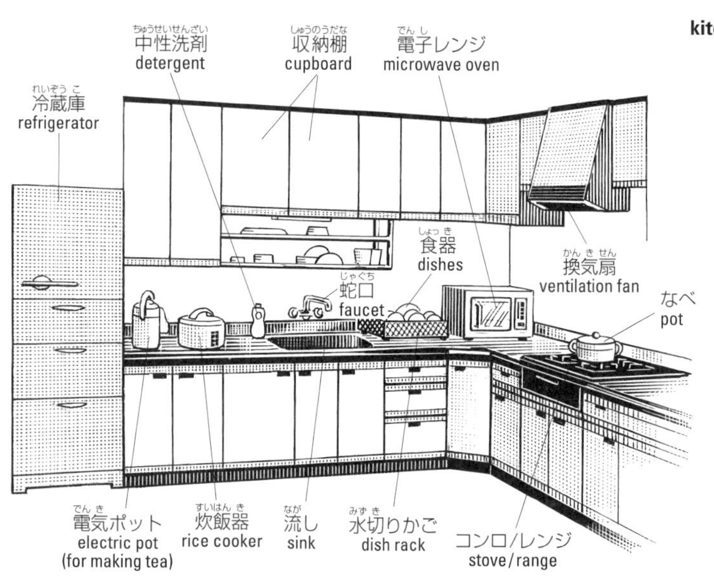

kitchen *n.* キッチン, 台所(だいどころ), (of restaurant) 調理場(ちょうりば) [→ picture above]

♦**kitchenette** *n.* 簡易台所(かんいだいどころ)

kite *n.* 凧(たこ)

fly a kite 凧揚(たこあ)げをする

kitten *n.* 子猫(こねこ)

kiwi *n.* (bird) キーウィ, (fruit) キーウィ

kleptomania *n.* 盗癖(とうへき)

♦**kleptomaniac** *n.* 盗癖(とうへき)のある人(ひと)

knack *n.* こつ, 技巧(ぎこう)

There's a knack to opening this door.
このドアをあけるには、こつが要(い)る。

knapsack *n.* リュック, ナップザック

knee *n.* ひざ [→ picture of BODY]

bend one's knees ひざを曲(ま)げる

The girl sat on her grandfather's knee.
女(おんな)の子(こ)はおじいさんのひざの上(うえ)に座(すわ)った。

kneecap *n.* ひざの(お)皿(さら), 膝蓋骨(しつがいこつ)

kneel *v.* ひざまずく

knife *n.* ナイフ, (large kitchen knife) 包丁(ほうちょう) [→ picture of COOKING UTENSILS], (jackknife) ジャックナイフ, (dagger) 短刀(たんとう), (scalpel) メス

v. ナイフで刺(さ)す

a knife and fork ナイフとフォーク

a sharp [dull] knife
鋭(するど)い [あまり切(き)れない] ナイフ

They pulled a knife on me.
私(わたし)はナイフを突(つ)きつけられた。

I cut the pumpkin with a large knife.
大(おお)きな包丁(ほうちょう)でカボチャを切(き)った。

He was knifed in the back.
その人(ひと)は背中(せなか)をナイフで刺(さ)された。

knight *n.* 騎士(きし)

knit *v.* 編(あ)む, (do knitting) 編(あ)み物(もの)をする

His wife knitted that sweater for him.

奥さんが彼のためにそのセーターを編んだ。

♦**knitted** ***adj.*** ニットの

knitting ***n.*** 編み物

♦**knitting needle** ***n.*** 編み棒, 編み針

knob ***n.*** (on door) 取っ手, ノブ, (on stereo) つまみ

turn the knob ノブ [つまみ] を回す

---

knock ***v.*** (rap: on door) ノックする, (strike hard) 打つ, (bump) ぶつける
n. (sound) ノックする音; (blow) 一撃

There's someone knocking on the door.
誰かがドアをノックしている。

I'll saw up the wood; you knock in the nails.
((*masculine*)) 僕が材木をのこぎりで切るから、君は釘を打ってくれ。

I knocked my head on the lampshade as I got up.
立ち上がった時、電灯の笠に頭をぶつけてしまった。

I heard a knock. ノックの音が聞こえた。

knock down ***v.*** (knock over) 倒す, (hit and cause to fall) 殴り倒す, (run over with a car) はねる; (demolish: building) 解体する; (lower: price) 下げる

He was knocked down by the force of the blow.
彼は殴られて倒れた。

I hear she was knocked down by a bus.
彼女はバスにはねられたらしい。

The city council has decided to knock down that building.
市議会はその建物を解体することを決めた。

They knocked the price down for us.
値引き [値下げ] してくれた。

knock out ***v.*** (with drug) 眠らせる, (with punch) 気絶させる, 失神させる, (in boxing) ＫＯする; (make inoperable) 使えなくする

The anesthetic knocked the patient out in a matter of minutes.
麻酔が効いて、患者はものの数分で眠り込んだ。

He was knocked out after only forty-five seconds in the ring.
彼はリングに上がって、たった４５秒でＫＯされた。

The storm knocked out the electricity.
嵐で停電した。

knock over ***v.*** ひっくり返す, (spill) こぼす [→ KNOCK DOWN]

Careful you don't knock anything over.
ひっくり返さないよう気をつけて。

---

knocker ***n.*** (on door) ドアノッカー

knockout ***n.*** (in boxing) ＫＯ

knot ***n.*** (in rope) 結び目; (unit of speed) ノット
v. (tie a knot in) 結ぶ

Can you untie this knot?
この結び目をほどけますか?

know ***v.***

1 HAVE KNOWLEDGE OF: 知っている, (**get to know**) 知る

2 UNDERSTAND/RECOGNIZE: わかる

3 EXPERIENCE: 味わう, (...の) 経験がある

1 Do you know where the place is?
場所は知っていますか?

K

I wouldn't have gone if I'd known he was going to be there.
あの人がそこにいるって知っていたら、行かなかったのに。

Does he know how to do it?
彼は、やり方を知って[わかって]いますか?

I knew it at one time, but I can't remember it now.
以前は知っていましたが、今は思い出せません。

Do they know each other?
あの人たちは、知り合いなのですか?

I'd like to get to know him more.
あの人のことをもっと知りたいんです。

He doesn't know a lot about electronics.
あの人は電気のことはよく知らない[電気関係に弱い]。

2 How was I to know it was a formal gathering?
正式の集まりだったなんて、私にわかるはずがないでしょう?

I'd know her anywhere.
彼女なら、どこで見かけてもわかる。

3 She's known suffering.
彼女は苦しみを味わったことがある。

as far as I know 私の知っている限り(では), 私の知る限り

As far as I know, that is correct.
私の知っている限りでは、それは正しい。

as you know ご存じのように

As you know, Tom is ill.
ご存じのように、トムは病気です。

before one knew it いつの間にか, あっという間に

It was dark before we knew it.
いつの間にか、暗くなっていた。

be known as …という名で知られている, …と呼ばれている

This flower is known as a Christmas rose.
この花はクリスマスローズという名で知られています。

be known for …で有名だ

He's known for his clumsiness.
あの人は不器用で有名だ。

be known to do …することがある

He's been known to drink a full bottle of scotch in one evening.
あの人は一晩でスコッチを1本空けてしまうことがある。

for all one knows もしかすると

For all I know, the man could be dead.
もしかすると、あの男は死んでいるかもしれない。

I know! わかった!, そうだ!

I know! Let's go see a movie!
そうだ、映画を見に行こう!

know best 一番知っている, 誰よりもわかっている

Suzuki always thinks he knows best.
鈴木さんはいつも、自分が一番わかっていると思い込んでいる。

know better (than to do) (…しないくらいの)分別がある

She wouldn't do such a thing. She knows better.
あの人はそんなことはしない。もっと分別があるよ。

You should know better than to do that.
そんなことをしないくらいの分別をもちなさい。

know by heart 暗記している, 覚えている

Akira knows his times tables by heart.
明君は九九を暗記している。

let one know (...に) 知らせる, 教える

Please let me know as soon as you hear something.
何か聞いたら、すぐ私に教えてください。

you know (pausing in mid-sentence) ええっと, あのう..., ちょっと, (trying to draw sb's attention to sth they know) ほら, あの, (used as a tag question) ...ね, ...よ, ...でしょ

Oh, you know, it was just an idea.
ああ、ちょっと思いついただけなんだ。

I was wondering if, you know, you'd like to go out for dinner sometime...
近いうちに、よかったらちょっと夕食でもいっしょに行かないかと思って...

know-how *n.* ノウハウ

have the know-how
ノウハウをもっている

knowing *adj.* (of look) 意味ありげな

know-it-all *n.* 知ったかぶりをする人

knowledge *n.* 知識, (understanding) 理解, (cognizance) 認識

common knowledge 常識

a knowledge of history 歴史の知識

to the best of one's knowledge (...の) 知る限り(では)

knowledgeable *adj.* 物知りの, 知識のある, (be knowledgeable about) よく知っている, (...に) 詳しい

be knowledgeable about grammar
文法に詳しい

known *adj.* 知られている, (famous, notorious) 有名な

a widely known story
広く知られている話

He's a known liar.
あの人はうそつきで有名だ。

knuckle *n.* 指の関節

koala *n.* コアラ

Koran *n.* コーラン

Korea *n.* 朝鮮, (South Korea) 韓国, (*(in abbr.)*) 韓, (North Korea) 北朝鮮

Korean *n.* (person) 朝鮮人, (South Korean person) 韓国人, (language) 朝鮮語, 韓国語, (script) ハングル

adj. (of culture) 朝鮮の, (of South Korea) 韓国の, (of person, South or North) 朝鮮人の, (of South Korean person) 韓国人の, (of language) 朝鮮語の, 韓国語の

kowtow *v.* (kowtow to) (...に) ぺこぺこする

kudos *n.* (fame) 名声, (honor) 栄誉

kumquat *n.* キンカン

Kuwait *n.* クウェート

L, l

lab → LABORATORY

label *n.* 札, ラベル, レッテル, (for parcels) 荷札; (record label) レーベル
v. (stick a label on) (…に) ラベルを貼る, (parcel) (…に) 荷札を付ける; (person: brand) (…に) レッテルを貼る
put on [take off] a label
ラベルを貼る [はがす]
The boy is labeled as a troublemaker.
その子はトラブルメーカーのレッテルを貼られている。

labor *n.* (hard work) 労働, (workers) 労働者; (stage of pregnancy) 陣痛
v. 働く, 仕事をする
physical/manual labor 肉体労働
labor and management 労使
go into labor 陣痛が始まる

♦**laborer** *n.* 労働者
labor of love *n.* 好きでする仕事
labor union *n.* 労働組合

laboratory *n.* (for scientific experimentation) 実験室, (for research in general) 研究所, (at university) 研究室
a language laboratory ＬＬ教室

Labor Day *n.* 労働者の日

laborious *adj.* 骨の折れる, 面倒な

labour → LABOR

♦**Labour Party** *n.* 労働党

lace *n.* (fabric) レース; (cord) ひも, (shoelace) 靴ひも
v. (shoes) (…の) ひもを結ぶ

lack *n.* 不足, 欠乏, 欠如
v. (be without enough of) (…が) 欠けている, 足りない, 不足している, (be totally without) (…が) ない
The school is unable to provide better facilities for lack of funds.
学校は資金不足のため、設備を充実させることができない。
They lack nothing.
あの人たちに足りないものなんて、一つもない。
The man lacks common sense.
あの人は常識がない。

KANJI BRIDGE

不足 ふそく/-ぶそく | LACK

lack of ability	能力不足
lack of exercise	運動不足
lack of nutrition	栄養不足
lack of sleep	睡眠不足, 寝不足
lack of sunshine	日照不足
lack of understanding	認識不足
shortage of goods	品不足
shortage of water	水不足

lacking *adj.* (be lacking in) (…が) 欠けている, 足りない

lacquer *n.* (varnish) ラッカー, (Japanese lacquer) 漆
v. (apply lacquer to) (…に) ラッカーを塗る, 漆を塗る

lacquerware *n.* 漆塗りの器, 漆器

lacrosse *n.* ラクロス

lad *n.* (boy) 少年, (young man) 若者
When I was a lad, I used to fish here.
若いころ、ここでよく釣りをした。

ladder *n.* (for climbing) はしご

climb up [down] a ladder
はしごを<u>登る</u> [下りる]

climb the corporate ladder 出世する

laden *adj.* (laden with) (=full of) (…で) いっぱいの, (=carrying a heavy load) (…を) いっぱい積んでいる

ladies' room *n.* お手洗い, トイレ

ladle *n.* (お)玉, 玉じゃくし, (in bathroom) ひしゃく [→ picture of COOKING UTENSILS, BATHROOM]

lady *n.* (woman) 女性, 女の人, 婦人, ((*polite*)) 女の方, ((*written*)) 淑女, (young lady) お嬢さん, (noble lady) 貴婦人, (**Lady**: form of address used in the U.K.) -夫人

Who's that lady over there?
向こうの、あの女の人は誰ですか？

Lady McDonald マクドナルド夫人

Ladies and gentlemen… 皆様

ladybug *n.* テントウムシ

lag *v.* (lag behind) 遅れる
n. (time lag) ずれ, 時間の遅れ

a lag of ten days 10日(の)遅れ

lager *n.* ラガー(ビール)

laggard *n.* (slow person) のろま, ぐず

lagoon *n.* 潟, 礁湖

laid-back *adj.* のんきな, 気楽な

lair *n.* (animal's) ねぐら, (person's) 隠れ家

laissez-faire *n.* 自由放任主義

laity *n.* 俗人

lake *n.* 湖, -湖

We went for a walk by the lake.
湖のほとりを散歩した。

Lake Biwa 琵琶湖

the Great Lakes 五大湖

lama *n.* ラマ僧

the Dalai Lama ダライ・ラマ

Lamaism *n.* ラマ教

lamb *n.* 子羊, (meat) ラム肉

lame *adj.* (of excuse) 下手な, まずい, (boring) つまらない, くだらない

lament *v.* 嘆く, 悲しむ, (sb's death) 悼む
n. 悲しみ, 悲嘆

lamentable *adj.* (deplorable) 嘆かわしい, (sad) 悲しむべき

laminated *adj.* ラミネート-, (of wood) 薄板を重ねた

laminated wood 合板

lamp *n.* 明かり, (electric lamp) 電灯, (oil lamp) ランプ, (desk lamp) 電気スタンド [→ LIGHT[1] 2]

turn on [off] a lamp
明かりを<u>つける</u> [消す]

an oil lamp 石油ランプ

We need a bedside lamp.
枕元に電気スタンドが必要だ。

lampoon *v.* 風刺する
n. 風刺文

lamppost *n.* 街灯の柱

lamprey *n.* ヤツメウナギ, 八目鰻

lampshade *n.* 電灯の笠

lance *n.* (weapon) やり, (for catching fish) もり [→ LANCET]

lance corporal *n.* (in U.S. Marine Corps) 兵長

lancet *n.* (surgical knife) ランセット

land

1 *n.* CRUST OF EARTH ABOVE SEA: 陸, 陸地

2 *n.* SOIL/PROPERTY/TERRITORY/REGION: 土地

3 *n.* NATION: 国, 国土

4 *v.* REACH GROUND: (after falling) 着地する,

(of airplane) 着陸する, (of boat) 着岸する

1 Are you traveling by land?
陸路で行くんですか？
It took weeks to reach land.
陸にたどり着くのに何週間もかかった。

2 fertile land 肥沃な土地
cultivate land 土地を耕す
This land will be used for residences.
この土地は宅地になります。
How much land does he own?
あの人はどのくらい土地を持っているんですか？
public [private] land 公有 [私有] 地

3 a land of everlasting summer 常夏の国
"land of the free, home of the brave"
「自由の地、勇者の国」

4 Cats always land on their feet.
猫はどんなときでも、足から着地する。
The plane landed safely.
飛行機は無事に着陸した。

landfill *n.* (site) ゴミ埋め立て地

landing *n.* (platform on staircase) 踊り場; (of airplane) 着陸, (of boat) 上陸
a crash landing 不時着

landlady *n.* (of apartment etc.) 大家(さん)

landlord *n.* (of apartment etc.) 大家(さん)

landmark *n.* (geographical feature) 目印, (historic building) 歴史的な建物, ランドマーク
adj. (significant) 画期的な
a landmark event 画期的な出来事

land mine *n.* 地雷

landowner *n.* 地主

landscape *n.* 景色, 風景, (painting) 風景画

landscape gardening *n.* 造園, 庭造り

♦**landscape gardener** *n.* 造園家, 庭師

landslide *n.* (falling of rocks/earth) 山崩れ, がけ崩れ, 地滑り; (overwhelming victory) 圧倒的な勝利, 圧勝

lane *n.* (narrow passage) 小道, 路地, (country lane) 田舎道, (driving space on road) 車線, (bowling lane) レーン

language *n.* 言語, -語, 言葉, (jargon) 専門用語, (wording) 言葉づかい, 言い方
the English language 英語
learn [master] the Japanese language
日本語を習う [習得する]
the spoken [written] language
話し [書き] 言葉
one's native language 母国語
a foreign language 外国語
colloquial language 口語
formal language 堅苦しい言葉
filthy language 汚い言葉
the language of politics 政治用語
watch one's language
言葉づかいに気をつける

languish *v.* (lose vitality) 元気がなくなる, 弱る, (of plants) しおれる, (suffer) 苦しむ, (of legislation) 棚上げされる

lanky *adj.* ひょろっとした

lantern *n.* (hand-held lantern) 手さげランプ, カンテラ, (paper lantern) ちょうちん
a stone lantern 石灯ろう

lap[1] *n.* (part of the body) ひざ
If she could sit on your lap, it would create more room.
その子をひざにのせてもらえれば、もう

少し席に余裕ができるんですが。

lap² *n.* (circuit in a race) 1周

He sprinted when he was on the last lap.
最後の1周で、彼はスパートをかけた。

lapdog *n.* 小犬

lapel *n.* (えりの) 折り返し, 折りえり

lapis lazuli *n.* ラピスラズリ, るり

lapse *n.* (passage of time) 経過; (failure) 過失, ミス

v. (**lapse into**) …してしまう, (…に) なる

a lapse of memory 度忘れ

a lapse of attention 注意散漫

a lapse of judgment 判断ミス

lapse into sleep 寝てしまう

after a lapse of …後

after a lapse of two months 2カ月後

laptop *n.* ノートパソコン, ラップトップ

larceny *n.* 窃盗, (crime) 窃盗罪

larch *n.* (tree) カラマツ, (wood) カラマツ材

lard *n.* ラード

larder *n.* (food storage room) 食料貯蔵室

large *adj.*

1 BIGGER THAN AVERAGE: 大きい, 大きな, (of space) 広い, 広大な

2 OF NUMBER / AMOUNT / DEGREE: (**a large number of**) たくさんの, 多くの, 多い, 多数の, (**a large amount of**) たくさんの, 多くの, 多い, 多量の, (**a large degree of**) かなりの, 相当の

3 OF CLOTHING / DRINK SIZE: Lサイズの

1 a large man 大きい [大柄な] 男性

a large car 大型車

a large field 大平原

How large is it?
どのくらいの大きさ [広さ] ですか？

a large living room 広いリビング(ルーム)

2 large numbers of birds たくさんの鳥

a large number of possibilities
多くの可能性

a large number of people
大勢 [たくさん] の人

a large amount of money
大金 [巨額の金]

3 Get the large size.
Lサイズにしたほうがいいよ。

largely *adv.* (to a great extent) 大部分は, 大いに; (mainly) 主に

large-scale *adj.* 大規模な, 大がかりな

a large-scale project 大規模なプロジェクト

lark¹ *n.* (bird) ヒバリ

lark² *n.* (prank) いたずら

larva *n.* 幼虫

laryngitis *n.* 喉頭炎

have laryngitis 喉頭炎になる

larynx *n.* 喉頭

laser *n.* レーザー

a laser beam レーザー光線

♦ **laser printer** *n.* レーザープリンター

lash *n.* (strike of a whip) むちの一打ち, (end of a whip) むちひも

v. (strike) 打つ, (whip) むちで打つ; (lash A to B: tie A tightly to B) (AをBに) 強く結び付ける

The boy was given five lashes of the cane.
少年は、むち打ち5回の刑に処せられた。

lash out at (criticize) 激しく非難する, ((*informal*)) …に食ってかかる

He lashed out at the referee.
彼は審判に食ってかかった。

lashing *n.* (punishment) むち打ち(の刑);

(**lashings**: ropes for tying) 縄, ひも

lasso *n.* 投げ縄

v. (投げ縄で) 捕らえる

last[1]

1 *adj.* FINAL: 最後の, 最終の, 終わりの

2 *adj.* MOST RECENT: この前の, (of night) 昨-, (of week, month) 先-

3 *adv.* MOST RECENTLY: 最後に

4 *n.* THE LAST: 最後

1 the last page 最後のページ

the last day of the term 学期の最終日

This is the last time I'm going to see him.
彼に会うのは、これが最後だ。

the last train 最終電車 [終電]

2 His last album was a flop.
彼のこの前のアルバムは失敗だった。

last Tuesday この前の火曜日

last night
昨日の夜 [ゆうべ, ((*formal*)) 昨夜]

last week 先週

last month 先月

last year 去年 [((*formal*)) 昨年]

the last year この1年

3 When did you last go there?
そこへ最後に行ったのはいつですか？

Taro came last.
太郎が最後にやって来た。

4 Maki was the last to arrive.
真紀が最後に到着した。

I'm sure we haven't heard the last of it.
この件はまだ終わっていませんよ。

I hope we've seen the last of him!
あの人に会うのはこれっきりにしたい！

at last とうとう, ついに, やっと

At last, the bus arrived.
やっと、バスが来た。

be the last to do (speaking about sb else) 一番…しそうにない, まさか…しないだろう, (speaking about oneself) 絶対…しない

Suzuki would be the last to complain.
まさか鈴木さんが文句を言うことはないだろう。

come in last (in a race) びりになる

last but not least (winding down a talk) 最後になりますが大切なこととして

to the last 最後まで

He battled on to the last and finished the marathon.
彼は最後までがんばり抜いて、マラソンを完走した。

♦ **last years of one's life** *n.* 晩年

last[2] *v.* (continue, endure) 続く, (of shoes etc.) 長持ちする, もつ, (of person) もちこたえる

How long did their relationship last?
二人の関係は、どのくらい続いたのですか？

The movie lasted over three hours!
その映画は3時間以上あったよ！

These shoes should last a few years.
この靴なら何年かもつだろう。

I don't know how he (= the boxer) lasted the last few rounds.
((*masculine*)) あのボクサー、終盤の数ラウンドをよくもちこたえたなあ。

last-ditch *adj.* どたん場の, 最後の

in a last-ditch attempt 最後の手段として

lasting *adj.* 永続的な, 恒久の, (enduring) 長く残る, (of impression) 消えない

a lasting peace 恒久平和

L

lastly *adv.* 最後に

last-minute *adj.* ぎりぎりの, 最後の

latch *n.* 掛け金, ラッチ

put down the latch 掛け金をかける

late

1 *adj.* TARDY: 遅い, 遅れた, 遅刻した

2 *adv.* AFTER THE USUAL TIME: 遅く, 遅れて

3 *adj.* TOWARD THE END OF: (of day) 遅い, (of period) 後期の, …の後半

4 *adv.* RECENTLY: 最近, このごろ, この間

5 *adj.* DECEASED: (**the late…**) 故…, 亡き…

1 have a late breakfast 遅い朝食をとる

If you don't hurry, you'll be late for your appointment.
急がないと、約束の時間に遅れますよ。

The boy was late for school.
その子は学校に遅刻した。

I was late getting up. 寝坊しました。

2 Do you go to bed late every night?
毎晩、寝るのが遅いんですか？

How late do you usually stay up?
いつもは何時まで起きてるの？

I realized my mistake too late.
間違いに気づくのが遅すぎた。

3 It's getting late.
遅くなってきた/もうこんな時間だ。

the late Victorian period
ビクトリア朝後期

late fall 晩秋

late at night 夜遅い時間

late 2006 2006年の後半

She's in her late forties.
彼女は40代後半です。

4 as late as last week つい先週

5 the late foreign minister 故外務大臣

one's late husband 亡き夫

of late 最近, このごろ

He hasn't been well of late.
最近、彼は具合がよくない。

lately *adv.* このごろ, 最近, 近ごろ

latent *adj.* (potential) 潜在的な, (hidden) 隠れた

a latent ability 潜在能力

later *adv.* あとで, 後に, ((*formal*)) 後ほど

adj. (subsequent) もっとあとの

Later I went up to my room for a nap.
そのあと、昼寝をしに2階の自分の部屋へ行った。

He came back two or three hours later.
彼は、2、3時間後に戻って来た。

If you could get here no later than 10 o'clock, I'd be grateful.
10時までに来ていただけると、ありがたいです。

It appeared in a later edition.
あとから出た版に載りました。

(see you) later あとでね

later on あとで, ((*formal*)) 後ほど

Later on we'll talk some more.
あとで、もっと話し合いましょう。

sooner or later 遅かれ早かれ, そのうちに

Sooner or later she's going to get caught.
遅かれ早かれ、彼女は捕まりますよ。

lateral *adj.* 横の

latest *adj.* (newest) 最新の, (last) 最後の

the latest technology 最新技術

The latest train from here to Tokyo is at 12:32 A.M.
東京駅までの最終電車は(午前)12時32分発です。

at the latest 遅くとも

Let's meet at 6 o'clock at the latest.
遅くとも6時には会うことにしよう。

latex *n.* ラテックス, (from rubber tree) 乳液

lath *n.* ラス, 木摺

lathe *n.* 旋盤

lather *n.* せっけんの泡

v. (apply lather to) (…に) せっけんの泡を塗る

Latin *n.* (language) ラテン語

adj. (of country, culture) ラテン系の

Latin America *n.* ラテンアメリカ

Latino *n.* ラテン系アメリカ人

latitude *n.* 緯度

longitude and latitude 経度と緯度

latrine *n.* 便所 [→ TOILET]

latter *adj.* 後の, 後者の

n. (**the latter**) 後者, ((*informal*)) 後のほう

Everything happens in the latter part of the novel.
すべては小説の後半に起こるんだ。

Of the two wines, I prefer the latter.
2本のワインのうち、後のほうが好きだ。

lattice *n.* 格子, (window) 格子窓, (latticework) 格子細工

laugh *v.* 笑う, (force a laugh) 苦笑する, (**laugh at**: make fun of) 笑い物にする

n. (act of laughing) 笑い, (sound of laughing) 笑い声, (source of fun) 笑いのたね

laugh uncontrollably
笑い転げる [げらげら笑う]

Don't laugh about him like that.
((*masculine*)) 彼のことをそんなふうに笑うなよ。

They all laughed at her.
みんなは彼女を笑い物にした。

I wouldn't want to be laughed at.
笑い物になりたくない。

have a good laugh 大笑いする

It was a good laugh.
実におかしかった。

burst out laughing どっと笑う, 吹き出す

laugh off 笑い飛ばす

He tried to laugh it off as a joke.
彼は、冗談として笑い飛ばそうとした。

laughable *adj.* こっけいな, 笑える, (silly) ばかばかしい

laughing *adj.* 笑っている, (of matter) 笑うような, おかしい

n. → LAUGH

It's no laughing matter.
笑い事じゃないよ。

laughter *n.* 笑い, (sound of laughter) 笑い声

launch[1] *v.* (ship) 進水させる, (rocket) 打ち上げる, (missile) 発射する; (project, attack, campaign) 始める, 開始する

launch[2] *n.* (small motorboat) ランチ

launchpad *n.* (for rocket) 発射台

Laundromat *n.* コインランドリー

laundry *n.* (business) クリーニング屋, (room) 洗濯場, (clothes to be washed/dried) 洗濯物

do the laundry 洗濯をする

♦**laundry basket** *n.* 洗濯かご

laurel *n.* (shrub) ゲッケイジュ, 月桂樹

lava *n.* 溶岩

a stream of lava 溶岩流

lavatory ***n.*** お手洗い, ((*both euphemistic*)) 洗面所, (for women) 化粧室

lavender ***n.*** (plant) ラベンダー, (color) 藤色, 薄紫(色)

lavish ***adj.*** (extravagant) ぜいたくな, 豪華な; (be lavish with: be generous with) 惜しまない

v. 惜しみなく与える

a lavish party 豪華なパーティー

be lavish with one's money

お金を惜しまない [気前よく使う]

law ***n.*** 法律, (rule) 規則, (of science) 法則, (custom) 習わし, おきて; (subject of study) 法学

law and order 治安

obey [break] the law 法律を守る [破る]

It's against the law to drink and drive.

飲酒運転は法律違反だ。

The law requires you to pay income tax.

所得税の納付は法律で義務づけられている。

Littering is forbidden by law.

ぽい捨ては法律で禁止されている。

The bill became law.

法案が法律になった。

go into law (=take up law as a profession) 法曹界に入る

Mrs. Wada practices law.

和田さんは弁護士をしています。

constitutional law 憲法

company law 会社法

criminal law 刑法

international law 国際法

the laws of nature 自然の法則

the law of gravity (万有)引力の法則

♦**law-abiding** ***adj.*** 法律を守る

law school ***n.*** ロースクール, 法科大学院

law court ***n.*** 裁判所

law enforcement ***n.*** (police) 警察

lawful ***adj.*** 合法の, 合法的な, 正当な

lawless ***adj.*** (of behavior) 不法な, 違法な

lawmaker ***n.*** (legislator) 議員

lawn ***n.*** 芝生

mow the lawn 芝を刈る

♦**lawn mower** ***n.*** 芝刈り機

lawsuit ***n.*** 訴訟

file a lawsuit against

...に対して訴訟を起こす

lawyer ***n.*** 弁護士

lax ***adj.*** (not strict) 厳しくない, (neglectful) 怠慢な

laxative ***n.*** 下剤

L

lay ***v.***

1 PUT: 置く, (lay A on top of B) (Bの上にAを)のせる, (lay down to rest) 寝かせる [→ LAY OUT]

2 CABLES/CARPETS: 敷く, (cables, lines) 敷設する

3 EGG: 産む

1 I laid my jacket carefully on the sofa.

上着をソファーにそっと置いた。

She laid her head on the pillow.

彼女は枕に頭をのせた。

The mother laid her baby down on the bed.

母親は赤ん坊をベッドに寝かせた。

2 How long will it take to lay the carpets?

じゅうたんを敷くのにどれくらい時間がかかりますか?

Mr. Tanaka runs a company that lays cables.
田中さんは、ケーブルを敷設する会社を経営している。

3 The chicken laid an egg.
鶏が卵を産んだ。

lay down *v.* (weapons, one's life) 捨てる

lay off *v.* (**be laid off**: be fired) 解雇される, リストラされる; (quit doing/consuming) やめる

He was laid off. 彼は解雇された。

You'd better lay off alcohol for a while.
しばらくお酒をやめたほうがいい。

Lay off! ((*masculine*)) やめろよ, ((*feminine*)) ちょっと!, やめてよ

L

lay out *v.* (spread out) 敷く

Let's lay the futons out.
布団を敷こう。

---

layer *n.* 層, (of paint) 一塗り, (of skin) 一皮, (of sandwich, cake) 段

a protective layer 保護層

layman *n.* (non-specialist) 素人

layoff *n.* (firing) 解雇, リストラ

layout *n.* (of page) レイアウト, 割り付け, (of building) 設計, (of house, apartment interior) 間取り

lazy *adj.* (of person) 怠惰な, 無精な, 怠け者の, (of day) けだるい

a lazy college student 怠け者の大学生

a lazy letter-writer 筆無精な人

This hot weather makes me lazy.
こう暑くては、だらけてしまう。

a lazy summer afternoon
けだるい夏の午後

♦ **laze around/about** *v.* だらける, のらくらする

lazybones *n.* 怠け者

LCD *abbr.* 液晶ディスプレー

lead[1]

1 *v.* DIRECT: (person) 案内する, ((*formal/also figurative*)) 導く, (orchestra) 指揮する

2 *v.* BE/WALK AT THE HEAD OF: (…の) 先頭に立つ/歩く, 先を行く

3 *v.* IN COMPETITION: (have points/advantage over) ((*also figurative*)) リードする

4 *v.* GO TO: (**lead to/into**: of road, door etc.) …に通じる, …に出る

5 *v.* BE A LEADER OF/FOR: 率いる, (…の) 指揮を取る

6 *v.* HAVE AS A CONSEQUENCE: (lead to) (…に) つながる, (= bring about) もたらす

7 *v.* LIVE: (lead a… life) (…生活を) 送る, 過ごす

8 *v.* IN DANCE: リードする

9 *n.* FOREMOST POSITION: 先頭, 首位, リード, トップ

10 *n.* IN PLAY/FILM: (lead role) 主役

11 *n.* CLUE: 手がかり

1 She led me along the corridor to the office.
廊下を通って、オフィスへ案内してくれた。

Ms. Ogawa leads tour groups through Kyoto.
小川さんは団体旅行客を京都に案内しています。

We were led by a guide.
私たちはガイドさんに案内された。

He led the horse into the stable.
彼は馬をきゅう舎へ引き入れた。

He led us safely through the crisis.
彼は危機を切り抜けて我々を安全に導いた。

Who led the orchestra?
オーケストラの指揮(者)は誰でした？

2 He led the way up the mountain path.
彼が先頭に立って山道を登った。

The mayor led the demonstration.
市長がデモの先頭に立った。

Bob was leading, and I was following.
ボブが先を行き、私はその後について歩いていた。

3 Germany is leading by five points.
ドイツが5点(差で)リードしている。

The U.S. leads the world in medical research.
医療研究では、アメリカが世界をリードしている。

4 This road leads to Ogikubo Station.
この道は荻窪駅に通じています/この道を行けば荻窪駅に出ます。

Where does this door lead to?
このドアはどこに通じているの？

5 Mr. Yamashita led the company for fifteen years.
山下氏が15年間、会社を率いた。

Who will lead us now?
我々の指揮を取ってくれるのは誰ですか？

6 The assassination of the prince led to war.
皇太子の暗殺が戦争につながった。

The whole affair led me to doubt his sincerity.
その一連のことがきっかけで、彼の誠実さを疑うようになった。

This leads me to my final point...
というわけで、結論といたしましては…

7 He leads a happy life.
彼は幸せな日々 [生活] を送っている。

8 The man is supposed to lead.
男性がリードすることになっています。

9 "Who's in the lead?"
"Takahashi is in the lead."
「誰が先頭なの？」
「高橋がトップだ」

10 The lead was played by De Niro.
主役はデニーロだった。

11 There were no leads for the police to follow.
警察には、何の手がかりもなかった。

lead the way (guide) 案内する, ((*formal/also figurative*)) 導く, 先導する, (pioneer) 先頭を切る

You lead the way. We'll follow.
案内してください。ついて行きますから。

The U.S. leads the way in space exploration.
アメリカが宇宙開発では先頭を切っている。

one thing led to another 次々にいろいろなことがあって, いろいろなことが次々に起きて

First he started shouting, then one thing led to another, and before we knew it, he'd slammed the door and left.
まず、彼がどなり出したんです。それから、いろんなことが次々に起きて、あっという間に、彼はドアをバタンと閉めて出て行ってしまったんです。

take the lead 先頭に立つ

lead[2] *n.* 鉛

Lead is a soft but heavy metal.

L

鉛は軟らかくて重い金属です。

♦ **lead-free** ***adj.*** 無鉛の

lead-free gasoline 無鉛ガソリン

leader ***n.*** 指導者, リーダー, (in race) トップをいく人

leadership ***n.*** 指導, (ability) 指導力, リーダーシップ

under the leadership of …の指導の下で

have leadership skills 指導力がある

leading ***adj.*** (main) 主な, (foremost) 先頭の, (influential) 有力な

a leading role 主役

leaf ***n.*** (of plant) 葉, 葉っぱ; (of book) 1枚

The leaves are falling.
落葉している/木の葉が落ちている。

turn over a new leaf 心機一転する

leaflet ***n.*** ビラ, ちらし

league ***n.*** (alliance) 連盟, (of teams) リーグ

the League of Nations 国際連盟

leak ***v.*** (let liquid or gas in/out) 漏れる, (of rain, roof) 漏る, (cause to become known) 漏らす

n. (seepage of liquid/gas) 漏れ, (hole) 漏れ穴, 漏れ口, (secret) 漏洩

Water is leaking from the washing machine.
洗濯機から水が漏れている。

The news was leaked to the press.
そのニュースは報道陣に漏れた。

leak a secret 秘密を漏らす

a gas leak ガス漏れ

How do we stop this leak?
この漏れをどうやって止めよう?

There's a leak somewhere.
どこかで漏れてる。

The pipe has sprung a leak.
パイプから漏れ出した。

♦ **leakage** ***n.*** 漏れ

lean[1] ***v.*** (incline) 傾く, (**lean over**) 身を乗り出す, (**lean on**) …に寄りかかる, (**lean against**) …にもたれる; (**lean to/toward**: tend toward) …に傾く

He leaned over me to get his papers.
彼は私のほうに身を乗り出して書類を取った。

Don't lean against the car, please.
車に寄りかからないでください。

The president's policies lean to the right.
大統領の政策が右傾化している。

lean[2] ***adj.*** (of person) やせた; (of meat) 赤身の, 脂肪の少ない

He's the lean, athletic sort.
彼はやせ形の運動選手タイプだ。

leap ***v.*** ぴょんと跳ぶ, はねる

The cat leaped over the puddle.
猫が水たまりを跳び越えた。

Will you stop leaping about on the sofa.
ソファーではね回るのはやめなさい。

leap year ***n.*** うるう年

learn ***v.*** (receive lessons in) 習う, 教わる, ((*formal*)) 学ぶ, (commit to memory) 覚える, (get to know) 知る

Ayako's learning to drive.
亜矢子さんは運転を習っています。

What new techniques did you learn at the workshop?
そのワークショップで、どんな新しい技術を教わったの?

I learned Japanese from Professor Ishida.

私は石田先生から日本語を学びました。

He learned French when he was a teenager.
彼は10代のころにフランス語を覚えた。

I learned yesterday that Mr. Matsumoto was promoted to section chief.
松本さんが課長になったことを、昨日知った。

learn a hard lesson (from) (…から) 苦い教訓を得る, (…で) こりる

learned ***adj.*** (of person) 学識のある

learner ***n.*** 学習者

a beginning-level learner 初学 [初心] 者

learning ***n.*** 学習, (scholarship) 学問, 学識

the learning process 学習過程

lease ***n.*** (contract) 賃貸借契約

v. (rent out) 貸す, 賃貸しする

on lease リースで, (being borrowed) 借りて

The car is on lease.
車は借りているんです。

leash ***n.*** ひも, (chain) 鎖

v. (put a leash on) ひもでつなぐ

least ***adj.*** (in size) 一番小さい, 最も小さい, 最小の, (in amount) 一番少ない

adv. 一番…ない

n. (**the least**) (in size) 最小のもの, (in degree) 最低限のもの, (= the worst) 最悪のもの

the least amount of 最少限の…

the least spicy 一番辛くない

She's the least selfish of all of them.
彼女は、その中で一番わがままを言わない人だ。

He works least.
あの人が一番、働かない。

The least I can do is drive you to the station.
せめて駅までお送りしますよ。

That is the least I expect.
最低限、それくらいは期待しているよ。

at least (drawing attention to the brighter aspect of a bad situation) とにかく, ともかく, (not less than) 少なくとも; (qualifying what one has just said) 少なくとも

At least you weren't late.
ともかく、遅刻はしなかったんだね。

We need five chairs at least.
少なくとも五つの椅子が要る。

I'll do it. Or, at least I'll do what I can.
私がするよ。まあ、少なくともできるだけのことはするよ。

least of all 特に…(ない)

I didn't think anyone would pass the exam—least of all you.
誰も試験に合格しないと思っていたよ—特に君はね。

not in the least 少しも…ない

I wasn't worried in the least.
少しも心配していなかった。

leather ***n.*** 革, レザー

leather products 革製品

---

leave[1] ***v.***

1 DEPART: 出る, (go away) 出て行く, 去る, (of train) 発車する, (on journey) 出発する, (=leave for) (…に) 向かう, (**leave the table/one's chair**) 席を立つ, 席を外す, (**leave the hospital**) 退院する

2 QUIT: (school, job) 辞める

3 ABANDON: 捨てる, 見捨てる

4 CAUSE TO REMAIN IN A PLACE: 残しておく, 置いておく, (leave a message) 残す, (leave in the care of) 預ける

5 CAUSE TO REMAIN IN A STATE/CONDITION: …ままにしておく

6 RESPONSIBILITY: (leave A to B) (AをBに) 任せる

7 MARK/EFFECT/IMPRESSION: 残す

8 FORGET: (leave sth somewhere) 置き忘れる

9 BEQUEATH: 残して死ぬ, 残す

1 He left a few moments ago.
彼はほんの少し前に出て行きましたよ。

(*announcement*) "The train leaves soon."
「(電車は)まもなく発車します」

What time does your flight leave?
何時の便ですか?

They're leaving for Rome next week.
彼らは来週、ローマに向けて出発します。

I left the table to make a phone call.
私は電話をかけるために席を外した。

2 He left his job and moved to the country.
彼は仕事を辞めて田舎へ引っ越した。

The girl left school at fourteen.
その子は14歳で学校を辞めた。

3 He left his wife and children.
彼は妻子を置いて出て行った。

She left him for another man.
彼女は彼を捨てて別の男に走った。

4 I left my bag in a locker at the station.
かばんは駅のロッカーに入れて来ました。

If you don't like the cabbage, just leave it.
キャベツが苦手なら、残したらいい。

I've only got ¥1,000 left.
1000円しか残っていない。

I'd like to leave the footnotes in.
脚注は残したい。

We left the key at the front desk.
かぎはフロントに預けておきました。

5 Who left the door open?
ドアをあけたままにしたのは誰?

Can I leave the light on?
明かりをつけたままにしておいてもいい?

The TV was left on.
テレビがつけっぱなしだった。

Don't leave things on the floor, please.
床に物を置きっぱなしにしないでください。

Let's leave that for the moment and move on to the next point.
それはとりあえず置いておいて、次(の点)に移りましょう。

6 Leave it to me. I'll do it.
任せてください。私がやります。

He left it to us to sort out.
あの人は私たちに解決させた。

It should be left to the police.
警察に任せるべきだ。

7 He left a bad impression.
彼は悪い印象を残した。

The wine has left a stain on the carpet.
ワインのしみがじゅうたんに残った。

8 I left my purse in the taxi.
バッグをタクシーに置き忘れた。

9 Mr. Inoue left a fortune.
井上さんは財産を残した。

leave alone (refrain from bothering)
ほうっておく, そっとしておく

Will you please leave me alone!

頼むからほうって[一人にして]おいて!

Leave the dog alone, will you!
犬にちょっかい出さないで!

leave out *v.* (omit) 省く, 抜く, ((*informal*)) 落とす, (exclude: person from group) のけ者にする

We'd better leave out this section.
この部分は省いたほうがいいね。

It was left out by mistake.
それは、間違って抜け落ちたんだ。

I don't want to be left out.
のけ者にされたくない。

---

leave[2] *n.* (holiday) 休暇, 休み
on leave 休暇(中)で, 休んで

Professor Shimizu is on leave—maternity leave—for the semester.
今学期、清水先生は産休を取っています。

lecture *n.* (presentation) 講義, 講演, (scolding) 説教, 小言
v. (give a lecture) 講義する, 講演する, (give a scolding to) (...に) 説教する

Professor Nakao gave a lecture on communications systems.
中尾先生は通信システムについて講演をした。

I've had enough of his lectures on quitting smoking.
たばこをやめろというお説教は、もうたくさんだ。

lecturer *n.* (instructor) 講師, (presenter of a lecture) 講演者

ledge *n.* (of cliff) 岩棚, (of window) 桟

ledger *n.* (in accounting) 元帳

leech *n.* (animal) ヒル, 蛭; (person) 寄生虫

leek *n.* リーキ, ニラネギ

leer *v.* (leer at) じろじろ見る, (...に) 色目を使う

leeway *n.* 余裕, ゆとり

left *n.* 左, (left side) 左側, (left turn) 左折; (**the Left**: political group) 左翼, 左派
adv. 左に, 左の方に

Take a left and go straight. Your hotel will be on the left.
左に曲がって、まっすぐ行ってください。ホテルは左側です。

On the left, you can see the imperial palace.
左手に、皇居がご覧いただけます。

Turn left at the intersection.
交差点で左に曲がってください。

left hand *n.* 左手
adj. (**left-hand**) 左側の

♦ **left-handed** *adj.* 左利きの

leftist *n.* 左翼の人

leftover *n.* (**leftovers**) 残り物
adj. 残りの, 余った

have leftovers for dinner
夕食の残り物がある

the leftover money 余ったお金

left-wing *adj.* 左翼の, 左派の

a left-wing organization 左翼団体

lefty *n.* (left-handed person) 左利き(の人)

leg *n.* (part of the body) 脚, 足, (of furniture) 脚; (of journey) 区間, 行程; (cooked bird) レッグ, もも肉

cross [bend, stretch] one's legs
脚を組む[曲げる, 伸ばす]

the first leg of the flight
フライトの最初の行程

pull sb's leg からかう

You're pulling my leg.

からかわないで。(lit.,"Don't kid me.")

legacy *n.* (of event, period) なごり; (bequeathed assets) 遺産

legal *adj.* (allowed by law) 合法的な, 適法の, (of law) 法律(上)の, 法的な

Is it legal to own a gun in this country?

この国では銃を所持することは合法ですか？

Who is the legal owner of this house?

この家の法律上の所有者は誰ですか？

a legal right 法的権利

legalize *v.* 合法化する

legally *adv.* (in terms of law) 法的に, 法律的に, (lawfully) 合法的に

legend *n.* 伝説

legendary *adj.* (of legend) 伝説の, (famous) 伝説的な

leggings *n.* レギンス

legible *adj.* 判読できる, 読みやすい

legion *n.* (army) 軍団; (large number) 多数, (of people) 大勢

legislate *v.* 法律を制定する, (**legislate for/against**) 法律で認める/禁止する

legislation *n.* (law) 法律, (lawmaking) 法律制定, 立法

pass legislation 法律 [法案] を通す

proposed legislation 法案

legislative *adj.* 立法の

the legislative branch of government

立法府 [機関]

legislator *n.* (in the U.S.) 州議会議員, (in Japan) 国会議員

legislature *n.* 立法機関, (in the U.S.: state legislature) 州議会

legitimate *adj.* (legal) 適法の, 合法の, (justifiable) 正当な; (of birth) 嫡出の; (reasonable) 筋の通った, もっともな

a legitimate excuse もっともな口実

leisure *n.* (free time) 暇, 余暇, 自由時間, (recreation) レジャー

Do it at your leisure.

時間のある [暇な] 時でいいですよ。

How do you spend your leisure time?

余暇はどんなふうにお過ごしですか？

Leisure has become an industry.

レジャーは一つの産業になった。

leisurely *adj.* ゆっくりした, のんびりした *adv.* ゆっくり(と), のんびり(と)

lemming *n.* レミング, タビネズミ

lemon *n.* レモン

a lemon pie レモンパイ

lemonade *n.* レモネード, レモン水, (clear, carbonated drink) レモンソーダ

lemongrass *n.* レモングラス

lend *v.* (allow to borrow) 貸す

Could you lend me your car?

車を貸してもらえませんか？

I wouldn't lend him a penny.

あいつには、一銭たりとも貸すもんか。

I'll lend you my umbrella.

((*polite*)) 傘をお貸ししますよ。

lend a hand → HAND

lender *n.* 貸し主

length *n.* (measurement, longness) 長さ, (**...in length**) 縦..., (duration) 期間, 長さ

It was two meters in length.

長さは2メートルでした。

the length of the essay エッセイの長さ

It was hot, and I couldn't walk for any length of time.
とにかく暑くて、とても歩くどころじゃなかった。

at length (finally) とうとう, やっと, (for a long time) 長時間

At length the shaking (due to the earthquake) stopped.
やっと揺れがおさまった。

We discussed the subject at length.
私たちはそのことについて長時間 [みっちり] 話し合った。

go to great lengths to do …するために大変な苦労をする

They went to great lengths to keep the matter secret.
彼らはそのことを秘密にしておくために、大変な苦労をした。

lengthen *v.* (make longer) 長くする, 伸ばす, (become longer) 長くなる

lengthy *adj.* (long) 長い, (too long) 長ったらしい

a lengthy discussion 長ったらしい議論

lenient *adj.* (not strict) 厳しくない, (generous) 寛大な, (too lenient) 甘い

lens *n.* (for camera) レンズ, (of eye) 水晶体

a telephoto lens 望遠レンズ

a wide-angle lens 広角レンズ

lentil *n.* レンズマメ, ヒラマメ

Leo *n.* (the Lion) 獅子座

leopard *n.* ヒョウ

leotard *n.* レオタード

leprosy *n.* ハンセン病

lesbian *n.* レスビアン

lesion *n.* (wound) 傷

less *adj.* (**less than**) …より少ない

adv. See examples below

Is a pint less than a liter?
1パイントは1リットルよりも少ないですか？

We are getting less and less information.
入ってくる情報が、減る一方だ。

I bought the less expensive one.
高くないほうを買いました。

Talk less and listen more. You might learn something.
もっと口数を減らして、人の話に耳を傾けなさい。何か得るものがあるよ。

It cost a little less than I thought it would.
思っていたより、少し安かった。

I know much less about it than you do.
それについては、私の知っていることは、あなたよりずっと少ないです。

less than (followed by a number) …足らず, …以内; (less than perfect/complete/helpful etc.) 全然…ない

It will take less than five minutes.
5分足らずです/5分はかかりません。

a little less than ten kilometers 10キロ弱

His grades were less than satisfactory.
彼の成績は全然満足のいくものじゃない。

less A than B AというよりむしろB

It's less the heat than the humidity that makes August miserable.
8月がきついのは、暑さより湿度のせいです。

less…than before 以前より…ない, 以前ほど…ない

less…than one had thought/expected 思っていた/予想していたほど…ない

L

no less A than B Bに劣らずA, Bと同じくらいA

She is no less qualified than any of the other applicants.
彼女は、ほかの応募者に劣らないくらい能力がある。

It's no less than I expected.
思ったとおりだ。

It's no less than you deserve!
それくらいの罰を受けて当然だ!

nothing less than まさに…, …にほかならない, …も同然

It was nothing less than a threat.
脅迫も同然だった。

not less than 少なくとも, …以上

If it isn't less than $200, don't buy it.
200ドル以上したら買わないでよ。

-less *suf.* (without) …のない

homeless 家のない

lessen *v.* (make less) 少なくする, 減らす, (become less) 少なくなる, 減る

lesser *adj.* (in amount) より少ない, (less significant) より重要でない

the lesser evil まだましなほう [悪事]

lesson *n.* (instruction, period of) 授業, -時間, -時限, (in art/music) レッスン, (お)けいこ, (in textbook) -課; (moral lesson) 教訓, (experience that leads to wisdom) 勉強

He did not go to the lesson.
彼は授業に出なかった。

I have three lessons today.
今日は授業が3時間ある。

The flower-arrangement lesson starts at 9 o'clock.
生け花のおけいこは9時から始まる。

Lesson 5 is by far the hardest.
第5課が明らかに一番難しい。

I learned quite a lesson from that experience.
あの経験からとてもいい教訓を得ました。

let *v.*

1 ALLOW: (…に) <causative form of verb>, (permit) 許可する

2 MAKING A SUGGESTION: (**let's**…) …しよう, ((*polite*)) …しましょう

3 → RENT, LEASE

1 Let me do it, please.
私にやらせてください。

Please let me know as soon as possible.
できるだけ早く知らせてください。

Are you going to let him do that to you?
彼にそんなことをされてもいいの?

I wouldn't let the children play so near the river, if I were you.
私なら子供たちを、川のそばで遊ばせたりしません。

The company is not going to let you take two weeks off work.
会社は、2週間もの休みは許可しないよ。

2 Let's go shopping today.
今日、買い物に行こう。

Let's not start arguing again.
もうけんかは、よそう。

"Shall we have dinner?"
"Yes, let's."
「晩ご飯を食べようか?」
「うん、そうしよう」

let alone → ALONE

let sb be そっとしておく, …にかまわな

いでおく

Will you just let her be.

とにかく彼女をそっとしておいてくれない？

let oneself go 羽目を外す

He really let himself go for once.

あの時ばかりは、彼もとことん羽目を外したよ。

let go of 放す

Why doesn't the dog let go of the stick?

犬は、どうして棒をくわえて放さないの？

Let go of me!

((*feminine*)) 放して / ((*masculine*)) 放せ!

let me see / let's see ええと…, うーん

let's wait and see → WAIT AND SEE

let by *v.* 通す

let down *v.* (disappoint) がっかりさせる, 失望させる; (let down from: lower) (…から) 下に下ろす

Don't let me down this time.

今度は頼むよ [がっかりさせないでよ]。

Hey! Let me down from here!

おおい! ここから下ろして!

let in *v.* (allow to enter) (中に)入れる, 中に通す, (allow to pass) 通す

Did they let you in?

中に入れてもらえましたか？

Are you going to let them in, or should I?

あの人たちを中に通してあげてくれる？ それとも私が出ようか？

let off *v.* (allow to explode) 爆発させる; (forgive) 許す, (let pass) 見逃す

It sounded like someone let off a firework.

誰かが花火を爆発させたような音だった。

I'll let you off this time, but don't do it again.

((*masculine*)) 今回は見逃してやるが、二度とやるんじゃないぞ。

let on *v.* (reveal) 口外する

let out *v.* (let outside) 外に出す, (release from confinement) 解放する, (from prison) 釈放する; (utter) (声を) 上げる

Will someone let the dog out?

誰か犬を外に出してくれない？

He was let out of prison about two months ago.

彼は2ヵ月ほど前に釈放された。

let out a cry [laugh, groan]

叫び声 [笑い声, うめき声] を上げる

let through *v.* (allow to pass) 通す

They let us through because we had press badges.

報道関係者のバッジをつけていたので、通してもらえた。

---

lethal *adj.* 致死の, 致命的な

a lethal dose 致死量

♦**lethal injection** *n.* (form of execution) 致死注射

lethargic *adj.* 無気力な, けだるい

lethargy *n.* (lack of energy) 無気力, (apathy) 無関心, (sleepiness) 眠気

letter *n.* (written message) 手紙, -状, ((*formal*)) 書簡 [→ p.1174], (to the editor of a newspaper) 投書; (character representing a sound) 字, 文字, (typed/printed character) 活字

write [send, receive] a letter

手紙を書く [送る, 受け取る]

a letter of request 依頼状

L

a letter of recommendation 推せん状
a business letter ビジネスレター
a personal letter 私信
The letters crossed in the mail.
手紙が行き違いになった。
The letter was about their new home.
手紙は新居について書かれていた。
We received a letter from your father.
お父様からお手紙をいただきました。
a capital [small] letter 大 [小] 文字
italic letters イタリック体(の文字)
Roman letters ローマ字

letterbox *n.* (mailbox) 郵便受け

lettuce *n.* レタス

leukemia *n.* 白血病

level

1 *n.* AMOUNT: 量, 値, -値
2 *n.* DEGREE: レベル, 程度, 水準
3 *n.* HEIGHT: 高さ
4 *adj.* EVEN: 平らな, 水平の, (at the same height) 同じ高さの
5 *v.* MAKE EVEN: 平らにする, ならす
6 *v.* DESTROY: 破壊する, (knock down: tall building, tree) 倒す
7 *v.* BE FORTHRIGHT: (**level with**) …に正直に言う, …に本当のことを言う
8 *n.* TOOL: 水準器

1 You'd better check the oil level.
オイルの量を調べたほうがいい。
The noise levels are high.
騒音が激しい。
a low [high] cholesterol level
低い [高い] コレステロール値

2 a high level of education 高度な教育
Word meanings sometimes change at sentence level.
単語の意味は、使われる文によって変化することがある。

3 ground level (of a building) 1階
water level 水位
two thousand meters above sea level
海抜2000メートル
The window is above eye level.
窓は目の高さより上にある。

4 a level surface 水平面
Are the boards level with each other?
板は同じ高さですか？

5 The ground has been leveled.
土地は、ならしてあります。

6 The town was leveled by a tornado.
その町は竜巻で破壊された。

7 Look, I'm trying to level with you here.
ねえ、本当のことを言うよ。

♦ **level off** *v.* (become even) 平らになる, (of prices) 横ばいになる

lever *n.* (handle on machine) レバー; (tool) てこ
Use a lever to open it.
てこを使ってあけなさい。

leverage *n.* (power with which sth can be lifted) てこの力; (influence) 力, 影響力

levy *v.* (tax) 徴収する, 取り立てる
n. (tax) 税金

lewd *adj.* みだらな, エッチな

lexicography *n.* 辞書学

lexicon *n.* (vocabulary) 語彙目録, (dictionary) 辞書

liability *n.* (impediment) 障害; (duty) 義務, (responsibility) 責任; (**liabilities**: debts) 負債

liable ***adj.*** (**be liable to do**: be likely to do) …しそう; (under legal obligation) (…する) 義務がある

She's liable to get into trouble.
彼女は問題を起こしそうだ。

The chair is liable to break if you sit on it that way.
そんな座り方をすると、椅子が壊れそうだ。

He's liable for his debts.
彼は借金を返済する義務がある。

liaise ***v.*** (liaise with) (…と) 連絡をつける, (act as a liaison) 連絡窓口になる

liaison ***n.*** (connection) (…との) 連絡, 接触, (go-between) 連絡役, 窓口; (extramarital relationship) 不倫

Mr. Hara acts as a liaison between the two companies.
原さんが2社の連絡窓口になっている。

liar ***n.*** うそつき

libel ***n.*** 名誉毀損

v. (…の) 名誉を毀損する

liberal ***adj.*** (open-minded) 心の広い, おうような, (of political affiliation) 自由主義の, (of Liberal party) 自由党の; (be liberal with: be generous with) 惜しまない, (of helping) たっぷりの

n. (person with liberal views) 偏見のない人, (used derogatively) 自由主義者, (**Liberal**: member of political party) 自由党員

♦ **Liberal Democratic Party** ***n.*** (Japanese political party) 自由民主党, 自民党

Liberal Party ***n.*** 自由党

liberal arts ***n.*** 一般教養科目

liberalism ***n.*** 自由主義

liberate ***v.*** 自由にする, 解放する

♦ **liberating** ***adj.*** (of experience) 解放されるような

liberation ***n.*** 解放, (movement) 解放運動

libertarian ***n.*** 自由論者

liberty ***n.*** (freedom) 自由, (freedom from confinement) 解放, (right) 権利

We fought for liberty.
我々は、自由のために戦った。

the Statue of Liberty 自由の女神

be at liberty to do 自由に…していい, 勝手に…できる

You are not at liberty to talk about this matter.
この件について、口外することを禁じます。

take the liberty of doing 勝手に…する

libido ***n.*** リビドー, (sexual desire) 性欲

Libra ***n.*** (the Balance) 天秤座

librarian ***n.*** 図書館員, 司書

library ***n.*** 図書館, (in school) 図書室, (in house) 書斎, (collection of books) 蔵書

borrow a book from the library
図書館から本を借りる

return a book to the library
図書館に本を返却する [返す]

lice ***n.*** シラミ

license ***n.*** (permission) 免許, 許可, ライセンス, (card, certificate) 免許証, 許可証

v. (permit) 認可する

a driver's license 運転免許証

a fishing license 漁業許可

♦ **license plate** ***n.*** (車の) ナンバープレート [→ picture of CAR]

lick ***v.*** なめる

n. (a single lick) 一なめ

licorice *n.* (plant) カンゾウ, 甘草, (root) カンゾウの根, (candy) カンゾウ入りキャンディー

lid *n.* (cover) ふた

take a lid off (…の) ふたをあける [取る]

put a lid on (cover) (…に) ふたをする, (keep secret) 隠す

lie[1] *v.* (**lie down**) 横たわる, 横になる, ((*informal*)) 寝転がる, (=on back) あお向けになる, (=on stomach) うつ伏せになる, (=on side) 横向きになる; (exist, be situated) ある

He was lying down on the sofa.
彼はソファーに寝そべっていた。

I think I'd better lie down.
横になったほうがよさそうだ。

The dog was lying on the bed.
犬がベッドの上に寝転がっていた。

B lies between A and C.
BはAとCの間にある。

The town lies just beyond that mountain.
町は、あの山の向こうにあります。

♦**lie ahead** *v.* 待ち受けている

the difficulties that lie ahead
この先に待ち受けている困難

lie around *v.* (be lazy) だらっとする, だらだらする, ごろごろする; (be scattered about) 散らかっている

Everything was lying around on the floor.
何もかも床に散らばっていた。

lie[2] *n.* (untruth) うそ, ((*written*)) 偽り
v. うそをつく, うそを言う, (lie about) ごまかす

It was a lie. (それは)うそだった。

He tells so many lies that he doesn't know what's true anymore.
あまりにうそが多いので、あの人は自分でも、もう何が本当だかわからなくなっている。

She lied about her age.
彼女は自分の年齢をごまかした。

lieutenant *n.* (in U.S. Navy) 大尉 [→ FIRST LIEUTENANT, SECOND LIEUTENANT]

lieutenant colonel *n.* (in U.S. Army/Air Force/Marine Corps) 中佐

lieutenant commander *n.* (in U.S. Navy) 少佐

lieutenant general *n.* (in U.S. Army/Air Force/Marine Corps) 中将

lieutenant junior grade *n.* (in U.S. Navy) 中尉

life *n.*

1 BIOLOGICAL EXISTENCE: 生命, 命
2 LIVING THINGS: 生き物, 生物
3 SOCIAL/DAILY LIFE: 生活, 暮らし, 人生, (way of life) 生き方, 暮らし方, 人生
4 DURATION OF LIFE: (person's life) 人生, (life span) 寿命, (one's whole life) 一生, 生涯, (of machine) 耐久期間, 寿命, (shelf life) (=of product) 貯蔵期間, (=of food) 賞味期限
5 PERSON: 人, 人命, 命
6 WORLD: 世界, 世
7 VITALITY: 生気, 活気, 元気
8 BIOGRAPHY: (in title of book) 伝記, -伝
9 CAREER: 人生, 生涯

1 How did life begin?
生命はどのようにして始まったのだろう?

Life is precious. 命は貴い。

2 animal life 動物

plant life 植物

insect life 昆虫

microscopic life 微生物

Is there life on Mars?
火星に生物はいるの？

3 Student life was great fun.
学生生活は最高に楽しかった。

Ms. Kimura leads a busy life.
木村さんは忙しい生活を送っている。

He spends his life watching TV.
あの人はテレビばかり見て暮らしている。

How do you enjoy life in Japan?
日本での暮らしはいかがですか？

Life is not always fair.
人生は必ずしも公平じゃない。

Gambling ruined his life.
あの人はギャンブルで身を滅ぼした。

4 His life was a sad story.
かわいそうな人生だった。

That's life! 人生なんて、そんなものだ。

He lived a long life. 彼は長生きした。

Smoking shortens your life.
喫煙は寿命を縮めるものだ。

She wrote her best novels in her early life.
あの作家は代表作となるすぐれた小説を、若いころに書いた。

In the latter part of his life, he became a recluse.
晩年、彼は隠とん生活に入った。

She worked all her life.
彼女は一生涯、働き続けました。

The machine has a life of three years.
その機械の寿命は3年だ。

This chocolate bar has a shelf life of two years.
このチョコバーの賞味期限は2年です。

5 save a life
命を救う[人命を救助する]

Hundreds of lives were lost.
何百人もの命が失われた。

6 this life この世

Do you believe in life after death?
死後の世界を信じますか？

7 She's full of life.
あの人は元気いっぱいだ/あの人は生き生きしている。

8 *The Life of Abraham Lincoln*
『エイブラハム・リンカーン伝』

9 He chose the life of a farmer.
彼は農民としての人生を選んだ。

a matter of life and death 生死にかかわる問題

It was a matter of life and death, so I called for an ambulance.
生死にかかわる問題だったので、救急車を呼んだ。

come to life 活気づく, 盛り上がる

The party suddenly came to life.
パーティーは、にわかに盛り上がった。

give one's life for …のために命をささげる

He gave his life for his country.
彼は祖国のために命をささげた。

life belt *n.* 救命帯

lifeboat *n.* 救命ボート

life cycle *n.* ライフサイクル, 生活環

life expectancy *n.* 平均余命

lifeguard *n.* 救助員, 監視員

life insurance *n.* 生命保険

life jacket *n.* 救命胴衣

lifeless *adj.* (of person: appears to be dead) 死んだ, (of planet) 生物のいない; (uninteresting) つまらない

lifelong *adj.* 生涯の, 一生の, 終生の
 a lifelong love 終生変わらぬ愛

life preserver *n.* 救命具

lifesaving *adj.* 人命救助の

life-sized *adj.* 実物大の

life span *n.* (duration of life) 寿命, (average length of life) 平均寿命

lifestyle *n.* 生き方, 生活様式

life support *n.* (system) 生命維持装置
 be on life support
 生命維持装置をつけている

lifetime *n.* (of person) 一生, 生涯, (of machine) 寿命; (long time) 長期間

♦ **lifetime employment** *n.* 終身雇用

lifework *n.* 一生の仕事, ライフワーク

lift

1 *v.* RAISE: 持ち上げる, (arm, head) 上げる

2 *v.* RISE: (of mist: rise and disappear) 晴れる

3 *v.* MAKE HAPPIER: (**lift one's spirits**) (…で) 元気が出る

4 *n.* MACHINE: (elevator) エレベーター, (ski lift) リフト

5 *n.* FREE RIDE IN A CAR: 乗せること

[1] I could hardly lift it.
とても持ち上げられなかった。
The crane lifted the steel girder into place.
クレーンは鋼鉄のけたを持ち上げて、所定の場所に置いた。
Does your foot hurt when you lift it?
足を上げると痛みますか？

[2] The mist seems to be lifting.
霧が晴れてきたようだ。

[3] The news lifted my spirits.
それを聞いて、元気が出た。

[4] Shall we take the lift?
エレベーターを使いましょうか？

[5] I gave the hitchhiker a lift.
そのヒッチハイカーを乗せてあげた。

liftoff *n.* (of rocket) 発射

ligament *n.* 靭帯

---

light[1]

1 *n.* BRIGHTNESS/RADIATION: 光, (ray of light) 光線, (sunlight) 日差し, 日光

2 *n.* SOURCE OF LIGHT: 明かり, (electric light) 電灯, 電気, ライト, (traffic light) 信号, (headlight) ヘッドライト

3 *adj.* NOT DARK: (of color: pale) 薄い, 浅い, (of sky: bright) 明るい

4 *v.* IGNITE: (…に) 火をつける, (oil lamp) つける, 点灯する, (match) 擦る

5 *v.* ILLUMINATE: (**be lit**) 照らされる [→ LIGHT UP]

[1] a strong [soft] light 強い [柔らかな] 光
The light from the window was enough to read by.
窓から差し込む光で十分読むことができた。
The sun's light was dazzling.
日差しがまぶしかった。
Too much light can harm plants.
過剰な日光は植物を傷める。

[2] In the old days, people read by candle-

L

light.
昔の人は、ろうそくの明かりで本を読んだ。

turn on [switch off] the lights
電灯のスイッチを入れる [切る]

The lights are on [off].
電気がついている [消えている]。

He shone a light in the direction of the woods.
彼は森の方をライトで照らした。

You're standing in my light.
そこに立たれると暗いんです。

Turn left at the third (traffic) light.
三つ目の信号を左に曲がってください。

3 light brown 薄茶色

light blue ライトブルー [水色, 薄い青]

It's still light outside.
外はまだ明るい。

4 light a cigarette たばこに火をつける

light a fire 火をつける [燃やす]

They lit a bonfire.
彼らはたき火に火をつけた。

light a match マッチを擦る

5 The church was lit with candles.
教会はろうそくで照らされた。

The room was poorly lit.
部屋は薄暗かった。

before light 夜明け前に

I usually get up before light.
私はたいてい夜明け前に起きます。

bring to light 明るみに出す, 暴露する

The truth was eventually brought to light.
結局、真実が明るみに出た。

come to light 明るみに出る

It came to light that the politician had taken a bribe.
その政治家がわいろを受け取っていたことが明るみに出た。

in (the) light of ...に照らして, ...によれば, ...を考慮して

In light of this new information, I'm afraid I have to ask you to resign.
この新情報によれば、あなたには辞めていただくほかありません。

see the light at the end of the tunnel 前途に光明が見える

throw/shed light on ...の解明に役立つ, 解明する

Can these discoveries throw any light upon this mystery?
このような発見が、このなぞの解明に役立ちますか?

light up *v.* (make/become bright) 明るくする/なる, (illuminate) 照らす, (of night sky, face) 明るくなる; (light a cigarette) たばこに火をつける

Floodlights lit up the stadium.
照明がついて、スタジアムを照らした。

L

light[2]

1 *adj.* NOT HEAVY: 軽い

2 *adj.* OF AMOUNT: (of traffic, rain) 少ない, (of sleep: shallow) 浅い

3 *adj.* OF FOOD: 軽い, あっさりした

4 *adj.* NOT SERIOUS: 軽い

5 *adj.* GENTLE: 軽い

6 *adv.* WITHOUT CARRYING A LOT: 身軽に, 軽装で

1 a light jacket 軽い上着

a light material 軽い生地

a light step 軽い足取り

2 a light rain 小雨

a light sleep 浅い眠り

3 a light lunch 軽い昼食

a light (= not oily) dish
軽い [あっさりした] 料理

4 light reading
軽い読み物 [肩の凝らない本]

a light injury 軽いけが

5 give it a light tap with a hammer
ハンマーで軽くたたく

6 I suggest you travel light.
身軽に旅行するのがいいですよ。

lightbulb *n.* 電球

lighten[1] *v.* (make/become brighter) 明るくする/なる

Lighten up! もっと気楽に, 落ち着いて, くよくよしないで

lighten[2] *v.* (make less heavy) 軽くする

lighter *n.* ライター

light-headed *adj.* (dizzy) めまいがする, 頭がふらふらする

lighthearted *adj.* (of person) 陽気な, のんきな, (of joke) 面白い

lighthouse *n.* 灯台

lighting *n.* 明かり, 照明

lightly *adv.* 軽く, (without consideration) 軽々しく; (of movement) そっと

It is not a matter to be taken lightly.
軽々しく考える問題ではない。

lightning *n.* 稲妻

light-year *n.* 光年

lignite *n.* 褐炭

likable *adj.* 好かれる, 好感のもてる

like[1] *v.*

1 BE FOND OF: (…が) 好きだ, (…を) 好む, (…が) 気に入る

2 EXPRESSING DESIRE: (**would like to do**) …したい, (speaking about sb else) …したがる, …したいみたい, (**would like sth**) (…が) 欲しい, (**would like sb to do**) …してほしい, …してもらいたい, ((*polite*)) …していただきたい

3 INVITING OR ASKING SB'S PREFERENCE: (**would you like…?**) See examples below

1 She likes jogging.
彼女はジョギングが好きだ。

Do you like seafood?
シーフード [魚介類] はお好きですか?

I like my coffee hot.
コーヒーは熱いのが好みです。

I like it when you do that to me.
君がそうしてくれるといいな。

I like this place.
この場所が気に入った。

2 I'd like to go one day.
いつか行きたい。

I'd like to see the manager, please.
支配人に会いたいのですが。

(*speaking to boss*) I'd like a vacation.
休暇をいただきたいのですが。

I think she would also like to go with us.
彼女もいっしょに行きたいみたいだ。

(*speaking to waiter*) I'd like one more cup of tea, please.
お茶をもう1杯下さい。

I'd like him to stop smoking.
彼にたばこをやめてもらいたい。

3 How would you like to go out for a meal tonight?
今晩、食事に行きませんか?

Would you like to come, too?

あなたもいらっしゃいますか？

Would you like Nakata to do it instead?
代わりに、中田さんにやってもらいましょうか？

if you like よかったら, ((*polite*)) よろしかったら

You can use our place if you like.
よろしかったら、うちを使ってもいいですよ。

I like that! (being ironic) あきれた！, よく言うよ

Him calling me an idiot. I like that!
((*masculine*)) あいつが、俺をばか呼ばわりするとはね。よく言えたもんだ！

like it or not いやでも, いやが応でも, 好き嫌いにかかわらず

Like it or not, you're going to have to study.
好き嫌いにかかわらず、勉強しなくちゃいけません。

like[2] ***prep.***

1 IN THE MANNER OF: …のように, …みたいに, …らしい

2 RESEMBLING: …のような, (**looks/sounds like**) …に似ている

3 IN KEEPING WITH: (sb's character) (いかにも)…らしい

1 You can swim like a fish.
魚みたいに泳げるんだね。

No, do it like this.
違います、こういうふうにやってください。

He dresses like a businessman.
彼は服装まで、ビジネスマンらしい。

2 It sounds like a duck. アヒルのようだ。

She looks like her mother.
彼女はお母さんに似ています [似です]。

3 It's like him to say that.
そんなことを言うなんていかにも彼らしい。

what's … like? …はどんなふうですか, …はどんな感じですか

What's it like working for a Japanese company?
日本の会社に勤めるのは、どんな感じですか？

What's your teacher like?
先生はどんな人？

-like ***suf.*** -的な, …のような, …みたいな, …らしい [→ -ISH]

businesslike 事務的な

a snakelike body 蛇みたいな体つき

childlike 子供らしい

likeable ***adj.*** → LIKABLE

likelihood ***n.*** 見込み, 可能性

The likelihood of our team winning is very remote.
うちのチームが勝つ可能性は、とても低い。

likely ***adj.*** (**be likely to do/happen**) (どうやら)…しそうだ/起こりそうだ, …する/起こる可能性がある; (plausible) もっともらしい, (promising) 見込みのある

adv. たぶん, おそらく

It's likely to snow later.
どうやらあとで雪になりそうです。

Your mother is likely to be up waiting for you.
たぶんお母さんは寝ないで、君を待っているよ。

He's not likely to forget this, is he?
彼はこのことを忘れそうにないですね。

I'll most likely be in bed at that time.
その時間には、もう床についてるでしょう。

a likely best-seller
ベストセラーになりそうな本

a likely story 眉つばの話, 信じられない話

That's a likely story if ever I've heard one.
そんな話、眉つば物だ。

liken *v.* (liken A to B) (AをBに) 例える

likeness *n.* 似ていること

bear a likeness to …に似ている

likewise *adv.* (similarly) 同じように; (also) …も(また)

I took off my coat, and he did likewise.
私がコートを脱ぐと、彼も同じようにした。

I hate cigarette smoke, and likewise loud children.
たばこの煙が嫌いだ。それにやかましい子供たちも。

L

liking *n.* 好み

be to one's liking …の好みだ, …の趣味に合う

She was not to Shinji's liking.
彼女は真治好みではなかった。

take a liking to (…が)気に入る

She took a liking to Sawada.
彼女は、沢田さんのことが気に入った。

lilac *n.* ライラック, リラ

lily *n.* ユリ, 百合

limb *n.* (leg, arm) 手足, (large branch) 大枝

go out on a limb 危険を冒す

limbo[1] *n.* (uncertain situation) どっちつかずの状態, (state of neglect) 無視された状態

limbo[2] *n.* (style of dance) リンボーダンス

lime[1] *n.* (fruit) ライム

♦ **lime green** *n.* 緑色

lime[2] *n.* (calcium oxide) 石灰

limeade *n.* ライムエード

limelight *n.* (**the limelight**) 注目の的

be in the limelight 注目の的になる, 脚光を浴びる

limestone *n.* 石灰岩

limit *n.* 制限, 限界, (of area: boundary) 境界

v. (restrict) 制限する, (…に)制限を設ける

a speed limit 制限速度

an age limit 年齢制限

There are limits to human endurance.
人間の忍耐力には限界がある。

A time limit was finally set.
ついに制限時間が定められた。

We'll have to limit the number of days guests can stay.
お客様の滞在日数に制限を設けざるを得ないだろう。

within limits 範囲内で

I'd do anything to have her back. Well, within limits.
彼女を取り戻すためなら何だってするよ。まあ、できる範囲内でってことだけど。

limitation *n.* (restriction) 制限, (**limitations**: limits) 限界

This (medical) treatment has its limitations.
この治療には限界があります。

limited *adj.* (not much) 限られた

♦ **limited company** *n.* 有限会社

limousine *n.* リムジン

♦ **limousine bus** *n.* リムジンバス

limp *v.* 足を引きずって歩く

line[1]

1 *n.* MARKING: 線, ライン

2 *n.* ROW OF PEOPLE/THINGS: 列, (of people waiting to buy/use sth) 行列

3 *n.* STRING/WIRE: (string) ひも, (rope) 綱, -線, (power line) 電線, (fishing line) 釣り糸 [→ CABLE, CORD]

4 *n.* TELEPHONE CONNECTION: See examples below

5 *n.* OF TEXT: 行, ライン

6 *n.* TRAIN LINE: 路線, -線, (railroad track) 線路

7 *n.* SPOKEN BY ACTOR/ACTRESS: せりふ

8 *n.* OF THOUGHT: 筋道, 方針

9 *n.* OF BUSINESS/WORK: 職種

10 *n.* BOUNDARY: 境界線

11 *n.*WRINKLE: (**lines**) しわ

12 *v.* FORM A ROW ALONG: (…に沿って) 並ぶ

1 draw a line 線を引く
a pencil line 鉛筆で書いた線
a dotted line 点線
a straight [curved] line 直[曲]線
a goal line ゴールライン
a starting [finish] line
スタート [ゴール] ライン

2 The students got into line.
生徒たちは1列になった。
We waited in line.
私たちは(列に)並んで待ちました。
There was a long line for the bathroom.
トイレの前には長い列ができていた。
There was a line outside the ramen shop.
ラーメン屋の外に行列ができていた。

3 a telephone line 電話線

4 The line is busy. お話し中です。
The line is dead. 電話が通じない。
Hold the line, please.
そのままお待ちください。

5 insert [delete] a line
1行挿入[削除]する
three lines from the top 上から3行

6 the Yamanote line 山手線
There was snow on the lines.
線路に雪が積もっていた。

7 The actor forgot his lines.
役者はせりふを忘れてしまった。

8 That negative line of thought will get you nowhere.
そんな消極的な考え方では、どうにもならないですよ。

9 What line of work is he in?
彼の職種は何ですか？

10 the state [county] line 州[郡]の境界線

11 He has deep lines on his face.
彼は顔に深いしわがある。

12 Trees lined the avenue.
大通りに沿って街路樹が植えられていた。

be in line for (a job etc.) 得る立場にある

be out of line (be overstepping one's bounds) 行き過ぎだ

draw the line 一線を引く, (**at…**) …の一線を越えない, (between A and B) (AとBを) 区別する

in line with …に沿った, …に従った
a project in line with policy
方針に沿った計画

line up *v.* (of people: form a line) 1列に並ぶ, ((*formal*)) 整列する, (arrange in a line: things) 1列に並べる

L

The soldiers lined up to be inspected.
兵士たちは閲兵のために整列した。

line² *v.* (apply an inner layer to) (…に) 裏を付ける

a kimono lined with bright silk
鮮やかな絹の裏地の付いた着物

linear *adj.* (shaped like a line) 線状の, (of movement) 直線的な

linen *n.* (material) リンネル, リネン, (**linens**) リンネル製品

liner *n.* (ship) 客船, 定期船

lineup *n.* (of people) 顔ぶれ, (of products, events) ラインアップ, 一覧

linger *v.* (of person) ぐずぐずする

lingerie *n.* ランジェリー

linguist *n.* (multilingual person) 語学の才能のある人, (specialist in linguistics) 言語学者

linguistic *adj.* 言語の

linguistics *n.* 言語学

liniment *n.* 塗り薬, ((*formal*)) 塗布剤

lining *n.* (of garment) 裏, 裏地; (of stomach) 内側

link *n.* (connection) つながり, 関連, (loop in chain) 輪

v. (link A to/with B: join A to B) (AをBに) つなぐ, 結ぶ, (**be linked**: be related) つながりがある, 関係がある

linoleum *n.* リノリウム

linseed *n.* アマの種子, アマニ

♦ **linseed oil** *n.* アマニ油

lint *n.* (balls of thread) 糸くず

lintel *n.* まぐさ

lion *n.* ライオン, 獅子

lip *n.* (of the mouth) 唇 [→ picture of FACE]; (of cup) へり, 縁

give sb lip (…に) 生意気な口をきく

lick one's lips 舌なめずりする, (get excited) わくわくする

liposuction *n.* 脂肪吸引

lip-read *v.* (…が) 読唇術でわかる

lip service *n.* 口先だけの支持

pay lip service to
…に口先だけいいことを言う

lipstick *n.* 口紅, リップスティック

put on lipstick 口紅をつける

liqueur *n.* リキュール

liquid *n.* 液体, (liquid content) 水分

adj. 液体の

Is it a solid, liquid or gas?
それは固体？ 液体？ それとも気体？

You should drink lots of liquids when you have a fever.
熱があるときは、水分を十分とらなくてはいけない。

liquid oxygen 液体酸素

liquid asset *n.* 流動資産

liquidate *v.* (business) 整理する, (assets) (資産を) 換金する, 清算する

liquid crystal *n.* 液晶

a liquid crystal display 液晶ディスプレイ

liquor *n.* 酒, アルコール, (Japanese liquor) 日本酒, (Western liquor) 洋酒, (distilled drink) 蒸留酒

He can hold his liquor.
あの人は、いくら飲んでも平気だ/あの人は、お酒が強い。

♦ **liquor store** *n.* 酒屋(さん)

list *n.* 表, リスト, 一覧表, (of names) 名

簿, (catalog) 目録

v. (make a list of) (…の) リストを作る, (enter in a list) リストに載せる

a shopping list 買い物リスト

an alphabetical list

アルファベット順の一覧表

Mori is on the list.

森さんはリスト [名簿] に載っています。

Let's put her name on the list.

彼女(の名前)をリストに入れよう。

Let's list all the names.

名前を全部リストアップしよう。

I was listed among those who were to go abroad.

海外へ行く人のリストに私が載っていた。

listen *v.* 聞く, (…に) 耳を傾ける, (listen to: follow the advice of) (…の) 言うことをきく, 言うとおりにする

Will you listen, please?

聞いてくれませんか？

Sorry, I wasn't listening.

ごめん、聞いてなかった。

I usually listen to the radio while cooking.

たいてい料理をしながらラジオを聴く。

Had the boy listened to his parents, the incident would never have happened.

その子が両親の言うことをきいていたら、あの事件は起こらなかったはずだ。

listener *n.* 聞き手, リスナー, (of radio program) 聴取者

a good listener 熱心に聞く人

liter *n.* リットル

literacy *n.* (ability to read and write) 読み書きする能力, ((*formal*)) 識字能力

a literacy rate 識字率

literal *adj.* (of meaning) 文字どおりの, (of translation) 逐語的な

literally *adv.* (to the letter) 文字どおりに; (in fact) 本当に

translate literally 直訳する

literary *adj.* 文学の, 文芸の, (of person) 文学に通じた, (of language) 文学的な

a literary magazine 文芸雑誌

literate *adj.* (able to read and write) 読み書きができる, (educated) 教養のある

literature *n.* 文学, (printed matter of any kind) 印刷物, 文献, (pamphlet) パンフレット, (data, documentation) 資料

Japanese literature 日本文学

The company sent its literature out to customers.

会社は顧客にパンフレットを送付した。

lithograph *n.* リトグラフ, 石版画

litigation *n.* 訴訟

litmus test *n.* ((*also figurative*)) リトマス試験, リトマステスト

litter *n.* (trash) ごみ, くず, (gravel for cats to urinate/defecate on) 猫砂

v. (drop garbage illegally) ごみを捨てる, (**be littered with**: be strewn with) (…が) 散らかっている,

Don't throw your litter on the ground like that! Look for a trash can.

そんなふうにごみを捨てちゃだめだよ! ごみ箱を探しなさい。

♦**litter box** *n.* (for cat) 猫用トイレ

little

1 *adj.* SMALL: 小さい, 小さな, ((*informal*)) ちっちゃな

2 *adj., adv.* OF AMOUNT/DEGREE: 少し(の),

ちょっと, 少々

3 ***adj.*** **PETTY:** つまらない, ささいな

4 ***adj.*** **HARDLY ANY:** ほとんどない, 少ししかない

5 ***adv.*** **NOT AT ALL:** 全く…ない

6 ***n.*** **SMALL AMOUNT:** 少し, わずか(のもの)

1 a little toy 小さいおもちゃ

a little shed 小さな小屋

a little boy ちっちゃな男の子

2 put a little sugar in

砂糖を少し [ちょっと] 入れる

add a little salt 塩を少々加える

There was a little rice left in the cooker.

炊飯器にご飯が少し残っていた。

I can speak a little Russian.

ロシア語をちょっと話せます。

Can you spare me a little more time?

もう少し時間を割いてもらえませんか？

Let's go a little further down this road.

この道をもう少し(先まで)行ってみよう。

I was a little put off by his comment.

彼の発言に、ちょっとうんざりした。

3 Here's a little something for you.

つまらないものですが、どうぞ。

I can't remember every little detail.

ささいなことを一々覚えていられません。

4 I have little experience in such matters.

そういう経験はほとんどありません。

I had little money set aside.

私には、ほとんど蓄えがなかった。

There's little chance of that happening.

そうなる見込みは、まずありません。

5 Little did I know what I was getting myself into.

自分が何に巻き込まれているのか、全く気づかなかった。

Little did I think he'd be back so soon.

彼がそんなに早く戻って来ようとは、考えもしなかった。

6 Give me a little, will you.

少し下さい/((*informal*)) ちょっとちょうだい。

The little that was left was gone by the next day.

わずかに残っていた物も、翌日にはなくなっていた。

Little seems to please him these days.

近ごろ彼は、楽しいことがほとんどないようだ/このところ彼は浮かない顔をしている。

I have little to do with them.

あの人たちとは、ほとんどかかわりがありません。

Our boss obviously thinks very little of us.

上司は明らかに私たちを軽く見ている。

just a little ほんの少し, ちょっとだけ

Could you pour me just a little bit more, please?

もう少しだけ入れていただけますか？

little better than …も同然

That sort of behavior is little better than criminal.

そういうふるまいは犯罪行為も同然だ。

little by little 少しずつ, だんだん

Little by little he began to get better (= recover).

彼は少しずつよくなり始めた。

little more than (of amount) …しか, …そこそこ(しか), (nothing but) (ほんの)…にすぎない

It'll take little more than half an hour.

３０分そこそこしか、かからないだろう。

It was little more than a prank.

ほんのいたずらにすぎなかった。

only a little ほんの少し

It's only a little way down the road.

この先をほんの少し行ったところです。

little finger ***n.*** 小指 [→ picture of HAND]

live

1 ***v.*** **RESIDE:** 住む, 住んでいる

2 ***v.*** **EXPERIENCE LIFE:** 生活をする, 暮らす, 生活を送る

3 ***v.*** **BE ALIVE:** 生きる

4 ***v.*** **SURVIVE:** 生き延びる, 生き続ける, 生き残る [→ LIVE THROUGH]

5 ***adj.*** **OF BAND/BROADCAST:** 生の, ライブの

6 ***adj.*** **LIVING:** (of animal) 生きている

7 ***adj.*** **OF WIRE:** 電流が流れている

1 He lives in Tokyo.

彼は東京に住んでいる。

How long have you lived in Nagoya?

名古屋にはどのくらいお住まいですか？

I'm living with my little sister in a two-bedroom apartment.

２ＤＫのアパートに妹といっしょに住んでいます。

Have you ever lived in London?

ロンドンに住んだことがありますか？

2 They live in fear of being caught.

彼らは、捕まるのではないかとびくびくしながら生活している。

The Inoues live very simply.

井上さん一家は、とても質素に暮らしています。

You ought to get out and live a little.

抜け出して少し人生を楽しみなさい。

3 We need water to live.

生きていくには水が必要です。

Women live longer than men.

女は男よりも長生きだ。

Samuel Pepys lived in the seventeenth century.

サミュエル・ピープスは１７世紀の人間だ。

4 He'll live, despite the seriousness of his injuries.

重傷を負ってはいますが、一命は取り留めるでしょう。

5 a live show ライブ

live coverage 生中継

6 a live snake 生きている蛇

7 a live wire 電流が流れている電線

live on ***v.*** (subsist on) …を食べて生きる; (remain in memory) 記憶に残る

They lived on berries and roots they found in the jungle.

彼らはジャングルで見つけた果実や木の根を食べて生き延びた。

live through ***v.*** (survive) 生き延びる

He lived through the war.

彼は戦争を生き延びた。

live together ***v.*** いっしょに住む, 同居する, (of lovers) 同棲する

livelihood ***n.*** 生計

lively ***adj.*** (of person) 元気な, はつらつとした, (of child, discussion) 活発な, (of place, event) 活気のある, にぎやかな, (of color) 鮮やかな, (of writing style) 生き生きした

Junko doesn't seem very lively today.

今日は純子はあまり元気がないね。

It was a lively debate.

活発な議論だった。

The town is not very lively in winter.
冬場は、その町はあまり活気がない。

a lively marketplace 活気のある市場

liven up *v.* (make/become more lively) 活気づける/活気づく, 面白くする/なる, 盛り上げる/盛り上がる

This should liven things up a bit.
これで少し活気づくはずです。

The party livened up when Kit arrived.
キットさんが着いて、パーティーは盛り上がった。

liver *n.* (organ) 肝臓, (of animal, as food) レバー

livestock *n.* 家畜

livid *adj.* (black-and-blue) 青黒い, (of face: pale) 青ざめた; (furious) 激怒した

living *n.* (livelihood) 生活, 生計, 暮らし
adj. (alive) 生きている, 生きた

living standards 生活水準
living conditions 生活状態
a living hell 生き地獄

be the living image of …の生き写しだ

make a living 生計を立てる, 生活する, 食べていく

Mr. Mori made a living selling jewelry.
森さんは宝石を販売して生計を立てた。

living room *n.* 居間, リビング(ルーム) [→ picture of APARTMENT]

lizard *n.* トカゲ

llama *n.* ラマ

load

1 *n.* GOODS: 荷, 積み荷

2 *n.* BURDEN: (physical or mental) 負担, (mental) 重荷, (workload) 仕事量

3 *v.* PUT (CARGO) INTO/ONTO: (load A into/onto B) (BにAを) 積み込む, 積む

4 *v.* BULLETS/FILM INTO GUN/CAMERA: 入れる, 装てんする

5 *v.* COMPUTER PROGRAM: ロードする, 取り込む

1 a heavy [light] load 重い [軽い] 荷
carry a load 積み荷を運ぶ

2 a load on one's mind 心の重荷

Let me take some of the load off your shoulders.
お手伝いしますから、肩の重荷を少し下ろしてください。

3 load up a truck トラックに荷を積み込む

load potatoes onto a truck
トラックにジャガイモを積み込む

4 load a gun 銃に弾を装てんする [入れる]

load film into a camera
カメラにフィルムを入れる

loaded *adj.* (full of goods) 荷を積んだ, (be loaded with) …でいっぱいだ; (of gun) 弾を込めた [→ DRUNK, RICH]

loaf *n.* (of bread) (パン) 1斤

loan *n.* (money) ローン, 借金, 貸付金, (act of lending) 貸し付け, 貸し出し
v. 貸す

make a loan to …に貸し付ける

take out a loan on
…のためにローンを組む

Have you repaid the loan?
ローンの返済は済みましたか？

on loan (being borrowed) 借りて, (being lent out) 貸し出し中で

It's on loan from the company.
それは会社から借りている物です。

It's on loan to the university.
それは大学に貸し出し中です。

lobby *n.* (of hotel) ロビー; (pressure group) 圧力団体, (group petitioning the government) 陳情団

v. (**lobby for/against**) ...に賛成/反対するよう働きかける, (petition) 陳情する

the antiabortion lobby
中絶反対の圧力団体

lobe *n.* (earlobe) 耳たぶ [→ picture of FACE]; (of brain, lung) 葉

lobotomy *n.* ロボトミー

lobster *n.* ロブスター, オマールエビ, (spiny lobster) 伊勢エビ

local *adj.* (regional) 地方の, 地元の, (in neighborhood) 近所の; (of anesthetic) 局部の

n. (person) 地元の人

a local newspaper 地方紙

a local government 地方自治体

a local supermarket 地元のスーパー

a local anesthetic 局部麻酔薬

They're locals. 彼らは地元の人です。

♦ **local train** *n.* 普通電車, 各駅停車

locality *n.* (place) 場所, (area) 地方

locally *adv.* 地元で, 現地で, (in this area) このあたりに

locate *v.* (find) 突き止める, 捜し出す, (**be located in**) (...に) ある, ((*formal*)) 位置する

locate the source 原因を突き止める

The investigators of the crash never did locate the black box.
墜落事故の調査団は結局、ブラックボックスを捜し出せなかった。

location *n.* 場所, 位置, (of film) ロケ

The movie was filmed on location in Cairo.
その映画はカイロでロケ撮影されました。

lock *n.* かぎ, 錠

v. (door) (...に) かぎをかける, (...を) ロックする, (sb/sth in a room) 閉じ込める

The lock is broken. かぎが壊れている。

The door is locked.
ドアには、かぎがかかっている。

We accidentally locked the kitten in the closet.
うっかり、押し入れに子猫を閉じ込めてしまった。

lock away *v.* (lock A away in B) (Bに) かぎをかけて (Aを) しまい込む [→ LOCK UP]

lock out *v.* (lock sb out) 締め出す

I was locked out of the house.
家に入れなくなった。

lock up *v.* (imprison) 刑務所に入れる, (put away: in safe etc.) かぎをかけてしまい込む; (lock doors) 戸締まりをする

The best thing you can do with people like that is lock them up in prison.
ああいう連中は、刑務所に入れておくしかない。

It's time to lock up.
戸締まりをする時間だ。

locker *n.* ロッカー, (coin locker) コインロッカー

locket *n.* ロケット

lockjaw *n.* 破傷風

locksmith *n.* かぎ屋, 錠前師

locomotive *n.* (engine) 機関車 [→ TRAIN]

locust *n.* イナゴ, バッタ

lodge *n.* (on mountain) 山小屋, ロッジ *v.* (lodge somewhere) (…に) 泊まる, (rent a room) 下宿する, 間借りする; (become embedded) とどまる; (lodge a complaint etc.) 申し立てる, 訴える

The bullet lodged in his right arm.
弾丸は彼の右腕にとどまった。

♦**lodger** *n.* 下宿人, 間借り人

lodging *n.* 宿, 宿泊所, (**lodgings**: rooms for rent in sb's house) 貸間, 下宿

loft *n.* (attic) 屋根裏, (elevated floor in room used for storage/sleeping) ロフト

log *n.* (for burning) まき, (for building) 丸太, 丸木

v. (record) 記録する

sleep like a log ぐっすり眠る

♦**log in/on** *v.* ログイン/オンする, 接続する

log out/off *v.* ログアウト/オフする, 終了する

logarithm *n.* 対数

logic *n.* 論理, (study of logic) 論理学

use logic 論理を使う

logical *adj.* 論理的な, 筋の通った, (natural) 当然の, (rational) 合理的な

♦**logically** *adv.* 論理的に, 必然的に

logistics *n.* (handling of details) 詳細を取り仕切る業務

logo *n.* ロゴ

loin *n.* (lower back) 腰, (of animal, as food) 腰肉

♦**loincloth** *n.* ふんどし

loiter *v.* うろつく, うろうろする

loll *v.* (loll about) ごろごろする, だらだらする

lollipop *n.* ぺろぺろキャンディー, 棒付きキャンディー

lone *adj.* (solitary) 単独の

lonely *adj.* (alone, sad) 寂しい, 心細い; (of place) 人里離れた

Although I lived by myself, I didn't feel lonely.
一人暮らしをしていたけど、寂しくなかった。

You must be lonely living so far from a town.
町からそんなに離れて暮らしてると、寂しいでしょう。

♦**loneliness** *n.* 寂しさ

lone wolf *n.* (person) 一匹狼

long[1]

1 *adj.* EXTENDED IN SPACE: 長い, (of distance: a long way to/from) (…まで/…から) 遠い

2 *adj., adv., n.* TIME: 長い, 長く, 長い間

1 The fabric is two meters long.
生地の長さは2メートルある。

These pants are too long.
このズボンは長すぎる。

How long is a city block?
街の1ブロックの距離はどのくらいですか?

It's a long way to walk.
歩くにはちょっと遠い。

It was a long way from home.
家から遠かった。

2 I haven't met him for a long time.
長い間会っていない。

"How long have you known her?"
"A long time."
「彼女とはいつからのお知り合いですか?」
「ずいぶん前からです/古い付き合いです」

It was not long before he changed his mind.
彼の気が変わるのに長くはかからなかった/まもなく彼は気が変わった。

It will be a long time before that happens.
当分、そういうことは起こらないよ。

It's been seven long years since we last met!
いやあ、7年ぶりだねえ!

It won't last much longer.
もうあまり長続きしないよ。

as long as (provided that) …さえすれば, …する限り; (being that) …なら

Let's drink as long as the money lasts.
お金が続く限り、飲もう。

As long as you don't mind, it's OK with me.
あなたさえよければ、私はかまわないよ。

As long as you're going out, could you mail this letter for me?
出かけるのなら、この手紙を出してくれない?

at the longest (いくら)長くても, せいぜい

It'll take an hour at the longest.
(長くても)せいぜい1時間でしょう。

before long まもなく, 近いうちに

He'll be here before long.
彼はまもなく、ここに来ます。

for long 長く, 長い間

You didn't stay there for long, did you?
長くはいなかったんでしょ?

in the long term 長い目で見ると, 長期的に見て

In the long term, the health risks could be serious.
長い目で見ると、健康に与える危険性は大きくなるだろう。

long time, no see お久しぶりです, ((*informal*)) 久しぶり(だね)

not any longer/no longer もう…ない

I don't want you to stay there any longer than is necessary.
用が済み次第、さっさと出て行ってもらいたい。

That is no longer my decision to make.
それはもう、私が決めることではない。

so long (good-bye) さよなら, じゃまた

so long as …さえすれば, …する限り

So long as he doesn't bother us, I don't mind.
じゃまさえしなければ、私はかまわない。

take (a) long (time) to do …するのに時間がかかる

You certainly took a long time to wash your hair.
髪を洗うのに本当に時間がかかったね。

long[2] *v.* (**long to do**) …したい, (speaking about sb else) …したがる, (long for) 待ちこがれる [→ WANT 1]

He longs to return home.
彼はしきりに家へ帰りたがっている。

The refugees are longing for peace.
難民たちは平和を待ちこがれている。

long-distance *adj.* 長距離の

make a long-distance phone call
長距離電話をする

longing *n.* (strong desire) 熱望, あこがれ

longitude *n.* 経度

long-range *adj.* (of missile) 長距離の, (of plan) 長期の

long-standing *adj.* 長く続いた, 長年の

a long-standing argument 長年の議論

long-term *adj.* 長期にわたる, (of loan) 長期-

long-time *adj.* 長年の, 昔からの

a long-time friend 長年の友達

long wave *n.* 長波

long-winded *adj.* 長ったらしい

a long-winded speech
長ったらしいスピーチ

---

look

1 *v.* USE VISION: 見る, ((*honorific*)) ご覧になる, ((*humble*)) 拝見する, (stare) 見つめる, (observe) 観察する

2 *n.* EXPRESSION: (in eyes) 目つき, (on face) 顔(つき), 表情

3 *v.* SEARCH: (**look for**) 探す, 求める

4 *v.* APPEAR TO BE: …ように見える, <adj. stem /-ますstem> + そうだ, …らしい, …みたいだ

5 *n.* APPEARANCE: (**looks**) 外見, 様子, 見かけ, 見た目, (=face) ルックス, 顔, (=dress) 身なり

1 Would you look at this, please?
ちょっとこれを見てくださいませんか？

I'd like you to look at this.
君にこれを見てもらいたい。

Have you looked at the paper today?
今日の新聞を見ましたか？

I looked out the window and saw a rainbow.
窓の外を見ると、にじが出ていた。

I like looking at antiques.
骨董品を見るのが好きです。

2 What a look he gave me!
彼の目つきといったら！

a look of surprise 驚いた顔 [表情]

You should've seen the look on her face!
彼女の顔を見せたかったよ！

3 I've been looking all over for you.
あちこち探してたんだよ。

Are you looking for work?
お仕事をお探しですか？

The UN is looking for peaceful means to end the dispute.
国連は、紛争を終結させるための平和的手段を模索しています。

4 It looks like oil. 油のようですね。

He looked Korean.
その人は韓国人のように見えた。

It looks as if someone has been here before us.
私たちより前に、誰かここにいたようだ。

She looked pleased. うれしそうだった。

It looks like it may rain. 雨が降りそうだ。

It looks like they've already left.
もう出かけたらしい。

You don't look well.
具合がよくないみたいですね。

5 I don't like the looks of him.
彼の見た目がいやなの。

I didn't like the look of the place, so I left.
そこの様子が気味悪かったので、その場を後にした。

The man doesn't care about his looks.
その男の人は身なりにむとんちゃくだ。

by the looks of …の様子からすると

You've had a nasty shock by the looks of it.
その様子からすると、だいぶショックを受

けたみたいだね。

give sb a…look …に…視線を送る, …に…顔をする

He gave her a warm look.
彼は彼女にあたたかい視線を送った。

She gave me a dirty look.
彼女は私にいやな顔をした。

look oneself いつもと同じに見える

You don't look your usual self.
いつもの君じゃないみたいだ。

look one's age 年相応に見える

He's beginning to look his age.
彼は年相応に見えるようになってきた。

look one's best 一番すてきに見える

She looks her best in that pink dress.
彼女はあのピンクのドレスを着ている時が、一番すてきに見える。

Try to look your best tomorrow.
明日は最高の自分を見せられるよう、がんばってね。

Look here! (trying to get sb's attention) ほら, あのね

look sb in the eye/face …の目/顔をまともに見る

The teacher looked me straight in the eye.
先生は、私の目をまっすぐ見た。

Look out! 気をつけて, ((*masculine*)) 注意しろ

look well (appear healthy) 元気そうだ, 顔色がいい

You're looking well today.
今日は元気そうだね。

throw sb a…look …に…視線を投げかける

look after *v.* (care for) …の世話をする, …の面倒を見る

Thank you for looking after us during our stay here.
滞在中いろいろとお世話になり、ありがとうございました。

Could you look after the children while I go out for a moment?
ちょっと外に出ている間、子供たちの面倒を見ていてもらえますか?

look ahead *v.* (think about the future) 将来を考える, 先のことを考える

You need to look ahead and plan for three or four years from now.
3、4年先のことを考えて、計画を立てなくちゃ。

look around *v.* (oneself) …の周りを見る, (a place) 見て回る, (look around for) 捜し求める

look away *v.* 目をそらす, 視線をそらす

She looked away from him.
彼女は彼から目をそらした。

Don't look away when I'm talking to you!
話しかけている時は目をそらさないで!

look back *v.* (turn around to have a look) 振り返る, (look back on the past) 振り返る, 思い出す

When I look back, I really wonder how we managed to cope at all.
振り返ってみると、よく対処できたものだと、つくづく思います。

look down on *v.* (from high place) 見下ろす; (think poorly of) 軽蔑する, 見下す

The window looks down on a playing field.
窓から運動場が見下ろせる。

There's no need to look down on people

like that.
人をそんなふうに軽蔑することはないでしょう。

look for *v.* (try to find) 捜す, 求める

"What are you looking for?"
"My car keys."
「何を捜しているの？」
「車のキー」

I didn't find what I was looking for, but I did find out something interesting.
求めていたものは見つからなかったけど、代わりに面白いことを発見した。

The police are looking for you.
警察が君を捜している。

You're looking for trouble.
あなたは自分で災いを招いている。

look forward to *v.* 楽しみにする, 楽しみに待つ, 期待する

I'm looking forward to my new job.
新しい仕事が楽しみです。

I'm looking forward to meeting Mr. Tominaga.
富永さんにお会いするのを楽しみにしています。

I'm really looking forward to the holidays.
休暇が待ち遠しくてならない。

look in *v.* (dictionary) (辞書を) 引く, (mirror) (鏡を) 見る

look in on …の所にちょっと立ち寄る

look into *v.* (investigate) 調べる, 調査する, 検討する

They told us they were going to look into the matter.
先方は、その件を検討してみると言っていました。

look out for *v.* (be careful of) …に注意する, …に気をつける [→ LOOK AFTER]

look over *v.* (read) 読む, (read quickly) ざっと読む, …に目を通す, (check for errors) チェックする

look over one's shoulder 振り返って見る, 肩越しに見る

look through *v.* (papers) …に目を通す

I didn't have time to look through the file.
ファイルに、目を通す時間がなかった。

look up *v.* (look upward) 見上げる; (search for) 調べる, 探す, (in dictionary) (辞書で) 引く; (of business conditions: improve) 上向く [→ IMPROVE]

You could try looking it up in the library.
図書館で調べてみてはどうですか。

I looked the word up a dictionary.
その言葉を辞書で引きました。

look up to *v.* 尊敬する [→ RESPECT]

---

lookout *n.* (watchman) 見張り人, 監視人, (lookout tower/platform) 監視塔/台

be on the lookout for 監視している, (wanted item) 探している

loom[1] *v.* (tower overhead/in the distance) そびえ立つ, (come into view) ぼうっと/ぬっと現れる, (of threat) 迫る

♦**looming** ***adj.*** (of threat) 迫り来る

loom[2] *n.* (for weaving) はた織り機

loony *n.* (insane person) 頭のおかしい人, ((*informal*)) いかれた人

adj. ((*informal*)) いかれた

loop *n.* (in string etc.) 輪, ループ, (in road) 環状道路, (in air) 宙返り

v. (loop A around B) (AをBに) 巻き付ける

throw sb for a loop/be thrown for a loop びっくりさせる/びっくりする

loophole ***n.*** 抜け道, 抜け穴

loose ***adj.***

1 NOT TIGHT: ゆるい, (of clothes) ゆったりした, (of rope: not taut) ゆるんだ, たるんだ

2 NOT FIRMLY IN PLACE: ゆるんだ, ぐらぐらの

3 NOT GATHERED TOGETHER: ばらばらの

4 NOT STRICT: (of translation) 不正確な, ずさんな, (of thinking) いいかげんな, (of behavior) だらしない

5 OF GRAVEL/SOIL: ぼろぼろした, さらさらした

1 This knot has come loose again.
この結び目が、またほどけてきた。
I like loose clothes.
ゆったりした服が好きです。

2 a loose tooth ぐらぐらの歯
a loose screw ゆるんでいるねじ

3 a loose sheet of paper ばらの紙
loosc puzzle pieces
ばらばらのパズルピース
loose change 小銭

4 loose conduct だらしない行動

5 loose snow さらさらした雪

break loose (escape) 逃げる

let loose (animal) 放す, (scream) (叫び声を) 上げる/出す

on the loose 逃亡中で, 逃走して
An elephant is on the loose.
象が逃走している。

loose end ***n.*** (of rope) 結んでいない端; (unfinished matter) 未解決の問題, 未処理の事項
The meeting went smoothly. There were no loose ends.
会議はスムーズに進んだ。未解決に終わった事項は一つもなかった。

loosely ***adv.*** (not tightly) ゆるく, 軽く, (in a not-very-exact manner) おおざっぱに

loosen ***v.*** ゆるめる
I ate so much I had to loosen my belt.
あんまりたくさん食べたので、ベルトをゆるめなくてはならなかった。
I couldn't loosen the lid.
ふたをあけることができなかった。

♦ **loosen up** ***v.*** (become relaxed) くつろぐ, リラックスする, 気楽にする, (talk freely) くつろいで話す; (stretch muscles) 筋肉をほぐす
Loosen up a little, will you.
もっと気楽に構えたら?

loot ***v.*** (steal) 略奪する, 強奪する
n. (stolen goods) 略奪品

♦ **looter** ***n.*** 略奪者

looting ***n.*** 略奪, 強奪

lopsided ***adj.*** 偏った

lord ***n.*** (**the Lord**: God, Jesus Christ) 神; (aristocrat) 貴族, (feudal lord) 領主, (**Lord**: title used in the U.K.) -卿, (also **Lord**: member of the House of Lords) 上院議員
the Lord Mayor of London ロンドン市長
Lord Butler of Billingsgate
ビリングズゲイトのバトラー卿

Oh Lord!/Good Lord! ああ, おお, ((*feminine*)) あら

lorry ***n.*** (truck) トラック

lose ***v.*** (misplace) なくす, ((*formal*)) 紛失

する, (be deprived of) 失う, (life) (命を)落とす, (chance) 逃す; (fail to win: game, contest) (…に) 負ける, 敗れる

I think I've lost my purse.
バッグをなくしたみたいだわ。

They lost everything in the typhoon.
あの人たちは台風で何もかも失った。

He lost his eyesight.
彼は視力を失った/彼は失明した。

He lost a leg in the war.
その人は戦争で片足を失った。

He lost a lot of money gambling.
彼はギャンブルで大金をすった。

Mori lost his chance for promotion.
森さんは昇進の機会を逃した。

The Giants lost the game.
ジャイアンツは試合に負けた。

have nothing to lose 失うものは何もない

I've nothing to lose by saying what I believe.
思ったとおりのことを口にしたからといって、私が失うものは何もない。

lose contact with → CONTACT

lose oneself in …に夢中になる

I really lost myself in that book.
あの本に、すっかり夢中になった。

lose one's head → HEAD

lose patience with → PATIENCE

lose sight of → SIGHT

lose one's temper → TEMPER

lose one's way → WAY

lose weight 体重を減らす/が減る, やせる

I'd like to lose weight, but I just don't have the discipline.
体重を減らしたいのですが、どうにも意志が弱くて…。(lit.,"but my will is weak")

loser *n.* (of game, fight) 敗者, 負けたほう, (social loser) だめな人, 負け犬

a sore loser 負け惜しみの強い人

loss *n.*

1 LOSING OF STH/SB: 失うこと, (of pride) 喪失, (of belonging) 紛失

2 DAMAGE: 損, (material loss) 損害, (material/spiritual loss) 損失

3 FAILURE TO WIN: 負けること, 負け, 敗北

4 DECREASE: 減少, 低下

1 a loss of pride 自尊心の喪失

memory loss 記憶喪失

He never recovered from the loss of his son.
彼は息子を失った痛手から、決して立ち直ることはなかった。

2 It was a terrible loss. ひどい損害だった。

It was a loss that the company could ill afford.
会社がもちこたえられないほどの損失だった。

3 The team had five losses and no wins.
5戦全敗だった。

4 a loss of body heat 体温の低下

be at a loss (for) (…に)困る, 途方に暮れる

I was at a loss for an answer.
返事に困った。

I was at a loss for words.
言葉に窮した [詰まった]。

lost *adj.* なくした, 失われた, (not knowing surroundings and unable to find one's way) 道に迷った, (spiritually/psy-

chologically lost) 途方に暮れた, (of person: missing) 行方不明の
 a lost book なくした本
 a lost civilization 失われた文明
 He's a lost cause.
 ((*masculine*)) 見込みのない奴だ。
 I suddenly realized I was lost.
 突然、道に迷ったことに気づいた。
 a lost child 迷子
 I felt very lost after my father died.
 父に死なれた後、ずいぶん途方に暮れました。
 Five people are feared lost in the avalanche.
 なだれで5人が行方不明となっているようです。

be lost in (be absorbed in) …に没頭している, …にふけっている, …に夢中になっている
 I was lost in thought.
 物思いにふけっていた。

♦**lost and found** *n.* 遺失物取扱所, 遺失物係, 忘れ物取扱所

lost article *n.* 落とし物, ((*formal*)) 遺失物

lot *n.*

1 MUCH: (**a lot, lots**) たくさん, いっぱい
2 TO A GREAT DEGREE: (**a lot**) 大変, とても, ((*formal*)) 大いに, (frequently) よく
3 PLOT OF LAND: 土地, 敷地, 1区画
4 FATE: 運命, 宿命, 巡り合わせ

1 There are lots of people who would like to be movie stars.
 映画スターになりたいと思っている人は、たくさんいます。
 There're lots of things we still need to do.
 まだやらなきゃならないことが、いっぱいある。
 He made a lot of friends over the holidays.
 休暇中に、彼は友達をいっぱいつくった。
 What a lot of trouble he's giving you!
 ((*masculine*)) 全くあいつは、君に迷惑をかけっぱなしじゃないか!

2 I like that restaurant a lot.
 あのレストランがとても好きです。
 She does the work a lot better than you do.
 彼女は、君よりずっときちんと仕事をしている。
 Thanks a lot. どうもありがとう。
 Ishikawa goes to that bar a lot.
 石川さんは、よくそのバーに行く。

3 There were two vacant lots.
 空き地が2ヵ所あった。
 There was no parking lot.
 駐車場はなかった。

4 His lot was not a happy one.
 彼の運命は幸せなものではなかった。

draw lots くじを引く

lotion *n.* ローション, 化粧水

lottery *n.* 宝くじ
 win a lottery 宝くじに当たる

lotus *n.* (plant) ハス, 蓮, (flower) スイレン, 睡蓮, ハスの花

♦**lotus position** *n.* (in yoga) 蓮華座

lotus root *n.* (food) レンコン, 蓮根, ハス

loud *adj.* (of voice) 大きい, (noisy) やかましい, うるさい, 騒々しい; (of fashion) 派手な
 He has a very loud voice.
 彼は声がとても大きい。
 The music is too loud! Turn it down,

please!
音が大きすぎる! 音量を下げて!

♦ **loudly** *adv.* 大きな声で, 大声で

Don't laugh so loudly.
そんなに大きな声で笑わないで。

loudspeaker *n.* 拡声器, スピーカー

lounge *n.* (in hotel, airport) ロビー, ラウンジ

v. (laze about) ごろごろする, ぶらぶら過ごす

louse → LICE

lousy *adj.* (terrible) ひどい, (unskillful) 下手な, (**feel lousy**: feel ill) 気分が悪い

louver *n.* (window) よろい窓

lovable *adj.* 愛らしい, 愛すべき

love

1 *v.* ENJOY VERY MUCH: (…が) 大好きだ, (**would love to do**) …したい [→ LIKE[1] 2]

2 *n.* STRONG AFFECTION/ATTRACTION: 愛, 愛情, (romantic love) 恋愛, 恋, (a love of/for: a passion) 愛好, (attachment) 愛着

3 *v.* FEEL LOVE FOR: 愛する, (…が) 好きだ, (love romantically) (…に) 恋する

4 *n.* LOVER: 恋人

5 *n.* FORM OF ADDRESS: (**Love**) ねえ

6 *n.* IN LETTER: (**Love…**) Usually not translated into Japanese [→ DEAR 1]

1 I love opera. オペラが大好きです。

I love playing tennis.
テニスをするのが大好きです。

I'd love to join you for tea.
ぜひ、お茶をごいっしょさせてください。

2 Most of his songs are about love.
その人の歌はほとんど、愛を歌っている。

Their love for each other is strong.
二人は強い愛情で結ばれている。

first love 初恋

His love is his work.
彼の恋人は仕事なんです。

My love for the city only grew with time.
町に対する愛着は、時がたつにつれて強くなるばかりだ。

3 Do you love her?
彼女を愛しているの?

They've been married a long time and still love each other.
二人は結婚して長いが、いまだに愛し合っている。

"I love you."
"And I love you, too."
((*masculine*))「愛してる/好きだよ」
((*feminine*))「私も」

4 She is the love of my life.
彼女は生涯の恋人だ。

5 Love, what are you doing?
ねえ、何してるの?

be in love (with) (…に) 恋をしている

Are you in love with her?
彼女に恋をしてるの?

fall in love 恋に落ちる, (at first sight) 一目ぼれする

They fell in love at first sight.
二人は一目ぼれだった。

We fell in love and married.
私たちは恋愛結婚です。

give my love to …によろしく(お伝えください)

Give my love to your family.
ご家族のみなさんによろしくね。

make love セックスする, 愛し合う

love affair *n.* 不倫

have a love affair (with) (…と) 不倫する

lovely *adj.* すてきな, (beautiful) きれいな, (cute) かわいい, (enjoyable) 楽しい

You look lovely today.

((*masculine*)) 今日の君は、すてきだよ。

It was such a lovely dress, I just had to buy it.

あんまりかわいいワンピースだったから、買わずにはいられなかった。

What a lovely day!

なんていいお天気なんだろう!

We had a lovely time in Europe.

ヨーロッパで楽しい [すばらしい] 時を過ごしました。

lover *n.* 恋人, (extramarital) 愛人; (enthusiast) -好き

a dog lover 犬好き

loving *adj.* 愛情に満ちた

loving parents 愛情に満ちた両親

low *adj.* 低い, (of heat) 弱い, (of price) 安い, (of quality) 悪い, 粗悪な, (insufficient) 不足している, 少ない

adv. 低く

a low bridge 低い橋

a low table 低いテーブル

low clouds 低い雲

a low note 低音

a low mark/grade 低い [悪い] 点数

One picture was lower than the other.

１枚だけ、ほかの絵より低い位置に飾られていた。

The issue was low on the list of priorities.

その問題は優先順位が低かった。

The car is low on oil.

車のオイルが少なくなっている。

low blood pressure *n.* 低血圧

lowbrow *adj.* (of book) 低俗な, 俗悪な

lower *adj.* (situated below another) 下の方の, (in rank) 下級の

v. 下ろす, (price, blood pressure, temperature) 下げる, (height of sth) 低くする, (voice) 小さくする [→ DECREASE]

the lower lip 下唇

The file is in the lower drawer.

ファイルは下の方の引き出しにあります。

The cargo was lowered onto the ship.

積み荷が船に下ろされた。

Retailers lowered their prices.

小売業者たちが値下げをした。

The main task was to lower the patient's blood pressure.

一番の課題は、患者の血圧を下げることだった。

lowercase *adj.* 小文字の

lower class *n.* 下層階級

adj. (**lower-class**) 下層階級の

low-fat *adj.* 低脂肪の

a low-fat diet 低脂肪食

low-grade *adj.* (of poor quality) 質の悪い

lowland *n.* (**lowlands**) 低地

low-level *adj.* 低レベルの

loyal *adj.* 忠実な, 忠誠心の強い

be loyal to …に忠実だ

loyalty *n.* 忠誠心

show one's loyalty (to)

(…に) 忠誠心を示す

LP *n.* (record) ＬＰ(盤)

LSD *n.* ＬＳＤ

lubricant *n.* 潤滑油, ((*informal*)) 油, (sth to help things happen) 滑らかにするもの

lubricate *v.* (grease) (…に) 油をさす, (help things along) 滑らかにする

lucid *adj.* (easy to understand) わかりやすい, (of person: coherent) 正気の

luck *n.* 運, (good luck) 幸運, ((*informal*)) つき

It was bad luck.
不運だった/運が悪かった。

This time we're going to need a bit of luck.
今度ばかりは、ちょっぴりつきが欲しいな。

Good luck! がんばって, ((*formal*)) 幸運を祈ります

push one's luck 図に乗る, 調子に乗る

luckily *adv.* 幸い, 幸運にも, 運よく

lucky *adj.* 幸運な, 運がいい, ((*informal*)) ついている, ラッキーな

Kawamoto is a very lucky man.
川本さんは本当に幸運な人です。

He was lucky catching that fish.
あの魚を釣るなんて、彼は運がいいよ。

You are lucky to be alive!
生きているなんて運がよかったね!

Today is not my lucky day.
今日は、ついてないなあ。

I was lucky to get a seat on the express train.
急行で座れるなんて、ラッキーだった。

lucrative *adj.* もうかる

ludicrous *adj.* ばかげた, (stupid) 愚かな, (laughable) こっけいな

lug *v.* (pull) (ぐいと) 引く, (drag) 引きずる

The porter lugged the heavy baggage into the room.
ボーイが重い荷物を引きずって、部屋に運び込んだ。

luggage *n.* 荷物, (handheld, carry-on) 手荷物, (suitcase) スーツケース

Our luggage has been sent on to Athens.
私たちの荷物は、アテネに送られてしまった。

lukewarm *adj.* (of temperature) ぬるい; (of reception) 気のない, いいかげんな

lull *n.* (in storm) なぎ, 静けさ, (in activity, conversation) とぎれ

v. (put to sleep) 寝かしつける, (cause to feel relaxed) (…に) 安心させる

We were lulled into a false sense of security.
うまいこと安心させられてしまった。

the lull before the storm 嵐の前の静けさ

lullaby *n.* 子守歌

lumbago *n.* 腰痛

lumber *n.* 材木, 木材

luminous *adj.* 輝く, (glow-in-the-dark) 夜光の

lump *n.* (piece of sth) かたまり, (swelling) しこり, こぶ

a lump of earth 土くれ [土のかたまり]

have a lump in one's throat 胸がいっぱいになる

lump sum *n.* (of money) 一時金

♦**lump-sum payment** *n.* 一括払い

lumpy *adj.* かたまりの多い

lunar *adj.* 月の

lunatic *n.* (insane person) 狂人

adj. (of idea) ばかばかしい, ばかげた, ((*informal*)) いかれた

lunch *n.* 昼食, (お)昼ご飯, ランチ, ((*masculine/informal*)) 昼飯, (packed lunch) (お)弁当

Let's have lunch tomorrow.
明日、昼食をいっしょにしましょう。

Don't forget to take your lunch.
お弁当を(持って行くのを)忘れないで。

♦ **lunch break / hour** *n.* (お)昼休み, 昼食時間

lunch box *n.* (お)弁当箱

luncheon *n.* (lunch) 昼食, (light lunch) 軽食, (formal lunch) 昼食会

lunchroom *n.* (in school) 食堂, ランチルーム

lunchtime *n.* 昼食時間, ランチタイム

lung *n.* 肺

lurch *v.* (stagger) よろめく, (of ship) 急に傾く

lure *n.* (attraction) 魅力; (decoy for trap) おとり, (bait for fish) ルアー, 擬似餌
v. (lure into) (…に) 誘い込む

the lure of the big city 大都会の魅力

The hunter lured the fox into the cage.
狩人はキツネをおりの中へ誘い込んだ。

lurid *adj.* (of bright colors) けばけばしい; (horrible) 恐ろしい

lurk *v.* 潜む, (hide) 隠れる

I thought I saw someone lurking in the bushes.
茂みの中に、誰か隠れているのが見えたような気がした。

luscious *adj.* (delicious) おいしい, (of fruit: sweet and delicious) 甘くておいしい, (ripe) 熟した; (sexy) 官能的な, セクシーな

lush *adj.* (verdant) 青々と茂った; (luxurious) 豪華な, ぜいたくな

lust *n.* (sexual desire) 性欲, 肉欲, (greed) 強い欲望

♦ **lust after** *v.* (person) …に欲情する

luster *n.* (shininess) 光沢, つや, (of mineral) 輝き

Her hair had a beautiful luster.
彼女の髪には美しいつやがあった。

Gold has a luster. 金には輝きがある。

lute *n.* リュート, (Japanese lute) 琵琶

Luxembourg *n.* ルクセンブルク

luxurious *adj.* ぜいたくな, 豪華な

luxury *n.* (style) ぜいたく, (thing) ぜいたく品
adj. ぜいたくな, 豪華-

That's a luxury we can do without.
なくても済ませられるぜいたく品です。

luxury items ぜいたく品

a luxury liner 豪華客船

lyceum *n.* (public hall) 文化会館, ホール

lymph *n.* リンパ

♦ **lymph node** *n.* リンパ腺

lynch *v.* リンチで殺す

lynx *n.* オオヤマネコ

lyre *n.* 竪琴

lyric *n.* (line of song) 歌詞, (poem) 叙情詩
adj. (of poem) 叙情的な

lyrical *adj.* 叙情的な

L

M, m

MA *abbr.* (qualification) 文学修士の学位

ma'am *n.* (young woman) お嬢様, (older woman) 奥様, (customer) お客様

macaroni *n.* マカロニ

macaroni and cheese マカロニチーズ

macaw *n.* コンゴウインコ

machete *n.* なた, 刀

machine *n.* 機械, -機

start [stop] a machine
機械を動かす [止める]

Can you operate this machine?
この機械を操作できますか？

a vending machine 自動販売機

a fare-adjustment machine 運賃精算機

♦ **machine gun** *n.* 機関銃

machine translation *n.* 自動翻訳

machinery *n.* 機械類

macho *adj.* 男っぽい, マッチョな

mackerel *n.* サバ, 鯖

macro- *pref.* マクロ-, (large) 大-, 巨大-, (long) 長-

macroeconomics マクロ経済学

macrobiotics マクロビオティック(ス)

mad *adj.* (angry) 怒った, (insane) 気の狂った, 狂気の

Don't be mad at me. 私に怒らないで。

My dad got very mad at me for scratching the car.
((*masculine*)) 車に傷をつけたことで、おやじは激怒した。

The king went mad. 王様は発狂した。

It's enough to drive you mad the way he keeps going on about his mother.
あの人がああやって母親のことばかりしゃべりまくるのでは、頭にくるのも無理はない。

like mad 狂ったように, 猛烈に

study like mad 猛勉強する

mad cow disease *n.* 狂牛病

madly *adv.* (in love) 熱烈に

be madly in love 熱烈な恋をしている

madman *n.* 狂人

madness *n.* (insanity) 狂気, (crazy behavior) 狂気の沙汰

maestro *n.* (of music) 大音楽家

Mafia *n.* マフィア

magazine *n.* 雑誌

a weekly [monthly, quarterly] magazine
週刊 [月刊, 季刊] 誌

a fashion magazine ファッション雑誌

Do you get the magazine every week?
毎週その雑誌を取ってるの？

magenta *n.* (color) 深紅色

maggot *n.* ウジ(虫)

magic *n.* (supernatural force) 魔法, 魔術, (art of creating illusions) 手品, マジック; (charm) 不思議な魅力

adj. 魔法の, (mysterious) 不思議な

Do you believe in magic?
魔法を信じますか？

It was like magic. 魔法のようだった。

As if by magic, the rain stopped.
(まるで)魔法のように、雨が上がった。

do magic 手品をやる

the magic of music 音楽の不思議な魅力

a magic hat 魔法の帽子

magical *adj.* (mysterious) 不思議な, (wonderful) すばらしい, 魅惑的な

magician *n.* 手品師, マジシャン

magistrate *n.* (government official) 行政官, (judge) 治安判事

magma *n.* マグマ

magnesia *n.* 酸化マグネシウム

magnesium *n.* マグネシウム

magnet *n.* 磁石

Magnets attract iron.
磁石は鉄を引き寄せる。

magnetic *adj.* 磁力の, 磁気の; (of personality) 魅力のある

♦ **magnetic field** *n.* 磁場, 磁界

magnetic tape *n.* 磁気テープ

magnetism *n.* 磁力, (of personality) 魅力

magnetize *v.* 磁化する

magnificent *adj.* (of size) 壮大な, (wonderful) すばらしい, 立派な

It was a magnificent performance.
すばらしい演技だった。

magnify *v.* 拡大する

♦ **magnifying glass** *n.* 拡大鏡, 虫めがね

magnitude *n.* (of earthquake) マグニチュード; (importance) 重要性, (immensity) 壮大さ

What was the magnitude of the quake?
地震のマグニチュードは、どのくらいだったの？

magnolia *n.* モクレン, 木蓮

magpie *n.* カササギ

mahjong *n.* マージャン, 麻雀

mahogany *n.* (tree) マホガニー, (wood) マホガニー材, (color) 赤褐色

maid *n.* お手伝い(さん), メイド

maiden *n.* 少女, (virgin) 処女

adj. (first) 初めての

a maiden voyage 処女航海

♦ **maiden name** *n.* 結婚前の名前, 旧姓

mail

1 *n.* ITEMS TO BE DELIVERED: 郵便物, (e-mail) メール

2 *n.* SYSTEM OF DELIVERY: 郵便

3 *v.* SEND BY POST: 送る, 郵送する, (a letter) (手紙を) 出す, 投函する

1 deliver mail 郵便物を配達する

get/receive mail 郵便物を受け取る

a mail delivery 郵便配達

Should we forward the mail to the previous occupier?
前の住人に郵便物を転送しますか？

2 express mail 速達郵便

registered mail 書留郵便

airmail 航空便

surface mail 船便

3 mail a package 小包を送る

♦ **mail order** *n.* 通信販売, 通販

mailbox *n.* (for collection) ポスト, (for delivery) 郵便受け, メールボックス [→ picture of HOUSE], (for e-mail) メールボックス

mail carrier *n.* 郵便屋(さん)

mailman *n.* 郵便屋(さん)

main *adj.* (chief) 主な, 主要な, 中心的な

n. (pipe) 本管

the main reason 主な理由

a main road 幹線道路

the main post office 中央郵便局

the main gate 正門

The company's main business is manufacturing software.

その会社の中心的な事業は、ソフトウェアの製造です。

The main thing is to be careful.
重要なことは、注意深くすることです。

a sewer main 下水本管

The water mains burst.
水道管が破裂した。

KANJI BRIDGE

本 ON: ほん KUN: もと | BOOK; MAIN

headquarters	本部
main building	本館
main issue	本題
mainland	本土
main office	本社
main purpose	本旨
main store	本店
mainstream	本流
main street	本通り
main text	本文

mainframe ***n.*** (computer) 汎用コンピューター

mainland ***n.*** 本土

mainly ***adv.*** 主に, ((*formal*)) 主として

mainstay ***n.*** 支え

mainstream ***adj.*** 主流の, 本流の
n. 主流, 本流

maintain ***v.*** 維持する, (building, machine) 管理する, (appearances, health) 保つ, (family) 養う, (belief) 主張する, 言い張る

It costs a lot to maintain a yacht.
ヨットを維持するには、多額の費用がかかります。

He earns just enough to maintain a reasonable standard of living.
彼の収入はごく普通の暮らしが、ちょうどできる程度です。

He maintains he's innocent.
男性は無実を主張している。

maintenance ***n.*** (of car) 整備, (of building, machine) メンテナンス, 管理, (of peace) 維持, (of safety) 管理

The car needs maintenance.
その車は整備が必要だ。

♦ **maintenance fee** ***n.*** 管理費

maize ***n.*** トウモロコシ

majestic ***adj.*** 堂々とした, 威厳のある

majesty ***n.*** (magnificence) 威厳, (**Your/His/Her Majesty**) 陛下

Her Majesty the Queen [Empress]
女王 [皇后] 陛下

His Majesty the King [Emperor]
国王 [天皇] 陛下

major

1 ***adj.*** RELATIVELY GREATER: 大きい, (important) 重要な, (main) 主な, 主要な, (substantial) 大幅な, (**a major part of**) …の大部分, …の大半

2 ***n.*** MAIN SUBJECT OF STUDY: 専攻

3 ***v.*** TAKE A DEGREE IN: (**major in**) 専攻する

4 ***n.*** MILITARY RANK: (in U.S. Army/Air Force/Marine Corps) 少佐

5 ***n., adj.*** IN MUSIC: (key) 長調(の)

1 a major improvement 大きな進歩

a major (natural) catastrophe 大災害

a major cause of …の主な原因

a major reason for …の主な理由

a major concession 大幅な譲歩

A major portion of the work has been finished.
仕事の大半は終わった。

2 Shinya's major is engineering.
慎也の専攻は工学です。

3 She is majoring in economics.
彼女は経済(学)を専攻している。

4 Major Johnson ジョンソン少佐

5 a sonata in F major ヘ長調ソナタ

majorette *n.* (baton twirler) バトンガール

major general *n.* (in U.S. Army/Air Force/Marine Corps) 少将

majority *n.* 大多数, 大部分, (of votes) 過半数

The majority was in favor.
大多数の人は賛成した。

The bill passed by a narrow majority.
法案は過半数ぎりぎりで通過した。

get/win a majority 過半数を得る

♦ **majority leader** *n.* 多数党の院内総務

make

1 *v.* CREATE: 作る, (manufacture) 作る, 製造する, (movie) 制作する, (trouble, disturbance) 起こす, (noise, plans) 立てる, (time) つくる

2 *v.* CAUSE TO DO: (**make sb/sth do**) (…を/に) <causative form of verb>

3 *v.* CAUSE TO BE/BECOME: (…を) …にする

4 *v.* EARN: (money) 稼ぐ, もうける, (profit) 得る

5 *v.* PREPARE: 用意する, (bed) 整える

6 *v.* AMOUNT TO: …になる

7 *v.* COMPOSE: (**be made of/from**) …で/から作られている, …で/からできている

8 *v.* SUCCEED: (**make it**) うまくいく, 成功する, (**make it through**: bad experience) うまく切り抜ける, (= survive) 生き延びる

9 *v.* BE ABLE TO ATTEND: (**make it**) 行ける, (**make it in time**) 間に合う

10 *n.* BRAND: メーカー, -製

1 make a model airplane
模型飛行機を作る

Can you make a paper crane?
折り鶴を<u>作れ</u> [折れ] ますか？

That company makes cars.
あの会社は車を製造している。

They made a movie about the disaster.
その災害を扱った映画が制作された。

He promised not to make any more trouble.
もうこれ以上、問題は起こさないと彼は約束した。

She made a great noise in the kitchen.
彼女は台所ですごい音を立てた。

Have you made plans for the summer?
夏の計画は立てた？

I need to make more time for studying.
勉強する時間を、もっとつくらなくてはいけない。

2 My mother made me go to bed early.
母は私を早く寝かせた。

He always makes me laugh.
彼は私をいつも笑わせる。

The teacher made him study harder.
先生はその子にもっと勉強させた。

Can't you make her understand that it's impossible?
無理だということを、彼女にわからせてくれないか？

The boy was made to stay after school.
その子は放課後、残された。

I was made to swear an oath.
私は誓約させられた。

3 She made him very happy.
彼女は彼をとても幸せにした。

They made him section chief.
彼を課長にした。

He made everyone angry.
彼はみんなを怒らせた。

Please make yourself comfortable.
どうぞ、くつろいでください。

I couldn't make myself heard above the noise.
騒音で、声が相手に届かなかった。

4 She makes a lot of money.
彼女はかなり[大金を]稼いでいる。

They make more in a day than I do in a month.
彼らは1日で私の1ヵ月分以上を稼ぐ。

The company made a huge profit this year.
会社は今年、巨額の利益を得た。

5 I made a quick dinner before leaving for work.
仕事に行く前に、手早く夕飯を作った。

Make the bed, will you. ベッドを整えて。

Shall I make some coffee?
コーヒーを入れましょうか？

6 Two and two makes four.
2足す2は4。

That'll make a good birthday present.
いい誕生日プレゼントになるだろう。

I doubt he would make a good husband.
彼がいいだんなさんになるかどうか疑わしい。

7 What is it made of?
(それは)何でできているの？

Plastic is made from petroleum.
プラスチックは石油から作られています。

This vase is made of bamboo.
この花びんは竹製です。

8 We made it! やった！/うまくいった！

I'm surprised he made it down from the mountain alive.
あの人が山から生還できたとは驚きだ。

9 I didn't make it to the wedding.
残念ながら結婚式に行けなかった。

Did you make it home in time for dinner?
晩ご飯に間に合った？

10 What make is the car?
その車はどこの製品ですか？

Is it a foreign make? 外国製ですか？

make believe (pretend) …のふりをする, (play make-believe) …ごっこをする

Let's make believe we're dead.
死んだふりをしよう。

Let's make believe we're cowboys.
カウボーイごっこをしよう。

make do (with) (…で)間に合わせる, 済ませる, やっていく

We'll have to make do with what we've got.
あるもので間に合わせるしかない。

We'll have to make do with $10 a day.
1日10ドルで済ませなくてはならない。

make into *v.* (make A into B) (AをBに)する, 変える

The book was made into a film.
その本は映画になった[映画化された]。

make of *v.* (interpret) 解釈する, 考える

What do you make of his story?
彼の話をどう考えますか？

make out *v.*

1 MANAGE TO SEE / HEAR: (see) 見える, (hear) 聞こえる

2 UNDERSTAND: わかる, 知る

3 CAUSE TO BELIEVE: See examples below

4 KISS AND TOUCH: いちゃつく, 愛撫し合う

5 WRITE: 書く

6 GET ALONG: うまくいく, やっていく

1 I could just make out Mt. Fuji in the distance.
遠くに富士山がかすかに見えた。

I could see his lips moving, but I couldn't make out what he was saying.
彼の唇が動いているのは見えたけど、何を言っているのか聞こえなかった。

2 As far as I can make out, the police are doing nothing.
私が知る限りでは、警察は全く何もしていない。

I can't make him out.
あの人のことは、わかりません。

3 The movie wasn't as good as everyone made it out to be.
その映画は皆が言うほどよくなかった。

Suzuki tried to make out that it was my fault.
鈴木さんは私のせいにしようとした。

4 There was a couple making out by the edge of the river.
川べりで一組の男女がいちゃついていた。

5 You can either make out a check, or pay by credit card.
小切手でも、クレジットカードでもいいですよ。

6 How're you making out with your new job?
新しい仕事は順調にいっているの？

make up *v.*

1 RESOLVE A QUARREL: 仲直りする

2 FABRICATE: (story) でっち上げる

3 APPLY MAKEUP TO: (…に) 化粧する

4 DO AT A LATER DATE: (**make up an exam**) 試験を受け直す, 追試を受ける

5 COMPENSATE: (**make it up to**) …に埋め合わせをする, …に償う [→ MAKE UP FOR]

6 CONSTITUTE: (**be made up of**) …から成る, …からできている

1 They argued and then made up.
二人はけんかをして、そして仲直りした。

2 She made up the whole story.
すべては彼女がでっち上げた話だった。

3 She made up her face with dark red lipstick.
彼女は濃い赤の口紅をつけて化粧をしていた。

4 I was able to make up the exam.
追試を受けることができた。

5 I'll make it up to you—I promise!
この埋め合わせはします——約束します!

6 Soil is made up of minerals and organic matter.
土はミネラルと有機物からできている。

make up one's mind 決心する, 決断する

You'd better make up your mind soon.
すぐに決断したほうがいい。

make up for *v.* (compensate for) …の埋め合わせをする, 補う

We made up for it by cleaning the house.
その埋め合わせに、家を掃除しました。

make up for lost time 遅れを取り戻す

M

make-believe *n., adj.* (imagining) 空想(の), (pretending) 偽り(の) [→ MAKE BELIEVE]

a make-believe world 空想の世界

maker *n.* (manufacturer) メーカー, 製造業者, (**the Maker**: God) 神

makeshift *adj.* 間に合わせの, 一時しのぎの, (temporary) 仮の

makeup *n.* (cosmetics) 化粧, メーキャップ, (cosmetic goods) 化粧品

making *n.* 作ること, (creating) 製作, (manufacturing) 製造

be in the making (being manufactured) 製作中だ

The new model is in the making.
ニューモデルは現在、製作中です。

have the makings of …になる素質がある

That student has the makings of a good business leader.
あの学生には優秀なビジネスリーダーになる素質がある。

maladjusted *adj.* (of person) (環境に)不適応の

malaria *n.* マラリア

Malaysia *n.* マレーシア

male *n.* 男, 男性, 男の人, (boy) 男子, (animal) おす

adj. 男の, 男性の, (of animal) おすの

She's popular among the male students.
彼女は男子生徒の間で人気がある。

a male chicken (= a rooster) おん鳥

malfunction *n.* 不調

v. 正常に機能しなくなる

malice *n.* 悪意, 恨み

out of malice 悪意で

malicious *adj.* 悪意のある, 意地の悪い

malign *v.* 中傷する

adj. 悪い, 有害な

malignant *adj.* (of tumor) 悪性の

a malignant tumor 悪性腫瘍

mall *n.* モール, ショッピングセンター

mallard *n.* マガモ, 真鴨

mallet *n.* (tool) 木づち, (used in sport) マレット

malnutrition *n.* 栄養失調

malpractice *n.* (medical) 医療過誤, 医療ミス

malt *n.* 麦芽, モルト

♦ **malt whiskey** *n.* モルトウイスキー

maltreat *v.* (abuse) 虐待する

mama *n.* ママ, (お)母ちゃん

mammal *n.* 哺乳動物

mammary *adj.* 乳房の

mammary glands 乳腺

mammoth *n.* (extinct elephant) マンモス

adj. (huge) 巨大な, ((*informal*)) でかい

man *n.*

1 ADULT MALE: 男, 男性, 男の人

2 HUMAN BEING: 人, 人間

3 WORKER: 従業員, 職員

4 SOLDIER: (**men**) 兵士

1 That man standing by the window is Kyoko's husband.
窓のそばに立っている男性 [男の人] は、京子さんのだんなさんです。

He's not a boy anymore. He's a man.
彼はもう子供じゃない。おとなたんだ。

Be a man!
((*masculine*)) 男らしくしろ / ((*feminine*))

男らしくしなさいよ!

2 a man from the Stone Age
石器時代の人間

All men are born equal.
人間はみな生まれながらにして平等です。

No man could live there.
あそこに住める人なんていない。

Tom is the man for the job.
トムはその仕事に適任だ。

3 The men aren't happy about their pay.
従業員たちは給料に満足していない。

the man from the telephone company
電話会社の人

4 Thousands of men were lost in battle.
何千人もの兵士の命が戦闘で奪われた。

be one's own man/woman (be independent) 人の干渉を受けない, (be free to act) 自由にできる

Kato is his own man. He doesn't need everyone's advice.
加藤さんは誰の干渉も受けない人だ。周りの忠告は必要としていない。

manage *v.*

1 DIRECT: (business) 経営する, (person, team) 監督する, (project) 指揮する, (be in charge of) 担当する

2 SUCCEED IN DOING: (**manage to do**) なんとか…する, どうにか…する, ((*ironic*)) 愚かにも…する, 結局…する, (**can't manage to do**) とても…できない

3 COPE: どうにかする

1 Mr. Suzuki manages his own company.
鈴木さんは自分の会社を経営している。

She managed a successful business.
彼女は順調な事業をやっていた。

Mr. Yamazaki manages the production line.
山崎さんは生産ラインを担当している。

2 She managed to become a lawyer.
彼女はどうにか弁護士になることができた。

He managed to alienate the entire staff.
結局、彼はスタッフ全員と仲たがいしてしまった。

I just can't manage to finish, what with all the noise going on.
あんまり騒がしくて、とても終わらせられない。

3 Can you manage on your own?
一人でどうにかできますか?

They manage to live on very little money.
彼らは、ほんのわずかなお金でなんとか暮らしている。

♦ **manageable** *adj.* (of task) 処理しやすい, (of person) 従順な

management *n.* (administration) 管理, 経営, (group of directors) 経営陣; (handling of things) 取り扱い, 処理

stress management ストレス管理

poor management まずい経営

upper management (of a company) (会社の)上層部

manager *n.* (of business) 経営者, (of hotel) 支配人, (of athlete, team) 監督, (of singer, performer) マネージャー, (person in charge) 責任者

a general manager 総支配人

I'd like to speak to the manager.
支配人と話がしたい。

Who is the manager here?
ここの責任者は誰ですか?

managerial *adj.* 管理の, 経営の

managing *adj.* 経営の, 首脳の

a managing director 常務取締役

a managing editor 編集長

mandala *n.* 曼荼羅

Mandarin *n.* (Chinese) 標準中国語

mandarin *n.* (orange) マンダリン

mandate *n.* (order) 命令, 指令

mandatory *adj.* 義務的な, 強制的な

Attendance is mandatory.
必ず出席しなければなりません。

♦ **mandatory retirement age** *n.* 定年 [NOTE: Usually age sixty in Japan]

mandolin *n.* マンドリン

mane *n.* たてがみ

maneuver *n.* (strategic move) 策略, (of car/airplane) 巧みな運転/操縦, (military exercise) 軍事演習

v. (cause to move) 動かす, 運ぶ, (car) うまく運転する

Military maneuvers began last month.
軍事演習は先月始まった。

We maneuvered the table out into the corridor.
テーブルを廊下へうまく運び出した。

manga *n.* (Japanese comic) 漫画

a manga book 漫画本

manganese *n.* マンガン

mango *n.* マンゴー

mangrove *n.* マングローブ

manhandle *v.* (treat roughly) 乱暴に扱う

manhole *n.* マンホール

manhood *n.* (male identity) 男らしさ, (adulthood) 壮年期

mania *n.* (enthusiasm, craze) 熱狂, (psychological disorder) そう病

♦ **-mania** *suf.* (craze) -狂

maniac *n.* (madman) 狂人, (fanatic) マニア, おたく, -狂

a baseball maniac 野球狂

like a maniac 狂ったように

manic-depressive *adj.* そううつ(病)の

manicure *n.* マニキュア, 爪の手入れ

♦ **manicurist** *n.* マニキュア師

manifest *adj.* 明らかな, はっきりした

v. (express) 表す, (show) 見せる

manifest itself (in) (…で)現れる

manifestation *n.* 現れ

be the manifestation of …の現れだ

manifestly *adv.* 明らかに

manifesto *n.* マニフェスト, 宣言書

manifold *adj.* (numerous) 多数の, (various) いろいろな

manipulate *v.* (person) 操る, (information, machine) 操作する

manipulation *n.* (of person) 巧みに操ること

manipulative *adj.* 人を巧みに操る

She's very manipulative.
彼女は人を巧みに操る。

mankind *n.* 人類, 人間

manly *adj.* 男らしい

man-made *adj.* 人工の, 人造の

mannequin *n.* マネキン(人形)

manner *n.* (**manner of doing**) やり方, <-ます stem>+方, (**manners**: etiquette) 行儀, 礼儀, マナー, (demeanor) 態度

a manner of speaking
話し方 [話しぶり]

He has no manners.

あの人は行儀が悪い [礼儀を知らない]。

That boy has good manners.
あの子は(お)行儀がいい [礼儀正しい]。

It's bad manners to pick your teeth in public.
人前で歯をほじるのは行儀が悪いよ。

She always has a very standoffish manner.
彼女はいつも、よそよそしい態度をとる。

all manner of あらゆる種類の

mannerism *n.* 癖

manor *n.* (mansion built in Middle Ages) 館, 屋敷

manpower *n.* 人力, 人手

mansion *n.* 屋敷, 大邸宅, -邸

manslaughter *n.* (involuntary) 過失致死罪

mantelpiece *n.* マントルピース

mantis *n.* カマキリ

mantle *n.* (cloak) 外套, マント

mantra *n.* マントラ

manual *n.* (instruction manual) 取扱説明書, マニュアル; (manual-transmission car) マニュアルカー

adj. (requiring muscle) 肉体の, (requiring hands) 手でやる, (of controls) 手動の

manual labor 肉体労働

♦ **manually** *adv.* (by hand) 手で

manufacture *v.* (make) 製造する, 生産する, (make up: story) でっち上げる

n. 生産, 製造

The company manufactures electronic goods.
その会社は電気製品を製造しています。

manufacturer *n.* 製造業者, メーカー

manufacturing *adj.* 製造の

the manufacturing industry 製造業

manure *n.* 肥料, 肥やし [→ DUNG]

manuscript *n.* 原稿

many

1 *adj.* **NUMEROUS:** たくさんの, 多くの, 多数の, 数々の, (of people) 大勢の, (**too many**) 多すぎる, (**not many**) あまり…ない, (of people) あまり…いない

2 *pron.* **NUMEROUS PEOPLE / THINGS:** たくさん, 多くの人/物

1 Why did you buy so many apples?
どうしてそんなにたくさんリンゴを買ったの？

So many people want to live here.
とても多くの人がここに住みたがっている。

Not many people were dancing.
踊っている人はあまりいなかった。

There are too many students in the class.
クラスの人数が多すぎる。

2 I wouldn't have given him that many.
私なら彼に、あんなにたくさんあげなかった。

Many of my coworkers went home sick.
同僚が何人も、具合が悪くて帰宅した。

a great many 非常に多く(の), かなりたくさん(の)

A great many of the buildings were damaged.
非常に多くの建物が被害を受けた。

as many as (used before a number) …もの

There were as many as fifty people in the restaurant.
レストランには５０人もの人がいた。

M

You can eat as many as you like.
好きなだけ食べていいんですよ。

There aren't as many bottles of beer in the fridge as I thought.
冷蔵庫には思ってたほど、ビールが残っていない。

how many...? 何 + counter [→ p. 1168 about "Counters"]

How many eggs are there in the fridge?
冷蔵庫の中に卵は何個入ってる？

How many brothers and sisters do you have?
ごきょうだいは何人いらっしゃいますか？

map *n.* 地図

v. (create a map of) (...の) 地図を作る

draw a map 地図をかく

a road map 道路地図

a map of Japan 日本地図

Excuse me, could you tell me where I am on this map?
すみませんが、この地図で今どこにいるのか教えていただけませんか？

♦ **map out** *v.* (make detailed plans for) (...の) 詳しい計画を立てる

If you could map out the itinerary, it would help me to visualize the trip.
詳しい旅行計画を立ててくれれば、もっとあれこれ思い描けるんだけど。

maple *n.* (tree) カエデ, モミジ, 紅葉, (wood) カエデ材

♦ **maple syrup** *n.* メープルシロップ

mar *v.* 台なしにする

mar someone's image
(...の) イメージを台なしにする

marathon *n.* マラソン

run a marathon マラソンをする

a marathon runner
マラソンランナー [選手]

marble *n., adj.* 大理石(の)

marbles *n.* (game) ビー玉遊び, (small balls) ビー玉

March *n.* 3月, 三月

march *v.* (of soldiers, band) 行進する, (of protesters) デモ行進をする, (strut) 胸を張って歩く, 堂々と歩く

n. (military march) 行進, (protest, demonstration) デモ, (march of protesters) デモ行進, (journey) 行程, (musical composition) マーチ, 行進曲

The band marched past the palace.
楽隊が宮殿の前を行進して通り過ぎた。

He marched into the room.
彼が、つかつかと部屋に入って来た。

a march for peace 平和デモ

a long march 長い行程

a funeral march 葬送行進曲

marchioness *n.* 侯爵夫人

mare *n.* (female horse) めす馬

margarine *n.* マーガリン

margin *n.* (of page) 余白, (edge) 縁, 端, (extra amount) 余裕, (profit margin) もうけ, マージン, (difference) 差

a 3-cm margin 3センチの余白

allow for a margin of error
誤差を見込む

win by a large [small] margin
大差 [僅差] で勝つ

marginal *adj.* (of ability, existence) 最低限の, (of cost) ぎりぎりの, 限界-

marginalize *v.* 軽んじる, 隅に追いやる

marginally *adv.* (just a little) ほんの

ちょっと

be only marginally better than
…よりほんのちょっといい

marigold *n.* マリーゴールド, キンセンカ

marijuana *n.* マリファナ, 大麻

marina *n.* マリーナ

marinade *n.* マリネ, マリネード

marinate *v.* マリネに漬ける, マリネにする

marinate the meat overnight
肉を一晩マリネに漬ける

marine *n.* (soldier) 海兵隊員 [→ MARINE CORPS]

adj. (of the sea) 海の, 海洋の

The marines' presence only aggravated the mounting tension in the region.
海兵隊の駐留は、地域の緊張を高めただけだった。

marine life 海洋生物

a marine biologist 海洋生物学者

Marine Corps *n.* 海兵隊

marionette *n.* マリオネット, 操り人形

marital *adj.* 結婚の, 夫婦の

maritime *adj.* 海の, (of insurance) 海上の, (near the sea) 海岸近くの, 沿岸の

a maritime museum 海事 [海の] 博物館

a maritime city 臨海都市

marjoram *n.* マージョラム, マヨラナ

mark

1 *n.* SPOT: (stain) しみ, (dirty spot) 汚れ, (bruise, birthmark) あざ, (scratch) 傷, (trace) 跡, 痕跡

2 *n.* PRINTED/WRITTEN SYMBOL: 記号, -符, (check) チェックの印, (cross) ×印

3 *n.* SIGN: しるし

4 *n.* TARGET: 的

5 *n.* SCORE ON HOMEWORK/EXAM: 点, 成績 [→ GRADE 4]

6 *n.* LEVEL: 水準

7 *v.* CORRECT: (exam) 採点する [→GRADE 1]

8 *v.* INDICATE WITH A MARK: (…に)印をつける

9 *v.* SIGNIFY: 示す, 意味する

10 *v.* CELEBRATE: 記念する

11 *v.* LABEL: (**be marked as**) …というレッテルを貼られる

12 *v.* BECOME DIRTY: 汚れる, 汚くなる

1 There's a mark on your hand.
手にしみがついていますよ。

There were dirty marks on the window.
窓に汚れがついていた。

a black mark 汚点

a burn mark やけどの跡

Their shoes left marks all over the floor.
彼らの靴跡が床一面に残っていた。

the mark of Roman civilization
ローマ文明の痕跡

2 a punctuation mark 句読点

a question mark 疑問符

quotation marks 引用符

an exclamation mark 感嘆符

3 a mark of respect 敬意のしるし

the mark of a true artist
本物の芸術家のしるし

4 His comments were off the mark.
彼の発言は的外れだった。

5 She got a mark of 80 out of 100.
彼女は100点満点で80点を取った。

6 Inflation is over the 4% mark.
物価上昇率が4 % を上回っている。

7 The teachers are busy marking the ex-

ams.
先生たちは採点にかかりっきりだ。

8 This spot marks the starting point.
ここがスタート地点です。

Mark the fragile goods with a red pen.
割れやすい物に、赤ペンで印をつけてください。

9 His death marked the end of an era.
彼の死は一時代の終わりを意味した。

10 They marked the occasion with a celebration.
彼らは記念にお祝いをしました。

11 His actions marked him as a dangerous individual.
彼はその行動から、危険人物というレッテルを貼られた。

12 This carpet marks easily.
このじゅうたんは汚れがつきやすい。

hit the mark 的中する, (succeed) 成功する

make one's mark 名を上げる, 成功する

miss the mark 的を外す, (fail) 失敗する

mark down *v.* (price) 値下げする

mark off *v.* (indicate with a mark) …に印をつける

mark out *v.* (area) 区画する

mark out the boundaries 境界線を引く

mark up *v.* (raise the price of) 値上げする; (scribble on) …に落書きする, (manuscript) …に赤字を入れる

---

marked *adj.* (noticeable) 著しい, 目立った; (sought after) ねらわれている

a marked difference
著しい [目立った] 違い

a marked man 目をつけられている人

marker *n.* (pen) マジック [→ picture of STATIONERY]; (grader of exams) 採点者

market *n.* (marketplace) 市場, 市, マーケット, (business, trade) 市場; (buyers) 購買層

v. (sell) 売り出す, 売りに出す

a fish market 魚市場

the stock market 株式市場

an open [a closed] market
公開 [非公開] 市場

What's on the market?
何が売られているの？

A new model has just come on the market.
ニューモデル [新型] が発売された。

the automobile market 車の購買層

market a new product
新製品を売り出す [市場に出す]

♦ **marketable** *adj.* よく売れる

market research *n.* 市場調査

marketing *n.* マーケティング

marketplace *n.* 市場

marking *n.* (pattern) 模様, (spots) 斑点; (grading, scoring) 採点

marksman *n.* 射撃の名手

marlin *n.* マカジキ

marmalade *n.* マーマレード

marmoset *n.* キヌザル

marmot *n.* マーモット

maroon[1] *n.* (color) えび茶色, 栗色

maroon[2] *v.* (leave stranded) 置き去りにする

marquis *n.* 侯爵

marriage *n.* (matrimony) 結婚, 結婚生活, (ceremony) 結婚式

a happy [an unhappy] marriage
幸せな [不幸せな] 結婚

a love marriage 恋愛結婚

an arranged marriage (お)見合い結婚

Their marriage ran into difficulties.
二人の結婚生活が危機に陥った。

married ***adj.*** 結婚している, ((*formal*)) 既婚の

They are married.
二人は結婚しています。

They are going to get married.
彼らは結婚する予定です。

Is he married?
あの人は結婚しているの？

a married person 既婚者

marrow ***n.*** (bone marrow) 骨髄

marry ***v.*** (…と) 結婚する, (perform wedding ceremony for) (…の) 結婚式を行う

Christopher married Etsuko.
クリストファーは悦子と結婚した。

They married two years ago.
二人は2年前に結婚した。

She married him for his money.
あの人は、お金のために彼と結婚した。

Reverend Smith married the couple.
スミス牧師が結婚式を執り行った。

He married his daughters into rich families.
彼は娘たちを裕福な家庭に嫁がせた。

Mars ***n.*** 火星

marsh ***n.*** 沼地, 湿地

♦**marshy** ***adj.*** 沼地の, 沼のような

marshal ***n.*** (sheriff) 連邦保安官, (field marshal) 陸軍元帥, (fire marshal) 消防本部長

marshmallow ***n.*** マシュマロ

marsupial ***n.*** 有袋動物

mart ***n.*** 市場

marten ***n.*** テン

martial ***adj.*** (of army) 軍隊の, (soldier-like) 軍人らしい

martial art ***n.*** 武術, 武道

martial law ***n.*** 戒厳令

The country is under martial law.
国に戒厳令が敷かれている。

martin ***n.*** イワツバメ, 岩燕

martini ***n.*** マティーニ

martyr ***n.*** 殉教者

marvel ***n.*** (wonder) 驚き, ((*emphatic*)) 驚異

v. (…に) 驚く, 感嘆する

It's a marvel that you were able to persuade her.
彼女を説得できたなんて、驚きです。

Your pep talk did marvels.
あなたの激励がよく効いたんです。

The whale is one of the marvels of creation.
クジラは驚異の創造物の一つです。

We marveled at the team's performance.
チームの活躍ぶりには驚いた。

marvelous ***adj.*** すばらしい, みごとな, (of progress, ability) 驚異的な

It was a marvelous performance of *Hamlet*.
みごとな『ハムレット』だった。

Marxism ***n.*** マルクス主義

Marxist ***n.*** マルクス主義者

mascara ***n.*** マスカラ

mascot ***n.*** マスコット

masculine *adj.* 男らしい, 男性的な, 男っぽい

♦ **masculinity** *n.* 男らしさ

mash *v.* (crush to a pulp) すりつぶす
n. (for brewing) マッシュ, (for feeding livestock) 飼料

♦ **mashed potatoes** *n.* マッシュポテト

masher *n.* マッシャー, すりつぶし器

mask *n.* ((*also figurative*)) 仮面, (worn by robber) 覆面, (theatrical) お面, (surgical) マスク [→ picture of FIRST-AID KIT]
v. (hide) 隠す
put on a mask マスクをする
a gas mask 防毒 [ガス] マスク

masking tape *n.* 保護テープ

masochism *n.* マゾヒズム, 被虐性愛

masochist *n.* マゾヒスト

mason *n.* 石工, 石屋

masquerade *n.* (costume) 仮装, (party) 仮面舞踏会; (pretense) 見せかけ, ふり
v. (pretend to be) (...に) 見せかける, (...の) ふりをする, (dress up in costume) 仮装する

Mass *n.* (religious ceremony) ミサ
celebrate Mass ミサを(執り)行う

mass *n.* (lump) かたまり, (large amount) 大量, (of people) 大勢, (**the masses**) (一般)大衆, 庶民; (amount of matter) 質量
adj. (on a large scale) 大量の, 大規模な, (for the masses) 大衆の
a shapeless mass 形のないかたまり
a mass of waste material 大量の廃棄物
a mass of red hair ふさふさした赤毛
a mass of people 大勢の人
mass murder 大量殺人
mass culture 大衆文化

♦ **mass-produce** *v.* 大量生産する

mass production *n.* 大量生産

mass transit *n.* 大量輸送

massacre *n.* 大虐殺
v. 虐殺する, (utterly defeat) 完敗させる, (...に) 圧勝する
It was a massacre. The people had no chance against the army.
大虐殺だった。人々が軍隊に対抗する手立てはなかった。
We were massacred. The other team was far superior.
完敗した。相手チームのほうがずっと、うわてだった。

massage *n.* マッサージ, あんま
v. マッサージする, あんまする, もむ

masseur, masseuse *n.* マッサージ師

massive *adj.* (large and heavy) どっしりした, (huge) 巨大な, (of debts) 膨大な
They have a massive oak dining table.
彼らの家には、オーク材のどっしりしたダイニングテーブルがある。
The company tried to conceal its massive debts.
その会社は、膨大な負債を隠ぺいしようとした。

mass media *n.* マスメディア, マスコミ

mast *n.* (of ship) 帆柱, マスト

master

1 *n.* HEAD OF HOUSEHOLD: 主人, (addressing one's master) だんな(さん)

2 *n.* OWNER: 持ち主, (of pet) 飼い主

3 *n., adj.* ORIGINAL: オリジナル(の), マスター-

4 *n.* SKILLED PERSON: 名人, 達人, マスター

5 *v.* **LEARN THOROUGHLY:** 身につける, 習得する, マスターする

6 *v.* **CONTROL:** (emotion) 抑える

1 master and servant 主人と使用人
the master of the house 家の主人

2 The dog obeyed its master.
犬は飼い主に従った。

3 the master copy 原本
Do you have the master key?
マスターキーを持っていますか？

4 a chess master チェスの名人
a master of aikido 合気道の達人

5 He mastered Arabic.
彼はアラビア語を<u>習得</u> [マスター] した。

6 You should try to master your anger.
できるだけ怒りを抑えなさい。

♦ **master plan** *n.* 総合計画
master's degree *n.* 修士号

masterful *adj.* (of person) 堂々とした, (of technique) みごとな

mastermind *n.* 立案者, (of plot) 首謀者
v. 立案する, 指揮する

masterpiece *n.* 名作, (painting, ceramic art) 傑作

mastery *n.* (great knowledge) 熟練, 熟達, (control) 支配

masticate *v.* (chew) かむ

masturbate *v.* マスターベーションをする, オナニーする

masturbation *n.* マスターベーション, オナニー, 自慰

mat *n.* (on floor) マット, (by door) ドアマット, (tatami mat) 畳, (on table) テーブルマット
a four-and-a-half mat room
四畳半の部屋

matador *n.* マタドール, 闘牛士

match[1]

1 *n.* **CONTEST:** 試合, 競技, -戦

2 *v.* **HARMONIZE (WITH):** (…と/に) 合う, マッチする, (…と) 調和する

3 *v.* **EQUAL:** (…に) 匹敵する, (**not match**) (…に) かなわない

4 *v.* **PAIR:** (match A with B) (BとAを) 合わせる, 組み合わせる

1 a soccer match サッカーの試合
It's the big match of the season.
今シーズンの大一番だ。

2 The tie didn't match the shirt.
ネクタイがシャツに合っていなかった。

3 The local team can't match the professionals.
地元チームはプロには、かなわない。

be no match for …にかなわない, …に歯が立たない
They're no match for our team.
相手は私たちのチームには、しょせんかなわない。

match[2] *n.* (small stick for starting a fire) マッチ
He lit the fire with a match.
彼はマッチで火をつけた。
The match went out.
マッチの火が消えた。

matchbox *n.* マッチ箱

matching *adj.* (of same color/design) (お)そろいの

matchmaker *n.* (of marriage) (お) 仲人(さん)

mate *n.* (friend) 仲間, 友達; (animal) つがいの片方, (partner) 連れ合い, 相手

M

v. (of animals) 交尾する, つがいになる

He's a good mate. 彼はいい友達です。

Hikaru is looking for a marriage mate. 光は結婚相手を探している。

Some animals only mate in spring. 春にだけ交尾する動物もいる。

material *n.* (substance) 物質, (resource, ingredient) 材料, (cloth) 生地; (information) 情報, (**materials**: data) 資料, (material for novel/news) 題材

adj. (not spiritual) 物質的な

raw materials 原料 [原材料, 素材]

What's this material made of? この生地は何でできているのですか?

research materials 研究材料

teaching materials 教材

It's said that material desires are an obstacle to spiritual development. 物欲は精神の成長の妨げになると言われている。

materialism *n.* 物質主義, (philosophy) 唯物論

materialize *v.* (become reality) 実現する, 現実化する, (appear) 現れる

His plans never seem to materialize. 彼のめざすことは実現しそうにない。

maternal *adj.* 母の, (motherly) 母親らしい, (on mother's side) 母方の

maternity *n.* (motherhood) 母であること, 母性

adj. 出産の, 産-

a maternity dress マタニティードレス

maternity leave 出産休暇 [産休]

a maternity hospital 産院

She works in the maternity ward. 彼女は産科で働いている。

mathematical *adj.* 数学の, 数学的な

a mathematical probability 数学的確率

mathematician *n.* 数学者

mathematics *n.* 数学, (in elementary school) 算数

matinee *n.* マチネ, 昼興行

matricide *n.* 母親殺し

matriculate *v.* 大学に入学する

matriculation *n.* 大学入学

matrimony *n.* 結婚

matrix *n.* 基盤, (in math) 行列, マトリックス

matte *n.* (kind of finish) つや消し

matter

1 *n.* AFFAIR: こと, 物事, 問題

2 *n.* SUBSTANCE: 物質, 素材

3 *n.* TROUBLE: 問題

4 *v.* MAKE A DIFFERENCE: (be important) 重要だ, (**not matter**) かまわない, 問題ではない, (=be unrelated) 関係(が)ない

1 a personal matter 私事 [個人的なこと]

a matter of life and death 生死の問題

You'd better discuss the matter with your parents. その問題は、ご両親と話し合ったほうがいい。

To make matters worse, he arrived late. さらに悪いことに、彼は遅れてやって来た。

2 liquid matter 液体

solid matter 固体

organic matter 有機物

reading matter 読み物

printed matter 印刷物

3 I went to see if anything was the matter with the car.
車に問題がないか見に行った。

There's nothing the matter.
何でもありません。

Is there anything the matter?
どうかしましたか？

What's the matter with Emiko?
恵美子はどうしたの/恵美子に何があったの？

4 The only thing that matters to me is that you're happy.
私にとって重要なのは、あなたの幸せだけです。

It doesn't matter which road you take. It takes the same amount of time.
どちらの道を選んでも変わりません。かかる時間は同じです。

as a matter of fact 実は

As a matter of fact, we're getting married next week.
実は私たち来週、結婚するんです。

no matter how どんなに…ても/でも

No matter how clever you are, you can't do your best unless you make an effort.
どんなに賢くても、努力なしには力を発揮できない。

no matter what 何があっても

I'll be there, no matter what.
何があっても [起ころうと]、行きます。

mattress *n.* マットレス [→ FUTON]

mature *adj.* (of person) おとなっぽい, おとならしい, (of wine) 熟成した
v. (of person) おとなになる, 成熟する

She's quite mature for her age.
彼女は年齢のわりに、ずいぶんおとなっぽい [おとなびている]。

It is said that women mature more quickly than men.
女性は男性より早熟だと言われている。

maturity *n.* 成熟

reach maturity 成熟する

show maturity おとなびる

mauve *n., adj.* 藤色(の), 薄紫色(の)

maxim *n.* 格言, 金言

maximum *n.* (limit) 最大限
adj. (greatest) 最大(限)の, 最高の

at the maximum 最大で

a maximum of three years 最長3年

a maximum speed 最高速度 [最速]

a maximum height 最高の高さ

a maximum capacity 最大収容力

a maximum-security prison
最も警備の厳しい刑務所

May *n.* 5月, 五月

may *aux.*

1 INDICATING POSSIBILITY: …かもしれない

2 GIVING/ASKING PERMISSION: (**you may…**) …して(も)いい, ((*formal*)) …して(も)よろしい, (**may I…?**) …して(も)いいですか

3 FORBIDDING SB TO DO STH: (**you may not …**) …してはいけない

1 He may have left already.
彼は出かけたかもしれない。

She may not have seen him.
彼女は彼を見ていないかもしれない。

We may have to wait a long time.
長く待つことになるかもしれない。

"Are you going to take a vacation next week?"
"Yes, I may, if all goes well."
「来週、休暇を取りますか？」

「はい、すべてが順調にいけば取るかもしれません」

This may or may not be the case.
これが真相かどうかわからない。

You may think it's silly, but that's what I want to do.
ばかげていると思うかもしれないけど、そうしたい。

You may say it's not important, but I think it is.
それは重要ではないとあなたは言うかもしれないけど、私は重要だと思います。

They may not be here, but we still have to take their opinions into consideration.
この場にいなくても、彼らの意見は考慮しなくてはいけない。

2 "May I use your dictionary?"
"Yes, certainly."
「辞書を使ってもよろしいですか？」
「ええ、どうぞ」

3 You may not smoke in here.
ここで喫煙してはいけません/ここは禁煙です。

however/whatever ... one may do どんなに/何を…ても/でも

However hard you may try, there's no way you can win.
どんなにがんばっても君に勝ち目はない。

Whatever people may say, my mind is made up.
人が何と言おうと、私の気持ちは決まっている。

maybe *adv.* もしかすると/もしかしたら…かもしれない

Maybe he's responsible.
もしかすると彼は責任があるかもしれません。

Well, maybe you're right.
もしかするとあなたは正しいかもしれない。

Maybe I ought to speak to him.
私が彼に話すべきかもしれません。

Maybe she's not as deaf as you think.
もしかしたらその人は、あなたが思うほど耳が遠くないかもしれない。

May Day *n.* メーデー

mayhem *n.* (confusion) 大混乱

mayonnaise *n.* マヨネーズ

mayor *n.* (of city) 市長, (of Tokyo) 都知事, (of town) 町長, (of village) 村長

maze *n.* 迷路

me *pron.* 私, ((*masculine*)) 僕, (as direct object) 私を, (as indirect object) 私に [→ I]

It's me. 私です/((*masculine*)) 僕です。

Who, me? 私ですか？

Do you remember me?
私(のこと)を覚えていますか？

He asked her to call me.
彼は、私に電話するよう彼女に頼んだ。

He told me about it.
彼はそのことを(私に)話してくれた。

Give me that book, please.
その本を下さい。

Are you coming with me?
いっしょに来る？

They went without me.
彼らは私を置いて行ってしまった。

meager *adj.* (not enough) 不十分な, (of income) わずかな, (of diet) 粗末な

meal *n.* (occasion of eating) 食事, ご飯, ((*masculine/informal*)) 飯

cook a meal 食事[ご飯]を作る
prepare a meal 食事[ご飯]の用意をする
eat/have a meal 食事をする
We enjoyed our meal.
食事がおいしかった。
serve a meal 料理を出す
make a meal for oneself 自炊する
three meals a day 1日3食
a light meal 軽食

mean[1] *v.*

1 SIGNIFY: 意味する
2 INTEND TO SAY: 言う, 言おうとする
3 INTEND: (**mean to do/be**) …する/なるつもりだ, …しよう/なろうと思う
4 MATTER: (**mean a lot**) 重要だ, (**not mean a thing**) どうでもいい
5 DESTINED: (**be meant to be/become**) …になるよう生まれつく, …になる運命だ
6 ENTAIL: …ことになる, (**not mean that…**) …(という)わけではない

1 What does this word mean?
この言葉はどういう意味ですか？
What does *kokoro* mean?
「心」とは、どういう意味ですか？
Does this mean anything to you?
これは、あなたにとって何か意味がありますか？
I know now what it means to be really ill.
今なら、実際に病気になるということがどういうことなのか、よくわかる。
She knew it meant trouble.
彼女はそれが面倒だってことを知っていた。

2 I know the place you mean.
あなたの言ってる場所はわかります。
I thought you meant he'd gone.
彼が行ってしまったと言っているのかと思った。
I mean it! 本気ですよ。
What the boss meant was that we should work harder.
上司が言おうとしていたのは、私たちがもっと一生懸命働くべきだということだ。
It was meant as a joke.
冗談のつもりだった。

3 I meant to come, but I was just too busy.
行くつもりだったけれど、忙しすぎて行けなかった。
I'm sorry, I didn't mean to be rude.
すみません、失礼になるとは思わなかったんです。
It wasn't meant to be thrown away.
捨てられるはずじゃなかった。

4 Money meant a lot to them.
お金は彼らにとってとても重要だった。
She meant nothing to him.
彼にとって彼女はどうでもよかった。

5 He was meant to become a doctor.
彼は医者になる運命だった。
They were meant for each other.
二人はまさにお似合いだった。

6 My limited speaking ability in Japanese doesn't mean that I can't understand what's being said to me.
日本語を話す能力が乏しいからといって、言われていることがわからないわけではない。

mean[2] ***adj.*** (malicious) 意地悪い, (stingy) けちな
be mean to people 人に意地悪をする
It was mean of her to do that.
そんなことをするとは、彼女は意地が悪い。

mean³ *adj.* (average) 平均の, 中間の
n. (average) 平均 [→ MEANS]

meander *v.* (of river, road) 曲がりくねる, (wander) あてもなくさ迷う
The river meanders.
川は曲がりくねっている。

meaning *n.* (sense) 意味
The character 気 has many meanings.
「気」という字には、いろんな意味がある。
I don't know the meaning of this sentence.
この文の意味がわかりません。
What's the meaning of this?
これは一体どういう意味ですか？
What is the meaning of life?
人生の意味は何ですか？

meaningful *adj.* 意味のある, 有意義な

meaningless *adj.* 意味のない, 無意味な

means *n.* (way) 手段, 方法; (income) 収入, ((*formal*)) 資力
As far as he was concerned, entering politics was just a means to an end.
彼にとっては、政界に入ることは目的を果たすための手段に過ぎなかった。
They're not rich, but they live comfortably within their means.
彼らはお金持ちではないけれど、収入の範囲で快適に暮らしている。

by all means (please do) どうぞ, ぜひ, (certainly) きっと, 必ず
By all means come earlier.
ぜひ早めに来てください。
By all means I'll be there.
必ず行きます。

by means of …によって, …で
You can only get there by means of helicopter.
そこへはヘリコプターで行くしかない。

by no means 決して…ない
It's by no means a weak album.
決して悪いアルバムじゃない。

meantime *n., adv.* その間(に)
"Mom was talking to a neighbor."
"What were you doing in the meantime?"
「母さんは近所の人とおしゃべりしてた」
「その間、何をしてたの？」

meanwhile → MEANTIME

measles *n.* はしか

measure *n.* (instrument) メジャー, 物差し, (way of judging) 尺度, (action) 処置, 対策, 手段
v. (determine) 測る, 測定する, (have a measurement of) …ある; (evaluate) 判断する, 評価する
a tape measure 巻き尺
a measure of ability 能力を測る尺度
Measures were taken to prevent the same accident from occurring again.
同じような事故が二度と起きないように対策が講じられた。
Jane measured the room.
ジェーンは部屋の大きさを測った。
Distance is measured in kilometers.
距離はキロメートル単位で測定される。
The test accurately measures a range of abilities.
その試験は、さまざまな能力を正確に測定します。
The carpet measures three meters by two.
じゅうたんは幅3メートル、長さ2メートルある。
The results were measured against pre-

vious findings.
結果は過去の調査結果に照らして判断された。

♦**measuring cup** *n.* 計量カップ [→ picture of COOKING UTENSILS]

measuring spoon *n.* 計量スプーン [→ picture of COOKING UTENSILS]

measurement *n.* (**measurements**: dimensions) 寸法, (act of measuring) 測定; (one's **measurements**) 体のサイズ

meat *n.* 肉
fresh meat 新鮮な肉
raw meat 生肉
tender [tough] meat 軟らかい [硬い] 肉
grilled meat 焼肉
chopped [minced] meat 細切れ [ひき] 肉
cut [slice] meat
肉を切る [薄切りにする, スライスする]

mechanic *n.* 修理工, (auto mechanic) 自動車整備士

mechanical *adj.* 機械の, 機械的な
a mechanical failure 機械の故障

♦**mechanical pencil** *n.* シャー(プ)ペン [→ picture of STATIONERY]

mechanics *n.* (branch of physics) 力学, 機械学; (operation of machines) 操作

mechanism *n.* (workings) 仕組み, メカニズム, (device) 機械装置, (system) 体系

medal *n.* メダル

medalist *n.* メダリスト

medallion *n.* 大メダル

meddle *v.* 干渉する
meddle in other people's affairs
他人のことに干渉する

media *n.* (**the media**: the mass media) (マス)メディア, マスコミ, 報道機関 [→ MEDIUM]

median *n.* (point) 中央値, (line) 中線
adj. (middle) 中央の

♦**median strip** *n.* 中央分離帯

mediate *v.* 調停する, 仲裁する

♦**mediation** *n.* 調停, 仲裁

mediator *n.* 仲裁人, 調停者

medic *n.* (doctor) 医者, (student doctor) 医学生, (army doctor) 軍医

medical *adj.* (of medicine) 医学の, (of treatment) 医学的な, (of practice) 医療の
n. (physical examination) 身体検査
medical care 医療
medical equipment 医療機器
for medical reasons 健康上の理由で

♦**medical examination** *n.* 健康診断

medical record *n.* カルテ

medical school *n.* 医科大学, 医大

medication *n.* (medicine) 薬, ((*formal*)) 薬品, (treatment) 薬の投与, ((*formal*)) 薬物治療
be on medication 薬物治療を受けている

medicine *n.* (substance) 薬, (subject of study) 医学
take medicine 薬を飲む
prescribe medicine 薬を処方する
practice medicine 医者をする
study medicine 医学を学ぶ

medieval *adj.* 中世の, (old) 古風な, 古めかしい
a medieval castle 中世のお城 [古城]

mediocre *adj.* 平凡な, 並の

meditate *v.* (think deeply) 深く考える,

M

(sit silently and contemplate) 瞑想する

meditation *n.* (thinking deeply) 熟考, (sitting silently and contemplating) 瞑想

Mediterranean Sea *n.* 地中海

medium *adj.* (of size, length etc.) 中くらいの, (of meat) ミディアムの

n. (means of communication) 媒体; (person who claims to communicate with the dead) 霊媒

medium heat 中火

medium height 中背

the happy medium 中庸, 中道

medium-rare *adj.* ミディアムレアの

I like my steak medium-rare.
ステーキはミディアムレアが好きです。

medium-sized *adj.* 中型の, 中くらいの, (of clothing) Mサイズの

a medium-sized car 中型車

medium wave *n.* 中波

medley *n.* (mixture) 寄せ集め, (tune) メドレー

♦ **medley relay** *n.* メドレー(リレー)

meek *adj.* おとなしい, 従順な, 素直な

meet *v.*

1 ENCOUNTER: (by chance) (…に) 出会う, 出くわす, (by arrangement) (…に) 会う, (unexpectedly: boyfriend, girlfriend) (…に) 巡り会う

2 HOLD A MEETING: 会合をもつ, 集まる

3 CONVERGE: (of eyes) 合う, (of road, river: join with) (…と/に) 交わる, 合流する

4 SATISFY: (requirements) 満たす, (…に) 応じる

1 I happened to meet her on the train.
電車で偶然、彼女に出会った。

We met each other in college.
私たちは大学で出会った。

I've never met her before.
彼女とは会ったことがありません。

Could you meet me at the station at 6:30?
6時半に駅で待ち合わせしませんか？

Mr. Ota came to meet me.
太田さんが会いに来ました。

We plan to meet up later in the day.
あとで会う約束をしています。

Kaoru met me at the airport.
薫が空港で出迎えてくれた。

2 The department meets once a month.
その部は月に一度、会合をもっている。

3 Our eyes met. 目が合った。

where the river meets the sea
川が海に合流する [流れ込む] 所

4 It meets our needs.
私たちの要望を満たしている。

meet sb halfway → HALFWAY

meet with (sth undesirable) …に遭遇する

They met with difficulties.
彼らは困難に遭遇した。

meeting *n.* 会, (assembly of people) 会合, ((*informal*)) 集まり, (business meeting) 会議, (informal business meeting) 打ち合わせ, ミーティング

call [call off] a meeting
会を招集する [取りやめる]

at a meeting 会合 [会議] で

have a (formal business) meeting
会議を開く

postpone a (business) meeting
会議を延期する

a departmental/faculty meeting
教授会

a general meeting of stockholders
株主総会

megabyte *n.* メガバイト

megahertz *n.* メガヘルツ

megaphone *n.* メガホン, 拡声器

melancholy *n.* 憂うつ

adj. (depressed) 憂うつな, 気がめいる, (sad) もの悲しい

mellow *adj.* (of flavor) まろやかな, (of music, color) 柔らかい, (of person) 温厚な

v. (of wine) 熟成する, まろやかになる, (of person) 柔らかくなる, 丸くなる

melodrama *n.* メロドラマ, (melodramatic behavior) おおげさな行動

melodramatic *adj.* 芝居がかった, おおげさな

melody *n.* メロディー, 旋律, (song) 歌, 曲

melon *n.* メロン

melt *v.* (lose shape in heat) 溶ける, (cause to melt) 溶かす

Sugar melts in water.
砂糖は水に溶ける。

The snow melted. 雪が解けた。

melt butter in a pan
フライパンにバターを溶かす

member *n.* メンバー, (one of a group) 一員, (of club) 会員, (of committee) 委員, -員

adj. 加入/加盟している, 会員の

a member of Congress/the Diet
国会議員

member countries 加盟国

membership *n.* 会員であること

♦ **membership card** *n.* 会員証

membrane *n.* 膜, 皮膜

memento *n.* 記念品, (keepsake) 形見, 思い出の品

memo *n.* (note) メモ, 控え, 覚え書き

a memo pad メモ帳

memoir *n.* (**memoirs**) 回顧録, 回想録, (biography) 伝記

write one's memoirs 回想録を書く

memorable *adj.* 思い出に残る, (great) 重大な, (unforgettable) 忘れられない

memorandum *n.* 覚え書き

memorial *n.* (monument) 記念碑, (building) 記念館

adj. (of service) 追悼の

a memorial service 追悼式

Memorial Day *n.* 戦没者追悼記念日

memorize *v.* 覚える, 暗記する

memory *n.* 記憶, (mental capacity) 記憶力, ((*informal*)) 物覚え, (thing remembered) 思い出; (of computer) メモリー

have a good [bad] memory for dates
日付に関する記憶力がいい [悪い]

I did it from memory.
記憶を頼りにやった。

Racial segregation is still within living memory.
人種差別は、今でも人々の記憶に残っている。

childhood memories
子供のころの思い出

I have pleasant memories of that trip.
あの旅行には、楽しい思い出がある。

M

in memory of (the dead) …をしのんで

The plaque is in memory of those who died during the war.
この銘板は戦没者をしのんで作られたものです。

men → MAN

menace ***n.*** (threat) 脅威, (dangerous person) 危険な人
v. (…に) 脅威を与える, (…を) 脅かす
a menace to society 社会に対する脅威

mend ***v.*** (restore to good condition) 直す, 修理する, (clothes) 直す, つくろう, (ways) 改める; (of wounds: heal) 治る

Did you mend the chair?
椅子を修理しましたか？

I mended it with glue.
接着剤で直した。

How much will it cost to be mended?
修理にいくらかかりますか？

It's time he mended his ways.
そろそろ彼は行いを改めるべきだ。

be on the mend 快方に向かっている

meningitis ***n.*** 髄膜炎, 脳膜炎

menopause ***n.*** 更年期, 月経閉止期

men's room ***n.*** トイレ

menstruate ***v.*** 生理がある

menstruation ***n.*** 月経, 生理 [→ PERIOD 4]

menswear ***n.*** 紳士服

mental ***adj.*** 精神の, 精神的な, 心の, (of sth done in the head) 頭の中で行う
a mental effort 精神的な努力
a mental breakdown 神経衰弱
a mental illness 精神病
a mental patient 精神病患者
mental arithmetic 暗算
mental gymnastics 頭の体操

mentality ***n.*** (attitude) 考え方

mentally ***adv.*** 精神的に
the mentally disabled 知的障害者

menthol ***n.*** メンソール, メントール

mention ***v.*** (say) 言う, 口にする, (touch on) (…に) 触れる, ((*formal*)) 言及する

Please don't mention this to anyone.
このことは誰にも言わないでください。

He mentioned your name.
彼はあなたの名前を口にしたよ。

don't mention it (you're welcome) どういたしまして

mentor ***n.*** (former teacher) 恩師, (teacher) 教師, 先生, (counselor) 指導者

menu ***n.*** メニュー

mercantile ***adj.*** (commercial) 商業の, (merchant) 商人の

mercenary ***n.*** (soldier) 外国人傭兵
adj. (greedy) (お)金目当ての

merchandise ***n.*** 商品, 品物

merchandising ***n.*** 販売促進

merchant ***n.*** (trader) 業者, 貿易商, 商人
adj. 貿易の, (of merchant ship) 商船の
a wine merchant ワイン業者
a merchant ship 商船

merciful ***adj.*** 情け深い, 慈悲深い
be merciful on …に情け深い

mercifully ***adv.*** (fortunately) 幸いにも

merciless ***adj.*** 無慈悲な, (cruel) 残酷な

Mercury ***n.*** 水星

mercury ***n.*** 水銀, (in thermometer) 水銀柱

mercy ***n.*** (compassion) 情け, 哀れみ, 慈悲, (forgiveness) 容赦

They showed no mercy.
彼らは情けをかけなかった。

They mocked us without mercy.
彼らは情け容赦なく私たちをあざけった。

be at the mercy of …のなすがままになる, …になすすべがない

We were at the mercy of the elements.
暴風雨に、なすすべもなかった。

mere *adj.* ほんの, ただの…にすぎない, (used before a number) たったの…だけ

He's a mere boy.
彼はほんの子供です。

a mere ¥10 たった(の) 10円

merely *adv.* (**merely doing**) (単に)…しているだけ, (ただ)…しているだけ

I am merely telling you what you need to know.
あなたが知っておかなきゃいけないことを、伝えているだけです。

merge *v.* (become one) 一つになる, (of companies) 合併する

♦ **merger** *n.* 合併

meridian *n.* 子午線, 経線

the prime meridian 本初子午線

merit *n.* 利点, 長所, メリット

v. (…に) 値する

merits and demerits 長所と短所

The merit of the plan is its practicality.
この計画の利点はその実用性にあります。

She merits much praise for her work.
彼女の仕事は多くの賞賛を受けるに値する。

mermaid *n.* 人魚, マーメイド

merry *adj.* (of person) 明るい, 陽気な, (of party) 楽しい

Merry Christmas! クリスマスおめでとう, メリークリスマス

merry-go-round *n.* メリーゴーラウンド, 回転木馬

mesh *n.* (of wire) 網の目

v. (**mesh with**: get along with) …とうまく合う

---

mess *n.* (state of disarray) 混乱, ((*informal*)) めちゃくちゃ

The place was a mess.
そこは混乱していた。

I don't know how the room got into such a mess.
どうやって部屋がこんなに散らかったのかわからない。

Let's clean up the mess.
きれいに片付けましょう。

Don't make a mess of things, OK?
めちゃくちゃにしないでくれる?

mess around *v.* (**mess around with**: fiddle with: machine) いじる

Who's been messing around with my computer?
私のコンピューターをいじっていたのは誰?

mess up *v.* (make untidy) 散らかす, (make disorderly) ごちゃごちゃにする, (ruin) めちゃくちゃにする, (spoil) 台なしにする; (make a blunder) へまをする, 失敗する, ((*informal*)) ドジを踏む

---

message *n.* (spoken piece of news) 伝言, ことづけ, (letter, fax) メッセージ, (of book, film: moral) 訴え, ねらい, メッ

セージ

I'm afraid he's not in. Can I take a message?
申し訳ありませんがただ今、外出しております。伝言をお預りしましょうか？

I wonder if you could give him a message?
じゃあ、お伝えいただけますか？

The film's message was clear.
その映画のメッセージは、はっきりしていた。

messenger *n.* 使者, メッセンジャー

messy *adj.* (untidy) 散らかっている, ごちゃごちゃの, (dirty) 汚い

metabolism *n.* 新陳代謝

metal *n.* 金属

metallic *adj.* 金属の, (shiny like mental) 金属のような

metallurgy *n.* 冶金学

metaphor *n.* 隠喩, 暗喩, メタファー

metaphorical *adj.* 隠喩の, 比喩的な

metaphysical *adj.* (abstract) 抽象的な

metaphysics *n.* 形而上学

mete *v.* (**mete out**) 与える

mete out punishment 罰を与える

meteor *n.* 流星

meteorite *n.* 隕石

meteorologist *n.* 気象学者

meteorology *n.* 気象学

meter *n.* (measure of distance) メートル; (machine) メーター, 計(量)器

a building thirty meters tall
高さ30メートルの建物

a parking meter パーキングメーター

a gas meter ガスメーター

What does this meter read?
このメーターの数字は何になっていますか？

methadone *n.* メタドン

methane *n.* メタン

methanol *n.* メタノール, メチルアルコール

method *n.* (means) 方法, 手段, やり方, (system) 方式

There must be a method of solving this problem.
この問題を解く方法があるに違いない。

methodical *adj.* (systematic) 規則正しい, (of person) きちょうめんな

methodology *n.* 方法論

meticulous *adj.* 細心の, 注意深い

metric system *n.* メートル法

metronome *n.* メトロノーム

metropolis *n.* 大都市

metropolitan *adj.* (of capital city) 首都の, (of big city) 大都市の

the metropolitan area 首都 [大都市] 圏

Mexico *n.* メキシコ

mezzo-soprano *n.* メゾソプラノ

micro- *pref.* マイクロ-, 小-, 微-

microbe *n.* 微生物, (germ) 細菌, (cause of disease) 病原菌

microbiology *n.* 微生物学

microchip *n.* マイクロチップ

microcosm *n.* 小宇宙, 小世界

microfilm *n.* マイクロフィルム

micron *n.* ミクロン

microorganism *n.* 微生物

microphone *n.* マイク

microprocessor *n.* マイクロプロセッサー

microscope *n.* 顕微鏡

microscopic *adj.* (small) 非常に小さい

microwave *n.* (microwave oven) 電子レンジ [→ picture of KITCHEN]; (electromagnetic wave) マイクロ波

midair *n.* 空中

midday *n.* 正午, 真昼

middle *n.* (center) 真ん中, 中央, (of month) 中旬, 中ごろ, (of game, campaign) 中盤, (of activity) 最中; (waist) 腰

adj. (center) 真ん中の

in the middle of the town 街の真ん中で

in the middle of the night 真夜中に

Junichiro's the oldest, Saburo the youngest, and Jiro's in the middle.
純一郎が一番上で、三郎が一番下、次郎は真ん中です。

the middle of December
12月の中ごろ [中旬]

in the middle of dinner 夕食の最中に

You're getting fat around the middle.
腰回りに肉がついてきたね。

KANJI BRIDGE

中 ON: ちゅう KUN: なか | MID-, MIDDLE, MEDIUM

center	中心
center, middle	中央
central figure/character	中心人物
core	中核
medium heat (in cooking)	中火
middle age	中年
middle ear	中耳
middle finger	中指
midmonth	中旬
midpoint	中点

middle-aged *adj.* 中年の

a middle-aged man
中年男性 [((*informal*)) おじさん]

a middle-aged woman
中年女性 [((*informal*)) おばさん]

Middle Ages *n.* 中世

middle class *n.* 中産階級, 中流

adj. (**middle-class**) 中産階級の, 中流の

Middle East *n.* 中東, 中近東

middle finger *n.* 中指 [→ picture of HAND]

middleman *n.* 仲介人, ブローカー

middle name *n.* ミドルネーム

middle school *n.* 中学校

a middle school student 中学生

midlife *n.* 中年

a midlife crisis 中年の危機

midnight *n.* (12 o'clock) 夜の12時, 午前0時, (middle of the night) 真夜中

at midnight 午前0時に

before [after] midnight
夜の12時前 [過ぎ]

midriff *n.* 胴の中央

midshipman *n.* 海軍兵学校生徒

midst *n.* (**in the midst of**) …の中に/の

midway *adj.* 中ほどの, 中間の

adv. 中ほどに

the midway point 中間地点

midweek *n. adj.* 週の中ごろ(の)

midwife *n.* 助産婦, 産婆

miffed *adj.* むっとする, しゃくにさわる

might[1] *aux.*

1 INDICATING POSSIBILITY: …かもしれない, ((*formal*)) …可能性がある

2 MAKING A SUGGESTION: (**you might…**)

M

…したらいかがですか

3 ASKING PERMISSION: (might I…?) …してもいいですか, …してもよろしいでしょうか

1 I might go—I don't know yet.
行くかも──でも、まだわからない。

Akiko might go to Canada.
晶子はカナダへ行くかもしれない。

He might have said that. I can't remember.
彼はそう言ったのかもしれないが、よく覚えていない。

You might be wrong.
あなたが間違っているかもしれません。

The wound might be infected.
傷口にばい菌が入った可能性がある。

2 You might want to ask a doctor.
お医者さんに聞いたらいかがですか？

3 Might I have a look at your notes?
あなたのメモをちょっと見てもいいですか？

might as well do …したほうがよさそうだ

We've got nothing else to do, so we might as well go.
ほかにやることがないから、行ったほうがよさそうだ。

might² *n.* (strength) 力

the might of the U.S. アメリカの力

mighty *adj.* 強力な, 強い, (in size) 巨大な

The pen is mightier than the sword.
ペンは剣よりも強し。

migraine *n.* 偏頭痛

migrant *n.* (worker) 出稼ぎ労働者

adj. (of bird) 渡り鳥の

migrate *v.* (of people) 移住する, (of bird) 渡る

migration *n.* 移住

mild *adj.* (not extreme) 軽い, (of climate) 穏やかな, (of taste) 口当たりのいい, マイルドな, (of curry) 甘口の, (of character) おとなしい, 優しい, 素直な

It's a mild case of Parkinson's.
パーキンソン病の軽い症例だ。

The weather's been unusually mild for this time of the year.
この時期にしては珍しく気候が穏やかだ。

a mild curry 甘口カレー

mildew *n.* かび, 白かび

mildly *adv.* (not extremely) 少々, 少し, (gently) 穏やかに

put it mildly 控え目に言えば

mile *n.* マイル [about 1.6 km]

thirty miles per hour 時速 30 マイル

How many miles is it from Boston to New York?
ボストンからニューヨークまでは何マイルありますか？

go the extra mile 一層努力する, がんばる

Carol went the extra mile for us.
キャロルは私たちのために、かなりがんばってくれた。

mileage *n.* (distance traveled) 走行距離, (miles one has traveled by airplane) マイレージ, (of car: efficiency) 燃費

milestone *n.* (important event) 画期的な出来事

militant *adj.* (of person) 戦闘的な, 好戦的な, (of country) 軍国主義的な

n. (person) 闘士, 活動家

military ***n.*** 軍隊

adj. 軍の, 軍事の, (of land forces) 陸軍の

The military was called in to sort things out.

紛争解決のために軍隊が出動した。

military power 軍事力

a military band 軍楽隊 [軍の吹奏楽隊]

military service 兵役

a military academy 陸軍士官学校

milk ***n.*** (cow's) 牛乳, ミルク, (other animal's) (お)乳, (mother's) 母乳

v. (obtain milk from) …の乳を搾る; (exploit) 搾取する

a glass of milk コップ1杯の牛乳 [ミルク]

coconut milk ココナッツミルク

powder milk 粉ミルク

♦**milk shake** ***n.*** ミルクシェイク

milky ***adj.*** 牛乳のような

mill ***n.*** (building for crushing grain) 製粉所, (grinder) 粉ひき器, ミル, (factory) 工場

a coffee mill コーヒーミル

millennium ***n.*** 千年間, ミレニアム

millet ***n.*** キビ

milligram ***n.*** ミリグラム, ミリ

milliliter ***n.*** ミリリットル

millimeter ***n.*** ミリメートル, ミリ

milliner ***n.*** 帽子屋(さん)

million ***n.*** 100万, (**millions**) 何百万, 多数, 無数

adj. 100万の, (many) 多くの, 無数の

a one-in-a-million chance

万に一つの可能性

What would you do if you won a million dollars?

もし100万ドル手に入ったら、何をする?

millionaire ***n.*** 億万長者, (very rich person) 大金持ち

millipede ***n.*** ヤスデ

millstone ***n.*** (burden) 重荷

mime ***n.*** (performer) パントマイム役者

v. (act using only gestures) パントマイムで演じる

mimic ***v.*** (…の)まねをする, (…を)まねる

mince ***v.*** 細かく切る, (meat) ひく, ひき肉にする, ミンチにする

minced beef 牛(の)ひき肉

mincemeat ***n.*** ミンスミート

make mincemeat (out) of こてんぱんにやっつける

mind

1 ***n.*** **THING THAT THINKS/FEELS:** 心, 精神, (intellect) 知性, 頭, (sanity) 正気; (thought, opinion) 考え, (mentality) 考え方, (intention) 意向, 気, 気持ち

2 ***v.*** **OBJECT:** かまう, 気にする, (asking a favor of sb: **would you mind doing …?**) …していただけませんか, (**do you mind if I…?**) …してもかまいませんか

3 ***v.*** **PAY ATTENTION TO:** (…に) 注意する, 気をつける

4 ***n.*** **INTELLIGENT PERSON:** 知識人

1 an open mind 広い心

Who's to say what makes the human mind tick?

何が人の心を動かすかなんて、誰にわかる?

In my mind, I imagine the place must be beautiful.

頭の中で、そこは美しい所に違いないと想像しています。

M

He keeps changing his mind.
あの人は、ころころ気が変わる。

focus the mind
心 [気持ち] を集中させる

2 I don't mind if you go.
(あなたが) 行ってもかまわないよ。

Nobody seemed to mind.
誰も気にしているようには見えなかった。

I decided to come early. I hope you don't mind.
早く来てしまいました。ご迷惑でなければいいのですが。

Would you mind leaving the room?
部屋から出ていただけませんか？

Would you mind not smoking in here?
ここでタバコを吸わないでいただけませんか？

"Do you mind if I close the window?" "No, I don't mind at all."
「窓を閉めてもかまいませんか？」
「ええ、どうぞ」

"Do you mind if I use the car tonight?" "Yes, I do mind."
「今夜車を使ってもいい？」
「いや、それは困る」

3 Mind your manners when the guests are here.
お客様がいらっしゃるときは、礼儀に気をつけなさい。

4 Some of the world's greatest minds will be there.
世界の一流の知識人たちがそこに集まるだろう。

bear in mind 心にとめておく, 忘れない

Well, just bear in mind that money doesn't grow on trees.
お金は木になるわけではないことを、心にとめておきなさい。

be in/of two minds about …について迷っている, …について決めかねている

I was in two minds about going because the weather wasn't good.
天気がよくなかったので、出かけるかどうか迷っていた。

be on one's mind 気にかかっている

That letter's been on my mind all week.
例の手紙のことが1週間ずっと気にかかっている。

call to mind 思い出させる

The name Kingston calls to mind a fantastic vacation we had in Jamaica.
キングストンという名は、ジャマイカでのすばらしい休暇を思い出させる。

change one's mind 気が変わる, 考えを変える

The boss has changed his mind three times already.
上司はすでに3度も考えを変えている。

Do you mind? (stop it) やめてくれませんか, いいかげんにしてくれない？

Do you mind? I'm trying to study.
やめてくれませんか？ 勉強してるんです。

go out of one's mind 気が変になる, 気が狂う

Has he gone completely out of his mind?
あの人は気が狂ってしまったの？

have a mind to do …する気がある

I have a good mind to speak to him about this.
この件については彼に話す気です。

have in mind 考えている

I'm not sure what the next step should be. Do you have anything in mind?

次はどうするべきか迷っています。何か考えはありますか?

keep in mind (that...) 忘れないでいる

make up one's mind 決心する, 決断する

Make up your mind quickly!
すぐに決心しなさい。

mind one's own business 人のことに余計な口出しをしない

That's a private matter, so I suggest you mind your own business.
それは私的な問題だから、余計な口出しをしないでください。

Mind your own business!
大きなお世話だ!

never mind ((*masculine*)) 気にするな, ((*feminine*)) 気にしないで

Oh, never mind, it's already too late to do anything about it.
((*masculine*)) 気にするな、今さら何をしても手遅れなんだから。

put one's mind at rest 安心させる

I tried to put her mind at rest and told her that everything was going fine.
彼女を安心させようとして、すべてうまくいっていると話した。

put one's mind to 決意する, 心に決める

You can do anything if you put your mind to it.
やろうと決意したら、どんなことでも成し遂げられるよ。

put out of one's mind ...のことを考えない, 忘れる

Try to put it out of your mind.
そのことは忘れるようにして。

speak one's mind 本心を打ち明ける, 本音を話す

There's nothing wrong with speaking your mind.
本音を話すのは悪いことではない。

take one's mind off ...のことを考えない, 忘れる

Try to take your mind off the situation for a few more hours.
あと数時間、そのことは考えないようにしたほうがいい。

to my mind 私が思うには, 私には (...と思える)

To my mind, the suggestion seems perfectly reasonable.
私には、その提案はとても理にかなっているように思える。

turn one's mind to ...に目/注意を向ける

He said he intends to turn his mind to a new venture, maybe oil painting.
彼は油絵か何か、新しい試みに目を向けてみるつもりだと言った。

mindless ***adj.*** (stupid) 愚かな, ばかな, (meaningless) 意味のない, (dull) 頭を使わない, 単純な

a mindless act of vandalism
愚かな破壊行為

mindless work 頭を使わない仕事

mindless of ...のことを考えない, ...のことを気にかけない

He pushed his way through the crowd, completely mindless of others.
彼は周りの人のことなど全く考えないで、人込みの中を押しのけて進んだ。

mine[1] ***pron.*** 私の(もの), 自分の(もの), ((*masculine*)) 僕の(もの) [→ I]

This is mine and that's yours.

M

これは私ので、あれがあなたのです。

This is a friend of mine.

こちらは私の友人です。

mine[2] *n.* (pit) 鉱山; (land mine) 地雷, (underwater mine) 機雷

v. (for ore) 掘り出す, 採掘する

a coal mine 炭坑

♦ **miner** *n.* (炭)坑夫

minefield *n.* 地雷原

mineral *n.* ミネラル, 鉱物

Minerals such as sulfur are formed naturally in rocks.

イオウなどの鉱物は、岩の中で自然に形成される。

♦ **mineral water** *n.* ミネラルウォーター, 鉱水

mineralogy *n.* 鉱物学

mingle *v.* (with people) (…と) 交わる, (talk) 会話を交わす; (become mixed) 混ざる

Let's mingle. みんなと話をしよう。

mini- *pref.* 小型-, ミニ-

a minibus 小型 [マイクロ] バス

a minivan ミニバン

a minibar ミニバー

miniature *adj.* 小型の

n. (smaller version of sth) 小型の模型, ミニチュア

minimal *adj.* 非常に低い, わずかな, (smallest allowed) 最低限の, 最小限の

The risk to your health is minimal.

健康への危険性は非常に低い。

minimalism *n.* ミニマリズム

minimize *v.* 最小限にする, (make light of) 過小評価する, 軽視する

minimum *adj.* 最低の, 最小の, (smallest allowed) 最低限の, 最小限の

n. (limit) 最低限, 最小限

a minimum cost 最低コスト

a minimum temperature 最低気温

The minimum number for a group is ten.

グループの最少人数は10人です。

Those are the minimum qualifications for the job.

それらがその仕事に就くための最低限の資格です。

It's the minimum I would expect in terms of a formal apology.

それが正式な謝罪として求める、最低限の内容です。

♦ **minimum wage** *n.* 最低賃金

mining *n.* 採掘

miniskirt *n.* ミニスカート

minister *n.* (government minister) 大臣; (Catholic) 聖職者, (Protestant) 牧師

the prime minister 首相 [総理大臣]

a Lutheran minister ルター派の牧師

ministry *n.* -省 [→ p.1178]

mink *n.* (animal) ミンク, (fur) ミンクの毛皮

minnow *n.* ハヤ, ウグイ, (small fish) 小魚

minor

1 *adj.* RELATIVELY LESSER: 小さな, (trivial) 大して重要ではない, ささいな

2 *n.* NON-ADULT: 未成年者

3 *n.* SECONDARY SUBJECT OF STUDY: 副専攻

4 *v.* TAKE A SECONDARY DEGREE IN: (**minor in**) 副専攻にする

5 *n., adj.* IN MUSIC: (key) 短調(の)

1 It was a matter of minor importance.

ささいなことだった。

The damage to the house was minor.
家への被害は小さかった。

2 Minors are not allowed to drink alcohol.
未成年者は飲酒を禁止されている。

3 My major is chemistry, and my minor is Japanese.
専攻は化学で、副専攻は日本語です。

4 She is minoring in English literature.
彼女は英文学を副専攻にしている。

5 in B minor ロ短調で

minority *n.* (small number of people) 少数, (minority party) 少数派, (ethnic minority) 少数民族, マイノリティー

♦ **minority leader** *n.* 少数党の院内総務

mint[1] *n.* (plant) ハッカ, (candy) ミント
adj. ハッカ入りの, ミントの

mint[2] *n.* (place where money is made) 造幣局

minuet *n.* メヌエット

minus *prep.* (take away) …引く [→ WITHOUT]
adj. (of temperature) 零下-; (of grade: below the mark) …の下, …マイナス
n. (demerit) 欠点; (minus sign) マイナス記号

Ten minus two is eight. 10引く2は8。

It was minus five degrees centigrade.
セ氏零下5度だった。

minute[1] *n.*

1 UNIT OF TIME: -分

2 BRIEF PERIOD OF TIME: ちょっと, 少しの間, (instant) 瞬間

3 AS SOON AS: (**the minute…**) (…したら) すぐに, 早速

4 OF MEETING: (**minutes**) 議事録

1 one minute [two minutes] 1分 [2分]

It's a five-minute walk from here to the convenience store.
ここからコンビニまで歩いて5分です。

2 Could you just wait a minute?
ちょっと待っていただけますか？

I'll be back in a minute.
すぐに戻ります。

3 I'll tell him the minute I see him.
彼に会ったら早速伝えます。

4 the minutes of the meeting
会議の議事録

any minute (now) 今すぐにでも, いつなんどきでも

He'll be back any minute now.
彼は今すぐにでも戻るはずです。

at the last minute 最後になって, どたん場で

Then, as usual, he turns up at the last minute.
そこへいつものように、彼が最後の最後[どたん場]で姿を見せる。

not for a minute 全く/少しも…ない

Not for a minute did I believe a word he was saying.
彼の言葉は全く信じられなかった。

this minute 今すぐ(に), ((*formal*)) ただちに

I want it done this minute!
今すぐやってほしい。

minute[2] *adj.* (very small) とても小さい, (of difference, improvement) わずかな; (detailed) 詳細な, 綿密な

a minute detail 詳細

minute hand *n.* (of clock) 長針, 分針

miracle *n.* 奇跡

It was a miracle anyone survived.
生き残った人がいたことは奇跡だった。

miraculous *adj.* 奇跡的な

a miraculous recovery (from an illness)
奇跡的な回復

mirage *n.* (natural phenomenon) しんき楼, (illusion) 幻覚

mirror *n.* (looking glass) 鏡, ミラー [→ picture of BATHROOM, PUBLIC BATH]

a rearview mirror
バックミラー [→ picture of CAR]

Don't you ever look at yourself in a mirror?
鏡を見ることはないの？

mirth *n.* (joy) 歓喜

misbehave *v.* 行儀が悪い, 無作法なことをする

Stop misbehaving!
行儀よくしなさい/いいかげんにしなさい!

miscalculate *v.* (miscount) 計算を間違える, (misjudge) (…の) 判断を誤る, 見込みを誤る

It looks as though we've miscalculated the costs.
費用の計算を間違えたようだ。

We miscalculated the result of the election.
選挙結果の見込みを誤った。

miscarriage *n.* 流産

have a miscarriage 流産する

miscarry *v.* (fail to give birth) 流産する; (of plan) 失敗する

miscellaneous *adj.* いろいろな, 種々雑多な

miscellaneous income 雑所得

mischief *n.* (devilry) いたずら, ちゃめっ気, (harm) 害, 被害

mischievous *adj.* (of person) いたずら好きの, 腕白な, (of look) いたずらっぽい, ちゃめっ気のある

misconduct *n.* (of public official) 職権乱用, (illegal behavior) 違法行為

misconstrue *v.* 誤解する, 取り違える

misdemeanor *n.* 軽犯罪

miser *n.* けち(な人), けちん坊

miserable *adj.* (unhappy) 不幸な, みじめな, 哀れな, (horrible) いやな, ひどい, 悲惨な, (of amount) わずかな

She had a miserable life.
彼女の人生は不幸だった。

Miserable weather, isn't it?
ひどい天気ですね。

We had a miserable vacation.
<u>悲惨な</u> [ひどい] 休暇だった。

misery *n.* (unhappiness) みじめさ, 不幸, (hardship) 苦難

put…out of his/her/its misery (kill) 安楽死させる

misfire *v.* (of gun) 不発になる, (of engine) 点火しない, (of plan) 失敗に終わる

The gun misfired.
銃は不発だった。

misfit *n.* 適応できない人, 不適格者

misfortune *n.* 不運, 不幸

It was his misfortune to be born during a civil war.
彼が内戦中に生まれたのは不運だった。

misgiving *n.* (apprehension) 不安, (doubt) 疑惑, 疑念

I have some misgivings about this plan.
この計画には少し疑問があります。

misguided *adj.* (of person) 心得違いの, (of opinion, effort) 見当違いの

misinform *v.* (…に) 誤った情報を伝える, (**be misinformed**: be told the wrong information) 間違って教わる

misinterpret *v.* 誤って解釈する, 誤解する

misjudge *v.* 誤って判断する, 誤解する

I misjudged his character.
彼の人柄を誤解していた。

mislay *v.* (misplace) 置き忘れる, (put down incorrectly) 置き違える

I seem to have mislaid the documents.
書類を置き忘れて来たらしい。

mislead *v.* (cause to believe) 思い込ませる, 信じ込ませる, (deceive) 欺く, (invite misunderstanding) 誤解を招く

We were misled into thinking the meeting was to begin at 7 o'clock.
会議は7時に始まるものと思い込まされていた。

misleading *adj.* 誤解を招く(ような)

mismanage *v.* (manage badly) (…の) 管理を誤る, (deal with badly) (…の) 処置を誤る

miso soup *n.* みそ汁

misprint *n.* 誤植, ミスプリント
v. 誤植する

There are misprints in this article.
この記事には誤植がある。

misread *v.* 読み違える, (mistake) 誤解する

misrepresent *v.* (misrepresent A as B) (AをBだと) 誤って伝える

miss[1] *n.* (younger woman) ((*polite*)) お嬢さん, ((*informal*)) おねえさん, (older woman) おばさん, (trying to get sb's attention) ちょっと, (**Miss**) -さん

Miss! You've dropped your handkerchief.
ちょっと! ハンカチを落としましたよ。

miss[2] *v.*

1 PASS UP: (opportunity) 逃す

2 BE ABSENT FROM: (school, work) 休む, (class, meeting) 欠席する

3 FAIL TO CATCH: (bus) (…に) 乗り遅れる, 間に合わない, (ball) 取り損なう, (meal) 抜く, 食べ損なう, (each other) 行き違う

4 FAIL TO NOTICE: (…に) 気がつかない, (not see) 見逃す, (not hear) 聞き逃す

5 FAIL TO HIT: 外す, (…に) 当たらない

6 KEENLY FEEL THE ABSENCE OF: (person) (…が) いなくて寂しい, 恋しくなる, (thing of the past) (…が) 懐かしい, (**be missing**: belonging) なくした

7 FAIL TO UNDERSTAND: (…が) わからない

1 He missed a golden opportunity.
彼は絶好の機会を逃してしまった。

2 I've missed two weeks at the office because of illness.
病気で会社を2週間も休んでいる。

She missed class this morning.
彼女は、けさ授業を欠席した。

3 I almost missed the train.
あやうく電車に乗り遅れるところだった。

I missed my stop.
停留所を乗り過ごした。

I was so late getting up, I had to miss breakfast.

寝坊したので朝食を抜かないといけなかった。

Despite our attempts to meet up, we seem to keep missing each other.
会おうとしているのに、行き違ってばかりいる。

4 I missed that TV program.
その(テレビ)番組を見逃した。

You can't miss it. It's a huge building.
見逃しようがありません/すぐにわかります。大きな建物ですから。

He doesn't miss much.
彼は、たいていのことは見逃さない。

He may have missed some of the details.
彼は、細かいことをいくつか聞き逃したのかもしれない。

5 I missed the target. 的を外した。

I threw the ball at him but missed.
彼にボールを投げたが、当たらなかった。

6 We all missed you so much.
あなたがいなくて、みんなとても寂しかったです。

The children missed not seeing their mother.
子供たちは母親を恋しがった。

I miss living in the country.
田舎暮らしが懐かしい。

Are you missing something?
何かなくしましたか？

7 He missed the point entirely.
彼は要点が全然わかっていなかった。

missile *n.* ミサイル, (guided missile) 誘導ミサイル, (ballistic missile) 弾道ミサイル

fire a missile ミサイルを発射する

a missile base ミサイル基地

a missile shield ミサイル防衛網

missing ***adj.*** (of person) 行方不明の, (of thing) 紛失した, なくなった, (omitted) 欠けている, 抜けている

thousands missing 大勢の行方不明者

go missing 行方不明になる

a missing book なくなった本

three missing pages 3ページの落丁

♦**missing link** ***n.*** 失われた環

missing person ***n.*** 行方不明者

mission ***n.*** (military) 任務, (personal) 使命, (group sent somewhere) 使節団, 派遣団, (religious mission) 伝道, 布教活動

missionary ***n.*** 宣教師

mist ***n.*** (vapor) 霧, もや, (spring mist) かすみ

v. (of windows) 曇る, (of air) 霧がかかる, もやがかかる, (of eyes) かすむ

A dense mist fell.
濃い霧がかかって [立ち込めて] いた。

The windows are misted over.
窓が曇っている。

mistake ***n.*** 間違い, ミス, ((*formal*)) 誤り, (misunderstanding) 誤解

v. (mistake A for B) (AをBと) 間違える

spelling mistakes
つづりの間違い [スペルミス]

There are a lot of mistakes in this translation.
この翻訳には間違い [誤り] が多い。

You've made very few mistakes.
ほとんど間違いをしていませんね。

I mistook her for her twin sister.
彼女を双子の妹[姉]と間違えてしまった。

I was mistaken for Tomoko.
智子に間違えられた。

by mistake 間違えて

I picked up someone else's umbrella by mistake.
間違えて、ほかの人の傘を取ってしまった。

mistaken ***adj.*** (of person) 間違っている, 勘違いしている, (of views) 間違った

a case of mistaken identity 人違い

mister ***n.*** (trying to get sb's attention) ちょっと [→ MR.]

mistletoe ***n.*** ヤドリギ

mistranslate ***v.*** 誤訳する

♦ **mistranslation** ***n.*** 誤訳

mistress ***n.*** (female lover of married man) 愛人, (boss) 女主人

mistrust ***n.*** 不信

v. 信用しない

misunderstand ***v.*** 誤解する, 間違って解釈する

I think they must've misunderstood what I said.
言ったことを誤解したんだと思う。

misunderstanding ***n.*** 誤解, 勘違い

It was all a big misunderstanding.
すべてが大きな誤解だった。

misuse ***v.*** 乱用する, 悪用する

mitigate ***v.*** 緩和する

mitten ***n.*** ミトン, 手袋

a pair of mittens 一組のミトン

wear mittens 手袋をはめる

mix

1 ***v.*** INGREDIENTS: (mix A with B) (AとBを) 混ぜる, (mix...together) 混ぜ合わせる, 混合する, (mix A into B) (BにAを) 入れる, 加える; (of combination) 合う

2 ***v.*** OF PEOPLE: (associate) 付き合う, (**mix with / in**: become involved with/in) …とかかわる

3 ***v.*** COCKTAIL/SALAD: 作る

4 ***v.*** MUSIC: ミキシングする

5 ***n.*** MIXTURE: 混ぜ合わせたもの, 混合物, (of ingredients for quick cooking) (…の) 素, (of music) ミキシング

1 Mix the flour with the egg.
小麦粉と卵を混ぜてください。

Mix the ingredients together.
材料を混ぜ合わせてください。

Mix the sauce into the pasta.
パスタにソースを加えて。

Coffee and sushi don't mix.
コーヒーとおすしは合わない。

2 She mixes with all sorts of people.
あの人はいろんな人と付き合いがある。

They mix very well together.
彼らはとても仲良くやっている。

Cats and dogs don't mix well.
猫と犬は相性があまりよくない。

I don't want you to mix with those ruffians.
あんな乱暴な連中とかかわってほしくない。

3 The barman mixed me a cocktail.
バーテンがカクテルを作ってくれた。

4 The album took about three months to mix.
そのアルバムをミキシングするのに3ヵ月くらいかかった。

5 miso soup mix みそ汁の素

mix up ***v.*** (mix A up with B) (AをBと) 間違える, 混同する, (ruin the order of) ごちゃ混ぜにする

M

I often get him mixed up with someone else.
よく、あの人をほかの人と間違えてしまう。

be/get mixed up (of person) 頭が混乱する, (of things) ごちゃごちゃになる

We got so mixed up we couldn't think straight.
頭が混乱して、きちんと考えられなかった。

It's all mixed up.
全部ごちゃごちゃになった。

---

mixed *adj.* (blended) 混じった, 混ざり合った, 混合の, (of assortment) 取り合わせの, 詰め合わせの; (of feelings: complex) 複雑な

assorted mixed nuts ナッツの取り合わせ

I have mixed feelings about it.
それについては複雑な思いがある。

♦ **mixed doubles** *n.* (in tennis) 混合ダブルス

mixture *n.* 混合物, (of emotions) 入り混じったもの

a mixture of spices
混合スパイス [調味料]

a mixture of admiration and disgust
賞賛と嫌悪の入り混じった思い

mix-up *n.* 混乱, ごたごた, (mistake) 手違い, (miscommunication) 食い違い

in the mix up 混乱の中で

There was a mix-up at the airport.
空港でごたごたがあった。

moan *v.* うめく, (of wind) うなる, (complain) 不平を言う, ぶつぶつ言う
n. うめき声, (of wind) うなり, (complaint) 不平, 不満, ((*informal*)) 文句

He's always moaning that he has too much homework.
あの人はいつも、宿題が多すぎると文句を言っている。

He gave out a moan of pain.
彼は痛くて、うめき声を上げた。

mob *n.* (mass of people) 群衆, (gang) 暴力団

mobile *adj.* (able to move) 動ける, (able to be moved) 動かせる, 移動-

♦ **mobile home** *n.* トレーラーハウス

mobile phone *n.* 携帯電話

mobility *n.* (movability) 可動性, 動きやすさ, (within society) 流動性

mobilize *v.* (people) 動員する

mobster *n.* ギャング, 暴力団員

moccasin *n.* モカシン

mock *v.* (ridicule) ばかにする, あざける, (mimic and laugh at) まねをしてからかう
adj. (fake) 見せかけの, 偽の, (of battle, exam) 模擬-

mockery *n.* (derision) あざけり

make a mockery of あざ笑う

mockingbird *n.* マネシツグミ

mode *n.* (method) ((*formal*)) 様式, (style, fashion) モード, 流行

model

1 *n.* PERSON/THING TO BE IMITATED: 模範, (お)手本

2 *n.* PERSON TO BE DRAWN/PHOTOGRAPHED: モデル

3 *n.* SOLID REPRESENTATION: 模型, (plastic model) プラモデル

4 *n.* MACHINE: 型, モデル

5 *v.* MAKE ACCORDING TO: (model A on B)

(Bを基にしてAを) 作る, (**model oneself on**) (お)手本にする

6 ***adj.*** **IDEAL:** 模範的な, 理想的な

7 ***v.*** **WORK AS A FASHION MODEL:** モデルをする

1 She's a model of good behavior.
彼女は品行方正のお手本のような人だ。

2 She's a world-famous model.
彼女は世界的に有名なモデルです。

3 The boys love to build those plastic models of aircraft.
子供たちが、ああいう飛行機のプラモデルを作るのが大好きなんです。

4 This is our company's new model.
これが当社の新製品です。

His car is the new model.
彼の車はニューモデルだ。

5 They don't want us to model it on previous designs.
過去のデザインを基にして作ってほしくないと言われた。

6 She is a model student.
彼女は模範的な学生だ。

modem ***n.*** モデム

moderate ***adj.*** (of views) 穏健な, 節度のある, (of climate) 穏やかな, (of amount) 中くらいの

n. (person) 穏健な人

have moderate views 穏健な考えをもつ

modern ***adj.*** (contemporary) 近代的な, モダンな, (recent) 現代の, 近ごろの, (of period) 近代の

They live in a modern apartment.
彼らはモダンなマンションに住んでいる。

It's a relatively modern idea.
それは比較的、現代的な考えだ。

modern history 近代史

modernize ***v.*** 近代化する

modest ***adj.*** (of behavior) 控え目な, 謙遜した, 謙虚な, (of income) ささやかな, (of amount) 少量の

He's very modest about his achievements.
彼は自分の業績に対してとても謙虚だ。

a modest income ささやかな収入

modesty ***n.*** 謙遜

modification ***n.*** 修正

modify ***v.*** (change) 修正する, 変更する, (make less extreme) 和らげる, 緩和する; (of word) 修飾する

The government's plan was too unpopular and had to be modified.
政府案はあまりに不評で、修正せざるを得なかった。

Adjectives modify nouns.
形容詞は名詞を修飾する。

module ***n.*** (course) モジュール, 履修単位; (of spacecraft) モジュール

mohair ***n.*** モヘア

moist ***adj.*** 湿っている, 湿った, (of air) 湿気を含んだ, (of eyes) 涙ぐんだ, 潤んだ

The soil was moist from the night's rain.
昨夜の雨で土が湿っていた。

I wiped the tabletop with a moist cloth.
湿ったふきんでテーブルをふいた。

My eyes went moist with laughter.
大笑いして目が潤んだ。

moisten ***v.*** (make moist) 湿らす, ぬらす

moisture ***n.*** (in air) 湿気, 水分, (in skin) 潤い

molar ***n.*** 臼歯

mold[1] ***n.*** (cast) 型, (type) タイプ

M

v. (shape) 形作る, 形成する

break the mold 型を破る

mold² *n.* (mildew) かび

moldy *adj.* (of food) かび臭い

mole¹ *n.* (on body) ほくろ

mole² *n.* (animal) モグラ

molecular *adj.* 分子の

a molecular structure 分子構造

molecule *n.* 分子

molest *v.* (sexually) (…に) いたずらをする

♦ **molester** *n.* 痴漢

mollusk *n.* 軟体動物

molten *adj.* 溶けた, 溶融した

molten lava 溶岩

M

mom *n.* (one's own) 母, (addressing one's own) お母さん, (sb else's) お母さん

moment *n.*

1 VERY BRIEF PERIOD OF TIME: ちょっと, 少しの間, (instant) 瞬間, 一瞬

2 POINT IN TIME: 時, (**at this moment**) 今

3 AS SOON AS: (**the moment…**) ちょうど…した時, …したらすぐ(に)

1 Just a moment, please.

ちょっと待ってください/((*polite*)) 少々お待ちください。

Could you wait a moment, please?

少々お待ちいただけますか？

I'll be there in a moment.

すぐ行きます/((*humble*)) すぐに参ります。

They were sitting there a moment ago.

ほんの少し前まで、そこに座っていましたが。

He said it wouldn't take but a moment.

さほど時間はかからないと言った。

I'm so busy, I scarcely have a moment to myself.

忙しすぎて自分の時間がほとんどない。

2 I'm busy at the moment. Could you call again later?

今、手が離せません。またあとで電話をしてもらえますか？

3 The moment I got into the bath, the phone rang.

ちょうどおふろに入った時、電話が鳴った。

The moment they get here, I'll let you know.

彼らが到着したらすぐお知らせします。

any moment (now) → ANY MINUTE

moment of truth 正念場, 試練の時

this moment 今すぐ(に) [→ THIS MINUTE]

momentarily *adv.* ちょっと, しばらく

momentary *adj.* 一瞬の, 瞬間的な, 一時的な

a momentary lapse of concentration

一瞬の気のゆるみ

momentous *adj.* 重大な

momentum *n.* 運動量, (impetus) 勢い, はずみ

monarch *n.* 君主

monarchy *n.* (country) 君主国, (system) 君主制, 君主政治

a constitutional monarchy 立憲君主国

monastery *n.* 修道院

Monday *n.* 月曜日

monetary *adj.* 貨幣の, 通貨の

monetary compensation 金銭的補償

money *n.* (お)金, (change) 小銭, (currency) 貨幣, 通貨, (assets) 財産

All he thinks about is money.
あの人は、お金のことしか考えていない。

Do you have any money on you?
お金の持ち合わせはありますか？

How much money did you bring?
いくら持って来ました？

What's the quickest way to make good money?
大金をもうけるのに一番手っ取り早い方法は何だろう？

It was easy money, but now I regret it.
楽に手に入れたお金だったが、今は後悔している。

change money 両替する

We'll change our money at the airport.
空港で両替しよう。

put money on …に(お金を)賭ける

money order *n.* 郵便為替

Mongolia *n.* モンゴル, ((*in abbr.*)) 蒙

mongoose *n.* マングース

mongrel *n.* 雑種

monitor *n.* (computer monitor) モニター; (supervisor) 監視人, (hall monitor) 学級委員

v. 監視する

UN officials are monitoring the voting.
国連職員が投票を監視している。

monk *n.* (Christian) 修道士, (Buddhist) 僧, 僧侶

monkey *n.* サル, 猿

monkey wrench *n.* 自在スパナ

monochrome *adj.* (black-and-white) 白黒の, モノクロの, (of one color) 単色の

monogamous *adj.* (of marriage) 一夫一婦制の

monogamy *n.* 一夫一婦制

monologue *n.* (in theater) 独白, モノローグ, (talk by one person) 一人の長話

monopoly *n.* 独占, (company with a monopoly on sth) 独占企業

have a monopoly on …の独占権をもつ

monorail *n.* モノレール

monotone *n.* 一本調子, 単調

monotonous *adj.* (boring) 退屈な, つまらない, (of tone) 単調な

monoxide *n.* 一酸化物

monsoon *n.* (seasonal wind) モンスーン, 季節風, (rainy season) 雨季

monster *n.* (imaginary creature) モンスター, 怪物, お化け, 化け物, (very large animal/thing) 巨大な動物/物, (evil person) 極悪人

adj. (huge) 巨大な, ((*informal*)) でかい

monstrous *adj.* (huge) 巨大な, (like a monster) 怪物のような, (awful) ひどい

month *n.* 月, (one month) 1ヵ月, 一月

this [last, next] month 今月 [先月, 来月]

the following month 翌月 [次の月]

the month before last 先々月

the month after next 再来月

every month 毎月

every other month 隔月 [1ヵ月おき]

a month ago 1ヵ月前

There are twelve months in a year.
1年は12ヵ月ある。

The month of February is quite cold, especially when the wind blows in off the lakes.
2月は寒い、それも湖から風が吹き付けると特に寒い。

The baby is only one and a half months old.
その赤ちゃんはまだ(生後)1ヵ月半です。

A month is not a long time if you're enjoying yourself.
楽しくやっていると、1ヵ月は長くない。

by the month 月ぎめで

for months 何ヵ月も

month after month 毎月毎月

monthly *adj.* (every month) 毎月の, (once a month) 月に1回の, (published monthly) 月刊の

adv. 月1回, 毎月, (by the month) 月ぎめで

a monthly salary 月給

a monthly magazine 月刊誌

monument *n.* (memorial) 記念碑, (remains, ruins) 遺跡

a monument to the great Victorian engineer Brunel
ビクトリア朝時代の偉大な技術者ブルーネルの記念碑

mood *n.* 気, 気分, 気持ち, 機嫌, (atmosphere) 雰囲気, ムード

Are you in the mood to talk now?
話す気になりましたか？

I'm not in the mood for going out.
出かける気分じゃない。

be in a good [bad] mood
機嫌がいい [悪い]

The mood was tense among the participants.
参加者たちの間に緊迫したムードが漂っていた。

moody *adj.* (temperamental) 気まぐれな, 気分の変わりやすい, (bad-tempered) 不機嫌な

a moody person 気分屋 [お天気屋]

moon *n.* (of Earth) 月, ((*informal*)) お月様, (of another planet) 衛星

a full [new] moon 満月 [新月]

How many moons does Jupiter have?
木星には衛星がいくつありますか？

once in a blue moon めったに…ない, ごくまれに

moonbeam *n.* 月光, 月の光線

moonlight *n.* 月光, 月明かり

moonshine *n.* (lies, nonsense) ばかげた考え; (illegal whiskey) 密造ウイスキー

moon-viewing *n.* (お)月見

moor[1] *n.* 荒野, 原野

moor[2] *v.* (tie to a dock) つなぎとめる, (be tied to a dock) 停泊する

moose *n.* ヘラジカ

mop *n.* モップ

v. モップでふく

mop the floor 床をモップでふく

mope *v.* (be gloomy) ふさぎ込む, 落ち込む

moped *n.* モペット, 原付き

moral *n.* (ethical content) 道徳, モラル, (of story) 教訓

adj. (concerning right and wrong) 道徳の, (of person) 品行方正な

He has no morals.
あの人には道徳心がない。

a moral vacuum モラルの欠如

the moral of the story 物語の教訓

A lot of people seem to think that moral standards are falling.
道徳基準が低下していると考えている

人が多いようだ。

morale *n.* 士気

The coach's pep talk helped boost the team's morale.
コーチの激励は、チームの士気を高めるのに役立った。

morality *n.* 道徳, 倫理

morbid *adj.* 病的な

a morbid fear of the dark
暗がりに対する病的な恐怖心

more

1 *adj.* GREATER IN AMOUNT/NUMBER: (…より) 多い, たくさん, もっと

2 *adv.* COMPARATIVE: …より(もっと), それ以上, さらに

3 *pron.* GREATER NUMBER OF THINGS/PERSONS: もっと

4 *adv.* IN PROPORTION: (**the more…the more**) …すればするほど

1 There are more students in this class than in the other.
このクラスは、あっちのクラスより生徒数が多い。

I have more books than him.
彼よりたくさん本を持っている。

Do we have any more coffee?
まだコーヒーはある?

We need more milk.
ミルクがもっと必要です。

I don't have any more money.
もうこれ以上お金がない。

2 This job is more interesting than the last.
今度の仕事は、前の仕事より面白い。

Are you more comfortable now?
今は少し楽になりましたか?

The party was more fun than I thought it would be.
パーティーは思っていたより楽しかった。

It might be more useful than you think.
あなたが考えているより役に立つかもしれないよ。

We need to work more efficiently.
もっと効率的に働かなくてはいけない。

The man is more than seventy years old.
その人は70歳を越えているよ。

She is studying more than before.
彼女は以前より勉強している。

I did my best. What more can they expect?
精一杯やった。これ以上どうしろというのだろう?

3 I want to know more. もっと知りたい。

How much more do you need?
あとどのくらい必要ですか?

4 The more you smoke, the more you'll want to smoke.
たばこは吸えば吸うほど、吸いたくなるものです。

The more you spend, the less you have.
お金は、使った分だけ減っていく。

a few/little more もう少し, あと少し

If there had been a few more people there, it would've been better.
あと数人いたら、もっと楽しかったはずだ。

I think you should do a little more to help your mother.
もう少しお母さんを手伝ってあげるべきだと思うな。

more and more ますます

More and more people are traveling.
旅行者はますます増えている。

M

more or less (approximately) おおよそ
What he said was more or less true.
彼が言ったことは、おおよそ真実です。

more than... (followed by a number) ...以上
The kids played together for more than three hours.
子供たちは、3時間以上もいっしょに遊びました。
He won by more than five points.
彼が5点以上差をつけて勝った。

no more/not any more これ以上...ない
I can't eat any more.
もうこれ以上食べられない。

no more than (emphasizing smallness of amount) たった, わずか
It's no more than five minutes on foot from the station.
駅から歩いてたった5分です。

not more than せいぜい, 多くても
The shop is not more than a kilometer away.
その店まではせいぜい1キロです。

once more もう一度
Do it once more. もう一度やって。

moreover *adv.* それに, その上, さらに

morgue *n.* 遺体安置所

morning *n.* (before noon) 朝, 午前
on the morning of ...の朝に
every morning 毎朝
yesterday [tomorrow] morning
昨日 [明日] の朝
in the morning 午前中 [朝のうち] に
from morning till night 朝から晩まで
a morning coffee モーニングコーヒー

♦ **morning paper** *n.* 朝刊

morning sickness *n.* つわり

morning glory *n.* アサガオ, 朝顔

morose *adj.* 不機嫌な

morphine *n.* モルヒネ

Morse code *n.* モールス信号

mortal *adj.* (cannot live forever) 死ぬ運命にある, (fatal) 致命的な, (human) 人間の
n. (person) 人間
We are all mortal.
人間は死ぬ運命にある。
He suffered a mortal injury.
彼は致命傷を負った。

♦ **mortal sin** *n.* 大罪
commit a mortal sin 大罪を犯す

mortality *n.* 死ぬ運命
the mortality rate 死亡率

mortgage *n.* 住宅ローン
v. (use as a guarantee) 抵当に入れる, 担保に入れる
Mortgage rates have gone up.
住宅ローンの金利が上がった。
They mortgaged their home to pay the debt.
借金を返済するために、彼らは自宅を抵当に入れた。

mortician *n.* 葬儀屋(さん)

mortuary *n.* (funeral home) 葬儀場

mosaic *n.* モザイク

mosque *n.* モスク, イスラム教寺院

mosquito *n.* カ, 蚊
I've been bitten by a mosquito.
蚊に刺された。

moss *n.* コケ, 苔

most

1 *adj.* GREATEST IN AMOUNT/NUMBER: 最も多くの, 一番多い, 一番たくさん

2 *adv.* SUPERLATIVE: (**the most**) 一番, 最も

3 *pron.* ALMOST ALL: ほとんど, 大部分

4 *adv.* VERY: とても, 大変, 本当に

1 The person with the most votes wins.
最も多くの票を得た人が勝ちます。

He has the most money.
彼が一番(多く)お金を持っている。

Most people would disagree.
たいていの人は賛成しないだろう。

2 This is the most difficult decision I've had to face in a long time.
これは長い間に直面した中で、最も難しい決断です。

Hiroko studies the most.
浩子が一番勉強している。

3 Some were acquaintances, but most were complete strangers.
知り合いもいましたが、ほとんどは全く知らない人たちでした。

4 Thank you, that's most generous of you.
とても親切にしていただいて、ありがとうございます/ご親切にどうも。

at (the) most 多くても, せいぜい

John is eighty-five kilos at most.
ジョンは多くても 85 キロだ。

for the most part 大部分は, ほとんど, 大半は

I slept through the film for the most part.
映画の上映中、ほとんど寝ていた。

His thesis was, for the most part, well written.
彼の論文は、大半はよく書けていた。

make the most of (take advantage of) できるだけ利用する, (enjoy thoroughly) 思い切り楽しむ

You'd better make the most of your time in Japan.
日本での滞在時間を、できるだけ有効に使ったほうがいいですよ。

Let's try to make the most of this vacation.
この休暇を思い切り楽しもう。

most of all 一番, とりわけ

I like different kinds of food, but most of all, I like Italian food.
いろんな料理が好きですが、イタリア料理が一番好きです。

Most of all, it was a good learning experience.
とりわけ、それはいい勉強になりました。

KANJI BRIDGE

最 ON: さい KUN: もっと(も) | THE MOST (THE "-EST")

best (situation)	最高の
best (selection)	最良の
(do one's) best	最善
fewest	最少の
final	最終の
first, beginning	最初
foremost	最先端の
height/midst of	最中
last	最後/最終
maximum	最大限
minimum	最小限
nearest	最寄りの
newest	最新の
recently	最近
worst	最悪の

M

mostly *adv.* 大部分は, 主に, たいてい

motel *n.* モーテル

stay a night at a motel
モーテルに1泊する

moth *n.* ガ, 蛾, (clothes moth) イガ, ((*informal*)) 虫

mothball *n.* 防虫剤

mother *n.* (one's own) 母, 母親, ((*masculine/informal*)) おふくろ, (addressing one's own) お母さん, (sb else's) お母さん, ((*polite*)) お母様

adj. 母の, (of country) 母国の

How old is your mother?
お母様はおいくつですか？

Mother! How could you say such a thing!
お母さん、なんてことを言うの！

♦ **motherland** *n.* 母国

motherly *adj.* 母親のような, 母親らしい

Mother's Day *n.* 母の日

mother tongue *n.* 母国語, 母語

mother-in-law *n.* しゅうとめ, 義理の母, ((*formal*)) 義母

motif *n.* モチーフ, (design) 基調, (theme) テーマ, 主題

motion *n.* 動き, 運動, モーション, (gesture) 身ぶり, 動作, (proposal) 動議

♦ **motion sickness** *n.* 乗り物酔い

motion picture *n.* 映画

motivate *v.* (…に) やる気を起こさせる, 動機を与える

It's hard to motivate the students.
生徒にやる気を起こさせるのは難しい。

motivation *n.* やる気, 意欲

have (the) motivation やる気がある

motive *n.* 動機

an ulterior motive 下心

motor *n.* (engine) モーター, エンジン, (car) 車, 自動車

♦ **motorized** *adj.* モーターの付いた, 電動-

motorbike *n.* (moped) 原付き

motorboat *n.* モーターボート

motorcade *n.* 自動車パレード

motorcycle *n.* オートバイ, バイク

motor home *n.* キャンピングカー

motorist *n.* 運転手, ドライバー

motorway *n.* 高速道路

motto *n.* 標語, モットー

mound *n.* (pile of earth) 盛り土, (ancient burial site) 古墳; (in baseball) マウンド

mount *n.* (Mount) -山

v. (horse, bike) (…に) 乗る; (picture in frame) 額に入れる; (of tension) 高まる, (of problems) 増える, (of debts) かさむ

Mount Fuji 富士山

He mounted his motorcycle and sped off.
彼はバイクに乗って走り去った。

You should consider mounting such a beautiful work of art.
このような美しい絵は、額に入れたらいかがですか。

The tension in the room mounted.
室内の緊張が高まった。

mountain *n.* 山

climb [come down] a mountain
山を登る [下りる]

a mountain hut 山小屋

mountain bike *n.* マウンテンバイク

mountaineer *n.* 登山者, (professional) 登山家

mountaineering *n.* 登山, 山登り

mountainous *adj.* 山の多い

mourn *v.* 悲しむ, 嘆く, (sb's death) (…の) 死を悼む

The nation mourned the loss of its popular princess.
国民は人気のあった王女の死を悼んだ。

in mourning 喪に服して

mouse *n.* ネズミ, ハツカネズミ, (for computer) マウス

mousse *n.* (chilled dessert) ムース; (styling foam) ムース

mouth *n.* 口 [→ picture of FACE], (way with words) 口のきき方, (**mouth to feed**) 扶養家族; (opening) 入口, (of river) 河口, (of volcano) 噴火口

a small mouth 小さな口 [おちょぼ口]

Don't eat with your mouth open, please.
口をあけて食べないで。

Watch your mouth!
口を慎みなさい！

He has four mouths to feed.
彼は扶養家族が4人いる。

by word of mouth 口コミで, 口伝えで

have a big mouth おしゃべりだ, 口が軽い

mouthful *n.* 口一杯, (long word) 長ったらしい言葉

---

move

1 *v.* CHANGE POSITION: 動く, (alter the position of) 動かす, 移動する, (move over/aside to make room) 詰める [→ MOVE OVER], (of traffic) 流れる, 進む, (of events: develop) 進展する

2 *v.* CHANGE RESIDENCE: 引っ越す, 移る, 移転する

3 *v.* FEELINGS: (**be moved**) 感動する

4 *n.* MOVEMENT: 動き, 移動

5 *n.* CHANGE: 変化

6 *n.* CHANGE OF RESIDENCE: 引っ越し

7 *n.* IN GAME: (change of position) 手, (turn) 番

1 The fish don't have much room to move about in their tank.
この水槽には、魚が泳ぎ回る余地があまりない。

Oh, I see you've moved the furniture around since I was last here.
あっ、前に来た時と違って家具を移動 [模様替え] したのね。

Good, the traffic has finally started moving again.
よかった、やっと車が流れ [動き] 出した。

Events started to move very quickly.
事態が急に進展し始めた。

2 They moved twice in one year.
彼らは1年で2度も引っ越しをした。

When do you expect to move?
いつ引っ越そうと思っているのですか？

The company moved to new premises.
会社が新しい建物に移転した。

3 I was moved to tears by the film.
その映画に感動して涙が出た。

4 He made a move for the door.
彼はドアの方に急いだ。

5 I think it's a move for the better.
良い方向に進んでいると思う。

6 The move will take two days.
引っ越しには2日かかる。

7 a good [bad] move いい [悪い] 手

Go ahead. It's your move.

どうぞ。あなたの番です。

get a move on (hurry up) 急ぐ

We haven't got all day. Get a move on, will you.
丸1日あるわけじゃないんだから、急いでくれない？

make a move 行動を起こす

If they don't make a move soon, it'll be too late.
彼らがすぐに行動を起こさなければ、手遅れになる。

move along *v.* (move) 移動する

The police told the demonstrators to move along.
警察官はデモ隊に移動するよう言った。

move away *v.* (leave one residence for another) 引っ越す

They've moved away.
彼らはもう引っ越しましたよ。

move in *v.* (begin to live in a different place) ...に引っ越して来る; (come in) ...に入って来る

Someone's moved in next door.
誰かが隣に引っ越して来た。

The police moved in to disperse the hooligans.
警察官が入って来て、フーリガンたちを追い払った。

move in on *v.* (get involved in) ...に参入する, ...に進出する

That new company is trying to move in on our market.
新しい会社が我々のマーケットに参入しようとしている。

move into *v.* (house) ...に引っ越す, ...に入居する

move on *v.* (continue moving) 先に進む; (**move on to**: sth new) ...に移る

Let's move on while there's still daylight.
まだ日のあるうちに先に進もう。

Let's move on now to the next topic.
さあ、次の話題に移りましょう。

move out *v.* (leave one residence for another) 引っ越す

I'm moving out next week.
来週、引っ越します。

move over *v.* (to make room) 詰める

Could you move over, please, so a few more people can fit in?
あと何人か入れるように、もう少し詰めてもらえませんか？

Could you move over a bit?
少し詰めていただけますか？

move up *v.* (rise) 上がる, (be promoted) 昇進する

I want to move up in the organization.
会社で昇進したいと思っている。

movement *n.* (action) 動き, 動作; (political movement) 運動

the peace movement of the 1960's
１９６０年代の平和運動

movie *n.* 映画 [→ FILM]

Let's go to the movies.
映画を見に行こう。

I didn't see that movie.
その映画は見なかった。

I saw that movie on video.
その映画はビデオで見た。

♦ **movie star** *n.* 映画スター

movie theater ***n.*** 映画館

moving ***adj.*** (of story) 感動的な; (of machine) 動く, (in motion) 動いている

mow ***v.*** (grass) 刈る

moxibustion ***n.*** (お)灸

apply moxibustion お灸をすえる

Mr. ***n.*** -さん, ((*polite*)) -様, ((*formal/written*)) -氏, (speaking to/of teacher) -先生, (in letter) -様, -殿

Mr. Smith スミスさん

Mrs. ***n.*** -さん, ((*polite*)) -様, (sb's wife) ((*formal*)) -夫人, ((*informal*)) -さんの奥さん, (in letter) -様

Mrs. Ishihara 石原さん

Ms. ***n.*** -さん, ((*polite*)) -様, (speaking to/of teacher) -先生, (in letter) -様

Ms. Robinson ロビンソンさん

MSc ***abbr.*** (qualification) 理学修士の学位

much

1 ***adj.*** OF AMOUNT: たくさんの, 多量の, 大量の, (of money) 多額の, (**too much**) 多すぎる, (**not much**) あまり…ない

2 ***pron., n.*** LARGE AMOUNT: たくさん, 多量, (a great part) 大部分

3 ***adv.*** GREATLY: とても, 大変, ((*informal*)) すごく

4 ***adv.*** WITH COMPARATIVE DEGREE: (…より) ずっと, もっと

1 Do you have much time?
時間は、たくさんありますか?

It's not much. あまりありません。

I couldn't do much work today.
今日はあまり仕事ができなかった。

2 What! Did you pay that much?
えっ! そんなに(たくさん)払ったんですか?

That's really a bit much.
それはあんまりだ。

He has far too much to say for himself.
彼はあまりにも自己主張が強い。

Much of our efforts were wasted.
私たちの努力は、ほとんどむだになった。

3 I liked it very much.
とても気に入りました。

However much you may try, you're not going to fool me.
いくらがんばっても、私をだませやしないよ。

4 It's much bigger than I imagined.
想像していたよりもずっと大きい。

We need to go much faster.
もっと急いで行かなければいけない。

It was much better than I thought it would be.
思っていたよりずっとよかった。

as much as (the same amount) …と同じ量の, …と同じくらいに, (before a number) …もの(量の), …ほども

That painting is worth as much as a Mercedes.
その絵はメルセデス1台分と同じくらいの価値がある。

It did not cost as much as I thought.
思っていたほど、お金はかからなかった。

how much…? どのくらい…, (of money) いくら…

How much rice is left?
お米はどのくらい残ってる?

How much money do you have on you?
今、いくらお金を持っている?

How much is that melon?

そのメロンはいくらですか？

How much do you need?

どのくらい必要ですか？

make much of 重視する, (make too much of) 大騒ぎする

It was a wonderful opportunity, but he didn't make much of it.

すばらしい機会だったのに、彼はあまり重視 [利用] しなかった。

much as (although) ...けど

Much as I like her, I'm not going to ask for a date.

彼女を好きだけど、デートに誘えない。

Much as I'd like to stay, I really must be going.

まだいたいのはやまやまなんですが、おいとましなくてはいけません。

much the same as ...と大体同じ, ...とほとんど同じ

He thinks much the same as I do.

彼は私とほとんど同じことを考えている。

not much of a 大した...ではない, ...と言えるものじゃない

Not much of a choice at all, really.

選択と言えるものじゃない。

so much for ...はここまで, ...はこれでおしまい

So much for our vacation! It rained almost every day.

休暇はこれでおしまいか！ ほとんど毎日雨だった。

So much for fair play!

フェアープレイはどこにあるんだ！

thank you very much → THANK

mucus *n.* 粘液

mud *n.* 泥

muddle *v.* (mix up) ごっちゃにする, 混同する

n. (mess) 混乱

muddy *adj.* 泥だらけの, ぬかるみの

muddy shoes 泥だらけの靴

mudflow *n.* 泥流

muffler *n.* (part of car) 消音器, マフラー

mug *n.* (cup) マグカップ [→ picture of CUP]

muggy *adj.* 蒸し暑い

♦ **mugginess** *n.* 蒸し暑さ

mulberry *n.* クワ, 桑

mule[1] *n.* (animal) ラバ

mule[2] *n.* (woman's slipper) ミュール

multi- *pref.* 多-

multicultural *adj.* 多文化の

multilateral *adj.* (between several nations) 多国間の

multimedia *n.* マルチメディア

multinational *adj.* 多国籍の

n. (company) 多国籍企業

multiple *adj.* (many) 多くの, (various) 多様な, (involving two or more) 複合的な

n. (number) 倍数

There was a multiple pileup on the expressway.

高速道路で玉突き事故があった。

Give me a multiple of twenty.

２０の倍数を答えなさい。

♦ **multiple-choice** *adj.* 多項式選択の

a multiple-choice test 多項式選択テスト

multiple sclerosis *n.* 多発性硬化症

multiplication *n.* (in math) 掛け算

multiply *v.* (do multiplication on) 掛ける; (increase) 増える, (breed) 繁殖する [→ INCREASE]

What's seven multiplied by nine?
7 × 9 は(いくつ)？

multipurpose *adj.* 多目的の

multiracial *adj.* 多民族の

mum *adj.* (**keep mum**) 黙っている

mumble *v.* ぶつぶつ言う

Stop mumbling and speak clearly.
ぶつぶつ言うのはやめて、はっきり話しなさい。

mumps *n.* おたふくかぜ

get the mumps おたふくかぜにかかる

munch *v.* むしゃむしゃ食べる

mundane *adj.* ありふれた, 平凡な

municipal *adj.* (of town) 町の, (of city) 市の, (of big city) 都市の

a municipal office 市役所

mural *n.* 壁画

murder *n.* (act of killing intentionally) 殺人, (murder case) 殺人事件

v. 殺す, ((*formal*)) 殺害する

attempted murder 殺人未遂

murderer *n.* 殺人者, 殺人犯

murmur *v.* (of person) つぶやく, (of wind, leaves) ざわめく, (of brook) さらさら流れる

n. (of person) つぶやき, (of wind, leaves) かすかな音, ざわめき

muscle *n.* 筋肉; (clout) 影響力

I think I've pulled a muscle.
筋を違えたようだ。

muscular *adj.* 筋肉の, (of build) たくましい, がっしりした

♦ **muscular dystrophy** *n.* 筋ジストロフィー

museum *n.* 博物館, (art museum) 美術館

mushroom *n.* キノコ, マッシュルーム

common Japanese mushrooms

エリンギ

music *n.* 音楽, ミュージック, (musical score) 楽譜

Do you mind if I put on some music?
音楽をかけてもいいですか？

Would you play some music for us?
私たちのために何か演奏してもらえませんか？

I like listening to music on the radio.
ラジオで音楽を聞くのが好きです。

musical *adj.* (of skills, sound) 音楽的な

n. (show) ミュージカル

a musical instrument 楽器

musician *n.* 音楽家, ミュージシャン

musk *n.* ジャコウ

musky *adj.* (of smell) ジャコウの香りのする

Muslim *n.* (believer) イスラム教徒, 回教徒

adj. イスラム教の, 回教の

a Muslim country イスラム教国

muslin *n.* 綿モスリン

mussel *n.* ムラサキイガイ, (for eating)

M

ムール貝

must

1 *aux.* HAVE TO: (**must do**) ...しなければならない, ...しなくてはいけない, ...しなくてはならない, ...しなければいけない, (**mustn't do**) ...してはいけない

2 *aux.* MOST PROBABLY: ...に違いない, ...はずだ

3 *n.* NECESSITY: 絶対必要なもの, なくてはならないもの

1 I must get back by 8 o'clock.
8時までに帰らなくてはならない。

It's an important interview so you must look your best.
大事な面接なんだから、きちんとした格好をしなくちゃね。

With streets as narrow as these, one must buy a small car.
こんなに道路が狭いんじゃ、小型車を買わないとだめだね。

You mustn't drink and drive.
飲酒運転をしてはいけない [ならない]。

You mustn't say such a thing.
そういうことを言ってはいけないよ。

This is a church so you mustn't speak too loudly.
ここは教会ですので、大きな声で話してはいけません。

2 He must be Chinese.
あの人は中国人に違いない。

She must be ready by now.
彼女はもう準備ができているはずです。

Mayumi must have broken up with her boyfriend.
真弓は彼氏と別れたはずです。

3 Vacuum cleaners are a must for every household.
掃除機は、どの家庭にもなくてはならない物です。

I must say... 全く, 本当に

I must say, I didn't expect this.
これは全く予期していませんでした。

mustache *n.* 口ひげ

mustard *n.* からし, マスタード

muster *v.* (energy to do) 奮い起こす

mutant *n.* 突然変異体

mutate *v.* 突然変異する

mutation *n.* 突然変異

mute *adj.* (does not speak) 口をきかない, 無言の, (can't speak) 口のきけない
v. (make silent) (...の) 音を消す

mutilate *v.* (...の) 手足を切断する, (...を) バラバラにする

mutiny *n.* 反乱, 反抗
v. 反乱を起こす, 反抗する

mutter *v.* ぶつぶつ言う

mutton *n.* マトン, 羊の肉

mutual *adj.* (reciprocal) (お)互いの, 相互の, (common) 共通の

Their love is mutual.
二人はお互いに愛し合っている。

The feeling is mutual.
気持ちが通じ合っている。

There needs to be a mutual understanding.
相互理解が必要です。

We have a mutual friend in Mayumi.
真由美は私たちの共通の友人です。

muzzle *n.* (device for dog's nose/mouth) 口輪; (nose) 鼻

my *adj.* 私の, 自分の, うちの, ((*masculine*))

僕の [→ I]

This is my umbrella. これは私の傘です。

my application 自分の申込書

my younger brother うちの弟

myna *n.* 九官鳥

myopia *n.* 近視, ((*figurative*)) 視野の狭さ

myriad *n.* 無数

a myriad of 無数の

myrtle *n.* ギンバイカ, 銀梅花

myself *pron.* 自分, (**I myself**) 私自身, 自分自身

I did it myself. 自分でやりました。

I can't go there myself.
私自身は行けません。

by myself (alone) 一人で, (without help) 自力で, 自分で

mysterious *adj.* 神秘的な, 不思議な

mystery *n.* 神秘, (riddle) なぞ, ミステリー, (novel film) ミステリー

I'd like to read a good mystery.
いいミステリーを読みたいなあ。

mystic *adj.* (mystical) 神秘的な

n. (person) 神秘主義者

mystify *v.* (**be mystified**) 当惑する, けむに巻かれる

mystique *n.* (aura) 神秘的雰囲気

There is a certain mystique about the old building.
その古い建物には、ある種の神秘的な雰囲気がある。

myth *n.* 神話

mythical *adj.* 神話の, (imaginary) 架空の, 想像上の

mythology *n.* 神話, (study) 神話学

N, n

nag *v.* (...に) がみがみ言う, うるさく言う
n. うるさい人, 口やかましい人

His mother is always nagging him to clean his room.
彼の母親は部屋の掃除をするように、いつもがみがみ言っている。

The neighbor has been nagging us about our dog.
隣の人が、うちの犬のことでずっとうるさく文句を言ってくる。

nail *n.* (fingernail) 爪 [→ picture of HAND], (tool) 釘 [→ picture of TOOL]
v. (fix together with nails) 釘で打ち付ける

cut one's nails 爪を切る

Stop biting your nails!
爪をかむのはやめなさい!

Hammer the nails in, will you.
釘を打ってくれる?

pull out a nail 釘を抜く

He nailed the floorboard down.
彼は床板を釘で打ち付けた。

♦ **nail clippers** *n.* 爪切り
nail file *n.* 爪やすり

nail polish *n.* マニキュア

♦ **nail polish remover** *n.* (マニキュア)除光液

naive *adj.* (ignorant of the way the world works) 世間知らずの, (simple-minded) 単純な, (考えの)甘い

I would describe her as naive.
彼女は世間知らずですね。

♦ **naivete** *n.* 世間知らず

naked *adj.* (unclothed) 裸の, (uncovered) おおいのない, (of wire) むき出しの; (of emotion) あからさまな, むき出しの

buck/stark naked 真っ裸で

The body was found naked.
遺体は全裸で発見された。

the naked eye 肉眼

You can't see it with the naked eye.
肉眼では見えませんよ。

the naked truth 赤裸々な事実, ありのままの真実

The naked truth was revealed.
赤裸々な事実が暴かれた。

name

1 *n.* PERSON'S NAME: 名前, ((*formal*)) 名, (surname) 名字, ((*formal*)) 姓, (full name) 氏名, 姓名, ((*informal*)) フルネーム, (first name) ファーストネーム

2 *n.* REPUTATION: 評判

3 *v.* PROVIDE WITH A NAME: (...に) 名前をつける, (name A B) (AをBと) 名づける

4 *v.* STATE: 言う, 指定する

5 *v.* APPOINT: 任命する, 指名する

1 Do you know his name?
あの人の名前を知ってますか?

Would you write your name and address here, please?
ここにお名前とご住所を記入していただけますか?

Yamada isn't her real name.
山田は彼女の本名ではありません。

a company name 会社名

a place name 地名

a stage name 芸名

a maiden name 旧姓

a pen name ペンネーム

N

a pet name 愛称

2 They have a good name for service.
あそこのサービスは評判がいい。

3 The first son was named Ichiro.
最初の男の子は一郎と名づけられた。

4 Just name a price. I'll buy it.
値段を決めてください。買いますから。

5 Hashimoto was named vice-president of the company.
橋本氏が会社の副社長に任命された。

be named after …にちなんで名づけられる

This street was named after a famous writer.
この通りは、有名な作家にちなんで名づけられた。

call sb names ののしる, …の悪口を言う

It's not nice to call people names.
人の悪口を言うのはよくない。

go by the name (of) …と呼ばれている

He goes by the name Wolf.
彼はウルフと呼ばれて［で通って］いる。

know by name 名前は知っている

I know him by name, though I've never met him.
会ったことはないけれど、名前は知っています。

put one's name down for (apply for) …に申し込む, …に応募する

Have you put your name down for the competition?
競技に参加を申し込みましたか？

take one's name off …から自分の名前を削除する

I took my name off the list.
リストから自分の名前を削除した。

nameless *adj.* (having no name) 名前のない, (obscure) 無名の, 名もない, (anonymous) 匿名の, (indescribable) 言いようのない

a nameless fear
何とも言いようのない恐怖

namely *adv.* 要するに, つまり, ((*formal*)) すなわち

nameplate *n.* (on door) 表札 [→ picture of HOUSE]

namesake *n.* 同名の人

name tag *n.* 名札

nanny *n.* (person who takes care of children) 子守, 乳母

nap *n.* (afternoon nap) (お)昼寝, (doze) うたた寝 [→ DOZE]

v. (have a nap) (お)昼寝する, (doze) うたた寝する

I had an afternoon nap. お昼寝をした。

napalm *n.* ナパーム

a napalm bomb ナパーム弾

nape *n.* (of neck) うなじ, 首の後ろ, 首筋, (hairline) えり足 [→ picture of FACE]

napkin *n.* ナプキン

nappy *n.* おむつ, おしめ

narcissism *n.* 自己愛, ナルシ(シ)ズム

narcissist *n.* ナルシスト

narcotic *n.* 麻酔薬, (illegal drug) 麻薬

The Mafia deals in narcotics.
マフィアは麻薬を売買している。

narrate *v.* 語る, 物語る, (movie, TV program) (…の) ナレーターを務める

narration *n.* ナレーション

narrative *n.* (story) 物語

narrator *n.* 語り手, ナレーター

narrow *adj.* (not wide) 狭い, 細い, (barely sufficient) ぎりぎりの, やっとの *v.* (become narrow) 狭くなる, 細くなる; (**narrow down**: possibilities etc.) 絞る
a narrow road 狭い [細い] 道
in the narrow sense 狭い意味 [狭義] では
a narrow majority ぎりぎりの過半数
The road narrows at the bottom.
その道は下の方で狭くなっています。
have a narrow escape 危機一髪で助かる

♦ **narrowness** *n.* 狭さ

narrowly *adv.* (avoid, escape) かろうじて, 危うく
The car narrowly missed the tree.
車は危うく木にぶつかるところだった。

narrow-minded *adj.* 心が狭い, 偏狭な

NASA *n.* ナサ, 航空宇宙局

nasal *adj.* 鼻の

♦ **nasal spray** *n.* (for decongestion) 点鼻スプレー

nasty *adj.* (unpleasant) いやな, (dirty) 汚い, (terrible) ひどい, (troublesome) 厄介な, (dangerous) 危険な, (vulgar) 下品な, (mean) 意地の悪い
a nasty smell いやなにおい
a nasty accident ひどい事故
a nasty bend in the road
道路の危険なカーブ
a nasty person 意地の悪い人
He has a tendency to turn nasty when he drinks.
あの人は酒癖が悪い。

nation *n.* 国, ((*formal*)) 国家, (people of a nation) 国民, 民族
as a nation 国家として
the United Nations 国連 [国際連合]
The nation was poised on the brink of anarchy.
その国は無政府状態に陥る寸前だった。

national *adj.* 国の, ((*formal*)) 国家の, (of the people) 国民の, (nationwide) 全国的な, (of institution) 国立の
n. (citizen) 国民
a national holiday (国の) 祝祭日
a national flag 国旗
a national anthem 国歌
a national university 国立大学
a national park 国立公園

nationalism *n.* (desire for independence) 民族(自決)主義, (belief that one's own country is best) 国家主義

nationalist *n.* 国家主義者
adj. 国家主義的な
a nationalist policy 国家主義的な政策

nationality *n.* (citizenship) 国籍, (national character) 国民性
What's her nationality?
彼女の国籍はどこですか？

nationalize *v.* (company) 国営にする, 国有化する
The banks have been nationalized.
銀行が国有化された。

nationally *adv.* 全国的に

nationwide *adj., adv.* 全国的な/に
on a nationwide scale 全国的な規模で

native *adj.* (**be native to...**) (=of person to place) ...生まれの, (=of plant to place) ...原産の; (of customs: local) 現地の,

地元の

n. (**a native of**) …生まれの人, …出身者, (a local) 地元の人, (**natives**: indigenous people) 先住民

Is this fruit native to this country?
この果物は、この国の原産ですか？

a native speaker of English
英語を母国語とする人

native customs 地元 [現地] の風習

one's native language 母国語

Native American *n.* アメリカ先住民, ネイティブアメリカン

natural

1 ***adj.*** **IN NATURE:** 自然の, 天然の

2 ***adj.*** **TO BE EXPECTED:** 普通の, 当然の, 当たり前の

3 ***adj.*** **USUAL:** ふだんの, いつもの, (**be one's natural self**) 気取らない, ふだんのままでいる, 自然体でいる

4 ***adj.*** **INNATE:** 生まれつきの, 生まれながらの, 天性の

5 ***n.*** **PERSON:** (best person for a job) 最適の人, ((*informal*)) うってつけの人, (talented person) 天才

1 a natural setting 自然環境

a natural disaster 自然災害 [天災]

a natural history museum 自然史博物館

natural science 自然科学

natural food 自然食品

natural gas 天然ガス

natural resource(s) 天然資源

2 It's quite natural for people to eat four times a day here.
ここでは1日4食(食べるの)が、ごく普通のことだ。

It's only natural that they feel tired.
彼らが疲れるのも当然だ [無理はない]。

It's only natural for children to play.
子供が遊ぶのは、ごく当たり前のことです。

3 Don't be tense. Just be natural.
緊張しないで。ふだんのままでいいんですよ。

4 He has a natural flair for acting.
彼には生まれつき演技の才能がある。

He's a natural athlete.
あの人は生まれながらのスポーツマンだ。

5 You're a natural!
あなたがうってつけだ！

♦ **natural selection** ***n.*** (Darwin's theory) (ダーウィンの)自然淘汰の法則

naturalism ***n.*** 自然主義

naturalist ***n.*** (scientist) 生物学者

naturally ***adv.*** (of course) もちろん, 当然; (without effort) 自然に, (unaffectedly) 気取らないで

Naturally, we expected you to arrive on time.
もちろん、時間どおりに着くと思っていました。

She's studied in Japan, so naturally she speaks good Japanese.
日本で勉強していたから、当然彼女は日本語を上手に話します。

Just try to behave as naturally as possible.
なるべく自然にふるまうようにして。

nature ***n.*** 自然, (the natural world) 自然界, (**Mother Nature**) 大自然; (essence) 本質, 特質, (character) 本来の性質, たち, (bad or hidden character) 本性 [→

N

KIND², SORT]

Let's let nature take its course.
自然の成り行きに任せよう。

Cloning seems to go against nature.
クローン技術は自然に反しているように思える。

Let's get back to nature.
自然に帰ろう。

the laws of nature 自然の法則

Steel is strong. That is its nature.
鋼鉄は強い。それが特質です。

It's not in her nature to be spiteful.
あの人は意地悪をするようなたちではない。

It's only human nature to want to improve one's lot.
自分の幸運を願うのが人情だ。

by nature 生まれつき, 生来, もともと

He's cheerful by nature.
彼はねっから明るい人だ。

naught → NOTHING, ZERO

all for naught むだに

naughty ***adj.*** いたずらな, 腕白な, 行儀の悪い

a naughty boy 腕白な子 [いたずらっ子]

Stop being naughty.
いたずらをするのはやめなさい。

It was very naughty of you to do that.
あんなことをするなんて、とても悪い子ですよ。

nausea ***n.*** 吐き気

nauseous ***adj.*** (**feel nauseous**) 吐き気がする

nautical ***adj.*** 航海の

♦ **nautical mile** ***n.*** 海里 [1852 m]

naval ***adj.*** 海軍の, (of warship) 軍艦の

naval warfare 海戦

a naval blockade 海上封鎖

navel ***n.*** (お)へそ [→ picture of BODY]

navigate ***v.*** (ship, airplane) 操縦する, (**navigate through**: traffic jam, maze) 通り抜ける; (give directions) 方向を指示する, ナビゲートする

The captain navigated the difficult straits.
船長は困難な海峡を通り抜けた。

navigation ***n.*** 航行, (of ship) 航海

navigator ***n.*** (of ship) 航海者, (person, device) ナビゲーター

navy ***n.*** 海軍

♦ **navy blue** ***n.*** 紺色, ネイビーブルー

Nazi ***n.*** ナチ, (believer in Nazism) ナチズム信奉者

♦ **Nazi Party** ***n.*** ナチス, ナチ党

near

1 ***adv.*** IN THE VICINITY: 近く(に)

2 ***adj.*** CLOSE: 近い, 近くの

3 ***prep.*** CLOSE TO: …の近くに

4 ***v.*** DRAW NEAR: (…に) 近づく, 近寄る, (of ship, typhoon) 接近する

5 ***adj.*** OF KINSHIP: 親しい, 近い [→ CLOSE²]

1 The cat came nearer.
猫が近寄って [近づいて] 来た。

2 It's very near. とても近いですよ。

the nearest post office
一番近い [最寄りの] 郵便局

The nearer the better.
近ければ近いほどいい。

3 The university is near the station.
大学は駅の近くにあります。

It's nowhere near here.

ここからはとても遠いよ。

4 We're nearing the end of our journey.
旅も終わりに近づいているね。

The typhoon is nearing the mainland.
台風が本土に接近して来ている。

5 a near relative 近親者

come near to (almost do) (…し)そうになる, もう少しで(…する)

She came near to tears.
彼女は泣きそうになった。

nearby *adj.* 近い, 近くの

adv. 近くに

nearly *adv.* (of condition) ほとんど, もう少しで, もうちょっとで, (of time) もうすぐ, まもなく

It's nearly empty. ほとんど空です。

He's nearly bald.
あの人は、ほとんど髪の毛がない。

We're nearly finished.
もうちょっとで終わります。

It's nearly 3 o'clock. もうすぐ3時だ。

It's nearly lunchtime.
まもなくお昼の時間です。

It's nearly time to go. もう行く時間だ。

not nearly 全然…ない

It's not nearly enough.
全然足りません。

near miss *n.* (narrowly averted collision) 異常接近, ニアミス

nearsighted *adj.* 近視の, 近眼の

neat *adj.* (clean and orderly) きちんとした, すっきりした, きれいな, (skillful) うまい, 巧妙な, (interesting) 面白い; (of drink) ストレートの

a neat room <u>きちんと</u> [すっきり] した部屋

a neat person (=person who likes things neat and clean) きれい好き

neat handwriting きれいな字

a neat trick 巧妙なトリック

I'll have a glass of whisky, neat.
ウイスキーをストレートで(下さい)。

♦ **neatly** *adv.* (tidily) きちんと

put away neatly きちんと片付ける

nebula *n.* 星雲

necessarily *adv.* (inevitably) 必ず, (**not necessarily**) 必ずしも…ない, …とは限らない

Money doesn't necessarily bring happiness.
お金が必ずしも、幸せを運んで来るとは限らない。

necessary *adj.* (required) 必要な, なくてはならない, (be necessary) 要る, (**be necessary to do**) …する必要がある, (**be not necessary to do**) …するまでもない, …しなくてもいい, …する必要がない [→ NEED]

a necessary condition 必要条件

A license is necessary.
許可が要ります。

Is it necessary for me to go?
私が行く必要はありますか？

Is it necessary to speak to him?
あの人に話さなくてはいけませんか？

It's a simple message, so it's not necessary to write it down.
簡単なことだから、書き留めるまでもないですよ。

I don't think it will be necessary for you to come today.
今日は来なくてもいいと思います。

necessity *n.* (thing) 必要不可欠なもの, 必需品, (need) 必要性

Food, clothing, and shelter are necessities.
衣食住は必要不可欠なものだ。

neck *n.* (part of the body) 首 [→ picture of BODY, FACE], (of garment) えり, えり元, 首回り, (of bottle, musical instrument) 首, ネック

a long neck 長い首
break one's neck 首の骨を折る
strain one's neck 首を痛める
a dress with a low neck えり元のあいた服
the neck of a bottle びんの首
the neck of a guitar ギターのネック

be up to one's neck in …をいっぱいかかえている, …を山ほどかかえている

He was up to his neck in work and didn't manage to sleep.
彼は仕事を山ほどかかえて、眠ることもできなかった。

breathe down sb's neck しつこく監視する

Her manager was always breathing down her neck.
マネージャーは、いつも彼女をしつこく監視していた。

neck and neck 互角で, 競り合って

The two candidates were neck and neck with voters.
二人の候補者は、選挙戦で競り合っていた。

risk one's neck 命がけでやる

It's the kind of job where you're always risking your neck for people.
人のために、常に命がけでやる仕事だ。

stick one's neck out for …のために危険を冒す

KANJI BRIDGE

首 ON: しゅ KUN: くび | NECK, HEAD

ankle	足首
capital	首都
execution by hanging	絞首刑
head (person)	首席
leading position	首位
necklace	首飾り
nipple	乳首
prime minister	首相
ruler, sovereign	元首
successfully	首尾よく
surrender	自首
wrist	手首

neckerchief *n.* ネッカチーフ, スカーフ

necklace *n.* ネックレス, 首飾り

wear a necklace ネックレスをする

necktie *n.* ネクタイ

wear a necktie ネクタイを締める

nectarine *n.* ネクタリン

née *adj.* 旧姓…

need

1 *v.* REQUIRE: (…が) 要る, 必要だ, 欲しい, (**need to do**) …する必要がある, …しなければならない, …しなくてはならない, (**not need to do**) …する必要はない

2 *aux.* MUST: …する必要がある, (**needn't**) …する必要はない, …しなくてもいい

3 *n.* COMPELLING REASON: 必要, 必要性, (**no need to do**) …する必要はない

4 *n.* SHORTAGE: 不足, 欠乏

5 *n.* REQUIREMENT: (**needs**) 要求, ニーズ, (necessary thing) 必需品, 必要なもの

1 Do you need any new clothes?
新しい服は要る？

"Do you need any sugar?"
"No thanks."
「お砂糖は要りますか？」
「いいえ、けっこうです」

If you need any help, please let me know.
助けが必要でしたら言ってください。

Who needs a break?
休憩が欲しい人はいますか？

We might need to see a specialist.
専門家に会う必要があるかもしれない。

We need to look into this matter more closely.
もっと詳しくこの問題を調べなくてはならない。

We need to sit down and think carefully.
腰を据えて慎重に考えなければならない。

In order to pass the test, you need to study hard.
試験に合格するには、一生懸命勉強しなくてはいけない。

He doesn't need to work.
彼は働く必要がない。

She didn't need to be admitted to the hospital.
彼女は入院する必要はなかった/彼女は入院しなくてもよかった。

2 You needn't have gone to the trouble.
わざわざそこまでする必要はなかったのに。

You needn't bother notifying him.
わざわざ彼に知らせなくてもいいよ。

It needn't happen, if we are careful.
注意すれば、そんなことは起こらないだろう。

3 There's no need to worry. Everything will work out fine.
心配する<u>必要</u>[こと]はない。すべてうまくいくよ。

There's no need to be nice to that slob.
あんな人に優しくすることはない。

There's no need to phone them.
彼らには電話するまでもないよ。

4 There is a desperate need for water.
水が絶対的に不足している。

5 meet consumers' needs
消費者のニーズに応える

basic needs 必需品

in need of 必要として

They were in need of medical supplies.
彼らは医薬品を必要としていた。

need hardly say 言うまでもない

need I say...? 説明する必要があるでしょうか

Gentlemen, need I say anything further?
みなさん、これ以上ご説明する必要があるでしょうか？

needle *n.* 針, (knitting needle) 編み棒, (syringe) 注射針

v. (annoy) いらいらさせる, いじめる

needless *adj.* (unnecessary) 不必要な, (wasted) むだな

needless to say 言うまでもなく

needlework *n.* (お)針仕事, (お)裁縫, (embroidery) 刺しゅう

negate *v.* (deny) 否定する, (nullify) 無効にする

negative *adj.* (of attitude) 消極的な, 悲観的な, (of response) 否定的な, (of

N

grammatical form) 否定の; (of electric charge) 陰の, (of medical test) 陰性の
n. (film for printing photographs) ネガ; (negative number) 負の数

She's a very negative person.
あの人は消極的な人だ。
a negative response 否定的な反応
a negative sentence 否定文

♦ **negative form** *n.* (Japanese verb form) ない形

negatively *adv.* (in a negative manner) 消極的に, 否定的に

neglect *v.* 無視する, ほうっておく, (one's duty) 怠る, おろそかにする, (**neglect to do**) …するのを忘れる, (**neglect to attend work/school**) ((*informal*)) サボる
n. 無視, 怠慢

He neglected his duties.
彼は職務を怠った。
The child's education was neglected.
その子の教育はほうっておかれていた。
The yard is in a state of neglect.
庭はほったらかしになっている。

negligée *n.* (women's sheer dressing gown) 部屋着, 化粧着

negligence *n.* 怠慢, 不注意

negligent *adj.* (neglectful of duty) 怠慢な, (careless) 不注意な, 気にしない

negligible *adj.* 取るに足らない, わずかな

The difference is negligible.
取るに足らない違いだ。

negotiable *adj.* 交渉できる

negotiate *v.* 交渉する, 協議する, 取り決める

The management refuses to negotiate with the trade union.
経営陣は労働組合との交渉を拒んでいる。
Are they going to negotiate a settlement?
彼らは和解に向けて協議するつもりですか？

negotiation *n.* 交渉, 折衝

enter into negotiations 交渉に入る

negotiator *n.* 交渉人

neighbor *n.* 近所の人, (next-door neighbor) 隣(の人), ((*written*)) 隣人

a next-door neighbor 隣の人
Shall we invite the neighbors?
近所の人も招きましょうか？
They've been good neighbors.
彼らはいい近所付き合いをしている。
Love your neighbor.
隣人を愛しなさい。

neighborhood *n.* 近所, 周囲, (area) 場所, 地域, (people) 近所の人

go for a walk around the neighborhood
近所を散歩する
live in a good neighborhood
いい場所に住んでいる

neighboring *adj.* (next to) 隣の

a neighboring country 隣国

neither

1 *adj.* NOT ONE OR THE OTHER: どちらの…も…ない

2 *adv., conj.* NOT EITHER: …も…ない, (**neither A nor B**) A も B も…ない

3 *pron.* NOT EITHER ONE: どちらも…ない

1 I support neither party.
どちらの党も支持していません。

2 Her paintings are neither good nor bad.
彼女の絵は良くも悪くもない。

The trip was neither too long nor too short. It was just right.
長すぎず、短すぎず、ちょうどいい旅だった。

Neither you nor I can answer that question.
あなたも私も、その質問には答えられません。

"I didn't enjoy the movie."
"Neither did I."
「映画、面白くなかった」
「私も」

3 Neither is capable of running this business.
どちらにも、この会社を運営する能力がない。

neon ***n.*** ネオン
a neon sign ネオンサイン

nephew ***n.*** (one's own) おい, (sb else's) おいごさん

Neptune ***n.*** 海王星

nerd ***n.*** オタク
a computer nerd コンピューターオタク

nerve ***n.*** 神経, (boldness) 勇気, 度胸, (impudence) 厚かましさ, ずうずうしさ
A nerve has been damaged beneath the tooth.
歯の根元の神経が傷んでいる。
He had the nerve to suggest I resign.
彼は厚かましくも私に辞職を求めた。
What nerve! なんてずうずうしい!

get on sb's nerves いらいらさせる
He gets on my nerves.
彼にはいらいらする。

lose one's nerve うろたえる, 気後れする
She lost her nerve and didn't call him.
彼女は気後れして彼に電話しなかった。

nervous ***adj.*** (jittery) びくびくする, (worried) くよくよする, (**get nervous**) あがる
Don't be nervous. びくびくするな。
a nervous feeling 落ち着かない気持ち

♦ **nervous breakdown** ***n.*** 神経衰弱
have a nervous breakdown
ノイローゼになる

nervous system ***n.*** 神経系

nervously ***adv.*** 神経質に, (timidly) おそるおそる, (uneasily) 落ち着きなく
laugh nervously 神経質に笑う
ask nervously おそるおそる尋ねる
look around nervously
落ち着きなく見回す

nest ***n.*** 巣
v. (build a nest) 巣を作る

♦ **nest egg** ***n.*** 貯金, (wife's secret savings) へそくり

net[1] ***n.*** (knotted material) 網, (in sport) ネット, (mosquito net) 蚊帳; (**the Net**: the Internet) インターネット
v. (catch) 網で捕らえる
a fishing net 魚網
a hair net ヘアーネット
cast a net 網を投げる
catch fish in a net 網で魚を捕る

net[2] ***adj.*** (of value) 純-, 正味の
n. (net profit) 純益, (net weight) 正味重量
v. (procure a net profit of) (…の) 純益をあげる

netball ***n.*** ネットボール

Netherlands ***n.*** オランダ, ((*in abbr.*)) 蘭

nettle ***n.*** イラクサ

network ***n.*** ネットワーク, (information

N

network) 情報網, (TV network) 放送網

v. (make business contacts) 人脈を作る

a communications network 通信網

a news network 報道ネットワーク

♦**networking** *n.* (making business contacts) 人脈作り

neuralgia *n.* 神経痛

neurology *n.* 神経学

neurosis *n.* ノイローゼ, 神経症

neurotic *adj.* ノイローゼの, 神経症の, (extremely anxious) 非常に神経質な

neuter *v.* (castrate) 去勢する

neutral *adj.* (of country) 中立の, (of color) 中間色の, (of electric charge) 中性の, (of substance) 中性の

n. (neutral gear) ニュートラル

neutrality *n.* 中立

maintain neutrality 中立を維持する

neutralize *v.* (make ineffective) 中和する

neutron *n.* 中性子, ニュートロン

never *adv.* (emphatic for "not") 決して…ない, 絶対(に)…ない, (speaking of experience: **have never done**) …したことがない, 一度も…ない, (speaking of habit: **never do**) …することはない

I will never forget this.
このことは決して忘れません。

He will never be a lawyer.
あの人が弁護士になることは絶対にない。

My bus never arrived.
バスはついに来なかった。

Never in my life have I seen such storms.
こんな嵐は生まれて初めてです。

He's never gotten angry.
あの人は怒ったことがありません。

I never eat meat on Sundays.
日曜日にお肉を食べることはありません。

never-ending *adj.* 果てしない, 終わりのない, 切りのない

nevertheless *adv.* それでもやはり, ((*formal*)) それにもかかわらず

"I hate going there."
"Nevertheless, I want you to go there."
「あそこに行くのはいやです」
「それでも、行ってほしいんです」

new *adj.*

1 NOT KNOWN/EXISTING BEFORE: 新しい, (of experience: first-ever) 初めての

2 NEXT: 新しい, 新たな, 次の

3 FRESH: 新鮮な, 新しい, 新たな

4 NEWLY ARRIVED: (new to) (…に)来たばかりの

5 NEWLY APPOINTED: 新任の

1 I bought a new stereo today.
今日新しいステレオを買った。

Skiing was a new experience for me.
スキーは初めての経験でした。

I am totally new to this sort of thing.
この種のことは全く初めての経験です。

2 a new era 新時代

He started on a new painting.
彼は次の絵に取りかかった。

3 new potatoes 新ジャガ

They started a new life together.
彼らは二人で新たな[新]生活を始めた。

4 Bill is new to this town.
ビルはこの町に来たばかりだ。

5 She's the new boss.
あの人が新任の上司です。

♦**new religion** *n.* 新興宗教

KANJI BRIDGE

新 ON: しん
KUN: あたら(しい), あら(た), にい | NEW

new article	新品
new bill/note	新札
new building	新築ビル
new car	新車
newcomer	新人
new employee	新入社員
new moon	新月
new product	新製品
new publication	新刊書
new student	新入生
new teacher	新任教師
new type/model	新型
nova	新星

newborn *n.* 新生児

newly *adv.* (recently) 最近, 近ごろ

newlywed *n.* 新婚の人, (**newlyweds**) 新婚夫婦

news *n.* (media information) ニュース, 報道, 情報, (tidings) 知らせ, 便り, 消息, (news program) ニュース番組

the international [domestic] news
海外 [国内] のニュース

The news about the economy is good.
景気に関するニュースは明るい。

Have you heard the latest news about China?
中国の最新情報を聞きましたか?

That's news to me. それは初耳です。

I've got some good news for you.
いい知らせがありますよ。

Is there any news of Tom?
トムの消息について何か知っていますか?

watch the news ニュースを見る

the 9 o'clock news 9時のニュース

break the news to …に打ち明ける

spread the news 情報を広める

news agency *n.* 通信社

news bulletin *n.* 臨時ニュース

newscaster *n.* ニュースキャスター

news flash *n.* ニュース速報

newsgroup *n.* (on the Internet) ニュースグループ

newsletter *n.* 会報

newspaper *n.* 新聞, (newspaper publisher) 新聞社

a daily newspaper 日刊新聞

buy [read] a newspaper
新聞を買う [読む]

a newspaper editor 新聞社の編集委員

a newspaper article 新聞記事

a newspaper headline 新聞の見出し

Your name was in the newspaper.
あなたの名前が新聞に載っていましたよ。

a newspaper delivery person 新聞配達員

Mr. Kawaguchi works for a newspaper.
川口さんは新聞社に勤めている。

newsstand *n.* 新聞販売店, 新聞屋(さん)

newt *n.* イモリ

New Year *n.* 新年 [→ HAPPY NEW YEAR!]

♦ **New Year's card** *n.* 年賀状

New Year's Day *n.* 元日, 元旦

New Year's Eve *n.* 大みそか

New Zealand *n.* ニュージーランド

next *adj.* (closest) 隣の, 次の, 一番近くの, (nearest in sequence/time) 次の, (of week, month, year) 来-

adv. 次に

n. (next person/thing) 次の人/もの

the next house (over) 隣の家

How far is it to the next town?

一番近くの町までは、どのくらいですか？

Next to the bank is a convenience store.

銀行の隣はコンビニです。

What time is the next bus?

次のバスは何時ですか？

next week 来週

the next day 翌日 [あくる日]

the next best policy 次善の策

What's the next best thing?

次にいいのは、どれですか？

the week [month, year] after next

再来週 [来月, 来年]

Would the next in line please come forward.

次にお並びの方は、前に来てください。

next time 今度, この次, ((*formal*)) 次回

Next time I see him, I'll tell him.

今度彼に会うときに、そう伝えます。

next to nothing ほとんど…ない

He probably earns next to nothing.

おそらく彼は、ほとんど稼ぎがないでしょう。

next door *adv.* 隣の家で/に, 隣で/に

adj. (**next-door**) 隣の

a next-door neighbor 隣の(家の)人

next of kin *n.* 近親者, 最も近い親戚

nibble *v.* (eat little by little) 少しずつかじる

nice *adj.*

1 PLEASANT: いい, 気持ちのいい, 感じのよい, (fun) 楽しい

2 KIND: 優しい, 親切な

3 CHARMING: すてきな, 魅力的な

1 nice weather いい天気

The bath was nice.

おふろは気持ちよかったです。

It was nice to have a rest.

休憩を取ってよかった。

We had a nice time in France.

フランスは楽しかった。

Thank you. It was nice talking to you.

ありがとう。お話できて楽しかったです。

It was nice meeting you.

お会いできてよかったです。

2 She's nice to children.

彼女は子供に優しい。

It was nice of you to help me.

手伝ってくださって、ありがとうございました。

He's such a nice man.

あの人は本当にいい人ですね。

3 That's a nice suit you're wearing.

すてきなスーツを着てらっしゃいますね。

nickel *n.* (element) ニッケル, (coin) 5セント硬貨

nickname *n.* あだ名, ニックネーム, ((*in a good sense*)) 愛称

v. (…に)あだ名をつける

nicotine *n.* ニコチン

niece *n.* (one's own) めい, (sb else's) めいごさん

night *n.* 夜, 晩, (nighttime) 夜間, (darkness) やみ, 暗やみ

a restless night 眠れない夜

on the night of September 7

9月7日の夜に

N

last night
昨日の夜 [ゆうべ, ((*formal*)) 昨夜]

tomorrow night
明日の夜 [((*formal*)) 明晩]

the night before last おとといの夜

spend a night at a hotel
ホテルで１泊する

a night flight 夜行便

a night train 夜行列車

a clear night 澄んだ夜空

a starry night 星の多い夜

a dark night やみ夜

all night (long) 一晩中, 夜通し

We stayed up all night long.
一晩中起きていた。

at night 夜に, ((*formal*)) 夜間に

At night I could hear the traffic.
夜は車の音が聞こえた。

by night 夜に

They work by night. 彼らは夜に働く。

every night 毎晩, 毎夜

He's out every night drinking.
あの人は毎晩外で飲んでいる。

for the night (in the past) その夜は, (tonight) 今夜は

And what are you going to do for the night?
今夜はどうする予定ですか？

have a good/bad night's sleep よく眠れる/眠れない

in the middle of the night 真夜中に, 深夜に

in/during the night 夜中に

I heard someone shouting next door in the night.
夜中に、隣の家で誰かがどなっているのが聞こえた。

night after night 毎晩, 毎夜, 夜ごと

Night after night my husband comes home drunk.
夫は毎晩酔って帰って来る。

night and day 昼も夜も, (all the time) 四六時中, いつも

I'm working night and day.
昼も夜も [四六時中] 働いています。

the other night この前の夜, 先日の夜

I spoke to Mr. Mori the other night.
この前の夜、森さんと話しました。

nightclub ***n.*** ナイトクラブ

nightdress ***n.*** (nightgown) ネグリジェ, (nightclothes) 寝巻き, パジャマ

nightfall ***n.*** 夕暮れ, 日暮れ

nightingale ***n.*** ナイチンゲール, サヨナキドリ

nightlife ***n.*** 夜遊び

nightly ***adj.*** 毎晩の, 夜ごとの
adv. 毎晩

nightmare ***n.*** 悪夢

have a nightmare 悪夢を見る

night school ***n.*** 定時制学校, 夜学

night shift ***n.*** 夜勤

nil ***n.*** (zero) ゼロ, (nothing) 皆無

We won five nil.
我々は５対０で勝った。

His chances of getting work are nil.
あの人が仕事をもらうチャンスはゼロ [ない] だろう。

nimble ***adj.*** (quick) 素早い, 敏しょうな, (skillful) 器用な, 上手な, (of mind) のみこみの早い

N

nine *n.* 9, 九 [also read く]
adj., pron. 9の, (people) 9人(の), (things) 9個(の), 九つ(の)

nineteen *n.* 19, 十九
adj., pron. 19の, (people) 19人(の), (things) 19個(の)

nineteenth *n.* 第19, (date) 19日
adj. 第19の, 19番目の

ninety *n.* 90, 九十, (**the nineties**) 90年代, (**one's nineties**) 90代

be ninety percent sure
90%自信がある

ninth *n.* 第9, 9番目, (date) 9日, (one-ninth) 9分の1
adj. 第9の, 9番目の

nipple *n.* 乳首 [→ picture of BODY]

nirvana *n.* 涅槃

N

nit *n.* (louse egg) シラミの卵

nitpick *v.* あら探しをする, けちをつける

nitrate *n.* 硝酸塩, 硝酸ソーダ

nitric acid *n.* 硝酸

nitrite *n.* 亜硝酸塩, 亜硝酸エステル

nitrogen *n.* 窒素

nitroglycerin *n.* ニトログリセリン

no[1]

1 *adv.* EXPRESSING NEGATION: いいえ, いえ, ((*informal*)) いや, (**no, thank you**) いいです, けっこうです

2 *adj.* NOT ONE/ANY: (thing) 何も…ない, 一つも…ない, (person) 誰も…ない, (place) どこも…ない

3 *adv.* USED BEFORE ADVERB AND ADJECTIVE: See examples below

4 *adj.* USED EMPHATICALLY: (definitely not a...) 絶対に/決して…ではない

5 *adv.* EXPRESSING AGREEMENT: はい, ええ, ((*informal*)) うん

6 *n.* NEGATIVE ANSWER: ノー, いいえ, ((*informal*)) いや

1 "Can you swim?" "No, I can't."
「泳げますか？」「いいえ、泳げません」

"Would you like a cookie?"
"No, thanks."
「クッキーはいかがですか？」
「いえ、けっこうです」

"Did you go?" "No, I didn't."
「行ったの？」「いや、行かなかった」

"It's too far." "No, it isn't."
「遠すぎるよ」「いや、そんなことないよ」

"Didn't you go?"
"No, I didn't"
「行かなかったの？」
「うん、行かなかった」

"Your name isn't Tom, is it?"
"No, it isn't—it's John."
「お名前はトムではないですよね」
「はい、違います。ジョンです」

2 She had no friends.
彼女には友達が一人もいなかった。

She has given no reason for not coming.
彼女は来ない理由を何も言わなかった。

I had no help at all.
全く助けがなかった。

No army could have survived such an attack.
どんな軍隊でも、あんな攻撃はくぐり抜けられなかっただろう。

3 Remember, no later than 6 o'clock.
いいね、6時より遅くならないのよ。

I have no particular plans for the weekend.

週末は、特に予定はありません。

The exams are of no great importance.
その試験は全然重要なものではない。

4 She's no fool, I can tell you.
彼女は決してばかじゃないよ。

He's no friend of mine.
あの人は友達なんかじゃない。

5 "It can't be difficult."
"No, of course it's not."
「難しいはずがない」
「うん、もちろん難しくはない」

6 Is that a no?
それはノーということですか？

Give me a yes or a no.
「はい」か「いいえ」で答えてください。

say no ノー[いや]と言う

no matter how/what → MATTER

No way! (expressing surprise) まさか, ((*informal*)) うそ！

KANJI BRIDGE

禁 ON: きん KUN: — | NO (AS ON SIGNS)

do not use	使用禁止
no crossing	横断禁止
no entry	立入禁止
no parking	駐車禁止
no photographs	撮影禁止
no shoes	土足厳禁
no smoking	禁煙
strictly forbidden	厳禁

no² *n.* 能, 能楽

Nobel Prize *n.* ノーベル賞

win the Nobel Prize
ノーベル賞を受賞する

nobility *n.* (**the nobility**) 貴族, (dignity) 心の気高さ

noble *adj.* (worthy of respect) 高貴な, ノーブルな, (of ambition) 気高い, (of aim) 崇高な

n. (aristocrat) 貴族

nobody *pron.* 誰も…ない, (**nobody else**) ほかに誰も…ない

n. (person without fame/influence) 名もない人

There was nobody there.
そこには誰もいなかった。

It's nobody's business but my own.
私だけのことですから、誰にも関係ありません。

Nobody could do that.
それは誰もできないよ。

I want to make my mark in this world. I don't want to be a nobody.
私はこの世に何か足跡を残したい。名もない人間になりたくないんだ。

nocturnal *adj.* 夜の, (of animal) 夜行性の

♦ **nocturnal emission** *n.* 夢精

nod *v.* (nod in agreement) うなずく, (bow slightly) 会釈する, (**nod off**) うとうとする

nod in assent うなずく

I nodded off on the train and went past my stop.
電車の中でうとうとして、乗り過ごした。

node *n.* (lump in the body) こぶ; (part of plant) 節; (on graph) 交点

Noh *n.* 能, 能楽

noise *n.* 音, 騒音, (commotion) 騒ぎ, ざわめき, (on TV, radio) 雑音, ノイズ

I couldn't stand the noise.

N

騒音に耐えられなかった。

What's all the noise about?
これは一体何の騒ぎですか？

noisy *adj.* うるさい, やかましい, 騒々しい

What a noisy pub!
なんてうるさいパブだ。

They are very noisy students.
とても騒がしい生徒たちです。

nomad *n.* 遊牧民

nomadic *adj.* 遊牧の

a nomadic tribe 遊牧民

no-man's land *n.* (situation) あいまいな状態; (between enemy lines) 中間地帯

nominal *adj.* (in name only) 名ばかりの, 名目上の; (of amount) ごくわずかな
n. (nounlike phrase) 名詞語句

He was charged a nominal amount.
彼は、ごくわずかな額を請求された。

nominate *v.* (nominate A as/for B) (= designate) (AをBに) 指名する, (= recommend) (AをBに) 推せんする, ノミネートする, (nominate A [person] as/to B [post]: appoint) (AをBに) 任命する

The committee nominated Mr. Hayashi as their candidate for the election.
委員会は、林さんを選挙の候補者に推せんした。

He was nominated president.
彼は大統領に任命された。

nomination *n.* 指名

the presidential nomination
大統領候補指名

nominee *n.* 指名された人

non- *pref.* 非-, (in-) 不-, (-less) 無-,

nonalcoholic *adj.* アルコールの入っていない, ノンアルコールの

nonchalant *adj.* 何気ない, (casual) 平気な, (cool) 平然とした, 冷静な

♦ **nonchalantly** *adv.* 何気なく, (coolly) 平然と, 冷静に

noncommissioned officer *n.* 下士官

none

1 *pron.* NOT ONE/ANY: 何も…ない, 一つも…ない, (**none at all**) 全然…ない

2 *pron.* NOBODY: 誰も…ない

3 *adv.* IN NO WAY: 少しも…ない, ((*informal*)) ちっとも…ない

1 "Do you have any cigarettes?"
"No, none."
「たばこある？」
「いや、1本もない」

"Is there a problem?"
"No, none at all."
「何か問題はありますか？」
「いいえ、全然ありません」

One is better than none.
一つでもないよりましだ。

2 None of us understood a word he was saying.
誰も、彼の言っていることを一言も理解できなかった。

None of them knew how to drive.
誰も運転の仕方を知らなかった。

3 He was none the smarter for all his schooling.
あれだけ学校に行っても、彼は少しも賢くならなかった。

She seemed none the worse for her accident.
彼女は事故にあったのに、大丈夫のようだった。

have none of (not accept) 受け入れない, 認めない

I'll have none of your excuses.
言い訳は認めません。

none other than ほかならぬ, まさしく

It was none other than Mr. Uno.
それは、ほかならぬ宇野さんだった。

nonessential *adj.* 不必要な

nonetheless *adv.* それにもかかわらず

nonexistent *adj.* 存在しない, 実在しない

nonfat *adj.* 脂肪分のない

nonfattening *adj.* (of food) 太らない

nonfiction *n.* ノンフィクション

noninterference *n.* 不干渉

non-past *n.* (tense) 現在形, 基本形

nonprofit *adj.* 非営利の

a nonprofit organization 非営利組織

nonsense *n.* (meaningless talk) ナンセンス, たわ言, (baloney) でたらめ, (foolishness) ばかなこと, くだらないこと

You're talking nonsense.
あなたの言っていることはでたらめだ。

"I shall be King." "Nonsense!"
「僕は王様になる」「ばかな!」

Stop this nonsense at once.
こんなばかなことは、今すぐやめなさい。

nonsmoker *n.* たばこを吸わない人

nonsmoking *adj.* 禁煙の

a nonsmoking section 禁煙席

(*at restaurant*) Smoking or nonsmoking?
たばこをお吸いになりますか?

nonstick *adj.* (of pan) 焦げ付かない

nonstop *adj.* (of train) 直行の, 直通の; (continuous) 絶え間ない

adv. 直行で, ノンストップで, (without pause) 休みなく

a nonstop flight 直行便

nontaxable *adj.* 課税対象外の

nontechnical *adj.* 非技術系の, 専門ではない

nonviolence *n.* (policy) 非暴力主義

noodles *n.* (in general) めん類, (**ramen noodles**) ラーメン, (**buckwheat noodles**) そば

noon *n.* (12 o'clock) 正午, (midday) 真昼

no one → NOBODY, NONE

nor *conj.* …も…も…ない [→ NEITHER]

Neither Kawamoto nor Saito was there.
川本さんも斉藤さんもいなかった。

It is neither hot nor cold today.
今日は暑くも寒くもない。

norm *n.* (standard) 標準, 基準, (**the norm**: the average) 平均, (**norms**) 規範

normal *adj.* (typical) 普通の, 通常の, ノーマルな, (not abnormal) 正常な, (standard) 標準的な, (average) 平均的な

live a normal life 普通の生活を送る

in normal circumstances 通常は

normal behavior 正常な行動

a normal child of three 平均的な3歳児

normality *n.* 正常

normally *adv.* 普通は, ふだんは

Normally, you would be fired for doing that.
普通は、そんなことをしたら首になるよ。

I normally don't eat meat.
ふだんは、お肉を食べません。

north *n.* 北, 北方, (northern part) 北部

adj. 北の, (north-facing) 北向きの

adv. 北に/へ

in [to, from] the north 北<ruby>に<rt>きた</rt></ruby> [へ, から]

The typhoon moved north.
<ruby>台風<rt>たいふう</rt></ruby>は<ruby>北上<rt>ほくじょう</rt></ruby>した。

♦ **North Pole** *n.* <ruby>北極<rt>ほっきょく</rt></ruby>

North Star *n.* <ruby>北極星<rt>ほっきょくせい</rt></ruby>

North America *n.* 北アメリカ, <ruby>北米<rt>ほくべい</rt></ruby>

northeast *n.* <ruby>北東<rt>ほくとう</rt></ruby>

adj., adv. <ruby>北東<rt>ほくとう</rt></ruby>の/に

northerly *adj.* (of wind) <ruby>北<rt>きた</rt></ruby>からの

northern *adj.* (in the north) <ruby>北<rt>きた</rt></ruby>の, (north-facing) <ruby>北向<rt>きたむ</rt></ruby>きの

♦ **Northern Hemisphere** *n.* <ruby>北半球<rt>きたはんきゅう</rt></ruby>

North Korea *n.* <ruby>北朝鮮<rt>きたちょうせん</rt></ruby> [→ KOREAN]

northward *adv.* <ruby>北<rt>きた</rt></ruby>の<ruby>方<rt>ほう</rt></ruby>へ, <ruby>北<rt>きた</rt></ruby>に<ruby>向<rt>む</rt></ruby>かって

adj. <ruby>北<rt>きた</rt></ruby>(へ)の

northwest *n.* <ruby>北西<rt>ほくせい</rt></ruby>

adj., adv. <ruby>北西<rt>ほくせい</rt></ruby>の/に

nose *n.* <ruby>鼻<rt>はな</rt></ruby> [→ picture of FACE]

blow one's nose <ruby>鼻<rt>はな</rt></ruby>をかむ

Your nose is bleeding.
<ruby>鼻血<rt>はなぢ</rt></ruby>が<ruby>出<rt>で</rt></ruby>ていますよ。

I've got a stuffed-up nose.
<ruby>鼻<rt>はな</rt></ruby>が<ruby>詰<rt>つ</rt></ruby>まっている。

I've got a runny nose today.
<ruby>今日<rt>きょう</rt></ruby>は<ruby>鼻水<rt>はなみず</rt></ruby>が<ruby>出<rt>で</rt></ruby>る。

♦ **nose around** *v.* かぎ<ruby>回<rt>まわ</rt></ruby>る, せんさくする

Stop nosing around in other people's business.
<ruby>他人<rt>たにん</rt></ruby>のことをせんさくするのはやめなさい。

nose out (detect) かぎつける

nosebleed *n.* <ruby>鼻血<rt>はなぢ</rt></ruby>

nostalgia *n.* <ruby>懐<rt>なつ</rt></ruby>かしさ, ノスタルジア, <ruby>郷愁<rt>きょうしゅう</rt></ruby>

feel nostalgia for (…が)<ruby>懐<rt>なつ</rt></ruby>かしい

nostalgic *adj.* <ruby>懐<rt>なつ</rt></ruby>かしい

nostril *n.* <ruby>鼻<rt>はな</rt></ruby>の<ruby>穴<rt>あな</rt></ruby>, ((formal)) <ruby>鼻孔<rt>びこう</rt></ruby>

not *adv.*

1 EXPRESSING NEGATION: (isn't)…ない, (isn't a…)…ではない, …じゃない, (not do)…しない, (isn't that one doesn't/isn't…)…ないことはない, (not only doesn't/isn't…)…ないだけではない

2 IMPERATIVE USAGE: (don't…)…するな, …しないで(ください)

1 It's not cold enough yet.
まだ<ruby>十分<rt>じゅうぶん</rt></ruby>冷えていない。

It's not that hot. そんなに<ruby>暑<rt>あつ</rt></ruby>くない。

It's not a kimono. It's a yukata.
<ruby>着物<rt>きもの</rt></ruby>じゃありません、ゆかたです。

There aren't any more.
もうありません。

He hasn't done it yet.
<ruby>彼<rt>かれ</rt></ruby>はまだやっていない。

Perhaps she won't notice.
<ruby>彼女<rt>かのじょ</rt></ruby>は<ruby>気<rt>き</rt></ruby>づかないかもしれない。

She didn't want to go.
<ruby>彼女<rt>かのじょ</rt></ruby>は<ruby>行<rt>い</rt></ruby>きたくなかった。

I told him not to come late.
<ruby>遅<rt>おく</rt></ruby>れて<ruby>来<rt>こ</rt></ruby>ないように<ruby>彼<rt>かれ</rt></ruby>に<ruby>言<rt>い</rt></ruby>っておいた。

2 Don't run. Walk.
<ruby>走<rt>はし</rt></ruby>らないで。<ruby>歩<rt>ある</rt></ruby>いてください。

isn't it? …ね

It's difficult, isn't it?
<ruby>難<rt>むずか</rt></ruby>しいですね。

not a bit → BIT

not all → ALL

not always → ALWAYS

not as…as …ほど…ない

It was not as difficult as I thought it would be.
<ruby>思<rt>おも</rt></ruby>ってたほど<ruby>難<rt>むずか</rt></ruby>しくなかった。

not at all (acknowledging gratitude) どういたしまして; (emphatic for "not") 決して/全然…ない

"Thank you." "Not at all."
「ありがとう」「どういたしまして」

"Sorry for making you wait."
"Not at all."
「お待たせしてすみません」
「いいえ、どういたしまして」

"Sorry to inconvenience you."
"Not at all."
「ご迷惑をおかけして申し訳ありません」
「いいえ、大丈夫です」

This job is not at all easy.
この仕事は決して簡単ではない。

I'm not at all pleased to hear this.
こんなことを聞いても、全然うれしくない。

not one 一つも…ない

Not one person came to the meeting.
会合に一人も来なかった。

Not one pen worked.
書けるペンは1本もなかった。

not only A but also B → ONLY

not quite どうも…ない

What he says is not quite convincing.
彼の言っていることは、どうも説得力がない。

not really/readily/easily なかなか…ない, 簡単には…ない

I haven't really had an opportunity to take a vacation.
休みを取る機会がなかなかありませんでした。

not that …というわけではない

It's not that I don't like sushi, I just prefer other food.
おすしが嫌いなわけではないけど、ほかの物が食べたい。

not to mention …はもちろん, …は言うまでもなく

She can speak Russian, not to mention German.
彼女はドイツ語はもちろん、ロシア語も話せる。

not very 大して/あまり…ない, それほどでもない

This program is not very interesting.
この番組は、あまり面白くない。

"Have you been busy lately?"
"No, not very."
「最近、忙しい？」
「ううん、それほどでもない」

or not …かどうか

I wonder if it will be successful or not.
成功するかどうか、気になりますね。

notable ***adj.*** (remarkable) 著しい, (of person) 著名な, (noteworthy) 注目に値する

notably ***adv.*** (in particular) 特に

notary public ***n.*** 公証人

notch ***n.*** (V-shaped opening) 刻み目, 切れ込み

note

1 ***n.*** WRITTEN MESSAGE: (memo) メモ, 覚え書き, (short letter) 短い手紙, (student's notes) ノート, (commentary) 注釈, (footnote) 脚注

2 ***v.*** NOTICE: (…に) 気づく, 注意する

3 ***v.*** WRITE DOWN: 書き留める, 書いておく, ((*formal*)) 記す

4 ***n.*** MONEY: 紙幣, (お)札

5 *n.* IN MUSIC: 音, 音符

1 I think you ought to take notes.
メモを取ったほうがいいと思う。

Do you have notes from last week's meeting?
先週の会議の覚え書きはありますか？

I left a note on the door.
ドアにメモを張っておいた。

a thank-you note (お)礼状

Can I borrow your notes from yesterday's lecture?
昨日の講義のノート、貸してくれない？

See note below. 下記の注釈参照。

2 Note that the verb comes at the end of the sentence.
文末に動詞が来ることに注意して。

3 I think you'd better note this one down.
これは書き留めておいたほうがいいと思います。

4 a crumpled note しわくちゃな紙幣

I'm sorry, I've only got a ¥10,000 note.
すみません、1万円札しかありません。

5 a high [low] note 高[低]音

notebook *n.* ノート

♦**notebook computer** *n.* ノートパソコン

notepad *n.* メモ帳

notepaper *n.* 便せん

nothing

1 *pron., n.* NOT ANYTHING: 何も…ない

2 *pron.* FOLLOWED BY ADJECTIVE: …ことではない, …ものではない

3 *adv.* IN NO WAY: 少しも…ない, 全然…ない

1 There was nothing in the room.
部屋には何もなかった。

There's nothing in the bag.
かばんには何も入っていません。

There is nothing to worry about.
心配することは何もない。

There's nothing to drink.
飲み物はありません。

He said nothing.
彼は何も言わなかった。

"What's wrong?" "Oh, nothing."
「どうしたの？」「いや、別に」

Nothing else came out.
ほかに何も出てこなかった。

Nothing happened when I pressed the button.
ボタンを押しても、何も起こらなかった。

He means nothing to me.
あの人は(私にとっては)何でもない/あの人のことは何とも思ってない。

They started arguing about nothing.
二人は、つまらないことで言い合いを始めた。

2 It's nothing special.
特別なことではない。

There's nothing new to report.
新しく報告することは、ありません。

There's nothing better than a warm fire on a cold winter's night.
寒い冬の夜の暖かい暖炉ほど、いいものはない。

I hope it's nothing serious.
大したことでないといいですね。

There's nothing so annoying as losing your house key.
家のかぎをなくすことほど、厄介なことはない。

There's nothing else to do, so why don't we see a movie?
ほかに何もすることがないから、映画

でも見ない？

3 It's nothing like that (which you are implying).
全くそういうことではありません。

It was nothing like what we had expected.
期待していたのと全然違った。

almost nothing ほとんど…ない

There was almost nothing left.
ほとんど何も残っていなかった。

come to nothing (be in vain) むだになる, (fail) 失敗に終わる, 何にもならない

In the end, it all came to nothing.
結局すべて、むだになった。

do nothing but ただ…するだけだ, …ばかりする

He does nothing but watch TV.
あの人はテレビばかり見ている。

for nothing (in vain) むだに; (for free) ただで, 無料で

All that effort was for nothing.
努力がすべてむだに終わった。

I got this bike for nothing.
ただでこの自転車を手に入れた。

have nothing to do with …と関係ない, …とかかわらない

That has nothing to do with it.
それは全く関係ない。

I'll have nothing to do with them.
彼らとかかわるつもりはない。

nothing but (no more than) ただの…, …にすぎない, (only) …しか…ない

He's nothing but a lazy bum.
あいつはただの怠け者だ。

There's nothing but butter in the fridge.
冷蔵庫にはバターしかない。

nothing less than → LESS

nothing like as…as …ほど…ない

It was nothing like as good as you said.
あなたが言ってたほどよくなかったよ。

nothing more than ただの…, …にすぎない

It's nothing more than a cold.
ただのかぜです。

He's nothing more than a liar.
あの人はうそつきにすぎない。

nothing short of → SHORT

nothing to… …ようなことではない

It's nothing to get excited about.
興奮するようなことじゃない。

there's nothing for it but to do …するよりほかない

There's nothing for it but to own up.
すっかり白状するよりほかない。

there's nothing like …ほどいいものはない, (…が) 一番だ

There's nothing like a hot bath after a long, hard day.
長くきつい一日の終わりの温かいおふろほど、いいものはない。

think nothing of it どういたしまして, 気にしないで

Oh, that's all right. Think nothing of it.
ああ、いいんですよ。気にしないで。

notice

1 ***n.*** **PRINTED/WRITTEN INFORMATION:** 通知, ((*formal*)) 告知, (on wall, bulletin board) 掲示, 張り紙, (warning) 警告

2 ***v.*** **OBSERVE:** (…に) 気がつく, 注意する

3 ***n.*** **ATTENTION:** 注意, 注目

1 a notice of change of address 移転通知

The door had a notice on it that said "Private."
ドアには「立入禁止」と書かれた掲示があった。

There was a notice on the bulletin board about next week's game.
掲示板に、来週の試合についての張り紙があった。

put up a notice 掲示を出す

take down a notice 掲示を外す

2 Did you notice the new car?
新車に気がついた?

She couldn't help noticing you staring at her.
君がじっと見ていることに、彼女はいやでも気づいていたよ。

3 He took no notice of what was being said.
彼は言われていることに何の注意も払わなかった。

If I were you, I wouldn't pay her any notice.
私があなただったら、あの人のことは気にかけないよ。

at/on short notice すぐに, 急に

I was told that I wouldn't be able to book a decent hotel on such short notice.
こんなに急に、きちんとしたホテルは予約できないと言われた。

be given notice 通知を受ける

We were given notice that as of next week our work hours would be cut.
来週から、労働時間が短縮されると通知を受けた。

give notice 通知する, 知らせる

I gave notice that I would vacate the apartment by the end of the month.
月末までに、アパートを引き払う予定だと知らせた。

noticeable *adj.* (easy to notice) 目立つ, 人目を引く, (evident) 明らかな

notice board *n.* 掲示板, 告知板

notification *n.* 通知

give notification 通知する

notify *v.* (inform) (...に) 知らせる, 通知する, (police) (...に) 通報する

The parents were notified of the accident.
両親に事故のことが知らされた。

notion *n.* (idea) 観念, 考え, (concept) 概念

the notion of reincarnation
霊魂は生まれ変わるという考え

notorious *adj.* 有名な, 悪名高い

a notorious thief [politician]
悪名高い泥棒 [政治家]

notwithstanding *prep.* ...にもかかわらず [→ DESPITE]

nougat *n.* ヌガー

noun *n.* 名詞

nourish *v.* 養う, 育てる, (feelings) いだく

nouveau riche *n.* 成金

novel[1] *n.* 小説

write a novel 小説を書く

a best-selling novel ベストセラー小説

a detective [historical] novel
推理 [歴史] 小説

novel[2] *adj.* (new) 新しい, 目新しい, 斬新な, (unusual, strange) 奇抜な [→ NEW]

novelist *n.* 小説家

novelty *n.* 目新しさ, 珍しさ

November *n.* 11月, 十一月

now

1 *adv.* PRESENTLY: 今, 現在, 今(で)は, 現在(で)は

2 *adv.* USED INTERJECTIONALLY: (to make a suggestion) さあ, さて, それでは, (to change the subject) ところで

3 *conj.* SINCE: (**now that...**) もう…から, もう…ので

4 *n.* THIS MOMENT: 今, 現在

5 *adv.* IMMEDIATELY: 今すぐに

1 It's now just past 7 o'clock.
今ちょうど7時を過ぎたところです。

I'm going out now.
今出かけるところです。

2 Now, just calm down.
さあ、落ち着いて。

Now then, let's go into the garden.
それでは、庭に行きましょう。

Now then, can we begin?
では、始めてよろしいですか？

Now then, where was I?
((*informal*)) えっと、どこまで話したっけ？

Now, how did the interview go?
ところで、面接はどうだった？

3 Now that everyone knows, there's no point in trying to keep quiet about it.
もうみんな知っているんだから、隠していてもしようがないよ。

Now that I'm retired, I can take things easy.
もう退職したので、のんびりできます。

4 Now is the time to decide.
今こそ決断する時ですよ。

Now's your chance.
今がチャンスです。

I don't know where I'll be a year from now.
今から1年後に、どこにいるかはわからない。

5 Do it now. 今すぐやりなさい。

any day/moment/time now まもなく

We should be hearing something from them any day now.
まもなく何か連絡があるはずだ。

as of now (from now on) これからは, 今後は, (at present) 今のところ

As of now, I want to see everyone working harder.
今後は、もっと一生懸命に働いてほしい。

come now さあさあ, まあまあ, ((*masculine*)) おいおい

even now 今でも, いまだに [→ EVEN[1]]

every now and again/then 時々 [→ EVERY]

for now 当分は, さしあたり

It'll do for now.
さしあたり、これでいこう/とりあえず、これで大丈夫。

For now, you'll just have to live with.
当分は、それでやっていくしかないよ。

from now on これからは, 今後は

From now on, things are going to be different.
これからは、事情が違ってきますよ。

just now たった今, ちょうど今

A fax came in just now.
たった今ファックスが届きました。

I was talking to him just now.
ちょうど今、彼と話していたところです。

now and then/again 時々

I visit my great-aunt now and again.

時々大おばを訪ねます。

now, now (to make sb calm) まあまあ, (to tell sb to stop sth) こらこら

Now, now! Let's not argue.

こらこら、けんかしないで。

now or never やるなら今, 最後のチャンス, 今しかない

You must decide. It's now or never.

決めるなら、今しかないよ。

up to/until/till now 今までは, 今までのところ

I've never thought about it much until now.

今までは、あまり考えたことはなかった。

nowadays *adv.* このごろ, 最近は, 今では

Nowadays, no one uses that word.

最近は、誰もその言葉を使わない。

nowhere *adv., n.* どこにも…ない, どこへも…ない

He was nowhere to be seen.

彼はどこにも見当たりませんでした。

Is nowhere sacred?

どこにも聖域はないのか？

There's nowhere else to hide.

ほかに隠れる場所はどこにもない。

I went nowhere yesterday.

昨日はどこへも行かなかった。

get nowhere (of person) うまくいかない, (of method) らちがあかない

We're getting nowhere doing it this way.

こんなやり方では、らちがあかない。

in the middle of nowhere 人里離れた所に, へんぴな所に

We got a flat tire in the middle of nowhere.

人里離れた所でタイヤがパンクした。

nowhere near …に程遠い, 到底…ない

You're nowhere near the answer.

正解には程遠いよ。

You're nowhere near as smart as he is.

頭のよさでは、あなたは彼には到底及ばない。

(from) out of nowhere 突然どこからともなく

He just popped up out of nowhere and became famous.

彼は突然<u>どこからともなく現れて</u> [全くの無名から] 有名になった。

nozzle *n.* ノズル, 発射口, ((*informal*)) 口

The nozzle of the hose is blocked.

ホースの口がふさがっている。

NSC *n.* 国家安全保障会議

nuance *n.* ニュアンス

nuclear *adj.* (of energy) 原子力の, (of atomic nucleus) 核の

a nuclear bomb 核爆弾

nuclear energy *n.* 原子力, 核エネルギー

nuclear family *n.* 核家族

nuclear power *n.* 原子力, 核エネルギー, (country) 核保有国

nuclear weapon *n.* 核兵器

nucleus *n.* (of atom) 原子核, (of cell) 細胞核, (of city) 中心, (core) 核心

nude *adj.* 裸の, (of painting, photo) ヌードの, 裸体の [→ NAKED]

n. (painting) 裸体画, (statue) 裸像

She appeared nude in a men's magazine.

彼女は男性誌にヌードで出ていた。

in the nude ヌードで, 裸で, ((*emphatic*)) 真っ裸で

nudge *v.* (push) ひじで軽くつつく, (encourage) 促す
n. (push) ひじで軽くつつくこと

nudism *n.* 裸体主義, ヌーディズム

nuisance *n.* (situation) 面倒なこと, 迷惑, 困ったもの, (person) 迷惑な人, 困り者
What a nuisance! 面倒だな!
That man is a nuisance.
あの人には困ったものだ。
Try not to make a nuisance of yourself.
人に迷惑をかけないようにしなさい。

nullify *v.* (render invalid) 無効にする, 取り消す, (legal decision) 破棄する

numb *adj.* (having no sensation) 感覚がない, (from cold) かじかんだ, (from not moving) しびれた; (be/feel emotionally numb) 呆然とする
My hands were numb from the cold.
寒さで手がかじかんでいた。
My legs are numb from sitting on my knees for so long.
長く正座をしていたせいで、足がしびれた。

number
1 *n.* FIGURE: 数字
2 *n.* QUANTITY: 数, 数量, (**a large number of**) たくさんの, 多数の, (=of people) 大勢の
3 *n.* NUMERAL IN A SERIES: 番号, -番, (telephone number) 電話番号, (room number) -号室
4 *v.* PROVIDE WITH A NUMBER: (…に) 番号をつける
5 *v.* AMOUNT TO IN NUMBER: (…に) 達する

1 The numbers were mind-boggling.
その数字は途方もないものだった。
an even [odd] number 偶数 [奇数]
a cardinal [an ordinal] number
基数 [序数]

2 A large number of people stood around doing nothing.
大勢の人が何もしないで立っていた。
Any number of people are welcome.
何人でも歓迎します。

3 Are you number eleven, or twelve?
あなたは１１番ですか、それとも１２番ですか？
What's your phone number?
電話番号は何番ですか？
It's room number 202.
２０２号室です。

4 Let's number them according to size.
大きさ順に番号をつけましょう。

5 The spectators numbered in the thousands.
観客の人数は数千にも達した。

♦ **number one** *n., adj.* 一番(の)
number plate *n.* (車の)ナンバープレート
[→ picture of CAR]

KANJI BRIDGE

数 ON: すう KUN: かず, かぞ(える) | NUMBER, SEVERAL, A NUMBER OF

amount .... 数量
commission .... 手数料
decimal .... 小数
decision by majority .... 多数決
fraction .... 分数
large number .... 多数
majority .... 大多数
many .... 数多くの

N

math(ematics)	数学
minority	少数
number of articles	品数
number of times	回数
number of trains	本数
plural	複数
points, score	点数
several days	数日
several fold	数倍
several kinds	数種類
several people	数人
several times	数回
total	総数

numeral ***n.*** 数字

numerical ***adj.*** 数の, 数的な

a numerical value 数値

numerous ***adj.*** (many) 多くの, 多数の, (of people) 大勢の

nun ***n.*** 尼僧, (Buddhist) 尼(さん), (Christian) 修道女

nurse ***n.*** 看護師(さん), ナース, (female) 看護婦(さん)

v. (ill person) 看病する, (baby) (…に) 授乳する, (wound) (…の) 手当てをする, (emotion) 心にいだく, (plant) 大事に育てる

She nursed him back to health.
彼女は彼が回復するまで看病した。

nursery ***n.*** (school) 保育園, (room) 子供部屋, 育児室; (for plants) 種苗場

She goes to the nearby nursery.
あの子は近くの保育園に通っている。

♦ **nursery rhyme** ***n.*** 童謡

nursery school ***n.*** 保育園

nursing ***n.*** (for ill people) 看病, 看護, (for the elderly) 介護

nursing home ***n.*** (for the elderly) 老人ホーム, (for ill people) 療養所

nurture ***v., n.*** 養育(する)

nut ***n.*** 木の実, (for eating: **nuts**) ナッツ; (for bolt) ナット [→ picture of TOOL]; (crazy person) 狂人, (eccentric person) 変人, (fan) ファン, -狂

an anime nut アニメファン

nuts and bolts (essentials) 基本, (practical details) 実務

nutcase ***n.*** 狂人

nutcracker ***n.*** クルミ割り器

nutmeg ***n.*** (seed, spice) ナツメグ, (tree) ニクズクの木

nutrient ***n.*** 栄養

nutrition ***n.*** 栄養, (study) 栄養学

This cereal contains a lot of nutrition.
このシリアルには栄養がたっぷり含まれている。

nutritious ***adj.*** 栄養のある

a nutritious breakfast 栄養のある朝食

nutshell ***n.*** 木の実の殻, (of walnut) クルミの殻

in a nutshell (to be brief) 簡単に言うと, 要するに

What is the book about, in a nutshell?
要するに、何に関する本ですか？

nylon ***n.*** (fiber) ナイロン, (**nylons**: stockings) ナイロンストッキング

O, o

oak *n.* (tree) オーク, カシ, ナラ, (wood) オーク材

oar *n.* オール, かい

pull the oars オールをこぐ

oasis *n.* ((*also figurative*)) オアシス

oat *n.* オートムギ, カラスムギ

oath *n.* 誓い, 宣誓 [→ SWEAR]

take an oath 誓う [宣誓する]

a written oath 誓約書

You are under oath to tell the truth.
あなたは真実を語ると宣誓しています。

oatmeal *n.* オートミール

obedience *n.* 服従, 素直に従うこと

obedient *adj.* (of child) 素直な, 従順な

obelisk *n.* オベリスク

obese *adj.* 肥満体の, 太りすぎの [→ FAT]

obesity *n.* 肥満症

obey *v.* (orders, instructions) (…に)従う, ((*formal*)) 服従する, (rules) 守る, (superiors) (…の)言うことをきく

The troops did not obey their orders.
軍隊は命令に従わなかった。

Obey the law. 法律を守りなさい。

obi *n.* (kimono waist wrap) 帯

put on an obi 帯を締める

obituary *n.* 死亡記事, (**the obituaries**) 死亡記事欄

object *n.* (thing) 物, 物体, (of interest, desire) 的, 対象, (aim) 目的 [→ AIM 3, GOAL]; (of verb) 目的語

v. (object to: oppose) (…に) 反対する, 異議を唱える

a solid object 固体

an object of ridicule 嘲笑の的

an object of desire 欲望の対象

Not all sentences have an object.
すべての文章に、目的語があるわけではない。

I object to that decision.
その決定には反対です。

objection *n.* 反対, 異議

raise objections 異議を唱える

have no objection (to) (…に) 異議はない

(*in court*) Objection, Your Honor!
裁判長、異議あり!

objective *adj.* 客観的な

n. (aim) 目的, 目標

Let's try to be objective about this problem.
この問題は客観的に見るようにしましょう。

objectively *adv.* 客観的に

obligate *v.* (**be obligated to do**) …する義務がある

obligation *n.* 義務, 義理

fulfill an obligation 義務を果たす

a sense of obligation 義務感

obligatory *adj.* (compulsory) 義務的な, 強制的な, (of course) 必修の

Medical insurance is obligatory in Japan.
日本では健康保険への加入が義務づけられています。

oblige *v.* (**be/feel obliged to do**) …せざるを得ない, …しなければならない, …するよう義務づけられている, (**oblige sb/me with**: help by providing) …してあげる/…してくれる, (**be obliged to**: be indebted to) …に義理がある, (**be obliged if**: feel grateful if) …していただければありがたい

We were obliged to see them off at the airport.
空港で、彼らを見送らなければならなかった。

Foreign students are obliged to undergo alien registration.
留学生は、外国人登録をするよう義務づけられている。

Now that they've helped us, we're obliged to return the favor.
助けていただいたのですから、彼らには義理があります。

We are obliged to you for coming.
お越しいただき、ありがとうございます。

Would you oblige us by playing the piano?
どうかピアノを弾いていただけませんか?

obliging *adj.* 親切な

oblique *adj.* (diagonal) 斜めの, 傾いた; (indirect) 間接の, (roundabout) 遠回しの

obliterate *v.* (destroy) 壊滅させる, (wipe out) 消す, 抹殺する

oblivion *n.* (state of unawareness) 無意識 (の状態), (state of having been forgotten) 忘れられている状態

drink oneself into oblivion 酔いつぶれる

fall into oblivion 忘れ去られる

oblivious *adj.* (be oblivious to/of) (…に) 気がつかない

oblong *n., adj.* (rectangular) 長方形(の), (elliptical) 楕円形(の)

obnoxious *adj.* いやな, うるさい

oboe *n.* オーボエ

obscene *adj.* (lewd) みだらな, ひわいな, (pornographic) わいせつな; (excessive) とんでもない

spend an obscene amount of money
とんでもない大金を使う

obscenity *n.* わいせつ, ひわい, (obscene utterance) ひわいな言葉

obscure *adj.* (unknown) あまり知られていない, 無名の, (unclear) はっきりしない *v.* (make difficult to see) 見えなくする, (blot out) おおい隠す, (make difficult to understand) あいまいにする, ぼかす

an obscure poet 無名の詩人

The mist obscured our view of the top of the tower.
塔のてっぺんは、もやがかかって見えなかった。

Don't let the main point be obscured by so many personal anecdotes.
個人の逸話を入れすぎて、主眼がぼやけないようにしなさい。

obscurity *n.* (namelessness) 無名

observance *n.* (of rules) 守ること; (celebration) 祝うこと, (ceremony) 行事, 式典

observation *n.* 監視, 観察, (opinion) 意見, (remark) 発言

under observation 監視中で

keep under observation 監視する

a brilliant observation すばらしい観察

♦ **observation platform** *n.* 展望台

observatory *n.* (astronomical) 天文台

observe *v.* (follow: rules) 守る, (pay attention to) よく見る, 観察する, (noticc) (…に) 気づく, (watch with a view to learn) 見学する, (comment) ((*formal*)) (… と) 述べる, (celebrate) 祝う

Try to observe the rules.
規則を守るよう心がけて。

Observe the animal's movements very

carefully.
動物の動きを、よく観察してみて。

The student teacher just sat at the back and observed.
教育実習生は、後ろに座って見学しているだけだった。

KANJI BRIDGE

観 ON: かん KUN: — | OBSERVE

audience	観客, 観衆
concept, idea	観念
intuitive	直観的な
objective	客観的な
observe	観察する
optimistic	楽観的な
pessimistic	悲観的な
sightseeing	観光
subjective	主観的な
survey	観測する
tourist	観光客
view of life	人生観
viewpoint	観点
visit (a school)	参観する
worldview	世界観

observer *n.* 観察者, 見る人, (nonparticipatory) オブザーバー, 立会人, 傍聴人

obsess *v.* (…に) 取り付く, (**be obsessed with**) …に取り付かれる, …で頭がいっぱいになる, (**obsess about / over**) くよくよ心配する

She was obsessed by the idea of being famous.
彼女は有名になりたいという思いに取り付かれていた。

He's obsessed with her.
彼は彼女のことで頭がいっぱいだ。

I wouldn't obsess over it (if I were you).
私だったら、そんなことをくよくよ心配しないよ。

obsession *n.* 取り付かれること, (fixed idea) 執念, (fantasy) 妄想

have an obsession with …に取り付かれる, …のことばかり考える

He has an obsession with money.
あの人はお金のことばかり考えている。

obsessive *adj.* (of person) 執拗な, 取り付かれる

♦ **obsessive-compulsive disorder** *n.* 強迫神経症

obsolete *adj.* (not used) 使われていない, (out-of-date) 時代遅れの, すたれた

This computer is now obsolete.
このコンピューターはもう時代遅れだ。

an obsolete word すたれた言葉 [廃語]

obstacle *n.* 障害, じゃま, 妨げ, (concrete thing) 障害物

His traditional conservative thinking was an obstacle to progress.
彼の古風で保守的な考え方が、進歩への妨げになっていた。

♦ **obstacle course** *n.* 障害物コース, ((*figurative*)) 難関

obstacle race *n.* 障害物競走

obstetrician *n.* 産科医

obstetrics *n.* 産科学, 助産学

obstinate *adj.* (of person) がんこな, 強情な, (of illness) 治りにくい

obstruct *v.* (road) ふさぐ, (sb's view) さえぎる, (sb's way, progress, justice) じゃまをする, 妨害する

O

Unfortunately, the building in front of us obstructs the view.
残念なことに、目の前の建物にさえぎられて景色が見えない。

They tried to obstruct the course of justice.
彼らは、裁判の進行を妨害しようとした。

obstruction *n.* (thing that obstructs) 障害物, (act of obstructing) 妨害

obstruction of justice 司法妨害

obtain *v.* 得る, 手に入れる [→ GET 6]

obtuse *adj.* (of person) 鈍い, 鈍感な, (of angle) 鈍角の

obvious *adj.* (clear) 明らかな, 明白な, (of lie) 見えすいた, (natural) 当然の

That's obvious. それは明らかだ。

It's obvious that he doesn't know what he's talking about.
あの人は自分の言っていることがわかっていないのは明らかだ。

The obvious conclusion is that they were involved in a relationship.
あの二人は関係があったというのが、当然の結論です。

obviously *adv.* (clearly) 明らかに, どう見ても, (naturally) 当然, もちろん

Obviously we're not welcome here.
どう見ても、私たちは歓迎されていないようだ。

occasion *n.* (timc) とき, 折, 時点, きっかけ, (situation) 場合, (chance) 機会, (event) 行事, 出来事, 催し [→ CHANCE 1, OPPORTUNITY]

His retirement provided the occasion for my promotion.
彼の退職で、私に昇進の機会が回って来た。

On that occasion, she said very little.
あのときは、彼女はほとんどしゃべらなかった。

If the occasion arises, I'll inform you.
((*polite*)) そういう場合には、ご連絡差し上げます。

I'd like to take this occasion to thank everyone here today.
((*polite*)) この場をお借りして、今日ここにお集まりの皆様にお礼を申し上げたいと存じます。

It was an important social occasion.
それは社交界の大切な催しだった。

on occasion 時々, 時折

I do enjoy a glass of brandy on occasion.
時々ブランデーを1杯程度飲むことはあります。

rise to the occasion 臨機応変に対処する

occasional *adj.* 時々の, たまの

an occasional mistake たまの誤り

occasionally *adv.* 時々, たまに, 時たま

Occident *n.* 西洋

occidental *adj.* 西洋の

occult *n.* オカルト

adj. オカルトの, (mysterious) 神秘的な

occupant *n.* (user of space) 使用者, (of house) 居住者

occupation *n.* (job) 職業 [→ JOB]; (military occupation) 占領

What's your occupation?
ご職業は何ですか？

be under occupation 占領下にある

♦ **occupation forces** *n.* 占領軍

occupied *adj.* (of room) 使用中だ

The bathroom was occupied.
トイレは使用中だった。

occupy *v.* (house) (…に) 入る, 住む, (area) 占める, (position, job) (…に) 就く, (country) 占領する; (take the place/space of) (…の場所を) 取る, (of activity: occupy one's time) (時間を) 取る, かける

When will you occupy the property?
ご入居の予定は、いつですか？

No one has occupied the house for years.
その家はもう何年も誰も住んでいない。

The new houses occupy an entire block.
新築の家が1区画全体を占めている。

Mr. Tanaka occupies a key position in the cabinet.
田中さんは内閣の要職に就いている。

After the war, the Allies occupied Germany and Japan.
戦後、連合軍はドイツと日本を占領した。

The cat occupied my seat.
猫が私の椅子を取った [占領した]。

Reading occupies a lot of my time.
読書に多くの時間をかけています。

occupy oneself with / be occupied with …に専念する, …に夢中になる, (be busy with) …で忙しい

He needs something to occupy himself with.
彼には、何か専念できるものが必要だ。

occur *v.* (happen) 起こる, 発生する; (**occur to**) ふと思う, 思いつく, 思い浮かぶ

The accident occurred late at night.
事故は夜遅くに起きた [発生した]。

The technological changes that have occurred in the last decade are staggering.
この10年間に起きた科学技術の変化は、驚異的です。

It occurred to me that he might be right, after all.
やっぱり彼は正しかったのかもしれないと、ふと思った。

The thought never occurred to me.
そんなことは思いつきもしませんでした。

occurrence *n.* 出来事

a rare occurrence まれな出来事

ocean *n.* 海

oceanfront *n.* 臨海地

adj. 海沿いの, 海辺の, 海に面した

an oceanfront cottage 海沿いの別荘

oceanography *n.* 海洋学

o'clock *adv.* -時

Our appointment is at 4 o'clock, isn't it?
約束は4時でしたよね？

octagon *n.* 八角形

octave *n.* オクターブ, 8度音程

October *n.* 10月, 十月

octopus *n.* タコ

oculist *n.* 眼科医

odd *adj.*

1 STRANGE: 変な, おかしな, 奇妙な, 変わった
2 BEING ONE OF TWO: 片方の, (being one of more than two) 半端な
3 A LITTLE MORE THAN: (**-odd**) …余りの
4 IRREGULAR: (of job) 不定期の, 臨時の, (of comment) 時たまの
5 OF NUMBER: (**odd number**) 奇数

1 It was odd of him to speak out like that.
彼があんなにはっきり言うなんて、変だ。

They're an odd couple.
あの二人は、おかしな組み合わせだね。

Personally, I find him rather odd.

個人的には、あの人はちょっと変わっていると思います。

It's odd that the clock should have stopped at the exact time of her death.
ちょうど彼女が息を引き取った時間に、時計が止まったなんて、不思議だね。

2 I found an odd sock under your bed.
ベッドの下で靴下を片方、見つけたよ。

3 A hundred-odd people were there.
100人余りがいました。

4 He does odd jobs to earn a bit more money.
いくらか余分に稼ぐために、彼は臨時の仕事もしています。

5 an odd number 奇数

oddball *n.* 変わった人

oddity *n.* (thing) 奇妙な物/こと

oddly *adv.* (strangely) 変に, 奇妙に

oddly enough おかしなことに

odds *n.* (chances of winning) 勝ち目, 勝算, (in poker) 賭け率, (probability) 確率, (likelihood) 可能性, 見込み

The odds of winning the lottery are one in twenty million.
その宝くじに当たる確率は、2000万分の1だ。

long [short] odds 低い [高い] 確率

What are the odds?
見込みは、どうですか?

be odds-on 勝ち目がある

It's odds-on that the Tigers will win.
タイガースに勝ち目がある。

by all odds どう見ても, はるかに

the odds are that... たぶん...だろう, ...見込みだ

The odds are that he will probably leave home and go to work in the city.
たぶん彼は家を出て、町で仕事に就くだろう。

odds and ends *n.* (odd jobs) 雑用, (miscellaneous things) がらくた, 半端物

There are just a few odds and ends to take care of.
やらなきゃならない雑用がまだあるんだ。

ode *n.* 頌歌, オード

odor *n.* におい, (foul odor) 臭さ, 悪臭 [→ SMELL 1]

Oedipus complex *n.* エディプスコンプレックス, ((*informal*)) マザコン

of *prep.*

1 BELONGING TO/RELATING TO/WITH RESPECT TO: ...の, (concerning) ...について, ...に対して

2 SPEAKING OF NUMBER/AMOUNT: ("a cup of ..." etc.) ...の

3 FROM AMONG: ...の

4 BY: ...の

5 MADE OF: ...でできている

6 INDICATING CAUSE: ...で

7 USED AFTER A VERBAL NOUN: ...の

8 INDICATING STH ONE IS DEPRIVED/MADE FREE OF: ...を, ...から

9 HAVING THE CHARACTERISTIC OF: ...の, ...である

10 CALLED: ...の, ...という

11 USED AFTER AN ADJECTIVE: See examples below

1 the first of October 10月1日
the cause of the accident 事故の原因
the north of Japan 日本の北部
south of the border 国境の南

What kind of images did you have of Japan before coming?
((*polite*)) 来日なさる前は、日本についてどういうイメージをおもちでしたか？

2 a liter of beer 1リットルのビール
a pint of milk 1パイントの牛乳
a pair of socks 靴下1足
hundreds of pounds 数百ポンド

3 one of my friends 友人の一人
one of the problems 問題の一つ

4 the works of Shakespeare
シェイクスピアの作品
the lies of the government
政府の(ついた)うそ

5 It's made of plastic.
それはプラスチックでできている[製だ]。
Do you know what it's made of?
何でできているか知っていますか？

6 She died of cancer.
彼女は、がんで亡くなった。
They died of hunger.
彼らは飢え死に[餓死]した。

7 the care of the ill 病人の看護
the removal of the tumor 腫瘍の除去
the running of the business 事業の経営

8 The athlete was stripped of his title.
その選手はタイトルを剥奪された。
It cured him of drinking.
それで彼の飲酒癖が治った。

9 a man of fifty 50歳の男性
a woman of refined taste
上品な趣味の女性

10 the city of Vancouver バンクーバーの街
the gift of life 命という贈り物

11 He is proud of his son.
彼は息子を自慢にしている。
She is critical of the plan.
彼女はその計画に批判的です。
I'm afraid of spiders. クモが怖い。
How kind of you to say so.
ご親切なお言葉ありがとうございます。

of course → COURSE

off

1 ***prep., adv.*** **DISTANT FROM:** (…から)それて, 離れて, (**off target**) 的を外れて, ((*figurative*)) 的外れで, (**off center**) 中心からずれて

2 ***adv.*** **SPEAKING OF THE FUTURE:** 先, (**long way off**) ずっと先

3 ***prep., adv.*** **REDUCED IN PRICE:** (…より)安く, -引きで, 負けて

4 ***adj., adv.*** **NOT OPERATING:** (of lights, TV) 消えて(いる), (of gas, electricity, water) 切れて(いる), 止まって(いる)

5 ***adj.*** **LEAVING:** 出かける, 出かけている, 出発する

6 ***adj.*** **NOT GOING TO HAPPEN:** 中止になった, 取りやめになった

7 ***adj., prep.*** **FREE FROM SCHOOL / WORK:** 休みを取って, 休んで, (from work) 欠勤して

8 ***prep.*** **NOT CONSUMING:** …をやめて

1 It's about two hundred meters off the road.
道路から200メートルほど離れた[入った]所にあります。
That was way off target.
それはかなり的外れだった。
It's a bit off the subject, but...
ちょっと話がそれますが...

2 Well, your birthday is only a few days

off now.
ほんの数日でお誕生日ですね。

Retirement seems a long way off.
引退なんてずっと先のことに思えます。

3 I bought the book for thirty percent off its regular price.
定価より30%安く本を買った。

They knocked twenty percent off the price of their TVs.
あの店はテレビを定価の2割引きにした。

I'll knock ¥100 off this fish.
この魚、100円負けておくよ。

4 Are the lights on or off?
電気は、ついてる？ 消えてる？

The heating is off. 暖房は切れている。

The water has been turned off.
水は止めてある。

5 He's off for New Zealand tomorrow.
彼は明日、ニュージーランドへ出発します。

6 I've just heard the game's off.
試合は中止になったと、たった今聞きました。

Did you hear their engagement is off?
二人が婚約を破棄したって、聞いた？

7 Can I have that day off?
その日休んでもいいでしょうか？

He had a year off work because of illness.
彼は病気で1年間休職した。

8 He's been off alcohol for a month.
彼は1ヵ月間も、お酒をやめている。

be better off (financially) 暮らしが豊かになる

We're better off now than we were before the war.
戦前よりも、私たちの暮らしは豊かになっている。

be better off doing …したほうがいい

You're better off buying a new computer.
新しいコンピューターを買ったほうがいい。

be not far off さほど遠くない, (from the truth) (…と) かけ離れていない

The children aren't far off.
子供たちは、それほど遠くへは行っていない。

be well off 裕福だ

They must be well off if they have a Ferrari.
フェラーリを持っているのなら、裕福に違いない。

off and on 時々

I see her off and on.
時々彼女に会います。

off the top of one's head → TOP

offal *n.* (of animal) 臓物, くず肉

off-center *adj.* 中心からずれた

off-duty *adj.* 非番の

an off-duty (police) officer
非番の警察官

offend *v.* 怒らせる, (…の) 気を悪くさせる

offender *n.* 犯罪者

a sex offender 性犯罪者

offense *n.* (minor crime) 軽犯罪, 違反, (insult) 気分を害すること, 侮辱; (in sport) 攻撃側, オフェンス

a driving offense 交通違反

a criminal offense 刑事犯罪

no offense (intended) 悪気はなかった

offensive *adj.* (of remark, manner) 失礼な, 無礼な, (insulting) 侮辱的な, (of smell) いやな, (in sport) 攻撃の

n. (attack) 攻撃, 攻勢, 攻め

go on the offensive 攻撃に出る

offer

1 *v.* SHOW READINESS TO GIVE: (**offer to do**) …しましょうと言う, …しましょうと申し出る, …しましょうと買って出る

2 *v.* PROVIDE: (one's seat) 譲る, (food, drink) 勧める, (advice, hope, comfort) 与える, (product, service) 提供する

3 *n.* SUM OF MONEY: 金額

4 *n.* PROPOSAL: 申し出, 提案

1 The bellhop offered to carry our suitcases.
ボーイは、スーツケースを持ちましょうと言ってくれた。

Ms. Ito has offered to take care of my children while I'm away.
伊藤さんは私が留守の間、子供たちの世話をしようと言ってくれた。

She offered to drive them to the station.
彼女は駅まで乗せて行ってあげようと申し出た。

2 You ought to offer your seat to elderly people.
お年寄りには席を譲るべきです。

Go and offer the guests some drinks.
お客様に飲み物を勧めてきて。

May I offer you some advice?
私からちょっとアドバイスしてもいいですか？

I was offered the job, not him.
採用されたのは私で、彼ではない。

I was offered a bribe.
私にわいろを贈ろうとする者がいた。

3 If they make a good offer, accept it.
いい金額だったら、受け入れなさい。

a final offer 最終的な金額

4 Their offer was rejected [accepted].
彼らの提案は、拒否された [受け入れられた]。

offhand *adj.* (unfriendly) そっけない, 無愛想な
adv. (impromptu) 即座に

office *n.*

1 PLACE OF BUSINESS: オフィス, 事務所, (**the office**: one's company) 会社, (**doctor's office**) 医院, (**dentist's office**) 歯科医院

2 ROOM FOR DOING WORK: 仕事場, (at company) 事務室, (CEO's/president's office) 社長室, (professor's office) 研究室

3 GOVERNMENT OFFICE: 役所, 官庁, (of U.S. government) -局, (of U.K. government) -省

4 PUBLIC POST: 公職, 官職

1 I have to go to the office.
会社に行かなくちゃ。

He's out of the office right now. May I take a message?
ただ今外出しております。ご伝言を承りましょうか？

2 The professor called me into his office.
教授は私を研究室に呼びました。

the Oval Office 大統領執務室

3 the ward office 区役所

the immigration office 移民局

4 the office of president of the United States アメリカ合衆国の大統領の職

be in office 公職に就いている, 在職している

He's been in office now for four years.
彼はもう4年在職している。

take office 就任する

The new managing director has taken

office.
新しい常務が就任した。

office boy *n.* 事務員

office girl *n.* 事務員, ＯＬ

office hours *n.* (of office) 業務時間, (of office worker) 勤務時間

officer *n.* (police officer) 警(察)官, (to get police officer's attention) お巡りさん , (military officer) 将校, 士官

a customs officer 税関職員

official *adj.* 公の/な, 公式の/な, (formal) 正式の/な

n. (government official) 役人, 公務員, (staff) 職員

an official letter 公式書簡

on official business 公用で

an official name 正式名称

his official biography
その人の正式な伝記

♦ **officialdom** *n.* 官僚

official residence *n.* 公邸, 官邸

officially *adv.* (formally) 正式に, (ostensibly) 表向きは, 表面上は

Officially, I'm not here.
表向きは、私はここにいないことになっている。

off-key *adj.* 音程の外れた

off-peak *adj.* ピークを過ぎた

the off-peak (travel) season
ピークを過ぎた(旅行)シーズン

offprint *n.* 抜き刷り

off-season *n.* シーズンオフ, 季節外れ

offset *v.* 埋め合わせる, (compensate for) 償う, (cancel out) 相殺する

Saving on travel expenses should offset some of our losses.
旅費を切り詰めれば、損失をいくらか埋め合わせられるはずだ。

offshore *adj.* (of funds, bank) 海外の, (of wind at sea) 沖に向かう

adv. (of wind) 沖に向かって

He has a lot of his money in offshore banks.
彼は多くの財産を海外の銀行に預けている。

The wind was blowing offshore.
風は沖に向かって吹いていた。

offside *adj.* (in sport) オフサイドの

The player was offside.
その選手はオフサイドだった。

offspring *n.* 子供, 子, ((*formal*)) 子孫, (of invention) 産物, (product, result) 結果

offstage *adj., adv.* (in theater) 舞台裏の/で, (in private life) 私生活の/で

off-the-record *adj., adv.* オフレコの/で, 非公式の/で

Is this off-the-record?
これはオフレコですか？

often *adv.* (frequently) よく, しょっちゅう, しばしば, (**not often**) あまり…ない

I often go swimming in the summer.
夏は、よく泳ぎに行きます。

We often get letters from our daughter in Australia.
オーストラリアにいる娘から、しょっちゅう手紙が来る。

It's not often that it snows here.
ここに雪が降ることはあまりありません。

How often do you need to see a doctor?
どのくらいの頻度で通院しなくてはならないんですか？(lit., "With about how much

frequency must you go to the hospital?")
The more often you do it, the more you get used to it.
何度もやればやるほど、慣れてきますよ。

as often as one can できるだけ(頻繁に)
During the cooler months, I go hiking as often as I can.
涼しい季節には、できるだけハイキングに行くようにしています。

as often as not たいてい, しょっちゅう

every so often 時々
We go there every so often.
私たちは、時々そこへ行きます。

more often than not たいてい, しょっちゅう
More often than not, they're late.
たいてい彼らは遅れて来る。

oh *interj.* (expressing surprise) あっ, えっ, おぉ, へえ, ああ, ほう, ((*feminine*)) まあ, あら, (changing topic) それで, じゃ, (hesitating) えーと, あのう
Oh, thanks. あっ、ありがとう。
Oh, no! そんな/まさか!
Oh, by the way, could you do me a favor?
あのう、ところで、お願いがあるんだけど。
Oh, I really don't think I ought to.
いえ、本当に遠慮します。

ohm *n.* オーム, Ω

oil *n.* 油, (petroleum) 石油, (**oils**: oil paint) 油絵の具
v. (lubricate) (...に) 油をさす
crude oil 原油
an oil slick 油膜
vegetable oil 植物油
paint with oils 油絵の具で描く
oil the brakes ブレーキに油をさす

♦**oil painting** *n.* (painting) 油絵, (art of painting with oils) 油絵画法
do oil painting 油絵を描く

oil-producing *adj.* 石油を産する, 産油-
an oil-producing country 産油国

oil field *n.* 油田

oil tanker *n.* (ship) オイルタンカー, (truck) タンクローリー

oily *adj.* (of food) 油っぽい, (like oil) 油のような

ointment *n.* 軟膏 [→ picture of FIRST-AID KIT]

OK, okay

1 *interj.* EXPRESSING APPROVAL: (all right) いいよ, ＯＫ, (understood) わかった, 了解, (said with irritation) わかったよ

2 *adj.* ASKING/GIVING PERMISSION: (**is it OK if...?**) ...してもいいですか, (**it's OK...**) いいよ

3 *adv.* CHANGING TOPIC: それでは, それじゃ, これで

4 *adj.* SO-SO: まあまあ

5 *adj.* SAFE: 大丈夫だ

6 *n.* APPROVAL: 承認, 了解, ＯＫ

7 *v.* APPROVE: いいと言う, 認める, 承認する

1 "Can we talk now?" "OK."
「今、話せる?」「いいよ」
OK, OK. I hear you.
わかった、わかった。聞いてるよ。

2 "Is it OK if I use the car?"
"It's OK, as long as you fill up the tank when you're done."
「車を使ってもいいかな?」
「あとで満タンにして返してくれるなら、いいよ」

Are you sure it's OK?
本当によろしいですか？

3 OK, now, let's talk about something different.
それじゃあ、何か別のことを話しましょう。

OK, let's finish up.
それでは、終わりにしましょう。

4 The food's OK. 食べ物はまあまあです。

5 "Are you hurt?" "I'm OK."
「けがをしたの？」「大丈夫です」

6 I got my boss's OK.
上司の了解を得ました。

7 The president OK'd the project.
社長はそのプロジェクトを承認した。

okra *n.* オクラ

old *adj.*

1 **OPPOSITE OF YOUNG:** 年をとった, (お)年寄りの, (ご)年配の, (of appearance) 老けた

2 **OPPOSITE OF NEW/MODERN:** 古い, 古びた, (ancient) 昔の, (antique) 古い時代の

3 **FORMER:** 昔の, 以前の, かつての

4 **FRIENDLY FAMILIARITY:** 昔なじみの, いつもの

1 old people 老人

a little old lady 小柄な老婦人

We must be getting old.
私たちも年をとったものだ。

"How old are you?" "Seventeen."
「いくつ[何歳]ですか？」「１７です」

How old are you, if you don't mind my asking?
差し支えなければ、年齢を教えていただけますか/失礼ですが、おいくつですか？

Hey, I'm not that old.
ちょっと、私はそんな年じゃありませんよ。

A man as old as he is should know better.
あの人ぐらいの年なら、もっと分別があってよさそうなものだ。

She's older than me.
彼女のほうが年上です。

Who's the oldest?
((*polite*)) 最年長の方は、どなたですか？

He looks old for his age.
あの人は年のわりに老けて見える。

2 a massive old building
どっしりした古い建物

old traditions 昔からの伝統

3 That was where the old road was.
そこが、旧道が通っていた所です。

I met up with an old friend the other day.
先日、昔の友達に会った。

the good old days 古き良き時代

4 good ol' John ジョンの奴

an old trick おなじみの手口

any old …なら何でも, どんな…でも

"Will this box do?"
"Yes, any old box."
「この箱でいい？」
「うん、箱なら何でもいい」

KANJI BRIDGE

古 **ON:** こ **KUN:** ふる(い) | **OLD, USED, ANCIENT**

ancient capital	古都
ancient tomb	古墳
archaic word	古語
old castle	古城
old magazines	古雑誌
old newspapers	古新聞
old temple	古寺
secondhand books	古本
secondhand clothes	古着

old age *n.* 老齢, 老年

old-fashioned *adj.* 古い, 古くさい, 時代遅れの, (out of fashion) 流行遅れの

old-timer *n.* (old person) 老人, (at workplace) 古参, 古株

oligarchy *n.* 少数独裁政治

olive *n.* (tree) オリーブの木, (berry) オリーブの実, (color) オリーブ色

♦ **olive oil** *n.* オリーブオイル, オリーブ油

Olympic *n.* (**the Olympics**) オリンピック, ((*written*)) 五輪

adj. オリンピックの

ombudsman *n.* オンブズマン, 行政監察官

omelette *n.* オムレツ

omen *n.* 前ぶれ, 前兆

ominous *adj.* 不吉な, 不気味な

omission *n.* 省略, 脱落

omit *v.* 抜く, 省略する, 省く, (by mistake) 抜かす

That's odd—the price has been omitted.
おかしいなあ—値段が抜けている。

omnibus *n.* (book) 選集

omnivore *n.* 雑食動物

♦ **omnivorous** *adj.* 雑食(性)の

on

1 *prep.* INDICATING LOCATION/PROXIMITY: …の上に/の/で, …に, …で

2 *prep.* INDICATING DATE/OCCASION/OCCURRENCE: …に, …のときに, (upon, whereupon) …するとすぐ, …するなり

3 *prep.* CONCERNING: …の, …について, …に関して, …に関する

4 *prep., adv.* APPEAR ON: (**be on**) (of TV program on TV) …でやっている, (of person on TV/stage) …に出ている, (of name on list) …に載っている

5 *prep., adv.* ON BODY: (**have on**) (=clothing) 着ている, 身につけている, (=money) 持っている, 持ち合わせている

6 *prep.* BASED ON: …に基づいて, …で

7 *prep.* INDICATING MEANS OF TRANSPORT: …で, …によって

8 *prep.* INDICATING BELONGING: (on a committee) …の一員で

9 *prep.* ON PAPER: …に

10 *adj., adv.* OPERATING: (of machine) 動いて(いる), (of lights, TV, gas) ついて(いる)

11 *adv.* CONTINUING: 続けて

1 a rug on the floor 床の上の敷物

There are lots of books on the shelf.
棚に本がたくさん、のっている。

He's on the third floor.
彼は3階です [にいます]。

Look at all the pigeons on the roof.
屋根の上の、あのたくさんのハトを見て。

Let's have a barbecue on the beach.
浜辺でバーベキューをしよう。

He has a house on the main road.
彼は大通り沿いに家を持っています。

On your left you can see Tokyo Tower.
左手に見えますのは、東京タワーでございます。

2 He usually comes on Sundays.
彼はたいてい日曜日に来ます。

We'll treat her on her birthday.
彼女のお誕生日に、ごちそうするんです。

He must be going on forty.
あの人は、もうすぐ40になるはずだ。

On his arrival, we all cheered.

彼が到着するなり、私たちはみな歓声を上げた。

3 a talk on meditation 瞑想についての話

a documentary on ancient Egypt
古代エジプトについてのドキュメンタリー

a lecture on economics
経済に関する講演

4 What's on TV tonight?
今晩のテレビは、どんな番組をやってる?

You're on in five minutes.
5分で出番です。

Here, look. It's on this list.
ここだ、ほら。このリストに載ってる。

5 He had no shirt on.
彼はシャツを着ていなかった。

She had nothing on.
彼女は何も身につけていなかった。

Do you have the car keys on you?
今、車のキーを持っていますか?

Do you have any change on you?
小銭の持ち合わせはありますか?

Really, it looks good on you.
とってもよく似合っているよ。

6 The story is based on fact.
その話は事実に基づいている。

Are you going to act on his advice?
彼の忠告に従うつもりですか?

7 Shall we go on foot?
歩いて行きましょうか?

on tiptoe つま先で

on hands and knees 四つんばいで

8 Ms. Kato is on the committee, isn't she?
加藤さんは委員会の一員ですよね?

That, I repeat, is not on the agenda.
繰り返しますが、それは議題にありません。

9 Please write it on a piece of paper.
紙に書いてください。

He signed his name on the back of the book.
彼は本の後ろにサインした。

10 The gas is on.
ガスが、ついている。

Someone left the lights on.
誰かが電気をつけっぱなしにした。

11 "It's just that..." "Go on."
「ただしそれは...」「続けて」

and so on ...など

Islamic countries—Indonesia, Saudi Arabia, Egypt, and so on
インドネシア、サウジアラビア、エジプトなどのイスラム諸国

have something on sb ...の弱みを握っている

Do the police have anything on you?
警察に何か弱みを握られているの?

on and on 長々と, 延々と

He went on and on about it.
彼はそのことを長々と話した。

We traveled on and on through an endless expanse of desert.
私たちは、果てしなく広がる砂漠を延々と進み続けた。

on time → TIME

on account of → BECAUSE OF

once

1 *adv.* A SINGLE TIME: 1度, 1回

2 *adv.* IN THE PAST: 前は, 以前, ((*formal*)) かつて, (long ago) 昔

3 *conj.* AS SOON AS: ...したらすぐ(に), ...したあとすぐ(に), ...するとすぐ(に)

4 *conj.* IF AT ANY POINT IN TIME: いったん...

したら, ...した以上は

1 once a week [month, year]
1週間 [1ヵ月, 1年] に1回

once every three months
3ヵ月ごとに [おきに]

I've only met her once.
彼女には1度しか会ったことがない。

I've only been to the Caribbean once.
カリブ海へは1回しか行ったことがありません。

Just try it once.
いいから、1回試してみたら。

I'd like to visit the botanical gardens once more.
植物園に、もう1度行ってみたい。

Not once did she ever say that.
彼女は1度もそんなことを言っていない。

2 I remember the story my grandmother once told me about that bridge.
あの橋について以前、祖母が語ってくれた話を覚えています。

Once, long ago, there lived a blind lute player called Semimaru.
昔々、蟬丸という盲目の琵琶法師がいました。

3 Once he arrives, let me know.
彼が着いたらすぐに知らせてください。

Once it gets dark, it gets cold.
日が落ちると、とたんに寒くなる。

4 Once you've made a promise to someone, you should keep it.
いったん約束したら [約束した以上は]、守らなくてはいけないよ。

all at once (suddenly) 突然, いきなり, (simultaneously) 一斉に

All at once the noise stopped.
突然、騒音がやんだ。

They started to speak all at once.
みんな一斉に話し始めた。

at once すぐに

Please come to the hospital at once.
すぐに病院に来てください。

just this once 今度だけは

For just this once will you do as I ask?
今度だけは、私の言うとおりにしてくれませんか？

more than once 一度や二度ではない, 再三

He's been in trouble at school more than once.
あの子が学校で問題を起こしたのは一度や二度じゃない。

once again もう一度, またしても

Could you say that once again?
もう一度言っていただけますか？

He made a mistake once again.
またしても、彼がミスをした。

once and for all きっぱり(と)

Once and for all, I'm not going.
きっぱりと言っておくが、行くつもりはない。

once in a while 時たま, たまに

I do go there, but only once in a while.
そこに行くことはありますが、ほんのたまにです。

once more もう一度

Sing it once more! もう一度歌って！

once upon a time 昔々, ((*written/literary*)) 今は昔

Once upon a time, there lived a beautiful princess.
昔々、ある所に美しいお姫様がいました。

one

1 ***n., pron.*** **NUMERAL:** 1, 一, (thing) 1個, 一つ, (person) 一人 [→ p.1168 about "Counters"]

2 ***adj.*** **INDICATING NONSPECIFIC TIME/PLACE:** (a certain...) ある, (the same...) 同じ

3 ***pron.*** **USED TO AVOID REPETITION:** See examples below

4 ***pron.*** **IMPERSONAL USAGE:** 人, 誰も

5 ***adj.*** **USED FOR EMPHASIS:** ただ一つの, 単一の, 唯一の

6 ***adj.*** **EMPHASIZING AN ADJECTIVE:** すごく, とても

1 Ten minus one is nine. 10引く1は9。

Every one was damaged.
一つ残らず損傷を受けた。

There are still one or two points that aren't clear.
明らかでない点が、まだ一つ二つあります。

One of them is German.
一人はドイツ人です。

One of my friends came.
友達が一人、来ました。

I spoke to no one. 誰とも話さなかった。

She'll be out of the hospital in one or two days.
彼女は、1日か2日で退院するでしょう。

2 One day... ある日...

One day he will be brought to justice.
いつか、彼は法の裁きを受けることになるだろう。

I can't stay in one place for long.
同じ場所に長くとどまっていられない。

We're doing five experiments at any one time.
我々は常に、五つの実験を同時に行っています。

3 I must get one. 手に入れなくちゃ。

I want a big one. 大きいのが欲しい。

"Which umbrella is yours?"
"The dark blue one."
「どれがあなたの傘？」
「紺のやつ」

4 One would hope so.
誰もがそう望むでしょう。

5 We are one nation. 我々は皆一国民だ。

Their one aim was to get rich.
彼らの目的はただ一つ、金持ちになることだった。

We believe in one path, one truth.
我々は、ただ一つの道、ただ一つの真実を信じています。

6 He is one strict teacher.
あの先生はすごく厳しい。

as one 一つになって, 一斉に

We worked as one.
我々は一つに [一丸と] なって働いた。

more than one 二つ以上の, 一つではない

There's more than one way of doing this.
やり方は一つだけではない。

one after another/the other あいついで, 次々に

The cities were bombed, one after another, until scarcely a building remained.
各都市が次々に爆撃を受け、建物はとうとうほとんど姿を消した。

one and only 唯一(無二)の, (irreplaceable) かけがえのない

my one and only daughter
かけがえのない一人娘

one and the same 全く同じ

As far as I'm concerned, they're one and the same thing.
私にしてみれば、どちらでも全く同じことです。

one another (お)互いに/の

They listened to one another carefully.
彼らはお互いの言葉にしっかりと耳を傾けた。

one by one 一つずつ

They entered the room one by one.
彼らは一人ずつ部屋に入った。

One by one, the balloons disappeared from view.
風船は、一つまた一つと視界から消えて行った。

one way or another → WAY

KANJI BRIDGE

単 ON: たん KUN: — | SINGLE, SIMPLE, MERE, UNI-

alone	単身の
alone, unaided	単独の
credit (for university course)	単位
simple	単純な
simple, brief	簡単な
single, sole	単一の
singular (not plural)	単数
unit price cost	単価
word, vocabulary	単語

oneself *pron.* 自分自身, 自ら

by oneself 一人で, (unassisted) 独力で, 自力で, (alone) 独り(ぼっち)で

It's not easy living by oneself.
一人暮らしは楽じゃない。

one-sided *adj.* (of view) 片寄った, (of decision) 一方的な

one-time *adj.* (former) かつての, (only once) 1回限りの

one-to-one *adj.* 1対1の

adv. マンツーマンで

one-way *adj.* 一方的な, (of street) 一方通行の, (of ticket) 片道の

ongoing *adj.* (in progress) 進行中の, (continuous) 継続中の

onion *n.* タマネギ

peel an onion タマネギの皮をむく

on-line *adj.* オンライン…

onlooker *n.* 見物人, 傍観者

only

1 ***adj.*** **SOLE:** ただ一つの, ((*emphatic*)) たった一つの, 唯一の, ただ…だけの

2 ***adv.*** **MERELY:** (used with a verb: **only do**) ただ…するだけ, (used with a noun: nothing more than...) ほんの…にすぎない

3 ***adv.*** **EXCLUSIVELY:** …だけ, …しか…ない, ((*formal*)) …のみ

4 ***adv.*** **OF SMALL AMOUNT:** たった, たかが, わずか, ((*emphatic*)) ごくわずか

5 ***adv.*** **RECENTLY:** つい…

6 ***adv.*** **ULTIMATELY:** (結局)…だけ

7 ***conj.*** **BUT:** …が, …でも, …けれども, …けど, …のに

1 an only child 一人っ子

one's only son [daughter] 一人息子 [娘]

He was the only one who heard the sound.
その音を耳にしたのは彼だけだった。

Her one and only aim in life is to become famous.
彼女の人生の目的はただ一つ、有名に

なることだ。

2 I was only joking. ただの冗談だよ。

He's only doing what he was told to.
彼は、言われたことをやっているにすぎません。

I could hear only their voices, not what they were actually saying.
彼らの声が聞こえただけで、何を話しているのかはわかりませんでした。

I will only do the minimum required.
要求されている最低限のことをやるだけだ。

He's only a kid.
あの子はほんの子供です。

This is only part of the story.
これは話のほんの一部にすぎない。

It was only a spider. ただのクモだった。

3 (*sign*) Women Only 女性専用

for those over 18 only 18歳以上のみ

At the time, only the Americans had the technology to do it.
当時、それをやる技術を持っていたのはアメリカだけだった。

I only read newspapers and magazines.
私は新聞と雑誌しか読まない。

I'm only interested in finding out the truth.
私は真実を知ることにしか興味がありません。

4 It was cheap—I only paid ¥100 for it.
安かったんだ——たった100円だった。

It was only worth ¥1,000.
たかが1000円の物だった。

The profit increase is only 2%.
利益の増加率はわずか2％です。

Of the many who play instruments, only a few are truly musicians.
楽器を演奏する者は多いが、真に音楽家と言える者はごくわずかだ。

5 The cure has only recently been discovered.
治療法はつい最近発見されたばかりだ。

I bought it only a week ago.
つい1週間前に買ったばかりなんです。

It was only after she left that he realized how much he missed her.
彼は彼女に去られてようやく、彼女がいないとどれほど寂しいかわかった。

6 That will only make things worse.
それは事態を悪くするだけだよ。

He ran all the way to the shop, only to find that it had closed.
彼は店までずっと走って行ったのに、店はすでに閉まっていた。

7 Cod and sea bream are both whitefish, only sea bream is much more expensive.
タラもタイも同じ白身の魚ですが、タイのほうがずっと値段が高いんです。

I would've told him, only you said not to.
彼に言おうと思ったのに、あなたがそうするなと言ったんじゃないですか。

have only to …さえすればいい

You have only to speak to me if any problems arise.
何か問題が持ち上がったら、私に話してくれさえすればいい。

if only → IF

not one's only …だけが…ない

Profit is not our only aim.
利益だけが我々の目的ではない。

not only A but also B AだけでなくBも, AばかりかBも

Not only were the teachers there, but also the parents and students.
教師だけでなく、父母と生徒も来ていた。

Not only didn't he come, he also didn't bother to call.
あの人は来なかったばかりか電話もしてこなかった。

Not only did he get drunk, he also made a complete fool of himself.
酔っ払っただけならまだしも、彼はとんでもないばかをやらかしたんだ。

only just なんとか, かろうじて, ぎりぎりで

It's only just enough, I think.
なんとか足りるとは思うけれどね。

He passed the exam, but only just.
彼はかろうじて試験に合格した。

I got there on time, but only just.
時間どおりに着いたといっても、ぎりぎりだった。

only too とても, 非常に

"Do you know George?"
"Yes, I do. Only too well, I'm afraid."
「ジョージとはお知り合いですか？」
「ええ。知りすぎているくらいです」

onomatopoeia *n.* 擬声語, 擬音語

on-screen *adj., adv.* 画面の/で

onset *n.* (of disease etc.) 始まり, 徴候

onshore *adj.* 陸上の, (of wind at sea) 陸に向かう

adv. (toward land) 陸に向かって

an onshore breeze 陸に向かって吹く風

onslaught *n.* 猛攻撃

The villagers were completely helpless against the onslaught of the enemy.
村人たちは、敵の猛攻撃にどうすることもできなかった。

onto *prep.* …の上に/へ, (**get onto**: bus etc.) …に乗る; (**be onto**: be aware of) …に感づいている, …をかぎつけている

The cat climbed up onto the roof.
猫は屋根の上に登って行った。

The media knew they were onto something big.
メディアは、何か大きなネタをかぎつけたことに気づいた。

onus *n.* (responsibility) 責任, (duty) 義務

onward *adv.* 先へ, 前へ

adj. (forward) 前方への

from…onward …から

oolong *n.* (tea) ウーロン茶, 烏龍茶

ooze *v.* 流れ出る, (of blood) にじみ出る, (ooze confidence etc.) 振りまく

opal *n.* オパール, 蛋白石

opaque *adj.* (not transparent) 不透明な, (unclear) はっきりしない

O

open

1 *adj.* NOT CLOSED: (of door) あいている/あいた, (of book) 開いた, (of flower) 咲いた, (of container) ふたのない

2 *v.* CAUSE TO OPEN: (door, shop, letter, present, eyes, mouth) あける, (book, hand) 開く, (umbrella) さす; (**open one's mind**) 心を開く, (**open one's eyes to**) …に目覚める

3 *adj.* AVAILABLE: (to the public) 公開している, 開放している, (**keep open**: day, time slot) あけておく

4 *v.* START: (business) 始める, (meeting, conference) 開く, 始める, (of movie, ceremony: **open with…**) …で始まる, (open a bank account) 開く, 開設する

5 ***adj.*** **NOT ENCLOSED:** (of space) 広々とした, 開けた, (of terrace) 屋根のない

6 ***adj.*** **READY TO DO BUSINESS:** 営業している, ((*informal*)) あいている, やっている

7 ***adj.*** **NOT RESTRICTED:** 指定のない, (of competition) 自由参加の, オープンの, (of discussion) 公開…

8 ***adj.*** **OF PERSON:** (frank) 率直な, あけっぴろげな, (willing to listen) 耳を傾ける, (of mind) 広い, (**be open with**: not hide anything from) …に隠しだてしない

9 ***adj.*** **SUSCEPTIBLE:** (**be open to**: criticism etc.) (…を) 受けやすい, (…に) さらされる

10 ***n.*** **OUTDOORS:** (**the open**) 外, 戸外

1 Come in. The door is open.
どうぞ。あいてますよ。

an open window あいた窓

I pushed the gate open.
門を押しあけた。

You left your diary open.
日記が開いたままになっていたよ。

an open wound 開いた傷口

2 Open the door, please.
ドアをあけてください。

The kids opened their presents straightaway.
子供たちはプレゼントをすぐにあけた。

Let's open a bottle of champagne.
シャンパンをあけましょう。

He opened his eyes.
彼は目をあけた。

Traveling through North Africa really opened my mind.
北アフリカを旅行して回ったことは、本当に私の心を開放してくれた。

3 The swimming pool is now open to the public.
そのプールは今、一般に開放されている。

Can you keep Tuesday open? They may want to meet us then.
火曜日はあけておいてもらえる? 彼らがその日に会いたいと言うかもしれない。

4 Last I heard, she opened an antique shop.
この前聞いたんだけど、彼女は骨董屋を始めたそうだ。

The new school is to open next week.
新しい学校は来週、開校予定です。

I'd like to open an account.
口座を開きたいのですが。

5 the open sea 外洋

an open field 広々とした野原

6 They're open for business from nine to five.
あそこは9時から5時まで営業している。

7 an open tournament オープントーナメント

an open lecture 公開講座

an open society 開かれた社会

8 The new section chief seems to be open to ideas from the staff.
新しい課長は、スタッフの意見に耳を傾ける人のようだ。

an open mind 広い心

9 The president's public statements on the issue have left him open to attack.
その問題についての声明で、大統領は攻撃にさらされた。

10 play out in the open 外で遊ぶ

open into/onto *v.* …に通じる

This door opens onto the garden.
このドアは庭に通じています。

open up *v.* (land for development) 切り

開く, 開発する; (open up to sb) (…と) うちとける, (…に) 心を開く

All of this area will be opened up for development.
この地域一帯は開発される予定です。

He's finally started to open up to others.
彼はようやく、周りの人たちに心を開き始めた。

KANJI BRIDGE

開 ON: かい KUN: ひら(く/ける), あ(く/ける) | OPEN

begin	開始する
development	開発
(*sign*) do not leave open	開放厳禁
open a meeting	開会する
open a new school	開校する
open a new store	開店する
opening and closing	開閉
opening ceremony	開会式
open to the public	公開する
reopen, resume	再開する

open-air *adj.* 戸外の, 野外の
an open-air bath 露天ぶろ

open-ended *adj.* (of question) 自由形式の, (without limits) 無制限の

It's an open-ended question, so there is no correct answer.
自由形式の質問なので、正解はない。

opener *n.* (bottle opener) 栓抜き, (can opener) 缶切り

openhanded *adj.* 気前のいい

opening *n.* (gap) すき間, ギャップ, 穴, (beginning) 初め, (of speech) 開始, (of shop, theater) オープン; (job opening) 就職口 [→ OPPORTUNITY]

The grand opening of the new supermarket takes place tomorrow morning.
明日の朝、スーパーが大々的にオープンします。

openly *adv.* (candidly) 率直に, あけっぴろげに, (publicly) 公然と

open market *n.* 公開市場

open-minded *adj.* 心の広い, (without bias) 偏見のない

open-necked *adj.* えりのあいた, 開襟…
an open-necked shirt 開襟シャツ

openness *n.* (frankness) 率直さ

opera *n.* オペラ, 歌劇

operate *v.* (work) 動く, 作動する, (manipulate) 動かす, 操作する; (perform surgery) 手術をする, 執刀する

This machine doesn't seem to be operating properly.
この機械は、ちゃんと作動していないようだ。

They have to operate because it's cancer.
がんだから、手術をしなくてはならない。

It's a difficult procedure, but one of our finest surgeons will operate.
難しい処置ではありますが、執刀するのは当院でも指折りの外科医です。

♦ **operating room** *n.* 手術室
operating table *n.* 手術台

operating system *n.* ＯＳ

operation *n.* (functioning) 操作, (surgery) 手術, (military action) 軍事行動, (business enterprise) 事業
have an operation 手術を受ける

operational *adj.* (of machine) 操作できる, 使用できる

O

operator ***n.*** オペレーター, 操作する人, 技師, (switchboard operator) 交換手

an X-ray operator 放射線技師

ophthalmology ***n.*** 眼科学

opinion ***n.*** (belief) 意見, 考え, ((*formal*)) 見解, (**public opinion**) 世論, (estimation) 評価

a difference of opinion 見解の相違

They are of the opinion that we should not try to climb the mountain.
私たちが山に登るのはやめたほうがいいというのが、彼らの意見です。

I should like to hear your opinions.
皆さんのご意見を伺いたいと思います。

I have no opinion on the matter.
それについては、別に考えはありません。

In her opinion, we're barking up the wrong tree.
彼女の考えでは、私たちは見当違いなことをしているということになる。

♦ **opinion poll** ***n.*** 世論調査

opinionated ***adj.*** 自説を曲げない, がんこな

opium ***n.*** アヘン

opponent ***n.*** (enemy) 敵, (in sport) 相手; (objector) 反対者

opportunist ***n.*** 日和見主義者

opportunity ***n.*** 機会, チャンス

take/seize the opportunity
機会をとらえる/チャンスをつかむ

You can't miss this opportunity.
こんないい機会は逃せないよ。

It's the opportunity of a lifetime.
一生に一度あるかないかのチャンスだ。

It was difficult to find an opportunity to talk about it.
それについて話す機会がなかなか、なかった。

oppose ***v.*** (…に) 反対する, 抵抗する, (**be opposed to**) …に反対している, …に反対だ

The majority opposed the proposed increases in income tax.
大多数が所得税引き上げ案に反対した。

as opposed to …と違って, …ではなくて

Socialism, as opposed to communism, is democratic.
社会主義は共産主義と違って民主的だ。

opposing ***adj.*** (opposite) 反対の, (of team) 相手の, 敵の

opposite ***adj.*** (reverse) 反対の, 逆の, (on the other side) 向こう側の

n. 反対(のこと), 逆(のこと), (antonym) 反対語, 反意語

prep., adv. (…の) 反対側に, (…の) 向かい(側)に

They drove off in the opposite direction.
彼らの車は反対方向へ走り去った。

The convenience store is on the opposite side of the street.
コンビニは通りの向こう側にあります。

They did the exact opposite of what you told them to do.
あの人たち、あなたが言ったのと正反対のことをしたんですよ。

The opposite is also true.
逆もまた真なり。

The opposite of "weak" is "strong."
「弱い」の反対語は「強い」です。

The post office is opposite the school.
郵便局は学校の向かい側にあります。

♦ **opposite sex** ***n.*** 異性

O

opposition *n.* (resistance) 反対, 抵抗, (**the Opposition**: political party) 野党

oppress *v.* 抑圧する, 虐げる

oppression *n.* 抑圧

oppressive *adj.* (of regime) 抑圧的な; (of heat) うだるような, 蒸し暑い

opt *v.* 選ぶ, 選択する

He opted for the easier of the two classes.
彼は二つの授業のうち楽なほうを選んだ。

optic *adj.* (of eye) 目の, 視覚の

the optic nerve 視神経

optical *adj.* (of eye) 目の, (of eyesight) 視力の; (of light) 光の, (of optics) 光学の

an optical illusion 目の錯覚

optician *n.* (maker of glasses) めがね技師, (seller of glasses) めがね屋(さん)

optics *n.* 光学

optimism *n.* 楽観, (doctrine) 楽観主義

optimist *n.* 楽観主義者, ((*informal*)) 楽天家

optimistic *adj.* 楽観的な, 楽天的な

optimum *adj.* 最高の, 最適な, 最善の

option *n.* (choice) 選択, (right to choose) 選択権, (thing that one can choose) 選択肢, (item, equipment) オプション; (button on keyboard) オプション(キー)

There are several options open to us.
私たちには、いくつかの選択肢がある。

We had no option but to accept.
私たちは、受け入れるほかなかった。

optional *adj.* 選択の, 任意の

an optional subject/course 選択科目

optometrist → OPTICIAN

opulent *adj.* ぜいたくな, 豪華な

opus *n.* (piece of music) 音楽作品

or *conj.*

1 INDICATING ALTERNATIVE: …か…, …または…, …それとも…, あるいは, ((*formal*)) もしくは, (presenting options: **you / we can do** this **or** that) …してもいいし…してもいい

2 IN OTHER WORDS: すなわち, つまり

3 OTHERWISE: そうしないと, そうしなければ, でないと

1 black or white 白か黒か

two or three times a day 日に2度か3度

I've only been there once or twice.
そこへは1、2回しか行ったことがない。

Should we go by taxi or subway?
タクシーで行く? それとも地下鉄で行く?

Work or no work, he'll have to pay the rent.
仕事があろうがなかろうが、彼は家賃を払わなければならない。

You can either do it now or later.
今やってもいいし、後にしてもいい。

We can rest now or carry on climbing.
今休憩を取ってもいいし、休まずに登ってもいい。

2 The town is twenty miles from here, or about thirty-two kilometers.
町はここから 20 マイル、つまり 32 キロの所にあります。

3 Better hurry, or you'll miss your bus.
急いだほうがいい、でないとバスに乗り遅れるよ。

Be quiet, or I'll tell on you.
静かにしないと言いつけるよ。

oral *adj.* 口頭の, 口述の, (of mouth) 口の, (of medicine) 経口の

O

The oral part of the exam only accounts for ten percent of your total grade.
<ruby>口頭<rt>こうとう</rt></ruby><ruby>試問<rt>しもん</rt></ruby> [<ruby>口述<rt>こうじゅつ</rt></ruby><ruby>試験<rt>しけん</rt></ruby>]の<ruby>評価<rt>ひょうか</rt></ruby>は、<ruby>全体<rt>ぜんたい</rt></ruby>の<ruby>成績<rt>せいせき</rt></ruby>の1<ruby>割<rt>わり</rt></ruby>を<ruby>占<rt>し</rt></ruby>めるにすぎない。

the oral cavity <ruby>口腔<rt>こうくう</rt></ruby>

♦ **orally** *adv.* (by word of mouth) <ruby>口頭<rt>こうとう</rt></ruby>で, (through the mouth) <ruby>経口<rt>けいこう</rt></ruby>で

oral sex *n.* オーラルセックス

orange *adj.* オレンジ<ruby>色<rt>いろ</rt></ruby>の, だいだい<ruby>色<rt>いろ</rt></ruby>の *n.* (color) オレンジ<ruby>色<rt>いろ</rt></ruby>, だいだい<ruby>色<rt>いろ</rt></ruby>; (fruit) オレンジ, (**mandarin orange**) みかん

orangutan *n.* オランウータン

orbit *n.* <ruby>軌道<rt>きどう</rt></ruby>

be in orbit around the earth
<ruby>地球<rt>ちきゅう</rt></ruby>を<ruby>周回<rt>しゅうかい</rt></ruby>する<ruby>軌道<rt>きどう</rt></ruby><ruby>上<rt>じょう</rt></ruby>に<u>ある</u> [いる]

orchard *n.* <ruby>果樹園<rt>かじゅえん</rt></ruby>

an apple orchard りんご<ruby>園<rt>えん</rt></ruby>

a satsuma orchard みかん<ruby>畑<rt>ばたけ</rt></ruby>

orchestra *n.* オーケストラ, <ruby>管弦楽団<rt>かんげんがくだん</rt></ruby>

orchestrate *v.* (music: compose/arrange) オーケストラ<ruby>用<rt>よう</rt></ruby>に<ruby>作曲<rt>さっきょく</rt></ruby>/<ruby>編曲<rt>へんきょく</rt></ruby>する, (campaign etc.) まとめる, <ruby>指揮<rt>しき</rt></ruby>する

orchid *n.* ラン, <ruby>蘭<rt>らん</rt></ruby>

ordeal *n.* <ruby>試練<rt>しれん</rt></ruby>

order

1 *n.* **INSTRUCTION:** <ruby>命令<rt>めいれい</rt></ruby>, <ruby>指示<rt>しじ</rt></ruby>, <ruby>指図<rt>さしず</rt></ruby>

2 *v.* **COMMAND:** <ruby>命令<rt>めいれい</rt></ruby>する, <ruby>命<rt>めい</rt></ruby>じる, ((*informal*)) <ruby>言<rt>い</rt></ruby>う

3 *n.* **REQUEST:** <ruby>注文<rt>ちゅうもん</rt></ruby>, (product requested) <ruby>注文<rt>ちゅうもん</rt></ruby>の<ruby>品<rt>ひん</rt></ruby>

4 *v.* **REQUEST:** <ruby>注文<rt>ちゅうもん</rt></ruby>する, (in restaurant) <ruby>注文<rt>ちゅうもん</rt></ruby>する, オーダーする, ((*informal*)) <ruby>頼<rt>たの</rt></ruby>む, (from retailer, maker) <ruby>取<rt>と</rt></ruby>り<ruby>寄<rt>よ</rt></ruby>せる

5 *n.* **SEQUENCE:** <ruby>順序<rt>じゅんじょ</rt></ruby>, <ruby>順番<rt>じゅんばん</rt></ruby>

6 *v.* **ARRANGE:** (put in order) <ruby>整理<rt>せいり</rt></ruby>する, (put

in a line) <ruby>並<rt>なら</rt></ruby>べる

7 *n.* **DISCIPLINE/STABILITY:** <ruby>秩序<rt>ちつじょ</rt></ruby>, (public order) <ruby>治安<rt>ちあん</rt></ruby>; (of nature/the universe) <ruby>道理<rt>どうり</rt></ruby>

8 *n.* **TAXONOMIC CATEGORY:** <ruby>目<rt>もく</rt></ruby>

1 give an order <ruby>命令<rt>めいれい</rt></ruby>を<ruby>出<rt>だ</rt></ruby>す

carry out an order <ruby>命令<rt>めいれい</rt></ruby>を<ruby>実行<rt>じっこう</rt></ruby>する

by order of the government
<ruby>政府<rt>せいふ</rt></ruby>の<ruby>命令<rt>めいれい</rt></ruby>で

He claims to have done it under orders.
<ruby>彼<rt>かれ</rt></ruby>は、<ruby>命令<rt>めいれい</rt></ruby>[<ruby>指示<rt>しじ</rt></ruby>]に<ruby>従<rt>したが</rt></ruby>ってやったんだと<ruby>主張<rt>しゅちょう</rt></ruby>している。

Papa quit smoking on doctor's orders.
パパは<u><ruby>医者<rt>いしゃ</rt></ruby>の<ruby>指示<rt>しじ</rt></ruby>で</u> [ドクターストップがかかって] たばこをやめた。

Kaneko only takes orders from his boss.
<ruby>金子<rt>かねこ</rt></ruby>さんは<ruby>上司<rt>じょうし</rt></ruby>の<ruby>指図<rt>さしず</rt></ruby>しか<ruby>受<rt>う</rt></ruby>けない。

2 Hayashi was ordered to go.
<ruby>林<rt>はやし</rt></ruby>さんは<ruby>行<rt>い</rt></ruby>くよう<ruby>言<rt>い</rt></ruby>われた。

The government ordered an investigation.
<ruby>政府<rt>せいふ</rt></ruby>は<ruby>調査<rt>ちょうさ</rt></ruby>を<ruby>命<rt>めい</rt></ruby>じた。

3 May I take your order?
ご<ruby>注文<rt>ちゅうもん</rt></ruby>はお<ruby>決<rt>き</rt></ruby>まりですか?

Your order has arrived.
ご<ruby>注文<rt>ちゅうもん</rt></ruby>の<ruby>品<rt>しな</rt></ruby>が<ruby>届<rt>とど</rt></ruby>きました。

4 I ordered a vegetarian meal.
ベジタリアン<ruby>用<rt>よう</rt></ruby>の<ruby>食事<rt>しょくじ</rt></ruby>を<ruby>注文<rt>ちゅうもん</rt></ruby>した。

I'll order some more kerosene.
<ruby>灯油<rt>とうゆ</rt></ruby>をもう<ruby>少<rt>すこ</rt></ruby>し<ruby>頼<rt>たの</rt></ruby>んでおこう。

5 in alphabetical order アルファベット<ruby>順<rt>じゅん</rt></ruby>に

In what order should we arrange these files?
このファイルはどういう<ruby>順番<rt>じゅんばん</rt></ruby>に<ruby>整理<rt>せいり</rt></ruby>したらいいだろう?

6 I've ordered the CDs according to genre.
CDをジャンル<ruby>別<rt>べつ</rt></ruby>に<ruby>並<rt>なら</rt></ruby>べた。

GIVING ORDERS

The way you command someone to do something in Japanese depends on your social status with respect to the other person. Generally, the older you are, or the higher your social status, the more blunt you can be. There are three levels of imperative: blunt, abrupt but polite, and polite.

LEVEL 1: blunt

Sit down!	座(すわ)れ！
Talk to me.	話(はな)せ。
Eat!	食(た)べろ！

This form is usually used by social superiors when speaking to social inferiors. It can sound extremely rude, so refrain from using it.

The blunt imperative is formed as follows: with Regular I verbs [→ p.1156], the final syllable of the dictionary form is altered to end in an *e* sound, e.g.,

洗(あら)う, "wash" → 洗(あら)え
急(いそ)ぐ, "hurry" → 急(いそ)げ

and with Regular II verbs [→ p.1158], the final syllable becomes ろ, e.g., 見(み)る, "see" → 見(み)ろ. The irregular verbs する, "do," and 来(く)る, "come," become しろ and 来(こ)い [→ p.1159].

LEVEL 2: abrupt but polite

Sit down.	座(すわ)りなさい。
Talk (to me).	話(はな)しなさい。
Look at this.	これを見(み)なさい。

This form is also used by social superiors when speaking to social inferiors, but it is much more polite than the blunt imperative (although it is still considered abrupt).

To form the abrupt-but-polite imperative, add なさい to the verb's -ます stem.

LEVEL 3: polite

Please sit down.	座(すわ)ってください。
Please talk (to me).	話(はな)してください。
Please come in.	どうぞ入(はい)ってください。[→ PLEASE 1]

> This imperative, formed by adding ください to the verb's -て form, is used among people for whom no particular vertical relationship exists.
>
> NOTE: ください is often dropped in informal speech, e.g.,
>
> ((*informal*)) Listen to what I have to say. 話を聞いて。
>
> To politely ask a social superior to do something, use the prefix お before the verb's -ます stem, and follow it up with ください, e.g.,
>
> ((*honorific*)) Please come in. どうぞお入りください。

7 law and order 法と秩序

maintain public order 治安を維持する

The riot police struggled to keep order on the streets.

機動隊は街の治安を保とうと奮闘した。

in order to do …するために

He studied hard in order to pass the exam.

試験に合格するために彼は猛勉強した。

We have to be competitive in order to succeed.

成功するには競争力がなくてはならない。

out of order 故障して

The photocopier is out of order.

コピー機は故障している。

put in order 整理する

orderly *adj.* 整然とした, きちんとした

Everyone left the theatre in an orderly manner.

みんな整然と劇場を後にした。

ordinal *n.* 序数

ordinance *n.* 条例, 規定

a city ordinance 市条例

ordinarily *adv.* 普通は, ふだんは

ordinary *adj.* (usual) 普通の, いつもの, (mediocre) 平凡な, (general) 一般の

It's an ordinary car—no frills or gimmicks.

ごく普通の車です――余分な飾りや新しい装置もありません。

It was just another ordinary day, or so it seemed until…

またいつもと同じ平凡な一日と思っていたのですが、それが…

Ordinary people aren't interested in politics.

一般の人々は政治に関心がない。

ore *n.* 鉱石

oregano *n.* オレガノ

organ *n.* (musical instrument) オルガン; (part of the body) 臓器

organic *adj.* 有機的な, (of farming) 有機の, (of food) 有機栽培の

organic farming 有機農業

organic vegetables 有機野菜

♦ **organic chemistry** *n.* 有機化学

organism *n.* 生物, 有機体

organization *n.* (organized body of people/things) 組織, (association) 団体, 協会; (act of arranging/preparing) まとめること, 準備, (skill) まとめる能力

a world banking organization

世界的な銀行組織

This organization was established to promote world peace.
この団体は、世界平和の促進を目的に設立されました。

This job requires organization.
この仕事は物事をまとめる力が必要だ。

organize *v.* (put in order) 整理する, まとめる, (**organize oneself**) 心の準備をする, 気を静める, (found) 設立する, ((*informal*)) 作る, (arrange) (...の) 手はずを整える, (...を) 準備する

We've been organized into small groups so that we can work more efficiently.
より効率的に仕事ができるよう、我々は小さなグループに編成された。

We're going to organize a society for the protection of trees.
私たちは、樹木を保護する団体を設立します。

It's OK. Everything's been organized.
大丈夫。手はずは、すべて整っています。

Frankly, I doubt if he could organize a banquet.
率直なところ、彼に宴会の準備ができるのか疑問です。

Who's going to organize the conference?
会議を運営するのは誰ですか？

organized *adj.* (made into a working system) 組織(化)された; (of person) てきぱき仕事をこなす

♦**organized crime** *n.* 組織犯罪

organizer *n.* (person) 担当者, 責任者; (book) 書類入れ

orgasm *n.* オルガスムス, オーガズム

orgy *n.* (sex party) 乱交パーティー

Orient *n.* 東洋, (East Asia) 東アジア

orient *v.* (**orient oneself**: find one's bearings) 自分の位置を知る; (**be oriented to/toward**) ...に適応する, ...に慣れる, (**-oriented**) ...志向の, ...優先の

oriental *adj.* (of East Asia) 東洋の, 東アジアの

orientation *n.* (induction) オリエンテーション, 研修; (direction sth faces) 方位, 方向, (inclination) 好み, (tendency) 傾向

origami *n.* 折り紙

origin *n.* 起源, 源, (start) 始まり, (birth) 生まれ

the origins of civilization 文明の起源

original *adj.* (first, earliest) 最初の, 元の, (new) 新鮮な, 斬新な, (imaginative) 独創的な

n. (work of art) 本物, (text) 原文, オリジナル

Is this an original idea, or have you copied it?
これはあなた自身のアイデアですか、それとも何かをまねたものですか？

This painting is an original.
この絵は本物だ。

The original is very different from this translation.
原文は、この翻訳とはかなり違います。

originality *n.* 独創性, オリジナリティー

originally *adv.* 最初は, 初めは, 元は

originate *v.* (begin from) (...から) 始まる, (create) 始める

ornament *n.* 飾り, 装飾品

ornamental *adj.* (used as decoration) 装飾用の

ornate *adj.* (of design) 飾りたてた

ornithology *n.* 鳥(類)学

orphan *n.* 孤児, ((*old-fashioned*)) みなし子

orphanage *n.* 孤児院

orthodontics *n.* 歯列矯正術

orthodontist *n.* 歯列矯正医, ((*informal*)) 矯正の歯医者(さん)

orthodox *adj.* 正統な, 伝統的な, (of sect) 正統派の

n. (member of the Greek Orthodox Church) ギリシャ正教徒

orthodox Judaism 正統派ユダヤ教

orthography *n.* 正書法, 正字法

orthopedics *n.* 整形外科

osprey *n.* ミサゴ

ostensibly *adv.* (not in fact) 表面上は

ostentatious *adj.* これ見よがしの, (conspicuous) 目立つ

osteopathy *n.* 整骨治療法

ostracize *v.* (banish) 追放する, (leave out of a group) 仲間外れにする, (shun) のけ者にする

♦ **ostracism** *n.* (exclusion) 仲間外れ, (exile) 追放, 排斥

ostrich *n.* ダチョウ, 駝鳥

other

1 *adj.* DIFFERENT/ALTERNATIVE/SECOND/ADDITIONAL: ほかの, 別の, 違った, もう一つの

2 *adj.* THE OPPOSITE: 反対の, (on or belonging to the opposite side) 向こう側の

3 *adj.* EARLIER: (the other...) この間の, (**the other day**) この間, ((*formal*)) 先日

4 *pron.* THE REST/REMAINING: (**the others**) (=people) ほかの人たち, 皆, みんな, (=things) ほかの物, 残り, あと

1 the other people in the group
グループのほかの人たち

I've got plenty of other things to do.
ほかにもすることが山ほどある。

I've got other things to think about than that.
そんなことよりも、ほかに考えないといけないことが、いろいろあるんだ。

Let's do it some other day.
別の日にしましょう。

Let's talk about other things.
違うことを話しましょうよ。

New York, London, Tokyo, and other major cities around the world
ニューヨーク、ロンドン、東京その他の世界の大都市

He is, among other things, an expert in investment.
彼はいろいろな得意分野があるけれど、特に投資が専門です。

No, not that one—the other one.
いいえ、それではなくて、もう一つのほうです。

2 the other side of the street
通りの向こう側

He was coming the other way.
彼は、向こうから来た。

The other team wore blue.
相手チームは青を着ていた。

3 the other evening この前の晩

I went shopping the other day.
この間、買い物に行きました。

4 We need to know what the others think.
みんながどう考えているのか、知る必要がある。

I'll wait till the others get here.

みんなが来るまで待ちます。

We picked ten apples, ate five, and gave the others to friends.
りんごを10個もいで、5個は自分たちで食べて、あとは全部、友達にあげました。

Well, what are you going to do with the others?
じゃあ、残りはどうするつもり？

each other お互い(に)

Try to be nice to each other.
お互いに思いやりをもってね。

every other 一つおきに

She visits her mother every other week.
彼女は1週間おきに母親を訪ねている。

There's a flea market in the park every other Sunday.
隔週の日曜日に、公園で蚤の市が開かれます。

one after the other 次々に

The students came into the classroom one after the other.
生徒たちは次々に教室に入って来た。

other than …以外, …とは別の/に

Other than James, I doubt if anyone else will come.
ジェームズ以外は、誰も来ないと思う。

the other way 逆方向に

No, it's no good that way. Try doing it the other way.
いや、そっちじゃだめだ。逆の方向にやってごらん。

this, that, and the other あれやこれや, 何やかや

What with this, that, and the other, how am I supposed make any progress?
あれやこれや、いろいろあるのに、どうやって先へ進めというんだ？

otherwise

1 *adv.* IF NOT: そうしなかったら, ((*informal*)) そうしなきゃ, (そう)でないと

2 *adv.* IN OTHER RESPECTS: ほかの点では, それ以外は

3 *adv.* IN ANOTHER WAY: ほかに, 別に

4 *adj.* CONTRARY: そうでない

1 Buy tickets in advance. Otherwise you will not be able to get in.
あらかじめチケットを買っておくこと。でないと、入れないよ。

Hurry up, otherwise we'll be late.
急がないと遅れるよ。

2 Kobayashi isn't a fast player, but otherwise he's OK.
小林さんは動きの速い選手ではないが、ほかの点では問題ない。

3 She was otherwise engaged.
彼女には、ほかに予定があった。

4 I wish it were otherwise.
そうでなかったらいいのに。

otter *n.* カワウソ

ouch *interj.* 痛い, あっ, わっ

Ouch! That's hot! わっ！ 熱い！

ought to *aux.*

1 EXPRESSING OBLIGATION: (**ought to do**) …するべきだ, …するのが当然だ, (**ought to have done**) …するべきだった(のに)

2 EXPRESSING DESIRABILITY: …といい, …ばいい, (**ought to have done**) …すればよかった(のに), (making a suggestion: **ought to do**) …したほうがいい

3 EXPRESSING PROBABILITY: …するはずだ, (surely) きっと…

1 You ought to apologize.

謝るべきです/謝るのが当然だ。

You ought to reconsider.
考え直すべきだよ。

I felt I ought to get your opinion first.
先にあなたのご意見を伺うべきだと思ったんです。

You oughtn't to have done it.
そうすべきじゃなかったんです。

2 She ought to become a politician.
彼女は政治家になるといい。

There ought to be more parks.
公園がもっとあればいいのに。

You ought to have told us earlier.
もっと早く私たちに話してくれればよかったのに。

3 Well, he ought to have arrived by now.
さて、彼はもう着いているはずだ。

She ought to pass the exam easily.
彼女なら、きっと簡単に合格するよ。

ounce ***n.*** オンス [about 28 grams]

our ***adj.*** 私たちの, 自分たちの, うちの, ((*masculine*)) 僕たちの, ((*formal*)) 我々の [→ WE]

Our house is the white one on the corner of the street.
うちは、通りの角の白い家です。

Our team won't be playing tomorrow.
私たちのチームは、明日は試合がない。

our company ((*formal*)) わが社, 当社, ((*humble*)) 弊社, 小社

our country/nation わが国

Our nation is committed to peace.
わが国は平和を誓約しています。

ours ***pron.*** 私たちの(もの), ((*masculine*)) 僕たちの(もの), ((*formal*)) 我々の(もの) [→ WE]

ourselves ***pron.*** 自分たち, (**we ourselves**) 私たち自身, 自分たち自ら, ((*formal*)) 我々自身

There's no point in worrying ourselves about that.
私たちが、心配したってしようがないよ。

We've often done so ourselves.
私たち自身、よくそうしました。

by ourselves 自分たちだけで

We did it by ourselves.
自分たちだけでやったんです。

oust ***v.*** 追い出す

out ***adv., adj.***

1 AWAY FROM THE INSIDE: 外へ/に, (**go out**) 出かける, (**be out**) 出かけている

2 RELEASED TO THE PUBLIC: (**come out**) (of news) 公になる, (of book) 出る, (**get out**) (of rumor) 広がる, (of information: be leaked) 漏れる

3 LACKING: (**be out of...**) (...が)ない, 切れている

4 DISTANT FROM ONESELF: 離れて

5 SO AS TO EXTINGUISH: (**put/turn out**: fire/lights) 消す

6 INDICATING COMPOSITION: (**out of...**) ...で, ...から [→ FROM 4]

7 BECAUSE OF: (**out of...**) ...から

8 OF SUN/MOON: (**be out**) 出ている, (**come out**) 出る

9 OUT LOUD: (**cry out**) 大声を出す, 叫ぶ

10 IN SPORT: アウトで

11 OUT OF FASHION: (**be out**) すたれている, 時代遅れだ

1 She went out about an hour ago.

彼女は1時間ほど前に出かけました。

I think he's out there playing in the street.
表の通りで遊んでいると思いますが。

I'm afraid he/she is out at the moment.
((*polite*)) 申し訳ありませんが、ただいま留守に [外出] しております。

Mr. Suzuki will be out of the office until two thirty this afternoon.
((*humble*)) 鈴木は、今日午後2時半まで外出しております。

out for lunch 昼食で外出中

2 The news is out.
ニュースが、公になった。

A new book of his just came out.
彼の新しい本が出た [出版された]。

If word gets out about this, we're in trouble.
このことについて情報が漏れたら、困ったことになるよ。

3 The car is out of gas. 車がガス欠だ。

We're out of coffee.
コーヒーが切れている。

4 They live out in the hills.
彼らは、山の中で暮らしている。

Way out over there you can see a water tower.
ずっと向こうに給水塔が見えるでしょう?

5 They tried to put the fire out.
彼らは火を消そうとした。

Turn out the light when you go to bed.
寝るときは明かりを消しなさい。

6 What is this made out of?
これは何でできているんですか？

7 I ask only out of curiosity.
ただ好奇心から聞きます。

8 The moon is out. 月が出ている。

When the sun comes out, the snow will melt.
日が出ると、雪は解ける。

9 He cried out for help, but nobody heard him.
彼は大声で助けを求めたが、誰にも聞こえなかった。

10 strike out (in baseball) 三振する

be out for oneself 自分のことだけ考えている

He's only out for himself.
彼は、自分のことしか考えてない。

be out to do …したがる, …しようとする

She's out to impress us all.
彼女は、私たちみんなを感心させようとしている。

go out of one's way わざわざ…する

He went out of his way to help.
彼はわざわざ手伝いに行った。

go out with (date) …と付き合う

He's going out with a different girl again.
あの人は、また別の女の子と付き合っている。

out of one's mind 気が狂って

Are you out of your mind!?
気でも狂ってるの！？

Out with it! 言ってしまいなさい!, 白状しなさい!

Out with it! You must tell us.
白状しなさい！ 私たちには話してよ。

outback *n.* 奥地, 未開拓地

outbox *n.* (for e-mail) 送信トレイ, 送信ボックス

outbreak *n.* (of war) 勃発, (of disease) 発生

outburst *n.* 爆発, 噴出

an outburst of anger 怒りの爆発

outcast ***n.*** 追放された人, 見捨てられた人

outcome ***n.*** 結果, 成果

Nobody knew what the outcome would be.
結果がどう出るか、誰にもわからなかった。

outcry ***n.*** (objection) 激しい抗議

There was a public outcry when the facts became known.
事実が明るみに出ると、世間から激しい抗議の声が上がった。

outdated ***adj.*** 時代遅れの

outdo ***v.*** (do better than) (…より) うまい, よくやる, (beat) (…に) 勝つ, (**outdo oneself**) 今までになくよくやる, いつになくうまい

On this occasion, he certainly outdid himself.
このときは、彼は確かに今までになく、いい出来だった。

outdoor ***adj.*** 外の, 屋外の, 野外の

outdoor sports 屋外スポーツ

an outdoor theater 野外劇場

outdoors ***adv.*** 外に/で, 屋外に/で, 野外に/で

n. 外, 屋外

Go on, go outdoors and play.
さあさあ、外に出て遊びなさい。

the great outdoors 野外

♦ **outdoorsman, -woman** ***n.*** アウトドア派

outer ***adj.*** 外の, 外側の

The outer casing is intact.
外装は無事だ。

The outer wall is damaged but the inside seems all right.
外壁は損傷を受けたが、内部は大丈夫のようだ。

outer space ***n.*** 宇宙(空間)

outfield ***n.*** (in baseball) 外野

♦ **outfielder** ***n.*** 外野手

outfit ***n.*** (set of clothes) 衣装, (set of equipment) 装備一式, (set of tools) 用具一式

That's a nice outfit you're wearing.
すてきな衣装を着てらっしゃいますね。

He turned up in a penguin outfit.
彼はペンギンの衣装で現れた。

outfitter ***n.*** (of sporting goods) スポーツ用品店, (of travel goods) 旅行用品店

outgoing ***adj.*** (sociable) 社交的な, 外向的な; (soon to retire) 辞任する

an outgoing person 外向的な人

the outgoing president 辞任する社長

outgrow ***v.*** (shoes) 大きくなってはけなくなる, (clothes) 着られなくなる, (activity, interest) (…が) なくなる

He's already outgrown his suit.
彼は体が大きくなって、今ある服がもう着られなくなってしまった。

outing ***n.*** 遠足, (day trip) 日帰り旅行

Our class is going on an outing.
クラスは遠足に出かけるんです。

outlandish ***adj.*** 奇妙な, 風変わりな

outlast ***v.*** (…より) 長持ちする, (outlive) (…より) 長生きする

outlaw ***n.*** 無法者, アウトロー

v. (make illegal) 違法とする, 禁じる

outlay ***n.*** (expenses) 支出, 経費

outlet ***n.*** (electrical socket) コンセント; (for feelings) はけ口

These teenagers need some kind of outlet for their frustrations.
このティーンエイジャーたちには、欲求不満のはけ口が何か必要だ。

outline *n.* (description of main points) あらまし, 概要, 概略; (line indicating contours) 輪郭
v. (summarize) 説明する, (…の) 概略を述べる, あらましを話す

Ms. Hayashi gave a brief outline of the history of medicine.
林さんは医学史の概略をざっと述べた。

He outlined the project for us.
彼は、私たちにプロジェクトのあらましを説明してくれた。

outlive *v.* (…より) 長生きする

outlook *n.* (point of view) 見解, 見方, (prospects) 見込み, 見通し, めど; (view) 見晴らし, 景色

The economic outlook is encouraging.
経済見通しは、明るそうだ。

outlying *adj.* 遠い所の, へんぴな

outmaneuver *v.* (…に) 策略で勝つ, (…を) 出し抜く

The prime minister was outmaneuvered by the Opposition parties.
首相は野党に<u>出し抜かれた</u> [裏をかかれた]。

outmoded *adj.* 時代遅れの, 流行遅れの

outnumber *v.* (…より) 数が多い, (…に) 数でまさる

They were outnumbered three to one.
3対1で、彼らのほうが数は少なかった。

out-of-date *adj.* 時代遅れの, 古くさい

outpatient *n.* 外来患者

outpost *n.* (military outpost) 前哨部隊; (remote settlement) 辺境の地

output *n.* 生産高, (of electricity) 出力, アウトプット

outrage *n.* (anger) 憤慨, (act of violence) 暴行

outrageous *adj.* (extraordinary) 思いも寄らない, とっぴな, (ridiculous) とんでもない, (of price) 法外な, べらぼうな

an outrageous idea とっぴな考え

an outrageous expenditure (of money) とんでもない出費

These prices are outrageous.
これは、どれも法外な値段だよ。

outright *adj.* (complete) 完全な, (thorough) 徹底的な; (direct, frank) 率直な
adv. (completely) 完全に, (thoroughly) 徹底的に; (directly, frankly) 率直に

an outright lie <u>全くの</u> [真っ赤な] うそ

outset *n.* 初め, 最初

at [from] the outset 最初<u>は</u> [から]

outside

1 *adv.* OUTDOORS: 外へ/に/で

2 *prep.* BEYOND: …の外へ/に/で

3 *n.* 外, (outer side) 外側, (exterior) 外部

4 *adj.* 外の, 外側の, (from the outer side) 外からの, (of person) 外部の

1 They are waiting outside.
((*polite*)) みなさんは、外でお待ちです。

Should I put all the chairs outside?
椅子を全部、外に出したほうがいいでしょうか？

Let's go outside. 外に出ましょう。

"Where is she?" "Outside."
「彼女はどこ？」「外だよ」

2 Outside London, the air is a lot cleaner.

ロンドンを一歩出れば、空気はずっときれいです。

3 the outside of the bottle びんの外側
the outside of the building 建物の外部

4 the outside world 外の世界 [外界]
outside assistance 外部からの援助
an outside consultant
外部のコンサルタント

on the outside (from outward appearances) 見かけは, 外見は

On the outside, he seems a normal sort of guy.
見かけは普通の男と変わらないのに。

outsider *n.* よそ者, 部外者, アウトサイダー; (person/horse in race) 勝ち目のない人/馬

As a foreigner, he was considered an outsider.
外国人なので、彼はよそ者と見なされた。

outskirts *n.* 外れ, 郊外

They live on the outskirts of Paris.
あの人たちはパリ郊外に住んでいます。

outspoken *adj.* 率直な, 遠慮なく言う, ずけずけ言う

He's very outspoken, and some people in the company don't like it.
彼はずけずけものを言うから、それを好ましく思っていない人も会社にはいます。

outstanding *adj.* (remarkable) 目立つ, (excellent) すぐれた, (wonderful) すばらしい; (of problem) 未解決の, (of debt) 未払いの

It was an outstanding (musical) performance.
すばらしい演奏だった。

Is there any debt outstanding?
未払い金がありますか？

outstretched *adj.* 伸ばした, 広げた

with outstretched arms 両腕を広げて

outstrip *v.* (…に) 勝る, (…を) 上回る

outward *adj.* (outer) 外側の, (toward the outside) 外に向かう, (of appearances) 外見の, うわべの

adv. 外へ/に, 外側へ/に

Do outward appearances count for much with you?
あなたは外見が気になるほうですか？

He spoke with an outward calm.
表向きは、彼は落ち着いて話した。

The door opens outward.
ドアは外側に開きます。

♦ **outwardly** *adv.* 表面上(は), 外見上(は), 表向きは

outweigh *v.* (…より) 重要だ, (…に) 勝る

Nothing outweighs peace.
平和に勝るものはない。

His obsession with that woman seemed to outweigh everything else.
彼はその女性に夢中で、ほかのことは一切二の次になっているようだった。

outwit *v.* 出し抜く, (…の) 裏をかく

oval *n.* (egg shape) 卵形の物, (ellipse) 長円形, 楕円形

adj. (egg-shaped) 卵形の, (elliptical) 長円形の, 楕円(形)の

ovary *n.* 卵巣

ovation *n.* 大かっさい, 大きな拍手

give a standing ovation
立ち上がって拍手を送る

oven *n.* オーブン, 天火

bake a cake in the oven

オーブンでケーキを焼く

over

1 *prep.* ABOVE OR ON TOP OF: …の上に/の, (**all over**: completely covering) …一面に, …中に/を

2 *prep.* MORE THAN: …以上, …ちょっと

3 *prep.* DURING (THE COURSE OF): …の間

4 *prep.* ABOUT/CONCERNING: …のことで, …をめぐって

5 *adv.* AGAIN: もう一度, もう一回 [→ OVER AND OVER AGAIN]

6 *adj.* FINISHED: (**be over**) 終わった

7 *adv.* TO THE OTHER SIDE: あっちに, 向こう側に [→ OVER HERE, OVER THERE]

8 *prep.* LOUDER THAN: (**can't hear** A **over** B) (Bが)うるさくて(Aが)聞き取れない

1 Watch out for the light over your head.
頭の上の明かりに注意して。

At least we have a roof over our heads.
少なくとも私たちには住む家がある。

Put this blanket over the bed.
ベッドの上にこの毛布をかけて。

There was snow all over the streets.
通りは一面、雪でおおわれていた。

2 He's over sixty kilos.
あの人は 60 キロ以上ありますよ。

It cost slightly over ¥10,000.
1万円ちょっとしました。

3 Did you get much done over the weekend?
週末で、はかどりましたか？

They spent a long time chatting over a cup of tea.
二人はお茶を飲みながら、長い間しゃべっていた。

4 They had a quarrel over something.
二人は、何かのことで言い争いをした。

It's no use crying over spilt milk.
覆水盆に返らず。

5 Let's start over.
もう一度始めよう/やり直そう。

If I could do things all over, I would do things differently.
もしもう一回始めからやり直せたら、違うやり方をすると思う。

6 The game is over.
試合 [ゲーム] は終わった。

It's all over now. もうおしまいだ。

7 Can we cross over now?
今なら渡れるかな？

She walked over to the door.
彼女はドアの方に歩いて行った。

8 I couldn't hear you over the sound of the traffic.
車の音がうるさくて、聞き取れませんでした。

be (all) over and done with すべて終わった

As far as I'm concerned, it's all over and done with.
私自身としては、もうすべて終わったことです。

be (all) over with …はもうだめだ, …はもう終わりだ

It's all over with Janet and me.
ジャネットと僕は、もう終わりだ。

over again もう一度(初めから)

I had to do it over again.
もう一度初めから、やり直さないといけなかった。

over and above …以外に, …に加えて

I don't expect you to do anything over and above what I've told you to do.
言ったこと以外は、やらなくていいんです。

over and over again 何度も何度も

We had to repeat it over and over again.
私たちは、何度も何度も繰り返さなければならなかった。

over here こっちに, ((*polite*)) こちらに

Step over here, please.
こちらにいらしてください。

If you bring that mouse over here, I'll scream.
((*feminine*)) あのネズミをここに持って来たりしたら、叫ぶわよ。

over there 向こうに, あっちに, ((*polite*)) あちらに

over- *pref.* (excessively) …すぎる, 過度に

overemphasize 強調しすぎる

overall *adj.* (total) 全体の, (general) 全般的な

adv. 全体として, 総合的に見て

Overall, I think the project is likely to succeed.
総合的に見て、このプロジェクトは成功するような気がします。

overalls *n.* オーバーオール

overboard *adv.* 船外に, 船から水中に

fall overboard 船から水中に落ちる

go overboard (do too much) やりすぎる

overcast *adj.* (cloudy) 曇っている, 雲でおおわれた

overcharge *v.* (…に) 高値をふっかける

overcoat *n.* コート, オーバー, 外套

overcome *v.* (difficulties) (…に) 打ち勝つ, (…を) 克服する, 乗り越える; (**be overcome:** with sadness etc.) (…に) 打ちひしがれる

He overcame all manner of difficulties.
彼は、ありとあらゆる困難を克服した。

She was overcome with grief.
彼女は悲しみに打ちひしがれた。

overconfident *adj.* 自信過剰な, うぬぼれの強い

overcook *v.* (broil too much) 焼きすぎる, (boil too much) 煮すぎる

overcritical *adj.* 批判的すぎる

overcrowded *adj.* (of room) 超満員の, (of school) 生徒の多すぎる, (be overcrowded with) (…で) あふれる, 混み合う

overcrowding *n.* 過密

overdo *v.* …しすぎる, やりすぎる, (**overdo it**: try to do too much) 無理をする

Don't overdo it or you'll make yourself ill.
体をこわすから、無理をしないで。

overdone *adj.* (broiled too much) 焼きすぎた, (boiled too much) 煮すぎた

overdose *v.* 飲みすぎる

n. 飲みすぎ

a drug overdose 薬の飲みすぎ

overdraft *n.* 当座借り越し

overdraw *v.* 引き出しすぎる, 借り越す

I'm overdrawn by about $500.
500ドルくらいの借り越しがある。

overdress *v.* 正装しすぎる

overdue *adj.* (late) 遅れた, 延び延びになった, (of payment) 支払い期限が過ぎた

These reforms are long overdue.
この改革は、どれも延び延びになって

いる。
an overdue fine
支払い期限が過ぎた罰金
The DVD I took out was overdue, so I had to pay a small amount.
ＤＶＤの返却期限が過ぎていたので、いくらか払わなければならなかった。

overeat *v.* 食べすぎる, 過食する

overestimate *v.* 過大評価する, 買いかぶる

overfeed *v.* (animal) (…に) えさをやりすぎる

overflow *v.* あふれる, (overflow into) (…に) あふれ出る, (flood) 氾濫する
The water tank seems to have overflowed.
タンクの水があふれ出したようだ。
The river has overflowed its banks.
川は堤防を越えて氾濫した。

overgrown *adj.* 生い茂った, 草ぼうぼうの
The garden was overgrown with weeds.
庭は一面、草ぼうぼうだった。

overhang *v.* (…の上に) かかる, (jut out over) (…の上に) 突き出す, 張り出す
n. (part of building) 張り出し, (part of rock face) 出っ張り

overhaul *v.* (repair) 修理する, (dismantle) 分解修理する, 整備する
n. (thorough repair) 修理, 分解, 整備
need an overhaul 分解修理が必要だ

overhead *adj., adv.* 頭上の/に
♦ **overhead projector** *n.* ＯＨＰ

overhear *v.* (ふと)耳にする, 小耳に挟む
I overheard him say something about the boss getting a divorce.
上司が離婚するとか何とか、彼が言っているのを耳にした。

overheat *v.* (of engine) オーバーヒートする, 過熱する

overindulge *v.* 甘やかしすぎる, (drink too much) 飲みすぎる

overjoyed *adj.* 大喜びする

overkill *n.* (excess) 過剰, 行きすぎ, やりすぎ

overland *adj., adv.* 陸上の/で, 陸路の/で

overlap *v.* 重なる, (of events) かち合う, (of interests) 共通する
n. 共通するところ, 重なり合う部分
The carpets overlap here.
じゅうたんは、ここで重なっている。
There's a certain amount of overlap between the two subjects.
この二つの分野には、ある程度共通するところがある。

overleaf *adv.* 裏ページに

overload *v.* (truck) (…に) 荷を積みすぎる, (person with information work) (…に) 詰め込みすぎる, 負担をかけすぎる
n. (too much information etc.) 詰め込み
♦ **overloaded** *adj.* (of car) 荷を積みすぎる, (of person) 負担をかけすぎる
The car was overloaded.
車は荷物を積みすぎていた。

overlook *v.* (allow a view of) 見渡せる, 見下ろせる; (fail to notice) 見落とす; (allow to go unpunished) 大目に見る, 見逃す
Our apartment overlooks the university.
うちのアパートから大学を見下ろせる。
The nuclear industry overlooks the problem of radioactive waste disposal.

原子力産業は、放射性廃棄物の処理の問題を見落としている。

The teacher was kind enough to overlook the fact that I was late (for class).
先生は遅刻したのを見逃してくれた。

overly *adv.* あまりにも, 過度に

overnight *adj.* 一晩中の, 夜通しの, (of guest, trip) 1泊の

adv. 一晩中, 夜通し, (suddenly) 一夜にして

an overnight train 夜行列車

They're working overnight to finish the road.
彼らは道路を完成させるために、夜通し働いている。

The situation changed overnight.
一夜にして状況が変わった。

stay overnight 泊まる, (at hotel for one night) 1泊する

overpass *n.* 陸橋, 高架道路

overpay *v.* (…に)余計に払う, 払いすぎる

overpopulated *adj.* 人口が多すぎる, 人口過密の

overpower *v.* (subdue) 取り押さえる, (overwhelm) 圧倒する

Two cashiers overpowered the bank robber until the police arrived.
警察が到着するまで、二人の出納係が銀行強盗を取り押さえていた。

overpowering *adj.* 強烈な

overprice *v.* (…に) 高値をつけすぎる

overproduce *v.* 過剰生産する

overprotective *adj.* 過保護の

overrated *adj.* 過大評価されている

That restaurant is overrated.
あのレストランは過大評価されている。

overreact *v.* 過剰反応する, 過度に反応する

Don't overreact.
過剰反応してはいけない。

override *v.* (take precedence over) (…に) 優先する, (overrule) くつがえす

overrule *v.* (decision) くつがえす, 却下する

The judge overruled the lower court's decision.
判事は、下級裁判所の判決をくつがえした。

overrun *v.* (of military: occupy) 占領する, (invade) 侵略する, (**be overrun with**) (=be occupied by in abundance) (…が) うようよいる, (=with weeds) (…が) はびこる

overseas *adv.* 海外に/で

adj. 海外の, 外国の

His company sent him to work overseas.
彼は海外勤務を命じられた。

oversee *v.* 監督する, 監視する

I was appointed to oversee the project.
私は、そのプロジェクトの監督役に任命されました。

overshadow *v.* ((*also figurative*)) (…に) 影を落とす, (**be overshadowed by**) …の陰になる, (=be dominated by) …に比べて見劣りする

The happiness of Christmas was overshadowed by the approach of war.
戦争が近づいていることが、楽しいクリスマスに影を落とした。

oversight *n.* (mistake) ミス, 見落とし

oversimplify *v.* 簡略化しすぎる, あまりにも簡単に扱う

oversleep *v.* 寝坊する, 寝過ごす

I overslept and missed my train.
寝坊して電車に乗り遅れた。

overspend *v.* 金を使いすぎる, 浪費する

overstaffed *adj.* 職員が多すぎる, 人員過剰の

overstate *v.* (exaggerate) おおげさに言う, 誇張する

overstay *v.* (visa) 不法(長期)滞在する, (**overstay one's welcome**) 長居する

overt *adj.* 公然の, あからさまな

overt criticism あからさまな非難

♦ **overtly** *adv.* 公然と, あからさまに

overtake *v.* (catch up with) (…に) 追いつく, (pass) 追い越す

It's not safe to overtake on a bend.
カーブで追い越すのは危険です。

overthrow *v.* (government) 転覆させる, 倒す

The two men were accused of plotting to overthrow the government.
二人の男性が、政府の転覆をはかった罪で告訴された。

overtime *n.* 残業, ((*formal*)) 超過勤務

I'm working overtime tonight.
今夜は残業だ。

overtone *n.* (**overtones**) 含み, ニュアンス

overture *n.* (musical prelude) 序曲

overturn *v.* (upturn) ひっくり返す, (capsize) 転覆する, (decision) くつがえす [→ OVERRULE]

overview *n.* 全般的な見解, 概観, (summary) 概要

overweight *adj.* 体重が標準より重い, 太りすぎの

He is two kilograms overweight.
彼は標準より2キロ重い。

overwhelm *v.* (beat) 圧倒する, (besiege, inundate) (…に) 殺到する, (**be overwhelmed with / by**: emotion) …に打ちのめされる

The state was overwhelmed by the invincible morale of the guerrilla fighters.
政府はゲリラの不屈の戦意に圧倒された。

We were overwhelmed with letters of sympathy and support.
我々の元に、同情と支援の手紙が殺到した。

She was overwhelmed with grief at the news of her son's death.
息子が死んだという知らせを聞いて、母親は悲しみに打ちのめされた。

overwhelming *adj.* (of number) 圧倒的な, (of reality) どうしようもない

♦ **overwhelmingly** *adv.* 圧倒的に

overwork *v.* (person) 働かせすぎる, (**overwork oneself**) 働きすぎる, (idea) 使いすぎる

He overworked himself and eventually had to take time off because of stress.
働きすぎた結果、彼はストレスのため休職せざるを得なくなった。

ovulate *v.* 排卵する

owe *v.* (be in debt to) (…に) 借りている, 借金がある, (have a moral obligation to) (…に) 恩がある, 借りがある, (**owe A [success etc.] to B**) (AはBの) おかげだ

How much do I owe you?
いくらお借りしていますか？

I owe him a lot.

彼にはたくさん恩がある。

Does he owe you anything?
彼はあなたに何か借りがあるの？

I think you owe him an apology.
彼に謝るべきだと思う。

He owes his success to his teachers.
彼の成功は先生たちのおかげです。

owing to *prep.* …のため(に), …が原因で, (implying blame) …のせいで

Owing to bad weather, all flights are canceled.
悪天候のため、全便が欠航です。

owl *n.* フクロウ

own

1 ***adj.*** **PERSONAL:** 自分の, 自分自身の, (peculiar) 独自の

2 ***v.*** **POSSESS:** 持つ, ((*formal*)) 所有する

3 ***pron.*** **ONE'S OWN THING:** 自分自身のもの

1 my own home 自分の家 [自宅]

He should mind his own business.
彼は、人のことに首を突っ込むべきではない。

She has her own ways of doing things.
彼女には独自のやり方がある。

2 He owns several properties.
彼は土地をいくつか持っている。

Who owns this place?
ここはどなたが所有しているのですか？

I may be your spouse, but you don't own me.
私は確かにあなたの配偶者だけど、あなたの所有物ではない。

3 The ideas are her own.
その考えは彼女自身のものです。

be one's own man/woman → MAN

on one's own (without help) 自力で, (alone) 一人で

It's time the boy did something on his own without your help.
あの子も、そろそろ君の助けを借りずに(自力で) 何かをやってもいいころだ。

♦**own up** *v.* 白状する, 認める

owner *n.* 持ち主, 所有者, オーナー, (landlord/landlady) 家主, (of business) 社長, 経営者, (of pet) 飼い主

ownership *n.* (fact of) 所有, (right of) 所有権

ox *n.* ウシ, 牛, (male cow) 雄牛

oxide *n.* 酸化物

oxygen *n.* 酸素

♦**oxygen mask** *n.* 酸素マスク

oyster *n.* カキ

raw oysters 生ガキ

ozone *n.* オゾン

♦**ozone hole** *n.* オゾンホール

ozone layer *n.* オゾン層

P, p

pace *n.* (speed) ペース, 速度, (walking speed) 歩調, (one step) 1歩, (distance of one step) 歩幅

v. (pace back and forth) 行ったり来たりする, (prowl) うろうろする; (**pace oneself**) 自分のペースでやる

He works at a good pace.
あの人はいいペースで仕事をしている。

Step forward a pace or two.
1、2歩、前へ進んでください。

She was pacing up and down the hall.
彼女は廊下を行ったり来たりしていた。

You'd better pace yourself or you'll get burned out.
自分のペースでやったほうがいい、でないと燃え尽きてしまうよ。

keep pace with …のペースについて行く, …の歩調に合わせる

pacemaker *n.* ペースメーカー

Pacific Ocean *n.* 太平洋

pacifism *n.* 平和主義

pacifist *n.* 平和主義者

pacify *v.* (person) なだめる, 静める, (country) 平定する, 平和な状態に戻す

pack

1 *v.* PUT INTO CONTAINER: (pack A into B) (AをBに) 詰める, 詰め込む, (pack one's belongings into: suitcase etc.) (…に) 荷物を詰める, (prepare for a trip) 旅行の用意をする, 旅支度をする, (prepare to move house by putting things in boxes) 荷造りをする

2 *v.* FILL WITH PEOPLE/THINGS: いっぱいにする, (**pack into**: of people into hall etc.) …にぎっしり入る [→ PACKED]

3 *n.* CONTAINER: (box) 箱, (bag) 袋, (backpack) リュック(サック), バックパック

4 *n.* GROUP: (of animals) 群れ, (of people) 集団

1 Let's pack these things away.
これをみんな、しまいましょう。

We'd better start packing our suitcases.
そろそろスーツケースに荷物を詰め始めないと。

If you're leaving tomorrow, you'd better start packing.
明日たつのなら、もう用意をしたほうがいいよ。

2 Hundreds of teens packed into the theater.
何百人もの10代の子が劇場にぎっしり入った。

3 a pack of cigarettes たばこ一箱

He had a pack on his back.
その人はリュックを背負っていました。

4 a pack of wolves オオカミの群れ

a pack of high schoolers 高校生の集団

♦**pack up** *v.* 荷物をまとめる

package *n.* (parcel) 小包, 包み, 荷物, (bundle) 一束

Let's unwrap [wrap up] the package.
小包をあけよう [作ろう]。

♦**package tour** *n.* パック旅行

packaging *n.* (materials used for packaging a product) 包装, パッケージ

packed *adj.* (crowded) 混んでいる, (of theater/train full of people) 満員の, (jam-packed) すし詰めの, (packed with…: filled with…) (…で) いっぱいの

The station was packed.
駅は混雑していた。

The train looks packed.
電車は満員のようですね。

The place was packed with people.
そこは人でいっぱいだった。

This book is packed with information.
この本には情報が満載されている。

packing *n.* (filling of boxes) 荷造り, (preparation for a trip) (旅行の)用意; (shipping material) 包装材料

pact *n.*(agreement) 協定, (promise) 契約, (treaty) 条約

make a pact with... ...と契約を結ぶ

pad *n.* (memo pad) メモ帳, (letter-paper pad) 便せん; (cushioning in garment/for protection of body) パッド; (launchpad) 発射台

v. (give padding to) (...に) 詰め物をする, パッドを入れる

Would you like to use my writing pad?
私のメモ帳をお使いになりますか?

♦ **padded** *adj.* パッド入りの

a padded bra パッド入りブラ

padding *n.* (cushioning) 詰め物, (in garment) パッド

paddle *n.* (for boat) かい, パドル, (for table tennis) (卓球の)ラケット

v. (row) こぐ

paddleboat *n.* 外輪船

paddock *n.* (field for horses) 牧草地, 小牧場, (at horse race) パドック

paddy *n.* (rice field) 水田, 稲田

padlock *n.* 南京錠

pagan *n.* 異教徒

page *n.* ページ, 頁

Now turn to the next page.
では次のページに進みましょう。

Look at page 2.
2ページを見てください。

Open your books to page 53.
53 ページを開いてください。

Some of the pages were missing.
何ページか欠けていた。

the top [middle, bottom] of the page
ページの上 [中央, 下]

the first [last] page 最初 [最後]のページ

pageant *n.* (beauty pageant) 美人コンテスト; (parade) 時代行列

pager *n.* ポケットベル, ポケベル

pagoda *n.* 塔, パゴダ

five-story pagoda
五重の塔

paid *adj.* (of vacation etc.) 有給の

Do you get paid vacations?
有給休暇はありますか?

pail *n.* (bucket) バケツ

pain *n.* 痛み, 苦痛, (unhappiness) 苦しみ, つらさ

v. (...が) 痛む, 痛い

Are you in pain? 痛いですか?

Is there any pain? 痛みはありますか?

menstrual pain 生理痛

The pain of separation was unbearable.
別れのつらさは耐えがたいものだった。

His back pained him.
彼は背中が痛かった。

go to great pains 非常に苦労する

painful *adj.* 痛い, (of experience, deci-

P

sion) 苦しい, つらい

♦**painfully** *adv.* 痛いほど, (extremely) ひどく

painkiller *n.* 鎮痛剤, 痛み止め

painless *adj.* 痛くない, 無痛の, (easy) 簡単な

painstaking *adj.* 骨の折れる

paint *n.* (for wall) ペンキ, ((*formal*)) 塗料, (as used by artists) 絵の具

v. (…に) ペンキを塗る, (paint a picture) (絵を) かく, (do paintings) 絵をかく

a can of red paint 赤ペンキの缶

(*sign*) Wet Paint ペンキ塗り立て

We painted the ceiling.
天井にペンキを塗った。

She painted a picture of the view.
彼女はその景色を絵にかいた。

paintbrush *n.* (painter's) はけ, ブラシ, (artist's) 筆, 絵筆

painter *n.* (artist) 画家, 絵かき, (person who paints things as a profession) ペンキ職人, ペンキ屋

painting *n.* (work of art) 絵, (creating pictures with paint) 絵をかくこと; (applying of paint) ペンキ塗り

an oil painting 油絵

pair *n.* (two of sth) 一組, 1対, ペア, (of people: a couple) カップル, (married couple) 夫婦, (two people) 二人

v. (pair A with B) (AとBを) 組み合わせる

a pair of glasses メガネ一つ

a pair of shoes 靴1足

a pair of pants ズボン1本

a pair of scissors はさみ1丁

an odd pair of socks
左右不ぞろいの靴下

They make a nice pair.
すてきなカップル [ご夫妻] だね。

Practice in pairs.
二人一組で練習してください。

♦**pair up** *v.* (for dance) ペアを組む

They paired up for the last dance.
二人は最後のダンスでペアを組んだ。

pajamas *n.* パジャマ

Pakistan *n.* パキスタン

pal *n.* 友達, 仲間

palace *n.* (monarch's) 宮殿, パレス, (Japanese Emperor's) 皇居, 御所, (president's) 官邸; (luxurious building) 大邸宅, 立派な建物

palate *n.* 口蓋

suit one's palate (…の) 口に合う

palatial *adj.* 宮殿のような

pale *adj.* (of face) 青白い, (ill-looking) 顔色が悪い; (of light) 薄い, 淡い

She has a very pale complexion.
あの人はとても青白い顔をしている。

He's so pale—I wonder if he's ill…
彼、顔色が悪いね――具合が悪いんじゃないかな。

a pale green 薄い緑色

pale in comparison to/with… …より見劣りがする

turn pale 青ざめる, 真っ青になる

paleontology *n.* 古生物学

Palestine *n.* パレスチナ

palette *n.* パレット

palm[1] *n.* (of hand) 手の平 [→ picture of HAND]

read someone's palm (…の) 手相を見る

P

palm² *n.* (tree) シュロの木, ヤシの木, (frond) シュロの葉

♦**palm oil** *n.* ヤシ油

palmist *n.* 手相見, 手相占い師

♦**palmistry** *n.* 手相占い

palpable *adj.* (obvious) 明白な, はっきりした, (tangible) 触ってわかる

a palpable lie 見え透いたうそ

pamper *v.* 甘やかす, ちやほやする

pamphlet *n.* パンフレット, 小冊子

pan *n.* (saucepan) (お)なべ, (frying pan) フライパン

put a pan on the stove

なべをレンジにかける

cover a pan なべにふたをする

empty a pan なべを空ける [空にする]

panacea *n.* 万能薬

pancake *n.* パンケーキ

pancreas *n.* すい臓

panda *n.* パンダ

pander *v.* (**pander to**) (=flatter) …のご機嫌を取る, …に迎合する, (=indulge, in order to take advantage of) …の弱みにつけこむ

Politicians usually pander to the public before elections.

政治家は、たいてい選挙前になると大衆のご機嫌を取るものだ。

pane *n.* (windowpane) 窓ガラス

panel *n.* (piece of wood) 羽目板; (group of people) 委員会, グループ; (**control panel**) コントロールパネル, 制御盤

One of the wooden panels was broken.

木の羽目板の一つが壊れていた。

Are you on the investigative panel?

(あなたは)調査委員の一人ですか?

a panel of experts 専門家の一団

♦**panel discussion** *n.* パネルディスカッション, 公開討論会

paneling *n.* パネル, 羽目板

panelist *n.* パネリスト

pang *n.* (sudden pain) 激痛, (of guilt) 苦しみ, 心の痛み

pangs of conscience 良心の呵責

panic *n.* パニック, 恐慌

v. パニック状態になる, うろたえる

Let's not panic. I'm sure everything's all right.

落ち着こう。きっと大丈夫だよ。

♦**panic disorder** *n.* パニック障害

panicky *adj.* うろたえた, パニック状態の

panorama *n.* パノラマ, 全景

pansy *n.* (plant) パンジー, 三色スミレ

pant *v.* 息が切れる, あえぐ

panther *n.* (black leopard) クロヒョウ, (cougar) ピューマ

panties *n.* パンティー, パンツ

pantomime *n.* パントマイム

pantry *n.* 食料貯蔵室

pants *n.* (trousers) ズボン [→ UNDERPANTS]

pantyhose *n.* (パンティー) ストッキング, パンスト

papa *n.* (お)父ちゃん, パパ

papaya *n.* (fruit) パパイヤ(の実), (tree) パパイヤ(の木)

paper

1 *n.* SHEET: 紙, 用紙, ペーパー

2 *n.* NEWSPAPER: 新聞

3 *n.* ESSAY: レポート, 論文

4 ***n.*** DOCUMENTS: (**papers**) 書類

5 ***v.*** COVER WITH WALLPAPER: (…に) 壁紙を張る

6 ***adj.*** MADE OF PAPER: 紙の, 紙製の

1 "How many sheets of paper do you have?"
"Only three."
「紙を何枚持っていますか？」
「3枚だけです」
Can I use some of this paper?
この紙を使ってもいい？
scratch/scrap paper 要らない紙

2 Where's today's paper?
今日の新聞はどこ？
Have you read this morning's paper?
今日の朝刊を読みましたか？

3 The paper is due next Monday.
レポートの提出は来週の月曜日です。
It will take at least a week to grade all the papers.
すべての論文に成績をつけるのに、少なくとも1週間はかかる。

4 All the papers were shredded.
書類はすべてシュレッダーにかけられた。
These papers are marked "important."
これらの書類には「重要」の印が押されている。

5 We papered the living room.
居間に壁紙を張った。

6 a paper cup 紙コップ [→ picture of CUP]
a paper bag 紙袋

paperback ***adj., n.*** ペーパーバックの(本)

paper clip ***n.*** クリップ, 紙挟み [→ picture of STATIONERY]

paperweight ***n.*** ペーパーウェイト, (used in Japanese calligraphy) 文鎮 [→ picture of CALLIGRAPHY]

paperwork ***n.*** (work) 事務処理, (documents) 書類

papier-mâché ***n.*** 張り子の材料

paprika ***n.*** パプリカ

par ***n.*** (in golf) パー

be below/under/not up to par (of feeling) 調子がよくない, (of anything in general: not so good) ((*informal*)) 今一だ
I'm feeling below par today.
今日はいつもより調子がよくない。
His writing is not up to par.
彼の書いたものは、今一だ。

be on a par with… …と同じ程度だ

parable ***n.*** 寓話, たとえ話

parabola ***n.*** 放物線

parachute ***n.*** パラシュート, 落下傘
v. パラシュートで降りる

parade ***n.*** (ceremony) パレード, 行進
v. パレードをする, 行進する

paradigm ***n.*** パラダイム, (example) 典型, 例

paradigmatic ***adj.*** (**be paradigmatic of**) …の典型的な例だ

paradise ***n.*** (heaven) 天国, (splendid place) 楽園, パラダイス

paradox ***n.*** (statement) 逆説, パラドックス, (contradiction) 矛盾

paraffin ***n.*** (for making candles) パラフィン; (kerosene) 灯油

paragliding ***n.*** パラグライディング

paragon ***n.*** (model) 模範, 手本

paragraph ***n.*** 段落, パラグラフ

parakeet ***n.*** インコ

parallel ***adj.*** (of lines) 平行の, 平行して

いる
adv. 平行に, 平行して
n. (equivalent/comparable thing) 匹敵するもの, (similarity) 類似点, 共通点; (parallel line) 平行線
The canal runs parallel to the river in places.
所々で、運河はその川と平行に流れている。
There were some parallels between the two crimes.
二つの犯罪には、いくつかの共通点があった。
be without parallel 匹敵するものがない, 類を見ない
The horror of this civil war is without parallel.
この内戦による惨劇は類を見ない。

parallelogram *n.* 平行四辺形

paralysis *n.* 麻痺

paralyze *v.* (**be paralyzed**) 麻痺する
His left side was paralyzed by the stroke.
脳卒中によって、彼は左半身が麻痺した。

paramedic *n.* 医療補助員

parameter *n.* (**parameters**) 範囲, 限界

paramilitary *adj.* 準軍事的な
a paramilitary operation 準軍事行動

paramount *adj.* (most important) 最重要の

paranoia *n.* 偏執病, 妄想症, パラノイア

paranoid *adj.* 偏執病の, 被害妄想の
Don't get paranoid.
被害妄想だよ/考えすぎだよ。

paraphernalia *n.* 道具一式

paraphrase *v.* わかりやすく言い換える
n. 言い換え, パラフレーズ

paraplegia *n.* 対麻痺

paraplegic *n.* (person) 対麻痺の人

parasite *n.* 寄生虫

parasol *n.* パラソル, (umbrella) 日傘

paratrooper *n.* 落下傘兵

paratroops *n.* 落下傘部隊

parcel *n.* 小包, 包み, 荷物

parched *adj.* (of throat) (のどが) からからの

pardon *v.* (criminal) 特赦する, (crime) 赦免する
n. 恩赦
The judge pardoned him.
裁判官はその男を特赦した。
The criminal was given a pardon.
その犯罪者は恩赦を受けた。
I beg your pardon? (could you repeat that?) すみませんが、もう一度言ってくださいますか?
pardon me (apologizing) ごめんなさい, 失礼しました
Pardon me? すみませんが、もう一度言ってくださいますか?
pardon me for asking/saying so, but... ちょっとお尋ねしますが.../失礼ですが...
pardon my French 品のない言葉ですが

pare *v.* (cut the skin off of) (...の) 皮をむく; (expenses) 切り詰める, 削減する
The university pared its budget.
大学が予算を削減した。

parent *n.* 親, (**parents**) 両親, (sb else's parents) ご両親
I don't see much of my parents these days.
最近、両親とはあまり会っていません。

Matsumoto's parents died when he was young.
松本さんは幼い時に両親を亡くした。

How are your parents doing?
ご両親はお元気ですか？

♦**parental** *adj.* 親の, 親としての, 親らしい

parent company *n.* 親会社

parenting *n.* 子育て, 育児

parenthesis *n.* (punctuation mark) (丸)かっこ, パーレン

The comment was in parentheses.
そのコメントはかっこでくくられていた。

parish *n.* 教区

parity *n.* (equality) 均等, 同等

park *n.* 公園

v. (car) 駐車する, 車を止めておく

There's a park just near here.
このすぐ近くに公園があります。

I go for a jog in the park every morning.
毎朝公園にジョギングに行きます。

It's very difficult to find a place to park around here.
このあたりで駐車する場所を探すのは、とても難しい。

You can park right here.
ここに車を止められますよ。

parking *n.* 駐車

(*sign*) No Parking 駐車禁止

♦**parking lot** *n.* 駐車場

parking meter *n.* 駐車メーター, パーキングメーター

parking ticket *n.* 駐車違反の切符

parkway *n.* パークウェイ

parliament *n.* 国会, 議会

parliamentary *adj.* 議会の

a parliamentary government 議会政治

parlor *n.* (business) -店, -院, -屋; (room) 居間

an ice-cream parlor アイスクリーム店

a massage parlor マッサージ店

a beauty parlor 美容院

a funeral parlor 葬儀屋

parochial *adj.* (narrow-minded) 狭い; (of school) 教区の

parody *n.* パロディー

parole *n.* 仮釈放

be on parole 仮釈放されている, 仮出所している

parrot *n.* オウム

parsley *n.* パセリ

part

1 *n.* PIECE/SEGMENT: 部分, 一片, 一部, 一部分, (of machine) 部品

2 *v.* SEPARATE: 別れる, (**be parted**) 離れ離れになる, (**part with**) 手放す

3 *n.* AREA: (region) 地方, 地域, (**these parts**) この辺, このあたり

4 *n.* ROLE: 役, 役割, 役目

5 *n.* EQUAL PORTION: 割合

6 *n.* DIVISION IN HAIR: (髪の)分け目

1 an engine part エンジン部分

It was one part of a bigger plan.
それは壮大な計画の一部だった。

It was a big part of my life.
それは私の人生の大きな部分を占めていた。

The first part was good, but the second part was terrible.
第1部はよかったけど、第2部はひどかった。

P

a spare part 予備部品

2 They parted on good terms.
二人は仲良く別れた。

We did not want to part.
私たちは別れたくなかった。

I didn't want to part with my car.
車を手放したくなかった。

3 You're not from around these parts, are you?
この辺の人じゃありませんね。

What part of LA are you from?
ロスのどのあたりのご出身ですか？

4 play/take the part of the villain
悪役を演じる

He had no part in what took place.
その出来事に、彼は何の役割も果たしていなかった。

5 one part soy sauce, two parts water
しょうゆ1に水2の割合

6 The part is in the middle.
分け目は真ん中です。

for my/our/your part 私/我々/あなたとしては

For my part, I was happy to go along with what the group decided.
私としては、みんなが決めたことに合わせて満足だった。

for the most part 大部分は, 大体は

For the most part, it was wonderful entertainment.
大部分は、すばらしいエンターテインメントだった。

on the part of …としては, …の側では

take part in …に参加する, (conference, competition) …に出る

Did you take part in the celebrations?
祝賀会に出ましたか？

till death do us part 死が二人を分かつまで

partial *adj.* (not all) 部分的な; (biased) 不公平な, えこひいきする

be partial toward えこひいきする

partially *adv.* 一部, (somewhat) 多少, ある程度 [→ PARTLY]

be partially responsible
一部 [多少] 責任がある

participant *n.* 参加者

participate *v.* 参加する, 加わる

I'm afraid I was unable to participate in this year's opening ceremony.
残念ながら、今年の開会式には参加できませんでした。

participation *n.* 参加

participation in politics 政治参加

participle *n.* 分詞

a past participle 過去分詞

a present participle 現在分詞

particle *n.* (minute piece) 粒子, (tiny grain) 小さな粒, かけら; (Japanese function word) 助詞

radioactive particles 放射性粒子

not a particle of …のかけらもない, …は少しもない

particular

1 *adj.* SPECIAL OR WORTH MENTIONING: (special) 特別な, (specific) 特定の, (**no particular…**) 別に…ない, 特に…ない

2 *adj.* FUSSY: 気難しい, やかましい, (**be particular about…**) …にうるさい, …にこだわる

3 *n.* DETAILS: (**particulars**) 詳細, 細かいこ

と, 詳しいこと

1 In this particular case, we chose to make an exception.
この場合に限り、例外とすることに決めた。

Foie gras is not a particular favorite of mine.
フォアグラは、特に好物というわけではありません。

I don't have any particular plans for today.
今日は別にこれといった予定はありません。

He has no particular likes or dislikes.
あの人は、特に好き嫌いはないよ。

2 He's very particular about his coffee.
彼はコーヒーにはとてもうるさい。

I'm not particular about what I eat.
あまり食べ物にはこだわりません。

3 The particulars of this case are interesting.
この事件は詳細が興味深い。

The broad thrust of your essay is fine, but it is lacking in particulars.
君の論文は、全体の主眼はいいが細かい部分が足りない。

in particular 特に, とりわけ

particularly *adv.* 特に, とりわけ, (**not particularly**) 特に…(というわけ)ではない

She is particularly interested in Heian-period literature.
彼女は特に、平安時代の文学に興味があります。

The movie wasn't particularly interesting.
その映画は、特に面白くはなかった。

parting *n.* (of people) (お)別れ, 別離, (in road) 分かれ目, 分岐点

adj. (お)別れの

a parting bow 別れのお辞儀

partisan *adj.* 特定の党派に偏った

n. (supporter) 党派心の強い人, (fighter) パルチザン

A partisan civil service would create problems.
公務員が特定の党派に偏っていたら、何かと問題があるだろう。

partition *n.* (for room) 仕切り

v. (room) 仕切る, (country, area) 分割する

partly *adv.* 少しは, 部分的に, (to an extent) ある程度, 多少

The fence was partly damaged.
フェンスは部分的に壊れていた。

The accident was partly due to the weather.
その事故は天候にも原因があった。

I'm sorry. It was partly my fault.
すみません。私にも責任の一端があります。

partner *n.* パートナー, 相手, (spouse) 伴侶, (business partner) 共同経営者, (buddy) 仲間, 相棒 [→ LOVER]

partnership *n.* (cooperative relationship) 協力, (in business) 提携

part of speech *n.* 品詞

partridge *n.* ヤマウズラ

part time *n.* パート(タイム), 非常勤

part-time *adj.* パート(タイム)の, 非常勤の

adv. パート(タイム)で, 非常勤で

Most of the housewives work part-time in this apartment complex.
この団地では、ほとんどの主婦がパート

P

で働いています。

♦ **part-time job** ***n.*** パート(タイム), (side job) アルバイト

part-timer ***n.*** パート, アルバイト, (young job-hopper) フリーター

party ***n.*** (celebration) パーティー, (gathering) 集まり, (among university students in Japan) コンパ; (political party) 政党, 党派, (group of people) 一行, 団体

v. (goof off a lot) 遊びほうける

We're going to have a party.
パーティーをやるよ。

Is it OK if I bring a friend along to your party?
パーティーに友達を連れて行ってもいい？

a welcome party 歓迎会

a farewell party 送別会 [お別れ会]

the ruling party 与党

We came across a party of tourists.
旅行者の団体に出くわしたよ。

throw a party パーティーを開く

pass

1 ***v.*** **MOVE PAST:** 通る, 通り過ぎる, (**pass through**) 通る, 通り抜ける

2 ***v.*** **GO AWAY:** 去る, 過ぎ去る

3 ***v.*** **OVERTAKE:** 追い越す, 追い抜く

4 ***v.*** **GIVE:** 渡す, 回す, 取る, (in sport: pass ball to) (…にボールを) パスする

5 ***v.*** **BE BEQUEATHED:** (**pass on to**) …の手に渡る

6 ***v.*** **TIME:** (時を) 過ごす, (aimlessly) 暇つぶしをする; (of time: elapse) 過ぎる, たつ

7 ***v.*** **BE SUCCESSFUL:** (pass an exam) (…に) 合格する, 受かる, パスする, (allow to pass an exam/a course) 合格させる

8 ***v.*** **EXCEED:** 超える

9 ***v.*** **BILL/LAW:** (get passed, become official) 通過する, (allow to pass) 可決する

10 ***n.*** **MOUNTAIN PASS:** 山道

11 ***n.*** **PERMIT:** 通行許可証, (boarding pass) 搭乗券

12 ***n.*** **PASSING OF A BALL:** パス

1 I have to pass this way to get to work.
仕事場に行くには、この道を通らないといけない。

I think we've passed the hotel.
ホテルを通り過ぎたみたいだ。

They wouldn't let us pass.
彼らは、私たちを通してくれなかった。

The water passes through these pipes.
水は、これらのパイプを通っています。

Do we pass through Osaka on the way to Kobe?
神戸へ行く途中、大阪を通りますか？

We passed through the temple grounds.
お寺の境内を通り抜けました。

2 The crisis passed and normality returned.
危機は去り、正常に戻った。

Fortunately, the storm passed.
幸い、嵐は過ぎ去った。

3 Can you pass the car in front?
前の車を追い越せますか？

He's going too fast for me to pass.
彼は速すぎて、追い抜けないよ。

4 Would you pass me that tray, please?
そのトレイを取っていただけますか？

The player passed the ball back to the goalkeeper.
選手はボールをゴールキーパーにパスした。

5 Most of his estate was passed on to his children.
彼の土地の大部分は、子供たちの手に渡った [に相続された]。

The country passed into the hands of the military.
その国は軍の手に渡った。

6 How did you pass the time while you were in the hospital?
入院中は、どうやって時間を過ごしていたんですか？

I passed the time reading and playing chess.
読書やチェスをして暇をつぶしました。

The first couple of months passed so quickly.
最初の2ヵ月は、あっという間に過ぎた。

7 I didn't pass the exam.
試験に合格できなかった。

He didn't pass his driving test.
彼は、運転免許の実地試験に受からなかった。

You need to pass with an A grade.
Aを取ってパスしなければなりませんよ。

8 Donations have already passed our target figure.
寄付金は、すでに目標額を超えている。

9 Congress passed the bill.
議会は、その法案を可決した。

10 They crossed into Tibet by a little-known mountain pass.
一行は、あまり知られていない山道を通ってチベット入りした。

11 Do you have your security pass?
通行(許可)証を持っていますか？

12 Nice pass! ナイスパス！

He missed the pass completely.
彼はパスを完全に取りそこなった。

make a pass at …に言い寄る

pass away/on *v.* (die) 亡くなる

He passed away last Sunday.
彼は先週の日曜日に亡くなりました。

pass by *v.* 通りかかる, 通り過ぎる; (of time) 過ぎる, たつ

Time passes by so quickly.
時がたつのは早い。

pass off as *v.* (pass A off as B) (AをBと) 偽る, (**pass oneself off as**) …のふりをする, …になりすます

He passed the painting off as an antique.
彼はその絵を骨董品だと偽った。

He tried to pass himself off as a doctor.
その男は、医者になりすまそうとした。

pass on *v.* (hand over) 渡す, 次に回す, (virus, infection) 移す, (tradition) 伝える [→ PASS AWAY]

Could you pass this letter on to Mr. Uno?
この手紙を宇野さんに渡してもらえませんか？

Take one and pass the rest on.
1部取って、残りを回していってください。

He's passed his cold on to me.
彼が私にかぜを移したんです。

pass out *v.* (lose consciousness) 気を失う, 気絶する

I thought I was going to pass out.
気を失うかと思ったよ。

pass up *v.* (not take advantage of) 逃す, 逃がす

He passed up a golden opportunity.
彼は、またとないチャンスを逃した。

passage ***n.***

1 PASSAGEWAY: (corridor) 廊下, (passageway, aisle) 通路

2 IN BOOK: 一節

3 JOURNEY: 旅, 旅行

4 OF TIME: 流れ, 経過

5 OF BILL / LAW: 通過, 可決

1 Paintings lined the walls of the passage.
廊下の壁に、絵が並んで掛けられていた。

Go down this passage and turn left at the end.
この廊下を進んで、突き当たりを左に曲がってください。

There was a narrow passage between the two buildings.
ビルとビルの間に、細い通路があった。

2 He quoted a passage from Shakespeare in his book.
彼は自分の本の中で、シェイクスピアからの一節を引用した。

3 The passage to India took weeks.
インドまでの旅は数週間もかかった。

4 Inside the cave, they had no sense of the passage of time.
洞窟の中では、彼らは時間の感覚がなくなっていた。

5 No one expected the passage of the bill to take so long.
法案が通過するのにそんなに時間がかかるとは、誰も予測していなかった。

passbook ***n.*** (bank book) 通帳

passenger ***n.*** 乗客

♦ **passenger seat** ***n.*** 助手席 [→ picture of CAR]

passerby ***n.*** 通行人

passing ***adj.*** (brief) 一時的な, つかのまの; (moving) 通り過ぎる, 通りがかりの
n. (of time) 経過, (of car) 通過

passing moments of joy つかのまの楽しみ

A passing bus blasted its horn.
通りがかりのバスが、クラクションを鳴らした。

in passing ついでに

He only mentioned it in passing.
彼はついでに言っただけです。

with each passing day 日がたつにつれて, 日を追うごとに

With each passing day, the police began to fear that the missing child had been abducted.
日を追うごとに、警察は行方不明の子供が誘拐されたのではないかと、懸念を強めた。

passion ***n.*** (strong emotion) 情熱, 激情, (anger) 激怒

a crime of passion 衝動的犯罪

have a passion for …に熱中している, …に夢中だ

Ms. Takeda has a passion for gardening.
武田さんはガーデニングに熱中している。

passionate ***adj.*** 熱烈な, 情熱的な

a passionate kiss 熱烈なキス

a passionate speech 情熱的な演説

passive ***adj.*** (unresponsive) 消極的な, 受け身の
n. (the passive voice) 受身, 受動態

That student is too passive. He needs to participate more in class.
あの生徒は消極的すぎる。もっと授業で活発に発言するべきだ。

♦ **passive form** ***n.*** (verb form) 受身形

Passover ***n.*** 過ぎ越しの祭

passport *n.* パスポート, ((*formal*)) 旅券〔りょけん〕

Your passport has expired and will have to be renewed.
あなたのパスポートは有効期限〔ゆうこうきげん〕が切〔き〕れていますので、更新〔こうしん〕する必要〔ひつよう〕があります。

◆ **passport control** *n.* 出入国〔しゅつにゅうこく〕管理〔かんり〕, (at airport) 出入国〔しゅつにゅうこく〕管理所〔かんりしょ〕

password *n.* 合い言葉〔あいことば〕, (for access to a computer) パスワード

past

1 *prep., adv.* **AFTER:** (…を) 過〔す〕ぎて, 越〔こ〕えて, (**half past**: hour) -半〔はん〕

2 *prep., adv.* **UP TO AND BEYOND:** (…を) 通〔とお〕り過〔す〕ぎて, 越〔こ〕えて

3 *n.* **EVENTS THAT HAVE HAPPENED:** 過去〔かこ〕, 昔〔むかし〕, 過去〔かこ〕のこと, (history) 歴史〔れきし〕, (career history) 経歴〔けいれき〕

4 *adj.* **BYGONE:** 過去〔かこ〕の, これまでの, (the past…) この前〔まえ〕の…, ここ…, 先〔せん〕-

5 *n.* **GRAMMATICAL:** (the past tense) 過去時制〔かこじせい〕, (verb form in the past tense) 過去形〔かこけい〕

1 As an athlete, he's past his prime.
スポーツ選手〔せんしゅ〕としては、彼〔かれ〕はもうピークを過〔す〕ぎた。

It's past the deadline.
締〔し〕め切〔き〕りを過〔す〕ぎています。

It's way past your bedtime.
寝〔ね〕る時間〔じかん〕をとっくに過〔す〕ぎている。

My alarm goes off at ten past six.
私〔わたし〕の目覚〔めざ〕まし時計〔とけい〕は、6時〔じ〕10分〔ろくじじゅっぷん〕に鳴〔な〕る。

Let's meet at half past seven.
7時半〔しちじはん〕に会〔あ〕いましょう。

2 I think we've just walked past the place.
そこは、たった今〔いま〕通〔とお〕り過〔す〕ぎたようだ。

Go past the river and you'll see the entrance to the farm.
川〔かわ〕を越〔こ〕えると農場〔のうじょう〕の入口〔いりぐち〕が見〔み〕えます。

Did you get past the first chapter?
1章〔いっしょう〕は終〔お〕わりましたか？

3 Have we learned the lessons of the past?
我々〔われわれ〕は過去〔かこ〕の教訓〔きょうくん〕を学〔まな〕んだのだろうか？

Her past has nothing to do with this.
彼女〔かのじょ〕の過去〔かこ〕は、この件〔けん〕とは関係〔かんけい〕がない。

Let's not dwell on the past.
過去〔かこ〕のことにこだわらないようにしよう。

We must look to the future and try to forget the past.
将来〔しょうらい〕に目〔め〕を向〔む〕けて、過去〔かこ〕のことは忘〔わす〕れるんだ。

4 Is this based on past experience?
これは過去〔かこ〕の経験〔けいけん〕に基〔もと〕づいているんですか？

Past events mustn't prevent future progress.
過去〔かこ〕の出来事〔できごと〕が、未来〔みらい〕の発展〔はってん〕を妨〔さまた〕げてはならない。

He's spent the past three years in Japan.
彼〔かれ〕は、この3年間〔さんねんかん〕を日本〔にほん〕で過〔す〕ごしている。

It happened this past weekend.
先週末〔せんしゅうまつ〕に起〔お〕こったんです。

in the past 過去〔かこ〕において, 以前〔いぜん〕は, (in the old days, in ancient times) 昔〔むかし〕は

not put it past sb (to do) …なら(…するくらいは)やりかねない

I wouldn't put it past him.
あの人〔ひと〕なら、やりかねない。

pasta *n.* パスタ

paste *n.* 練〔ね〕り粉〔こ〕, (glue) のり, (cooking ingredient) ペースト

v. (paste A on to B) (AをBに) 張〔は〕る, (paste A and B together) (AとBを) 張〔は〕

り合わせる

pastel *n.* パステル, (drawing) パステル画, (color) パステルカラー

pasteurize *v.* 低温殺菌する

pasteurized milk 低温殺菌牛乳

pastille *n.* トローチ

pastime *n.* 気晴らし, 趣味

Her favorite pastime is the piano.
彼女の趣味はピアノです。

pastoral *adj.* (of priest's work) 牧師の, (of scenery, life) 田園の

pastrami *n.* パストラミ

pastry *n.* ペーストリー, (on pie) パイ生地

pasture *n.* 牧草地, 放牧地, 牧場

pat *v.* 軽くたたく

pat someone on the back
(…の) 肩を軽くたたく

patch *n.* (of cloth) 継ぎ, 継ぎはぎ, (for eye) 眼帯, (badge) 記章; (of ground) 小さな畑, (on animal) まだら

v. (patch a hole in) (…に) 継ぎを当てる

He's got lots of patches on his jeans.
彼のジーンズは継ぎはぎだらけだ。

This is the patch I'll use for planting vegetables.
ここが野菜を植える畑です。

The dog's got a white patch on its tail.
その犬のしっぽには、白いまだらがある。

♦**patch up** *v.* (repair) 修理する, (injuries) (…の)手当てをする, (**patch things up**: make up) 仲直りする

patchwork *n.* (quilt-making) パッチワーク, (jumble) 寄せ集め

patchy *adj.* (of material) 継ぎはぎだらけの; (of work) むらのある

pâté *n.* パテ

pâté de foie gras フォアグラのパテ

patent *n.* (permission) 特許, (exclusive right) 特許権

get/take out a patent on …の特許を取る

♦**patented** *adj.* 専売特許の

paternal *adj.* 父の, (fatherly) 父親らしい, (on father's side) 父方の

path *n.* (walkway) 小道, 道, (pavement) 歩道, (line of movement) 通り道, (of typhoon) 進路, (flight path) 飛行経路, (orbit) 軌道

the path to the school 学校までの道

a path through the woods 森を抜ける道

the path to heaven 天国への道

The man deliberately stepped in front of me and blocked my path.
男はわざと私の前に歩み出て、通り道を阻んだ。

pathetic *adj.* (despicable) 情けない, ひどい, (pitiable) かわいそうな, 痛ましい

It was a pathetic attempt at a joke.
どうしようもない [ひどい] 冗談だった。

It was a pathetic sight that brought tears to my eyes.
涙が出るほど痛ましい光景だった。

pathological *adj.* (of pathology) 病理学の; (of behavior) 病的な

a pathological liar 病的なうそつき

pathology *n.* 病理学

pathos *n.* ペーソス, 悲哀

patience *n.* がまん, 辛抱, 忍耐, がまん強さ

lose one's patience with …にがまんで

きなくなる, …に辛抱できなくなる

run out of patience with …に愛想を尽かす

patient *adj.* (uncomplaining) がまん強い, 辛抱強い, 忍耐強い

n. (in hospital) 患者(さん)

She is very patient with her meddlesome mother-in-law.
彼女は、お節介なしゅうとめにも辛抱強く接している。

Please be patient while I find out the reason for the delay.
遅れの原因がわかるまでご辛抱ください。

The ward was full of patients.
病棟は患者であふれていた。

The patients were eagerly waiting their turn to see the doctor.
患者は今か今かと診察の順番を待っていた。

The nurses are looking after the patients.
看護師たちは、患者さんの世話をしています。

patiently *adv.* がまん強く, 辛抱強く

patiently await 辛抱強く待つ

patio *n.* テラス, パティオ

patriot *n.* 愛国者

patriotic *adj.* 愛国の, 愛国的な

a patriotic heart 愛国心

patriotism *n.* 愛国心

patrol *n., v.* 巡回(する), パトロール(する)

be on patrol パトロール中だ

♦**patrol car** *n.* パトカー

patrolman, -woman *n.* 巡査

patron *n.* (of arts) パトロン, 後援者; (regular customer) 常連, ひいき客

patronize *v.* (look down on) (…に) 偉そうにする, 恩着せがましい態度をとる; (support) 後援する

♦**patronizing** *adj.* (of attitude, remark) 偉そうな, 恩着せがましい

patter *v.* (of rain) パラパラと降る, (of feet) パタパタと音を立てる

The rain pattered on the window.
雨が窓にパラパラと降りかかっていた。

pattern

1 *n.* ORNAMENTAL DESIGN: 模様, 柄, 形

2 *n.* WAY OF BEHAVING / MOVING: 型, パターン, 様式, (tendency) 傾向

3 *n.* MODEL DRAWING: (for dress etc.) 型紙

4 *v.* MAKE SIMILAR TO: (pattern A after B) (Bにならって Aを) 作る, (**pattern oneself on/after**) (お)手本とする

1 draw a pattern 模様を描く

a crisscross pattern 十字模様

a pattern of dots and stars
水玉と星の模様

the pattern of the wallpaper 壁紙の柄

a busy pattern ごてごてした柄

2 Our work pattern will change starting next week.
仕事の形態が来週から変わる。

behavior patterns 行動様式 [パターン]

a consistent pattern 一貫した傾向

3 It was a difficult pattern to work from.
縫いにくい型紙だった。

sewing patterns 裁縫用の型紙

4 The program was patterned on similar successful programs in the United States.
それは、アメリカで成功した同種のプログラムにならって制作された。

He patterned himself after the teacher

P

he most admired.
彼は最も尊敬する先生をお手本としていた。

paulownia *n.* キリ, 桐

pause *v.* ちょっと止まる, 間を置く, (take a break) 休憩する, 一息つく

n. (break in conversation) 中断, 途切れ, 間, (silence) 沈黙; (break) 休憩

He paused to fill his glass with water.
彼はちょっと間を置いてから、自分のグラスに水をついだ。

We paused for a break.
みんなで一休みした。

He carried on working without pausing.
彼は休憩せずに働き続けた。

There was a long pause before she continued to speak.
彼女が再び話し始めるまでには長い沈黙があった。

without pause 休みなく, 一息つく間もなく, 途切れることなく

The Opposition candidate spoke for about half an hour without pause.
反対陣営の候補者は、途切れることなく３０分間話し続けた。

pave *v.* 舗装する

pave the way for …への道を開く, 可能にする

pavement *n.* (paved road) 舗道, (sidewalk) 歩道

pavilion *n.* (for exhibition) 展示館, パビリオン

paw *n.* 足

There was a splinter in the dog's paw.
犬の足にとげが刺さっていた。

pawn *n.* (pawned article) 質, 質草; (person being manipulated by another) 手先

v. 質に入れる

pawnshop *n.* 質屋

pay *v.* (…にお金を) 払う, 支払う

n. (salary) 給料

We paid someone to repair the roof.
お金を払って屋根を修理してもらいました。

I haven't paid for it yet.
まだお金を払っていません。

Is it all right if I pay by credit card?
クレジットカードで支払ってもいいですか？

Have you been paid for your work?
仕事の報酬はもらった？

You'll receive your pay on the twenty-fifth of each month.
給料は毎月２５日に支払われます。

pay attention to → ATTENTION

pay back *v.* (return money to) …にお金を返す, …に返済する, (punish in retribution) …に仕返しをする

pay for *v.* …の代金を払う

pay off *v.* (debt) 借金をすべて返す, (person: bribe) …にわいろを贈る; (be profitable) うまくいく, 利益をもたらす

Did your business plan pay off?
事業計画は、うまくいきましたか？

payable *adj.* (payable to…) (…に) 支払う

payday *n.* 給料日

payload *n.* 有料荷重

payment *n.* (act of paying) 支払い, (amount paid) 支払い金額, 支払額, (monthly payment) 月賦

(*customer service speaking*) When do you expect to make the payment?
お支払いは、いつがよろしいですか？

a tax payment 納税

installment plan payments 分割払い

The payment is overdue.
支払いが遅れている。

Payments are debited from my account each month.
支払額は、毎月私の口座から引き落とされています。

payroll ***n.*** 従業員名簿

be on the payroll 雇われている

PC ***abbr.*** (personal computer) パソコン; (politically correct) 差別的ではない

pea ***n.*** エンドウ, エンドウ豆

peace ***n.*** 平和, (peace and quiet) 静けさ, (peace of mind) 心の平和, 安らぎ, 安心, (law and order) 治安

Japan has been at peace since the end of World War II.
日本は第二次大戦の終結以降、平和が続いている。

If you don't mind, we'd like to be left in peace.
できれば、そっとしておいていただきたいのです。

I love the peace of the countryside.
田舎の静けさが、とても好きなんです。

She seemed totally at peace with her surroundings.
周りの環境に、彼女は心がすっかり安らいだようだった。

Peace of mind—you can't buy that.
心の安らぎ——これぱかりは、お金では買えない。

These hoodlums disturb the peace of the neighborhood.
あの不良たちが、この近辺の治安を乱している。

peaceful ***adj.*** 平和な, (of place) 穏やかな, のどかな, (calm and quiet) 静かな

a peaceful country 平和な国

a peaceful demonstration 静かなデモ

peach ***n.*** (fruit) モモ, 桃, (tree) 桃の木

peacock ***n.*** クジャク, (male peafowl) 雄クジャク

peak ***n.*** (of mountain) 山頂, 峰, (of career, success) 頂点, ピーク, 絶頂, (rush-hour peak) 真っ最中, ピーク; (of hat) つば, ひさし

v. ピークに達する, 頂点に達する

Will the climbers reach the peak before the weather worsens?
天気が悪くなる前に、登山者たちは山頂にたどり着くだろうか？

Mr. Tamiya had reached the peak of his career.
田宮さんは仕事の絶頂期にあった。

I left the office at the peak of rush hour.
ラッシュのピーク時に会社を出ました。

Consumer buying had peaked.
消費者の購買力はピークに達していた。

peanut ***n.*** ピーナッツ, 落花生

peanut butter ***n.*** ピーナッツバター

pear ***n.*** 洋梨, (Japanese pear) ナシ, 梨

pearl ***n.*** 真珠, パール

peasant ***n.*** (farmer) 農夫, (farmer who rents land) 小作農, (bumpkin) 田舎者

peasantry ***n.*** 農民, 小作農

pebble ***n.*** 小石

peck ***v.*** つつく, (kiss on the cheek) (…の)ほおに軽くキスをする

peculiar *adj.* (odd) 変な, おかしな, 変わった; (**peculiar to**: unique to) …独特の, (special) 特別の

He's a peculiar fellow.
あの人はおかしな人だ。

This way of thinking seems to be peculiar to Asian countries.
こうした考え方は、アジアの国々独特のものだろう。

He managed to do it in his own peculiar way.
彼は独自のやり方でなんとか処理した。

peculiarity *n.* (habit) 癖, (bad habit) 奇癖, (characteristic) 特徴, 特色

pedal *n.* ペダル
v. (on bike) ペダルをこぐ

peddle *v.* (goods) 売り歩く, 行商する, (drugs) 密売する

peddler *n.* (itinerant seller) 行商人, (of sth bad) 売人

pedestal *n.* 台, 台座
put sb on a pedestal 尊敬する, 奉る

pedestrian *n.* 歩行者
adj. (for walkers) 歩行者の

♦**pedestrian crossing/crosswalk** *n.* 横断歩道

pediatrician *n.* 小児科医

pediatrics *n.* 小児科, 小児科医学

pedigree *n.* (person's) 家系, (animal's, person's) 血統, (list of animal's ancestors) 血統書

The dog has a long pedigree.
その犬は長く続いた血統です。

pee *n., v.* おしっこ(する)

peek *v.* のぞく, のぞき見する
n. のぞき見
take a peek at のぞき見する

peel *n.* (of fruit, vegetable) 皮
v. (fruit) (…の) 皮をむく, (label) はがす; (of skin) むける, (of wallpaper) はがれる, (of paint) はげる, はげ落ちる

an orange peel オレンジの皮

Could you help me to peel the apples?
リンゴの皮をむくのを手伝ってくれませんか?

My suntan's peeling.
日焼けで皮がむけてきた。

The paint is peeling off.
塗料がはげ落ちてきています。

peep[1] *v.* のぞく, (steal a glance) 盗み見する
n. のぞき見

peep[2] *n.* (sound) ピーピー(いう音), (utterance) 一言

peer[1] *n.* (person of the same age) 同輩, (classmate) 同級生, (fellow) 仲間; (member of the nobility) 貴族, (member of the House of Lords) 上院議員

peer pressure 仲間の圧力

♦**peerage** *n.* (the Lords) 貴族階級

peer[2] *v.* (gaze) じっと見る

peerless *adj.* 無類の, 無比の

peg *n.* (hook for clothes) 掛け釘, (spike for tent) くい, (small wooden pin) 木釘, (clothespin) 洗濯挟み
v. (**peg down**) くいで留める

pejorative *adj.* 軽蔑的な

pelican *n.* ペリカン

pellet *n.* (bullet) 小弾丸

pelt[1] *v.* (pelt A with B) (AにBを) 投げ

つける

♦**pelt down** *v.* (of rain) 激しく降る

pelt[2] *n.* (animal skin) 生皮, (untanned animal skin) なめしていない毛皮

pelvis *n.* 骨盤

pen *n.* ペン, (ballpoint pen) ボールペン, (fountain pen) 万年筆 [→ picture of STATIONERY]

♦**pen name** *n.* ペンネーム, 筆名

penalize *v.* 罰する, (**be penalized**) 罰せられる

penalty *n.* 罰, (fine) 罰金, (in sport) ペナルティー

a stiff penalty 厳しい罰 [厳罰]

the death penalty 死刑

He paid the penalty for his dishonesty. 彼は不正行為をして報いを受けた。

The referee gave a penalty. 審判はペナルティーを課した。

♦**penalty kick** *n.* ペナルティーキック

pencil *n.* 鉛筆, (mechanical pencil) シャー(プ)ペン [→ picture of STATIONERY]

♦**pencil sharpener** *n.* 鉛筆削り

pendant *n.* (piece of jewelry) ペンダント

pending *adj.* (undecided) 未決定の, ペンディングの, 保留中の, (of lawsuit) 係争中の

prep. (awaiting) …まで

A lawsuit is pending. 訴訟は係争中です。

They said they'd still consider me for the job, pending the results of my exam. 試験の結果が出るまで、私の採用を考えてくれると言っていました。

pendulum *n.* 振り子

penetrate *n.* (pierce) 貫通する, (permeate) 浸透する, (infiltrate) 潜入する, (see through) 見抜く

penetration *n.* 貫通, (of enemy lines) 突破, (of liquid) 浸透, (sexual) 挿入

penguin *n.* ペンギン

penicillin *n.* ペニシリン

peninsula *n.* 半島

penis *n.* ペニス, 陰茎, 男根, (as spoken by child) おちんちん, チンポ

penitent *adj.* 後悔している, 悔い改めている

penitentiary *n.* (prison) 刑務所

penniless *adj.* (very poor) すごく貧しい, (totally broke) 一銭もない, 無一文の

penny *n.* (coin) ペニー, 1セント硬貨

pen pal *n.* ペンパル, ペンフレンド

pension[1] *n.* (retirement allowance) 年金

♦**pensioner** *n.* 年金受給者

pension[2] *n.* (resort lodge) ペンション

pentagon *n.* (five-sided figure) 五角形; (**the Pentagon**) アメリカ国防総省

penthouse *n.* 屋上住宅, マンションの最上階

pent-up *adj.* (of emotion) うっ積した

penultimate *adj.* 最後から2番目の

peony *n.* シャクヤク

people *n.* 人, 人々, 人たち, (inhabitants) 住民, (citizens) 市民, (all persons of a nation) 国民, (all persons of a race) 民族, (**the people**: the masses) 庶民

How many people came? 何人来ました / ((*polite*)) 何人お見えになりました?

There were too many people trying

to get in.
入場しようとする人が多すぎました。

This bus can carry forty-eight people.
このバスの定員は　48　人です。

It's no good putting up your stall where there are no people.
人けのない場所に屋台を出してもむだだよ。

The people who live here do not want to move.
ここの住民は、引っ越したくないんです。

the people of Timor チモールの島民

The government needs to listen to the people.
政府は国民の声に耳を傾けるべきだ。

pepper *n.* (peppercorn) コショウ, 胡椒 [NOTE: red-pepper powder 唐辛子, red pepper with six other spices 七味唐辛子, Japanese hot pepper 山椒]

Do you mind if I sprinkle some pepper on the salad?
サラダにコショウを振ってもいいですか？

Excuse me, could we have some pepper, please?
すみません、コショウをいただけますか？

peppermint *n.* ペパーミント, ハッカ, (candy) ペパーミントキャンディー

per *prep.* (for each) …につき, …当たり, …ごとに

two people per room 1室につき2人

fifty kilometers per hour 時速 50キロ

income per person 1人当たりの収入

♦ **per annum** *adv.* 1年につき

per capita *adj.* 1人当たりの

perceive *v.* (notice) (…に) 気がつく, (understand, recognize) (…と) わかる

percent *n.* パーセント [NOTE: 10% =1 割, 20%=2 割, 30%=3 割 etc.]

a 25% increase 25　%　増

a 10% mark up
10　%　[1 割] の値上げ

Only 55% of the population bothered to vote.
人口の55　%　しか投票しなかった。

Gross profits surged 32%.
総利益が　32　%　に上昇した。

percentage *n.* パーセント, 割合, 比率

What percentage of the students are foreign?
生徒の何　%　が外国人ですか？

A high percentage of car accidents is attributable to drunk driving.
交通事故の原因のうち、高い割合を占めるのは飲酒運転です。

perception *n.* (seeing, perceiving) 知覚, (recognizing, discerning) 認識, (understanding) 理解; (belief, idea) 概念

Einstein changed the world's perception of time.
アインシュタインは人類の時間の概念を変えた。

perceptive *adj.* (observant) 直観力が鋭い, 敏感な

Women are often more perceptive than men.
女性は概して男性より直観が鋭い。

perch *n.* (for bird) 止まり木, (elevated place in general) 高い所
v. 止まる

percussion *n.* (instrument) 打楽器, (**the percussion**: drum players) 打楽器部

percussionist *n.* 打楽器奏者

perennial *adj.* (of problems) 絶えることのない, 絶えず起こる; (of plant) 多年生の
n. (plant) 多年生植物

perfect *adj.* (flawless) 完璧な, 申し分のない, (complete) 完全な, (of couple, pair) ぴったりの, (お)似合いの
v. (master) マスターする, (refine, polish) (…に) 磨きをかける
n. (grammatical tense) 完了時制

Nobody's perfect.
完璧 [完全無欠] な人などいない。

He speaks perfect French.
彼は完璧なフランス語を話します。

The room looked just perfect.
部屋は申し分なかった。

a perfect gentleman 申し分のない紳士

a perfect match (=person)
お似合いの相手

They say English is easy to learn but difficult to perfect.
英語を学ぶのは簡単だがマスターするのは難しい、と言われている。

He's trying to perfect his technique.
彼は自分の技術に磨きをかけようとしている。

perfection *n.* (state of perfection) 完璧, 完全, (act of perfecting) 完成

perfectionist *n.* 完全主義者

perfectly *adv.* (used emphatically: quite) 全く, 十分; (faultlessly) 完璧に

You know perfectly well what I mean.
私の言っていることは、十分おわかりですね。

The new computer runs perfectly.
新しいコンピューターは完璧に動いている。

perform *v.*

1 CARRY OUT: 行う, ((*informal*)) する, やる, (duty) 果たす

2 ACT ON STAGE: (perform a role) (役を) 演じる, (do a stage performance) 上演する, 公演する, (do a musical performance) 演奏する

3 OF MACHINE: (function) 機能する, (of car: run) 走る

1 The ceremony is performed every year.
式は毎年行われます。

These charity organizations perform an important service.
これらの慈善団体は重要な活動を行っています。

He has performed more operations than any other doctor in this hospital.
あの先生は、この病院で他のどの医師よりも多くの手術をやってきました。

2 He performed the role of Hamlet.
彼はハムレットを演じた。

They're performing at The National Theater of Japan.
彼らは国立劇場で公演しています。

3 This car performs well on the track.
この車は、わだちの上をよく走る。

performance *n.* (on stage) 公演, 上演, (of music) 演奏; (carrying out) 実行, 遂行; (of machine) 性能

It was a fantastic performance.
すばらしい公演だった。

work performance 職務の遂行

a high-performance car 高性能の車

performer *n.* (entertainer) 芸能人, (ac-

P

tor/actress) 役者

perfume *n.* (liquid) 香水, (smell) 香り

perhaps *adv.* もしかしたら…かもしれない, もしかして, たぶん

Perhaps she'll change her mind.
もしかしたら、彼女は気が変わるかもしれないよ。

"Are you going?" "Perhaps."
「あなたは行くの？」「もしかしたらね」

Has the venue been changed, perhaps?
もしかして会場が変わりましたか？

Nobody will be there, except, perhaps, Keiko.
誰もそこにいないよ、たぶん恵子以外はね。

I waited for perhaps twenty minutes.
たぶん２０分くらい待ちました。

peril *n.* 危険 [→ DANGER]

be in peril 危険にさらされている

perimeter *n.* 周囲, 周り

period *n.*

1 STRETCH OF TIME: (short period) 間, 時間, (long period) 期間, 時期, (historical period) 時代 [→ p. 1176], (geologic period) -紀

2 LESSON: 授業, -時限, -時間, (in university) -コマ

3 FULL STOP: ピリオド, 終止符

4 MENSTRUATION: 生理, 月経

1 a twenty-four-hour period ２４時間

He was away for a period of months.
彼は数ヵ月間、離れていました。

The work was done over a period of several years.
その仕事は数年かけて行われた。

It was an important period for the company.
それは会社にとって重要な時期だった。

The art of that period is very religious.
その時代の芸術は宗教色がとても強い。

the Edo period 江戸時代

2 What's the first period? History?
１時限目は何？ 歴史？

I've got two periods in the morning and one in the evening.
午前中に２時間、午後に１時間授業がある。

She teaches four periods a week at the university.
その先生は大学で週４コマ教えています。

3 This sentence is missing a period.
この文はピリオドが抜けている。

4 She has heavy periods.
彼女は生理が重いんです。

periodic *adj.* (happening regularly) 定期的な

It's best to have periodic health checks.
定期的に健康診断を受けることが大切です。

♦ **periodically** *adv.* 定期的に

periodical *n.* 定期刊行物, (monthly) 月刊誌, (weekly) 週刊誌

periodic table *n.* (of elements) 周期表

peripheral *adj.* 周辺の

n. (peripheral equipment) 周辺機器

peripheral vision 周辺視野

periphery *n.* 周囲, 周辺

periscope *n.* 潜望鏡

perish *v.* 死ぬ [→ DIE]

perjury *n.* 偽証, (crime) 偽証罪

perk[1] *v.* (ears) ぴんと上げる

perk[2] *n.* (perquisite) 役得, 特典

Unlimited use of the company car is one of the perks.
会社の車を無制限に利用できるのは、役得の一つです。

perm ***n.*** パーマ

get/have a perm パーマをかける

permafrost ***n.*** 永久凍土層

permanent ***adj.*** (lasting forever) 永久の, (of conditions: unchanging) 変わらない, いつも…, (will not heal) 治らない, (will not go away) 消えない, (of stain) 取れない

n. (hair style) パーマ

a permanent peace 永久平和

a permanent job 定職

He's in a permanent state of drunkenness.
あの人はいつも酔っ払っている。

The stain is permanent.
このしみは取れない。

♦**permanent employment** ***n.*** 終身雇用

permanent resident ***n.*** 永住者

permanent tooth ***n.*** 永久歯

permanently ***adv.*** 永久に, いつまでも

permeate ***v.*** 行き渡る, 浸透する

permissible ***adj.*** 許される, 差し支えない

permission ***n.*** 許可, 許し, 承認

Did you get permission?
許可を取り [許しを得] ましたか？

Permission was not given.
許可はおりなかった。

You need his permission to do that.
それをするには、彼の承認が必要です。

permissive ***adj.*** (lenient) 寛容な, 甘い

permit ***v.*** (allow) 許す, (**permit to do**) (…に) <causative form of verb>, (**if … permits**/used in the subjunctive mood) (… が) よければ, 許せば

n. (document) 許可証

Her father would not permit her to stay out later than 10 o'clock.
彼女のお父さんは彼女が10時以降、外出しているのを絶対許さない。

Had time permitted, I would have explained everything in more detail.
時間が許せば、もっと詳しく説明したのですが。

If the weather permits, we'll go to the beach.
天気がよければ、海に行きます。

You can't get in without a permit.
許可証なしに中には入れません。

perpendicular ***adj.*** 垂直の

a perpendicular line 垂線

perpetrate ***v.*** (crime) 犯す

perpetrator ***n.*** 犯人

perpetual ***adj.*** (continual) 永久の, 永遠に続く, (constant) ひっきりなしの, 絶え間のない

perpetual motion 永久運動

These creatures live in perpetual darkness.
これらの生物は常にやみの中で生息している。

perpetuate ***v.*** (cause to continue) 永続させる

perplexed ***adj.*** 途方に暮れた, 当惑した

persecute ***v.*** 迫害する, 虐げる

They were persecuted for their beliefs.
彼らは、その信念のために迫害された。

persecution ***n.*** 迫害

persevere *v.* (persist) がんばり通す, やり抜く, (work hard) 一生懸命やる

Sachiko didn't give up. She continued to persevere.
佐知子さんはあきらめなかった。最後までがんばり通した。

persimmon *n.* (fruit) カキ, 柿, (tree) 柿の木

persist *v.* (continue to exist) 続く, (continue doing in spite of opposition) やり抜く [→ CONTINUE]

persistence *n.* (of person) 粘り強さ

persistent *adj.* (pushy) しつこい, (dogged) 粘り強い; (continuous) 永続的な

person *n.* 人, 者, ((*honorific*)) 方; (type of pronoun) 人称

He's a popular person.
彼は人気者です。

Do you know that person?
あの人を知ってますか/((*polite*)) あの方をご存じですか?

He's the type of person who can't say no.
彼はノーとは言えない人です。

She's a charming person.
あの人はすてきな人です。

She's quite a famous person in literary circles.
文学(の世)界では、彼女はとても有名な人です。

Only five persons are allowed in this elevator.
このエレベーターの定員は、わずか5人です。

first [second, third] person
一人称 [二人称, 三人称]

in person 本人が, 自分で, じかに

You must register in person.
本人が登録しなければなりません。

Did you meet him in person?
あの人に、じかに会ったんですか?

KANJI BRIDGE

家 ON: か, け KUN: いえ, や | PERSON, EXPERT, -ER, -IST

activist	活動家
cartoonist	漫画家
composer	作曲家
devotee	愛好家
novelist	小説家
potter	陶芸家
specialist	専門家
translator	翻訳家

personal *adj.* (private) 個人的な, 私的な, 個人の, (of belongings) 自分の, 自分自身の, (of the body) 体の, 身なりの
***n.* (personals)** 恋人募集コーナー, パーソナルズ

a personal letter 個人的な手紙

As this is a personal matter, I'd prefer it if you told no one.
これは個人的なこと [私事] なので、誰にも話さないでほしい。

Is that your personal opinion?
それは、あなた個人の意見ですか?

It's only a matter of personal preference.
単に個人の好みの問題です。

She's his personal secretary.
あの女性は彼の個人秘書です。

Keep your personal belongings with you at all times.
自分の持ち物は、常に肌身離さず持っていてください。

P

personal hygiene 身だしなみ

personality *n.* 性格, 人格, パーソナリティー; (TV personality) タレント

personalize *v.* (design to meet an individual's needs) 個人の需要に合わせる, 個別対応する

personally *adv.* (in person, on a personal level) 個人的に, ("as far as I'm concerned") 私としては; (directly, not through an intermediary) じきじきに, 直接に

I'll see to the matter personally.
その件は個人的に引き受けましょう。

Personally, I thought the film was boring.
私としては、あの映画は退屈だと思った。

She said she wanted to speak to you personally.
彼女はあなたに直接話したいと言った。

take it personally 当て付けと取る

I wouldn't take it personally if I were you.
私があなたなら、当て付けとは取らない。

personification *n.* 象徴, 典型, ((*used negatively*)) 権化

personify *v.* 象徴する, (...の) 典型だ

personnel *n.* (employees) 職員, (personnel division) 人事課

perspective *n.* (viewpoint) 見方, (standpoint) 立場; (drawing technique) 遠近(画)法

Let's try and look at this problem from their perspective.
彼らの立場に立って、この問題を見てみよう。

This evening we were taught about perspective in painting.
今晩は、絵画における遠近法について習った。

put in/into perspective 公平な目で見る, 客観的に見る

To put things in perspective…
客観的に見ると…

perspiration *n.* (sweat) 汗, (act of perspiring) 発汗作用

perspire *v.* 汗をかく

persuade *v.* (convince) 説得する, 納得させる, (**persuade to do**) (...に) ...するよう説得する, ...するよう説き伏せる

Don't try to persuade me. I've already made up my mind.
説得しようとしてもむだだよ。もう決めたんだから。

Did you manage to persuade her to come?
彼女に来るように説得できた？

I had no difficulty in persuading them to agree.
同意するよう説き伏せるのは難しくなかった。

Somewhat against my better judgment, I was persuaded to join the club.
あまり気は進まなかったのに、勧められてそのクラブに入ってしまった。

persuasion *n.* 説得

have powers of persuasion
説得力がある

persuasive *adj.* 説得力のある

pertinent *adj.* 関係のある

pervade *v.* (...に) 広がる, 行き渡る, (of smell) (...に) 充満する

pervasive *adj.* 広がる, 浸透する

perverse *adj.* ひねくれた, 片意地な, (spiteful) 意地が悪い

perversion *n.* (sexual) (性的)倒錯; (of

the truth etc.) 曲解

pervert *n.* (sexually deviant person) 変質者, 変態, (on train: one who sexually molests women) 痴漢, (sexually playful person) すけべえ, エッチ

v. (distort: the truth etc.) ゆがめる

perverted *adj.* (sexually) 倒錯した

pessimism *n.* 悲観, (doctrine) 悲観主義, 悲観論

Enough of your pessimism!
そういう悲観論は、うんざりだ！

pessimist *n.* 悲観主義者, ((*informal*)) 悲観的な人

pessimistic *adj.* 悲観的な

pest *n.* (person) いやな人, うるさい人, 厄介な人; (insect) 害虫

pester *v.* しつこく頼む, (of child) せがむ

pester someone for money
(…に)お金をせびる

Stop pestering me to buy you ice cream.
アイスクリームを(買ってと)せがむのはやめなさい。

pesticide *n.* 殺虫剤

pestle *n.* すりこぎ

v. すりつぶす

pet *n.* (animal) ペット, 愛玩動物

v. (pet an animal) かわいがる, なでる

Do you have any pets?
何かペットを飼っていますか？

♦**pet project** *n.* 長年あたためている企画

petal *n.* 花びら

a single [double] petal 一重 [八重]

peter *v.* (**peter out**) (=come to an end) なくなる, 尽きる, (=become weaker and disappear) 弱くなってなくなる

petite *adj.* (of woman) 小柄な, (of clothing size) 小さい

petition *n.* 請願書, 陳情書

v. (…に) 請願する, 陳情する

petrol *n.* (gasoline) ガソリン

a petrol station ガソリンスタンド

petroleum *n.* 石油

petticoat *n.* ペチコート

petty *adj.* つまらない, ささいな

Don't bother me with petty details.
((*masculine*)) つまらないことで、煩わせないでくれ。

♦**petty cash** *n.* 小口現金

petulant *adj.* 怒りっぽい

petunia *n.* ペチュニア

pew *n.* 教会の座席

pewter *n.* スズ合金, しろめ

phallic *adj.* 男根の, ペニスの

phallus *n.* (penis) ペニス, (image of a penis) 男根像

phantom *n.* お化け, (illusion) 幻影, 幻想

adj. 幻の, (fake) 見せかけの

pharmaceutical *adj.* 薬学の, 薬剤の

pharmacist *n.* 薬剤師

pharmacology *n.* 薬学, 薬理学

pharmacy *n.* (drugstore) 薬局, 薬屋, (study) 薬学

---

phase *n.* (stage of development) 段階, 時期

the final phase 最終段階
a dangerous phase 危険な時期
It's just a phase. He'll grow out of it.
今の状態は一時的なものにすぎない。
彼はいずれそこから抜け出るよ。

in phase 一致して, 同調して

out of phase 一致しないで, 同調しないで

phase in *v.* (bring in gradually) 徐々に導入する, 段階的に採用する

The new curriculum will be phased in over the next two years.
新しいカリキュラムは、今後2年間で段階的に導入される。

phase out *v.* (remove gradually) 徐々に廃止する, 段階的にやめる

The old analog systems will be phased out.
昔ながらのアナログ式は、徐々に廃止されていくだろう。

PhD *n.* (qualification) 博士号

She's got a PhD in engineering.
彼女は工学の博士号をもっている。

pheasant *n.* キジ

phenomenal *adj.* (incredible) ものすごい

phenomenon *n.* 現象

Philippines *n.* フィリピン, ((*in abbr.*)) 比

philosopher *n.* 哲学者

philosophical *adj.* 哲学の, 哲学的な

a philosophical question 哲学的な問い

philosophy *n.* (subject of study) 哲学, (way of thinking) 思想, 考え方, (view of life) 人生観

phlegm *n.* たん

phobia *n.* 病的恐怖, 恐怖症

phoenix *n.* フェニックス, 不死鳥

phone *n.* 電話 [→ TELEPHONE]

v. (…に) 電話する

phone book *n.* 電話帳

phonetics *n.* 音声学

phony *adj.* (false, fake) 偽の

a phony ID card 偽の身分証明書

phosphate *n.* リン酸塩

phosphor *n.* リン光体, 蛍光体

phosphorescence *n.* (glow) リン光

phosphorus *n.* リン

photo → PHOTOGRAPH

photocopier *n.* コピー機, 複写機

photocopy *n., v.* コピー(する), 複写(する)

photogenic *adj.* 写真写りがいい

photograph *n.* 写真

v. (…の) 写真を撮る

It's a good photograph.
いい写真ですね。

Why not take several photographs of the view?
この景色の写真を何枚か撮ったらどうですか？

Excuse me, would you mind taking a photograph of us?
すみませんが、写真を撮っていただけませんか？

How long will it take to have the photographs developed?
現像にどのくらい時間がかかりますか？

(*sign*) No Photographs 撮影禁止

I don't like being photographed.
写真を撮られるのは好きじゃない。

photographer *n.* カメラマン, 写真家

photographic *adj.* 写真の, (for photo) 写真用の; (of memory) 鮮明な

a photographic lens 写真用レンズ

He has a photographic memory.
彼には鮮明な記憶がある。

photography *n.* 写真撮影

photosynthesis *n.* 光合成

phrase *n.* (expression) 表現, 言い方, 言い回し, (fixed expression) 慣用句, 成句 [NOTE: a 4-kanji character idiomatic expression 四字熟語], (sequence of words in a sentence) 句

v. (express) 言い表す, 表現する

It's a phrase I came across in a book on medicine.
医学書で見つけた表現です。

I think you should phrase your argument in a different way.
君の主張は、別の言い方で表現するほうがいいと思う。

♦**phrase book** *n.* (for travelers) 会話表現集

phylum *n.* (taxonomic category) 門

physical *adj.* (material) 物質的な, 物質の, (scientific) 自然科学の, 物理的な, (of the body) 身体的な, 身体の, 肉体的な

the physical world around us
我々を取り巻く物質界

the physical properties of the substance
物質の物理的性質

physical and emotional
肉体的・精神的な

get physical (=violent) 手荒なことをする

♦**physical education** *n.* 体育

physical examination *n.* 身体検査

physically *adv.* 肉体的に

be physically attractive
肉体的魅力がある

physician *n.* (doctor) 医者, (practitioner of general medicine) 内科医

physics *n.* 物理学

physiognomy *n.* (facial features) 人相

examine someone's physiognomy
(…の) 人相を見る

physiology *n.* 生理学

physiotherapist *n.* 理学療法士

physiotherapy *n.* 物理療法

physique *n.* 体格, 体つき

pi *n.* (Greek letter) パイ; (mathematical ratio) 円周率

pianist *n.* ピアニスト

piano *n.* ピアノ

play the piano ピアノを弾く

piccolo *n.* ピッコロ

---

pick[1] *v.*

1 GRAB AND LIFT UP: 摘み取る, 摘む

2 SELECT: 選ぶ, 選び取る, 取る

3 OBTAIN: 取る, 手に入れる [→ PICK UP 2]

4 CLEAN/REMOVE WITH FINGERS: つまみ取る, (nose, teeth) ほじる

1 How nice of you to pick flowers for me.
花を摘んで来てくれるなんて、どうもありがとう。

Let's go and pick some strawberries.
いちご狩りに行こう。

2 Which course did you pick?
どのコースを<u>選び</u> [取り] ました？

I couldn't have picked a better partner.
これ以上ないパートナーを選んだと思っています。

Pick whichever most suits you.
どれでも一番ぴったりのものを取ってください。

At your age you can pick and choose as you like.
君の年なら、自分の好きなようにやれば

いい。

3 I picked it off the shelf.
棚から取ったんです。

4 The monkey was picking fleas off another monkey.
猿は別の猿のノミをつまみ取って(毛づくろいをして)いた。

Don't pick your nose.
鼻をほじるのは、よしなさい。

You should cover your mouth when you pick your teeth.
歯をほじるときは、手で口をおおいなさい。

pick a fight with …にけんかを売る

He picked a fight with another boy.
彼はほかの男の子にけんかを売った。

pick a lock 錠をこじあける

The thief picked the lock.
泥棒は錠をこじあけた。

pick at food ほんの少し食べる, 食べ物にちょっと手をつける

Junko was picking at her food and seemed to have no appetite.
純子はちょっと食事に手をつけたが、食欲がなさそうだった。

pick sb's brains (…の) 知恵を借りる, ((*humble*)) お知恵を拝借する

I would love to pick your brains sometime.
そのうちぜひ、お知恵を借りたいです。

pick sb's pocket(s) (…の) 財布をする, (…に) すりを働く

pick on *v.* (tease) からかう, (bully) いじめる, (find fault with) (…の) 揚げ足を取る

Stop picking on me.
((*masculine*)) からかうのはよせ / ((*feminine*)) からかうのはやめて。

Why do they always pick on our boy?
((*feminine*)) どうしてあの子たちは、うちの子をいつもいじめるの?

pick out *v.* (select) 選ぶ, (discern from among a crowd) 見分ける

pick up *v.*

1 LIFT: (suitcase) 持ち上げる, (telephone) 取る, (object from the ground) 拾う

2 GET/BUY: 手に入れる, (buy and bring back) 買って来る, (go and get) 取りに行く

3 PERSON: (go to meet and provide transport for) 迎えに行く, (allow in as a passenger) 乗せる

4 CLEAN UP: (mess, room) 片付ける, (**pick up after**) …の後片付けをする

5 FOR SEXUAL RELATIONSHIP: ひっかける

6 ILLNESS: (…に) かかる

7 LEARN: 覚える, 身につける

8 GET BETTER: (of sales, economy) よくなる, 上向く, (of person: recover) 回復する

9 DETECT: (sound) 拾う, 捕らえる, (signal) 受信する, キャッチする, (scent) かぎつける

10 CONTINUE: (conversation) (話を) また続ける, (…の) 続きをやる

11 ARREST: (**be picked up**) 捕まる

12 SPEED: (スピードを) 上げる

1 The box was too heavy for me to pick up.
その箱は重すぎて持ち上げられなかった。

I picked up the receiver.
受話器を取った。

Pick up those cigarette butts.

散らばっている吸い殻を拾って。

2 I picked up this very old book at that secondhand bookshop.
この古書は、あの古本屋で手に入れた。

I'll pick up some pizzas on the way home.
帰りがけにピザを買って来るよ。

I'll pick up the package at the post office tomorrow.
明日郵便局に小包を取りに行きます。

3 Who is going to the station to pick him up?
誰が彼を駅まで迎えに行くの？

I'll pick her up on my way home from work.
仕事から帰る途中で、彼女を乗せるよ。

4 Before you go out, I want you to pick up all this mess on the floor.
出て行く前に、床に散らかした物を全部片付けて。

I'm sick of picking up after you!
あなたの後片付けは、もううんざりだ。

5 He was trying to pick up some girl at a bar.
あの人はバーで女の子をひっかけようとしてたよ。

She was picked up by some smooth-talking guy.
彼女は口のうまい男にひっかかった。

6 He picked up hepatitis in India.
彼はインドで肝炎にかかった。

7 After only a couple of weeks, she started to pick up some Spanish.
ほんの2週間で、彼女は片言のスペイン語を覚え始めた。

Where did you pick up that (bad) habit?
どこでそんな(悪い)癖がついたの？

8 Sales are picking up.
売れ行きが上がっている。

She hasn't been well, but she's beginning to pick up now.
彼女は体調がよくなかったみたいだけど、今は回復に向かっているよ。

9 We couldn't pick up any radio stations.
どのラジオ局も受信できなかった。

10 Let's pick up this conversation later.
あとで、この話の続きをやろう。

He picked up where he left off yesterday.
昨日終わったところから、話を続けた。

11 He was picked up by the police for drug dealing.
あの男は麻薬売買で警察に捕まった。

12 I began to feel sick as the airplane picked up speed for take-off.
離陸のため飛行機がスピードを上げるにつれて、気分が悪くなっていった。

pick up on *v.* (notice) …に気づく

I didn't pick up on that.
そのことに気づかなかった。

---

pick² *n.* (pickax) つるはし, (plectrum) ピック

a guitar pick ギターのピック

pickax *n.* つるはし

picket *n.* (labor union picket) ピケ隊

v. (…に) ピケを張る

♦**picket line** *n.* ピケ

pickle *n.* (お)漬物, ピクルス [NOTE: 漬物 refers to vegetables such as radish, eggplant or cucumber that have been pickled in salt or rice-bran paste and which are commonly eaten with Japanese rice.]

v. 漬ける, ピクルスにする

pickpocket *n.* すり

Be careful. There are a lot of pickpockets in this area.
気をつけて。この辺は、すりが多いので。

pickup truck *n.* 小型トラック

picnic *n.* ピクニック

v. ピクニックをする

no picnic 容易ではない

pictorial *adj.* (of book) 絵入りの

a pictorial history of Japan
絵入りの日本の歴史書

picture *n.* (painting) 絵, (photo) 写真, (image on TV screen) 画像, (imagined image) イメージ, 心象

v. (imagine) 想像する, 心に描く

That's a good picture. いい絵ですね。

The frame is better than the picture.
額のほうが写真より立派だ。

the big picture 全体像

I can just picture myself now in the Bahamas—the sun is setting…
想像できるよ、バハマにいるところが—ちょうど日が暮れる時で…

get the picture 状況がのみこめる, 事態を理解する, 状況を把握する

Do you get the picture?
状況がのみこめましたか？

in/out of the picture (relevant/irrelevant) 関係がある/関係がない

shoot/snap pictures 写真をパチパチ撮る

picturesque *adj.* 絵のように美しい

pidgin *n.* 混成語, ピジン語

♦**pidgin English** *n.* ピジン英語

pie *n.* パイ

♦**pie chart** *n.* 円グラフ

piebald *n.* (horse) 白黒まだらの馬

piece *n.* (fragment) 破片, かけら, (slice) 一切れ, (of paper) 1枚, (game piece) こま, (**a piece of**: a part/share of) …の1部 [→ COIN]

v. (**piece together**: facts, information) つなぎ合わせる

a piece of cake ケーキ1個 [一つ]

a piece of furniture 家具1点

a piece of advice [information]
一つの助言 [情報]

There were pieces of glass on the floor.
床にはガラスの破片が落ちていた。

rip to pieces びりびりに破く, ずたずたに引き裂く

I ripped the letter to pieces.
その手紙をびりびりに破いた。

piecemeal *adv.* (a little at a time) 少しずつ; (in pieces) ばらばらに

adj. 少しずつの

The work was done in a piecemeal fashion.
その仕事は少しずつ進められた。

pier *n.* 埠頭, 桟橋

pierce *v.* (penetrate) 突き通す, 貫通する, (put a hole through) (…に) 穴をあける, (with knife) 刺す; (of sound) つんざく, 破る

The enemy has pierced our defenses.
敵は我々の防御線を突破した。

She's decided to get her ears pierced.
彼女、耳にピアスの穴をあけることにしたんだって。

piercing *adj.* (of scream) 甲高い, (of

wind) 身を切るような, (of eyes) 鋭い

pig ***n.*** (animal) ブタ, 豚, (meat) 豚肉; (greedy person) 欲張り

pigeon ***n.*** ハト, 鳩

pigeonhole ***n.*** (for documents) 書類棚; (for pigeons) ハトの巣箱

pigeon-toed ***adj.*** 内またの

piggyback ***adv., adj.*** おんぶして/た, 背負って/た

n. おんぶ

give someone a piggyback おんぶする

piggy bank ***n.*** 貯金箱

pigment ***n.*** (used as paint) 顔料, (in animal, plant) 色素

pigtail ***n.*** (**pigtails**) お下げ(髪)

pike¹ ***n.*** (fish) カワカマス

pike² ***n.*** (weapon) 矛, やり

pike³ ***n.*** (turnpike) 有料道路

pile ***n.*** (heap) 山, 積み重ね, (**a pile of/piles of**: lots of) たくさん, いっぱい

v. (heap together) 積み重ねる, 山と積む, 積み上げる

a pile of books 本の山

a pile of sand 砂の山

a pile of dishes お皿の山

I have a pile of homework to do by tomorrow.
明日までにやらなきゃならない宿題がいっぱいある。

Just pile everything you don't need over there.
要らない物は全部あそこに積み重ねておいて。

He was piling food onto his plate.
彼は取り皿に料理を山ほど盛っていた。

My desk was piled with papers.
机の上に、書類を山と積んでいた。

♦**pile into** ***v.*** (room) ...にどやどや入る, (car) ...にどやどや乗り込む

piles ***n.*** (hemorrhoids) 痔

pileup ***n.*** (car accident) 玉突き衝突

pilgrim ***n.*** 巡礼者, (**the Pilgrim Fathers**) ピルグリム・ファーザーズ

pilgrimage ***n.*** 巡礼の旅, 聖地巡礼

pill ***n.*** (medicine) 薬, 錠剤, 丸薬, (**the pill**: oral contraceptive) ピル, 経口避妊薬

Take two pills a day.
１日２錠飲んでください。

Are you on the pill?
ピルを飲んでいますか？

pillar ***n.*** ((*also figurative*)) 柱

She's a pillar of our association.
彼女は私たちの協会の柱です。

pillow ***n.*** 枕 [→ picture of FUTON]

pillowcase ***n.*** 枕カバー

pilot ***n.*** (flier of aircraft) パイロット, 操縦士; (pilot episode) 実験番組

v. (fly) 操縦する, (be the pilot of) (...の) 水先案内をする

adj. (test) 試験的な

Yoshiko wants to be a pilot.
良子はパイロットになりたいと思っている。

It's a pilot project and the first of its kind.
これは試験的なプロジェクトで、その手のものとしては初の試みです。

pilot light ***n.*** 種火, 口火

pimp ***n.*** ひも, ぽん引き

pimple ***n.*** にきび, 吹き出物

pin ***n.*** (needle) 針, ピン, (piece of jewelry) ピンブローチ; (in bowling) ピン

v. 針で留める, ピンで留める

a safety pin 安全ピン

There was a pin sticking out of the chair.
椅子から針が突き出ていた。

Could you pin the notice up on the board, please?
そのお知らせを、掲示板にピンで留めておいてもらえますか？

be on pins and needles そわそわしている, びくびくしている

get/have pins and needles しびれる

pinafore *n.* (apron) エプロン, 前掛け

pincers *n.* (tool) 釘抜き, やっとこ; (of animal/insect) はさみ

pinch *n.* (tiny amount) 一つまみ, 少量
v. つねる

a pinch of salt 塩一つまみ

How dare you pinch my butt!
お尻をつねるなんて、ひどいじゃない！

pincushion *n.* 針刺し, 針山

pine[1] *n.* (tree) マツ, 松, (wood) マツ材

pine[2] *v.* (long for) 恋しく思う

pineapple *n.* パイナップル

pine cone *n.* 松かさ, 松ぼっくり

pink *n., adj.* ピンク色(の), 桃色(の)

a pink cherry blossom
ピンク色の桜の花

pinkie *n.* (finger) 小指 [→ FINGER]

pinnacle *n.* (of success) 頂点, 絶頂, (summit) 高峰

pinpoint *v.* (identify precisely) 正確に示す, 的確に指摘する
n. (pin's point) ピンの先

He pinpointed the difficulties the company was facing.
彼は会社が直面している難題を、的確に指摘した。

pint *n.* (unit of measure) パイント

A pint of beer, please.
ビールを1パイント下さい。

pinup *n.* (image) アイドルの写真, ピンナップ, (girl) グラビアアイドル

pioneer *n.* (early settler) 開拓者, (first person) パイオニア, 先駆者

Freud was a pioneer in psychology.
フロイトは心理学の先駆者です。

pioneering *adj.* 先駆的な

pious *adj.* 信心深い, 敬けんな

pip *n.* (in fruit) 種

pipe *n.* (metal tube) パイプ, 管, (for tobacco) パイプ, キセル; (**pipes:** musical instrument) 管楽器 [→ BAGPIPE(S)]

a water [gas] pipe 水道 [ガス] 管

One of the hot water pipes has burst.
温水パイプの一つが破裂した。

Smoking your pipe again?
またパイプを吸っているの？

the sound of pipes 管楽器の音

pipeline *n.* パイプライン

in the pipeline (under preparation) 準備中で

piracy *n.* (of copyrighted material) 著作権侵害

piranha *n.* ピラニア

pirate *n.* 海賊, (pirate ship) 海賊船
v. (books, DVD) (…の) 海賊版を出す

♦**pirated** *adj.* 海賊版の

Pisces *n.* (the Fishes) 魚座

piss *n., v.* 小便(をする)

♦**piss off** *v.* (anger) 怒らせる; (**Piss off!**) 出て行け

pistachio *n.* ピスタチオ

pistol *n.* ピストル

He fired the pistol five times.
彼はピストルを5回撃った。

piston *n.* ピストン

pit *n.* (hole) 穴, (depression) くぼみ, (coal mine) 炭坑, (orchestra pit) オーケストラボックス, (for racecar) ピット; (**the pits**: misery) 最低, 最悪

a bottomless pit 底なしの穴

pitch *n.* (sound level) ピッチ, 調子; (sports ground) グラウンド, 競技場; (throw of a ball) 投球

v. (throw) 投げる, (throw away) 捨てる; (pitch a tent) (テントを)張る

pitch-black *adj.* 真っ暗な

pitcher[1] *n.* (in baseball) ピッチャー, 投手

pitcher[2] *n.* (of beer) ピッチャー

pitchfork *n.* くまで

v. (throw as if with a pitchfork) 投げ上げる

pitfall *n.* 落とし穴

the pitfalls of the life of a job-hopping part-time worker
フリーターの生活の落とし穴

pitiful *adj.* (lamentable) かわいそうな, 哀れな; (meager) わずかな, (undeserving of respect) くだらない

pitted *adj.* (holed) 穴だらけの, (uneven) でこぼこの; (without seeds) 種なしの

pity *n.* (disappointment) 残念なこと, 惜しいこと, (pitiable thing) かわいそうなこと, 気の毒

v. かわいそうに思う, 気の毒に思う

It's a pity you can't come.
あなたが来られないのは残念です。

Pity you missed the party.
あのパーティーに出られなかったなんて、惜しいことをしましたね。

What a pity it rained on their wedding day.
結婚式の日に雨が降ったなんて、本当に気の毒だ。

Frankly, I pity him losing his wife in that awful accident.
正直な話、あんな悲惨な事故で奥さんを亡くして彼も気の毒だよ。

take pity on 気の毒に思う, …に同情する

pivot *n.* (axis of rotation) 回転軸; (most important thing/person) 中心, かなめ

v. 回転する

pivotal *adj.* (very important) きわめて重要な, 中枢の

The role of the Air Force was pivotal to success.
空軍の働きが成功のかぎを握っていた。

pixie *n.* 小妖精

pizza *n.* ピザ

placard *n.* プラカード

placate *v.* (person) なだめる, 静める

place

1 *n.* LOCATION/AREA: 場所, 所, (city) 都市, (town) 町, (village) 村, (country) 国

2 *v.* PUT: 置く

3 *n.* ROLE: 役割, 立場

4 *n.* IN BOOK: (point where one has stopped reading) 読んでいたところ, 読みさしの箇所

5 *n.* RANK IN RACE: -着, -位

6 *n.* SEAT TO SIT IN: 席, 座る場所

7 *n.* IN LINE: 場所, 所

8 ***n.*** **HOME:** 家, うち

9 ***v.*** **REMEMBER:** 思い出す

1 a place for playing 遊び場

a meeting place 集合 [待ち合わせ] 場所

a place of business 事業所

Make sure to put things back in their proper place.
必ず元の場所に戻しておいてね。

a sore place 痛い所

a place called Phoenix
フェニックスという町

2 The missing keys were placed on the desk.
なくなったかぎは、机の上に置いてあった。

The boy was placed in a foster home.
男の子は里親の所に預けられた。

3 It's not your place to criticize her.
彼女を非難する立場ではないですよ。

Matsui lost his place on the team.
松井はチームを外された。

4 I've lost my place in the book.
どこまで読んだかわからなくなった。

5 The horse came in second place.
その馬は2着だった。

6 There's no place to sit.
座る場所がない。

7 I lost my place in line.
行列の中の元いた場所に戻れなかった。

8 Whose place are you staying at tonight?
今夜、誰の家に泊まるの？

9 The man looks familiar, but I can't place his face.
見覚えはあるんだけど、誰なのか思い出せない。

change places with …と交替する, …と入れ替わる

I wouldn't mind changing places with him for a day.
1日だけあの人と入れ替わってもいいな。

in place of …の代わりに

I went in place of John.
僕がジョンの代わりに行った。

in places 所々, あちこちに

The walls were crumbling in places.
壁は所々、はがれ落ちていた。

in the first place まず第一に

In the first place, I have no intention of going, and in the second, I couldn't even if I wanted to.
まず第一に行く気などないですし、第二に仮に行きたくても行けないんです。

out of place 合わない, 場違いの

Do you think this vase looks out of place on the table?
その花びんは、このテーブルに合わないと思う?

put sb in his/her place (…に) 身の程を思い知らせる

placement ***n.*** (placing of things) 置くこと, 配置; (job placement) 就職あっせん

placenta ***n.*** 胎盤

placid ***adj.*** 穏やかな, 落ち着いた

plagiarism ***n.*** 盗用, 盗作

plagiarize ***v.*** 盗用する, 盗作する

plague ***n.*** 疫病, (epidemic) 伝染病, (the bubonic plague) ペスト

plaice ***n.*** カレイ

plaid ***n.*** (pattern) 格子じま, チェック

plain

1 ***adj.*** **CLEAR:** 明らかな, 明白な, はっきりした

2 ***adj.*** **SIMPLE:** 素朴な, 簡単な, (banal, run-of-the-mill) ありふれた, (of clothes) 地味な, (without pattern) 無地の, (not mixed with other ingredients) 混ぜ物のない, プレーンな

3 ***n.*** **AREA OF FLAT LAND:** 平原, 平野

4 ***adj.*** **CANDID:** 率直な, ありのままの

5 ***adj.*** **OF LOOKS:** 魅力のない, きれいでない

6 ***adv.*** **FOR EMPHASIS:** 全く

1 The facts are plain enough.
事実は明白だ。

It was plain that we were not welcome there.
そこで歓迎されていないのは、明らかだった。

I made it plain to him that he was not to park there.
そこに駐車してはいけないことを、彼にはっきりと言っておいた。

2 The food was very plain.
料理の味は、とてもありふれたものだった。

She has plain taste in clothing.
彼女は服の趣味が地味だ。

He wore a plain tie.
彼は無地のネクタイをしていた。

You'd better use a plain envelope.
無地の封筒を使ったほうがいいよ。

I'll have a plain omelette.
プレーンオムレツを下さい。

3 the Kanto Plain 関東平野

There are many flowers that are only found on the high plains.
高原でしか見られない花は、たくさんあります。

4 I told him the plain truth, nothing more.
ありのままの真相を、あの人に言っただけです。

5 Her looks are kind of plain for a model.
彼女の容姿は、モデルにしては魅力に欠ける。

6 That's just plain stupid.
全くばかげている。

plainly ***adv.*** (candidly) 率直に; (obviously) 明らかに

If I may speak plainly...
率直に言わせていただくと...

He was plainly lying.
彼は明らかにうそをついていた。

plaintiff ***n.*** 原告

plait ***n.*** (**plaits**) 三つ編み, お下げ, (French plait) 編み込み

v. (hair) 編む

The girl wore her hair in plaits.
その子は髪を編んでお下げにしていた。

plan

1 ***n.*** **ARRANGEMENT:** 計画, プラン, 予定, (business plan, project) 企画

2 ***v.*** **MAKE ARRANGEMENTS:** 計画する, 計画を立てる, プランを練る, 企画する, (**plan to do**) ...する予定だ, ...するつもりだ

3 ***n.*** **OUTLINE DRAWING OR DIAGRAM:** 図, 図面, (for building) 設計図

1 We've had to change our plans.
計画を変更しなければならなかった。

What's the plan for tomorrow?
明日の予定は？

That's a good plan.
それはいい企画だ。

2 It was planned last year.
それは去年計画されたものです。

We must plan ahead.

前もって計画を立てなくちゃ。

We didn't plan for this to happen.
こんな事が起こるとは想定していなかった。

Are you planning to go?
行く予定ですか？

They are planning to hold a festival.
フェスティバルを開催する予定らしい。

3 Show me the plans, why don't you.
図面を見せてください。

according to plan 予定どおりに, 計画どおりに

Everything is going according to plan.
すべて計画どおりに進んでいます。

plane¹ *n.* (airplane) 飛行機; (flat surface; also in math) 平面, (horizontal surface) 水平面, (level of thought/existence) 次元
adj. (level) 平らな

We went by plane.
飛行機で行きました。

I watched a film on the plane.
機内で映画を見た。

Shc's on a different plane than he is.
彼女は彼とは次元が違うんだ。

plane² *n.* (tool) かんな [→ picture of TOOL]

planet *n.* 惑星

plank *n.* (thick board) 厚板

walk the plank (be made to resign) 辞職させられる

plankton *n.* プランクトン

planner *n.* (person) 立案者, (notebook, daily planner) 手帳

planning *n.* 計画

family planning 家族計画
town planning 都市計画

My husband has no sense of planning.
主人には計画性が全然ない。

plant

1 *n.* ORGANIC LIFE GROWING IN THE GROUND: 植物, 草木, (indoor plant) 観葉植物
2 *v.* PUT (SEEDS) IN THE GROUND: 植える, (sow) まく
3 *n.* FACTORY: 工場
4 *v.* PUT IN POSITION: 仕掛ける, 配置する

1 What's this plant called?
これは何という植物ですか？

This plant likes a shady spot.
この植物は日陰を好みます。

2 And when do they plant the rice?
それで稲はいつ植えるんですか？

We planted lots of roses in our garden.
庭にたくさんのバラを植えた。

3 a cement plant セメント工場
a chemical plant 化学工場

4 A bomb had been planted near the house.
その家の近くに爆弾が仕掛けられていた。

plantation *n.* 大農園, プランテーション

a banana plantation バナナ農園

plaque *n.* 飾り板, (commemorative) 記念額; (on teeth) 歯垢

plasma *n.* (blood plasma) 血しょう; (state of matter) プラズマ

plaster *n.* しっくい, (plaster of Paris) 石膏
v. (apply plaster to: wall) (…に) しっくいを塗る

The plaster was falling off the walls.
壁からしっくいがはがれ落ちていた。

♦**plaster cast** *n.* ギブス, ギプス

plastic *n., adj.* プラスチック(の), 合成樹

P

脂(の)

plastic toys プラスチックのおもちゃ

the plastics industry プラスチック産業

♦**plastic bottle** *n.* ペットボトル [NOTE: ペット is short for *p*oly*e*thylene *t*erephthalate.]

plastic surgery *n.* (to repair tissue) 形成外科, (to improve looks) 美容整形

plate

1 *n.* FOR/OF FOOD: (お)皿, (small serving plate) 取り皿, (a plateful) 一皿分, (plate of food) 料理, (gold-plated/silver-plated tableware) 金/銀食器, (**plates**: dishes) 食器類

2 *n.* CONTAINING INFORMATION: (license plate) ナンバープレート, (nameplate) 表札 [→ picture of HOUSE]

3 *n.* OF EARTH'S CRUST: プレート

4 *v.* COAT WITH GOLD/SILVER: (…に) 金/銀めっきする

5 *n.* IN BASEBALL: (home plate) 本塁, ホームプレート

6 *n.* METAL PLATE: 金属板, 鉄板

1 Do we have enough plates?
お皿は足りる?
Would you pass me a plate, please?
お皿を取っていただけますか?
I'll have the shrimp plate.
えび料理を食べよう。

2 Did you get the plate number?
車のナンバーを見ましたか?

3 the theory of plate tectonics
プレートテクトニクス理論
the Pacific plate 太平洋プレート

4 a bracelet plated in gold
金めっきのブレスレット

5 reach home plate ホームインする

6 a steel plate 鉄板

♦**plating** *n.* めっき

silver plating 銀めっき

plateau *n.* 高原

v. (level off) 横ばいになる

platform *n.* (at train station) ホーム, -番線; (lecture platform) 演壇, (teacher's platform) 教壇

"Excuse me, which platform does the train for Osaka leave from?"
"It's platform 5."
「すみません、大阪行きの電車は何番線ですか?」
「5番線[ホーム]です」

platinum *n.* プラチナ, 白金

platitude *n.* 陳腐な言葉, 決まり文句

platonic *adj.* プラトニックな, 精神的な

platonic love プラトニックラブ [純愛]

platoon *n.* (of soldiers) 小隊

platter *n.* (big plate) 大皿, (meal served on a big plate) 大皿に盛った料理

platypus *n.* カモノハシ

plausible *adj.* もっともらしい

play

1 *v.* HAVE FUN: 遊ぶ

2 *v.* DO: (sport) する, やる

3 *v.* HAVE A COMPETITION: (play against) (…と) 対戦する

4 *n.* FUN: 遊び

5 *n.* THEATRICAL PIECE: (stage performance) (お)芝居, 演劇, (script for stage considered as literature) 戯曲

6 *v.* INSTRUMENT: 弾く

7 *v.* PERFORM: (role on stage) (…の) 役をやる, (…を) 演じる, (music before audience) 演奏する, (drama before audience) 上演する, (film) 上映する, (position in game) (…に) つく, (**play a trick on**) (…に) いたずらをする

8 *v.* AUDIO/AUDIO-VISUAL MEDIA: (put on: CD etc.) かける, (press play button and allow to be heard/seen) 再生する

9 *n.* MOVEMENT IN SPORT/GAME: プレー, 動き

10 *n.* BUTTON ON MACHINE: 再生(ボタン)

1 The children are playing quietly in the other room.
子供たちは、向こうの部屋でおとなしく遊んでいるよ。

2 We play tennis every weekend.
週末はいつも、テニスをします。

Do you play golf?
ゴルフは、やりますか？

3 Who is the team playing against next week?
来週はどこと対戦するんですか？

4 Children need play.
子供には遊びが必要です。

5 It's a fine play. Do go and see it.
いい芝居だから、ぜひ見に行くといいよ。

He's written a lot of plays.
あの人はたくさんの戯曲を書いています。

6 Can you play the piano?
ピアノを弾けますか？

7 Who played the main part?
主役をやったのは誰ですか？

What part did Michael play?
マイケルは何の役を演じたの？

Tosca is playing at the Opera House.
『トスカ』がオペラハウスで上演されている。

8 We played a CD. ＣＤをかけた。

9 a bad play まずいプレー

♦ **play back** *v.* (video, DVD) 再生する, (CD) もう一度かける

playback *n.* 再生, (playback button) 再生(ボタン)

playboy *n.* 道楽者, 遊び人

player *n.* (athlete) 選手, プレーヤー, (musician with instrument) 奏者

a baseball player 野球選手

John Coltrane ranks as one of the best sax players of all time.
ジョン・コルトレーンはサックスの不滅の名奏者の一人です。

playful *adj.* (of person) ちゃめっ気のある, いたずら好きの, (of kitten) じゃれる

playground *n.* 遊び場, (at school) 運動場

playing field *n.* 競技場, グラウンド

playmate *n.* 遊び友達

play-off *n.* 決勝試合, (**the play-offs**) 王座決定戦

playpen *n.* ベビーサークル

playtime *n.* (during school) 休み時間

playwright *n.* 劇作家, 脚本家

plaza *n.* 広場

plea *n.* (appeal) 嘆願, (in court) 申し立て, 抗弁

make a plea (in court) 申し立てをする

♦ **plea-bargain** *n., v.* 司法取引(をする)

plead *v.* (appeal) 嘆願する, ((*informal*)) 頼む, (in court) 申し立てをする

I pleaded with him not to do it, but he wouldn't listen.

P

そんなことはしないでと、必死になって頼んだけど、彼は耳を貸そうとしなかった。

pleasant *adj.* (of experience) 楽しい, 愉快な, (of climate, scent) 気持ちのいい, (of person) 感じのいい

We had a pleasant afternoon.
楽しい午後を過ごしました。

He's a very pleasant young man.
彼はとても感じのいい青年だね。

KANJI BRIDGE

快 ON: かい KUN: こころよ(い) | PLEASANT

agreeable, comfortable	快適な
cheerful, lively	快活な
clear, lucid	明快な
complete recovery	全快
light, nimble	軽快な
pleasant, merry	愉快な
pleasure	快楽
unpleasant	不愉快な

pleasantries *n.* (small talk) 雑談, (social etiquette) 社交辞令, かたいあいさつ

exchange pleasantries 雑談を交わす

dispense with pleasantries
社交辞令を抜きにする

please

1 *adv.* MAKING A REQUEST: どうぞ, (by all means) ぜひ, (**please...**) ...してください, (**please do not...**) どうか...しないでください, (**would/could you...please?**) ...していただけますか, (shopping: ... please) (...を)下さい, お願いします

2 *v.* MAKE HAPPY: 喜ばせる, (cause to have fun) 楽しませる, (satisfy) 満足させる

3 *interj.* EXPRESSING IRRITATION: ((*feminine*)) やめてよ, よしてよ, ((*masculine*)) やめろよ

1 Please do come to Japan.
ぜひ日本へいらしてください。

Please don't ask that question again.
その質問はもうしないでください。

Could you walk a bit faster, please?
もう少し速く歩いていただけますか?

Would you turn the radio down, please?
ラジオの音量を下げてくださいますか?

The red one, please. 赤いのを下さい。

A return ticket, please.
往復切符をお願いします。

2 It will please you to know that...
...を知ってうれしいでしょう。

It pleased me to hear you were coming.
あなたが来るって聞いて、うれしかった。

What can we do to please them?
あの人たちを満足させるのには、何をしたらいいだろう?

3 Please! Stop pushing!
押すのはやめて!

as one pleases 好きなように, ((*used negatively*)) 勝手に

You can eat as much as you please.
好きなだけ食べてくださいね。

please oneself 好きなようにする, 勝手にする

pleased *adj.* (happy) うれしい, (satisfied) 満足した, (**be pleased to do**) 喜んで...する

She wasn't at all pleased by your remark.
あなたが言ったことを、彼女はちっともうれしく思っていなかったよ。

pleased to meet you (初めまして)どうぞよろしく

pleasurable *adj.* (fun) 楽しい, 快い

pleasure *n.* (recreation) 楽しみ, 喜び, (satisfaction) 満足

study for pleasure
楽しみとして勉強する

I get a lot of pleasure from fishing.
釣りが楽しくて仕方ありません。

I take pleasure in my work.
仕事が楽しい/仕事にやりがいを感じる。

What a pleasure it would be to see them together again!
二人がまたいっしょにいるのを見ることができたら、どんなにうれしいだろう。

it's a pleasure/the pleasure is mine どういたしまして、こちらこそ

“Thank you for helping us.”
“Don't mention it. It was a pleasure.”
「手伝ってくれてありがとう」
「いえいえ、どういたしまして」

with pleasure 喜んで

I'll do it with pleasure.
喜んでやります。

pleat *n.* (in skirt) ひだ, プリーツ

plectrum *n.* ピック, つめ

pledge *n.* 誓約, 固い約束, (token) しるし
v. (**pledge to do**) …することを誓う

plenipotentiary *n.* 全権大使, 全権委員

plentiful *adj.* (of resources) 豊富な, 豊かな

plenty *n.* (a lot) たくさん, いっぱい, (sufficient) 十分, たっぷり

We've got plenty of drink but not much food.
飲み物はたくさんあるけど、食べ物はあまりありません。

There's plenty of time, so there's no need to rush.
時間はたっぷりあるから、急ぐ必要はないよ。

pleurisy *n.* 肋膜炎

pliers *n.* ペンチ [→ picture of TOOL]

plight *n.* みじめな状況, 苦境

plod *v.* (trudge) とぼとぼ歩く, (work slowly) こつこつ働く
n. (heavy steps) 重い足取り

The children plodded along behind the teacher.
子供たちは教師の後をとぼとぼ歩いて行った。

plot

1 *n.* SECRET PLAN: 陰謀, 計画
2 *v.* DEVISE: たくらむ, 企てる
3 *n.* AREA OF LAND: 土地, 場所
4 *v.* MARK OUT: (on graph) 記入する, (on map) 書き込む
5 *n.* SEQUENCE OF EVENTS IN NOVEL/FILM: 筋, プロット, 筋書き

1 a plot to overthrow the government
政府転覆の陰謀
an assassination plot 暗殺計画

2 They look as if they were plotting something.
彼らは何かをたくらんでいるかのようだ。

3 I use this plot for vegetables.
この土地を野菜作りに使っています。
a building plot 建設場所

4 Plot the numbers on the graph.
数値をグラフに記入してください。

5 The plot was good, but the characters were unconvincing.

筋書きはよかったけど、登場人物は説得力に欠けていた。

plover *n.* チドリ

plow *n.* (piece of farming machinery) すき, (snowplow) 除雪車

v. (field) 耕す, (street) 除雪する

plowman *n.* (farmer) 農夫

ploy *n.* 策略, たくらみ, 手

pluck *v.* (bird) (…の) 羽をむしり取る, (fruit) もぐ, (eyebrows) 抜く, (string of instrument) かき鳴らす

plug *n.* (electrical device) プラグ, 差し込み; (stopper) 栓

v. (stop up) ふさぐ [→ ADVERTISE]

The plug came out. プラグが外れた。

This sink doesn't have a plug.
この流しには栓がない。

♦**plug in** *v.* (connect) つなぐ, 接続する

Is the antenna plugged in?
アンテナは、つないであるの？

plum *n.* プラム, (Japanese plum) 梅; (color) 濃い紫色

♦**plum wine** *n.* 梅酒

plumber *n.* 水道屋, 配管工

plumbing *n.* (pipelaying) 配管; (drainage system) 排水設備

The plumbing in this building doesn't work.
このビルの排水設備が故障している。

plummet *v.* (fall quickly) 急落する, 暴落する

Stock prices plummeted.
株価が暴落した。

plump *adj.* ふっくらした, ぽっちゃりした, (of baby) 丸々とした

plunder *v.* (place) 荒らして略奪する

plunge *v.* 突っ込む, (into water) 飛び込む

take the plunge (and do) 思い切って(…する)

plural *adj.* (more than one) 複数の, (in the plural form) 複数形の

n. (plural form) 複数形

plus *prep.* (in addition to) …足す, …を加えて, …をプラスして, …と

adj. プラスの, (of grade: above the mark) …の上, …プラス

n. (merit) プラス, 利点; (plus sign) プラス記号

eight plus two 8足す2

Take away travel expenses plus your hotel costs.
旅費とホテル代を引いてください。

All of us, plus John, made it here on time.
僕たち全員とジョンは、時間どおりにここに着きました。

a plus factor プラスの要素

I got a C+ on my homework.
宿題の成績はCプラスだった。

There are plusses and minuses to the plan.
その計画には利点もあるが不利な点もある。

plush *adj.* (luxurious) 豪華な, ぜいたくな

Pluto *n.* 冥王星

plutocracy *n.* 財閥, 富豪階級

plutonium *n.* プルトニウム

ply *n.* (layer) 層, -重

two-ply 2重 [2枚重ね] の

plywood *n.* ベニヤ板, 合板

P.M., p.m. *abbr.* (afternoon) 午後…

2:40 P.M. 午後2時40分

pneumatic *adj.* 圧搾空気の

♦**pneumatic drill** *n.* 空気ドリル

pneumonia *n.* 肺炎

have pneumonia 肺炎にかかる

poach[1] *v.* (fish) 密漁する, (animals) 密猟する

♦**poacher** *n.* (hunter) 密猟者

poach[2] *v.* (egg) 割ってゆでる

a poached egg 落とし卵[ポーチドエッグ]

PO Box *n.* 私書箱

pocket *n.* (of garment) ポケット, (of car seat) 小物入れ; (small area) 狭い地域 *v.* (put in one's pocket) ポケットに入れる, (money) ごまかす, ((*formal*)) 着服する

I'm sure I put it in my pocket.
確かにポケットに入れたんだ。

pocketbook *n.* (handbag) ハンドバッグ, (wallet) 札入れ

pocketknife *n.* 小型ナイフ

pocket money *n.* (お)こづかい

pod *n.* (of bean) さや

podgy *adj.* ずんぐりした

podiatry *n.* (treatment) 足の治療

podium *n.* (speaker's) 演壇, (teacher's) 教壇, (conductor's) 指揮台

poem *n.* 詩, (haiku) 俳句

write a poem 詩を書く

poet *n.* 詩人

poetic *adj.* 詩的な

poetry *n.* 詩, 詩歌

read poetry 詩を読む

poignant *adj.* (moving) 感動的な, (sad) 胸を刺すような, 心が痛む

I have poignant memories of this place.
この場所には心が痛む思い出がある。

point

1 *n.* SHARP EXTREMITY: 先, 先端

2 *v.* INDICATE/AIM: (with finger) 指さす, (aim: gun etc.) 向ける, (**point out**: indicate) 指す, 示す, 指摘する

3 *n.* EXACT MOMENT/PLACE: (in time) 時, 時点, (in space: place) 所, 場所, 地点, (on graph) 点

4 *n.* PURPOSE: 目的, (meaning) 意味

5 *n.* ESSENTIAL IDEA/ARGUMENT: 要点, ポイント, 核心, (item) 点

6 *n.* EXTENT: 程度

7 *n.* CRITICAL LEVEL/STAGE: 段階

8 *n.* IN GAME: 得点, 点数, -点

9 *n.* PENINSULA: (**Point**) …岬

10 *n.* EXPRESSING DECIMAL: 点

1 the point of a needle 針の先端
the point of a sword 剣の先

2 It's rude to point at people.
人を指さすのは失礼ですよ。

He pointed at the cat.
彼はその猫を指さした。

Point the light over here.
明かりをこっちに向けて。

She pointed out a few mistakes.
彼女はミスをいくつか指摘した。

3 Let's stop at this point and take a break.
ここで一息入れましょう。

It was the high point of his career.
それは、彼の仕事が絶好調の時期でした。

It was here at this point that the Battle of Sekigahara took place.
関ヶ原の合戦があったのは、まさにこの場所でした。

P

Draw a line through these points.
これらの点を結ぶ線を引いてください。

4 What's the point in that?
その目的は何ですか/何のためですか？

There's no point in trying to have a discussion with them.
彼らと話し合おうとしてもむだだ。

5 get [miss] the point 要点をつかむ [外す]

Your point is well taken.
あなたの考えは十分に伝わっている。

The point I am trying to make is that we mustn't be dogmatic.
私が言おうとしているのは、独断に陥ってはならないということです。

That's not the point—I told you not to tell anyone.
それは関係ない——誰にもしゃべらないでと言ったんです。

That's a good point and one that deserves consideration.
それは大事な点で、一考の価値があります。

6 I can agree with him only up to a point.
彼には、ある程度までしか同意できない。

7 the point of no return 引き返せない段階

a point of critical mass 臨界点

8 ten points against eight 10対8

How many points do you have?
何点取ってる？

9 Point Barrow, Alaska アラスカのバロウ岬

10 Pi is 3.14.
円周率は3．14である。

beside the point (irrelevant) 見当違いで, 関係ない, (not important) 重要ではない, どうでもいい

The question of whether he wants to go or not is beside the point.
あの人が行きたいかどうかなんて、どうでもいいことだ。

get to the point 核心に触れる, 要点を言う

Please get to the point!
要点を言ってください！

make a point of doing 必ず…することにしている, …するようにする

He made a point of arriving early.
彼は早めに到着するようにした。

make one's point 主張を通す, 言いたいことを言う

OK, OK! You've made your point.
わかった、わかった。もう言いたいことはわかったよ。

on/at the point of doing まさに…しようとして, …するところで

I was just on the point of leaving.
ちょうど今、帰ろうかと思っていたところです。

Mother was on the point of calling the police when my sister finally came home.
お母さんが警察に電話しようとしていたところに、お姉ちゃんが帰って来た。

point of view 立場

Let's look at this from their point of view.
彼らの立場に立って、これを見てみよう。

point-blank *adj.* 直射の, 至近距離からの; (direct and blunt) あけすけな *adv.* (at close range) 至近距離から; (directly) あけすけに, 単刀直入に

at point-blank range 至近距離で

She asked point-blank if I was interested in the job.
私がその仕事に興味があるかどうか、

彼女は単刀直入に聞いてきた。

pointed ***adj.*** (sharp) とがった, (of remark: too direct) 当てつけの

pointer ***n.*** (advice) 助言, 指針, (hint) ヒント; (needle on a dial) 針; (hunting dog) ポインター

Did he give you any pointers?
彼は何か助言してくれた？

pointless ***adj.*** (senseless) 無意味な

poise ***n.*** (calm) 落ち着き, 平静

poised ***adj.*** (**be poised to do**) …する態勢にある, …しようと構えている

poison ***n.*** (substance) 毒

v. (put poison in) (…に) 毒を盛る, (murder with poison) 毒殺する

a deadly poison 猛毒

The fish were poisoned by pollution.
汚染によって、魚は死んだ。

poisonous ***adj.*** 有毒な

a poisonous snake 毒蛇

poke ***v.*** (prod) 突っつく, (protrude) 突き出す

He poked me in the back.
((*masculine*)) あいつは僕の背中を突っついた。

A man poked his head out the window.
男が窓から頭を突き出した。

poke fun at からかう

poker[1] ***n.*** (hearth tool) 火かき棒

poker[2] ***n.*** (card game) ポーカー

polar ***adj.*** 極地の, (of the North/South Pole) 北極の/南極の; (**polar opposite**) 正反対の

pole ***n.*** (length of wood) 棒, さお

a bamboo pole 竹ざお

polecat ***n.*** (weasel-like animal) ケナガイタチ [→ SKUNK]

polemic ***n.*** (attack) 批判, (rebuttal) 反論, (**polemics**) 論争術

pole vault ***n.*** 棒高跳び

v. (**pole-vault**) 棒高跳びをする

police ***n.*** 警察

v. (keep order in) 取り締まる, (…の) 治安を維持する

Are you going to call the police?
警察を呼ぶつもりですか？

the secret police 秘密警察

It's difficult to police this area.
この地域の治安を維持するのは難しい。

♦**police officer** ***n.*** 警官, 巡査, ((*informal*)) お巡りさん

police station ***n.*** 警察署

policy[1] ***n.*** 方針, (political measure) 政策, (countermeasure) 対策; (way of doing sth) やり方, ポリシー

Government policy seems to change by the day.
政府の方針は毎日のように変わっているようだ。

The schools need to develop a policy to combat bullying.
学校は、いじめと闘うための対策を立てる必要がある。

It's not his policy to interfere in other people's business.
他人のことに首を突っ込むのは、彼のやり方ではない。

policy[2] ***n.*** (insurance document) 保険証書

polio, poliomyelitis ***n.*** ポリオ, 小児麻痺

polish ***v.*** (shoes, surface, skill) 磨く, (fingernails) (…に) マニキュアを塗る, (writing) 推こうする, (...に) 磨きをかける

n. (substance) つや出し, (sheen) つや, 光沢, (refinement, style) 洗練

You've forgotten to polish your shoes.
靴を磨くのを忘れてますよ。

polish one's writing
文章を推こうする [に磨きをかける]

♦ **polished** *adj.* (refined) 洗練された

polished writing 洗練された文章

polite *adj.* 丁寧な, (good-mannered) 礼儀正しい, (of child's behavior) (お)行儀がいい

a polite expression 丁寧な表現

He's always so polite.
彼はいつでも礼儀正しい。

It's only polite to ask permission first.
先に許可をもらうのが礼儀というものだ。

♦ **politeness** *n.* 礼儀正しさ, 丁寧さ

politely *adv.* 礼儀正しく,丁寧に

to put it politely 丁寧に言えば

political *adj.* 政治の, 政治的な, (of person: active/interested in politics) 政治に関心のある, 政治的な

politically *adv.* 政治的に

a politically motivated action
政治的動機に基づいた行動

politician *n.* 政治家

politics *n.* (statecraft) 政治, (subject of study) 政治学, (world of politics) 政界, (power dynamics within an organization) 駆け引き, 策略

local politics 地方政治

He studied politics at Princeton.
彼はプリンストン大学で政治学を学んだ。

"Don't go into politics"—that was my father's advice to me.
「政界には入るな」──というのが父の忠告だった。

He was fired because of politics, not because of lack of competence.
あの人は能力不足だからではなく、策略によって辞めさせられた。

polka dot *n.* 水玉模様

poll *n.* (voting) 投票, (votes cast) 投票数, (**the polls**: voting place) 投票所; (opinion poll) 世論調査

v. (receive: votes) (票数を) 得る, (survey for opinions) (...の) 世論調査をする

Who polled the most votes?
得票数が一番多かったのは誰ですか?

pollen *n.* 花粉 [NOTE: In Japan, an abundance of pollen in the air each spring causes hay fever 花粉症 among a considerable number of people, especially in big cities.]

The pollen in the air is exceptionally bad this year.
空中に飛散する花粉が、今年は特にひどい。

♦ **pollen count** *n.* 花粉数

pollute *v.* 汚染する, 汚す

pollution *n.* 汚染, (damage caused by pollution) 公害

pollution of the atmosphere 大気汚染

pollution disease 公害病

Pollution damaged the habitat of many wild birds.
公害が、たくさんの野鳥の生息地を破壊した。

polo *n.* ポロ, (water polo) 水球, ウォーターポロ

polyester ***n.*** ポリエステル

polygamy ***n.*** 一夫多妻制

polygon ***n.*** 多角形

polymer ***n.*** ポリマー, 重合体

pomegranate ***n.*** ザクロ

pompous ***adj.*** きざな, もったいぶった

poncho ***n.*** ポンチョ

pond ***n.*** 池

ponder ***v.*** じっくり考える, 熟考する

pony ***n.*** ポニー, 小型の馬

ponytail ***n.*** ポニーテール

put one's hair in a ponytail
髪をポニーテールにする

poodle ***n.*** プードル

pool¹ ***n.*** (puddle) 水たまり, (swimming pool) プール

The rain had left large pools of water.
雨が上がると、大きな水たまりができていた。

The hotel has a pool.
ホテルにはプールがあります。

pool² ***n.*** (joint investment) 共同出資, (in poker) 総賭け金; (billiards) プール

♦**pool table** ***n.*** 玉突き台

poor ***adj.***

1 HAVING LITTLE MONEY: 貧しい, 貧乏な, 貧困な

2 EXPRESSING SYMPATHY: かわいそうな, (お)気の毒な, 哀れな

3 NO GOOD: よくない, 悪い, ひどい, (of goods) 粗末な, (of skill) 下手な

4 INSUFFICIENT: 不十分な, 乏しい

1 He comes from a poor background.
彼は貧しい生い立ちです。

They're very poor.
彼らは、とても貧乏です。

2 Poor fellow. He has no money.
かわいそうに。あの人、お金がないんだ。

Her poor mother died in a car accident.
彼女のお母さんは、お気の毒に交通事故で亡くなりました。

3 The results were poor.
結果はひどいもんだった。

The quality was very poor, so I took it back to the shop.
質が非常に悪かったので、店に返品した。

That's a poor excuse.
下手な言い訳だ。

4 a country poor in oil resources
石油資源に乏しい国

poorly ***adv.*** (badly) まずく, ひどく

He did very poorly on the exam.
彼はテストでしくじった。

pop¹ ***n.*** (sound) ポンという音; (soda pop) サイダー

v. (balloon) ポンと破裂させる, (cork) ポンと抜く; (make a popping sound) ポンと鳴る, (of ears) ツーンとなる, 痛くなる

Pop went the champagne.
シャンパンをあけるとポンと音が鳴った。

My ears popped as the plane rose.
飛行機が上昇する時、耳がツーンとなった。

pop into one's head (of idea) ふっと頭に浮かぶ

pop up (appear suddenly) ひょいと現れる, (in conversation) ポンと出る

pop² ***n.*** (music) ポップス

adj. (of the masses) 大衆の, (for the

P

masses) 大衆向きの [→ POPULAR]

♦**pop art** *n.* ポップアート

popcorn *n.* ポップコーン

pope *n.* ローマ法王, (**Pope**: title) 教皇

poplar *n.* ポプラ

poppa → PAPA

poppy *n.* ケシ, ポピー

populace *n.* (of country) 大衆, (of area) 住民

popular *adj.* (well liked) 人気のある, (fashionable) はやっている, 流行の, (for the masses) 大衆向きの

It's a popular bar with young people.
若い人たちの間で人気のバーだよ。

a popular TV show
人気のあるテレビ番組

He's popular with all the girls at school.
彼は学校で女の子にすごくもてる。

popularity *n.* 人気

popularize *v.* 普及させる, 大衆化する

popularly *adv.* 一般に, 広く

populate *v.* (inhabit) (…に) 住む, (colonize) (…に) 移住する

population *n.* 人口, (inhabitants) 住民

population growth 人口増加

porcelain *n.* 磁器

porch *n.* (space at the entrance to a house) 玄関, ポーチ, (veranda) ベランダ

porcupine *n.* ヤマアラシ

pore *n.* (in skin) 毛穴

pork *n.* 豚肉

pornography *n.* ポルノ

porous *adj.* (having many small holes) 穴だらけの, 多孔性の, (= through which air/water can pass) 通気/通水性のある

porpoise *n.* ネズミイルカ

porridge *n.* オートミール

port[1] *n.* (harbor) 港, (harbor town) 港町

The ship entered port without any difficulty.
船は難なく入港した。

port[2] *n.* (left side of a ship) 左舷

port[3] *n.* (type of wine) ポートワイン

portable *adj.* 携帯用の, ポータブルの

portend *v.* (…の) 前兆になる

porter *n.* (at hotel) ボーイ(さん), ポーター, (at station) 赤帽

I need a porter to help me with this luggage. Porter!
この荷物を運ぶのに、ボーイの手が要るな。ボーイさん！

portfolio *n.* (artist's) 作品集, (photographer's) 写真集; (of stocks) 有価証券; (minister's area of responsibility) 大臣の職務

portion *n.* (one part of sth) 部分, 一部, (amount of food for one person) 1人前, (a share) 分け前, 割り当て

v. (**portion out**) 分配する, (work) 振り分ける

the front portion 前の部分

He accepted a portion of the blame.
彼は責任を一部認めた。

His land was divided into three portions.
彼の土地は3分割された。

She was not entitled to a portion of the profits.
彼女には利益の分配を受ける権利がなかった。

portrait *n.* (painting) 肖像画, ポートレート, (description) 描写

portray *v.* (paint) 描く, (describe) 描く, 表現する

The media portrayed him as an evil genius.
マスコミは彼を「悪の天才」と表現した。

portrayal *n.* 描写

Portugal *n.* ポルトガル, ((*in abbr.*)) 葡

pose *v.* (for photo) ポーズをとる, (pose as: pretend to be) (…の) ふりをする, (try to look good) 気取る, 格好をつける

n. ポーズ

We posed for photographs.
写真撮影のため、ポーズをとった。

The model posed for the painter.
モデルは画家のためにポーズをとった。

The man was posing as a priest.
その男は聖職者のふりをしていた。

She was photographed in a number of poses.
彼女はいくつかのポーズで写真を撮られた。

pose a question 質問をする

poser *n.* 気取り屋

posh *adj.* (stylish) しゃれた, (expensive-looking) 豪華な

position

1 *n.* LOCATION: 位置, 場所, (position of readiness) 定位置, 所定の位置

2 *n.* POSTURE OF THE BODY: 姿勢, (for photo opportunity: pose) ポーズ

3 *n.* JOB: 職, ポスト, (job vacancy) 勤め口

4 *n.* RELATIVE RANK: 地位, ポジション

5 *n.* POINT OF VIEW: 意見, ((*formal*)) 見解

6 *n.* SITUATION: (of person) 立場, (of company, organization) 状態, 状況

7 *n.* IN SPORT: (position on team) ポジション, (in race) 順位, -位

8 *v.* PLACE: 置く

1 It won't work if it's not in the right position.
正しい位置に置かないと動きません。

He was in a perfect position to score a goal.
彼はゴールを決めるのに最適の位置にいた。

The steel beam was lifted into position.
鉄骨が所定の位置に引き上げられた。

The riot police are in position.
機動隊が所定の位置についている。

2 That's not a good position for your back.
その姿勢は背中によくないよ。

Could you hold that position for a moment?
もうちょっとそのポーズでいてくれますか?

3 She has an important position in the company.
彼女は会社の要職にあります。

What's Mr. Takada's position?
高田さんのポストは何ですか?

4 Japan's position as a major economic power
経済大国としての日本の地位

5 What's your position on abortion?
中絶について、どういうご意見ですか?

It seems the company's position has changed once again.
会社の見解がまたしても変わったようだ。

6 If I had been in your position, I would have done the same thing.
私があなたの立場だったとしても、同じことをしたでしょう。

7 What position do you play?
ポジションはどこですか？

He moved into a scoring position.
彼はスコアリング・ポジションに進んだ。

8 We positioned it in the corner.
隅に置きました。

positive *adj.* (of attitude) 積極的な, (of response) 肯定的な; (of electric charge) 陽の, (of medical test) 陽性の

n. (photograph) ポジ; (positive number) 正の数

She has a positive attitude toward work.
彼女は仕事に対して積極的です。

He tested HIV positive.
彼はＨＩＶ検査で陽性だった。

be positive about/that... ...に自信がある/...と確信している

I think I locked the door, but I'm not positive.
ドアにかぎをかけたと思うけど、自信がない。

positively *adv.* (in a positive manner) 肯定的に, 前向きに, (beyond doubt) 確かに

possess *v.* 持つ, 持っている, ((*formal*)) 所有する/している [→ OWN]

possession *n.* (thing owned) 持ち物, 所持品, (ownership) 所有, 保有, (**possessions**: wealth) 財産

Keep your possessions with you at all times.
所持品は常に持ち歩いてください。

come into one's possession 手に入れる

possessive *adj.* (of person) 所有欲の強い, 独占欲の強い

n. (grammatical case) 所有格

♦**possessive pronoun** *n.* 所有代名詞

possibility *n.* 可能性

There's a good possibility that...
...という可能性が高い

possible *adj.* (reasonable) 可能な, できる, ありうる

It just isn't possible.
とにかく不可能 [無理] だ。

It's a possible scenario.
その線は、ありうるね。

Is it possible that he could have written such a good paper?
彼に、こんないいレポートが書けただろうか？

as ... as possible できるだけ...

Do it as quickly as possible.
できるだけ早くやって。

would it be possible to...? ...は可能でしょうか, ...はできますか

Would it be possible to be paid in advance?
前払いは可能でしょうか？

possibly *adv.* ひょっとすると, ことによると, ...かもしれない, (**not possibly**) とうてい...ない, とても...ない

I can't possibly go.
とても行けません。

possum *n.* フクロネズミ

play possum (pretend to be asleep) 眠ったふりをする

post[1] *n.* (postal service) 郵便, (delivery of mail) 郵便配達, (sending in the mail) 郵送

v. (send) 出す, 送る, 郵送する, (put in a mailbox) 投函する, (pin up on a bulletin board, the Internet) 載せる

The post is late [early].
郵便の配達が遅い [早い]。

How long will it take if I send it by post?
郵送にしたら、どのくらい時間がかかりますか？

I still haven't posted the letter.
まだ手紙を投函してない。

post² ***n.*** (pole, pillar) 柱, 支柱 [→ POLE]

post³ ***n.*** (job) 職, ポスト, 地位

v. 配置する, 派遣する

post- ***pref.*** (after) 後の, (beyond) …以後の

postage ***n.*** (shipping fee) 郵便料金, 郵送料, 送料

postal ***adj.*** (of post office) 郵便の, 郵送の

a postal worker 郵便局員

♦**postal code** ***n.*** 郵便番号

postbox ***n.*** (郵便)ポスト

postcard ***n.*** 葉書

postdate ***v.*** (come after) (…の) 後にくる; (put later date on) (…の) 日付を遅らせる

poster ***n.*** ポスター

posterity ***n.*** 後世

postgraduate ***n.*** 大学院生

adj. 大学院の

posthumous ***adj.*** 死後の

postman, -woman ***n.*** 郵便配達人, ((*informal*)) 郵便屋(さん)

postmark ***n.*** 消印

v. (…に) 消印を押す

postmaster ***n.*** 郵便局長

postmortem ***n.*** 検死

adj. (of examination) 検死の; (occurring after death) 死後の

post office ***n.*** 郵便局

postpone ***v.*** 延期する, 延ばす, 後回しにする

What! Has the meeting been postponed again?
えっ? また会議が延期になったんですか?

The match was postponed because of bad weather.
試合は悪天候のために延期された。

postscript ***n.*** (in letter) 追伸, (in book, journal) あとがき, 後記

posture ***n.*** 姿勢

postwar ***adj.*** 戦後の

the postwar period 戦後

posy ***n.*** (bouquet) 花束, (single flower) 花

pot ***n.*** (cooking pot) なべ [→ picture of KITCHEN], (teapot) ティーポット, (Japanese teapot) 急須, (flower pot) 植木鉢, (earthenware pot) つぼ

v. (plant in a pot) 鉢に植える

potash ***n.*** (potassium carbonate) カリ, (potassium hydroxide) 水酸化カリウム

potassium ***n.*** カリウム

potato ***n.*** ジャガイモ, ポテト [NOTE: sweet potato サツマイモ, Japanese yam とろろ芋, 長芋, grated Japanese yam とろろ, taro 里芋, roasted/baked sweet potato 焼き芋]

mashed potatoes マッシュポテト

potato chips ***n.*** ポテトチップ(ス)

potent ***adj.*** (strong) 強い, (effective) 強力な, 効き目がある

Information is a potent weapon in the war against terrorism.
テロとの戦いには、情報が強力な武器となる。

This medicine is extremely potent.
この薬はすごく効き目がある。

potential *adj.* 可能性のある, 潜在的な
n. 可能性, 潜在力, (of person) 素質
a potential problem 潜在的な問題
This land has a lot of potential for development.
この土地は開発の可能性が大いにある。
Jim has potential, but he's lazy.
ジムは素質はあるけど、怠け者なんだよ。

♦**potential form** *n.* (verb form) 可能形

potentially *adv.* (possibly) もしかすると

potion *n.* 薬
a love potion 媚薬

potter *n.* 陶芸家, 陶工

pottery *n.* (activity) 陶芸, (ware) 陶器

pouch *n.* (small bag) ポーチ, 小袋; (mammal's) 袋, のう, (kangaroo's) 育児のう

poultry *n.* 飼い鳥, (bird meat) 鳥肉

pounce *v.* (**pounce on**) 襲う, …に飛びかかる

pound[1] *n.* (unit of money/weight) ポンド

pound[2] *v.* (beat) たたく, 打つ, (crush) すりつぶす; (of heart: beat fast) どきどきする, (of head due to headache) がんがんする [→ HEADACHE]

pound[3] *n.* (place for dogs) おり

pour *v.* (liquid into cup) つぐ, 注ぐ, (sauce etc. on/over food) かける; (**pour into**: crowd) …にどっと押し寄せる, (**pour out of**: leave) …からどっと出て来る, (of rain) 激しく降る, どしゃ降りだ
pour beer into a glass
ビールをグラスにつぐ
Pour it down the drain.
下水に流して。
Commuters poured out of the station.
通勤客が駅からどっと出て来た。
It's pouring outside.
外はどしゃ降りだ。

pour oneself/sb a drink 自分で/人に飲み物をつぐ

poverty *n.* 貧乏, 貧困, 貧しさ

♦**poverty-stricken** *adj.* 極貧の, とても貧しい

powder *n.* (substance) 粉, 粉末, (for face) おしろい, パウダー
v. (apply powder to: face) (…に) おしろいをつける; (in cooking: cover with powder) (…に) 粉を振り掛ける
a fine powder 細かい粉末
She powdered her face.
彼女は顔におしろいをつけた。

♦**powdered milk** *n.* 粉ミルク

power
1 *n.* STRENGTH: 力, (physical strength) 体力, (ability) 能力, (willpower) 精神力, (authority) 権力, 権限, (military power) 軍事力
2 *n.* ENERGY: (mechanical power) 動力, パワー, (electric power) 電力, (electricity) 電気
3 *n.* CONTROL: 政権, 支配権
4 *v.* GIVE MECHANICAL POWER TO: (**be powered by**) …で動く
5 *n.* COUNTRY: 強国, 大国
6 *n.* EXPONENT: 累乗, -乗
7 *n.* OF LENS: 倍率

1 the power to influence people
人への影響力

supernatural powers 超能力

They don't have the military power to challenge the government.
彼らには、政府に立ち向かうだけの軍事力はない。

2 solar power 太陽熱 [エネルギー]

The power went out [came on] almost an hour ago.
1時間前に停電した [電気が復旧した]。

a power outage 停電

3 Which party is in power?
どの党が政権を握っているんですか？

a power struggle 権力闘争 [勢力争い]

4 This car is powered by the sun.
この車は太陽エネルギーで動く。

5 a nuclear power 核保有国

6 six to the tenth power 6の10乗

raise to the third power 3乗する

♦**power line** *n.* 送電線

power plant/station *n.* 発電所

KANJI BRIDGE

力 ON: りょく, りき KUN: ちから | FORCE, POWER, ENERGY

electric power	電力
horsepower	馬力
nuclear power/energy	原子力
physical strength	体力
power of imagination	想像力
powers of concentration	集中力
power to influence	影響力
vitality, energy	活力
waterpower	水力
wind power	風力

powerful *adj.* (strong) 力強い, 強力な, (influential) 影響力のある, 権力のある

powerless *adj.* 無力な, (**be powerless to do**) ...する力はない

be powerless to stop someone from...
(人が)...するのをやめさせる力はない

practical *adj.* (realistic) 現実的な, 実際的な, (useful) 実用的な

Such a plan is not practical.
そういう計画は現実的ではない。

There's no substitute for practical experience.
実際の経験に勝るものはない。

practically *adv.* (almost) ほとんど, ほぼ

practice

1 *n.* REPEATED ACTION: (exercise) 練習, (お)けいこ [NOTE: (お)けいこ is usually used in reference to traditional arts]; (custom, habit) 習慣

2 *v.* DO/TRAIN TO GET BETTER (AT): 練習する, (...の)けいこをする

3 *v.* HAVE AS A PROFESSION: (**practice law/medicine**) 弁護士/医者をしている

1 Practice makes perfect.
習うより慣れろ。

There's practice tonight at the gym.
今夜ジムで練習がある。

I have dance practice on that day.
その日はダンスの練習がある。

It's good to make a practice of taking notes.
ノートを取る習慣をつけるといい。

2 We practiced aerobics for an hour.
1時間エアロビクスをしました。

Don't disturb him while he's practicing.
練習している間は、あの人のじゃまをしないで。

P

You should practice the piano more.
ピアノのけいこを、もっとやらないとだめだよ。

3 He practices law.
その人は弁護士をしています。

She practices medicine at the local hospital.
彼女は近くの病院で医者をしている。

in practice 実際には

out of practice 練習不足で

put into practice 実行する

practitioner *n.* 開業者

a general practitioner 開業医

a legal practitioner 弁護士

KANJI BRIDGE

士,師 ON: し KUN: — | PRACTITIONER, -ER

accountant	会計士
attorney	弁護士
barber	理容師
dietician	栄養士
engineer	技師
fortune teller	占い師
magician	手品師
maintenance worker	整備士
masseur/masseuse	マッサージ師
missionary	宣教師
pastor	牧師
pilot	操縦士
samurai	武士
sumo wrestler	力士
swindler	詐欺師
teacher	教師
tuner (of instruments)	調律師

pragmatic *adj.* (practical) 実際的な

a pragmatic approach
実際的なアプローチ

pragmatism *n.* (philosophy) 実用主義

pragmatist *n.* 実用主義者

prairie *n.* 大草原

praise *v.* ほめる, 賞賛する
n. 賞賛

He was praised for his hard work.
彼は、よくがんばったのでほめられた。

She deserves praise for what she did.
彼女のやったことは、賞賛に値する。

praise to the skies 絶賛する

pram *n.* 乳母車

prattle *v.* ぺちゃくちゃしゃべる

prawn *n.* エビ, 海老, (tiger prawn) 車海老

pray *v.* 祈る, お祈りをする, 祈願する, (observe a minute's silence) 黙とうする

We prayed for his safe return.
彼が無事に戻ってくることを祈りました。

prayer *n.* (act of praying) (お)祈り, (words of prayer) 祈りの言葉

not a prayer (no chance at all) 見込みは全くない

praying mantis *n.* カマキリ

pre- *pref.* (before) …前の, …以前の, (in advance) 前もって…

preach *v.* (lecture) (お)説教する, (the gospel) 伝道する

Don't preach to me!
お説教はたくさんだ!

prearrange *v.* 前もって取り決める

♦**prearranged** *adj.* 事前に取り決められた, 前もって決めた

a prearranged meeting spot

前もって決めていた待ち合わせ場所

prearrangement *n.* 事前の打ち合わせ

precarious *adj.* (uncertain) 不安定な, (risky) 危険な

precaution *n.* (preventative measures) 予防策, 用心

It's just a precaution.
予防策です/用心のためです。

precede *v.* (come before) (…の)前に来る, (…に)先行する

precedence *n.* (importance) 重要, (order) 優先

take precedence over …に優先する, …より重要だ

precedent *n.* 前例, 先例

a dangerous precedent 危険な前例

set a precedent 前例をつくる

precinct *n.* (district) 区域, (electoral precinct) 選挙区

precious *adj.* (valuable) 貴重な, 高価な, (important) 大切な, 大事な

a precious brooch 高価なブローチ

Life is the most precious thing of all.
命は何よりも大切です。

precipitate *v.* (bring on) 引き起こす, (quicken) 早める

precise *adj.* 正確な, 的確な

Please tell me the precise details.
詳細を正確に教えてください。

The precise time was not known.
正確な時間はわからなかった。

At that precise moment, the door opened.
まさにその時、ドアがあいた。

precisely *adv.* (exactly) 正確に, (in reference to time) ぴったりに, きっかりに; ("exactly as you say") そのとおり

precisely because …からこそ

precision *n.* (exactness) 正確さ, 精密, (of work) ち密

precocious *adj.* ませた, 早熟な, おとなびた

preconceived *adj.* 予想していた

a preconceived idea/notion 先入観

preconception *n.* 先入観

precondition *n.* 必要条件

precursor *n.* (forerunner) 先駆者; (sign) 前兆

predator *n.* 捕食動物

predecessor *n.* 前任者, (previous person/thing) 以前の人/もの

predetermined *adj.* 前もって決めた, 事前に定めた

Do you think our lives are predetermined?
私たちの人生は、あらかじめ決まっていると思いますか？

predicament *n.* 苦境, 困難な状態

get into a predicament 苦境に陥る

predicate *n.* (of sentence) 述部, 述語
v. (**be predicated on**) …に基づいている

predicative *adj.* 叙述的な

predict *v.* 予言する, 予測する

Nobody could have predicted that this would happen.
こんなことが起こるとは、誰にも予測できなかった。

predictable *adj.* 予測できる, (of person, thing) ありきたりの, 目新しさのない

prediction *n.* 予言

predispose *v.* (**be predisposed to/to-**

ward) …に傾く

♦**predisposition** ***n.*** 傾向

predominant ***adj.*** (noticeable) 特に目立つ, (dominant) 支配的な

♦**predominantly** ***adv.*** (mainly) 主に

predominate ***v.*** (prevail) 勝る, 優位に立つ

preelection ***n.*** 予選

preemptive ***adj.*** (of war) 先制の

a preemptive strike 先制攻撃

prefabricated ***adj.*** (of building) プレハブ式で建てた

preface ***n.*** はしがき, 前書き, ((*formal*)) 序文

prefecture ***n.*** -県, -府

Chiba Prefecture 千葉県

prefer ***v.*** (prefer A to B) (BよりAのほうが) 好きだ, (**prefer doing/to do**) (どちらかと言えば) …したい

I prefer staying at home to going out.
外出するより家にいるほうが好きです。

Which do you prefer, scotch or brandy?
スコッチとブランデーのどちらがいいですか？

I prefer not to speak to him.
あの人とは話したくない。

I would prefer it if you did not do that.
そうしないでいただきたいのですが。

preferable ***adj.*** (better) (…のほうが) いい, (desirable) 望ましい, (better but not great) (…のほうが) ましだ

That would be preferable.
それのほうがいい。

preferably ***adv.*** できれば

preference ***n.*** 好み

give preference to 優先的に扱う

preferential ***adj.*** 優先の, 特別の

prefix ***n.*** (of word) 接頭辞

pregnancy ***n.*** (being pregnant) 妊娠, (period of) 妊娠期間

♦**pregnancy test** ***n.*** 妊娠検査

pregnant ***adj.*** 妊娠中, 妊娠している

preheat ***v.*** 前もって温めておく

prehistoric ***adj.*** 有史以前の

prehistory ***n.*** 先史時代

prejudge ***v.*** 前もって判断する

prejudice ***n.*** (negative dislike) 偏見, (bias) 先入観

racial prejudice 人種的偏見

He seems to have a prejudice against foreigners.
彼は外国人に偏見をもっているようだ。

prejudiced ***adj.*** 偏見のある

a prejudiced view 偏見

preliminary ***adj.*** (initial) 予備の, (of remarks) 前置きの

n. (**the preliminaries**: qualifying games) 予選

a preliminary examination [investigation, negotiation]
予備テスト [調査, 折衝]

prelude ***n.*** (song) 前奏曲, プレリュード; (forerunner) 前触れ, 前兆

premarital ***adj.*** 結婚前の

premarital sex 婚前交渉

premature ***adj.*** (of baby) 早産の, (too early) 早すぎる

The baby was born premature.
その赤ちゃんは早産だった。

premier ***adj.*** (most) 最高の

n. (prime minister) 総理大臣, 首相

premiere *n.* (film) 封切り, (play) 初演

v. (of film/play) 初公開/初演される

premise *n.* 前提; (**premises**) 敷地, 構内, (=land and buildings) 土地建物

v. (assume) 前提とする

premium *n.* (extra payment) 割増金, (money paid to an insurance company) 保険料

adj. (higher in price) 高価な, (of higher quality) 高級な

at a premium (difficult to get) なかなか手に入らない, 貴重だ, (at a higher price than usual) 額面以上で, プレミアム付きで

premonition *n.* 予感, (omen) 前兆

have a premonition 予感がする

prenatal *adj.* 出産前の

prenatal diagnosis 出生前診断

preoccupation *n.* 没頭, 夢中

preoccupy *v.* (**be preoccupied with**) …のことで頭がいっぱいだ, …のことばかり考えている

preparation *n.* (act of preparing) 準備, (**preparations**) 手はず, 段取り

prepare *v.* (make ready) 準備する, 用意する, (food) (…の) 支度をする, (for class) 予習する, (**prepare oneself**) (= for bad news) 心構えをする, (= for the worst) 覚悟する

We've prepared your room.
お部屋の用意ができました。

Have you prepared dinner yet?
もう、晩ご飯の支度をした？

You'd better sit down and prepare yourself for a shock.
腰を下ろして、心の準備をして。

Export companies have to prepare themselves for a steep downturn in orders.
輸出会社は、注文の激減を覚悟しなければならない。

prepared *adj.* (of thing) 準備された, 用意された, (made in advance) 事前に作られた, (of person) 準備ができている, (**be prepared for / to do**) …の/…する用意ができている, (=be resolved to do) …する覚悟をする

It was a prepared speech.
あらかじめ準備されたスピーチだった。

prepay *v.* 前払いする

♦**prepaid phone card** *n.* テレホンカード, ((*informal*)) テレカ

preposition *n.* 前置詞

preposterous *adj.* (ridiculous) ばかげた

prerecorded *adj.* (audio) 前もって録音した, (TV program) 事前に収録した

prerequisite *n.* 必要条件

prerogative *n.* 特権, 特典

preschool *n.* (nursery school) 保育園

prescribe *v.* (medicine, treatment) 処方する

prescription *n.* (order for medicine) 処方せん, (prescribed medicine) 処方薬

presence *n.* (attendance) 出席, (existence) 存在

present[1]

1 *adj.* OF PERSON: (**be present**: be in attendance) いる, 出席している

2 *n.* NOW: (**the present**) 今, 現在

3 *adj.* CURRENT: 今の, 現在の

4 ***adj.*** **OF SUBSTANCE:** (**be present**: exist) 存在する, ある

5 ***n.*** **GRAMMATICAL:** (the present tense) 現在時制, (verb form) 現在形

1 Most of the students were present.
生徒の大半は出席していた。

He was present at the meeting.
彼は会議に出席していました。

2 the past, present, and future
過去、現在、そして未来

We live in the present.
私たちは今を生きている。

3 The present system is too rigid.
今の制度は厳しすぎる。

The present government is weak and ineffective.
現政府は、弱くて無能だ。

4 Titanium is present in ores.
チタンは鉱石中にある。

Alcohol was present in his blood.
アルコールが彼の血液中に含まれていた。

5 a verb in the present 現在形の動詞

at present 現在, 今(は)

At present, there aren't enough nurses.
現在、看護師が不足しています。

for the present 当面(は), さしあたり

For the present, we will have to make do with what we have.
当面は、あるもので何とかするしかないだろう。

present[2]

1 ***n.*** **GIFT:** プレゼント, 贈り物

2 ***v.*** **GIVE:** (present A with B) (AにBを) 贈る, プレゼントする, ((*polite/humble*)) 差し上げる, ((*formal*)) 贈呈する, (bestow) 授与する

3 ***v.*** **GIVE RISE TO:** 引き起こす, もたらす, 生じさせる

4 ***v.*** **SUBMIT:** (report) 差し出す, 提出する, (vision, ID card) 提示する, 示す

5 ***v.*** **IDEA/INFORMATION:** (explain) 説明する, (present a paper at a conference) 発表する

6 ***v.*** **BEFORE AN AUDIENCE:** (present a play) 上演する

7 ***v.*** **ONESELF:** (put in an appearance) 出る, 出席する, (at court) 出廷する; (**present oneself as**: in a particular light) 自分を…のように見せる

8 ***v.*** **ITSELF:** 到来する, (of opportunity) 訪れる, (of solution: come to mind) 心に浮かぶ

1 Did you get any presents?
何かプレゼントはもらった？

What are you going to buy him as a present?
彼にどんなプレゼントを買うんですか？

Here's a small present for you.
つまらないものですが、どうぞ。

2 He was presented with a prize.
彼に賞が贈られた。

They presented him with a medal for bravery.
彼の勇敢さをたたえて、勲章が授与された。

3 This plan for a new road presents a number of problems.
この新道路の建設計画は、いくつもの問題を引き起こしています。

4 I'd like to present an alternative proposal.
代案を示したいのですが。

5 Dr. Suzuki will present a paper at the conference.
鈴木教授は、会議で論文を発表する予定です。

6 The play is being presented by the university.
そのお芝居は大学によって上演されている。

7 It all depends how you present yourself at the interview.
すべては面接でいかにアピールするかにかかっていますよ。

He presented himself as an honest person.
彼は自分を正直な人間のように見せた。

8 A good opportunity presented itself.
絶好の機会が訪れた。

presentation *n.* (talk) 発表, プレゼンテーション, (way of talking) 発表の仕方; (appearance) 見栄え, 体裁; (submission) 提出; (conferral) 贈呈, 授与

presently *adv.* (at present) 現在, 今(は); (soon) もうすぐ, まもなく

preservation *n.* 保存, (protection) 保護

preservation of the environment
環境保護

preservative *n.* 保存料, 防腐剤

preserve *v.* 保存する, (protect) 守る, 保護する, (maintain) 維持する

n. (nature preserve) 自然保護区; (**preserves**: fruit) 果物の砂糖煮, (jam) ジャム

presidency *n.* (of company) 社長の地位, (term of office of president of a country) 大統領の任期

president *n.* (of company) 社長, 会長, (of country) 大統領, (of university) 学長, 総長

presidential *adj.* 大統領の

a presidential election 大統領選挙

press

1 *v.* PUSH: (button) 押す, (press against) (…に) 押し付ける

2 *v.* PRESSURE: (**press into doing**) (…に) …するよう強制する/強要する, (**press for**) 強く要求する, 主張する

3 *n.* NEWSPAPERS/MEDIA: (**the press**) 報道機関, マスコミ, (=media employees) 報道陣, (media coverage) 批評, 論評

4 *v.* FLATTEN/CRUSH: (fruit) 絞る, ((*formal*)) 圧搾する, (garlic) つぶす

5 *v.* IRON: (…に) アイロンをかける

6 *n.* MACHINE: (for pressing fruit) -絞り機; (printing press) 印刷機

1 He pressed the button and waited.
彼はボタンを押して待った。

Don't press too hard. It might break.
あまり強く押さないで。壊れるかもしれないから。

I pressed myself against the warm sand.
私は熱い砂に体を押し付けた。

It was so crowded we were pressed up against each other.
混雑がひどくて、ぎゅうぎゅう詰めだった。

2 I was pressed into doing more overtime.
もっと残業するよう強要された。

The workers pressed for higher wages.
従業員は賃金引き上げを強く要求した。

The UN continued to press for a political solution.
国連は政治的解決を主張し続けた。

Don't press me on this point. I need time to think about it.

このことについて問い詰めないで。考える時間が欲しい。

3 The story was leaked to the press.
その話はマスコミに漏れた。

The press have arrived.
報道陣が到着しました。

Any press is good press.
どんな批評でもいい宣伝になる。

The play got good [bad] press.
その演劇は新聞、雑誌で好評だった[悪評を買った]。

4 Have you ever pressed grapes?
ブドウを絞ったことはありますか？

5 Did you press your pants?
ズボンにアイロンをかけた？

6 a cider press リンゴ絞り機

♦**press conference** *n.* 記者会見
hold a press conference
記者会見を開く

pressed *adj.* (of clothes) アイロンのかかった; (**be pressed for**: have no) (…が)ない

pressing *adj.* (urgent) 緊急の

pressure *n.* 圧力, (air pressure) 気圧; (coercion) 強制, (stress) プレッシャー
blood pressure 血圧

He did it, but only under pressure from his boss.
彼はやったけど、上司から圧力をかけられただけなんだ。

There's high pressure to the north of Japan.
日本の北は高気圧におおわれています。

be under pressure プレッシャーがかかっている, (**be under pressure to do**) …するよう迫られている

The editors were under serious pressure to finish the dictionary.
編集者は、辞書を完成させるよう厳しく迫られていた。

put pressure on …に圧力をかける, …にプレッシャーをかける

Don't you think you're putting too much pressure on him?
彼にプレッシャーをかけすぎているとは思わない？

pressure cooker *n.* 圧力がま

pressure group *n.* 圧力団体

prestige *n.* 威信, (reputation) 名声, (honor) 名誉

prestigious *adj.* (reputable) 名誉ある, 評判の高い, (of school) 名門の

presumably *adv.* おそらく…だろう, たぶん…だろう

Presumably he went straight home.
たぶん彼はまっすぐ家に帰ったでしょう。

presume *v.* (…と)思う, 推測する

I presume that is not what you mean.
それはあなたが言っている意味と違うでしょう。

presumption *n.* 推測, 推定

presumptuous *adj.* おこがましい, せんえつな

pretend *v.* (act as if) (…)ふりをする, (…ように)見せかける, 装う

He pretended to be working.
彼は仕事をしているふりをした。

It's no good pretending to be sorry.
申し訳なさそうなふりをしてもむだだよ。

pretense *n.* (act) 見せかけ, ふり, (excuse) 口実, 言い訳

under false pretenses 偽って, うそをついて

They obtained the money under false pretenses.
彼らは、うそをついて金を手に入れた。

pretension ***n.*** (conceit) うぬぼれ, (affectation) 気取り

pretentious ***adj.*** (of person) うぬぼれた, (of manner) もったいぶった

pretext ***n.*** 口実, 弁解

pretty ***adj.*** (beautiful) きれいな, (cute) かわいい

adv. (fairly) かなり, なかなか, 相当, すごく

She's pretty and intelligent.
あの人はかわいくて頭もいい。

The garden's very pretty.
とてもきれいなお庭ですね。

I thought the book was pretty good.
なかなかいい本だと思いました。

I think this is all pretty stupid, don't you?
こんなの、すごくばかげてると思わない？

prevail ***v.*** (win) 打ち勝つ; (be common) 広く行き渡っている, 広がっている

prevailing ***adj.*** (existing at a particular time) 広く行き渡っている, 一般的な

prevalence ***n.*** 普及, 流行

prevalent ***adj.*** 広く行き渡っている, 流行している

prevent ***v.*** (**prevent from doing**) (…が) …しないようにする, (**prevent from happening**) (…が) 起きないようにする, (disaster) 予防する [→ STOP]

They tried to prevent me from speaking.
彼らは、私がしゃべらないようにした。

I was prevented from entering the meeting.
会議に出席するのを妨害された。

We've tried to prevent this from happening again.
二度とこんなことが起きないよう、努めてきました。

preventative ***adj.*** 予防の

a preventative measure 予防策

prevention ***n.*** 予防, 防止

prevention of crime 犯罪防止

preview ***n.*** (of film) 試写, (trailer) 予告編

v. (…の) 試写を見る

previous ***adj.*** (earlier) 前の, 先の, 以前の

On a previous occasion, I seem to remember you said the exact opposite.
前は、全く反対のことを言ってたような気がするんだけど。

I spent the previous year studying Greek.
その前の年は、ギリシャ語を勉強していました。

All previous attempts have failed.
これまでの試みは、すべて失敗している。

previously ***adv.*** (formerly) 前に, 以前に, (in advance) 先に, あらかじめ

prewar ***adj.*** 戦前の

prey ***n.*** 獲物, えじき

prey on/upon (of animal) 捕って食べる, (of person) 食い物にする

price

1 ***n.*** COST: 値段, 価格

2 ***n.*** PENALTY: 代償, 代価

3 ***v.*** GIVE A PRICE TO: (…に) 値段をつける

4 ***v.*** OBSERVE AND COMPARE THE PRICES OF: (…の) 値段をあちこち調べる

1 What's the price?

値段はいくらですか？

The price of gasoline has risen.
石油の値段が上がっている。

The price of computers has fallen.
コンピューターの価格が下がっている。

The price hasn't changed much over the years.
値段は、ここ何年もの間ほとんど変わっていません。

a price list 値段表

a bargain [list] price 特価 [定価]

the market price 市価

the asking [buying] price
言い値 [買い値]

price increase [decrease]
値上げ [値下げ]

2 The price of progress may be the destruction of our environment.
発展の代償は、環境破壊なのかもしれません。

He paid a terrible price for his mistake.
彼は自分の犯したあやまちに、大きな代償を払った。

Prison was the price he paid for his dishonesty.
詐欺行為の償いとして、彼は刑務所行きとなった。

3 The painting will be priced at around ten million yen.
その絵は1千万円程度の値がつけられるだろう。

4 I priced computers carefully before deciding to buy this one.
このコンピューターを買う前に、値段をあちこちで調べて比較した。

at any price どんなことがあっても, ぜひとも

priceless ***adj.*** (can't buy with money) (お)金で買えない, (valuable) 非常に貴重な

prick ***v.*** ちくりと刺す

n. (thorn) とげ, (sharp pain) ちくちくする痛み, うずき

prickly ***adj.*** とげの多い, (of texture) ちくちくする

pride ***n.*** (satisfaction) 誇り, (self-respect) 自尊心, プライド, (arrogance) 横柄さ, 傲慢さ, 思い上がり

v. (**pride oneself on**) …に誇りをもつ

He looked with pride upon his work.
彼は自分の作品に誇りをもっていた。

How could you do such a thing? Don't you have any pride?
どうしてそんなことができるの？ あなたには、プライドというものがないの？

His pride wouldn't allow him to admit it.
彼の自尊心が、それを認めることを許さなかった。

He prides himself on his workmanship.
彼は自分の腕前に誇りをもっている。

pride and joy 自慢のたね

She's her mother's pride and joy.
彼女はお母さんの自慢のたねなんです。

priest ***n.*** 聖職者, (Catholic) 司祭, (Buddhist) 僧侶, ((*informal*)) (お)坊さん

priestess ***n.*** (of Shinto shrine) 巫女

priesthood ***n.*** 聖職

prim ***adj.*** 上品ぶった, (とり)すました

Ms. Watanabe is always so prim and proper.
渡辺さんはいつも、とりすましていて堅苦しい。

primal ***adj.*** (primeval) 原始の, (first) 最

初の

primarily ***adv.*** 第一に, 主に

primary ***adj.*** (leading) 第一の, (fundamental) 基本的な, (main) 主要な, 重要な; (of education) 初等の

n. (election) 予備選挙

Young people were the primary target of drug pushers.
若者は麻薬の売人の最大のターゲットだった。

One of the government's primary concerns was rising unemployment.
政府の主要な懸案の一つは、失業率の上昇だった。

primary education 初等教育

the Democratic [Republican] primary
民主党 [共和党] 予備選挙

primary school ***n.*** 小学校

primate ***n.*** 霊長類の動物

prime ***adj.*** (most important) 最も重要な, 主要な, 第一の, (greatest in degree) 最大の; (classic, archetypal) 典型的な; (best) 最高の, (of meat) 極上の

n. (heyday) 全盛期, 最盛期, (zenith) 盛り

He was the prime suspect in the case.
あの男は事件の第一容疑者でした。

It was a prime example of what not to do.
それは、やってはいけないことの典型的な例だった。

It was prime beef.
極上の牛肉だった。

He should be dropped from the team. He's way past his prime.
あの人をチームから外すべきです。全盛期はとっくに過ぎています。

He was in the prime of his life when he decided to quit the firm.
働き盛りに、彼は退職を決意した。

♦**prime time** ***n.*** ゴールデンアワー

adj. **(prime-time)** ゴールデンアワーの

a prime-time TV show
ゴールデンアワーのテレビ番組

prime minister ***n.*** 総理大臣, 首相

primer ***n.*** (book) 入門書; (substance) 下塗り剤

primitive ***adj.*** (unsophisticated) 原始的な, 未開の; (basic) 基本的な

primitive tribes 未開の部族

Compared to our present-day technology, their methods are primitive.
今日のテクノロジーに比べて、あの人たちのやり方は原始的です。

primrose ***n.*** サクラソウ, 桜草, プリムラ

prince ***n.*** プリンス, 王子, (crown prince) 皇太子, (Japanese prince) ((*formal*)) 親王

princess ***n.*** プリンセス, 王女, (crown princess) 皇太子妃, (Japanese princess) ((*formal*)) 内親王

principal ***adj.*** (most important) 主要な, 最も重要な

n. (head of a school) 校長

principality ***n.*** 公国

principally ***adv.*** 主に

principle ***n.*** (basic truth) 原理, 原則, (moral principle) 主義, 信念, (scientific principle) 原理, 法則, (essence) 本質

These principles have formed the basis of our creed.
これらの原則が、我々の信条の基礎となっています。

It was a matter of principle: I had to support him.

P

私の主義として彼を支える必要があったのです。

There's a big difference between what people say their principles are and the extent to which they follow them.
人が掲げる信念と、その信念にどの程度従っているかには、大きな差がある。

as a matter of principle 主義として

in principle 原則として

print

1 *n.* TYPE: 文字, 活字, (condition of type) 印刷

2 *v.* PRODUCE IN TYPESET FORM: 印刷する, 刷る, プリントする

3 *v.* PUBLISH: 出版する

4 *v.* WRITE IN CAPITALS: 活字体で書く

5 *n.* PHOTOGRAPH: 写真

6 *n.* MARK: 跡, 痕跡

7 *n.* ENGRAVING: 版画

8 *n.* FABRIC/PATTERN: (fabric) プリント地, (pattern) プリント模様

1 The print is too small. I can't read it.
文字が小さくて読めないんです。

The print is not very clear.
印刷があまり鮮明じゃないですね。

2 They printed a hundred thousand copies of the book.
その本は10万部印刷された。

Could you print it out and give me a copy, please?
プリントアウトしてコピーを1部くれますか。

3 And who do you think is going to print your story?
それでどこが、君の話を出版してくれると思う?

No newspaper would print such a story.
そんな話は、どの新聞も記事にしないだろう。

4 I'd like you to print the title and subtitles.
タイトルとサブタイトルを活字体でお書きください。

5 black-and-white prints
白黒 [モノクロ] 写真

6 a tire print タイヤの跡

7 a woodblock print 木版画

in print 発売中で, 入手可能で

out of print 絶版になって

The book is out of print.
その本は絶版になっている。

printed matter *n.* 印刷物

printer *n.* (company) 印刷業者, (printing press) 印刷機, (for computer) プリンター

printing *n.* (process) 印刷, (print run) 印刷部数

a printing press 印刷機

printout *n.* プリントアウト

prior *adj.* 前の, 先の, 事前の

No prior knowledge is required.
予備知識は一切、必要ありません。

prior to …の前は, …に先立って

Prior to electricity, people used oil lamps for lighting.
電気になる前は、照明にランプが使われていた。

prior to my departure…
出発に先立って…

priority *n.* 優先権

Military projects were given top priority.
軍事計画が最優先された。

I don't see why they should have priority over us.

どうして彼らが私たちより優先されるのか、わからない。

give priority to 優先する, …に優先権を与える

prism *n.* プリズム

prison *n.* 刑務所

prisoner *n.* 囚人, (serving a prison sentence) 受刑者

♦ **prisoner of war** *n.* 捕虜

prisoner-of-war camp *n.* 捕虜収容所

pristine *adj.* (fresh, clean) 新鮮な, (in mint condition) 新品の, (as good as new) 新品同様の

privacy *n.* プライバシー

private

1 *adj.* PERSONAL: 私的な, 個人の, 個人的な, プライベートの

2 *adj.* PRIVATELY OWNED/MANAGED: (of property) 私有の, (of school) 私立の [also read わたくしりつ], (of company) 民間の

3 *adj.* NOT FOR THE GENERAL PUBLIC: (of hearing) 非公開の, (of club) 会員制の

4 *adj.* SECRET: 秘密の, 内密の, 内々の

5 *adj.* QUIET: 静かな, 人目につかない

6 *n.* SOLDIER WITHOUT RANK: 兵卒, (**Private** ...) …二等兵

1 He never spoke about his private life.
彼は私生活について全く話さなかった。

I've already expressed my private feelings about this issue.
この件に関しては、すでに私の個人的な考えを申し上げました。

2 This is private property.
ここは私有地です。

She went to a private school.
彼女は私立の学校へ行った。

3 There's going to be a private hearing tomorrow.
明日、非公開の審問が行われる予定です。

He belongs to a private golf club.
彼は会員制のゴルフクラブに入っている。

4 This matter must be kept private.
この問題は内密にしなくてはならない。

This is strictly private, so tell no one.
((*masculine*)) これは極秘だから、誰にも言うなよ。

5 It's a private place ideal for reading.
読書にはぴったりの静かな場所です。

6 Private Smith スミス二等兵

in private (not publicly) 非公開に, (in confidence) 内密に

privately *adv.* (in secret) 内密に, (unofficially) 非公開に; (personally) 個人的に

privatize *v.* (company) 民営化する

♦ **privatization** *n.* 民営化

privilege *n.* 特権

The managers don't have any special privileges.
支配人には、これといった特権はない。

prize *n.* (reward) 賞

Yoshikawa received first prize.
吉川さんが1等賞をもらった。

He got a consolation prize.
彼は残念賞をもらった。

the Akutagawa Prize 芥川賞

♦ **prize money** *n.* 賞金

prizewinner *n.* 受賞者

pro[1] *n.* (argument for) 賛成論

the pros and cons 賛否両論

P

pro[2] ***n., adj.*** (professional) プロ(の)

a pro tennis player
プロのテニスプレーヤー

pro baseball プロ野球

probability ***n.*** 可能性, 見込み, ((*formal*)) 公算

probable ***adj.*** ありそうな, 可能性のある, 見込みがある

probably ***adv.*** たぶん, おそらく

He's probably wrong.
あの人はたぶん間違ってるよ。

She'll probably give us a call tonight.
たぶん今夜彼女から電話があるはずだ。

probation ***n.*** (for delinquent) 保護観察; (trial apprenticeship) 見習い期間

be on probation 保護観察中だ

♦**probation officer** ***n.*** 保護観察官, 保護司

probe ***v.*** (investigate) 探る, 調べる

problem ***n.*** 問題, (homework problem) 課題, (source of worry) 悩みのたね

adj. (of child) 扱いにくい, 問題の

I don't know how you can cope with all these problems.
こんなにたくさんの問題に、どうやって対処できているのか私にはわからない。

solve a problem 問題を解決する

a problem child 問題児

procedure ***n.*** 手続き, 手順

What's the procedure for getting a work permit?
労働許可を得るには、どんな手続きが必要ですか？

The proper procedure has to be followed.
正規の手順に従わなければなりません。

♦**procedural** ***adj.*** 手続き上の

proceed ***v.*** (proceed to do after doing sth else) (...してから) 取りかかる, する, (proceed with) (...を) 進める [→ CONTINUE, GO[1] ON 1]

proceedings ***n.*** (of meeting) 議事録

proceeds ***n.*** (profit) 収益金

The proceeds from the concert will go to charity.
コンサートの収益金は慈善団体に寄付されます。

process ***n.*** 過程, プロセス, (manufacturing process) 工程

v. (materials) 加工する, (information, data) 処理する

a process of trial and error
試行錯誤の過程 [プロセス]

a chemical process 化学作用

It's a long and difficult process.
時間がかかるし、難しい工程です。

processed foods 加工食品

in the process of doing (in the middle of doing) ...している最中で, ...しているところで

procession ***n.*** 行列, 行進

a wedding procession 婚礼の行列

processor ***n.*** (machine) 加工機

a food processor フードプロセッサー

pro-choice ***adj.*** 中絶合法化に賛成の

proclaim ***v.*** 宣言する

proclamation ***n.*** 宣言, 布告

proctor ***n.*** 試験監督官

v. (...の) 試験監督をする

procure ***v.*** 入手する, 手に入れる

prod ***v.*** (encourage) 促す, (**prod into doing**) 刺激して...させる, (stick with a sharp object) 突き刺す

prodigy *n.* (genius) 天才

a child prodigy 天才児 [神童]

produce

1 *v.* MAKE: 作る, (manufacture) 製造する, 生産する, (movie) 制作する, プロデュースする, (offspring) 産む

2 *v.* GIVE RISE TO: 引き起こす, もたらす [→ BRING ABOUT]

3 *v.* SHOW/SUBMIT: (show) 提示する, (submit) 提出する, (from pocket) 取り出す

4 *n.* AGRICULTURAL YIELD: 農産物

1 They produce car components.
そこでは自動車の部品を製造しています。

The factories are producing more than they ever have.
工場の生産量は過去最高です。

The film was produced by a production company in Mexico.
その映画はメキシコにある制作会社によって作られた。

2 Burning fossil fuels produces global warming.
化石燃料の使用は地球の温暖化を引き起こします。

3 He produced the evidence.
彼は証拠を提示した。

4 dairy produce 乳製品

the produce section (of supermarket) (スーパーの)生鮮食料品売場

producer *n.* (of films) 制作者, プロデューサー

product *n.* (manufactured) 製品, (for sale) 商品, (agricultural) 産物; (result) 結果

a new product 新製品

production *n.* 生産, (amount produced) 生産量

♦**production line** *n.* 流れ作業

productive *adj.* 生産的な, 生産力がある, (of discussion) 建設的な, 実りある

a productive day 実りある1日

Let's have a productive discussion.
建設的な議論をしよう。

♦**productivity** *n.* 生産力

prof. → PROFESSOR

profess *v.* (declare) はっきり言う, 明言する, (**profess to be/do**: claim to be/do) …だと/…すると言い張る

profession *n.* 職業, 専門職

professional *adj.* (expert) 専門家の, プロの

I got professional advice.
専門家にアドバイスしてもらった。

She's a professional singer.
彼女はプロの歌手です。

It was done in a very professional manner.
いかにもプロらしいやり方で行われた。

professionalism *n.* 職人かたぎ, プロ意識

professor *n.* 教授

a professor of English Literature
英文学の教授

Professor Wilkins ウィルキンス教授

proficiency *n.* 熟練, 熟達

a proficiency test 習熟度テスト

proficient *adj.* (in language) たんのうな, (in vocation) 熟練した

She's quite proficient in Arabic.

彼女はアラビア語がたんのうです。

profile *n.* (side view) 横顔, (outline) 輪郭; (biography) 人物紹介, プロフィール

profit *n.* (money gained) もうけ, 利益

v. (**profit from**) (=gain money by) …でもうける, …で利益を得る, (=gain an advantage from/by) (…が) ためになる, 役に立つ

How much profit did you make?
もうけは、どの程度出たんですか？

profit and loss 損益

They made a profit of 50%.
彼らは 50 % の利益をあげた。

We profited from the deal.
その取引で利益を得ました。

We profited from her advice.
彼女のアドバイスが役に立ちました。

profitability *n.* もうけ, 利益

profitable *adj.* もうかる, 利益になる

a profitable business もうかる事業

profound *adj.* (deep) 深い, (of knowledge) 深遠な, 奥深い

The news left her in a state of profound shock.
その知らせに、彼女は深いショックに陥った。

Professor Kato's knowledge of that period is profound.
加藤教授はその時代について奥深い知識をもっている [造詣が深い]。

profuse *adj.* たくさんの, おびただしい

prognosis *n.* (of illness) 予後

program *n.* (TV program) 番組, (concert, computer program) プログラム; (agenda) 予定, 計画

v. (**program to do**) (…に) …するようプログラムする

What a stupid (TV) program!
なんてくだらない番組だ。

This (computer) program has a bug.
このプログラムには、欠陥がある。

OK, what's the program for today?
じゃあ、今日の予定は？

♦**programmer** *n.* プログラマー

programming *n.* (computer programming) プログラミング, プログラム作成; (for TV) 番組編成

progress

1 *n.* FORWARD MOVEMENT: 前進, 進行, (of industry) 進歩, 発展, 発達, (of person: getting better at sth) 上達, (in negotiations) 進展

2 *v.* MOVE FORWARD: 進む, (of person at work) はかどる, (of industry: develop) 進歩する, 発展する, 発達する, (of person: move up in rank) 昇進する

3 *v.* OF TIME: たつ, 経過する

1 There has been great progress in biotechnological research.
生物工学の研究は大きく進歩している。

She's made good progress in math recently.
最近、彼女は数学がよくできるようになりましたね。

According to the paper, progress has been made in solving the dispute.
新聞によると、論争の解決に進展があったそうだ。

2 Can cloning progress much further?
クローン技術は、さらに進歩していくのでしょうか？

3 As the day progressed, the weather got worse.
時間がたつにつれて、天気が悪くなった。

in progress 進行中で

an investigation in progress
進行中の調査

make progress (at work) はかどる

progression *n.* (development) 発展, (forward movement) 前進; (one thing after the next) 連続

progressive *adj.* 進歩的な, (of art, music) モダンな, (of reform) 段階的な
n. (grammatical tense) 進行形

Not all social change can be described as “progressive.”
社会の変化がすべて「進歩」と言えるわけではない。

prohibit *v.* 禁止する, 禁じる

prohibition *n.* 禁止, (in U.S. history: **Prohibition**) 禁酒法時代

project *n.* (scheme) 計画, プロジェクト
v. (film) 映写する, (voice) はっきり出す

The project was a great success.
計画は大成功に終わった。

Do we have a screen to project the film on to?
映写用のスクリーンはありますか？

projection *n.* (image projected) 映像; (sales projection) 見積もり, 予測

projector *n.* 映写機

proletarian *n.* 無産階級の者, プロレタリア
adj. 無産階級の, プロレタリアの

pro-life *adj.* 中絶合法化に反対の

proliferate *v.* (spread quickly) 激増する, (of animals) 繁殖する

proliferation *n.* (rapid increase) 激増, (of animals) 繁殖

prolific *adj.* (of writer) 多作の

prologue *n.* (to event) 前触れ, (to book) 序文, プロローグ

prolong *v.* 引き延ばす

prolonged *adj.* (for a long time) 長期の

prominent *adj.* (sticking out) 突き出ている, (noticeable) 目立つ; (distinguished) 著名な

promiscuous *adj.* 誰とでも関係をもつ, (of woman) 尻が軽い

promise *v.* (**promise to do**) ...すると約束する
n. (pledge) 約束, (potential) 有望, 見込み

You promised to be back by 11 o’clock.
11時までには戻ると約束したでしょう?

I promise I’ll pay for it if I break it.
壊したら弁償します。

I promised him I’d return it within a week.
1週間で返すと彼に約束したんだ。

I’ve been promised a salary increase.
昇給を約束されています。

He broke his promise.
あの人は約束を破った。

have/show promise 見込みがある, 有望だ

His son shows a lot of promise.
彼の息子さんはとても有望だ。

promising *adj.* 見込みのある, 有望な

promote *v.* (product) 宣伝する, (...の)販売促進をする, (of person: **be promoted**) 昇進する; (encourage) 促進す

P

る, 広める

How do you aim to promote the product?
その製品をどのように宣伝するつもりですか？

Ms. Ishii was promoted to manager.
石井さんは部長に昇進した。

promote democracy around the world
世界中に民主主義を広める

promotion ***n.*** (advancement in career) 昇進; (in market) 宣伝, 販売促進, プロモーション

promotional ***adj.*** 宣伝用の, 販売促進の

prompt ***adj.*** (without delay) 迅速な, 素早い

Prompt action is needed.
迅速な行動が必要とされる。

We received a prompt reply.
即答をいただきました。

promptly ***adv.*** すぐに, 即座に, ((*formal*)) 速やかに

prone ***adj.*** (**be prone to do**) …しやすい, (とかく)…しがちだ; (lying flat on one's stomach) うつ伏せに

He's accident prone.
あの人はよく事故にあう。

She lay prone on the bed.
彼女はベッドでうつ伏せになっていた。

pronoun ***n.*** 代名詞

pronounce ***v.*** (utter clearly) 発音する [→ ANNOUNCE]

I'm afraid I don't know how to pronounce this word.
この単語の発音がわからないんですが。

pronounced ***adj.*** (clear) はっきりした, (noticeable) 目立つ

pronouncement ***n.*** (public statement) 宣言

pronunciation ***n.*** 発音

have good [bad] pronunciation
発音がいい [悪い]

proof ***n.*** (evidence) 証拠; (trial copy of a manuscript) ゲラ, 校正刷り

Do you have any proof?
何か証拠はありますか？

The proofs have arrived, so we can begin checking them.
ゲラが出たので、チェックを始められる。

♦**proof-of-purchase** ***n.*** 買ったことを証明する物

-proof ***suf.*** (-resistant) (…に) 強い, 防-, 耐-

rainproof 防水の

shockproof 耐震性の

proofread ***v.*** 校正する

prop ***n.*** (on stage) 小道具

v. (prop A against B) (AをBに) もたせかける

♦**prop up** ***v.*** 支える

propaganda ***n.*** プロパガンダ, 宣伝

propagate ***v.*** (plants) 繁殖させる; (idea) 広める, 宣伝する

♦**propagation** ***n.*** (of plants) 繁殖; (of idea) 宣伝

propane ***n.*** プロパン

propel ***v.*** (drive forward) 前進させる, 進ませる, 駆り立てる

The country was propelled into war.
国は戦争へと駆り立てられていった。

propeller ***n.*** (of ship) スクリュー, (of airplane) プロペラ

propensity ***n.*** (tendency) 傾向, 癖

proper ***adj.*** ちゃんとした, きちんとした, まともな, (correct) 正しい, (appropriate) 適切な, ふさわしい, (polite) 礼儀正しい

If we had proper facilities, this business would flourish.
きちんとした設備があれば、このビジネスは成功しますよ。

That's what I call a proper dinner.
こういうのを、夕食と言うんだよ。

He's never had a proper job.
あの人はまともな職に就いたことがない。

That is not the proper way to do things.
それは正しいやり方ではない。

Do you think this is the proper thing to do?
これが適切な行動だと思いますか？

That's not proper attire for a wedding.
それは、結婚式にふさわしい服装ではありませんよ。

He's always very proper.
あの人はいつだって礼儀正しい。

properly ***adv.*** ちゃんと, きちんと, (correctly) 正しく, (appropriately) 適切に

The rules were never properly explained to us.
その規則は一度も我々に、きちんと説明されたことはなかった。

proper noun ***n.*** 固有名詞

property ***n.*** (land) 土地, (real estate) 不動産; (characteristics) 特性, 特質; (possessions) 財産, 所有物

His parents left him some property.
彼の両親は、彼に土地を遺した。

public [private] property 公有 [私有] 地

What are the main properties of hydrogen?
水素の主な特性は何ですか？

♦ **property tax** ***n.*** 固定資産税

prophecy ***n.*** 予言

prophesy ***v.*** 予言する

prophet ***n.*** (predictor of things) 予言者, (interpreter of God's will) 預言者; (**the Prophet**) マホメット

proponent ***n.*** 提案者

proportion ***n.*** (ratio) 割合, 比率, (share) 部分

What's the proportion of flour to sugar?
小麦粉と砂糖の割合はどのくらいですか？

What proportion of these earnings is taxable?
この所得のどの程度が、課税対象になりますか？

A vast proportion of what you hear and see on TV is nonsense.
テレビで見聞きしていることの大部分は、たわごとだ。

in proportion バランスよく, 客観的に

Now don't exaggerate. We must try and keep things in proportion.
事をおおげさにしてはいけないよ。客観的に判断するようにしよう。

in proportion to …に比例して, …につれて

Your salary will go up in proportion to the responsibility you take on.
責任が重くなるにつれて、給料が上がる。

proportional ***adj.*** 比例する, 対応する

♦ **proportional representation** ***n.*** 比例代表制

proposal ***n.*** (plan) 提案, 申し込み, (offer of marriage) プロポーズ, 結婚の申し込み

It was a ridiculous proposal.
ばかげた提案だった。

The proposal was accepted [refused].
その提案は受け入れられた[拒絶された]。

propose *v.* (suggest) 提案する, (recommend) 推せんする, (marriage) プロポーズする

A new bridge has been proposed.
新しい橋の建設が提案されている。

What methods do you propose using?
どんな方法を取るよう提案しますか？

Did he propose to you on bended knees?
彼はひざまずいてプロポーズしたの？

proposition *n.* (plan) 提案, 計画

proprietary *adj.* (sold under a trade name) 専売の, (as if owned by) 所有者のような, わが者顔の, (of rights) 所有する

proprietor *n.* オーナー, 所有者

prosaic *adj.* (dull) 退屈な

prose *n.* 散文

prosecute *v.* 起訴する

Do you think they'll prosecute?
検察は起訴するだろうか？

Shoplifters will be prosecuted.
万引き犯は起訴されます。

prosecution *n.* (prosecuting) 起訴, (**the prosecution**) 検察側

prosecutor *n.* 検察官, 検事

prospect *n.* (outlook) 見通し, 展望, めど, (possibility) 見込み, (expectation) 期待

The prospects are bright.
見通しは明るい。

They have no prospect of winning tonight's match.
彼らが今夜の試合に勝つ見込みはないね。

I don't relish the prospect of having another interview.
また面接を受けることを考えると、気が重いよ。

prospective *adj.* (likely to become) 将来の, …になりそうな

a prospective client 顧客になりそうな人

prospectus *n.* (of school/company) 学校/会社案内書, (of business) 趣意書

prosper *v.* 栄える, 成功する, (of business) 繁盛する, (of city, culture) 繁栄する

prosperity *n.* 繁栄

prosperous *adj.* (of business) 成功する, (flourishing) 繁栄する

prostate *n.* (gland) 前立腺

prostitute *n.* 売春婦, 娼婦

prostitution *n.* 売春

protagonist *n.* 主人公

protect *v.* 守る, (preserve, conserve) 保護する

The law is intended to protect us.
法律とは本来私たちを守るためのものだ。

We want to protect the wildlife here, but how?
ここにいる野生動物を保護したいが、どうすればいいのか？

This vaccination should protect you for five years.
この予防接種は5年間効き目があります。

protection *n.* 保護, (shade from the sun) 日よけ; (contraception) 避妊具, コンドーム

protective *adj.* 保護の, 防護の, (**be protective of/toward**) 守る, かばう

protective clothing 防護服

protective custody 保護拘置

Hiroshi is very protective of his autistic

sister.
浩は自閉症の妹をとてもかばっている。

protectorate *n.* (country) 保護国, 保護領

protégé(e) *n.* (young person helped/guided by older person) 被保護者, (of great artist) 弟子

protein *n.* タンパク質

protest *n.* (objection) 抗議, 反対, (demonstration) デモ

v. (raise an objection against) (…に) 反対する, 抗議する, 異議を申し立てる, (assert) 主張する

The protests carried on for days.
デモは何日も続いた。

The demonstrators protested against tax increases.
デモ参加者は増税に反対していた。

I protested my innocence.
私は無実を主張した。

Protestant *n., adj.* プロテスタント(の), 新教(の)

protester *n.* 反対者, 抗議者, (in demonstration) デモ参加者

protocol *n.* (etiquette among diplomats/statespeople) 外交儀礼, (code of conduct) 礼儀作法, 習わし

follow protocol 外交儀礼に従う

proton *n.* 陽子, プロトン

prototype *n.* (original model) 原型, (typical example) 典型

prototypical *adj.* 典型的な

protracted *adj.* (drawn out) 長引く

protractor *n.* (instrument) 分度器

protrude *v.* (stick out) 突き出る, 出っ張る, (of eyes) 飛び出る

proud *adj.* (showing pride) 誇りに思う, 満足した, 自慢に思う, ((*informal*)) 鼻が高い, (having self-respect) 誇り高い, (arrogant) 傲慢な, いばっている, (conceited) うぬぼれた, 思い上がった

He's proud of his son's achievements.
彼は息子の成功を誇りにしている。

I felt proud of what I'd done.
私は自分のしたことに満足感を覚えた。

He's too proud to admit that he was wrong.
あの人は思い上がっているから自分の過失を認めないよ。

♦**proudly** *adv.* 誇らしげに, 自慢げに, (arrogantly) 横柄に, 高慢な態度で

prove *v.* 証明する, 立証する, (**prove to be**: turn out to be) 結果的に…とわかる

It's been scientifically proven.
それは科学的に証明されている。

This proved that he was right.
これで彼が正しかったことが証明された。

Forensic evidence proved him guilty.
科学的証拠によって、彼が有罪であることが立証された。

It proved to be just the right choice.
結果的に正しい選択だった。

Mr. Endo proved to be a fine manager.
遠藤さんはいい部長であることがわかった。

She proved herself an able leader.
彼女は有能なリーダーであることを証明した。

♦**proven** *adj.* 立証された, ((*informal*)) 折り紙付きの

proverb *n.* ことわざ

proverbial *adj.* (related to proverb) ことわざの, (well-known) よく知られている

provide *v.* (supply) 供給する, 支給する, (necessities, information) 提供する, 与える

The Middle East provides most of the world's oil.
中東が、世界中で使われる石油のほとんどを供給している。

Blankets were provided.
毛布が支給された。

The conference provided me with the opportunity to visit New York.
その会議は、ニューヨークを訪問する機会を与えてくれた。

This information doesn't provide us with any clues as to his whereabouts.
この情報は、彼の行方を知る手がかりにはならない。

♦ **provide for** *v.* (family) 養う, (future event) …に備える

Is the pension enough to provide for our old age?
年金だけで老後の備えは十分だろうか?

provider *n.* 供給する人, (Internet service provider) プロバイダー

provided *conj.* (so long as) …なら(ば), もし…のなら(ば), …という条件で

I will accept, provided accommodation is included in the package.
宿泊も含まれているのなら、申し込みます。

You can bring your children, provided you look after them.
自分でお子さんの面倒を見るのなら、連れて来てもいいですよ。

province *n.* (of country) 州, (**the provinces**: the countryside) 地方, 田舎; (field of knowledge) 分野

provincial *adj.* 地方の, 田舎の

provision *n.* (suppliance) 供給, 支給, (allowance) 配給, (preparation) 用意, 準備; (**provisions**: food) 食料; (condition) 条件, 条項

Make sure you have enough provisions for the entire journey.
目的地に着くまでの十分な食料を持って行きなさい。

There are several provisions in the bill to help the elderly.
その法案には、高齢者を援助する条項がいくつか盛り込まれている。

provisional *adj.* 一時的な, 暫定的な, 仮の, 臨時の

a provisional government 暫定政府

a provisional contract 仮契約

♦ **provisionally** *adv.* とりあえず

proviso *n.* (condition) 条件, 条項

provocation *n.* 挑発

provocative *adj.* 挑発的な

provoke *v.* (anger) 怒らせる, (give rise to) 巻き起こす, 引き起こす

Don't provoke him by talking about that.
その話題を持ち出して、彼を怒らせないで。

Price increases provoked a rash of protests.
値上げは抗議の嵐を巻き起こした。

prowl *v.* うろつく, うろつき回る

prowler *n.* (burglar) こそ泥, (creep) 不審者

proximity *n.* (closeness) 近いこと, 近接

proxy *n.* (person) 代理人, (authority) 代

理

by proxy 代理で

♦**proxy vote** *n.* 代理投票

prude *n.* 上品ぶる人, 気取り屋

prudent *adj.* (careful) 慎重な, 用心深い

prune[1] *n.* (fruit) プルーン

prune[2] *v.* (cut off) 切り取る, (trees, bushes) 刈り込む, せん定する

pry[1] *v.* (be nosy) せんさくする

pry[2] *v.* (**pry up**) てこで上げる, (**pry open**) こじあける

P.S. → POSTSCRIPT

psalm *n.* 聖歌, 賛美歌

pseudonym *n.* (of writer) 筆名, ペンネーム, (of poet, calligrapher) 雅号, (false name) 偽名

psych *v.* (**get psyched up**) 気合いを入れる

psyche *n.* 精神, 魂

psychiatric *adj.* 精神医学の

a psychiatric hospital 精神科病院

psychiatrist *n.* 精神科医

psychiatry *n.* 精神医学

psychic *n.* 霊能者

adj. (of phenomenon) 心霊の, (of person) 超能力のある

a psychic phenomenon 心霊現象

psychoanalysis *n.* (study) 精神分析学, (treatment) 精神分析療法

psychoanalyst *n.* 精神分析医, 精神分析学者

psychoanalyze *v.* (…の) 精神分析をする

psychological *adj.* 精神的な, 心理的な

psychologist *n.* 心理学者

psychology *n.* (psychological behavior) 心理, (subject of study) 心理学

psychopath *n.* 精神病質者

psychosis *n.* 精神病

psychotherapist *n.* 精神療法家, (サイコ) セラピスト

psychotherapy *n.* 心理療法, 精神療法

psychotic *adj.* 精神病の

n. 精神病患者

pub *n.* パブ

puberty *n.* 思春期

pubic *adj.* 陰部の

pubic hair 陰毛

public *adj.* (of/for the people) 一般の人々の, 公衆の, 公共の

n. (**the public**) 一般の人々, 一般市民, 大衆, 世間

The movement has a lot of public support.
その運動は、一般の人々から多くの支援を得ている。

a public lecture 公開講座

a public telephone 公衆電話

a public toilet 公衆トイレ

Public interest is waning.
一般市民の関心は薄れつつある。

The house is not open to the public.
その家は、一般公開されていない。

They're not listening to what the public wants.
彼らは国民の要望に耳を傾けていない。

go public 公表する, ((*slang*)) ばらす; (of company) 株式を公開する, 上場する

If she goes public with that, we're dead.
((*masculine*)) 彼女がそのことをばらし

P

たら、俺たちはおしまいだ。

in public 皆の目の前で, 人前で, 公然と

publication ***n.*** (act of publishing) 出版, 発行, 刊行, (published thing) 出版物

She oversees the publication of several titles.
彼女は数冊の本の出版を監督している。

Do you know the date of publication?
発行日をご存じですか？

public bath ***n.*** 銭湯 [NOTE: Public bathhouses have dwindled drastically in number in modern times, with the advent of apartments and homes equipped with baths. → picture below]

publicity ***n.*** (promotion) 宣伝, (evaluation by media) 評判

good [bad] publicity 好評 [悪評]

publicize ***v.*** (promote) 宣伝する, (make known to the public) 公表する

publicly ***adv.*** 公に, 公的に, (openly) 公然と

public opinion ***n.*** 世論

public relations ***n.*** ＰＲ, 宣伝, 広報活動

public school ***n.*** (in U.S.) 公立学校, (in U.K.) (私立の) パブリックスクール

public transportation ***n.*** 交通機関

publish ***v.*** (print and distribute) 出版する, 発行する, (article/story in book/newspaper) 載せる, 掲載する

Do we dare publish this?
思い切ってこれを出版しようか？

This book was published in 1957.
この本は１９５７年に出版された。

It's published by Kodansha.
講談社発行です。

They have just published the sequel.

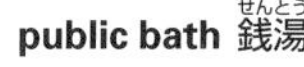

public bath 銭湯

The procedure for using a public bath is:
① Remove shoes and store in shoe locker.
② Pay cashier.
③ Remove clothes and store in basket/locker.
④ Shower. Scrub down and wash away suds.
⑤ Get in bathtub.

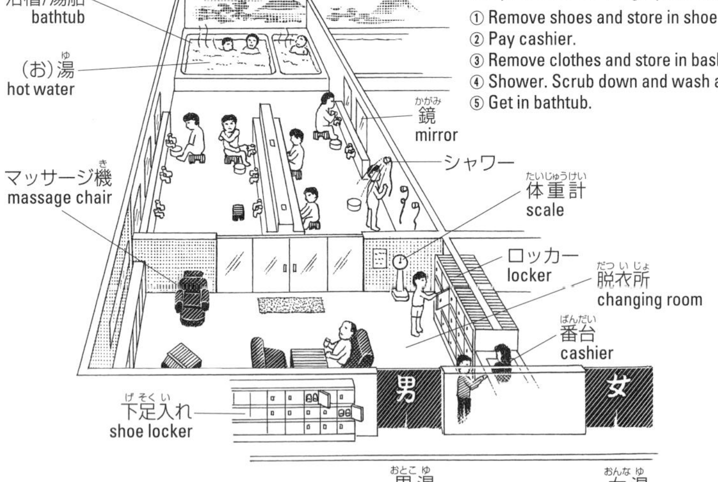

続編が刊行されたばかりです。

I was very pleased to have my letter published.
手紙が掲載されて、とてもうれしかった。

publisher *n.* 出版社, 発行元

publishing *n.* (business) 出版業

pudding *n.* プディング, プリン

puddle *n.* 水たまり

pudgy *adj.* ずんぐりした

puff *v.* (on pipe) プカプカ吹かす, (of train: puff smoke) (煙を) パッと吐く; (be out of breath) 息を切らす, 息切れする
n. (**a puff of**) 一吹きの

He was puffing on his pipe.
彼はパイプをプカプカ吹かしていた。

"I'm coming," she puffed.
「今、行くわ」と彼女は息を切らしながら言った。

puffin *n.* ツノメドリ

puffy *adj.* (swollen) はれた, 膨れた

puke *v.* (vomit) 吐く
n. げろ

pull

1 *v.* TUG/DRAW: 引っ張る, 引く, (curtain) 引く, (pull near to) 引き寄せる
2 *n.* ACT OF PULLING: 引くこと, 引っ張ること
3 *v.* STRAIN: (muscle) 痛める, (筋を)違える
4 *v.* ROW: こぐ
5 *v.* GUN: (pull trigger) 引く, (pull out a gun) 引き抜く, (pull a gun on) (…に) 突き付ける
6 *n.* INFLUENCE: 影響力

1 Don't pull so hard.
そんなに強く引っ張らないで。

The boy pulled at the girl's hair.
少年が女の子の髪の毛を引っ張りました。

He pulled on the rope.
彼はロープを引いた。

The horse pulled the cart.
馬は荷馬車を引いた。

She pulled the curtains over.
彼女はカーテンを引いた。

Pull your chair over here.
椅子をこっちに寄せてください。

She pulled herself out of the water.
彼女は水中からあがった。

2 We all gave a great pull.
全員で思い切り引っ張った。

When I shout, "OK," give the rope a pull.
私が「ＯＫ」と声を上げたら、ロープを引っ張って。

3 I've pulled a muscle in my back.
背中の筋肉を痛めてしまった。

4 We pulled on the oars.
オールをこいだ。

5 She pulled the trigger.
彼女は引き金を引いた。

The man pulled a gun on me.
その男は私に銃を突き付けた。

6 He's got a lot of pull in the local community.
あの人は地元では有力者です [顔が利く]。

pull away *v.* (of car) 動き出す; (detach) 引き離す, (tear up/off) はがす

pull back *v.* (retreat) 撤退する

pull down *v.* (demolish) 壊す, 破壊する; (lower) 下げる

That building is going to be pulled down next week.

そのビルは来週壊されます。

pull in *v.* (arrive) 到着する, (draw to a halt) 止まる

The bus pulled in. バスが到着した。

Just pull in here, would you?
ここに止めてください。

pull off *v.* (clothes) 脱ぐ, (things) はぎ取る; (stunt) やってのける, (victory) 勝ち取る, つかむ

Here, pull off your wet clothes and put on these.
ここで、ぬれた服を脱いでこれを着て。

Pull the blankets off the bed, would you.
ベッドから毛布を取ってくれる？

I don't know how they managed to pull off that stunt.
あの人たちは、どうやってあの離れ業をやってのけたんだろう。

He pulled off three wins in a row.
彼は続けざまに3勝を勝ち取った。

pull on *v.* (clothing) 着る, (shoes) はく, (gloves) はめる

He pulled on his boots and then his gloves.
彼はブーツをはき、それから手袋をはめた。

pull out *v.*

1 REMOVE: 取る, 取り出す, (tooth) 抜く, (page from book) 抜き取る

2 OF VEHICLE: (of car) 出る, (of train) 発車する

3 RETREAT: (of person) 手を引く, (of army) 撤退する

1 Someone's pulled a page out here.
誰かがここのページを抜き取ってる。

One tooth has been pulled out.
1本の歯が抜かれた。

2 The car pulled out right in front of me, and I couldn't stop.
車がちょうど目の前に出て来たので、止まることができなかった。

The train slowly pulled out of the station.
電車はゆっくりと駅を出発した。

3 I pulled out of the project.
そのプロジェクトから手を引いた。

UN troops began to pull out of Ethiopia.
国連軍はエチオピアから撤退し始めた。

pull over *v.* (of car) 止まる, (of police: cause to pull over) (...に) 停車させる

A car pulled over and a couple got out.
車が止まり、中から一組の男女が出て来た。

We got pulled over for speeding.
スピード違反で停車させられた。

pull up *v.* (of car) 止まる, (chair) 引き寄せる

pullet *n.* めん鳥

pulley *n.* (machine) ベルト車

pullover *n.* (sweater) セーター

pull-up *n.* 懸垂

pulmonary *adj.* 肺の

a pulmonary artery 肺動脈

pulp *n.* (wood pulp) パルプ, (soft wet substance) どろどろしたもの, (of fruit) 果肉

v. (fruit) (...から) 果肉を取り除く, (books etc.) パルプにする, 再生資源にする

crush to a pulp 粉砕してパルプにする

be beaten to a pulp (of person) こてんぱんにやっつけられる

pulsate *v.* (beat) 鼓動する, 脈打つ

pulse *n.* 脈, 脈拍

take someone's pulse (...の)脈を取る

puma *n.* ピューマ

pump *n.* ポンプ, (bicycle pump) (自転車の) 空気入れ

v. (water) ポンプでくみ出す, (bicycle tire) (...に) 空気を入れる

pumpkin *n.* カボチャ, 南瓜

pun *n.* だじゃれ, 語呂合わせ

punch *v.* (...に) パンチを食らわす, ぶん殴る

n. (one punch) 一撃, パンチ

throw a punch パンチを食らわす

punctual *adj.* 時間どおりの, 時間を守る, 時間を厳守する

Akiko is always punctual.
明子はいつも時間を守る。

punctuation *n.* (marks used in writing) 句読点, (use of) 句読法

puncture *v.* (pierce) 刺す, (put a hole in) (...に) 穴をあける, (of tire) パンクする

n. (in tire) パンク, (small hole) 穴

pundit *n.* (expert) 専門家, (learned person) 物知り

punish *v.* 罰する, 処罰する, (for nonlegal matters) こらしめる, ひどい目にあわせる, (children) (...に) お仕置きをする

The man was punished for stealing.
男は窃盗で罰せられた。

Criminals should be punished.
犯罪者は処罰されるべきだ。

punishment *n.* 罰, 処罰

severe punishment 厳罰

punk *n.* (violent young man) ちんぴら; (music) パンクロック

pup *n.* 子犬

pupa *n.* さなぎ

pupil[1] *n.* (in school) 生徒, (from teacher's standpoint) 教え子; (apprentice) 弟子

pupil[2] *n.* (part of the eye) ひとみ, (medical) 瞳孔

puppet *n.* 操り人形, (person) 手先, (government) かいらい

a puppet regime かいらい政権

puppy *n.* 子犬

purchase *v.* 買う, ((*formal*)) 購入する [→ BUY]

n. 買い入れ, ((*formal*)) 購入, (**purchases**) 買った物, 買い物

♦**purchaser** *n.* 買い手, ((*formal*)) 購入者

pure *adj.* 純粋な, (of substance: unmixed) 混じり気のない, 純-, (of air, water: clear, beautiful) きれいな, 澄んだ; (used emphatically: plain and simple) 単なる, 全くの

pure gold [wool] 純金 [純毛]

The air is pure. 空気が澄んでいる。

The water here is pure—you can drink it.
ここの水はきれいなので、飲めますよ。

That's pure nonsense! 全くたわごとだ!

purée *n., v.* ピューレ(にする)

purely *adv.* (completely) 全く, 完全に, (simply) 単に

It was purely coincidental.
単なる偶然だった。

purge *v.* (purge A [organization] of B [people]) (AからBを) 追放する, 一掃する

purifier *n.* 浄化装置

P

purify *v.* (water, air) きれいにする, 浄化する, (rid of impurities/evil) 清める

purist *n.* 純粋主義者

puritan *n.* (person of strict morals) 厳格な人, (in the past: **Puritan**) 清教徒, ピューリタン

♦**puritanical** *adj.* (strict) 厳格な

purity *n.* 純粋, (cleanliness) 清浄, きれいさ

purple *n., adj.* 紫色(の)

purport *n.* 趣旨, 意味

purpose *n.* (aim) 目的, 意図, (meaning) 意味

The purpose of the meeting was to choose a new chairperson.
会議の目的は新議長を選ぶことでした。

The house wasn't built for that purpose.
その家は、そういう意図で建てられたわけではない。

I just can't see the purpose in going.
私には行く意味がわかりません。

for the purpose of …のために

on purpose わざと, 故意に

serve a purpose ためになる

purr *v.* (of cat) ゴロゴロとのどを鳴らす

purse *n.* (handbag) (ハンド)バッグ

a change purse 小銭入れ

pursue *v.* (chase) 追う, 追跡する, (try to get) 追い求める, (court) 追いかける, (advance: policy) 進める, (follow: plan, course of action) (…に) 従う

The police are pursuing the whereabouts of the man.
警察はその男の行方を追っている。

The government is pursuing a policy of low inflation.
政府は低インフレ政策を進めている。

pursuit *n.* (chasing) 追跡, (trying to get) 追求; (hobby) 気晴らし, 楽しみ

pursuit of happiness 幸福の追求

purveyor *n.* (supplier) 調達人, 供給者

---

push

1 *v.* PRESS/SHOVE: 押す, (push out of the way) 押しのける, どける

2 *v.* URGE: 駆り立てる, (**push into doing/to do**) (…に) …するよう無理強いする; (put pressure on) (…に) 迫る

3 *n.* ACT OF PUSHING: 押し, 突き

1 Did you push the button?
ボタンを押しましたか？

Let's push all these books out of the way.
この本を全部どけよう。

He pushed past me in his rush to get to the train.
その人は電車にあわてて飛び乗ろうとして、私を押しのけた。

2 Don't try to push me into something I don't want to do.
やりたくもないことを無理強いしないで。

The parents pushed their children very hard to do well at school.
その両親は、子供が学校でいい成績を取るよう尻をたたいた。

She pushed him for an answer.
彼女は彼に返答を迫った。

3 Could you give me a push? I can't start my car.
すみませんが、押してもらえませんか？エンジンがかからないんです。

when push comes to shove いざとい

うときは

push around *v.* (order around) こき使う, あごで使う

I'm not going to let him push me around.
あの人にこき使われてたまるか。

push in/into *v.* …に押し入る, (into line) …に割り込む

Hey! Don't push in! There is a line, you know.
ちょっと! 割り込まないで。並んでるんですよ。

push on *v.* (carry on) 進める, 続ける, 続行する

He pushed on with the work.
彼はその仕事を続けた。

push up *v.* (prices) 押し上げる

Demand was pushing up prices.
需要が価格を押し上げていた。

---

pushover *n.* (person) 言いなりになる人, 弱い人

pushpin *n.* 画びょう [→ picture of STATIONERY]

push-up *n.* 腕立て伏せ

pushy *adj.* (impudent) 厚かましい, (aggressive) 押しの強い, (forward) でしゃばりの

---

put *v.*

1 SET/PLACE: 置く, (put A on B) (AをBに) のせる, (put A into B) (AをBに) 入れる, (write) 記入する, 書いておく

2 EXPRESS: 言う, 言い表す

3 INTO SITUATION/CIRCUMSTANCE: (…に) する, (put into a bad position) (…の立場に) 追い込む, (**put oneself in sb else's position**) (…の) 立場に立つ

4 INVEST: (**put energy into**) …に力を注ぐ, (**put time into**) …に時間をかける, (**put money on**) …にお金をかける

1 I put the new coasters on the coffee table.
コーヒーテーブルの上に新しいコースターを置いた。

She put her head on my shoulder.
彼女は僕の肩に頭をのせた。

Could you put my glasses in their case?
めがねをケースに入れてくれる?

I put some money into my account this morning.
けさ、口座に少しお金を入れた。

Put your name and address at the top, please.
上に名前と住所を記入してください。

2 I wouldn't have put it like that.
私なら、そんなふうには言わなかった。

Try to put it in your own words.
あなた自身の言葉で言い表してみてください。

I don't quite know how to put this to you, but…
これをどう伝えればいいのか、よくわからないけれど…

Let me put this question to you…
お尋ねしたいのですが…

3 This puts me in a difficult position.
これで私は難しい立場に立たされる。

Try to put yourself in her situation.
彼女の立場に立って考えてみて。

4 We put a lot of time and energy into this project.
私たちは、このプロジェクトに多大な時

間と労力を注いだ。

put across *v.* (communicate) 伝える, 納得させる, わからせる

How are we going to put this across to the public?
これを世間にどうやって伝えよう?

put aside *v.* (money) 蓄える, 取っておく, (time) あけておく, (proposal, argument) 棚上げする, ほうっておく, (thought) 考えないでおく, (**put to the side/out of the way**) わきに置く

She has some savings which she has put aside.
彼女には蓄えた貯金がいくらかある。

The proposal should be put aside until more market research is done.
もっと市場調査が行われるまで、その提案は棚上げするべきです。

put away *v.* (return to proper storage place for keeping) 片付ける, しまう; (send to prison) 刑務所に入れる

Let's put all these toys away, shall we?
みんなでこのおもちゃを全部片付けましょう。

Could you put the chairs away, please?
椅子を片付けていただけますか?

He should be put away for life.
あの男は、一生刑務所に入れておくべきだ。

put back *v.* (return to original place/position) 戻す; (postpone) 延期する, 遅らせる

If you take a book off the shelf, please put it back where you found it.
棚から本を取り出したら、必ず元あった場所に戻してください。

One cannot put back the clock.
時計の針を元に戻すことはできない。

The meeting has been put back.
会議は延期になりました。

put before *v.* …よりも優先する, …よりも大事に考える

Are you putting your social life before your work?
仕事よりも付き合いを大事にしているの?

put down *v.*

1 SET DOWN: 置く

2 WRITE DOWN: (jot down) 書き留める, (fill in) 記入する

3 QUELL: 鎮圧する

4 PAY: (as deposit) 払う, 前払いする

5 BELITTLE: ばかにする, こき下ろす

1 He put down the paper.
彼は用紙を置いた。

You can put that box down over there.
箱はあそこに置いてもいいよ。

Put that gun down! 銃を下に置け!

2 I'd put that down if I were you—it's important.
重要なことは、私なら書き留めておくよ。

Put your name down here.
ここにお名前を記入してください。

3 The rebellion was put down.
反乱は鎮圧された。

4 How much do we need to put down as a deposit?
手付け金として、いくら払えばいいんですか?

5 She may not be a great cook, but you shouldn't put her down because of it.
彼女はあまり料理がうまくないかもしれないけど、だからってばかにすることは

ないよ。

put forward *v.* (propose) 出す, 提出する; (date) 早める, (time) 進める

It's time to put forward a new proposal.
新しい提案を出す時だ。

put in *v.*

1 SUBMIT: 出す, 提出する

2 SAY: (add) 付け加える, 添える, (interject) 差し挟む

3 SPEND TIME: (時間を) 費やす, (put in extra hours at work) 残業する

4 INSTALL: (appliance) 取り付ける

5 PUT ONESELF IN → PUT 3

1 The most important thing is to put your application in on time.
一番大事なのは、期限までに申請書を提出することです。

2 He put in a good word for you.
彼は君のために推せんの言葉を添えて [口添えをして] くれたんだ。

3 I put in more than twenty hours of overtime this week.
今週、20時間以上残業をした。

4 Who put the plumbing in?
誰が配管設備を取り付けたんですか？

put in for *v.* (apply for) 申し込む, 応募する

Are you going to put in for this new job?
この新しい仕事に応募するんですか？

put off *v.* (meeting etc.) 延期する, (**put off doing until...**) ...まで...しない; (discourage) (...の) 気をそぐ, (**be put off by**: be turned off/offended by) (...が) いやだ, うんざりする

What! You're not going to put off going again, are you?
えっ！ まさか、また行くのを延期するつもりじゃないでしょうね？

Don't let them put you off.
彼らのことは気にするな。

Oddly enough, I wasn't put off by his manner.
おかしなことに、彼の態度はいやじゃなかった。

put on *v.*

1 CLOTHING: (coat, shirt) 着る , (shoes, pants) はく, (hat) かぶる, (**put on makeup**) (お)化粧する [→ WEAR 1]

2 TURN/SWITCH ON: (lights) つける, (music: CD etc.) かける

3 PERFORMANCE: (produce: theatrical performance) 上演する, (**put on an act**) (お)芝居をする, 見せかける

4 GAIN: (weight) (体重が) 増える [→ FAT]

5 ADD ON: (extra cost) 上乗せする

1 Put on some clothes, will you.
服を着たら？

Aren't you going to put some makeup on?
お化粧をしないの？

2 Could you put the lights on, please?
電気をつけてもらえますか？

Shall I put on some music?
音楽をかけようか？

3 They're putting on *Romeo and Juliet* at the National Theater.
国立劇場で『ロミオとジュリエット』を上演して [やって] いる。

He's always putting on a macho act.
あの人はいつも男らしく見せている。

4 Have you put on weight?
((*informal*)) 体重が増えた？/太った？

P

5 You can expect them to put another ¥1,000 on the bill—a so-called "table charge."
いわゆるテーブルチャージとして、勘定に1000円上乗せしてくると思うよ。

put out *v.*

1 EXTINGUISH: 消す

2 PLACE OUTSIDE: 外に出す

3 ANNOY: (**be put out**: feel upset) 気を悪くする, 怒る

4 PUBLISH/PRODUCE: 出す, 発行する

5 ISSUE: (announcement) 出す, 発表する

6 STICK OUT: (hand) 差し出す

1 I want the lights put out when you leave.
出る時は電気を消してもらいたい。

Put that cigarette out, please.
たばこの火を消してください。

2 Did you put the trash out?
ごみを出してくれた?

Better put the dog out.
犬は外に出しておいたほうがいい。

3 She seemed put out by your not telephoning.
あなたが電話しなかったから、彼女は気を悪くしたみたいだったよ。

4 That singer recently put out a new album.
あの歌手は最近、新しいアルバムを出した。

5 The government put out a terrorist alert.
政府はテロに注意するよう警報を出した。

6 He put his hand out to me and I shook it.
彼が手を差し出したので握手しました。

put through *v.* (put sb through: connect by telephone) 電話でつなぐ, (requesting sb: **put me through to Mr./Ms...., please**) ...さんをお願いします

Could you put me through to Mr. Hara, please?
原さんをお願いします。

put sb through hell/a lot (...に) 地獄の/大変な思いをさせる

put together *v.* (assemble) 組み立てる, (make) 作る; (ideas) まとめる

I think we can put together a plan before the deadline, don't you?
締め切りまでにみんなで企画をまとめられそうだね。

put our heads together みんなで考える

put two and two together あれこれ考え合わせる

put up *v.*

1 ERECT: (building) 建てる, (tent) 張る

2 RAISE: 上げる

3 PROVIDE LODGING FOR: 泊める

4 PLACE IN PUBLIC VIEW: (notice, poster) 張り出す, 掲示する, (on Internet) 出す

5 PUT UP FOR SALE: (売りに)出す

1 I hope to put a shed up here.
ここに物置を建てたい。

I'll put some shelves up for the books.
本棚を取り付けよう。

2 More than half the crowd put up their hands.
半数以上の人が手を挙げた。

Surely you haven't put your prices up again?
また値上げしたんじゃないでしょうね?

3 We can't put her up here.
彼女をここに泊めるわけにはいかない。

4 I put my resume up on various Web sites.

いろいろなウェブサイトに履歴書を出した。

5 They had to put their house up for sale.
彼らは自宅を売りに出さなければならなかった。

put up with *v.* (tolerate) がまんする, …に耐える

I don't know why you put up with him.
どうしてあの人のことをがまんするのか、わからない。

At his age, how can you expect him to put up with this cold weather?
彼の年齢で、この寒さに耐えられると思いますか？

I can't put up with this noise any longer.
この騒音にはこれ以上耐えられない。

putt *n., v.* パット(する)

putty *n.* パテ

puzzle *n.* (difficult question) 難問, (riddle) なぞ, (toy) パズル

v. (confuse) 当惑させる, (…の) 頭を悩ます; (**puzzle over**: ponder) …のことで頭を絞る

Why he didn't come is a puzzle to me.
どうして彼が来なかったのか、なぞです。

Why don't you buy him a jigsaw puzzle?
ジグソーパズルを買ってあげたら？

That's been puzzling me all day.
そのことで一日中、頭を悩ましている。

puzzled *adj.* (of look) 困惑した, けげんそうな

be puzzled by …に困惑する

puzzling *adj.* 理解できない, 訳のわからない

pyjamas → PAJAMAS

pylon *n.* 鉄塔

pyorrhea *n.* 歯槽膿漏

pyramid *n.* (**the Pyramids**) ピラミッド; (shape) ピラミッド型

pyromania *n.* 放火癖

pyromaniac *n.* 放火狂

pyrotechnic *adj.* 花火の

n. (**pyrotechnics**) 花火技術 [→ FIREWORKS]

python *n.* ニシキヘビ, 錦蛇

P

Q, q

quack *v.* ガーガー鳴く
n. ガーガー鳴く声, ガーガーいう鳴き声

quadrangle *n.* (4-sided figure) 四角形; (inner courtyard) 中庭

quadrant *n.* 四分円

quadrilateral *n.* 四辺形

quadruple *n., adj.* 4倍(の)
v. (multiply by four) 4倍にする, (increase fourfold) 4倍になる

quadruplet *n.* 四つ子の一人, (**quadruplets**) 四つ子

quail *n.* ウズラ, (meat) ウズラの肉

quaint *adj.* 風変わりな, (old-fashioned) 古風な

quake *v.* (of ground) 揺れる, 震動する, (of person) ガタガタ震える
n. (earthquake) 地震

qualification *n.* (**qualifications**) 資格, (=skills) 技能, (=license) 免許; (condition) 条件, (restriction) 制限

qualified *adj.* (of person for job) 資格のある, 免許のある, 資格を持っている, (be qualified for: be suited for) (…に) 適任だ; (conditional) 条件付きの

He's a qualified ski instructor.
あの人は資格のあるスキーインストラクターです。

I'm not qualified to enter the competition.
その競技に参加する資格はありません。

She is highly qualified for the post.
彼女はそのポストに適任だ。

get qualified as …の資格を取る

qualify *v.*

1 GET/HAVE PROPER QUALIFICATIONS: (get qualified) 資格を取る, (be qualified) 資格がある, (**qualify for**: be fit for) …に向いている [→ QUALIFIED], (= for competition) …の出場権を得る

2 MODIFY: (statement) 修正する, (attach a condition to) (…に) 条件をつける

3 BE REGARDED AS: (**qualify as**) …とみなす, …と言える

1 She qualified as an ESL instructor.
彼女はＥＳＬの先生の資格を取った。

You don't qualify to vote.
あなたには投票する資格がない。

Does that mean you qualify for the job?
あなたはその仕事に向いているということですか？

Our team qualified for the semifinals.
我々のチームは準決勝の出場権を得た [に進んだ]。

2 I'd better qualify what I just said.
今の私の発言は修正したほうがよさそうですね。

3 That qualifies as the worst pick-up line I've ever heard.
今まで聞いた中で最悪の口説き文句だと言える。

qualitative *adj.* (pertaining to quality) 性質上の, 質的な

qualitative differences 質的な相違

quality

1 *n.* HOW GOOD/BAD STH IS: 質, (of goods) 品質 [→ QUANTITY]

2 *n.* CHARACTERISTIC: (of person) 資質, (of substance) 特性 [→ ASPECT]

3 *n.* EXCELLENCE: 良質

4 *adj.* OF PRODUCT: (high-quality) 質の高い, 良質の, 高級な

1 The quality of the material was poor.
その材料は質が悪かった。

We need to improve the quality of service.
サービスの質を向上させる必要がある。

Everybody seems to be talking about "quality of life" these days.
近ごろ「生活の質」ということが、よく話題になっているようですね。

2 He's generous and kind. In fact, he has many good qualities.
あの人は寛大で優しい。実際たくさん長所がある。

Can you name some of the qualities of copper?
銅の特性をいくつか挙げられますか?

3 We only deal in products of true quality.
当店では良質の商品しか取り扱っておりません。

4 It was printed on quality paper.
上質紙に印刷されていた。

qualm *n.* (uneasiness) 不安, 心配

have qualms 気がとがめる

have no qualms about 何とも思わない

quandary *n.* 困惑

be in a quandary 途方に暮れる, 困る

quantifier *n.* 数量詞

quantitative *adj.* (pertaining to quantity) 量的な

quantity *n.* 量, (large quantity) 大量, 多量, (small quantity) 少量

Quality comes before quantity.
量より質。

A large quantity of junk mail was found behind the door.
ドアの後ろに大量のダイレクトメールがあった。

We only need a small quantity of salt.
塩は、ほんの少量しか要りません。

in quantity/large quantities 大量に

quantum *n.* 量子

♦ **quantum leap** *n.* めざましい飛躍

quantum theory *n.* 量子論

quarantine *n., v.* 隔離(する)

quarrel *v.* (argue) 口げんかする, けんかする, 言い争う, 口論する, (disagree) ((*formal*)) 異論がある

n. (argument) けんか, 口げんか, 言い争い, 口論

I do wish you two would stop quarreling.
けんかをやめてくれない?

Do you know what they were quarreling about?
あの人たちが何について言い争っていたか知っていますか?

I would quarrel with your definition of "safe."
あなたの言う「安全」の定義に対して異論があります。

a marital quarrel 夫婦げんか

It's a long-standing family quarrel.
長年の骨肉の争いなのです。

quarrelsome *adj.* けんか好きな, けんかっ早い

quarry *n.* (mine) 採石場

v. 採石する

quart *n.* クォート

quarter

1 *n.* FOURTH PART: 4分の1, (of hour) 15分, (of year) 四半期, (of academic year)

Q

学期, (of game) クオーター

2 *n.* AREA OF CITY: 地区, -街

3 *n.* ARMY RESIDENCE: (**quarters**) 宿舎, 兵舎

4 *v.* DIVIDE INTO FOUR: 四つに分ける, 4 等分する

5 *n.* COIN: 2 5 セント硬貨

1 three quarters 4 分の 3

It's quarter past one.
(今、) 1時15 分です。

Let's divide the cake into quarters.
ケーキを4 等分しよう。

Profits were up in the first quarter.
利益は第 1 四半期で上昇した。

2 These are the residential quarters.
ここは住宅街です。

The French Quarter (in New Orleans)
フランス人街

3 The soldiers were told to return to their quarters.
兵士たちは宿舎に戻るよう命じられた。

4 The nicotine content of these cigarettes has been quartered.
このたばこのニコチン含有量は4 分の1 になった。

5 Do you have a quarter? I need to use a pay phone.
2 5 セント持ってる？ 公衆電話を使いたいんだ。

quarterfinal *n.* 準々決勝

quarterly *n.* (publication) 季刊誌
adj. 3 カ月ごとの, 年 4 回の
adv. 3 カ月ごとに, 年 4 回

quartet *n.* (piece for four) 四重奏曲, (band of four) 四重奏団, カルテット

quartz *n.* クオーツ

quash *v.* (officially reject) 却下する, (make invalid) 無効にする; (put down: rebellion) 鎮圧する, 抑える

quasi- *pref.* (semi-) 準-, 半-

a quasi-religious movement
半宗教的な運動

quaver *v.* (of voice) 震える
n. (eighth note) 8 分音符

quay *n.* 波止場, 埠頭

queasy *adj.* (nauseated) 吐き気がする, 気持ちが悪い

queen *n.* 女王, ((*polite*)) 女王様, (wife of king) 王妃; (playing card) クイーン

Queen Elizabeth I 女王エリザベス1 世

a beauty queen 美の女王

king and queen 王様と王妃

♦ **queen bee** *n.* 女王バチ

queer *adj.* (strange) 変な, 奇妙な, おかしい

It was a very queer feeling, talking to her after all those years.
何年かぶりに、彼女と話をするのはとても奇妙な気分だった。

quell *v.* (suppress) 抑える, 鎮める

quench *v.* (thirst) いやす

quench one's thirst のどの渇きをいやす

query *n.* 質問, (doubt) 疑問
v. 質問する

quest *n.* 探究

question

1 *n.* INQUIRY: 質問, ((*formal*)) 問い, (on exam) 問題

2 *v.* THROW QUESTIONS AT: (…に) 聞く, 質問する, 尋ねる, (interrogate) 尋問する

3 *v.* DOUBT: 疑う, (…に) 疑問をもつ

4 *n.* DOUBT: 疑い, 疑問

5 ***n.*** **ISSUE:** 問題

■1 She certainly asked a lot of questions.
確かにあの人は質問をたくさんしました。

We couldn't answer half the questions.
質問の半分も答えられなかった。

That's a difficult question.
それは難しい質問ですね。

The exam consists of fifty true-or-false questions.
試験は50問の○×問題から成っている。

■2 Our teacher questioned us as to our whereabouts.
どこにいたのかと先生に聞かれた。

Don't question me about my love life.
異性関係については質問しないでください。

The man was questioned by the police.
その男は警察に尋問された。

■3 It's not a bad thing for youngsters to question authority.
若者が、権威に対して疑問をもつのは悪いことではない。

Are you questioning her credibility?
彼女が信用できるかどうか、疑っているんですか？

Frankly, I question his judgment in this matter.
正直言って、この件に関する彼の判断には疑問を感じる。

■4 There are still a number of questions in my head about this so-called plan .
この計画というものには、今でも多くの疑問をもっています。

Are you calling his character into question?
彼の品性の問題だと言うのですか？

■5 The question has been debated for years.
その問題は何年も議論されている。

out of the question (unacceptable) 問題外で, (impossible) 全く不可能で

No, I'm sorry, that's out of the question.
申し訳ありませんが、それはとても不可能です。

without question (undoubtedly) 間違いなく, 疑いなく; (without arguing) 何も言わずに, あれこれ言わずに

He is without question the best candidate.
あの人は間違いなく最有力候補です。

questionable ***adj.*** (suspicious) 怪しい, うさんくさい, (doubtful) 疑わしい

questioning ***n.*** (by police) 尋問

question mark ***n.*** クエスチョンマーク, 疑問符

questionnaire ***n.*** アンケート

queue ***n.*** (line) 列, (of people waiting to buy/use sth) 行列
v. (line up) 並ぶ, 列を作る

quibble ***v.*** (say this and that) つべこべ言う, (argue) へ理屈を言う [→ QUARREL]
n. へ理屈, こじつけ

quick

1 ***adj.*** **RAPID:** (of movement, action) 速い, 素早い, ((*formal*)) 迅速な, (nimble) すばし(っ)こい, (quick and efficient) てきぱきした, (**be quick to do**) すぐ…する

2 ***adj.*** **BRIEF:** ちょっとした, 簡単な

3 ***adj.*** **CLEVER:** 理解が早い, 頭の回転が速い

4 ***adj.*** **OF TEMPER:** (**have a quick temper**) 気が短い, 短気だ

5 ***adv.*** **RAPIDLY:** 速く, 急いで, (quick and

efficiently) てきぱきと

1 It's probably quicker to go by train.
電車で行ったほうがたぶん速いですよ。

Be quick! We'll be late otherwise.
急いで！ じゃないと遅れるよ。

He's quick to criticize and slow to praise.
あの人はすぐ人を非難するけど、なかなかほめないね。

2 Shall we go and have a quick look?
ちょっと見てきますか？

Shall we have a quick drink?
軽く一杯やっていきませんか？

3 He's so quick at math, he's finished the book already.
あの子は数学の理解が早いから、もう問題集を終わらせてしまったよ。

This dog's quick to learn.
この犬は物覚えがいい。

4 He has a quick temper.
彼は短気だ。

5 I can't do it any quicker.
これ以上速くできません。

quicken *v.* (get faster) 速まる, (make faster) 速める

quickly *adv.* 速く, (straightaway) すぐ(に), (hurriedly) 急いで

quiet

1 *adj.* NOT NOISY: 静かな

2 *adj.* OF PERSON: おとなしい, 静かな, 物静かな

3 *adj.* OF COLOR: 地味な, 落ち着いた

4 *adj.* RELAXED: ゆっくりした, くつろいだ, (of setting: peaceful) 穏やかな, のどかな, 平穏な

5 *adj.* OF BUSINESS: 忙しくない, 暇な

6 *n.* QUIET STATE/CONDITION: 静けさ, (peace) 平穏

7 *v.* MAKE/BECOME QUIET: 静かにさせる/なる

1 a quiet street 静かな通り

It's a quiet spot not many people know about.
あまり知られていない静かな所です。

The office was quiet today.
今日は会社が静かだった。

2 He's a quiet person.
あの人は物静かだ。

3 She prefers quiet colors.
彼女は落ち着いた色が好きです。

4 Let's just have a quiet time at home.
家でゆっくりしよう。

5 Business is quiet at the moment, but it'll pick up next month.
今は仕事が暇だけど、来月は忙しくなる。

6 Can't we have some peace and quiet around here!
ここは、もう少し静かにならないもんでしょうか！

7 The class quieted down.
クラスは静かになった。

keep quiet about sth / keep sth quiet 黙っておく, 内緒にする, ((*formal*)) 内密にする

Could you keep it quiet and not tell anyone?
内緒にして誰にも話さないでくれる？

on the quiet (secretly) こっそり, ひそかに

quietly *adv.* 静かに, そっと

Let's speak more quietly.
もっと静かに話しましょう。

Some students quietly made their exit before the lecture was over.
何人かの学生は、講義が終わる前にそっと退席した。

quill *n.* (pen) 羽ペン

quilt *n.* キルト [→ COMFORTER]

♦**quilted** *adj.* キルトの

quince *n.* (plant) マルメロ, (fruit) マルメロの実

quip *n.* (funny remark) しゃれ, 気の利いた言葉, (ironic remark) 皮肉
v. (make a funny remark) 気の利いたことを言う, (make an ironic remark) 皮肉を言う

quirk *n.* (odd habit) 癖, (whim) 気まぐれ
a quirk of fate 運命の気まぐれ

quirky *adj.* (odd) 変わった, 変な, 奇妙な
That guy has a quirky sense of humor.
あの人には変わったユーモアのセンスがある。

quit *v.* (work, school, task, smoking) やめる [→ RESIGN, RETIRE]
This must be the hundredth time you've quit smoking.
あなたがたばこをやめたって言うのは、これで100回目だよ。
I couldn't stand the job any longer, so I quit.
仕事がいやでたまらなくなったので、辞めたんです。
Quit trying to tell me how to live my life!
いかに生きるべきかなんて話は、やめて。
call it quits これまでとする, 切り上げる
OK, let's call it quits for the day.
よし、今日のところはこれまでとしよう。

quite *adv.*
1 ENTIRELY: すっかり, 全く, 完全に
2 RATHER: かなり, 相当, ずいぶん, なかなか
3 TO AN EXCEPTIONAL DEGREE: (**quite a...**) 大した..., すごく...

1 I quite agree.
全くそのとおりです。
I'm quite certain of it.
絶対そうだと思います。
Could you wait a minute? I'm not quite done yet.
ちょっと待っていただけますか？ まだ完全に終わっていませんので。

2 It's quite windy today.
今日は風がかなり強いですね。
He's quite handsome, don't you think?
あの人、なかなかハンサムだと思わない？

3 You really are quite a girl.
君は本当に大した子だ。
You've made quite a lot of progress.
すごく上達したね。
The main course wasn't that good, but the dessert—that was quite something.
メインディッシュは、それほどおいしくなかったけど、デザートはすばらしかった。

quiver[1] *v.* (tremble) 震える
n. 震え

quiver[2] *n.* (case for arrows) 矢筒, えびら

quiz *n.* (short test) 小テスト, (question designed to test one's knowledge) クイズ
v. (give a quiz to) (...に) 簡単なテストをする, (quiz A about B: ask A questions about B) (AにBについて) 質問する
a quiz show クイズ番組
a pop quiz 抜き打ちテスト

quota *n.* (share) 割り当て(分)

quotation *n.* (passage) 引用語句 <ruby>引<rt>いんよう</rt></ruby>; (price estimate) 見積もり <ruby><rt>みつ</rt></ruby>

quotation mark *n.* 引用符 <ruby><rt>いんようふ</rt></ruby>

quote *v.* (from book) 引用する <ruby><rt>いんよう</rt></ruby>, (from less formal source) 引き合いに出す <ruby><rt>ひ あ だ</rt></ruby>; (give as a price estimate) (...と) 見積もる <ruby><rt>みつ</rt></ruby>

n. (passage) 引用語句 <ruby><rt>いんようごく</rt></ruby>, (quotation mark) 引用符 <ruby><rt>いんようふ</rt></ruby>; (estimate) 見積もり <ruby><rt>みつ</rt></ruby>

He can quote long passages from Shakespeare.
あの人は、シェークスピアの長文を引用して言うことができる。

Don't quote me on this, but...

このことで私を引き合いに出さないでほしいんだけど...

Could you quote me a price for the repair?
修理の見積もりをしていただけますか?

They quoted me ¥7,000 for the repair of my watch.
時計の修理は7000円と見積もりが出た。

The president predicts, quote, "The economy will revive," unquote.
大統領は「経済は回復する」と予測している。

quotient *n.* (number) 商 <ruby><rt>しょう</rt></ruby>

R, r

rabbi *n.* ラビ, (expert on Jewish law) ユダヤの律法学者

rabbit *n.* ウサギ, 兎

rabble *n.* (crowd) 群衆, 野次馬, (**the rabble**) 下層階級

rabid *adj.* (of dog) 狂犬病の, (of person: fanatical) 過激な, 狂信的な

rabies *n.* 狂犬病

raccoon *n.* アライグマ

race[1]

1 *v.* RUSH: 急ぐ, (race somewhere) 急いで行く, (**race around**) 走り回る, (**race over to**) …に駆け寄る, (of feeling: **race through** one's body) 駆け抜ける, (of heart: beat fast) どきどきする

2 *v.* COMPETE IN A RACE: レースに出る, (race against/sb) (…と) 競走する

3 *v.* DOG/CAR: レースに出す

4 *n.* COMPETITION: レース, 競走, ((*also figurative*)) 競争

1 We raced out of the room and down the stairs.
私たちは急いで部屋を出て、階段を駆け下りた。

We had to race to get the job finished.
大急ぎで仕事を終わらせなくてはならなかった。

I saw him racing around the neighborhood in his new car.
彼が新車で近所を走り回っているのを見たよ。

Inflation is racing ahead again.
インフレがまた急激に進んでいる。

2 Are you going to race at the next meet?
次の大会はレースに出ますか？

Who is she racing against?
彼女は誰と競走しているんですか？

Let's race each other to the top.
あのてっぺんまで競走しよう。

3 He races greyhounds.
あの人はグレーハウンドをレースに出している。

4 a horse race 競馬

I finished second in the race.
競走で2着でした。

an arms race 軍拡競争

a race against time 時間との闘い

race[2] *n.* (of human) 人種, -族

the human race 人類

the Caucasian [Mongolian] race
白色 [黄色] 人種

♦**race relations** *n.* 人種関係

racehorse *n.* 競走馬

racetrack *n.* (for cars) サーキット, (for horses) 走路

racial *adj.* 人種の

racial discrimination 人種差別

racing *n.* (of cars) 自動車レース, (of horses) 競馬, (of boats) 競艇

racism *n.* 人種差別

racist *n.* 人種差別主義者

rack *n.* (for luggage) 棚, (for hanging things on) -掛け

Would you put your luggage on the rack, please?
荷物は棚に置いていただけませんか？

a magazine rack マガジンラック

a hat rack 帽子掛け

a towel rack タオル掛け

a slipper rack スリッパ立て

racket[1] *n.* (for tennis/badminton) ラケット

racket[2] *n.* (noise) 騒音, 大騒ぎ; (dishonest business) 不正な商売

radar *n.* レーダー

radiance *n.* 輝き

radiant *adj.* (bright, emitting light) 輝く, (happy-looking) うれしそうな

radiate *v.* 放射する, 発する, (extend in raylike fashion from a central point) 放射状に伸びる

radiation *n.* 放射線, 放射物

radiator *n.* (in car) ラジエーター

radical *adj.* (fundamental) 根本的な, 抜本的な; (leftist) 急進的な, ラジカルな, (extreme) 過激な

n. (person) 過激論者, (politician) 急進党員; (part of Chinese character) 部首

radical reforms 抜本的な改革

a group of radical students
過激派の学生たち

radically *adv.* (completely) 根本的に, 完全に

be radically different 根本的に違う

radio *n.* ラジオ

v. (contact by radio) 無線連絡する, (send by radio) 無線で送る

Do you listen to the radio much?
ラジオはよく聴きますか？

turn on [off] the radio
ラジオをつける [消す]

The ship radioed for help.
その船は無線で助けを求めた。

♦ **radio-controlled** *adj.* ラジコンの, 無線制御の

radio station *n.* ラジオ局

radioactive *adj.* 放射性の, 放射能のある

radioactive waste 放射性廃棄物

♦ **radioactivity** *n.* 放射性, 放射能

radiology *n.* 放射線科, 放射線学

radio wave *n.* 周波数帯

radish *n.* ラディッシュ, 二十日大根, (daikon) 大根

radium *n.* ラジウム

radius *n.* 半径

We were within a ten-kilometer radius of our destination.
目的地から半径10キロ以内の所にいた。

radon *n.* ラドン

raft *n.* いかだ, (life raft) 救命ボート

rafter *n.* (wooden beam for ceiling) 垂木

rafting *n.* いかだ乗り, 川下り

go rafting いかだ乗りに行く

rag *n.* ぼろきれ, (for cleaning window) ぞうきん, (**rags**: ragged clothes) ぼろぼろの服, ぼろ服

an old rag 古いぼろきれ

He was dressed in rags.
その人は、ぼろぼろの服を着ていた。

rags to riches 無一文から大金持ちに

rage *n.* (anger) 怒り, 激怒

v. (of storm) 荒れ狂う, (of battle, argument) 激しく続く; (of person: rage about sth) 激怒する

The teacher was trembling with rage.
先生は怒りに震えていた。

The battle raged. 戦闘は激化した。

be all the rage 大流行だ, 大はやりだ

ragged *adj.* (of clothes) ぼろぼろの, (of

badly dressed person) ぼろを着た; (of edge) ぎざぎざの

raid *n.* 襲撃

v. 襲撃する, (of army) (…に) 奇襲攻撃をする, (of police) (…に) 踏み込む

an air raid 空襲

The police raided the place for drugs. 警察は麻薬捜査でそこに踏み込んだ。

rail *n.* (handrail) 手すり, (railroad track) レール, 線路, (railway) 鉄道

I leaned against the rail and stared out over the ocean.
手すりに寄りかかって海を眺めていた。

go by rail 列車で行く

go off the rails (of train) 脱線する

railing *n.* (handrail) 手すり, (guardrail) ガードレール, (fence) さく

railroad *n.* 鉄道

When was the first railroad built?
いつ最初の鉄道が敷かれたのですか?

a railroad company 鉄道会社

♦**railroad crossing** *n.* 踏切

railroad station *n.* 駅

railroad track *n.* 線路

railway *n.* 鉄道

rain *n.* 雨, (rainwater) 雨水, (fall of rain) 雨降り

v. 雨が降る

heavy rain 大雨 [どしゃ降り, 豪雨]

light rain 小雨

The rain is coming through the roof.
屋根から雨が漏っている。

It's raining heavily [lightly].
大雨 [小雨] だ。

Do you think it will rain today?
今日、雨が降ると思う?

It's started raining. 雨が降り出した。

It looks like it's going to rain.
雨になりそうです。

It looks like it's going to stop raining.
雨は上がりそうです。

rainbow *n.* にじ

A rainbow appeared. にじが出た。

rainbow trout *n.* ニジマス

raincoat *n.* レインコート

raindrop *n.* 雨のしずく, 雨だれ

rainfall *n.* (quantity of rain) 雨量

rain forest *n.* 熱帯雨林

rainproof *adj.* 防水の

rainy *adj.* 雨の, 雨の多い

a rainy day 雨の日

♦**rainy season** *n.* (in Japan) 梅雨, (in other countries) 雨季

raise

1 *v.* LIFT/PUT UP: (lift to a higher position) 上げる, 高くする, 持ち上げる, (flag) 揚げる; (**raise oneself**) 腰を上げる; (**raise one's voice**) 大声を出す, 声を張り上げる

2 *v.* INCREASE THE LEVEL OF: 引き上げる, (bolster, improve) 高める

3 *v.* GATHER: (money, support) 集める

4 *v.* REAR: (child) 育てる, ((*formal*)) 養育する

5 *v.* OFFER FOR CONSIDERATION: (question, point, topic) 挙げる, 持ち出す

6 *v.* PROVOKE: (suspicion, fear) いだかせる, (laughter) 引き起こす

7 *v.* GROW: (crops) 作る, 栽培する

8 *v.* BREED: (animals) 飼う

9 *v.* ERECT: (building, statue) 建てる

10 *n.* SALARY INCREASE: 昇給, 賃上げ

1 The level of the work surface needs to be raised a couple of centimeters.
作業台をもう2、3センチ高くする必要がある。

Everyone who agrees, raise your hand.
賛成の人は手を挙げてください。

She raised her head when the teacher called her name.
先生が名前を呼ぶと彼女は頭を上げた。

At last he raised himself from the sofa.
ようやく彼はソファーから腰を上げた。

There's no need to raise your voice like that.
そんなに大声を出す必要はありません。

2 The government's trying to raise the employment rate.
政府は雇用率を引き上げようとしている。

The standard of education can't be raised overnight.
教育水準は一朝一夕には高められない。

raise morale 士気を高める

3 We're trying to raise money for the relief effort.
救援活動のための資金を集めようとしているんです。

Politicians will promise anything to raise support.
支持を集めるためなら、政治家は何でも約束する。

4 Raising a child is no easy matter.
子供を育てるのは簡単なことではない。

He was born and raised in Brooklyn.
彼はブルックリンで生まれ育った。

5 That's an interesting point you've raised.
今挙げられた点は面白いですね。

I wouldn't raise the issue.
私なら、その問題を持ち出さない。

6 His comments raised quite a storm.
彼の発言は、波乱を引き起こした。

It raised a laugh.
それは笑いを誘った。

7 She raises corn and soybeans.
彼女はトウモロコシと大豆を栽培している。

8 He raises cattle in North Dakota.
彼はノースダコタ州で牛を飼っている。

9 A monument was raised to honor the fallen.
戦死者の栄誉をたたえて、記念碑が建てられた。

10 Did you get the raise you hoped for?
期待どおりの昇給でしたか？

raisin *n.* 干しブドウ, レーズン

rake *n.* (tool) くま手

v. はく

I'm going to rake the leaves this afternoon.
午後、落ち葉をはきます。

rally *n.* (gathering) 集会; (continuous series of shots in tennis) ラリー; (car race) ラリー

v. (gather: support) 集める

a political rally 政治集会

The Opposition could not rally enough support.
野党は十分な支持を集められなかった。

RAM *n.* (random-access memory) RAM

ram *n.* (male sheep) 雄羊

v. (crash into) (…に)ぶつかる, 激突する

He was drunk and rammed his car into a wall.
彼は酔っ払って、車で塀に激突した。

ramble *v.* (go for a long walk) 散歩する, ぶらつく, (talk in a confused fashion) とりとめもなく話す

n. (long walk) 散歩

rambling *adj.* (digressive) とりとめのない, まとまりのない

rambunctious *adj.* (of child) 手に負えない

ramen *n.* (Chinese noodles) ラーメン

ramification *n.* (**ramifications**: results) 結果

ramp *n.* ランプ, (leading to a building) スロープ

rampage *n.* 狂暴な行為

go on a rampage 暴れ回る

rampant *adj.* (of growth) 生い茂る, (of disease) はびこる, 猛威をふるう

ramshackle *adj.* 今にも倒れそうな

ranch *n.* (where animals are raised) 大牧場, (where crops are grown) 大農場

♦**rancher** *n.* 牧場主, 農場主

rancid *adj.* (bad-smelling) 腐ったにおいのする, (bad-tasting) 腐った味のする

R&B *n.* (music) リズム・アンド・ブルース

random *adj.* 行き当たりばったりの, ((*formal*)) 任意の, 無作為の

a random comment 出まかせの発言

a random guess 当てずっぽう

a random sampling 無作為抽出

random shooting 銃の乱射

at random でたらめに, ((*formal*)) 無作為に

select at random 任意に選ぶ

range

1 *n.* SCALE/VARIETY: 幅, 範囲

2 *v.* VARY: (range from A to B) (AからBに) 及ぶ, わたる

3 *n.* DISTANCE: 距離, 範囲, (firing range) 射程距離; (earshot) 聞こえる距離

4 *n.* HILLS/MOUNTAINS: (of hills) 連なり, (of mountains: **mountain range**) 山脈

5 *n.* STOVE: レンジ [→ picture of KITCHEN]

6 *n.* PLACE FOR SHOOTING GUNS: 射撃場

1 What's the price range?
値段の幅 [価格帯] はどのくらいですか？

It costs somewhere in the range of one to two hundred dollars.
費用は100ドルから200ドルの範囲 [間] です。

a wide range of choice 幅広い選択肢

The age range varies a great deal.
年齢層が非常に広い。

2 Proficiency levels range from elementary to advanced.
技能のレベルは初級から上級にわたっています。

The talk ranged over various issues.
話し合いは、さまざまな問題に及んだ。

3 long [short] range 遠 [近] 距離

This gun has a range of a hundred meters.
この銃は射程距離が100メートルです。

4 a range of hills 山並み [小山の連なり]

5 a gas range ガスレンジ

6 practice shooting at a range
射撃場で射撃の練習をする

at close range 至近距離で/から

He was shot at close range.
彼は至近距離から撃たれた。

out of range 射程外に

within range 射程内に

ranger *n.* レンジャー, (forest ranger) 森

林警備員, (park ranger) 国立公園警備員

rank[1] *n.* (level in hierarchy) 位, 階級, (official position) 地位, (social standing) 身分; (**the ranks**: the soldiers as opposed to the officers) 兵士, 兵卒

v. (assess) 位置づける, 評価する

What's his rank?
あの人はどういう地位ですか？

He's an officer who has risen from the ranks.
一兵卒から将校になった人です。

I don't rank it very highly.
私はあまり高く評価していません。

the rank and file 一般人, (in company) 一般社員, (in society) 一般会員

rank[2] *adj.* (of odor) 悪臭のする, 臭い

ranking *n.* ランキング, 順位

a low [high] ranking 低い [高い] 順位

ransack *v.* (plunder, pillage) 荒らす, (…から) 略奪する

ransom *n.* 身代金

hold to/for ransom 人質にして身代金を要求する

rant *v.* わめく

rant and rave わめき散らす

rap *n.* (sound) ノックする音; (music) ラップ

v. (hit) トントン/コツコツたたく; (perform rap music) ラップを歌う

♦ **rapper** *n.* ラッパー

rape *n.* レイプ, 強姦

v. レイプする, 強姦する

a rape victim レイプ被害者

rapid *adj.* (speedy) 速い, 急速な

n. (**rapids**) 急流, 早瀬

a rapid recovery 早い回復

She's made rapid progress in math.
彼女は数学でめざましい進歩を遂げた。

The situation has shown rapid improvement.
事態は急速に収拾に向かった。

Those rapids look dangerous.
あそこの急流は危なそうだ。

♦ **rapidly** *adv.* 速く, 急速に, 素早く

The temperature is dropping rapidly.
気温は急速に下がっている。

rapport *n.* (relationship) 関係

Mr. Fujita has a good rapport with his students.
藤田先生は、生徒たちといい関係を築いている。

rapt *adj.* (of audience) 没頭している, 夢中になっている

with rapt attention 一心不乱に, 夢中で

Everyone was watching with rapt attention.
みんな、夢中になって見ていた。

rapture *n.* 大喜び, 狂喜, 有頂天

The winning goal sent the crowd into raptures.
決勝ゴールに観衆は狂喜した。

rapturous *adj.* (joyful) 大喜びの, 狂喜の, (feverish) 熱狂的な

The president was greeted with rapturous applause.
大統領は、熱狂的な拍手かっさいで迎えられた。

rare[1] *adj.* (infrequent) 珍しい, めったにない, まれな, ((*formal*)) 希少な

It's a rare bird. 珍しい鳥です。

Mr. Goto collects rare plants.
後藤さんは珍しい植物を収集している。

It's a rare sight these days.
近ごろは、めったに見られない光景だ。

rare² *adj.* (lightly cooked) 生焼けの, レアの

I'll have my steak rare.
ステーキはレアでお願いします。

rarely *adv.* めったに…ない

I rarely go to bed before midnight these days.
このごろは、12時前に寝ることはめったにない。

rarity *n.* (rare person/thing) 珍しい人/物, (rare occurrence) まれなこと

rascal *n.* いたずらっ子, (scoundrel) ならず者

rash¹ *adj.* (hasty) 軽率な, 軽はずみな, 性急な

Don't make rash promises.
軽はずみな約束をするものではない。

He made a rash decision to marry.
彼は性急に結婚を決めた。

♦ **rashly** *adv.* 軽率に

rash² *n.* 発疹, 吹き出物, (heat rash) あせも; (outbreak of sth) 多発, 頻発

rasp *v.* (make awful sound) ギシギシ/ギーギー音がする, (of person: say with a rasp) しゃがれ声で言う

The gate rasped on its hinges.
門がギーギー音を立てた。

raspberry *n.* キイチゴ, ラズベリー, (color) 暗い赤紫 (色)

rat *n.* ネズミ, ドブネズミ, (as laboratory animal) ラット

rate

1 *n.* RATIO: 率, 割合

2 *n.* MANNER OF PROCEEDING: 進み具合, (speed) 速度, 速さ

3 *n.* QUALITY: (**-rate**) -級, -流

4 *n.* EXCHANGE RATE: 為替相場, 換算レート

5 *n.* COST: 料金, 代金

6 *v.* REGARD: 評価する, みなす, 考える, ((*informal*)) 思う

7 *v.* BE RANKED: (…と) ランク付けされる, 評価される

1 the mortality rate 死亡率
the rate of progress 成長率
a discount rate 割引 [値引] 率
interest rates 金利 [利率]

2 We'll never get there at this rate.
この調子では、着くのは無理だ。

a rate of thirty kilometers per hour
時速30キロの速度

3 That was a first-rate meal.
あれは第一級の料理でした。

It was a second-rate performance.
二流の演技だった。

4 the yen-to-dollar exchange rate
ドルに対する円の為替レート [相場]

5 water rates 水道料金
telephone rates 電話料金

6 How would you rate his chances of success?
彼がうまくやれる公算は、どのくらいだと考えますか?

7 On a scale of one to five, it rated four.
5段階評価で4だった。

at any rate とにかく, いずれにせよ

rather *adv.*

1 AS OPPOSED TO: (**rather than**) …というよりも, …よりむしろ

2 SOMEWHAT: ちょっと, かなり, なかなか

3 PREFERABLY: (**would rather do**) …より(も)…したい, むしろ…するほうがいい

4 THAT IS: (**or rather…**) というより(は)…

1 It's a coat rather than a jacket.
ジャケットというよりコートですね。

This text is for classroom use rather than self-study.
このテキストは自習用というより、教室で使うためのものです。

2 It is rather cold today.
今日は、ちょっと冷えますね。

It was rather difficult.
かなり難しかった。

3 I'd rather have a dog than a cat.
猫より犬を飼いたい。

I think I'd rather stay at home.
私は、家にいるほうがいい。

"Would you like to join us for a drink?" "Thanks, but I'd rather not."
「いっしょに一杯どうですか？」
「せっかくですが、遠慮しておきます」

4 He failed the class—or rather he was kicked out.
彼は落第した──というより追い出されたんだ。

ratify *v.* (treaty) 批准する

♦**ratification** *n.* 批准

rating *n.* 評価, 格付け, (approval rating) 支持率, (credit rating) 信用度; (**ratings**) (=of TV show) 視聴率, (=of radio show) 聴取率; (of film: PG, R etc.) 指定

The president's approval rating has soared in recent months.
大統領の支持率は、この数ヵ月で急上昇した。

What's his credit rating?
彼の信用度はどんなもんですか？

The show's ratings have dropped.
その番組の視聴率が落ちた。

ratio *n.* 割合, 比率

a ratio of one teacher to thirty students
生徒３０人に先生１人の割合

The ratio of old people to young is changing rapidly in developed countries.
先進諸国では、高齢者と若者の比率が急速に変化している。

ration *n.* (amount) 配給量, 割当量, (**rations**: food) 配給食料

v. (**ration out**: distribute) 配給する

♦**rationing** *n.* 配給

rational *adj.* 理性的な, 合理的な

For God's sake, let's try to be rational about this.
頼むから、ここは理性的になろうよ。

There was no rational explanation for it.
それに対して合理的な説明はなかった。

rationale *n.* (reason) 理由

rationalism *n.* 合理主義

rationalist *n.* 合理主義者

rationalization *n.* (justifying) 正当化

rationalize *v.* (justify) 正当化する

rationally *adv.* 合理的に

Let's think rationally.
合理的に考えよう。

rattle *v.* (make a short sharp sound) ガタガタ/ガラガラ音を立てる, (cause to make a sharp sound) ガタガタ/ガラガラさせる

n. (sound) ガタガタ/ガラガラ(いう音); (child's toy) ガラガラ

There's something rattling outside.
外で何かガタガタ音がしている。

Did you hear that rattle?
今、ガタガタいう音が聞こえた？

be rattled by (be unnerved by) …に当惑する

rattlesnake ***n.*** ガラガラヘビ

raucous ***adj.*** しわがれた, 耳障りな

ravage ***v.*** (damage) 破壊する, 荒らす, 荒廃させる

The country has been ravaged by war for decades.
国はここ十数年の戦争で、荒廃した。

rave ***v.*** わめく; (**rave about**: praise to the skies) ほめちぎる

raven ***n.*** ワタリガラス, 大ガラス

ravine ***n.*** 峡谷

raw ***adj.*** (of food) 生の, (=not cooked enough) 生焼けの, (of materials: unprocessed) 加工されていない, 未処理の

raw fish 生魚

The meat was raw. 肉は生だった。

raw data 生の [加工されていない] データ

raw sewage 未処理の下水

♦ **raw materials** ***n.*** 原料, 原材料

ray ***n.*** (sun's ray) 光線, ((*figurative*)) 一筋の光

The sun's rays had never penetrated the cave.
太陽光線が、洞窟に差し込んだことはなかった。

a ray of hope 一筋の希望の光

rayon ***n.*** レーヨン

raze ***v.*** 破壊する

The entire building was razed to the ground.
建物は全壊した。

razor ***n.*** かみそり

Do you sell razors here?
かみそりは置いていますか？

razor-sharp ***adj.*** ((*also figurative*)) かみそりのように鋭い

The edge was razor sharp.
刃は、かみそりのように鋭かった。

re- ***pref.*** 再-, 再び, もう一度/一回/一遍

[NOTE: 再- can only attach to Sino-Japanese nouns or "noun + する" verbs; the others can attach to verbs of any kind.]

reach

1 ***v.*** ARRIVE AT/IN: (…に) 着く, 到着する, (of letter) (…に) 届く, (of typhoon: come ashore) (…に) 上陸する

2 ***v.*** USING ARM: (**reach for**) (…に) 手を伸ばす, (touch by stretching) (…に) 届く

3 ***v.*** A STAGE/LEVEL: (…に) なる, 達する, (agreement, conclusion) (…に) 達する, 到達する

4 ***v.*** CONTACT: (…に) 連絡する

5 ***n.*** DISTANCE/LIMIT SB CAN STRETCH: リーチ, 手の届く範囲

6 ***n.*** EXPANSE: (**reaches**) 広がり

1 We reached Tokyo by evening.
夜には東京に着きました。

They reached the summit at sunrise.
一行は日の出に頂上に到達した。

Did the letter reach you?
手紙は届きましたか？

By noon, the typhoon had reached the mainland.
正午には、台風は本土に上陸していた。

2 She reached for her bag.

彼女はバッグに手を伸ばした。

He reached over for the salt.
彼は塩を取ろうと手を伸ばした。

If I stretch my arm upward, I can reach the ceiling.
手を伸ばせば天井に届く。

3 reach adulthood 成人 [おとな] になる

Unemployment has reached a high level.
失業率は高いレベルに達した。

The figures reached a new low.
数値が過去最低に達した。

The coat reached down to her ankles.
コートは足首にまで達していた。

We reached an agreement after consultation.
話し合いの結果、合意に達しました。

A decision was reached at the eleventh hour.
どたん場で結論が出た。

4 I tried to reach you several times by phone, but you weren't in.
((*polite*)) 何度か、お電話を差し上げたんですが、ご不在だったんです。

The senator could not be reached for comment.
上院議員にコメントを取ろうとしたが、連絡がつかなかった。

5 He has a long reach.
あの人は手 [リーチ] が長い。

6 the outer reaches of our solar system
太陽系の外れ

within reach (nearby) 近く, (attainable) 手が届く, 手に入れられる

It's within easy reach of the station.
駅から、すぐ [目と鼻の先] です。

out of reach 手が届かない

Keep the medicine out of reach of the children.
薬は子供の手の届かない所にしまっておくように。

react *v.* 反応する, 反応を示す, (**react against**) (…に) 反発する, 反抗する

I wonder how he'll react to the new boss.
新しい上司に、彼はどういうふうに反応するだろう。

Phosphorus reacts to high temperatures.
リンは高温に反応する。

It's natural for teenagers to react against the values of their parents.
10代の子が親の価値観に反発するのは、自然なことです。

reaction *n.* 反応, (**reactions**: reflexes) 反射神経, 反作用

a chemical reaction 化学反応

an allergic reaction アレルギー反応

It was a reaction against the times.
時代に対する反動だった。

quick reactions 素早い反応

reactionary *adj.* 反動的な

reactivate *v.* 復活させる, 再活性化する

reactor *n.* (nuclear reactor) 原子炉

read *v.*

1 UNDERSTAND WRITING: 読む, (read aloud) 声に出して読む, (recite, narrate) 朗読する

2 INTERPRET: 読む, 判読する, (read into) (…の中に) 読み取る, (**read between the lines**) 行間を読む

3 INDICATE: 示す, 表示する

1 I was reading the paper while waiting.
待っている間、新聞を読んでいました。

I remember reading about that in the

newspaper.
それは新聞で読んだ覚えがあります。

How do you read this kanji?
この漢字は何と読みますか？

Can you read French?
フランス語が読めますか？

Could you read this to me, please?
これを読んでいただけませんか？

Would you read that out aloud?
声に出して読んでいただけますか？

I do enjoy listening to stories read on the radio.
ラジオで物語の朗読を聴くのが楽しいんです。

2 Can you read music? 楽譜が読める？

How do you know? Can you read his mind?
どうして知ってるの？ 彼の心が読めるの？

She can read people's palms.
あの人は手相を見ることができます。

A deeper meaning can be read into it.
もっと深い意味を読み取ることもできます。

3 What does the meter read?
メーターは何と表示されてる？

reader *n.* (of magazines) 読者; (book for learning to read) リーダー, 読本

readily *adv.* (willingly) 進んで, 喜んで; (easily) 容易に, 簡単に

Internet access is readily available at stations and airports.
インターネットへのアクセスは、駅や空港でも簡単にできます。

reading *n.*

1 ACT OF READING: 読書, 本を読むこと, (narration) 朗読, (way of reading) 読み方

2 MATERIAL: 読み物

3 INTERPRETATION: 解釈

4 INDICATION: 表示

1 Reading is fun. 読書は楽しい。

I do a lot of reading in the summer.
夏はたくさん本を読みます。

That reading of Eliot's poetry was excellent.
あのエリオットの詩の朗読はみごとだった。

Do you know the reading of this kanji?
この漢字の読み方を知っていますか？

2 This is good reading.
これはいい読み物です。

3 What is your reading of the situation?
この状況をどう解釈します [見ます] か？

4 The machine gave the wrong reading.
器械の表示が間違っていた。

♦ **reading circle** *n.* 読書会

reading glasses *n.* 老眼鏡, 拡大鏡

reading room *n.* 読書室, (in library) 閲覧室

readjust *v.* (settings) もう一度調整する, 調整し直す; (of person to surroundings) もう一度 (...に) 慣れる

readmit *v.* (**be readmitted** to school) 再入学する, 復学する

♦ **readmission** *n.* (to school) 再入学

ready *adj.*

1 PREPARED: (**be ready for / to do**) ...の/する準備ができた, (mentally ready) 覚悟ができた, (of dinner) でき上がっている, (**get ready**: prepare) 用意する, (**get oneself ready**) 身支度をする

2 WILLING: (**be ready to do**) 喜んで...する

3 ABOUT TO DO: (**be ready to do**) (今にも) ...しようとする

R

1 Everything's ready. All we need to do now is wait for the guests to arrive.
準備はすべて整った。あとは、お客さんの到着を待つばかりだ。

I don't think she's ready to start dating yet.
あの子はまだ、男の子と付き合う心の準備ができていないと思う。

Dinner will be ready in half an hour.
あと 30 分で晩ご飯ができるよ。

Hurry up and get ready, will you.
さっさと支度をしてくれない？

2 He's always ready to lend a hand.
彼はいつでも喜んで手を貸してくれる。

They are only too ready to criticize.
あの人たちは、すぐに批判をする。

A lot of people are ready to move to the capital to find work.
職を求めて首都に移り住もうとしている人たちが、大勢いる。

3 I was ready to head out the door when the phone rang.
出かけようとしていたところに、電話が鳴った。

ready-made *adj.* 既製の, 出来合いの

reaffirm *v.* (declare anew) 再び断言する, (commitment) 再確認する

real

1 *adj.* GENUINE: 本物の, 本当の, 真の

2 *adj.* EXISTING IN THE REAL WORLD: 実際の, 現実の, 実在する

3 *adj.* SERIOUS: 大変な

4 *adj.* COMPLETE: ((*informal*)) 全くの, すごい

5 *adv.* REALLY: 本当に, ものすごく

1 This is real silk. これは本物の絹です。

I can't tell whether it's real butter or not.
本物のバターかどうかわかりません。

If you want the real thing, you'll have to pay for it.
本物が欲しいなら、それに見合う金額を払わなくてはなりません。

That is not the issue. The real issue is...
それは問題ではない。本当の問題は...

I have no idea what her real opinion of me is.
彼女が僕のことを、本当はどう思っているのか、全然見当がつかない。

That's not the real reason you're calling me.
それは、電話をかけてきた本当の理由じゃないでしょ。

I think they are real heroes.
あの人たちは真のヒーローだと思う。

2 Are these real people, or just fictional characters?
これは実在する人たちですか？ それとも架空の人物ですか？

The events described here are real.
ここで語られた出来事は、実話 [本当にあったこと] です。

3 That boy is in real trouble.
その子は、かなり困った立場になっている。

4 He's a real jerk.
全くむかつく奴だ。

5 It was real nice of him to come.
彼が来てくれて本当によかった。

for real 本当に, 本気で

Get real! 現実的になれよ

real estate *n.* 不動産

real estate agent *n.* 不動産屋

realign *v.* (regroup, reorganize) 再編成する; (tires) (...の) 位置を再調整する

♦ **realignment** *n.* (regrouping) 再編成; (of tires) 再調整

realism *n.* 現実主義, (artistic realism) 写実主義, リアリズム

realist *n.* 現実主義者

realistic *adj.* 現実的な, (of story) 写実主義の, (true to life) 写実的な, リアルな

reality *n.* 現実, (thing) 現実のこと

You need a reality check.
あなたの考えが、現実的かどうか検討することが必要だ。

in reality 実際は, 現実は

realization *n.* (understanding) 理解, 認識; (making real) 実現

come to/be hit with the realization that... ...と気づく, ...とわかる

realize *v.* (understand) わかる, 知る, (become aware of) (...に) 気がつく; (make real) 実現する, (**realize a dream**) 夢をかなえる

Do you realize you're the first person I've spoken to about this?
このことを話すのは、あなたが初めてだということをわかっている?

I didn't realize at the time that he was married.
あのときは、彼が結婚しているなんて知りませんでした。

I realized the importance of the job too late.
その仕事の大切さに気づいたが、後の祭りだった。

She's a lot smarter than most people realize.
人が思っているより、彼女はずっと頭がいいんです。

really

1 *adv.* **IN FACT:** 本当に, 実際に

2 *adv.* **USED EMPHATICALLY:** 本当に, 実に, 全く

3 *adv.* **VERY:** すごく, 本当に, 実に

4 *interj.* **EXPRESSING SURPRISE/DISBELIEF:** (Is that so?) そうですか, えっ, 本当?, (I can't believe it!) うそ!, まさか

1 Is that really true? 本当ですか?
Is that really you speaking?
今話しているのは本当にあなたなの?

2 I really ought to be going now.
本当に、もう行かなくてはなりません。
It's really a tragedy.
実に気の毒なことだ。

3 That is really interesting.
すごく面白いよ。
The houses around here are really expensive.
この辺の家は、ものすごく高い。

4 Really? You won first prize?
本当? 1位を取ったの?
Really! How extraordinary!
まさか! すごい話だねえ!

realm *n.* (kingdom) 王国, (world, sphere) 世界, (subject area) 分野

a small realm 小さな王国
in the realm of fantasy 空想の世界で

real time *n.* リアルタイム

real world *n.* (**the real world**) 実社会, 現実の世界

In the real world, such idealism is useless.
実社会で、そんな理想主義は通用しない。

ream *n.* (quantity of paper) 連, リーム; (**reams of**: lots of) たくさんの, 多量の

reap *v.* 刈る, 刈り入れる, (harvest) 収穫する, (obtain) 得る, 受ける

reap the corn トウモロコシを刈り入れる

reap one's rewards 報酬を得る

reappear *v.* また出てくる, 再び現れる, (of characters on TV, in film) 再登場する

♦**reappearance** *n.* 再出現, (on TV, in film) 再登場

reapply *v.* (for school) 再出願する, (for job) もう一度応募する, (for loan) 再び申し込む; (sunscreen etc.) 塗り直す

reappoint *v.* 再任する

reappraisal *n.* 再検討

reappraise *v.* 再検討する

rear[1] *adj.* (back) 後ろの, 裏の

n. (back) 後ろ, 裏, (buttocks) (お)尻

the rear of the building

ビルの後ろ [裏手]

the rear entrance 裏口

rear[2] *v.* (raise: child) 育てる

rear admiral *n.* (in U.S. Navy) 少将

rear end *n.* (of car) 後部, (of person) (お)尻

v. (**rear-end**: hit from behind) (…に) 追突する

rearm *v.* 再武装する, 再軍備する

♦**rearmament** *n.* 再武装, 再軍備

rearrange *v.* 配列し直す, (room) (…の) 模様替えをする, (schedule) 立て直す

♦**rearrangement** *n.* 再配列, 再整理

rearview mirror *n.* バックミラー [→ picture of CAR]

reason

1 *n.* LOGICAL CAUSE OR MOTIVE: 理由, 訳, (grounds) 根拠, (motive) 動機

2 *n.* FACULTY: 理性

3 *n.* RIGHT THINKING: 道理

4 *v.* THINK: (use reason) (…と) 論理的に考える, (**reason that…**) (=conclude) (…と) 考える, ((*formal*)) 推論する, (=argue) (…と) 論じる

5 *v.* PERSUADE: (**reason with**) 説得する

1 It's usual to give reasons for your absence.

欠席の理由を言うのが普通です。

It was for this reason, and this reason alone, that I quit soccer.

僕がサッカーをやめたのは、ひとえに、そういう理由からだった。

I have reasons for saying this.

これを言うのには訳があるんです。

For some reason or other, he keeps making excuses.

どういう訳か、あの人は弁解ばかりする。

She had every reason to doubt his word.

彼女が彼の言葉を疑うには、十分な根拠があった。

2 Reason, not emotion, is needed here.

ここは感情的にならず、理性を働かせましょう。

3 Listen to reason, will you.

道理をわきまえなさいよ。

4 The teacher reasoned that humorous presentations help people to learn and remember.

その先生は、ユーモアたっぷりに説明することが、理解と記憶を助けるのではないかと論じた。

5 See if you can reason with him.

彼を説得できるかどうかやってみて。

within reason 常識の範囲内で

R

He'll do anything for money—within reason, of course.
お金のためならあの人は何でもしますよ。と言っても、もちろん常識の範囲内でですが。

reasonable ***adj.*** (sensible) もっともな, 妥当な, (of person) 分別のある, 道理をわきまえた; (of price) 手ごろな, リーズナブルな

It seemed a reasonable request.
もっともな要求に思えた。

We are all reasonable people.
私たちはみんな、分別のある人間です。

Let's be reasonable.
道理をわきまえようよ。

I don't mind doing what you ask as long as it's reasonable.
無理なことでない限り、やってあげるよ。

I got it at a reasonable price.
手ごろな値段で手に入れました。

reasonably ***adv.*** (to a fair extent) けっこう, かなり; (sensibly) 分別をもって

reasoning ***n.*** (thinking) 考え方, (logic) 論理

reassess ***v.*** (reevaluate) 再評価する, (reconsider) 見直す

♦**reassessment** ***n.*** 再評価

reassure ***v.*** 安心させる

He reassured us that the terms of the contract would be favorable.
契約条件が有利になりますと言って、彼は私たちを安心させた。

♦**reassured** ***adj.*** (at ease) 安心する, 心強い

feel reassured 安心する

rebate ***n.*** 払い戻し

rebel ***v.*** (...に) 反抗する, 反発する, 背く ***n.*** (person) 反逆者, 反抗する者

As an adolescent he rebelled against his father's authority.
思春期のころ、彼は父親の権威に反抗した。

rebellion ***n.*** 反乱

start a rebellion 反乱を起こす

rebellious ***adj.*** (of youth) 反抗的な

a rebellious stage (in growing up) 反抗期

rebirth ***n.*** (revival) 復活, リバイバル; (after death) 再生

reborn ***adj.*** (be reborn) 生まれ変わる

rebound ***v.*** (bounce back) はね返る, (from illness) (...から) 回復する, (from depression) 立ち直る

rebroadcast ***v.*** 再放送する

rebuff ***v.*** (reject: suggestion, request) はねつける, 拒絶する

rebuild ***v.*** (house) 建て直す, 再建する, (country, life, economy) 立て直す, 再建する, (trust, confidence) 取り戻す

rebuke ***v.*** 叱責する, 非難する

recall ***v.*** (recollect) 思い出す, (call to mind) 思い起こさせる; (product) リコールする, 回収する

recapture ***v.*** (steal back) 奪い返す, 奪還する, (rearrest) 再逮捕する, 再び捕まえる; (call to mind: memories, atmosphere) 思い出させる

The army recaptured the bridge.
軍隊は橋を奪還した。

The thief was recaptured by the police.
泥棒は、再び警察に捕まった。

recast ***v.*** (mold again) 鋳直す, (make

R

again) 作り直す; (give another role to) (...の) 配役を変える

recede *v.* 後退する, (of tide, flood) 引く, (of hair) はげてくる

His hairline is receding.
あの人は額が、はげてきている。

receipt *n.* (proof of payment) 領収書, レシート

Don't throw away the receipt.
領収書を捨てないでね。

receive *v.*

1 BE GIVEN: 受け取る, 受ける, もらう, ((*humble*)) いただく

2 WELCOME: 受け入れる, (**be well received**) 評判がいい

3 EXPERIENCE: (injury) 負う, (education, treatment) 受ける

4 RADIO SIGNAL: 受信する

1 Did you receive your money?
お金を受け取りましたか？

We've received a lot of complaints.
苦情をたくさん受けた。

I received your present. Thank you.
プレゼント、いただきました。どうもありがとうございました。

2 His latest book was well received.
あの作家の最新作は評判がよかった。

3 He received minor injuries.
彼は軽傷を負った。

receiver *n.* (part of telephone) 受話器, (radio) 受信機; (person) 受取人, (in sport) レシーバー

recent *adj.* 最近の, 近ごろの, この前の

They were talking about their recent vacation.
彼らは、この前の休暇の話をしていた。

in recent times 近年, このところ

in recent years 近年, ここ数年

recently *adv.* 最近, 近ごろ, このごろ

They recently bought a new car.
彼らは最近、新しい車を買った。

receptacle *n.* 入れ物, 器, 容器

reception *n.*

1 IN BUILDING: 受付, フロント

2 RESPONSE: 反応, 受け入れ

3 PARTY: 歓迎会, レセプション, (wedding reception) (結婚) 披露宴

4 OF TV/RADIO: (receiving of signals) 受信, (picture on TV) 映り

1 We'd better sign in at the reception.
受付で記帳しなくてはいけないね。

Excuse me, could you tell me where the reception desk is?
すみません。受付はどこでしょうか？

2 How was the book's reception abroad?
その本の外国での反応は、いかがでしたか？

She got a warm reception.
彼女はあたたかく迎えられた。

3 The wedding reception was held in a hotel near the church.
結婚披露宴は、教会の近くのホテルで催された。

4 The proximity of the airport sometimes interferes with the TV reception.
空港が近いので、時々テレビの映りが悪くなる。

receptionist *n.* 受付の人, 受付係

receptive *adj.* (to new ideas) 受容力がある, よく受け入れる

recess *n.* (break) 休憩, (playtime) 休み

時間, (of congress) 休会

recession ***n.*** 不景気, 景気後退

recharge ***v.*** (battery) 再充電する

recharge one's batteries ((*figurative*)) 充電する

recipe ***n.*** 作り方, 調理法, レシピ

follow a recipe レシピに従う

a recipe for success 成功の秘訣

recipient ***n.*** 受取人, ((*written*)) 受領者

reciprocal ***adj.*** 相互の

a reciprocal relationship 相互の関係

reciprocate ***v.*** (action) (...に) 報いる, お返しをする

recital ***n.*** (reading) 朗読, 暗唱; (piano recital) リサイタル

recite ***v.*** (poem etc.) 朗読する, (from memory) 暗唱する

reckless ***adj.*** むちゃな, 無謀な

reckless driving 無謀な運転

reckon ***v.*** (think) (...と) 思う; (calculate) ざっと計算する

About one third of all marriages are reckoned to end in divorce.

約3分の1の結婚が、離婚に終わると見られている。

reclaim ***v.*** (waste products) 再生利用する, (land from the sea) 干拓する, (marsh) 埋め立てる, (uncultivated land) 開墾する; (take back) 取り戻す

reclassify ***v.*** 再分類する, 分類し直す

♦**reclassification** ***n.*** 再分類

recline ***v.*** (lie down) 横になる, 体を横たえる, (in chair) 深くもたれて座る

recliner ***n.*** (chair) リクライニングチェア

recluse ***n.*** 隠とん者, 世捨て人

recognition ***n.*** (awareness) 認識, (acknowledgement, acceptance, endorsement) 承認, (praise) 評価, たたえること

in recognition of 認めて

He received a medal in recognition of his bravery.

勇敢さを認められて、彼はメダルをもらいました。

recognize ***v.*** (...と) わかる, (tell apart) 見分ける; (admit as true/legal/valid) 認める, 承認する, (recognize A as B) (Aを Bと) みなす, 認める

I didn't recognize her at first.

初めは、彼女だとわかりませんでした。

Do you think you would recognize him if you saw him again?

もう一度会ったら、彼の顔がわかると思いますか？

They refused to recognize that it was their mistake.

彼らは自分たちのミスだったことを認めようとしなかった。

His was recognized as an exceptional case.

彼の場合は例外とみなされた。

♦**recognizable** ***adj.*** 目に見える, 見分けがつく

There's a recognizable difference between the two paintings.

2枚の絵画には目に見える違いがある。

recollect ***v.*** 思い出す [→ REMEMBER]

recollection ***n.*** (memory) 記憶, (a memory) 思い出

recommend ***v.*** (suggest as good) 推せんする, 勧める, (advise) ...したほうがいいと言う, 勧める, ((*formal*)) 勧告する

R

Would you recommend him?
あの方を推せんなさいますか？

The restaurant was recommended to me by a friend.
そのレストランは友人が勧めてくれた。

I'd recommend you take a vacation.
休みを取ったほうがいいと思いますよ。

The board recommended a merger.
理事会は合併を勧告した。

recommendation *n.* (suggestion) 推せん, (advice) 勧め

on the recommendation of
...の推せん [勧め] で

recompense *v.* 償う [→ COMPENSATE]

reconcile *v.* (opposing beliefs: reconcile A with B) (AとBを) 調和させる, (AとBの) 折り合いをつける, (legal dispute) 調停する

It's a pity they can't reconcile their differences.
両者の折り合いがつかないとは残念だね。

reconciliation *n.* (restoration of relations) 和解

reconfirm *v.* 再確認する

reconnaissance *n.* (military) 偵察

reconnect *v.* 再びつなぐ, (machine to machine, computer to Internet) 再接続する

The electricity has been reconnected.
電気が元どおりつながった。

reconsider *v.* 考え直す, 再考する, (take up for review) 再検討する

Would you at least reconsider?
考え直していただけませんか？

reconsideration *n.* 再考

reconstruct *v.* (rebuild) 再建する, (house) 建て直す, 改築する; (crime) 再現する

reconstruction *n.* (rebuilding) 再建, (restoration) 復元, 復旧

reconvene *v.* 再招集する

record

1 *n.* VINYL RECORD: レコード

2 *v.* COPY: (sound) 録音する, レコーディングする, (picture) 録画する, 記録する

3 *v.* MAKE A NOTE OF: 記録する, 書き留める

4 *n.* NOTE: 記録

5 *n.* BEST PERFORMANCE: 最高記録, 新記録

6 *n.* HISTORY: 経歴

1 She has cut several hit records.
彼女はヒットしたアルバムが数枚ある。

He has lots of jazz records.
彼はジャズのレコードをたくさん持っている。

2 Are you going to record the program?
その番組を録画するの？

The events were recorded on film.
その一連の出来事は撮影された。

Is this interview being recorded?
このインタビューは録音していますか？

3 From now on you're going to have to record all income.
これからは、収入をすべて記録する必要があります。

The secretary recorded the minutes of the meeting.
秘書は議事録を書き留めた。

4 These records date back a century.
この記録は、1世紀以上前にさかのぼります。

There is no record of it in this book.

この本にはそういう記録[記載]はない。

It was the hottest summer on record.
記録的に暑い夏でした。

5 He broke the world long-jump record.
彼は幅跳びの世界記録を破った。

She broke the record again.
彼女は再び記録を更新した。

It was a record time. 新記録でした。

6 an academic record 学歴

a criminal record 犯罪歴 [前科]

off the record オフレコで, 非公式に, 非公開に

Is this off the record?
これは非公開ですか？

recorder *n.* (musical instrument) リコーダー

recording *n.* (sound) 録音, (picture) 録画

a video recording ビデオ録画

record player *n.* レコードプレーヤー

recount *v.* (tell) 順を追って話す, (relate) 列挙する

re-count *v.* (votes) 数え直す
n. 数え直し

recoup *v.* (get back) 取り戻す, 埋め合わせる

He never managed to recoup his losses.
彼は、損失を二度と取り戻すことができなかった。

recourse *n.* 頼ること

have recourse to …に頼る

recover *v.* (get better) 回復する, (recover from shock) 立ち直る; (losses, stolen goods, ability) 取り戻す, (health, composure) 回復する, (corpse) 収容する

The patient finally recovered.
患者はようやく回復した。

Will he recover in time for the match?
彼は試合までに治るでしょうか？

The economy is gradually recovering from recession.
経済は徐々に不景気から回復している。

She never recovered from the loss of her son.
彼女は、息子をなくしたショックから立ち直ることはなかった。

Did the police ever recover the stolen paintings?
結局、警察は盗まれた絵画を取り戻したのですか？

He never recovered the use of his legs.
彼の足の機能は回復しなかった。

A body was recovered from the river.
遺体が川から引き上げられた。

recovery *n.* (getting better) 回復; (retrieving) 取り戻すこと

make a full recovery 完全に回復する

re-create *v.* (sth from the past) 再現する

♦**re-creation** *n.* (reenactment) 再現

recreation *n.* レクリエーション, 娯楽

recrimination *n.* 非難の応酬

recruit *v.* (employ) 採用する, (seek to employ) 募集する, (for service in army) 入隊させる

n. (new company employee) 新入社員, (army recruit) 新兵

We need to recruit a flexible workforce.
臨時従業員を入れる必要がある。

This year we recruited ten new college graduates.
今年は大学の新卒者を10人採用した。

The army is trying to recruit more wom-

R

en.
<ruby>陸軍<rt>りくぐん</rt></ruby>は<ruby>女性兵<rt>じょせいへい</rt></ruby>をもっと<ruby>入隊<rt>にゅうたい</rt></ruby>させようとしている。

♦ **recruitment** *n.* (for company) <ruby>新入社<rt>しんにゅうしゃ</rt></ruby><ruby>員募集<rt>いんぼしゅう</rt></ruby>, (for army) <ruby>新兵募集<rt>しんぺいぼしゅう</rt></ruby>

rectangle *n.* <ruby>長方形<rt>ちょうほうけい</rt></ruby>

rectangular *adj.* <ruby>長方形<rt>ちょうほうけい</rt></ruby>の

rectify *v.* <ruby>直<rt>なお</rt></ruby>す, <ruby>修正<rt>しゅうせい</rt></ruby>する

rectum *n.* <ruby>直腸<rt>ちょくちょう</rt></ruby>

recuperate *v.* (get better) <ruby>回復<rt>かいふく</rt></ruby>する; (get back: money) <ruby>取<rt>と</rt></ruby>り<ruby>戻<rt>もど</rt></ruby>す

recur *v.* (happen again) <ruby>再発<rt>さいはつ</rt></ruby>する

recurrence *n.* (return, re-emergence) <ruby>再発<rt>さいはつ</rt></ruby>, (repetition) <ruby>繰<rt>く</rt></ruby>り<ruby>返<rt>かえ</rt></ruby>し

recurrent *adj.* (of illness) <ruby>再発<rt>さいはつ</rt></ruby>する, (of theme) <ruby>繰<rt>く</rt></ruby>り<ruby>返<rt>かえ</rt></ruby>し<ruby>起<rt>お</rt></ruby>こる
a recurrent illness <ruby>再発<rt>さいはつ</rt></ruby>する<ruby>病気<rt>びょうき</rt></ruby>
a recurrent theme
<ruby>繰<rt>く</rt></ruby>り<ruby>返<rt>かえ</rt></ruby>し<ruby>出<rt>で</rt></ruby>て<ruby>来<rt>く</rt></ruby>るテーマ

recycle *v.* リサイクルする, <ruby>再利用<rt>さいりよう</rt></ruby>する
Aluminum cans are recycled.
アルミ<ruby>缶<rt>かん</rt></ruby>はリサイクルされている。

recycling *n.* リサイクル, <ruby>再利用<rt>さいりよう</rt></ruby>

red *adj.* <ruby>赤<rt>あか</rt></ruby>い, <ruby>赤<rt>あか</rt></ruby>くなった
n. <ruby>赤<rt>あか</rt></ruby>
red wine <ruby>赤<rt>あか</rt></ruby>ワイン
His face was red with drink.
お<ruby>酒<rt>さけ</rt></ruby>で<ruby>彼<rt>かれ</rt></ruby>の<ruby>顔<rt>かお</rt></ruby>は<ruby>赤<rt>あか</rt></ruby>かった。
Her face was red with embarrassment.
<ruby>彼女<rt>かのじょ</rt></ruby>は<ruby>恥<rt>は</rt></ruby>ずかしさで<ruby>顔<rt>かお</rt></ruby>を<ruby>赤<rt>あか</rt></ruby>らめていた。
Red and black go well.
<ruby>赤<rt>あか</rt></ruby>と<ruby>黒<rt>くろ</rt></ruby>は、よく<ruby>合<rt>あ</rt></ruby>う。
in the red <ruby>赤字<rt>あかじ</rt></ruby>で
That company has been in the red for three full years.
その<ruby>会社<rt>かいしゃ</rt></ruby>は、まる3<ruby>年<rt>ねん</rt></ruby><ruby>赤字<rt>あかじ</rt></ruby><ruby>続<rt>つづ</rt></ruby>きだ。

♦ **Red Cross** *n.* <ruby>赤十字<rt>せきじゅうじ</rt></ruby>

redden *v.* <ruby>赤<rt>あか</rt></ruby>くなる, (with embarrassment) <ruby>顔<rt>かお</rt></ruby>を<ruby>赤<rt>あか</rt></ruby>らめる, <ruby>赤面<rt>せきめん</rt></ruby>する

redecorate *v.* (room) リフォームする, (store) <ruby>改装<rt>かいそう</rt></ruby>する

redeem *v.* (redeem oneself) <ruby>名誉<rt>めいよ</rt></ruby>を<ruby>挽回<rt>ばんかい</rt></ruby>する

redefine *v.* <ruby>定義<rt>ていぎ</rt></ruby>し<ruby>直<rt>なお</rt></ruby>す
The Beatles redefined pop music.
ビートルズはポップスの<ruby>概念<rt>がいねん</rt></ruby>を<ruby>変<rt>か</rt></ruby>えた。

redesign *v.* (...の) デザインを<ruby>変更<rt>へんこう</rt></ruby>する

redevelop *v.* (area) <ruby>再開発<rt>さいかいはつ</rt></ruby>する

♦ **redevelopment** *n.* <ruby>再開発<rt>さいかいはつ</rt></ruby>

redhead *n.* <ruby>赤毛<rt>あかげ</rt></ruby>の<ruby>人<rt>ひと</rt></ruby>

red-hot *adj.* (of metal) <ruby>真<rt>ま</rt></ruby>っ<ruby>赤<rt>か</rt></ruby>に<ruby>焼<rt>や</rt></ruby>けた, (very hot) ものすごく<ruby>熱<rt>あつ</rt></ruby>い
a red-hot poker
<ruby>真<rt>ま</rt></ruby>っ<ruby>赤<rt>か</rt></ruby>に<ruby>焼<rt>や</rt></ruby>けた<ruby>火<rt>ひ</rt></ruby>かき<ruby>棒<rt>ぼう</rt></ruby>

redirect *v.* (person) (...の) <ruby>方向<rt>ほうこう</rt></ruby>を<ruby>変<rt>か</rt></ruby>える, (mail) <ruby>転送<rt>てんそう</rt></ruby>する

rediscover *v.* <ruby>再発見<rt>さいはっけん</rt></ruby>する

♦ **rediscovery** *n.* <ruby>再発見<rt>さいはっけん</rt></ruby>

redistribute *v.* <ruby>再分配<rt>さいぶんぱい</rt></ruby>する

♦ **redistribution** *n.* <ruby>再分配<rt>さいぶんぱい</rt></ruby>

red light *n.* (traffic signal) <ruby>赤信号<rt>あかしんごう</rt></ruby>
go through a red light <ruby>赤信号<rt>あかしんごう</rt></ruby>を<ruby>突破<rt>とっぱ</rt></ruby>する

redouble *v.* (strengthen, bolster) <ruby>強<rt>つよ</rt></ruby>める, (double) <ruby>倍加<rt>ばいか</rt></ruby>する
We'll need to redouble our efforts to succeed.
<ruby>成功<rt>せいこう</rt></ruby>するには2<ruby>倍<rt>ばい</rt></ruby>の<ruby>努力<rt>どりょく</rt></ruby>が<ruby>必要<rt>ひつよう</rt></ruby>だろう。

red pepper *n.* トウガラシ [→ PEPPER]

redraw *v.* (picture) かき<ruby>直<rt>なお</rt></ruby>す, (line) <ruby>引<rt>ひ</rt></ruby>き<ruby>直<rt>なお</rt></ruby>す

redress *v.* (make right) <ruby>正<rt>ただ</rt></ruby>す

redress the balance 不均衡を正す

reduce *v.* (make less) 減らす, (price) 下げる, (speed) 落とす [→ DECREASE]

The government is trying to reduce the size of its current deficit.
政府は、経常赤字を削減しようとしている。

There's talk of reducing our overtime.
我々の残業を減らすといううわさだ。

reduction *n.* (decrease) 減少, (in scale) 縮小; (discount) 割引

redundant *adj.* (unnecessary) 余分な, 不要な, (of wording) くどい

redwood *n.* 赤杉, セコイア, アメリカスギ

reed *n.* アシ, 葦

reeducate *v.* 再教育する

reef *n.* (coral reef) サンゴ礁, (rock reef) 岩礁

reek *v.* ひどいにおいがする
n. 悪臭

reel[1] *n.* (spool) 糸巻き, (fishing reel) リール; (reel of film) フィルム一巻き

♦**reel in** *v.* (line) 巻く, (fish) リールで釣り上げる

reel off *v.* (recite) すらすら挙げる

reel[2] *v.* (stagger) よろめく; (be shocked) 動揺する

reelect *v.* 再選する
be reelected 再選される

♦**reelection** *n.* 再選

reenact *v.* 再現する

♦**reenactment** *n.* 再現

reenter *v.* 再び入る, (country) 再入国する, (company) 再就職する, (competition) 再出場する

♦**reentry** *n.* (into country) 再入国
a reentry permit (to get into Japan)
(日本への) 再入国許可

reevaluate *v.* 再評価する

reexamine *v.* (review, reconsider) 再検討する, 見直す, (medically) 再検査する

♦**reexamination** *n.* (review) 再検討

refer *v.*

1 TURN TO FOR INFORMATION: (refer to) 参考にする, 参照する

2 SPEAK OF: (refer to) (…のことを) 言う, 話す, (…に) 触れる, (refer to A as B) (AをBと) 呼ぶ

3 DIRECT TO: (refer A to B) (AをBに) 差し向ける, 回す, (Bに問い合わせるよう/照会するよう、Aに) 言う

1 We can refer back to this information when we need it.
必要なときには、この資料を参照すればいいね。

You'll find out how it works by referring to the manual.
説明書を見れば、しくみがわかりますよ。

I want you to do this work without referring to any dictionary.
この課題は辞書を引かずにやってほしい。

2 I was referring to his father.
彼の父親のことを言っていたんだ。

I'm not allowed to refer to them by name.
彼らの名前を挙げて話すことはできません。

Elvis is often simply referred to as "the King."
エルビスは、よく「キング」と一言で呼ばれる。

3 Mr. Suzuki referred me to you.

R

そちらに問い合わせるよう、鈴木さんから言われました。

referee *n.* レフェリー, 審判

v. 審判をする

referee a match 試合の審判をする

reference *n.*

1 LOOKING FOR INFORMATION: 参考, 参照

2 MENTION: 言及

3 FOR JOB: (statement) 推せん状, (person) 身元保証人

4 IN BOOK: (source listed in bibliography) 出典, 参考文献; (cross-reference) 相互参照

1 just for your reference

((*polite*)) ご参考までに

reference books 参考図書

2 make a passing reference to

…にちょっと言及する [触れる]

3 References provided upon request.

推せん状は、必要であれば用意いたします。

4 a reference list 参考文献一覧

referendum *n.* 国民投票

hold a referendum 国民投票を実施する

referral *n.* (referring to sth) 参照, (sending sb somewhere for information) 照会; (recommendation) 推せん

refill *v.* 補充する, 詰め替える

n. (of drink) お代わり

Would you like a refill ?

お代わりは [もう一杯] いかがですか？

refine *v.* (oil) 精製する, (process, machine) 改良する

refined *adj.* (genteel) 上品な, (sophisticated) 洗練された; (of substance) 精製した

refined oil 精油

refined salt 精製塩

refinement *n.* (of manner, taste) 洗練; (of substance) 精製, 純化

refinery *n.* 精製所

refit *v.* (repair) 修理する

reflect *v.*

1 THROW BACK/BE THROWN BACK: 映す/映る, 反射する

2 BE AN INDICATION OF: 反映する, 映す, 示す

3 THINK: (**reflect on**) じっくり考える, (=on one's conduct) 振り返る

1 I saw myself reflected in the mirror.

鏡に映っている自分の姿が目に入った。

The sunlight reflected off the water.

日の光が水面から反射していた。

2 These grades don't reflect your true ability.

この成績は、あなたの本当の実力を反映していない。

The novel reflects the changes that have taken place in British society since the 1950s.

その小説は、１９５０年代以降イギリス社会で起きた変化を映している。

3 I haven't had time to reflect on the experience yet.

その経験について、じっくり考える時間がまだありません。

reflection *n.*

1 IMAGE: 姿

2 BENDING OF LIGHT: 反射

3 INDICATION: 反映, 表れ

4 BLEMISH: 不名誉, 汚点

5 THOUGHTS: (**reflections**) 考え

1 I can see your reflection in the window.
窓にあなたの姿が映っている。

2 I saw a bright reflection over there.
向こうの方で、ピカッと光が反射した。

3 a reflection of one's knowledge
知識の反映

a reflection of one's sincerity
誠実さの表れ

4 a poor reflection on America
アメリカの<u>汚点</u> [名誉を傷つけるもの]

5 reflections on the war in Iraq
イラク戦争に対する考え

reflex *n.* (action) 反射運動, (**reflexes**) 反射神経

reform *v.* 改善する, 改革する
n. 改革

The system needs to be reformed.
この制度は改善すべきです。

tax reforms 税制改革

♦**reformer** *n.* 改革者

reform school *n.* 少年院

reformat *v.* (hard drive) 初期化する

reformation *n.* (act of reforming) 改善, (in European history: **the Reformation**) 宗教改革

refract *v.* (light) 屈折させる

refrain *v.* (**refrain from doing**) …するのを控える, …するのをやめる

refresh *v.* すっきり/さっぱりさせる, (one's memory) よみがえらせる, (**refresh oneself**) 元気を取り戻す, 気分がさわやかになる

Maybe these photos will help to refresh your memory.
この写真を見たら、<u>記憶がよみがえる</u> [思い出す] かもしれませんよ。

refreshed *adj.* すっきりした, さっぱりした

I feel refreshed now that I've had a shower.
シャワーを浴びて、さっぱりした。

refreshing *adj.* (of air, drink) さわやかな, (of idea, situation) 斬新な

refreshment *n.* (soft drink) 飲み物, (**refreshments**: food and drink) 軽食

refrigerate *v.* 冷やす, 冷蔵する

♦**refrigeration** *n.* 冷蔵

refrigerator *n.* 冷蔵庫 [→ picture of KITCHEN]

refuel *v.* (…に) 燃料を補給する, 給油する

The jets refueled in flight.
ジェット機は空中給油をした。

refuge *n.* (shelter) 避難所

take/seek refuge in doing …して難を逃れる

refugee *n.* 難民

refund *n.* 払い戻し, 返金, (repaid money) 払い戻し金
v. 払い戻す, 返金する, 返済する

Did you get a refund?
払い戻してもらいました？

If you bought it on sale, they are unlikely to refund your money.
バーゲンで買ったのなら、たぶん返金してもらえないでしょう。

refurbish *v.* (room) 改造する, (building) 改装する, 一新する

refusal *n.* 拒否, 拒絶

refusal to go to school 登校拒否

refuse[1] *v.* (decline) 断る, 拒否する, 拒絶する, (**refuse to do**: not do) …しない

They refused our offer.

我々の申し出を断った。

I refuse to believe that.
そんなことは信じない。

They were fired for refusing to do the work.
彼らは仕事を拒否したことでクビになった。

pupils who refuse to go to school
不登校児童

refuse² *n.* (garbage) ごみ, ((*formal*)) 廃棄物

regain *v.* (health, trust) 回復する, 取り戻す, (**regain one's breath**) 息を整える

He never regained consciousness.
彼の意識が戻ることはなかった。

regal *adj.* (of manner) 堂々とした, (of clothing, house) 豪華な

regard

1 *n.* GREETINGS: (**regards**) よろしく, (at the end of a letter) 敬具 [→ DEAR 1]

2 *n.* CONSIDERATION: 配慮, 気づかい

3 *n.* ESTEEM: 尊敬, 敬意

4 *v.* THINK OF: (regard A as B) (AをBと) 考える, みなす, (regard with: respect/suspicion etc.) (敬意/疑いを) もって見る, (**regard highly**) 高く評価する

1 Please give my regards to your family.
どうぞご家族によろしくお伝えください。

(*in letter*) Kind / Warm regards 敬具

2 He shows no regard for other people's feelings.
あの人は、他人の気持ちに何の気づかいも示さない。

3 Doctors are held in high regard by society.
医者は社会的にとても尊敬されている。

4 She was regarded as the prime suspect in the case.
彼女は、その事件の第1容疑者とみなされた。

He was not as highly regarded as he thought.
彼は自分で思っているほど、高く評価されていなかった。

as regards …に関しては, …については

As regards your allowance, I never said I would increase it.
おこづかいについては、上げると言った覚えはない。

in this/that regard この/その点では

In this regard, he's an exceptional salesman.
この点では、彼はセールスマンとして群を抜いている。

in/with regard to …に関しては

With regard to this other matter, I think it would be best to await developments.
もう一つの件に関しては、成り行きを見守るのが一番だと思います。

regarding *prep.* → AS REGARDS

regardless *adv.* それでも

regardless of …とは関係なく, …にかかわらず

regatta *n.* レガッタ, ボートレース

regenerate *v.* (rebuild) 再建する, (improve, develop, grow anew) 再生する

♦**regeneration** *n.* 再生

regent *n.* (government official) 摂政, (of U.S. university) 理事

reggae *n.* レゲエ

regime *n.* (government) 政権, (system) 体制, 制度

regiment ***n.*** (army) 連隊, (large group of people) 大勢の人

region ***n.*** (area) 地域, (particular area within a country) 地方, (zone) 地帯, (part) 部分, (range) 範囲 [→ RANGE]

It's a region of the country that has changed very little.
国内でも、昔とほとんど変わらない地域です。

the Kansai region 関西地方

a mountainous region 山岳地帯

a region of the brain that little is known about
脳の中の、ほとんど解明されていない部分

regional ***adj.*** 地域の, 地方の

regional differences in language
言葉の地域差

register

1 *v.* **SUBMIT NAME/INFORMATION:** 登録する, (at hotel) 宿泊者名簿に名前を記入する, (to vote) 選挙人名簿に登録する

2 *v.* **MAKE AN IMPRESSION IN THE MIND:** 印象に残る

3 *v.* **MAIL:** 書留にする

4 ***n.*** **OFFICIAL RECORD:** 登録, (school register) 出席簿, (family register) 戸籍

5 ***n.*** **CASH REGISTER:** レジ

1 You have to register first, then you get the application forms.
まず登録して、それから申込書を受け取ってください。

register for a divorce 離婚届を出す

2 The man's words did not register in my mind.
その人の言葉は印象に残らなかった。

3 If it's important, you'd better register the letter.
大切な手紙なら、書留にしたほうがいい。

4 Have you signed the register yet?
もう登録しましたか？

5 Who's working the register?
誰がレジをやっているんですか？

registered ***adj.*** (of letter) 書留の; (accredited, authorized) 公認の

a registered nurse 正看護師

♦**registered mail** ***n.*** (system) 書留郵便

registration ***n.*** 登録

a vehicle registration number
車両登録番号

a registration fee 登録料

regress ***v.*** 後退する

♦**regression** ***n.*** 後退

regret ***v.*** 後悔する, 悔やむ, ((*formal*)) 遺憾に思う, (have regrets) 未練がある, 心残りがある; (declining an offer: **I/we regret that/to say that...**) 残念ながら...

n. 後悔, ((*formal*)) 遺憾, (sth one can't put behind one) 未練, 心残り

I regret what I said.
あんなこと言わなければよかった。

I don't regret giving up city life.
都会生活に未練はない。

We regret that we will not be able to attend your wedding.
ご結婚式に出席することができなくて、とても残念に思います。

Do you feel any regret about quitting your job?
仕事を辞めて後悔していませんか？

We informed them with regret of our decision.

我々の決定を、遺憾の意と共に先方に伝えた。

I have no regrets about retiring early.
早期退職をしたことに、全く心残りはありません。

regretful *adj.* 後悔している, 残念な

regrettable *adj.* 残念な, ((*formal*)) 遺憾な

It is extremely regrettable that…
…はとても残念です。

♦**regrettably** *adv.* 残念ながら, 残念なことに

regroup *v.* (of people) 再編成する

regular

1 *adj.* COMING AT STEADY INTERVALS: (periodic) 定期的な, 定例の, 一定の, (frequent) しばしば起こる/来る, (of customer) よく来る, 常連の

2 *adj.* CONFORMING TO A PATTERN: 規則的な, 規則正しい

3 *adj.* ORDINARY: 普通の

4 *adj.* PERMANENT: 正規の, (of player) レギュラーの

5 *adj.* USUAL: いつもの

6 *adj.* OF SIZE: レギュラーの

7 *adj.* OF FACIAL FEATURES: 整った, 均整のとれた

8 *n.* CUSTOMER: 常連

1 You should check the brakes at regular intervals.
ブレーキは定期的に点検すべきです。

We took regular breaks to avoid getting too tired.
疲れすぎないように、時々休憩を取った。

2 a regular verb 規則動詞

a regular pulse 正常な脈拍

I can't wait to get back to a regular schedule of sleep.
規則正しい睡眠のリズムに戻るのを待てない。

3 I'm just a regular guy with a regular job.
僕は普通の仕事をしている普通の男にすぎない。

4 He became a regular member of the golf club.
彼はゴルフクラブの正会員になった。

5 I was unable to see my regular doctor.
いつもの先生に診察してもらえなかった。

6 I'll have a regular ice coffee.
レギュラーのアイスコーヒー(を下さい)。

7 He has regular features.
彼は整った顔立ちをしている。

8 Bill's a regular at this pub.
ビルはこのパブの常連だ。

regularly *adv.* (periodically) 定期的に, (customarily) 通常, (frequently) よく

regulate *v.* (control) 規制する, (adjust) 調節する

regulation *n.* (rule) 規則, (law) 法規

It's against the regulations.
それは規則に反します。

regurgitate *v.* 吐く, もどす

rehabilitate *v.* (drug addict, alcoholic) 社会復帰させる, (criminal) 更生させる, (injured person) (…に) リハビリを施す

rehabilitation *n.* リハビリ

a rehabilitation center リハビリセンター

rehearsal *n.* リハーサル

rehearse *v.* リハーサルをする

reheat *v.* (food) 温め直す

reign *v.* 統治する, 支配する, (of monarch) 君臨する
n. 統治, 支配, (of monarch) 君臨

reimburse *v.* 返済する, 払い戻す, (compensate) 弁償する

reimbursement *n.* (repayment) 返済, (compensation) 弁償

rein *n.* 手綱

pull (on) the reins 手綱を引く

reincarnate *v.* (**be reincarnated**) 生まれ変わる

reincarnation *n.* 生まれ変わり, 化身, (Buddhist concept) 輪廻(転生)

Do you believe in reincarnation?
輪廻を信じますか？

reindeer *n.* トナカイ

reinforce *v.* 強める, (roof, bridge) 補強する, (army) 増強する

♦ **reinforced concrete** *n.* 鉄筋コンクリート

reinforcement *n.* (strengthening) 補強; (**reinforcements**: troops) 援軍

reinstate *v.* (person to previous job) 復職させる, (law) 復活させる

reinsure *v.* (…に) 再び保険をかける

reinvent *v.* 再発明する

reinvent the wheel 一からやり直す

There's no need to reinvent the wheel.
わざわざ一からやり直す必要はないよ。

reissue *v.* 再発行する

reiterate *v.* 繰り返す

reject *v.* 断る, 拒絶する, (throw out) 捨てる

n. (rejected person/thing) 拒絶された人/もの

rejected a peace plan 和平案を拒絶する

She rejected him.
彼女は彼を<u>拒絶した</u> [はねつけた]。

rejection *n.* 拒否, 拒絶

He's afraid of rejection.
彼は断られるのが怖いんだ。

My son applied to three universities and got rejections from all of them.
息子は三つの大学に出願して、すべて不合格だった。

rejoice *v.* 大いに喜ぶ, 非常にうれしく思う

rejoin *v.* (club) (…に) 復帰する, 再入会する, (group) (…に) またあとで会う, (return to) (…に) 戻る

rejuvenate *v.* (**be rejuvenated**: return to health) 元気を回復する

rekindle *v.* (debate, quarrel) 再燃させる, (interest) 再びかきたてる

relapse *v.* (become ill again) 病気をぶり返す

n. (return to illness) ぶり返し, 再発

My father had a relapse after the operation.
手術後に父の病気は再発した。

relate *v.*

1 HAVE TO DO WITH: (relate to) (…と) 関係がある, かかわる

2 UNDERSTAND: (**can relate**) (=to sb's feelings) 理解できる, (=to each other) 心が通じ合う

3 RECOUNT: 順を追って話す, ((*formal*)) 列挙する

1 That relates to what I was saying earlier.
それは、さっき申し上げたことと関係があります。

2 People need to be able to relate to one another.
人はお互いに、心が通じ合うようになることが必要だ。

3 Can you relate in detail what happened after you left work that day?
その日、退社した後何が起こったか、順を追って話してくれますか？

relating to …に関する, …に関連した

related *adj.* 関係のある, (of family) 親類関係にある, 親戚の

The two events are not related.
二つの事件は関係がありません。

We're related. 私たちは親戚です。

relation *n.*

1 BETWEEN PEOPLE/COUNTRIES: (**relations**) 関係

2 BETWEEN THINGS: 関係, 関連

3 KIN: 親戚, 親類

1 The two countries have maintained diplomatic relations for a long time.
両国は長年、外交関係を結んできた。

Relations are strained between those countries.
2国間の関係は緊迫している。

2 This story has no relation to the facts.
この物語は事実と全く関係がない。

There must be a relation between crime and poverty.
犯罪と貧困との間には、関連があるに違いない。

3 She's a distant relation.
彼女は遠い親戚です。

They are blood relations.
あの人たちは親類 [血縁] です。

in relation to (compared to) …と比べて, …のわりに

Wages are low in relation to the cost of living.
生活費のわりに賃金が安い。

relationship *n.* (connection) 関係, 関連, (friendship) 関係, (sexual relationship) (性的) 関係

It's said there is a relationship between mad cow disease and CJD.
狂牛病とヤコブ病との間には、関連があると言われている。

They seem to have a good relationship.
あの人たちは、いい関係にあるようです。

The relationship between the two countries is stronger than ever.
両国の結び付きは、今までになく強い。

She's in a relationship right now.
彼女は今、付き合ってる人がいる。

relative *n.* (member of extended family) 親戚, 親類

Do you have a lot of relatives?
親戚は多いですか？

Is he a relative of yours?
あの方は、あなたのご親戚ですか？

relatively *adv.* 比較的, わりあい

She's relatively well off.
あの人は、わりあい豊かな生活をしている。

There's relatively little rainfall during the summer months.
夏は比較的雨が少ない。

relativism *n.* 相対主義

relativity *n.* (theory) 相対性理論

relax *v.* (take it easy) リラックスする, くつろぐ, のんびり/ゆっくりする, 楽にする, (rules) ゆるめる, ((*formal*)) 緩和する, (muscles) ほぐす, 和らげる

Just relax, will you.
頼むから、まあ落ち着けよ。

I like to relax at home.

家でのんびりするのが好きです。

Try to relax your whole body.
全身を楽にしてください。

The rules have been relaxed recently.
規則が最近ゆるくなった。

relaxation *n.* くつろぎ, 息抜き, 気晴らし

relaxed *adj.* のんびりした, (unhurried) ゆったりした

relaxing *adj.* くつろげる, リラックスする, ゆったりする

Did you have a relaxing vacation?
お休みは、ゆったり過ごしましたか？

relay *n.* (relay race) リレー; (electrical relay) 中継装置
v. (broadcast) 中継する

relearn *v.* 学び直す

release

1 *v.* **ALLOW TO GO FREE:** 自由にする, 解放する, (animal) 解き放つ, (prisoner) 釈放する, (patient) 退院させる

2 *v.* **LET GO OF:** (balloon) 放つ, (remove hand from) (…から) 手を離す

3 *v.* **NEW PRODUCT:** 発売する, (film) 封切る, (album) リリースする

4 *v.* **INFORMATION:** (news) 発表する, (documents) 公開する, 出す

5 *v.* **EMOTIONS:** 開放する

6 *v.* **GASES:** 放出する

7 *n.* **FREEING:** 解放, (of prisoner) 釈放, (of patient) 退院, (of emotions) 解放, 発散

8 *n.* **SEEPAGE:** (of gases) 放出

9 *n.* **MAKING AVAILABLE:** (of product) 発売, (of film) 封切り, (of album) リリース, (of news) 発表, (of documents) 公開

1 The prisoner was released last week.
その囚人は先週、釈放されました。

The bear was released into the wild.
熊は野生に戻された。

2 One hundred white balloons will be released at the end of the ceremony.
式典の最後に100個の白い風船が放たれます。

3 The book is being released in August.
本は8月に発売されます。

4 A statement has been released by the Foreign Ministry.
声明は外務省から出された。

5 Exercise is a good way to release stress.
運動は、ストレスを発散するのにいい方法です。

6 Harmful gases were released into the air.
有毒なガスが空中に放出された。

7 The prisoner's release was approved.
囚人の釈放が承認された。

stress release ストレスの発散

8 The release of ozone-depleting gases continues.
オゾンを減少させる気体の放出が続いている。

9 The film's release was delayed.
映画の封切りが遅れた。

♦ **sense of release** *n.* 解放感

relegate *v.* (task to person) 任せる, (person to position) 左遷する

relent *v.* 態度を和らげる, ((*informal*)) 折れる

Father relented and let the children stay up late for just one night.
父親は折れて、子供たちに一晩だけ夜更かしを許した。

relentless *adj.* (merciless) 容赦のない,

(fierce) 厳しい, (persistent) 執拗な

relevance *n.* 関連(性), (applicability) 適切さ

I don't see what relevance that has.
それがどんな関連があるのか、わからない。

relevant *adj.* (pertinent) 関係のある, (applicable) 適切な, 当を得た

It wasn't relevant to our situation.
それは、私たちの現状には関係がありませんでした。

I don't think that's relevant.
それは関係ないと思います。

reliability *n.* 信頼性

reliable *adj.* 信頼できる, 頼りになる, (of information) 確かな

He's totally reliable.
彼はすごく信頼できる人です。

reliance *n.* (dependence) 依存, 頼ること, (trust) 信頼

reliant *adj.* (be reliant on) (…に) 頼っている

relic *n.* (idea) なごり, (object) 遺物

relief *n.*

1 EASE OF MIND: 安心, 安堵

2 REDUCTION: (alleviation) 軽減, 緩和, (elimination) 除去

3 HELP: 救援, 救済, (relief supplies) 救援物資, (relief money) 救済金

1 feel relief ほっと [安心] する

breathe a sigh of relief
ほっと安堵のため息をつく

What a relief! I thought you'd never get here.
ほっとした! もう来ないんじゃないかと思ったよ。

2 pain relief 痛みの軽減
stress relief ストレスの緩和

3 relief workers 救援隊
relief measures 救済対策

relieve *v.* (alleviate) 和らげる; (allow to be free: person from duty) 解放する; (**relieve oneself**: use toilet) 用を足す

relieved *adj.* (at ease) ほっとした, 安心した

religion *n.* (institution) 宗教, (faith) 信仰

What religion are you?
何の宗教を信じていますか?

religious *adj.* 宗教の, 宗教上の, (of person) 信心深い

a religious experience 宗教的体験

She's religious, although she doesn't go to church.
彼女は教会へはあまり行かないけれど、信心深い。

relinquish *v.* (right) 放棄する, (hope) 捨てる

relish *v.* (enjoy) 楽しむ, (like) 好む

relive *v.* (past experience) 再び経験する, (through imagination) 追体験する

reload *v.* (gun) (…に) 弾丸を詰め直す, (truck) (…に) 荷を積み直す

relocate *v.* (move somewhere) 移転する

♦**relocation** *n.* 移転

reluctant *adj.* いやがる, やりたがらない, 渋る, 気が進まない

They were reluctant to help.
彼らは手伝うのをいやがった/彼らは手伝いたがらなかった。

rely on *v.* (depend on) …に頼る, …に依

存する, (put one's hopes on) 当てにする

You can't rely on her to help.
彼女の援助に頼ることはできませんよ。

The Japanese economy relies too much on exports.
日本経済は輸出に依存しすぎている。

Can we rely on Tanabe?
田辺さんは当てにできますか？

remain *v.*

1 IN CONDITION: See examples below
2 BE LEFT OVER: 残る
3 STAY BEHIND: 居残る, とどまる, 残る

1 He remained silent.
彼は黙ったままだった。

This affair must remain a secret.
この件は内密にしておかなくてはいけません。

We remained good friends despite our different views.
考え方が違っても、私たちは相変わらずいい友達だった。

2 Much still remains to be done.
やるべきことが、まだたくさん残っている。

The fact remains that he still hasn't apologized.
彼が謝罪をしていないという事実は、変わらない。

What remained of his money was divided among his children.
残された彼の財産は、子供たちで分け合った。

3 Even though everybody else went out, she remained at home.
ほかの人はみんな出かけたけど、彼女は家に残った。

remain to be seen まだわからない

"Can he win?"
"Well, that remains to be seen."
「彼は勝てますか？」
「それは、まだわかりませんね」

remainder *n.* (that which remains) 残り, (in math) 余り

remaining *adj.* 残った, 残りの, (other) その他の

remains *n.* 残り, (of building: ruins) 遺跡, (of person: corpse) 遺体

remake *v.* 作り直す, 作り変える, (movie) リメークする
n. (of movie) リメーク(版)

remark *n.* (comment) コメント, (utterance) 発言
v. (remark that...) (...と) 言う, (**remark on**: express one's thoughts about) ...について感想を言う

a rude remark 失礼な発言

She made some remark about the film, but I forget what she said.
彼女は映画について何か感想を言ってたけど、何て言ったのか忘れた。

His opening remarks were relevant.
彼の開会のあいさつは当を得ていた。

If anyone remarks on her appearance, she gets mad.
容姿のことを言われると、彼女は怒る。

remarkable *adj.* (noteworthy) 注目すべき, (surprising) 驚くべき, (fantastic) すごい, すばらしい, (outstanding) すぐれた, 優秀な, (rare, strange) 珍しい

a remarkable discovery 注目すべき発見
a remarkable achievement 驚くべき業績

It's remarkable that no one noticed.
誰も気づかなかったとは驚きだ。

He's a remarkable student.
彼は非常に優秀な生徒だ。

remarkably *adv.* (unusually) 異常に, (strikingly) 著しく, (extremely) 非常に, (used at the beginning of a sentence: surprisingly) ((*formal*)) 驚くことに

remarry *v.* 再婚する

♦**remarriage** *n.* 再婚

rematch *n.* 再試合

remedial *adj.* (of medical treatment) 治療の

remedy *n.* (means of putting right) 改善法, (cure) 治療法

v. 治療する, 治す

remember *v.*

1 KEEP IN MEMORY: 覚えている, ((*formal*)) 記憶している

2 RECALL: 思い出す

3 NOT FORGET: (important fact for future contingency) 忘れずに覚えておく, (**remember to do**) 忘れずに…する

1 Kyoko always remembers my birthday.
京子は、私の誕生日をいつも覚えていてくれます。

He said he remembered you.
彼はあなたのことを覚えていると言っていたよ。

Do you remember playing down by the river?
川の近くで遊んだのを覚えていますか？

I remember being told to turn off the oven after an hour, but not to put a pie in.
1時間後にオーブンを切ってとは言われたけれど、パイを入れてとは言われた覚えがない。

Nehru, you remember, was educated at Oxford.
ネルーは、ほら、オックスフォードで教育を受けたでしょ。

2 I can't remember his name for the life of me.
どうしても彼の名前が思い出せない。

What is the last thing you can remember?
思い出せる最後のことは何ですか？

3 Please remember to mail this letter.
どうか忘れずにこの手紙を投函してください。

Remember, you have to lock the front door when you go out.
出かけるときは、玄関のかぎをかけるのを忘れないでよ。

remembrance *n.* (commemoration) 記念

in remembrance of …を記念して, …の思い出に

remind *v.* (remind A of/about B) (AにBを) 思い出させる, (say so that one does not forget) 忘れないように言う

She reminded him that she was married.
彼女は自分が結婚していることを、彼に思い出させた。

Please, don't remind me. It's something I'd rather forget.
頼むから思い出させないでほしい。忘れたいことなんだ。

This song reminds me of my father.
この歌を聞くと父を思い出します。

You should've reminded me earlier.
もっと早く言ってくれたらよかったのに。

Remind me to mail this, will you.
これを投函するのを忘れないよう、言ってもらえますか？

reminder ***n.*** (letter, note) 催促状

reminisce ***v.*** (tell of the past) 思い出話をする, (think fondly of the past) 懐かしむ

reminiscence ***n.*** (story about the past) 思い出, 思い出話

reminiscent ***adj.*** (be reminiscent of) 思い出させる, しのばせる

remission ***n.*** (of illness) 小康状態

remit ***v.*** (send money) (お金を) 送る

remnant ***n.*** (leftover) 残り, (cloth) 半端物, 端切れ; (vestige) なごり, 面影

remorse ***n.*** 深い後悔, 悔恨, 良心の呵責 [→ REGRET]

feel remorse ひどく後悔する

show remorse 深い後悔の念を示す

remote ***adj.*** (distant) 遠い, (secluded) 人里離れた, へんぴな

He lives in a remote village.
彼は人里離れた村に住んでいる。

remote control ***n.*** (device) リモコン, (operating remotely) 遠隔操作

removal ***n.*** (removing) 除去, (dismissal from office) 解任, 免職

remove ***v.*** 取り除く, 取り払う, 除去する, (clean up) 片付ける, (stain) 消す, 落とす, (shoes, clothes) 脱ぐ

The homeless people's tents were removed from the park.
ホームレスの人々のテントが公園から取り払われた。

A cleanup crew removed the broken glass.
清掃班が壊れたガラスを片付けた。

The graffiti was removed from the wall.
壁の落書きが消された。

It says on the label that it can remove the nastiest of stains.
どんなにしつこい汚れも落ちる、とラベルに書いてある。

You're supposed to remove your shoes before entering.
入る前に靴を脱ぐことになっています。

renaissance ***n.*** (**the Renaissance**) ルネッサンス, (of style) ルネッサンス様式; (revival) 復興, 復活

rename ***v.*** (…に) 新しい名をつける, (rename A as B) (AをBと) 改名する

render ***v.*** (render A B) (AをBに) する [→ MAKE 3]; (provide) 与える [→ PROVIDE]; (translate) 訳す [→ TRANSLATE]

render useless 使えなくする

rendezvous ***n.*** (place) 待ち合わせ場所, (meeting) 待ち合わせ

v. (meet) 会う, 待ち合わせする

rendition ***n.*** (musical performance) 演奏, (play) 演出, (translation) 翻訳

renegade ***n.*** (rebel, traitor) 反逆者

renege ***v.*** (go back on a promise) 約束を破る

renegotiate ***v.*** 再交渉する

We had to renegotiate the contract.
契約の再交渉をしなければならなかった。

renew ***v.*** 新しくする, (license) 更新する, 書き換える, (subscription) 継続する

I have to renew my work permit.
就労許可証を更新しなくてはならない。

renewable ***adj.*** (of contract, permit etc.) 更新可能な

renewal ***n.*** (extension, update) 更新, (revival) 再生, 回復, (of shop, restaurant) リニューアル

a renewal fee 更新料

renounce *v.* (give up) 放棄する, (belief, religion) 捨てる, (the world) (…と) 縁を切る

renovate *v.* (rebuild) 建て直す, (redecorate) 改装する, (restore) 修復する, (repair) 修理する

renown *n.* 名声

renowned *adj.* 有名な, 著名な

a renowned scholar 著名な学者

rent *v.* (pay to use) 借りる, (allow to use in exchange for money) 貸す, 賃貸しする

n. (payment for house/apartment) 家賃, (room charge) 部屋代

I'm going to rent an apartment.
アパートを借りるつもりです。

Where can I rent a car in this town?
この町でレンタカーを借りられるのはどこですか？

Ms. Yamada rents rooms to students.
山田さんは学生に部屋を貸している。

My parents pay the rent.
両親が家賃を払っています。

The rent has gone up.
家賃が上がった。

for rent 賃貸の

a room for rent 貸室

rental *n.* (amount) 賃貸料, (process) 賃貸

adj. 賃貸の

a rental fee (for DVD etc.)
レンタル [貸出] 料

♦**rental car** *n.* レンタカー

reopen *v.* (shop) 再び開店する, (debate) 再開する

reorder *v.* 再注文する

reorganization *n.* 再編成, 再編

reorganize *v.* 再編成する, 再編する

repair *v.* (mend) 直す, 修理する, 修繕する

n. (mending) 修理, 修繕, 直し

The man at the shop says he can repair my watch.
店の人は、私の腕時計を修理できると言っている。

Repairing this window is not going to be easy.
この窓を直すのは簡単にはいかない。

The landlady says she'll pay for the repairs.
大家さんが修理代を出すと言っている。

The cottage looks like it needs repair.
別荘は修繕が必要なようだ。

That table is beyond repair.
あのテーブルは直しようがない。

♦**repairer** *n.* 修理する人, 修理工

repatriate *v.* 本国に送還する

♦**repatriation** *n.* 本国送還, 帰還

repay *v.* (money) 返す, 返済する, (**repay the favor**) (ご)恩返しをする

Did you repay the money on time?
お金を期日までに返しましたか？

One day I'll repay the favor.
((*polite*)) いつかご恩返しします。

repayment *n.* (paying back) 返済

repeal *v.* (law) 廃止する

repeat

1 *v.* SAY AGAIN: 繰り返し言う, (**repeat after**) …の後について言う

2 *v.* DO AGAIN: 繰り返す

3 *v.* TELL TO ANOTHER: 口外する, 人に言う

4 ***n.*** **ANOTHER OF THE SAME:** 繰り返されるもの, (TV program) 再放送, (performance) 再演

1 He kept repeating, "I didn't do it."
彼は「僕はやっていない」と繰り返し言い続けた。

The picture, I repeat, is not for sale.
((*polite*)) 重ねて申し上げますが、その絵はお売りできません。

Repeat after me.
後に続けて言ってください。

2 I repeated the same exercise in the evening.
夜にも同じ運動をやった。

Try not to repeat the mistake.
あやまちを繰り返さないようにしなさい。

3 Don't repeat this to anyone else.
このことは誰にも言わないでください。

4 This is a repeat. I've seen this show twice before.
これは繰り返し放送している。同じのを前に2度も見た。

repeated ***adj.*** 繰り返される, 度重なる
repeated requests 度重なる要求

repeatedly ***adv.*** 繰り返し, 何度も, (without stopping) 絶えず

repellent ***n.*** (insect repellent) 防虫剤, 虫よけ

repent ***v.*** 悔やむ, 後悔する

repercussion ***n.*** (**repercussions**) (=bad influence) 影響, (=consequences) 結果

repertoire ***n.*** レパートリー

repetition ***n.*** 繰り返し, 反復

repetitive ***adj.*** 繰り返しの

replace ***v.***

1 **INSTALL IN PLACE OF:** 取り替える, 置き換える

2 **SUPERSEDE:** (...に) 取って代わる

3 **PUT BACK:** (元に)戻す, 元の場所に置く

4 **EXCHANGE:** (merchandise) 交換する

1 It'll cost a lot of money to replace these doors.
このドアをみんな取り替えると、だいぶお金がかかる。

I bought it to replace the old one, which broke.
古いのが壊れたので、買い換えました。

2 He's a genius. Nobody can replace him.
彼は天才だ。取って代われる者は、どこにもいない。

3 Don't forget to replace the receiver.
受話器を元に戻すのを忘れないでね。

4 Did they replace it for you?
それを交換してくれた?

replacement ***n.*** 代わり, (thing) 取り替え品, (person in organization) 後任

replay ***v.*** (DVD) 再生する

replenish ***v.*** 補充する, 補給する

replica ***n.*** 複製, 模造品, レプリカ

reply ***v.*** (respond) 答える, 返事する, (reply that...) (...と) 答える
n. (response) 返事, 答え, ((*formal*)) 回答, 返答, (face-to-face response) 応答

He never replies to our letters.
私たちの手紙には、彼は絶対に返事をよこさない。

Did you get a reply?
返事をもらいましたか / ((*formal*)) 回答はありましたか?

I rang the doorbell but there was no

R

reply.
ベルを鳴らしたが、応答はなかった。

report

1 *n.* SUMMARY/ACCOUNT: 報告, (written report) 報告書

2 *n.* PIECE OF NEWS: ニュース, (news broadcast) 報道, (news article) 記事

3 *v.* GIVE AN ACCOUNT OF: 報告する

4 *v.* INFORM: (report A [crime/danger] to B [authorities]) (AをBに) 通報する

5 *v.* PRESENT AS NEWS: (on TV) 報道する, ((*formal*)) 報じる

6 *v.* PRESENT ONESELF: 出向く, 顔を出す, (**report for work/duty**) 出勤する

1 There have been a number of reports of UFO sightings.
ＵＦＯを目撃したという報告が、何件もある。

I want that report on my desk by tomorrow morning.
明日の朝までに、報告書を私の机の上に置いておくように。

The commission's report was over five hundred pages long.
委員会の報告書は500ページ以上あった。

2 This report just in...
たった今入ったニュースですが...

a report in the *New York Times*
ニューヨークタイムズの記事

3 I have nothing else to report.
ほかに何も報告することはありません。

4 Have you reported this to the police?
このことを警察に通報しましたか？

5 No casualties were reported.
死傷者はいないと報道された。

6 We had to report to the desk on arrival.
着いてすぐ、デスクのところに顔を出さなければならなかった。

♦**report card** *n.* (at school) 通知表, 成績表

reportedly *adv.* 伝えられるところによると

reporter *n.* 記者, レポーター

reporting *n.* 報道

repository *n.* (storage place) 保管場所, (of knowledge, information) 宝庫

repossess *v.* 取り戻す, (property) 回収する, 引き取る

♦**repossession** *n.* 回収, 再所有

represent *v.* (symbolize) 表す, 象徴する, (indicate) 示す, 表す; (act in place of) 代表する, (speak for) 代弁する

Peace is often represented by the symbol of a dove.
平和の象徴によくハトが使われる。

The cancellation of the road-building project represented a change in transport policy.
道路建設計画の中止は、交通政策の転換を表していた。

Over a hundred countries were represented at the Olympics.
オリンピックに100ヵ国以上から代表団が送られた。

The organization represents the views of small businesses.
その団体は零細企業の意見を代弁している。

representation *n.* (legal representation) 代理; (explanation, account) 説明

representative *n.* (person acting for another) 代表, (politician) 代議士
adj. 代表する, 代表的な

repress *v.* (feeling) 抑える, (rebellion) 鎮圧する

repressed *adj.* 抑圧された

a repressed childhood
抑圧された子供時代

repression *n.* 抑圧

repressive *adj.* (of government) 抑圧的な

reprieve *n.* (postponement of death sentence) 死刑執行延期, (warrant for) 死刑執行延期令状

v. (...の) 死刑執行を猶予する

reprimand *n., v.* 叱責(する)

reprint *n.* (reprinting) 増刷, 重版, (reprinted book) 再版本, リプリント

v. 重版する

reprisal *n.* 報復

take reprisals 報復する

reproach *v.* 非難する, とがめる

n. 非難 [→ BLAME]

reprocess *v.* (materials) 再加工する

reproduce *v.* (breed) 繁殖する, (sound) 再生する, (picture, document) 複写する [→ COPY 3]

reproduction *n.* (process of producing babies/plants) 生殖, (of cells, sound) 再生; (photocopy) 複写, (copy of antique) 複製

sexual reproduction 有性生殖

reptile *n.* は虫類

republic *n.* 共和国, (system) 共和制

republican *n.* (believer in republic) 共和主義者, (**Republican**: Republican Party member) 共和党員

adj. (of government) 共和制の, (**Republican**: of Republican Party) 共和党の

♦ **Republican Party** *n.* 共和党

republish *v.* 再版する

repudiate *v.* (negate) 否認する, 拒否する

repulsive *adj.* ぞっとする, 吐き気のする, 胸の悪くなる

That's repulsive! ぞっとするよ!

reputable *adj.* (having a good reputation) 評判のよい, (respectable) 立派な

a reputable car dealer
評判のいい車のディーラー

reputation *n.* 評判, (good name) 名声

The company has a good reputation.
その会社は評判がいい。

His reputation was ruined.
彼の名声は台なしになった/彼の面目は丸つぶれだった。

reputed *adj.* (rumored) ...と言われている

request

1 *n.* THING TO ASK: お願い, 依頼, (demand) 要求, (desire) 要望

2 *v.* ASK FOR: 頼む, 依頼する, ((*humble*)) お願いする, (**request to do**) (...に) ...するよう頼む

3 *n.* SONG: リクエスト

1 I have a small request...
ちょっとお願いがあるんですが...

Our request for a loan was turned down.
ローンを申し込んだが、断られた。

It's only a request. ほんの要望です。

Unfortunately we cannot accommodate your request.
残念ながら、ご要望にはお応えできません。

2 I requested an extension.

R

延期するよう頼んだ。

You are requested not to park on campus.
構内での駐車はご遠慮ください。

3 The next request goes to Linda.
次のリクエストはリンダさんからです。

requiem *n.* (religious ceremony) レクイエム, (song) 鎮魂歌

require *v.* (need) (...が) 必要だ, (...を) 必要とする, (demand: **require to do**) (...に) ...するよう要求する, (**be required to do**) ...しなければならない, ...しなくてはいけない

I don't require any help.
手伝いは必要ではありません。

Should you require anything else, just ring the bell.
もし何かほかに入り用でしたら、ベルを鳴らしてください。

A suit and tie are required.
スーツとネクタイを着用のこと。

I'm required to attend the meeting.
会議に出席しなくてはなりません。

requirement *n.* (necessary thing) 必要なもの, (condition) 必要条件

What are the requirements for this job?
この仕事に必要なものは何ですか？

reread *v.* 読み直す, 読み返す

rerun *n.* (TV show) 再放送

rescue *v.* 救う, 救い出す, 救助する, 助ける *n.* 救助, 救出, 助け

The passengers were rescued from the sinking ship.
乗客は沈みかけた船から救助された。

Luckily a passerby came to our rescue.
幸い、通りがかりの人が助けてくれた。

research *n.* 研究, 調査, リサーチ *v.* 研究する, 調査する, 調べる

scientific research 科学研究

He plans to do some research on modern sculpture.
彼は近代彫刻を研究する予定です。

The documentary had been carefully researched.
そのドキュメンタリーは、綿密な調査を行っていた。

♦ **researcher** *n.* 研究者

resell *v.* 転売する

resemblance *n.* (similarity) 似ているところ, 類似点

There's a striking resemblance between the brothers.
あの兄弟は驚くほど似ている。

resemble *v.* (...に) 似ている

Takuya resembles his mother whereas Miho takes after her father.
拓也は母親似だが、美穂は父親に似ている。

They (=the two people) certainly don't resemble each other.
確かに、あの二人は似ていませんね。

resent *v.* (...に) 憤慨する, 腹を立てる

He resents being spoken to as if he were a child.
彼は、子供扱いするような話し方をされると、憤慨する。

resentment *n.* 憤慨, 憤り

feel resentment toward ...に対して憤りを感じる

reservation *n.* (booking) 予約; (land for Native Americans) 特別保留地

reserve

1 *v.* MAKE A RESERVATION FOR: 予約する
2 *v.* SET ASIDE: 取っておく
3 *v.* HAVE: (right) 保有する, 所有する, もっている
4 *n.* SUPPLIES: (**reserves**: of natural resources) 埋蔵量
5 *adj.* SPARE: 予備の
6 *n.* SOLDIER: 予備軍
7 *n.* SELF-RESTRAINT: 遠慮
8 *n.* PROTECTED LAND: 保護区

1 Have you reserved a hotel?
ホテルを予約しましたか？
I'd like to reserve a table for six, for 8 o'clock.
8時に6名で予約をお願いします。

2 I reserved this seat for you.
あなたのためにこの席を取っておいたよ。
This room is reserved for members only.
この部屋は会員専用です。

3 We reserve the right to pursue happiness.
我々は幸福を追求する権利があります。
All rights reserved. 著作権所有

4 This country has huge oil reserves.
この国は石油の埋蔵量が豊富です。

5 The bank is getting low on reserve funds.
銀行は予備資金の残高が減ってきている。

6 naval reserves 海軍予備兵
the U.S. Air Force Reserve 米空軍予備軍

7 show reserve 遠慮する

8 a nature reserve 自然保護区

reserved *adj.* (of seat, table) 予約した; (of person: quiet, unassuming) 控え目な, 遠慮がちな

reservoir *n.* 貯水池

reset *v.* (machine) リセットする, (hair) セットし直す, (bone) 継ぎ直す

reshuffle *v.* (cards) 切り直す, (government cabinet) 改造する

reside *v.* 住む, ((*formal*)) 居住する

residence *n.* 住宅, 住居, 住まい

resident *n.* 住民, 居住者
local residents 地元の住民
a permanent resident 永住者

residential *adj.* 居住の, (suitable for residence) 住宅向きの
a residential district 住宅地

residual *adj.* (remaining) 残りの
residual effects 残留効果

residue *n.* 残留物

resign *v.* (quit) 辞任する, 辞職する; (**resign oneself to**: uncomplaining acceptance) 仕方なく受け入れる, (**resign oneself to doing**) あきらめて…する
Ambassador Chiba resigned his post.
千葉大使は役職を辞任した。
The chairman threatened to resign.
会長は辞任すると脅した。
She seems resigned to the fact that her children have left home.
彼女は子供たちが家を出てしまったという事実を、仕方なく受け入れているようだ。

resignation *n.* (quitting) 辞任, 辞職; (uncomplaining acceptance) あきらめ

resigned *adj.* (be resigned to: a situation) あきらめる [→ RESIGN]

resilience *n.* (ability to recover) 回復力; (of substance) 弾力

resilient *adj.* (mentally) 立ち直りの早い, (physically) 回復の早い; (of substance)

R

弾力のある

resin *n.* 樹脂, (artificial) 合成樹脂

resist *v.* (stand up to) (...に) 抵抗する, 逆らう, (stop) 阻止する, (fight: temptation, urge) こらえる, がまんする

They did everything they could to resist our demands for an inquiry.
我々の調査要求を阻止しようと、彼らはありとあらゆることをした。

He was charged with resisting arrest.
彼は逮捕に抵抗したかどで告訴された。

I can't resist sweet things.
甘い物を見たらがまんできない/甘い物には目がない。

can't resist doing ...せずにはいられない

I couldn't resist eating one more piece of cake.
ケーキをもう一切れ食べずにはいられなかった。

resistance *n.* 抵抗, (ability to resist) 抵抗力; (resistance movement) レジスタンス

resistance to disease
病気に対する抵抗力

resistant *adj.* (opposed) 抵抗する; (**-resistant**) 耐-

They are resistant to change.
彼らは変化に抵抗する。

This material is water-resistant.
この素材には耐水性があります。

resolution *n.*

1 DECISION/RESOLVE: 決意, 決心, (by legislature) 決議

2 FORMAL PROPOSAL: (put before legislature) 決議案

3 SOLUTION: 解決

4 OF IMAGE: 解像度

1 He made a New Year's resolution to give up smoking.
新年を機に、彼は禁煙を決意した。

a UN resolution 国連決議

2 The resolution to ban the sale of handguns was passed by the House.
拳銃の売買を禁止する決議案が、下院を通過した。

3 All we can do is hope for a quick resolution.
私たちができることは、早期解決を祈ることだけです。

4 high [low] resolution 高[低]解像度

resolve *v.* (decide) 決心する, 決意する, (**be resolved to do**) ...しようと決心している; (solve) 解決する

How are we going to resolve this problem?
この問題をどうやって解決しよう?

resonance *n.* (sound) 共鳴, (echo) 反響

resonate *v.* (make a deep sound) 鳴り響く, 響きわたる

resort *v.* (have recourse) 頼る, 訴える

n. (vacation place) リゾート(地), 行楽地

In the end, they resorted to violence.
最後には、彼らは暴力に訴えた。

a summer resort 避暑地

as a last resort 最後の手段として

As a last resort, he saw a psychiatrist.
最後の手段として、彼は精神科医に診てもらった。

resounding *adj.* (loud, echoing) 鳴り響く; (total) 完全な

The toolbox fell to the floor with a resounding crash.

道具箱が大きな音を鳴り響かせて床に落ちた。

Our appeals were met with a resounding "no."
我々の訴えは、大反対にあった。

The concert was a resounding success.
コンサートは大成功だった。

resource *n.* (wealth potential) 資源, (source material, data) 資料

Canada is rich in natural resources.
カナダは天然資源が豊富だ。

This will be a good resource for my thesis.
これは論文のいい資料になる。

resourceful *adj.* (of person) 機転の利く, 臨機応変の

respect

1 *v.* FEEL/SHOW REVERENCE FOR: 尊敬する, 偉いと思う, 高く評価する, (…に) 一目置く

2 *v.* SHOW UNDERSTANDING OF: 尊重する, 考慮する, 考えに入れる

3 *n.* REVERENCE: 尊敬, 敬意, 尊重

4 *n.* REGARD: 点

1 I respect him as a scholar, but I do not like the way he conducts his classes.
学者としては尊敬していますが、指導の仕方は好きではありません。

I respect her because she's a hard worker.
彼女はとてもがんばり屋なので、偉いと思います。

I respect him for his integrity.
彼の誠実さを高く評価している。

Mr. Hashimoto respects you.
橋本さんはあなたに一目置いていますよ。

2 We must respect the family's wishes.
ご家族の希望を尊重すべきです。

Let's try to respect the local customs.
地元のしきたりを考慮しよう。

3 He has no respect for his parents.
あの人には親を敬う気持ちが全くない。

4 In this [that] respect…
この [その] 点で…

pay one's respects to …に敬意を表する

with respect to …に関しては

With respect to this second paragraph, I think it might as well be deleted.
この第2段落に関しては、削除してしまっていいと思います。

respectable *adj.* (admirable) 立派な, 偉い, ちゃんとした; (of amount: considerable) かなりの, 相当な, いい

a respectable member of society
社会の立派な一員

respected *adj.* (高く) 評価されている

respectful *adj.* 丁寧な, 礼儀正しい, 敬意を表する

respective *adj.* それぞれの, 各自の

respectively *adv.* それぞれ, 各自

give A and B to X and Y respectively
AはXに、BはYにそれぞれ与える

respiration *n.* 呼吸

respirator *n.* 人工呼吸器

be on a respirator
人工呼吸器をつけている

respiratory *adj.* 呼吸器の

the respiratory system 呼吸器系

respite *n.* (cessation) 休止, 停止

respond *v.* (answer) 返事をする, 答える, (react) 反応する, 応じる

Let me respond to that question.
その質問に答えさせてください。

respondent *n.* 回答者, ((*formal*)) 応答する人

response *n.* (answer) 返事, (reaction) 反応

There was very little response to the advertisement.
広告への反応は、ほとんどなかった。

The audience's response was to boo.
観客からはブーイングの反応があった。

responsibility *n.* 責任, (duty) 義務

You're in a position of responsibility.
あなたは責任のある地位にいらっしゃいます。

I made the mistake, and I take full responsibility for it.
私が間違ったんですから、全責任を取ります。

The responsibilities of parents cannot be underestimated.
親としての義務を軽くみてはいけない。

responsible *adj.*

1 DESERVING BLAME: 責任がある

2 OF PERSON: (having a sense of responsibility) 責任感のある, (trustworthy) 信頼できる

3 IMPORTANT: 責任の重い

1 Who's responsible for this mess?
こんなことになったのは、誰の<u>責任</u> [せい] ですか？

She's the one responsible for this mix-up.
この手違いの責任は、あの人にあります。

2 He's the most responsible person I know.
彼ほど責任感の強い人に会ったことがありません。

3 She holds a very responsible job.
彼女はとても責任の重い仕事に就いている。

be held responsible for …の責任を負わされる

She was held responsible for the accident.
彼女はその事故の責任を負わされた。

be responsible to …に対して責任がある

Now, let's get this straight. You're responsible to me.
いいかい、これははっきりさせておこう。君は私に対して責任があるんだよ。

rest

1 *n.* RELAXATION: (recuperation) 休息, 休養, (sleep) 眠り, 睡眠, (break) 一休み, 休憩

2 *v.* RECUPERATE: 休養を取る, (take a break) 休む, 休憩する, 一休みする

3 *n.* REMAINDER: (**the rest**) 残り, (=the excess) 余分, (=the remaining people/things) ほかの人/もの

4 *v.* SET DOWN: 置く

5 *v.* BECOME RECUMBENT: (lie down) 横になる, (lie against) もたれる

1 Sunday is my day of rest.
日曜日は私の休息日です。

I'm going to have a rest on the sofa.
ソファーでちょっと休みます。

We didn't even have time to take a rest.
一休みする時間さえなかった。

2 The doctor told me to rest.
医者から休養を取るよう言われた。

If we rest for fifteen minutes every two hours, we should still reach the campsite by 1 o'clock.
2時間ごとに15分間の休憩を取っても、1時にはキャンプ場に着くだろう。

I'm not going to rest until I find the man who did this.
これをやった人を見つけるまで、休んでなんかいられない。

3 What did you do the rest of the time?
残りの時間は何をしましたか？

What was it Hamlet said?—"The rest is silence"?
ハムレットは何と言ったんだっけ？——「あとは沈黙」？

You're just like all the rest.
あなたも、ほかのみんなと同じですね。

Wada went, but the rest of us didn't.
和田さんは行ったけど、ほかは誰も行きませんでした。

4 Rest it on the piano, will you.
ピアノの上に置いてくれる？

Mother rested her foot on the chair.
母は足を椅子にのせた。

5 Here's something you can rest on.
ほら、これにもたれればいい。

♦**rest area** ***n.*** (on highway) 休憩所

restart ***v.*** (computer) 再起動する, (car) 再び走らせる, (talks) 再開する

restate ***v.*** 言い直す, 言い換える

restaurant ***n.*** レストラン, (cafeteria, canteen) 食堂, (traditional, expensive Japanese restaurant) 料亭

restful ***adj.*** (of place) ゆっくりできる, 心の安らぐ, (of scenery) のどかな

restless ***adj.*** (nervous) 落ち着かない, そわそわしている, (uneasy) 不安な

restock ***v.*** (restock A with B) (AにBを) 補充する

restoration ***n.*** (of building, painting) 修復, 復元, (of order, confidence) 回復, (of railroad) 復旧; (in Japanese history: **the Meiji Restoration**) 明治維新

restore ***v.*** (building, painting) 修復する, 復元する, (health, confidence) 回復する, 取り戻す [→ BRING BACK 3]

The palace was restored to its former glory.
宮殿は昔の美しい姿に修復された。

We need to restore consumer confidence in food safety.
食品の安全性に対する消費者の信頼を回復しなくてはいけない。

restrain ***v.*** 抑える, こらえる, (**restrain sb from doing**) (…に) …させないようにする

Try to restrain your anger.
怒りを抑えるようにしなさい。

I could not restrain my tears.
涙を抑えられなかった。

I tried to restrain myself from laughing.
笑いを懸命にこらえた。

♦**restraining order** ***n.*** 禁止命令, 差し止め命令

restraint ***n.*** (control) 抑制, (calm/controlled behavior) 遠慮, 控え目

restrict ***v.*** 制限する, 限定する, 限る

These narrow streets restrict the movement of traffic.
こういう細い道は通行が制限されている。

Membership is restricted to those over fifty.
会員は50歳以上に限定されています。

restricted ***adj.*** 制限された, 限られた

♦**restricted area** ***n.*** 立入禁止区域

restriction ***n.*** 制限, 限定, 制約

restrictive ***adj.*** (limiting) 限定する, 制限

的な

a restrictive clause 制限節

rest room *n.* お手洗い, 洗面所, (for women) 化粧室 [lit., "makeup room"]

restructure *v.* (reassemble) 編成し直す, 再編する, (…の) 構造改革をする

♦**restructuring** *n.* (of company) リストラ, 再編

result *n.* (outcome) 結果, 結末 [→ GRADE 4]

v. (**result from**) (…が) 原因で起こる, (**result in**) …に終わる, …という結果になる, もたらす

The flooding was a direct result of deforestation.
その洪水は、森林伐採の直接的な結果だった。

The new tax system was introduced with disastrous results.
新しい税制の導入は、ひどい結果をもたらした。

And what do you think would be the result of that?
で、結果はどうなると思います？

As a result, he resigned.
その結果、彼は辞任した。

The change in personnel resulted in chaos.
人事異動が大混乱をもたらした。

The firm's restructuring resulted in layoffs.
その会社の再編は、結果的に一時解雇を招いた。

resume *v.* 再び始める, 再開する

♦**resumption** *n.* 再開

resurgence *n.* 復活, 再起

resurrect *v.* (dead person) 生き返らせる, (idea) 復活させる

resurrection *n.* (**the Resurrection**) キリストの復活; (return) よみがえること, 復活

resuscitate *v.* 生き返らせる, 蘇生させる

retail *n., adj.* 小売り(の)

v. (retail for) (…で) 売られている

the retail price 小売価格

♦**retailer** *n.* 小売店

retailing *n.* (business) 小売業

retain *v.* (keep) 保つ, 保持する, 維持する, (employ) 雇う

retainer[1] *n.* (servant) 召し使い, (attendant to high-ranking samurai) 家来; (device for mouth) 固定装置

retainer[2] *n.* (fee) 顧問料

retaliate *v.* 仕返しする, 復讐する, ((*formal*)) 報復する

retaliation *n.* 仕返し, 復讐, ((*formal*)) 報復

retard *v.* (slow) 遅らせる

retarded *adj.* (mentally) 知能の遅れた

retell *v.* (story) 形を変えて語る

rethink *v.* 考え直す, ((*formal*)) 再考する

reticent *adj.* 口の重い, 無口な

retina *n.* 網膜

retinue *n.* 随行員, 側近

retire *v.* (give up work) 引退する, 退職する [NOTE: retire at mandatory retirement age 定年退職する]; (retire to: somewhere quiet) (…に) こもる

When do you intend to retire?
((*polite*)) いつ引退なさるおつもりですか？

He retired early at fifty-six.
彼は５６歳で、早期退職した。

I'm not going to retire until I'm eligible for my full pension.
年金が満額もらえるまで退職しません。

He retired to the library.
彼は書斎にこもった。

♦ **retired** *adj.* 引退した, 定年退職した

a retired professor 定年退官した教授

retiree *n.* 定年退職者

retirement *n.* (act of retiring) 定年退職, 引退, (post-retirement life) 引退後の生活, 老後

retort *v.* (…と) 言い返す, やり返す

retrace *v.* (one's way) 引き返す, 後戻りする

Try to retrace your steps.
引き返してみてください。

retract *v.* (take back: statement) 撤回する, (pull back) 引っ込める

retrain *v.* 再訓練する, 再教育する

retreat *v.* (of troops) 退却する, 撤退する, (step back) 引き下がる, ((*also figurative*)) 後退する, (**retreat into**: room) …に引っ込む

n. (withdrawal of troops) 退却, 撤退; (quiet place) 静養先, (**mountain retreat**) 山荘

The troops retreated to a safer position.
軍隊は、より安全な地点まで退却した。

The government seems to be retreating from its original policy.
政府は当初の政策から手を引いているように思う。

We stayed at the mountain retreat for two weeks.
山荘には2週間滞在しました。

retrial *n.* 再審

retribution *n.* 天罰, 報い [→ REVENGE]

retrieval *n.* (of information from computer) 検索, (of belongings) 回収

retrieve *v.* (data) 検索する, (get back) 取り戻す, 回収する

retriever *n.* (dog) レトリバー

retro *adj.* レトロの, リバイバルの

retroactive *adj.* さかのぼる

♦ **retroactively** *adv.* さかのぼって

retrograde *adj.* 後退する

a retrograde step 後退

retrospect *n.* 回想, 回顧, 追想

in retrospect 振り返ってみて

retrospective *adj.* 回顧的な

n. (exhibition) 回顧展

retry *v.* (in court) 再審する

return

1 *v.* COME/GO BACK: 戻る, 帰る, (to speaker's location) 戻って来る, 帰って来る

2 *n.* ACT OF COMING BACK: 帰り, 帰って来ること

3 *v.* TAKE/SEND BACK: 返す, (library book, rented DVD) 返却する, (product to store/maker) 返品する, (put back) 戻す

4 *v.* RESUME: (return to) (…に) 戻る, (**return to doing**) 再び…し続ける

5 *v.* RECIPROCATE: (…に) 答える, (**return a phone call**) 折り返し電話する, (**return a/the favor**) お返しをする

6 *n.* PROFIT: 収益, 利潤, 利益

7 *n.* BUTTON ON KEYBOARD: リターン(キー)

1 I decided to return to the hotel.
ホテルに戻ることにした。

He returned from his service in the

R

Peace Corps in 1991.
彼は１９９１年に平和部隊の勤務から戻った。

My husband didn't return until the next morning.
夫は翌朝まで帰って来なかった。

2 Upon his return, he went straight to bed.
彼は帰るとすぐに寝た。

His parents are looking forward to his return.
ご両親は、彼が帰って来るのを心待ちにしています。

3 Please return the book when you've finished it.
本は読み終えたら、返してください。

He still hasn't returned the money.
あの人はまだ、お金を返していない。

Please return the document to its proper place in the filing cabinet when you are finished with it.
済んだら、書類はキャビネットの元の位置に戻しておいてください。

4 I'd like to return to this point later in the lesson.
この点については、またあとで戻りたいと思います。

5 He never returned my phone call.
電話をしても、(彼は)折り返してかけてくることはなかった。

6 The return was good.
収益は、よかった。

7 press return リターンキーを押す

in return for (in exchange for) …の代わりに, (favor) …のお礼に

♦**return match** *n.* リターンマッチ

return ticket *n.* 帰りの切符, (round-trip ticket) 往復切符

returnable *adj.* (of deposit) 返却してもらえる, (of bottles) 買い取ってもらえる

returnee *n.* (person who has returned to Japan after living abroad) 帰国子女

reunification *n.* 再統一

reunion *n.* 再会, (class reunion) クラス会, 同窓会

reunite *v.* (people) (…に) 再会する, (organization) 再結合する

reuse *v.* 再利用する

revamp *v.* 改造する, 刷新する

reveal *v.* 明らかにする, 明かす, (betray, lay bare) 暴露する, さらけ出す, (leak) 漏らす, (show) 見せる

The whole sordid affair was revealed in the tabloids.
その卑劣な事件の一部始終が、タブロイド紙に暴露された。

Who revealed the secret?
誰が秘密を漏らした？

revealing *adj.* (enlightening) 啓発的な; (of clothes) 肌を露出する

revel *v.* (**revel in**) 楽しむ, 満喫する

revelation *n.* (surprise) 意外なこと, (disclosure) 漏らすこと, 暴露; (religious) 黙示

revelry *n.* ばか騒ぎ

revenge *n.* 復讐, 仕返し, 報復

They're out for revenge.
彼らは復讐をしようとねらっている。

in revenge for …の仕返しに, …の報復として

He was killed in revenge for Yamaguchi's death.
山口が死んだ報復として彼は殺された。

revenue *n.* 歳入, (tax revenue) 税収, (earnings) 収益

reverberate *v.* (of sound) 反響する, 響きわたる

revere *v.* あがめる, 敬愛する

reverend *n.* 牧師, ...師

reversal *n.* (of situation) 逆転

reverse *n.* (**the reverse**) (=the opposite) 逆, 反対, (=the back side) 裏, 裏側; (gear) バックギア

v. (situation, process) 逆にする, (decision) くつがえす, (**reverse oneself**: change one's opinion) 意見を変える [→ BACK UP 2]

adj. (opposite) 逆の, (back) 裏の

No, quite the reverse. I think things are getting better.
いいえ、全く逆です。事態は、いいほうに向かっていると思います。

He says one thing and does exactly the reverse.
あの人は言うこととやることが全く逆だ。

The front was all right, but the reverse was filthy.
表は大丈夫だったけど、裏は汚かった。

Two months later, the courts reversed the decision.
2ヵ月後、法廷は決定をくつがえした。

reverse discrimination 逆差別

reversible *adj.* (can be reversed) 逆にできる, (of clothes) リバーシブルの

revert *v.* (revert to) (...に) 戻る

review *v.* (comment on, criticize) 批評する, 評論する, (reexamine) 再検討する, (for class, exam) 復習する

n. (of book) 書評, (of film) 批評, (reexamination) 再検討, (for class, exam) 復習

write a book review 書評を書く

under review 検討中

The matter is under review.
その件は検討中です。

reviewer *n.* 評論家

a book reviewer 書評家

revise *v.* (alter) 改める, 変える, 変更する, (modify) 修正する, (book) 改訂する, (essay) 書き直す

♦**revised** *adj.* 改訂された

a revised edition 改訂版

revision *n.* (of text) 改訂, (to text) 修正, (revised edition) 改訂版

revisit *v.* (visit again) 再び訪れる

revitalize *v.* 復興させる, 再生する

revitalize the economy 経済を復興させる

♦**revitalization** *n.* 復興, 再生

revival *n.* 復活, リバイバル, (new performance) 再上演

revive *v.* (bring back to life) 生き返らせる, (bring back to consciousness) 意識を取り戻す, (reinvigorate) 復活する

revolt *v.* (start a rebellion) 反乱を起こす, (revolt against: defy) (...に) 反抗する

n. (rebellion) 反乱

revolting *adj.* むかむかする, 吐き気のする

revolution *n.* (radical political change) 革命, (great change) 大変革; (full cycle) 回転

the French Revolution フランス革命

The industrial revolution took far longer than the microelectronic revolution.

R

産業革命は、超小型コンピューターの大変革よりもずっと時間がかかった。

Darwin's theory of evolution caused a revolution in our thinking.
ダーウィンの進化論は、我々のものの考え方に大変革をもたらした。

33 1/3 revolutions per minute
毎分 3 3 1/3 の回転

revolutionary *adj.* (of revolution) 革命の, (involving radical change) 革命的な, 画期的な
n. (person) 革命家

revolutionize *v.* (...に) 革命をもたらす, 革命を起こす

revolve *v.* 回転する, 回る [→ GO[1] AROUND]
The earth revolves around the sun.
地球は太陽の周りを回る [公転する]。

♦ **revolving door** *n.* 回転ドア

revolver *n.* リボルバー, ピストル

revue *n.* レビュー

reward *n.* 報酬, 謝礼, お礼, (given to child) (ご)ほうび, (money) 謝礼金, (for providing information to authorities) 懸賞金
v. (...に) 報いる, 報酬を与える
How much was the reward?
報酬は、いくらだったんですか？
There ought to be more rewards for hard workers.
よく働いた人には、もっと報奨があるべきだ。
There's a reward of $100,000 for information about the suspect.
容疑者についての情報には10万ドルの懸賞金が支払われる。
Their efforts were rewarded.
彼らの努力は報いられた。

rewarding *adj.* やりがいのある
The pay wasn't good, but it was rewarding work.
給料は低かったけど、やりがいのある仕事だった。

rewind *n.* (button/function) 巻き戻し
v. 巻き戻す

rewire *v.* (building) 配線し直す

rewrite *v.* 書き直す, リライトする
n. 書き直し, リライト

rhapsody *n.* ラプソディー, 狂詩曲

rhetoric *n.* 修辞学, (rhetorical language) 美辞麗句, おおげさな言葉

rhetorical *adj.* 修辞的な
a rhetorical question 修辞疑問

rheumatism *n.* リウマチ

rhinestone *n.* ライン石, 模造ダイヤモンド

rhinoceros *n.* サイ

rhododendron *n.* シャクナゲ

rhubarb *n.* ルバーブ, 大黄

rhyme *n.* (kind of poem) 韻
v. (sound similar) 韻を踏む

rhythm *n.* リズム

♦ **rhythm and blues** *n.* リズム・アンド・ブルース

rib *n.* (bone) 肋骨, あばら骨, (meat on a bone) あばら肉; (in knitted cloth) リブ編み

ribbon *n.* リボン

riboflavin *n.* リボフラビン

rice *n.* (お)米, (cooked rice) ご飯, (as served on a plate in Western restaurants) ライス, (rice plant) 稲
brown rice 玄米

R

white rice 白米

foreign rice 外米

rinse rice (お)米をとぐ

cook rice ご飯を炊く

fried rice チャーハン

plant rice 田植えをする

harvest rice 稲を刈り入れる

♦**rice cake** *n.* (お)もち

rice cooker *n.* 炊飯器 [→ picture of KITCHEN]

rice dealer *n.* (お)米屋(さん)

rice field *n.* 水田, ((*informal*)) 田んぼ

rich *adj.*

1 WEALTHY: 金持ちの, 裕福な, (**the rich**) 金持ち, (of country) 豊かな

2 ABUNDANT: 豊かな, (be rich in) (…が) 豊富だ, (…に) 恵まれている

3 OF FOOD: (oily) 油っこい, こってりした, (containing lots of fat) 脂肪分の多い, (of chocolate, wine) 濃厚な

4 OF SOIL: 肥えた, 肥沃な

5 OF COLOR: 濃い

1 She's a very rich woman.
あの人は大金持ちだよ。

He got rich by buying land when it was cheap.
彼は、値段が安かった時に土地を買って金持ちになった。

The richer you get, the busier you are.
裕福になればなるほど、忙しくなる。

Are the rich happier than the poor?
金持ちは貧乏人より幸せだろうか？

Only the rich could afford a house like that.
ああいう家を持てるのは金持ちだけだよ。

It's a very rich country.
とても豊かな国です。

2 The author's rich vocabulary results in vivid descriptions.
著者の豊かな語彙が、活き活きとした描写を生んでいる。

Saudi Arabia is rich in oil.
サウジアラビアは石油資源が豊富です。

3 The sauce was too rich for my liking.
私の好みとしては、あのソースはこってりしすぎていた。

4 This is rich soil.
ここの土地は肥えている。

5 a deep rich red 深みのある濃い赤

riches *n.* (wealth) 富, (property) 財産

build up riches and fame
富と名声を築く

richly *adv.* (amply) 十分に, (lavishly) 豊富に

rickshaw *n.* 人力車

ricochet *v.* はね返る

The ball ricocheted off the wall.
ボールは壁に当たってはね返った。

rid *v.* (rid A of B) AからBを取り除く

An exterminator was called to rid the house of cockroaches.
家からゴキブリを退治するため、害虫駆除業者が呼ばれた。

be rid of 追い払う, …から解放される

I'm glad to be rid of that old bed.
古いベッドを処分して、すっきりした。

get rid of (spot, cough) 取る, (garbage) 捨てる, 処分する, (person) 追い払う

How do you get rid of these spots?
このしみは、どうすれば取れますか？

We've got to get rid of all this trash.

このごみを全部処分しなくちゃならない。

It was difficult to get rid of him, but I managed in the end.
彼を追い払うのには苦労したけど、最後はなんとかうまくいった。

riddle ***n.*** なぞ

riddled ***adj.*** (riddled with) …だらけの

a translation riddled with errors
間違いだらけの翻訳

ride ***v.*** (…に) 乗る

n. (act of riding) 乗ること, (amusement park ride) 乗り物

The kids love riding their bikes.
子供たちが自転車に乗るのが大好きなんだ。

This car is comfortable to ride in.
この車は乗り心地がいい。

Riding the crowded trains every morning must be tough.
毎朝、満員電車に乗るのは大変でしょう。

Can you ride a horse?
馬に乗れますか？

He gave me a ride into town.
彼は街まで車に乗せて行ってくれた。

Do you like scary rides?
怖い乗り物は好きですか？

rider ***n.*** (of motorcycle) 乗り手, 乗っている人, ライダー

ridge ***n.*** (of mountain) 尾根, 山の背, (of roof) 棟, (under sea) 海嶺

a mountain ridge 山の尾根

the ridge of a wave 波頭

the ridge of one's nose 鼻筋

ridicule ***n.*** あざけり, あざ笑い, 嘲笑

v. あざける, あざ笑う, 嘲笑する

an object of ridicule 物笑いのたね

ridiculous ***adj.*** ばかげた, ばかばかしい, おかしな, (of appearance) こっけいな, (of price) とんでもない

It was an absolutely ridiculous demand.
全くばかげた要求だった。

It's a ridiculous price to pay.
とんでもない値段だ。

riding ***n.*** (horseback riding) 乗馬

rife ***adj.*** 横行している, 広まっている

rifle ***n.*** ライフル(銃)

shoot a rifle ライフルを撃つ

rift ***n.*** (serious difference) 対立, 亀裂; (in earth, rock) 断層

Serious rifts developed within the cabinet.
閣内で深刻な対立が起きた。

rig ***v.*** (fix) 不正に操作する

n. (oil rig) 油田掘削装置; (truck) トラック; (arrangement of sails etc. on ship) 艤装

The election was rigged.
選挙が不正に操作された。

rig a horse race 競馬で八百長をする

right

1 ***adj.*** CORRECT: 正しい, 間違っていない, 合っている, (used as a tag question) …ね

2 ***adj.*** SUITABLE: ちょうどいい, ふさわしい, ぴったりの

3 ***n.*** DIRECTION OPPOSITE LEFT: 右, (right side) 右側, (right turn) 右折

4 ***adv.*** TO THE RIGHT: (giving directions) 右に, 右の方に

5 ***n.*** GOOD: 正しいこと, 正義

6 ***adv.*** CORRECTLY: 正確に, 間違いなく, ずばり, (in a morally correct way) 正しく

7 ***adv.*** DIRECTLY: まっすぐ(に), 直接

8 *adv.* **IMMEDIATELY:** すぐ(に)

9 *adv.* **USED EMPHATICALLY:** See examples below

10 *adv.* **SUITABLY:** See examples below

11 *n.* **ENTITLEMENT:** 権利

12 *v.* **MAKE RIGHT:** 正す

13 *n.* **POLITICAL GROUP:** (**the Right**) 右翼, 右派

1 That's not the right answer.
それは正しい答えではありません。

Are you sure you're right?
間違いない？

I think you were right to do as you did.
あなたがそうしたのは、正しかったと思うよ。

I think that's right.
そのとおりだと思います。

Is that the right time?
その時間は合っていますか？

You're Polish, right?
ポーランドの方ですよね？

2 I just happened to be in the right placc at the right time.
私はたまたま、ちょうどいい時にちょうどいい所にいただけです。

I don't think she's the right person to talk to about this.
彼女は、この件を話すのにふさわしい相手じゃないと思う。

That's just the right tie for that shirt.
そのシャツにぴったりのネクタイだよ。

You've got the right attitude.
その心構えですよ。

3 To the right and left are tall buildings.
右側にも左側にも高いビルがある。

You'll notice a castle to your right.
右手にお城が見えます。

Take the second right.
２本目の道を右折してください。

4 Turn right at the next stop sign, please.
次の一時停止の標識で、右に曲がってください。

5 Children ought to be taught the difference between right and wrong.
子供には、善悪の区別を教えなくてはいけない。

6 She guessed right.
彼女はずばり言い当てた。

Some of them got it right, others didn't.
きちんとわかった人もいれば、わかってない人もいた。

7 I suggest you go right there.
まっすぐ行ったほうがいい。

8 I'll be right back. すぐ戻ります。

He came right out with it.
彼はすぐに言ってしまった。

9 It fell right down to the bottom.
一番下まで落ちた。

He was right on time.
彼はちょうど時間どおりに現れた。

10 It serves him right. 自業自得だ。

It fits you just right.
あなたにぴったりです。

11 We have a right to know.
私たちには知る権利がある。

equal rights 平等の権利

human rights 人権

12 right a wrong 不正を正す

all right → ALL RIGHT

be in the right 正しい, 道理があ

He said he was in the right and th

other driver was in the wrong.
彼は自分が正しくて、向こうの運転手が間違っているのだと言った。

by right of …の権限で, …による

He has diplomatic immunity by right of the Vienna Convention.
彼にはウィーン条約による外交特権がある。

get right (correctly understand) 正しく理解する, (correctly answer) 正解する

He got the answer right the first time.
彼は1回目で正解した。

right and wrong 善悪, 善し悪し [→ 5]

right away/off すぐに

I want this done right away.
これをすぐにやってください。

right now 今すぐ

I want an answer right now.
今すぐ返事がほしいんです。

set/put right (repair) 直す, (make fair) 矯正する

the rights and wrongs of …の善悪, …の善し悪し

Let's not argue about the rights and wrongs of the situation.
事の善し悪しを言い争うのはよそう。

ight angle *n.* 直角

hteous *adj.* (of person) 正義の, 公正, (of decision) 正しい, 公正な

tful *adj.* 正当な, 正しい

e car was returned to its rightful ner.
は、正当な持ち主に返された。

hand *n.* 右手

◆ **handed** *adj.* 右利きの

ri hand man *n.* 右腕, 片腕

rightly *adv.* 正しく, 当然, 間違いなく

He was sacked, and quite rightly, too.
彼はクビになったが、それも当然のことだ。

rightly or wrongly 良かれ悪しかれ, 是非はともかく

Rightly or wrongly, he has decided to return to America.
是非はともかく、彼はアメリカに戻ることにしている。

right-wing *adj.* 右翼の, 右派の

rigid *adj.* (stiff) 堅い, (fixed) 固定した, (strict) 厳しい

rigidly *adv.* (tightly) 堅く, (strictly) 厳しく, 堅苦しく, 厳格に

There's no need to follow the rules so rigidly.
そんなに厳しく規則に従う必要はない。

rigor *n.* (strictness) 厳しさ, (exactness) 厳密さ

rigor mortis *n.* 死後硬直

rigorous *adj.* (of investigation) 厳密な, (of work) 厳しい

rim *n.* 縁, へり

the rim of the cup カップの縁

The metal rim was rusted.
金属の縁の部分がさびていた。

rind *n.* 皮

ring[1] *n.* (circle) 輪, 円形, (piece of jewelry) 指輪; (boxing ring) リング, (sumo ring) 土俵

Let's form a ring. 輪になろう。

They danced in a ring.
彼らは輪になって踊った。

a wedding [an engagement] ring
結婚 [婚約] 指輪

R

a ring collection 指輪のコレクション

♦ **ring finger** *n.* 薬指 [→ picture of HAND]

ring² *v.* (make a ringing sound) 鳴る, (cause to ring) 鳴らす [→ CALL 4]

n. (ringing sound) 鳴る音

The telephone is ringing.
電話が鳴っている。

Did you ring the doorbell?
ドアのベルを鳴らした?

ringleader *n.* 首謀者

ringworm *n.* 白癬, たむし

rink *n.* スケートリンク, スケート場

rinse *v.* ゆすぐ, すすぐ, すすぎ洗いする, (hair) リンスする

n. すすぎ, ゆすぎ, (hair conditioner) リンス

Be sure to rinse the dishes thoroughly after washing them.
お皿を洗ったら、しっかりすすいでね。

I'll just give these glasses a quick rinse.
グラスをさっと、ゆすいできます。

riot *n.* 暴動

v. 暴動を起こす

There was a riot in the prison.
刑務所で暴動があった。

The sharp increase in food prices caused a riot.
食品の急激な値上がりが暴動を招いた。

♦ **riot police** *n.* 機動隊

rip *v.* (tear) 裂く, 引きちぎる, 引き裂く, (become torn) 裂ける, ほころびる, (**rip away/down**) はぎ取る

n. 裂け目, ほころび

You ripped your shirt.
シャツが裂けてるよ。

I ripped open the letter.
手紙をビリッと破いて開封した。

Let's rip down the wallpaper.
壁紙をはぎ取ろう。

There's a rip in the curtain.
カーテンにほころびがある。

♦ **rip off** *v.* (steal) 盗む, (con) だます

You've been ripped off.
あなたは、だまされたんだよ。

ripe *adj.* 熟した, 熟れた

The strawberries were ripe enough for picking.
イチゴは、もいでもいいくらい熟していた。

The bananas were too ripe.
そのバナナは、熟れすぎていた。

ripen *v.* 熟する

ripple *n.* さざ波, (ripple marks) 波紋

v. (of water) さざ波が立つ

rise

1 *v.* GO UPWARD: 上がる, (stand up) 立ち上がる, (of sun) 昇る, (of temperature, level) 上昇する, (of hill: slope upward) 上り坂になる, (of balloon) 飛ぶ

2 *v.* GET UP: (from sleep) 起きる, ((*formal*)) 起床する

3 *v.* INCREASE IN AMOUNT: 増加する, (of price) 値上がりする, (of dough) 膨れる

4 *v.* BECOME SUCCESSFUL: (be promoted) 昇進する, (rise in rank) 地位が上がる, (rise in the world) 出世する

5 *v.* OF FEELING: (well up) 募る, わき上がる

6 *v.* EMERGE: 起こる, 生まれる

7 *v.* REBEL: 立ち上がる, 反乱を起こす

8 *v.* LOOM: そびえ立つ

9 *n.* INCREASE: 上昇, 上がること

R

10 *n.* **EMERGENCE:** (in history: the rise of…) (…の) 台頭, 興隆, (of sun, moon) 出ること [→ SUNRISE]

1 As the elevator rose, a spectacular view of the city unfolded below.
エレベーターが上がるにつれて、眼下に街のすばらしい眺めが広がった。

Smoke rose from the fire.
火から煙が立ち昇った。

I rose to shake his hand.
彼と握手するために立ち上がった。

Would the audience please rise.
みなさんどうぞ、ご起立ください。

The sun rises in the east.
太陽は東から昇る。

The rivers have risen a lot since the snow started melting.
雪解けが始まってから、川の水位はかなり上昇した。

2 He rises at 7 o'clock every morning.
彼は毎朝7時に起きる。

3 Prices are constantly rising.
物価が絶えず上がっている。

The dough should rise after an hour or so.
1時間かそこらで生地が膨らむはずだ。

4 Many of my former schoolmates have risen to high positions.
かつての級友の多くが、高い地位に昇りつめている。

He rose rapidly within the company.
彼は会社でみるみる出世した。

5 I could feel the frustration rising in me.
しだいに、いらだちが募るのがわかった。

6 A new Europe rose from the ruins of war.
戦後のがれきの中から、新生ヨーロッパは生まれた。

7 The poor rose in protest.
貧しい人たちが抗議して立ち上がった。

8 The mountain rose in the distance.
遠くに山がそびえ立っていた。

9 a rise in stock prices 株価の上昇

a rise in living standards
生活水準の向上

10 the rise and fall of the Roman Empire
ローマ帝国の興亡

risk *n.* (danger) 危険, 危機, リスク; (uncertain factor) 賭け, 冒険

v. (**risk doing**) 危険を冒して…する, (**risk one's life to do**) 命がけで…する

It's the elderly who are most at risk from influenza.
インフルエンザにかかった場合、一番危険なのはお年寄りです。

More jobs have been put at risk.
さらに多くの人が、失業の危機にさらされている。

She considered the investment a risk.
彼女はその投資は賭けだと思った。

That's quite a big risk.
それはかなり大きな冒険だね。

He risked his life to save someone from drowning.
彼は命がけで、おぼれかけている人を救った。

run the risk 危険を冒す

If you smoke, you run the risk of getting cancer.
喫煙すると、がんになる危険を冒すことになる。

risky *adj.* 危ない, 危険な

rite *n.* 儀式

ritual *n.* (ceremony) 儀式, (custom of a particular society) しきたり, 風習, (individual's habit) 習慣

a religious ritual 宗教儀式

a daily ritual 日常の習慣

rival *n.* 競争相手, ライバル

v. (be equal/not inferior to) (…に) 匹敵する/劣らない

rivalry *n.* 競争, 対抗

a long-standing rivalry

長年にわたる競争

river *n.* 川, (of other substances) 流れ

Let's cross the river. 川を渡ろう。

the River Edo (in Tokyo)

(東京の) 江戸川

riverbank *n.* 川岸, 川堤

riverboat *n.* 川船

rivet *n.* リベット, びょう

road *n.* (street) 道, 道路, 通り, (in names of streets) …街道; (way) 方法, ((*figurative*)) 道

the main road 幹線道路

the road that leads to the station

駅へ行く道

the London Road ロンドン街道

a road map 道路地図

a road sign 道路標識

the road to success [ruin]

成功 [破滅] への道

on the road (traveling) 旅行中で, (touring) 巡業中で

the end of the road 終わり, おしまい, 年貢の納め時

It looks like it's the end of the road for him.

どうやら彼もおしまいのようだ。

road show *n.* (of play) 地方公演, (of movie) ロードショー

roadside *n.* 道端

roadworks *n.* 道路工事

roar *v.* (of animal) ほえる, うなる, (shout) どなる, (scream) 叫ぶ, わめく, (**roar with laughter**) 大笑いする, (of thunder) とどろく, (of machine) 轟音を立てる

n. (of animal) うなり声, (of angry person) どなり声, (of wind) うなり

The lion roared.

ライオンがほえた [うなり声を上げた]。

The teacher roared at the class to be quiet.

先生は生徒たちに向かって、静かにしろとどなった。

We roared with laughter.

私たちは大笑いした。

The crowd roared with delight.

群集が喜びにどよめいた。

A motorcycle roared past.

オートバイが轟音を立てて走って行った。

roast *v.* (meat) 焼く, ローストする, (coffee beans, tea leaves) いる, ほうじる; (criticize harshly) こき下ろす

adj. ローストした, 焼いた

n. (barbecue party) バーベキューパーティー

roast chestnuts 焼き栗

♦**roast beef** *n.* ローストビーフ

rob *v.* (steal money from) (…から) お金を奪い取る, (rob A of B) (AからBを) 奪う, 脅し取る, 略奪する, (rob a bank) (…に) 強盗に入る

The store was robbed.
店は強盗に入られた。

He was robbed as he got out of his car.
彼は、車から降りようとしたところを襲われた。

robber *n.* 強盗, 泥棒

robbery *n.* (act of robbing) 強盗, 略奪

armed robbery 凶器を使った強盗

robe *n.* (bathrobe) バスローブ

robin *n.* コマツグミ

robot *n.* ロボット

robust *adj.* (strong) 強い, 頑丈な

rock *n.* (stone) 岩, 岩石, (small stone) 石; (music) ロック

v. (sway) 揺り動かす, 揺らす, 振動させる, (move gently) 揺れる

He fell onto the rocks and cut his hand.
彼は岩に落ちて手を切った。

The boy threw a rock into the pond.
男の子は池に石を投げた。

Don't rock the boat.
ボートを揺らすんじゃない/((*figurative*)) 事を荒立てるな。

♦**rock garden** *n.* 石庭, ロックガーデン

rock climbing *n.* ロッククライミング, 岩登り

rocket *n.* (spaceship) ロケット, (missile) ミサイル, (firework) 打ち上げ花火

v. (of prices) 急上昇する

rocking chair *n.* ロッキングチェア, 揺り椅子

rock 'n' roll *n.* ロックンロール

rocky *adj.* (having many rocks) 岩の多い, (of surface) 岩のごつごつした, (rock-like) 岩のような

rod *n.* (stick) 棒, つえ, (for fishing) さお, 釣りざお

rodent *n.* げっ歯動物

rodeo *n.* ロデオ

roe *n.* (fish eggs) 魚の卵

rogue *adj.* (of animal) 群れを離れた

n. (bad person) 悪党, ならず者

a rogue elephant はぐれ象

role *n.* (part in play) 役, (function) 役割, 任務, 役目

She has the lead role, and I've been given a small supporting role.
彼女が主役で、私は小さなわき役をもらった。

What exactly is his role in this company?
この会社での、彼の正確な役割は何なのですか?

♦**role model** *n.* 理想の姿, (employee) 模範社員, (student) 模範生

roll

1 *v.* MOVE CYCLICALLY: 転がる, (roll away) 転がって行く, (**roll off**) (…から) 転げ落ちる, (cause to roll) 転がす, 動かす

2 *v.* FORM BY ROLLING: 丸める, 巻く

3 *n.* CYLINDRICAL BUNDLE: 巻物, 一巻き

4 *v.* SWAY: 揺れる, (of ship) 横揺れする, (of person) よろよろ歩く, (=drunkenly) 千鳥足で歩く, (of waves) うねる

5 *v.* GO WITH SMOOTH MOVEMENT: (of car) 進む, 走る

6 *v.* OF DRUMS/THUNDER: 鳴る

7 *n.* BREAD: ロールパン

8 *n.* ROLL CALL: 出席を取ること, 出欠調べ

1 The ball rolled down the road.
ボールは道路を転がって行った。

I rolled off the sofa onto the floor.
ソファーから床に転げ落ちた。

Let's roll it under the table.
テーブルの下まで転がしましょう。

roll a wheelchair 車椅子を動かす

2 It'd be easier to carry if you roll it into a bundle.
一まとめに丸めたほうが、持ち運びが楽ですよ。

3 a roll of toilet paper
トイレットペーパー<u>1個</u>[一巻き]

a roll of cloth 1反の布

a roll of carpet カーペット<u>1本</u>[一巻き]

a roll of fat 脂肪のかたまり

4 The ship rolled on the heavy seas.
船は荒波にもまれて大きく揺れた。

The drunk rolled along the platform.
酔っ払いがホームをよろよろ歩いていた。

5 The car rolled along quietly.
車は静かに走って行った。

6 The thunder began to roll.
雷がゴロゴロ鳴り出した。

7 Shall I bring some more rolls?
ロールパンをもう少しお持ちしましょうか?

8 take roll 出席を取る

be on a roll うまくいっている, 波に乗っている

start/get the ball rolling 始める

It's time to get the ball rolling on this project.
このプロジェクトを始める時です。

roll down *v.* (fall) 転がり落ちる, (of sweat) したたり落ちる, (of tear) 伝って落ちる; (sleeves) (まくり上げたそでを) 下ろす, (car window) 下げる, あける

The sweat rolled down off my forehead.
汗が額からしたたり落ちた。

A tear rolled down her cheek.
涙が彼女のほおを伝って落ちた。

roll in *v.* (of money) 転がり込む; (of person: appear) 現れる

roll out *v.* (dough) 伸ばす, (map, carpet) 広げる

Once you've rolled out the dough for the pie crust, the rest is easy.
パイ皮用の生地を伸ばしてしまえば、あとは簡単ですよ。

roll over *v.* (in bed) 寝返りを打つ

roll up *v.* (sleeves) まくり上げる, (car window) 上げる, 閉める; (of car) 近づいて来る

OK, roll up your sleeves and let's get to work.
じゃあ、腕まくりして仕事に取りかかろう。

A black car rolled up.
黒い車が近づいて来た。

---

roll call *n.* 出席を取ること, 点呼

roller *n.* ローラー

♦**roller coaster** *n.* ローラーコースター, ジェットコースター

Rollerblade *n.* ローラーブレード

roller skate *n.* ローラースケートの靴
v. (**roller-skate**) ローラースケートをする

roller skating *n.* ローラースケート

ROM *n.* (read-only memory) ROM

roman *adj.* (**Roman**) (of Rome) ローマの, (of people) ローマ人の; (of alphabet) ローマ字の

♦**Roman Catholic** *n.* カトリック教徒

roman numeral *n.* ローマ数字

romance *n.* 恋愛, ロマンス, (story) 恋愛物語

romanize *v.* ローマ字で書く

romanized Japanese
ローマ字で書かれた日本語

♦**romanization** *n.* ローマ字表記

romantic *adj.* ロマンチックな

a romantic atmosphere
ロマンチックな雰囲気

He's a very romantic person.
あの人はすごくロマンチックな人です。

romanticism *n.* ロマン主義

romp *v.* (of children: romp around) はね回る

roof *n.* (of building) 屋根 [→ picture of HOUSE, CAR]; (of mouth) 口蓋
v. (…に) 屋根をつける, (…の) 屋根をふく

The roof is leaking. 屋根が漏っている。

rooftop *n., adj.* 屋上(の)

a rooftop terrace 屋上テラス

rook *n.* (bird) ミヤマガラス

rookie *n.* ルーキー, 新人

room *n.* (in house) 部屋, -室 [→ picture below], (space in general) 場所, 余地, スペース, (possibility) 余地

This room is very small.
この部屋はとても狭い。

The house has a bedroom, a kitchen, and a living room.
その家には寝室一つと台所、居間があ

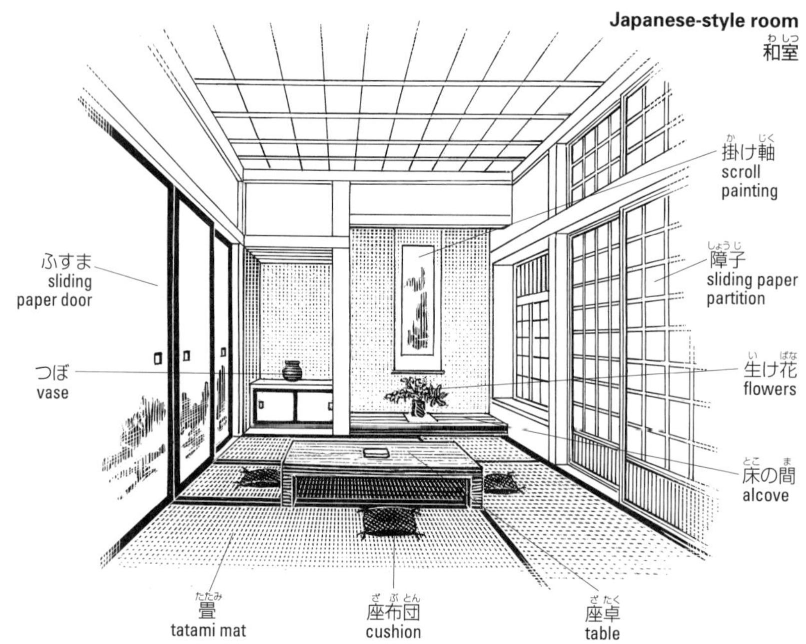

ります。

Do you have a room for rent?
貸し部屋はありますか？

All the rooms are booked.
全室、予約済みです。

There's plenty of room for furniture.
家具を置く場所はたっぷりある。

There's not enough room in the car for you.
車に乗せてあげる余地がない。

Can we make room for one more?
もう1人分、詰められる？

His testimony leaves no room for doubt.
その人の証言には疑問の余地がない。

♦**room number** *n.* 部屋番号, ルームナンバー

room service *n.* ルームサービス

KANJI BRIDGE

室 ON: しつ KUN: むろ | ROOM

bedroom	寝室
chamber music	室内楽
classroom	教室
dressing room	試着室
greenhouse	温室
guest room	客室
indoors	室内
Japanese-style room	和室
reception room	応接室
study	研究室
tea-ceremony room	茶室
vacant room	空室
waiting room	待合室
Western-style room	洋室

roommate *n.* ルームメイト

roomy *adj.* 広々とした, ゆったりした

roost *n.* ねぐら

rooster *n.* おんどり

root[1] *n.* (of tree) 根, ((*informal*)) 根っこ, (of thing) 根元, 付け根, (of hair) 毛根; (**roots**) (=origin) 根源, 根底, 根本, (=ancestry) ルーツ, (main cause) 原因; (in math) 根, ルート

adj. 根本的な, 根本の

v. (**root out**) 根こそぎにする, 根絶する

The tree is big but its roots are shallow.
木は大きいけど、根は浅い。

The root of your tooth is rotten.
あなたの歯は根元が腐っています。

Let's get to the root of this problem.
問題の核心をつかみましょう。

The root cause of crime is not clear.
この犯罪の根本原因は明らかではない。

the square root 平方根

take root 根付く, 定着する

root[2] *v.* (root for) 応援する

rooted *adj.* (be rooted in) (…に) 根ざしている

rootless *adj.* 根のない, (of person) よりどころのない, 根なし草の

rope *n.* 縄, 綱, ロープ

rosary *n.* ロザリオ

rose *n.* (flower) バラ, (color) バラ色

a bouquet of roses バラの花束

rosemary *n.* ローズマリー

roster *n.* 勤務当番表

rosy *adj.* ((*also figurative*)) バラ色の

rot *v.* (decay) 腐る, だめになる

n. 腐敗

R

rotary *adj.* (of motion) 回転する, (of machine) 回転式の

n. (roundabout) ロータリー

♦**rotary engine** *n.* ロータリーエンジン

rotary telephone *n.* ダイヤル式の電話

rotate *v.* (turn around) 回転する, (cause to turn) 回転させる, 循環させる; (take turns) 交替する, 循環する

rotation *n.* (circular motion) 回転, (of earth) 自転; (circulation) 循環, (changeover) 交替, 輪番

rotten *adj.* 腐った, 腐敗した, 悪くなった, (unskilled) 下手な, (unpleasant) いやな

a rotten egg 腐った卵

What rotten luck!
なんて不運なんだろう!

feel rotten 気分が悪い [→ FEEL GUILTY]

rough *adj.*

1 OF SURFACE: きめの粗い, ざらざらした

2 APPROXIMATE: 大体の, おおよその, おおまかな

3 VIOLENT: (of person) 乱暴な, 荒っぽい, (of place) 不用心な

4 HAVING NO CLASS/GRACE: がらの悪い, 品のよくない, 荒っぽい

5 OF SEA/WEATHER: 荒れた

6 SIMPLE: 質素な, 粗末な

7 OF EXPERIENCE: ひどい, つらい, いやな

1 His skin is rough.
彼の肌はきめが粗い。

It has a rough surface.
表面がざらざらしている。

2 As a rough guide, keep bearing north.
大体の目安として、常に北へ向かってください。

Could you give me a rough estimate of how long it will take to complete the repairs?
修理を終えるのにどのくらいの時間がかかるか、おおよその見積もりを出していただけますか?

3 I suppose I was a bit rough with her.
確かに彼女にちょっと荒っぽくしすぎた。

He lives in a rough neighborhood.
彼は不用心な地域に住んでいる。

4 That's a rough bar.
あそこは、がらの悪い飲み屋だ。

5 The sea is rough today.
今日は海が荒れている。

6 The home they'd built was rough, but they liked it.
建てた家は質素だったが、彼らは気に入っていた。

7 We had a rough time.
つらい思いをしました/苦労しました。

♦**rough draft** *n.* 下書き, 草稿

This is a rough draft.
これが下書き [草稿] です。

roughage *n.* (fiber) 繊維質, 食物繊維

roughly *adv.* (approximately) 大体…くらい/ぐらい [→ ABOUT 2]; (without due care) ぞんざいに, いいかげんに, (badly) 荒々しく, (violently) 乱暴に

roughly speaking おおざっぱに言えば

roulette *n.* ルーレット

round

1 *adj.* OF SHAPE: (circular) 丸い, 円形の, (spherical) 球形の, (of surface: curved) 丸みを帯びた

2 *n.* BOUT: (of game) 一勝負, (in sport)

一試合, (in golf/boxing) ラウンド, (in tournament) -回戦

3 *n.* **SET: (a round of)** (=of meetings) 一連の, (=of drinks) 全員に一渡り分の

4 *v.* **GO AROUND:** (of car: round a bend) (カーブを) 曲がる

5 *v.* **MAKE ROUND:** 丸くする

6 *prep., adv.* → AROUND

1 a round shape 丸い形 [円形]
a round hole 丸い穴
a round face 丸顔

2 play a round of bridge
ブリッジを一勝負する
a round of golf ゴルフの1ラウンド
He was knocked out in the third round.
彼は第3ラウンドでノックアウトされた。

3 a round of meetings 一連の会談
a round of drinks
全員に一渡りする分の飲み物

4 The car rounded the corner to the right.
車は角を右に曲がった。

5 We can round the edges off with sandpaper.
紙やすりで角を丸くできる。

♦ **round number** *n.* 概数, おおよその数
round-trip ticket *n.* 往復チケット, 往復切符

round up *v.* (gather together) 集める, (animals) 駆り集める, (criminals) 逮捕する; (round up figures) 切り上げる
The suspects were rounded up by the police.
容疑者たちが警察に逮捕された。
Round up the number so that we don't have any decimals.
小数点以下は切り上げてください。

KANJI BRIDGE

丸 ON: がん KUN: まる, まる(い), まる(める) | **ROUND**

bullet	弾丸
cajole, coax	丸め込む
clear profit	丸もうけ
Japanese flag	日の丸
log	丸太
log cabin	丸太小屋
parentheses	丸かっこ
pill	丸薬
plump	丸々とした
roundness	丸み
round shape	丸形
unarmed	丸腰
whole	丸ごと
whole year	丸1年

roundabout *adj.* (of route) 遠回りの, (of expression) 遠回しの、婉曲の
n. (traffic circle) ロータリー

rounded *adj.* 丸い

rouse *v.* (awaken) 呼び起こす, (excite) かき立てる
rouse someone's curiosity
(人の)好奇心をかき立てる

route *n.* ルート, 路線, 道筋
Route 66 (国道) 66 号線

routine *n.* 決まってやること, (the things one does every day) 毎日やること, (daily routine) 日課
adj. 決まりきった, (periodic) 定期的な; (uninteresting) つまらない, 退屈な

R

It's a routine.
決まってやることです。
a boring routine 単調な日課
routine work 決まりきった仕事
a routine check 定期点検

routinely *adv.* いつものように

rove *v.* (wander) さまよう, ((*used negatively*)) うろつく, (travel) 流浪する, (of eyes) きょろきょろ見回す

row¹ *n.* (line) 列, 並び
a row of seats 座席の列
the front [back] row 前列 [後列]
row upon row of desks 何列も並んだ机
in a row (continuously) 連続して, 続けて, 立て続けに
He won the championship four times in a row.
彼は4回続けてチャンピオンになった。
She drank five glasses of wine in a row.
彼女は立て続けにワインを5杯飲んだ。

row² *v.* (propel with oars) こぐ, (row a boat) ボートをこぐ
We rowed the boat back to shore.
ボートをこいで岸まで戻った。
Do you enjoy rowing?
ボートをこぐのは好きですか？

rowdy *adj.* やかましい, 騒々しい

royal *adj.* (of family) 王室の, (of king/queen) 王の/女王の
♦**royal family** *n.* 王室, (in Japan) 皇室
royal highness *n.* 殿下

royalty *n.* (members of a royal family) 王族; (payment) 印税

rub *v.* こする, (to clean: with cloth) 磨く, (rub together) こすり合わせる, (rub A into B) (AをBに) すり込む, (rub against: of two surfaces against each other) すれる, (massage) もむ
He rubbed himself down with a towel.
彼はタオルで体をこすった。
She rubbed her glasses with a dry cloth.
彼女は乾いた布でめがねを磨いた。
He rubbed his hands to keep them warm.
彼は手をこすり合わせて暖めた。
If you rub oil into your scalp, that should prevent dandruff.
頭皮に油をすり込めば、ふけを予防できるよ。
These new shoes are rubbing my heels.
この新しい靴は、かかとがすれる。
Rub my shoulders, will you.
肩をもんでくれる？
♦**rub out** *v.* (erase) 消す

rubber *n.* (substance) ゴム, (condom) コンドーム, ((*informal*)) ゴム [→ ERASER]
♦**rubber band** *n.* 輪ゴム, ゴムバンド [→ picture of STATIONERY]
rubber stamp *n.* ゴム印 [→ picture of STATIONERY]

rubbery *adj.* ゴムのような

rubbish *n.* (waste material) ごみ, ごみくず [→ GARBAGE]; (worthless nonsense) くだらないこと, ばかげたこと [→ NONSENSE]

rubble *n.* (after disaster) がれき, (stones) 荒石

rubella *n.* 風疹

ruble *n.* (currency) ルーブル, R

ruby *n.* ルビー

rucksack *n.* リュックサック

rudder *n.* かじ

rude *adj.* (impolite) 失礼な, 無礼な, (ill-mannered) 行儀の悪い, (gross) 下品な

He was rude to the guests.
彼はお客さんに対して失礼だった。

It's rude to talk with your mouth full.
口をいっぱいにしたまま話すのは、行儀が悪いよ。

♦**rudely** *adv.* 失礼にも, 無礼にも, ぞんざいに

He rudely interrupted me.
失礼にも彼は口を挟んできた。

rudeness *n.* 行儀の悪さ

rudimentary *adj.* 基本の

rue *v.* 後悔する [→ REGRET]

ruffle *v.* (hair, feelings) かき乱す

ruffle sb's feathers いら立たせる

ruffled *adj.* (of hair) 乱れた, (of blouse) フリルのついた

rug *n.* 敷物, じゅうたん

rugby *n.* ラグビー

rugged *adj.* (uneven) でこぼこの, (of features) ごつごつした, (of coastline) ぎざぎざの

ruin

1 *v.* DESTROY: 破壊する, 崩壊させる

2 *v.* SPOIL: 壊す, だめにする, 台なしにする, (make a mess of) 荒らす

3 *n.* COMPLETE DESTRUCTION: 崩壊, 破滅, 荒廃

4 *n.* BROKEN DOWN BUILDINGS: (**ruins**) 廃墟, (of ancient civilization) 遺跡

5 *n.* CAUSE OF DOWNFALL: (of person) 身を滅ぼすもと, 破滅の原因

6 → BANKRUPT

1 The city was ruined by war.
その都市は戦争で破壊された。

2 You're ruining your health.
体を壊すよ。

His drunk relatives ruined our wedding.
彼の親戚が酔っ払って、私たちの結婚式をぶち壊した。

Don't put in too much salt—you'll ruin the flavor.
塩を入れすぎないで—味が台なしになるから。

Raccoon dogs ruined our cabbage patch.
タヌキが、うちのキャベツ畑を荒らした。

3 The regime collapsed in total ruin.
政権は完全に崩壊した。

The church lay in ruins.
教会は荒れ果てていた。

4 the ruins of a castle 城跡 [お城の跡]

You can still see Roman ruins.
今もローマの遺跡を見ることができます。

5 Drugs were his ruin.
ドラッグが彼の破滅の原因だった/彼はドラッグで身を滅ぼした。

ruined *adj.* 破壊された, 崩壊した, (of civilization) 滅びた

rule

1 *n.* REGULATION: 規則, ルール, 規定 [→ LAW]

2 *v.* GOVERN: 治める, 統治する, 支配する

3 *v.* DECIDE: (of judge) (…と) 裁決する, 判決を下す

1 according to the rules 規則によると
obey the rules 規則を守る
break the rules 規則を破る
bend the rules 規則を曲げる
stretch the rules 規則を拡大解釈する

R

Could you explain the rules to me?
ルールを教えていただけますか？

2 Who's ruling this country?
この国を統治しているのは誰ですか？

That country is ruled by a military dictatorship.
その国は軍事独裁政権に支配されている。

3 The judge ruled that the accused should serve three years in prison.
裁判官は、被告に懲役3年の判決を下した。

as a rule 原則として, (usually) 普通は, (generally) 概して

As a rule, we don't like people smoking in here.
原則として、ここでは喫煙をご遠慮いただきたい。

ruler *n.* (person) 支配者; (measuring instrument) 定規, 物差し, ルーラー

ruling *n.* (court ruling) 判決

adj. (having control) 支配している

♦**ruling class** *n.* 支配階級

ruling party *n.* 与党

rum *n.* ラム酒

rumble *v.* ゴロゴロ鳴る

♦**rumbling** *n.* ゴロゴロいう音

rummage *v.* (rummage through) かき回して捜す

rumor *n.* うわさ

v. (**be rumored that...**) ...といううわさが流れる, ...といううわさだ

Rumor has it that they are going out (=seeing each other).
あの二人は付き合ってるといううわさだよ。

The rumors are flying.
うわさが飛び交っている。

rump *n.* (part of animal's body) (お)尻

run

1 *v.* MOVE FAST: 走る, 駆ける, (**run around/all over the place**) 駆けずり回る

2 *v.* COMPETE: (in race) 出場する, ((*informal*)) 出る, (in election) 選挙に出る, 立候補する, 出馬する

3 *v.* FLEE: 逃げる, 逃亡する, 逃走する [→ RUN AWAY, RUN OFF 1]

4 *v.* MANAGE: (business) やる, 運営する, 経営する, 営む

5 *v.* OF BUS/TRAIN: (depart) 出る, (be in service) 走る, 運行する

6 *v.* OPERATE: 動かす, 操作する, 運転する, (of machine) 動く, 作動する

7 *v.* DRIVE: (run sb somewhere by car) 車に乗せる, 車で送る

8 *v.* EXTEND: (cable) 引く, (thread through) 通す, (of road: run to) (...まで) 延びている, 続いている

9 *v.* OF SHOW: (of play) 上演し続ける, (of film) 上映し続ける

10 *v.* OF LIQUID: 流れる, (of nose) (鼻水が) 出る, (of color) 落ちる, (of ink on paper) にじむ [→ RUN OFF 2]

11 *v.* OF TIGHTS: 伝線する

12 *n.* JOG: 走ること, 走り

13 *n.* DAMAGE TO TIGHTS: 伝線

1 I can run faster than you.
君より速く走れるよ/足は君より速いよ。

Don't run. Walk.
走らないで歩きなさい。

I ran downstairs to answer the phone.
電話に出ようと、階段を駆け下りた。

I've been running all over the place trying to find you.
あなたを捜して、あちこち駆けずり回っていたんですよ。

2 I'm running in the marathon this year.
今年、マラソンに出場します。

Are you going to run in tomorrow's race?
明日のレースに出るの？

He ran in the election.
あの人は選挙に出馬した [立候補した]。

I think I'll run for president.
大統領選に立候補しようと思う。

3 He ran away rather than face up to the situation.
彼は現実に立ち向かわずに、逃げた。

You'd better run for it, before the police come.
警察が来る前に、逃げたほうがいい。

4 He runs his own business.
彼は自分で事業をやっている。

Who's going to run the company when you leave?
あなたが辞めたら、誰が会社を経営することになりますか？

5 Trains run every thirty minutes.
電車は 30 分ごとに出ています。

The busses have stopped running.
バスが運休した。

6 How do you run this machine?
この機械はどうやって操作するの？

The engine was running smoothly.
エンジンは滑らかに動いていた。

7 I'll run you to the station.
駅まで車で送る [乗せてあげる] よ。

8 This road runs all the way into town.
この道は町までずっと続いている。

9 That play has been running for years.
その芝居は何年も前からずっと上演されています。

10 The color ran.
色落ちした。

11 My pantyhose have run.
パンストが伝線した。

in the long run (in the end) 結局は, 最後には, (viewing things in the long term) 長い目で見れば

In the long run, I think it'll turn out all right.
最後には、いい結果が出ると思います。

on the run (escaping) 逃走中で

He's on the run from the police.
彼は警察から逃走中だ [追われている]。

run across *v.* (encounter) …に出会う, …に出くわす, (find) 偶然見つける

Did you run across any problems?
何か問題を見つけましたか？

run after *v.* (pursue) 追いかける

The dog ran after her.
犬は彼女を追いかけた。

run away *v.* 逃げる, (from home) 家出する, (**run away with**) (=steal) 持ち逃げする, (=with lover) …と駆け落ちする [→ RUN OFF 1]

She ran away from home.
彼女は家出した。

run down *v.*

1 HIT WITH A CAR: 突き倒す, ひく

2 BATTERY POWER: (deplete) 使い切る, (cause to deplete) 切れる

3 CRITICIZE: こき下ろす, けなす
4 SCAN WITH EYES: …にざっと目を通す

1 He ran down a cyclist.
彼は自転車に乗っていた人をひいてしまった。

2 Try not to run down the batteries.
電池を使い切らないようにね。

3 You're always running me down.
あなたはいつも私のことをけなしている。

4 run down a list　リストにざっと目を通す

run into *v.* (collide with) …と/に衝突する, (problem) …にぶつかる, (meet by chance) …に偶然会う

The bus ran into a wall.
バスは塀に衝突した。

We ran into a slight problem.
ちょっとした問題にぶつかった。

Fancy running into you here!
ここでお会いするなんて!

run off *v.*

1 ESCAPE: 逃げる, (**run off with**) (=steal) 持ち逃げする
2 OF LIQUID: 流れ落ちる, 流れ出す
3 MAKE: (copy) 取る

1 He ran off with the money.
彼は金を持ち逃げした。

2 Water was running off the roof.
水が屋根から流れ落ちていた。

3 Could you run off copies for everyone?
全員のコピーを取ってくれますか?

run out *v.* (become used up) 切れる, なくなる, 尽きる, (**run out of**) 切らす, 使い果たす

The lease runs out in a month.
あと1ヵ月で賃貸契約が切れる。

The radio has run out of batteries.
ラジオのバッテリーが切れた。

I've run out of ideas.
もうアイデアが尽きました。

We've run out of coffee.
コーヒーを切らしてしまった。

We ran out of funds.
資金を使い果たした [が底をついた]。

run over *v.* (hit with a car) ひく; (scan with eyes) …にざっと目を通す, (quickly review) ざっとおさらいする, (confirm) ざっと確認する [→ OVERFLOW]

He ran over a dog.
彼は犬をひいた。

Let's run over the plan again.
もう一度、計画をざっと確認しておこう。

run through *v.*

1 READ QUICKLY: ざっと読む, …にざっと目を通す
2 PRACTICE: (drill) する, やる, (scene) ざっとけいこする, リハーサルする
3 PERVADE: …に一貫して流れる, …に行き渡る
4 USE UP QUICKLY: すぐに使い果たす

1 Let's run through the contract once more.
もう一度、契約書にざっと目を通しましょう。

2 It won't take but a couple of minutes to run through the drill.
訓練をやるのに2、3分しかかからないはずです。

3 The theme of loneliness runs through all of his works (=books).
孤独というテーマは、彼のすべての作品に一貫して流れている。

4 She ran through her inheritance in a month.
彼女は1ヵ月で遺産を使い果たした。

run up *v.* (debts) ためる, かかえ込む, (expenses) 増やす

He ran up a lot of debts.
彼は多額の借金をかかえ込んだ。

run up against *v.* (problem) …にぶつかる [→ RUN INTO]

---

runaway *n.* (person who has left home) 家出人, (fugitive) 逃亡者

run-down *adj.* (exhausted) 疲れきっている; (of place) うらぶれた, 荒れ果てた

rung *n.* (of ladder) 横木

run-in *n.* (argument) けんか

runner *n.* 走者, ランナー

runner-up *n.* 2位になった者

running *n.* (exercise) ランニング

adv. (consecutively) 連続して, 続けて

adj. (of joke) 繰り返し使われる

be in the running (might win) 勝算がある, 見込みがある

be out of the running (cannot win) 勝算がない, 見込みがない

runny *adj.* (of liquid: runs/flows easily) 流れやすい, (of nose) 鼻水の出る

I have a runny nose today.
今日は鼻水が出る。

runway *n.* 滑走路

rupture *v.* 破裂する, (**rupture oneself**: have a hernia) ヘルニアを起こす

n. (hernia) ヘルニア, (of blood vessel) 破裂, (in diplomatic relations) 決裂, 断絶

rupture a blood vessel
血管が切れる

rural *adj.* 田舎の, 地方の

a rural life 田舎暮らし

rural Alabama アラバマ州の田舎の方

ruse *n.* 策略

rush

1 *v.* HURRY: 急ぐ, (rush somewhere) 急いで行く, 駆け付ける, (**rush out** of/from) (…から) 飛び出す, (rush sb) せかす, せきたてる, (rush sth) 急いでやる, (rush sth/sb somewhere) 急いで運ぶ

2 *n.* NEED TO BE SOMEWHERE: (**be in a rush**) 急いでいる

3 *n.* SURGE: (of people) 殺到, (of water) 奔流

4 *n.* OF EMOTION: (**rush of excitement**) 興奮, (**rush of anger**) 激怒

5 *n.* EFFECT OF DRUG: 快感

1 They rushed to get the job done.
彼らは早く仕事を終わらせるために、急いでやった。

I have to rush, as I'm on my way to an appointment.
今、人に会いに行くところなので、急がないといけないんです。

He rushed out of the office to meet a client.
彼は顧客に会うために、オフィスから飛び出した。

He doesn't like to be rushed.
彼はせかされるのが嫌いだ。

Don't rush the work, otherwise you'll make mistakes.
急いでやらないほうがいいよ、ミスをするから。

She was rushed off to the hospital.

彼女は大急ぎで病院に運ばれた。

2 I'm in a rush—I can't talk right now.
急いでいるんです——今は話ができません。

3 There was a rush for the door.
ドアに人が殺到した。

4 There was a rush of excitement.
興奮が高まった。

♦ **rush hour** *n.* ラッシュアワー
rush-hour traffic
ラッシュアワー時の交通

rushed *adj.* (of job) 急ぎの, (of person: under pressure to do) せかされる

Russia *n.* ロシア, ((*in abbr.*)) 露

Russian *n.* (person) ロシア人, (language) ロシア語
adj. (of country, culture) ロシアの, (of person) ロシア人の, (of language) ロシア語の

rust *n.* さび
v. さびる

rustic *adj.* 田舎の, (of cabin) 田舎風の

rustle *v.* (of leaves, paper) サラサラ/カサカサという音を立てる
n. サラサラ/カサカサ(いう音)
High above we could hear the sound of leaves rustling in the trees.
はるか頭上で、木の葉がカサカサいう音がしていた。
Stop rustling your newspaper, will you.
新聞をガサガサさせるのは、やめてくれない?

rusty *adj.* (corroded) さびた, (of color) さび色の; (of person, skill: out of practice) 腕が鈍った, 下手になった

rut[1] *n.* (wheel track) わだち, (ditch) 溝
be in a rut 型にはまった生活をしている, マンネリになっている

rut[2] *n.* (period when deer etc. are sexually active) 発情期, さかりがつく時期

ruthless *adj.* (cold-blooded) 冷酷な, (merciless) 情け容赦のない, 非情な
a ruthless killer 冷酷な殺人鬼

rye *n.* ライ麦

♦ **rye bread** *n.* ライ麦パン, 黒パン

S, s

Sabbath *n.* 安息日

saber *n.* (in fencing) サーベル, (cavalry sword used in the past) 軍刀

rattle one's saber 武力で威嚇する

sable *n.* (animal) クロテン

sabotage *n.* (destruction) 破壊行為, (obstruction) 妨害行為

v. (destroy) 破壊する, (obstruct) 妨害する

The bridge had been sabotaged by the enemy.
橋は敵に破壊されていた。

saccharin *n.* サッカリン

sachet *n.* におい袋

a sachet of scented, dried flowers
ドライフラワー入りのにおい袋

sack *n.* (large bag) 袋; (**the sack**: dismissal from one's job) 解雇, 首切り

v. (fire) 解雇する, (…の) 首を切る; (put into a sack) 袋に入れる

a sack of rice 一袋の米

She was sacked. 彼女は解雇された。

get the sack 首になる

He got the sack for screwing up.
失敗したため、彼は首になった。

sacred *adj.* (holy) 神聖な, (inviolable) 神聖不可侵の, 侵すことのできない [→ HOLY]

a sacred text 聖典

As far as the media is concerned, nothing's sacred.
マスコミに、聖域はない。

sacrifice *n.* (to a deity) ささげ物, (of living animals) いけにえ; (giving up sth of value) 犠牲

v. (give up) 犠牲にする, (offer to a deity) ささげる, (live animal) いけにえをささげる

Taeko's always sacrificing herself for the family.
多恵子はいつも、家族のために自分を犠牲にしている。

They sacrificed their free time to help the sick.
彼らは空き時間をなげうって、病人の世話をした。

sacrifice one's life for …のために命をささげる

Would you sacrifice your life to save another?
人を救うために命をささげられますか?

He sacrificed his life for his country.
彼は戦死した。

sacrilege *n.* (blasphemous behavior) 冒とく行為

sacrilegious *adj.* 冒とくする

sacrosanct → SACRED

sad *adj.* (unhappy) 悲しい, (of things and third persons) かわいそうな, 悲しそうな, (miserable) みじめな, (tragic) 悲惨な [→ PATHETIC]

The ending of the movie was very sad.
映画の結末はとても悲しかった。

We were sad to hear of her death.
彼女が死んだことを聞いて悲しかった。

He looks sad. 彼は悲しそうだ。

a sad state of affairs 悲惨な状況

♦**sadden** *v.* 悲しませる

It saddens me to think…

…と思うと悲しい。

saddle ***n.*** (on animal) 鞍, (on bike) サドル
v. (…に) 鞍をつける

sadism ***n.*** サディズム

sadist ***n.*** サディスト

sadistic ***adj.*** サディスト的な, サディスティックな

sadly ***adv.*** (unfortunately) 不運にも, 残念にも; (pitiably) 悲しそうに

sadness ***n.*** 悲しみ, 悲哀

sadomasochism ***n.*** サドマゾヒズム

safari ***n.*** サファリ

safe

1 ***adj.*** FREE FROM DANGER: 安全な, (of place: having law and order) 治安がいい

2 ***adj.*** UNHARMED: 無事な/に

3 ***n.*** SECURE PLACE/BOX FOR VALUABLES: 金庫

4 ***adj.*** IN BASEBALL: セーフの

1 Is nuclear power safe?
原子力は安全ですか？

It's not exactly safe to swim in this river.
この川で泳ぐのは安全とは言い切れない。

That neighborhood is not safe at night.
あのあたりは夜は、危ない。

The streets are safe again.
街は再び治安がよくなった。

2 My wife called to let me know she got home safe.
妻は無事に家に着いたことを、電話で知らせてくれた。

3 You'd best put your valuables in the safe.
貴重品は金庫に入れておくほうがいい。

4 He's safe on first base.
一塁はセーフだった。

be on the safe side 大事をとる

We'd better be on the safe side and take the early train.
大事をとって [念のため]、早めの電車に乗ったほうがいい。

keep sth safe 安全な場所に保管する

Would you keep this ring safe for me?
この指輪を安全な所に保管していただけますか？

safe and sound 無事(に)

The children arrived home safe and sound.
子供たちは無事、帰宅した。

safeguard ***n.*** (device) 安全装置, (strategy) 安全策, 保護対策
v. 守る, 保護する

These measures will safeguard the interests of minorities.
この対策で、少数民族の利益が守られるだろう。

safely ***adv.*** (in a safe/secure manner) 安全に, (unharmed) 無事(に)

safely say …と言って差し支えない

safe sex ***n.*** 安全なセックス

practice safe sex 安全なセックスをする

safety ***n.*** 安全

safety first 安全第一

♦ **safety belt** ***n.*** 安全ベルト, シートベルト

safety deposit box ***n.*** 貸金庫

safety net ***n.*** ((*also figurative*)) 安全網

safety pin ***n.*** 安全ピン

saffron ***n.*** サフラン, (color) サフラン色, 濃い黄色

saga ***n.*** (story) 物語, (long novel) 大河小説

sagacious ***adj.*** 賢明な [→ WISE]

sage[1] ***n.*** (wise man) 賢人

sage[2] ***n.*** (herb) セージ

Sagittarius ***n.*** (the Archer) 射手座

sail ***v.*** (move on water in a boat) 船で行く, 船旅をする, 航海する, (set sail) 出航する, 船出する, (sail a boat) (船を) 操縦する [→ FLY[1]]

n. (canvas used for sailing) 帆; (pleasure trip) セーリング, 帆走

We sailed to Australia on a luxury cruise.
オーストラリアへ豪華な船旅をしました。

She sailed across the Atlantic single-handed.
彼女は単独で大西洋を航海 [横断] した。

We sailed around the cape.
船で岬を回った。

They're preparing to sail to the Caribbean.
彼らはカリブ海へ出航する準備をしている。

Can you sail? 船を操縦できますか？

The main sail was pulled in.
主帆が下ろされた。

Let's go for a sail.
セーリングに出かけよう。

♦**sailboat** ***n.*** ヨット

sailing ***n.*** セーリング, 帆走

sailing ship ***n.*** (clipper) 帆船

sailor ***n.*** 船乗り, 船員, (in navy) 水兵

♦**sailor uniform** ***n.*** (worn by sailor) 水兵服, (worn by schoolgirl) セーラー服

saint ***n.*** ((*also figurative*)) 聖人, (**Saint**) 聖-

He has the patience of a saint.
あの人は聖人のように忍耐強い。

Saint Paul 聖パウロ

sake ***n.*** (**for sb's / sth's sake, for the sake of**) ...のために

I kept quiet for your sake.
あなたのために黙ってたんだよ。

For the children's sake, I would prefer it if we dropped the subject.
子供のために、この話はやめにしよう。

For the sake of argument, let's assume that inflation does increase.
議論のために、インフレが進むと仮定しよう。

saké ***n.*** (Japanese liquor) 酒, 日本酒

salad ***n.*** サラダ

make a salad サラダを作る

♦**salad bar** ***n.*** (in restaurant) サラダバー

salad dressing ***n.*** (サラダ)ドレッシング

salad oil ***n.*** サラダ油, サラダオイル

salamander ***n.*** サンショウウオ, 山椒魚

salami ***n.*** サラミ

salary ***n.*** 給料, (monthly salary) 月給, 月収, (annual salary) 年収, 年俸

She gets a high [low] salary.
彼女は給料が高い [安い]。

He earns a salary of a hundred thousand dollars a year.
彼は10万ドルの年収を稼いでいる。

♦**salary cut** ***n.*** 減給

salary increase ***n.*** 昇給

sale ***n.***

1 **ACT OF SELLING:** 販売, 売却, セールス

2 **QUANTITY SOLD OR MONEY MADE:** 売上高, (**sales**) 売り上げ

3 **DEPARTMENT:** (**Sales**) 販売部, 営業部

4 **EVENT:** セール, 特売, 安売り

5 **DISAPPEARING FROM SHELVES:** 売れ行き

1 Is it for sale?
それは売り物ですか？

S

They've put their house up for sale.
彼らは家を売りに出した。

sales promotion 販売促進

2 Sales are up from last year.
昨年から売り上げが伸びている。

Sales this year were better than ever.
今年の売上高は今までより、よかった。

3 Sales would never approve such a proposal.
そんな提案を販売部が聞き入れるはずがない。

4 a New Year's sale 初売りセール

a bargain sale バーゲンセール

5 Sales have been slow this month.
今月は売れ行きが鈍い。

on sale (available for purchase) 発売中で, (discounted) 特売で, 安売りで

This dress is on sale.
この服は特売です。

salesman, -person, -woman *n.* (in shop) 店員, 販売員, (in company: person in charge of sales) セールスマン, 営業部員

sales slip *n.* 売上伝票

salient *adj.* 目立つ, 顕著な

saline *adj.* (containing salt) 塩分を含んだ

a saline solution 塩水

saliva *n.* つば, ((*formal*)) 唾液

salmon *n.* サケ, 鮭, ((*informal*)) しゃけ

smoked salmon スモークサーモン

♦**salmon roe** *n.* イクラ

salon *n.* (hair salon) 美容院

salt *n.* 塩, (table salt) 食塩

v. (preserve with/in salt) 塩漬けにする

add salt 塩を加える

salt and pepper 塩とコショウ

I salted the fish to preserve it.
保存するために、魚を塩漬けにした。

♦**salty** *adj.* (of taste) 塩辛い, ((*informal*)) しょっぱい

salt water *n.* (ocean water) 海水, (water containing salt) 塩水 [also read えんすい]

adj. (**saltwater**) (of lake) 塩水の, (of fish) 海水にすむ

saltwater fish 海水魚

salutary *adj.* (of experience) 有益な

salutation *n.* あいさつ

salute *v.* (officer, flag) (…に) 敬礼する [→ GREET]

salvage *n.* (salvage operation) 引き揚げ作業

v. (raise: a ship) 引き揚げる [→ SAVE 1]

salvation *n.* 救済, 救い

♦**Salvation Army** *n.* 救世軍

salve *n.* (ointment) 軟膏

same *adj.* 同じ, ((*formal*)) 同様の, (one and the same) 同一の

pron. (**the same**) 同じ物, 同じこと

adv. (**the same**) 同じように

They wore the same tie.
二人は同じネクタイをしていた。

It's not the same person.
同一人物ではありません/違う人です。

I feel the same way about sports as you do about studying.
私のスポーツに対する気持ちは、あなたの勉強に対する気持ちと同じです。

I'll have one more of the same.
同じ物をもう一つ下さい。

I would have done the same.

私も同じことをしただろう。

all/just the same それでもやはり

Just the same, I'd rather you went.
それでもやはり、行ってもらいたい。

be all the same (to) (…にとって) 同じことだ, どうでもいい

If it's all the same to you…
もしあなたにとって同じことなら…

one and the same 全く同一の

same here こっちも同じだ

thanks all the same でもどうもありがとう

the same as …と同じ

It will be the same as last year.
昨年と同じになります。

I'll have the same as you.
あなたと同じ物をいただきます。

He did exactly the same as she had done.
彼は彼女がしたのと全く同じようにした。

KANJI BRIDGE

同 ON: どう KUN: おな(じ) | IDENTICAL, SAME, CO-

alumni association	同窓会
associate, colleague	同僚
at the same time	同時に
classmate	同級生
club, association of like-minded people	同好会
cohabitation	同棲, 同居
contemporary	同時代の
same name	同名
sympathy	同情
synonym	同義語
tie (in game)	同点

samisen *n.* (three-string lute) 三味線

play the samisen 三味線を弾く

sample *n.* サンプル, 見本

v. (take a sample of) (…の) 見本を取る, (food) 試食する, (drink) 試飲する

Did you get a free sample?
無料サンプルをもらった?

I sampled the wine.
ワインを試飲した。

sampler *n.* (for mixing music) サンプラー; (of food) 盛り合わせ

a sashimi sampler (お)刺身の盛り合わせ

samurai *n.* 侍

sanatorium *n.* サナトリウム, 療養所

sanction *n.* (permission) 認可, 許可; (**sanctions**: political, economic) 制裁

v. (permit) 認める, 許可する; (apply sanctions to) (…に) 制裁を加える

During apartheid, South Africa was subject to frequent economic sanctions.
アパルトヘイト時代、南アフリカはしばしば経済制裁を受けた。

♦**sanctioned** *adj.* 認められている, 公認されている

sanctuary *n.* (sacred place) 聖域, (place for refuge/asylum) 避難所, (for wildlife) サンクチュアリ, 野生動物保護区域

seek sanctuary in …に逃げ込む

sand *n.* 砂

v. (smooth by rubbing) 紙やすりで磨く

♦**sandbar** *n.* 砂州

sandcastle *n.* 砂の(お)城, ((*figurative*)) 砂上の楼閣

sand dunes *n.* 砂丘

sand trap *n.* (in golf) バンカー

sandal *n.* サンダル

sandalwood *n.* ビャクダン, 白檀(びゃくだん)

sandpaper *n.* 紙(かみ)やすり, サンドペーパー [→ picture of TOOL]

sandstone *n.* 砂岩(さがん)

sandwich *n.* サンドイッチ
v. 挟(はさ)む
I was sandwiched between two drunk salarymen on the train.
電車(でんしゃ)の中(なか)で二人(ふたり)の酔(よ)っ払(ぱら)いのサラリーマンに挟(はさ)まれた。

sandy *adj.* (of beach) 砂(すな)の, (of color) 砂(すな)のような色(いろ)の, 薄茶色(うすちゃいろ)の, (covered in sand) 砂(すな)だらけの
a sandy beach 砂浜(すなはま)

sane *adj.* 正気(しょうき)の, 狂(くる)っていない

sanguine *adj.* (optimistic) 楽天的(らくてんてき)な; (of color) 紅(くれない)の,(of complexion)血色(けっしょく)のいい

sanitarium → SANATORIUM

sanitary *adj.* 衛生的(えいせいてき)な
a sanitary bathroom 衛生的(えいせいてき)なお手洗(てあら)い
♦ **sanitary landfill** *n.* ごみ埋(う)め立(た)て地(ち)
sanitary napkin/towel *n.* 生理用(せいりよう)ナプキン

sanitation *n.* 公衆衛生(こうしゅうえいせい)

sanity *n.* 正気(しょうき)
lose one's sanity
正気(しょうき)を失(うしな)う [気(き)が狂(くる)う]

sansei *n.* (third-generation immigrant from Japan) 三世(さんせい)

Sanskrit *n.* サンスクリット語(ご), 梵語(ぼんご)

Santa Claus *n.* サンタクロース

sap[1] *n.* (of tree) 樹液(じゅえき)

sap[2] *v.* (cause to deplete) 徐々(じょじょ)になくさせる, (weaken) しだいに弱(よわ)らせる

sapling *n.* 若木(わかぎ), 苗木(なえぎ)

sapphire *n.* (gem) サファイア, (color) サファイア色(いろ), 薄青色(うすあおいろ)

Saran wrap *n.* ラップ, サランラップ

sarcasm *n.* 嫌(いや)み, 皮肉(ひにく), 当(あ)てこすり

sarcastic *adj.* 皮肉(ひにく)な, 嫌(いや)みな
Don't be sarcastic. 皮肉(ひにく)はやめなさい。
a sarcastic remark 嫌(いや)みな発言(はつげん)

sardine *n.* イワシ, 鰯(いわし)
a can of sardines イワシの缶詰(かんづめ)

sardonic *adj.* (of smile, laugh) 冷笑的(れいしょうてき)な, あざけるような

sarong *n.* サロン

sash *n.* サッシュ, 飾(かざ)り帯(おび), (kimono sash) 帯(おび); (window sash) サッシ

sashimi *n.* (sliced raw fish) (お)刺身(さしみ)

Satan *n.* 悪魔(あくま), 魔王(まおう), サタン

satanic *adj.* 悪魔(あくま)の

satchel *n.* 学生(がくせい)かばん

satellite *n.* 人工衛星(じんこうえいせい), (moon) 衛星(えいせい)
put up a satellite 人工衛星(じんこうえいせい)を打(う)ち上(あ)げる
♦ **satellite broadcasting** *n.* 衛星放送(えいせいほうそう)
satellite dish *n.* パラボラアンテナ [→ picture of HOUSE]

satin *n.* サテン, しゅす

satire *n.* 風刺(ふうし), 皮肉(ひにく)

satirical *adj.* (sarcastic) 皮肉(ひにく)な, 嫌(いや)みな, (of novel etc.) 風刺的(ふうしてき)な, 風刺(ふうし)の利(き)いた

satisfaction *n.* 満足(まんぞく)
to one's satisfaction 満足(まんぞく)するように

satisfactory *adj.* 満足(まんぞく)な, 満足(まんぞく)のいく, 十分(じゅうぶん)な
a satisfactory answer 満足(まんぞく)のいく答(こた)え

satisfied *adj.* (contented) 満足(まんぞく)した
a satisfied customer 満足(まんぞく)した客(きゃく)
Now that you have what you want, are

you satisfied?
欲しいものが手に入って、満足ですか？

Some people are never satisfied.
決して満足しない人もいる。

satisfy *v.* (make contented) 満足させる, (answer, fulfill) 満たす [→ CONVINCE]

We try to satisfy our customers.
私たちは、お客様にご満足いただけるよう努めていきます。

These conditions don't satisfy us.
こういう条件は、のめない。

To join the club, you must satisfy certain conditions.
入会するには、一定の条件を満たさなくてはなりません。

♦ **satisfying** *adj.* (of experience) 十分な, 確かな, (of meal) 十分な, 満足な, (of job, life) 充実した

saturate *v.* (completely soak) びしょぬれにする, (**saturate the market**) 市場に過剰供給する

saturated *adj.* (completely soaked) びしょぬれになる, (of market: full of a particular product) 過剰供給の; (of solution) 飽和した

saturation *n.* (process of soaking) 浸透, (of market: being completely full of a particular product) 過剰供給; (in chemistry) 飽和(状態)

Saturday *n.* 土曜日

Saturn *n.* 土星

sauce *n.* ソース, (used in Japanese recipes) たれ

Worcestershire sauce ウスターソース

saucepan *n.* (お)なべ [→ picture of KITCHEN]

saucer *n.* (plate) 受け皿, (for green tea) 茶托 [→ picture of CUP]; (saucerlike object) 円盤

saucy *adj.* (cheeky) 生意気な

Saudi Arabia *n.* サウジアラビア

sauerkraut *n.* ザウアークラウト

sauna *n.* サウナ

saury *n.* サンマ, 秋刀魚

sausage *n.* ソーセージ

sauté *n.* ソテー

v. ソテーにする

adj. ソテーの

a chicken sauté チキンソテー

savage *adj.* (cruel) 残酷な, むごい, (wild) 野蛮な

n. (cruel person) 残酷な人, (uncivilized person) 野蛮人

♦ **savagery** *n.* 残忍さ, (cruel behavior) 残酷な行為

save *v.*

1 RESCUE: 救う, 助ける

2 PUT/SET ASIDE: (for future purpose) 取っておく, (**save money**) お金をためる, 貯金する

3 CONSERVE: (strength) セーブする, 蓄える, (energy, time) 節約する

4 MAKE UNNECESSARY: (**save sb doing sth**) …せずに済む

5 PREVENT: (goal kick) 阻む, 阻止する

6 PRESERVE IN COMPUTER: 保存する

1 He saved that man's life.
彼はあの男性の命を救った。

She saved him from drowning.
彼女は彼がおぼれているところを助けた。

S

Were the doctors able to save the patient?
お医者さんは、その患者さんを助けることができたんですか？

2 Are you going to save those letters?
その手紙は取っておくの？

He saves ¥50,000 every month.
彼は毎月５万円ずつ貯金している。

Have you saved up enough to buy that car you wanted?
欲しかった車が買えるぐらい、お金はたまった？

3 Save your strength for the match tomorrow.
明日の試合のために、力を蓄えておきなさい。

If you switch off the lights when you're not using them, you'll save energy.
使わない時は電気を消せば、エネルギーを節約できるよ。

If we take the shortcut, it'll save time.
近道をすれば、時間の節約になる。

4 That phone call saved us wasting a lot of time.
あの電話のおかげで、時間をむだにせずに済んだ。

5 The goalkeeper saved a penalty kick.
ゴールキーパーがペナルティーキックを阻止した。

6 Did you save the file before quitting the program?
終了する前にファイルを保存しましたか？

savings *n.* 貯金, 貯蓄, 蓄え, (wife's secret savings) へそくり; (amount not spent) 得

one's life savings 老後の蓄え

a savings of ¥1,000 1000円の得

savings account *n.* (普通)預金口座

savior *n.* (messiah) 救世主, (**the Savior**: Jesus) キリスト; (person to whom one owes one's life) 命の恩人

savor *v.* (enjoy the taste of) 味わう

savory *adj.* (tastes good) 味のいい, (salty) 塩味の利いた

saw *n.* (tool) のこぎり [→ picture of TOOL]

v. (cut with a saw) のこぎりで切る

sawdust *n.* おがくず

saxophone *n.* サキソホン

play the saxophone サキソホンを吹く

♦**saxophonist** *n.* サキソホン奏者

say *v.* (…と) 言う, ((*honorific*)) (…と) おっしゃる, ((*humble*)) (…と) 申し上げる, (talk about) 話す

"Come in," he said.
「お入りなさい」とその人が言った。

"What did you just say?"
"I said I would like to start the meeting as early as possible."
「今、何ておっしゃいました？」
「できるだけ早く会議を始めたいと言ったのです」

I told her that I never said that.
そんなことは言っていないと彼女に言った。

He said something about having dropped his wallet.
彼は財布を落としたというようなことを言った。

She says she would like to come.
彼女は行きたいと言っている。

Only this morning my husband said the very same thing.
ちょうどけさ、夫が全く同じことを言った。

He said no. 彼はノーと言った。

Did he say he was sorry?
彼は謝ったの?

I can't say what's going to happen.
これから何が起きるのか何とも言えない。

If she doesn't like it, she can say so.
気に入らないのなら、そう言えばいい。

I couldn't think of anything to say.
話すことが何も思いつかなかった。

having said that (qualifying a statement) だから(とい)って, そうはいうものの

I love art, but, having said that, I'm not a very artistic person.
美術は大好きなんだけど、だからってそんなに芸術的な人間じゃないよ。

if I may say so 言わせてもらえば

If I may say so, I don't think that was fair.
言わせてもらえば、今のはフェアじゃなかったと思う。

I must say 全く, 本当に

Well, I must say, you look beautiful in that dress.
ほんと、そのドレスを着るとすてきだよ。

it's said that ...と言われている, ...そうだ

It's said that Cleopatra was a woman of unparalleled beauty.
クレオパトラは、絶世の美女だったと言われている。

let's say (let's pretend) ...ことにしよう, (let's suppose) (仮に)...としよう

Let's say it was an accident.
事故だったことにしよう。

Let's say you don't find a job. What will you do?
もし就職できなかったら、どうする?

people/they say ...と言われている

People say the house is haunted.
あの家は幽霊が出ると言われている。

They say that Elvis died of an overdose.
エルビスの死因は、薬物の過剰摂取だったと言われている。

say to oneself ...と(心の中で)思う

I said to myself, "I won't smoke another cigarette."
「もう二度とたばこは吸わない」と心の中で思った。

say what you like 何と言おうと

Say what you like about him. Personally, I still think he's innocent.
彼のことを何と言おうと、彼は潔白だと思う。

that is to say つまり, ((*formal*)) すなわち

The government may decide to reinstate conscription—that is to say, compulsory enrollment—in the armed forces.
政府は徴兵制度の復活を決定するかもしれない——つまり、軍隊への強制入隊だ。

to say nothing of さらに, おまけに

The beaches were great, to say nothing of the seafood and local crafts.
ビーチはよかったし、おまけに海産物や地元の工芸品も最高だった。

what do you say to...? (making a suggestion or inviting) ((*polite*)) ...についてはどうですか, ...しませんか, ((*informal*)) ...は/をどう?, (asking sb's opinion) ...についてどう思う?

What do you say to dinner tonight?
今夜、夕食をどう?

saying *n.* (popular adage) 格言, 言い習わし, ことわざ

scab *n.* かさぶた

scabbard *n.* さや

scaffold *n.* (for building/repairing sth) 足場; (for hanging) 絞首台

put up [take down] a scaffold 足場を<u>組む</u> [解体する]

scaffolding *n.* 足場

scald *v.* やけどする

scalding *adj.* やけどするような

scalding-hot water やけどするほど熱いお湯

scale[1] *n.* (on fish, reptile) うろこ

scale[2]

1 *n.* SIZE/SCOPE: スケール, 規模

2 *n.* NUMBERS ON INSTRUMENT: 目盛り

3 *n.* OF MAP: 縮尺

4 *n.* IN MUSIC: 音階

5 *v.* CLIMB: 登る

1 the scale of the task 仕事の規模

a large scale 大規模

2 the scale of a thermometer 温度計の目盛り

3 What's the scale of the map? この地図の縮尺はどのくらいですか？

a map with a scale of 1:150,000 縮尺15万分の1の地図

4 What scale is this piece? この曲の音階は何？

5 They scaled Mt. Blanc. 一行はモンブランに登った。

♦**scale down** *v.* 一定の基準で下げる, 縮小する

scale up *v.* 一定の基準で上げる, 拡大する

scale[3] *n.* (for measuring weight) はかり, (bathroom scale) 体重計 [→ picture of BATHROOM, PUBLIC BATH]

get/climb on a scale 体重計に乗る

scallion *n.* (spring onion) 春タマネギ, (shallot) エシャロット

scallop *n.* ホタテガイ, 帆立貝

scalp *n.* 頭皮

scalpel *n.* メス

scamper *v.* 駆け回る, はね回る

scan *v.* (read quickly) (...に) ざっと目を通す, (look carefully at) じっと見る; (scan using a scanner) スキャンする

scan a photograph 写真をスキャンする

scandal *n.* スキャンダル, 醜聞

cause a scandal スキャンダルを起こす

scandalous *adj.* 恥ずべき, みっともない, (shocking) ひどい

scanner *n.* (for computer) スキャナー, (at airport) 手荷物検査装置

scant *adj.* (insufficient) 足りない, 乏しい, (**a scant...**) わずかな

scantily *adv.* (**scantily clad**) ほとんど裸の

scanty *adj.* (insufficient) 不十分な, 足りない; (of clothing) 肌の見える

scapegoat *n.* 身代わり, 犠牲

scapula *n.* 肩甲骨

scar *n.* 傷跡

v. (...に) 傷跡を残す

a scar on one's arm 腕の傷跡

He was scarred for life. 彼は一生残る傷を負った。

scarce *adj.* 足りない, 不十分だ

♦**scarcity** *n.* (shortage) 不足

scarcely *adv.* (hardly) ほとんど...ない, (used with a number: **scarcely...**) ...そ

S

こそこ [→ HARDLY]

The light was so bad I could scarcely read.
明かりがとても暗かったので、ほとんど読めなかった。

Scarcely anyone was there.
ほとんど誰もいなかった。

There were scarcely ten people in the audience.
聴衆は10人そこそこだった。

scare *v.* (frighten) 怖がらせる, (surprise) びっくりさせる
n. 脅威, (fear) 恐怖

You didn't scare me at all.
全然怖くなかったよ。

Sorry, did I scare you?
失礼、びっくりさせましたか/((*informal*)) ごめん、びっくりした?

My God! You scared me.
なんだ、驚かさないでよ。

the mad cow scare 狂牛病の脅威

♦ **scare away/off** *v.* 怖がらせて追い払う

scarecrow *n.* かかし; (haggard person) みすぼらしい人

scared *adj.* (speaking of oneself) 怖い, (speaking of sb else) 怖がる

Are you scared of him? 彼が怖いの?

She was too scared to move.
彼女はあまりにも怖くて動けなかった。

I was scared stiff.
怖くて体が硬直していた。

scarf *n.* (worn around neck) マフラー, えり巻き

wear a scarf マフラーを巻く

scarlet *adj.* 緋色の, 深紅の

scarlet fever *n.* 猩紅熱

scary *adj.* 怖い, 恐ろしい

a scary movie 怖い映画

scathing *adj.* 容赦のない, 痛烈な

scathing criticism 痛烈な批判 [酷評]

scatter *v.* (move in different directions) 散らばる, (of crowd) ちりぢりになる, (throw in various directions) ばらまく, まき散らす

The crowd scattered.
群衆はちりぢりになった。

scatterbrain *n.* そそっかしい人, 注意散漫な人

♦ **scatterbrained** *adj.* そそっかしい, 注意散漫な

scattered *adj.* 散らかっている, 散らばっている, (of people over area) まばらな

There were clothes scattered all over the room.
部屋中に衣類が散らばっていた。

scattered showers にわか雨

scavenge *v.* あさる

scavenge the garbage ごみをあさる

scavenger *n.* (animal) 腐食動物, (person) ごみあさりをする人

scenario *n.* (plot outline) 筋書き, (script) シナリオ, 脚本; (situation) 状況, 想定

a worst-case scenario 最悪の事態の想定

scene *n.*

1 VIEW: 景色, 風景, 光景

2 SITE OF EVENT: 現場, 場所

3 SECTION OF PLAY/FILM: 場, 場面, シーン

4 SPHERE OF ACTIVITY: 分野, 方面, ...界

5 PUBLIC DISPLAY OF EMOTION: 大騒ぎ, 醜態

1 It was a scene of indescribable beauty.

S

言葉に表せない美しい景色でした。

scenes of life in Kenya ケニアの生活風景

2 the scene of an accident 事故現場

The police arrived on the scene too late.
警察が現場に到着したのは、あまりにも遅かった。

3 Act 4, scene 3 第四幕第三場

The play comes to a climax in the final scene.
この劇は最終場面でクライマックスを迎える。

4 the art scene 芸術の分野

5 Don't make a scene.
((*masculine*)) 大騒ぎするな。

You didn't have to make a scene in front of all those people.
あんなに大勢の人の前で醜態をさらすことはなかったんだよ。

behind the scenes 裏で(は), 舞台裏で

Behind the scenes, things were very different.
裏では事情が全く違っていた。

He worked behind the scenes.
彼は裏で動いた。

scenery ***n.*** (natural setting) 景色, 風景, (stage setting) 舞台装置, 背景

scenic ***adj.*** 景色のいい

a scenic view すばらしい景色

scent ***n.*** におい, (good smell) 香り [→ SMELL]

the scent of roses バラの香り

schedule ***n.*** スケジュール, 予定, (train schedule, timetable) 時刻表

v. 予定する, (**be scheduled to do/take place**) …する/行われる予定だ

What's your schedule today?
今日の(ご)予定は?

He has a very busy schedule.
彼は予定がぎっしり詰まっている。

The plan was carried out according to schedule.
計画は予定どおりに実行された。

ahead of schedule 予定より早く

behind schedule 予定より遅れて

on schedule 予定どおりに, 時間どおりに

Are the trains running on schedule?
電車は時間どおりに動いていますか?

scheme ***n.*** (devious plan) 陰謀, たくらみ

v. (plot) たくらむ

schism ***n.*** 分裂

schizophrenia ***n.*** 統合失調症

schizophrenic ***adj.*** 統合失調症の

scholar ***n.*** 学者, (scholarship recipient) 奨学生

a Rhodes Scholar ローズ奨学生

scholarly ***adj.*** (of person) 学者らしい, (of writing) 学問的な

scholarship ***n.*** 奨学金

receive a scholarship 奨学金をもらう

scholastic ***adj.*** 学校の

scholastic achievements 学校の成績

school ***n.*** 学校, (division of university) 学部; (sect) 派, 流派

v. (**be schooled**) (=receive education) 教育を受ける, (=be trained) 訓練される, しつけられる

attend school 学校に通う

change schools 転校する

What time do you go to school?
何時に学校に行くの?

School starts at 9:00 A.M. and finishes

at 3:30 P.M.
学校は午前９時に始まって、午後３時半に終わります。

Did you go to school with him?
彼と同じ学校に通っていたの？

The school was built in 1864.
その学校は　１８６４　年に創立された。

an international school
インターナショナルスクール

the School of Modern Languages
現代語学部

a school of thought 学派

♦**schoolbook** *n.* 教科書

schoolboy *n.* 男子生徒

school building *n.* 校舎

school bus *n.* スクールバス

schoolchild *n.* 学童

school day *n.* (day of classes) 授業のある日, (**school days**: years spent in school) 学生時代, 学校時代

school festival *n.* 文化祭

school gate *n.* 校門

schoolgirl *n.* 女子生徒

school grounds *n.* 学校の構内

schooling *n.* 学校教育

school lunch *n.* 学校給食

school outing *n.* 遠足

school playground *n.* 運動場, 校庭

school rules *n.* 校則

schoolteacher *n.* (学校の) 先生, 教師

school trip *n.* (one-day) 遠足, (multi-day) 修学旅行

schoolwork *n.* 学業, ((*informal*)) 学校の勉強, (homework) 宿題

schoolyard *n.* 校庭

school year *n.* 学年(度)

science *n.* 科学, 学問

the importance of science 科学の重要性

arts and science 人文科学と自然科学

science fiction *n.* ＳＦ

scientific *adj.* 科学的な

a scientific experiment 科学実験

scientific research 科学的研究

the scientific method 科学的方法

scientist *n.* 科学者

scintillate *v.* (shine) きらめく

scissors *n.* はさみ [→ picture of STATIONERY, FIRST-AID KIT]

Why don't you use scissors to cut it open.
はさみで開いてみれば？

scoff *v.* (scoff at) あざ笑う, あざける

scold *v.* しかる [→ TELL OFF]

scoop *n.* (small shovel) スコップ, (big spoon) 大さじ, (scoopful) 一すくい; (story) スクープ, 特ダネ

v. (**scoop up**) すくう, すくい取る, (**scoop out**) すくい出す

scooter *n.* (type of motorbike) スクーター, (child's toy) キックボード

scope *n.* (range) 範囲, (breadth) 幅, (room, space) 余地

The scope of the course was too narrow.
そのコースの範囲は狭すぎた。

We need to broaden the scope of education.
教育の幅を広げなければいけない。

That is beyond the scope of this discussion.
それは話し合いの範囲外だ。

♦**scope out** *v.* (area) よく見る

scorch *v.* 焦がす, 焼く [→ BURN]

scorching *adj.* (of weather) 焼けつくような

score *n.* (in sport/game) 得点, スコア, (on test) 成績; (musical writing) 楽譜, スコア

v. (in sport/game) (点を) 取る

"What's the score?"
"Two to three, with the Mariners in the lead."
「(スコアは) 今、何点？」
「2対3でマリナーズが勝ってる」

No one has scored yet.
まだ得点がない。

He scored sixteen goals in five games.
彼は5試合で16点取った[を挙げた]。

He scored well on the test.
彼は試験でいい点を取った。

scoreboard *n.* スコアボード, 得点掲示板

scorn *n., v.* 軽蔑(する) [→ CONTEMPT]

scornful *adj.* 軽蔑した

Scorpio *n.* (the Scorpion) さそり座

scorpion *n.* サソリ

Scotch *n.* (whiskey) スコッチ

Scotch tape *n.* セロテープ [→ picture of STATIONERY]

Scotland *n.* スコットランド

Scottish *n.* (person) スコットランド人, (language) スコットランド英語

adj. (of Scotland, Scottish culture) スコットランドの, (of language) スコットランド英語の

a Scottish accent スコットランドなまり

scour *v.* (**scour for**: look carefully for) 捜し回る; (scrub) ごしごし磨く

scout *n.* (soldier) 偵察兵, (talent scout) スカウト; (**Boy Scout**) ボーイスカウト, (**Girl Scout**) ガールスカウト

v. (an area) 偵察する, (**scout around for**) 探し回る, (=for talent) スカウトする

scowl *v.* (wrinkle one's brow) 顔をしかめる, (scowl at) にらみつける

scramble

1 *v.* CLIMB: (**scramble up/over**) 登る, (using hands) よじ登る, (**scramble down**) はい下りる

2 *v.* MIX UP: ごちゃごちゃにする, (eggs) かき混ぜる, (code) かく乱させる

3 *v.* RUSH: (**scramble for**) 奪い合う, (**scramble to do**) 急いで…する

4 *n.* HARD CLIMB: 登はん

5 *n.* RUSH: 奪い合い

6 *n.* MOTORCYCLE SPORT: スクランブルレース

1 The hikers had to scramble over rocky terrain for several kilometers.
ハイカーは、数キロの岩山を登らなければならなかった。

I scrambled down the ladder as quickly as I could.
できる限り早く、はしごを下りた。

2 Now scramble the cards.
さあ、トランプを混ぜてください。

I like my eggs scrambled.
スクランブルエッグが好きだ。

3 Everyone scrambled for the door.
みんな戸口に殺到した。

I scrambled to finish my tax returns.
急いで税金の申告を済ませた。

4 a 500-meter scramble
500メートルの登はん

♦**scrambled eggs** *n.* いり卵, スクランブ

ルエッグ

scrap ***n.*** (**a scrap of**) 一片の..., ...切れ, (=of paper) 紙切れ, (=of cloth) 切れ端, (scrap metal) くず鉄, スクラップ, (**scraps:** remaining bits of food) 残り物, 残飯, 食べ残し

v. (throw away) 捨てる, (proposal) 取りやめる, ご破算にする

I couldn't even sell it for scrap.
くず鉄としても売れなかった。

The whole plan should be scrapped.
計画そのものをご破算にすべきだ。

♦ **scrap heap** ***n.*** ゴミの山

scrap iron ***n.*** くず鉄

scrape ***v.*** (**scrape off**: layer of sth) こすり取る, こすり落とす, (**scrape oneself**) すりむく; (make an awful noise) こすって音を立てる, (drag against) こする, (scratch) かく

Have you scraped the paint off yet?
もうペンキをこすり取った？

I scraped my knee on the door.
ドアでひざをすりむいた。

I can't stand the sound of fingernails scraping down a chalkboard.
黒板を爪でこする音は、耐えられない。

♦ **scrape by** ***v.*** (financially) かつかつの暮らしをする

scratch ***v.*** (cause damage to: surface) (...に) 傷をつける, (scrape) かく, (scrape forcefully) 引っかく

n. (minor injury) かすり傷, (minor damage to a surface) 引っかき傷

Don't scratch the furniture.
家具に傷をつけないで。

The cat scratched me.
猫に引っかかれた。

I like having my back scratched.
背中をかいてもらうのが好きなんです。

Oh, it's only a scratch.
ほんのかすり傷だよ。

not up to scratch 調子がよくない, ((*informal*)) 今一だ

scrawl ***v.*** なぐり書きする [→ SCRIBBLE]

scream ***v.*** 悲鳴を上げる, (キャーと) 叫ぶ

n. 悲鳴, 叫び声

Stop screaming, will you.
大声を出すのはやめてくれない？

The fans screamed wildly.
ファンが絶叫した。

The baby is screaming again.
赤ちゃんがまたギャーギャー泣いている。

a scream for help 助けを求める悲鳴

screech ***v.*** 甲高い声を上げる, (of brakes, machine) キーと音を立てる

The car screeched to a halt.
車がキーと音を立てて止まった。

screen

1 ***n.*** FOR PROJECTING IMAGES: (screen for viewing films/slides) スクリーン, (TV screen, computer display) 画面

2 ***n.*** FOR WINDOW: 網戸

3 ***n.*** PANEL: (folding screen) 屏風

4 ***v.*** SHOW: (film) 上映する

5 ***v.*** JOB APPLICANTS: 審査する, 選考する, (**screen out**) ふるい落とす

1 a TV [computer] screen
テレビ [コンピューター] 画面

2 There's a hole in this screen.
この網戸に穴があいている。

3 Where can I get a screen like that?
そういう屏風は、どこで手に入れられますか？

4 The movie will not be screened.
その映画は上映されないことになっている。

5 Applicants will be thoroughly screened.
応募者はじっくり審査されることになる。

screening *n.* (of film) 上映; (of applicants for a job) 審査, 選考

screenplay *n.* 映画のシナリオ

screen saver *n.* スクリーンセーバー

screenwriter *n.* シナリオライター

screw *n.* (metal peg) ねじ, ねじ釘 [→ picture of TOOL], (act of twisting/turning) 一ひねり, 一回し

v. (screw A to/on B) (AをBに) ねじで取り付ける, (**screw on/in**) ねじ込む, (**screw shut/down**) ねじで締める

You'll need a bigger screw than that.
それよりもっと大きなねじが必要だ。

Give it another screw.
もう1度回して。

Have you screwed it down tight?
ねじをきつく締めましたか？

have a screw loose ちょっとおかしい, どうかしている

♦**screw around** *v.* (fool around) ふざける, (**screw around with**) いじる; (sleep around) 誰とでも寝る

screw over *v.* だます

screw up *v.* (commit a blunder) 大失敗する

screwdriver *n.* ドライバー, ねじ回し [→ picture of TOOL]

scribble *v.* (write all over) 落書きする, (jot down) 走り書きする

n. 落書き, 走り書き

script *n.* (for film, play) 脚本, 台本; (writing) 文字, (typeface) 書体

The script was excellent but the acting left something to be desired.
脚本はすばらしかったけど、演技が今一つだった。

the Japanese script 日本語の文字

scripture *n.* (**Holy Scriptures**) 聖書, (**Buddhist Scriptures**) 仏典

scriptwriter *n.* 脚本家, シナリオライター

scroll *n.* (paper scroll) 巻物

v. (through text) スクロールする

scroll up [down] (the screen)
(画面を) 上に [下に] スクロールする

♦**scroll bar** *n.* スクロールバー

scrotum *n.* 陰のう

scrounge *v.* せびる, たかる, (**scrounge around for**: try to find) 探し回る, あさる

scrounge for change つり銭をせびる

♦**scrounger** *n.* たかり屋

scrub[1] *v.* (scrub clean) こすってきれいにする, ごしごし洗う

n. ごしごし洗うこと

scrub the dishes 食器をごしごし洗う

scrub oneself down in the shower
シャワーで体をごしごし洗う

scrub[2] *n.* (bushes) やぶ, 低木の茂み

scruff *n.* (nape) えり首, 首筋

take by the scruff of the neck
えり首をつかまえる

scruffy *adj.* (of person) だらしない, (of clothes) みすぼらしい

scrum *n.* (in rugby) スクラム

scruple *n.* 良心の呵責

have no scruples about doing 平気で…する

He has no scruples about lying to her. 彼は彼女に平気でうそをつく。

scrupulous *adj.* (honest) 実直な, (meticulous) きちょうめんな

scrutinize *v.* 綿密に調べる, 吟味する

scrutiny *n.* 精査, 吟味

be under scrutiny (of person) 監視されている

scuba diving *n.* スキューバダイビング

♦**scuba diver** *n.* スキューバダイバー

scud *v.* (of cloud) 飛んで行く

scuff *v.* (a surface) (…に) 傷をつける

scuffle *n.* 取っ組み合い

get into a scuffle 取っ組み合いになる

sculpt *v.* 彫刻する

♦**sculptor** *n.* 彫刻家

sculpture *n.* (art of sculpture) 彫刻, (statue) 彫像

scum *n.* (on surface of liquid) あく; (rotten person) 人間のくず

He's scum! あいつは人間のくずだ!

scurry *v.* ちょこちょこ走る

scurvy *n.* 壊血病

scuttle[1] *n.* (coal bucket) 石炭入れ

scuttle[2] *v.* ちょこちょこ走る, (**scuttle off / away**) 急いで逃げる

scythe *n.* 草刈りがま

sea *n.* (also **seas, the seas**) 海

land and sea 陸と海

go by sea 船で行く

a calm [rough] sea 穏やかな [荒れた] 海

a house by the sea 海辺の家

the open sea 外洋

seabird *n.* 海鳥

seaboard *n.* 海岸

seafood *n.* シーフード, 海産食品, 魚介類

seafront *n.* 海岸通り, 臨海地区

seagull *n.* カモメ

seal[1]

seal 印鑑

Seals are used instead of signatures in Japan.

印鑑/はんこ seal

印肉 inkpad

1 *n.* INSIGNIA: はんこ, 印鑑

2 *n.* ON PACKAGE: 封, 封印

3 *v.* CLOSE: (container) 密封する, (envelope) (…に) 封をする

1 Put your seal here, please. ここに、はんこを押してください。

2 The seal was broken. 封が破られていた。

3 He sealed the envelope. 彼は封筒に封をした。

seal[2] *n.* (animal) アザラシ

sea level *n.* 平均海面

a thousand meters above sea level 海抜1000メートル

seam *n.* (line of stitches) 縫い目, (layer of coal) (石炭の) 層

come apart at the seams →COME APART

seaman *n.* 船員, 船乗り

seamless *adj.* とぎれのない, (without stitches) 縫い目のない, (of stockings) シームレスの

seamy *adj.* (dark) 暗黒の, 裏の

the seamy side of society 社会の裏側

séance *n.* 降霊術の会

S

seaplane ***n.*** 水上飛行機

seaport ***n.*** (harbor) 港, (port town) 港町

search

1 ***v.*** **LOOK FOR: (search for)** 捜す, (on Internet) 検索する, (=seek) 求める, (the truth) 探求する

2 ***v.*** **OF AUTHORITIES:** (search sb) ボディーチェックする, (search a place) 捜索する, (search sb's belongings) 検査する, 調べる

3 ***n.*** **ACT OF SEEKING:** (search for a missing person) 捜索, (Internet/library search) 検索, (investigation) 調査

1 What are you searching for?
何を捜しているの？

They're still searching for survivors.
まだ生存者を捜索中だ。

I've searched everywhere, but it's nowhere to be found.
くまなく捜したけど、どこにも見当たらない。

Let's search for a solution to the problem.
問題の解決策を探そう。

2 search a house 家宅捜索する

Customs searched my luggage.
税関で荷物を調べられた。

3 It was a long and unsuccessful search.
長時間にわたる、不毛な捜索だった。

The search for gold continues.
金の探索は続けられている。

♦ **search engine** ***n.*** 検索エンジン, 検索ソフト

search party ***n.*** 捜索隊

search plane ***n.*** 捜索機

searing ***adj.*** (so hot it could burn) 焼けつくような

seashore ***n.*** 海岸, 海辺

seasick ***adj.*** 船酔いした

♦ **seasickness** ***n.*** 船酔い

seaside ***n.*** 海辺, 浜辺

a seaside resort 海辺のリゾート

season

1 ***n.*** **DIVISION OF THE YEAR:** 季節

2 ***n.*** **PERIOD FOR A PARTICULAR ACTIVITY:** シーズン, 時期, (for food) 旬

3 ***v.*** **FLAVOR:** (…に) 味を付ける, 味付けする

1 What's your favorite season?
好きな季節は、いつですか？

The island of Honshu has four clearly defined seasons.
本州は四季がはっきりしている。

the rainy season (in Japan) 梅雨

2 the baseball season 野球のシーズン

the tourist season 観光シーズン

Tomatoes are in season now.
トマトは今が旬です。

When is it pumpkin season?
カボチャの時期はいつですか？

3 What spices are you going to season it with?
どんな香辛料で味付けするの？

♦ **season tickets** ***n.*** 通し切符

seasonal ***adj.*** (of season) 季節の, (happening/needed during a season) 季節的な

seasoned ***adj.*** (experienced) 熟練した, ベテランの, (treated, dried) よく乾燥した

a seasoned teacher ベテラン教師

seasoning ***n.*** 味付け, (for soba/udon)

薬味

seat

1 *n.* PLACE TO SIT: (in public place) 席, (in general) 座席, (chair) 椅子, (for elderly/pregnant/disabled person on train/bus) 優先席, (on bicycle) サドル, (toilet seat) 便座 [→ picture of TOILET]

2 *v.* SIT: (**seat oneself**) 座る, 腰をかける

3 *v.* PROVIDE SEATING FOR: (of theater) 収容できる

4 *n.* PART OF GARMENT: (お)尻

5 *n.* POLITICAL POSITION: (legislative seat) 議席

1 Is there a spare seat here anywhere?
どこかに空席はありますか？

How many seats are there in the room?
部屋に椅子はいくつありますか？

You can use this box as a seat if you like.
よかったら、この箱を椅子代わりに使って。

2 She seated herself opposite me.
彼女は私の向かい側に座った。

3 The theater seats over a hundred people.
その劇場は100人以上収容できる。

4 He tore the seat of his pants.
彼のズボンの(お)尻の所が破けた。

5 The government lost a lot of seats in the local elections.
地方選挙で与党は多くの議席を失った。

seat belt *n.* シートベルト, 安全ベルト [→ picture of CAR]

seating *n.* (capacity) 収容力

sea urchin *n.* ウニ

seaweed *n.* 海草, (kelp, edible seaweed) 昆布

dried seaweed のり

secede *v.* 脱退する

secluded *adj.* (of place) 人里離れた, 人けのない

a secluded beach 人里離れたビーチ

live a secluded life 隠とん生活をする

seclusion *n.* 隔離

second[1] *adj.* (next after first) 第2の, 2番目の, 2度/2回目の

n. 第2, 2番目, (date) 2日

adv. 第2に, 2番目に, 次に

He came in second place.
彼は2位だった。

That's the second time you've asked me.
あなたにその質問をされるのは2度目だ。

It was his second marriage.
彼は2度目の結婚 [再婚] だった。

the Second World War
第二次世界大戦

the second tallest person
2番目に背の高い人

First, shall we sit down? And second, how about a drink?
まずは座りましょう。それで飲み物はどうします？

second to none 勝るものはない

The outdoor hot springs there are second to none.
あそこの露天ぶろに勝るものはない。

♦**second base** *n.* (in baseball) 二塁

second opinion *n.* セカンドオピニオン

get a second opinion
セカンドオピニオンを取る

second person *n.* 二人称

second thoughts *n.* 再考, 考え直すこと

second[2] *n.* (sixtieth part of a minute) 秒,

S

瞬間

Does your watch show the seconds?
あなたの腕時計は、秒を表示しますか？

It only took about thirty seconds.
ほんの３０秒くらいしか、かからなかった。

A second later it was raining.
次の瞬間には雨が降り出していた。

secondary *adj.* (of less importance) 第２の, ２番目の; (of education) 中等の

second best *n.* ２番目によいもの, 次善のもの

adj. (**second-best**) 次善の, ２位の

She'll never settle for second best.
彼女なら決して２番に甘んじない。

second-class *n.* (quality) 二流, (accommodation) ２等

adj. (**second-class**) ２等の

second hand *n.* (of clock) 秒針

secondhand *adj.* (used) 中古の; (of information) また聞きの, 人づての

second lieutenant *n.* (in U.S. Army/Air force/Marine Corps) 少尉

secondly *adv.* 第二に, 次に

second-rate *adj.* (of poor quality) 二流の, 二級の

a second-rate restaurant 二流レストラン

secrecy *n.* 秘密を守ること

secret *adj.* 秘密の, ((*informal*)) 内緒の

n. 秘密, (official secret) 機密

a secret garden 秘密の花園

a secret door 秘密の扉

Let me tell you a secret.
秘密を打ち明けよう。

Can you keep a secret?
内緒にしてもらえますか？

The results remain a secret.
結果は明かされていない。

in secret こっそり, ひそかに

They met in secret.
二人はこっそり会った。

♦**secret police** *n.* 秘密警察

secret service *n.* 秘密諜報機関

secretariat *n.* (administrative department) 事務局

secretary *n.* (personal assistant) 秘書, (official in charge of correspondence) 書記官, (government official) 長官, 大臣

the Secretary of Defense [State]
<u>国防</u> [国務] 長官

secrete *v.* (bodily fluid) 分泌する

♦**secretion** *n.* 分泌

secretive *adj.* 秘密主義の, 隠し立てする

secretly *adv.* こっそり, ひそかに

sect *n.* (religious) 宗派, (of church) 教派, (political) 派閥

♦**sectarian** *adj.* 宗派の, 派閥の

section *n.* (department) 部, 課, 部門, セクション, (part) 部分, パート, (of book) 節, 項

Which section are you working in now?
今は、どこの部で働いていますか？

You'll find it in the section entitled "Immigration."
「入国管理」の項に書いてありますよ。

The report was divided into four sections.
報告書は四つの項に分かれていた。

sector *n.* (of economy) 部門, セクター, (of city) 区域

the public [private] sector

公的 [民間] 部門

secular *adj.* (nonreligious) 非宗教的な, (worldly) 世俗の

secure

1 ***adj.*** **SAFE:** 安全な, 大丈夫な

2 ***adj.*** **STABLE:** (of job, income) 安定した, (of foothold) しっかりした

3 ***adj.*** **CONFIDENT:** (positive, sure of oneself) 確信している, (not worried, at ease) 安心している

4 ***v.*** **OBTAIN:** 確保する

1 Is this website secure?
このサイトは安全ですか？

2 Is your job secure?
あなたの仕事は安定していますか？

3 Do you feel secure in your relationship?
あなたはその関係に安心感をもっていますか？

4 The UN's efforts secured a ceasefire.
国連の努力で停戦が実現した。

♦**securely** ***adv.*** 安全に, (firmly) しっかりと

Please make sure your seat belts are securely fastened.
シートベルトがしっかり締まっていることをお確かめください。

security *n.* (safety) 安全, (protection) 警備, (feeling of being safe) 安心; (collateral) 担保

sedan *n.* セダン

sedate *v.* (…に) 鎮静剤を与える, (**be sedated**) 鎮静剤を飲んで落ち着いている

sedative *n.* 鎮静剤

sedentary *adj.* (always sitting) いつも座っている, 座りっぱなしの

a sedentary job デスクワーク

sediment *n.* 沈殿物, おり, かす

seduce *v.* 誘惑する, 口説く, (entice) そそのかす

seduction *n.* 誘惑

seductive *adj.* 誘惑するような, 魅惑的な

---

see *v.*

1 **HAVE/USE THE POWER OF SIGHT:** (**can see**) (…が) 見える

2 **VIEW:** 見る

3 **UNDERSTAND:** わかる

4 **MEET TO TALK TO:** (…に/と) 会う, 会って話をする

5 **ESCORT:** 送って行く

6 **LEARN FROM OBSERVATION:** わかる

7 **HAVE AN OPINION:** 考える, 見る, 見方をする

8 **REFER TO:** 参照する, 見る, (read) 読む

1 Can you see that building over there?
あそこのビルが見えますか？

It was so dark, I couldn't see a thing.
とても暗くて、何も見えなかった。

I can't see without my glasses.
めがねがないと見えない。

Can you see over that fence?
塀の向こうが見えますか？

The window is so dirty I can barely see through it.
窓がひどく汚れていて、ほとんど向こうが見えない。

2 I saw her in the restaurant.
レストランで彼女を見た。

Can I stop by to see your new apartment?
新しいアパートを見に寄ってもいい？

I went to London to see the exhibition.

展覧会を見にロンドンに行きました。

They want to see all your documents.
あなたの書類を全部見たいそうです。

"I can't get this lid off!"
"Here, let me see it."
「ふたがあかない！」
「ちょっと見せて」

3 Do you see what I'm getting at?
私の言おうとしていることがわかりますか？

"The machine should be switched off before 7 o'clock."
"I see."
「7時前には機械のスイッチを切っておいてください」
「わかりました」

4 Are you seeing your friends tonight?
今晩、友達に会うの？

She said she'd come over to see us later.
彼女はあとで会いに来ると言ってた。

Can I see you tomorrow?
明日、会える？

5 Did he see you home?
彼に家まで送ってもらったの？

I saw him to the station.
彼を駅まで送った。

6 I see from this article that not all sides feel the same way about the issue.
その問題に対して、みんなが同じ考えをもっているわけではないことが、この記事からわかる。

7 You'll be seeing things differently in a week or so.
1週間もすれば見方も変わるよ。

8 (*written*) See below for further details.
詳細は以下をご覧ください。

as far as I can see 私の見るところ(では)

As far as I can see, the mistake is on their end.
私の見るところ、間違っているのは向こうのほうだ。

as I see it / the way I see it 私の見るところ(では), 私の考えでは

The way I see it, she should have told him earlier.
私の考えだと、彼女はもっと早く彼に言うべきだった。

I'll / we'll (have to) see 考えておきます, 様子を見てから決めます

"Can you go tomorrow?"
"We'll see."
「明日、行けそうですか？」
「考えておきます」

let me see / let's see えーっと, うーん, そうねー

see a lot of / a great deal of (see often) ...としょっちゅう会う

We saw a lot of each other over the summer.
夏の間、しょっちゅう会っていた。

see for oneself 自分で見てみる, 自分の目で確かめる

Here, see for yourself. The fridge is empty.
ほら、見てみて。冷蔵庫が空っぽよ。

seeing as / that ...ので, ...から

Seeing that you've worked so hard, the least I can do is treat you to lunch.
仕事をがんばってくれたから、せめて昼食でもおごらせて。

see nothing / little of 全然会わない, ほとんど会わない

We saw little of him while he was writ-

ing his dissertation.
彼が博士論文を書いている間は、ほとんど会わなかった。

see to it that 必ず…する, …よう取り計らう, …ようにする

Would you see to it that this work is finished before you go home?
帰るまでに、この作業を終わらせるようにしてもらいたいんだが。

see you (later/soon/again) じゃあまた, また会いましょう

See you tomorrow. じゃ、また明日。

see about *v.* (**see about doing**) …する手配をする

I'll see about selling the car.
車を売る手配をします。

we'll see about that (being ironic) そんなこと、させるもんか

see off *v.* (at airport, station) 見送る

We saw them off at the airport.
空港で彼らを見送った。

see out *v.* (the door) 玄関まで見送る

see through *v.* 見抜く, 見通す

---

seed *n.* (of plant) 種

v. (remove seeds from) (…の) 種を取り除く, (plant seeds in) (…に) 種をまく

grass seeds 草の種

plant seeds 種をまく

♦ **seedless** *adj.* 種なしの

seedling *n.* 苗木

seedy *adj.* (shabby) みすぼらしい, (disreputable) いかがわしい, 怪しげな

Seeing Eye dog *n.* 盲導犬

seek *v.* 求める [→ LOOK FOR, SEARCH]

seek approval for …への賛成を求める

seek compensation for …に対する補償を求める

seem *v.* …ように見える/思われる, …そうだ, …ようだ, …らしい, …みたいだ

It seemed important at the time.
当時は重要に思えたんです。

She seemed so friendly.
彼女はとても親切そうに見えたのに。

There don't seem to be many people working today.
今日は働いている人は多くないようだ。

He seems to be in a bad mood.
彼は今、機嫌が悪いみたい。

can't seem to do …できそうもない

I can't seem to get the hang of this.
こつをつかめそうもない。

it would seem that どうやら…ようだ, どうも…ようだ

It would seem that you're mistaken.
どうやらあなたは間違っているようだ。

there seems to be …があるようだ

There seems to be a misunderstanding.
誤解があるようです。

seemingly *adv.* 一見(したところ), 表面上は

a seemingly endless dispute
一見、果てしないと思われる論争

seep *v.* 漏れる, しみ出る [→ LEAK]

seesaw *n.* シーソー

play on a seesaw シーソーで遊ぶ

seethe *v.* (with anger) 煮えくり返る

see-through *adj.* シースルーの, 透けて見える

segment *n.* (part) 部分, (fragment,

piece) 一片, (slice) 切片, (of straight line) 線分, (of circle) 弧

segregate *v.* 分離する

segregation *n.* (racial) 人種差別

seismic *adj.* 地震の

seismic activity 地震活動

seismograph *n.* 地震計

seize *v.* (grab hold of) つかむ, 握る, (opportunity) 捕らえる, つかむ

He seized me by the arm.
彼は私の腕をつかんだ。

♦**seize up** *v.* (go stiff) 動かなくなる

seizure *n.* (illness) 発作

seldom *adv.* (rarely) めったに…ない

We seldom see him these days.
このごろめったに彼に会わない。

select *v.* (choose) 選ぶ, 選択する, (select from among) 選び出す

adj. (best) えり抜きの, (top-class) 高級な, (high-quality) 極上の

Try to select a good university.
いい大学を選びなさい。

Which candidate did you select for the job?
その仕事にどの候補者を選んだのですか?

He was selected from among twenty applicants.
彼は20人の応募者の中から選ばれた。

select players えり抜きの選手

a select restaurant 高級レストラン

select wines 極上ワイン

♦**select committee** *n.* 特別委員会

selection *n.* (choice) 選択; (selection of goods) 精選品, 特選品, (selection of literary works) 選集

That was a good selection you made.
いい選択をしたね。

That store has the best selection of foreign books in Tokyo.
その店は東京で一番、洋書の品ぞろえがいい。

a fine selection of French cheese
フランス産チーズの特選品

a selection of modern poetry
現代詩の選集

selective *adj.* (careful in choosing) 慎重に選ぶ, こだわりがある, (fussy) 好みがうるさい

have a selective memory 都合のいいことだけ覚えている

self *n.* 自己, 自分自身

pref. (**self-**) 自-, 自己-

He was his usual cheerful self.
彼は相変わらず陽気だった。

self-addressed *adj.* 返信用の, 自分あての

a self-addressed envelope 返信用封筒

self-centered *adj.* 自己中心的な, わがままな

self-confessed *adj.* …と自認する, …と公言する

self-confidence *n.* 自信

♦**self-confident** *adj.* 自信のある

self-conscious *adj.* 人目を気にする, 自意識過剰の

be self-conscious about 気にする

self-contained *adj.* (of community) 必要な物を完備した, (of person) 自制心のある

S

self-control *n.* 自制心

self-critical *adj.* 自己批判する

self-defense *n.* 自己防衛, (art of defending oneself) 護身術

♦ **Self-Defense Forces** *n.* 自衛隊

Air [Ground, Maritime] Self-Defense Forces
航空 [陸上, 海上] 自衛隊

self-determination *n.* 自己決定

self-discipline *n.* 自己鍛練, 自制(心)

have self-discipline 自制心をもつ

self-educated *adj.* 独学の

self-employed *adj.* 自営(業)の
n. (**the self-employed**) 自営業者

self-esteem *n.* 自尊心

have [lack] self-esteem
自尊心がある [欠けている]

self-evident *adj.* 自明の

self-explanatory *adj.* 自明の, 明らかな

self-expression *n.* 自己表現

self-fulfilling *adj.* 自己実現の

♦ **self-fulfillment** *n.* 自己実現

self-governing *adj.* 自治の

♦ **self-government** *n.* 自治

self-help *n.* 自助, 自立

self-image *n.* 自己像, 自己イメージ

have a poor self-image
自分について貧相なイメージをもっている

self-importance *n.* うぬぼれ, 尊大

♦ **self-important** *adj.* 尊大な, うぬぼれた

self-improvement *n.* 自己改善

self-indulgent *adj.* 勝手気ままな, 好き勝手な

self-inflicted *adj.* 自ら招いた

a self-inflicted injury
自傷行為によるけが

self-interest *n.* 私利私欲

be motivated by self-interest
私利私欲が動機である

self-introduction *n.* 自己紹介

selfish *adj.* わがままな, 自分勝手な, 身勝手な

That was a selfish thing to do.
身勝手なことをした。

♦ **selfishly** *adv.* わがままに, 自分勝手に

selfishness *n.* (self-centeredness) 自己中心, わがまま

selfless *adj.* 無欲の, 無私の

selfless devotion 無私の献身

self-made *adj.* (of successful person) 自力/独力で成功した

♦ **self-made person** *n.* たたき上げの人

self-pity *n.* 自己憐憫

self-portrait *n.* 自画像

self-possessed *adj.* 冷静な, 落ち着いた

self-preservation *n.* (instinct) 自衛本能

self-proclaimed *adj.* 自称…

the self-proclaimed "King of Pop"
自称「ポップスの王」

self-respect *n.* 自尊心

♦ **self-respecting** *adj.* 本当の, まともな

self-restraint *n.* (reserve) 遠慮, (control) 自制

show/exercise self-restraint 遠慮をする

self-righteous *adj.* 独りよがりの, 独善的な

self-sacrifice *n.* 自己犠牲

♦ **self-sacrificing** *adj.* 自己を犠牲にする, 献身的な

self-satisfied *adj.* 自己満足の

S

a self-satisfied smirk 自己満足の笑み

self-service *n.* セルフサービス [→ BUFFET[1]]

self-styled *adj.* 自称…

self-sufficient *adj.* 自給自足の

♦**self-sufficiency** *n.* 自給自足

self-taught *adj.* 独学の, 独習の

sell *v.* (sell A to B/sell B A) (AをBに) 売る, ((*formal*)) 売却する, (=try to get B to buy A) (AをBに) 売り込む, (offer for sale) 売っている, 販売している, (be sold) 売れる

Did you sell your car?
車を売ったの？

I couldn't sell all of the fruit.
果物が売れ残った。

He tried to sell his house.
彼は家を売却しようとした。

Do you sell yogurt?
ヨーグルトは売っていますか？

These plants are selling for $4 apiece.
ここの植木は一株4ドルです。

Are they selling well? 売れてる？

sell one's soul 魂を売る

♦**seller** *n.* 売る人, 売り手

a seller's market 売り手市場

selling *n.* 販売

buying and selling 売買

sell out *v.* 売り切れる

semantic *adj.* 意味の

semantics *n.*(subject of study) 意味論

semaphore *n.* 手旗信号

semblance *n.* (outward appearance) うわべ, 見せかけ

a semblance of normality
うわべだけ正常な状態

semen *n.* 精液

semester *n.* 学期, (**first semester**) 前期, (**second semester**) 後期

semi- *pref.* (half) 半-, (of competition) 準- [→ SEMIFINAL]

semicircle *n.* 半円(形)

semicolon *n.* セミコロン

semiconductor *n.* 半導体

semifinal(s) *n.* 準決勝

advance to the semifinals
準決勝に進出する

semiformal *adj.* (of clothing) 略式の, (of event) 準公式の

seminal *adj.* (influential) 将来大きな影響力をもつ

seminar *n.* ゼミ

Semitic *adj.* (of Arabic/Hebrew language) セム語の, (of speaker of Arabic/Hebrew) セム族の, (Jewish) ユダヤ人の

senate *n.* (**the Senate**) 上院

senator *n.* 上院議員

---

send *v.*

1 MAIL: 送る, 出す, (letter) 郵送する, (package) 発送する, (e-mail) 送信する, (money) 送金する

2 PERSON/PEOPLE: (cause to go) 行かせる, (dispatch) 派遣する, (transfer: to a branch office etc.) 転勤させる

3 CAUSE TO FLY: (**send flying**) 飛ばす

1 I sent the package yesterday.
昨日、小包を送りました。

Did you send them a thank-you card?
礼状を出しましたか？

This has come to the wrong address. We'll have to send it back.
配達先を間違えている。返送しなきゃ。

I sent money by electronic transfer.
電信で送金した。

2 The government sent a special envoy.
政府は特使を派遣した。

He's been sent to the Osaka office.
彼は大阪支社へ転勤になった。

3 The wind sent my hat flying.
風で帽子が飛ばされた。

♦**sender** *n.* (of letter) 差出人, (of parcel) 発送人, 送り主

send along *v.* (send) (…を添えて) 送る, (send A along with B) (B) といっしょに (Aを) 送る

Send along some flowers, too.
お花も添えて送ってください。

She sent a gift along with some money.
彼女はお金といっしょに贈り物を送った。

send away *v.* 追い払う, 追い返す

Send those door-to-door salespeople away.
あの訪問販売の人たちを追い返して。

♦**send away for** *v.* (product, catalog) 取り寄せる

send for *v.* 呼ぶ, (ask/order to come by means of a messenger) 呼びにやる

Send for a doctor!
お医者さんを呼んで！

send in *v.* (mail) 出す, 送る, (bring in: person to fix a situation) 送り込む

I sent my essay in a week ago.
1週間前に論文を送りました。

send off *v.* (mail) 送る [→SEND AWAY FOR]

I sent off a quick fax.
急いでファックスを送った。

send out *v.* (send A [person] out of B [room]) (AをBの) 外に出す; (radio wave) 発信する, (smoke, gas) 出す, 放つ

The teacher sent him out of the room.
先生はその子を教室の外に出した。

The machine sends out a signal so people know where you are.
居場所がわかるように、その機械から信号が発信されます。

---

senile *adj.* ぼけている, もうろくしている

become senile もうろくする

senility *n.* もうろく

senior

1 *adj.* HIGH-RANKING: 地位が上の, 上級の

2 *n.* OLDER PERSON: 年長者, (one's senior) 年上, (at company, school) 先輩, (elderly person) 高齢者, (お)年寄り

3 *n.* FOURTH-YEAR STUDENT: 4年生, (12th grader in Japan's 3-year high school system) 高校3年生

4 → SR.

1 He's senior to me, so I can't do anything about it.
あの人は地位が上なので、私には何もできません。

senior management 上級管理職

senior officials 高官

2 He's five years my senior.
彼は5歳年上です。

Admission is half price for seniors.
高齢者の入場料は半額です。

3 a senior in college 大学4年生

senior chief petty officer ***n.*** (in U.S. Navy) 上等兵曹

senior citizen ***n.*** 高齢者

senior master sergeant ***n.*** (in U.S. Air Force) 曹長

seniority ***n.*** (being older) 年上であること, 年長であること, (having higher rank) 地位が上であること

♦**seniority system** ***n.*** 年功序列制度

sensation ***n.*** (ability to feel) 感覚; (public reaction) センセーション, 大評判

a pleasant sensation 快感

He lost all sensation on his left side.
彼は左半身の感覚をすべて失った。

The movie caused a sensation.
その映画はセンセーションを巻き起こした[大評判になった]。

sensational ***adj.*** (of news, event) センセーショナルな, 世間をあっと言わせる, (of article, film: intended to excite/upset) 扇情的な; (fabulous) すばらしい

sensational news
世間をあっと言わせるニュース

a sensational article 扇情的な記事

sense

1 ***n.*** ONE OF THE FIVE SENSES: 感覚

2 ***v.*** FEEL/NOTICE: 感じる, (…に)気づく, 感づく

3 ***n.*** GOOD JUDGMENT: 分別, 良識

4 ***n.*** AWARENESS: 認識, 感覚, 観念 [→ FEELING]

5 ***n.*** ABILITY TO UNDERSTAND: 感覚, センス

6 ***n.*** NORMAL STATE OF MIND: (**senses**) 正気

7 ***n.*** MEANING: 意味

1 the five senses 五感

the sense of sight [hearing, smell, taste, touch]
視覚 [聴覚, 嗅覚, 味覚, 触覚]

If it weren't for our senses, we wouldn't know we were here.
感覚がなければ、こうやって生きていることもわからないだろう。

2 Sensing he wasn't wanted, he left.
彼は歓迎されていないことに気づいて、引き揚げた。

I'm beginning to sense trouble.
厄介なことになってきたようだ。

3 It's good you had the sense to refuse any more drink.
君に、あれ以上の酒を断るだけの分別があってよかったよ。

She has a strong sense of right and wrong.
彼女は善悪の分別をきちんとわきまえている。

I thought you had more sense than that.
あなたには、もっと良識があると思っていた。

4 a sense of duty 義務感

a sense of direction 方向感覚

5 He has a good sense of humor.
彼はユーモアのセンスがある。

6 come to one's senses 正気に返る

lose one's senses 気が狂う

7 In what sense do you mean that?
どういう意味でしょうか？

in a sense ある意味で

In a sense, we were all wrong.
ある意味で、私たちはみんな間違っていた。

make sense (have meaning) 意味を成す, (be rational) 筋が通っている

His explanation made no sense at all.
彼の説明は全く意味を成さなかった。

What she said just didn't make sense.
彼女の話はまるで筋が通っていなかった。

You're not making any sense at all.
あなたの言ってることは全く訳がわからないよ。

make sense of (…が)理解できる, わかる

Could you make sense of what he was saying?
あの人の言っていることが理解できましたか？

talk sense 筋の通ったことを言う, まともなことを言う

If you can't talk sense, shut up.
まともなことを言えないのなら、黙っていなさい。

there's no sense in doing …しても意味がない, …してもむだだ

There's no sense in talking to her if she won't listen.
彼女が聞く耳をもたないのなら、話しても意味がない。

senseless *adj.* (foolish) ばかげた, (meaningless) 無意味な

a senseless act of violence
無意味な暴力行為

sensibility *n.* (ability to experience deep feelings) 繊細な感受性, (concerning art) 鋭い感性; (**sensibilities**) 感情

offend someone's sensibilities
(…の)感情を傷つける

sensible *adj.* (showing good sense) 良識のある, 分別のある, 賢明な

Now there's a sensible fellow.
あれは分別のある男だ。

I thought it was very sensible of her not to marry him.
彼女が彼と結婚しなかったのは、とても賢明だと思った。

sensitive *adj.* 敏感な, デリケートな, 繊細な, (easily hurt) 傷つきやすい, (be sensitive about/to) 気にする, (…に) 神経質だ

sensitive skin <u>敏感な</u> [デリケートな] 肌

My eyes are very sensitive to light.
私の目は光にとても敏感です。

He's too sensitive to criticism.
彼は批判を気にしすぎる。

sensitivity *n.* (understanding with respect to another's feelings) 思いやり; (of skin, eyes etc.) 敏感さ, (ease with which one is upset/offended) 感じやすさ, 感受性

sensor *n.* センサー

sensory *adj.* (related to the senses) 感覚の, 知覚の

sensory perception 知覚

sensual *adj.* (sexual) 官能的な, (physical) 肉体的な

sensuous *adj.* (of art, music) 感覚的な, 心地よい

sentence *n.* (grammatical unit) 文, センテンス; (punishment) 判決, (prison sentence) 懲役

v. (…に) 判決を下す, 宣告する

This sentence doesn't make sense.
この文は意味を成さない/((*informal*)) この文はちんぷんかんぷんだ。

The judge's sentence was harsh.
裁判官が下した判決は厳しかった。

He was sentenced to life in prison.
彼は終身刑の判決を受けた。

sentiment *n.* (emotion) 感情

sentimental *adj.* 感情的な, センチメンタルな

sentry *n.* (soldier) 歩哨

separate

1 *adj.* APART: 別々の, 分かれた

2 *v.* DIVIDE: 分ける, 分離する, (two people) 引き離す

3 *v.* OF COUPLE: 別れる, (live separately) 別居する [→ DIVORCE]

4 *adj.* DIFFERENT: 異なった, 別の, 別個の

1 Keep your luggage separate from ours.
荷物は、私たちのと別々にしてください。

The garage is separate from the house.
車庫は家と分かれている。

2 There's a knack to separating the yolk from the egg white.
卵の黄身と白身を分けるには、こつがある。

Those two are always together. You can't separate them.
あの二人はいつもいっしょだ。引き離すことはできない。

3 They separated two or three years ago.
二人は2、3年前に別れた [別居した]。

4 We face two separate problems.
私たちは二つの異なった問題に直面している。

That's a separate issue.
それは別問題だ。

♦ **separately** *adv.* 別々に, 別個に

pay (a restaurant bill) separately
(レストランの勘定を)割り勘にする

separation *n.* (of couple) 別居; (act of separating: things) 分離

separatism *n.* 分離主義

separatist *n.* 分離主義者

sepia *adj.* (color) セピア色の

September *n.* 9月, 九月

septic *adj.* (of wound) 敗血症の

septic tank *n.* 汚水浄化槽

sequel *n.* (continuation) 続き, (to book, movie etc.) 続編

sequence *n.* (series) 連続, (**a sequence of**) 一連の, (order) 順序

a sequence of events 一連の行事

be out of sequence 順序が狂っている

sequin *n.* スパンコール

serene *adj.* 落ち着いた, 平静な

sergeant *n.* 軍曹

sergeant first class *n.* (in U.S. Army) 一等軍曹

sergeant major *n.* (in U.S. Marine Corps) 上級曹長

serial *n.* (part of story) シリーズ

adj. 連続の, (of novel) 連載の

a serial killer 連続殺人犯

a serial novel 連載小説

♦ **serial number** *n.* 通し番号, 連番

serialize *v.* (novel) 連載する

series *n.* シリーズ, 連続, (**a series of**) 一連の, 連続の

a TV series 連続テレビ番組

a series of lectures 連続講義

serious *adj.*

1 CAUSE FOR WORRY: (of illness) 重い, 重大な, 深刻な

2 EARNEST/SINCERE: 真剣な, 本気の, 真面目な

3 DIFFICULT/HIGHBROW: かたい, シリアスな

1 a serious illness 重い病気 [重病]

Crime is one of the most serious problems facing society.
犯罪は最も重大な社会問題の一つだ。

A serious situation has developed in the nation's capital.
首都で深刻な事態が起きている。

2 I'm serious. 私は真剣なんです。

They are engaged in a serious discussion right now.
彼らは今、真剣に話し合っているところです。

I thought it was a joke, but no, they were serious.
冗談だと思ったら、彼らは本気だった。

She's a serious student.
彼女は真面目な学生です。

Is it a serious relationship?
真面目なお付き合いですか？

3 a serious movie かたい映画
serious literature 純文学

seriously *adv.* (sincerely) 真面目に, 本気で, (truly) 本当に; (terribly) ひどく, (deeply) 深く

Are you seriously suggesting I ask her out on a date?
彼女をデートに誘ったらいいって、本気で言っているのか？

The dog was seriously injured.
犬はひどいけがをした。

sermon *n.* 説教

serpent *n.* ヘビ, 蛇

serum *n.* 血清

servant *n.* (maid) メイド, お手伝い, (retainer) 使用人, 召し使い, (servant girl) 女中

serve

1 *v.* **PERFORM DUTIES FOR:** (…に) 奉仕する, (…のために) 働く, (company) (…に) 勤務する, (military) (…に) 服する

2 *v.* **IN RESTAURANT:** (take orders from customers) (…の) 注文を聞く, (bring out food/drink) (料理/飲み物を)出す

3 *v.* **BE USABLE AS:** (**serve as**) …として使える, …になる

4 *v.* **SPEND TIME:** (in military) 軍務に服する, (in prison) 服役する

5 *n., v.* **IN TENNIS:** サーブ(する)

1 He served his country in two world wars.
2度の世界大戦で、彼は国のために戦った。

She has served the company loyally for more than twenty years.
彼女は20年以上も会社に忠実に働いている。

We served in the same regiment.
私たちは同じ連隊で兵役に就いていた。

2 Have you been served yet?
もう、ご注文は伺いましたか？

You'll wait ages to be served in that restaurant.
あのレストランは、料理が出てくるまですごく待たされるよ。

We were served Peking duck.
北京ダックが出された。

3 This book will serve as a useful reference for scholars.
この本は学者にとって役に立つ資料になるだろう。

4 He served twenty-five years in prison.
その人は25年間、刑務所で服役した。

5 That player has a strong serve.
あの選手はサーブが強いね。

serve a purpose 役に立つ

serve the needs of …の要求に応える

service

1 *n.* SYSTEM TO SUPPLY PUBLIC NEEDS: 事業, 業務

2 *n.* WORK DONE TO HELP OTHERS: 奉仕, (commercial/customer service) サービス

3 *n.* MAINTENANCE: 点検

4 *v.* MAINTAIN: 点検する

5 *n.* FORM OF WORSHIP: 礼拝

6 *n.* GOVERNMENT DEPARTMENT/BRANCH: 官庁, 省庁

7 *n.* ARMED FORCES: 軍隊, (**the service/services**) 陸海空軍

1 the train service 鉄道事業
the postal service 郵便事業
welfare services 福祉事業

2 a service to the community
地域社会への奉仕活動
It's a free service. 無料サービスです。
The service in that restaurant is good.
あのレストランはサービスがいい。
the service industry サービス業

3 The car needs a service every year.
車は毎年、点検が必要だ。

4 You'd better get the car serviced.
車を点検に出したほうがいい。

5 There's a service every Sunday.
毎週日曜日に礼拝がある。

6 I took the civil service exam.
公務員試験を受けた。

7 join the service 入隊する

at your service 何なりとお申し付けください

be of service (to) (…の) 役に立つ
Not at all. I'm glad I could be of service.
どういたしまして。お役に立ててうれしいです。

no longer in service (of phone number) 現在使われていない

out of service (of machine) 休止中で, (of bus, train) 回送中で

service charge *n.* 手数料

serviceman, -woman *n.* 軍人

servile *adj.* 卑屈な

serving *n.* (of food) 1人前, (of drink) 1杯

sesame *n.* ゴマ, 胡麻

♦**sesame oil** *n.* ゴマ油

session *n.* 会, 会議, 会合, (of court) 開廷, (of congress) 会期, (of music etc.) セッション
a group-therapy session 集団療法の会
an emergency session of the UN
国連の緊急会議
a jam session ジャムセッション

in session (of court) 開廷中で
The court is still in session.
裁判所はまだ開廷中です。

set

1 *n.* NUMBER OF THINGS THAT GO TOGETHER: セット, 一組, 一そろい

2 *v.* PUT: 置く

3 *v.* BE LOCATED: (**be set in**) …にある, …に位置している

4 *v.* TAKE PLACE: (**be set in**: of play, novel, film) …を舞台にしている

5 *v.* **SCHEDULE/FIX:** 決める, 取り決める

6 *v.* **OF SUN:** 沈む

7 *v.* **CLOCK/MACHINE:** セットする, 合わせる, (alarm clock) かける

8 ***adj.*** **FIXED/DECIDED:** 所定の, 決まった

1 a chess set チェスセット

Do you have another set of coasters?
コースターは、もう一組ありますか？

2 Set it on the table, will you.
テーブルに置いてください。

You can set that box down right here.
その箱はここに置けるよ。

3 The building is set within a beautiful park.
その建物は美しい公園の中にあります。

4 The novel is set in nineteenth-century Japan.
その小説は 19 世紀の日本を舞台にしている。

5 Have you set a date for the wedding?
結婚式の日取りを決めた？

6 The further north you go, the earlier the sun sets in winter.
北へ行くほど、冬に日が沈むのが早くなる。

7 I set the alarm clock every day.
毎日目覚まし時計をかけている。

8 a set fee 所定の料金

a set phrase 慣用句 [成句]

COMMON EXPRESSIONS WITH "SET"

set a bone 骨接ぎをする
set a clock 時間/時計を合わせる
set a (sports) record 記録を樹立する
set a target 目標を定める
set at ease 安心させる
set a time/date 時間/日を決める
set a trap わなを仕掛ける
set fire to ...に火をつける
set free 自由にする, 解放する
set one's hair 髪をセットする
set the table 食卓の用意をする
set to work 仕事を始める

be set in one's ways 自分のやり方に固執する, (be stubborn) がんこだ

set an example (of behavior) 模範になる

You need to set an example for the children.
子供たちの模範にならなくてはいけない。

set about *v.* (start doing) ...に取りかかる

They set about their work.
彼らは仕事に取りかかった。

set apart *v.* (cause to be different or stand out) 区別する, 際立たせる

His accent sets him apart from the others.
アクセントだけで、彼の声だとわかる。

set aside *v.* (money, time) 取っておく; (differences) 無視する

set back *v.* (delay) 遅らせる, (hinder) 妨げる [→ COST]

A lack of funds has set back the film's production.
資金不足で、映画製作が遅れた。

set off *v.*

1 **DEPART:** 出発する, 出かける

2 **TRIGGER:** (alarm) 鳴らす, (panic, chain reaction) 引き起こす

3 **CAUSE TO EXPLODE:** (bomb) 爆発させる, (fireworks) 打ち上げる

1 They set off early in the morning.
彼らは朝早く出発した。

2 Someone set off the fire alarm.
誰かが火災報知器を鳴らした。

3 set off a bomb 爆弾を爆発させる
set off fireworks 花火を打ち上げる

set out *v.*

1 AIM: めざす

2 ARRANGE ITEMS/FACTS/POINTS: 並べる

3 BEGIN A JOURNEY: 出発する, 出かける

1 They failed to achieve what they had set out to do.
彼らは、めざしたことを成し遂げられなかった。

2 The excavated tools were set out on the table.
発掘された道具が台に並べられた。

3 They set out for the North Pole in late August.
8月の終わりに、彼らは北極に向けて出発した。

set up *v.*

1 ESTABLISH: (business) 設立する, 起こす, (set A [person] up in B [business]) (AのBを) 援助する, 支援する

2 PREPARE FOR USE: (stereo) セットアップする, (board in board game) …の準備をする, (tent) 張る

3 PUT UPRIGHT: 立てる

1 They set up a business three years ago.
彼らは3年前に事業を起こした。

2 Have you set up the computer?
コンピューターをセットアップした?

3 Set the chest of drawers up against the wall, please.
たんすを壁際に立ててください。

set up shop 開業する, 店を出す

setback *n.* (hindrance) 妨げ, (defeat) 敗北, (delay) 遅れ

It was a grave setback for the government.
それは政府にとって大きな敗北だった。

setting *n.* (surroundings) 環境, (of play, film, novel) 舞台, 設定, 背景; (of computer, machine) 設定

The setting was beautiful.
環境はすばらしかった。

The setting of the novel was the twenty-second century.
小説の舞台は22世紀だった。

How do you change the settings?
環境設定はどうやって変更するの?

settle *v.*

1 REACH AN AGREEMENT CONCERNING: (problem, dispute) 解決する, (…に) 決着をつける, (settle a case out of court) 示談にする, 和解する

2 PAY: 支払う, 払う

3 MAKE ONE'S HOME IN: (settle in) (…に) 落ち着く

4 COME TO REST: (of dust) 積もる, たまる, (of impurities in a liquid) 沈殿する

1 They seem to have settled their differences.
互いの食い違いを解決したようだ。

That issue has already been settled.
その問題はすでに決着がついた。

Eventually, the case was settled out of court.
結局、その件は示談になった。

2 He still hasn't settled the bill.
彼はまだ勘定を払っていない。

3 They moved around a lot, but finally settled in the south of France.
彼らは住まいを転々としたが、最終的に南フランスに落ち着いた。

4 Dust has settled on the furniture.
家具に、ほこりが積もっている。

settle down *v.* (relax) くつろぐ, ゆっくりする, (calm down) 落ち着く

They settled down in front of the fire.
火の前でくつろいだ。

Come on now, settle down and find a book to read.
さあさあ、落ち着いて本でも読みなさい。

settle down and marry/get married and settle down 身を固める

I wish he'd settle down and marry.
彼には身を固めてほしいと思っている。

---

settled *adj.* (of people, life) 落ち着いた; (of matter/issue concerning which an agreement has been reached) 決着済みの, 解決した

settlement *n.* (agreement concerning a legal dispute) 和解, 合意; (place) 入植地

settler *n.* 入植者, 移民

seven *n.* 7, 七 [also read しち]
adj.,pron. 7の, (people) 7人(の), (things) 7個(の), 七つ(の)

seventeen *n.* 17, 十七
adj., pron. 17の, (people) 17人(の), (things) 17個(の)

seventeenth *n.* 第17, 17番目, (date) 17日
adj. 第17の, 17番目の

seventh *n.* 第7, 7番目, (date) 7日, (one seventh) 7分の1
adj. 第7の, 7番目の

seventy *n.* 70, 七十, (**the seventies**) 70年代, (**one's seventies**) 70代
adj., pron. 70の, (people) 70人(の), (things) 70個(の)

sever *n.* (cut off) 切る, 切断する, (ties) 断つ

several *adj.* (two or more) いくつかの, 何-, 数-

There were several messages on the answering machine.
留守電にいくつかの伝言が入っていた。

severe *adj.* (strict) 厳しい, 厳格な, (terrible, serious) ひどい, 深刻な

severe punishment 厳しい刑罰

I think you were too severe with him.
あなたは彼に厳しすぎたと思う。

severe damage ひどい被害

severely *adv.* (strictly) 厳しく, (terribly) ひどく, 大変

be severely injured
ひどいけがをする [重傷を負う]

severity *n.* 厳しさ, 厳格さ

sew *v.* 縫う, (sew A on B) (AをBに) 縫い付ける, (sew A and B together) (AとBを) 縫い合わせる, (do sewing) 縫い物をする, 裁縫をする

Thanks for sewing the button on my sleeve.
そでのボタンを付けてくれてありがとう。

Can you sew? 裁縫ができますか?

sewage *n.* 下水

♦**sewage disposal** *n.* 下水処理

sewer *n.* 下水管

sewing *n.* 裁縫, 縫い物

♦ **sewing machine** *n.* ミシン

sex *n.* (gender) 性, 性別, 男女, (of animal) 雌雄; (sexual intercourse) セックス, 性交

What sex is this rabbit?
このウサギの性別はどちらですか？

a book about sex セックスに関する本

Did you have sex with him?
彼とセックスしたの [寝たの]？

sexism *n.* 性差別

sexist *adj.* (of behavior, remark) 性差別的な, (of person) 性差別をする

sexual *adj.* 性的な

a sexual relationship 性的な関係

♦ **sexual assault** *n.* 婦女暴行

sexual discrimination *n.* 性差別

sexual harassment *n.* セクシャルハラスメント, セクハラ

sexual intercourse *n.* 性交

sexual orientation *n.* 性的嗜好

sexuality *n.* (being male or female) 性別, (sexual desire) 性欲, (sexual interest) 性的関心

sexy *adj.* セクシーな, 色っぽい, 色気のある

sh *interj.* (be quiet!) しっ!, 静かに!

shabby *adj.* (of appearance) みすぼらしい, ぼろぼろの, (of building) 古ぼけた

shack *n.* 掘っ建て小屋

shade

1 *n.* SHADOW: 日陰, 陰

2 *v.* PROTECT/BLOCK FROM SUNLIGHT: 日差しから守る, おおう

3 *n.* WINDOW SHADE: ブラインド, 日よけ

4 *n.* DEGREE/DEPTH OF DARKNESS: 影, 陰影, (color) 色合い

5 *v.* DARKEN WITH PENCIL LINES: (shade in) (…に) 陰影をつける

6 *n.* SUNGLASSES: (**shades**) サングラス

1 It was so hot I had to stand in the shade.
あまりに暑かったので、日陰に入らずにはいられなかった。

The shade was nice and cool.
日陰は涼しくて気持ちがよかった。

There's some shade over there, under those trees.
向こうの木の下に日陰があるよ。

2 The sun was so bright I had to shade my eyes.
太陽がまぶしくて、手をかざして目をおおわなければならなかった。

3 Pull the shades down, will you.
ブラインドを下ろしてくれる？

4 The shade is too dark in that picture.
あの絵は陰影が強すぎる。

5 I'd like you to shade in the background.
背景に陰影をつけてほしい。

6 Nice shades. Where did you get them?
おしゃれなサングラスだね。どこで買ったの？

shadow *n.* (area of shade) 影, (partial darkness) 陰, 暗がり; (eye shadow) アイシャドー

dark shadows 暗い影

The shadow of the tree grew longer as the sun set.
太陽が沈むにつれて、木の影が長くなっていった。

The whole room is in shadow.

部屋全体が陰になっている。

shadowy ***adj.*** (full of shadows) 陰の多い, (shadowlike) 影のような

shady ***adj.*** (having shade) 木陰の, 日陰の; (suspicious) 怪しい

shaft ***n.*** (of cylindrical object) 柄, (in machine) シャフト

shake

1 ***v.*** **CAUSE TO MOVE:** 振る, (in hands) 揺する, 揺さぶる, (cocktail) シェークする

2 ***v.*** **TREMBLE:** (of person) 震える, (of building) 揺れる, 振動する

3 ***v.*** **SHAKE HANDS:** 握手する, (shake sb's hand) (…の) 手を握る

4 ***n.*** **MOVEMENT:** (a shake) 一振り

5 ***n.*** **MILK SHAKE:** ミルクシェイク

1 He shook his head.
彼は首を横に振った。

Go ahead and shake the dice.
先にさいころを振って。

Did you shake the salad dressing?
ドレッシングを振った?

2 I was so cold I couldn't stop shaking.
寒くて震えが止まらなかった。

Her voice shook with emotion.
彼女は感極まって声が震えた。

The whole building shook.
建物全体が揺れた。

3 They shook hands after the first round of talks.
初会談後、彼らは握手をした。

He shook my hand and congratulated me.
彼は私の手を握って祝ってくれた。

4 Give the spray a good shake.
スプレーをよく振ってください。

5 I'll take a chocolate shake.
チョコレートシェイクを下さい。

shake off ***v.*** (cause to fall by shaking) 振り落とす, (brush off) 振り払う

The kids were trying to shake the apples off the branches.
子供たちは木を揺すって、リンゴを振り落とそうとしていた。

shake up ***v.*** (**be shaken up**: of person: be disturbed) 動揺する, 混乱する

shakeup ***n.*** (change of personnel) 刷新, 整理

shakuhachi ***n.*** (flute) 尺八

play the shakuhachi 尺八を吹く

shaky ***adj.*** (of voice) 震える, (of desk: wobbly) ぐらぐらする, ガタガタの, (of position, venture: not stable) 不安定な, (of language skill) たどたどしい

shall ***aux.***

1 **EXPRESSING INTENTION:** …します, …するつもりです

2 **EXPRESSING EXPECTATION:** …します, …でしょう, (**shall have done**) …したでしょう

3 **IN COMMAND:** …すべし, …するものとする, (**shall not**) …するべからず, …してはならない [→ WILL¹ 6]

4 **OFFERING TO DO:** (**shall I…?**) …しましょうか

1 I shall visit Mr. Inoue first.
まずは井上さんのお宅に伺います。

Successful candidates shall be notified in writing.

合格者には書面にて通知します。

2 We shall be landing in fifteen minutes.
あと15分で着陸します。

I shall miss you. 寂しくなるよ。

3 No, you shall not go tomorrow, nor the next day.
いや､明日もあさっても行ってはならない。

4 Shall I mail this letter for you?
この手紙を出しましょうか？

shallow ***adj.*** 浅い, (of person) 浅はかな, 深みのない

a shallow pond 浅い池

It's shallower over here.
こっちのほうが浅いですよ。

He strikes me as rather shallow.
あの人は、あまり深みのない男だという気がする。

♦**shallowness** ***n.*** 浅さ, (of person) 浅はかさ

sham ***n.*** (deception) ごまかし, 見せかけ, (imitation) 偽物

adj. ごまかしの, 偽の, 見せかけの

shambles ***n.*** (confused mess) 大混乱, めちゃくちゃ

shame ***n.***

1 EMBARRASSMENT: 恥, 恥ずかしさ

2 DISHONOR: 不名誉, (person/thing that brings disgrace) 恥, 恥さらし

3 PITY: 残念, 気の毒

1 I almost died of shame when I heard what he'd done.
彼がしたことを聞いて、死ぬほど恥ずかしかった。

2 You've brought shame on the family.
((*masculine*)) お前は一家の恥さらしだ。

3 What a shame.
それは残念ですね。

♦**shameful** ***adj.*** 恥ずかしい

shameless ***adj.*** 恥知らずな

shampoo ***n.*** シャンプー [→ picture of BATHROOM]

shamrock ***n.*** シロツメクサ

shank ***n.*** (meat) すね肉

shape

1 ***n.*** FORM: 形

2 ***v.*** GIVE FORM TO: (…で) 形を作る, 形作る, (idea, plan) 具体化する, 形にする, 形成する

3 ***n.*** PHYSICAL CONDITION: 調子, 状態

4 ***n.*** SHADOW: 影

1 a rectangular shape 長方形

What an odd shape!
なんて奇妙な形だ！

Do you have a bowl the same shape but with a different design?
同じ形で違う柄のボウルはありませんか？

2 I shaped the clay into a reclining figure.
粘土で横たわる人間の姿を作った。

It was ancient Greece and Rome that shaped Western thinking most.
西洋思想を形成したのは、主に古代ギリシャ・ローマだった。

3 You're in no shape to play tonight.
今夜は出場できる状態ではないよ。

be out of shape (in poor physical condition) 体がなまっている

I'm totally out of shape.
すっかり体がなまっている。

get into shape 体を鍛える

You'd better get into shape quick.

S

早く体を鍛えたほうがいい。

take shape 具体化する, 形になる

It was rewarding to see our ideas begin to take shape.
我々のアイデアが具体化していくのを見て、報われる気がした。

shaped *adj.* (shaped like) …のような形の, (**-shaped**) …形の

a U-shaped pipe U字形のパイプ

shapeless *adj.* 形がはっきりしない, 形のない

share

1 *v.* USE JOINTLY: 共用する, 共同で使う, (own jointly) 共有する

2 *v.* DIVIDE: 分ける, (**share among/between**) …の間で分け合う, (cost, work) 分担する

3 *n.* PORTION: 分, 分け前

4 *n.* BURDEN: (of work) 分担, 役割

5 *n.* STOCK: (in company) 株

1 He shares an apartment with two other students.
彼はほかの二人の学生とアパートを共同で使っている。

2 He shared the candy with the other kids.
彼はほかの子供たちにお菓子を分けた。

They share the cost between them.
二人は費用を分担している。

3 Where's my share? 私の分は？

He's had more than his fair share of bad luck.
あの人は人一倍運が悪い。

4 You haven't done your share yet.
君はまだ自分の分担をやっていない。

5 We bought shares in the company.
私たちは、その会社の株を買った。

shareholder *n.* 株主

shark *n.* サメ, 鮫; (swindler) 詐欺師, (greedy person) 欲張りな人

a loan shark 高利貸し [サラ金]

sharp

1 *adj.* NOT BLUNT: (of blade) 鋭い, よく切れる, (of point, corner) とがった

2 *adj.* DEFINITE: はっきりした, 明確な

3 *adj.* CHANGING DIRECTION QUICKLY: 急な

4 *adj.* SHRILL: 甲高い

5 *adj.* OF MUSICAL NOTE: 嬰-, -シャープ

6 *adj.* QUICK-WITTED: 頭の切れる, 聡明な

7 *adj.* OF TASTE: ぴりっとした

8 *adj.* OF PAIN: 鋭い, 激しい

9 *adj.* WELL DRESSED: おしゃれな, かっこいい

10 *adj.* BITING: (of criticism) しんらつな, 痛烈な, (of wind) 身を切るような

11 *adv.* ON THE DOT: (of time) きっかりに, ちょうど

1 The blade is very sharp.
刃がとても鋭い。

sharp claws 鋭い爪

a sharp knife よく切れるナイフ

a sharp pencil 先のとがった鉛筆

2 a sharp distinction はっきりした区別

draw a sharp line between
…の間に明確な線引きをする

3 a sharp bend (in the road) 急カーブ

4 a clear, sharp voice よく通る甲高い声

5 B sharp 嬰ロ音

6 The boy is very sharp.
とても頭のいい子です。

S

7 a sharp taste ぴりっとした味

8 a sharp pain 鋭い痛み

9 You look sharp tonight.
今夜はかっこいいですね。

10 sharp criticism しんらつな批評
sharp words きつい言葉

11 at 5 o'clock sharp 5時きっかりに

♦**sharpness** *n.* (of blade) 鋭さ; (of image) 鮮明さ; (cleverness) 利口

sharpen *v.* (knife) 研ぐ, (pencil) 削る, とがらす

sharply *adv.* (rise, fall) 急に; (criticize) 厳しく; (pointed) 鋭く

shatter *v.* (break into small pieces) 粉々に割る, (dreams, hopes) 打ち砕く, (spoil, ruin) 台なしにする, (**be shattered by**: bad news) …に取り乱す

shave *v.* (face) ひげをそる, 顔をそる, (legs) 足の毛をそる; (wood) 削る
n. (cutting of a beard) ひげそり
He's so hairy he has to shave twice a day.
あの人は1日に2度そらないといけないほど、ひげが濃い。
When you're done shaving, I need to use the mirror.
ひげそりが済んだら、そこの鏡を使わせて。
He's shaved off his beard.
彼はあごひげをそり落とした。
You need a shave.
ひげをそったほうがいいよ。

shaving *n.* (act of cutting a beard) ひげそり; (**shavings**: of wood) 削りくず

♦**shaving cream** *n.* シェービングクリーム, ひげそりクリーム

shawl *n.* ショール

she *pron.* 彼女は/が, あの人は/が [NOTE: Avoid using 彼女 in reference to social superiors. Use the person's name, followed by さん, or job title instead.]
She's a teacher. 彼女は教師です。
Who is she? あの人は誰?

shear *v.* (fleece from a sheep) (…の) 毛を刈る
n. (**shears**) 大ばさみ

sheath *n.* (for sword) さや

sheathe *v.* (put in a sheath) さやに納める; (**be sheathed in**) …でおおわれている

shed[1] *v.* (tears) 流す, (of dog: shed hair) 毛が抜ける, (of snake: shed skin) 脱皮する
shed blood 血を流す [→ KILL]
shed light on → LIGHT[1]

shed[2] *n.* (building) 物置, 小屋

sheep *n.* ヒツジ, 羊

sheepish *adj.* (of smile) 気弱そうな, 恥ずかしそうな

sheer *adj.* (used emphatically: complete) 全くの, 完全な; (thin) ごく薄い; (vertical) 垂直の
sheer nonsense 全くばかげたこと
sheer silk ごく薄いシルク
a sheer drop 垂直な落下

sheet *n.* (**sheets**: bed linens) シーツ, 敷布; (a single sheet) 1枚
Have you changed the sheets?
シーツを取り替えた?
clean sheets きれいなシーツ
a sheet of paper 紙1枚
a sheet of metal 金属板

as white as a sheet (of surprised/ill-looking face) 顔が真っ青になって

sheikh *n.* 首長

shelf *n.* 棚, (bookshelf) 本棚

Could you put it back on the shelf?
棚に戻してくれる？

The supermarket shelves are full of processed food.
スーパーの棚は、加工食品であふれている。

shell *n.* (of egg, nut, oyster) 殻, (of turtle, crab) 甲羅, (of pea) さや; (framework) 骨組み, (exterior) 外観

v. (nuts/peas) 殻/さやから取り出す, (…の) 殻/さやを取る

walnut shell クルミの殻

crack open the shell 殻を割る

Shell the beans and boil them for ten minutes.
豆をさやから出して10分ゆでます。

shellfish *n.* (mollusk) 貝, (crustacean) 甲殻類

shelter *n.* (refuge) 避難所, (hut) 小屋

v. (criminal) かくまう, (child) 守る [→ PROTECT]

a bus shelter バス待合所

We built a shelter. 小屋を建てた。

The family sheltered him from the police.
その家族が警察の手から彼をかくまった。

The trees sheltered us from the rain.
木の下で雨宿りした。

food, shelter, and clothing 衣食住

sheltered *adj.* (of person, life) 守られた, 保護された

live a sheltered life 守られた生活をする

shelve *v.* 棚に置く, (postpone) 延期する, 棚上げにする

shepherd(ess) *n.* (女の) 羊飼い

sherbet *n.* シャーベット

sheriff *n.* 保安官

sherry *n.* シェリー酒

shiatsu *n.* 指圧

shield *n.* 盾

v. (protect) 守る, (cover) おおう

shift *n.* シフト, (work period) 勤務時間, (**shifts**) 交替

v. (move) 移す, (change) 変える

What shift are you working next week?
来週のシフトはどうなってる？

There are two shifts here—the day shift and the night shift.
ここは日勤と夜勤の2交替制です。

shift into second [third] (gear)
ギアをセカンド [サード] に変える

shifty *adj.* (deceitful) ずるい, (suspicious) 怪しい

shimmer *v.* (of water) チラチラ光る, かすかに光る

shin *n.* 向こうずね, すね [→ picture of BODY], (shinbone) けい骨

shine

1 *v.* GIVE/REFLECT LIGHT: 照る, 光る, 光り輝く, (of face) 輝く, (of candlelight) ともる

2 *v.* DIRECT A BEAM OF LIGHT: (shine a light in/on) (ライトで…を) 照らす

3 *n.* LUSTER: 光沢, つや

4 *v.* POLISH: 磨く

1 The sun's shining today.
今日は太陽が照っている。

A candle shone in remembrance.

S

記念にろうそくがともっていた。

2 Do you mind not shining that flashlight in my face?
懐中電灯で顔を照らすのをやめてくれませんか？

3 The brass had a good shine to it.
真ちゅうは、すばらしい光沢を放っていた。

Your shoes have a good shine.
靴がぴかぴかだね。

4 It'll take all morning to shine the floors.
床を磨くには午前中いっぱいかかる。

shingle[1] *n.* (for roof) 屋根板

shingle[2] *n.* (small stones on seashore) 小石, 砂利, (stretch of seashore) 砂利の浜

shingles *n.* (infection) 帯状疱疹

Shinto *n.* 神道

♦**Shinto priest** *n.* 神主(さん)

Shinto shrine *n.* 神社

shiny *adj.* ぴかぴかの, (of fabric) てかてかの, (bright) 明るい

ship *n.* (vessel) 船

v. (send by sea) 船便で送る, (send by air) 飛行機で送る, 空輸する

They traveled around the world by ship.
彼らは船で世界中を旅行した。

The cargo was loaded onto a ship.
貨物が船積みされた。

♦**shipbuilding** *n.* 造船

shipment *n.* (mailing) 発送, 輸送, (cargo) 積み荷

shipping *n.* (postal fee) 発送料, (act of mailing) 発送, 輸送; (shipping industry) 海運業, (ships) 船舶

shipshape *adj.* きちんとした

shipwreck *n.* 難破船

shipyard *n.* 造船所

shirk *v.* (avoid: responsibility, duty) 回避する; (slack off) 怠ける

shirt *n.* シャツ, (dress shirt) ワイシャツ, (T-shirt) Tシャツ

put a clean shirt on きれいなシャツを着る

♦**shirttail** *n.* シャツのすそ

shit *n.* (feces) 大便, (animal's) ふん, (human's) ((*informal*)) うんこ, (rubbish) ごみ; (nonsense) でたらめ

v. (defecate) ((*informal*)) うんこする

interj. くそっ, ちくしょう

That's a crock of shit!
それはでたらめだ!

shiver *v.* 震える, 身震いする

n. 身震い

He gives me the shivers.
あの人には身震いする。

get the shivers 身震いする, ぞっとする

shoal[1] *n.* (underwater sandbar) 砂州

shoal[2] *n.* (of fish) 群れ, 大群

shock *n.* (electric shock) 電気ショック, 感電, (blow) ショック, 打撃, 衝撃

v. (…に) 衝撃を与える, ショックを与える, (give an electric shock to) (…に) 電気ショックを与える

The death of his son came as a terrible shock.
息子の死は彼に大きな衝撃を与えた。

shocked *adj.* (upset) ショックを受けた, (surprised) びっくりした, (astounded) あきれた

They were shocked by the news.
そのニュースに彼らはショックを受けた。

shocking *adj.* (upsetting) 衝撃的な,

S

(causing offense) ひどい, とんでもない

shock wave *n.* 衝撃波

shoddy *adj.* (of goods) 粗末な, 質の悪い, (of work) いいかげんな

shoe *n.* (**shoes**) 靴

a pair of shoes 靴 1 足

no shoes allowed 土足禁止

♦ **shoeshine** *n.* (shining of shoes) 靴磨き

shoe shop *n.* 靴屋

shoelace *n.* 靴ひも

tie one's shoelaces 靴ひもを結ぶ

shogi *n.* (board game) 将棋

shogun *n.* (military dictator) 将軍

♦ **shogunate** *n.* 幕府

---

shoot

1 *v.* FIRE A GUN (AT): (銃で) 撃つ, 銃撃する, (shoot a gun) (銃を) 撃つ

2 *v.* TRY TO SCORE A GOAL: シュートする

3 *v.* DASH: 素早く走る, 突進する

4 *v.* FILM: 撮影する, 撮る

5 *n.* FILMING OR TAKING OF PHOTOGRAPHS: (filming) 撮影, (photo shoot) 写真撮影

6 *n.* YOUNG PLANT: 新芽, 若い芽

1 The journalist was shot in the leg.
ジャーナリストは足を撃たれた。

They were ready to shoot.
彼らは銃を構えていた。

We were being shot at.
我々は銃撃を受けていた。

2 He shot at the goal from close range.
彼は至近距離から、ゴールめがけてシュートした。

3 We shot up the stairs when we heard the noise.
物音を聞いて、階段を駆け上がった。

4 The movie will be shot on location in Paris.
その映画はパリでロケ撮影されます。

5 The shoot will take thirty minutes.
(写真)撮影は 30 分くらいかかるでしょう。

6 bamboo shoots 竹の子

shoot down *v.* (aircraft) 撃墜する, (person) 撃ち殺す, 射殺する; (idea) はねつける, 拒絶する

They shot down an aircraft.
飛行機を撃墜した。

It was a good idea, but it was shot it down.
いいアイデアだったけど、はねつけられた。

shoot for *v.* (aim for) ねらう, めざす

shoot up *v.* (rapidly increase) 急上昇する, (grow tall in a short period) 急に成長する

---

shooting *n.* (firing of a gun at sb) そ撃, 発砲, (firing of a gun for sport) 射撃

♦ **shooting range** *n.* 射撃練習場

shooting star *n.* 流星, 流れ星

shop *n.* (place to buy goods) (お)店, -屋
v. 買い物する, ショッピングする

There weren't many customers in the shop.
店には、あまり客が入っていなかった。

Who's going to close the shop today?
今日は誰が店を閉めるの？

He works in the shoe shop on the corner.
彼は角の靴屋で働いています。

She usually shops for fresh vegetables on Monday.

彼女は、たいてい月曜日に新鮮な野菜を買っている。

♦ **shop around** *v.* 見て回る, (**shop around for**) 探し回る

shopkeeper *n.* 店主

shoplift *v.* 万引きする

♦ **shoplifter** *n.* 万引き(犯)

shoplifting *n.* 万引き

shopper *n.* 買い物客

shopping *n.* 買い物, ショッピング

Are you going shopping this afternoon?
今日の午後、買い物に行く?

♦ **shopping bag** *n.* 買い物袋, ショッピングバッグ

shopping mall/center *n.* ショッピングセンター

shopping street *n.* 商店街

shore *n.* (of sea) 海岸, (of lake) 湖畔, 岸辺, (land as viewed from sea) 陸地

short

1 *adj.* NOT LONG: 短い, (**a short distance**) 近い

2 *adj.* OF PERSON: 背の低い

3 *adj.* DEFICIENT: 不足の, 不十分な, (**be short of/on**) (…が) 足りない [→ SHORT OF]

4 *n.* PANTS: (**shorts**) 半ズボン, 短パン

1 She has short hair.
彼女はショートヘアです [髪が短い]。

The paper was shorter than expected.
論文は予想していたより短かった。

Didn't the day seem short?
一日が短く感じなかった?

That was the shortest letter I've ever read.
これまでに読んだ中で、一番短い手紙だった。

The station is a short distance from the house.
駅は家から近い。

2 He's short. 彼は背が低い。

3 Vegetables are in short supply.
野菜が品薄です。

He's in no way short of cash.
現金が足りないということは、彼には絶対にない。

I was short of breath.
息切れしていた。

for short (in abbreviation) 略して

His name is Alexander, but people call him Alex for short.
彼の名前はアレグザンダーだけど、略してアレックスと呼ばれている。

in short 要するに, つまり

In short, we succeeded.
要するに、私たちは成功したんです。

nothing short of 全く…, ((*formal*)) まさに…

That they survived was nothing short of a miracle.
彼らが生き延びたのは、まさに奇跡だ。

short of (other than) …以外で, (without going so far as to) …まではしないで

Short of being rude, how am I to get rid of him?
失礼にならずに、どうやって追い払えというんですか?

shortage *n.* 不足

shortcake *n.* ショートケーキ

shortchange *v.* (…に) つり銭をごまかす, (cheat) だます

short circuit *n.* ショート

v. (**short-circuit**) ショートする

shortcoming *n.* 欠点, 短所

shortcut *n.* 近道

shorten *v.* 短くする, 縮める

shortfall *n.* (shortage) 不足

shorthand *n.* 速記

short-lived *adj.* つかのまの, はかない

shortly *adv.* (soon) まもなく

shortsighted *adj.* (lacking foresight) 先見の明のない [→ NEARSIGHTED]

short-term *adj.* 短期間の

shortwave *n.* 短波

shot *n.*

1 FIRING OF A GUN: 発砲, (sound of gunfire) 銃声

2 IN GAME: (in soccer, basketball) シュート, (in tennis, golf) ショット

3 PHOTOGRAPH: 写真

4 INJECTION OF A DRUG: 注射

5 OF ALCOHOL: (a single shot) 1杯

6 CHANCE: 見込み, 勝ち目

1 How many shots were fired?
何発、発砲されましたか？

Several shots were heard.
銃声が何度か聞こえた。

2 Nice shot! ナイスショット！

His second shot made it to the green.
彼の第2打はグリーンまで届いた。

3 That's a nice shot of your daughter among the sunflowers.
ヒマワリに囲まれたお嬢さんの写真、すてきですね。

4 I hate getting shots.
私は注射が大嫌いなんです。

5 a shot of tequila 1杯のテキーラ

6 Do you think he's got a shot?
彼に見込みがあると思う？

give it a shot やってみる, 試してみる

I'll give it a shot.
ちょっとやってみよう。

shotgun *n.* ショットガン, 散弾銃

♦**shotgun wedding/marriage** *n.* できちゃった結婚

should *aux.*

1 SAYING WHAT ONE OUGHT TO DO: …するべきだ, …したほうがいい

2 EXPRESSING EXPECTATION/PROBABILITY: …する, …だろう, (with a feeling of certainty) …はずだ

3 POLITE USAGE: See example below

4 EXPRESSING SURPRISE/ANGER: (that one should…) …するとは, …するなんて, (who/what should one… but) 一体, なんと

1 You should leave immediately.
すぐに出るべきだ。

I should sack him, but I won't.
彼を首にすべきだが、私はしない。

I'm sorry, I should've explained that before.
すみません、先に説明しておくべきでした。

It's not the kind of job she should be doing.
彼女がするような仕事じゃない。

You shouldn't have gone to so much trouble.
そこまでしていただかなくてもよかったのに。

How should I write the letter?
どういうふうに手紙を書けばいいんだろう？

■2 We should be there soon.
もうすぐ、着きます。

"I'm so pleased."
"So you should be."
「本当にうれしいです」
「そうでしょうね」

You should have heard from him by now.
もう彼から連絡があっていいはずだ。

■3 I should be most grateful if those invited arrive by 7:30, before the honored guest is due.
貴賓が到着予定の7時半までに、ほかの招待客が着いてもらえるとありがたい。

■4 It's strange he should say that.
彼がそんなことを言うなんて不思議だ。

And who should I meet at the hotel but Mrs. Kawahara.
なんとそのホテルで、河原夫人に会ったんですよ。

shoulder ***n.*** 肩 [→ picture of BODY], (meat of shoulder) 肩肉; (of road) 路肩

♦ **shoulder blade** ***n.*** 肩甲骨

shoulder strap ***n.*** ストラップ, 肩ひも

shoulder width ***n.*** 肩幅

shout ***v.*** 叫ぶ, 大声を出す, (say in a loud voice) (…と) 大きな声で言う, (shout at) (…に) どなりつける, どなる

n. 叫び声

We had to shout to be heard.
大声を出さないと聞こえなかった。

Do you have to shout?
どなる必要があるの？

The teacher shouted at us for talking.
おしゃべりしていたので先生にどなりつけられた。

a shout for help 助けを呼ぶ叫び声

shouts of joy 歓声

shove ***v.*** 押し合う, (shove A into B) (AをBに) 押し込む, (**shove aside**) 押しのける

n. 一押し

Everyone was shoving to get onto the train.
みんな、電車へ乗り込もうと押し合っていた。

Give it another shove. もう一押し。

shovel ***n.*** シャベル, スコップ

v. シャベルですくう

shovel earth into a wheelbarrow
シャベルで土をすくって手押し車にのせる

---

show

1 ***v.*** PRODUCE TO BE SEEN: 見せる, (TV program) 放映する, (movie) 上映する, (art) 展示する, 陳列する

2 ***v.*** INDICATE: 示す, 表す, 意味する

3 ***v.*** ESCORT: (**show around**) 案内する, (**show in**: to room) 中に通す, (**show out the door**) 玄関先まで送る

4 ***v.*** TEACH BY DEMONSTRATING: (…に) 教える, 説明する

5 ***n.*** PERFORMANCE: ショー, (TV program) 番組, (exhibition) 展覧会, 展示会

6 ***v.*** BE NOTICEABLE: 目立つ

7 ***v.*** EXPRESS: (emotion) 表す, 顔に出す

■1 Could you show me the apartment?
アパートを見せてくれませんか？

I'll show you my room.
部屋を見せるよ。

The photograph shows her when she was only twelve years old.

写真は、彼女がまだ12歳の時の姿を写している。

The program was also shown in the evening.
その番組は夕方にも放映された。

The movie is showing until Friday.
映画は金曜日まで上映している。

2 These figures show that inflation is falling.
この数字はインフレが鈍化していることを示している。

This graph shows changes in the birthrate over the past decade.
このグラフは、過去10年間の出生率の変化を表しています。

This shows that he's not interested.
これは彼が関心をもっていないことを意味する。

The survey showed that many people were in favor of the bill.
調査で、多くの人々がその法案を支持していることが明らかになった。

3 I showed them around the city.
彼らを市内に案内した。

He showed me out.
彼は玄関先まで送ってくれた。

4 Can you show me how to set the timer?
タイマーのかけ方を教えてくれない？

Want me to show you a better way?
もっといいやり方を説明しようか？

5 It was an excellent show.
すばらしいショーだった。

a flower show フラワーショー

a talk show トークショー

There was an interesting show on TV last night.
ゆうべテレビで面白い番組があった。

6 The stain doesn't show.
そのしみは目立たないね。

This carpet doesn't show the dirt so much.
このカーペットは、それほど汚れが目立たない。

7 He was upset but didn't show it.
彼は動揺していたけど、顔には出さなかった。

have sth/nothing to show for …に対して見るべき成果がある/ない

it (just) goes to show よくわかる, よく表している

This just goes to show how important good manners are.
行儀がいいことがどんなに大切か、このことからよくわかる。

steal the show 人気をさらう

show off *v.* (try to look good) かっこつける, 目立ちたがる, (show sth off) 見せびらかす, ひけらかす

He's always showing off.
彼はいつもかっこつけている。

show up *v.* (appear) 現れる, やって来る

show up on time (for)
(…に) 時間どおりにやって来る

show business *n.* ショービジネス, (world of) 芸能界

go into show business 芸能界に入る

showdown *n.* 対決

shower

1 *n.* BRIEF RAIN: にわか雨, (summer afternoon shower) 夕立

2 *n.* FIXTURE IN BATHROOM: シャワー [→ picture of BATHROOM, PUBLIC BATH]

3 *v.* WASH ONESELF: シャワーを浴びる

1 showers and thunderstorms
にわか雨と雷雨
There were several heavy showers today.
今日は何度か、激しいにわか雨があった。

2 Does the apartment have a shower?
アパートにシャワーはありますか？
take a shower シャワーを浴びる

3 I like to shower in the summer and bathe in the winter.
夏はシャワー、冬はおふろがいい。

♦**shower cap** *n.* シャワーキャップ
shower gel *n.* ボディーソープ

showoff *n.* 目立ちたがり, 自慢屋

showroom *n.* ショールーム, 展示室

showy *adj.* 派手な, 目立つ

shrapnel *n.* 爆弾の破片

shred *v.* 切り刻む, (document) シュレッダーにかける
n. 切れ端

shredder *n.* シュレッダー

shrew *n.* (animal) トガリネズミ

shrewd *adj.* (clever) 賢い, 鋭い, (of businessperson) 如才ない

shriek *v.* 悲鳴を上げる
n. 悲鳴

shrill *adj.* 甲高い
a shrill voice 甲高い声

shrimp *n.* エビ, 海老

♦**shrimp cocktail** *n.* 小エビのカクテル

shrine *n.* (Shinto place of worship) 神社, (in Japanese home) 神棚, (portable shrine used in festivals) おみこし
go to a shrine 神社にお参りする
(pay) one's first visit of the year to a shrine 初詣(に行く)

shrink *v.* (become/make smaller) 縮む/縮める, 小さくなる/小さくする, (decrease) 減る/減らす
Will this shirt shrink in the wash?
このシャツは洗濯で縮みますか？

♦**shrinkage** *n.* (in size) 縮小

shrivel *v.* (of plant) しなびる

shroud *n.* (for the dead) 経かたびら
v. (**be shrouded in**) …に包まれている
be shrouded in mystery
なぞに包まれている

shrub *n.* 低木

shrug *v.* (shoulders) すくめる
n. すくめること

♦**shrug off** *v.* (forget) 忘れる

shudder *v.* (of person: shake) 震える, (of building) 揺れる
shudder to think (that) …と思うとぞっとする

shuffle *v.* (cards) 切る, シャッフルする; (**shuffle along**) 足をひきずって歩く
n. (act of shuffling cards) シャッフル

shun *v.* 避ける

---

shut *v.* (cause to close) 閉める, 閉じる, (become closed) 閉まる [→ CLOSE[1]]
Would you shut the door, please?
ドアを閉めてもらえますか？
I shut my eyes and dozed off.
目を閉じてうとうとした。
The doors shut automatically.
ドアは自動的に閉まります。

shut down *v.* (business) 閉鎖する, (machine) 止(と)める

The factory was shut down.
工場(こうじょう)が閉鎖(へいさ)された。

shut off *v.* (turn off) 切(き)る, (gas, faucet) 止(と)める; (of machine) 止(と)まる

shut out *v.* (shut A out of B) (BからA を) 締(し)め出(だ)す

shut up *v.* (stop talking) 黙(だま)る; (**shut oneself up in**) …に閉(と)じこもる

Just shut up, will you!
黙(だま)って/うるさい!

Takeshi wanted to study, so he shut himself up in his room.
武(たけし)は勉強(べんきょう)したかったので、部屋(へや)に閉(と)じこもった。

---

shutter *n.* (on camera) シャッター; (on house) シャッター, よろい戸(ど), 雨戸(あまど) [→ picture of HOUSE]

shuttle *n.* (for weaving) 杼(ひ), シャトル; (space shuttle) スペースシャトル

♦ **shuttle bus** *n.* シャトルバス

shy *adj.* (bashful) 内気(うちき)な, シャイな, 恥(は)ずかしがりの, (of smile, glance) はにかんだ, (timid) 引(ひ)っ込(こ)み思案(じあん)の, 人見知(ひとみし)りする, (of animal: easily frightened) 臆病(おくびょう)な

He's always been shy.
彼(かれ)はもともと内気(うちき)だ。

She was too shy to talk to anyone.
彼女(かのじょ)は恥(は)ずかしがり屋(や)で誰(だれ)とも話(はな)せなかった。

a shy look はにかんだ表情(ひょうじょう)

The tapir is a very shy animal.
バクというのは、とても臆病(おくびょう)な動物(どうぶつ)だ。

♦ **shy away from** *v.* (avoid) 避(さ)ける

shyness *n.* 内気(うちき), はにかみ

sibling *n.* きょうだい

sick *adj.* (ill) 具合(ぐあい)が悪(わる)い, 気分(きぶん)が悪(わる)い, (nauseous) 気持(きも)ちが悪(わる)い, 吐(は)き気(け)がする; (nasty, unpleasant) いやな

He's very sick.
彼(かれ)はとても具合(ぐあい)が悪(わる)い。

Are you feeling sick?
気分(きぶん)でも悪(わる)いの?

Half the class is out sick with the flu.
クラスの半分(はんぶん)がインフルエンザで休(やす)んでいる。

I think the custard made me sick.
あのカスタードにあたったんだと思(おも)う。

a sick joke いやな冗談(じょうだん)
a sick movie 気持(きも)ちの悪(わる)い映画(えいが)

be sick and tired of …にはすっかり飽(あ)きている, …にはうんざりだ

I'm sick and tired of your complaints.
君(きみ)のぐちはもう、うんざりだ。

get sick 病気(びょうき)になる

I got sick during my vacation.
休暇中(きゅうかちゅう)に病気(びょうき)になった。

sicken *v.* (cause to feel ill) 吐(は)き気(け)を催(もよお)させる, (disgust) むかつかせる, うんざりさせる

♦ **sickening** *adj.* (causing anger, disgust) 吐(は)き気(け)のする, うんざりする, ひどい

sickle *n.* かま

sickly *adj.* (of person) 病気(びょうき)がちの, 病弱(びょうじゃく)な

sickness *n.* (illness) 病気(びょうき), (nausea) 吐(は)き気(け)

side

1 *n.* SURFACE: 面(めん), 側(がわ)

2 *n.* INDICATING LOCATION: 側(がわ), (**this side/**

that side) こっち側/あっち側, (**left side/right side**) 左側/右側, (**the side of**) (= the area next to) …のそば, …の隣, …の横, (=the edge) …の端

3 *n.* SLOPE: 斜面

4 *n.* OF BODY: わき腹

5 *n.* OPPOSING GROUP: (**the other side**) 相手, 先方, (**both sides**) 両者

6 *n.* IN ARGUMENT/WAR: 味方, 側

7 *n.* OF FAMILY: (**mother's side**) 母方, (**father's side**) 父方

8 *n.* ASPECT: 面, 側面

9 *v.* SUPPORT: (**side with**) …に味方する, …に賛成する

1 Just paint one side.
片面だけペンキを塗って。

This side is smooth, but the other is rough.
この面は滑らかだけど、裏はざらざらしている。

2 This side of the country is much warmer.
国のこっち側はだいぶ暖かい。

The wall on the left side of the classroom was decorated with children's paintings.
教室の左側の壁には、子供たちの絵が飾られていた。

Let's meet at the south side of the station.
駅の南側で待ち合わせしよう。

There were people on all sides.
四方八方 [そこらじゅうに] 人がいた。

There's a garage on the side of the house.
家の横に車庫がある。

3 The sides of the valley were steep.
渓谷の斜面は急だった。

4 My left side aches. 左のわき腹が痛い。

5 The other side would not agree to a compromise.
先方は和解に応じなかった。

Both sides reached an agreement.
両者は合意に達した。

6 Whose side are you on, mine or his?
私と彼と、どっちの味方なの？

7 He gets his musical ability from his mother's side.
彼の音楽の才能は、母方から受け継いだものだ。

8 There's another side to this problem.
この問題には別の側面がある。

9 We sided with Harry.
私たちはハリーに味方した。

at/by one's side …のそばに, ((*figurative*)) …の側に, …の味方に

She stood by my side.
彼女は私のそばに立った。

be on sb's side …の側に立つ, …の味方をする

be on the right side of …に気に入られる

Try to keep on the right side of him.
なるべく、彼に気に入られるようにしておくほうがいい。

change sides 立場を変える, 寝返る

from all sides 四方八方から, (from all aspects) あらゆる面から

from side to side 左右に

The boat swayed from side to side.
船が左右に揺れた。

on either side (on both sides) 両側に

on the side (extra) 余分に, (as a separate job) 副業に

side by side 並んで

walk side by side 並んで歩く

take sides 一方の側につく, 一方に味方する

I'm not taking sides.
私は誰の味方もしない。

sideboard *n.* サイドボード

sideburns *n.* もみあげ

side effect *n.* (of drug) 副作用

sideline *n.* (**the sidelines**) (in sport) サイドライン; (job) 副業

v. (**be sidelined**) (in sport) 出場できなくなる; (in life: be prevented from doing sth) 主流から外される

sidelong *adj.* (sideways) 横の, (sloping) 斜めの

give someone a sidelong glance
横目で見る

sidestep *v.* (avoid) 避ける

side street *n.* 横道, わき道

sidetrack *v.* (**get sidetracked**) 脱線する, わき道にそれる

sidewalk *n.* 歩道

sideways *adv.* (to the side) 横に, (from the side) 横から, (diagonally) 斜めに

siding *n.* (railroad track) 側線, 待避線

siege *n.* 包囲攻撃

v. (lay siege to) 包囲攻撃する

siesta *n.* シエスタ, 昼寝

sieve *n.* ふるい

v. ふるいにかける

sift *v.* (put through a sieve) ふるいにかける

♦ **sift through** *v.* 取捨選択する, ふるい分ける

sigh *n., v.* ため息(をつく)

sight

1 *n.* POWER OF SEEING: 視力, (one of the five senses) 視覚

2 *n.* VIEW: 光景, 景色

3 *n.* SPECTACLE: 見もの, (**sights**: places worth seeing) 名所

4 *v.* DISCOVER: 見つける [→ CATCH SIGHT OF]

5 *n.* DEVICE ON A GUN: 照準器

1 Miraculously, she regained her sight.
奇跡的に、彼女の視力は戻った。

He's lost his sight.
彼は視力を失った [失明した]。

2 The meteor showers were an awesome sight.
流星群はすばらしい光景だった。

3 They were a sight—arguing in front of everyone like that!
見ものだったよ──あんなふうにみんなの前でやり合うなんて。

see the sights 名所を見物する

4 sight a new star 新しい星を見つける

A UFO was sighted last night.
昨夜ＵＦＯが目撃された。

at first sight 一見, 一目で

It seemed easy at first sight, but it turned out to be quite difficult.
一見簡単そうだったけど、やってみるとかなり難しかった。

It was love at first sight!
一目ぼれだった!

catch sight of 見つける, (...が) ちらっと見える

We caught sight of the president passing in his limousine.
大統領がリムジンで通り過ぎる姿が、ちらっと見えた。

in sight (viewable) 見える所に, (in the

foreseeable future) 間近に, 近いうちに

There's no end in sight to this mess.
この混乱は、近いうちには終わりそうにない。

keep in sight (keep in perspective) 見失わない

Let's keep our objectives in sight.
目標を見失わないようにしよう。

lose sight of 見失う

We lost sight of them when they turned the corner.
彼らが角を曲がった所で、見失ってしまった。

Don't lose sight of your purpose.
目的を見失ってはいけない。

out of sight 見えない所に

Don't go out of sight.
見えない所へ行ってはいけませんよ。

sightseeing *n.* 観光, 見物

go sightseeing 見物に行く

sign

1 *n.* BOARD PROVIDING INFORMATION: 標示(板), (road sign) 標識, (shop sign) 看板

2 *n.* SYMBOL: サイン, しるし, 記号

3 *n.* GESTURE: 身振り, 合図, しるし

4 *v.* PUT ONE'S NAME TO: (...に)サインする, 署名する, はんこを押す [=put one's seal to; → SEAL[1]], (**sign a contract**: enter into an agreement) 契約する

5 *n.* INDICATION: 兆し, 兆候, 気配

6 *n.* ZODIAC SIGN: 星座

1 an exit sign 出口の標示

The sign says "one way."
標識には一方通行と書いてあります。

I missed the exit because I couldn't read the sign.
標示が読めなかったので出口を通り過ぎてしまった。

2 a minus sign マイナス記号

an equal sign 等号

semiotics—the science of signs
記号論—記号の科学

3 He nodded as a sign of approval.
彼は同意のしるしにうなずいた。

4 They both signed the contract.
双方が契約書にサインした。

5 a sign of spring 春の兆し

a sign of old age 老化の兆候

There's no sign of any improvement in the economy.
景気回復の兆しは全くない。

They say he's mean, but I've seen no sign of it.
彼は意地悪だと言われているけど、そんな気配は全くない。

6 "What sign are you?"
"I'm a Libra."
「星座は何？」
「天秤座」

♦**sign in** *v.* 署名して入る

sign out *v.* 署名して出る

sign up (for) *v.* (...に)登録する, (...に)参加する

Have you signed up for the course yet?
もうそのコースに登録しましたか？

signal

1 *n.* GESTURE/SOUND: 合図, サイン, 身振り(手振り)

2 *v.* MAKE A GESTURE/SOUND: (...に)合図する

3 *n.* INDICATION: 兆候, 兆し, サイン

4 *v.* INDICATE: 表す, (...の)しるしだ

5 *n.* TRAFFIC SIGNAL: 信号

6 *n.* FROM RADIO/RADAR: 信号

1 Divers use signals to communicate underwater.
ダイバーは身振り手振りで水中でコミュニケーションする。

2 He raised his hand to signal us to stop.
彼は(私たちに)止まるよう手で合図した。

3 What kind of signals did you get from her?
彼女には、どんな兆候がありましたか？

4 The pension problems signal an aging society.
年金問題は高齢化社会のしるしだ。

5 When the signal turns green, go.
信号が青に変わったら進みなさい。

signatory *n.* 署名者

signature *n.* 署名, サイン

significance *n.* (importance) 重要性, (meaning) 意義

At the time, no one fully appreciated the significance of his discovery.
当時は誰も、彼の発見の重要性を十分に認識していなかった。

The significance of this law cannot be underestimated.
この法律の意義は軽視できません。

significant *adj.* (important) 重要な, (meaningful) 意義深い; (considerable) かなりの

significantly *adv.* (considerably) かなり; (used at beginning of a sentence: meaningfully) 意義深いことに

signify *v.* (indicate) 示す, (mean) 意味する

sign language *n.* 手話

Sikh *n.* シーク教徒

silence *n.* (absence of sound) 静けさ, (absence of words) 沈黙, 無言, (lapse in correspondence) 音信不通

v. (cause to be silent) 静かにさせる

the silence of the forest 森の静けさ

They were sworn to silence.
彼らは沈黙を誓わせられた。

the virtue of silence 沈黙の美徳

I apologize for the long silence (convention used in letter writing) ごぶさたしております

silent *adj.* (quiet) 静かな, (not speaking) 無言の, 沈黙を守る; (not pronounced) 発音されない

a silent *p* 黙字のP

silent majority 声なき声, サイレントマジョリティー

silently *adv.* (quietly) 静かに, (by not speaking) 黙って

silhouette *n.* シルエット, (outline) 輪郭, (drawing) 影絵

v. (...の) 輪郭を見せる, (**be silhouetted against**) ...を背景にくっきり浮かび上がる

Mt. Fuji was silhouetted against the orange sky.
オレンジ色の空を背景に、富士山がくっきり浮かび上がっていた。

silicon *n.* ケイ素, シリコン

a silicon chip シリコンチップ

silicone *n.* シリコン

silk *n.* シルク, 絹

silkworm *n.* カイコ, 蚕

sill *n.* (windowsill) 窓台

silly *adj.* (foolish) ばかな, ばかみたいな

That was a silly thing to say.

あんなことを言うなんて、ばかだった。

You silly boy. おばかさん。

Don't be silly! そんなばかな!

silo *n.* サイロ

silt *n.* 沈泥

v. (**silt up**) 沈泥でふさがる

silver *n.* 銀, シルバー, (color) 銀色

adj. 銀の, (of color) 銀色の

a silver medal 銀メダル

♦**silver age** *n.* 銀時代

silversmith *n.* 銀細工師

silverware *n.* (eating utensils) 銀食器, カトラリー

similar *adj.* 同じような, 似た, 似ている

There was a similar accident last month.
先月も同じような事故があった。

Their house is very similar to ours.
彼らの家は、うちとよく似ている。

similarity *n.* 類似点, 似ているところ

The similarities were striking.
類似点が目立った。

similarly *adv.* 同じように, 同様に

I was treated similarly.
私も同じように扱われた。

simile *n.* 直喩

simmer *v.* ぐつぐつ煮える, (allow to boil on low heat) とろ火で煮る, 弱火で煮る

simple *adj.*

1 NOT COMPLEX: やさしい, 簡単な

2 NOT HIGHLY DEVELOPED: 単純な

3 PLAIN: 質素な, シンプルな

4 VERY ORDINARY: ごく普通の, ごく平凡な

1 It's a simple question.
簡単な質問です。

There is no simple answer.
簡単な答えはありません。

The exam was simple.
試験はやさしかった。

Wouldn't it be simpler to pay someone to do it?
お金を払って誰かにやってもらうほうが、簡単じゃない?

2 It's a simple invention.
単純な発明です。

a simple instrument 単純な道具

a simple pattern 単純な模様

3 He lives a simple life.
彼は質素な暮らしをしている。

"What do you want to have for dinner?" "Something simple."
「夕食は何が食べたい?」
「何か簡単なものがいい」

4 My parents are simple people.
うちの両親は、ごく普通の人間です。

the simple fact 紛れもない事実, 純然たる事実

The simple fact is, we have no choice.
我々に選択の余地がないのは、紛れもない事実だ。

simplicity *n.* (easiness) 簡単さ, (absence of sophistication) 単純さ

simplify *v.* 簡単にする, ((*formal*)) 簡素化する

simplistic *adj.* 短絡的な, あまりにも単純な

take a simplistic view of things
物事を短絡的に考える

simply *adv.* 簡単に, 単に

simply put 簡単に言えば

Simply put, there is no better choice.

簡単に言えば、これ以上の選択はない。

simulate *v.* (imitate) まねる, (re-create) (…の)模擬実験をする, シミュレーションをする

simulation *n.* シミュレーション

simulator *n.* シミュレーター

simultaneous *adj.* 同時の, 同時に起こる

simultaneously *adv.* 同時に

sin *n.* 罪

v. 罪を犯す

since

1 *prep., conj.* AFTER: …から(ずっと), …以来, …以後

2 *conj.* BECAUSE: …ので, …から

3 *adv.* SUBSEQUENTLY: それ以来, それ以後, その後

1 I've been up since 6 o'clock.
6時から(ずっと)起きている。

I haven't seen them since Christmas.
クリスマス以来、彼らに会っていない。

A long time has passed since we last met.
この前会ってから、ずいぶんたちましたね/本当にお久しぶりですね。

I've been wearing glasses since I was sixteen.
16の時から、めがねをかけています。

That's the first time since I've known you that you've been late.
あなたが遅刻して来るのは、知り合って以来初めてだ。

2 Since we really needed the money, I had to sell the car.
どうしてもお金が必要だったので、車を売らなければならなかった。

3 The house has since been rebuilt.
家はその後、建て直された。

ever since (from a point in the past until now) それ以来, (from a point in the past when) …の時からずっと

We came in 1974, and we've been here ever since.
１９７４年に来て、それ以来ずっとここにいます。

Ever since I was seven years old, I have wanted to become a doctor.
7歳の時からずっと、お医者さんになりたかった。

long since ずっと前に, とっくに

The master tapes have long since been lost.
マスターテープがずっと前からない。

sincere *adj.* 誠実な, 真面目な, 心からの

She strikes me as a very sincere person.
彼女はとても誠実な人という印象を受ける。

You have my sincere apologies.
心からおわびいたします。

sincerely *adv.* 心から, (at the end of a letter) 敬具 [→ DEAR 1]

sincerity *n.* 誠実さ, 誠意

show/express sincerity 誠意を示す

sinecure *n.* 閑職

sinew *n.* (tendon) 腱

♦**sinewy** *adj.* 引き締まった

sinful *adj.* 罪深い

sing *v.* 歌う, (**sing along**) いっしょに歌う, (**sing along with/to**) …に合わせて歌う, (of bird) 鳴く, さえずる

Can you sing? 歌える?

We all sang together.
みんなでいっしょに歌った。

Will you sing to us?

歌っていただけますか？

She sang the baby to sleep with a lullaby.
子守唄を歌って子供を寝かしつけた。

The birds started singing when the sun came up.
日が昇ると鳥がさえずり出した。

Singapore ***n.*** シンガポール

singer ***n.*** 歌手, シンガー

singing ***n.*** 歌うこと

single

1 ***adj.*** ONE: たった一つの, (**not a single person/thing**) 一人も/一つも…ない [→ p. 1168 about "Counters"]

2 ***adj.*** FOR ONE PERSON: 一人用の, シングルの

3 ***adj.*** NOT IN A RELATIONSHIP: 恋人がいない, (not married) 独身の, シングルの

4 ***adj.*** USED EMPHATICALLY: (**every single…**) 毎-, (**the single most…**) 最も, 一番

5 ***n.*** RECORD: (CD, LP) シングル盤

6 ***n.*** IN SPORT: (**singles**) シングルス

7 ***n.*** ROOM/BED/BEVERAGE: シングル

8 ***n.*** UNMARRIED PEOPLE: (**singles**) 独身者

1 I finished the book in a single day.
たった1日でその本を読み終えた。

It won't cost you a single cent.
1銭もかからないよ。

There wasn't a single person there.
そこには誰一人いなかった。

I couldn't think of a single thing to say.
話すことが何一つ思い浮かばなかった。

2 a single room シングル(の部屋)

a single bed シングルベッド

3 Is he still single? あの人はまだ独身？

a single woman 独身女性

4 every single day 毎日毎日

every single time 毎回

the single most important reason
一番の理由

5 He collects pop singles from the 80s.
彼は80年代のポップスのシングル盤を集めている。

6 Let's play singles. シングルスをやろう。

7 Do you have any singles available?
シングルの部屋は、あいていますか？

8 a singles party 独身者のパーティー

♦**single out** ***v.*** 選び出す

be singled out for criticism
やり玉に挙げられる

single-handed ***adv.*** (also **single-handedly**) 一人で, 独力で
adj. 単独の, 独力の

single-minded ***adj.*** ひたむきな

♦**single-mindedly** ***adv.*** ひたすら, いちずに

single mother ***n.*** シングルマザー

single parent ***n.*** 片親

singular ***adj.*** (remarkable) 並外れた; (not plural) 単数の, (in the singular form) 単数形の; (only one) 唯一の
n. (singular form) 単数形

sinister ***adj.*** (evil) 邪悪な, (ominous) 不吉な

sink

1 ***n.*** BASIN: 流し, シンク [→ picture of KITCHEN]

2 ***v.*** GO DOWN: 沈む, (of boat) 沈没する, (of heart) 落ち込む, 意気消沈する

3 ***v.*** DECREASE: 減る, 減少する, 下がる

4 ***v.*** WORSEN: 悪化する, 傾く

5 ***v.*** DEFEAT: (enemy boat) 撃沈する, (proj-

S

ect, proposal) だめにする, つぶす

1 Dirty dishes are piling up in the sink.
流しに汚れたお皿が山積みになっている。

The bathroom sink needs cleaning.
洗面所(の流し)は掃除が必要だ。

2 The ship sank with all hands aboard.
船は全乗組員を乗せたまま沈没した。

Our spirits sank. 意気消沈した。

3 The number of applicants has sunk to a new low.
志願者数が記録的に減少した。

4 His business is sinking.
彼の事業は悪化している。

5 We were ordered to sink the ship.
我々は船を撃沈するよう命令された。

sink in *v.* (of words, warning) 十分理解される, 心にしみ込む

What she told me just didn't sink in.
彼女が私に言ったことは、十分心にしみていなかった。

sink into *v.* (debt, despair) …に陥る

We sank further and further into debt.
どんどん借金地獄に陥った。

sinus *n.* 洞

sip *n.* 一すすり, 一口

v. ちびりちびり飲む

siphon *n.* サイフォン

sir *n.* (customer) お客様; (title given to a knight / baronet: **Sir**) -卿

Dear Sir… 拝啓 [→ DEAR 1]

siren *n.* サイレン, 警笛

sirloin *n.* サーロイン

a sirloin steak サーロインステーキ

sister *n.* (one's own older sister) 姉, (sb else's) お姉さん, (one's own younger sister) 妹, (sb else's) 妹さん, (**sisters**) 姉妹, 女きょうだい; (title given to a nun: **Sister**) シスター

♦ **sister city** *n.* 姉妹都市

sister-in-law *n.* 義理のきょうだい, (older) 義理の姉, (younger) 義理の 妹

sit *v.* 座る, 腰(を)かける, 腰を下ろす, (cause to sit) 座らせる; (of object: be placed somewhere) ある, 置いてある

Sit down, please.
((*polite*)) どうぞお座りください。

We were sitting right in front of the stage.
私たちは舞台の真ん前に座っていました。

He sat down in his usual seat.
彼はいつもの席に着いた。

Sit! (speaking to dog) お座り!

I sat him down and asked him a few questions.
彼を座らせて、いくつか質問した。

A table sat in the middle of the room.
テーブルは部屋の真ん中にあった。

sit cross-legged あぐらをかく

You don't have to sit upright. Feel free to sit cross-legged.
正座しなくてもいいですよ。どうぞあぐらをかいて、くつろいでください。

sit around *v.* (do nothing) のらくらする, ぶらぶらする

sit back *v.* ゆったり座る, (relax) くつろぐ

sit by *v.* (not take action) 傍観する

sit by and watch 傍観 [静観] する

sit for *v.* (pose for) …のモデルになる, …のポーズをとる

S

How many models must have sat for Picasso!
どれだけの人が、ピカソのモデルになっただろう。

sit in on *v.* (meeting) 傍聴する, (lecture) 聴講する

sit through *v.* (lecture) 最後まで聞く, (movie) 終わりまで見る

sit up *v.* (move into a nonrecumbent position) 起き上がる, (stay up late) 起きている, (sit straight) 背筋を伸ばして座る, きちんと座る

They were still sitting up chatting when we got home.
私たちが家に着いたら、まだ起きてしゃべっていた。

Sit up properly at the table, will you.
テーブルではきちんと座りなさい。

site *n.* (place) 場所, 現場, (for new building) 用地, (historical site) 遺跡, (website) (ウェブ)サイト

work on a construction site
建設現場で働く

a camp site キャンプ場

sitting room *n.* (living room) 居間 [→ picture of APARTMENT]

situation *n.* 状況, 事態, 状態

What should I do in a situation like this?
こういう状況では、どうすればいい？

The situation is getting worse.
状況は悪化している。

It's a ridiculous situation.
とんでもない事態だ。

What a situation to find yourself in!
なんてことになったの！

sit-up *n.* 腹筋運動

six *n.* 6, 六

adj., pron. 6の, (people) 6人(の), (things) 6個(の), 六つ(の)

sixteen *n.* 16, 十六

adj., pron. 16の, (people) 16人(の), (things) 16個(の)

sixteenth *n.* 第16, 16番目, (date) 16日

adj. 第16の, 16番目の

sixth *n.* 第6, 6番目, (date) 6日, (one sixth) 6分の1

adj. 第6の, 6番目の

sixty *n.* 60, 六十, (**the sixties**) 60年代, (**one's sixties**) 60代

adj., pron. 60の, (people) 60人(の), (things) 60個(の)

size *n.* 大きさ, (of clothing) サイズ, (scale) 規模

It's about the size of a mouse.
ネズミくらいの大きさです。

The size of the population has almost doubled.
人口がほぼ2倍に増えた。

"What size shoe do you wear?"
"Size 25."
「靴のサイズはいくつ？」
「25(センチ)です」

I take a size 9.
私は9号です [を着ています]。

This dress is about one size too big.
このドレスはワンサイズ大きいみたいね。

Can I try it on for size?
試着してもいいですか？

♦**sizable** *adj.* かなり大きな

a sizable loss かなりの損害

sizzle *v.* ジュージューいう
n. ジュージュー(いう音)
♦**sizzling** *adj.* (of food) ジュージューいう, (of weather) 焼けつくような
skate *v.* スケートをする
n. スケート
Let's go skating. スケートに行こう。
a pair of skates スケート靴1足
skateboard *n.* スケートボード
♦**skateboarding** *n.* スケートボード乗り
skeleton *n.* 骸骨, (of building) 骨組み
a human skeleton 人間の骨格
skeleton in the closet 内輪の恥
sketch *n.* (rough drawing) スケッチ
v. スケッチする, 写生する, 描く
The detective made a quick sketch of the house.
探偵はその家をざっとスケッチした。
The artist sketched a disturbing portrait of the accused.
画家は、怖そうな被告人の似顔絵を描いた。
sketchbook *n.* スケッチブック
sketchy *adj.* (incomplete, not thorough) おおざっぱな, 簡単な
skewer *n.* 串
v. 串に刺す
ski *n.* スキー板
v. スキーをする
Can you rent skis there?
そこでスキー板は借りられる?
a pair of skies スキー一組
Do you go skiing every winter?
冬は毎年スキーに行きますか?
♦**ski boot** *n.* スキー靴
skier *n.* スキーヤー
ski instructor *n.* スキーインストラクター
ski lift *n.* スキーリフト
ski pole *n.* (スキーの) ストック
ski resort *n.* スキー場
skiwear *n.* スキーウェア
skid *n.* 横滑り
v. (of car) 横滑りする, スリップする
The car skidded to a stop.
車はスリップして、キーッと音を立てて止まった。
♦**skid mark** *n.* (tire mark) タイヤ跡
skill *n.* (expertise) 技術, 技能, (ability) 手腕
This work requires skill.
この作業は技術が要る。
The more skills you have, the easier it is to find a job.
もっている技術が多いほど、仕事は見つけやすい。
He certainly showed a lot of skill in the way he handled the situation.
その状況に対処するのに、彼はすばらしい手腕を発揮した。
skilled *adj.* (of person) 熟練した, うまい
skillful *adj.* 腕のいい, うまい, 上手な
skim *v.* (read quickly) ざっと読む; (**skim off**: remove from a surface) すくい取る
skim milk *n.* スキムミルク
skimp *v.* (economize) けちる, 節約する
skimpy *adj.* (not enough) 不十分な, (of clothing) 小さすぎる
skin
1 *n.* OF THE BODY: 肌, 皮膚
2 *n.* ANIMAL HIDE: 皮
3 *n.* PEEL OF A FRUIT/VEGETABLE: 皮

4 *v.* REMOVE THE SKIN FROM: (animal) (…の)皮をはぐ, (fruit) (…の) 皮をむく

5 *v.* DAMAGE THE SKIN ON: (knee etc.) すりむく

1 You'd better put cream on to protect your skin.
肌を守るためにクリームをつけたほうがいい。

She has sensitive skin.
彼女は敏感肌だ。

2 a tiger skin トラの皮
animal skins 動物の皮

3 a banana skin バナナの皮
peel the skin off 皮をむく

4 skin a fish 魚の皮をはぐ

5 I've skinned my elbow.
ひじをすりむいた。

♦**skin care** *n.* スキンケア
skin cream *n.* スキンクリーム

skin diving *n.* スキンダイビング

skinflint *n.* けちん坊

skinny *adj.* (of person) やせた

skip *v.*

1 HOP: 跳びはねる, (**skip along**) スキップする, (**skip around**: hop around) はね回る, (using jump rope) 縄跳びをする

2 NOT ATTEND: (class) サボる, (**skip a year** in school) 飛び級する

3 OMIT: 省く, 飛ばす, 抜かす

4 CAUSE TO BOUNCE ON WATER: (skip stones) 水切り遊びをする

1 The girls were skipping in the playground.
少女たちが、運動場で縄跳びをしていた。

The children were skipping along in front of us.
子供たちは私たちの前をスキップして行った。

2 I skipped last week's lecture.
先週の講義をサボった。

3 Let's skip the formalities.
堅苦しいことは抜きにしましょう。

I skipped that chapter and went on to the next.
その章は飛ばして次に進んだ。

skipper *n.* (of ship) 船長

skirmish *n.* (minor battle) 小競り合い
get into a skirmish 小競り合いになる

skirt *n.* スカート
wear a skirt スカートをはく

skull *n.* 頭蓋骨, (head) 頭

skunk *n.* スカンク

sky *n.* 空
a blue sky 青空
a cloudy sky 曇り空

skydiving *n.* スカイダイビング

skylark *n.* ヒバリ

skylight *n.* (window) 天窓 [→ picture of HOUSE]

skyscraper *n.* 超高層ビル, 摩天楼

slab *n.* (of wood, stone) 厚板

slack *adj.* (loose) ゆるい
v. (not do work) 怠ける, サボる

slacken *v.* (rope) ゆるめる

slacks *n.* スラックス

slam *v.* (shut noisily) バタンと閉める, (put down noisily) ドシンと置く, (slam A against B) (AをBに) ゴツンとぶつける, (slam into: collide with) (…に) ドンとぶつかる

Don't slam the door!
ドアをバタンと閉めないで!

He slammed the book onto the table and left the room.
彼はテーブルにドシンと本を置いて、部屋を出て行った。

I slammed on the brakes.
急ブレーキをかけた。

slander *n.* 中傷, 誹謗, ((*formal*)) 名誉毀損
v. 中傷する, ((*formal*)) (…の) 名誉を毀損する

slang *n.* スラング, 俗語

slant *n.* (angle, viewpoint) 観点, 見解
v. (lean) 傾く, 斜めになる
a different slant 別の観点

slap *v.* (hit) ぶつ, ピシャリとたたく, ひっぱたく, (knee, back) ポンとたたく
n. 平手打ち

She slapped me across the face.
彼女は私の顔をピシャリとたたいた。

He slapped his knees as he roared with laughter.
彼は大笑いしながら、ひざをたたいた。

I slapped him on the back and wished him the best of luck.
彼の背中をたたいて、幸運を祈った。

slash *v.* (cut) 切る, 切り裂く, (…に) 深く切りつける, (prices) 大幅に下げる
n. (cut) 切り傷; (punctuation mark) スラッシュ

Someone's slashed the tires.
誰かがタイヤを切り裂いた。

slate *n.* (type of stone) 粘板岩, (used as roofing) スレート

slaughter *v.* (people) 虐殺する, (animals) 殺す

slaughterhouse *n.* 食肉処理場

slave *n.* 奴隷
v. (**slave away**) 奴隷のように働く, あくせく働く

♦ **slavery** *n.* 奴隷制度

sleazy *adj.* (cheap-looking) 安っぽい, (sordid) 下品な, (dirty) 汚い, (of person) 気持ちの悪い

sled *n.* そり

sledgehammer *n.* 大づち, 大ハンマー

sleek *adj.* (smooth) すべすべした, 滑らかな, (shiny) つやのある; (stylish) おしゃれな

sleep *v.* 寝る, 眠る, (**can/could sleep**) 眠れる, (nod off) うとうとする, (**sleep out in the open/underneath the stars**) 野宿する, (sleep with) (=sleep beside) (…に) 添い寝する, (=have sex with) (…と) 寝る
n. 睡眠, 眠り

I slept from twelve till seven.
12時から7時まで寝た。

Did you sleep well?
よく眠れましたか?

I haven't been getting enough sleep recently.
最近は十分睡眠をとっていない。

I haven't had a good sleep for days.
ここ数日よく眠れない。

get to sleep 寝つく

I can't get to sleep. 寝つけない。

in one's sleep 眠りながら

put to sleep (cause to sleep) 寝つかせる, (euthanize) 安楽死させる

sleep in 寝坊する

sleep well/deep よく眠る, 熟睡する

sleeping *n.* 寝ること, 眠り, 睡眠

♦**sleeping bag** *n.* 寝袋, シュラフ

sleeping car *n.* 寝台車

sleeping pill *n.* 睡眠薬

sleepless *adj.* 眠れない

♦**sleeplessness** *n.* 睡眠不足

sleepy *adj.* 眠い, 眠たい, (of face) 眠(た)そうな

♦**sleepiness** *n.* 眠気

sleet *n.* みぞれ

sleeve *n.* (part of garment) そで, (kimono sleeve) たもと; (covering for record) ジャケット

roll up one's sleeves そでをまくり上げる

short sleeves 半そで

sleigh *n.* そり

slender *adj.* (of figure) すらりとした, ほっそりした, スマートな, (of waist) 引き締まった

sleuth *n.* (detective) 探偵

slice *n.* (flat piece) 一切れ, スライス

v. (cut) スライスする, 切る

slice of the cake/pie 利益の分け前

slick *adj.* (good at persuading) 口のうまい, (clever) 巧みな; (of hair) てかてかした

slide

1 *n.* PIECE OF PLAYGROUND EQUIPMENT: 滑り台

2 *n.* IMAGE: スライド

3 *v.* MOVE SMOOTHLY: 滑る

4 *v.* SLIP AND FALL: (**slide down/off**) (…から) 滑り落ちる, 転落する

5 *v.* MOVE STEALTHILY: (**slide out**) (…から) こっそり抜け出す, 逃げる, (**slide in/into**) (…に) こっそり入る

6 *v.* IN BASEBALL: 滑り込む

1 Children like to play on slides.
子供たちは滑り台で遊ぶのが好きだ。

a water slide 水上滑り台

2 a slide show スライド上映会

a slide projector (スライド)映写機

3 I slid on the ice and fell.
氷の上で滑って転んだ。

The doors slide open.
このドアは引き戸になっています。
(lit., "These are sliding doors.")

4 Three climbers slid down the mountain to their deaths.
3人の登山者が山から転落して死んだ。

5 The burglar must have slid out the back door.
泥棒は、裏口からこっそり逃げたに違いない。

6 The runner slid to third base.
走者は三塁に滑り込んだ。

♦**sliding door** *n.* 引き戸, (used to partition a room) ふすま, 障子 [→ picture of ROOM]

slight *adj.* (insignificant) 少しの, ちょっとの, わずかな

We had a slight advantage.
我々のほうが、ちょっと有利だった。

I've got a slight cold. かぜ気味です。

♦**slightly** *adv.* わずかに, 少し

slim *adj.* 細い, (of figure) すらりとした, スリムな, ほっそりした; (of chance) わずかな

v. (**slim down**: lose weight) やせる

She is slim. 彼女はすらっとしている。

There is only a slim chance of winning.
勝つ見込みは、ほんのわずかだ。

slime *n.* (soft mud) 軟泥, (in river) ヘドロ

slimy *adj.* (of substance) どろどろした, (of person) 卑屈な

slip

1 *v.* LOSE BALANCE: 滑る, (slip and fall) 滑って転ぶ

2 *v.* SLIDE/COME LOOSE: (slip from one's hands) (手から)滑り落ちる, (of socks) ずり落ちる

3 *v.* GIVE/HAND TO: (secretly) こっそり渡す

4 *v.* PUT INTO: (slip A into B) (AをBに) こっそり/さっと入れる

5 *v.* MOVE WITH SUBTLETY: (**slip away**) こっそり抜け出す, (**slip by/past**) こっそり/さっと通り過ぎる

6 *v.* PUT ON/TAKE OFF CLOTHES: (**slip into/on**) さっと着る, (**slip off/out of**) さっと脱ぐ

7 *n.* FALSE STEP: (tumble) 滑って転ぶこと, (error) 誤り, 間違い, しくじり

8 *n.* PIECE OF PAPER: 紙切れ

9 *n.* PIECE OF UNDERWEAR: スリップ

❶ He slipped on the ice.
彼は氷の上で滑って転んだ。

She slipped and fell off the edge of the cliff.
彼女は滑って、がけから落ちた。

❷ My hand slipped. 手が滑った。

The ball slipped out of my hand.
ボールが手から滑り落ちた。

Your socks have slipped down.
靴下がずり落ちてますよ。

❸ I saw him slipping the man some cash.
彼がその男に現金をこっそり渡しているのを見た。

She slipped me a note.
彼女はメモをそっと渡してきた。

❹ I slipped the document into the drawer and closed it.
書類をさっと引き出しに入れて閉めた。

❺ They must have slipped past us.
彼らは、私たちの前をさっと通り過ぎたに違いない。

❻ She slipped out of her clothes and got in the bath.
彼女は服をさっと脱いでおふろに入った。

❼ One small slip and you're in trouble.
ちょっとでもしくじったら、大変なことになる。

❽ It's on a slip of paper by the phone.
電話の横の紙切れに書いてある。

♦**slipped disk** *n.* 椎間板ヘルニア

slipper *n.* スリッパ, 上ばき

♦**slipper rack** *n.* スリッパ立て

slippery *adj.* 滑りやすい

slit *n.* (in clothes) 切り込み, スリット, (in flesh) 切り口

slither *v.* (of snake) するすると滑って行く

slob *n.* だらしない人

slobber *v.* よだれを垂らす

n. よだれ

slog *v.* (trudge) とぼとぼ歩く, (**slog through**: boring/difficult work) こつこつ働く

n. (difficult work) つらい仕事

slogan *n.* スローガン

slope *n.* (area of rising/falling ground) 坂, 坂道, (downward slope) 下り坂, (upward slope) 上り坂, (ski slope) スロープ, 斜面

a steep slope 急な坂

♦**sloping** *adj.* (of road) 坂になった, (of

roof) 傾斜した

sloppy ***adj.*** (of job) いいかげんな, ぞんざいな, (of person, appearance) だらしない, (of food) 水っぽくてまずそうな

slot ***n.*** (hole) 差し入れ口

a coin slot コイン投入口

♦**slot machine** ***n.*** スロットマシーン

sloth ***n.*** (laziness) 無精, 怠惰; (animal) ナマケモノ

♦**slothful** ***adj.*** 無精な, 怠惰な

slouch ***v.*** (sit lazily) だらーっと座る

slovenly ***adj.*** だらしない, 汚らしい

slow

1 ***adj.*** NOT QUICK: ゆっくりした, 遅い, のろい, (time-consuming) 時間のかかる

2 ***adj.*** OF CLOCK: 遅れている

3 ***v.*** REDUCE SPEED: 速度を落とす

4 ***adj.*** NOT QUICK TO LEARN: 飲み込みが遅い, 物覚えが悪い, 鈍い, とろい

5 ***adv.*** NOT QUICKLY: ゆっくり(と)

1 Tanaka is a slow worker.
田中さんは仕事が遅い。

He threw a slow curve.
彼はスローカーブを投げた。

We seem to have taken the slow route.
時間のかかるルートを取ったようだ。

2 I think my watch is slow.
時計が遅れているようだ。

3 You'd better slow down.
速度を落としたほうがいい。

The train slowed as it approached the station.
電車は駅に近づくと、速度を落とした。

4 He's slow to learn./He's a slow learner.
あの人は飲み込みが遅い。

She was slow to understand the joke.
彼女はその冗談を理解するのに、時間がかかった。

5 Would you walk a little slower, please?
もう少しゆっくり歩いてもらえませんか？

♦**slow down** ***v.*** (reduce speed) 速度を落とす; (live less hectically) ゆっくりやる, のんびりする

slowdown ***n.*** (of work) 怠業, サボタージュ

slowly ***adv.*** ゆっくり, のろのろ, 徐々に

slow motion ***n.*** スローモーション

adj. (**slow-motion**) スローモーションの

sludge ***n.*** (mud) 泥

slug[1] ***n.*** (animal) ナメクジ

slug[2] ***v.*** (hit hard) 殴る, (ball) 強打する

slugger ***n.*** (in baseball) 強打者

sluggish ***adj.*** (of feeling) けだるい

slum ***n.*** スラム街

slumber party ***n.*** パジャマパーティー

slump ***v.*** (fall) ドスンと落ちる, (of prices) 暴落する, 急落する

n. スランプ, 不調

slur ***v.*** (speak indistinctly) 不明瞭に発音する, (of drunk person) ろれつが回らない

n. (offensive remark) 中傷, 非難

He was drunk and slurring.
彼は酔っ払って、ろれつが回らなかった。

a racial slur 人種的な中傷

slurp ***v.*** (make noise while eating/drinking) 音を立てて食べる/飲む

slurp one's noodles (お)うどんをすする

slut ***n.*** 尻軽女, ふしだらな女

sly ***adj.*** ずるい

smack *v.* (slap) ピシャリとたたく

n. (slap) 平手打ち(ひらてうち)

He smacked the horse with his whip.
彼(かれ)は馬(うま)にむちを入(い)れた。

She gave her son a smack across the buttocks.
彼女(かのじょ)は息子(むすこ)のお尻(しり)をピシャリとたたいた。

small *adj.*

1 **OF SIZE:** 小(ちい)さい, 小(ちい)さな, ((*informal*)) ちっちゃな

2 **NOT A LOT:** (**a small number of**) 少(すこ)しの, 少数(しょうすう)の, (**a small amount of**) 少(すこ)しの, 少量(しょうりょう)の, (**a small degree of**) わずかな

3 **INCONSEQUENTIAL:** ささいな, さまつな

4 **OF CLOTHING/DRINK SIZE:** S(エス)サイズの

1 a small house 小(ちい)さな家(いえ)

a small mountain village 小(ちい)さな山村(さんそん)

a small business 零細企業(れいさいきぎょう)

Is the cat smaller than ours?
その猫(ねこ)はうちの猫(ねこ)より小(ちい)さい？

2 We've only got a small amount of butter left.
バターがあと少(すこ)ししか残(のこ)っていない。

Even a small effort can help a great deal.
少(すこ)しの努力(どりょく)でも、とても役(やく)に立(た)つ。

A small number of people showed up.
少(すこ)しの人(ひと)しか来(こ)なかった。

3 It's a small problem, but it needs attention.
ささいな問題(もんだい)ですが、注意(ちゅうい)が必要(ひつよう)です。

Small changes were made to the safety procedures manual.
安全(あんぜん)の手引書(てびきしょ)にわずかな修正(しゅうせい)が加(くわ)えられた。

4 Get the small size. S(エス)サイズを下(くだ)さい。

KANJI BRIDGE

小 ON: しょう KUN: ちい(さい), こ, お | SMALL

dwarf	小人(こびと)
elementary school	小学校(しょうがっこう)
little/pinkie finger	小指(こゆび)
small build	小柄(こがら)
small change (= coins)	小銭(こぜに)
small intestine	小腸(しょうちょう)
small island	小島(こじま)
small/lowercase letters	小文字(こもじ)
small package	小包(こづつみ)

smallpox *n.* 天然痘(てんねんとう), ほうそう

small print *n.* (details) 詳細(しょうさい), (part in smaller print) 細字部分(ほそじぶぶん)

small-scale *adj.* 小規模(しょうきぼ)な

smart *adj.* (clever) 頭(あたま)のいい, 賢(かしこ)い, 利口(りこう)な; (fashionable) かっこいい, おしゃれな, (dressed up) ぱりっとした

She's a very smart woman.
彼女(かのじょ)はとても頭(あたま)のいい人(ひと)ですよ。

He thinks he's smart.
彼(かれ)は自分(じぶん)を賢(かしこ)いと思(おも)っている。

You look smart tonight.
今夜(こんや)はかっこいいね。

smash *v.* (break into small pieces) 粉々(こなごな)に砕(くだ)く, 粉々(こなごな)にする, (shatter) 割(わ)る, (break by bashing against or with a hard surface/object) 壊(こわ)す, たたき壊(こわ)す, (**smash into**: collide with) …に激突(げきとつ)する

The boat had been smashed to pieces by the storm.
船(ふね)は嵐(あらし)で粉々(こなごな)に壊(こわ)れていた。

The window has been smashed.

窓を割られた。

The firefighters smashed their way into the house.

消防士たちは家の中に突入した。

smattering ***n.*** (superficial knowledge) 生かじりの知識; (**a smattering of**: a small amount of) 少しの

smear ***v.*** (create a smudge on) 汚す, (spread thickly) 塗りつける; (hurt the reputation of) 中傷する

smell

1 ***n.*** ODOR: におい, (good smell) 香り, (stink) 臭いにおい

2 ***n.*** ONE OF THE FIVE SENSES: 嗅覚

3 ***v.*** GIVE OUT AN ODOR: においがする, におう

4 ***v.*** PERCEIVE WITH THE NOSE: (...の)においを感じる, (put one's nose near and inhale) (...の)においをかぐ

1 What's that smell? 何のにおい?

the smell of curry カレーのにおい

a horrible smell ひどいにおい

2 Dogs have an excellent sense of smell.

犬は嗅覚がすぐれている。

3 The room smelled of smoke and beer.

部屋はたばことビールのにおいがした。

The fish in the refrigerator is beginning to smell.

冷蔵庫の中の魚がにおってきた。

4 Do you smell gas? ガス臭くない?

Smell this flower—it's wonderful!

この花のにおいをかいで――いいにおい!

smelly ***adj.*** 臭い

smile ***n.*** 笑顔, ほほえみ

v. ほほえむ, にこにこする, にっこりする

She has a lovely smile.

彼女の笑顔はすてきだ。

a knowing smile したり顔

He was smiling at her the whole time.

彼はずっと、彼女にほほえんでいた。

smirk ***v.*** にやにや笑う

n. (forced smile) 作り笑い

smog ***n.*** スモッグ

smoke ***n.*** 煙

v. (give out smoke) 煙を出す, (smoke tobacco) たばこを吸う

Smoke rose from the burning building.

燃えているビルから煙が上がった。

The room was full of cigarette smoke.

部屋にたばこの煙が充満していた。

secondhand smoke 副流煙

The chimney was smoking.

煙突から煙が出ていた。

Do you smoke?

たばこを吸いますか?

My father smokes a pipe.

父はパイプを吸う。

smokestack ***n.*** 煙突

smoking ***n.*** 喫煙

passive smoking 受動喫煙

(*sign*) No Smoking 禁煙

smoky ***adj.*** (of room: filled with cigarette smoke) 煙が立ち込める

smolder ***v.*** ((*also figurative*)) くすぶる

smooth

1 ***adj.*** OF SURFACE: 滑らかな, すべすべの, つるつるの

2 ***adj.*** OF LIQUID: 滑らかな, むらのない

3 ***adj.*** OF PROCESS/OPERATION: 順調な, 滑らかな

4 ***v.*** MAKE SMOOTH: (**smooth out**: surface)

滑らかにする, (make even) ならす

❶ smooth skin すべすべの肌
smooth stone つるつるの石

❷ Stir until the mixture becomes smooth.
滑らかになるまでかき混ぜます。

❸ a smooth-running car 順調に走る車

❹ Smooth out the bumps with your hands.
手で、でこぼこをならしてください。

smoothly *adv.* 滑らかに, スムーズに, (of progress) 円滑に, 順調に
Everything's going smoothly.
すべて順調にいってます。

smorgasbord *n.* バイキング料理

smother *v.* (person) 窒息死させる; (fire: smother with) (…をかけて火を) 消す

smudge *n.* しみ, 汚れ
v. (dirty) 汚す, (smear) (…に)しみをつける, (become smeared) しみになる

smug *adj.* (of person) 独りよがりの, (of look) 気取った

smuggle *v.* (contraband goods) 密輸する, (**smuggle in**: secretly bring in) こっそり持ち込む

♦**smuggler** *n.* 密輸業者
smuggling *n.* 密輸

smut *n.* (obscene words) みだらな言葉, (obscene literature) わいせつな文学

snack *n.* 軽食, おつまみ, おやつ
v. (eat between meals) 間食する, おやつを食べる

snack bar *n.* (refreshment stand) 軽食堂

snag *n.* (problem) 問題
v. (snag A [=clothing] on B) (AをBに引っ掛けて) かぎ裂きをつくる
snag one's skirt on a nail
スカートを釘に引っ掛けて、かぎ裂きをつくる

snail *n.* カタツムリ

snake *n.* ヘビ, 蛇

snap

1 *v.* BREAK: (of branch) ポキッと折れる, (of rope) プツンと切れる

2 *v.* COME TOGETHER: (of pieces: **snap together**) カチッと合う, (of device: **snap shut**) パチンと閉まる

3 *v.* CLICK FINGERS: 指をパチンと鳴らす

4 *v.* TRY TO BITE: かみつこうとする

5 *v.* SAY/SPEAK ANGRILY: 怒って言う

6 *v.* LOSE CONTROL OF ONESELF: 度を失う, 取り乱す

7 *v.* PHOTOS: パチリと撮る

8 *n.* SOUND: (of breaking) ポキッ, (of pieces coming together) カチッ, (of fingers clicking) パチン

❶ The rope snapped.
ロープがプツンと切れた。

❷ The lid snaps shut.
ふたがパチンと閉まる。

❸ He snapped his fingers to the beat.
彼はビートに合わせて、パチパチ指を鳴らした。

❹ The dog snapped at the child.
犬が子供にかみつこうとした。

❺ "Quiet!" the teacher snapped.
「静かに!」と先生は怒って言った。

❻ He snapped when he heard the news of his son's death.
息子の死の知らせを聞いて、彼は取り乱した。

❼ He was snapping pictures one after the other.

彼はパチパチ写真を撮っていた。

8 the snap of wood 木がポキッと折れる音

with a large snap パチンと

snapdragon *n.* キンギョソウ, 金魚草

snapshot *n.* スナップ写真

take a snapshot (of)

(…の) スナップ写真を撮る

snare *n.* ((*also figurative*)) わな

v. ((*also figurative*)) わなにかける

snarl[1] *v.* (of dog) 歯をむいてうなる, (of person: shout) どなる

snarl[2] *v.* (of hair) もつれる

n. (tangle) もつれ

snatch *v.* (steal) ひったくる, (quickly grab) 急いで取る

A thief snatched her purse.

泥棒が彼女のバッグをひったくった。

sneak *v.* (**sneak in/out**) こっそり入る/出る, (**sneak away** from/out of: party, lecture) (…から) こっそり立ち去る, こっそり抜け出す, (**sneak sth in/out**) こっそり持ち込む/持ち出す, (**sneak sb in/out**) こっそり連れ込む/連れ出す

♦**sneak up on** *v.* …にそっと近づく

sneaker *n.* スニーカー

sneaky *adj.* ずるい

sneer *v.* あざ笑う, せせら笑う

sneeze *n., v.* くしゃみ(をする)

sniff *v.* (…の) においをかぐ, (wine) (…の) 香りをかぐ, (glue) 吸う

sniffle *v.* 鼻をすする

snip *v.* チョキンと切る

sniper *n.* 狙撃者, スナイパー

snob *n.* 気取り屋, お高くとまった人, 偉ぶった人

♦**snobbery** *n.* 気取り

snobbish *adj.* 気取った, お高くとまった

snoop *v.* こそこそかぎ回る

n. かぎ回る人

snooze *v.* うたた寝する, 居眠りする

n. うたた寝, 居眠り

snore *n., v.* いびき(をかく)

snorkel *n.* シュノーケル

snorkeling *n.* シュノーケリング

snort *v.* 鼻を鳴らす; (take through the nose: cocaine etc.) 吸い込む

n. (noise) 鼻を鳴らす音; (a single snort: of cocaine etc.) 吸飲

snot *n.* 鼻くそ

snow *n., v.* 雪(が降る)

Snow lay on the ground.

地面に雪が積もっていた。

It was snowing. 雪が降っていた。

♦**snow blower** *n.* 除雪機

snowplow *n.* 除雪車

snow tire *n.* スノータイヤ

snowball *n.* 雪の玉

v. 雪だるま式に大きくなる

snowboard(ing) *n.* スノーボード

v. (**snowboard**) スノーボードをする

♦**snowboarder** *n.* スノーボードをする人

snowfall *n.* (falling of snow) 降雪, (amount of snowfall) 降雪量

snowflake *n.* 雪, 雪片

snowman *n.* 雪だるま [→ ABOMINABLE SNOWMAN]

snowstorm *n.* 吹雪

snowy *adj.* 雪の多い

snowy streets 雪の道

snub *v.* (treat rudely) 鼻であしらう, (de-

S

liberately ignore) わざと無視する

snub-nosed *adj.* しし鼻の

snuff *v.* (**snuff out**) (=extinguish) 消す, (hopes etc.) 奪う, (=kill) 殺す

snug *adj.* (of place: cozy) 居心地のいい, (of clothing: close-fitting) ぴったり合う

♦**snugly** *adv.* (cozily) 居心地よく, (of fitting) ぴったり

snuggle *v.* (**snuggle up with/against**) …に寄り添う

so

1 *adv.* REFERRING TO WHAT HAS ALREADY BEEN SAID: そう, それ

2 *conj.* THEREFORE: …から, …ので

3 *adv.* EXTREMELY: すごく, とても, 本当に

4 *adv.* TO THAT EXTENT: そんなに

5 *conj.* IN ORDER THAT: …よう(に), …ために

6 *adv.* SIMILARLY: …も

7 *interj.* CHANGING TOPIC: ところで, さあ, さて

1 "You're not allowed to do that."
"Who says so?"
「そんなことは許されない」
「誰がそう言ってるの？」

"Is it snowing?"
"Yes, I'm afraid so."
「雪が降ってる？」
「うん、残念ながらそうみたい」

"Do you like wine? If so, I recommend this one."
「ワインはお好きですか？ それならこちらをおすすめします」

"Do you want to go?"
"No, I don't think so."
「行く？」
「いや、やめておく」

"The door's open." "So it is."
「ドアがあいてる」「ほんとだ」

"You look terrible."
"So would you, if you'd been through what I have."
「ひどい顔をしているね」
「同じことを経験すればこうなるよ」

2 This is important, so listen.
これは重要ですから、聞いてください。

He didn't speak much English, so we spoke in French.
彼は英語があまり話せなかったので、フランス語で話した。

3 I'm so nervous around her, I don't know what to do.
彼女といるととても緊張して、どうしたらいいかわからなくなる。

I'm so glad you could come.
来てくれて本当にうれしい。

4 Don't walk so fast.
そんなに速く歩かないで。

5 I write down what I need to do so I don't forget.
やらないといけないことを忘れないよう、書き留めている。

The bikes are here so people can use them.
ここの自転車は誰でも使えるように置いてある。

Turn the TV down so it doesn't wake him.
彼を起こさないよう、テレビの音を小さくして。

6 "He was late." "So were you."
「彼は遅刻した」「あなたもね」

7 So, how have you been?
ところで、どうしてるの？

So, what shall we have for dinner to-

night?
さて、晩ご飯は何にしようか？

and so on …など

You can go skiing, skating, and so on.
スキーやスケートなどができます。

go so far as to say → FAR

like so こうやって, こういうふうに

You tie it like so.
こうやって結ぶんですよ。

so far → FAR

so long → LONG[1]

so long as → LONG[1]

so many/much たくさんの, とても多くの

There were so many people there we couldn't get a ticket.
人がとても多くて、チケットが買えなかった。

so what それがどうしたっていうんだ, だから何？

So what if I'm always late!
いつも遅刻するからって、それがどうだっていうんだ！

"You quit your job." "So what?"
「仕事を辞めたんだね」「だから何？」

soak *v.* (put in liquid) 浸す, つける, (sit in liquid) つかる, (**become soaked**) ずぶぬれになる, びしょぬれになる; (**soak up**: liquid) 吸い込む

I've left the dishes to soak.
お皿を水につけておいた。

I like to soak in a hot bath after a long, hard day of work.
一日中きつい仕事をした後、熱いおふろにつかるのが好きです。

Our clothes were soaked.
服はずぶぬれだった。

♦**soaking-wet** *adj.* ずぶぬれの, びしょぬれの

so-and-so *n.* (unnamed person) なんとかさん, 誰それ, (thing) 何々

soap *n.* せっけん [→picture of BATHROOM]

soap opera *n.* 連続メロドラマ

soar *v.* (fly high in the sky) 空高く舞い上がる, (rise into the sky) 空高く上がる; (rise/increase suddenly) 急に上がる

sob *v.* 泣きじゃくる [→ CRY]

soba *n.* (buckwheat noodles) そば, 蕎麦

sober *adj.* (not drunk) しらふの, 酔っていない

v. (**sober up**) 酔いがさめる

sobering *adj.* (of experience: causing one to think) 考えさせる

so-called *adj.* いわゆる, 俗に言う

the so-called domino effect
いわゆるドミノ効果

soccer *n.* サッカー

sociable *adj.* 社交的な, 人付き合いのいい

social *v.* (involving interaction with people) 社交の, 付き合いの, (sociable) 社交的な, (connected with society) 社会の

a social occasion 社交の場

She's not a very social person.
彼女はあまり社交的な人じゃない。

a social problem 社会問題

♦**social life** *n.* 社会生活

social security *n.* 社会保障

social service *n.* 社会事業

social welfare *n.* 社会福祉

social work *n.* 社会福祉事業

social worker *n.* ソーシャルワーカー

socialism *n.* 社会主義

socialist *n.* 社会主義者

socialize *v.* (interact with people) 交流する, (socialize with) (…と) 交際する

social science *n.* 社会科学

social studies *n.* (in school) 社会科

society *n.* (social community) 社会, 世間, (organization) 協会

a capitalist society 資本主義社会

a primitive society 原始社会

a multiracial society 多民族社会

a drama society 演劇協会

sociological *adj.* 社会学的な

sociologist *n.* 社会学者

sociology *n.* 社会学

sock *n.* (**socks**) 靴下, ソックス

a pair of socks 靴下1足

put on [take off] one's socks

靴下をはく[脱ぐ]

socket *n.* 差し込み口

soda *n.* 炭酸飲料, ソーダ(水)

sodium *n.* ナトリウム

sofa *n.* ソファー

soft *adj.*

1 YIELDING: 柔らかい, ソフトな

2 SMOOTH: 滑らかな, 柔らかい, (of texture: soft to the touch) 肌触りのいい

3 OF SOUND: 優しい, 静かな, 穏やかな

4 GENTLE: 優しい, おとなしい, 物静かな

5 OF COLOR: 柔らかい, ソフトな

6 FEEBLE: 弱い, 軟弱な

7 NOT STRICT: (**be soft on**) …に甘い

1 a soft mattress 柔らかいマットレス

a soft collar 柔らかいえり

a soft toothbrush 柔らかい歯ブラシ

2 soft fur 滑らかな毛皮

soft skin 柔らかい肌

a soft towel 肌触りのいいタオル

3 a soft voice 優しい声

soft music 静かな音楽

4 a soft, caring person

優しくて思いやりのある人

a soft heart 優しい心

5 soft green hues 柔らかい緑色

6 a soft person 軟弱な人

7 There's no need to be soft on him.

あの人に甘くする必要などない。

♦**soft drug** *n.* 中毒性のない薬

softness *n.* (to touch) 柔らかさ, (gentleness) 穏やかさ

soft water *n.* 軟水

softball *n.* ソフトボール

soft drink *n.* 清涼飲料, ソフトドリンク

soften *v.* (food) 柔らかくする, (attitude, tone of voice, blow) 和らげる

softly *adv.* (quietly) 静かに, (tenderly) 優しく

soft-spoken *adj.* 穏やかに話す

software *n.* ソフト(ウェア)

soggy *adj.* (soft, spongy) ねっとりした, ベチャッとした, (of ground) 水浸しの

soggy cereal ベチャッとしたシリアル

soil *n.* (earth) 土, ((*formal*)) 土壌

soiled *adj.* (dirty) 汚れた, (stained) しみのついた

solace *n.* (comfort) 安堵, 慰め

find solace in …に慰めを見出す

solar *adj.* 太陽の

♦**solar energy/power** *n.* 太陽エネルギー, 太陽光発電

solar panel *n.* ソーラーパネル, 太陽電池

solar-powered car ***n.*** ソーラーカー

solar system ***n.*** 太陽系

solder ***v.*** はんだ付けにする

n. はんだ

soldier ***n.*** 兵士, 兵隊, 軍人

sole[1] ***adj.*** 唯一の, たった一つの, (of person) たった一人の [→ SINGLE 1]

the sole survivor 唯一の生存者

I went with the sole purpose of meeting him.
彼に会うためだけに行った。

sole[2] ***n.*** (of foot) 足の裏, (of shoe)(靴の)底

solely ***adv.*** (exclusively) もっぱら

My trip to Italy was solely for pleasure.
イタリアへの旅は、もっぱら観光のためだった。

solemn ***adj.*** 厳粛な, 厳かな

a solemn ceremony 厳粛な式典

solicit ***v.*** 求める, 請う; (of prostitute) 客を引く

♦**soliciting** ***n.*** (crime) 客引き

solicitor ***n.*** (person who solicits) 勧誘員

solid

1 ***n., adj.*** NOT LIQUID/GAS: 固体(の)

2 ***adj.*** HARD: かたい

3 ***adj.*** STRONG: しっかりした, (of physique) がっしりした, (of evidence) 確かな

4 ***adj.*** CONTINUOUS: ぶっ通しの, (**a solid...**: week, month, year etc.) まる...

5 ***adj.*** PURE: 純粋の, 純-

6 ***n.*** SHAPE: (geometric shape) 立体

1 Is glass a liquid or a solid?
ガラスは液体ですか、固体ですか?

a solid object 固体

2 solid rock 堅い岩

solid ice 堅い氷

3 a solid foundation しっかりした土台

a solid build (referring to physique)
がっしりした体つき

There is no solid evidence to suggest that.
そう思わせるような確かな証拠は、ありません。

4 I studied for three solid hours.
3時間ぶっ通しで勉強した。

It took two solid weeks for them to reply.
向こうは返事をするのに、まる2週間かかった。

5 solid gold 純金

solidarity ***n.*** 連帯, 団結

a feeling of solidarity 連帯感

solidify ***v.*** (make/become solid) 固める/固まる, 堅くする/堅くなる

solidly ***adv.*** (continuously) ぶっ通しで; (strongly) しっかりと

solitaire ***n.*** (card game) 一人遊び

solitary ***adj.*** (alone) 孤独な, 独りぼっちの, (enjoys being alone) 孤独を好む, (of activity) 一人でする, (of place) 寂しい, 人里離れた

♦**solitary confinement** ***n.*** 独房監禁

solitude ***n.*** 孤独

solo ***n.*** ソロ, (song) 独唱曲, (instrumental) 独奏曲, (dance performance) 独演

adj. ソロの, (done alone) 単独の

adv. 一人で, 単独で

sing a solo 独唱する

play a solo 独奏する

fly solo 単独飛行する

♦**soloist** *n.* ソリスト, (singer) 独唱者, (musician) 独奏者

solstice *n.* 至

the summer solstice 夏至

the winter solstice 冬至

soluble *adj.* (dissolvable) 溶ける

solution *n.* (answer to problem) 解決, (remedy) 解決法, 解決策; (liquid solution) 溶液, -水

It seemed there was only one solution.
解決法は一つしかないようだった。

Is there a solution to this problem?
この問題の解決策はありますか？

a solution of salt and water 食塩水

solve *v.* 解く, 解決する [→ ANSWER]

Have you solved the question yet?
問題は解けた？

This raises more questions than it solves.
解決するどころか、さらなる疑問を招く。

solvent *n.* 溶媒

adj. (able to pay debts) 支払い能力がある

somber *adj.* (serious) 深刻な, (dark) 薄暗い, (of color) 地味な, (of news) 暗い, (of mood) 憂うつな

sombrero *n.* ソンブレロ

some

1 *adj.* A NONSPECIFIC AMOUNT/NUMBER OF: (referring to a countable noun) いくつかの, (referring to an uncountable noun) いくらかの, 多少の [NOTE: Not always translated into Japanese. See examples below.]

2 *pron.* NONSPECIFIC AMOUNT/NUMBER: (referring to a countable noun) いくつか, (**some people**) 何人か, (**some places**) 何ヵ所か, (referring to an uncountable noun) いくらか, 多少

3 *adj.* A CERTAIN: ある, 何かの, 何らかの

4 *adv.* APPROXIMATELY: 約, およそ, …くらい, (used after a number) …数-, …あまり

5 *adv.* TO A CERTAIN EXTENT: (to a minor extent) 少し, (considerably) かなり

1 We had some bread. パンを食べた。

Some friends are coming over later.
友達が(何人か)あとで来ます。

I've got some presents for you.
あなたに贈り物があるんです。

I haven't been to a movie for some years.
ここ何年か、映画を見に行ってない。

2 I gave some to you, didn't I?
いくつかあげたよね？

Some of them refused to accept the offer.
何人かは申し出を断った。

I've visited some of those places.
そのうちの何ヵ所かは訪ねたことがある。

Some of the food was spoiled.
腐った食物もあった。

3 To some extent, that's true.
ある程度まで、それは真実だ。

For some reason, the experiment didn't work.
何らかの理由で、実験はうまくいかなかった。

4 The nearest town is some ten kilometers away.
隣町までは10キロくらいある。

Twenty some people were at the party.
２０数人 [２０人あまり] がパーティーに出席していた。

S

5 The swelling has gone down some.
はれが少しひいてきた。

somebody *pron.* 誰か, ある人 [→ SOMEONE]

someday *adv.* いつか, そのうち

We'll meet again someday.
いつかまた会いましょう。

Someday we'll be able to afford a cruise.
そのうち、クルーズに行ける余裕もできるだろう。

somehow *adv.* (in a way not known) なんとかして, どうにかして, (for a reason not understood) どういう訳か, どうも

We'll manage somehow.
なんとかなりますよ。

He managed it somehow or other.
彼は、どうにかこうにかやり遂げた。

Somehow I just couldn't bring myself to say so.
どういう訳か、どうしてもそれを口に出せなかった。

Somehow I just don't trust him.
どうもあの人は信用できない。

someone *pron.* 誰か, ある人, ((*formal*)) ある人物

There's someone at the door.
誰かが訪ねて来たよ。

Someone wants to speak to you.
あなたと話したがっている人がいます。

There was a panic, and someone got hurt.
パニック状態になり、けが人が出た。

She's writing a book about someone—a famous politician, I think.
彼女はある人物に関する本を書いている—それは有名な政治家だと思いますが。

someplace → SOMEWHERE

somersault *n.* 宙返り, とんぼ返り *v.* 宙返りする, とんぼ返りする

something *pron.* 何か, あること, あるもの

Something was moving in the distance.
何かが遠くで動いていた。

I knew I'd forgotten something.
何か忘れてると思った。

I have something to tell you.
ちょっと話したいことがあるんです。

I was going to tell her, but she started talking about something else.
言おうと思ったら、彼女が何かほかのことを話し始めた。

I can't remember exactly what he said, but it was something like this...
彼が何て言ったか正確には思い出せないけど、こんなようなことだった...

I think she's thirty something.
彼女は 30 いくつだと思う。

Oh, what's she called? Sarah something.
彼女の名前は何だっけ？ サラなんとかさん。

have something to do with ...と/に関係がある

He has something to do with sales.
彼は営業関係の仕事をしている。

or something ...か何か

He couldn't come. His car broke down, or something.
彼は来られなかった。車がえんこしたか何からしい。

something like a ...のような, ...に似た

The Celtic harp is small and something like a lyre.
ケルト族のハープは小さくて、竪琴のようなものだ。

something of a ちょっとした

She's something of a celebrity around here.
彼女はこのあたりでは、ちょっとした有名人だ。

something tells me …ような気がする

Something tells me that all is not well.
何かが、おかしいような気がする。

sometime *adv.* (referring to the past) いつだったか, ある時, (referring to the future) いつか, そのうち

I met them sometime last year.
去年のいつだったか、彼らに会った。

It'll all end sometime.
そのうちすべて終わるよ。

sometimes *adv.* 時々, 時たま, たまに

Sometimes I wonder if they know what they're doing.
時々、彼らは自分たちがしていることをわかっているのだろうかと思う。

"Do you visit them every day?"
"No, just sometimes."
「毎日訪ねているのですか？」
「いいえ、ほんのたまにです」

somewhat *adv.* ちょっと, 多少, やや [→ RATHER 2]

somewhere *adv.* (in/at a place) どこかに/で, (to a place) どこかへ/に

The restaurant is somewhere in Ginza.
レストランは銀座のどこかにあります。

"Do you have some toothpicks?"
"Yes, they're somewhere in that drawer."
「爪楊枝はある？」
「ええ、その引き出しのどこかにあるよ」

I read about that somewhere.
どこかでそのことを読んだ。

get somewhere (in life) 成功する, うまくいく

I expect he'll get somewhere in life.
あの人はきっと成功すると思う。

somewhere between/in the range of おおよそ [→ APPROXIMATELY]

son *n.* (one's own) 息子, ((*humble*)) せがれ, (sb else's) 息子さん, (お)坊ちゃん

How old is your son?
息子さんは何歳ですか？

This is our eldest son, and this is our youngest.
これが長男で、こっちが末の息子です。

one's first-born son 長男

one's second-born son <u>次男</u> [二男]

the next-youngest son
下から2番目の息子

sonar *n.* ソナー

song *n.* 歌, 曲, (of bird, animal) 鳴き声

It was a beautiful song.
美しい歌だった。

We all burst into song.
私たちみんなで一斉に歌い出した。

the canary's song カナリアの鳴き声

♦**songwriter** *n.* (composer of songs) 作曲家, (composer of lyrics) 作詞家

sonic *adj.* 音の, 音響の

♦**sonic boom** *n.* ソニックブーム, 衝撃波音

son-in-law *n.* (one's own) 娘婿, 婿, 義理の息子, (sb else's) お婿さん

soon *adv.*

1 IN A SHORT TIME: もうすぐ, まもなく, すぐ(に), そろそろ

2 EARLY: 早く

1 "What time are you leaving?" "Soon."

「何時に出かけるの？」「もうすぐ」

Soon it will start snowing.
まもなく雪が降り始めるだろう。

They started going out soon after they met.
出会ってすぐに、付き合い始めた。

It'll soon be time to start packing.
もうそろそろ荷造りする時だ。

2 It's too soon to start talking about getting married.
結婚の話をするには、まだ早すぎます。

I should finish this work in a couple of weeks, if not sooner.
この仕事は、あと数週間か、あるいはもう少し早く終わるはずだ。

How soon do you think you will finish?
あと、どのくらいで終わると思う？

as soon as …するとすぐ(に), …したらすぐ(に)

Let me know as soon as you arrive.
到着したらすぐに、知らせてください。

as soon as possible できるだけ早く

I want you to do it as soon as possible.
できるだけ早くやってほしい。

no sooner had one done … than …したらすぐ(に), …したとたん(に)

No sooner had I gotten into the bath than the phone rang.
おふろに入ったとたん、電話のベルが鳴った。

sooner or later 遅かれ早かれ

Sooner or later, he'll get what's coming to him.
遅かれ早かれ、彼は報いを受けるだろう。

would just as soon (どちらかといえば) …したい

Thank you, but I'd just as soon walk.
ありがとう。でも歩きたい気分なんです。

soot *n.* すす

soothe *v.* (cause to feel relaxed) なだめる, 静める, 落ち着かせる, (pain) 和らげる

soothe the pain 痛みを和らげる

sop *n.* (bribe) わいろ

v. (**sop up**: remove moisture from) 吸い取る

sophisticated *adj.* (of person) あかぬけた, 洗練された, (of machine) 精巧な, 高性能の

sophistication *n.* (of person) 洗練, (of machine) 精巧さ

sophomore *n.* 2年生

soprano *n.* ソプラノ

sordid *adj.* (dirty) 汚い, (squalid, shabby) みすぼらしい, (unpleasant) いやな

sore *adj.* (painful) 痛い

sorely *adv.* (badly) ひどく, (very much) 大いに, すごく

He will be sorely missed.
彼がいなくなると、すごく寂しくなるよ。

sorority *n.* (society of female university students) 女子学生社交クラブ

sorrow *n.* 悲しみ

sorrowful *adj.* 悲しい, 悲しそうな

sorry *adj.*

1 APOLOGIZING: すみません, ごめんなさい, ((*formal*)) 申し訳ありません [→ PARDON]

2 EXPRESSING SYMPATHY: 気の毒だ, かわいそうだ, (**feel sorry for**) …に同情する

3 FEELING REGRET: 後悔している, すまないと思う

4 EXPRESSING DISAPPOINTMENT: 残念だ

5 PITIFUL: かわいそうな, 気の毒な, みじめな

1 I'm sorry I'm late. 遅れてすみません。

I'm sorry if I upset you.
気を悪くしたのなら謝ります。

Sorry about the mess in my room.
部屋が散らかっていてごめんね。

(*on phone*) "I'd like to speak to Mr. Ito, please."
"Sorry, but he's not in right now."
「伊藤さんを、お願いします」
「申し訳ありませんが、ただ今席を外しております」

I'm sorry, but you're mistaken.
失礼ですが、それは違います。

2 I wasn't a bit sorry to hear he'd been sacked.
あの人が首になったと聞いても、ちっともかわいそうとは思わなかった。

"I'm afraid she died last week."
"Oh, I'm sorry."
「残念ながら、彼女は先週亡くなりました」
「お気の毒に」

I don't know whether to feel sorry for her or not.
彼女に同情すべきかどうかわからない。

3 He seems sorry about the trouble he's caused.
彼は面倒を起こしたことを後悔しているようだ。

4 I'm sorry to hear that you didn't pass.
合格できなくて残念だったね。

5 a sorry state of affairs みじめな状態

say (one is) sorry 謝る

Say you're sorry. 謝りなさい。

---

sort *n.* (type) 種類, タイプ, 種, (**this sort of**) こういう, (**that sort of**) そういう, ああいう, (**all sorts of**) あらゆる, (**what sort of**) どんな, どういう

v. (arrange) 分ける, 分類する

It's a mushroom of some sort.
ある種のキノコです。

This sort of journalism irritates me.
こういう記事にはいらいらする。

Are you interested in this sort of thing?
こういったことに興味がありますか？

All sorts of people were there.
あらゆるタイプの人がいた。

What sort of cheese do you like?
どんなチーズが好きですか？

What sort of person is she?
彼女はどんな人ですか？

Let's sort them into two piles.
二つの山に分けましょう。

The mail is sorted by department.
郵便物は部門別に分類される。

sort out *v.* (arrange) 整理する, (decide) 決める, (solve) 解決する, (bring to a conclusion) まとめる, 収拾する

It took me three hours to sort out the stuff in my desk.
机の中の物を整理するのに3時間かかった。

It's about time you sorted out your priorities.
そろそろ優先順位を整理する時だよ。

Exactly how this will be done has not yet been sorted out.
実際にどうやるかは、まだ決まっていない。

Someone's going to have to sort out this mess you've caused.

君が巻き起こしたこの混乱は、誰かが収拾しなくてはいけないんだよ。

sort through *v.* (papers, photos) 仕分ける, えり分ける

---

sortie *n.* (military) 出撃, 突撃

so-so *adv., adj.* まあまあ(の)

soufflé *n.* スフレ

sought-after *adj.* 引っ張りだこの

soul *n.* (spirit) 魂, 精神, (emotional and intellectual energy) 情熱; (soul music) ソウル

Obon is a time when we pray for the souls of our ancestors.
お盆は、先祖の魂に祈る時です。

His soul wasn't in the job anymore.
彼は仕事に情熱がなくなった。

soulful *adj.* 感情のこもった

sound[1]

1 *n.* SOMETHING HEARD: 音, 音響, (referring to music) サウンド, (sound level) 音量

2 *v.* SEEM: ...ようだ, <adj. stem /-ますstem> +そうだ, ...ように思える, (based on sound/words) ...ように聞こえる

3 *v.* PRODUCE SOUND: 音を立てる, 鳴る, (sound an alarm etc.) 鳴らす

4 *v.* PRONOUNCE: (**sound out**) 発音する

1 What sort of sound does the instrument make?
その楽器はどんな音が出るの?

I heard what I thought was the sound of a garage door closing.
車庫の扉が閉まるような音が聞こえた。

The band has its own kind of sound.
そのバンドは独特のサウンドをもっている。

Could you turn down [up] the sound?
音量を下げて[上げて]もらえますか/音を小さく[大きく]してくれる?

2 Did he sound happy?
彼は幸せそうだった?

She sounded as if she wasn't that keen on the idea.
彼女はその案に乗り気ではないように聞こえた。

You sound just like your father.
あなたの話しぶりは、お父さんにそっくりだ。

"He says he wants to move to Alaska." "Sounds crazy to me."
「彼はアラスカに移住したいと言ってる」「どうかしてるよ」

3 The buzzer sounded. ブザーが鳴った。

Someone sounded the alarm.
誰かが非常ベルを鳴らした。

4 Sound it out slowly, please.
ゆっくり発音してみて。

♦**sound barrier** *n.* 音速の壁

sound effect *n.* 音響効果

sound[2]

1 *adj.* COGENT/VALID: もっともな, 妥当な

2 *adj.* THOROUGH: 十分な, きちんとした, 徹底的な

3 *adj.* HEALTHY AND GOOD: 健全な, 健康な

4 *adv.* DEEPLY: (of sleep) ぐっすり(と)

1 The president put forth sound reasons for going to war.
大統領は、戦争をするもっともな理由を挙げた。

The argument is sound.
その議論はもっともだ。

2 The boy has a sound grasp of basic ge-

ometry.
あの子は幾何学の基礎をきちんと理解している。

3 Are you of sound health in body and mind?
心身ともに健康ですか？

4 I was sound asleep and didn't even notice the earthquake.
ぐっすり眠って [熟睡して] いたので地震にさえ気づかなかった。

soundproof ***adj.*** 防音の
a soundproof room 防音室

soundtrack ***n.*** サウンドトラック, ((*informal*)) サントラ

sound wave ***n.*** 音波

soup ***n.*** スープ, 汁
miso soup みそ汁

sour ***adj.*** (having a sharp taste) すっぱい, (rotten) 腐った
n. (cocktail) サワー
sour grapes 負け惜しみ

source ***n.*** 源, (of problem) もと, 原因, (of information) 出所, (of river) 水源, 源流
a source of friction 摩擦の原因
Could you tell me the source of your information?
その情報源を教えてもらえませんか？
News sources confirmed fighting had broken out in the capital.
消息筋は、首都で戦闘が勃発したことを確認した。
The source of the Nile remained a mystery for a long time.
ナイル川の水源は長い間、なぞに包まれていた。

KANJI BRIDGE

源 ON: げん KUN: みなもと | **ORIGIN, BEGINNING, ROOT, SOURCE**

beginning, origin	起源
etymology	語源
focus, hypocenter	震源
power source	電源
resources	資源
revenue source	財源
source of information	情報源
water source	水源

south ***n.*** 南, 南方, (southern part) 南部
adj. 南の, (south-facing) 南向きの
adv. 南に/へ
Which way is south?
南はどっちですか？
The window in the bedroom faces south.
寝室の窓は南向きです。
The south of England boasts a warmer climate than the north.
イギリス南部は北部よりも気候が温暖だ。
A warm, south wind was blowing.
暖かい南風が吹いていた。
We went south through Memphis.
メンフィスを通って南へ向かった。

♦**South Pole** ***n.*** 南極

South Africa ***n.*** 南アフリカ

South America ***n.*** 南アメリカ, 南米

southeast ***n.*** 南東
adj., adv. 南東の/に

Southeast Asia ***n.*** 東南アジア

southerly ***adj.*** (of wind) 南からの

southern ***adj.*** (in the south) 南の, (south-facing) 南向きの

S

♦**Southern Hemisphere** *n.* 南半球

South Korea *n.* 韓国 [→ KOREAN]

southward *adv.* 南の方へ, 南に向かって

adj. 南(へ)の

southwest *n.* 南西

adj., adv. 南西の/に

souvenir *n.* おみやげ, 記念品

sovereign *n.* 主権者, (monarch) 君主, (ruler) 統治者

adj. 主権を有する

a sovereign nation 主権国家

♦**sovereignty** *n.* 主権

have sovereignty over ...の主権をもつ

sow *v.* (seeds) ((*also figurative*)) 種をまく

soybean *n.* 大豆

soy milk *n.* 豆乳

soy sauce *n.* しょうゆ

spa *n.* 温泉

space *n.*

1 ROOM: 場所, 広さ, スペース

2 AREA FOR A SPECIFIC PURPOSE: 場所, 場, スペース

3 OUTER SPACE: 宇宙

4 THREE-DIMENSIONAL SPACE: 空間

5 PERSONAL FREEDOM: 自由

1 There's not much storage space.
収納場所があまりない。

Leave a bit of space for me.
私のために場所を少しあけておいて。

There was just enough space to get the table into the room.
テーブルを部屋に入れるのに、ぎりぎりの広さだった。

The space between the lines is too wide.
行間が広すぎる。

2 a space for a refrigerator
冷蔵庫を置く場所

a play space for children
子供たちの遊び場

a parking space 駐車スペース

3 Somewhere in space, there's got to be another planet like Earth.
宇宙のどこかに、地球のような惑星がきっとあるはずだ。

4 time and space 時間と空間

5 He won't give me any space.
彼といると、自由なんかない。

♦**space age** *n.* 宇宙時代

space bar *n.* (button on keyboard) スペースキー, スペースバー

spaceflight *n.* 宇宙飛行

space shuttle *n.* スペースシャトル

space suit *n.* 宇宙服

space travel *n.* 宇宙旅行

space walk *n.* 宇宙遊泳

spaceship *n.* 宇宙船

spacing *n.* (between lines) 行間

spacious *adj.* 広い, 広々とした

a spacious room 広い部屋

spade[1] *n.* (tool) すき

spade[2] *n.* (**spades**: suit of cards) スペード

spaghetti *n.* スパゲッティ

Spain *n.* スペイン, ((*in abbr.*)) 西

spam *n.* (unwanted e-mail) 迷惑メール

span *n.* (length) 長さ, 全長, (of time) 間, 期間

v. (of bridge: extend across) (...に) かかっている

a span of six months 6ヵ月間

spaniel *n.* スパニエル犬

Spanish *n.* (person) スペイン人, (language) スペイン語

adj. (of country, culture) スペインの, (of person) スペイン人の, (of language) スペイン語の

spank *v.* ピシャリとたたく

spanner *n.* スパナ, レンチ [→ picture of TOOL]

spar[1] *n.* (mast of a ship) スパー, 円材

spar[2] *v.* (practice boxing) スパーリングする, (argue) 口論する

spar[3] *n.* (mineral) スパー, へげ石

spare

1 *adj.* ADDITIONAL TO WHAT IS NEEDED: 予備の, 余分な, スペアの [→ SPARE TIME]

2 *v.* ALLOW TO HAVE: (cash) 貸す, (time) さく

3 *v.* HAVE MERCY ON: (…の) 命を助ける

4 *v.* NOT FORCE TO TOLERATE: 勘弁する

1 a spare tire スペアタイヤ

Do we have any spare scissors?
予備のはさみは、ある?

Don't forget to take a spare shirt.
予備のシャツを持っていくのを忘れないように。

There's enough spare blankets should you feel cold during the night.
夜中に寒いと思われたときのために、毛布は十分に用意してありますから。

2 Can you spare me a dollar?
1ドル貸してもらえませんか?

I'm afraid I don't have any money to spare.
悪いけど、余分なお金はないんだ。

Do you have five minutes to spare?
5分、時間をさいてもらえますか?

I finished the exam with ten minutes to spare.
10分の余裕をもって試験を終えた。

3 My life was spared.
命を助けてもらった / 命拾いした。

4 Can you spare me the lecture?
お説教は勘弁してくれる?

♦ **spare part** *n.* スペア, 予備部品, 交換部品

spare time *n.* 暇, 余暇, 時間のゆとり

I have no spare time.
時間のゆとりが全然ない。

sparing *adj.* (be sparing with: not use so much of) 節約する, 控える, (be sparing of) 惜しむ

♦ **sparingly** *adv.* 控え目に

spark *n.* 火花

v. (give off sparks) 火花を散らす

♦ **spark plug** *n.* 点火プラグ

sparkle *v.* (give off sparks) 火花を散らす, (shine) ((*also figurative*)) 光る, 輝く

sparkling *adj.* ((*also figurative*)) 光る, 輝く, きらめく

♦ **sparkling wine** *n.* スパークリングワイン, 発泡ぶどう酒

sparrow *n.* スズメ, 雀

sparse *adj.* (of population, audience) まばらな, (of hair) 薄い

spartan *adj.* (simple) 質素な; (**Spartan**: of people of Sparta) スパルタ人の

spasm *n.* けいれん, ひきつけ, 発作

spatial *adj.* 空間の

spatter *v.* (spatter A on B/spatter B with A) (BにAを) はねかける, まき散らす

spatula *n.* へら, フライ返し [→ picture of COOKING UTENSILS]

S

spawn *v.* (give rise to) 生じる, 引き起こす

n. (eggs) 卵

---

speak *v.*

1 UTTER LANGUAGE: 話す, しゃべる, 言う, 口をきく

2 KNOW/USE A LANGUAGE: 話す, (**can speak**) 話せる, しゃべれる

3 DISCUSS: 話す, 話をする, 相談する

4 DECLARE: 言う, ((*formal*)) 述べる

5 GIVE A SPEECH: 演説する, 講演する

1 She spoke with an Australian accent.
彼女はオーストラリアなまりで話した。

I didn't have a chance to speak.
話す機会がなかった。

Have you spoken to him?
彼に話した?

He stared at me without speaking.
彼は何も言わずに私を見つめた。

"Hello, Henry speaking."
「もしもし、ヘンリーです」

2 Do you speak English?
英語を話せますか?

He speaks Urdu and English fluently.
あの人はウルドゥー語と英語を流ちょうに話す。

3 She often speaks of life during the war.
彼女はよく戦時中の生活の話をする。

I spoke with him about that matter this morning.
そのことについてけさ、彼と相談した。

4 Speak your views!
((*masculine*)) 自分の考えを言えよ!

She spoke her mind.
彼女は自分の意見を述べた。

5 The mayor spoke, as did one or two other dignitaries.
市長と、ほかに一人か二人の要人も演説した。

How long did he speak?
彼はどのくらい講演したんですか?

as we speak ちょうど今

generally speaking 一般的に言えば

speak ill of 悪く言う, けなす, (...の) 悪口を言う

speaking of ...と言えば

Speaking of Fred, is it true he's gone abroad?
フレッドって言えば、彼、外国へ行ったって本当?

speak for *v.* ...の意見を代弁する

speak for itself 物語っている, 明らかだ

The evidence speaks for itself.
証拠を見れば明らかだ。

Speak for yourself! 自分といっしょにするな!

speak out (against) *v.* (...に反対して) 意見を述べる

speak up *v.* 大きな声で話す, (**speak up for**) かばう, 弁護する

---

speaker *n.* (person talking) 話す人, (speech giver) 演説者, (**the Speaker of the House**) 議長; (piece of stereo equipment) スピーカー

the Speaker of the House 下院議長

spear *n., v.* やり (で突く)

spearhead *v.* (lead) (...の) 先頭に立つ

spearmint *n.* スペアミント

special ***adj.*** 特別な, 特殊な, (unique) 独特の

n. (dish at a restaurant) 特別料理, おすすめ料理, (TV program) 特別番組

special preparations 特別な準備

Professor Ueda has a special interest in Renaissance art.
上田先生はルネッサンス美術に特別な関心がある。

He was a special adviser to the prime minister.
あの人は首相の特別顧問だった。

They've got something special planned.
彼らには何か特別な企画がある。

She did it for us as a special favor.
彼女は私たちのために、特別にやってくれた。

This cake was made from my mother-in-law's special recipe.
このケーキは義理の母の特製レシピで作りました。

She shows a special talent in learning languages.
彼女には、言語の習得に特殊な才能がある。

What's so special about the film?
その映画の何がそんなに独特なの？

♦**special effect** ***n.*** 特殊効果

specialist ***n.*** 専門家, スペシャリスト

specialize ***v.*** 専門とする

specialized ***adj.*** 専門の

specialized knowledge 専門知識

specially ***adv.*** 特別に

specialty ***n.*** (area of expertise) 専門; (famous product of a place) 名物, (famous food of a particular restaurant) おすすめ, 自慢料理

species ***n.*** 種類, (taxonomic category) 種

And what species does this creature belong to?
この生き物は何の種に属していますか？

specific ***adj.*** (concrete) 具体的な, はっきりした, 明確な, (particular) 特定の

n. (**specifics**) 細かいこと, 詳細, 細部

Could you give us a specific example?
具体的な例を挙げてもらえませんか？

for a specific purpose ある特定の目的で

Let's not discuss the specifics right now.
今は細かいことを議論するのはやめよう。

the specifics of the job 仕事の詳細

to be more specific もっと具体的に言えば, もっとはっきり言うと

A boy, or to be more specific, my son…
男の子、もっとはっきり言うと私の息子は…

specifically ***adv.*** (clearly) はっきり, 明確に, (qualifying a statement) 特に, とりわけ

I specifically told you not to do that.
それはやっちゃいけないと、はっきり言ったでしょ。

specification ***n.*** (**specifications**) 仕様書

specify ***v.*** 具体的に述べる, 指定する, 明確に述べる

specimen ***n.*** 見本, (of plant, animal, mineral) 標本, (of blood, urine) サンプル

speck ***n.*** (spot) しみ, 小さな汚れ, (small grain of sth) 細かい粒

speckled ***adj.*** まだらの, 斑点のある

spectacle ***n.*** (magnificent sight) 壮観, (event) ショー, スペクタクル

make a spectacle of oneself 恥をさらす

spectacular *adj.* 壮大な, 豪華な
a spectacular view 壮大な眺め
spectator *n.* 観客, 見物人
♦**spectator sport** *n.* 大観衆を集めるスポーツ
specter *n.* (ghost) 幽霊, お化け, 妖怪
spectrum *n.* スペクトル
speculate *v.* (conjecture) 推測する, 見当をつける; (risk money) 投機をする
speculation *n.* (conjecturing) 推測, 憶測; (risking of money) 投機
speech *n.* (public) スピーチ, ((*formal*)) 演説, (act of speaking) 話すこと, (spoken words) 話し言葉, (way of speaking) 話し方
Mr. Kaji gave a speech at the wedding.
梶さんは結婚式でスピーチをした。
That was a fine speech.
すばらしい演説だった。
Is the boy capable of speech?
その子は話すことができますか？
Speech is very different from writing.
話し言葉は書き言葉とはまるで違う。
Nakajima's speech is not very clear.
中島さんの話し方はあまり明瞭ではない。
the right to free speech 言論の自由
♦**speech recognition** *n.* 音声認識
speech therapy *n.* 言語障害治療
speechless *adj.* 口がきけない, 言葉が出ない
be left speechless 言葉を失う
speechwriter *n.* (for politician) スピーチ原稿を書く人
speed
1 *n.* RATE OF MOTION: スピード, 速度, 速さ
2 *v.* MOVE QUICKLY: 速く走る, スピードを出す, 飛ばす, (**speed up**) 加速する
3 *v.* DRIVE TOO FAST: スピードを出しすぎる, (drive at an illegal speed) スピード違反をする
4 *v.* CAUSE TO MOVE QUICKLY: (**speed up**) スピードアップする
5 *n.* DRUG: スピード
1 He was traveling at a speed of fifty kilometers per hour.
彼は時速50キロ(の速さ)で走っていた。
This car can travel at high speeds.
この車は高速で走れる。
the speed and accuracy of a computer
コンピューターの速度と精度
2 We sped along the expressway.
私たちは高速道路を飛ばした。
The motorcycle sped up and passed us.
バイクは加速して私たちを追い越した。
3 You're speeding. You'd better slow down.
スピードの出しすぎだ。速度を落としたほうがいい。
She was caught speeding.
彼女はスピード違反で捕まった。
4 Is there a way to speed up the process?
工程をスピードアップする方法は、ありますか？
5 Speed is an amphetamine.
スピードというのはアンフェタミンだ。
♦**speed freak** *n.* スピード狂
speedily *adv.* 速く, すぐに, ((*formal*)) 速やかに
speed limit *n.* 制限速度
You're breaking the speed limit.
制限速度を超えているよ。

S

speed of light *n.* 光の速さ

speed of sound *n.* 音速

speedboat *n.* 高速モーターボート

speedometer *n.* スピードメーター [→ picture of CAR]

speed skating *n.* スピードスケート

spell[1] *v.* (name/write the letters of) つづる, (...の)つづりを言う/書く; (portend) もたらす, (...に)なる

Can you spell *committee*?
「コミッティー」のつづりを書けますか?

Sean is spelled *S-E-A-N*.
ショーンは、*S-E-A-N*とつづります。

The earthquake following a long rain spelled disaster.
長雨の後の地震が災害をもたらした。

spell[2] *n.* (words used as a charm) 魔法, 呪文

They say the witch cast a spell on him.
魔女が彼に魔法をかけたと言われている。

spell[3] *n.* (period of time) しばらくの間, 一時期

There was a hot spell last week.
先週は暑い日がしばらく続いた。

spellchecker *n.* スペルチェッカー

spelling *n.* つづり, スペル, (ability to spell) スペリング能力

♦ **spelling bee** *n.* つづり字競技

spend *v.*

1 MONEY: (お金を)使う, 費やす, (on investment) (...にお金を)かける, つぎ込む

2 TIME: 過ごす, 費やす, かける

3 ENERGY: 使う, 使い果たす, 費やす

1 How much did you spend?
いくら使った?

I only spent $12 on this bag.
このバッグは、たった12ドルだった。

I spend a lot of money on books.
私は、本にかなりお金をかける。

If you're going to renovate the house, count on spending a fortune.
家を改装するなら、ひと財産つぎ込むつもりでね。

They spend money left and right.
彼らは金づかいが荒い。

2 We spent most of the time listening to music.
ほとんどの時間を音楽を聴いて過ごした。

I spent five years writing that book.
その本を書くのに5年を費やした。

3 We spent a lot of energy getting the garden to look nice.
庭の見栄えをよくするために、多くのエネルギーを費やしました。

spending *n.* 支出

government spending 財政支出

spending money *n.* (お)こづかい

spendthrift *n.* 浪費家, 金づかいの荒い人

sperm *n.* (cell) 精子, (semen) 精液

sphere *n.* 球, (celestial body) 天体, (domain) 領域, (field) 分野

sphinx *n.* スフィンクス

spice *n.* スパイス, 香辛料, (interest) 面白み

♦ **spiced** *adj.* (containing spices) スパイス入りの

spicy *adj.* (hot) 辛い, ピリッとした

spider *n.* クモ

spike *n.* (large nail) 大釘; (**spikes**) (=athletic shoes) スパイクシューズ, (=high heels) 高いかかと

v. (in volleyball: hit downward) スパイクする; (add strong alcohol to) (…に) 強い酒を加える

spill *v.* こぼす

Careful you don't spill the drinks.
飲み物をこぼさないように気をつけて。

Wine has been spilled on the carpet.
じゅうたんにワインがこぼれた。

I didn't spill a drop.
一滴もこぼさなかった。

spill one's guts → GUT

spill the beans → BEAN

spin *v.*

1 MOVE AROUND AND AROUND: (cause to move in circles) 回転させる, ぐるぐる回す, (ball) (…に) スピンをかける, (move in circles) 回転する, ぐるぐる回る

2 FORM BY TWISTING: 紡ぐ, (web) つくる, 張る, (**spin a story**) 作り話をする

1 spin a top こまを回す

He spun the ball.
彼はボールにスピンをかけた。

The child was spinning around.
子供がぐるぐる回っていた。

My head was spinning with ideas.
頭の中をいくつかのアイデアが巡っていた。

2 Who taught you how to spin wool?
羊毛の紡ぎ方を誰に教わったの？

The spider spun its web.
クモが巣を張った。

put a spin on …に解釈を加える

spinach *n.* ホウレンソウ

spin dryer *n.* 脱水機

spine *n.* 背骨, (courage) 気骨

♦**spinal cord** *n.* 脊髄

spineless *adj.* (cowardly) 意気地のない

spin-off *n.* (TV program) 続編, (product) 副産物

spiral *n.* らせん, 渦巻き

adj. らせん状の

v. (move spirally) らせん状に動く

♦**spiral staircase** *n.* らせん階段

spire *n.* 尖塔

spirit

1 *n.* SOUL: 魂, 霊魂

2 *n.* GHOST: 霊, 幽霊

3 *n.* ATTITUDE/MOOD: 機嫌, 気分

4 *n.* MIND/HEART: 精神, 心, (courage) 勇気, 元気, 意気込み

5 *n.* ALCOHOL: (**spirits**) アルコール, (strong alcohol spirits) 蒸留酒

6 *v.* TAKE AWAY: (**spirit sb away**) 連れ去る, (**spirit sth away**) 持ち去る

1 They believe our spirits go to heaven.
彼らは 魂 が天国へ行くと信じている。

2 It's said that evil spirits dwell here.
悪霊がここに住みついていると言われている。

3 You seem in good spirits today.
今日は気分がよさそうだね。

4 the spirit of the age 時代精神

A community spirit still exists in this small town.
この小さな町には、まだ共同体意識が息づいている。

But surely you must admire the man's spirit, his courage?
でも、その男性の意気込み、勇気はすごいと思うでしょう?

5 No spirits are sold here.
ここではアルコールは売っていない。

6 The man was spirited away by his friends before the police came.
警察が来る前に、男は友達に連れ去られた。

spirited *adj.* (vigorous, full of life) 活発な, (of place, event) 活気のある

spiritual *adj.* 精神的な, (of the soul) 霊魂の, (religious) 宗教上の, (supernatural) 超自然的な

♦**spiritual leader** *n.* 宗教指導者

spiritualism *n.* 精神主義

spiritually *adv.* 精神的に

spit *n.* つば

v. つばを吐く, (**spit out**) 吐く, 吐き出す

It's rude to spit in public.
人前でつばを吐くのは失礼だ。

He spit out his gum on the sidewalk.
彼は歩道にガムを吐き捨てた。

spite *n.* (ill will) 悪意

in spite of …のに, …にもかかわらず

In spite of the cold weather, they still went camping.
寒いにもかかわらず、彼らはキャンプに出かけた。

in spite of oneself 意志に反して, 思わず

He became nervous in spite of himself.
彼は意志に反してあがってしまった。

out of spite 腹いせに

He did it out of spite.
彼は腹いせにやった。

spiteful *adj.* 意地の悪い

a spiteful laugh 意地の悪い笑い

♦**spitefully** *adv.* 意地悪く

splash *n.* ザブン(という音)

v. (splash A on B/splash B with A) (BにAを) はねかける, かける, (of liquid) はねかかる, 飛び散る, (**splash around**: play in water) バチャバチャ水しぶきを上げる

The stone fell into the water with a big splash.
石は、ザブンと大きな音を立てて水の中に落ちた。

I splashed some cold water on my face.
冷たい水をピチャピチャ顔にかけた。

I got splashed by a big wave.
大波をかぶった。

The children were splashing around in the pool.
子供たちはプールでバチャバチャ水しぶきを上げていた。

splatter *v.* (of rain, paint) 飛び散る, はねる, (splatter A on B/splatter B with A) (AをBに) はね散らす

splendid *adj.* (magnificent) すばらしい, みごとな [→ EXCELLENT]

It was a splendid idea.
すばらしい案 [名案] だった。

The town hall is a splendid old building.
町役場は古いみごとな建築物です。

splendor *n.* 豪華, 華麗

splice *v.* (rope) よってつなぐ, (film, tape) つなぎ合わせる, 継ぎ合わせる

splinter *n.* とげ, 破片

v. (become broken) 割れる, 粉々になる, (break) 割る, 粉々にする

split

1 *v.* TEAR/BREAK: (cloth) 裂く, (wood) 割る, (lip) 切る

S

2 *v.* DIVIDE: 分ける

3 *n.* CRACK/TEAR: 割れ目, 裂け目

4 *n.* RIFT: (among people) 不和, 分裂, 対立

5 *adj.* DIVIDED: (of groups of people) 分裂した, 割れた

6 *n.* STRETCHING OF LEGS: (**the splits**) 開脚

1 Split the wood up, would you?
木を割ってくれる?
I split my lip. 唇を切った。

2 Let's split the profits fifty-fifty.
もうけを半々に分けよう。

3 There's a split in your trousers.
ズボンが裂けてるよ。

4 a split in the Cabinet 内閣の分裂
The split between the rich and the poor is getting wider.
貧富の差が広がっている。

5 The community was split over the issue.
町は、その問題で分裂していた。

6 Can you do the splits?
開脚ができる?

♦**split ends** *n.* (damaged hair) 枝毛

split second *n.* ほんの一瞬

split up *v.* (of couple) 別れる

The newlyweds split up after only three months.
その新婚夫婦は、たった3ヵ月で別れた。

splurge *v.* ぜいたくをする

splutter *v.* (speak hastily and incoherently) 訳のわからないことをしゃべる

spoil *v.* 台なしにする, だめにする, (child) 甘やかす, だめにする; (of food) 腐る

She was angry with him for spoiling the evening.
彼にその夜を台なしにされて、彼女は怒っていた。

You'll spoil the children if you keep on giving them presents all the time.
いつも物を与えてばかりいたら、子供たちをだめにしてしまいますよ。

spoiled *adj.* だめになった, 台なしになった, (of child) わがままな

It's spoiled now that you've put too much sugar in.
砂糖を入れすぎたから、味が台なしになったじゃない。

spokesman, -person, -woman *n.* スポークスマン, 代弁者

sponge *n.* (porous material) スポンジ

sponger *n.* (scrounger) たかり屋

sponsor *n.* スポンサー, 後援者, (of competition) 主催者, (TV program sponsor) 番組提供者, (guarantor) 保証人

v. (be a sponsor for) (…の) スポンサーになる, (…を) 提供する, (be a guarantor for) (…の) 保証人になる

Do you have a sponsor for your balloon flight?
気球飛行にスポンサーは、いるんですか?

Most of the TV programs are sponsored by large companies.
大半のテレビ番組は、大企業がスポンサーになっている。

sponsorship *n.* 後援

spontaneity *n.* 自発性

spontaneous *adj.* 自発的な, 任意の, (natural) 自然な, 自然に起きる

a spontaneous offer 自発的な申し出
spontaneous combustion 自然発火

spontaneously *adv.* (naturally) 自然に, (by itself) ひとりでに

spoof *n.* パロディー, ちゃかし

spook *v.* (frighten) びっくりさせる

n. (spy) スパイ

spooky *adj.* 気味の悪い

spool *n.* 糸巻き

spoon *n.* (utensil) スプーン, (お)さじ

sporadic *adj.* (intermittent) 散発的な, 時々起こる, (of outbreak) 突発生の

spore *n.* 胞子

sport *n.* スポーツ, 運動

Which sports do you like best?
どのスポーツが好きですか？

My favorite sport is tennis.
一番好きなスポーツはテニスです。

♦ **sports car** *n.* スポーツカー

sports paper *n.* スポーツ新聞

sportswear *n.* スポーツウェア

sportswriter *n.* スポーツ記者

sports jacket *n.* 上着

sportsman, -woman *n.* アウトドア派, (athlete) スポーツマン

sportsmanship *n.* スポーツマンシップ

show sportsmanship
スポーツマンシップを見せる

sporty *adj.* スポーティーな

spot

1 *n.* DIRTY MARK: しみ, 汚れ

2 *n.* PARTICULAR PLACE/AREA: 場所, 所, (on the body) 部分

3 *n.* PATTERN: (**spots**) 斑点, ぶち, (polka dots) 水玉模様

4 *v.* PICK OUT: 見つける, 見つけ出す

5 *v.* HELP TO LIFT WEIGHTS: サポートする

1 Can you get this spot off?
このしみは取れますか？

There's a damp spot on the wall.
壁に湿った汚れがついている。

2 a spot in the shade 日陰の場所

a nice fishing spot 絶好の釣り場

a tourist spot 観光地

"Where does it hurt?"
"This spot here."
「どこが痛むの？」
「この部分です」

3 She was wearing a colorful dress with spots.
彼女は、水玉模様の色鮮やかなワンピースを着ていた。

4 I spotted you straightaway.
すぐにあなたを見つけました。

5 Could you spot me?
サポートしてくれますか？

spotless *adj.* (immaculate) 汚れ一つない, きれいな

spotlight *n.* スポットライト, ((*figurative*)) 脚光

v. (put a spotlight on) (…に) スポットライトを当てる, (give special attention to) 大々的に取り上げる

spotty *adj.* (having many spots) 斑点の多い, (of animal) ぶちの

spouse *n.* 配偶者

spout *v.* (water) 噴き出す

n. (fixture for pouring water) 口, 注ぎ口, (stream of water etc.) 噴出, ほとばしり

♦ **spout off** *v.* (talk on and on) とうとうとしゃべる

sprain *v.* くじく, ねんざする

Did you sprain your ankle badly?
足首をひどくねんざしたの？

S

sprawl *v.* (spread out arms and legs) 手足を投げ出す; (of city) 無秩序に広がる
n. (urban sprawl) スプロール現象

spray *v.* (spray A on B/spray B with A) (BにAを) 吹きかける, かける; (of cat: urinate) おしっこをかける
n. (splash of liquid) しぶき, (device, container, substance) スプレー

The old woman sprayed the leaves with water.
おばあさんは葉っぱに水を吹きかけた。

The gardener sprayed the trees with insecticide.
植木屋さんは木に殺虫剤をかけた。

The spray from the vehicles in front covered the windshield.
前の車の水しぶきがフロントガラスにかかった。

♦ **spray paint** *n.* スプレー塗料
v. (**spray-paint**) スプレー塗装する

spread

1 *v.* UNFOLD AND LAY OUT, OPEN WIDE, OR DISSEMINATE: 広げる, (news, rumor) 広める
2 *v.* FOOD: 塗る
3 *v.* BECOME WIDESPREAD: (of fire, disease) 広がる, (of rumor) 広まる
4 *n.* EXPANSION/DIFFUSION: 広がり, (of products) 普及, (of disease) まん延
5 *n.* PASTE FOR BREAD/CRACKERS: スプレッド

1 We spread the blanket out over the grass.
芝生の上に毛布を広げた。

Spread your arms wide.
両手を大きく広げてください。

Don't spread rumors.
うわさを広めないでください。

2 The first thing to do is to spread mayonnaise on both pieces of bread.
まず最初に、2枚の食パンにマヨネーズを塗ります。

3 The firefighters were unable to prevent the fire from spreading.
消防士は、炎の広がりを食い止めることができなかった。

Some diseases spread very quickly.
きわめて急速に広がる病気もある。

4 the spread of AIDS
エイズのまん延

5 What kind of spread is that?
そのスプレッドは何ですか。

spreadsheet *n.* スプレッドシート

spree *n.* (**shopping spree**) 派手な買い物

spring

1 *n.* SEASON: 春
2 *n.* COILED WIRE: ばね, スプリング
3 *n.* PLACE WHERE WATER COMES FROM THE GROUND: 泉
4 *v.* COME ABOUT: (spring from/out of) (…から) 生じる, 起こる
5 *v.* BOUNCE: (**spring back**) はね返る

1 Spring has come at last.
ようやく春が来た。

2 This mattress has springs in it.
このマットレスにはスプリングが入っている。

3 a mountain spring 山の泉
hot springs 温泉

4 These problems all spring from a bad upbringing.
こうした問題は、すべてしつけの悪さから生じる。

5 Be careful, the wire might spring back.
気をつけて、針金がはね返るかもしれ

ないから。

♦**springtime** *n.* 春, ((*formal*)) 春期

spring water *n.* わき水

It's as clear as spring water.
わき水と同じぐらい澄んでいる。

springboard *n.* (in gymnastics) 跳躍台

spring-cleaning *n.* 大掃除

spring onion *n.* 春タマネギ

spring roll *n.* 春巻

springy *adj.* (elastic) 弾力性のある

sprinkle *v.* (water) まく, かける, (salt) かける, 振りかける

sprinkler *n.* スプリンクラー

sprint *v.* 全速力で走る

n. 全力疾走

sprout *v.* 芽をふく, 芽が出る, 発芽する

n. 芽

spruce[1] *n.* トウヒ, エゾマツ

spruce[2] *v.* (**spruce up**: make neater) こぎれいにする, (**spruce oneself up**) 身なりを整える

spunk *n.* 勇気, 元気

spur *v.* (urge) (…に) 拍車をかける, (encourage) 駆り立てる, 勇気づける

n. (spiked wheel) 拍車

His encouragement spurred me on.
彼の励ましに勇気づけられた。

Exports were spurred on by a weak currency.
通貨が弱いことで、輸出に拍車がかかった。

on the spur of the moment 時のはずみで, とっさに

spurious *adj.* (of comment) まやかしの, 偽の

spurn *v.* (reject) はねつける

spurt *v.* (of water) 噴き出す, 噴出する; (dash) スパートをかける

n. (of water) 噴出

sputter → SPLUTTER

spy *n.* スパイ

v. (work as spy) スパイを働く, スパイする

an industrial spy 産業スパイ

A long time ago, he spied for the KGB.
ずっと昔、彼はＫＧＢのスパイだった。

♦**spy on** *v.* (watch secretly) ひそかに見張る

squabble *n., v.* 口げんか(をする)

squad *n.* (team) チーム

squadron *n.* (navy squadron) 小艦隊, (air force squadron) 飛行中隊

squalid *adj.* (dirty) 汚い, (dirty-looking) 汚らしい, (unpleasant to live in) むさくるしい

squall *n.* スコール

squalor *n.* (dirtiness) 汚らしさ, むさくるしさ

live in squalor むさくるしい生活をする

squander *v.* 浪費する, むだづかいする

square

1 *n.* SHAPE: 正方形, 四角

2 *adj.* SQUARE-SHAPED: 正方形の, 四角い

3 *adj.* MEASUREMENT: (square meter etc.) 平方-, (meters etc. square) -平方

4 *n.* OPEN FOUR-SIDED AREA IN A TOWN: 広場

5 *n.* IN MATH: (product of a number multiplied by itself) 2乗, 平方

6 *v.* RAISE TO THE SECOND POWER: 2乗する

1 a square and a triangle
正方形と三角形

The pattern consisted of linked squares.
その模様は、つなげた正方形でできていた。

Fold the handkerchief into a square.
ハンカチを四角にたたんでください。

2 a square building 四角い建物

3 three square kilometers
3平方キロメートル

The room is six meters square.
部屋は6メートル平方です。

4 People gathered in the square.
人々が広場に集まった。

5 What is the square of four?
4の2乗はいくつですか？

go back to square one 一からやり直す

squarely *adv.* (directly) 正面から, まともに, まっすぐに

look someone squarely in the eyes
人の目をまっすぐに見る

square root *n.* 平方根

squash[1] *v.* (crush) 押しつぶす, (flatten) ぺちゃんこにする

n. (game) スカッシュ

squash[2] *n.* (pumpkin) カボチャ, 南瓜, (vegetable of the marrow family) ウリ類

squat *v.* しゃがむ, うずくまる

squatter *n.* (person who occupies a building illegally) 不法占拠者

squeak *v.* キーキー音を立てる

n. キーキー(いう音), (of mouse) チューチュー(鳴く声)

squeal *v.* (of person) キャーキャー言う, (of brakes) キーキーいう

n. (of person) キャッと言う声, (of brakes) キーッという音

squeamish *adj.* (easily made to feel sick) すぐに気持ちが悪くなる

squeeze *v.* (press: towel, fruit) 絞る, (**squeeze out**: juice, contents of a package) 絞り出す, (sb's hand) かたく握る; (**squeeze through**: a crowd) 押し分けて進む, (**squeeze into**) ...に割り込む

n. (crowded situation) ぎゅうぎゅう詰め, すし詰め

Squeeze the water out of the cloth.
ぞうきんを絞ってください。

Can you squeeze past?
何とか通り抜けられる？

Everyone tried to squeeze onto the bus.
皆がバスに乗り込もうとした。

It was a tight squeeze to fit everyone into the car.
全員が車に乗り込んだために、ぎゅうぎゅう詰めだった。

squeezer *n.* (for fruit) 絞り器

squid *n.* イカ

squint *v.* (strain to see) 目をこらす, 目を細めて見る

n. (medical) 斜視

squirm *v.* もがく

squirrel *n.* リス

squirt *v.* 噴出する, ほとばしる, (squirt A with water) (Aに水を) かける, (**squirt out**) 噴出させる

♦ **squirt gun** *n.* (toy) 水鉄砲

Sr. *adj.* 父親のほうの, -シニア

stab *v.* 突き刺す, 刺す

The victim was stabbed several times.
被害者は何度か刺された。

stabbing *n.* 刺すこと

adj. (of pain) 鋭い, 刺すような

stability *n.* 安定

have stability in one's life
生活の安定を得ている

stabilize *v.* (become stable) 安定する, (make stable) 安定させる

stable[1] *adj.* (unchanging) 安定した, 変わらない, (steady) しっかりした

Prices have been stable recently.
このごろ、物価が安定している。

a politically stable country
政情が安定した国

a stable work surface
しっかりした作業台

stable[2] *n.* (building for horses) 馬小屋, (horse-raising facility) きゅう舎

He works at a stable.
あの人はきゅう舎で働いている。

staccato *adj.* スタッカートの

stack *n.* (pile) 積み重ね, 山, (**a stack of/stacks of**) 大量の…, …の山

v. (put in an orderly pile) 積み重ねる

a stack of plates 積み上げられたお皿

stacks of papers 書類の山

The shelves were stacked with boxes.
棚に箱が積み重ねてあった。

stadium *n.* 競技場, スタジアム

staff *n.* (group of workers) スタッフ, 職員; (walking stick) つえ

Is he a member of the staff?
あの人はスタッフの一員ですか？

She joined the staff last year.
彼女は昨年、職員に加わった。

In all, there's a staff of fifty-five.
職員は総勢 ５５ 人です。

staff sergeant *n.* (in U.S. Army/Marine Corps) 二等軍曹, (in U.S. Air Force) 三等軍曹

stag *n.* (male deer) 雄ジカ

stage

1 *n.* PERFORMANCE PLATFORM: 舞台, ステージ

2 *n.* THEATER: (**the stage**) 演劇, (お)芝居

3 *n.* POINT IN TIME/PROCESS: 段階, 一歩, (**in stages**) 徐々に, 段階的に, (**one stage at a time**) 一歩ずつ

4 *v.* PRODUCE ON STAGE: 上演する

5 *v.* CARRY OUT: 行う

1 The cast came out onto the stage.
出演者全員が舞台に登場した。

On stage she looks very different.
彼女はステージに上がると違って見える。

2 The story's been adapted for the stage.
その物語は舞台化されている。

3 It's a difficult decision to make at this stage.
この段階では難しい決断だ。

Let's consider that at a later stage.
そのことは、もっと後の段階で考えよう。

Children develop in stages.
子供は徐々に成長する。

We can accomplish our aims one stage at a time.
目標は一歩ずつ達成すればいい。

4 It was first staged at the Kabuki-za.
歌舞伎座で初めて上演された。

5 stage a demonstration デモを行う

♦ **stage left** *n.* 上手

stage right *n.* 下手

stagecoach *n.* 駅馬車

staged *adj.* (not real, but acted out to

seem real) 仕組まれた, やらせの

stage fright *n.* 人前で上がること

stagger *v.* よろめく, ふらつく, (stagger drunkenly) 千鳥足で歩く

The drunk staggered along the platform.
酔っ払いが駅のホームをふらふら [千鳥足で] 歩いていた。

staggering *adj.* (astounding) 信じられないほどの, すごい

stagnant *adj.* (of water, air) 流れない, よどんだ; (of economy) 停滞した

stagnate *v.* (of water, air) よどむ, (of business) 活気がなくなる

stagnation *n.* (economic) 停滞

stain *n.* (mark) しみ, 汚れ

v. (become discolored) しみがつく, 汚れる

The stain won't come out.
しみがなかなか取れない。

The wallpaper is stained.
壁紙が汚れている。

stained glass *n.* ステンドグラス

stainless steel *n.* ステンレス(鋼)

S

stair *n.* (also **stairs**) 階段

go up [down] the stairs
階段を上る [下りる]

staircase *n.* 階段

stake *n.*

1 *n.* MONEY RISKED: 賭け金

2 *n.* INTEREST: (vested interest) 利害関係, (personal involvement) かかわり

3 *n.* POST: (used as a marker or support) くい, (**the stake**) はりつけ柱, (=execution by burning) 火あぶりの刑

4 *v.* BET: 賭ける

1 They're playing for high stakes.
彼らは大ばくちをしている。

2 We have a big stake in the business.
我々はその事業に大きな利害関係がある。

3 tent stakes テントのくい

He was burned at the stake for his Christian faith.
その人はキリスト教信仰のかどで、火あぶりの刑に処せられた。

4 He staked a fortune on a rise in the stock market.
彼は株式市場の高騰に大金を賭けた。

stalactite *n.* 鍾乳石

stalagmite *n.* 石筍

stale *adj.* (of bread) 古くなった, (of beer) 気の抜けた

stale bread 古くなったパン

stalemate *n.* (in chess) ステイルメイト, 手詰まり, (in negotiations) 行き詰まり

stalk[1] *n.* (part of plant) 茎

stalk[2] *v.* (pursue stealthily) (...に) 忍び寄る, そっと近寄る, (...を) こっそり追跡する

stalker *n.* ストーカー

stall[1] *n.* (stand) 屋台, 露店

v. (of car) 止まる, エンストする

Let's eat at that stall.
あの屋台で食べよう。

The engine stalled as we reached the stop sign.
一時停止の場所でエンストした。

stall[2] *v.* (delay) ごまかして時間稼ぎをする

stallion *n.* 種馬

stalwart *adj.* (staunch) 忠実な, 揺るぎない, (strong) 頑健な

n. (loyal supporter) 忠実な支持者

stamina *n.* スタミナ, 体力, 持久力

stammer *v.* どもる, 口ごもる

stamp

1 *n.* THING STUCK TO LETTERS: 切手, (thing stuck to documents) 印紙

2 *n.* OBJECT WHICH STAMPS: スタンプ, 印, 押し型 [→ picture of STATIONERY]

3 *v.* MARK WITH A STAMP: (…に) 印を押す, スタンプを押す

4 *v.* BRING FOOT DOWN ON: 踏み鳴らす, (crush with foot) 踏みつける, 踏みつぶす

5 *v.* EXTINGUISH: (**stamp out**: fire) 踏み消す

6 *v.* QUELL: (**stamp out**: rebellion) 鎮圧する

1 I bought some stamps and postcards.
切手と葉書を買った。
a book of stamps 切手帳
a ¥5,000 revenue stamp
5000円の収入印紙

2 Have you seen the stamp?
スタンプを見なかった?
a rubber stamp ゴム印

3 Did they stamp your passport?
パスポートにスタンプを押してもらった?
These papers need to be stamped.
この書類には印が必要です。

4 The boy stamped the floor.
男の子は床をドンと踏み鳴らした。
He threw the letter on the floor and stamped on it.
彼は床に手紙を投げ捨てて踏みつけた。

5 Did you stamp out the fire?
火を踏んで消した?

6 The government is still trying to stamp out the insurgency.
政府は今も反乱を鎮圧しようとしている。
stamp one's feet in anger 怒ってじだんだを踏む

♦**stamping ground** *n.* たまり場

stampede *n.* (of horses) 暴走, (of shoppers) 殺到
v. (of horses) どっと暴走する, (of people) どっと押し寄せる, 殺到する

stance *n.* (attitude) 姿勢, (opinion) 意見, (in sport: position of readiness) スタンス, 構え

---

stand

1 *v.* STAND UPRIGHT: (be in a standing position) 立っている

2 *v.* RISE TO ONE'S FEET: 立ち上がる, 立つ, ((*formal*)) 起立する

3 *v.* OF BUILDING/STRUCTURE: ある, 建っている, (remain) 残っている

4 *v.* REMAIN UNCHANGED: (of tradition) 続いている, 生きている, (of record) 破られていない, (of offer) 生きている, 有効だ

5 *v.* ENDURE: がまんする

6 *v.* BE IN A POSITION/SITUATION: 立場/状態にある

7 *v.* BE TALL: (**stand…feet** etc. **tall**) (of person) 身長…だ, (of tower) 高さ…だ

8 *n.* SALES DISPLAY: 売り場

9 *n.* DEVICE FOR SUPPORTING: -台, -立て

10 *n.* IN STADIUM: (**the stands**) スタンド

1 He was so ill he couldn't stand.
彼はあまりにも具合が悪くて、立っていられなかった。
I stood still and watched.
私はじっと立って見つめた。

S

Lots of people were standing in the cold waiting for the train.
寒い中、大勢の人が立って電車を待っていた。

Don't just stand there—do something!
そこにただ立ってるんじゃなくて——何かしなさい！

2 The president (= CEO) stood up to speak.
社長は話そうと立ち上がった。

The teacher asked me to stand up.
先生に立つように言われた。

3 In the middle of the town, there stands a castle.
街の真ん中にお城が建っている。

At least the fence is still standing.
少なくとも、垣根はまだ残っている。

4 The tradition still stands today.
その伝統は今も続いている。

My offer still stands.
私の提案はまだ生きています。

5 I couldn't stand it any longer, so I left.
がまんできなくなって、そこを出た。

6 How do things stand with your girlfriend?
彼女とは<u>どうなの</u> [うまくいってるの]？

7 He stands 180 centimeters tall.
彼は身長 180 センチです。

8 various publishers' stands
いろいろな出版社の売り場

9 a music stand 譜面台

an umbrella stand 傘立て

10 The ball landed in the stands.
ボールはスタンドに入った。

it stands to reason that... ...は当然だ

stand a chance 見込みがある，可能性がある

stand in line 並ぶ，行列をつくる

stand in sb's way ...のじゃまをする

stand on one's own (two) feet (be independent) 自立する

take a stand (on) (...について) はっきりした態度をとる

take/make a stand (against) (...に反対の) 立場をとる

stand around *v.* ぼんやり立っている，(do nothing) 傍観する

stand aside *v.* (move out of the way) わきに寄る

stand back *v.* (remain at a distance) 後ろに下がる

Stand back, please. 下がってください。

stand by *v.* (observe passively) 傍観する; (support) (...の) 力になる，味方をする

I couldn't just stand by and do nothing.
何もしないで傍観しているなんて、できなかった。

If there's trouble, we'll stand by you.
困ったことがあれば、力になりますよ。

stand for *v.* (tolerate) がまんする; (represent) 意味する，表す，(advocate) 主張する

I'm not going to stand for it!
そんなこと許せない！

What does *UNHCR* stand for?
UNHCR は何の略ですか？

What does this party stand for?
この政党は、どういうことを主張しているのですか？

stand in for *v.* ...の代わりをする，...の代役を務める

Would you stand in for me just this once?

今回だけ代わりをしてもらえませんか？

stand out *v.* (be noticeable) 目立つ, 人目につく

The company's name stands out in the ad. 広告には企業の名前が目立つ。

She certainly stands out in a crowd. 彼女は人込みの中でもほんとに目立っている。

stand up *v.* 立ち上がる, (stand sb up: not meet) (…に) 待ちぼうけを食わせる

stand up for *v.* (defend) 弁護する, …に味方する

stand up to *v.* (resist) …に立ち向かう, …に抵抗する

He's afraid to stand up to his boss. 彼は上司に立ち向かうのを怖がっている。

---

standard *n.* (level) 標準, 水準, (norm) 基準

adj. (normal) 標準の, 普通の, 標準的な

be below standard 標準を下回る

living standards 生活水準

moral standards 道徳基準

a standard medical procedure 標準的な治療

♦ **standard Japanese** *n.* (日本の) 標準語

standard time *n.* 標準時

standardize *v.* 標準化する

♦ **standardization** *n.* 標準化

standby *n.* (person/thing that can be used if needed) 頼りになる人/物; (waiting for the availability of a seat on an airplane) キャンセル待ち

on standby 待機して

stand-in *n.* (performer) 代役, (substitute) 代用品

standing *n.* (position in society) 地位, 身分, (reputation) 名声

adj. (upright) 立っている

♦ **standing ovation** *n.* 立ち上がっての拍手

standoff *n.* (deadlock) 行き詰まり

standoffish *adj.* つんとした, よそよそしい

standpoint *n.* 立場, 観点

standstill *n.* 停止, (of talks) 行き詰まり

staple[1] *n.* (basic food) 必需食品, (product) 主要産物

♦ **staple diet** *n.* 主食

staple[2] *n.* (metal holder for papers) ホッチキスの針

v. ホッチキスで留める

stapler *n.* ホッチキス [→ picture of STATIONERY]

star

1 *n.* OBJECT IN THE SKY: 星

2 *n.* RATING: …星

3 *n.* SHAPE: 星

4 *n.* FILM STAR: スター

5 *v.* TAKE A LEADING ROLE IN: (**star in**) 主演する, 主役を務める

6 *v.* HAVE AS A LEADING ACTOR/ACTRESS: 主役にする

1 The sky was full of stars. 空にいっぱい星が出ていた。

There are billions of stars in our galaxy. この銀河系には無数の星がある。

2 a three-star hotel 三つ星ホテル

a five-star restaurant 五つ星のレストラン

3 a star pattern 星の柄

4 a movie star 映画スター

5 He starred in *2001: A Space Odyssey.*

S

彼は『2001年宇宙の旅』に主演した。

6 The movie stars Jack Nicholson.
映画はジャック・ニコルソンを主役にしている。

♦ **star-shaped** *adj.* 星形の

starch *n.* でんぷん, (**starches**: foods with high starch levels) でんぷん食品

stare *v.* 見つめる, じっと見る

The child was staring into space.
その子は宙を見つめていた。

She was staring at me.
彼女は私をじっと見ていた。

stark *adj.* (utter) 全くの
adv. 全く, 完全に

It was in stark contrast to his earlier paintings.
それは彼の初期の絵とは全く対照的だった。

He was stark naked.
彼は真っ裸だった。

starlight *n.* 星明かり, 星の光

starling *n.* ムクドリ

starry *adj.* (of sky) 星の多い, 星明かりの

start

1 *v.* BEGIN: 始める, 開始する, (**start doing/to do**) …し始める, …し出す, …しかける, (begin to happen) 始まる

2 *n.* BEGINNING: 始め, 最初, 出だし

3 *v.* TURN ON: (car) スタートさせる, (computer) 立ち上げる, 起動させる

4 *v.* SET OUT: (**start for**) 出発する, たつ

5 *v.* GIVE RISE TO: 引き起こす, 発生させる

6 *v.* ESTABLISH: (business) 始める, 開く

1 What time do we start work tomorrow?
明日は何時に仕事を始めますか？

They started the journey at 9:00 A.M.
彼らは午前9時に旅行に出発した。

It's starting to rain. 雨が降り出した。

It sounds like he's starting to understand English.
彼は英語がわかりかけてきたようだね。

The concert didn't start till after dark.
コンサートは暗くなってから始まった。

2 the start of this century 今世紀初め

It was terrible from start to finish.
最初から最後まで最悪だった。

At the very start, I realized it was a big mistake.
出だしでそれが大きな間違いであることに気づいた。

3 Start the car, will you.
車をスタートさせて。

To start the computer, press this button.
コンピューターを立ち上げるには、このボタンを押します。

4 We started for the airport together.
私たちは空港に向けていっしょに出発した。

5 The lightning started a forest fire.
落雷によって山火事が発生した。

6 He started a restaurant when he came back to England.
彼はイギリスに戻って来てから、レストランを始めた。

for a start まず手始めに

start off *v.* (begin) 始める, (begin to happen) 始まる, (set out: on journey) 旅行に出かける; (**start A off on/with B**) (AにBを) 始めさせる, (AにBから) やらせる

We started off early in the morning.

私たちは朝早く旅行に出かけた。

Let's start him off on something easier.
彼には、もっと簡単なことからやらせよう。

start on *v.* (begin work on) …に取りかかる

start out *v.* (begin) 始める, (set out: on journey) 旅行に出かける

start over *v.* (begin again) やり直す

start all over again 一からやり直す

start up *v.* (business) 起こす, 始める; (turn on) 始動させる, (computer) 起動させる

---

starter *n.* (**starters**: appetizers) 前菜, オードブル; (engine starter) スターター

for starters まず(始めに), 第一に

We need to get the money together for starters.
まず始めに資金を集めなくてはならない。

starting line *n.* スタートライン

starting point *n.* 出発点

startle *v.* びっくりさせる

You startled me!
びっくりさせないでよ。

♦**startling** *adj.* 驚くべき, びっくりするような

starve *v.* (die of hunger) 飢え死にする, 餓死する, (suffer from hunger) 飢えている [→ STARVING]

If aid doesn't get there soon, thousands of people may starve.
援助物資が早く届かなければ、何千人もの人が飢え死にするかもしれない。

♦**starvation** *n.* 餓死

starving *adj.* (dying of hunger) 飢えに苦しんでいる, (hungry) おなかがすいている, おなかがペコペコだ, ((*masculine*)) 腹が減った

stash *v.* (hide) 隠す, しまっておく

n. (**a stash of**) 隠していた…

state

1 *n.* CONDITION: 状態, 事態, 様子, 情勢, (bad condition) ありさま

2 *n.* ORGANIZED POLITICAL COMMUNITY: (country) 国家, (part of federation) 州

3 *v.* SAY: 言う, 述べる

4 *adj.* RUN BY STATE: (rather than by federal government) 州の, 州立の

1 The building was in a reasonable state.
その建物は、まずまずの状態だった。

She was in a state of shock.
彼女はショック状態にあった。

The state of his health is not good.
彼の健康状態はよくない。

A state of emergency has been declared.
緊急事態が宣言された。

What a state this country is in!
この国はなんてありさまなんだ!

state of affairs 現状

2 a Palestinian state パレスチナ国家

What state (in the U.S.) are you from?
(アメリカの)どこの州の出身ですか?

3 State your case, and state it clearly.
自分の意見をはっきり言いなさい。

4 a state school 州立学校

a state government 州政府

stately *adj.* 堂々とした, (dignified) 威厳のある

statement *n.* (pronouncement) 声明, (view) 意見, (report) 報告

The government is due to make a statement shortly.
政府はまもなく声明を出すはずだ。

It's not an opinion, it's a statement of fact.
これは意見ではなく事実です。

a bank statement (銀行の)取引明細書

state of the art *n.* 最新技術

adj. (**state-of-the-art**) 最新の, 最先端の

statesman, -woman *n.* 政治家

static *adj.* 静止の, 動かない

n. (noise) 雑音

♦ **static electricity** *n.* 静電気

station

1 *n.* PLACE OF ARRIVAL/DEPARTURE: (train station) 駅, (bus station) 発着所

2 *n.* PLACE WHERE A SERVICE IS ORGANIZED: -署, (TV/radio station) テレビ/ラジオ局, 放送局

3 *n.* WORKSTATION: 持ち場

4 *v.* ASSIGN TO A POST: 駐在させる

1 Shinjuku Station 新宿駅

"Do I get off at the next station?"
"No, yours is the one after that."
「次の駅で降りればいいですか？」
「いいえ、次の次の駅です」

2 a police [fire] station
警察 [消防] 署

a TV station テレビ局

3 Return to your station.
持ち場に戻りなさい。

4 He was stationed in Germany for several years.
彼は数年間ドイツに駐在していた。

♦ **station master** *n.* 駅長

station wagon *n.* ステーションワゴン

stationary *adj.* (not moving) 動かない

stationery *n.* 文房具, 文具 [→ picture below]

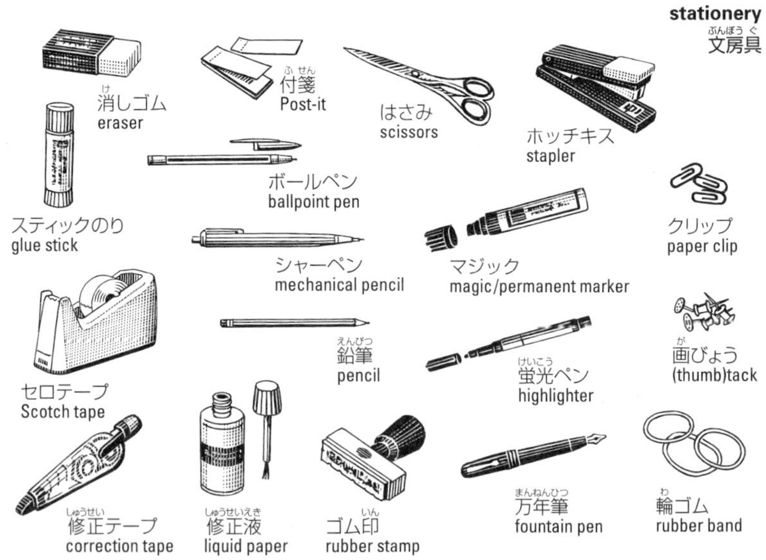

S

statistic ***n.*** (**statistics**) (=numerical data) 統計, (=subject of study) 統計学; (figure) 統計値

statue ***n.*** 像, 彫像

a statue of Buddha 仏像

stature ***n.*** (height) 身長, 背, 背丈; (reputation) 評判, 名声

status ***n.*** (position in society) 地位, 身分, (position) 立場

the social status of teachers
教師の社会的地位

Switzerland's status as a neutral country
スイスの中立国としての立場

status quo ***n.*** 現状

go against the status quo 現状に逆らう

statute ***n.*** 法令, 法規

statutory ***adj.*** 法定の

staunch ***adj.*** (loyal) 忠実な, 信頼できる

stave off ***v.*** (stop from occurring) 防ぐ, 食い止める

stay

1 ***v.*** **REMAIN:** いる, とどまる

2 ***v.*** **BE A GUEST:** 泊まる, ((*formal*)) 滞在する, (**stay overnight**) 1泊する, 一晩泊まる

3 ***v.*** **CONTINUE IN A CERTAIN STATE:** …ままでいる, …っぱなしだ

4 ***n.*** **BEING A GUEST:** (lodging) 宿泊, (being somewhere for a period) 滞在, (period of being somewhere) 滞在期間

1 She doesn't like staying at home.
彼女は家にいるのが好きではない。

Do you plan to stay at that company for the rest of your life?
このまま一生、あの会社にいるつもりですか？

You go on. We'll stay here.
どうぞ行って。私たちはここに残るから。

2 We stayed at their house for the weekend.
週末に彼らの家に泊まった。

We stayed the night in a cheap motel.
夜は安いモーテルで1泊した。

3 I stayed awake all night.
一晩中起きていた。

If it stays sunny out, let's go for a walk.
このまま晴れてたら、散歩に出かけよう。

I stayed crouched in the same position for a good half-hour.
少なくとも３０分は、しゃがみっぱなしだった。

4 I enjoyed my stay in Kyoto.
京都(の滞在)は楽しかった。

a stay of two nights 2泊

stay behind ***v.*** 後に残る

We stayed behind to clean up.
後片付けをするため、後に残った。

stay in ***v.*** 家にいる

I stayed in and did some housework.
家にいて家事をしました。

stay out ***v.*** 外出している, 出かけている

Don't stay out too late.
あまり夜遅くまで外出しないでね。

stay up ***v.*** (be awake) 起きている, (**stay up all night**) 徹夜する, (stay up late) 夜更かしをする

I stayed up all night working.
徹夜で仕事をした。

stay with ***v.*** …と(いっしょに)いる

Would you stay with the baby while I

go and make a phone call?
電話をかけてくる間、赤ちゃんといっしょにいてくれる？

I'll stay with the bags while you get the car.
車を取りに行っている間、私はここで荷物をみておくよ。

steadfast *adj.* ぐらつかない, (**be steadfast in** one's faith) (信念を) 曲げない

steadily *adv.* (consistently) 着実に, どんどん

steady *adj.* (stable) 安定した, 着実な, (not varying) 変わらない, 決まった, (firmly fixed: not wobbly) しっかりした, ぐらつかない

v. (make firm) 安定させる

I'm looking for a steady job.
安定した仕事を探している。

There's been a steady rise in the birth rate.
出生率は着実に上昇している。

Does Kazuo have a steady girlfriend?
和夫には決まった彼女がいるの？

Is the ladder steady?
そのはしごは、ぐらつかない？

Steady the boat, will you.
ボートを安定させて。

steak *n.* ステーキ

How would you like your steak? Rare, medium or well-done?
ステーキの焼き具合はどう致しましょうか？ レアかミディアムかウェルダンか？

steal *v.* (take from) 盗む, ((*informal*)) とる, (commit theft) 盗みを働く; (base in baseball) 盗塁する

He stole that watch.
彼はあの時計を盗んだんだ。

I think my camera has been stolen.
カメラをとられたみたいです。

He's in trouble for stealing.
あいつは盗みを働いてとがめられている。

stealth *n.* ひそかなやり方

♦ **stealthily** *adv.* ひそかに, こっそり(と)

steam *n.* (from bath, cooking) 湯気, (from machine) 蒸気, スチーム

v. (give out vapor) 湯気を立てる, (cook using steam) 蒸す, (of boat, train: move by the power of steam) 蒸気で進む

The kitchen was full of steam.
台所は湯気でいっぱいだった。

The kettle was steaming.
やかんが湯気を立てていた。

Let's steam the dumplings.
お団子を蒸しましょう。

The ship steamed into harbor.
汽船が入港した。

let off steam うっぷんを晴らす, ストレスを発散させる

steamer *n.* (steamship) 汽船; (cooking appliance) 蒸し器

steel *n.* 鋼鉄, スチール

a steel frame 鉄骨

It was built with steel.
鋼鉄で造られていた。

steep[1] *adj.* (rising/falling sharply) 急な, (of cliff: dangerous) 険しい, (of prices: high) 異常に高い

a steep hill 急な坂

a steep increase 急増

steep[2] *v.* (food) つける, 浸す

steer *v.* (car) 運転する, ハンドルを握る, (boat) (...の) かじをとる

Can you steer for a while?
しばらく運転してくれる?

♦**steering wheel** *n.* ハンドル [→ picture of CAR]

stellar *adj.* (of stars) 星の; (fabulous) すばらしい

stem *n.* (of plant) 茎, 幹, (root or main part of word) 語幹

♦**stem cell** *n.* 幹細胞

stench *n.* 悪臭

stencil *n.* ステンシル, 型紙
v. ステンシルで刷り出す

stenography *n.* 速記

step

1 *n.* MOVEMENT OF THE FOOT: 1歩, ステップ

2 *v.* MOVE: (take a step) 一歩踏み出す, (walk) 歩く

3 *v.* PRESS FOOT ON/IN: (**step on/in**) 踏む, 踏みつける, ((*informal*)) 踏んづける

4 *n.* STAIR: (a single step) 踏み段, (**steps**: stairs) 階段, (**stone steps**) 石段

5 *n.* FOOTING: (area around the feet) 足元, (place to put one's foot) 足場

6 *n.* FOOTSTEP: (sound) 足音

7 *n.* FOOTPRINT: 足跡

8 *n.* STAGE/PHASE IN PROCESS: 段階, 一歩, (**in steps**) しだいに, (**one step at a time**) 一歩ずつ

1 take a step forward 1歩前に出る

It's just a few steps away.
ほんの数歩の所にある。

a step to the left 左に1歩

2 I stepped back a couple of paces.
2、3歩後ろに下がった。

Step over here, please.
こちらに来てください。

3 Someone stepped on my foot.
誰かが足を踏んだ。

I've just stepped in some dog poo.
犬のふんを踏んづけてしまった。

4 The steps were slippery.
階段は滑りやすかった。

5 Watch your step.
足元に気をつけて。

6 I could hear the mailman's steps on the path.
小道から郵便屋さんの足音が聞こえた。

7 There were steps in the snow leading up to the car.
車へと続く雪の道に足跡がついていた。

8 Let's take things one step at a time.
一歩ずつ片付けよう。

step by step 一歩一歩, 一歩ずつ, 少しずつ

Step by step, we moved closer to achieving our goal.
目標達成に一歩一歩近づいて行った。

take steps 対策を講じる, 手を打つ

Steps had been taken to prevent a similar accident from happening again.
二度と同じ事故が起きないように、対策が講じられていた。

step aside *v.* よける, わきに寄る [→ STEP DOWN]

I stepped aside to let them pass.
わきに寄って、彼らを通した。

step down *v.* (resign) 辞職する, 辞任する

S

step in *v.* (between two people, to break up a fight) …に割って入る, (become involved) …に乗り出す, …に介入する

step up *v.* (increase the intensity of) 強化する

step- *pref.* まま-, 義-, 義理の

stepbrother *n.* 義理の兄弟 [→ HALF BROTHER/SISTER]

stepchild *n.* まま子

stepfather *n.* まま父, 義父

stepladder *n.* 踏み台, 脚立

stepmother *n.* まま母, 義母

steppe *n.* ステップ, 大草原

stepping-stone *n.* 踏み石, 飛び石, (to success) 足がかり

stepsister *n.* 義理のきょうだい [→ HALF BROTHER/SISTER]

stereo *n.* ステレオ

stereotype *n.* ステレオタイプ, 固定観念
v. 型にはめる, 固定観念をもって見る

sterile *adj.* (free of bacteria) 無菌の; (unable to produce offspring) 不妊の

♦**sterility** *n.* (absence of bacteria) 無菌; (inability to produce offspring) 不妊

sterilization *n.* 殺菌; (for women) 不妊手術, (for men) 断種手術

sterilize *v.* (disinfect) 殺菌する

sterilized *adj.* (disinfected) 殺菌した; (of animal) 不妊手術をした, 断種した

sterling *n.* (U.K. currency) 英国の通貨, 英貨
adj. みごとな, すばらしい

sterling silver *n.* 純銀, (sterling silver items) 純銀製品

stern[1] *adj.* (strict, severe) 厳しい

stern[2] *n.* (of ship) 船尾

sternum *n.* 胸骨

steroid *n.* ステロイド

stethoscope *n.* 聴診器

stew *n.* シチュー
v. とろ火で煮る, 煮込む

steward *n.* スチュワード

stewardess *n.* スチュワーデス

stick

1 *n.* PIECE OF WOOD: (branch) 枝, (small branch) 小枝, (used as firewood) まき, (used for support: **walking stick**) つえ, ステッキ

2 *n.* ROD-SHAPED OBJECT: 棒, (gear lever in car) シフトレバー [→ picture of CAR]

3 *v.* ATTACH: (stick A to/on B) (AをBに) くっつける, 貼る, 貼り付ける, (cling) くっつく, 貼り付く

4 *v.* THRUST SO AS TO PIERCE: 突き刺す, 刺す

5 *v.* PUT: 置く

6 → STUCK

1 Will you stop waving that stick around?
その枝を振り回すのはやめてくれない？
a pile of sticks まきの山
Do we have enough sticks to make a fire?
火をおこすのに十分なまきはある？

2 a stick of dynamite ダイナマイトの棒
a stick of butter バター1個
a stick of celery セロリ1本

3 Stick a label on it. ラベルを貼って。
This stuff sticks to your hands.
これは手にくっつきますよ。

4 I stuck the fork into the meat.

S

肉にフォークを突き刺した。

5 Just stick it over there in the corner.
向こうの隅に置いてくれればいいよ。

stick around *v.* (stay here/there) ここ/そこにいる, (wait) 待つ

stick by *v.* (stay loyal to) ...に忠実だ

stick out *v.* (tongue etc.) 出す, 突き出す, (be prominent) 突き出る, 出っ張る, (jut out overhead) 張り出す

The dog stuck its head out of the car window.
犬が車の窓から頭を出した。

The cupboard sticks out too far.
この戸棚は出っ張りすぎている。

The branches of the tree are sticking out into the road.
木の枝が道路に張り出している。

stick it out (endure) がまんする

stick to *v.* (idea, opinion) 変えない, 貫く, (rules) 守る, ...に従う, (promise) 守り通す, (path) ...からそれない

We stuck to the original plan.
最初の計画を貫いた。

Let's stick to the rules.
規則はきちんと守ろう。

stick together *v.* (of group: be together) いっしょにいる, (of glue etc.) くっつく

stick up for *v.* (support) 応援する, ...の味方をする, (defend) 守る

I stuck up for my friends.
友達の味方をした。

---

sticker *n.* ステッカー

stick shift *n.* (manual transmission car) マニュアル車, (gear shift) 変速レバー, シフトレバー [→ picture of CAR]

sticky *adj.* べとべとの, ねばねばした

sticky hands べとべとの手

This candy is very sticky.
このキャンディーは、すごくねばねばしている。

♦ **stickiness** *n.* 粘着性, 粘り

stiff *adj.* (not flexible) かたい, (of muscle) 張っている, (of shoulder) 凝っている, (of behavior) 堅苦しい, (severe) 厳しい

adv. (used emphatically) 全く, ひどく

stiff new shoes 新しくてかたい靴

a stiff door 堅いドア

My muscles are stiff from yesterday's game.
昨日の試合のせいで、筋肉が張っている。

stiff shoulders 肩凝り

I find him rather stiff.
あの人はちょっと堅苦しい人だ。

I was bored stiff by the lecture.
その講義には全くうんざりした。

♦ **stiffly** *adv.* (not flexibly) かたく, (of manner) 堅苦しく

stiffen *v.* (become stiff) かたくなる, (of muscle) 張る, こわばる, (make stiff) かたくする, (make stronger) 強める

stifle *v.* (repress: laugh etc.) 抑える; (kill by suffocating) 窒息死させる

stifling *adj.* (stuffy) 息苦しい

stigma *n.* 汚名

stigmata *n.* 聖痕

stigmatize *v.* (**be stigmatized**) 汚名を着せられる

stiletto *n.* (knife) 短剣, (stiletto heel) ピンヒール

still

1 *adv.* EVEN NOW: まだ, 今でも, いまだに

2 *adj.* MOTIONLESS: (of person) じっとした, (of sea) 静かな, 穏やかな

3 *adv.* YET: (**still another**) さらにもう一つ, (**still more**) もっと, さらに

4 *adv.* HOWEVER: でも, それでも, しかし

5 *n.* QUIET: (of night) しじま, 静けさ

6 *n.* PHOTOGRAPH: スチール写真

1 I'm still waiting for her to call.
まだ彼女からの電話を待っているんです。
He's still a good friend.
彼は今でもいい友達です。
I still don't understand.
いまだにわからない。
Remember, they could still change their minds.
まだ彼らの気が変わるかもしれないんだよ。

2 We stood still and watched.
私たちはじっと立って見ていた。
The children couldn't sit still.
子供たちはじっと座っていられなかった。
The sea was still. 海は穏やかだった。

3 There was still another reason for his absence.
彼がいない理由はさらにもう一つあった。
There's still more food to come.
料理はもっと出てきますよ。

4 "Our team lost."
"Still, it was a good game."
「うちのチームは負けた」
「でも、いい試合だった」

♦**stillness** *n.* 静けさ, 静寂

stillborn *adj.* (of baby) 死産の

still life *n.* (picture) 静物画

stilted *adj.* (stiff, formal) 堅苦しい, (affected) わざとらしい

stilts *n.* (for play) 竹馬, (for building) 支柱

stimulant *n.* 興奮剤, 刺激物

stimulate *v.* 刺激する

stimulating *adj.* 刺激的な, いい刺激になる
a stimulating experience 刺激的な経験

stimulation *n.* 刺激

stimulus *n.* 刺激

sting *v.* (of bee) 刺す, (of wound: be a source of pain) ひりひり/ちくちく痛む
n. (sharp poisonous organ) 針, とげ, (sharp pain) 刺すような痛み
Have you ever been stung by a bee?
ハチに刺されたことはありますか？
Some rays have a nasty sting.
エイの中には、危険な針を持っているものもいる。

stinger *n.* (on animal) 針, とげ

stingy *adj.* けちな

stink *v.* (give off a foul odor) いやなにおいがする, 臭い

stint *n.* (period of time) 期間, (of job) 任期

stipend *n.* 俸給, 給料

stipulate *v.* 条件として要求する, 規定する

stir *v.* (mix up: liquid) かき混ぜる
n. (commotion) 大騒ぎ [→ MOVE]
You have to keep stirring it.
絶えずかき混ぜていないといけないのよ。
The scandal created quite a stir.
そのスキャンダルで大騒ぎになった。

♦**stir up** *v.* (cause) 引き起こす
His comments stirred up trouble.

彼の発言は騒ぎを引き起こした。

stirring *adj.* (stirring the emotions) 感動的な

n. (**stirrings**: beginnings) 始まり, 芽生え

stirrup *n.* あぶみ

stitch *n.* (of thread) 縫い目, (of wool) 編み目, (**stitches**: lengths of thread for closing a wound) 針

v. (sew) 縫う

I had five stitches in my forehead from the accident.
事故で、額を5針縫いました。

stock

1 *n.* AVAILABLE SUPPLY: 在庫, ストック

2 *n.* LIQUID USED IN COOKING: だし

3 *n.* SHARE IN A BUSINESS: 株

4 *v.* CREATE A SUPPLY OF: (**stock up on**) 蓄える, 貯蔵する, (buy) 買う

5 *v.* FILL: 詰める, いっぱいにする

6 *v.* HAVE FOR SALE: 扱っている, 置いている

7 *n.* LIVESTOCK: 家畜

1 check the stock 在庫を確認する

goods in stock 在庫品

They don't have any in stock right now.
今は在庫がないそうです。

2 fish stock 魚のだし

chicken stock とりがらスープ

3 Stock prices have fallen.
株価が下がった。

4 We'd better stock up on canned food.
缶詰を蓄えておいたほうがいい。

5 The refrigerator was stocked with beer.
冷蔵庫には、ビールがいっぱい詰まっていた。

6 They don't stock clothes.
衣類は扱っていない。

be/have in stock 在庫がある

stockbroker *n.* 株式仲買人

♦**stockbroking** *n.* 株式仲買

stock exchange *n.* 株式取引所

stockholder *n.* 株主

stocking *n.* ストッキング, (Christmas stocking) クリスマスの靴下

stock market *n.* 株式市場

stockpile *n., v.* 備蓄(する)

stocky *adj.* (of build) ずんぐりした, がっしりした

stockyard *n.* 家畜置き場

stoic *adj.* (of look) 平然とした

n. (person who perseveres) がんばり屋, ストイックな人, (philosopher) ストア哲学者

stoke *v.* (fire: stir up) かき立てる, (stoke A [fire] with B [wood, coal]) (AにBを) くべる

stoke up a fireplace with wood
暖炉にまきをくべる

stole *n.* (article of clothing) 肩掛け, ストール

stomach *n.* (part of the body) おなか, 腹, 胃 [→ picture of BODY]

v. (endure) がまんする

lie heavy on one's stomach 胃にもたれる

stomachache *n.* 腹痛, 胃痛

have a stomachache
腹痛がする [おなかが痛い]

stomp *v.* 足を踏み鳴らす, (stomp foot) じだんだを踏む, (**stomp on**) 踏んづける

♦**stomping ground** → STAMPING GROUND

stone ***n.*** (solid material) 石; (center of fruit) 種

The walls are built of stone.
壁は石でできている。

He threw a stone at the wave.
彼は波に石を投げた。

a peach stone 桃の種

♦**Stone Age** ***n.*** 石器時代

stony ***adj.*** 石の多い, 石ころだらけの

stool ***n.*** (piece of furniture) スツール, 椅子 [→ picture of BATHROOM]; (bowel movement) 便通, (feces) 大便

stoop ***v.*** かがむ

---

stop

1 ***v.*** QUIT: やめる, 中断する, ストップする, (**stop doing**) …するのをやめる, よす

2 ***v.*** COME/BRING TO A HALT: 止まる/止める, 停止する/停止させる, (of rain) やむ, (**stop and stand, stop to do**) 立ち止まる, (stop sb: cause to stop walking) 呼び止める, (**be stopped**: be forced by police to stop one's car) 停止させられる

3 ***v.*** PREVENT: やめさせる, 止める, 阻む

4 ***v.*** STAY: (at hotel) 泊まる

5 ***n.*** HALTING PLACE: (for bus) 停留所, (for train) 駅, (for car: rest stop) パーキングエリア

1 Stop it, will you! やめなさい!

I told them to stop it.
彼らにやめるように言った。

I stopped eating to hear the news.
ニュースを聞くために食事を中断した。

We all stopped talking.
私たちは皆、しゃべるのをやめた。

Can you stop doing that for a minute?
少しの間、それをやめてもらえますか?

2 The truck couldn't stop.
トラックは止まれなかった。

The trains have stopped because of a signal failure.
電車が信号機故障で止まっている。

The music stopped all of a sudden.
音楽がふいに止まった。

Did anyone try to stop you?
誰かに止められなかった?

I was stopped by the police for speeding.
スピード違反で警官に停止させられた。

3 I tried to stop him from going there.
彼がそこに行くのをやめさせようとした。

Nothing could stop him from becoming a successful businessman.
彼が事業で成功するのを阻むものは、何もなかった。

The Green Party's lobbying stopped the bill from getting congressional approval.
緑の党の陳情運動が、法案の議会承認を阻止した。

4 We stopped at a motel for the night.
その夜はモーテルに泊まった。

5 We get off at the next stop.
次の停留所で降ります。

Which stop do you get off at?
どこの駅で降りるの?

It's five stops from hcrc.
ここから五つ目の駅です。

bring to a stop 止める, 終わらせる, 中断させる

It brought the whole game to a stop.
(そのために) 試合が中断された。

cannot stop doing やめられない, 止め

られない, ...せずにはいられない

I can't stop smoking.

たばこをやめられない。

I couldn't stop laughing.

笑わずにはいられなかった。

stop to/and think ちょっと待って考える

Let's just stop and think about it for a moment.

ちょっと待って、考えてみましょう。

without stopping 止まらずに, (without resting) 休まずに

The car drove on without stopping.

車は休まずに走っていた。

stop by *v.* (…に) 立ち寄る

If you have time later, why don't you stop by for a cup of coffee?

あとで時間があったら、うちに寄ってコーヒーでも飲んでいかない？

stop off *v.* (break a journey) 寄る, (get off a train) 途中下車する

We stopped off in Moscow for a couple of nights on our way to Japan.

日本へ行く途中でモスクワに寄って、2泊した。

stopgap *n.* 間に合わせ

stopover *n.* 立ち寄り, 短期滞在, (getting off of an airplane) ストップオーバー, 途中下車

I made a one-day stopover in Paris.

途中で降りて、パリに1日滞在しました。

stoppage *n.* 停止, (of work, in protest) 操業停止, ストライキ

storage *n.* (act of preserving) 貯蔵, (act of keeping) 保管, (act of storing) 収納; (storage facility) 倉庫, 貯蔵所

storage space 収納スペース

store

1 *v.* KEEP/PUT IN STORAGE: しまっておく, 蓄える, (food) 貯蔵する, (clothes, document) 保管する, 収納する, (data) 収める

2 *n.* SHOP: 店

3 *n.* SUPPLY: 蓄え, 貯蔵

1 I store firewood in the shed.

物置にまきを蓄えている。

Where do you store your wine?

ワインはどこに貯蔵していますか？

I need a spare room to store things in.

物を収納する余分な部屋が必要だ。

2 a convenience store

コンビニ(エンスストア)

a corner store 角の店

What time does the store close?

店は何時に閉まりますか？

3 We have a good store of wine in the cellar.

地下室にワインをたくさん貯蔵している。

The store of water is almost gone.

水の蓄えが、ほとんどなくなった。

in store for (prepared for) …に備えて, (awaiting) 待ち構えて

storefront *n.* 店頭

stork *n.* コウノトリ

storm *n.* (violent weather) 嵐, 暴風, (violent outburst of feeling) 嵐

The storm went away. 嵐は去った。

a storm of protest 反対の嵐

stormy *adj.* 嵐の, 荒れた

a stormy night 嵐の夜

stormy weather 荒れた天候

story[1] *n.* (fictional account of events) 物語, (お)話, (=novel) 小説, (nonfictional account of events) 話, (=report) 記事, (=rumor) うわさ

Children love bedtime stories.
子供は、寝る前に物語を聞くのが大好きだ。

a short [detective] story <u>短編</u> [推理] 小説

a true story <u>本当の話</u> [実話]

That was a good story. いい話だった。

He told me the story of his ill-fated marriage.
彼は自分の不幸な結婚の話をした。

There was an interesting story in today's paper.
今日の新聞に面白い記事が載っていた。

spread stories うわさを広める

story[2] *n.* (level of building) 階

a three-story building 3階建てのビル

stout *n.* (kind of beer) スタウト, 黒ビール
adj. (strong) 強い, 丈夫な, (fat) 太った

stove *n.* (for cooking) レンジ, こんろ [→ picture of KITCHEN], (for heating a room) ストーブ

turn on the stove
<u>こんろの火</u> [暖房] をつける

S

stow *v.* しまう, のせる

♦ **stow away** *v.* (go abroad secretly) 密航する

straddle *v.* (have legs on both sides of) (...に) またがる

straight

1 *adj.* NOT CURVED/BENT: まっすぐな, 直線の

2 *adv.* DIRECTLY: (in a straight line) まっすぐ(に), 一直線に, (without making any detours) じかに, 直接, ストレートに, (immediately) すぐ(に); (of speech: not roundabout) 率直に, 単刀直入に

3 *adj.* CONSECUTIVE: 連続した

4 *adv.* UPRIGHT: (of posture) まっすぐ(に)

5 *adj.* HONEST AND FORTHRIGHT: 率直な, 正直な

6 *adj.* OF FACE: 真面目くさった

7 *adj.* OF DRINK: ストレートの, 割ってない

8 *adj.* HETEROSEXUAL: 同性愛でない

[1] a straight road まっすぐな道路

a straight line 直線

straight hair ストレートヘア

[2] I saw the car coming straight at me.
車が、私めがけてまっすぐ走って来るのが見えた。

I went straight to the doctor's.
医者へ直行した。

I went straight back to bed.
またすぐに寝た。

He got straight to the point and asked about promotion.
彼は昇進について、単刀直入に尋ねた。

[3] four straight wins 4連勝

get straight As オールAを取る

[4] Sit up straight, will you!
まっすぐ座りなさい!

[5] I couldn't get a straight answer from her.
彼女から率直な返事をもらえなかった。

[6] I couldn't keep a straight face.
真面目くさった顔をしていられなかった。

[7] I like my whiskey straight.
ウイスキーはストレートが好きだ。

see straight まっすぐに見る

straight off (immediately) すぐに, ただちに

straight out (bluntly) 率直に

think straight 筋道立てて考える

straightaway *adv.* すぐ(に), 早速, ただちに

When you get to Tokyo, call me straightaway.
東京に着いたらすぐ電話してください。

straighten *v.* まっすぐにする, きちんとする

♦**straighten up** *v.* (stand straight) まっすぐに立つ; (clean up) 片付ける; (improve behavior) まっとうになる

straightforward *adj.* (simple) 簡単な, (easy to understand) わかりやすい, (not complicated) 複雑ではない; (frank) 率直な

strain

1 *n.* TENSION/STRESS: 緊張, ストレス, (burden: mental or physical) 重荷, 負担, (pressure) 重圧, プレッシャー

2 *v.* INJURE: 痛める, (**strain a muscle**) 筋を違える

3 *v.* TRY: (**strain to do**) …しようと全力を尽くす, 精一杯…する, (**strain to see**) 目を凝らす, (**strain to hear**) 耳を澄ます

4 *n.* INJURY: 筋違い, 痛めること

1 The strain began to take its toll on her.
彼女はストレスで参ってきた。

It was a real strain studying for the exam.
試験勉強は本当に重荷だった。

He cracked up under the strain.
彼はプレッシャーで心身共におかしくなった。

2 I think I've strained a muscle in my back.
背中の筋を違えたようだ。

3 I had to strain to reach the pipe.
手を精一杯伸ばさないと、パイプに届かなかった。

I strained forward to see the procession.
行列を見ようと前に身を乗り出した。

4 I feel a strain in my left shoulder.
左肩に痛みを感じる。

strained *adj.* (of relations) 緊迫した, 緊張した; (unnatural) 不自然な

strait *n.* (of sea) 海峡

strand[1] *n.* (beach) 浜, 岸

v. (**be stranded**) 座礁する, (岸に)乗り上げる, (at airport) 立ち往生する

be stranded on a desert island
無人島に乗り上げる

strand[2] *n.* (single thin piece: of hair, thread etc.) 1本; (part of story) 筋

strange *adj.* (peculiar) 変な, 奇妙な, おかしな, 不思議な, (unfamiliar) 知らない

A strange thing happened the other day.
この前おかしなことがあった。

It was strange to meet him again.
彼にまた会うなんて奇妙だった。

He gave me a strange look and walked away.
彼は私を不思議そうな目で見て、立ち去った。

♦**strangely** *adv.* 変に, (used at the beginning of a sentence) 不思議なことに

stranger *n.* (unfamiliar person) 知らない人, よそから来た人, (person unfamiliar with a place) 初めての人, 不案内の人

I'm a stranger here.
ここは初めて [不案内] です。

strangle *v.* 絞め殺す, 絞殺する

♦**stranglehold** *n.* (control) 締め付け

strangulation *n.* (type of murder) 絞殺

S

strap *n.* ひも, ストラップ, (leather strap) 革ひも, (shoulder strap on dress) 肩ひも
v. (**strap oneself in**: put on one's seat belt) シートベルトを締める, (**be strapped in**) (ひもで) 固定される
hold onto a strap つり革につかまる

stratagem *n.* 戦略, 計略

strategic *adj.* 戦略の, 戦略的な, (militarily important) 戦略上重要な, (of weapon) 戦略…

strategy *n.* 作戦, 戦略
military strategy 軍事作戦

stratified *adj.* (of society) 階層化した, (of rock) 層になった

stratosphere *n.* 成層圏

stratum *n.* 層, (in society) 階層

straw *n.* (stalk of wheat/barley) わら, 麦わら; (tube for sucking liquid) ストロー
a straw hat 麦わら帽子
drink through a straw ストローで飲む

strawberry *n.* イチゴ, 苺

stray *v.* (stray from: a path) (道から)それる, はぐれる
adj. (of animal) 野良の
We seem to have strayed from the path.
道からそれてしまったようだ。
a stray cat 野良猫

streak *n.* (line) 筋; (**a streak of**: a series of) …続き
streaks of paint ペンキの筋
His hair had a distinguished gray streak in it.
彼の髪には目立つしらがが一筋あった。
a winning streak 連勝
a streak of good luck 幸運続き

stream *n.* (brook) 川, 小川, (steady flow) 連続, 流れ
v. (flow freely) 流れる
There's a small stream at the back of the garden.
庭の奥に小さな小川がある。
a steady stream of traffic
切れ目のない車の流れ
a stream of inquiries
ひっきりなしの問い合わせ
a never-ending stream of people
絶え間ない人の流れ
a stream of air 空気の流れ
Tears streamed down her face.
彼女の顔を涙が流れた。

streamlined *adj.* (simplified) 簡素化された, (efficient) 能率的な; (of car) 流線型の

street *n.* 通り, 街路, 道路
Which street does he live on?
彼はどの通りに住んでいるんですか？
a narrow street 狭い通り
a street map 道路地図

streetcar *n.* 路面電車

streetlight *n.* 街灯

strength *n.* 力, 強さ, (power, influence) 力, 威力, (advantage) 強み
I didn't have the strength to lift a finger.
指1本上げる力もなかった。
He pulled with all his strength.
彼は全力で引っ張った。
the strength of the yen 円の強さ
The organization has lost much of its strength.
その団体は力がかなりなくなっている。

the strength of popular opinion
世論の威力

Their greatest strength is their ability to work as a team.
彼らの最大の強みはチームワークだ。

strengthen *v.* 強める, 強化する

strenuous *adj.* (of exercise) 激しい, 力の要る

stress

1 *n.* MENTAL STRAIN: ストレス, (pressure) 重圧

2 *v.* EMPHASIZE: 強調する

3 *n.* OF SYLLABLE/WORD: アクセント, 強勢

4 *n.* FORCE/PRESSURE: 圧力, (force that deforms a body) ひずみ

1 the stress of work 仕事のストレス

Stress builds up.
ストレスはたまるものだ。

She's under stress right now.
彼女は今ストレスをかかえている。

He does yoga to rid himself of stress.
彼はストレス解消にヨガをやっている。

He couldn't cope with the stress of his parents' expectations, and cracked.
彼は両親の期待の重圧に耐えきれずに、だめになった。

2 My parents always stressed the importance of good manners.
両親はいつも礼儀の大切さを強調した。

3 Where is the stress on this word?
この単語のアクセントはどこですか？

4 There is a lot of stress on that beam.
あのはりには、かなりの圧力がかかっている。

structural stresses 構造上のひずみ

◆ **stress management** *n.* ストレス対策

stress mark *n.* 強勢記号, アクセント記号

stressed *adj.* (of person: under pressure) ストレスのたまった; (of syllable: accented) 強勢のある, アクセントのある

stressful *adj.* ストレスの多い

stretch

1 *v.* EXTEND: 伸ばす, (rope: make taut) 張る, (become extended) 伸びる, (stretch arms/legs) 手/足を伸ばす

2 *v.* EXERCISE: ストレッチする, (**stretch one's legs**: go for a walk) ちょっと歩いて足を伸ばす

3 *v.* CONTINUE FOR A DISTANCE: 続く, 広がる

4 *n.* LENGTH/EXPANSE: (of sea, forest) 広がり, 一帯, (of road) 一筋, (of racecourse: **the final stretch**) ゴール前の直線コース

5 *n.* PERIOD: 間, 期間

6 *n.* FORM OF EXERCISE: ストレッチ

1 I stretched myself to get rid of the stiffness in my shoulders.
体を伸ばして肩の凝りをほぐした。

We stretched a rope between the trees.
木と木の間にロープを張った。

Elastic stretches easily.
ゴムは簡単に伸びる。

Will the rope stretch that far?
縄はそこまで伸ばせるかな？

The salesman stretched to get the book.
店員は本を取るため、手を伸ばした。

2 It's good to stretch before and after exercising.
運動の前後にストレッチすることはいいことだ。

3 The forest stretched for miles.
森は何マイルも続いていた。

4 a stretch of forest 森林地帯

a stretch of open road
一筋の広々とした道路

5 He studied abroad for a stretch.
彼はしばらくの間、海外で勉強した。

stretcher *n.* 担架, ストレッチャー

be carried off the field on a stretcher
競技場から担架で運び出される

strict *adj.* (stern) 厳しい, 厳格な, (rigid, exact) 厳密な

a strict teacher 厳しい先生

strict discipline 厳しいしつけ

strict rules 厳格な規則

a strict Muslim 厳格なイスラム教徒

in the strict sense of the word
厳密な意味では

in strict confidence 極秘に/で

I told him in strict confidence.
彼に極秘で言った。

strictly *adv.* (with strict adherence: to rules) 厳しく, 厳密に; (totally, completely) 全く; (**strictly for**: only for) …のためだけに

Cell phones are strictly forbidden here.
ここでは携帯電話の使用は、かたく禁じられている。

strictly speaking 厳密に言うと

stride *v.* (walk with big steps) 大またで歩く

n. (big step) 大また

make great strides (make progress) 大きな進歩を遂げる

strident *adj.* (loud, unpleasant to hear) 甲高い, 耳障りな

strife *n.* (conflict) 争い, 闘争

strike

1 *v.* HIT: 打つ, (person) 殴る, ぶつ

2 *v.* ATTACK: ((*also figurative*)) 攻撃する, 襲う

3 *n.* REFUSAL TO GO TO WORK: スト(ライキ)

4 *v.* IMPRESS: (**strike one as…**) (…に) …という印象を与える

5 *v.* OF CLOCK: (strike…) 打つ

6 *n.* MILITARY OPERATION: 攻撃

7 *v.* DISCOVER: (gold, oil) 掘り当てる, 発見する, (**strike upon**: idea) 思いつく

8 *n.* IN BASEBALL: ストライク

1 He fell and struck his head on the sidewalk.
彼は倒れて歩道で頭を打った。

His wife struck him across the face.
奥さんは彼の顔を殴った。

2 The army struck the town at dawn.
軍は夜明けに町を攻撃した。

The earthquake struck the area at 4:08 A.M.
午前4時8分に地震がその地域を襲った。

3 There's a strike on, so no one's at the office.
ストライキ中で、会社には誰もいない。

Everyone's on strike.
全員ストライキに入っている。

The union has decided to call a strike.
組合はストの実施を決定した。

4 He strikes me as an honest person.
彼は正直な人という印象を受けた。

5 The clock struck five.
時計が5時を打った。

6 an air strike 空爆 [爆撃]

a preemptive strike 先制攻撃

7 The company struck oil in the South China Sea.
その会社は南シナ海で石油を掘り当てた。

8 Strike two! ツーストライク!
He was called out on strikes.
彼は三振を取られた。

strike a balance 折り合いをつける
strike a chord 心の琴線に触れる, 胸を打つ
strike a deal 合意する
strike a pose ポーズをとる
strike gold/oil ((*figurative*)) 一山当てる
strike it rich 思わぬ大もうけをする

strike down *v.* (opponent) 打ちのめす, 倒す, (verdict) 無効にする

strike out *v.* (delete) 消す, 削除する; (fail) 失敗する; (in baseball) (of batter) 三振する, (of pitcher) 三振に打ち取る

---

striking *adj.* 際立った, 著しい, 人目を引く
The differences are striking.
相違点が著しい。
There is a striking resemblance between her and her mother.
彼女とお母さんは、そっくりだ。

string
1 *n.* CORD: ひも, (on instrument) 弦, (**strings**: musical instruments) 弦楽器
2 *n.* SERIES: (**a string of**) 一連の…
3 *v.* HANG: つるす, (in a row on a line) 並べる, (between/on two points) 張る

1 tie with a string ひもで縛る
the violin and other strings
バイオリンその他の弦楽器
2 a string of events 一連の行事
a string of victories 連勝
3 string Christmas lights on a tree
クリスマスツリーにライトをつるす

no strings attached (付帯) 条件なしで, ひも付きでなく

string bean *n.* サヤエンドウ, サヤインゲン [→ picture of BEAN]

stringent *adj.* (strict) 厳しい, 厳格な
stringent laws 厳しい法律

strip[1] *v.* (remove: paper, paint etc.) はがす, はぐ, (take clothes off) 服を脱ぐ
They stripped the paint from the wood.
木材の塗装をはがした。
He stripped off his clothes and dived into the water.
彼は服を脱いで水に飛び込んだ。

♦**stripper** *n.* ストリッパー
strip show *n.* ストリップショー

strip[2] *n.* 一切れ, 細長いもの
a strip of cloth 端切れ
cut it into strips 細長く切る

stripe *n.* (band of color) しま, ストライプ, (badge on uniform) 記章, そで章
red and blue stripes
赤と青のしま模様 [ストライプ]

♦**striped** *adj.* しま模様の

striptease *n.* ストリップショー

strive *v.* (**strive for**) …を求めて懸命に努力する

stroke[1] *n.*
1 CEREBRAL HEMORRHAGE: 脳卒中, (attack, spasm) 発作
2 SOUND OF CLOCK: 打つ音
3 MOVEMENT OF PEN/BRUSH: 一筆, (counting strokes of kanji: a single stroke) 1画

1 My mother had a stroke.
母は脳卒中を起こした。

2 At the stroke of midnight, they began to sing.
夜の12時ちょうどに、彼らは歌い始めた。

3 The monk made some rapid strokes with a brush.
お坊さんは筆でさっと一筆書いた。

The character for "tree" has four strokes.
「木」という字は4画です。

at a stroke (in one stroke) 一挙に

stroke² *v.* (rub, pet) なでる [→ SMOOTH 4]

The cat likes to be stroked.
その猫は、なでられるのが好きだ。

stroll *v.* (walk) 散歩する
n. 散歩

stroller *n.* ベビーカー, バギー

strong *adj.*

1 HAVING STRENGTH: 強い, (robust) 丈夫な, (intense) 激しい, (of will: unwavering) 強固な, (of support) 強力な, 有力な

2 PROFICIENT: (**be strong in**) (…が) 上手だ, 得意だ, …に強い

3 OF ARGUMENT: (convincing) 説得力のある, (legitimate) もっともな

4 OF OPINION: (definite, clear) はっきりした

5 OF POSSIBILITY: 高い

6 OF DRINK: 強い

7 OF CURRENCY: 強い

1 Ryoko was strong for her size.
良子さんは体つきのわりに強かった。

Satoshi wasn't as strong as I had thought he was.
聡君は思っていたほど強くなかった。

a strong rope 丈夫なロープ

There was strong criticism of the role he played in the affair.
彼がその件で果たした役割について、激しい非難があがった。

Yagi's a strong supporter of the bill.
八木さんは法案の強力な支援者です。

2 She's strong in math.
彼女は数学が得意だ。

3 There's a strong case for banning the sale of arms.
武器の販売禁止には、もっともな言い分がある。

4 She doesn't seem to have any strong views on the matter.
彼女にはその問題について、はっきりした意見はないようだ。

5 There's a strong possibility things will get worse before they get better.
物事は、よくなる前に悪くなるという可能性が高い。

6 This liquor is too strong for me.
このお酒は私には強すぎる。

7 The yen is strong now.
円は今、強い。

♦ **strongly** *adv.* 強く

stronghold *n.* 本拠地, 拠点

structural *adj.* 構造(上)の

structural damage 構造上の損傷

♦ **structural engineering** *n.* 構造工学

structuralism *n.* 構造主義

structure *n.* 構造, 構成
v. 体系づける, 組織化する

a light structure made of aluminum
アルミニウム製の軽い構造

the structure of the (human) body
人体の構造

the structure of our society 社会構造

The course structure is outlined in the syllabus.
講座の構成は講義概要に示されている。

We must structure the business to meet customer needs.
顧客のニーズにあった形に、ビジネスを組織化しなくてはいけない。

struggle *v.* (fight) 闘う, (**struggle to do**) ...しようと苦心する, ...しようと奮闘する, (exert energy: scrabble, twist) もがく, あがく, (struggle with: grapple with: person, problem) (...に) 取り組む

n. (fight) 闘い, (fight in which people grapple) 取っ組み合い, (resistance) 争い, (difficulty) 困難, 苦労

The people struggled to achieve independence.
人々は独立を勝ち取ろうと闘った。

They struggled to make ends meet.
彼らは収入の範囲内でやりくりしようと苦心した。

They literally struggled to survive.
彼らは生き残ろうと奮闘した。

Don't give up the struggle against injustice.
不正との闘いをあきらめてはいけない。

There was a struggle as the police tried to arrest him.
警察が男を逮捕する時、取っ組み合いになった。

We had very little money, and life was a constant struggle.
お金がなくて、苦労の連続だった。

strum *v.* (guitar) つま弾く

strut *v.* 気取って歩く

n. 気取って歩くこと

strut one's stuff ひけらかす

stub *n.* (of cigarette) 吸い殻, (of ticket) 半券

v. (toe) ぶつける

♦**stub out** *v.* (cigarette) もみ消す

stubble *n.* (beard) 無精ひげ, (remainder of harvested crops) 刈り株

stubborn *adj.* がんこな, 一徹な, (hard to deal with) 扱いにくい

stuck *adj.* (jammed) 動かない, 詰まった, (stumped) 行き詰まる, (unable to move) 動けない, 身動きできない, (unable to leave a place) 足止めを食う, (of car: stuck in mud etc.) 立ち往生する

The door was stuck.
ドアが動かなかった。

If you're stuck on a particular problem, ask for help.
何か問題に行き詰まったら、言ってください。

I'm stuck in a boring job.
つまらない仕事で行き詰まっている。

I was stuck at the airport for eight hours.
空港で8時間も足止めを食った。

stuck-up *adj.* うぬぼれた, 横柄な

stud[1] *n.* (small piece of metal) びょう, スタッド, (earring) ピアス

stud[2] *n.* (horse) 種馬; (man who is popular with women) もてる男

student *n.* 学生, (primary and middle school) 生徒

a university student 大学生
a high school student 高校生
a middle school student 中学生

♦**student union** *n.* (building) 学生会館, (association) 学生自治会

student teaching *n.* 教育実習

♦**student teacher** *n.* 教育実習生, 教生

studio *n.* (TV/film/radio studio) スタジオ, (artist's studio) アトリエ, 工房; (studio apartment) ワンルームマンション

studious *adj.* 勉強好きな

study

1 *v.* LEARN: 勉強する, ((*formal*)) 学ぶ

2 *n.* SCHOOLWORK: (**studies**) 勉強

3 *n.* RESEARCH: 研究

4 *v.* EXAMINE CAREFULLY: よく見る, 詳しく検討する

5 *n.* ROOM: 書斎, (child's study) 勉強部屋, (university teacher's office) 研究室

1 What's she studying?
彼女は何を勉強しているの？

He says he'd rather work than study.
彼は勉強するより働くほうがいいと言う。

Did you study for the exam?
試験勉強はした？

I'm studying how to start a business.
起業の方法を学んでいる。

2 I think I need a break from my studies.
勉強には休憩が必要だと思う。

3 a study on dolphins イルカの研究

The results of the study were announced.
研究結果が発表された。

4 I studied the report before making any comments.
報告書を詳しく検討してから意見を言った。

5 He's probably in his study.
彼はたぶん書斎にいる。

♦**study hall** *n.* (period for studying) 自習時間

stuff *n.* (material, substance) 物, 材料, (things) こと

v. (stuff A with B) (AにBを)詰める, (stuff A in B) (AをBに) 詰め込む, (**stuff oneself**: eat too much) おなかいっぱい食べる

What's this stuff called?
この材料は何と言うんですか？

That's my stuff! それは私の物だ！

I have lots of stuff to do today.
今日はやること [用事] がいっぱいある。

What's it stuffed with?
何が詰まってるの？

stuffed *adj.* (of person: full of food) おなかいっぱいだ, (of dead animal) 剥製の

♦**stuffed animal** *n.* (toy) ぬいぐるみ

stuffing *n.* 詰め物

stuffy *adj.* (of room with poor ventilation) 風通しの悪い, (stifling) 息苦しい, むっとする, (of person) 堅苦しい, (of nose) 詰まった

have a stuffy nose 鼻が詰まっている

stumble *v.* (trip) つまずく, よろめく; (in speech) つかえる, しどろもどろになる

♦**stumble on** *v.* (discover by chance) 偶然見つける

stumbling block *n.* 障害(物)

stump *n.* (of tree) 切り株

v. (**be stumped**) 困る, 当惑する

I was stumped by the third problem.
3問目の問題に困ってしまった。

stun *v.* (surprise) びっくりさせる, (cause to lose consciousness) 気絶させる

♦**stun gun** *n.* スタンガン

stunning *adj.* (extremely beautiful) もの

すごくきれいな, とても美しい, (splendid) すばらしい, (astonishing) 驚くべき
a stunning performance すばらしい演技

stunt ***n.*** (feat) みごとな技, 妙技, スタント
v. (**stunt growth**) (...の) 発育を止める, 成長を妨げる

stuntman, -woman ***n.*** スタントマン

stupefy ***v.*** (**be stupefied**: be amazed) びっくりする

stupid ***adj.*** ばかな, ばかげた, ばからしい
a stupid question <u>ばかな質問</u> [愚問]
That was really stupid of you.
全くばかげたことをしたもんだね。
It's stupid to even think it.
そんなことは、考えるだけでばからしい。
He made us look stupid.
あの人のせいで私たちは恥をかいた。

stupidity ***n.*** (behavior) ばかげた行為, (thought) 愚かな考え

stupor ***n.*** 意識もうろう, (drunken stupor) 泥酔

sturdy ***adj.*** がっしりした, 頑丈な

stutter ***v.*** どもる

♦**stutterer** ***n.*** どもる人

sty[1] ***n.*** (pigsty) 豚小屋, (dirty place) 汚い場所
His room is a sty. 彼の部屋は汚い。

sty[2] ***n.*** (on eyelid) ものもらい

style ***n.*** (manner) やり方, (elegance) 上品, 優雅, (fashion) 流行, ファッション, (design of art/building) 様式, -風, -流, -式
v. (hair) (髪を) 整える
I don't like his style of doing things.
あの人のやり方が気に入らない。
She's got style. 彼女は品がある。
the Gothic style ゴチック様式
Japanese [Western] style <u>和</u> [洋] 風
in style 流行している, はやっている
Baggy pants are back in style.
バギーパンツがまた流行している。

stylish ***adj.*** かっこいい, いきな, おしゃれな

stylist ***n.*** (hair stylist) 美容師

stylized ***adj.*** 様式化された, 型にはまった

stylus ***n.*** (writing tool) 鉄筆, (needle for record player) レコードの針

suave ***adj.*** (of man) 物腰は柔らかい, (表面上) 丁寧な

sub → SUBMARINE, SUBSTITUTE

subcategory ***n.*** 下位区分

subcommittee ***n.*** 小委員会, 分科会

subconscious ***adj.*** 無意識の, 潜在意識の
n. 潜在意識

♦**subconsciously** ***adv.*** 無意識のうちに

subcontract ***n.*** 下請け, 下請け契約
v. 下請けに出す

♦**subcontractor** ***n.*** 下請け人, 下請け業者

subculture ***n.*** サブカルチャー, (minority culture) 少数文化

subdivide ***v.*** 細分する

subdue ***v.*** 征服する, 抑える

subdued ***adj.*** (quiet) 静かな, (of lighting) 柔らかい

subheading ***n.*** 小見出し

subhuman ***adj.*** 人間以下の

subject ***n.*** (issue) こと, 事柄, 件, (topic of discussion) 話題, 主題, (grammatical) 主語, (course of study) 学科, 科目
v. (subject A [person] to B [criticism

etc.]) (AをBに) さらす, (AをBのような目に) あわせる

It's not a subject I particularly want to talk about.
特に話したい事柄ではありません。

I don't really have an opinion on that subject.
その件については特に意見はありません。

Can we change the subject, please?
話題を替えませんか？

What's the subject of this sentence?
この文の主語は何ですか？

What's your best subject at school?
一番得意な科目は何？

I wouldn't want to subject him to that.
彼をそんな目にあわせたくない。

♦ **subject matter** *n.* (content) 内容, (theme) 主題, テーマ

subjective *adj.* 主観的な, (personal) 個人的な

a subjective opinion 個人的な意見

♦ **subjectively** *adv.* 主観的に

subjunctive *adj.* 仮定法の

n. (subjunctive mood) 仮定法

submarine *n.* 潜水艦; (sandwich) サブマリーンサンドイッチ

submerge *v.* (put underwater) 沈める, 水中に入れる, (inundate) 水浸しにする

The houses were submerged by the hurricane.
家がハリケーンで水浸しになった。

submission *n.* (proposal, proposing) 提案; (accepting of defeat) 服従, 降伏

submissive *adj.* (obedient) 従順な, (passive) 受け身の

submit *v.* (hand in) 出す, 提出する; (give up) 屈服する

Have you submitted your application yet?
もう願書を提出した？

subnormal *adj.* 普通以下の

subordinate *adj.* (junior, lower in rank) 下の, 目下の

n. (in company) 部下

Is he subordinate to you?/Is he your subordinate?
その人はあなたの部下ですか？

♦ **subordinate clause** *n.* 従属節

subplot *n.* わき筋

subpoena *n.* 呼び出し状, 召喚状

v. 召喚する

subscribe *v.* (to newspaper, magazine) 予約購読する, 定期購読する, (to newsgroup) (...に) 加入する; (agree) 同意する, 賛同する

I used to subscribe to that magazine.
以前、その雑誌を定期購読していました。

I don't subscribe to that view.
その意見には賛同できない。

♦ **subscriber** *n.* (to newspaper, magazine) (予約)購読者

subscription *n.* (to newspaper, magazine) 予約購読, 定期購読

subsection *n.* (of document) 条項

subsequent *adj.* その後の, 次の [→ AFTER 1]

Subsequent findings have disproved the original theory.
その後の調査結果で、当初の説はくつがえされた。

subsequent to → AFTER 1

subsequently *adv.* その後, すぐあとで

subservient *adj.* 卑屈な

subside *v.* (of water, flood) 引く, (of earth) 陥没する, 沈下する, (of pain, feeling) 引く, 治まる, (of noise) 静まる, 治まる

♦**subsidence** *n.* (of earth) 陥没, 沈下

subsidiary *adj.* 補助の, 付随する

n. (company) 子会社

a subsidiary role 補助的な役割

subsidize *v.* (…に) 補助金を支給する

subsidy *n.* 補助金, 助成金

subsist *v.* (live) 生存する

♦**subsistence** *n.* 生存

the subsistence level 最低生活水準

substance *n.* (matter) 物質, (content) 内容, 中身

harmful substances 有害物質

an unknown substance 未知の物質

There was no substance to the argument.

主張には中身がなかった。

substandard *adj.* 標準以下の, 不十分な

substantial *adj.* (considerable) かなりの, 相当な

substantially *adv.* (considerably) かなり, 相当

substantiate *v.* (prove) 実証する

substitute *n.* (person/thing that takes the place of another) 代わりの人/物, (teacher) 代用教員, (actor) 代役, (athlete) 補欠選手, (product) 代用品

v. (substitute A for B: use A in place of B) (Bの)代わりに(Aを)使う, (BをAで)代用する, (**substitute for**) (=do sb else's job) …の代わりをする, (=teach in place of) …の代わりに教える

A substitute came in for the injured player.

負傷した選手の代わりに補欠選手が出場した。

Can red-wine vinegar be substituted for white?

赤のワインビネガーを白の代わりに使えますか？

be no substitute for …の代わりにならない

TV is no substitute for the real thing.

テレビは実物の代わりにはならない。

subterranean *adj.* (underground) 地下の

subtitle *n.* (for book) サブタイトル, 副題; (**subtitles**: for movie) 字幕

subtle *adj.* 微妙な, (of color) 淡い, (of odor) ほのかな

a subtle change in mood

雰囲気の微妙な変化

a subtle smile 微笑

a subtle color 淡い色

♦**subtlety** *n.* 微妙さ

subtly *adv.* 微妙に

subtract *v.* 引く

subtract 7 from 91　9 1 から7を引く

subtraction *n.* 引き算

suburb *n.* 郊外, 住宅地

Richmond is a suburb of London.

リッチモンドはロンドンの郊外です。

a large suburb on the edge of town

街外れの大きな住宅地

♦**suburban** *adj.* 郊外の

suburbia *n.* 郊外

subvert *v.* (ruin) 破壊する, (overthrow)

転覆させる

subway *n.* 地下鉄

The subway is the quickest form of transport in the city.
地下鉄は都心で一番速い移動手段です。

succeed *v.* 成功する, 成し遂げる, (**succeed in doing**) ...するのに成功する, ...することができる, (go up in life) 出世する; (replace) 継ぐ, 継承する, (kabuki actor) 襲名する [→ INHERIT]

She succeeded in becoming a top lawyer.
彼女は一流の弁護士になることができた。

I didn't expect to succeed, but I did.
思いもよらず、成功した。

Who'll succeed the managing director?
常務を継ぐのは [の後任は] 誰だろう?

success *n.* 成功, (of film, play) 大当たり

Success eluded him.
彼は成功を逃した。

Her success was short-lived.
彼女の成功は、つかのまだった。

That company has had a lot of success in developing new products.
あの会社は新製品を次々開発して、大成功している。

The movie was a great success.
映画は大当たりだった。

♦ **success story** *n.* 成功談, (person) 大成功した人

successful *adj.* 成功した, (renowned) 有名な, (of attempt: well done) うまくいった

successfully *adv.* うまく, みごとに

succession *n.* (series) 連続, (being next for a job) 後任, 後継, (being next for a title) 継承

five wins in succession 5連勝

The president's (=CEO's) succession was in doubt.
社長の後任は確定していなかった。

successive *adj.* (consecutive) 連続した, 続いての

successor *n.* 後継者, 後任

succinct *adj.* 簡潔な

succulent *adj.* (fresh and juicy) みずみずしい, (juicy) 水分の多い

succumb *v.* (give in) 負ける, (to illness) 倒れる, (die) 死ぬ

such

1 *adj.* REFERRING TO STH ALREADY MENTIONED: そのような, このような, あのような, ((*informal*)) そんな, こんな, あんな

2 *adv.* USED EMPHATICALLY: See examples below

1 Such disasters could be avoided.
そのような災害は避けられるだろう。

The principal expelled the boy, but most of us wondered whether such an action was necessary.
校長は男子生徒を退学させたが、私たちのほとんどは、そのような処分が必要だったのか疑問をいだいていた。

2 It's such a wonderful/fine day!
なんていい天気なんだろう!

I didn't expect to find such a splendid hotel in such a tiny village.
こんな小さな村に、こんなに豪華なホテルがあるとは思わなかった。

He's such a nice guy.
彼はとてもいい人よ。

as such (in itself) それ自体は

I'm not against free expression as such,

but the group openly promotes racial violence.
表現の自由、それ自体には反対ではないが、あのグループは人種間暴力を公然とあおっている。

or some such …とかなんとか, …かそんなような

It was someone called McGregor, or some such name.
マクレガーとかなんとかいう名前の人だった。

such and such これこれの, しかじかの

They'll meet at such and such a time, and at such and such a place.
いつか、どこかで彼らは会うでしょう。

such as …などの, …のような

countries such as France, Italy, and Spain…
フランス、イタリア、スペインなどの国

such… (that) あまりにも…ので

It was such a shock, I had to take time off work.
あまりにもショックだったので、仕事を休まなくてはならなかった。

suck *v.* (draw in air) 吸う, (stick in mouth: thumb etc.) しゃぶる, (**suck up**: of vacuum cleaner) 吸い上げる; (be no good) ひどい, 最悪だ

suck the juice from an orange
オレンジの果汁を吸う

suck through a straw
ストローで<u>吸う</u> [飲む]

He still sucks his thumb.
あの子はまだ親指をしゃぶっている。

sucker *n.* (easily deceived person) かも, (person who has a weakness for sth) (…に) 弱い人; (suction cup) 吸着盤, (on octopus) 吸盤

suckle *v.* (breast-feed) (…に) 乳を飲ませる

sucrose *n.* しょ糖

suction *n.* (action) 吸い上げ, 吸引, (force) 吸引力

♦ **suction cup** *n.* 吸着盤

sudden *adj.* 突然の, 急の/な

a sudden jump in prices 価格の急上昇

a sudden change in the weather
天候の急変

all of a sudden 突然, 不意に, いきなり

Things got ugly all of a sudden.
突然、事態が悪化した。

All of a sudden, I realized I'd forgotten my keys.
不意に、かぎを忘れてきたことに気づいた。

suddenly *adv.* 急に, 突然, いきなり

sue *v.* 訴える, 告訴する, 訴訟を起こす

He was sued for libel.
その人は名誉毀損で訴えられた。

She sued for damages.
彼女は損害賠償の訴訟を起こした。

suede *n.* スエード

suffer *v.* 苦しむ, 苦労する, (from illness) 患う, (suffer injury) (傷を) 負う, (けがを) する, (suffer damage) (被害を) こうむる, (痛手を) 受ける

He has suffered a lot over the years.
彼は長年にわたり、かなり苦労してきた。

She is suffering from cancer.
彼女はがんを患っている。

The patient was suffering from multiple injuries.

患者は、あちこちにけがをしていた。

As usual, it was the commuters that suffered most during the transport strike.
例によって、交通機関のストで一番迷惑をこうむったのは、通勤通学の人たちだった。

The research suffered when no new funding could be found.
新たな資金提供を見出せず、研究は痛手を受けた。

♦**suffering** *n.* 苦しみ, 苦痛, 苦労

suffice *v.* (be enough) 十分だ, (**will suffice**: will do) …でいい

suffice it to say …と言えば十分だ

sufficient *adj.* 十分な, 足りる

a sufficient condition 十分な条件

♦**sufficiently** *adv.* 十分に

suffix *n.* 接尾辞

suffocate *v.* (die) 窒息死する, (be stifled) 息が詰まる

The baby suffocated to death.
赤ちゃんが窒息死した。

suffrage *n.* (right to vote) 選挙権, 参政権

sugar *n.* (お)砂糖, シュガー

suggest *v.* (propose) 提案する, 言い出す, (say) 言う, (recommend) 勧める, (imply) ほのめかす, (indicate) 示す

suggest an alternative 代案を提案する

She suggested eating out.
彼女は外食しようと言い出した。

I'm not suggesting that you should leave him.
彼と別れたほうがいいとは言ってない。

What do you suggest we do?
何をしたらいいですか？

Can someone suggest a good restaurant?
誰か、いいレストランを知らない？

There is evidence suggesting that the government was wrong.
政府が間違っていたことを示す証拠があるんです。

suggestion *n.* (proposal) 提案, 案, (implication) 示唆, ほのめかし

suggestive *adj.* (causing one to think of sex) 挑発的な, (be suggestive of: be reminiscent of) 思わせる, 示唆する

suicidal *adj.* (of behavior) 自滅的な, (of person) 自殺したいと思う

suicide *n.* 自殺, (of entire family) 一家心中, (of lovers) 心中

attempted suicide 自殺未遂

commit suicide 自殺する

suit

1 *n.* CLOTHING: スーツ, (men's) 背広

2 *v.* BE CONVENIENT FOR: (…に) 合う, 都合がいい

3 *v.* LOOK GOOD ON: (…に) 似合う

4 *n.* SET OF CARDS: (トランプの) 組札

5 *n.* LAWSUIT: 訴訟

1 He's always dressed in either a gray or blue suit.
あの人は、いつもグレーかブルーのスーツを着ている。

2 That system doesn't suit people's needs.
そのシステムは、人々の需要に合っていません。

What time would suit you best?
一番ご都合がいいのは何時ですか？

"How about Friday?"
"Friday suits me fine."
「金曜日はいかがですか？」
「金曜日でいいですよ」

3 That jacket suits you.
そのジャケット、似合うね。

4 Which suit of cards do you have?
どの組札を持ってるの？

5 file a suit 訴訟を起こす

suit yourself 好きにしなさい, ((*rude*)) 勝手にしなさい

suitable ***adj.*** 適している, 向いている, ふさわしい, 適当な

This location is not suitable for a restaurant.
この場所はレストランにふさわしくない。

♦**suitably** ***adv.*** ぴったり合って, ふさわしく

suitcase ***n.*** スーツケース

suite ***n.*** (set of rooms) スイートルーム

suited ***adj.*** (be suited to/for) (…に) 合っている, 向いている

He isn't suited to the job.
彼はその仕事に向いていない。

suitor ***n.*** (for marriage) 求婚者

sukiyaki ***n.*** すき焼き

sulfur ***n.*** イオウ, 硫黄

sulk ***v.*** すねる, ぶすっとする
n. (bad mood) 不機嫌

sulky ***adj.*** すねた, 不機嫌な

sullen ***adj.*** (in a bad mood) 不機嫌な

♦**sullenly** ***adv.*** 不機嫌に, ブスッとして

sultan ***n.*** サルタン, イスラム教国君主

sultry ***adj.*** (hot and humid) 蒸し暑い; (sexually arousing) 官能的な

sum ***n.*** (total) 合計, (amount of money) 総額, 金額, (**sums**: problem in arithmetic) 計算問題

What's the sum of 5, 10 and 12?
5と10と12の合計は？

a huge sum of money 巨額のお金

I couldn't do the sums.
計算問題が解けなかった。

to sum up (to conclude) 要するに, 結論として

summarize ***v.*** 要約する

summary ***n.*** 要約, 概要

summation ***n.*** (total) 合計, 総数; (in court) 最終弁論

summer ***n.*** 夏

♦**summer school** ***n.*** サマースクール, 夏期講習

summertime ***n.*** 夏, ((*formal*)) 夏期

summery ***adj.*** 夏の, 夏らしい

summit ***n.*** 頂上, (zenith) 頂点; (meeting of world leaders) サミット, 首脳会談

The climbers reached the summit.
登山者たちは、頂上にたどり着いた。

the G8 Summit 主要8カ国首脳会談

summon ***v.*** (send for) 呼び出す, (order to appear in court) (…に) 出頭を命じる

summons ***n.*** (order to appear in court) 出頭命令, 召喚状

sumo ***n.*** 相撲

♦**sumo wrestler** ***n.*** 相撲取り, 力士

sun ***n.*** 太陽, 日, (sunlight) 日光, 日差し

the sun, the moon, and the earth
太陽、月、そして地球

The sun went behind a cloud.
太陽は雲の陰に隠れた。

The sun was in my eyes.
日差しが目に入っていた。

get some sun (expose oneself to sunlight) 日光に当たる, (get sunburned) 日焼けする

S

Looks like you got some sun.
日焼けしたね。

sunbathe *v.* 日光浴をする

sunblock *n.* 日焼け止め

sunburn *n.* 日焼け

♦**sunburned** *adj.* 日焼けした

sundae *n.* サンデー

Sunday *n.* 日曜日

♦**Sunday best** *n.* (clothes) よそ行き, 晴れ着

Sunday school *n.* 日曜学校

sun-dried *adj.* 天日干しの, 日干しにした

sun-dried cuttlefish 天日干しのイカ

sundries *n.* 雑貨, 小物

sundry *adj.* いろいろな, 種々の

sunflower *n.* ヒマワリ

sunglasses *n.* サングラス

sun hat *n.* 日よけ帽

sunken *adj.* (of ship) 沈没した, (of eyes) 落ちくぼんだ

sunlight *n.* 日光, 日差し

hours of sunlight 日照時間

sunny *adj.* (of weather) 晴れた, (of room) 日当たりのいい

a sunny day 晴れた日

It's sunny today. 今日は晴れている。

sunny-side up *adj.* (of eggs) 目玉焼きの/で

sunrise *n.* 日の出

sunscreen *n.* (lotion, cream) 日焼け止め

sunset *n.* (time) 日没, 日暮れ, (sight) 夕焼け

sunshine *n.* 日光, 日差し

sunstroke *n.* 日射病

suntan *n.* 日焼け

♦**suntan lotion** *n.* 日焼け止め

super *adj.* (very good) すごくいい, すばらしい, (fabulous, splendid) とびきりの *adv.* (very) すごく

super- *pref.* 超-

supermodern 超モダンな

superb *adj.* (splendid) すばらしい, とびきりの, (of the highest quality) 超一流の, (gorgeous) 豪華な

supercilious *adj.* 傲慢な, 横柄な

superficial *adj.* (of knowledge, analysis) 浅い, 表面的な, (of changes) うわべだけの, 形式的な, (of person) 浅はかな, (of differences, resemblance) 外見上の, (of wound) 浅い

Watanabe has only a superficial knowledge of jazz.
渡辺さんは、ジャズについて浅い知識しかない。

Superficial changes won't solve the problem.
うわべだけの変更では問題を解決できない。

There is a superficial resemblance.
外見上、似ているところがあります。

superfluity *n.* (excess) 過剰, 余分

superfluous *adj.* 不必要な

superhuman *adj.* 超人的な

superimpose *v.* 重ね合わせる

superintendent *n.* (official in charge) 監督者, 管理者

superior *adj.* (excellent) すぐれた, (of high quality) 質のいい, (of person: **thinks oneself superior**) 自分を偉いと思っている, (higher in rank) 上の位の, (of officer) 上級の, (greater in number) 数が多い

n. (person of higher rank) 上司, 上役, (**social superiors**) 目上の人

a superior instrument すぐれた道具

He thinks he's superior to everyone.
あの人は自分が誰よりも偉いと思っている。

Their superior numbers were cause for concern.
相手のほうが数が多いことが、悩みのたねだった。

His superior gave him a good evaluation.
上司は彼を高く評価した。

superiority *n.* 優位, 優越, (excellence) 卓越していること

♦ **superiority complex** *n.* 優越感

superlative *adj.* (the best) 最高の

n. (in grammar: "-est," "most") 最上級

superman *n.* スーパーマン, 超人

supermarket *n.* スーパー(マーケット)

supermodel *n.* スーパーモデル

supernatural *adj.* 超自然の, (miraculous) 神秘的な

n. (**the supernatural**) 超自然的なもの

a supernatural phenomenon 超常現象

superpower *n.* 超大国

supersede *v.* (take the place of) (…に) 取って代わる

supersonic *adj.* (of aircraft) 超音速の

a supersonic jet 超音速ジェット機

superstar *n.* スーパースター

superstition *n.* 迷信

superstitious *adj.* (of person) 迷信を信じる

He is so superstitious.
彼はすごく迷信を信じる [縁起を担ぐ]。

supertanker *n.* 超大型タンカー

supervise *v.* 監督する, 管理する

supervise an exam 試験を監督する

supervision *n.* 監督, 管理

The boy needs supervision.
その少年は監督が必要だ。

supervisor *n.* 監督, 管理人, (academic supervisor) 指導教官

supper *n.* (evening meal) 夕食, (late meal) 夜食

supplant *v.* (…に) 取って代わる

supple *adj.* (of object) よく曲がる, (of body) 柔軟な, しなやかな

supplement *n.* 補足, (to newspaper) 特集ページ, (vitamin/herbal supplement) サプリメント

v. 補う

You should supplement your diet with vitamins.
食事にビタミンを補ったほうがいいよ。

♦ **supplementary** *adj.* 追加の, 補足の

supplier *n.* (company) 供給会社, (country) 供給国, (person) 供給者

supply *v.* (provide) (…に) 供給する, 与える, 支給する

n. (stock, amount available) 供給

The Middle East supplies industrialized nations with most of their oil.
中東諸国は工業国が消費する石油の大部分を供給している。

The refugees were supplied with tents and blankets.
難民はテントと毛布を支給された。

supply and demand 需要と供給

be in short supply (…の供給が) 不足

S

している, (...が) 足りない

Bananas are in short supply.
バナナの供給が不足している。

support

1 *v.* **BACK:** 支持する, 支援する, 後押しする, (encourage) 応援する, 支える, (by providing money/necessities) 援助する

2 *n.* **BACKING:** 支持, 支援, 後押し, 支え, (aid) 援助

3 *v.* **CAUSE TO KEEP UPRIGHT:** 支える, 維持する

4 *n.* **PART OF BUILDING/STRUCTURE:** (pillar) 支柱, (thing that supports) 支える物

5 *v.* **MAINTAIN:** (family) 養う, 支える, 扶養する

6 *v.* **PROVE:** (back up) 裏付ける, (substantiate) 立証する

1 Which party do you support?
どの政党を支持しますか？

They don't support the mayor.
彼らは市長を支援しない。

Your family will support you during hard times.
苦しい時はご家族が支えてくれますよ。

2 Support for the government is declining.
政府への支持が低下している。

You have our support.
我々が支援します。

We got no support from the locals.
地元の後押しを全く得られなかった。

They need government support.
彼らには政府の援助が必要だ。

financial support 経済援助

moral support 精神的支え

3 These poles support the roof.
これらの柱が屋根を支えている。

A good pair of crutches will support up to two hundred kilograms.
しっかりした松葉づえなら、200キロまで支えられる。

4 steel supports スチール製の支柱

We'll need some supports to keep the wall up.
この塀を立てておくには何か支えが必要だ。

5 He has a large family to support.
あの人は大家族を養っている。

6 That incident supported his claim.
あの事件で彼の主張が裏付けられた。

be in support of 支持する

Are you in support of the motion?
その動議を支持しますか？

supporter *n.* 支援者, 支持者, (of sports team: fan) サポーター

supporting *adj.* (of actor/actress) わき役の, 助演の

supportive *adj.* (be supportive of) 支持する, 支援する

suppose *v.*

1 **ASSUME:** (...と) 予想する, 思う

2 **GUESS:** (...と) 思う, (making a suggestion) (...したら) どうですか

3 **SHOULD/OUGHT:** (**is supposed to**) ...ことになっている, ...はずだ

4 **IF:** (**suppose you/we had...**) もし...していたら, 仮に...していたら [→ IF]

1 I suppose they'll raise taxes again.
また増税があるだろう。

I didn't suppose he would like it.
彼が気に入るとは思わなかった。

I suppose you think that's funny?

さぞかし面白いでしょう?

The course was even worse than I had supposed.
その授業は、予想していたよりさらにひどかった。

Let's suppose there was a conspiracy. How could it have been kept secret for so long?
陰謀があったとしよう。しかしどうしてこんなに長い間、隠しておけるだろう?

2 "Was it worth going?"
"I suppose so."
「行く価値があった?」
「あったと思うけど」

I suppose we should've written a letter.
手紙を書いておくべきだったんでしょうね。

Suppose we go out for dinner tonight?
今夜は外食でもどう?

3 We're supposed to get there by 6 o'clock.
6時までに行くことになっている。

They're supposed to let us know where we should go.
どこへ行けばいいか、知らせてくれるはずです。

4 Suppose you had gone. You would have been dead by now.
もし行っていたら、今ごろ死んでいたよ。

supposed *adj.* (alleged) ...と思われている, ...とされている

supposedly *adv.* おそらく, ...と思われる

This is supposedly one of the best restaurants in Tokyo.
ここはおそらく、東京で一番いいレストランの一つだ。

supposing *conj.* → SUPPOSE 4, IF

suppository *n.* 座薬

suppress *v.* (rebellion) 鎮圧する, (feelings) 抑える, (the truth) 隠す

♦ **suppression** *n.* (of rebellion) 鎮圧, (of feelings) 抑制, (of the truth) 隠ぺい

supremacist *n.* ...至上主義者

supremacy *n.* (dominance) 支配, 優位, (power) 支配権

supreme *adj.* 最高の

♦ **Supreme Court** *n.* 最高裁判所

surcharge *n.* 追加料金

sure

1 *adj.* CONFIDENT: 確かだ, 自信がある, 確信している, (**be not sure**) わからない

2 *adj.* BOUND: (**be sure to do**) きっと...する, 必ず...する

3 *adj.* CERTAIN: 確実な, 確かな

4 *adv.* USED EMPHATICALLY: 本当に, 確かに

5 *adv.* OF COURSE: もちろん

1 He's sure he's going to win.
彼には勝つ自信がある。

I feel sure it was the right thing to do.
正しいことをしたと確信している。

I wasn't sure what to think.
何を考えていいのかわからなかった。

I'm not sure about going this evening.
今晩行くかどうかわからない。

2 Don't worry, you're sure to see her again.
大丈夫、きっとまた彼女に会えるよ。

He's sure to be back.
彼は必ず戻って来るよ。

3 a sure win 確実な勝利

a sure remedy for cancer
がんの確かな治療法

4 Sure is humid today, isn't it?
本当に蒸し暑いですね。

5 "Can I come, too?"

“Sure.”
「私も行っていい？」
「もちろん」

be sure to do (asking sb to do sth: don’t forget to do) 必ず…して(ください)

Be sure to call us once you arrive.
着いたら必ず電話してね。

for sure 確実に, 絶対に

I’m going, and that’s for sure.
行くよ、絶対に。

make sure (check that) 確かめる, (**make sure to do**: remember to do) 必ず…する

Make sure the door’s locked.
かぎが、かかっていることを確かめて。

Make sure to send this letter.
この手紙を必ず出してね。

sure enough 案の定, 思ったとおり

And sure enough, there was Ralph, leaning up against the bar.
案の定、ラルフはバーにいてカウンターにもたれかかっていた。

surely *adv.* (indicating one’s belief that sth ought to be the case) …でしょう, (used emphatically: definitely) きっと, 間違いなく, 絶対, (**surely not**) まさか

She’ll surely pass her driving test.
彼女はきっと、運転免許試験に受かるでしょう。

Surely he won’t be late this time.
まさか今度は遅れないでしょう。

surety *n.* (money) 保証金; (confidence) 自信, (certainty) 確信

surf *n.* 打ち寄せる波

v. サーフィンをする, (**surf the Internet**) ネットサーフィンする

The surf was good.
波はよかった。

Do you surf?
サーフィンをやるの？

surface *n.* (of object) 表面, (of body of water) 水面, (of person: outward appearance) 見かけ, 外見

The surface has to be dry before painting.
ペンキを塗る前に、表面が乾いていないといけない。

The surface of the pond was covered in algae.
池の水面が藻でおおわれていた。

On the surface he seems tough, but beneath it all he has a heart of gold.
彼は見かけは怖そうだけど、内面は優しい心の持ち主だ。

surfboard *n.* サーフボード

surfer *n.* サーファー

surfing *n.* サーフィン, (of Internet) ネットサーフィン

surge *v.* (suddenly increase) 急増する; (**surge up**: of emotion) 込み上げる; (of crowd) 殺到する

n. (sudden increase) 急増; (sudden movement of people) 殺到

surgeon *n.* 外科医, (army surgeon) 軍医, (ship’s surgeon) 船医

surgery *n.* (medical operation) 手術

surgical *adj.* (of treatment) 外科の, 外科的な, (of equipment) 手術用の

surmise *v.* 推測する, 推量する

surname *n.* 名字, ((*formal*)) 姓

surpass *v.* (…より) 勝る, (…を) 超える

The results surpassed all our expectations.

結果は予想をはるかに超えていた。

surplus ***n.*** (excess) 余分, (amount of money) 剰余金
adj. 余分の, 余った
be in surplus 余る
Rice is in surplus this year.
今年はお米が余っている。

surprise ***v.*** 驚かす, びっくりさせる
n. (state of being surprised) 驚き, (act of surprising) 驚かすこと
adj. 突然の, 不意の
Let's surprise them!
びっくりさせようよ!
It wouldn't surprise me if it snows later.
いつ雪が降ってもおかしくない天気だ。
It came as a surprise to everyone.
誰にとっても驚きだった。
I want it to be a surprise, so don't tell her.
驚かせたいから彼女には言わないで。
What a lovely surprise! I didn't expect a present.
なんてすてきなんでしょう! プレゼントをもらえるとは思わなかった。
a surprise visit 不意の訪問
a surprise attack 奇襲(攻撃)
in surprise びっくりして, 驚いて
He looked at me in surprise.
彼はびっくりして私を見た。
take by surprise 不意に襲う
to one's surprise 驚いたことに, 意外にも
To my surprise, he immediately agreed.
驚いたことに、彼はすぐに同意した。

surprised ***adj.*** 驚いた, びっくりした
a surprised look 驚いた様子
I was surprised to see Kubota there.
久保田さんがそこにいてびっくりした。

surprising ***adj.*** 驚くべき, びっくりするような, 思いがけない
a surprising turn of events
びっくりするような展開
It was a surprising result.
思いがけない結果だった。

♦**surprisingly** ***adv.*** 驚くほど, (used at the beginning of a sentence) 驚いたことに, 意外にも

surreal ***adj.*** 超現実的な

surrealism ***n.*** シュールレアリスム, 超現実主義

surrender ***v.*** (to enemy) 降伏する, (to police) 自首する

surrogate ***adj.*** 代理の

♦**surrogate mother** ***n.*** 代理母

surround ***v.*** 囲む, 取り巻く, 取り囲む
A high wall surrounded the house.
高い塀が家を取り囲んでいた。
We were surrounded by a hostile crowd.
敵意に満ちた群衆に取り囲まれた。

surroundings ***n.*** (environment) 環境, (area around oneself) 周囲

surveillance ***n.*** 監視, 見張り
a surveillance camera 監視カメラ
under surveillance 監視下に

survey ***n.*** (study) 調査, (geological survey) 測量
v. (land) 測量する; (people: ask opinions of) (…に) 意見を聞く, (=using questionnaire) (…に) 世論調査する; (area: scope out) 見渡す
a public opinion survey 世論調査

survival ***n.*** 生き延びること, 生き残ること

the survival rate 生存率

There's only a small chance of survival.
生き残る見込みは、わずかしかない。

survival of the fittest 適者生存

survive *v.* (continue to live) 生き延びる, (after accident) 生き残る, (live through) 生存する, (outlive) (…より) 長生きする; (overcome) 乗り越える, 切り抜ける, (endure) 耐える

I doubt if the tiger will survive to the end of this century.
トラが今世紀最後まで生き延びられるか疑問だ。

Only one person survived the crash.
墜落事故で生存したのは、一人だけだった。

She survived her husband by another twelve years.
彼女は夫より12年長生きした。

He has survived so many difficulties.
彼はとても多くの困難を乗り越えてきた。

I wonder how she can survive with the noise those children make.
あの子たちの騒がしさに、彼女はどうやって耐えられるのかしら。

survivor *n.* 生存者, (person who perseveres through life) 困難を切り抜けていく人

There were no survivors.
生存者はいなかった。

sushi *n.* 寿司, 鮨

suspect *n.* 容疑者

v. 疑う, 思う

adj. 疑わしい

The police have arrested a suspect.
警察が容疑者を逮捕した。

The police suspect he is the culprit.
警察は、彼が犯人ではないかと疑っている。

I suspect they went out drinking last night.
彼らはゆうべ飲みに出かけたかも。

suspect data 疑わしいデータ

suspend *v.* (stop for a time) 一時停止する, (**be suspended from school**) 停学になる, (delay, postpone) 延期する; (hang) つるす

He was suspended for a week.
彼は1週間、停学になった。

suspenders *n.* (straps to hold up trousers) サスペンダー, ズボンつり, (straps to hold up stockings: garters) ガーター

suspense *n.* (uneasiness) 気がかり, 不安, (excitement) はらはらする状態; (genre) サスペンス

suspension *n.* (of car) サスペンション; (stoppage) 停止, (removal from school) 停学; (act of hanging) つるすこと

♦ **suspension bridge** *n.* つり橋

suspicion *n.* 疑い, 疑惑, 不審

throw suspicion on …に疑いをかける

suspicious *adj.* 怪しい, 疑わしい, 不審な

sustain *v.* (support) 支える, (bear) (…に) 耐える, (maintain) 維持する, 持続する/させる, (accept: decision, ruling, law) 認める, (suffer) 受ける, こうむる

♦ **sustainable** *adj.* (of economy) 持続可能な

sutra *n.* (Buddhist text) (お)経, 経典

recite a sutra お経をあげる

swagger *v.* いばって歩く

swallow[1] *v.* 飲み込む, (absorb) 吸収する, (believe: a far-fetched story etc.) うのみにする

n. 一口

I couldn't swallow it.
私は飲み込めなかった。

The small companies were swallowed up by the big ones.
中小企業が大企業に吸収された。

He took it down in one swallow.
彼は一口で飲み込んだ。

swallow[2] *n.* (bird) ツバメ, 燕

swamp *n.* 沼, 沼地

swan *n.* ハクチョウ, 白鳥

swap *v.* 交換する, 取り替える, (swap lovers) スワッピングする

Let's swap seats.
席を交換しよう。

♦**swap meet** *n.* フリーマーケット, 古物市

swarm *n.* 群れ, 大群

v. (of insects, people) 群がる

swastika *n.* (ancient symbol) 卍, (of the Nazi Party) かぎ十字

swat *v.* (insect) ピシャリと打つ, パチッとたたく

sway *v.* (rock to and fro) 揺れる [→ INFLUENCE]

The trees swayed in the wind.
木々が風で揺れた。

swear *v.* (use filthy language) 口汚い言葉を使う, ののしる; (take an oath) 誓う, (**be sworn into office**) 宣誓する

He swore at the other man.
その人は相手の男をののしった。

Stop swearing like that!
そんな口汚い言葉を使うのはやめなさい!

He swore that he would never drink again.
彼はもう二度とお酒は飲まないと誓った。

The president was sworn into office.
大統領は宣誓して就任した。

♦**swear by** *v.* (believe firmly in) 信頼しきっている

swear to *v.* (be certain of) 確信している, (**swear to God**) 神にかけて誓う

swearword *n.* 口汚い言葉

sweat *n.* (moisture) 汗

v. (produce moisture through skin) 汗をかく; (worry) 気をもむ

He was covered in sweat.
彼は汗まみれだった。

I wiped the sweat from my face.
顔の汗をぬぐった。

Everyone was sweating from the heat.
みんな暑くて汗をかいていた。

♦**sweat gland** *n.* 汗腺

sweating *n.* 発汗

sweatband *n.* 汗止め (バンド)

sweater *n.* セーター

sweatpants *n.* スウェットパンツ

sweatshirt *n.* トレーナー

sweaty *adj.* 汗まみれの, 汗くさい

Sweden *n.* スウェーデン

♦**Swede** *n.* スウェーデン人

sweep *v.* (clean with a broom) はく, (sweep the house) 掃除する, (sweep crumbs off a table) 払う; (spread quickly) さっと広がる; (win overwhelmingly) 圧勝する [→ MOVE, RUSH] *n.* (act of sweeping with a broom) はくこと, 掃除; (search of an area) 捜索

I've swept the hall.
廊下は、はきました。

I started sweeping up the leaves.
落ち葉の掃除を始めた。

make a sweep of (area: search for criminals) さっと見回す

sweep under the carpet 隠す

sweeping *adj.* (of changes) 大胆な, (of generalization) おおざっぱな

sweet *adj.* (of food, smell) 甘い, (of wine) 甘口の; (kind) 優しい, (cute) かわいい, (agreeable) 感じのいい

n. (**sweets**) 甘いもの, お菓子

The cake was so sweet.
ケーキはとても甘かった。

There was a sweet smell of roses in the air.
バラの甘い香りが漂っていた。

What a sweet baby!
なんてかわいい赤ちゃんでしょう!

sweeten *v.* (food) 甘くする

sweetener *n.* (sweetening ingredient) 甘味料

sweetheart *n.* (lover) 恋人, (addressing lover) ((*feminine*)) あなた, ((*masculine*)) 君

sweetness *n.* 甘さ, 甘味, (of person) 優しさ

sweet pepper *n.* ピーマン

sweet potato *n.* サツマイモ

swell *v.* (of bruise) はれる, (of river) 増水する, (of wave) うねる

n. (wave) うねり

The bruise has swelled up.
打ったところがはれている。

♦**swelling** *n.* (of wound) はれ

sweltering *adj.* 蒸し暑い

swerve *v.* (suddenly change direction) 急にそれる, 外れる, 急に曲がる, (of drunk driver) 蛇行運転する

The car swerved to avoid the child.
車は子供をよけようとして急に曲がった。

swift *adj.* 速い, 素早い, 迅速な

♦**swiftly** *adv.* 速く, 素早く, 早速

swim *v.* (move through the water) 泳ぐ; (of head: be in a daze) (頭が)くらくらする, めまいがする

n. 水泳, 泳ぎ

It's too cold to swim today.
今日は、泳ぐには寒すぎる。

Want to go for a swim?
泳ぎに行かない?

swimmer *n.* 泳ぐ人, (athlete) 競泳選手

swimming *n.* 水泳, 泳ぎ

adj. 水泳用の

♦**swimming cap** *n.* 水泳帽

swimming pool *n.* プール

swim suit *n.* 水着

swindle *v.* (swindle A out of B) (AからBを)だまし取る, (practice fraud) 詐欺を働く

She swindled him out of ¥10,000.
彼女は彼から1万円をだまし取った。

♦**swindler** *n.* 詐欺師

swing

1 *v.* MOVE IN A CURVE: (sway) 揺れる, 揺れ動く, (**swing open**) ぱっと開く, (**swing shut**) ぱっと閉まる, (of car: turn quickly to left/right, or into parking lot) 急に

曲がる

2 *v.* **CAUSE TO MOVE IN A CURVE:** (arms, bat) 振る, 振り回す, (rotate) 回転させる, (car: turn quickly to left/right) 急に (左/右に) カーブさせる

3 *n.* **SEAT FOR SWINGING:** ぶらんこ

4 *n.* **ATTEMPTED PUNCH:** 殴ろうとすること

5 *n.* **CHANGE:** 変化, 変動

6 *n.* **MUSIC:** (swing music) スイング

1 The lantern was swinging in the breeze.
ちょうちんが風に揺れていた。

The door swung open.
ドアがぱっと開いた。

2 Will you please stop swinging your arms around?
腕を振り回すのをやめてもらえませんか？

He swung his chair around.
彼は椅子をくるっと回転させた。

3 Would you like to have another go on the swing?
ぶらんこにもう1回乗りたい？

4 He took a swing at me.
((*masculine*)) 彼は俺に殴りかかってきた。

5 a mood swing 気分の変化

a swing in public opinion 世論の変動

6 Do you listen to swing?
スイングは聴きますか？

♦ **swing vote** *n.* 浮動票

swing voter *n.* 浮動票の有権者

swipe *v.* (steal) 盗む; (strike with fist) ぶん殴る, (take a swing at) (…に) 殴りかかる

n. (attempted punch) 殴ろうとすること

take a swipe at (try to hit) 殴ろうとする; (criticize) 非難する

swirl *v.* (of water, air) 渦巻く; (of boat, car, airplane) 旋回する

n. (of water, air) 渦

swish *v.* (expressing sound) ヒュッと音を立てる, (expressing movement) ヒュッと動く

n. (sound) ヒュッ(という音)

Swiss *n.* (person) スイス人; (cheese) スイスチーズ

switch

1 *n.* **ELECTRICAL CONNECTOR:** スイッチ

2 *v.* **TURN ON/OFF:** (**switch on**) つける, (**switch off**) 切る

3 *v.* **CHANGE:** (switch from A to B) (AからBに) 切り替える, 変える, (**switch sides**) 反対側に回る

4 *v.* **SWAP:** 取り替える, (secretly) すり替える, (switch A with B) (AをBと) 交換する

5 *n.* **CHANGE:** 変更, (from one thing to another: switchover) 切り替え, 転換

1 I can't find the switch.
スイッチが見つからない。

It's the switch on the right.
右側のスイッチです。

2 Switch on the radio, would you.
ラジオをつけて。

Who switched off the lights?
誰が電気のスイッチを切ったの？

3 We're in the process of switching to the new operating system.
新しいＯＳに切り替えているところです。

4 The two men switched suitcases.
２人の男がスーツケースを取り替えた。

5 the switch to digital TV

S

デジタルテレビへの切り替え

switchboard *n.* 電話交換台

♦ **switchboard operator** *n.* 電話の交換手

Switzerland *n.* スイス

swivel *v.* (turn around on an axis) 回転する, (cause to turn around) 回転させる

♦ **swivel chair** *n.* 回転椅子

swollen *adj.* (of body part) はれた, (of river) 増水した

Look how swollen the river has become.
川があんなに増水してるよ。

swoon *v.* 気絶する

swoop *v.* (of bird) 急降下する, 舞い降りる, (suddenly attack) 急襲する, (**swoop in**: of police) 家宅捜索する

sword *n.* 刀

swordfish *n.* メカジキ

sworn *adj.* (absolute) 絶対の

sworn secrecy 極秘

sycamore *n.* (tree) スズカケの木

syllable *n.* シラブル, 音節

syllabus *n.* (outline of course) 講義概要

symbol *n.* シンボル, 象徴

The dove is a symbol of peace.
ハトは平和の象徴です。

symbolic *adj.* シンボルの, 象徴的な, (be symbolic of) 象徴する

symbolism *n.* (in literature) 象徴主義

symbolize *v.* 象徴する

symmetrical *adj.* 左右対称の, (balanced) 均整のとれた

symmetry *n.* 左右対称, (balance) 均整

sympathetic *adj.* (kind) 思いやりのある, (of voice, comment) 同情的な

be sympathetic to (person) …に同情する, (cause, proposal) …に共感する, …に好意的だ

sympathize *v.* 同情する, 気の毒に思う, (approve of) 賛成する, 同意する, (understand) 理解する, 共感する

Well, I sympathize with your situation, but there's really not much I can do to help.
その状況には同情するけど、あまり力になれないんです。

I can't sympathize with their methods.
彼らのやり方には賛成できない。

♦ **sympathizer** *n.* (supporter) 支持者, 同調者

sympathy *n.* 同情, (kindness) 思いやり, (understanding and affection) 共感, (**sympathies** for sb's death) お悔やみ

You have our sympathies (for the death in your family).
お悔やみ申し上げます。

have sympathy for (feel sorry for) …に同情する, (understand and share: sb's proposal) …に共感する

symphony *n.* 交響曲, シンフォニー

♦ **symphony orchestra** *n.* 交響楽団

symposium *n.* シンポジウム, 討論会

symptom *n.* (of illness) 徴候, 症状

symptomatic *adj.* (be symptomatic of) 示す, 表す

synagogue *n.* ユダヤ教の教会

sync *n.* 同調

be in sync 合う, 一致する

be out of sync 合わない, 一致しない

synchronize *v.* (synchronize A with B) (AをBに)合わせる, (clocks) (…の)時間を合わせる

♦ **synchronized swimming** *n.* シンクロナイズド・スイミング

syndicate *n.* シンジケート

syndrome *n.* 症候群, シンドローム

synonym *n.* 同義語, 類義語

synonymous *adj.* (of words) 同義の, (be synonymous with) (…と) 同じ意味だ

synopsis *n.* 粗筋

syntax *n.* シンタックス, (subject of study) 統語論

synthesis *n.* (combining of ideas) 総合

synthesize *v.* (ideas) 総合する

synthetic *adj.* 合成の, (not genuine) 本物ではない

synthetic leather 合成皮革

syphilis *n.* 梅毒

syringe *n.* (medical instrument) 注射器

syrup *n.* シロップ

system *n.* システム, (organization) 組織, 体制, (institution) 制度, (method) 方法, やり方; (of the body) -系

There doesn't seem to be any system for complaints in this company.
この会社には苦情処理の体制がないようだ。

He rebelled against the system.
彼は体制に反抗した。

the legal system 法制度

The system seems to work, so let's not change it.
このやり方はうまくいっているようだから、変えるのはやめよう。

SYSTEMS OF THE BODY

the circulatory system 循環器系
the digestive system 消化器系
the nervous system 神経系
the respiratory system 呼吸器系

systematic *adj.* (of approach, method) 体系的な, 組織的な

T, t

tab[1] *n.* (on can) タブ, つまみ

tab[2] *n.* (restaurant bill) 付け, 勘定; (tab key) タブキー

pick up the tab (pay for a meal) ごちそうする, おごる

table *n.* (piece of furniture) テーブル, (dining table) 食卓; (chart) 表

The book's on the table.
本はテーブルの上にあります。

Your dinner is on the table.
晩ご飯は食卓に出してあるよ。

The table was set for dinner.
食卓には夕食の用意ができていた。

tablecloth *n.* テーブルクロス

tablespoon *n.* 大さじ [→ picture of COOKING UTENSILS]

tablet *n.* (pill) 錠剤

Take two tablets a day.
１日２錠、飲んでください。

This medicine comes in tablet form.
この薬は錠剤になっています。

table tennis *n.* 卓球, ピンポン

tabloid *n.* タブロイド紙

taboo *n.* タブー

tacit *adj.* (of agreement) 暗黙の

♦**tacitly** *adv.* 暗黙のうちに, (**tacitly approve**) 黙認する

tack *n.* (thumbtack) 画びょう, (nail) びょう

tackle *v.* (deal with) (…に) 取り組む; (in football: run down: another player) (…に) タックルする

n. (fishing tackle) 釣り道具

How do you intend to tackle this problem?
この問題にどう取り組むつもりですか？

He was tackled before he could score.
得点する前に、彼はタックルされた。

tacky *adj.* (lacking in taste) やぼったい, さえない, 安っぽい

tact *n.* (thoughtfulness) 機転, 気配り, 如才なさ

He certainly doesn't show much tact.
あの人は本当に機転が利かないね。

♦**tactless** *adj.* 機転の利かない, 気の利かない, 無神経な

tactic *n.* (strategy) 作戦, 戦術, 戦略, (countermeasure) 対策, (method) 方法

What sort of tactics do you expect them to adopt?
彼らはどんな作戦を取ると思う？

delaying tactics 牛歩戦術

tactile *adj.* 触覚の

tadpole *n.* オタマジャクシ

tag[1] *n.* (price tag) 値札, (label on clothing) タグ, (name tag) 名札

v. (attach a label to) (…に) 名札をつける

tag[2] *n.* (game) 鬼ごっこ

v. 捕まえる

Let's play tag. 鬼ごっこしようよ。

Tagalog *n.* タガログ語

tail *n.* (part of animal's body) しっぽ, 尾; (of shirt) すそ, (back part of sth) 後ろ, (**tails**: side of coin) 裏

Look at the dog wagging its tail.
見て、あの犬しっぽを振ってるよ。

This breed has its tail cut off when it's a puppy.
この種類は、子犬の時にしっぽを切ってしまうんです。

♦**tail away/off** *v.* (become smaller) しだいに小さくなる, (become weaker) 少しずつ弱まる

tailgate *n.* (back door of car) 後部ドア, 後尾扉

v. (...の) 後ろにぴったりつけて走る

taillight *n.* テールライト, テールランプ [→ picture of CAR]

tailor *n.* (shop) 仕立屋(さん)

v. (tailor A to/for B) (AをBに) 仕立てる, 合わせる

♦**tailor-made** *adj.* (of clothes) あつらえの, オーダーメイドの

tailspin *n.* (of aircraft) きりもみ降下

tailwind *n.* 追い風

taint *v.* (reputation) 傷つける

Taiwan *n.* 台湾, ((*in abbr.*)) 台

take

NOTE: See also COMMON EXPRESSIONS WITH "TAKE" on p. 987.

1 *v.* BRING SOMEWHERE: (person) 連れて行く, 送る, (thing) 持って行く

2 *v.* GET INTO HANDS: 取る, (**take by the hand**) 手を取る, (**take into one's hands**) 手に取る, (**take in one's arms**) 抱く

3 *v.* REMOVE: (take without permission or by mistake) 持って行く, 持ち出す, (steal) とる, 盗む

4 *v.* HAVE: (day off) 取る

5 *v.* BUY: 買う, (**I'll take...**) 下さい [→ SUBSCRIBE]

6 *v.* RECEIVE/ACCEPT: 受け取る, (employ) 雇う, 採用する

7 *v.* REQUIRE: (...が) 要る, 必要だ, かかる

8 *v.* CAPTURE: (**take prisoner**) 捕虜にする, (**take hostage**) 人質にする, (of military: occupy) 占領する

9 *v.* CONSIDER: 受け取る, 思う, 理解する

10 *v.* ENDURE: 耐える, がまんする

11 *v.* HOLD/CARRY: 持つ

12 *v.* TRAVEL BY: (...に) 乗る, (...で) 行く, (...に) 乗って行く

13 *v.* INGEST: (medicine) 飲む, ((*formal*)) 服用する

14 *v.* SUBTRACT: 引く

15 *n.* SEGMENT: テイク, (of film) 1回分の撮影, (of sound recording) 1回分の録音

16 *n.* MONEY: (profit) 利益, (share) 取り分, 分け前

17 *n.* POINT OF VIEW: 見方, 解釈

1 Where are you taking me?
私をどこに連れて行くつもり?

I took Kumiko to the station.
久美子を駅まで送りました。

I offered to take her home.
家まで送ろうかと彼女に言った。

Don't forget to take your lunch with you.
お弁当を持って行くのを忘れないで。

Can you take this parcel to the post office?
この小包を郵便局に出して来てくれる?

He gave her some work to take home.
彼は持ち帰りの仕事を彼女に渡した。

2 He took me by the hand.
彼は私の手を取った。

The witch took the apple into her hands.
魔女はリンゴを手に取った。

He took the baby in his arms.
彼は赤ん坊を抱いた。

3 Someone has taken my umbrella.
誰かが私の傘を持って行ってしまった。

You took it from my desk, didn't you!
私の机から持ち出したでしょう！

He took my idea for a novel.
あの人は私の小説のアイデアを盗んだ。

4 I took a day off work last week.
先週は休みを1日取った。

OK, let's take a break.
じゃ、一息いれましょう。

5 I'll take the lunch special.
日替わりランチを下さい。

6 Did you take the money?
そのお金を受け取ったの？

He took a job in the Foreign Office.
彼は外務省に就職しました。

They won't take people without a college degree.
あそこは大卒でない人は採用しない。

7 It takes guts to do that.
それをするには勇気が要る。

It takes a lot of money to set up a business.
ビジネスを始めるには、多額の資金が必要です。

It'll take a day to do all this work.
この仕事をするのに1日かかるだろう。

How long do you think it'll take?
どのくらいかかると思いますか？

8 He was taken prisoner.
彼は捕虜になった。

They were taken hostage.
彼らは人質になった。

The city was taken without loss of life.
町は死者を出すことなく占領された。

9 Don't take it so seriously.
そんなに深刻に受け取るなよ。

What do you take me for—an idiot?
私を何だと思ってるの、ばかだとでも思ってるの？

So, can I take it that 9 o'clock is OK for you?
では、9時でOKだと思っていいんですね？

I took it to mean that he couldn't come.
彼は来られないんだと理解した。

10 I really can't take much more of this.
もうがまんの限界だ/もうたくさんだ。

11 Can I take your bags?
荷物を持ちましょうか？

Let me take your coat.
コートをお預かりしましょう。

12 Let's take a taxi. タクシーに乗ろう。

We took a bus to the zoo.
動物園までバスで行った。

13 You're supposed to take two tablets twice a day.
1日2回2錠を飲むことになっています。

14 Take 17 from 45 and what do you have?
45から17を引くといくつになる？

15 The director wrapped after two takes.
監督は2テイクで終わりにした。

16 The agent's take is 10%.
代理人の取り分は10%です。

17 What's your take on the situation?
この状況をどう見ますか？

take ... as is ありのまま受け取る

take it from me 本当だよ, 間違いないよ

Take it from me, that restaurant is overrated.
本当だよ、あのレストランは言われてるほどよくないって。

take it or leave it (buy or not) 買うか買わないか決める, (accept or not) 受けるかどうか好きにする
That's my final offer. You can take it (=buy it) or leave it.
これ以上、まけられません。それで買うか買わないか決めてください。

take it out on ...に八つ当たりする

take it upon oneself to do 勝手に...することに決める, 思い切って...することにする
She took it upon herself to tell the boss.
彼女は思い切って上司に言うことにした。

take (some) doing なかなか難しい, とても大変だ
Winning that race took some doing.

COMMON EXPRESSIONS WITH "TAKE"

take a bath おふろに入る, 入浴する
take a break/rest 休憩する
take a bus/train バス/電車に乗る
take a call 電話に出る
take account of 考慮する
take a chance 一か八かやってみる
take a class/course コースを取る
take a crack/whack at やってみる
take advantage of 利用する
take sb's advice (...の) アドバイスに従う
take aim (at) (...に) ねらいを定める
take a joke 冗談を受け流す
take a look (at) 見る, 見てみる
take a nap 昼寝する
take an interest (in) (...に) 興味をもつ
take a picture/photo 写真を撮る
take a poll 世論調査を行う
take a seat 座る
take a shower シャワーを浴びる
take a sip 一口飲む
take a test 試験を受ける
take a vote (on) 採決する
take a walk 散歩をする
take care 気をつける
take care of ...の世話をする
take charge 担当する, 主導権を握る
take cover 隠れる
take effect 効く, 効果が出る
take for granted 当たり前のことと思う
take heart 元気を出す
take into account 考慮に入れる
take issue with ...に反対する
take kindly to 快く受け入れる
take medicine 薬を飲む
take notes ノートを取る
take offense (at) (...に) 腹を立てる
take office 就任する
take part in ...に参加する
take place 行われる, 催される
take power 権力を握る
take pride in ...に誇りをもつ
take prisoner 捕虜にする
take sides 一方の側につく
take sugar 砂糖を入れる
take sb's temperature (...の) 体温を計る
take the blame 責任を取る, 責任を負う
take the trouble to do わざわざ...する
take time 時間がかかる
take one's time ゆっくりする
take turns (at) 交替でする

あの競走に勝つことは、なかなか大変だった。

take after *v.* (resemble) …に似ている

The second son takes after his father.
次男の方はお父さんに似ています。

take along *v.* 持って行く

You'd better take along an umbrella.
傘を持って行ったほうがいいよ。

take apart *v.* (disassemble) 分解する, バラバラにする

take away *v.* (subtract) 引く; (remove) 運び去る, よそに移す, 片付ける, (person) 連れ去る, (toy) 取り上げる

Take away two from ten.
10から2を引きます。

I took away the bookshelves to create more space.
場所をもっとあけるために、本棚をよそに移した。

take back *v.*

1 RETURN: (library book, rented DVD) 返す, 返却する, (purchased product) 返品する

2 RETRACT: (words) 取り消す

3 CAUSE TO RECALL: (**takes me back**) (…が) 懐かしい

4 LOVER: 受け入れる, 迎え入れる

1 Have you taken the books back yet?
もう本を返しましたか?

They say they won't take it back because it was on sale.
バーゲン品だから返品できないって。

2 I'm sorry, I take back everything I said.
ごめんなさい、言ったことを全部取り消します。

3 This Michael Jackson sure takes me back.
マイケル・ジャクソンのこの曲、懐かしいなあ。

4 She took her boyfriend back because he stopped drinking.
彼女は、お酒をやめた彼氏を迎え入れた。

take down *v.*

1 DISASSEMBLE AND/OR REMOVE: 取り壊す, 取り払う, (remove) 取り除く

2 JOT DOWN: 書き留める

3 PULL DOWN: (pants) 下げる

1 When are they going to take down the scaffolding?
いつ足場を取り払うんだろう?

Let's take the poster down.
ポスターを外そう。

2 Just take down the main ideas, please.
要点だけを書き留めてください。

3 He took down his pants in front of us all.
彼はみんなの前でズボンを下げた。

take in *v.*

1 ALLOW TO STAY: 泊める, 迎え入れる

2 ABSORB: (moisture, information) 吸収する, 取り込む, (understand) 飲み込む

3 INCLUDE: 含む, 入れる

4 DECEIVE: (**be taken in**) だまされる

1 Thanks for taking me in.
泊めていただいてありがとう。

2 This material takes in moisture.
この素材は水分を吸収します。

I can't take in all that information at once.
一度にその情報を全部吸収するなんてできないよ。

3 Many tours try to take in both Thailand and Cambodia.
多くのツアーが、タイとカンボジアの両

T

方を日程に入れている。

4 I was completely taken in by his smooth talking.
彼の口のうまさに、まんまとだまされた/彼の口車に乗ってしまった。

take off *v.*

1 REMOVE: (lid, cover) 取る, (clothing) 脱ぐ
2 LEAVE THE GROUND: 離陸する
3 LEAVE: 立ち去る, (for home) 帰る
4 NOT WORK: 休む

1 Please take off your shoes before coming in.
靴を脱いでからお入りください。

2 What time are we due to take off?
離陸予定は何時ですか？

3 They took off without so much as a "good-bye."
さよならも言わずに彼らは帰った。

4 I took last Friday off.
先週の金曜日は休みました。

take on *v.*

1 UNDERTAKE OR AGREE TO DO: 引き受ける
2 EMPLOY: 雇う, 採用する
3 SEAT: (passengers) 乗せる

1 The truth is, you took on too much work.
要は、君が仕事を引き受けすぎたんだよ。

2 I took him on as an assistant.
彼を助手として雇った。

3 This bus cannot take on any more passengers.
このバスは、これ以上乗客を乗せることはできません。

take out *v.*

1 DRAW OUT: 取り出す, 持ち出す, (dog) 連れ出す, (money) 引き出す, (tooth) 抜く
2 TAKE ON A DATE: (…と) デートする
3 DELETE: (text) 削除する

1 I took out my wallet to pay.
支払いをするため、財布を取り出した。

Don't take those papers out of the drawer.
その書類を引き出しから持ち出さないように。

Who took the dog out?
犬を連れ出したのは誰？

I've just had a tooth taken out.
歯を抜いたばかりなんです。

2 He wants to take her out, but he's too scared to ask.
彼は彼女とデートしたいんだけど、怖くて誘えないんだ。

3 Why don't we take this section out?
この部分を削除してはどう？

take over *v.* (assume control of) 引き継ぐ, (company) 買収する, 乗っ取る

Who's going to take over the direction of this project?
誰が、この事業の指揮を引き継ぐんですか？

The company was taken over by a rival.
その会社はライバル企業に買収された。

take up *v.*

1 ADOPT AS A PASTIME/JOB: 始める, やる
2 OCCUPY TIME/SPACE: 占める, 取る
3 CONTINUE: 続ける, 再開する

1 He's taken up golf as a hobby.
彼は趣味でゴルフを始めました。

She's taken up swimming.
彼女は水泳を始めた。

2 This table takes up too much space.
このテーブルは場所を取りすぎる。

3 Let's take up where we left off.

やめたところから続けましょう。

takeoff ***n.*** (of airplane) 離陸

takeout ***n.*** (food) 持ち帰り(料理), テイクアウト

takeover ***n.*** (buyout) 買収

tale ***n.*** (お)話, 物語, (lie) うそ, 作り話

a tale of medieval times 中世の物語

an old tale 昔話

It's hard to separate the tales from the truth.

本当のことと作り話を見分けるのは、難しい。

tell a tale 話をする

talent ***n.*** 才能

She has a talent for creative cooking.

彼女には創作料理の才能がある。

talented ***adj.*** 才能のある

talisman ***n.*** お守り

talk

1 ***v.*** **SPEAK:** 話す, しゃべる, (have a discussion) 話し合う, 話をする, (**talk in one's sleep**) 寝言を言う, (**talk to oneself**) 独り言を言う

2 ***n.*** **DISCUSSION:** 話, 話し合い, (**talks:** among nations) 会談, 協議

3 ***n.*** **SPEECH:** 講義, 講演

4 ***n.*** **EMPTY TALK WITHOUT ACTION:** 口先だけの話, 空論

5 ***n.*** **MANNER OF SPEAKING:** 話し方, 言葉づかい

1 Can your baby talk yet?

赤ちゃんは、もうしゃべれるようになった?

Have you talked to your father about this?

これについてお父さんと話した?

I talked with Mr. Harris for over an hour.

ハリスさんと1時間以上話しました。

What were they talking about?

彼らは何を話していたの?

Don't all talk at once!

一度に全員がしゃべらないで。

We need to talk.

話し合う必要がありますね。

The old man is talking to himself again.

あのおじいさん、また独り言を言っているよ。

2 This talk about moving, is it for real?

引っ越しの話、本当なの?

It's time we had a serious talk.

そろそろきちんと話し合いをしよう。

Bilateral talks resulted in a new immigration agreement.

2ヵ国協議の結果、新しい移民協定が生まれた。

3 Mr. Ozaki gave a talk on altitude sickness.

尾崎さんは高山病について講演しました。

4 There's too much talk and not enough action here.

口先ばかりで、行動が伴っていない。

5 I don't want to hear that kind of talk in our home!

うちでは、そんな言葉づかいはやめなさい!

talk one's way out of うまく言い逃れをして切り抜ける

He talked his way out of trouble.

彼はうまく言い逃れをして、トラブルを切り抜けた。

talk around *v.* (persuade) 説得する

talk back *v.* 口答えをする

Don't you talk back to me!
口答えをするな！

talk down to *v.* …に対して見下した態度で話す

talk into *v.* (**talk into doing**) (…に) …するよう説得する, …させようとする

The salesman tried to talk me into buying a new car.
セールスマンは僕に新車を買わせようとした。

talk out of *v.* (**talk out of doing**) (…に) …するのをやめるよう説得する

We couldn't talk him out of going.
彼に行くのをやめるよう説得できなかった。

I talked her out of quitting her job.
彼女を説得して、仕事を辞めるのを思いとどまらせた。

talk out of turn ずけずけ話す, 考えなしに話す

talk over *v.* (discuss) 話し合う [→ TALK AROUND]

---

talkative *adj.* おしゃべりな, 話し好きな, 口数の多い

talk show *n.* トークショー

tall *adj.* (of person) 背が高い, (giving height of a person) 身長…, (of thing) 高い, (giving height of a thing) 高さ…

Kikuchi is over 180 centimeters tall.
菊池さんは身長が180センチ以上あります。

Is she taller than you?
彼女はあなたより背が高いの？

Gosh! You've grown taller since we last met.
わあ！前に会った時より､背が伸びたね。

How tall would you say that building is?
あのビルはどのくらいの高さだと思いますか？

a tall order 無理な注文

tally *v.* (calculate the total number of) 計算する; (match, correspond) 合う

keep a tally (of) (…の) 記録をつける

Talmud *n.* タルムード

talon *n.* 爪

tambourine *n.* タンバリン

play the tambourine
タンバリンを鳴らす

tame *adj.* (domesticated) 飼いならされた, (gentle) おとなしい

v. (convert from a wild state) 飼いならす

Tame hawks are used in hunting.
飼いならしたタカは、狩猟に使われます。

You can't really tame tigers.
トラを本当に飼いならすことはできません。

tamper *v.* (**tamper with**) 勝手にいじくる

tampon *n.* タンポン

tan *n.* (suntan) 日焼け; (color) 小麦色

v. (become suntanned) 日焼けする; (turn hide into leather) (皮を) なめす

You certainly got a good tan.
日焼けしたね。

Do you tan easily?
日焼けしやすいですか？

♦**tanned** *adj.* 日焼けした

tanning salon *n.* 日焼けサロン

tandem *n.* (bicycle) 二人乗り自転車

ride tandem 二人乗り自転車に乗る

in tandem (simultaneously) 同時に,

(together) いっしょに

tangent ***n.*** タンジェント, 接線

tangential ***adj.*** (not really related) あまり関係ない

tangerine ***n.*** タンジェリンオレンジ

tangible ***adj.*** (clear) 明白な, (certain) 確実な, (real) 実際の, 具体的な

tangible evidence 明白な証拠

tangle ***v.*** (become tangled) もつれる, からまる

n. (predicament) ごたごた, 混乱

tangled ***adj.*** もつれた, からまった, (of affairs) 込み入った

My hair is tangled.
髪の毛がもつれてる。

tango ***n.*** タンゴ

v. (do the tango) タンゴを踊る

tank ***n.*** (container) タンク; (armored vehicle) 戦車

a gasoline tank ガソリンタンク
a fish tank 魚の水槽

tanka ***n.*** (5-7-5-7-7 syllable poem) 短歌

a tanka poet 歌人

tankard ***n.*** ジョッキ

T

tanker ***n.*** (ship) タンカー

tank top ***n.*** タンクトップ

tannin ***n.*** タンニン

tantalize ***v.*** じらす

♦**tantalizing** ***adj.*** じれったい

tantamount ***adj.*** (be tantamount to) (…と) 同じだ, ((*formal*)) (…に) 等しい

This is tantamount to murder.
これは人殺しに等しい。

tantrum ***n.*** かんしゃく

The little boy threw a tantrum.
男の子は、かんしゃくを起こした。

Taoism ***n.*** 老荘思想, (the Way) 道教

tap[1] ***v.*** (strike gently) (軽く) たたく, (on door) ノックする

n. (gentle strike) 軽くたたくこと, (on door) ノック, (sound) ノックする音

Was that someone tapping at the window?
誰かが窓をたたかなかった？

I tapped him on the shoulder to get his attention.
注意を引こうと、肩をたたいた。

I thought I heard a tap at the door.
ドアをノックする音がしたように思った。

♦**tap dancing** ***n.*** タップダンス

tap[2] ***n.*** (water tap) 蛇口 [→ picture of BATHROOM, KITCHEN], (gas tap) ガス栓, (main tap) 元栓

v. (tap A [person] for B [money]) (Aに Bを) せびる, 無心する; (tap a phone) 盗聴する

Someone's left the tap on.
誰かが蛇口を閉め忘れて行った。

Is there an outside tap?
外に蛇口はありますか？

turn on [off] the tap 栓を<u>開く</u> [閉める]

My son tapped me for a few bucks.
息子がおこづかいを無心してきた。

The phone's been tapped.
電話は盗聴されています。

on tap (of beer) たる詰めで, 生で

What kind of beer is on tap?
どのビールが生ビールですか？

tape ***n.*** (material for recording) テープ, (cassette tape) カセットテープ, (video tape) ビデオテープ; (strip of sticky paper) テープ

v. (record sound/video) テープに取る, 録音/録画する; (fasten with tape) テープで留める

a blank tape 生テープ

Do you have any Scotch tape?
セロテープはありますか？

Did you tape yesterday's interview?
昨日のインタビュー、録音した？

♦**tape deck** *n.* テープデッキ

tape measure *n.* 巻き尺

taper *v.* (become narrower) 細くなる

♦**taper off** *v.* (become weaker) 弱まる

tape-record *v.* 録音する

♦**tape recorder** *n.* テープレコーダー

tape recording *n.* 録音

tapestry *n.* タペストリー

tapeworm *n.* サナダムシ

tapioca *n.* タピオカ

tar *n.* タール

tarantula *n.* タランチュラ

tardy *adj.* (slow) 遅い, (late) 遅れた

Don't be tardy for class!
授業に遅れてはいけません！

target *n.* (object/person aimed at) 的, ターゲット, 標的, (goal) 目標 [→ GOAL, PURPOSE]

v. (take aim at) (…に) ねらいを定める, (…を) ターゲットにする, (set as a goal) 目標とする [→ AIM]

I haven't hit the target yet.
まだ的に当たっていないよ。

Large gatherings have become a target for terrorist attacks.
大集会はテロ攻撃の標的になっている。

What's the production target for next year?
来年の生産目標はどのくらいですか？

We're targeting the teen market.
10代をターゲットにしています。

tariff *n.* (trade tariff) 関税

tarnish *v.* (ruin: reputation etc.) 汚す

♦**tarnished** *adj.* (of reputation) 傷ついた

tarpaulin *n.* (sheet) 防水シート

tart[1] *adj.* (of taste) すっぱい

tart[2] *n.* (kind of dessert) タルト

tartan *n.* (pattern) タータンチェック, 格子じま

tartar *n.* (substance that forms on teeth) 歯石

task *n.* 仕事

The first task was to recruit capable people.
有能な人材を採用することが、最初の仕事だった。

♦**task force** *n.* 対策本部

taste

1 *v.* HAVE FLAVOR: 味がする

2 *v.* SENSE THE FLAVOR OF: (**can taste**) (…の) 味がする

3 *v.* TEST THE FLAVOR OF: 味見する, 食べてみる

4 *n.* FLAVOR: 味

5 *n.* SAMPLING OF FOOD/DRINK: 一口, 味見

6 *n.* ONE OF THE FIVE SENSES: 味覚

7 *n.* LIKING: 趣味, 好み

8 *n.* SENSE FOR THINGS: センス, 趣味

1 It tasted of nuts. ナッツの味がした。

It tasted like chicken.

とり肉のような味がしました。

2 Can you taste the garlic?
ニンニクの味はしますか？

3 I tasted the fish. 魚を味見した。
Here, taste this.
ちょっとこれを食べてみて。

4 It has a sweet taste. 甘い味ですね。
The taste of this wine is hard to describe.
このワインの味は、言葉で説明できない。

5 Can I have a taste of your ice cream?
そのアイスクリーム、一口くれる［ちょっと味見させてくれる］？

6 The sense of taste is closely linked to that of smell.
味覚は嗅覚と密接に結び付いています。

7 You seem to have acquired a taste for opera.
オペラが好きになったようですね。

8 She has good taste in clothes.
彼女は洋服のセンスがいい。
He has bad taste in music.
彼は音楽の趣味が悪い。

tasteful *adj.* 趣味のいい

tasteless *adj.* (flavorless) 味のない; (lacking sense) 趣味の悪い, (vulgar) 品のない
a tasteless joke 品のない冗談

tasty *adj.* (delicious) おいしい, ((*masculine*)) うまい

tatami *n.* (straw mat) 畳 [→ picture of ROOM, FUTON], (one-tatami size) -畳 [→ MAT]

tattered *adj.* (ragged) ぼろぼろの

tatters *n.* ぼろ
be in tatters (of plan) ずたずただ, (of cloth) ぼろぼろだ

tattoo *n.* 入れ墨, タトゥー
get a tattoo 入れ墨を入れる［する］

taunt *v.* あざける

Taurus *n.* (the Bull) 牡牛座

tavern *n.* バー, (Japanese-style) 居酒屋

tax *n.* 税金, タックス
v. (…に) 税金をかける
How much do you get paid after taxes are taken out?
税金を引くと、手取りでいくらもらっていますか？
raise [lower] taxes 増税［減税］する
make a tax return 確定申告をする
income tax 所得税
consumption/sales tax 消費税
inheritance tax 相続税

♦**taxable** *adj.* 課税対象となる
tax-deductible *adj.* 税控除の
tax-free *adj.* 免税の, 非課税の

taxation *n.* 課税

taxi *n.* タクシー
v. (of airplane) 滑走する, 移動する
Should I call a taxi?
タクシーを呼びましょうか？
The plane slowly taxied to the gate.
飛行機はゆっくりと搭乗口まで移動した。

♦**taxi driver** *n.* タクシー運転手
taxi fare *n.* タクシー代［料金］
taxi stand *n.* タクシー乗り場

taxidermy *n.* 剥製術

taxpayer *n.* 納税者

tea *n.* お茶, (green tea) 緑茶, (black tea) 紅茶
Which do you prefer, coffee or tea?

コーヒーと紅茶のどちらがいいですか？

Let's have another cup of tea.
お茶をもう1杯飲みましょう。

Is there any tea left in the pot?
ポットにお茶は残っていますか？

♦**tea bag** *n.* ティーバッグ

tea ceremony *n.* 茶道

teach *v.* 教える, (**be taught**) 教わる, (**teach oneself**) 独学する

"What do you teach?"
"Right now I'm teaching art, but I also teach drama."
「((*polite*)) 何を教えておられるんですか？」
「今は美術を教えていますが、演劇も教えます」

He was taught how to ski when he was five years old.
彼は5歳の時にスキーを教わった。

I was taught French by a professor from Guadeloupe.
グアドループ出身の先生にフランス語を教わりました。

I taught myself how to drive.
独学で運転を覚えた。

teach one (a lesson) …に思い知らせる, こらしめる

That'll teach 'em!
少しは思い知ればいい/ざまあ見ろ！

teacher *n.* 教師, 先生

teaching *n.* (act of teaching) 教えること, (profession) 教職

♦**teaching assistant** *n.* 補助教員

teaching staff *n.* 教職員

teacup *n.* ティーカップ, (for green tea) (お)湯飲み [→ picture of CUP]

teak *n.* (tree) チークの木, (wood) チーク材

teakettle *n.* やかん, 湯沸かし

team *n.* (persons playing together) チーム, (group) 一団

He only joined the team last year.
彼は去年チームに入ったばかりです。

a rugby team ラグビーチーム

How many people are in a baseball team?
野球のチームは何人ですか？

Japan's soccer team
日本代表のサッカーチーム

teammate *n.* チームメイト

teamwork *n.* チームワーク

teapot *n.* 急須, ティーポット

tear[1]

1 *v.* RIP/SHRED: 破る, 引き裂く, 引きちぎる, (**tear to pieces/shreds**) びりびりに破る, ずたずたに引き裂く, (**tear a hole in**) …に穴をあける, (become torn) 破れる, (split open) 裂ける

2 *v.* MOVE AT GREAT SPEED: すごいスピードで走る/駆ける, (**tear down**) (stairs) 猛スピードで駆け下りる, (road) 突っ走る

3 *n.* RIP: 破れ, 裂け目

1 I tore the paper in half.
紙を半分に破いた。

The dog tore the stuffed animal to pieces.
犬は縫いぐるみをずたずたに引きちぎった。

I tore a muscle while playing tennis.
テニスをしている時、肉離れを起こした。

It tears very easily, so be careful.
とても破れやすいから、気をつけて。

2 He tore around the bend.
彼はすごいスピードでカーブを曲がった。

He tore down the steps in an effort to make the last train.
終電に乗ろうとして、彼は階段を猛スピードで駆け下りた。

The motorcycle was tearing down the road.
バイクは道を突っ走っていた。

3 There's a tear in your shirt.
シャツがちょっと破れているよ。

♦**tear down** *v.* (demolish) 取り壊す; (pull off, rip away) 引きはがす [→ 2]

tear up *v.* (rip up) 引き裂く

tear² *n.* (drop from the eye) 涙

A tear rolled down her cheek.
涙が彼女のほおを伝った。

burst into tears わっと泣き出す

When her name was called out as the winner, she burst into tears.
自分の名が勝者として告げられると、彼女はわっと泣き出した。

in tears 泣いて, 泣きながら

He was in tears as he told us what happened.
彼は泣きながら、何があったのかを話した。

T

tearful *adj.* (about to cry) 泣きそうな, (while crying) 涙ながらの [→ SAD]

tear gas *n.* 催涙ガス

tease *v.* (playfully) からかう, 冷やかす, (nastily) いじめる, いびる

teaspoon *n.* (spoon for serving tea) ティースプーン, (cooking measure) 小さじ [→ picture of COOKING UTENSILS]

teat *n.* 乳首

teatime *n.* お茶の時間

technical *adj.* (relating to technology) 技術的な, (specialized) 専門的な

technical skills 技能

technicality *n.* (point of detail) 細かい規則

technically *adv.* (strictly speaking) 厳密には; (in terms of technology) 技術的に

technical sergeant *n.* (in U.S. Air Force) 二等軍曹

technician *n.* 技術者, 技師

technique *n.* (skill) テクニック, 技術, 技, (ability) 腕, 腕前

technological *adj.* 科学技術的な

technological advances
科学技術の進歩

technology *n.* テクノロジー, 科学技術

tedious *adj.* (boring) 退屈な, つまらない, (too long) 長たらしい

tedium *n.* 退屈

tee *n.* (in golf: area) ティー(グラウンド), (small peg) ティー

♦**tee off** *v.* (in golf) ティーからボールを打つ

teem *v.* (**be teeming with**) (…が) いっぱいいる

teenage *adj.* 10代の

a teenage girl 10代の女の子

teenager *n.* 10代の子, (**teenagers**) ティーンエイジャー

teens *n.* 10代, (**early teens**) ローティーン, (**late teens**) ハイティーン

teeter-totter *n.* シーソー

teethe *v.* 歯が生える

telecommunications *n.* 電気通信, (subject of study) 電気通信学

telegram, telegraph *n.* 電報

send a telegram 電報を打つ

telemarketing *n.* テレマーケティング, 電話による販売/営業

♦ **telemarketer** *n.* 電話営業員, テレフォンアポインター

telepathy *n.* テレパシー

telephone *n.* 電話

v. (…に) 電話をする, 電話をかける

a telephone call 電話

a public telephone 公衆電話

Did you answer the telephone?
電話を受けましたか？

I've been on the telephone all morning.
朝からずっと電話に出ている。

a long-distance telephone call
長距離電話

I telephoned the New York office.
ニューヨークオフィスに電話した。

I telephoned to make a reservation.
予約をするために電話をした。

♦ **telephone bill** *n.* 電話料金, 電話代

telephone booth *n.* 電話ボックス

telephone card *n.* テレホンカード, ((*informal*)) テレカ

telephone directory *n.* 電話帳

telephone jack *n.* 電話の差し込み口

telephone number *n.* 電話番号

telephone pole *n.* 電柱

telescope *n.* 望遠鏡

televise *v.* テレビ放送する

television *n.* テレビ [→ TV]

tell *v.*

1 INFORM: (…に) 伝える, 知らせる, 教える, ((*formal*)) 告げる, (reveal to) (…に) 打ち明ける, (**be told**) (…と) 言われる, (= hear) (…と) 聞く

2 SAY TO: (…に) 言う, (try to convince) (…に) 言い聞かせる

3 RECOUNT FOR: (…に) 語る, 話す

4 ORDER: (**tell to do**) (…に)…するよう言う

5 UNDERSTAND: (…が) わかる

1 So, when will you tell him?
それで、いつ彼に伝えますか？

You might have told me sooner.
もっと早く教えてくれればよかったのに。

He told me that he was an accountant.
会計士だと彼は言いました。

I was told you didn't attend the meeting.
あなたは会議に出なかったと聞いているけど。

2 "Do as you wish," I told my son.
「好きなようにしなさい」と息子に言った。

There's no need to panic, I told myself.
あわてることなんかない、と自分に言い聞かせた。

3 He told me about his experiences in Mongolia.
彼はモンゴルでの経験について語ってくれた。

Now tell me again what happened.
何があったのか、もう一度話してみて。

4 I told you not to do that.
それをするなと言ったじゃないか。

I told them to get off our land.
我々の土地から出て行けと、奴らに言った。

5 I couldn't tell what they were rattling on about.
彼らが何をしゃべっているのか、わからなかった。

You could tell she was lying.

彼女がうそをついていることがわかったはずです。

as far as I can tell 私の知る限り(では)

As far as I can tell, the car's in reasonable condition.
私の知る限り、車はまずまずの状態です。

I'll tell you what いい考えがある, こうしようよ

I'll tell you what, let's celebrate by going out to dinner tonight.
いい考えがあるよ、今夜は外食してお祝いしよう。

there's no telling よくわからない, 何とも言えない

There's no telling what will happen if the UN pulls out.
国連が引き上げたらどうなるか、誰にもわかりません。

There is no telling how he'll react.
彼がどういう反応をするか予測できない。

tell apart *v.* 見分ける, 区別する

I can't tell the twins apart.
あの双子の見分けがつかないよ。

tell off *v.* (scold) しかりつける, (speak harshly to) (...に) がみがみ言う

He's always getting told off by his teachers.
彼はしょっちゅう先生にしかられている。

tell on *v.* ...のことを告げ口する

I'll let you in on my secret if you promise not to tell on me.
告げ口しないと約束するなら、秘密を教えてあげるよ。

teller *n.* (bank clerk) 銀行の窓口係

telling *adj.* 効果的な, 効き目のある

temp *n.* 臨時雇いの人, (person supplied by an employment agency) 派遣社員
v. 臨時雇いで働く, 派遣で働く

temper *n.* (emotional condition) 気性, (ご)機嫌, (bad temper) かんしゃく, (short temper) 短気
v. (moderate) 和らげる

He's got a bad temper.
あの人は気が短い。

have a temper tantrum かんしゃくを起こす

The little girl had a temper tantrum in the middle of the supermarket.
その女の子はスーパーの中でかんしゃくを起こした。

lose one's temper 頭に来る, かっとなる

The teacher lost his temper.
教師はかっとなった。

This time try not to lose your temper.
今度は、かっとならないようにするんだよ。

temperament *n.* 気質, 性分, 性格

a good [bad] temperament
いい [悪い] 性格

temperamental *adj.* (short-tempered) 短気な, (has mood swings) 気まぐれな

temperate *adj.* (of climate) 温暖な, (mild, gentle) 穏やかな

Temperate Zone *n.* 温帯

temperature *n.* 温度, (body temperature) 体温, (air temperature) 気温

The temperature now is thirty degrees.
今の気温は３０度です。

template *n.* 型板, (file) テンプレート

temple[1] *n.* (religious building) (お)寺, 寺院

go to a temple お寺にお参りする

temple[2] ***n.*** (part of the head) こめかみ

tempo ***n.*** テンポ

temporarily ***adv.*** 一時的に, 臨時に

temporary ***adj.*** 一時的な, 臨時の, 仮の

a temporary job 臨時の仕事

a temporary worker → TEMP

tempt ***v.*** 誘う, 引き込む, 誘惑する, (**tempt to do**) …する気にさせる, (**be tempted to do**) …したくなる

Tempted by the smell, I entered the restaurant.
においに誘われて、そのレストランに入った。

I was tempted to eat the cake, but I decided I didn't need the extra calories.
ケーキを食べたくなったけれど、余分なカロリーをとるのはやめた。

We were tempted to go sailing, until the weather turned cloudy.
セーリングに出たいなと思っていたら、天気が曇ってしまった。

I was tempted to take the job, but I didn't.
その仕事に就こうかと思いましたが、やめました。

temptation ***n.*** 誘惑

resist the temptation to do …したい気持ちを抑える

tempting ***adj.*** 心をそそる, 魅力的な

tempura ***n.*** 天ぷら

ten ***n.*** 10, 十

adj., pron. 10の, (people) 10人(の), (things) 10個(の)

tenant ***n.*** 借り主, ((*formal/written*)) 賃借人, (of office, large premises) テナント

tend ***v.*** (**tend to do**) …しがちだ, …する傾向がある

Grandpa tends to stay at home these days.
おじいちゃんは最近、家に閉じこもりがちだ。

tendency ***n.*** 傾向

have a tendency to do …しがちだ, …する傾向がある

Miura has a tendency to become loud after drinking.
三浦さんは、お酒を飲むとうるさくなる(傾向がある)。

tender[1] ***adj.*** (of food: soft) 柔らかい, (of injured body part: hurts when one touches) 触ると痛い; (of person: caring) 優しい, 思いやりのある

What children need is tender loving care.
子供に必要なのは、優しく愛情をこめてかまってもらうことです。

tender[2] ***n.*** (bid) 入札

v. (formally offer) 提出する, 申し出る

tenderhearted ***adj.*** 思いやりのある, 心の優しい

tenderize ***v.*** 柔らかくする

tenderloin ***n.*** テンダーロイン

tendon ***n.*** 腱

tenet ***n.*** (of religion) 教義

tennis ***n.*** テニス

play tennis テニスをする

♦**tennis ball** ***n.*** テニスボール

tennis court ***n.*** テニスコート

tennis shoes ***n.*** テニスシューズ

tenor ***n.*** テノール

tense[1] ***adj.*** (nervous) 緊張した, ぴりぴりした, (of situation) 緊迫した

v. (of muscle) 硬くなる, 張る

Since the divorce, he's been so nervous

and tense.
離婚して以来、彼はとても神経質になってぴりぴりしている。

It was a very tense situation.
非常に緊迫した状況でした。

tense[2] ***n.*** (form of verb) 時制

the past tense 過去形 [時制]

the present tense 現在形 [時制]

tension ***n.*** (among people) 緊張, (in rope) 張り

The tension mounted.
緊張が高まった。

Tensions between the two countries have increased along the border.
国境沿いにおける両国の緊張は増している。

tent ***n.*** テント

put up [take down] a tent
テントを張る [たたむ]

tentacle ***n.*** (of octopus) 足

tentative ***adj.*** (provisional) 一時的な, 仮の, (of settlement) 暫定的な

We made a tentative arrangement to meet sometime next week.
私たちは来週中に会おうと、仮の申し合わせをした。

♦**tentatively** ***adv.*** 一応, 仮に

tenth ***adj.*** 第10の, 10番目の
n. 第10, 10番目, (date) 10日, (one tenth) 10分の1

ten thousand ***n.*** 1万

tenuous ***adj.*** 弱い, 薄弱な

tenure ***n.*** (period in office) 任期, (of academic post) 終身在職権

tepee ***n.*** ティピー, テント小屋

tepid ***adj.*** (lukewarm) ぬるい, なまぬるい

term

1 ***n.*** PERIOD: 期間, (of academic year) 学期, (=**first term**) 前期, (=**second term**) 後期, (of president) 任期, (of imprisonment) 刑期

2 ***n.*** CONDITIONS OF AGREEMENT: (**terms**) 条件

3 ***n.*** WORD/EXPRESSION: (word) 言葉, (one of a group of words having special usage) 用語, (expression) 表現, 言い方

4 ***v.*** REFER TO AS: (term A B) (AをBと) 呼ぶ, 言う

1 The term of the loan is sixteen years.
ローンの期間は16年です。

When does the term begin?
学期はいつ始まりますか？

2 The general terms of the contract are clear. However, we'd better reexamine the small print.
契約の全体的な条件は明確です。しかし、詳細については再検討したほうがいいでしょう。

3 a politically correct term
差別的でない言葉

a technical term 専門用語

4 It was termed "the worst accident in aviation history."
それは「航空史上、最悪の事故」と言われた。

be on good terms with …と仲がいい

We're on good terms with our neighbors.
ご近所とは仲がいいです。

come to terms with (accept) 受け入れる, (get used to) …に慣れる, (compromise with) …と折り合いがつく

After the accident, he had to come to terms with life in a wheelchair.

事故の後、彼は車椅子での生活を受け入れなければならなかった。

in terms of …という点では, …という面では

The pay is not good, but in terms of job satisfaction, I'm happy.
給料はよくないですが、仕事のやりがいという点では満足しています。

in the long term 長期的に見れば

Our company will see profits in the long term.
長期的に見れば、わが社は利益を得ることになるでしょう。

in the short term 短期的に見れば

terminal *n.* (air/bus terminal) ターミナル, (computer) 端末機
adj. (of disease) 末期の

♦**terminal velocity** *n.* 終端速度

terminate *v.* (bring to an end) 終わらせる, (come to an end) 終わる; (fire) 解雇する

terminate a contract 解約する

terminology *n.* 専門用語

terminus *n.* (last station) 終点

termite *n.* シロアリ, 白蟻

term paper *n.* 期末レポート

terrace *n.* テラス [→ picture of HOUSE], (roof terrace) ルーフバルコニー; (row of houses) テラスハウス

♦**terraced fields** *n.* 段々畑

terraced house *n.* テラスハウス

terra-cotta *n.* (clay) テラコッタ

terrain *n.* 地形

terrestrial *adj.* 地球の

terrible *adj.* (extremely bad) ひどい, (tragic) 悲惨な, (frightening, horrifying) 怖い, 恐ろしい

My grades this semester were terrible.
今学期の成績はひどかった。

In retrospect, I feel terrible about what I did.
思い返すと、ひどいことをしたと思う。

a terrible accident 悲惨な事故

a terrible crime 恐ろしい [凶悪な] 犯罪

terribly *adv.* (very) ものすごく, 非常に

terrier *n.* テリア

terrific *adj.* (very good) すごくいい

terrify *v.* ぞっとさせる

♦**terrified** *adj.* 怖い, 恐れる

terrifying *adj.* 恐ろしい, ぞっとする

territorial *adj.* 領土の

territory *n.* 地域, 地方, (of nation) 領土, (of animal) 縄張り

enemy-occupied territory 占領地域

Both nations claim rights to the territory.
両方の国が、その地域の領有権を主張している。

terror *n.* (great fear) 恐怖

terrorism *n.* テロ

terrorist *n.* テロリスト

♦**terrorist organization** *n.* テロ組織

terrorize *v.* (scare) 恐れさせる

terse *adj.* ぶっきらぼうな, そっけない

tertiary education *n.* 高等教育

test *n.* (exam) 試験, テスト, (medical check) 検査, (experiment) 実験 [→ EXAM]
v. 試験する, テストする, 試す, (**be tested:** of person) 試験を受ける, (theory) 実験する; (carry out a medical test on) 検査する, (**test positive/negative for**)

…の検査で陽性/陰性と出る

take a test 受験する

Eighty percent of them passed the test.
8割が試験に合格した。

The test was easy [difficult].
テストは簡単だった[難しかった]。

a blood test 血液検査

This machine has been tested and approved.
この機械は試験され、認可されています。

We'll be tested at the end of the term.
学期末には試験があります。

Are you testing me?
私を試しているんですか？

The label says the product hasn't been tested on animals.
ラベルには、この製品は動物実験をせずに作られたと書いてある。

put to the test 試す, 試験する

testament *n.* (**the Old Testament**) 旧約聖書, (**the New testament**) 新約聖書; (proof) 証拠; (will) 遺言

testicle *n.* こう丸

testify *v.* 証言する

testify in court 法廷で証言する

testimonial *n.* (tribute) 推せん状 [→ REFERENCE 3]

testimony *n.* 証言

testing *n.* 試験, (experiment) 実験, (check) 検査

nuclear testing 核実験

drug testing 薬物検査

testosterone *n.* テストステロン

test run *n.* 試運転, テスト走行

test tube *n.* 試験管

♦**test-tube baby** *n.* 試験管ベビー

tetanus *n.* 破傷風

get a tetanus shot
破傷風の予防接種を受ける

text *n.* (written material) テキスト, (main body of book) 本文 [→ TRANSCRIPT]

textbook *n.* 教科書, テキスト

textile *n.* (fabric) テキスタイル, 織物, 布地, (**textiles**: business) 織物業

texture *n.* (feel) 手触り, 感触, (of fabric) 生地, 織り方, (of food) 食感, 歯ごたえ

Thailand *n.* タイ

than *prep., conj.* …より(も) [→ "MAKING COMPARISONS" on p. 189]

She's much older than me.
彼女は私よりずっと年上です。

His voice is better than yours.
彼は君よりもいい声をしている。

Hikaru has a lot more CDs than I do.
光は私よりもずっとたくさんCDを持っている。

I prefer to travel by train rather than car.
車よりも電車で旅行するほうが好きです。

less than → LESS

more than… → MORE

no sooner…than → SOON

thank *v.* (**thank you**) ありがとう, ((*polite*)) ありがとうございます, (say words of gratitude to) (…に) (お)礼を言う, (feel grateful toward) (…に) 感謝する [→ THANKS, THANK YOU]

Thank you for coming.
来てくれてありがとう。

Don't forget to thank them.
お礼を言うのを忘れないでね。

I thanked him for all his help.
いろいろ助けてくれたことに対し、彼にお礼を言った。

You have Naoko to thank for that.
直子に感謝しなくちゃね [のおかげだよ]。

We have much to thank him for.
彼にはずいぶんお世話になった。

thank God/goodness やれやれ, よかった, ほっとした

Thank God you've finally arrived.
やれやれ、やっと来たね。

Thank goodness you got my letter in time.
手紙が間に合ってよかったよ。

thank you very much どうもありがとう, ((*polite*)) 本当にありがとうございます

I thank you very much for your patience.
辛抱してくれてどうもありがとう。

Thank you very much for your time and effort.
((*formal*)) これまでのご努力に、心から感謝いたします。

thankful *adj.* (grateful) ありがたい, 感謝している, (happy) うれしい

I was very thankful for their help.
彼らの協力が、ありがたかった。

Just be thankful you're in good health.
健康であるだけで感謝しなくちゃ。

♦ **thankfully** *adv.* 感謝して, (used at the beginning of a sentence) ありがたいことに

thankless *adj.* 感謝されない, 報われない
a thankless task 報われない仕事

thanks *interj.* ありがとう, すみません, (**no thanks**) いいです, けっこうです [→ THANK YOU]

n. (gratitude) 感謝の気持ち

Thanks a lot for your help.
手伝ってくれてどうもありがとう。

"Here's your coat and umbrella."
"Thanks."
「コートと傘をどうぞ」
「すみません」

"Would you like another chocolate?"
"No thanks."
「チョコレートをもう1個いかがですか？」
「いえ、けっこうです」

I expressed my thanks to them for their help.
彼らの助力に対し、感謝の気持ちを述べた。

thanks to …のおかげで

thanks to you (used ironically) あなたのおかげで, あなたのせいで

Thanksgiving Day *n.* 感謝祭

thank you *interj.* (どうも) ありがとう, ((*polite*)) (どうも) ありがとうございます, すみません, (**no, thank you**) いえ、けっこうです/いいです

"Would you like a cup of tea?"
"Thank you."
「お茶はいかがですか？」
「どうもありがとう」

"Would you like a lift to the station?"
"Thank you. It's kind of you to offer."
「駅まで車でお送りしましょうか？」
「どうもありがとうございます、お気づかいいただいて」

"Would you like something to eat?"
"No, I'm not hungry, thank you."
「何か召し上がりますか？」
「ありがとうございます、でもおなかはすいていないんで」

"After you..." "Thank you."
「お先にどうぞ」「すみません」

"Did you enjoy your stay?"
"Yes, thank you."
「楽しく過ごせましたか？」
「はい、おかげさまで」

"Can I get you a cup of coffee?"
"No, thank you. I don't drink coffee."
「コーヒーを入れましょうか？」
「いえ、けっこうです。コーヒーは飲まないものですから」

thank-you letter ***n.*** お礼の手紙, 礼状

that

1 ***demonstrative pron.*** それ/あれ, ((*polite*)) そちら/あちら, (as opp. to "this") そっち/あっち, (referring to a matter under discussion) そのこと/あのこと, (referring to a place) そこ/あそこ, (**like that**) そのように, そんなふうに

2 ***relative pron.*** See examples below [NOTE: No equivalent in Japanese.]

3 ***adj.*** その/あの

4 ***conj.*** こと

5 ***adv.*** それほど, そんなに

1 Is that supposed to be a joke?
それって冗談のつもり？

"I didn't feel well."
"Is that why you didn't call?"
「気分がよくなかったんだ」
「それで電話しなかったの？」

"I hate classical music."
"Does that mean you're not coming to the concert?"
「クラシックは嫌いなんだ」
「それはつまり、コンサートには行かないってこと？」

"Shall I gift-wrap it for you?"
"Yes, that'll be fine."
「プレゼント用に包装いたしましょうか？」
「ええ、そうしてください」

Who's that over there?
向こうにいるあの人は誰？

2 the house that I lived in
前に住んでいた家

a car that won't start
エンジンがかからない車

Did you hear about the disaster that happened in Kuwait?
クウェートで起きた災害のことを聞きましたか？

The bananas that I bought are not ripe.
買ったバナナが熟してない。

There's one last point that I'd like to bring up.
最後にお話ししたい点が一つあります。

3 Hey, look at that snake!
ほら、あのヘビを見て！

That teacher retired.
((*honorific*)) あの先生は退職なさいました。

4 Can you prove that you weren't there?
そこにいなかったことを証明できますか？

It says here that they went to Brazil.
彼らはブラジルに行ったと、ここに書いてある。

It's important that you understand exactly what I'm saying.
私が言っていることを的確に理解することが大切だ。

5 It wasn't that bad.
それほど悪くはなかった。

It isn't that expensive.
そんなに高くないよ。

I didn't think you were that interested.

あなたがそんなに興味をもっているなんて思わなかった。

in that …という点で

He was right in that no one actually complained.
実際に誰も不平を言わなかったという点では、彼は正しかった。

so…that あまりにも…ので

It was so crowded that I decided to leave.
あまりにも混んでいたので帰ることにした。

that is (to say) すなわち, つまり

Semantics—that is to say, the study of meaning—is a part of linguistics.
意味論、すなわち意味の学問は、言語学の一分野です。

that's that (ending a discussion) そういうことだ, 以上だ

I'm going, and that's that.
私は行くんです、それだけのことです/((*informal*)) 行くといったら行くんだ。

She's the woman I want to marry, and that's that.
僕が結婚したいのは彼女だということさ。

thatched *adj.* (of roof) わらぶきの

thaw *v.* (food) 解凍する, (of ice, snow: melt) 解ける

Thaw it out in the microwave.
電子レンジで解凍して。

Has the meat thawed yet?
お肉はもう解凍した？

The lake is beginning to thaw.
湖の氷は解け始めています。

the *article*

NOTE: No equivalent in Japanese except その (→ **1** below).

1 IDENTIFYING ONE AMONG OTHERS: その [NOTE: Usually not translated into Japanese.]
2 THE ONLY ONE RELEVANT
3 USED WITH A SUPERLATIVE
4 THE ONLY ONE EXISTING
5 OF A PARTICULAR INVENTION: (the computer, the telephone etc.)
6 USED WITH NUMBERS AND AMOUNTS

1 the man with the red hat
赤い帽子をかぶった男

Our office is in the brick building in front of the post office.
うちの事務所は、郵便局の前のレンガ造りの建物の中にあります。

The star was named after the man who first discovered it.
その星は最初に発見した人にちなんで名づけられた。

"It's downtown."
"You mean the old part of town?"
「それはダウンタウンにあるんですよ」
「旧市街にですか？」

2 the clock on the wall 壁に掛かった時計

the river by the railroad tracks
鉄道の線路のそばの川

How's the baby? 赤ちゃんは元気？

The future is uncertain.
未来は不確かなものだ。

3 I think Ms. Suzuki is the best teacher.
鈴木先生が一番いい先生だと思う。

Physics is the hardest subject for me.
物理は一番苦手な科目なんだよ。

This is one of the most difficult jobs I've ever had.
これは今までやった中で、一番難しい仕事の一つです。

4 the Atlantic Ocean 大西洋
the Ninth Symphony 第九交響曲
the Middle East 中東

5 The computer has had an enormous influence on society.
コンピューターは社会に非常に大きな影響を与えてきた。

Do you play the piano?
ピアノを弾きますか？

6 the 15th of August ８月１５日

It was the first time I'd been to India.
インドに行ったのは、その時が初めてでした。

In the 1960s there were a lot of good rock bands.
６０年代には、いいロックバンドがたくさんいた。

It gets ten kilometers to the liter, roughly.
大体1リッター当たり10キロ走ります。

the more ... the more ...すればするほど...

The more I hear about this, the more I like it.
この話を、聞けば聞くほど好きになる。

The quicker the better.
早ければ早いほどいい。

theater *n.* (building) 劇場, シアター, (movie theater) 映画館, (drama) 演劇
♦ **theater-goer** *n.* 芝居好き, 芝居の常連

theatrical *adj.* (of behavior) 芝居がかった; (for use on stage/in drama) 舞台の, 演劇用の

theft *n.* 盗難, 盗み, (crime) 窃盗

their *adj.* 彼らの, あの人たちの, 自分たちの, (referring to a group of women) 彼女らの [NOTE: Often not translated into Japanese.]

Their interest is mountain climbing.
あの人たちの趣味は山登りです。

Most people leave their cars at home and go by train.
ほとんどの人は車を自宅に置いて、電車で行きます。

Old people find it difficult to change their ways.
年をとった人は、自分たちのやり方をなかなか変えられない。

theirs *pron.* 彼らの(もの), あの人たちの(もの), 自分たちの(もの), (referring to a group of women) 彼女らの(もの)

It's not ours, it's theirs.
それは私たちのものではなく、あの人たちのものです。

It's neither his fault, nor theirs.
彼の責任でもなければ、彼らの責任でもない。

theism *n.* 有神論

them *pron.*

1 REFERRING TO PEOPLE: 彼ら, あの人たち, (referring to a group of women) 彼女たち, (as direct object) 彼らを, (as indirect object) 彼らに

2 REFERRING TO THINGS: それ, (as direct object) それらを, (as indirect object) それらに

1 I told them we had to be going home.
そろそろ帰らないといけないって、彼らに言った。

Couldn't you talk to them?
あの人たちに話してもらえませんか？

I was not with them at the time.
その時は彼らといっしょではなかった。

2 Don't put them in that drawer, please.
その引き出しには入れないでください。

Yes, I did leave some keys here, but that's not one of them.
確かにここにかぎを置いたけど、そのかぎじゃない。

theme *n.* テーマ, 主題

♦**theme park** *n.* テーマパーク

theme song *n.* テーマソング, 主題歌

themselves *pron.* 自分たち, (used emphatically) …自身, (**they themselves**) 彼ら自身

They only care about themselves.
あの人たちは、自分たちのことにしか関心がない。

Do you think they'll be able to look after themselves while we're away?
私たちが留守の間、あの子たちは自分たちだけでちゃんとできると思う?

Let's hear what the protesters themselves have to say.
抗議している人たち自身の主張を聞きましょう。

by themselves 自分たちで

then

1 *adv.* AT THAT TIME: その/あの時, その/あのころ

2 *n.* THAT TIME: その時, (**before then**) それ以前, (**since then**) それ以来

3 *adv.* AFTERWARD: それから, そのあとで

4 *adv.* IN THAT CASE: では, それでは, それなら

5 *adv.* FURTHERMORE: それに, その上, しかも

6 *adj.* AT THE TIME: (**the then…**) 当時の

1 He was in New York on a business trip then.
その時、彼は出張でニューヨークにいました。

Just then someone coughed.
ちょうどその時、誰かがせきをした。

I thought it was stupid then, and I still think so now.
あの時はばかげていると思いましたし、今でもそう思っています。

2 Up until then, I had no idea what they wanted me to do.
その時まで、彼らが私に何をしてほしいのか見当もつかなかった。

Before then, most stores stocked only domestic wine.
それ以前は、ほとんどのお店は国産ワインしか置いていなかった。

I haven't written to her since then.
それ以来、彼女に手紙を書いていない。

3 I'm going to take a bath, read a bit, and then watch some TV.
おふろに入って、ちょっと本を読んで、それからテレビでも見るよ。

I hung up and then I remembered all the things I should have said.
電話を切ったあとで、言いたかったことを思い出した。

4 "Are you an engineer?"
"No."
"What do you do then?"
「エンジニアですか？」
「いえ」
「では、何をなさっているんですか？」

"Can't I stay up a little later? There's no school tomorrow."
"Oh all right then."
「もう少し起きてちゃだめ？ 明日は学校

がお<ruby>休<rt>やす</rt></ruby>みだから」

「それならかまわないよ」

"I'm afraid the bus has left."

"Well then, when's the next one?"

「バスは<ruby>出<rt>で</rt></ruby>てしまいました」

「それじゃ、<ruby>次<rt>つぎ</rt></ruby>は<ruby>何時<rt>なんじ</rt></ruby>ですか？」

5 Then there's the dog to think of, don't forget.

それに<ruby>犬<rt>いぬ</rt></ruby>のことも<ruby>忘<rt>わす</rt></ruby>れちゃだめだよ。

6 the then prime minister Koizumi

<ruby>当時<rt>とうじ</rt></ruby>の<ruby>小泉首相<rt>こいずみしゅしょう</rt></ruby>

and then (adding to what one has just said) すると, そうしたら

We get there, and then he isn't even there.

<ruby>到着<rt>とうちゃく</rt></ruby>してみると、<ruby>彼<rt>かれ</rt></ruby>はまだ<ruby>来<rt>き</rt></ruby>てもいなかった。

every now and then <ruby>時々<rt>ときどき</rt></ruby> [→ EVERY]

then again …し, いや

They may come. Then again, they may not.

<ruby>彼<rt>かれ</rt></ruby>らは<ruby>来<rt>く</rt></ruby>るかもしれないし、<ruby>来<rt>く</rt></ruby>ないかもしれない。

then and there その<ruby>場<rt>ば</rt></ruby>で

He dropped his pants then and there.

<ruby>彼<rt>かれ</rt></ruby>はその<ruby>場<rt>ば</rt></ruby>でズボンを<ruby>下<rt>お</rt></ruby>ろした。

thence *adv.* (from that place) そこから

theocracy *n.* <ruby>神権政治<rt>しんけんせいじ</rt></ruby>, <ruby>神政政治<rt>しんせいせいじ</rt></ruby>

theologian *n.* <ruby>神学者<rt>しんがくしゃ</rt></ruby>, <ruby>宗教専門家<rt>しゅうきょうせんもんか</rt></ruby>

theology *n.* <ruby>神学<rt>しんがく</rt></ruby>

theorem *n.* <ruby>定理<rt>ていり</rt></ruby>

theoretical *adj.* <ruby>理論<rt>りろん</rt></ruby>の, <ruby>理論上<rt>りろんじょう</rt></ruby>の

theoretical physics <ruby>理論物理学<rt>りろんぶつりがく</rt></ruby>

theoretically *adv.* <ruby>理論的<rt>りろんてき</rt></ruby>に, (used at the beginning of a sentence) <ruby>理論的<rt>りろんてき</rt></ruby>には, <ruby>理論上<rt>りろんじょう</rt></ruby>は

theorize *v.* <ruby>理論化<rt>りろんか</rt></ruby>する, <ruby>理論<rt>りろん</rt></ruby>を<ruby>立<rt>た</rt></ruby>てる,

(speculate) <ruby>推測<rt>すいそく</rt></ruby>する

theory *n.* <ruby>理論<rt>りろん</rt></ruby>, (general principle) …<ruby>論<rt>ろん</rt></ruby>, (reasoned explanation) <ruby>学説<rt>がくせつ</rt></ruby>, <ruby>説<rt>せつ</rt></ruby>, (sth conjectured, not proved) <ruby>推測<rt>すいそく</rt></ruby>, (pet theory) <ruby>持論<rt>じろん</rt></ruby>

the theory of evolution <ruby>進化論<rt>しんかろん</rt></ruby>

There's a theory that says people who eat lots of carrots see better in the dark.

<ruby>人参<rt>にんじん</rt></ruby>をたくさん<ruby>食<rt>た</rt></ruby>べると、<ruby>暗<rt>くら</rt></ruby>い<ruby>所<rt>ところ</rt></ruby>でもよく<ruby>見<rt>み</rt></ruby>えるという<ruby>説<rt>せつ</rt></ruby>があります。

He's full of nonsensical theories.

あの<ruby>人<rt>ひと</rt></ruby>はばかげた<ruby>理屈<rt>りくつ</rt></ruby>ばかり<ruby>言<rt>い</rt></ruby>っている。

therapeutic *adj.* (of medicine) <ruby>治療<rt>ちりょう</rt></ruby>のための, <ruby>病気<rt>びょうき</rt></ruby>に<ruby>効<rt>き</rt></ruby>く, (of activity: good for one) <ruby>心<rt>こころ</rt></ruby>が<ruby>休<rt>やす</rt></ruby>まる, いやされる

therapeutic treatment <ruby>治療<rt>ちりょう</rt></ruby>

therapist *n.* <ruby>療法士<rt>りょうほうし</rt></ruby>, セラピスト

therapy *n.* <ruby>治療<rt>ちりょう</rt></ruby>, (psychotherapy) <ruby>心理療法<rt>しんりりょうほう</rt></ruby>, セラピー

get therapy <ruby>心理療法<rt>しんりりょうほう</rt></ruby>を<ruby>受<rt>う</rt></ruby>ける

there

1 *pron.* USED WITH A LINKING VERB: (**there is**) (of inanimate object) (…が) ある, (of animate object) (…が) いる, (**there is not**) (of inanimate object) (…が) ない, (of animate object) (…が) いない, (**is there a…?**) (of inanimate object) …はありますか, (of animate object) …はいますか

2 *adv.* IN/TO A PLACE: そこに, あそこに

3 *adv.* IN GREETING: (**hello / hi / hey there**) ((*masculine*)) やあ, よう, ((*feminine*)) まあ, (**you there**) ちょっと, ((*masculine/rude*)) おい

4 *interj.* See examples below

5 ***adv.*** **CONCERNING THAT POINT/MATTER:** その点で, そのことで

6 ***adv.*** **FOLLOWED BY A MOTION VERB AND A NOUN:** See example below

1 There was a photo I hadn't seen before in the album.
見たことのない写真がアルバムの中にあった。

There are still lots of unanswered questions.
まだ答えの出ていない質問がたくさんあります。

Look! There's a butterfly.
ほら！ ちょうちょがいる。

There's a guard at the gate.
門には警備員がいます。

There are twenty families in that apartment building.
あのマンションには20世帯が暮らしている。

There isn't any bread in the house.
家にパンはないよ。

There aren't any more chocolates.
チョコレートはこれ以上ありません。

How many books are there in that box?
その箱には本が何冊入っていますか？

Isn't there anyone in charge here?
ここに責任者はいませんか？

2 I went over there and bought a ticket.
そこに行って、切符を買った。

He climbed up there but couldn't get down.
彼はそこまで登ることはできたけど、下りられなくなったんです。

I walked there and back in about two hours.
約2時間で、そこに歩いて戻って来ました。

He was just standing there staring at us.
彼はただそこに立って、私たちをじっと見ていました。

Don't just sit there!
そこにただ座っているんじゃない！

I used to live there, and I still go back occasionally to visit.
昔あそこに住んでいたんで、今でも時々遊びに行きます。

3 "Hello there, Nick." "Hi there!"
((*masculine*))「やあ、ニック」「よう！」

4 There, there. Everything is all right now.
さあさあ。もう大丈夫だよ。

There! I told you you could do it.
ほら、言ったでしょ、できたじゃない。

There, I'm done! ああ、できた！

5 I don't agree with you there.
その点で同意しかねる。

6 There goes the train!
電車が行ってしまった！

there you are/go (emphasizing that one is right about sth) ほら(ね), やっぱり, 言ったとおりでしょ; (giving sb sth) (さあ)どうぞ; (admitting that the situation could not be otherwise) 仕方ない, どうしようもない

There you are. It's raining.
ほら、やっぱり雨が降っている。

It wasn't a very good film, but there you are, it was better than staying at home.
大して面白い映画じゃなかったけど、仕方ない。家にいるよりはよかったじゃない？

there we were そんな訳で

So, there we were, feeling like a bunch of idiots.
そんな訳で、まあ私たちはばかを見た

気分でしたよ。

thereabouts *adv.* (**or thereabouts**: referring to a place) …か(どこか)そのあたり

thereafter *adv.* それ以来, その後

thereby *adv.* それによって

therefore *adv.* (as a result) …ので, (used at the beginning of a sentence) ((*formal*)) したがって

Water is scarce. Therefore we need to ration our use of it.
水が不足しています。したがって使用を制限しなければなりません。

thermal *adj.* (warm) 熱の

thermal energy 熱エネルギー

♦ **thermal underwear** *n.* 防寒用下着

thermodynamics *n.* 熱力学

thermometer *n.* 温度計

Thermos *n.* ポット, 魔法びん

thermostat *n.* サーモスタット

thesaurus *n.* 類語辞典, シソーラス

these *adj.* これらの [NOTE: In practice the plural is often not translated and instead この is used.]

pron. これら [NOTE: In practice これ is used.], (opposite of "those") こっち

These ideas need to be considered.
これらの案は検討する必要があります。

These mountains are famous for their wildlife.
この山々は、野生動物がすんでいることで有名です。

These monkeys are intelligent.
ここのサルはみんな利口です。

These can be used, but I doubt if those can.
こっちは使えるけれど、あっちはたぶんだめだと思う。

thesis *n.* 論文

thespian *n.* 役者, 俳優

they *pron.* (referring to people) 彼らは/が, あの人たちは/が, (referring to a group of women) 彼女らは/が, (referring to things) それらは/が

They didn't seem to be enjoying the party.
彼らは、パーティーを楽しんでいないようだった。

Are they old enough to get into the club?
彼らは、そのクラブに入れる年齢になっているの?

thiamine *n.* チアミン, ビタミンB_1

thick *adj.* 厚い, ((*emphatic*)) 分厚い, (of body part) 太い, (of undergrowth) 生い茂った, (of hair) (量の) 多い, (of liquid, fog) 濃い, (of sauce) こってりした, (of accent) すごい

a thick layer of ice 厚い氷の層

These walls are thick. この壁は厚い。

This piece of wood is too thick.
この板は厚すぎる。

a thick book 分厚い本

a thick neck 太い首

thick undergrowth 生い茂った草むら

He has thick red hair.
あの人の髪は赤毛で量が多い。

a thick, creamy soup
濃厚でクリーミーなスープ

A thick fog descended on the lake.
濃い霧が湖に立ち込めていた。

He speaks with a thick French accent.

あの人はすごいフランスなまりで話す。

through thick and thin いい時も悪い時も, 終始変わりなく

thicken *v.* (make/become thick: food) 濃くする/なる, (of fog) 深くなる

thicket *n.* やぶ, 茂み

thickly *adv.* (so as to produce a thick layer, piece etc.) 厚く, (densely) 濃く

thickness *n.* (dimension, quality) 厚さ, 太さ, (viscosity, density) 濃さ

thick-skinned *adj.* 図太い, 鈍感な

thief *n.* 泥棒, (sneak thief) こそ泥

The police caught the thief red-handed.
警察は泥棒を現行犯で逮捕した。

thigh *n.* もも, 太もも [→ picture of BODY]

thin *adj.* 薄い, (thin and flat) ((*emphatic*)) 薄っぺらな, (of person) やせた

v. (water down: sauce etc.) 薄める, (**thin out**: of crowd) まばらになる

This paper is too thin.
この紙は薄すぎます。

The ice was very thin.
氷はとても薄かった。

I'd like to use a thin material for the curtains.
カーテンには薄い素材を使いたいんです。

a thin slice of bread 薄切りのパン

a thin dress 薄手のドレス

The carpet has worn thin.
カーペットはすり切れて薄くなっている。

A thin mist covered the hilltop.
丘の上には薄くもやが、かかっていた。

He's looking very thin.
あの人はとてもやせて見える。

You've gotten thin! やせたね!

thing *n.*

1 MATERIAL OBJECT: 物, ((*informal*)) やつ

2 BELONGINGS: (**things**) 物, 持ち物, ((*formal*)) 所持品

3 SUBJECT: こと

4 CIRCUMSTANCES: (**things**) 物事, 事態

5 ANIMATE OBJECT: (person) 人, (child) 子, (animal) 動物, (living thing) 生き物

1 What's this soft thing called?
この柔らかい物は何と言うんですか?

There were all these things you could experiment with.
実験に使える物がいろいろそろっていた。

There were all sorts of things in the room.
部屋には、ありとあらゆる物があった。

A ball and a sphere are not the same thing.
球と球体とは同じものではありません。

2 Where did you put your things?
持ち物をどこへ置いたの?

Do you have all your things?
自分の物は全部持った?/忘れ物はない?

3 I couldn't think of a single thing to say.
言うことが何一つ思いつかなかった。

I wouldn't even think of such a thing.
そんなことは考えもしません。

There are one or two things I want to ask you about.
一つ、二つ聞きたいことがあります。

Now that's one thing I do not want to talk about.
それについては話したくありません。

He only talks about one thing and that's baseball.
あの人が話すことといったら一つだけ、

T

野球のことだよ。

4 Your fretting is only making things worse.
心配しても、事態は悪くなるだけだ。

Things couldn't be better.
絶好調です/万事順調です。

5 What a sweet thing you are.
あなたはなんて優しい人なんだ。

as things are/stand 現状では, 今のところ(は)

As things are, I would prefer not to go.
今のところは、行きたくないんです。

a thing of the past 過去の物/こと

Video tapes are fast becoming a thing of the past.
ビデオ(テープ)は急速に過去の物になりつつある。

do one's own thing (act selfishly) 自分のしたいようにする, (do what one likes) 自分の好きなことをやる

He just does his own thing.
あの人はただ自分のしたいようにするだけさ。

Everyone is doing their own thing and it is complete chaos.
みんながやりたいようにやっているから、もうめちゃくちゃだ。

first thing (in the morning) (朝)一番に, 真っ先に

for one thing 一つには

I'm not interested in the job. For one thing, the commute is too far.
その仕事に興味はありません。一つには、通勤時間がかかりすぎるんです。(lit., "the commuting time is too long")

have a thing about (like) (…が) 大好きだ, (hate) (…が) 大嫌いだ

Jeff has a thing about Asian women.
ジェフはアジア女性が大好きだ。

She seems to have a thing about spiders.
彼女はクモが大嫌いらしい。

how're things (going)? 最近どうですか, 調子はどうですか

Hey, Rick. How're things going?
やあ、リック。最近どう?

just the thing 必要なこと/もの

A vacation will be just the thing for Tom.
トムに必要なのは休暇なんです。

make a thing of/about 騒ぎ立てる

OK, I was wrong. But there's no need to make such a big thing of it.
((*masculine*)) わかった、俺が悪かった。でもそんなに騒ぎ立てることはないだろう。

of all things よりによって, こともあろうに

Well, of all things, it's you again!
おいおい、こともあろうにまた君か。

one thing led to another 次から次に広がって, いろいろあって

First they started squabbling about whose toys were whose. Then one thing led to another, and soon they were crying.
最初子供たちは、どのおもちゃが誰のかについてけんかを始めて、次から次に広がって結局泣き出した。

the thing is (the problem is) 問題は, (the point is) 肝心なのは

The thing is, what do I do?
問題は、何をすればいいかだ。

The thing is, if you panic, you'll make everyone else upset.
肝心なのは、あなたがパニックになったら、ほかのみんなが動揺するということだ。

think *v.* 思う, (believe) 信じる, (**think about**: consider) …のことを考える, (presume) 思い込む [→ THINK OF]

I think he's a very nice person. Don't you think so?
いい人ですね。そう思いませんか？

(*being ironic*) How old do you think I am?
私をいくつだと思ってるの？

Don't you think it's a bit late for that?
それにはちょっと遅いと思わない？

I'm not sure, but I think it starts at 7 o'clock.
確かじゃないけど、7時に始まると思う。

What did you think of her performance?
彼女の演技、どう思いました？

They thought the sun and moon were gods.
当時の人々は太陽と月を、神だと考えていました。

It all makes sense when you stop and think about it.
じっくり考えれば、つじつまが合うよ。

do you think you could…? …してくれませんか

Do you think you could give me a wake-up call?
モーニングコールしてくれない？

think again 考え直す

I'd think again if I were you.
私だったら、考え直すね。

think aloud/out loud 考え事を口に出す, 声に出して考える

Must you think aloud? It's really distracting.
声に出して考えなきゃだめなの？ すごく気が散るんだよ。

think badly of 悪く思う

I don't think badly of him.
彼のことを悪くは思わない。

think better of 見直す, (**think better of doing**) …しないことにする

Now that I've actually been to the country, I think better of it.
あの国に実際に行ってみて、見直しました。

She thought better of taking the job when she heard about the salary.
給料を聞いて、その会社に就職しないことにした。

think highly of 高く評価する

He is thought highly of in the field of medicine.
彼は医学の分野で高く評価されている。

think little of (not think much about) 何とも思わない, (not think highly of) あまり評価しない, 軽視する

I think very little of that time now.
今となれば、あのころのことを何とも思わない。

think nothing of it お気になさらずに, とんでもありません, どういたしまして

"Thank you so much."
"Really, think nothing of it."
「ありがとうございました」
「いえ、お気になさらずに」

think to oneself 内心思う, 心の中で思う, (ひそかに) 思う

think back *v.* 振り返る, 思い出す

think of *v.* (think about) 考える, 思う, (call to mind) 思い出す, (imagine, think up) 思いつく, 考えつく, 考え出す

I can't think of anything except him.
彼のこと以外は考えられない。

I thought of it just the other day.
つい先日思いついたんです。

Who was it that thought of satellites in the first place?
最初に人工衛星を考え出したのは、誰ですか？

think over *v.* じっくり考える, よく考える, ((*formal*)) 熟考する

I'd like to think this over for a couple of days before I make a final decision.
最終的な結論を出す前に、2、3日よく考えたいと思います。

think up → THINK OF

---

thinker *n.* (person who thinks carefully about things) よく考える人, (academic type) 思想家

thinking *n.* (ideas, opinions) 考え, 考え方, (act of considering) 思考, (ideology) 思想

What was the thinking behind this plan?
この計画の背景には、どういう考えがあったんですか？

This is going to require some serious thinking.
これについては、じっくり考えなければならないだろう。

Clear thinking seems to be a rare commodity in this office.
このオフィスでは、冷静な判断というものが珍しいようだ。

To my way of thinking, they're wrong.
私の考えでは彼らが間違っています。

third *n.* 第3, 3番目, (date) 3日, (one third) 3分の1

adj., adv. 第3の/に, 3番目の/に

♦ **third base** *n.* (in baseball) 三塁

third party *n.* (person) 第三者

third person *n.* 三人称

third dimension *n.* 第3次元

third world *n.* 第3世界

thirst *n.* (need for a drink) のどの渇き; (strong desire) 切望, 渇望

thirsty *adj.* のどが渇いた

Boy, am I thirsty!
いやあ、のどが渇いた！

thirteen *n.* 13, 十三

adj., pron. 13の, (people) 13人(の), (things) 13個(の)

thirteenth *n.* 第13, 13番目, (date) 13日

adj. 第13の, 13番目の

thirtieth *n.* 第30, 30番目, (date) 30日

adj. 第30の, 30番目の

thirty *n.* 30, 三十, (**the thirties**) 30年代, (**one's thirties**) 30代

adj., pron. 30の, (people) 30人(の), (things) 30個(の)

this

1 *pron.* これ, ((*polite*)) こちら, (as opp. to "that") こっち, (referring to a matter under discussion) このこと, (referring to a place) ここ, (**like this**) このように, こんなふうに

2 *adj.* この, ((*formal*)) 当-, 本-

3 *adv.* このくらい, こんなに

1 He handed me a book and said, "This will help you learn German."

T

彼は本を渡してくれて「これはドイツ語を学ぶのに役立つよ」と言った。

This is for you. It's a present.
これをどうぞ。プレゼントです。

This is terrible news.
これはひどいニュースだね。

Please don't tell this to anyone.
このことは誰にも言わないでください。

You may not believe this, but…
信じられないかもしれないけど…

This is my favorite place.
ここが私のお気に入りの場所です。

What day is this? 今日は何曜日？

Sorry to interrupt like this, but I have something important to tell you.
こんなふうにじゃまをして申し訳ありませんが、大切なことをお伝えしなければならないんです。

2 This student shows promise, but the rest do not.
この生徒は見込みがあるが、残りはだめだ。

This shirt is still damp.
このシャツはまだ湿っている。

In this case I've got to agree.
この場合、私も賛成です。

This store has the cheapest milk.
この店の牛乳が一番安い。

It happened this morning, I hear.
けさ起こったらしいよ。

This case is the exception.
本件は例外です。

3 It was about this big.
このくらいの大きさでした。

I didn't think the snow would be this deep.
雪がこんなに積もるなんて思わなかった。

this and that あれこれ

thistle ***n.*** アザミ

thorax ***n.*** 胸部

thorn ***n.*** とげ

thorny ***adj.*** (of plant) とげのある, (of problem) 厄介な

thorough ***adj.*** (exhaustive) 徹底的な, (well done) 申し分のない, 完璧な, (of person: methodical) きちょうめんな

The police carried out a thorough investigation.
警察は徹底的な捜査を行った。

This is a very thorough essay.
これは申し分のないエッセイです。

♦ **thoroughness** ***n.*** (of action) 完全, 徹底

thoroughbred ***n.*** サラブレッド

thoroughfare ***n.*** 道路, (main road) 幹線道路

thoroughly ***adv.*** (completely) すっかり, 全く, (carefully) 綿密に, 細かく, (to a great degree) 存分に, とことん

I was thoroughly bored throughout the entire movie.
映画は初めから終わりまで、全く退屈だった。

Read it thoroughly. 精読しなさい。

I thoroughly enjoyed the play.
お芝居を存分に楽しんだ。

those

1 ***adj.*** それらの/あれらの [NOTE: In practice the plural is often not translated and instead その or あの is used.]

2 ***pron.*** それら/あれら [NOTE: In practice それ or あれ is used.], (as opp. to "these") そっち/あっち, (**those who…**)

…する人, ((*polite*)) …する方

1 Those books should be on the other shelf.
そっちの本はもう一つの棚に入る本です。

Look at those fish! あの魚を見て！

Those boys are on the school team.
あの少年たちは、学校のチームに入っています。

Back then, those kinds of delays were frequent.
当時は、あのような遅れは日常茶飯事でした。

2 What are those? あれは何ですか？

I prefer these to those.
あっちより、こっちのほうがいいです。

Those who can play an instrument, raise your hand.
楽器ができる人は、手を挙げてください。

though *conj., adv.* …けれど(も), ((*informal*)) …けど, ((*formal*)) …が

Though we'd been walking all day, I wasn't very tired.
一日中歩いたけれど、あまり疲れていなかった。

Though he didn't say anything, he was obviously angry.
何も言わなかったけど、彼は明らかに腹を立てていた。

Though it looks delicious, I'm already stuffed.
おいしそうだけど、もうおなかがいっぱいです。

The room is small, though not too small.
部屋は小さいけど、小さすぎることはない。

Though she's never been to Japan, Lena can speak Japanese very well.
レナさんは日本に行ったことはないですが、とても上手に日本語を話せます。

I thought they were right, though many others did not.
ほかの大勢の人はそう思わなかったが、私は彼らが正しいと思った。

as though まるで…かのように

She acted as though she knew me.
彼女はまるで、僕を知っているかのようにふるまった。

even though たとえ…ても/でも

Even though I never win, I enjoy chess.
たとえ勝てなくても、チェスは楽しい。

thought *n.*

1 IDEA: 考え

2 PROCESS OF THINKING: 考え, 考慮, 思考

3 CONSIDERATION TOWARD OTHERS: 思いやり, 心づかい

4 INTENTION: 考え, 意図

1 The thought suddenly occurred to me that he might have been lying.
彼はうそをついていたのかもしれないという考えが、ふと心に浮かんだ。

You'd better keep your thoughts to yourself.
考えは人には言わないほうがいい。

I couldn't bear the thought of her being with him.
彼女が彼といっしょだと思うと、たまらなかった。

Do you have any thoughts on what happened?
何があったのか、思い当たることはないですか？

2 We were deep in thought when there was a sudden knock at the door.
考え事に浸っていると、突然ドアをノックする音がした。

We'd better give this matter some

thought.
この件については、少し考えたほうがよさそうだ。

3 He put a lot of thought into that gift, don't you think?
心のこもった贈り物だと思いませんか？

4 My one thought was to get out as quickly as possible.
一刻も早く抜け出すことしか、頭になかった。

on second thought (でも)やっぱり

thoughtful ***adj.*** (considerate) 思いやりのある, 親切な

thoughtless ***adj.*** (inconsiderate) 思いやりのない, 無神経な

thousand ***n.*** 1000, 千, (**thousands of**) 何千もの…

adj. 1000の, (people) 1000人の, (things) 1000個の

a thousand-yen note 千円札

I must have told you this a thousand of times.
このことは何千回も言ったはずだよ。

thread ***n.*** (spun cotton) 糸; (of thought, conversation, argument) 筋道

v. (thread A through B) (AをBに) 通す, (**thread a needle**) 針に糸を通す

I lost the thread of his argument.
彼の議論の筋道がわからなくなった。

threadbare ***adj.*** (of carpet, clothing) すり切れた

threat ***n.*** (intention to hurt) 脅迫, (menace) 脅威

a terrorist threat テロの脅威

a threat to national security
国の安全に対する脅威 [を脅かすもの]

threaten ***v.*** (give a warning to) 脅す, 脅迫する, (**threaten to do**) …する(ぞ)と脅す, …する(ぞ)と脅迫する; (seem likely to happen) 起こりそうだ

Don't threaten me.
脅迫しないでください。

He threatened to tell the police.
そいつは警察に知らせるぞと脅した。

It was threatening to rain when we left.
出発した時、雨が降りそうだった。

The demonstration threatened to get out of hand.
デモは収拾がつかなくなるおそれがあった。

Yet again, famine threatened.
またもや、ききんが起こりそうだった。

three ***n.*** 3, 三

adj., pron. 3の, (people) 3人(の), (things) 3個(の), 三つ(の)

three quarters 4分の3

three-dimensional ***adj.*** 3次元の

threesome ***n.*** (group of three) 3人組

threshold ***n.*** (entrance) 敷居, 入口

be on the threshold of …の出発点にいる

We're on the threshold of a medical breakthrough.
我々は医療の飛躍的な発展の出発点にいる。

thrift ***n.*** (frugality) 質素, (economy) 節約

♦**thrift shop** ***n.*** リサイクルショップ

thrifty ***adj.*** 質素な

thrill ***v.*** (excite) わくわくさせる, (cause to feel joy) 大喜びさせる

n. (excitement) わくわくする感じ, (joy) 大喜び, (fear) スリル

T

I was thrilled to be there.
そこにいてわくわくした。

thriller *n.* (book) スリラー小説, (movie) スリラー映画

thrilling *adj.* わくわくする

thrive *v.* (go well) うまくいく, (be successful) 成功する, (flourish) 繁盛する

Business is thriving.
商売は繁盛しています。

thrive on …に生きがいを感じる

She's the sort who thrives on competition.
彼女は競争に生きがいを感じるような人間だ。

throat *n.* のど

Do you have a sore throat?
のどが痛いんですか？

clear one's throat せき払いをする

It got stuck in my throat.
のどに詰まった。

throb *v.* (of heart) どきどきする, (of body part, with pain) ずきずきする

My heart throbbed with excitement.
興奮で胸がどきどきした。

My foot throbbed with pain.
足がずきずき痛んだ。

throne *n.* (seat for monarch) 王座, (**the throne**: kingship) 王位

throng *n.* (crowd) 群衆

throttle *n.* スロットル, 絞り弁

through

1 ***prep., adv.*** FROM ONE SIDE TO THE OTHER (SIDE OF): (…を) 通って, 通り抜けて, 通して [→ GO[1] THROUGH]

2 ***prep.*** BY MEANS OF: …で, (person) …を通して, (thing, person) …によって

3 ***prep., adv.*** DURING THE ENTIRE PERIOD (OF): …中, …の間ずっと, (from A through to B) (AからB)まで, (AからB)にかけて

4 ***prep.*** IN: …の中を

5 ***prep., adv.*** PAST: (a barrier) (…を) 通り抜けて, 通して, 通って

1 Once you go through the first door, it's the third door on your left.
最初のドアを通り抜けて、左手にある３番目のドアです。

We drove through Glasgow.
グラスゴーを通り抜けた。

The train went through a tunnel.
電車はトンネルを抜けて行った。

I can see you through the window.
窓越しにあなたが見えますよ。

We traveled through Russia by train.
列車でロシアを横断しました。

The Danube flows through several countries.
ドナウ川は数ヵ国を流れています。

Moths had eaten a small hole right through my suit.
虫に食われて、スーツに小さい穴があいていた。

The prisoners broke through the wall of their cell.
囚人らは独房の壁を打ち破った。

2 I could see a bird through the binoculars.
双眼鏡で鳥が見えた。

I found out you were here through sheer coincidence.
あなたがここにいることは、全くの偶然で知ったんです。

I was introduced to him through Mr.

Takahashi.
高橋さんを通して彼に紹介されました。

We spoke through an interpreter.
通訳を通して話しました。

3 The bombing continued through the night.
爆撃は一晩中続いた。

All through February, I worked on finishing my dissertation.
2月はずっと、博士論文の仕上げにかかりっきりだった。

I slept through most of it.
その間ほとんど、寝ていた。

It is warm from May through to September.
5月から9月にかけては、暖かい。

4 The Frisbee flew through the air.
フリスビーは空中を飛んで行った。

We walked home through the darkness.
真っ暗な中を歩いて帰った。

5 It took an hour to get through the road construction.
道路工事を通り抜けるのに、1時間もかかった。

We couldn't get through because of the crowds.
混雑していて、通り抜けられなかった。

They let us through once we showed them our IDs.
ＩＤを見せると、通してくれた。

be through with (sick of and ready to give up) …に飽きる, …にうんざりする, (done using) 使い終わる, (…が) 済む, (has ended one's relationship with) …と別れる

I'm through with painting.
絵をかくのに飽きてしまった。

When you're through with the computer, please turn it off.
コンピューターを使い終わったら、電源を切ってください。

I'm through with him. 彼とは別れた。

get through → GET

go through → GO[1]

halfway through …途中で

I was halfway through my talk when the power went out.
話の途中で、停電してしまった。

throughout ***prep.*** (in all parts of) …中で/に, …の至る所で/に, (during the entire period of) …中, …の間ずっと
adv. (everywhere) 至る所で/に, (during the entire time) ずっと

Throughout the country, everyone is talking about this new invention.
国の至る所で、みんなこの新発明の話をしている。

The World Cup is broadcast throughout the world.
ワールドカップは世界中に放送されます。

The fire kept burning throughout the night.
火は一晩中 [夜通し] 燃え続けた。

throw ***v.*** 投げる, (**throw in/into**) 投げ込む, 投げ入れる, (of horse: fling off: rider) 振り落とす, (**throw oneself from/off**: jump off/from) …から飛び降りる, (throw carelessly: chuck) ほうり投げる
n. (of ball) 投球, 送球

They threw snowballs at us.
彼らは僕らに雪玉を投げてきた。

The boy threw the ball into the river.

男の子はボールを川へ投げ入れた。

Maki was thrown off a horse.
真希は馬から振り落とされた。

The man threw himself off a tall building.
その男性は高層ビルから飛び降りた。

I threw the papers down onto the desk.
書類を机にほうり投げた。

Don't throw your clothes on the floor!
服を床に脱ぎ捨てないで!

throw a fit → FIT

throw one's arms around (embrace) …に抱きつく

throw oneself into (work) …に没頭する

throw light on → LIGHT[1]

throw away *v.* (chance) 見逃す, むだにする, (thing) 捨てる

Don't throw away this chance.
((*masculine*)) このチャンスをむだにするな。

Our neighbor is a hoarder who can't throw away anything.
隣の人は物を捨てられずに、ため込むたちだ。

throw out *v.* (discard) 捨てる, (force to leave) 追い出す, ほうり出す, (**be thrown out of school**) 退学させられる

Why don't you throw these old clothes out?
この古い服は捨てたらどう?

He was thrown out of the bar for fighting.
あの人は、けんかをしてバーからほうり出された。

throw up *v.* (vomit) 吐く

Someone threw up all over the carpet.
誰かがカーペットのあちこちに吐いていた。

thrush *n.* (bird) ツグミ

thrust *v.* (thrust A into B) (AをBに) 押し付ける; (stab) 刺す

n. (main point) 要点 [→ PUSH 3]

thud *n.* ドサッ/ドスン(という音)

v. (fall) ドサッ/ドスンと落ちる

thug *n.* ちんぴら, (gangster) やくざ

thumb *n.* 親指 [→ picture of HAND]

This thumb was bruised.
この親指を痛めた。

rule of thumb 経験則

thumbs-up *n., adj.* (sign) 賛成の(合図)

He gave the thumbs-up sign.
彼は親指を立てて賛成の合図を送った。

thumbtack *n.* 画びょう, 押しピン [→ picture of STATIONERY]

thump *v.* (tap with fist) ドン/ゴツンとたたく, (thump against) (…に)ドンとぶつかる, (of heart) どきどきする, (of head: throb with pain) ずきずきする

thunder *n.* 雷

You could hear the thunder in the distance.
遠くで雷が鳴っているのが聞こえた。

thunder and lightning 雷と稲妻

thunderbolt *n.* 雷鳴と稲妻

thunderstorm *n.* 雷雨

Thursday *n.* 木曜日

thus *adv.* (in this/that way) この/そのように, (therefore) したがって

thwart *v.* (prevent) 妨害する, 妨げる

thyme *n.* (herb) タイム, (plant) タチジャコウソウ

thyroid *n.* 甲状腺

tiara *n.* ティアラ

T

Tibet *n.* チベット

tic *n.* (twitch) けいれん, チック

tick[1] *n.* (sound of a clock) カチカチ(いう音); (check mark) チェック(の印)

v. (of clock) カチカチいう

♦**tick off** *v.* (anger) 怒らせる

tick[2] *n.* (parasite) ダニ

be bitten by a tick ダニに食われる

ticket *n.* 券, (for travel) 切符, チケット, ((*formal*)) 乗車券, (for movie, concert) チケット, ((*formal*)) 入場券

Have you bought your ticket yet?
切符はもう買いましたか?

I have two tickets for tonight's show.
今夜の公演のチケットが2枚あるんだ。

an airplane ticket 航空券

There was a parking ticket when I got back to my car.
車に戻ったら、駐車違反のステッカーが張られていた。

♦**ticket gate** *n.* 改札口

ticket office *n.* 切符売り場

tickle *v.* くすぐる, (cause a tickling sensation) くすぐったい, こそば(ゆ)い

That tickles! くすぐったい!

♦**ticklish** *adj.* くすぐったい

tidal wave *n.* 津波

tidbit *n.* (piece of information) ちょっとした情報, 一片の情報; (food) 一口

tide *n.* (of sea) 潮; (of opinion) 傾向, 風潮, 流れ

high [low] tide 満[干]潮

The tide is coming in [going out].
潮が満ちて[引いて]いる。

The tide of public opinion is changing.
世論の流れが変わりつつある。

♦**tide over** *v.* (of food) (...で) 済ませる, (of money) (...で) やっていける

These potato chips should tide you over.
このポテトチップスで、なんとか済ませられるでしょう。

tidy *adj.* きちんとした, (of room: organized) 整理された, 片付けられた, (of person: cleanly) きれい好きな, (of appearance) こぎれいな

v. (make neat) 片付ける, きちんとする

He keeps his room very tidy.
彼は自分の部屋をいつもきちんとしている。

Kaori's a tidy person.
香さんはきれい好きな人です。

♦**tidiness** *n.* (state) 整然, 整とん

---

tie

1 *n.* ARTICLE OF CLOTHING: ネクタイ

2 *v.* FASTEN: (shoelaces, ribbon) 結ぶ, (hair) くくる, 縛る, (necktie) 締める, (tie A to B) (AをBに) 結び付ける, (dog, horse) つなぐ

3 *v.* RESTRICT: (**be tied**) 縛られる

4 *n.* RELATIONSHIP: (**ties**) つながり, 関係

5 *n.* EQUAL SCORE: 同点, 引き分け

6 *v.* SCORE EQUALLY: 同点になる, 引き分ける

1 I lent him one of my ties.
僕のネクタイを彼に1本貸した。

You'd better wear a tie.
ネクタイをしたほうがいいよ。

2 tie a knot 結び目を作る

The boy still can't tie his shoelaces.
その子はまだ、靴ひもを結べない。

Her hair was tied back.
彼女は髪を後ろで縛っていた。

3 I'm not tied to one task at work.
職場では、一つの仕事に縛られているわけではありません。

4 Japan has close ties with the United States.
日本はアメリカと密接なつながりがある。

family ties 家族のきずな

5 The result was a tie.
結果は引き分けでした。

In the event of a tie, there'll be a play-off match.
同点の場合には、決勝戦を行います。

6 They (=the two people) tied for first place.
二人は同点で1位だった。

tie around *v.* (tie A around B) (AをBに)巻き付ける

The fisherman tied the rope around the anchor.
漁師はロープをいかりに巻き付けた。

tie down *v.* (restrict) 束縛する, ((*figurative*)) 縛る

He felt tied down with his job.
彼は仕事に縛られていると感じた。

tie up *v.* (person, parcel) 縛る, くくる, (animal to a fixed point) つなぐ, (**be tied up**: be busy) 忙しい, 手が離せない

Do you have any string to tie this up with?
何か、これを縛るひもはありますか？

I'm tied up right now. Can I call you back?
今、手が離せないので、折り返しかけていいですか？

tiger *n.* トラ, 虎

tight

1 *adj.* FIRMLY IN PLACE: 堅い, きつい

2 *adv.* FIRMLY: しっかり(と), きつく

3 *adj.* TOO SMALL: きつい, 窮屈な, ぴったりした

4 *adj.* TAUT: ぴんと張った

5 *adj.* SHARP: (of curve in road) 急な

6 *adj.* OF SCHEDULE: ぎっしり詰まった, きつい

7 *adj.* OF CHEST/THROAT: 締め付けられるような

8 *adj.* OF COMPETITION: 接戦の

9 *adj.* STRICT: 厳しい

1 The door was closed tight.
ドアは堅く閉ざされていた。

The nut was so tight I couldn't loosen it.
ナットはきつくて、ゆるめることができなかった。

2 Hold on tight! しっかりつかまれ！

Don't hold my hand so tight.
そんなにきつく手を握らないで。

3 Your jeans look tight on you.
そのジーンズ、きつそうだね。

She wore a tight skirt.
彼女は、ぴったりしたスカートをはいていた。

4 Is the rope tight?
ロープはぴんと張ってる？

5 Slow down. There's a tight curve up ahead.
スピードを落として。この先に急カーブがあるから。

6 I have a tight schedule this week.
今週は予定がぎっしり詰まっている。

7 My chest feels tight.
胸が苦しい。

8 It was a tight race.
接戦だった。

9 Security was tight at the airport.
空港での警備は厳しかった。

♦**tightly** ***adv.*** きつく, しっかり(と)

tighten ***v.*** (rope) ぴんと張る, (belt, screw) しっかり締める, (knot) 堅く結ぶ

tight-fisted ***adj.*** (stingy) けちな

tights ***n.*** (tight pants for dancers, acrobats) タイツ, (pantyhose) パンティーストッキング, ((*informal*)) パンスト

tile ***n.*** (for roof) かわら, (for floor) タイル
v. タイルを張る
a tile floor タイル張りの床

tiled ***adj.*** タイル張りの

till → UNTIL

tilt ***v.*** (lean) 傾く, (cause to lean) 傾ける
Don't tilt it too far or it'll fall.
あんまり傾けると倒れてしまうよ。

timber ***n.*** 材木, 木材

time

1 ***n.*** TIME OF DAY: 時間, 時刻

2 ***n.*** POINT IN LIFE: 時, (in a broad sense; being nonspecific) ころ, 時期

3 ***n.*** INSTANCE: …回, …度, (**this time**) 今回, (**last time**) この間, (**next time**) 今度, この次, ((*formal*)) 次回, (**first time**) 初めて, (**every time**) 毎回, (**how many times**) 何度

4 ***n.*** TIME AVAILABLE: 時間, 暇

5 ***n.*** STRETCH OF TIME: 時間, 期間, (in race: minutes etc. for covering a distance) タイム

6 ***n.*** PERIOD OF HISTORY: 時代, (**the times**: the present) 現代

7 ***n.*** OPPORTUNE TIME: 時間, 時, 時機

8 ***n.*** EXPERIENCE: (経験した)時間, 時

9 ***n.*** USED WITH NUMBERS: (multiplying: ... **times**) …倍 [→ TIMES]

10 ***v.*** CHOOSE THE MOMENT FOR: (…の) タイミングを見計らう, 時間を定める

11 ***v.*** MEASURE THE TIME FOR: (…の) タイムを計る

1 The time is 5 P.M.
時間 [時刻] は午後5時です。
local time 現地時間
What's the time? 今何時ですか？
What time did you arrive?
何時に着いたんですか？
See you the same time tomorrow.
じゃあ、明日の同じ時間に。
It's almost lunch time.
もうお昼(の時間)だ。

2 There were good times and bad times.
いい時もあれば悪い時もありました。
This time next year I'll be in France.
来年の今ごろはフランスにいます。
During my time at the embassy, I got the chance to meet many prominent people.
大使館に勤務していたころ、たくさん著名人に会う機会がありました。

3 This time it's going to be different.
今度は違ってくる。
Next time, please be here a few minutes earlier.
この次は少し早めに来てください。
It's the first time I've ever been here.
ここに来たのは初めてです。
That's the second time that's happened today.
今日それが起きたのは2度目です。

4 How do you find time to do all these things?
これだけのことをやる時間を、どうやって見つける？

She spends most of her time studying.
彼女は、ほとんどの時間を勉強に費やしている。

There's no time for that.
そんな時間ないですよ。

I don't think we'll have time to visit the museum.
美術館に行く暇はないと思う。

5 It was the best movie I've seen in a long time.
こんなにいい映画を見たのは久しぶりです。

He has a fast time in the 100-meter sprint.
彼は100メートル走で速いタイムを出している。

6 the time of the dinosaurs 恐竜時代

The times are changing.
現代は変化が激しい。

7 It's time for a break. 休憩時間です。

It's time for us to go home.
もう帰る時間だ。

The time has come to review what we've done.
これまでやったことを確認しよう。

8 Thank you for a wonderful time.
すばらしい時間をありがとう。

Did you have a fun time in New York?
ニューヨークは面白かったですか？

I had a tough time settling in.
引っ越して落ち着くまで、苦労しました。

9 It cost three times as much as I thought it would.
思っていたより3倍もお金がかかった。

10 You timed your remark perfectly.
絶妙なタイミングで発言しましたね。

The lights were timed to go off at 6 P.M.
電気は午後6時に消えるようになっていた。

11 Time me. タイムを計って。

ahead of time 予定よりも早く

I think the project will be finished ahead of time.
計画は予定よりも早く終わると思います。

all the time しょっちゅう, いつも

any time → ANYTIME

at a time 一度に

Please speak one at a time.
一度に一人ずつお話しください。

at the best of times 一番いいときですら

He's not very polite at the best of times.
あの人は一番いいときですら、礼儀正しいとは言えない。

at the same time (simultaneously) 同時に, (together) いっしょに; (used at the beginning of a sentence) しかし, 一方で

They both arrived at the same time.
二人とも同時に到着しました。

at times 時々, 時には

At times, I feel like taking a long, solitary walk through the park.
時には、一人で公園をゆっくり散歩したくなる。

be ahead of one's time 時代を先取りする, 時代に先駆ける

Einstein was ahead of his time.
アインシュタインは時代を先取りしていた。

before one's time (before one was

born) 生まれる前に

The Beatles were before your time.
ビートルズは君が生まれる前のバンドだ。

for the time being ここしばらくは, とりあえず, さしあたり

The room is small, but it'll do for the time being.
部屋は狭いけれど、ここしばらくは問題ないと思う。

(*at a restaurant*) "Anything else you'd like to order, sir?"
"No, that'll do for the time being."
「ほかにご注文はございませんか？」
「とりあえず、それでけっこうです」

from time to time 時々, 時折

She visits this cemetery from time to time.
その女性は時々この墓地を訪れます。

half the time (often) しばしば, よく, (in half as much time) 半分の時間で

Half the time, he's not even awake.
彼は起きてさえいないことがよくある。

We could do the job in half the time.
我々なら、半分の時間でその仕事をやれます。

in no time あっという間に, すぐに

It seems like a year has passed in no time at all.
1年があっという間に過ぎてしまった感じです。

in time (without being late) 間に合って, 時間までに, (in due time) そのうちに

Do you think we'll get there in time?
間に合うと思う？

In time, he will understand.
そのうち彼にもわかるよ。

it's about time (at last) やっと, (**it's about time for one to do**) (...が) そろそろ...するころだ

"Dinner's ready!"
"It's about time."
「夕食ができたよ」
「やっとできたね」

lose time 時間をむだにする, ぐずぐずする

Hurry up, we mustn't lose any more time.
急いで。これ以上、ぐずぐずしてはいられない。

make time 時間をつくる

I'm going to have to make time to see a dentist tomorrow.
明日、時間をつくって歯医者に行かなくちゃいけない。

nine times out of ten 十中八九, たいてい(の場合)

Nine times out of ten, he's right.
十中八九、あの人が正しい。

no time to lose 一刻を争う, 一刻の猶予もない

Quick! There's no time to lose.
急いで！ 一刻を争うよ。

only a matter of time 時間の問題

It's only a matter of time before the public hears the news.
世間に知れ渡るのは時間の問題です。

on one's own time 暇な時に, あいてる時間に

He took the work home to finish it on his own time.
彼は、あいてる時間にやって終わらせるため、仕事を家に持ち帰った。

on time 時間どおりに, 予定どおりに, 定刻に

Did you get there on time?
時間どおりに着いた？

You're only just on time.
ぴったり定刻ですね。

pass the time 時間をつぶす, 時間を過ごす

I passed the time window-shopping.
ウインドーショッピングをして時間をつぶした。

time after time 何度も

Time after time, I wonder what would have happened if I hadn't called.
電話していなかったらどうなっていただろうと、何度も考えます。

time bomb *n.* 時限爆弾

timecard *n.* タイムカード

time-consuming *adj.* 時間のかかる

a time-consuming process
時間のかかる方法

time frame *n.* 期間

time keeper *n.* 計時係, タイムキーパー

timeless *adj.* 永久の, 時間を超越した

a timeless classic (=work of fiction)
不朽の名作

time limit *n.* 制限時間

timely *adj.* 時宜を得た, タイムリーな

in a timely manner
タイムリーに [ちょうどいい時に]

timer *n.* (used in kitchen) (キッチン)タイマー [→ picture of COOKING UTENSILS]

times *prep.* (multiplied by) 掛ける

Six times eight is forty-eight.
６掛ける８は ４８ です。

timescale *n.* 期間

timetable *n.* (transportation timetable) 時刻表, (personal/work timetable) 予定表

time zone *n.* 時間帯

timid *adj.* (shy) 内気な, (cowardly) 臆病な

♦**timidly** *adv.* (nervously) おどおどして, こわごわ

timing *n.* タイミング, 好機の選択

The timing couldn't be better.
これ以上の好機はない。

timpani *n.* ティンパニー

tin *n.* (metal) スズ

tinder *n.* 火口

tinfoil *n.* アルミホイル, アルミ箔

tinge *v.* (**tinged with**: color) …がかった, …をおびた

n. (slight coloring) 色合い

flowers tinged with red
赤みがかった花

tingle *v.* (of body part) ぴりぴりする; (from excitement) ぞくぞくする

tinker *v.* (tinker with) いじる

tinsel *n.* 金銀糸

tint *n.* 色合い

a greenish tint 緑がかった色

♦**tinted** *adj.* 色付きの, 着色した

tiny *adj.* 小さな, ちっちゃな

tip[1] *n.* (pointed end) 先, 先端, (top) てっぺん

the northern tip of Japan 日本の北端
the tip of one's tongue 舌の先
the tip of the sword 刃の先端 [刃先]
the tip of the iceberg 氷山の一角

tip[2] *n.* (payment) チップ; (piece of advice) 助言, アドバイス, こつ, 秘訣, (clue)

手がかり, (information) 情報

v. (give money to) (…に) チップをあげる

That customer left a very poor tip.

その客は、ほんのわずかのチップしか置かなかった。

I gave him a tip on how to fit the door.

その戸のはめ方のこつを彼に教えました。

So far the police haven't received any tips.

今までのところ、警察は何の手がかりも得ていない。

Did you tip the porter?

ポーターにチップは払った？

♦**tip off** *v.* (police) (…に) 密告する

n. (**tip-off**) 密告

tip[3] *v.* (**tip over**) ひっくり返す, (cause to lean) 傾ける, (**tip forward/backward**) 前に/後ろに倒す

In his drunken stupor, he tipped over his glass.

泥酔して、彼はグラスをひっくり返した。

You can tip the seat back.

シートを後ろに倒すことができますよ。

tipsy *adj.* ほろ酔いの

tiptoe *v.* つま先で歩く

n. つま先

on tiptoe つま先で, (stealthily) 忍び足で, そっと

stand on tiptoe つま先立ちする

tire[1] *v.* (become/make weary) 疲れる/疲れさせる, くたびれる/くたびれさせる

Don't tire yourself out.

無理はしないでね。

tire[2] *n.* タイヤ [→ picture of CAR]

The tire is flat.

タイヤがパンクしている。

pump up a tire タイヤに空気を入れる

tired *adj.* (fatigued) 疲れている, 疲れた, (be tired of) 飽きた, うんざりした

You look tired. お疲れのようですね。

I'm tired, so I think I'll go to bed early tonight.

疲れたから、今夜は早く寝ようと思う。

I'm tired of the same thing for breakfast every day.

毎朝、同じ物ばっかり食べてるから飽きたよ。

I'm tired of going to school.

学校へ行くのはうんざりだ。

tireless *adj.* (of worker) 疲れを知らない, (of effort) たゆみない

tiresome *adj.* (tedious) 退屈な

tiring *adj.* 疲れる, くたびれる

tissue *n.* (tissue paper) ティッシュペーパー; (skin tissue) 組織

a box of tissues ティッシュペーパー一箱

titanium *n.* チタン

titillate *v.* (excite) 刺激する

title *n.* (of book, film) 題名, タイトル, (of chapter, heading) 題; (in sports: championship) 選手権; (aristocratic title) 爵位

What's the title of the book?

その本の題名は何ですか？

He has a title, I believe.

その人は確か爵位をもっていると思う。

titular *adj.* (nominal) 名ばかりの

TNT *n.* トリニトロトルエン

to *prep.*

1 INDICATING DIRECTION OF MOVEMENT: …へ, …に, (as far as) まで

2 INDICATING LOCATION: …に

3 INDICATING INDIRECT OBJECT: …に

4 FOR: …にとって

5 UNTIL: …まで

6 IN, MAKING UP: …につき [NOTE: Often omitted.]

7 TELLING TIME: …前

8 USED WITH RATIOS: …対

9 IN ORDER TO: …ために, …のに

1 I'm going to the post office.
郵便局に行ってきます。

He wandered from town to town.
彼は町から町へ流れ歩いた。

Let's drive to town.
車で町まで行こう。

It's only a short walk from the office to the station.
オフィスから駅までは歩いてすぐです。

We ride our bicycles to school.
自転車で通学しています。

2 He was in the middle, and I stood to his right.
彼が真ん中で、私は彼の右側にいました。

It's to your left as you walk in the door.
ドアを入って左手にあります。

3 I gave the package to Mr. Ogura.
包みは小倉さんに渡しました。

I had to pay $15,000 in taxes to the government.
国に1万5000ドルの税金を支払わなければならなかった。

4 To me, it didn't seem that important.
私にとっては、さほど重要とは思えませんでした。

It's beginning to make sense to me.
わかりかけてきました。

5 There are only a few days left to the end of the semester.
学期末まで、あと数日しかない。

You can reach me at home in the afternoon from 2 o'clock to 5 o'clock.
午後2時から5時までは、自宅にいます。

6 How many kilometers are there to the mile?
1マイルは何キロですか？

7 It's now ten to nine.
9時10分前です。

8 We won five to one.
私たちは5対1で勝った。

9 We could use this wood to make a fire.
火をおこすのに、この木を使えるよ。

to and fro 行ったり来たり

The movers have been going to and fro all morning.
けさはずっと、引越屋さんが行ったり来たりしている。

toad *n.* ヒキガエル, ガマ

toadstool *n.* 毒キノコ

toast¹ *n.* トースト

v. (cook in a toaster) 焼く, トーストにする

toast² *n.* (raising of glasses) 乾杯, (speech in honor of) 乾杯のあいさつ

v. 乾杯する

drink a toast to (…のため)に乾杯する

propose a toast (to sth/sb) (…を祝して/…のために) 乾杯の音頭を取る

toaster *n.* トースター

tobacco *n.* たばこ

toboggan *n.* トボガン, そり

today *n., adv.* (this day) 今日(は), ((*formal*)) 本日(は), (at the present time) このごろ(は), 最近(は), ((*formal*)) 今日では, 現代

What're you doing today?
((*informal*)) 今日の予定は？

I heard from your older brother today.
今日、お兄さんから連絡があったよ。

Young people today face hard choices.
最近の若い人は厳しい選択に直面している。

The world is different today.
現代の世界は昔と違う。

toddle *v.* よちよち歩く

toddler *n.* よちよち歩きの子

toe *n.* 足の指, (of sock, shoe) つま先

I stubbed my toe. 足の指をぶつけた。

I stood on my toes to see the show.
つま先立ちで舞台を見た。

tofu *n.* 豆腐 [→ p.1168 about "Counters"]

together *adv.*

1 IN ONE ANOTHER'S COMPANY: いっしょに, ((*formal*)) 共に
2 SO AS TO BE ONE UNIT: See examples below
3 SO AS TO BE COMBINED: (全部)合わせて, いっしょに
4 SIMULTANEOUSLY: 同時に, 一斉に

1 Let's go together.
いっしょに行きましょう。

We all work together at the same company.
私たちは全員、同じ会社でいっしょに働いています。

We had lunch together just the other day.
ついこの間、お昼ご飯をいっしょに食べたんです。

2 The monkeys seem to want to stick together.
あの猿たちは、いっしょにくっついていたいようです。

Don't pack them too close together.
ぎゅうぎゅうに詰め込まないでね。

That knot should hold it together.
ああやって結んでおけば大丈夫でしょう。

3 Mix the ingredients together.
材料を全部混ぜ合わせます。

One is supposed to put all these parts together.
この部品を全部組み立てるんです。

4 They quit their jobs together.
彼らは同時に仕事を辞めた。

get it/one's act together ちゃんとやる, きちんとする

Get your act together, will you!
ちゃんとやりなさい！

toil *v.* あくせく働く, こつこつ仕事をする
n. 骨折り, 苦労

toilet *n.* トイレ, お手洗い [→ picture below], ((*sign*)) 便所

a public toilet 公衆トイレ

toilet トイレ

A "washlet" features an integrated bidet system, which includes an adjustable jet of warm water for cleaning the anus or vulva, a hot-air drier, and usually seat-heating. Buttons and knobs control the bidet nozzle (on/off, positioning, water temperature and pressure), drier, and seat temperature. More than half of all households in Japan are equipped with this modern wonder.

♦ **toilet paper** *n.* トイレットペーパー

toiletries *n.* 洗面道具

toilet seat *n.* 便座

token *n.* (coin) コイン [→ COUPON]

as a token of …のしるしに

as a token of our appreciation
感謝のしるしに

by the same token 同じ理由で, 同様に

tolerance *n.* (broad-mindedness) 寛容(さ); (endurance) 忍耐力, がまん

have a low [high] tolerance for alcohol
お酒に弱い [強い]

tolerant *adj.* (broad-minded) 寛大な, 心の広い

tolerate *v.* (bear) がまんする, (…に) 耐える, (allow for, overlook) 大目に見る

I can't tolerate this noise any longer.
この騒音には、もうがまんできない。

♦ **tolerable** *adj.* がまんできる, 耐えられる

toleration *n.* がまん, 忍耐

toll *n.* (charge) 使用料; (number of victims) 被害者数

take its toll (on) (…に) 大きな打撃を与える, 害をもたらす

tomato *n.* トマト

tomb *n.* 墓

tomboy *n.* おてんば

tombstone *n.* 墓石 [→ picture of GRAVE[1]]

tomorrow *n., adv.* (the next day) 明日(は), 明日, ((*formal*)) 明日(は), (in the future) 将来(は), 未来(は)

What day is tomorrow?
明日は何曜日ですか？

Where are you going tomorrow?
明日はどこに行きますか？

Who knows what tomorrow will bring.
未来のことは誰にもわからない。

the day after tomorrow あさって

ton *n.* (measure of weight) トン, (**tons of**: lots of) たくさんの, いっぱい

tone *n.* (sound) 音, 音色, 音質, (atmosphere) 雰囲気, (manner) 気品, 品格, (color) 色調, 色合い, (of speech) 口調, 口ぶり

I didn't like the tone of his voice.
あの人の口ぶりが嫌いだった。

♦ **tone-deaf** *adj.* 音痴の

tone down *v.* (make less extreme/bright) 抑える, 和らげる

tongue *n.* 舌, (of cow etc., to be eaten) タン; (language) 言語, 国語

one's mother tongue 母国語

♦ **tongue twister** *n.* 早口言葉

tonic *n.* (quinine water) トニックウォーター

tonight *n., adv.* 今夜(は), 今晩(は)

We're going to a party tonight.
今晩パーティーへ行きます。

What's on TV tonight?
今夜はテレビで何をやるの？

tonsils *n.* 扁桃腺

too *adv.*

1 ALSO: …も

2 IN A HIGHER DEGREE THAN ALLOWABLE: <adj. stem>+…すぎる, あまりにも, あまりにも…<adj. stem>+すぎる

3 MOREOVER: しかも

1 You can come, too.
あなたも来ていいよ。

I plan to study economics and interna-

tional trade, too.
経済と国際貿易についても学ぶつもりです。

"I'm Irish." "Me, too."
「私はアイルランド人です」「私もです」

While it was comical, there was a tragic element, too.
こっけいだったけど、悲劇的な要素も入っていた。

I, too, am behind you.
私もあなたの味方です。

2 It's too far to walk.
歩くには、遠すぎます。

It's too late for that now.
それにはもう遅すぎます。

It's too hot to play tennis.
テニスをするには暑すぎる。

He cooked the pasta for too long.
彼はパスタをゆですぎた。

There were too many people there.
人が多すぎました。

I left too late. 出かけるのが遅すぎた。

This essay is too long.
このエッセイはあまりにも長すぎる。

3 Then, too, there is the problem of what to keep and what to leave out.
しかもまだ、何を残して何を取るかという問題がある。

cannot be too いくら…してもしすぎることはない

One cannot be too careful about safety.
安全については、いくら用心してもしすぎることはない。

tool *n.* (instrument) 道具 [→ picture below], (means) 手段

♦**toolbar** *n.* (on computer screen) ツールバー

tooth *n.* (in the mouth) 歯 [→ picture of FACE], (of machine) 歯, (of saw) 目

brush one's teeth 歯を磨く

false teeth 入れ歯

have good (=straight) teeth
歯並びがよい

wisdom teeth 親知らず

toothache *n.* 歯痛, 歯の痛み

toothbrush *n.* 歯ブラシ

toothpaste *n.* 歯磨き

top[1]

1 *n.* HIGHEST PART: 一番上, 最上部, (peak, zenith) 頂上, てっぺん

tools 大工道具

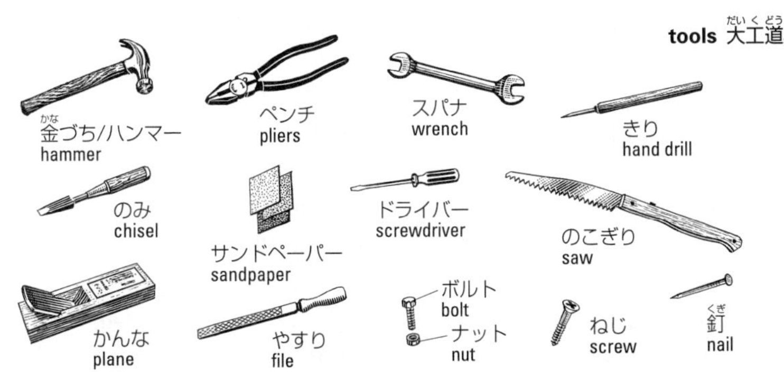

2 ***adj.*** **UPPERMOST:** 一番上の, 最も高い

3 ***n.*** **COVER:** ふた, 栓

4 ***adj.*** **MAXIMUM:** 最高の, 最大の

5 ***adj.*** **IN RANK:** 上位の, 首位の, トップの

6 ***adj.*** **MOST IMPORTANT:** 最優先の

7 ***v.*** **SURPASS:** 超える, 上回る

8 ***n.*** **CLOTHING:** (for upper body) 上の服

9 ***n.*** **PART OF A PLANT:** 葉(の部分), 葉っぱ

1 at the top of the stairs 階段の最上段

the top of the page ページの上段

He filled my glass to the top.
彼はグラスいっぱいについでくれた。

The top of the mountain was covered in clouds.
山の頂上は雲でおおわれていた。

2 It's in the top drawer.
一番上の引き出しに入っています。

We live on the top floor.
私たちは最上階に住んでいます。

3 Where's the top to this bottle?
このびんのふたはどこ?

Take the top off and see what's inside.
ふたを取って、中身を見て。

4 What's its top speed?
最高速度はどのくらいですか?

5 the top twenty albums
上位20枚のアルバム

the top people in the company
企業のトップ [首脳陣]

the top prize トップ賞

6 The environment is the top item on the agenda.
環境問題が最優先の議題です。

7 Can you top that?
あれを超えられる?

8 That's a nice top you're wearing.
その上の服、すてきですね。

9 Now remove the carrot tops.
では、人参の葉っぱの部分を切り落としてください。

be on top of (be in control of) 把握している

He's on top of things now.
彼は今や事情をすべて把握している。

be over the top (extreme) 度が過ぎている, (exaggerated) おおげさだ

Her reaction was over the top.
彼女の反応はおおげさだった。

from top to bottom 上から下まで, (thoroughly) すっかり, 徹底的に

The company has been reorganized from top to bottom.
その企業は、上から下まで組織が再編された。

off the top of one's head ふと思い浮かんだだけで, (instantly) 即座には, すぐには

It was right off the top of my head.
それが、ふと頭に浮かんだだけです。

Off the top of my head, I don't really know.
すぐには、わからない。

top² ***n.*** (toy) こま

topaz ***n.*** トパーズ

topcoat ***n.*** (coat) コート, オーバー; (finish) 上塗り

topic ***n.*** トピック, 話題

topical ***adj.*** 話題になっている, 時事的な

topical news 時事ニュース

topless ***adj.*** (bare-breasted) トップレスの

topnotch ***adj.*** 最高の, 一流の

T

topography *n.* (shape of land) 地形

topple *v.* (cause to fall) 倒す, (fall down/over) 倒れる

Torah *n.* モーセの五書

torch *n.* (flaming stick) たいまつ, (metal-cutting torch) トーチ, トーチランプ [→ FLASHLIGHT]

torment *n.* 苦痛, 苦悩
v. 苦しめる, 悩ませる

tornado *n.* 竜巻, トルネード

torpedo *n.* 魚雷
v. 魚雷で攻撃する

torque *n.* トルク, 回転力

torrent *n.* 急流

Torrid Zone *n.* 熱帯

torso *n.* (part of the body) 胴, (statue) トルソー

tortoise *n.* カメ, 亀

torture *n.* (mental/physical pain) 苦痛, (physical pain as punishment) 拷問
v. ひどく苦しめる, (inflict pain on as punishment) 拷問する

toss *v.* 投げる, ほうり上げる

total

1 *n.* TOTAL AMOUNT: 合計, 全部, 総計

2 *v.* ADD UP: 合計する

3 *adj.* UTTER: 完全な, 全くの

4 *adj.* ENTIRE: 全部の, 統計の

1 The total comes to ¥15,250.
合計　１５,２５０　円になります。

I borrowed a total of ten books from the library.
図書館から全部で10冊、本を借りた。

2 What does it total up to?
合計するといくつになりますか？

You'll need a calculator to total it up.
合計するのに電卓が必要でしょう。

3 a total waste of time 全くの時間のむだ

It was a total success [failure].
大成功 [失敗] だった。

4 The total workforce only amounted to ten.
全従業員を合わせても10人しかいなかった。

What's the total cost?
総費用はいくらですか？

in total 全部で, 総計で

In total, there were representatives from over eighty nations present.
全部で 80 カ国以上の代表が、出席していた。

totalitarian *adj.* 全体主義の

a totalitarian regime 全体主義体制

♦**totalitarianism** *n.* 全体主義

totally *adv.* (used emphatically) 全く, すっかり, 完全に

totem *n.* トーテム

touch

1 *v.* PUT HAND ON: (…に) 触る, 触れる

2 *v.* COME/BE IN CONTACT WITH: (…に) 接触する, 触れる

3 *n.* ACT OF TOUCHING: 触れること

4 *n.* FEEL: 手触り

5 *n.* ONE OF THE FIVE SENSES: 触覚

6 *v.* STIR THE EMOTIONS OF: (**be touched by**) …に感動する

7 *v.* MENTION: (**touch on**) …に触れる

8 *v.* NOT DEAL WITH: (**not touch**) かかわらない

9 *n.* SMALL AMOUNT: (**a touch of**) 少量の…, (=tinge) …ぎみ, …めいたもの

1 It was too hot to touch.
熱すぎて触れなかった。

That man tried to touch me.
あの男が私に触ろうとしました。

Don't touch anything till the police arrive.
警察が来るまで一切、手を触れないように。

2 The refrigerator shouldn't be touching the wall.
冷蔵庫は壁に接触してはいけない。

Our knees were touching.
私たちのひざが触れ合った。

3 I felt his touch.
彼が触れたのを感じました。

It works with the touch of a button.
ボタンに触れると作動します。

4 the touch of silk シルクの手触り

5 the sense of touch 触覚

6 I was touched by the final scene of the movie.
映画のラストシーンに感動しました。

7 Did he touch on the problem of insurance?
彼は保険の問題に触れましたか？

8 I wouldn't touch it with a ten-foot pole.
私なら、その件には一切かかわらない。

9 a touch of salt 少量の塩

a touch of irony 皮肉めいたもの

be/keep in touch (with) (…と) 連絡を取り合っている, (お)付き合いをしている

Are you still in touch with Professor Suzuki?
鈴木先生とは今でも連絡を取り合っていますか？

I intend to keep in touch with them, even after the move.
引っ越した後も、あの人たちとはお付き合いをしていくつもりです。

be out of touch (with the times) (時代の) 事情にうとい, (時代に) 遅れている

be touch and go (be very close/undecided) ぎりぎりだ, きわどい

get in touch (with) (…と) 連絡を取る

I've been trying to get in touch with you all day.
一日中、連絡を取ろうとしていたんです。

keep in touch (with) (…と) 連絡を取り合う

lose touch (with) (…と) 連絡がとだえる, 疎遠になる

We lost touch with them about five years ago.
5年ほど前から彼らと連絡がとだえてしまった。

wouldn't touch with a ten-foot pole (…に) かかわりたくない [→ 8]

touching ***adj.*** (stirring the emotions) 感動的な

touchy ***adj.*** (easily upset) すぐ気にする

tough ***adj.*** (of meat) かたい, かみ切れない, (durable) 丈夫な, 頑丈な, (able to endure hardship) タフな, (difficult) 難しい, (of time, experience) きつい, つらい

This meat is tough.
この肉はかたい。

This leather is tough and will resist wear and tear.
この革は丈夫なので、磨耗に強いです。

That's a tough question.
それは難しい質問だ。

toughen ***v.*** (make stricter) 厳しくする,

強化する

toupee ***n.*** (wig) かつら, (hairpiece) ヘアピース

tour ***n.*** (brief visit) ツアー, 観光旅行, 旅, (round of official visits) 視察, 見学
v. 旅行する

He went on a tour of Asian capitals.
彼はアジアの首都巡りの旅に出かけた。

♦**tour guide** ***n.*** 添乗員, 観光ガイド

tourism ***n.*** (business) 観光事業

tourist ***n.*** 観光客, 旅行者

♦**tourist route** ***n.*** 観光コース, 観光ルート

touristy ***adj.*** (popular among tourists) 観光客に人気のある

tournament ***n.*** トーナメント

the spring sumo tournament
相撲の春場所

tourniquet ***n.*** 止血帯

tow ***v.*** (car) レッカー移動する, (boat) 曳航する

I got my car towed away for parking it illegally.
違法駐車したから、車をレッカー移動された。

toward ***prep.***

1 IN THE DIRECTION OF: …の方へ/に/を
2 WITH THE GOAL OF ACHIEVING: …に向けて, …のために
3 CLOSE TO (A TIME): …近くに
4 CLOSE TO (A PLACE): …の方に
5 AS REGARDS: …に対して, …に対する

1 He pointed toward the park.
公園の方を指さした。

I glanced toward the exit.
出口の方に目をやった。

2 We're working toward a compromise.
我々は和解へ向けて努力している。

3 Toward evening, it starts to get cold.
夕方近くには、冷えてきます。

4 I would prefer to sit toward the back.
後ろの方に座りたいんです。

5 Attitudes toward religion have changed.
宗教に対する見方が変わりました。

towel ***n.*** タオル [NOTE: お絞り are the small, damp towels offered to customers in Japanese restaurants.]

tower ***n.*** タワー, 塔

Tokyo Tower 東京タワー

town ***n.*** 町, (big town) 都会, (main commercial center) 中心地

It's a small country town.
そこは小さな田舎町です。

It's the best restaurant in town.
そのお店は町で一番のレストランです。

How far out of town is it?
そこは町からどのくらい離れていますか？

Will you be in town next week?
来週は、こちらにいらっしゃいますか？

♦**town hall** ***n.*** (municipal office) 市役所

town-planning ***n.*** 都市計画

toxic ***adj.*** 有毒な

toxic waste 有毒廃棄物

toy ***n.*** おもちゃ

play with toys おもちゃで遊ぶ

trace ***v.*** (copy) なぞる, トレースする, (draw: line etc.) かく; (of police: follow: criminal) 追跡する, (discover) 見つけ出す, (ascertain) 突き止める, (**trace back**: one's way, ancestry) たどる
n. (mark, sign) 跡, 足跡, 痕跡, (vestige)

なごり; (**a trace of**: a small amount of) ほんのわずかの

We traced our way back to find the glove I'd dropped.
落とした手袋を見つけるために、私たちは来た道をたどった。

They could find no trace of her.
彼女の足跡をたどることはできなかった。

There were traces of arsenic in the water.
その水にはヒ素の痕跡があった。

trace a (phone) call 逆探知する

without a trace 跡かたもなく

He disappeared without a trace.
彼は跡かたもなく姿を消した。

trachea ***n.*** 気管

track

1 ***n.*** PATH: 道, 小道

2 ***n.*** USED FOR RACING: トラック

3 ***n.*** TRAIN TRACK: (**tracks**) 線路

4 ***n.*** MARK: 跡, (**tracks**) (=footprints) 足跡, (=tire tracks) タイヤの跡

5 ***n.*** RECORDED PIECE: 曲

6 ***v.*** FOLLOW: 追う, (using radar) (…の) 動きを追跡する [→ TRACK DOWN]

7 → TRACK AND FIELD

1 If we follow this track, it may lead us to the river.
この道をたどって行けば、川に出るかもしれない。

2 All the athletes gathered at the track.
選手が全員トラックに集まった。

3 The train was delayed because of damage to the tracks.
線路の破損により、電車は遅れた。

4 These are strange tracks.
奇妙な足跡だ。

5 How many tracks are on the CD?
そのＣＤには何曲入ってますか？

6 It was easy tracking the prisoner in the snow.
雪の中で囚人を追うのは簡単だった。

be on the right track 正しい方向に向かっている

I think we're on the right track now to solving the problem.
問題解決に向けて、正しい方向に向かっていると思います。

keep track of (follow) 絶えず追う, (be aware of: time) (常に) 意識する

Trying to keep track of an animal's movements is not easy.
動物の動きを絶えず追うのは、容易ではありません。

Please keep track of the time.
時間の経過を(常に)意識してください。

lose track of 忘れる, わからなくなる

We quickly lost track of the time.
時間がたつのをすぐに忘れてしまった。

♦**track down** ***v.*** 見つけ出す, 捜し出す

The police are trying to track down the suspect.
警察は容疑者を見つけようとしている。

track and field ***n.*** 陸上競技

track event ***n.*** トラック競技

track record ***n.*** 実績, 業績

tracksuit ***n.*** トラックスーツ, トレーニングウェア

traction ***n.*** (pulling action) けん引, (of shoes: grip) 静止摩擦

These shoes have good traction.
この靴は滑らない。

tractor ***n.*** トラクター

trade *n.* (buying/selling of goods) 商売, 取引, 商業, (between countries) 貿易; (occupation) 職業
v. (exchange) 交換する, (trade A for B) (AをBと) 取り替える
a trade balance 貿易収支

♦**trade in** *v.* 下取りに出す
I traded in my old car for a new one.
古い車を下取りに出して新車を買った。

trader *n.* 商人, 貿易商

trade-in *n.* (transaction) 下取り, (thing traded in) 下取り品

trademark *n.* 商標, トレードマーク

trade union *n.* 労働組合

trading *n.* (international) 貿易 [→ TRADE]

♦**trading company** *n.* 商社, 貿易会社

tradition *n.* 伝統, 習わし, しきたり
The people here certainly value their traditions.
ここの人たちは、確かに伝統を重んじていますね。

traditional *adj.* 伝統的な

♦**traditionally** *adv.* 伝統的に

traffic *n.* 交通, 通行, 往来
one-way traffic 一方通行
The traffic never stops.
車の往来はやむことがない。

♦**traffic accident** *n.* 交通事故

traffic jam *n.* 交通渋滞

traffic light *n.* 信号

tragedy *n.* 悲劇, (disaster) 惨事, 災難
Shakespeare's tragedies
シェークスピア作の悲劇
It was a tragedy what happened.
それは確かに悲劇だった。
It was the worst tragedy in the airline's history.
その航空会社の歴史上、最悪の惨事だった。

tragic *adj.* 悲惨な, 痛ましい, 悲劇的な
a tragic mistake 悲惨な誤り

trail

1 *n.* PATH: 道, 小道, (made by animal) 獣道

2 *n.* SERIES OF MARKS: 足跡

3 *n.* SUCCESSIVE NUMBER OF THINGS: (**a trail of**) 次々に, あちこちに

4 *v.* FOLLOW: 追跡する, (...の) 跡をつける, (of detective) 尾行する, (tracks) (...の) 足跡をたどる, (scent) (...の) 臭跡を追う

5 *v.* FLUTTER: (trail in the wind) なびく

6 *v.* OF PLANT: はう

1 a forest trail 森の小道
a mountain trail 山道

2 follow a trail 足跡をたどる
Where does this trail lead?
この足跡はどこに通じているんですか？

3 The tornado left a trail of destruction.
竜巻は次々に破壊していった。

4 We're being trailed.
私たちは跡をつけられている。

5 Her hair was trailing in the wind.
彼女の髪は風になびいていた。

6 The ivy trailed up the wall.
ツタは壁をはっていた。

trailer *n.* トレーラー, (trailer house) トレーラーハウス

♦**trailer park** *n.* トレーラーハウス用駐車場

train

1 *n.* LOCOMOTIVE: 電車, (for long journey) 列車, (steam engine) 汽車

2 *v.* **TEACH:** (person) 教育する, (animal) 調教する

3 *v.* **PRACTICE:** 訓練する, 練習する, トレーニングする

1 When does the train leave, and from what platform?
その電車はいつ、何番線から発車しますか？

Are you going to catch a train to work?
仕事場まで電車に乗って行くの？

(*announcement*) "The train will be departing shortly."
「まもなく(電車は)発車いたします」

2 Who is going to train these new recruits?
誰がこの新入社員を教育するんですか？

I don't believe lions can be trained.
ライオンを調教できるとは思えない。

3 He's training for the Olympics.
彼はオリンピックに向けてトレーニングしている。

train of thought 考えの脈絡

I lost my train of thought.
考えの脈絡を失った。

♦ **train fare** *n.* (鉄道)運賃, ((*informal*)) 電車賃[代]

TYPES OF TRAINS

a local train 普通電車, 各駅停車
an express train 急行(電車)
a semiexpress 準急
a limited express 特急電車
a rapid-service train 快速電車
a special rapid 特別快速, 特快
a freight train 貨物列車

trained *adj.* (qualified) 訓練を受けた

a trained physician 訓練を積んだ医師

trainee *n.* 訓練生

trainer *n.* (of athlete) トレーナー, (of animal) 調教師

training *n.* (athletic) トレーニング, 訓練, (in-service) 研修

trait *n.* 特性, 特徴, (in genetics) 形質

a genetic trait 遺伝形質

traitor *n.* (against government) 反逆者, (against friends) 裏切者

tram *n.* 路面電車, ((*informal*)) チンチン電車

tramp *n.* (vagrant) 放浪者, 宿なし

trample *v.* 踏みつける

trampoline *n.* トランポリン

trance *n.* 催眠状態

put someone into a trance
催眠術にかける

tranquil *adj.* 静かな, 平穏な

tranquilize *v.* 静める, 落ち着かせる

tranquilizer *n.* 精神安定剤, 鎮静剤

transact *v.* 取り引きする

transaction *n.* (act of buying/selling) 取引, (**transaction of business**) 事務処理

transcend *v.* 越える, (…に)勝る

transcribe *v.* 書き写す

transcript *n.* (copy) コピー, 写し, (proof of academic qualifications) 成績証明書

transfer *v.* 移る, (from one bus/train to another) 乗り換える, (from one office to another) 転任する, 転勤する, (from one team to another) 移籍する, (to another school) 転校する, (money) 振り込む

He's been transferred to the Osaka office.
彼は大阪支社に転勤させられました。

KANJI BRIDGE

転 ON: てん KUN: ころ(がる/げる/がす/ぶ) | CHANGE, TRANSFER

be transferred .... 転入する
change houses .... 転居する
change jobs .... 転職する
change schools .... 転校する
convert .... 転換する
forward mail .... 転送する
relocate .... 移転する
transfer to another office 転任/転勤する
turning point .... 転機

transference ***n.*** (moving of things) 移動, 移転

transform ***v.*** (change) 変える

transformation ***n.*** 変化

transformer ***n.*** トランス, 変圧器

transfusion ***n.*** (blood transfusion) 輸血

transient ***adj.*** (impermanent) 一時的な, つかのまの, はかない

transistor ***n.*** トランジスター, (transistor radio) トランジスターラジオ

transit ***n.*** (passing through) 通過, (shipping) 輸送

a transit lounge
通過 [トランジット]ラウンジ

in transit 輸送中(の)

luggage in transit 輸送中の手荷物

transition ***n.*** (change) 変化, (of season) 移り変わり, (from one stage/phase to another) 変わり目, 過渡期

in transition 過渡期に

make the transition to …に移行する

transitional ***adj.*** 移行する

a transitional period 移行期間[過渡期]

transitive ***adj.*** (**transitive verb**) 他動詞

transitory ***adj.*** (impermanent) 一時的な, つかのまの, はかない

translate ***v.*** 訳す, 翻訳する

Could you translate this for me, please?
これを訳してもらえますか？

It's a classic that's been translated into many languages.
それは、いろいろな言語に翻訳されている名著です。

translation ***n.*** 翻訳, (business) 翻訳業

in translation 翻訳で

read (a book) in translation 翻訳で読む

translator ***n.*** (of particular text) 翻訳者, (professional) 翻訳家

translucent ***adj.*** (partially transparent) 半透明の

transmission ***n.*** (sending) 伝達, (of disease) 伝染; (in car) トランスミッション, 変速機

transmit ***v.*** 送る, (disease) うつす, 伝染させる, (information, knowledge) 伝える

transmitter ***n.*** (machine) 送信機

transparency ***n.*** (quality of being transparent) 透明(度); (slide) スライド

transparent ***adj.*** 透明な, 透き通った

transplant ***v.*** 移植する

n. (operation) 移植

have a heart transplant
心臓移植を受ける

transport ***v.*** 輸送する, 運送する

n. 輸送, 運送

The goods are now ready for transport.
品物は輸送の準備ができました。

T

transportation *n.* (moving of goods) 輸送, 運送, (public transportation system) 交通機関, (means of transport) 交通手段

transsexual *n.* 性転換した人

transverse *adj.* 横の

trap *n.* ((*also figurative*)) わな
v. (animal) わなで捕らえる, (person: deceive) だます, (**feel trapped**) がんじがらめにされていると感じる
set a trap わなを仕掛ける
They felt trapped by the system.
彼らは制度にがんじがらめにされているように感じた。

trapezoid *n.* 台形

trash *n.* ごみ, くず, がらくた

trauma *n.* トラウマ

traumatic *adj.* (of experience) トラウマになるような, 心の傷となる

travel *v.* 旅行する, 旅をする, (travel to) (…に) 行く, (=commute) 通勤する, 通う
n. (act of traveling, activity) 旅行, 旅, (travel industry) 旅行業
He has travelled all over the world.
あの人は世界中を旅している。
I travel to work by car.
車で通勤しています。
air travel 飛行機の旅
space travel 宇宙旅行

♦ **travel agency** *n.* 旅行会社, 旅行代理店
travel expenses *n.* (for business trip) 出張旅費

traveler *n.* 旅行者

♦ **traveler's check** *n.* トラベラーズチェック

traveling *n.* 旅行

travesty *n.* (of justice) 曲解

trawl *v.* (search: through a large volume of information) くまなく探す; (catch fish using a large net) トロール漁業をする
n. (search) 探査, 捜査; (net) トロール網

trawler *n.* トロール船

tray *n.* (for food) (お)盆, トレー, (for paper) 書類入れ

treacherous *adj.* (disloyal) 裏切りの, (dangerous) 危険な
a treacherous mountain path
危険な山道

treachery *n.* 裏切り, 背信

tread *v.* (walk) 歩く
tread water 立ち泳ぎする

treadmill *n.* (for running) トレッドミル, ランニングマシーン
run on a treadmill トレッドミルで走る

treason *n.* 反逆罪
commit treason 反逆罪を犯す
high treason 大逆罪

treasure *n.* (store of valuables) 財宝, (highly valued item) 宝, 宝物
v. 宝物のように大切にする, 大事にする
a treasure chest 宝石箱
It's a memory that I shall treasure.
大切な思い出です。

treasurer *n.* (in company) 経理部長, (in association, organization) 会計係

Treasury *n.* (in the U.S.) 財務省, (in the U.K.) 大蔵省

treat

1 *v.* BEHAVE IN A CERTAIN WAY TOWARD: 扱う

2 *v.* GIVE MEDICAL CARE TO: 治療する, (…の) 手当てをする

3 *v.* **CONSIDER:** (treat A as B) (AをBと) みなす

4 *v.* **DEAL WITH:** 扱う

5 *v.* **PUT THROUGH A PROCESS:** 処理する

6 *n.* **THING THAT GIVES PLEASURE:** (food that has been paid for) おごり, (form of fun) 楽しみ, (reward) (ご)ほうび

7 *v.* **PAY:** (treat A to B) (AにBを) おごる, ごちそうする

1 She was badly treated.
彼女は不当な扱いを受けた。

They treated me like a king.
私を王様のようにもてなしてくれました。

I was treated very well by my host family.
ホストファミリーにとてもよくしてもらった。

2 He's being treated for shock.
ショックのため、彼は治療を受けている。

Your injury needs to be treated.
その傷は手当てが必要だ。

3 They seem to be treating the whole matter as a joke.
この問題を冗談とみなしているようだ。

4 They say they'll treat the matter as confidential.
先方は、この問題を内密に扱うと言っています。

These expenses can be treated as tax deductible.
この支出は控除の対象になります。

5 Sewage needs to be treated before it is discharged into the sea.
下水は、海に排出する前に適切な処理をしなければなりません。

6 No, no. This is my treat.
いえいえ、ここは私のおごりです。

It was a real treat to go to the theater.
劇場に行くことができて本当に楽しかった。

7 Mr. Sato treated me to lunch.
佐藤さんはお昼をおごってくれました。

I treated the kids to ice-cream.
子供たちにアイスをごちそうした。

treatment *n.* 扱い, 待遇, (medical) 治療, 手当て, (for hair) トリートメント

treaty *n.* 協定, 条約

The government has signed a new treaty with South Korea.
政府は韓国と新しい協定を結んだ。

treble *adj.* (triple) 3倍の, 3重の
n. (highest sound) 最高音部, ソプラノ

♦**treble clef** *n.* ト音記号

tree *n.* 木

trek *n., v.* トレッキング(する)

tremble *v.* (of hand, body) 震える

tremendous *adj.* ものすごい, 大変な, (extremely good) とてもすばらしい

There was a tremendous noise.
ものすごい音がした。

He has a tremendous advantage over the other player.
彼は相手選手よりかなり優勢だ。

It was a tremendous waste of time.
大変な時間のむだづかいだった。

tremor *n.* (earthquake) (地面の) 震動, (trembling) 震え

trench *n.* 溝, 堀, (**the trenches:** in war) ざんごう

dig a trench 溝を掘る

trench coat *n.* トレンチコート

trend *n.* 傾向, (fashion) 流行, はやり

follow a trend 流行を追う

trendy *adj.* はやりの, 流行の, おしゃれな

trespass *v.* 不法侵入する

(*sign*) No Trespassing 立入禁止

trial *n.* (court trial) 裁判; (test) 試験

adj. (experimental) 試験的な

Will the suspect be brought to trial?
容疑者は裁判にかけられるだろうか？

The man was put in prison without a trial.
その人は裁判を受けずに投獄された。

The initial trial of the new jet went very well.
新型ジェット機の１回目の試験飛行は、大成功に終わった。

be on trial (in court) 裁判にかけられている, 公判中だ

He is on trial for murder.
彼は殺人容疑で公判中だ。

trial and error 試行錯誤

triangle *n.* 三角形

triangular *adj.* 三角形の

tribe *n.* 部族, -族

tribunal *n.* 裁判所, 法廷

a military tribunal 軍事法廷

tributary *n.* 支流

tribute *n.* (sign of respect/gratitude) 敬意/感謝のしるし

pay (a) tribute to …に敬意を表す

trick

1 *n.* THING DONE TO DECEIVE: わな, 策略

2 *v.* DECEIVE: ごまかす, だます

3 *adj.* DECEPTIVE: トリックの, (of question) 落とし穴のある

4 *n.* FEAT OF SKILL: (knack) こつ, 秘訣, (magic trick) 手品

1 It was a trick to divert my attention while his accomplice stole my wallet.
連中の仲間が私の財布をとる間、注意をそらすためのわなだった。

2 They tricked us into believing it was a solid investment.
だまされて、手堅い投資だと信じ込まされたんです。

3 trick photography トリック写真
a trick question 落とし穴のある問題

4 There's a trick to opening this door.
このドアをあけるには、こつがあるんだ。

That was a good trick he did with the rabbit coming out of the hat.
帽子からウサギを出す手品は、みごとだったね。

play a trick on …にいたずらをする

trickle *v.* (of water) したたる, (**trickle in**) (of people) 少しずつ来る, (of information) 徐々に伝わる

tricky *adj.* (difficult) 難しい; (sly) ずるい

tricycle *n.* 三輪車

trifling *adj.* くだらない, つまらない

trigger *n.* 引き金

v. 引き起こす, (…の) 引き金になる

pull the trigger 引き金を引く

The earthquake triggered a tsunami.
地震は津波を引き起こした。

trigonometry *n.* 三角法

trillion *n.* １兆

trilogy *n.* 三部作

trim *v.* (hedge) (…の) 手入れをする, (…を) 刈り込む, (hair) 少し切る

n. (haircut) カット

It's time I trimmed the hedge.
そろそろ生け垣の手入れをしなければ。

I'd like a trim, please.
カットをお願いします。

♦**trimmings** ***n.*** (decorations) 飾り, 装飾; (of bush) 刈り取った物

trimester ***n.*** (three months) 3カ月間, (one of three terms) 3学期制の1学期

a trimester system 3学期制

trinket ***n.*** 小さなアクセサリー; (trivial thing) つまらない物

trio ***n.*** トリオ

trip ***n.*** (journey) 旅行, 旅, (business trip) 出張; (act of stumbling) つまずき

v. (fall, stumble) つまずく, (cause to fall, stumble) つまずかせる

It was on that trip that I met my wife.
妻に出会ったのは、その旅の途中でした。

How was your trip to Chicago?
シカゴ旅行はどうでした？

He's on a business trip to Australia.
彼はオーストラリアに出張中です。

The mailman took a nasty trip as he was coming down the steps.
郵便屋さんは階段を下りている時に、ひどくつまずいた。

I tripped on the step and fell over.
段差につまずき、転んでしまった。

The waiter tripped over your purse.
ウェーターがあなたのハンドバッグにつまずいたよ。

♦**trip up** ***v.*** (cause to make an error: of problem) 間違わせる, 引っかける

tripe ***n.*** (cow's stomach) 牛の胃

triple ***n., adj.*** 3倍(の), 3重(の)

v. (make/become three times as much) 3倍にする/なる

♦**triple jump** ***n.*** 3段跳び

triple play ***n.*** (in baseball) トリプルプレー

triplet ***n.*** 三つ子の一人, (**triplets**) 三つ子

tripod ***n.*** 三脚

triumph ***v.*** 勝利を収める

n. 勝利

It was a triumph for democracy.
それは民主主義の勝利だった。

triumphant ***adj.*** (of smile etc.) 勝ち誇った [→ SUCCESSFUL]

trivia ***n.*** つまらないこと, ささいなこと

trivial ***adj.*** (insignificant) つまらない, ささいな

trolley ***n.*** (street car) 路面電車

trombone ***n.*** トロンボーン

troop ***n.*** (**troops**: soldiers) 軍隊

send troops 軍隊を派遣する

trooper ***n.*** (state police officer) 州警察官

trophy ***n.*** トロフィー

win a trophy トロフィーを獲得する

tropic ***n.*** (**the tropics**) 熱帯地方

♦**Tropic of Cancer** ***n.*** 北回帰線

Tropic of Capricorn ***n.*** 南回帰線

tropical ***adj.*** 熱帯の, トロピカルの

a tropical climate 熱帯気候

a tropical rainforest 熱帯雨林

tropical fish 熱帯魚

trot ***v.*** (of horse) 速足で駆ける, (of person: hurry) 小走りする, 足早に歩く

trotter ***n.*** (foot of pig) 豚の足

trouble

1 ***n.*** PROBLEM: 問題, (**troubles**: personal worries) 悩み, 心配事, (difficulty) 困難, (labor) 手間, 面倒, (**have no trouble...**) 難なく...

2 ***n.*** ILLNESS: 病気, 不調

3 ***n.*** NUISANCE: 迷惑

4 *n.* **CONFLICT:** (dispute, disagreement) もめごと, (commotion) 騒動

5 *v.* **INCONVENIENCE:** (…に) 迷惑をかける

6 *v.* **CAUSE DISTRESS TO:** 悩ます, (**trouble oneself**) 悩む, 心配する

1 The trouble with this city is the heavy traffic.
この街の問題は激しい交通量です。

His trouble is he drinks too much.
あの人の問題は酒を飲み過ぎることだ。

I thought all my troubles were over, but then this letter came.
問題は全部解決したと思っていたら、この手紙が来た。

If you're having any trouble, just tell me.
何か問題があったら、言ってください。

He's always going on about his troubles.
あの人はいつも自分の心配事を言ってばかりいる。

It'll save everyone a lot of trouble.
みんなの手間がずいぶん省けます。

Did you have any trouble finding your hotel?
ホテルは難なく見つかりましたか？

2 My teacher has heart trouble.
先生は心臓が悪い。

3 He stayed with us for a while and was no trouble at all.
彼はしばらくうちにいましたが、少しも迷惑ではありませんでした。

4 If there is trouble at the match, the police will be there to deal with it.
試合で騒動が起これば、警察が対処するでしょう。

5 I wouldn't want to trouble him.
彼に迷惑をかけたくありません。

6 This troubles me a great deal.
このことで、ずいぶん悩んでいます。

ask/look for trouble 自ら災難を招く

He's asking for trouble taking part in that demonstration.
彼はあんなデモに参加して、自ら災難を招こうとしている。

be in trouble (be subject to a scolding) しかられている, (**be in trouble with**: the police) ごたごたを起こしている; (in need of help) 困っている

He's in trouble again for being late.
あの人は遅刻して、またしかられている。

get into trouble 面倒を起こす

Now be a good boy and don't get into trouble.
面倒は起こさずに、おとなしくしているんだよ。

go to a lot of trouble 骨を折る, とても苦労する

I went to a lot of trouble for the company and got no thanks.
会社のためにとても苦労したのに、ありがとうの一言もなかった。

make trouble (cause a disturbance) 騒ぎを起こす

The hooligans are making trouble again.
フーリガンが、また騒ぎを起こしている。

put to a lot of trouble …に大変な迷惑をかける

I'm sorry I put you to a lot of trouble by not contacting you earlier.
早くご連絡しなかったため、大変ご迷惑をおかけしてしまい、申し訳ありませんでした。

take the trouble to do わざわざ…する

It was nice of him to take the trouble to help us with our move.
彼はわざわざ引っ越しの手伝いをしてくれた。

the trouble is 困ったことに…

The trouble is, he's always so unreliable.
困ったことに、あの人は全く当てにならない。

troubled ***adj.*** (distressed) 困った, (worried) 心配な, (of look) 心配そうな

troublemaker ***n.*** ごたごたを起こす人, 問題を起こす人

troublesome ***adj.*** 面倒な, 厄介な

trough ***n.*** 水桶, (feed box) えさ入れ

troupe ***n.*** 一座, 一団

trousers ***n.*** ズボン

wear trousers ズボンをはく

trout ***n.*** マス, 鱒

trowel ***n.*** (for gardening) 移植ごて, (for plastering) こて

truant ***n.*** 不登校児

adj. 無断欠席する

play truant 学校をサボる, ずる休みする

truce ***n.*** 休戦, 停戦

call a truce 休戦する

truck ***n.*** トラック

trudge ***v.*** のろのろ歩く, とぼとぼ歩く

true ***adj.*** (agreeing with fact) 本当の, 真実の, (genuine) 本物の, 真の

adv. (in fact) 確かに

It's a true story.
本当の話 [実話] です。

Is it true that you were there?
そこにいたというのは本当ですか？

He's a true artist.
彼は本物の芸術家です。

Mr. Tajima was a true friend who supported me throughout the ordeal.
田島さんは、苦しい時期にも私を支えてくれた真の友人でした。

True, he hasn't turned up yet, but I'm sure he will.
確かに彼はまだ来ていないけれど、きっと現れます。

come true 実現する

My dream of visiting Paris came true last year.
パリに行くという夢が、去年実現しました。

true to …のとおり, …らしく; (**be true to one's word**) 約束を守る

True to his nature, he skirted the issue of marriage.
いかにも彼らしく、結婚の問題には触れなかった。

Was she true to her word?
彼女は約束を守りましたか？

truffle ***n.*** トリュフ

truly ***adv.*** 本当に

trump ***n.*** 切り札

trumped-up ***adj.*** でっち上げられた

trumpet ***n.*** (instrument) トランペット; (noise made by elephant) 象の甲高い鳴き声

v. (of elephant) 甲高い鳴き声を上げる

play the trumpet トランペットを吹く

blow one's own trumpet ほらを吹く

trunk ***n.*** (large container) トランク, (main stem of tree) 幹, (nose of elephant) 象の鼻, (body) 胴体, (part of car) トランク [→ picture of CAR]

truss ***v.*** (tie up) きつく縛る

trust

1 *v.* BELIEVE IN OR HAVE CONFIDENCE IN: 信用する, 信頼する, 信じる

2 *n.* CONFIDENCE: 信頼, 信用

3 *v.* EXPECT: (**I trust...**) …と思う

4 *n.* RESPONSIBILITY: 責任

5 *n.* ARRANGEMENT FOR HANDLING MONEY: 信託

1 You can't trust politicians.
政治家は信用できない。

Everybody trusted him.
誰もが彼を信じていた。

Trust your own instincts.
直感を信じなさい。

I couldn't trust him to do the job properly.
彼にはその仕事を任せられなかった。

You can't trust him with a secret.
あの人には秘密を打ち明けてはだめだよ。(lit.,"You mustn't tell him secrets.")

2 I have trust in her.
彼女を信頼しています。

Trust is the foundation of human relations.
信頼は人間関係の基礎だ。

He put his trust in me, and I won't betray that trust.
彼は私を信じてくれているので、その信頼は裏切らない。

3 I trust you had an enjoyable evening.
きっと楽しい夜を過ごされたことと思います。

4 a position of trust 責任ある立場

5 a trust fund 信託資金

trustee *n.* 役員, 理事

trustworthy *adj.* 信頼できる

trusty *adj.* (reliable) 頼りになる, 当てになる

truth *n.* (that which is true) 本当のこと, 真実, (verity) 真理

He's probably telling the truth.
おそらく彼は本当のことを言っている。

Only one person knew the truth.
真実を知っていたのはたった一人でした。

a scientific truth 科学的事実

a universal truth 普遍の真理

in (all) truth 実は, 実のところ

In all truth, I thought she was dead.
実のところ彼女は死んだと思っていた。

moment of truth 正念場, 試練の時

to tell you the truth 実は, 実を言うと

To tell you the truth, I can't remember what I said.
実を言うと、何を言ったか思い出せないんだ。

truthful *adj.* (of person) 正直な, (of remark) 真実の, うそのない

try

1 *v.* MAKE AN ATTEMPT: (**try to do**) …しようとする, …しようと努める, (**try not to do**) …しないようにする, …しないように努める

2 *v.* DO IN ORDER TO LEARN: やってみる, してみる [→ TRY ON]

3 *v.* TEST: 試す, 試してみる

4 *v.* APPLY THE PROCESS OF LAW: (put on trial) 裁判にかける, (try a case) 審理する

5 *v.* STRAIN: (…に)負担をかける

6 *n.* ATTEMPT: 試し, やってみること

7 *n.* SCORE IN RUGBY: トライ

1 I tried to reach you, but you weren't in. ((*polite*)) ご連絡しようとしましたが、ご不在だったんです。

I was trying to get in through the back door, when the dog started barking. 裏口から入ろうとしていたら、犬がほえ始めた。

We tried time and time again, but the car wouldn't start. 何度もやってみたけれど、車は動かなかった。

She tried her best. 彼女は最善を尽くしました。

Don't try to fool me. ((*masculine*)) だまそうなんて思うな。

Try not to fall asleep. 寝ないようにね。

He tried not to lose his temper. 彼は怒らないようにした。

I tried hard not to show my disappointment. がっかりしていることを顔に出さないよう努めた。

2 Have you ever tried skiing? スキーをしたことはありますか？

Why not let him try, if he thinks he really wants to become a dancer? 彼が本当にダンサーになりたいと思っているなら、やらせてあげましょうよ。

Try this fish—it's delicious! この魚を食べてみて——おいしいよ。

I like trying new foods. 新しい食べ物を試食するのが好きです。

3 I tried the battery again. もう一度バッテリーを試した。

Try it to see if it works. 使えるかどうか試してみて。

4 The suspect was tried and convicted. 容疑者は裁判にかけられ、有罪判決を受けた。

The man will be tried in Germany. その男はドイツで裁判にかけられます。

Which judge will try the case? その事件を審理するのは、どの判事ですか？

5 He tries my patience. 彼は私をいらいらさせる。

6 Give this (phone) number a try. この電話番号にかけてみて。

Here—have a try. さあ——やってみて。

try on *v.* (clothes) 着てみる, 試着する

Can I try these on, please? これを試着してもいいですか？

I tried the pants on, but they were too small. ズボンを試着してみたけど、小さすぎた。

try out *v.* (test) 試す, 試してみる; (try out for: audition for) (…の) オーディションを受ける

---

trying *adj.* (tough) つらい, (hard) 苦しい

tsar *n.* 皇帝

T-shirt *n.* Tシャツ

tsunami *n.* (seismic ocean wave) 津波

tub *n.* (bathtub) 湯船, 浴槽, (for washing clothes) 桶, たらい

tube *n.* (hollow cylinder) 筒, 管, -管, (containing paste) チューブ; **(the tube)** (= the underground) 地下鉄, (=TV) テレビ

a tube of toothpaste 歯磨きチューブ

♦**tubing** *n.* 管, -管

T

glass tubing ガラス管

tuberculosis ***n.*** 結核

tuck ***v.*** (**tuck in**) (…の端を) 入れる, (**tuck away**) しまい込む, (conceal) 隠す

Tuck your shirt in, will you.
シャツのすそを入れなさいよ。

Tuck the sheets in.
シーツの端をたくし込んでください。

He tucked the money under a floorboard.
彼は床下にお金を隠した。

♦ **tuck in** ***v.*** (child) 布団でくるむ

Tuesday ***n.*** 火曜日

tuft ***n.*** (of hair) 房

tug ***v.*** (pull) ぐいと引っ張る

tugboat ***n.*** タグボート

tug-of-war ***n.*** ((*also figurative*)) 綱引き

play tug-of-war 綱引きをする

tuition ***n.*** (fee for education) 授業料, (instruction) 授業

a tuition fee 授業料

tulip ***n.*** チューリップ

tumble ***v.*** (fall) 転ぶ, 転げ落ちる

tumbler ***n.*** (glass) タンブラー

tummy ***n.*** おなか

tumor ***n.*** 腫瘍

tumultuous ***adj.*** (of events) 騒がしい, 騒然とした

tuna ***n.*** マグロ, 鮪, (canned tuna) ツナ

tundra ***n.*** ツンドラ

tune ***n.*** (melody) 曲, メロディー

v. (machine) チューニングする, (piano) 調律する

That's a lovely tune.
きれいなメロディーですね。

It's one of my favorite tunes.
私の大好きな曲の一つです。

The piano needs to be tuned.
ピアノは調律する必要がある。

♦ **tune in** ***v.*** (to TV program) (…に) チャンネルを合わせる

tune out ***v.*** (stop listening) 耳を貸さない

tuner ***n.*** (machine) チューナー

tungsten ***n.*** タングステン

tunic ***n.*** チュニック

tunnel ***n.*** トンネル

v. (…に) トンネルを掘る

the Channel Tunnel 英仏海峡トンネル

build a tunnel トンネルを掘る

♦ **tunnel vision** ***n.*** 視野狭窄症

Tupperware ***n.*** タッパー(ウェア)

a Tupperware container タッパー

turban ***n.*** ターバン

turbine ***n.*** タービン

turbojet ***n.*** ターボジェットエンジン

turbulence ***n.*** (air turbulence) 乱気流, (political turbulence) 混乱

turbulent ***adj.*** (of events) 騒がしい, 激動の

turf ***n.*** 芝生; (territory) 縄張り

turkey ***n.*** (bird) 七面鳥, ターキー; (very bad movie) 失敗作

a turkey dinner 七面鳥の食事

turmoil ***n.*** (confusion) 混乱, (commotion, stir) 騒ぎ

turn

1 ***v.*** **MOVE BODY/HEAD:** 向く, 向きを変える, (**turn around**) 振り向く, 振り返る, (**turn toward**) …の方を向く

2 *v.* **CHANGE THE POSITION OF:** (so as to be facing a different direction) (…の) 向きを変える

3 *v.* **ROTATE:** 回る, (cause to rotate) 回す [→ TURN DOWN, TURN UP]

4 *v.* **CHANGE DIRECTION:** 曲がる, 曲がって行く, 向きを変える, (**turn back**) 引き返す

5 *v.* **FLIP:** (page) めくる, (pancake) ひっくり返す, (**turn to**: specific page) 開く

6 *v.* **BECOME:** ("turn"+adjective) <い-adj. stem> + くなる, <な-adj. stem> + になる

7 *n.* **SHIFT OF DIRECTION:** (**right turn**) 右折, (**left turn**) 左折, (in swimming) ターン, 折り返し

8 *n.* **OCCASION FOR DOING:** 番

9 *n.* **BEND IN ROAD:** 曲がり角, カーブ

1 He turned to me and started telling me off.
彼は私の方を向くと、小言を言い始めた。

She turned to look the other way.
彼女は反対の方を見ようと、向きを変えた。

They kept turning around and staring at us.
彼らは何度も振り返っては、私たちを見つめていた。

The kids turned around to wave good-bye.
子供たちは振り返って手を振った。

2 Let's turn the table around so it faces the door.
テーブルの向きを変えて、ドアの方に向くようにしましょう。

Turn the box on its side.
箱を横向けにして。

3 The baggage carousel continued to turn, though it was practically empty.
ほとんど何ものっていないのに、手荷物のベルトコンベヤーは回り続けていた。

I can't seem to turn this key.
このかぎを、なかなか回せない。

Today we turn our clocks forward an hour.
今日は時計を1時間早めます。

4 The river turns here.
川はここで曲がります。

Turn left here, then right at the next corner.
ここで左折して、次の角で右折してください。

We turned onto the main street.
大通りに入った。

5 I turned the page and carried on reading.
ページをめくって、読み続けた。

Turn to page 52.
52ページを開いて。

6 Her face turned red from embarrassment.
きまりが悪くて彼女の顔は赤くなった。

The weather turned cloudy again.
天気はまた曇った。

7 Was I supposed to take a right turn or a left turn back there?
さっきは右か左か、どっちに曲がるはずだったの?

8 It's your turn to drive now.
今度はあなたが運転する番だ。

It was my turn to look after the kids.
私が子供の面倒を見る番でした。

9 a sharp turn 急カーブ

in turn(s) 順番に, 交替で

We ate in turns because we only had two chairs.
椅子が二つしかなかったので、交替で食

べた。

out of turn 順番を間違えて

You're out of turn. He goes before you.
順番を間違えてるよ。彼のほうが先だよ。

take a turn for the better 好転する, よくなる

take a turn for the worse 悪化する, 悪くなる

take turns doing 交替で…する

Let's take turns washing the dishes.
交替で皿洗いをしよう。

turn one's back on → BACK

twists and turns 紆余曲折

Life is full of twists and turns.
人生は紆余曲折でいっぱいだ。

turn away *v.* (send away) 断る; (look away) 目をそむける

We were so busy, we had to turn away customers.
あまりに忙しくて、お客様をお断りしなければならなかった。

turn back *v.* (reverse direction) 引き返す, (drive back: people) 追い返す; (clock) 遅らせる

The weather was so bad, we had to turn back.
天気があまりにも悪かったので、引き返さざるを得なかった。

The refugees were turned back at the border.
難民は国境で追い返された。

The clocks are turned back one hour in winter.
冬になると、時計を1時間遅らせます。

turn down *v.* (volume) (…の) 音を下げる, 音を小さくする, (heat) 弱くする; (refuse) 断る

Could you turn the TV down a bit?
テレビの音をちょっと小さくしてもらえますか?

Turn the gas down to low.
(火を) 弱火にしてください。

The company turned down our offer.
先方は私たちの申し出を断った。

turn in *v.* (hand in) 提出する, (**turn oneself in**: to police) 自首する; (go to bed) ベッドに入る, 寝る

turn into *v.* (become) …になる

He turned into a very mature young man.
彼はとてもしっかりした青年になった。

turn off *v.* (switch off) 消す; (cause to be uninterested in) うんざりさせる

Would the last person out please turn off the lights and lock up.
最後に出る人は、電気を消して戸締まりをしてください。

That kind of behavior really turns me off.
ああいう行動には、本当にうんざりする。

turn on *v.* (switch on) つける; (sexually arouse) 興奮させる

It's a bit dark. Would you turn on the light, please?
ちょっと暗いですね。電気をつけてもらえますか?

whatever turns you on お好きなように

turn out *v.*

1 SPEAKING OF RESULT: …になる

2 SWITCH OFF: 消す

3 OF CROWDS: (show up) 集まる, 繰り出す, 出かける

4 PRODUCE: 作る, 生み出す

5 EVICT: (tenant) 追い出す

T

1 Nothing ever turns out right for me.
何事も自分の思うようにはならないよ。

It turned out to be a very pleasant evening, much to our surprise.
意外なことに、とても楽しい夜になりました。

Despite the rush, everything turned out fine on the night itself.
急だったにもかかわらず、当日の夜はすべてがうまくいった。

2 Remember to turn out the light when you go to sleep.
寝る時に電気を消すのを忘れないで。

3 A record number of people turned out to vote.
記録的な数の人々が選挙に出かけた。

4 That band continues to turn out great albums.
あのバンドは、すばらしいアルバムを作り続けている。

5 She was turned out of her apartment for not paying rent.
彼女は家賃を滞納して、アパートを追い出された。

turn over *v.* (flip) ひっくり返す, 裏返す, (capsize) 転覆する, (change the position of one's body) 体を回転させる, (while sleeping) 寝返りを打つ; (hand over) 渡す

I turned it over to see if anything was written underneath.
裏返して、下に何か書かれていないか調べた。

I turned over and lay on my stomach.
体を回転させて、うつ伏せになった。

turn to *v.* (for help) …に頼る

Who will you turn to when things don't work out?
うまくいかないときは、誰に頼るの？

turn up *v.* (volume) (…の) 音量を上げる, 音を大きくする, (heat) 強める; (appear) 現れる, やって来る

Turn up the volume, will you.
音を大きくしてくれる？

Don't turn the heat up too much.
火を強くしすぎないでください。

He turned up the next morning with one hell of a hangover.
次の日の朝、彼はひどい二日酔いでやって来た。

turning *n.* (rotation) 回転

turning point *n.* 転機, 分かれ目

turnip *n.* カブ

turnout *n.* (attendance) 出席者(数)

a low turnout 少ない出席者

turnover *n.* (profit) 売り上げ, 売上高, (rate at which customers/goods move through a restaurant/shop) 回転率, (rate at which staff leave a company) 離職率

turnpike *n.* (toll road) 有料高速道路

turn signal *n.* ウインカー [→ picture of CAR]

turntable *n.* (revolving table) 回転台, (record player) ターンテーブル

turpentine *n.* テレピン油

turquoise *n.* (mineral) トルコ石, (color) 青緑色

adj. (of color) 青緑色の

turtle *n.* カメ, 亀

turtledove *n.* キジバト

turtleneck *n.* タートルネック

tusk *n.* きば

tutor *n.* 家庭教師

tutorial *n.* (lesson) 個別指導, (computer program) 取扱説明のプログラム

tuxedo *n.* タキシード

TV *n.* テレビ

Did you watch TV last night?
昨日の夜はテレビを見た？

turn on [off] the TV
テレビをつける [消す]

tweed *n.* ツイード

tweet *n.* さえずり

v. さえずる

tweezers *n.* ピンセット, 毛抜き [→ picture of FIRST-AID KIT]

twelfth *n.* 第12, 12番目, (date) 12日

adj. 第12の, 12番目の

twelve *n.* 12, 十二

adj., pron. 12の, (people) 12人(の), (things) 12個(の)

twentieth *n.* 第20, 20番目, (date) 20日

adj. 第20の, 20番目の

twenty *n.* 20, 二十, (**twenty years old**) 二十歳, (**the twenties**) 20年代, (**one's twenties**) 20歳代, 20代

adj., pron. 20の, (people) 20人(の), (things) 20個(の)

twice *adv.* (two times) 2回, 2度, (double) 2倍

I've been to Dublin twice.
ダブリンへは2度行ったことがあります。

They get together twice a week.
彼らは週2回集まります。

That's twice as much.
それは2倍です。

once or twice 1、2度

Oh, I've been there once or twice.
そこなら1、2度行ったことがあるよ。

think twice よく考える

You'd better think twice before you quit that job.
その仕事を辞める前に、よく考えたほうがいい。

twice as… (as) (…の)倍, 2倍

The trip was twice as expensive as I thought it'd be.
旅費は予想の2倍かかった。

twig *n.* 小枝

twilight *n.* (early evening) たそがれ, (dim light) 薄明かり

twin *n.* 双子の一人, (**twins**) 双子, ((*formal*)) 双生児

They're twins.
彼らは双子です。

She gave birth to twins.
彼女は双子を生みました。

They're identical twins.
二人は一卵性双生児です。

♦ **twin(-size) bed** *n.* ツインベッド

twin (hotel) room *n.* ツインルーム

twinkle *v.* きらきら輝く

twirl *v.* (rotate rapidly) くるくる回る, (cause to rotate) くるくる回す

twist

1 *v.* TURN: 回す, (by putting force into: screw etc.) ねじる, (faucet) ひねる

2 *v.* BEND: 曲げる, (of river, road) 曲がりくねる, 蛇行する

3 *v.* CONTORT/DISTORT: (body part) ゆがめる, (words) 歪曲する

4 *v.* TWINE AROUND: (**twist around**) (twist

A around B) (AをBに) からませる, (=coil about) (…に) からみつく

5 *v.* INJURE: (ankle) ねんざする

6 *n.* TURNING MOTION: (of body part) ひねり, (of cap, screw) ねじり, 回すこと

7 *n.* BEND: (in river, road) 湾曲, カーブ

8 *n.* UNEXPECTED DEVELOPMENT: 意外な展開

1 Just twist the dial to the left.
ダイヤルを左に回してください。

I had to twist myself around to see what was happening.
何が起きているのかを見るため、体をねじらなければならなかった。

2 Only Superman could twist those bars.
その棒を曲げられるのは、スーパーマンくらいだ。

The road twists across the mountains.
道は山々を曲がりくねって通っている。

3 He twisted his face to show his displeasure.
彼は顔をゆがめて、不快感をあらわにした。

Don't twist my words!
私が言ったことを歪曲しないで。

4 The weeds had twisted around the plant.
雑草がその植物にからみついていた。

5 I twisted my ankle.
足首をねんざした。

6 Give it another twist.
もう1回、回して。

7 a twist in the road 道路の湾曲

8 There was a twist at the end of the novel.
その小説の最後に意外な展開があった。

twisted *adj.* (bent out of shape) ねじれた; (evil) ねじ曲がった, ひねくれた

twister *n.* (tornado) 竜巻

twitch *v.* けいれんする, ぴくっと動く *n.* けいれん

two *n.* 2, 二
adj., pron. 2の, (people) 2人(の), (things) 2個(の), 二つ(の)

Only two people came.
2人しか来なかった。

There are two things I would like to bring up at the meeting.
会議で取り上げたいことが二つあります。

This will only take two minutes.
これはたった2分でできます。

put two and two together あれこれ考え合わせる

two-dimensional *adj.* 2次元の

twofold *adj.* 2倍の, 2重の

twosome *n.* 2人, 2人組

two-way *adj.* 2方向の, (of traffic, road) 両面交通の

tycoon *n.* 大物, ((*informal*)) ドン

tympanum *n.* 中耳, 鼓膜

type

1 *n.* KIND: 種類, タイプ, (**all types of**) あらゆる種類の

2 *n.* TYPEFACE: (printed letters/characters) 活字, (font) 書体

3 *v.* USE A KEYBOARD: (hit keys) タイプを打つ, 入力する, (**type in**) 挿入する, (**type out/up**) タイプする

1 It's a type of seaweed.
海草の一種です。

I'm not much of an outdoorsy type.
野外活動は、それほど好きなタイプではありません。

This type of problem comes up all the time.

T

この種の問題は、しょっちゅう起こる。

They sell all types of cameras at that store.

その店ではあらゆる種類のカメラを売っています。

2 The type is too small.

この活字は小さすぎる。

Put the word *sale* in bold type.

「セール」の文字を太字にしてください。

3 Can you type?

タイプは打てますか？

She can type very fast.

彼女はタイプを打つのがとても速い。

♦**typing** *n.* タイプで打つこと, 入力

be fast at typing タイプを打つのが速い

typeface *n.* 書体

typewriter *n.* タイプライター

typhoid *adj.* 腸チフスの

♦**typhoid fever** *n.* 腸チフス

typhoon *n.* 台風

typical *adj.* 典型的な, (**be typical of**) いかにも…らしい

a typical British summer

典型的なイギリスの夏

It was typical of her to turn up late.

遅れて来るとは、いかにも彼女らしかった。

That's typical of Kenji to forget his own mother's birthday.

自分の母親の誕生日を忘れるとは、いかにも賢治らしい。

typically *adv.* (usually) 一般的に, 大体は

typify *v.* (…の) 典型になる, (represent) 代表する

typist *n.* タイピスト

typography *n.* (appearance of text) (印刷の) 体裁

tyrannical *adj.* (of person) 暴君のような, 横暴な, (of government) 専制的な

tyranny *n.* (tyrannical government) 専制政治

tyrant *n.* 暴君, 専制君主

U, u

ubiquitous *adj.* (of thing) 至る所にある, (of animal, person) どこにでもいる

udder *n.* 乳房

UFO *n.* ＵＦＯ, 未確認飛行物体

ugly *adj.* 醜い, 不格好な, (of situation) 厄介な, 醜悪な

an ugly building 不格好なビル

It was a very ugly situation.
とても厄介なことになっていた。

♦**ugliness** *n.* 醜さ

UHF *abbr.* (ultrahigh frequency) ＵＨＦ, 極超短波

uh-huh *interj.* ええ, ((*informal*)) うん

uh-oh *interj.* (after having made a mistake) ああ, あれっ

uh-uh *interj.* ううん

U.K. *abbr.* (United Kingdom) 英国, ＵＫ

ukiyoe *n.* (woodblock print) 浮世絵

ukulele *n.* ウクレレ

ulcer *n.* 潰瘍

a stomach ulcer 胃潰瘍

ulterior *adj.* (hidden) 隠れた

♦**ulterior motive** *n.* 下心, 魂胆

have ulterior motives 魂胆がある

ultimate *adj.* (final) 最終の, (fundamental) 根本的な, (greatest) 最高の, 最大の, 最大限の, (worst) 最悪の

the ultimate goal/aim 最終目的

The ultimate success of this project depended on teamwork.
最終的にこのプロジェクトがうまくいくかどうかは、チームワークにかかっていた。

The ultimate cause of the accident was human error.
事故の根本原因は人為ミスだった。

It was the ultimate example of modernity.
それは現代的なものの最たる例だった。

ultimately *adv.* (in the end) 最終的に; (basically) 基本的に

ultimatum *n.* (final warning) 最後通告, 最後通牒

ultrasound *n.* (sound therapy) 超音波

ultraviolet *adj.* 紫外線の

ultraviolet radiation 紫外線

umbrella *n.* 傘; (company, organization) 包括的組織

open an umbrella 傘を差す [開く]

a folding umbrella 折りたたみ傘

Drat! I left my umbrella at the restaurant.
しまった! レストランに傘を忘れてきた。

under the umbrella of …の傘下に

umpire *n.* 審判(員), アンパイア, レフリー
v. (…の) 審判をする

un- *pref.* (in-) 不-, (non-) 非-, (-less) 無-, (not yet) 未-

unpleasant 不愉快な

unofficial 非公式の

unconscious 無意識の

unfinished 未完成の

unable *adj.* (**be unable to do**) …することができない, ((*formal*)) …しかねる

He was unable to walk after the accident.
彼は事故の後歩くことができなくなった。

I'm afraid I'll be unable to come this evening.
あいにく今晩は伺えそうにありません。

unabridged *adj.* (of book) 無削除の, 完全な

an unabridged edition 無削除版

unacceptable ***adj.*** (difficult to accept) 受け入れられない, 認めることができない, (no-good) だめな

unaccustomed ***adj.*** 不慣れな, (be unaccustomed to) (…に) 慣れていない

unaffected ***adj.*** (unassuming) 気取らない; (uninfluenced) 影響を受けていない

unanimity ***n.*** 全員一致

unanswered ***adj.*** (of letter) 返事のない, (of question) 答えのわからない

There are still several unanswered questions.
まだ答えのわからない質問がいくつもある。

unappetizing ***adj.*** まずそうな, 食欲をそそらない

unarmed ***adj.*** 武器を持たない, 丸腰の

unashamed ***adj.*** 人目をはばからない, (be unashamed of) 恥ずかしく思わない

unassisted ***adj.*** (by oneself) 一人での, (without help) 助けなしで

walk unassisted 助けなしで歩く

unattractive ***adj.*** 魅力のない [→ UGLY]

unauthorized ***adj.*** 無認可の, 許可されていない

unavailable ***adj.*** (cannot be obtained) 手に入らない

unavoidable ***adj.*** 避けられない, やむを得ない

unaware ***adj.*** 気づいていない, 知らない ***adv.*** (**unawares**) 思いがけなく, 不意に

He seemed completely unaware of what was happening around him.
彼は自分の周りで起こっていることに、全く気づいていないようだった。

I was unaware there was a problem.
問題があるとは知らなかった。

unbalanced ***adj.*** 不つり合いな, アンバランスな, (mentally) 精神的に不安定な

unbearable ***adj.*** 耐えられない, がまんできない

unbeatable ***adj.*** 太刀打ちできない, 無敵の

unbeaten ***adj.*** (of record) 破られていない, (of person) 負け知らずの

unbelievable ***adj.*** 信じられない

♦ **unbelievably** ***adv.*** 信じられないほど

unbiased ***adj.*** 偏見のない

unborn ***adj.*** (of fetus) まだ生まれていない, (**the unborn**) 胎児

unbreakable ***adj.*** 壊れない, 壊すことのできない, (of spirit) くじけない

unbroken ***adj.*** (of line) とぎれていない, (of silence, record) 破られていない

unbutton ***v.*** (…の) ボタンを外す

uncanny ***adj.*** (strange) 異様な, 無気味な

uncensored ***adj.*** 検閲されていない

uncertain ***adj.*** (unsure) わからない, 知らない, (unclear) はっきりしない, 確かではない

I was uncertain about whether I should go or not.
行くべきかどうか、わからなかった。

We were uncertain of the outcome.
結果は、はっきり知らなかった。

in no uncertain terms ずけずけ(と), きっぱり(と), はっきり(と)

uncertainty ***n.*** (feeling of anxiety) 不安, (lack of certainty) 不確かさ, 不確定

unchallenged ***adj.*** (of position, record)

揺るぎない

unchanged ***adj.*** 元のままの, 変化のない

uncharacteristic ***adj.*** (not typical of) ...らしくない

uncharitable ***adj.*** (not kind) 不親切な

unchecked ***adj.*** (of disease) 抑えられない; (of baggage) 機内持ち込みの

uncle ***n.*** (one's own) おじ, (sb else's) おじさん [NOTE: People, especially children, use おじさん of middle-aged men, too, in place of the person's name.]

one's great uncle 大おじ(さん)

unclear ***adj.*** はっきりしない, あいまいな, (of print) 不鮮明な

uncombed ***adj.*** ぼさぼさの, とかしていない

uncomfortable ***adj.*** 快適ではない, 不快な, (in/of chair) 座り心地の悪い, (in/of bed) 寝心地の悪い, (in/of social setting) 居心地の悪い, (uneasy) 落ち着かない

The train was crowded and uncomfortable.
電車は混んでいて不快だった。

This chair is really uncomfortable.
この椅子は本当に座り心地が悪い。

These shoes are uncomfortable to walk in.
この靴は歩きづらい。

She's uncomfortable around him.
彼女は彼のそばにいると気詰まりなんだ。

I felt very uncomfortable in front of all those people.
あれだけの人を前にして、とても落ち着かない気分だった。

♦ **uncomfortably** ***adv.*** 心地悪く, (nervously) 落ち着かなく

uncommitted ***adj.*** (of voter) 無党派の

uncommon ***adj.*** 普通ではない, 珍しい

uncomplicated ***adj.*** 複雑ではない, 単純な

uncompromising ***adj.*** 妥協しない

unconcerned ***adj.*** 関心がない, 無関心だ

unconditional ***adj.*** 無条件の

unconditional surrender 無条件降伏

unconfirmed ***adj.*** 未確認の

unconnected ***adj.*** (not linked) 無関係の, 関連していない, (lacking social connections) コネのない; (of machine) 接続していない

unconscious ***adj.*** (not conscious) 意識を失った, (be unconscious of: be unaware of) (...に) 気づいていない

n. (**the unconscious**) 無意識

He lay unconscious for a few moments.
彼は少しの間、意識を失って倒れていた。

He seemed unconscious of her presence.
彼は彼女がいることに気づいていないようだった。

When we sleep, images rise from the unconscious.
人は眠ると無意識からイメージがわき起こります。

♦ **unconsciously** ***adv.*** 無意識に, 思わず

unconstitutional ***adj.*** 憲法違反の

uncontrollable ***adj.*** (of person) 手に負えない, (of laughter, anger) 抑えられない

uncontrolled ***adj.*** 制御されていない, (of laughter, anger) 抑えられない

unconventional ***adj.*** 型破りな, 因襲にとらわれない

U

unconvincing *adj.* 説得力のない, 納得いかない

uncooked *adj.* (only half-cooked) 生煮えの, (raw) 生の

uncooperative *adj.* 非協力的な, 協力的ではない

uncouth *adj.* やぼな, 粗野な

uncover *v.* (take cover off of) (...の) おおいを取る, (expose) 暴露する

undaunted *adj.* (fearless) 恐れない

undecided *adj.* (of issue) 未解決の, 未定の, (of person) まだ決めていない

undecided voters 浮動票層

undemocratic *adj.* 非民主的な, 民主的ではない

undeniable *adj.* 否定できない

under

1 *prep.* UNDERNEATH: ...の下に/で/を

2 *prep.* LESS THAN: ...未満, ...より少ない, ...足らず, ...以下

3 *prep.* IN THE PROCESS OF: ...中, ...しているところ

4 *prep.* UNDER THE INSTRUCTION/LEADERSHIP/LAWS OF: ...の下で

5 *prep.* UNDER THE HEADING OF: ...の項目に/で

6 *prep.* OWING TO: ...で(は), ...のもとで

7 *prep.* LOWER IN RANK THAN: ...の下に/で

8 *adv.* UNDERWATER: 水中に

1 The wastepaper basket is under the desk.
くずかごは机の下にあります。

The boys hid under the bed.
少年たちはベッドの下に隠れた。

We stood under the canopy to keep out of the rain.
ひさしの下に立って雨宿りをした。

"Where shall I put it?"
"Oh, just put it under the chair for the moment."
「どこに置きましょうか？」
「ああ、とりあえず椅子の下に置いといてください」

Are you wearing anything under that sweater?
そのセーターの下に何か着ていますか？

The kids crawled under the fence.
子供たちは、さくの下をくぐった。

2 There isn't a man on the team under 180 centimeters.
チームに身長が１８０センチ未満の者は一人もいない。

He's under twenty and not allowed to smoke.
彼は20歳未満だから喫煙は許されない。

It's under a kilo.
１キロ足らずですよ。

3 The bridge is under construction.
橋は建設中です。

Your pay is under review.
あなたの給料については検討中です。

The issue is under discussion.
その問題は討議しているところです。

4 I studied pottery under an old master.
陶芸を老齢の師匠の下で習いました。

Britain changed under Thatcher's government.
イギリスはサッチャー政権の下で変わった。

Under the laws of this country, you could be jailed for smoking marijuana.
この国の法律では、マリファナを吸ったら刑務所行きもありうるんだよ。

5 Dolphins are listed in the index under "mammals."

イルカは索引の「哺乳類」の項目に載っています。

Look under the noun to find that idiom.
そのイディオムは名詞の項目で引いてください。

6 Under the circumstances, I must decline.
こういう状況では、辞退しなければなりません。

7 The manager has four people under him.
部長には4人の部下がいる。

8 The ship went under.
船は沈没した。

underage ***adj.*** 未成年の
underage drinking 未成年者の飲酒

underbelly ***n.*** (of animal) 下腹部; (of thing: weakest part) 弱点

underbrush ***n.*** 下生え

undercharge ***v.*** (…に) 料金以下の金額を請求する

underclass ***n.*** (**the underclass**) 下層階級(の人々)

underclothes ***n.*** 下着

undercover ***adj.*** (secret) 秘密の
adv. (**work undercover**) おとり捜査をする
an undercover cop 秘密捜査員

undercurrent ***n.*** ((*also figurative*)) 底流

undercut ***v.*** (price) (…より) 安く売る

underdeveloped ***adj.*** (of country) 開発途上の, (of person) 未発達の

underdog ***n.*** (in competition) 勝ち目のない人, (in society) 弱者

underdone ***adj.*** (not broiled enough) 生焼けの, (not boiled enough) 生煮えの

underdress ***v.*** 略式すぎる服装をする

underestimate ***v.*** 過小評価する, 軽く見すぎる

undergo ***v.*** (receive) 受ける, (experience) 経験する
undergo surgery 手術を受ける

undergraduate ***n.*** 大学生

underground ***adj.*** 地下の, (secret) 秘密の, (of art) アングラの
adv. 地下に
n. (**the Underground**) 地下鉄
an underground parking lot
地下駐車場
an underground organization
地下 [秘密] 組織
The movement was forced to go underground.
その運動は地下に潜ることを余儀なくされた。

undergrowth ***n.*** 下生え

underhand ***adj.*** (dishonest) 不正な, ずるい; (**underhand throw**) 下手投げ
underhand tactics ずるい作戦

underlie ***v.*** (be the basis of) (…の) 基礎となる

underline ***v.*** (…に) 下線を引く, (emphasize) 強調する

underlying ***adj.*** (basic) 基本的な; (lower) 下にある

undermine ***v.*** (weaken) 弱める, (health) 害する

underneath ***adv., prep.*** (…の) 下に/で/を, (…の) 下の方に
n. 下, 底
I've put your bag underneath the seat, sir.
おかばんは、座席の下に置きました。

He was standing underneath the clock.
彼は時計の下に立っていた。

How many layers are you wearing underneath your coat?
コートの下に何枚着てる？

You'd better check underneath as well.
下も見たほうがいい。

underpants *n.* 下着, パンツ

underpay *v.* (…に) 十分支払わない

underrate *v.* 過小評価する

underscore → UNDERLINE

undershirt *n.* シャツ

underside *n.* (bottom) 下, 底面

understaffed *adj.* 職員が足りない, 人手不足の

understand *v.* (…が) わかる, (…を) 理解する, (**I understand…**: I hear…) (…と) 聞いている

I don't quite understand the question.
ご質問の意味がよくわかりません。

"Did you understand me?"
"I understood you perfectly."
「私の言うことがわかりましたか？」
「よくわかりました」

Well, I could easily understand why he wanted to leave that job.
まあ、私には彼がなぜあの仕事を辞めたかったのかよくわかるよ。

She doesn't understand him at all.
あの人は彼のことを全く理解していない。

I don't understand what he's talking about.
彼が何のことを言っているのか、理解できない。

I understood from her tone that she meant what she said.
あの口ぶりから、彼女は本気だとわかった。

As I understand it, Yuka's intending to study art.
私の聞いたところでは、由佳さんは美術を勉強するつもりらしい。

I understand he's a diplomat.
その人は外交官だと聞いています。

KANJI BRIDGE

解 ON: かい, げ KUN: と(く/かす/ける) | UNDERSTAND, SOLVE

answer	解答
excuse	弁解
explanation, commentary	解説
interpretation	解釈
misunderstanding	誤解
opinion	見解
solution	解決
understanding	理解
unsolved	未解決の

understandable *adj.* 理解できる

understanding *n.* 理解, (ability to understand) 理解力, (knowledge) 知識; (agreement) 了解, 合意

adj. (sympathetic) 理解がある

It is/was my understanding that…
私の理解では…

He seems to have a real understanding of the current political situation.
彼は現在の政治状況についてよく理解しているようです。

That was not the understanding!
話が違います！

She was very understanding and just listened to what I had to say.
彼女はとても理解があって、私の言うことにただ耳を傾けてくれました。

understate *v.* 控え目に述べる

♦**understated** *adj.* 控え目な, 抑えた

understatement *n.* 控え目な表現

undertake *v.* (accept, take on) 引き受ける; (begin) 始める

undertaker *n.* 葬儀屋

undertaking *n.* (task) 仕事

undertow *n.* 引き波

undervalue *v.* (not appreciate enough) 過小評価する, 軽視する

underwater *adj.* 水中の, 水面下の

underway *adj.* (in progress) 進行中で

The project is underway.
計画は進行中です。

underwear *n.* 下着

underweight *adj.* 体重が標準より軽い, やせすぎの

underworld *n.* (**the underworld**) (=criminal underworld) 暗黒街, (=place for the dead) 黄泉の国

underwrite *v.* (insure) (…の) 保険を引き受ける, (guarantee) 保証する

undesirable *adj.* (unpleasant) 不快な, (unwanted) 望ましくない

undisclosed *adj.* 明らかにされていない, (secret) 秘密の

undisputed *adj.* 異議のない, (clear) 明白な

undisturbed *adj.* (not interrupted) じゃまされない, 乱されない, (of tomb) 元のままの, (of slumber) 静かな

undo *v.* (knot, rope) ほどく, (button) 外す, (loosen) ゆるめる, (reverse the effects of) 元どおりにする

Can you undo this knot for me?
この結び目をほどいてくれる?

He undid his pants.
彼はズボンをゆるめた。

It can't be undone.
元どおりにはならないよ/もう元には戻せないよ。

undoing *n.* (cause of ruin) 破滅の原因

Alcohol was his undoing.
お酒が彼の破滅の原因でした。

undoubtedly *adv.* 疑いなく

undress *v.* (remove clothes) 服を脱ぐ, (undress sb) (…の) 服を脱がせる

You'd better undress.
服を脱いだほうがいい。

The nurse helped undress the patient.
看護師は患者が服を脱ぐのを手伝った。

unearth *v.* (dig up) 発掘する, 掘り出す, (secret) 暴く

unease *n.* 不安

uneasy *adj.* 不安な, 落ち着かない

uneducated *adj.* (has not had schooling) 教育を受けていない

unemotional *adj.* 感情を表さない

unemployed *adj.* 失業した, 無職の
n. (**the unemployed**) 失業者

unemployment *n.* 失業, (unemployment rate) 失業率

unemployment benefits 失業手当

rising [falling] unemployment
失業率の上昇 [低下]

unending *adj.* 終わりのない, 果てしない [→ ETERNAL, PERPETUAL]

unequal *adj.* (of rights) 不平等な, (of amount) 同じではない

unequivocally *adv.* 明確に, はっきりと

unethical *adj.* 倫理に反する, 不道徳な

uneven *adj.* (bumpy) でこぼこの, (of performance) むらのある, (of surface) (= not flat) 平らではない, (= not smooth) 滑らかではない

unexpected *adj.* 思いがけない, 意外な, 予想外の

an unexpected guest 思いがけない客

You could hardly describe their marriage as unexpected.
二人の結婚は全然意外ではなかった。

The results were totally unexpected.
結果は全く予想外のものだった。

Well, this is a most unexpected visit.
いやあ、あなたが訪ねて来てくれるとは思いも寄らなかった。

♦ **unexpectedly** *adv.* 思いがけなく, 意外に, 不意に, 予想外に

unexplained *adj.* 説明のつかない

an unexplained phenomenon
説明のつかない現象

unexplored *adj.* 未踏の

unfair *adj.* 不公平な, 不正な, アンフェアな, フェアではない

He had an unfair advantage.
彼は不正に便宜を受けていた。

It's unfair to expect them to compete on equal terms.
あの二人を同じ条件で競わせるのは、不公平です。

You're being unfair to her.
彼女に対してフェアではないですよ。

♦ **unfairly** *adv.* 不公平に, 不正に

be treated unfairly 不公平な扱いを受ける

unfaithful *adj.* (to lover) 浮気をする

unfamiliar *adj.* なじみのない, よく知らない

unfashionable *adj.* ださい, やぼったい

unfavorable *adj.* (critical) 批判的な, (undesirable) 好ましくない

unfinished *adj.* 未完成の

♦ **unfinished business** *n.* やりかけの事

I have some unfinished business to attend to.
やりかけの仕事が残っている。

unfit *adj.* (be unfit for) (…に) 適さない, ふさわしくない, 向いていない; (out of shape, in poor physical condition) 体がなまっている

unfold *v.* (open) 広げる, 開く, (reveal) 明らかにしていく; (of events) 展開する

unforeseen *adj.* 予期しない, 思いがけない

an unforeseen event
思いがけない出来事

unforgettable *adj.* 忘れられない

unfortunate *adj.* 不運な, 運の悪い, 不幸な

it is unfortunate that …とは残念です

unfortunately *adv.* あいにく, 残念ながら, 運悪く

Unfortunately, the weather changed and we had to cancel our outing.
あいにく [運悪く]、天気が変わって遠足を取りやめなければならなくなった。

Mr. Aoki says he can't join us tonight, unfortunately.
青木さんは、残念ながら今夜は来られないとのことです。

unfounded *adj.* (groundless) 根拠のな

い, 理由のない

unfriendly *adj.* とっつきにくい, 無愛想な, 親しみにくい

unfulfilled *adj.* (of wish) 果たされていない, (of person) 充実していない

unfurnished *adj.* 家具付きではない

It's an unfurnished, two-room apartment.
家具付きでない２ＬＤＫのマンションです。

ungrammatical *adj.* 文法的に正しくない

ungrateful *adj.* 恩知らずの

unhappy *adj.* (in general) 不幸な, 不幸せな, (of mood: sad) 悲しい, (miserable) みじめな, (unsatisfied) 不満な

an unhappy life 不幸な人生

She was terribly unhappy in her old job.
前の職場で、彼女は実にみじめな思いをした。

He seemed very unhappy with his exam grade.
彼は試験の結果に、ひどく不満なようだった。

What's up? You seem unhappy.
どうしたの？ 浮かない顔だね。

♦ **unhappiness** *n.* 不幸, 不幸せ

unharmed *adj.* 無事な, けがのない, 無傷の

unhealthy *adj.* 健康によくない, (bad for the mind/soul) 不健全な, よくない

unheard-of *adj.* (unprecedented) 聞いたことがない; (shocking) とんでもない

unhelpful *adj.* 助けにならない, 役に立たない

unhurt *adj.* 無事な, けがのない, 無傷の

unidentified *adj.* 正体不明の, 未確認の [→ UFO]

unification *n.* 統一, 統合

uniform *n.* (outfit) 制服, ユニフォーム *adj.* (the same) 同じの, 同一の, (constant) 一定の, (consistent) 首尾一貫した

a school uniform 学校の制服

The guards were all in uniform.
警備員は皆, 制服を着ていました。

unify *v.* (make into one) 一つにする, (consolidate, make consistent) 統一する

♦ **unified** *adj.* 統一された

unilateral *adj.* (of decision) 一方的な

unimaginable *adj.* 想像できない, 考えられない, 思いも寄らない

unimaginative *adj.* (of person) 想像力に欠ける, (of thing, idea) 独創性のない

unimportant *adj.* 重要ではない, 大切ではない, (petty) ささいな

unimpressed *adj.* 感動していない

uninhabited *adj.* 人の住んでいない, 無人の

an uninhabited island 無人島

uninhibited *adj.* (straight in one's manner of speaking) 率直な, ストレートな, (of laughter) 遠慮のない

unintelligent *adj.* 頭のよくない, 利口ではない

unintelligible *adj.* 理解できない

unintentional *adj.* わざとではない, 故意ではない

uninteresting *adj.* 面白くない, つまらない

uninterrupted *adj.* (continuous) 連続した, とぎれない

union *n.* (association) 組合, 同盟, 連合, (**labor union**) 労働組合, (**student union**)

学生自治会; (being united) 結合

Are you a member of the trade union?
労働組合の組合員ですか？

unique *adj.* 珍しい, ユニークな, 独特な, (be unique to) (…に) 特有の

It was a unique experience.
珍しい経験だった。

These problems aren't unique to any one country.
こうした問題はどこか一つの国に特有というものではない。

unisex *adj.* 男女兼用の, 男女両用の

a unisex restroom 男女兼用トイレ

unison *n.* (**in unison**) (=at the same time) 一斉に, (=in agreement) 一致して, 調和して

unit *n.* (of measurement, academic study) 単位, (family unit) 世帯, (division in organization) 部署, (in hospital) 科; (device) 装置, 設備 [→ APPLIANCE]

unite *v.* (come/bring together) 団結する/団結させる

The question was whether the Opposition could unite in time.
問題は、時間内に野党が団結できるかどうかだった。

united *adj.* (of people) 団結した, (unified) 統一された

United Kingdom *n.* 英国, イギリス

United Nations *n.* 国際連合, ((*in abbr.*)) 国連

United States of America *n.* アメリカ合衆国 [→ AMERICA]

unity *n.* 統一性

universal *adj.* 万人に共通の, 普遍的な

The movie is of universal interest.
その映画には誰もが興味がわく。

a universal truth 普遍の真理

universe *n.* (**the universe**) 宇宙

Few people now believe that earth is at the center of the universe.
今日では地球が宇宙の中心であると思っている人は少ない。

university *n.* 大学

He doesn't want to go on to university.
彼は大学に進学する気がない。

Izawa is soon to graduate from university.
伊沢さんはもうすぐ大学を卒業します。

unjust *adj.* 不正な, 不公平な

unjustified *adj.* 正当化されていない

unkind *adj.* (not considerate) 思いやりのない, 不親切な, (spiteful) 意地の悪い

unknown *adj.* (not known) 知られていない, (not famous) 有名ではない, (mysterious) 未知の

n. (unknown thing) 知らないこと, (person who is not famous) 無名の人; (**the unknown**) 未知のもの

He's well known in the U.S. but virtually unknown in Europe.
その人はアメリカでは有名ですが、ヨーロッパではほとんど知られていません。

a bone of unknown origin 身元不明の骨

unlawful *adj.* 違法の, 非合法の

unleaded *adj.* (of gasoline) 無鉛の

unless *conj.* …ない限り, (もし)…なければ, …なかったら

Don't call me unless it's an emergency.
緊急でない限り、電話をかけないで。

Unless you come clean with me right

now, this relationship is over.
今すぐはっきりさせない限り、この関係は終わりだよ。

Unless I misunderstood, she should have left by now.
(もし)私の思い違いでなければ、彼女は今ごろはもう出発しているはずです。

unlike ***prep.*** (different from) …と違って, (in appearance) …に似ていない, (in demeanor) …らしくない
adj. 似ていない, 違う

Unlike John, Paul worked hard.
ジョンと違って、ポールはよく働いた。

It was quite unlike any other animal I'd ever seen before.
それまでに見たどんな動物とも全く違っていた。

Though they're not unlike in appearance, their personalities are very different.
外見は似てなくもないが、二人の性格は全く違う。

It's unlike you to complain so much.
そんなに文句を言うなんて、あなたらしくない。

unlikely ***adj.*** …そうにない, (**be unlikely to do**) …することはないだろう, (improbable) ありそうもない, 思いも寄らない

It's unlikely they'll win.
彼らは勝ちそうにない。

He's unlikely to show up early.
彼が早く来るなんてことはないでしょう。

It was an unlikely gathering of academics, workers, and artists.
学識者、労働者、それに芸術家が集うという、思いも寄らない会合だった。

unlimited ***adj.*** 無限の, 無制限の

unload ***v.*** (luggage) 下ろす, (dishwasher) (…から) 食器を取り出す

They took a long time to unload our luggage.
荷物を下ろすのに、ひどく時間がかかっていた。

unlock ***v.*** (…の) かぎをあける

He unlocked the door and let himself in.
彼はドアのかぎをあけて中に入った。

unloved ***adj.*** 愛されていない

unlucky ***adj.*** 運の悪い, 不運な, ((*informal*)) ついてない, (inauspicious) 縁起の悪い

If you're unlucky enough to miss the train, you'll have to walk.
運悪く電車に乗り遅れたら、歩かなくてはなりませんよ。

unmarked ***adj.*** (having no identifying marks) 標示のない

an unmarked police car 覆面パトカー

unmarried ***adj.*** 未婚の, 独身の

unmistakable ***adj.*** (easy to recognize) 明白な, 明らかな

unmoved ***adj.*** 動じない, 冷静な

unnamed ***adj.*** 誰ともわからない, 名前が明らかになっていない

unnatural ***adj.*** 不自然な, 異常な

unnecessary ***adj.*** 不必要な, 必要のない, 余計な, むだな

It was a totally unnecessary remark.
それは全く余計な口出しだった。

unnerve ***v.*** 不安にさせる, (discourage) (…の) 気力をくじく

unnoticed ***adj.*** 気づかれない, 注目されない

unobtrusive ***adj.*** 目立たない, 控え目な

unoccupied ***adj.*** (of room) あいている
unofficial ***adj.*** 非公式の
♦**unofficially** ***adv.*** 非公式に
unoriginal ***adj.*** 独創性のない, ありきたりの
unorthodox ***adj.*** 正統派ではない
unpack ***v.*** (suitcase) あけて中身を取り出す, (clothes from suitcase) (スーツケースから) 取り出す; (take things out of boxes) 梱包を解く, 荷を解く
unpaid ***adj.*** (of work) 無給の, (of bill) 未払いの

It was unpaid work.
それは無給の仕事だった。

There were several bills that had been left unpaid.
未払いのままの請求書がいくつかあった。

unparalleled ***adj.*** 空前の, またとない
unpatriotic ***adj.*** 愛国心のない
unpleasant ***adj.*** いやな, 不愉快な, 不快な, (disgusting) 気持ちの悪い, (of person) 無愛想な

It was a very unpleasant smell.
とってもいやなにおいだった。

He's always so unpleasant.
あの人はいつも無愛想だ。

unplug ***v.*** (...の)栓を抜く, プラグを抜く
unpopular ***adj.*** 人気のない, 不評の
unprecedented ***adj.*** 前例のない
unpredictable ***adj.*** (of event) 予測できない, (of person) 気まぐれな
unprepared ***adj.*** (not ready) 用意ができていない, (mentally) 心構えができていない
unproductive ***adj.*** 非生産的な
unprofitable ***adj.*** もうけが出ない, 利益の上がらない
unprotected ***adj.*** 危険にさらされた, 無防備の, (of sex) コンドームを使わない
unprovoked ***adj.*** いわれのない
unpublished ***adj.*** (of manuscript) 未刊の, 未発表の, (of author) 作品が出版されていない
unqualified ***adj.*** 無資格の, 資格のない
unquestionable ***adj.*** (without a doubt) 疑いのない
♦**unquestionably** ***adv.*** 疑いなく
unravel ***v.*** (thread, knot) ほどく, (mystery) 解く, 解明する
unreadable ***adj.*** 読みにくい, 読めない
unreal ***adj.*** (very strange) 非現実的な, 現実とは思えない
♦**unreality** ***n.*** 非現実性
unrealistic ***adj.*** 非現実的な, 現実的ではない
unreasonable ***adj.*** 無茶な, 無理な, 理不尽な, (of price) 法外な
unrelated ***adj.*** 無縁の, 無関係の
unrelenting ***adj.*** (ceaseless) 絶え間ない, (relentless) 容赦しない
unreliable ***adj.*** 当てにできない, 信用できない
unremarkable ***adj.*** 目立たない
unrepentant ***adj.*** 後悔しない
unresolved ***adj.*** 未解決の

an unresolved dispute 未解決の紛争

unrest ***n.*** 不安
unrestricted ***adj.*** 制限のない, (free) 自由な
unrivaled ***adj.*** 比べられない, 無比の

unruly *adj.* (of child) 手に負えない

unsafe *adj.* 安全ではない, 危険な

unsanitary *adj.* 不衛生な, 清潔ではない

unsatisfactory *adj.* 不満足な, 不十分な

unsatisfied *adj.* 不満足な, 満足していない

unsavory *adj.* (unpleasant) 不快な

unscathed *adj.* 無傷で

unscheduled *adj.* 予定外の, 臨時の

unscrew *v.* (...の) ねじを抜く

unscrupulous *adj.* (dishonest) 悪徳の, あくどい

unseen *adj.* 目に見えない

unselfish *adj.* 利己的ではない

unsettled *adj.* 不安定な

unsettling *adj.* (causing concern) 人を動揺させる

unshaven *adj.* ひげをそっていない

unsightly *adj.* (ugly) 醜い, 見苦しい

unskilled *adj.* (of labor) 熟練を要しない, (skill-less) 未熟な, 技術のない

unsociable *adj.* 非社交的な, 社交的ではない, 付き合いが苦手の

unsolicited *adj.* (of mail, phone call) 迷惑な, 頼んでいないのに来る, (of advice) お節介な

unsolved *adj.* 未解決の

an unsolved mystery
未解決のミステリー

unsophisticated *adj.* (unrefined) やぼったい, (of machine) 複雑ではない

unsound *adj.* (of argument) 理屈の通らない, (of structure: likely to collapse) 不安定な

unspeakable *adj.* (awful) 言いようのない, ひどい

unspecified *adj.* (vague) はっきりしない, (not made clear) 明示されていない

unspoiled *adj.* (of scenery) 損なわれていない, (of person) 甘やかされていない

unspoken *adj.* 無言の, 暗黙の

unstable *adj.* 不安定な, 安定しない

unsteady *adj.* (wobbly) ぐらぐらする, (of person: shaky) ふらふらする

unstressed *adj.* (of syllable) アクセントのない

unsubstantiated *adj.* 確証のない, 立証されていない

unsuccessful *adj.* 成功しなかった, 失敗の

unsuitable *adj.* ふさわしくない, 向かない

unsuited *adj.* 合わない, 不つり合いな

unsure *adj.* わからない

be unsure of oneself (自分に) 自信がない

unsuspecting *adj.* (unwary) 怪しまない, 疑わない

unsympathetic *adj.* 同情心のない, 思いやりのない, (cold) 冷淡な

untamed *adj.* 飼いならされていない

unthinkable *adj.* (unimaginable) 考えられない, (improbable) あり得ない, (ridiculous) とんでもない

do the unthinkable
考えられないことをする

untidy *adj.* (of person) だらしのない, (of place) 散らかった

He's just so untidy.
あいつは全く、だらしのない奴だ。

Look how untidy everything is.

なんてひどい散らかりようなの!

untie *v.* (knot) ほどく, 解く, (person who has been tied up) 解放する

until *prep., conj.* …まで(は)

I work from 9 o'clock in the morning until 11 o'clock at night.
朝9時から夜11時まで働いています。

I waited for you until 7:30.
7時半まで待っていました。

We have until Tuesday to think about it.
考える時間は火曜日まである。

Until recently, that was certainly the case.
最近までは、確かにそうでした。

You get free dental care until you're 16.
16歳まで無料で歯の治療が受けられます。

untimely *adj.* (of remark) タイミングの悪い, (of death) 早すぎる

untold *adj.* (countless) 数えられない, 無数の

untouched *adj.* (unaltered) 元のままの, 手つかずの, (unmoved) 心を動かされない [→ UNHARMED]

untrained *adj.* 訓練されていない

untreated *adj.* (of disease) 治療していない, 放置した

U

untrue *adj.* (not the truth) 事実に反する, 事実ではない, (not correct) 正しくない [→ INACCURATE]

untrustworthy *adj.* 信用できない, 信頼できない

unused *adj.* (not being used) 使われていない, (new) 新しい; (be unused to) (…に)慣れていない

unusual *adj.* 珍しい, 変わった, 普通ではない

It's not unusual for him to come home late.
彼が夜遅く帰宅するのは珍しいことじゃない。

That's an unusual name.
それは珍しい名前ですね。

unusually *adv.* 異常に, 珍しく

an unusually hot summer 異常に暑い夏

He's unusually cheerful today.
今日、彼は珍しく明るい。

unveil *v.* (remove the veil from) (…の)ベールを取る; (new product) 発表する, 公開する

unwanted *adj.* 要らない, 不必要な, 不要な [→ UNLOVED]

an unwanted child
望まれずに生まれた子供

unwarranted *adj.* (unreasonable) 不当な, (unnecessary) 不要な

unwelcome *adj.* ありがたくない, いやな, (of guest) 招かれざる

unwell *adj.* 調子がよくない

unwieldy *adj.* (cumbersome) 扱いにくい

unwilling *adj.* (**be unwilling to do**) …したがらない

He was unwilling to talk about it.
彼はそのことは話したがらなかった。

unwind *v.* (cause to unravel) ほどく, (become unraveled) ほどける; (relax) くつろぐ, 緊張をほぐす

unwise *adj.* 分別に欠ける, 賢明ではない, 愚かな

unwitting *adj.* 気づかない, 無意識の

♦**unwittingly** *adv.* 気づかずに, 無意識に

unworkable *adj.* 実際的ではない, 実行不可能な

unworthy *adj.* (be unworthy of: not deserve) (…に) 値しない

unwrap *v.* あける

unwritten *adj.* (of agreement) 暗黙の

♦ **unwritten rule** *n.* 不文律

unzip *v.* (…の) ファスナー/チャックをあける

up

1 *adv.* IN A HIGHER POSITION: 上へ/に, 上の方へ/に

2 *adv.* UPRIGHT/UPWARD: 上がる/上げる

3 *prep.* INDICATING DIRECTION OF MOVEMENT: …を上がって, …を登って

4 *prep.* INDICATING LOCATION: (along road, river etc.) …に沿って, …沿いに/を

5 *adv.* UNTIL OR THROUGH TO: (**up to**) …まで

6 *adv.* INDICATING LEVEL/DISTANCE REACHED OR COVERED: (**up to**) …まで

7 *adv.* DEPENDS ON: (**be up to**) …次第だ

8 *adv.* DOING: (**be up to**) …している, (= scheming) たくらんでいる

9 *adv.* IN THE MOOD FOR/TO DO: (**be up for/to doing**) …したい

10 *adj.* OF TIME: 切れた, 終わりだ

11 *adj.* AWAKE: 起きている

12 *v.* RAISE: 上げる

1 Just put it up on that shelf.
その棚の上に置いて。

"Where's Taro?"
"He's up in his room."
「太郎は？」
「2階の自分の部屋にいるよ」

2 Please stand up and introduce yourself.
立って自己紹介をしてください。

She got up from her seat and walked up onto the stage.
彼女は席から立ち上がって、舞台へと登って行った。

The kite just wouldn't go up.
凧はどうしても揚がらなかった。

She looked up and gazed straight into my eyes.
見上げると、私の目をじっと見つめた。

Lift your head up so I can have a look at the cut.
傷がよく見えるよう、頭を上げて。

3 The children ran up the hill.
子供たちは丘を駆け上がった。

We walked up the stairs to take a look at the bedrooms.
寝室を見るために、階段を上がって行きました。

4 Further up the road there was a parking lot.
道のもっと先の方に駐車場があった。

It's a little greener up the river aways.
川沿いをずっと行くと、いくらか緑が多くなります。

5 Up to now, she's done very well.
今までのところ、彼女は実によくやっています。

These rituals have been practiced from ancient times right up to the present.
こうした儀式は古代から現代に至るまでずっと、執り行われてきました。

6 The water came up to our knees.
水はひざまでありました。

I've read up to Chapter 10.
10章まで読みました。

7 "Which one should I buy?"

"It's up to you."
「どれを買ったらいい？」
「それは君次第だよ」

8 "So, what have you been up to lately?"
"Not much."
「それで最近何をしているの？」
「相変わらずだよ」

9 He's just not up to taking on that kind of responsibility.
彼はそういう責任を負いたくないだけだ。

10 Time's up. Put your pens down.
時間切れです。ペンを置いてください。

11 He's up, at last.
彼、ようやく起きたよ。

12 They upped my salary two percent.
給料を2 % 上げてもらった。

be up against (be facing) …に直面している

We are up against a lot of opposition.
私たちは多くの反対に直面している。

up and down 上がったり下がったり

The roller coaster went up and down.
ジェットコースターは上がったり下がったりした。

up close 間近で, すぐ近くで

Up close, the picture didn't look nearly as good.
間近で見ると、絵はそんなによくなかった。

ups and downs (in life) 浮き沈み

Life has its ups and downs.
人生には浮き沈みがある。

up until …まで

Up until then, I had no idea what hard work really was.
その時まで、きつい仕事とはどういうものか、全然知らなかった。

what's up (How's it going?) どうしてる?, 元気?

up-and-coming *adj.* 成功する見込みのある, 有望な

upbeat *adj.* 明るい, 楽しい

upbringing *n.* しつけ, 育てられ方, (education) 教育

She had a good upbringing.
彼女は、育ちがいい。

Parents should share in the upbringing of their children.
子供の教育には、両親ともかかわるべきだ。

upcoming *adj.* (of events) もうすぐやって来る, 来たるべき

update *n.* 最新情報

v. 最新のものにする, (book) 改訂する, (software) 更新する, アップデートする, (provide new information to) (…に) 最新情報を提供する

up-front *adj.* (frank) 率直な

adv. (**up front**) (=in advance) 前もって, 前金で; (=frankly) 率直に

upgrade *v.* (hardware) アップグレードする, (airline ticket) 格上げする

upheaval *n.* 大変動

uphill *adj.* 上りの, (of path, slope) 上り坂の; (difficult) 苦しい, 骨の折れる

an uphill battle 苦戦

uphold *v.* (support) 支持する

upholstery *n.* 室内装飾品, (business) 室内装飾業

upkeep *n.* (maintenance) 維持, (cost of upkeep) 維持費

uplifting *adj.* 元気にさせる, 気持ちを高

揚させる

upload *v.* アップロードする

upon *prep.* (on) …の上に; (**upon doing**) …したとたん, …するなり

The girl sat upon his knees.
女の子は、彼のひざの上に座った。

Upon entering the room, he heard everyone shout, "Congratulations!"
部屋に入ったとたん、彼はみんなが一斉に「おめでとう!」と叫ぶのを聞いた。

once upon a time → ONCE

upper *adj.* (situated above another) 上の方の, (higher in rank) 上級の

The fog made it impossible to see the upper half of the building.
霧のせいで建物の上半分は見えなかった。

have the upper hand 優勢だ, 優位に立つ

The other team has the upper hand.
相手チームのほうが優勢だ。

uppercase *adj.* 大文字の

upper class *n.* 上流階級, 上流社会
adj. (**upper-class**) 上流階級の

upright *adj.* (vertical) まっすぐに立った

sit in an upright position
まっすぐな姿勢で座る

uprising *n.* (rebellion) 反乱

uproar *n.* 騒ぎ, 騒動

uproot *v.* (pull up: plant) 引き抜く, 引っこ抜く

upscale *adj.* 高級な

upset

1 *adj.* UNHAPPY: 気が動転した, 取り乱した, (**get upset**) うろたえる

2 *v.* CAUSE TO FEEL UNHAPPY: 動揺させる, 悲しませる

3 *v.* KNOCK OVER: ひっくり返す

4 *n.* DISTURBANCE: 混乱, 乱れ

5 *adj.* OF STOMACH: 調子が悪い, 具合が悪い

6 *n., adj.* OF VICTORY: 逆転(の)

1 She looked extremely upset when she hung up the phone.
彼女は電話を切った時、ひどく動転していた。

Come on, don't be upset.
がんばれ、落ち着いて。

2 Now you've gone and upset the children.
あなたのせいで、子供たちが動揺してしまいましたよ。

3 Careful you don't upset the chess pieces.
チェスの駒をひっくり返さないように気をつけて。

4 The misunderstanding caused quite an upset.
誤解から、大変な混乱が生じた。

5 I've got an upset stomach.
胃の調子が悪い。

The Conservative Party scored an upset election victory.
保守党は選挙で逆転勝利を収めた。

upset the applecart 台なしにする

upside down *adv.* 逆さに, ひっくり返して

Turn the jar upside down.
びんをひっくり返して。

upstairs *adv.* 上に/へ, 2階に/へ
adj. 上の, 2階の
n. 上の階, 2階

He's already gone upstairs to bed.
彼はもう2階に休みに上がった。

There is more storage space upstairs.
2階にはもっと収納スペースがあります。

There's a fine view from the upstairs

window.
2階の窓は眺めがいい。

upstart *n.* 成り上がり(者)

upstream *adv., adj.* 川上に/の, 上流に/の

upsurge *n.* (sudden increase) 急増

uptight *adj.* (tense) 緊張する, ぴりぴりする, (**get uptight**) 怒る

up-to-date *adj.* 最新の

uptown *n.* 山の手, 住宅街, (suburbs) 郊外

upturn *n.* 上向き, 好転
v. 上に向ける, ひっくり返す

upward *adv.* (to a higher position) 上の方へ [→ UP]
adj. 上向きの

Sales are showing an upward trend.
売り上げは、上向き傾向を示している。

uranium *n.* ウラン

Uranus *n.* 天王星 [also read てんおうせい]

urban *adj.* 都会の, 都市の, (urbanlike) 都会風の

an urban sprawl 都会の乱開発

urge *v.* (**urge to do**) (…に)…するよう勧める, ((*formal*)) …するよう促す, (**urge on**) せき立てる
n. (strong desire) 衝動

I urged her to continue with her singing lessons.
彼女に歌のレッスンを続けるよう勧めました。

I wish you'd stop urging him on.
彼をせき立てるのは、やめてほしい。

She fought the urge to go shopping.
彼女は買い物に出かけたい衝動と闘った。

have the urge for/to do …したい衝動に駆られる

When you get the urge for something sweet, try a piece of fruit instead.
甘い物を食べたい衝動に駆られたら、代わりに果物を食べてみるといい。

urgent *adj.* 緊急の, 至急の

There's an urgent message for you.
緊急の伝言が届いていますよ。

The roof is in urgent need of repair.
屋根は至急、修理が必要です。

Mr. Takada is out on urgent business.
((*humble*)) 高田は急用で出ております。

♦ **urgently** *adv.* 緊急に, 至急

urinal *n.* 便器

urinary *adj.* 尿の

the urinary tract 尿管 [尿路]

urinate *v.* ((*formal*)) 排尿する, ((*masculine/informal*)) 小便する

urine *n.* ((*formal*)) 尿, ((*masculine/informal*)) 小便

URL *n.* ＵＲＬ

urn *n.* (for ashes, bones) 骨つぼ

U.S. *abbr.* (the United States) アメリカ [→ AMERICA]

us *pron.* 私たち, ((*masculine*)) 僕たち, ((*formal*)) 我々, (as direct object) 私たちを, (as indirect object) 私たちに [→ WE] [NOTE: If it is clear that "us" 私たち is the object of the sentence, it is omitted.]

The guide showed us around the palace.
ガイドが、宮殿の中を案内してくれた。

Why's he telling us this?
なぜ彼は、このことを私たちに話したのだろう?

usable *adj.* 使える, 利用できる

usage *n.* (of words) 使い方, 用法

U

use

1 *v.* **MAKE USE OF:** 使う, ((*formal*)) 用いる, 使用する, (utilize) 利用する, 活用する, (adopt) 採用する

2 *v.* **CONSUME:** 使う, 消費する

3 *v.* **TAKE ADVANTAGE OF:** 利用する

4 *n.* **USING:** 使用, 利用

1 Can I use it now?
もう使ってもいい？

It hasn't been used for a long time.
長い間使われていません。

I can't use my watch anymore. It's broken.
腕時計はもう使えない。壊れている。

If you use a chisel, you might get the job done faster.
のみを使えば、もっと手早く仕事を片付けられるんじゃないかな。

What do you use this closet for?
この押し入れは何に使うの？

It's easy to use. I'll show you.
使い方は簡単です。お見せしましょう。

Use your brains!
頭を使えよ！

2 The developed countries use most of the world's resources.
先進諸国が世界の資源の大半を消費している。

He uses drugs.
彼は麻薬をやっている。

3 She uses people.
彼女は人を利用する。

4 The scanner is in use right now.
スキャナーは今、使用中です。

This is for use only in an emergency.
これは非常用です。

be no use むだだ

There's no use getting angry now.
今さら怒ってもむだだよ。

It's no use grumbling.
ぼやいたって始まらない。

be of use to (…が) 使う, …の役に立つ

Is this chalk of any use to anyone?
このチョークは誰か使いますか？

bring back into use 復活させる

They're thinking of bringing trams back into use.
路面電車を復活させることが検討されています。

come into use 使われるようになる, 使われ出す, 実用化される

Solar-powered forms of mass transit have not come into use yet.
太陽エネルギーを利用した大量輸送の方法は、まだ実用化されていない。

go out of use 使われなくなる, 使用されなくなる

It went out of use years ago.
もう何年も前に使われなくなりました。

have no use for (…は) 必要ない

I've no use for these bookshelves.
私には、この本棚は必要ありません。

lose the use of (arm, leg etc.) …の自由を失う, (…が) 利かなくなる

make use of 使う, 利用する, 活用する

Try to make better use of your free time.
余暇をもっと有効に活用するようにしなさい。

put to use 使う, 利用する

I'm sure we'll be able to put it to some use.
きっと何かに利用できると思います。

what's the use of doing …して/…したって何になる

What's the use of talking to him? He won't agree.
あの人に話したって何になる? うんと言いやしないよ。

♦**use up** *v.* 使い果たす, 使い切る

Next time you use up all the toilet paper, change the roll.
今度トイレットペーパーを使い切った時は、新しいロールに差し替えておいてください。

used *adj.* (secondhand) 中古の, お古の

a used car 中古車

a used bookstore 古本屋

used to (expressing past practice) よく…したものだ, (**be used to**) …に慣れている, (**get used to**) …に慣れる

We used to fish in this river.
昔はこの川でよく魚を釣ったものです。

Did you use to meet at this place often?
この場所で、よく会ったのですか?

I didn't use to work as hard as I do now.
昔は、今ほど仕事をがんばっていたわけではなかった。

He's used to meeting people from all walks of life.
彼は、あらゆる職業の人と会うのに慣れています。

I doubt if we will ever get used to these terrorist attacks.
こうしたテロ攻撃に慣れることは、決してないだろう。

useful *adj.* (handy) 便利な, 役に立つ, ためになる

It's a useful phrase book to have when you travel.
旅行する時、持っていると便利な会話表現集ですよ。

It'd be useful for all of us to get together again later in the week.
全員が今週中にもう一度、集まれるといいのですが。

Try and make yourself useful.
人の役に立とうと努めなさい。

♦**usefully** *adv.* 有効に, 役立つように

usefulness *n.* 便利さ, ((*formal*)) 有用性

useless *adj.* (of no use) 役に立たない, (ineffectual, pointless) むだな

The bike's useless without wheels.
自転車は、車輪がないと何の役にも立たない。

He's completely useless.
あいつは、全くの役立たずだ。

It's useless to try to argue with him.
彼と議論しようとしてもむだです。

user *n.* 使用者, 利用者

♦**user group** *n.* ユーザーグループ

user name *n.* ユーザー名

user-friendly *adj.* 使いやすい, わかりやすい

usher *n.* 案内係

usual *adj.* いつもの, 普通の

Mr. Matsumoto came around at his usual time.
松本さんは、いつもの時間にやって来た。

It's usual to greet people with a smile where I come from.
私の生まれ育った所では、笑顔であいさつするのが普通です。

It's not usual for it to be so hot at this time of the year.
この時期にこんなに暑いのは普通じゃない。

as usual いつものように, いつもどおり, 相変わらず

You're late, as usual.
相変わらず遅刻だよ。

usually *adv.* いつもは, 普通は, ふだんは, たいてい

I usually skip breakfast on weekdays.
平日はたいてい、朝ご飯を抜きます。

usurp *v.* 奪う

utensil *n.* (kitchen utensil) 台所用品, (cooking utensil) 調理器具 [→ picture of COOKING UTENSILS]

uterus *n.* 子宮

utilitarian *adj.* (practical) 実用的な

utility *n.* (usefulness) 役に立つこと; (important service for everyone) 公益事業

utilize *v.* 利用する, 活用する

utmost *n., adj.* 最大限(の), 最大(の)

do one's utmost 全力を尽くす, 最善を尽くす

The paramedics did their utmost to revive the man.
救急救命士たちは、その男性を生き返らせようと最善を尽くした。

utopia *n.* ユートピア, 理想郷

utopian *adj.* (like a utopia) ユートピアのような; (unrealistic) 非現実的な, 夢物語の

utter[1] *adj.* 全くの, 完全な

It was an utter failure.
全くの失敗だった。

utter[2] *v.* (word) 口に出す, (cry, groan etc.) 出す, 上げる

utter a cry [moan]
叫び声 [うめき声] を上げる

utterance *n.* 発言

utterly *adv.* 全く, すっかり, 完全に

U-turn *n.* Uターン

V, v

vacancy *n.* (room) 空室, 空き室, (job) 欠員

vacant *adj.* (of room) あいている, (of look) うつろな [→ EMPTY]

a vacant room 空室

a vacant seat 空席

♦ **vacantly** *adv.* ぼんやり(と)

stare vacantly ぼんやり見つめる

vacate *v.* (room) 出る, あける, (apartment) 引き払う, (place) 立ち退く

vacation *n.* 休暇, 休み

take a vacation 休暇 [休み] を取る

go on (a) vacation 休暇に出かける

get back from (a) vacation 休暇から戻って来る

be (away) on vacation 休暇中です

a summer vacation 夏休み

Where are you going for your vacation?
休みには、どこへ行く予定ですか？

He was given a two-week paid vacation.
彼は2週間の有給休暇をもらった。

vaccinate *v.* (…に) 予防接種をする, (**be vaccinated**) 予防接種を受ける

be vaccinated against smallpox
種痘を受ける

♦ **vaccination** *n.* 予防接種

vaccine *n.* ワクチン

vacillate *v.* 揺れ動く, ぐらつく

♦ **vacillator** *n.* 優柔不断な人

vacuum *n.* 真空; (feeling that sth is missing) 空虚, ぽっかり穴があいた感じ

vacuum cleaner *n.* 電気掃除機

vagina *n.* 膣, バギナ

vagrant *n.* 放浪者, 浮浪者

vague *adj.* あいまいな, はっきりしない, あやふやな, 漠然とした

a vague reply あいまいな返事

He was deliberately vague.
彼は、わざとあいまいな言い方をした。

The instructions were too vague.
指示が漠然としすぎていた。

vaguely *adv.* (unclearly) あいまいに, 漠然と; (somehow) なんとなく

I vaguely expected I would be asked to do overtime.
なんとなく、残業を頼まれそうな気がした。

vain *adj.*

1 WITHOUT RESULT/USE/VALUE: むだな

2 CONCEITED: うぬぼれの強い, 虚栄心の強い, (**be vain about**) 鼻にかける

1 So does this mean that all our efforts have been in vain?
すべてはむだな努力だったというのか？

These soldiers did not die in vain.
兵士たちは、むだ死にしたわけではない。

It was a vain attempt to rescue the situation.
事態を収拾しようとしたが、むだだった。

vain words むなしい言葉

2 He's so vain.
うぬぼれの強い人だ。

take the Lord's name in vain みだりに神の名を挙げてののしる

valentine *n.* (card) バレンタインカード, (lover) 恋人

♦ **Valentine's Day** *n.* バレンタインデー

valiant *adj.* 勇敢な

valid *adj.* (effective) 有効な, (justifiable)

正当な, (appropriate, legitimate) 妥当な, もっともな

Is this ticket valid?
この券は使えますか？

Your membership card is valid for one year.
会員カードは1年間有効です。

Your train pass is no longer valid.
その定期券は期限が切れていますよ。

The reasons he gave were perfectly valid.
彼が挙げた理由は全く妥当なものだった。

validate *v.* (give credence to) 認める, 認可する, (make valid) 有効とする

validity *n.* (condition of being in effect) 有効性, (of argument) 妥当性

valley *n.* 谷, 谷間

a deep valley 深い谷

valuable *adj.* 価値のある, 高価な, (of advice) 有益な, (of experience) 貴重な

n. (**valuables**) 貴重品

It proved to be a very valuable painting.
とても高価な絵であることがわかった。

Thank you for the valuable advice.
有益なアドバイスをありがとう。

I count it as a valuable experience and one that I won't forget easily.
貴重な、忘れがたい経験だったと思っています。

valuation *n.* (assessing of value) 評価, 査定, (estimated value) 見積価格

value

1 *n.* WORTH: 価値, 値打ち

2 *n.* PRICE: 値段, 価格, 値

3 *n.* PRINCIPLES: (**values**) 価値観

4 *v.* VIEW AS IMPORTANT: 大切に思う, 高く評価する

5 *v.* ESTIMATE THE COST OF: 見積もる

1 the value of an education 教育の価値

You don't seem to put much value on art.
あなたは芸術にあまり重きを置いてないようですね。

Is it of value?
これは値打ちのある物ですか？

His services were of great value to society.
彼の功績は社会にとって大変意味のあるものだった。

2 The value of land in Hong Kong is extremely high.
香港の土地の値段は非常に高い。

The value of the dollar has gone up.
ドルの値が上がった。

3 traditional values 伝統的な価値観

moral values 道徳観

4 Mai certainly values her independence.
麻衣は自分の自立をとても大切に思っている。

5 The house was valued at ¥50 million.
その家は5000万円と見積もられた。

♦ **value judgment** *n.* 価値判断, 主観的判断

valueless *adj.* 価値のない, つまらない

valve *n.* 弁, バルブ

turn on a valve バルブをあける

vampire *n.* 吸血鬼

van *n.* バン

vandal *n.* (delinquent) 不良, (hooligan) フーリガン

vandalism *n.* 破壊行為

vandalize *v.* 破壊する

vanguard *n.* (troops at the front) 前衛, 先遣隊

in the vanguard (of) (in the lead) (…の)

先頭に立って

vanilla *n.* バニラ

vanish *v.* 消える, 消えていく, (from sight) 見えなくなる, (of pen etc.: become lost) なくなる, (become extinct) 消滅する

The pickpocket vanished in the crowd.
すりは人込みに紛れて見えなくなった。

That's odd—my keys seem to have vanished.
おかしいな、かぎがなくなったみたいだ。

If we are not more careful, a lot more animals and plants will vanish from the earth.
もっと考えなければ、さらに多くの動植物が地球上から消滅するでしょう。

vanity *n.* (conceitedness) うぬぼれ, 虚栄心

vanity publishing *n.* 自費出版

vantage point *n.* (place from which one can easily see things) 見晴らしの利く場所

vapid *adj.* (unimaginative, boring) つまらない

vapor *n.* 蒸気

water vapor 水蒸気

vaporize *v.* (become vapor) 蒸発する, 気化する

variable *adj.* (changes easily) 変わりやすい, (inconsistent) むらのある

n. (unpredictable factor) 変わりやすいもの, 不確定要素; (in math: letter representing a quantity) 変数

variant *n.* 変形, (word) 異形

variation *n.* バリエーション, 変化, 変動, 幅 [→ CHANGE]

There's not a lot of variation in their act.
彼らの芸には、あまり幅がない。

There's too much variation in the temperature to provide a stable environment for the experiment.
気温の変動が激しすぎて、安定した実験環境が得られない。

varicose veins *n.* 静脈瘤

varied *adj.* さまざまな, いろいろな, 多様な

variety *n.* バラエティー, 多様性, (change) 変化, (kind) 種類; (kind of entertainment) バラエティー

Variety is the spice of life.
いろいろあるからこそ人生は楽しい。

This dull routine is no good for you. You need some variety in your life.
こんな単調な毎日を過ごしていてはよくないよ。君の生活には変化が必要だ。

This variety of mushroom only grows in a very limited area.
この種類のキノコは、ごく限られた地域にしか生えません。

a variety of (many different types of) いろいろな, さまざまな, 多様な

There's an amazing variety of butterflies on the island.
島には、驚くほど多様なチョウが生息しています。

for the sake of variety 変化をつけるため, 目先を変えて

various *adj.* いろいろな, さまざまな, 多彩な

There are various reasons why I can't go.
行けない理由はいろいろある。

There are various methods you can use.
いろいろな方法が使えますよ。

various Asian countries アジア諸国

♦**variously** *adv.* いろいろと, さまざまに

varnish *n.* (for wood) ニス

v. (…に) ニスを塗る

vary *v.* (differ) 違う, 異なる, (change) 変わる, (cause to change) 変える, (give variety to) (…に) 変化をつける

People's likes and dislikes tend to vary according to their age group.
好き嫌いは、年齢層によって異なる傾向がある。

His opinion seems to vary from day to day.
あの人の意見は日によって変わるようだ。

The estimates for this job vary a great deal, don't you think?
この仕事の見積額には、かなりの差があると思いませんか？

We need to try to vary our approach.
アプローチを変えてみる必要がある。

varying *adj.* さまざまな, いろいろな

varying levels of language proficiency
言語のさまざまな習熟度

vase *n.* (for flowers) 花びん, (earthenware) つぼ [→ picture of ROOM]

Would you arrange the flowers in that vase, please?
花をその花びんに生けてもらえますか？

vast *adj.* (large, spacious) 広大な, (of number, amount) 莫大な, (of degree) ものすごい, 大変な

Asia is a vast continent.
アジアは広大な大陸だ。

the vast majority of the people
圧倒的多数の人々

vastly *adv.* (very) 非常に, とても

vat *n.* たる, 大桶

vault[1] *n.* (curved ceiling) アーチ形天井, (curved roof) アーチ形屋根; (storage space for money) 金庫

The diamonds were kept in the bank's vault.
ダイヤ(モンド)は銀行の金庫に保管されていた。

vault[2] *v.* (jump over) 飛び越える

VCR *n.* ビデオカセットレコーダー, ビデオデッキ

veal *n.* 子牛の肉

vector *n.* (quantity) ベクトル

veer *v.* (of car) 向きを変える [→ SWERVE]

veer off a road 道からそれる

vegan *n.* 絶対菜食主義者

vegetable *n.* 野菜, (as opp. to "mineral" and "animal") 植物; (person in a coma) 植物人間

adj. (derived from plants) 植物性の

vegetable juice 野菜ジュース

vegetable soap 植物性石けん

vegetarian *n.* 菜食主義者, ベジタリアン

vegetate *v.* (do nothing) ぼうっと時を過ごす

vegetation *n.* (plants) 植物, 草木

vehement *adj.* 激しい

♦**vehemence** *n.* 激しさ

vehemently *adv.* 激しく

vehicle *n.* (for transport) 乗り物; (for ideas) 伝達手段

veil *n.* ベール

veiled *adj.* (wearing a veil) ベールをかぶった, (hidden) 隠された

vein *n.* (blood vessel) 血管, 静脈

in the same vein 同じ調子で

KANJI BRIDGE

脈 ON: みゃく KUN: — | VEIN, PULSE, CONNECTION

artery .... 動脈
(literary) context .... 文脈
gold vein .... 金脈
mountain range .... 山脈
personal connections .... 人脈
pulse rate .... 脈拍
vein .... 静脈
vein of ore .... 鉱脈

Velcro *n.* マジックテープ
velocity *n.* 速度 [→ SPEED 1]
velvet *n.* ベルベット, ビロード
velvety *adj.* ベルベット [ビロード] のような
vendetta *n.* 長年にわたる抗争
 have a vendetta against ...と長い間争う
vending machine *n.* 自動販売機
vendor *n.* 売り主
veneer *n.* (overlay of fine wood) 化粧板; (superficial display) 虚飾, 見せかけ
venerable *adj.* 尊敬すべき
venereal disease *n.* 性病
vengeance *n.* 復讐
 take vengeance on ...に復讐する
venison *n.* シカの肉
venom *n.* 毒
venomous *adj.* (of animal) 毒を出す, 毒-
 a venomous snake 毒蛇
vent *n.* (opening for air) 通気孔, (of volcano) 噴火口
 v. (vent anger) (怒りを)ぶちまける
ventilate *v.* (...の)換気をする, 空気を入れ替える
ventilation *n.* 換気
ventilator *n.* (for room) 換気装置, (for person: machine that helps one breathe) 人工呼吸器
ventriloquist *n.* 腹話術師
venture *n.* (business) 新事業
 v. (go in spite of risks) (危険を冒して)行く, 進む, (say in spite of risk of criticism) あえて言う, 思い切って言う
 The water was deep, so I didn't venture any further out.
 水深が深かったので、それ以上先へは進まなかった。
 venture a question 思い切って質問する
♦**venture capital** *n.* 危険投下資本, 投機資本
venue *n.* 開催地, 会場
Venus *n.* (planet) 金星; (goddess in Roman mythology) ビーナス
veranda *n.* ベランダ, (traditional Japanese veranda) 縁側
verb *n.* 動詞
 an auxiliary verb 助動詞
verbal *adj.* (spoken) 言葉による, 口頭の; (relating to verbs) 動詞の
 a verbal agreement 口約束
 verbal abuse 言葉の暴力
 a verbal warning 口頭注意
verbalize *v.* 言葉で表す, 言葉にする
verbatim *adv.* 一字一句そのまま
verdict *n.* (in court) 評決, (in general: judgment) 判断
 The police were not happy with the verdict: they thought the sentence was too

V

lenient.
警察は刑が軽すぎるとして、評決に不満だった。

Well, what's your verdict? Was the party a success?
で、感想は？ パーティーは成功だったと思う？

verge *n.* (edge) 端
v. (**verge on**) …に近い

Michiko was on the verge of tears.
美智子は今にも泣きそうだった。

be on the verge of doing …しそうになっている, …しかけている

I was on the verge of quitting, but I was persuaded to give it one more try.
仕事を辞めかけていたけど、もう一度やってみたらどうかと説得された。

verify *v.* (prove the truth of) 立証する, (check) 確かめる

♦ **verifiable** *adj.* 立証できる

vernacular *n.* 方言, 土地の言葉

versatile *adj.* (talented) 多才な, (of performer) 多芸の, (of tool) 何にでも使える, 万能の

verse[1] *n.* (of poem) 行, (of the Bible) 節

verse[2] *v.* (**verse oneself in**) …に精通している

version *n.* (explanation) 説明, 見解, (edition, adaptation: of book, film, software) -版, バージョン, (translation) -訳

Your version of events seems to differ from hers.
あなたの説明は、彼女の話とは違うようです。

There are two versions of this film and I prefer the earlier one.
この題の映画は2バージョンあって、私は古いほうが好きです。

This is a different version—it's the Russian version.
これは違う版、ロシア語版ですよ。

the Japanese version of *War and Peace*
『戦争と平和』の日本語版

versus *prep.* (against) …対; (in contradistinction to) …に対して, …か…か

It's Brazil versus Italy.
ブラジル対イタリアだ。

country life versus city life
田舎暮らしか都会生活か

vertebra *n.* 脊椎

vertebrate *n.* 脊椎動物
adj. 脊椎のある

vertical *adj.* 縦の, 垂直の
n. (line) 縦の線, 垂直線, (plane) 垂直面

vertical writing 縦書き

The walls were not vertical but sloping.
塀は垂直ではなく、傾いていた。

vertigo *n.* めまい

experience/suffer vertigo めまいがする

very

1 *adv.* TO A HIGH/FREQUENT DEGREE: とても, すごく, 大変, 非常に, 全く, なかなか, (**very best**) 最高の, (**very newest/latest**) 最新の, (**not very…**) あまり…ない, (**very little**) ほとんど…ない

2 *adj.* EXTREME: See examples below

3 *adj.* EXACT: まさにその

1 That's a very good idea.
とてもいい考えだ。

It's very loud in here.
この中はすごくうるさい。

It will be very difficult to convince him.
彼を納得させるのは非常に難しい。

That's very true. 全くそのとおりです。

I think it's one of his very best works.
これは彼の最高傑作の一つだと思う。

the very latest technology 最新の技術

He's not there very often.
あの人がそこにいることはあまりない。

"Why don't you tell her to get lost?"
"I can't very well tell her that."
「どこかへうせろと言ったらどう?」
「そうもいかないよ」

"Is the work interesting?" "Not very."
「仕事は面白い?」「いや、あまり」

I'm sorry, I know very little about this industry.
申し訳ありませんが、この業界についてはほとんど知りません。

2 The president's (=CEO's) office is at the very end of the hall.
社長室は廊下の突き当たりです。

I climbed to the very top.
てっぺんまで登りきった。

3 Those were her very words.
それがまさに彼女の言った言葉だった。

You're the very man we're looking for.
あなたこそ私たちの探していた人です。

at the very least せめて

At the very least, you could have called.
せめて電話ぐらいくれればよかったのに。

very much so (yes) ええとても, (expressing agreement) まさにそのとおり

"So, now you have a home of your very own. You must be proud."
"Oh, yes. Very much so."
「マイホームを手に入れて、さぞかしうれしいでしょう」
「それはもう、とても」

"He needs to learn a lesson."
"Yes, very much so."
「あいつは痛い目にあわないとだめだね」
「ああ、全くそのとおりだ」

very well わかりました, ((*polite*)) 承知しました, ((*humble*)) かしこまりました

"Would you bring him in?"
"Very well, sir."
「その方を連れて来てくれますか」
「承知しました」

vessel ***n.*** (ship) 船; (container) 入れ物, 容器

vest ***n.*** ベスト, チョッキ

vested interest ***n.*** 既得権, 利権

vestige ***n.*** (trace) なごり, 跡

veteran ***n.*** (ex-serviceperson) 退役軍人, (old hand) ベテラン

adj. (experienced) ベテランの

a veteran Japanese language teacher
ベテランの日本語教師

Veteran's Day ***n.*** 復員軍人の日

veterinarian ***n.*** 獣医

veto ***n.*** 拒否, (right of veto) 拒否権

v. 拒否する

The president vetoed the bill.
大統領は法案を拒否した。

vex ***v.*** 悩ませる, 困らせる

via ***prep.*** (by traveling through) …を経て, …経由で, (by means of) …を通して

We flew to Japan via Los Angeles.
ロス経由で日本行きの便に乗った。

I got the news via his secretary.
彼の秘書を通してそのことを知りました。

V

viable *adj.* 現実的な, 実行可能な

♦ **viability** *n.* (of plan) 実行可能性

viaduct *n.* 陸橋

vial *n.* 小びん

vibe *n.* (**vibes**) (=feeling) 感じ, (=atmosphere) 雰囲気

good [bad] vibes いい [悪い] 感じ

vibrant *adj.* (of personality) 活発な, (of city) 活気のある, (of color) 鮮やかな

vibrate *v.* 振動する, 揺れる

vibration *n.* 振動 [→ VIBE]

vicar *n.* 牧師

vice *n.* (moral vice) 悪徳, (character flaw, weakness) 欠点, 弱点

vice- *pref.* 副-

vice admiral *n.* (in U.S. Navy) 中将

vice president *n.* (of country) 副大統領, (of company) 副社長, (of bank) 副頭取

vice-versa *adv.* 反対に, 逆に

vicinity *n.* 近所, 近辺, 周辺

in the vicinity (of) (…の) 近くに

vicious *adj.* (violent and cruel) 残酷な, 凶悪な, (of animal) どう猛な

a vicious criminal 凶悪な犯罪者

a vicious dog どう猛な犬

♦ **vicious circle** *n.* 悪循環

viciously *adv.* 残酷に

viciousness *n.* (cruelness) 凶悪さ, 残忍さ

victim *n.* (of accident, war) 犠牲者, (of crime, natural disaster) 被害者

a rape victim レイプ事件の被害者

victimize *v.* (treat unjustly) 不当に苦しめる

♦ **victimization** *n.* 不当に苦しめること

victimless *adj.* 被害者のいない

victor *n.* (in sport, game) 勝った人, 勝者, (in war) 戦勝者

Victorian *adj.* (of architecture) ビクトリア様式の, (of people, values) ビクトリア朝の

n. (**Victorians**) ビクトリア朝時代の人

victorious *adj.* 勝利を得た

victory *n.* 勝利

It was a victory for peace.
平和の勝利だった。

video *n.* (videotape) ビデオ(テープ)

video camera *n.* ビデオカメラ

video conferencing *n.* テレビ会議

video game *n.* テレビゲーム, ビデオゲーム

video jockey *n.* ビデオジョッキー, ＶＪ

videotape *n.* ビデオ

v. 録画する

vie *v.* 競い合う, 争う

The two giant electronic companies vied with each other for supremacy in the video game market.
巨大な電気メーカー2社は、テレビゲームの市場で優位に立とうと競い合っていた。

view

1 *n.* SCENE: 眺め, 見晴らし, 景色

2 *n.* WAY OF LOOKING AT THINGS: 考え方, 見方, (**views**: opinions) 見解, 意見

3 *v.* LOOK AT: 見る, 眺める

4 *v.* CONSIDER: 考える

1 The view from the window was excellent.
窓からの眺めは最高だった。

The new building will block our view.
新しく建つビルが、この眺めをさえぎるでしょう。

V

an oceanfront view 海に面した眺め

2 She has a very warped view of the world.
彼女は世界について、ゆがんだ見方をしている。

His views are not shared by everyone.
あの人の意見に誰もが賛成しているわけではない。

3 Viewed from the air, the city looks beautiful.
空から眺めると、この街は美しい。

4 I don't view it that way.
私はそんなふうに考えない。

come into view 見えてくる

The ship came into view.
船が見えてきた。

in full view of …の面前で

He did it in full view of the public.
彼は公衆の面前でやったんです。

in view of …を考えると, …を考慮して

In view of the fact that it's raining, we'd better call off the barbecue.
雨が降っていることを考えると、バーベキューはやめたほうがよさそうだ。

on view 展示されて, 公開されて

There's a lot of modern art on view.
たくさんの現代美術が展示されています。

take a dim view of よく思わない, …に感心しない

The teachers took a dim view of his behavior.
教師たちは、その生徒の態度をよく思わなかった。

with a view to doing …するつもりで, …するために

I went with a view to explaining our side of the matter.
私たちの立場を説明するために行った。

viewer *n.* (of TV program) 視聴者

viewpoint *n.* 観点, 見地, 立場

vigilance *n.* (care) 用心

vigilant *adj.* 油断のない

vigor *n.* 元気, 活気, 精力

vigorous *adj.* (lively) 活気のある, (active) 活発な, (healthy) 元気な, (intense) 激しい, (enthusiastic) 積極的な

♦ **vigorously** *adv.* (strongly) 強く, (enthusiastically) 積極的に

vile *adj.* いやな

villa *n.* 別荘

village *n.* 村, (remote mountain village) 山里

♦ **villager** *n.* 村の人, 村人

villain *n.* (bad person) 悪人, 悪者, 悪漢, 悪党, (in movie) 悪役

vindicate *v.* (prove the truth of) (…が) 正しいことを証明する, (…の) 正当性を立証する, (prove the innocence of) (…の) 潔白を証明する

The government's decision to raise interest rates was vindicated.
政府による利率引き上げの決定は、正しいことが立証された。

♦ **vindication** *n.* 証明, 立証するもの

vindictive *adj.* (spiteful) 悪意のある, 意地の悪い

vine *n.* (grapevine) ブドウの木, (in general) つる植物

vinegar *n.* 酢, ビネガー

vineyard *n.* ブドウ園

vintage *adj.* (of wine) 極上の, (in general: classic) 名作の, 傑作の, (of clothing) ビンテージものの

n. (of wine) ワイン醸造年度(じょうぞうねんど)

vintage clothing ビンテージ古着(ふるぎ)

vinyl *n.* ビニル基(き) [NOTE: ビニール means "plastic."]; (LP records) レコード

viola *n.* ビオラ

♦ **violist** *n.* ビオラ奏者(そうしゃ)

violate *v.* (law) (…に) 違反(いはん)する, (…を) 破(やぶ)る

violation *n.* (of law) 違反(いはん), (of rights) 侵害(しんがい)

violence *n.* 暴力(ぼうりょく), 暴行(ぼうこう)

It's a pity that violence is the only thing some people understand.
暴力(ぼうりょく)しか知らない人がいるのは、情(なさ)けないことだ。

violent *adj.* (of behavior) 暴力的(ぼうりょくてき)な, 乱暴(らんぼう)な, (of storm) 激(はげ)しい
violent movies 暴力的(ぼうりょくてき)な映画(えいが)

violently *adv.* (intensely) 激(はげ)しく, (roughly) 乱暴(らんぼう)に

violet *n.* (flower) スミレ, (color) スミレ色(いろ)

violin *n.* バイオリン

♦ **violinist** *n.* バイオリニスト, バイオリン奏者(そうしゃ)

VIP *n.* 要人(ようじん), ビップ

virgin *n.* 処女(しょじょ), バージン
adj. (of forest) 未踏(みとう)の, 未開発(みかいはつ)の

♦ **virgin forest** *n.* 原生林(げんせいりん)

virginity *n.* (of female) 処女(しょじょ), (of male) 童貞(どうてい)

lose one's virginity 処女(しょじょ) [童貞(どうてい)] を失(うしな)う

Virgo *n.* (the Virgin) 乙女座(おとめざ)

virile *adj.* (masculine) 男性的(だんせいてき)な, (having sexual prowess) 性的能力(せいてきのうりょく)のある

virtual *adj.* 実際(じっさい)の, 事実上(じじつじょう)の

♦ **virtual reality** *n.* バーチャルリアリティ

virtually *adv.* 実質的(じっしつてき)に, 事実上(じじつじょう), ほとんど

virtue *n.* (moral virtue) 美徳(びとく), (advantage, good point) 利点(りてん), 長所(ちょうしょ) [→ ADVANTAGE, GOOD 11]

Modesty is a virtue.
謙虚(けんきょ)さは美徳(びとく)です。

The job has its virtues, the main one being the company car.
この仕事(しごと)にも利点(りてん)はある。第一(だいいち)は、会社(かいしゃ)の車(くるま)を使(つか)えることだ。

by virtue of …のおかげで, …の力(ちから)で

He won by virtue of his size.
体格(たいかく)のおかげで彼は勝(か)った。

virtuoso *n.* 名手(めいしゅ), 大家(たいか)

virtuous *adj.* (principled) 高潔(こうけつ)な, 立派(りっぱ)な

virulent *adj.* (vicious) 悪意(あくい)のある, (of disease) 悪性(あくせい)の, (of poison) 毒性(どくせい)の強い

♦ **virulence** *n.* (viciousness) 憎悪(ぞうお)

virus *n.* ウイルス

visa *n.* ビザ, 査証(さしょう)
a cultural visa 文化(ぶんか)ビザ
a work visa 就労(しゅうろう)ビザ

A tourist visa allows you to stay here for three months.
観光(かんこう)ビザで滞在(たいざい)できる期間(きかん)は3ヵ月(さんげつ)です。

Did you get your visa extended?
ビザの期限(きげん)を延長(えんちょう)してもらえましたか？

viscosity *n.* 粘性(ねんせい), (stickiness) 粘着性(ねんちゃくせい)

viscount *n.* 子爵(ししゃく)

viscountess *n.* 子爵夫人(ししゃくふじん)

viscous *adj.* 粘(ねば)り気(け)のある, どろどろした

visibility *n.* 視界(しかい)

good [poor] visibility

良好な [不良な] 視界

visible *adj.* (can be seen) 見える, 目に見える, (clear) 明らかな [→ SEE]

Mt. Fuji is visible from Tokyo in the winter months.
冬は東京から富士山が見える。

vision *n.* (ability to see) 視力, (foresight) 見通し, 先見の明; (thing seen in a dream/trance) 幻, 幻影

have good [bad] vision
視力がいい [悪い]

a vision of the future 将来の見通し

a man of vision 先見の明のある人

Blake, it is said, frequently had visions of paradise.
ブレークは頻繁に、楽園の幻影を見たと言われている。

visionary *n.* (person who can tell the future) 予言者, (clairvoyant) 透視者, (person with foresight and determination) 先見の明のある人

visit *v.* (go to see) 訪ねる, (go to meet) (…に) 会いに行く, ((*formal*)) 訪問する, (visit for sightseeing) (…に) 見物に行く, (…を) 訪れる

n. (act of visiting) ((*formal*)) 訪問, (sightseeing) 見物, (stay, sojourn) 滞在

We visited Grandma about a year ago.
1年ほど前に祖母を訪ねた。

No one ever seems to visit me.
誰も私に会いに来てくれない。

Would you like to visit us next Friday?
今度の金曜日に遊びに来ませんか？

They are expecting the president to visit next year.
大統領が来年訪問する予定になっています。

Thousands of people visit the Grand Canyon every year.
毎年何千人もの人が、グランドキャニオンを訪れる。

This is our first visit to London.
ロンドンに来たのは初めてです。

We had a very nice visit with our relatives.
親戚と会って楽しく過ごした。

We didn't stay long. It was just a brief visit.
私たちは長くはいなかった。ほんの短い滞在だった。

a three-day visit 3日間の滞在

♦**visiting hours** *n.* (at hospital) 面会時間

visiting professor *n.* 客員教授

visitation *n.* 訪問, (visitation rights: of parent) 面接交渉権

visitor *n.* 客, ((*polite*)) お客さん, ((*formal*)) 来客, (tourist) 観光客

visor *n.* (on helmet) バイザー, (in car) サンバイザー [→ picture of CAR]

vista *n.* (view) 眺め

visual *adj.* 視覚の, 視覚的な

♦**visual aid** *n.* 視覚教材

visual arts *n.* 視覚芸術

visualize *v.* (imagine) 想像する, 思い描く

vital *adj.* (crucial) きわめて重要な, (essential) 絶対必要な, 不可欠な

It's of vital importance that we get that information.
その情報を手に入れることがきわめて重要だ。

It was vital that we break the enemy's code.
敵の暗号を解読することが不可欠だった。

vitality ***n.*** 元気, バイタリティー

vitamin ***n.*** ビタミン

vitamin C ビタミンC

vivacious ***adj.*** (lively) 活発な, 元気な, (cheerful) 陽気な

viva voce ***n.*** 口頭試験, 口述テスト

vivid ***adj.*** (of color) 鮮やかな, ビビッドな, (of description) 生き生きとした, (of memory) 鮮明な, (of imagery) 生々しい

vivisection ***n.*** 生体解剖

viz. ***adv.*** ((*written*)) すなわち

VJ ***n.*** ＶＪ, ビデオジョッキー

V-neck ***n.*** Ｖネック

vocabulary ***n.*** 語彙, ボキャブラリー, (all the words in a language) 総語彙, (list of words) 単語集, 用語集

vocal ***adj.*** (of voice) 声の, (of person: outspoken) 声高に主張する, 口やかましい

n. (part of band) ボーカル

There was some vocal opposition to the plan.
その計画には、いくつかの反対の声があった。

Who's on vocals?
ボーカルは誰ですか？

♦ **vocal chords** ***n.*** 声帯

vocalist ***n.*** ボーカリスト, 歌手

vocation ***n.*** (job that one was meant to do) 天職

vocational ***adj.*** (pertaining to one's job) 職業の; (of course) 職業指導の

vocational training 職業訓練

vociferous ***adj.*** (strident) 大声で叫ぶ, うるさい

vodka ***n.*** ウオッカ

vogue ***n.*** 流行

be in vogue 流行している, はやっている

voice ***n.*** 声, (right to express one's opinion) 発言権

His voice was so quiet I could hardly hear what he was saying.
あの人の声はあまりに小さくて、何を言っているのか、ほとんど聞き取れなかった。

Keep your voices down, will you!
声を抑えて！

Hey now, there's no need to raise your voice.
もう声を荒げる必要はないよ。

Don't take that tone of voice with me, young man!
((*feminine*)) あんた、私に向かってそんな口のきき方はないでしょう！

In a democracy, everyone has a voice.
民主主義においては、誰もが発言権をもっている。

lose one's voice 声が出なくなる

with one voice (in unison) 口をそろえて

void

1 ***n.*** EMPTINESS: (empty space) 空間; (empty feeling) 空虚感, むなしさ

2 ***adj.*** NOT VALID: 無効の

3 ***v.*** NULLIFY: 無効にする

1 No one can fill the void left by his death.
彼が死んでからの心のむなしさは、誰も埋めることはできない。

In Buddhism, "the Void" is a concept.
仏教では「空」は一つの観念である。

2 The contract is void. 契約は無効です。

3 The application must be filled in completely or it will be voided.

申請書は、全部きちんと記入されていないと無効になります。

be void of (have no…) (…が) ない

The defendant's voice was void of all emotion.
被告の声には、感情というものが全くなかった。

null and void 無効の

volatile ***adj.*** (of substance) 揮発性の, (of relations, situation) 一触即発の; (of person) 激しやすい

volcanic ***adj.*** 火山の

a volcanic rock 火山岩

volcano ***n.*** 火山

The volcano erupted. 火山が噴火した。

volition ***n.*** 意志, 決断

of one's own volition 自らの意志で

volitional ***adj.*** (of action) 意志に基づく

♦ **volitional form** ***n.*** (verb form) 意志形

volley ***v.*** (in sport) ボレーをする

volleyball ***n.*** バレーボール

volt ***n.*** ボルト

voltage ***n.*** 電圧, ボルト数

volume ***n.*** (loudness) ボリューム, 音量, (amount) 量, ボリューム, (cubic capacity) 容積, 容量; (one of a set of books) -巻, -冊

Could you turn down the volume, please?
音量を下げてもらえますか？

The volume of trade between the two countries has decreased.
2国間の貿易量は減少した。

Can you tell me what the volume of this container is?
この容器の容量はどれくらいか、教えていただけますか？

How many volumes are there in the complete works?
全集は何巻あるのですか？

I've read the first two volumes, but there are still two more to read.
初めの2巻は読んだけれど、まだ2巻残っている。

voluminous ***adj.*** (of book) 膨大な, (of container) 大きい [→ BAGGY]

voluntary ***adj.*** (of work) ボランティアの, (of action: of one's own volition) 自発的な, 任意の, 自主的な

It was voluntary work to help the disabled.
体の不自由な人を援助するための、ボランティア活動だった。

You don't have to go. It says attendance is voluntary.
別に行かなくてもいいんだよ。出席は任意と書いてある。

It's all run on a voluntary basis.
すべて自主的に運営されている。

We don't get paid—it's a voluntary organization.
報酬はもらっていません——任意団体なんです。

volunteer ***n.*** ボランティア, 有志, (for military service) 志願兵

v. (**volunteer to do**) 買って出る, 進んで…する, …しようと申し出る, (volunteer for: do volunteer work for) (…の) ボランティア活動をする

a volunteer nurse ボランティアの看護師

volunteer work ボランティア活動

I volunteered to clean up after the party.
パーティーの後片付けを買って出た。

vomit *v.* 吐く, もどす

n. 吐いた物, ((*informal*)) げろ

The cat vomited on the carpet.
猫は、じゅうたんの上に吐いた。

voracious *adj.* (of eater) 大食の, もりもり食べる, (of appetite) 旺盛な

vote *n.* (expression of choice) 票, (act of voting) 投票, (total number of votes) 得票数

v. (express one's views by voting) (…に) 票を入れる, 投票する, (**vote for/against**) …に賛成の/反対の票を入れる, (suggest: **I vote…**) …しよう, …しない?

It's time to count the votes.
開票の時間だ。

It was decided that we should take a vote on it.
多数決で決めることになった。

the right to vote 選挙権

I vote we order a pizza.
ピザを注文しようよ。

♦ **vote of confidence** *n.* 信任投票

vote of no confidence *n.* 不信任投票

voting booth *n.* 投票記入所

voting machine *n.* 投票機

voter *n.* 投票者, 有権者

vouch *v.* (**vouch for**) 保証する

voucher *n.* 券, (travel voucher) クーポン

vow *n.* 誓い

v. 誓う, (make a vow) 誓いを立てる

vowel *n.* 母音

voyage *n.* (sea voyage) 航海, 船旅, (air voyage) 空の旅, (space voyage) 宇宙旅行

v. 旅をする

bon voyage よいご旅行を, 気をつけて

voyeur *n.* のぞき魔

vulgar *adj.* (of language, joke) 下品な, いやらしい, (of taste) 悪趣味な, (of TV program, magazine) 低俗な, 俗悪な [→ LEWD]

I'd rather you didn't use that vulgar expression.
その下品な表現は使わないでほしい。

He wears flashy clothes and really has the most vulgar taste.
彼は派手な服を着て、実に趣味が悪い。

I thought the program was vulgar.
低俗な番組だと思った。

vulgarity *n.* (tastelessness) 下品, (sleaziness) 低俗; (filthy expression) 下品な表現

vulnerable *adj.* (easy to hurt) 傷つきやすい, (weak) 弱い, もろい, (open to attack) 攻撃を受けやすい, (susceptible to illness) 病気にかかりやすい

The nation had no navy and was vulnerable to attack.
その国は海軍を持たず、攻撃を受けやすかった。

Old people are particularly vulnerable to illness.
お年寄りは特に、病気にかかりやすい。

♦ **vulnerability** *n.* (weak point) 弱み, もろさ

vulture *n.* (bird) ハゲワシ; (person) 強欲な人

vulva *n.* 外陰部

W, w

wad *n.* (bundle) 束, (mass of soft material) かたまり

a wad of bills 札束

wade *v.* (through water/mud) (…の中を) 歩く, (across river) 歩いて渡る

wade across a river 川を歩いて渡る

wafer *n.* (thin cracker) ウエハース

waffle *n.* ワッフル

waft *v.* (drift) 漂う

n. (odor) 漂うにおい, (fragrance) 漂う香り

a waft of fresh air 新鮮な空気の香り

wag *v.* (tail) 振る

The dog wagged its tail.
犬はしっぽを振った。

wage *n.* 賃金, 給料 [→ PAY, SALARY]

v. (war, campaign) する, 行う

low [high] wages 低 [高] 賃金

Wages are low in the service sector.
サービス業は賃金が低い。

an hourly [a weekly, a monthly] wage
時給 [週給, 月給]

The United States waged war on Iraq.
アメリカはイラクと戦争をした。

wager *n.* (a bet)賭け, (money bet) 賭け金

v. 賭ける

wager money on …にお金を賭ける

wagon *n.* (four-wheeled vehicle) 四輪車, (horse-drawn) 荷馬車, (hand-drawn, for child) おもちゃの荷車

wail *v.* 泣き叫ぶ

n. 泣き叫ぶ声

waist *n.* (part of the body) ウエスト, 腰, (of article of clothing) 胴着

What is your waist measurement?
ウエストのサイズはいくつですか？

waistline *n.* ウエストライン

wait

1 *v.* REMAIN IN STATE OF ANTICIPATION: 待つ, ((*polite*)) お待ちになる, ((*humble*)) お待ちする

2 *n.* PERIOD OF WAITING: 待ち時間

3 *v.* BE PUT OFF: (**can wait**) 延ばせる, 急がない, (**will have to wait**) 延ばすしかない

4 *v.* WORK AS A WAITER: (**wait tables**) 給仕をする

1 How long have you been waiting?
どのくらい待っていますか？

Do you want me to wait here for you?
ここで待っててほしい？

I waited up till midnight, but our daughter still hadn't come home.
夜12時まで寝ずに待ったけど、娘は帰って来なかった。

Sorry to keep you waiting.
((*polite*)) お待たせしてすみません。

Could you wait just a minute, please?
ちょっと待ってくれる？

I'm tired of waiting around for him to make up his mind!
彼が決心するのを待つだけなんて、うんざりだ。

Dinner is waiting for you.
夕食ができていますよ。

2 The wait for a table was forty-five minutes.
席の待ち時間は45分だった。

It was a long wait.
ずいぶん待たされたよ。

There was a five-hour wait to get inside.
入るのに5時間待った。

3 I'm sorry, but this matter cannot wait.
申し訳ありませんが、この件は延ばせないんです。

"The meeting can wait."
"No, it cannot."
「打ち合わせは、急ぎませんよ」
「いいえ、後回しにできません」

The phone call will have to wait till Monday.
電話は月曜日まで延ばすしかない。

4 Mikami has a job waiting tables.
三上さんは給仕の仕事をしている。

can't wait to do 早く…したい, …したくてたまらない

I can't wait to see the movie.
あの映画を早く見たい。

wait and see 成り行きを見守る, 様子を見る

Let's wait and see what the results are before making a decision.
決定を下す前に、その結果の成り行きを見守りましょう。

Let's just wait and see, shall we?
しばらく様子を見ることにしようか。

wait one's turn 順番を待つ

wait around *v.* (…で)待つ

We had to wait around the airport for hours.
何時間も空港で待たなければならなかった。

wait on *v.* (customer) …に給仕する, …の接客をする

waiter *n.* ウェーター [NOTE: To get a waiter's attention, call out すみません.]

waiting list *n.* (at restaurant) 順番待ちのリスト, (for flight) キャンセル待ちの名簿

be on the waiting list 順番を待っている

waiting room *n.* 待合室

waitress *n.* ウェートレス [→ WAITER]

waive *v.* (cancel) 放棄する

wake[1]

1 *v.* FROM SLEEP: (stop sleeping, open eyes) 目が覚める, 目を覚ます, (cause to wake up) 目覚めさせる, (rise from bed) 起きる, (cause to rise from bed) 起こす

2 *v.* COME TO ONE'S SENSES: 目覚める, (**wake up to**) …に気がつく, …を悟る

3 *n.* CEREMONY: (お)通夜

1 I woke up early this morning.
けさは早く目が覚めた。

Wake up! You'll be late for work.
起きて！ 仕事に遅れるよ。

Could you wake me up at 6 o'clock tomorrow morning?
明日の朝6時に起こしてくれますか？

What! Are they still in bed? I'll wake them up.
えっ、まだ寝てるの？ 起こしてくるよ。

2 The patient woke up from a long coma.
患者は長い昏睡状態から目覚めた。

One day he'll wake up to the fact that he's no longer young.
いずれ、あの人も自分はもう若くないってことに気がつくでしょう。

3 Did you go the wake?
お通夜に行きましたか？

wake² ***n.*** (track of waves behind boat etc.) 航跡

in the wake of (in the aftermath of) …の結果

walk

1 ***v.*** MOVE USING FEET: 歩く, (walk somewhere) 歩いて行く, (go for a stroll) 散歩する

2 ***n.*** STROLL: 散歩, ウォーキング

3 ***v.*** TAKE FOR A WALK: (dog) 散歩させる

4 ***v.*** ESCORT: 送る, (…に)付き添う

5 ***n.*** DISTANCE TO WALK: 道のり

6 ***n.*** PATH: 道, 歩道, 散歩道

7 ***n.*** MANNER OF WALKING: 歩き方

1 Don't walk so quickly.
そんなに速く歩かないで。

They walked together arm in arm.
二人は腕を組んで歩いた。

I walk to work every morning.
毎朝、歩いて仕事に行きます。

I prefer to walk rather than take the bus.
バスに乗るより歩いて行くほうがいい。

I like walking.
散歩するのは [歩くのは] 好きです。

I walked around the park for about an hour.
1時間くらい、公園をぶらぶらした。

2 Want to go for a walk?
ちょっと歩きませんか？

I was taking a walk around the neighborhood.
近所を散歩していたんです。

I'll take the dog for a walk.
犬を散歩に連れて行ってくるよ。

3 We'd better walk the dog.
犬を散歩させたほうがいいね。

4 I'll walk you home if you like.
よかったら、家まで送って行くよ。

5 It's a three-minute walk to the station from my house.
家から駅までは歩いて3分(の道のり)です。

6 "The Philosopher's Walk" is one of the nicest walks in Kyoto.
「哲学の道」は京都の最もすばらしい散歩道の一つです。

7 He has a funny walk.
あの人は変な歩き方をする。

♦ **walkable** ***adj.*** 歩いて行ける

Is it a walkable distance?
歩いて行ける距離ですか？

walk away ***v.*** 立ち去る, (from situation, person) 逃げ出す [→ WALK OFF WITH]

She just walked away without saying a word.
彼女は一言も言わずに立ち去った。

walk into ***v.*** (enter) …に入る, (bump into) (うっかりして) …にぶつかる

The students walked into the classroom one after an other.
学生は次々と教室に入って行った。

I accidentally walked straight into him.
うっかりして彼にまともにぶつかってしまった。

walk off with ***v.*** (take) 取る, 持って行く, (steal) 持ち逃げする

Didn't he just walk off with your umbrella?
あの人があなたの傘を持って行ったんじゃない？

walk out *v.* (go on strike) スト(ライキ)をする; (leave) 立ち去る, 出て行く, (**walk out on**: abandon) 見捨てる, 捨てる

The whole workforce has walked out.
全従業員がストをしている。

He walked out on his wife.
あの人は奥さんを捨てた。

walk over *v.* (**walk all over**: treat badly) …にひどい扱いをする, こき使う

walking *n.* 散歩

walking stick *n.* つえ

walkout *n.* 退席, (strike) スト(ライキ)

walkway *n.* 散歩道

wall *n.* ((*also figurative*)) 壁, (outside) 塀 [→ picture of HOUSE]

Can you climb over that wall?
あの壁を乗り越えられる?

The bulldozer knocked down a huge wall.
ブルドーザーが巨大な塀を突き崩した。

come up against a wall 壁にぶつかる, 壁に突き当たる

wallaby *n.* ワラビー

wallet *n.* (お)財布, (お)札入れ

Oh no, I think I've lost my wallet.
しまった、財布をなくしたみたいだ。

wallow *v.* (**wallow in**) (=roll around in) …の中を転げ回る, (=in misery) …に浸る

wallpaper *n.* 壁紙

walnut *n.* クルミ

walrus *n.* セイウチ

waltz *n.* ワルツ

wand *n.* つえ

a magic wand 魔法のつえ

wander *v.* (walk around aimlessly) ぶらぶら歩き回る, ぶらつく, さまよう, (**wander off/from**: path, topic) (…から) それる, 外れる, (of thoughts: meander) とりとめがなくなる

I wandered around wondering what to do.
何をしようかと考えながら、ぶらぶら歩き回った。

I wandered around the shopping arcade.
商店街をぶらぶらしました。

I think we may have wandered from the path.
道から外れてしまったような気がする。

His (=that teacher's) lectures tend to wander.
あの先生の講義はよく横道にそれる。

wane *v.* (decline) 衰える, 弱まる, (of the moon) 欠ける

The church's influence has waned.
教会の影響力は衰えた。

want

1 *v.* DESIRE: (…が) 欲しい, (speaking about sb else) 欲しがる, ((*formal*)) 望む, 求める, (**want to do**) …したい, (speaking about sb else) …したがる, (**I want you to…**) …してほしい, …してもらいたい

2 *v.* NEED: (…する) 必要がある

3 *n.* DESIRES: (**wants**) 欲しい物

1 I want a day off. 休みが欲しい。

Do you want a cup of coffee?
コーヒーを飲みますか?

I don't want anymore cake.
ケーキはもうけっこうです。

An electric foot massager—just what I've always wanted!
(電動の) フットマッサージャーは、ずっと欲しかったんだ！

She wants a new handbag.
彼女は新しいバッグを欲しがっている。

What do you want? (=Why are you bothering me?)
((*rude*)) 何の用？

Both countries want peace.
両国とも和平を望んでいます。

I want to be a singer.
歌手になりたいんです。

He wanted to talk to the girl.
彼はその子と話したがっていた。

What do you want me to do?
私に何をしろというの / ((*polite*)) 何をしてほしいの？

I didn't want him to go.
彼に行ってほしくなかった。

I want you to stay here till I get back.
私が戻るまで、ここにいてほしい。

2 You'll want to book early to get a good seat.
いい席を取るには、早く予約する必要があります。

3 There are wants and there are needs.
欲しい物と必要な物があるんです。

for want of …の不足のために, (**for want of a better…**) ほかにいい…がないから

He didn't pass the exam, but it wasn't for want of trying.
彼は試験に合格しなかったが、努力不足だったわけではない。

if you want よかったら, 必要なら

If you want, I'll show you the way there.
よかったら、道を教えてあげますよ。

want nothing more than to do …したいだけだ

wanted *adj.* (by authorities) 指名手配の

That man is a wanted terrorist.
あの男は指名手配中のテロリストだ。

the FBI's Ten Most Wanted Fugitives list
ＦＢＩの重要指名手配者10名のリスト

war *n.* (armed conflict) 戦争, (struggle) 戦い

civil war 内戦

be at war 交戦 [戦争] 中だ

go to war (with) (…と) 戦争を始める

wage war on …と戦争をする

win [lose] a war 戦争に勝つ [負ける]

the First [Second] World War
第一次 [第二次] 世界大戦

before [after] the war 戦前 [戦後]

a cold war 冷戦

a trade war 貿易戦争

War broke out. 戦争が勃発した。

♦ **war crime** *n.* 戦争犯罪

ward *n.* (in hospital) 病棟, (in prison) 監房; (administrative division of a city) 区

warden *n.* (of prison) 刑務所長

wardrobe *n.* (collection of clothes) ワードローブ, 持ち衣装

Ms. Ando has a large wardrobe.
安藤さんは衣装持ちです。

warehouse *n.* 倉庫

The warehouses had been converted into luxury condominiums.
倉庫は、高級マンションに改造されていた。

warfare *n.* 戦争

psychological warfare 心理 [神経] 戦

warm

1 ***adj.*** **NOT COLD:** (of weather, clothes) 暖かい, (of bath) 温かい, (lukewarm) ぬるい

2 ***v.*** **HEAT:** 暖める, (food) 温める

3 ***adj.*** **KIND:** あたたかい, 優しい, (of words) 心のこもった

1 It was a warm day.
暖かい日でした。

I'd put some warm clothes on. It's going to be cold today.
暖かい服を着たほうがいいな。今日は寒くなりそうだから。

It's too warm in here. Mind if I open a window?
ここはちょっと暑いですね。窓をあけてもいいですか？

2 Let's warm the room up first.
まず部屋を暖めよう。

We warmed ourselves by the stove.
ストーブのそばで体を暖めた。

3 He's a very warm person.
彼はとても優しい [あたたかい] 人だ。

We got a warm welcome from the locals.
地元の人たちから、あたたかい歓迎を受けました。

♦ **warm up** *v.* (before exercise) 準備体操をする, ウォーミングアップをする; (make/become warmer) 暖める/暖まる

You'd better warm up first with some stretching exercises.
先にストレッチをしてウォーミングアップしたほうがいいよ。

warmly ***adv.*** あたたかく

We were greeted warmly by our waiter.
ウェーターから、あたたかくあいさつされた。

warmth ***n.*** 暖かさ, (of heart) (心の) あたたかさ, ぬくもり, (kindness) 思いやり

warn ***v.*** (tell) (…に) 前もって言う, 知らせる, 予告する, (advise) (…に) 警告する, 注意する

I'm warning you—keep out of my way.
(前もって)言っておくが、じゃまはするなよ。

I did warn you to expect trouble.
もめごとがあるかもしれないって、注意したのにねえ。

They were warned not to do it again.
彼らは二度としないよう注意された。

warning ***n.*** 警告, 注意, 通告, (of bad weather) 警報

a flood warning 洪水警報

warp ***v.*** ((*also figurative*)) ゆがめる, (become distorted) ゆがむ

warrant ***n.*** (for arrest) 逮捕状

warrant officer ***n.*** (in U.S. Army/Air Force/Marine Corps) 准尉, (in U.S. Navy) 兵曹長

warranty ***n.*** 保証, (warranty card) 保証書

warrior ***n.*** 戦士, (samurai) 武士

warship ***n.*** 軍艦, 戦艦

wart ***n.*** いぼ

have warts いぼがある

wartime ***n.*** 戦時

wary ***adj.*** (be wary of) (…に) 気をつける, 用心する

was → BE

wash ***v.*** 洗う, (clothes) 洗濯する

n. (**the wash**) 洗濯, (=clothes to be washed) 洗濯物

I'll use these rags to wash the car.

このぼろきれは洗車するときに使おう。

You'd better go wash your hands first.
先に手を洗ってらっしゃい。

Whose turn is it to wash the dishes?
お皿洗いの当番は誰？

My husband does the wash every Sunday.
夫が日曜日ごとに洗濯をしてくれる。

♦ **wash out** *v.* (of stain) 洗って落ちる

Do you think this stain will wash out?
このしみは洗って落ちると思う？

wash up *v.* (on shore) 打ち上げる; (clean oneself) 体を洗う

washable *adj.* 洗える, 洗濯の利く

washcloth *n.* 手ぬぐい

washing machine *n.* 洗濯機 [NOTE: Usually read せんたっき.] [→ picture of BATHROOM]

wasp *n.* スズメバチ

waste

1 *v.* SQUANDER: むだにする, 浪費する, (**waste money on**) …にお金をつぎ込む, (opportunity) 逃す

2 *n.* GARBAGE: (domestic waste) ごみ, (industrial waste) 廃棄物

3 *n.* POOR USE OF TIME/MONEY/ENERGY: 浪費, むだづかい

1 Don't waste it! Use it again.
むだにしないで。もう一度使ってちょうだい。

The man wasted his life savings on gambling and women.
男は貯金を全部、ギャンブルと女につぎ込んだ。

You're just wasting everyone's time.
あなたはみんなの時間をむだにしているだけだ。

He wasted a good chance for scoring a goal.
得点する絶好のチャンスを逃した。

You can't afford to waste opportunities like this.
こういう機会を逃すわけにはいかない。

2 waste products 廃棄物

nuclear waste 核廃棄物

3 a waste of time and energy
時間と労力のむだづかい

What a waste!
何というむだづかい/もったいない！

be left to waste (of food) 手をつけずにむだになる

wastebasket *n.* ごみ箱, くずかご, 紙くず箱 [→ picture of BATHROOM]

wasteful *adj.* むだの多い, むだな, 浪費する

wasteland *n.* 荒れ地

watch

1 *n.* TIMEPIECE: 時計, (wristwatch) 腕時計

2 *v.* LOOK AT: 見る, (stare at) 見つめる, (keep a close eye on) 見守る, (guard) 見張る

3 *v.* BE CAREFUL OF/WITH: (…に)気をつける, 注意する

4 *v.* SPY ON: 監視する, 見張る

1 wear a watch 腕時計をする

My watch has stopped.
時計が止まった。

Your watch is fast [slow].
あなたの時計は進んで[遅れて]いるよ。

2 I'm going to stay in tonight and watch TV.
今夜は家でテレビでも見るよ。

He was just standing there watching me.

彼はただそこに立って私を見ていた。

Let's watch the sunset.
夕焼けを見ましょう。

Now watch carefully as I do this.
では私がやるのをよく見ていてください。

Will you watch my bag while I use the restroom?
お手洗いに行ってる間、バッグを見てててくれる？

3 Watch your head as you go in.
入るときに頭に気をつけて。

Watch your step.
((*polite*)) 足元にご注意ください。

4 The house was being watched.
その家は監視されていた。

keep a watch on (observe closely) 監視する, (guard) 見張る

The troops kept a watch on the bridge.
兵士たちは橋を見張った。

watch oneself 慎重に行動する, 自重する

You better watch yourself.
慎重に行動しないといけないよ。

watch it/out 危ない！, ((*masculine*)) 気をつけろ

watch one's mouth 言葉に気をつける

watch out for (be wary of) …に用心する, …に気をつける

Watch out for pedestrians.
歩行者に気をつけて。

watchdog *n.* (dog) 番犬, (organization) 監視機関

watchman *n.* (night watchman) 夜警

water

NOTE: Japanese distinguishes "cold water" (お)水 from "hot water" お湯.

1 *n.* LIQUID: (お)水, (hot water) お湯, (drinking water) 飲み水, ((*formal*)) 飲料水

2 *v.* GIVE WATER TO: (plant) (…に) 水をやる, (**water the ground**) 地面に水をまく [NOTE: In Japan, people sometimes water the pavement in front of their homes or shops in order to clean it or keep it cool on hot summer days.]

3 *v.* SECRETE BODY FLUID: (of eyes) 涙が出る, (of mouth) よだれが出る

4 *n.* ZONE OF WATER: (**waters**) 水域

5 *n.* PUBLIC FACILITY: 水道

1 a glass of water コップ1杯の水

a bowl of hot water ボウル1杯のお湯

a water shortage 水不足

The boy was up to his knees in water.
その子はひざまで水につかっていた。

How do you turn the water off [on]?
水を止める [出す] には、どうすればいいですか？

I could see a coin sparkling in the water.
水の底でコインが光っているのが見えた。

2 Has anyone watered the plants yet?
もう誰か植木に水をやった？

3 My eyes are watering.
涙が出てきた。

4 uncharted waters 海図にない水域

territorial waters 領海

5 water and electricity 水道と電気

♦ **water bill** *n.* 水道料金請求書

water main *n.* 水道本管

water pipe *n.* 水道管

water pistol *n.* 水鉄砲

water power *n.* 水力

water supply ***n.*** 水道, 給水

watercolor ***n.*** (paint) 水彩絵の具, (work of art) 水彩画

watercress ***n.*** クレソン

waterfall ***n.*** 滝

waterfront ***n.*** (district) 海岸通り, ウォーターフロント

water lily ***n.*** スイレン, 睡蓮

waterlogged ***adj.*** 水浸しになった, (of house) 浸水した

watermelon ***n.*** スイカ, 西瓜

water mill ***n.*** 水車小屋

waterproof ***adj.*** 防水性の, 防水-

waterskiing ***n.*** 水上スキー

♦ **water-ski** ***v.*** 水上スキーをする

watersports ***n.*** ウォータースポーツ, 水上スポーツ

watertight ***adj.*** 水を通さない, 防水の

waterway ***n.*** (canal) 運河, (sea route) 水路

waterwheel ***n.*** 水車

waterworks ***n.*** 給水施設, 浄水場

watery ***adj.*** (like water) 水のような, (of food) 水っぽい

watt ***n.*** ワット

wave

1 ***v.*** CAUSE TO MOVE BACK AND FORTH: 振る, (in greeting: wave one's hand) 手を振る, (**wave a flag**) 旗を振る

2 ***n.*** OF WATER: 波

3 ***n.*** GESTURE: (**give a wave**) 手を振る

4 ***n.*** OF HAIR: ウェーブ, 縮れ

5 ***n.*** SURGE: (of emotion, protest) 波, 高まり

6 ***n.*** PATTERN: 波形模様

1 They waved good-bye to us.
別れ際、彼らは手を振った。

I waved to her to stop.
彼女に止まるよう手を振った。

The children lined the streets waving flags as the president's motorcade passed.
子供たちは通りに並んで、通過する大統領の車列に旗を振った。

2 The wave went right over me.
波をまともにかぶってしまった。

a tidal wave 津波

3 The queen gave a wave to the crowd.
女王は群衆に向かって手を振った。

4 He has lots of waves in his hair.
彼の髪の毛はとても縮れている。

5 a wave of dread 恐怖の高まり

a wave of protest 抗議の波

waveband ***n.*** 周波数帯

wavelength ***n.*** ((*also figurative*)) 波長

be on the same wavelength 波長が合う

waver ***v.*** (hesitate) ためらう, (vacillate) ぐらつく

wavy ***adj.*** (of hair) ウェーブのかかった, 縮れ毛の, (of pattern) 波形の

♦ **wavy line** ***n.*** 波線

wax ***n.*** ろう, (for floor) ワックス

v. (floor) (…に) ワックスをかける; (of moon) 満ちる

a wax candle ろうそく

way

1 ***n.*** PATH/ROUTE: ((*also figurative*)) 道, (route) 道順, 行き方

2 ***n.*** DIRECTION: 方向, (**this way**) こっちへ, ((*polite*)) こちらへ, (**that way**) あっちへ, ((*polite*)) あちらへ, (**which way**) どっちへ, ((*polite*)) どちらへ

3 *n.* DISTANCE: (also **ways**) 道のり, 距離

4 *n.* METHOD: 方法, やり方

5 *n.* MANNER: やり方, <-ますstem>＋方/ぶり

6 *n.* OF LIFE/LIVING: (**ways**: customs) 習慣, しきたり, (**way of living**) 生き方

7 *n.* RESPECT: 点

8 *n.* CONDITION: 状態, 状況

9 *adv.* EMPHASIZING DEGREE/AMOUNT/DISTANCE: かなり, ずっと

1 I went the wrong way. 道を間違えた。

I think I've lost my way.
道に迷ってしまった。

I came the short way.
近道を通って来ました。

The brothers went their different ways in life.
兄弟はそれぞれ別の道を歩んだ。

I can't get past with all the garbage in the way.
こんなにごみが置いてあったら、通れないよ。

Could you tell me the way to the station?
駅に行きたいんですが、道を教えてもらえませんか？

She was kind enough to show me the way.
彼女は親切に道を案内してくれた。

Someone asked me the way to the post office.
郵便局への道順を聞かれた。

Do you know the way to the cafeteria?
食堂への行き方をご存じですか？

2 Please come this way. こちらへどうぞ。

Which way did the car go?
車はどっちへ行きました？

Are you going the same way?
同じ道を行きますか？

3 Is it a long way? 遠いですか？

A little ways off the road there's a church.
道路からちょっと入った所に、教会があります。

We still have quite a ways to go.
まだかなりの距離がある/((*figurative*))まだまだ先は長い。

4 It's a useful way to get the paint off.
ペンキを落とすのに便利な方法です。

You can do it in two ways.
やり方は二つあります。

My sister's way of doing things is different from mine.
姉のやり方は、私とは違う。

5 She spoke in a polite way.
彼女の話し方は丁寧だった。

There are two ways of looking at this.
これについては、二つの見方ができる。

6 You must try to change your ways.
生活習慣を改める努力をしなければいけません。

The ways of our grandparents are long gone.
祖父母の時代のしきたりは、ずいぶん前になくなってしまった。

7 In some ways you're right, but in others I think you miss the point.
いくつかの点であなたは正しいと思いますが、一方で肝心な点を見落としていると思います。

In some ways I'd like to join, but in other ways I'd rather not.
参加したいという気持ちの反面、したくない気もするんです。

8 The company is in a good way financially.

会社の財政状態はいい。

9 It's way too expensive. かなり高い。

(*in boat*) We are way off course.
コースからかなり外れているよ。

all the way ずっと

I walked all the way home.
家までずっと歩いて帰りました。

as is the way with …はそんな感じだ, …によくあることだ

As is the way with young people these days.
近ごろの若者はそんな感じですよ。

be/stand in the way (of) (…の) じゃまになっている, 妨げになっている

All these rules and regulations stand in the way of progress.
こうした規則や規制が、発展の妨げになっている。

by the way ところで, それはそうと

By the way, did you remember to call Koizumi?
それはそうと、ちゃんと小泉さんに電話した?

by way of (via) …を経由して, (by means of) …で

The president went by way of Honolulu.
社長はホノルルを経由して行きました。

come a long way 大いに進歩する, はるかによくなる

get in the way じゃまをする

We don't like him. He just gets in the way.
あの人は好きじゃない。じゃまするだけだから。

get out of the way どく, 道をあける

Get out of the way and let the cars pass.
道をあけて車を通して。

give way (break) 折れる

give way to …に屈する, …に譲歩する

go out of one's way to do わざわざ…する

He went out of his way to help us.
彼はわざわざ手伝ってくれた。

go one's own way わが道を行く, 自分の思いどおりにやる

have it both ways 両方やる, 二またかける

You can either go swimming or fishing, but you can't have it both ways.
泳ぎに行っても釣りに出かけてもいいけど、両方やるわけにはいかないよ。

have/get one's way 思いどおりにする

She usually gets her way.
彼女はふだん思いどおりにやっている。

in a bad way 困って, (of business) 悪化して

He's in a bad way—alcohol, gambling …you name it.
彼は困ったもんだ——酒、ギャンブル、悪いことすべてやってるよ。

in a way ある意味で(は)

In a way, I think Mom's right.
ある意味では、お母さんは正しいと思う。

keep out of sb's way …にかかわらない, …を避ける

Try to keep out of his way.
彼にはかかわらないようにしなさい。

lead the way 先に立って案内する, 先導する

You lead the way. We'll follow.
ついて行きますから、先に立って案内してください。

lose one's way 道に迷う

Have you lost your way?
道に迷われたのですか？

make one's way (**through**: crowd etc.) …の中を進む, (**in the world**) 道を切り開く, 世の中を渡る

He's an adult now, so he'll have to make his own way in the world.
彼ももうおとななんだから、自分で世の中を渡って行かなければならない。

(there are) no two ways about it 間違いない

No two ways about it. She's the one.
間違いない。彼女だよ。

one way or another なんとかして, なんとしてでも

One way or another, I'm going to find out his name.
なんとかして、彼の名前を調べるよ。

One way or another, I'm going to win this prize.
なんとしてでも、この賞を取るつもりです。

on the way 途中で

On the way home, I stopped to have a drink.
帰宅途中に、寄り道して一杯飲んだ。

on one's way (to) (…に) 向かって

Mr. Nakata is on his way to Osaka.
中田さんは大阪に向かっています。

on one's way out the door 出かけるところ

I was just on my way out the door when the phone rang.
電話が鳴った時、ちょうど出かけるところだった。

out of the way (in an inaccessible/inconvenient location) へんぴな所にある, (away from civilization) 人里離れた所にある

The store is well stocked, but a little out of the way.
そのお店は品物は豊富だけど、ちょっとへんぴな所にあるんだ。

the easy way out 楽な道, (easy solution) 安易な解決策

Don't take the easy way out.
楽な道を取らないで。

ways and means 方法

There are ways and means of persuading him.
彼を説得する方法はある。

we *pron.* 私たちは/が, ((*formal*)) 我々は/が, 私たちは/が, ((*polite*)) こちらは/が, ((*masculine*)) 僕たちは/が, ((*masculine/informal*)) 僕らは/が, 俺たちは/が, ((*feminine/informal*)) あたしたちは/が

You may think so, but we don't.
あなたはそう思うかもしれないが、我々はそうは思わない。

We Japanese… 私たち日本人は…

weak *adj.*

1 LACKING STRENGTH: 弱い, (physically) 虚弱な, ひ弱な, (mentally) 軟弱な, (of thing: fragile) もろい

2 NOT PROFICIENT: (**be weak in**) (…が) 苦手だ, 弱い

3 OF ARGUMENT: (not persuasive) 説得力のない

4 OF DRINK: 薄い, 弱い

5 OF CURRENCY: 安い, 弱い

1 I'm weak. I should start lifting weights.

僕はひ弱だから、ウエートリフティングでもやらなきゃ。

He's a weak leader.
彼は<u>弱い</u> [無力な] リーダーです。

Young men these days are weak.
最近の若い男は軟弱だ。

The bridge was weak and ready to collapse.
橋はもろくて、今にも崩れそうだった。

2 He's weak in math.
彼は数学が苦手です。

His French is weak.
彼はフランス語が弱い。

3 That's a pretty weak argument.
全く説得力のない議論だ。

4 I prefer my tea weak.
紅茶は薄いのが好きです。

a weak cocktail 弱いカクテル

5 The yen is weak right now.
今、円は安い。

♦**weak point** *n.* 弱点

weaken *v.* (make/become weaker) 弱める/弱まる, 弱くする/なる

weakling *n.* 体の弱い人, 虚弱な人

weakness *n.* (condition/quality of being weak) 弱さ, (flaw) 欠点

have a weakness for …に弱い, …には目がない

She has a weakness for sweets.
あの人は甘い物には目がない。

wealth *n.* 財産, ((*formal*)) 富, (resources) 産物, 資源

It was a period of wealth and prosperity.
富と繁栄の時代でした。

wealthy *adj.* (お)金持ちの, 裕福な, 経済力のある, (of family, country) 豊かな

wean *v.* (stop breast-feeding) 乳離れさせる, (wean A off B) (AにBを) 断ち切らせる

weapon *n.* 武器, (used to commit a crime) 凶器, (military weapon) 兵器

Did the police ever find the murder weapon?
結局、警察は殺人の凶器を発見したのですか？

weapons of mass destruction
大量破壊兵器

wear

1 *v.* **HAVE ON:** (shirt, coat, kimono) 着る, (shoes, socks, pants, stockings) はく, (hat, wig, helmet) かぶる, (scarf) する, 巻く, (glasses) かける, する, (make-up) する, (lipstick) つける, (glove, ring) する, はめる, (wristwatch) する

2 *v.* **DETERIORATE:** (of clothing, carpet) すり切れる, (of shoes) すり減る

3 *v.* **BE RESISTANT TO USE:** (**wear well**) 持つ, 長持ちする

4 *n.* **CLOTHES:** -服, -ウェア

1 What are you going to wear today?
今日は何を着ていくつもり？

The clothes she wore didn't match.
彼女の着ていた服は、組み合わせが合っていなかった。

I don't like wearing formal clothes.
正装をするのは好きじゃない。

I wear contact lenses.
私はコンタクトを<u>して</u> [着けて] います。

wear perfume 香水をつける

Do you wear lipstick [nail polish, mascara]?
口紅[マニキュア, マスカラ]をつけますか?

She wears her hair up for work.
彼女は仕事のときは髪をアップにします。

2 The carpet's beginning to wear near the door.
カーペットが、ドアのあたりですり切れ始めた。

3 This material doesn't wear as well as cotton.
この素材は木綿ほど持ちません。

4 men's [women's] wear 紳士 [婦人] 服
formal wear フォーマルウェア [礼服]
casual wear カジュアルウェア
beach wear ビーチウェア

wear and tear 消耗

wear away *v.* (of material: become worn) すり減る

wear down *v.* (cause to diminish by rubbing etc.) すり減らす; (exhaust) 疲れさせる

wear off *v.* (fade and disappear) なくなる, 取れる

The pain gradually wore off.
痛みは徐々になくなった。

wear out *v.* 使い古す, (shoes) はき古す, はきつぶす; (**be worn out**: be exhausted) 疲れ切っている, ひどく疲れている

You've worn out your shoes.
靴をはきつぶしたね。

You look completely worn out.
ひどく疲れてるようだね。

wear out one's welcome 長居する

weariness *n.* (fatigue) 疲労

weary *adj.* (exhausted) 疲れ切った, ひどく疲れた

v. (**weary of**) …にうんざりする, …に飽きる

♦ **wearily** *adv.* 疲れ切った様子で

weather

1 *n.* ATMOSPHERIC CONDITIONS: (お)天気, 天候, 空模様, (climate) 気候

2 *v.* BECOME WEATHER-BEATEN: (lose color) 外気で変色する, (erode) 風雨にさらされて傷む

3 *v.* ENDURE OR LIVE THROUGH: (difficult situation) 乗り切る, 切り抜ける

1 The weather's been very bad recently.
このところずっと、天気がとても悪い。

Good morning. Fine weather we're having, don't you think?
おはようございます。いいお天気ですね。

The forecast is for cold weather.
天気予報によると寒くなるらしい。

The mail is delivered in all kinds of weather.
郵便はどんな天候であっても配達される。

2 The statue has weathered beyond recognition.
彫像は風雨にさらされて傷んで、見る影もなかった。

3 Japan has weathered more than a decade of recession.
日本は10年以上の不況を乗り切った。

under the weather (not feeling well) 具合が悪い

weather forecast *n.* 天気予報

♦ **weather forecaster** *n.* 気象予報士

weave *v.* (cloth) 織る, (basket) 編む

n. 織り方, -織り

My wife wove that rug.
その敷物は妻が織りました。

The blind weave these baskets.
盲目の人たちが、このかごを編んでいます。

♦ **weaving** *n.* 織ること

web *n.* (spider web) クモの巣; (**the Web**: the Internet) ウェブ

webbed *adj.* (of feet) 水かきのある

webcam *n.* ウェブカム

webmaster *n.* ウェブマスター

web page *n.* ウェブページ, ホームページ

website *n.* ウェブサイト, ホームページ

wedding *n.* (ceremony) 結婚式, 婚礼, (anniversary) 結婚記念日

a wedding day 結婚式の日
a wedding present 結婚祝い(の品)
a golden [silver] wedding 金[銀] 婚式

♦ **wedding cake** *n.* ウェディングケーキ

wedding dress *n.* ウェディングドレス, (Japanese-style) 花嫁衣装

wedding ring *n.* 結婚指輪

wedge *n.* (tool) くさび, (piece of fruit etc.) くさび形の物

v. (wedge A into B) (AをBに) 押し込む, (**wedge a door**) ドアをくさびで留める

Wednesday *n.* 水曜日

weed *n.* (wild plant) 草, 雑草

v. (take weeds out of) (...の) 草を取る, 草むしりする

♦ **weeding** *n.* 草取り, 草むしり

weed killer *n.* 除草剤

week *n.* 週, (one week) 1 週間

this [last, next] week 今週 [先週, 来週]
the following week 翌週 [次の週]
the week before last 先々週
the week after next 再来週
every week 毎週
every other week 隔週 [1 週間おき] に
a week from today 今日から 1 週間
a week ago 1 週間前

by the week 週ぎめで

for weeks 何週間も

week after week 毎週毎週

weekday *n.* 平日, ウィークデー

weekend *n.* 週末, ウィークエンド

weekly *adj.* (every week) 毎週の, (once a week) 週に 1 度の

adv. 週 1 回, 毎週, (by the week) 週ぎめで

n. (weekly magazine) 週刊誌

♦ **weekly pay** *n.* 週給

weeknight *n.* 平日の夜

weep *v.* 泣く, 涙を流す

weigh *v.* (measure the weight of) (...の) 重さを量る, (have as weight) (...の) 重さがある, (**weigh the pros and cons of**) ...に対する賛否両論を検討する, (consider seriously) 慎重に考慮する

Let's weigh it. 重さを量ろう。

Have you weighed the package?
その包みの重さを量りましたか？

This machine weighs about two tons.
この機械は約2トンの重さがあります。

He weighs about seventy kilos.
彼の体重はおよそ70キロある。

We're going to have to weigh the pros and cons of such a course of action.
そのような行動に対する賛否両論を、検討しなければならないだろう。

We need to weigh the situation first.
まず状況を慎重に考慮する必要がある。

weigh (heavily) on one's shoulders (…の) 肩に(重く)のしかかる

The responsibility weighed heavily on his shoulders.
責任は彼の肩に重くのしかかった。

weight ***n.***

1 HEAVINESS: (of the body) 体重, (of object) 重さ, 重量

2 HEAVY OBJECT: 重い物

3 IN WEIGHTLIFTING: (dumbbell) ダンベル, (barbell) バーベル

4 PIECE OF METAL USED ON A SCALE: おもり

5 BURDEN: 重荷, 重圧

6 IMPORTANCE: 重き, 重要性, (**give weight to**) …に重きを置く, 重要視する, (**carry weight**: be influential) 影響力がある

1 What's your weight?
体重は、どのくらいありますか？

I haven't put on any weight this week.
今週は体重が増えていない。

lose weight やせる (lit.,"get thin")

gain weight 太る (lit.,"get fat")

2 My doctor told me I'm not to lift heavy weights.
医者から、重い物を持ち上げてはならないと言われた。

3 Do you lift weights?
ウエートリフティングをやりますか？

4 That weight is too heavy. Take it off the scale.
そのおもりは重すぎる。はかりから取って。

5 I felt an enormous weight lifted from my shoulders.
肩から大きな重荷が取れた感じがした。

6 I wouldn't give much weight to the review.
その批評は重要視しなくてもいいと思う。

weightless ***adj.*** (in space) 無重力の

♦**weightlessness** ***n.*** 無重力(状態)

weightlifting ***n.*** (sport) ウエートリフティング, 重量挙げ

weighty ***adj.*** (heavy) 重い, (serious, important) 重要な

weird ***adj.*** (strange) 変な, おかしな, (creepy) 気味の悪い

weirdo ***n.*** 変な人, おかしな人

welcome

1 ***interj.*** いらっしゃい, ようこそ

2 ***v.*** RECEIVE WITH PLEASURE: 喜んで迎える, あたたかく迎える, 歓迎する, 迎える

3 ***n.*** RECEPTION: 歓迎, もてなし

4 ***adj.*** FREE: (**you are welcome to…**) 自由に…してよい

5 ***adj.*** BEING CAUSE TO REJOICE: ありがたい, うれしい

1 Welcome to Japan! 日本へようこそ！

Welcome back/home! お帰りなさい！

2 The host family welcomed me into their home.
ホストファミリーは私をあたたかく迎えてくれた。

The prime minister was welcomed by the president.
総理大臣は大統領の歓迎を受けた。

We went to the airport to welcome them.
私たちは空港まで、彼らを出迎えに行きました。

We welcome your comments.
ご意見をお待ちしています。

3 Let's give a warm welcome to our guest.

ゲストをあたたかく迎えましょう。
What a welcome! すごい歓迎だね！

4 You're welcome to use our kitchen.
自由に台所を使ってくださいね。

5 welcome rain ありがたい [恵みの] 雨

you're welcome どういたしまして，とんでもありません

"Thank you for the compliment."
"You're welcome."
「おほめいただいてありがとう」
「どういたしまして」

♦ **welcome party** *n.* 歓迎会

weld *v.* 溶接する

♦ **welder** *n.* 溶接工

welfare *n.* (well-being) 福祉，(aid given by government) 生活保護

be on welfare 生活保護を受けている

♦ **welfare state** *n.* (country) 福祉国家

welfare system *n.* 福祉制度

well[1]

1 ***adv.*** IN A GOOD MANNER: (skillfully) 上手に，うまく，よく，(conscientiously) 丁寧に，ちゃんと，(smoothly) うまく

2 ***adv.*** TO A CONSIDERABLE EXTENT: 十分に，ずっと

3 ***adj.*** HEALTHY: 元気な，(after illness: feeling better) 治った，元気になった

4 ***interj.*** EXPRESSING EMOTION: (surprise) へえー，えっ，((*feminine*)) まあ，(relief) やれやれ，(doubt) さあ，(reluctance, resignation) じゃ，まあ，いやもう

5 ***interj.*** CHANGING SUBJECT: それじゃ，ところで，((*formal*)) さて

6 ***interj.*** PAUSING TO CHOOSE WORDS: えーっと，うーん，(to be less direct or to sound less rude) まあ，そうですねー

7 ***interj.*** QUALIFYING A STATEMENT: いや，というより

8 ***adv.*** KINDLY: (**speak well of**) 良く言う，ほめる，(**think well of**) 良く思う

9 ***adj.*** GIVING ADVICE: (**be/do well to do**) …したほうがいい

1 You dance very well.
踊りがすごく上手ですね。

He did pretty well in the interview.
彼は面接がかなりよかった。

Well done! よくやった！/よくできた！

I want this job done well.
この仕事は丁寧にやってもらいたい。

You didn't do the work very well.
その仕事は、あまりちゃんとできていなかったよ。

The test went well.
試験はうまくいった。

They get along well with one another.
彼らは互いに仲良くやっている。

2 It's well worth a visit.
行く価値は十分にあるよ。

The gymnasium is well equipped.
体育館には十分な設備が整っています。

Make sure you stand well away from the edge of the platform.
プラットホームの端から、十分下がって立つんですよ。

I'm well aware of that, thank you.
それは十分承知していますから、ご心配なく。

We woke up well before 7 o'clock.
7時よりずっと前に起きました。

3 You don't look very well.
あまり元気そうじゃないね。

I'm pleased to hear that you're well again.

治ったと聞いて安心しました。

4 Well, I'm glad that's over!
やれやれ、終わってうれしい!

Well, I'm not sure, but let's try it anyway.
さあ、どうかわからないけど、ともかくやってみよう。

5 Well then, let's go.
それじゃ行きましょう。

Well, what's the next step?
ところで、次の段階は何ですか?

6 It was, well, a bit stupid.
まあ、ちょっとまぬけだったよ。

The story was, well, too clichéd.
話は、そうですねー、とてもありきたりのものでした。

7 We—well, I should say some of us—think otherwise.
我々は—いや、我々の何人かはと言うべきだが—そうは思わない。

8 Everyone speaks well of him.
みんな彼のことを良く言う。

9 It would be well to start early.
早く出発したほうがいいだろう。

You'd do well to e-mail them about your concerns.
心配ならメールを送ったほうがいいでしょう。

as well (also) …も, その上

Are you going as well?
あなたも行きますか?

A as well as B BだけでなくAも, AもBも

She's an actress as well as a director.
彼女は監督だけでなく女優でもある。

That author has written fiction as well as nonfiction.
その作家はフィクションもノンフィクションも書いた。

it is just as well (that) …とは幸運だ, …が好都合だ

It is just as well that the bill didn't pass.
法案が通らなかったのは幸運だ。

may/might as well do まだ…したほうがいい, …したほうがましだ

We may as well stay at home.
家にいたほうがましだよ。

may/might well (with good reason) …するのも無理はない, …するのももっともだ, (possibly) …かもしれない

You may well laugh. I thought it funny too.
笑うのも無理はないよ。私だっておかしかったもの。

He might well turn up.
彼は現れるかもしれない。

well² *n.* (hole in the ground) 井戸
v. わき出る, あふれる, こみ上げてくる

The well is dry. 井戸はかれています。

Tears welled in her eyes.
彼女の目から涙があふれた。

A feeling of disgust welled up inside me.
嫌悪感が心にこみ上げてきた。

well-advised *adj.* (sensible) 分別のある

well-balanced *adj.* バランスのとれた

a well-balanced diet
バランスのとれた食事

well-behaved *adj.* (of child) (お)行儀のいい

well-being *n.* (happiness) 幸福, (health) 健康, (welfare) 福祉

well-bred *adj.* 育ちのいい

well-built *adj.* (of person) 体格のいい; (of building) しっかりした造りの

W

well-done *adj.* (of meat) よく焼けた, ウェルダンの

well-dressed *adj.* 身なりのよい, 立派な服装の

well-educated *adj.* いい教育を受けた

She's a well-educated young lady.
彼女はいい教育を受けたお嬢さんです。

well-established *adj.* 定着した, 確立した

well-informed *adj.* (be well-informed about) (...に)詳しい

well-known *adj.* よく知られた, 有名な

He's a well-known figure around here.
彼はこの辺ではよく知られた人物です。

It's a well-known fact.
それは周知の事実です。

well-off *adj.* (お)金持ちの

well-paid *adj.* 給料のいい

well-read *adj.* 多読の, (knowledgeable) 博識の

were → BE

werewolf *n.* オオカミ人間

west *n.* 西, 西方, (western part) 西部; (**the West**: Europe and America) 西洋, 欧米

adj. 西の, (west-facing) 西向きの

adv. 西に/へ

from the west 西から

the West Coast アメリカ西海岸

a west wind 西風

westerly *adj.* (of wind) 西からの

western *adj.* (in the west) 西の, (west-facing) 西向きの; (**Western**: European/American) 西洋の

n. (**Western**: cowboy movie) 西部劇, ウェスタン

♦ **Westerner** *n.* 西洋人

Western-style *adj.* 洋式の

Westernize *v.* 西洋化する

♦ **Westernization** *n.* 西洋化

westward *adv.* 西の方へ, 西に向かって

adj. 西(へ)の

wet

1 *adj.* COVERED IN WATER: ぬれている, ぬれた, (**soaking-wet**) ずぶぬれの, びしょぬれの [→ FLOODED]

2 *adj.* DAMP: 湿っている, 湿った, (not yet dry) まだ乾いていない

3 *adj.* RAINY: 雨の, 雨が降っている

4 *v.* MAKE WET: ぬらす, 湿らせる

5 *v.* URINATE IN: (**wet the bed**) おねしょをする, ((*masculine*)) 寝小便をする, (**wet one's pants**) おしっこを漏らす, ((*formal*)) 失禁する

1 wet clothes ぬれた服

The grass is wet. 芝生がぬれている。

I don't want to get wet. ぬれたくない。

The bench is wet.
ベンチがぬれている。

I got soaking wet.
ずぶぬれになってしまった。

2 The laundry is still wet.
洗濯物がまだ湿っている。

Be careful of the wet paint.
ペンキ塗りたてだから気をつけて。

3 a wet day 雨の日

We're going to have wet weather for the next week.
これから来週にかけて雨が降るでしょう。

4 Wet the walls first, so the paper will

come off more easily.
先に壁をぬらして、紙をはがしやすくするんだ。

The spray from the side of the boat wet the back of my shirt.
ボートのへりからの水しぶきで、シャツの後ろがぬれてしまった。

5 As a child, he used to wet the bed.
子供のころ、彼はよくおねしょをした。

wetland ***n.*** (**wetlands**) 湿地帯, (= marshlands) 沼地

wet nurse ***n.*** 乳母
v. (**wet-nurse**) (…の) 乳母になる

wet suit ***n.*** ウェットスーツ

whack ***v.*** (hit) ピシャッと打つ
n. ピシャッと打つこと

whale ***n.*** クジラ, 鯨
♦ **whale meat** ***n.*** 鯨肉
whaling ***n.*** 捕鯨

wharf ***n.*** 埠頭, 波止場

what

1 ***interrogative pron.*** 何
2 ***interrogative adj.*** 何の, どんな, どの, (**what kind of**) どんな, どのような, (**what time**) 何時, (**to what extent**) どの程度, どれほど
3 ***interrogative pron./adj.*** INTRODUCING A WHAT-CLAUSE: 何/何の…か
4 ***adj.*** IN EXCLAMATIONS: なんと, なんて
5 ***relative pron.*** See examples below [NOTE: No equivalent in Japanese.]
6 ***interj.*** ええっ!, 何だって!, ((*feminine*)) あらっ [→ YOU WHAT?]

1 What happened? 何があったの？
What is it? それは何ですか？
What's his name?
彼は何という名前ですか？
What's the matter? You look pale all of a sudden.
どうしたんですか？ 急に顔色が悪くなりましたよ。
What did you say you had to do tomorrow?
明日やらなければいけないことは、何だっけ？
"What?"
"I said, can you pass the sugar."
「えっ、何？」
「お砂糖を取ってくれる？(って言ったのよ)」

2 What time is it? 今、何時ですか？
What price did you pay?
いくら払ったんですか？
What books of his have you read?
その作家のどんな本を読みました？
What Beatles CDs do you have?
ビートルズのどのＣＤを持っているの？
To what extent do you agree with their argument?
どの程度まで彼らの議論に賛成ですか？

3 I don't know what it's called.
それを何と言うのかわかりません。
Do you know what an octant is?
八分儀って何だかわかりますか？
I don't know what this word is in Japanese.
この言葉を、日本語で何というのかわかりません。
Tell me what's wrong.
どうしたのか話してよ。

4 What nerve! なんと、ずうずうしい！
What a lovely day!

W

なんて気持ちのいい日なんでしょう!

What a beautiful view!
なんてきれいな眺めだ!

5 You can do what you like.
好きなことをしていいですよ。

Don't repeat what I've said.
私が言ったことを繰り返すな。

What you need is sleep.
君に必要なのは睡眠だ。

6 What! (=What did you say?)
何だって!

so what → so

what about …はどう?, ((*polite*)) …はどうですか

What about her? (=What should we do about her?)
彼女はどうする?

"Thursday any good?"
"No."
"Well, what about Friday?"
「木曜日は大丈夫?」
「いえ、ちょっと…」
「じゃ、金曜日はどう?」

what for (for what purpose) 何のため(に), (why) なぜ

What is this for?
これは何のための物ですか?

"I hid the book from him."
"What for?"
「彼から本を隠したんだ」
「なぜ?」

what have you など, その他

The closet's full of skis and camping gear, and what have you.
押し入れは、スキーやキャンプ用品などでいっぱいだ。

what if (もし…し)たらどうする/どうなる

What (will we do) if they don't come?
彼らが来なかったら(どうする)?

What if we don't finish in time?
時間どおりに終わらなかったら、どうなりますか?

What would have happened if Kennedy hadn't been assassinated?
ケネディが暗殺されていなかったら、どうなっていただろうか?

what it takes to do …するのに必要な資質

She has what it takes to be a leader.
彼女はリーダーになるのに必要な資質を備えている。

what of it? それがどうしたというんだ, だから何

"You cheated." "What of it?"
「ずるしたね」「それがどうかした?」

what's it called? 何て言うんだっけ

Oh, what's it called? It's an instrument used to measure pressure.
あの、何て言うんだっけ? 気圧を測るのに使う道具だよ。

what's what ものの道理, (the truth) 事の真相

He knows what's what.
あの人は、ものの道理をわきまえている。

what with one thing and the other 何やか(ん)やで, あれやこれやで

What with one thing and the other, I forgot to tell you about it.
何やかやで、そのことを話すのを忘れていた。

you what? 何だって, 何て言った, まさか

"I bought a new car."
"You what? You just bought one last year!"
「新車を買ったよ」
「えっ、何だって? 去年買ったばかりじゃないか」

whatever

1 *adj.* ANY: どんなに…でも, …は何でも

2 *pron.* NO MATTER WHAT: 何を/が…ても/でも, 何を…と, どんな…にしろ

3 *relative pron.* ANYTHING/EVERYTHING THAT: …は何でも

4 *interrogative pron.* WHAT: ((*emphatic*)) 一体何

5 *adj.* SOME…OR ANOTHER: 何かの, 何らかの

1 Whatever nonsense they print, people will read.
どんなにばかげた内容でも、出ると人々は読むんです。

We had to survive on whatever food we could find.
手に入る食料は何でも食べて、生き延びるしかありませんでした。

2 Whatever they may say, you must hold your head high.
彼らが何と言おうと、堂々としていなさい。

We've decided to go, whatever the circumstances.
どんな状況にしろ、我々は行くと決めたんです。

3 I'll do whatever I can to help.
できることは何でもします。

Do whatever you like. I don't care.
好きなようにやりなさい。私は気にしないから。

I read whatever I could find on the topic.
その話題に関するものは、手当たり次第に読みました。

4 Whatever do you mean?
一体どういう意味ですか?

5 For whatever reason, the problem seems to have gone away.
何らかの理由で、問題は解決したようだ。

or whatever …その他(何でも), …とか何とか(そういったもの)

desks, chairs, bookshelves, or whatever
机、椅子、本棚、その他何でも

whatsoever *adv.* **(nothing/none whatsoever)** 全く…ない

Lazy bum! He's done nothing whatsoever.
なんて怠け者だ! 全く何もしなかった。

wheat *n.* 小麦

wheedle *v.* ねだる, (**wheedle into doing**) (…に)ねだって…させる

wheel *n.* 車輪, (**the wheel**: the steering wheel) ハンドル

v. (pull) 引く, (push) 押す, (person in wheelchair, on stretcher) 運ぶ

a potter's wheel ろくろ
a spinning wheel 糸車

reinvent the wheel → REINVENT

wheelbarrow *n.* 手押し車

wheelchair *n.* 車椅子

be wheelchair accessible
車椅子で利用できる

when

1 *interrogative adv.* AT WHAT TIME: いつ, (at what hour) 何時に, (in what situation) どんな場合に

2 *interrogative adv.* INTRODUCING A WHEN-CLAUSE: いつ…か

3 ***relative adv.*** AT/DURING WHICH TIME: See examples below [NOTE: No equivalent in Japanese.], (..., when) その時(に)

4 ***pron.*** WHAT TIME: いつ

5 ***conj.*** AT THE TIME WHEN: ...時, ((*written*)) ...際

6 ***conj.*** ONCE/AFTER: (**when sb/sth does sth**) ...したら, ...と

7 ***conj.*** WHENEVER: ...と, ...する時は(いつも)

8 ***conj.*** ALTHOUGH: ...けれども, ((*informal*)) ...けど, ...のに

9 ***conj.*** GIVEN THAT: (expressing dissatisfaction) ...のに

1 "I have to go out later."
"When?"
「あとで出かけないといけない」
「いつ？」

When was the last time you went back home (to visit your family)?
実家に帰ったのは最近ではいつですか？

When did she get that job?
いつ彼女はその仕事に就いたんですか？

When will the meeting begin?
会議は何時に始まりますか？

2 I don't know when I'll be back.
いつ戻るかわかりません。

I can't remember when I said that.
いつそれを言ったか、思い出せません。

Tell me when we can give him an answer.
彼にいつ返事ができるか教えて。

3 Sunday's the day when I play golf.
日曜日はゴルフをする日です。

Do you remember the time when we went skiing in France?
フランスにスキーに行った時のことを、覚えていますか？

George will be here on Monday, when he'll explain everything.
ジョージは月曜にここへ来て、その時にすべてを説明します。

4 Till when can you stay?
いつまでいられる？

By when do you want this translation finished?
いつまでに、この翻訳を終わらせたらよろしいでしょうか？

Since when is this area off-limits to employees?
いつからここは、従業員の立ち入りが禁止になったんですか？

5 When I was in China, I studied Chinese.
中国にいた時に、中国語を学びました。

When I was your age, things were different.
私が君と同じ年ごろだった時は、事情が違っていた。

I was quietly reading the morning paper and sipping my tea when all of a sudden I heard a loud bang on the door.
静かに朝刊を読んでお茶を飲んでいた時、突然戸口でバーンと大きな音がした。

"When did you first fall in love?"
"When I was sixteen years old."
「初恋はいつだった？」
「16の時だった」

6 When I finish my homework, I'll watch TV.
宿題が終わったら、テレビを見よう。

I'll let you know when the first guest arrives.
最初のお客さんが見えたら、お知らせします。

When I got home, I went straight to bed.

家に着くと、すぐ寝た。

7 When the sun goes down, the temperature drops rapidly.
太陽が沈むと、気温は急速に下がる。

When it rains, it pours.
降るときはいつもどしゃ降り。

8 You say she's not qualified, when in fact she is.
彼女は資格がないと言うけど、実際はそうじゃないよ。

9 How can we save money when we're taxed so heavily?
こんなにたくさん税金を取られているのに、どうやって貯金すればいいというのか？

whenever

1 ***conj.*** ANYTIME: いつでも, …時にいつでも

2 ***conj.*** EVERY TIME: …と(いつも), …時は必ず, …たびに

3 ***adv.*** WHEN: ((*emphatic*)) 一体いつ

1 You can do it whenever you like.
いつでも好きな時にやっていいよ。

Come to see me whenever you have the time.
時間がある時にいつでも遊びに来てください。

2 He calls me whenever he comes to Osaka.
彼は大阪に来るといつも電話をくれる。

Whenever we come here, it rains.
ここに来る時は必ず雨が降る。

Whenever we go to the pool, we eat at that restaurant.
プールに行くたびに、あのレストランで食べます。

3 Whenever did you stop smoking?
一体いつ、たばこをやめたの？

or whenever (not sure when) …かそのころ, (anytime) …でもいつでも

I must have left the message a couple weeks ago, or whenever.
2週間前かそのころに、メッセージを残したんだと思います。

You can come tomorrow, or whenever.
来るのは明日でもいつでもいいよ。

whenever possible できる時はいつでも, 可能な限り

where

1 ***interrogative adv.*** (in/to what location/position) どこに/へ, ((*polite*)) どちらに/へ

2 ***interrogative adv.*** INTRODUCING A WHERE-CLAUSE: どこに…か

3 ***relative adv.*** IN WHICH: See examples below [NOTE: No equivalent in Japanese.], (…, where) そこで, (introducing a noun clause: the place/point in/at which) …ところ, …点

4 ***conj.*** IN THE PLACE WHERE: …所に/で, …場所に/で

1 Where's Jeff? ジェフはどこですか？

Where's my hat?
帽子はどこにあります？

Where did Emiko go?
恵美子はどこへ行ったの？

Where are you going for your vacation?
休みはどこへ行くの？

Where does he live?
彼はどちらに住んでいるんですか？

Where were we before we got interrupted?
中断される前はどこまでいってたっけ？

Where are you in the textbook?
教科書はどこまでいってる？

W

2 How did you know where to find me?
私(わたし)がどこにいるか、どうしてわかったんですか？

I forget where it was.
どこだったか忘(わす)れたよ。

I didn't know where to look.
どこを捜(さが)せばいいのかわからなかった。

I have no idea where he comes from.
彼(かれ)がどこの出身(しゅっしん)なのか、見当(けんとう)もつきません。

3 We live in an apartment complex where there are lots of kids.
私(わたし)たちは、子供(こども)がたくさんいる団地(だんち)に住(す)んでいます。

We walked to Shinjuku Station, where we got on a train.
新宿駅(しんじゅくえき)まで歩(ある)いて、そこで電車(でんしゃ)に乗(の)った。

We got into a situation where there was no going back.
後戻(あともど)りできない状況(じょうきょう)になってしまった。

This is where I disagree with them.
ここが彼(かれ)らに賛成(さんせい)できないところです。

4 Add extra paint where the stains show.
汚(よご)れの目立(めだ)つ所(ところ)にちょっと多(おお)めにペンキを塗(ぬ)ってください。

I found my glasses where I left them.
置(お)き忘(わす)れた場所(ばしょ)にめがねはありました。

whereabouts *adv.* どの辺(へん)に, どのあたりに
n. (the place where sb/sth is) 行方(ゆくえ), 所在(しょざい)
whereabouts unknown 行方不明(ゆくえふめい)

whereas *conj.* (while on the contrary) ...のに, ...け(れ)ど, ...に対(たい)し(て)

He's good at sports, whereas I'm not.
彼(かれ)はスポーツが得意(とくい)だけれど、僕(ぼく)は苦手(にがて)だ。

My wife wants to go to Thailand, whereas I would prefer Scotland.
妻(つま)はタイに行(い)きたがっているけど、僕(ぼく)はスコットランドのほうがいい。

wherever
1 *conj.* ANY PLACE: どこに...ても/でも, どこでも...所(ところ)に
2 *conj.* EVERYWHERE: ...所(ところ)はどこでも, (**wherever one goes**) どこへ行(い)っても, 行(い)く先々(さきざき)に
3 *adv.* WHERE: ((*emphatic*)) 一体(いったい)どこ

1 You can sit wherever you like.
どこでも好(す)きな所(ところ)に座(すわ)ってください。

We need to get to Hino, wherever that is.
どこだか知(し)りませんが、日野(ひの)という所(ところ)に行(い)かなければなりません。

2 Wherever there's water, there's life.
水(みず)がある所(ところ)はどこでも、生命(せいめい)が存在(そんざい)する。

He seems to make friends wherever he goes.
彼(かれ)は行(い)く先々(さきざき)で友達(ともだち)ができるようだ。

3 Wherever have you been?
一体(いったい)どこにいたの？

or wherever ...かどこか

I don't care if you're going to a disco or wherever, just be back by midnight.
ディスコかどこかに行(い)くのはかまわないけど、12時(じゅうにじ)までには帰(かえ)りなさい。

whether *conj.* ...かどうか, (whether A or B) A(の)かB(の)か, (expressing indifference, or saying that an outcome will be the same no matter what) ...であろうとなかろうと, ...ても/でも...なくても

I wasn't sure whether to go.
行(い)くべきかどうか、よくわかりませんでした。

Could you check whether or not there's a meeting scheduled in this room now?

この部屋で今から会議の予定があるかどうか、調べてもらえますか？

I don't know whether the Tigers won or lost.
タイガースが勝ったのか負けたのか、知らない。

I asked him whether he might reconsider.
考え直してくれないかと、彼に尋ねた。

Whether we go or stay, it's all the same to me.
行っても行かなくても、私にとっては全く同じことです。

He's your teacher, whether you like it or not.
好むと好まざるとにかかわらず、彼はあなたの先生です。

which

1 ***interrogative pron.*** (among two) どっち, ((*polite*)) どちら, (among three or more) どれ, ((*polite*)) どちら

2 ***interrogative adj.*** (among two) どっちの, ((*polite*)) どちらの, (among three or more) どの, どこの, ((*polite*)) どちらの

3 ***interrogative adj./pron.*** INTRODUCING A WHICH-CLAUSE: どの/どっち…か

4 ***relative pron.*** See examples below [NOTE: No equivalent in Japanese.]

5 ***relative adj.*** (そして) その

1 Which is better, the green one or the red one?
緑のと赤のと(では)、どっちがいいかな？

Which would you like: beer, wine, or whiskey?
ビール、ワイン、あるいはウイスキー、どれになさいますか？

2 Which brand do you think is better?
どっちのブランドがいいと思う？

Which department are you looking for?
どちらの課をお探しですか？

3 Do you know which company he works for?
彼がどの会社に勤めているか、わかりますか？

I had no idea which one was right.
どっちが正しいのか、さっぱりわからなかった。

4 The houses are all old, except for one, which is built in a bizarre, futuristic style.
どの家もみんな古いですが、1軒だけ例外で、奇抜で超現代的な設計になっています。

The book from which you took the quote is full of misprints.
君が引用に使った本は誤植だらけだよ。

It was hard work which kept us ahead of the competition.
競争をリードし続けられたのは、我々の勤勉な努力の結果です。

5 She lived in Japan for ten years, during which time she learned to speak fluent Japanese.
彼女は10年間日本に住んでいた。そしてその間に流ちょうな日本語をしゃべれるようになった。

whichever

1 ***adj.*** NO MATTER WHICH: どの/どっちの…ても/でも, ((*polite*)) どちらの…ても/でも, (**whichever one**) …ほう

2 ***pron.*** WHICHEVER ONE: (どっちでも)…ほう

3 ***pron.*** NO MATTER WHICH: どれを/が…ても/でも, どれを…と, どれを/が…にしろ

1 Whichever way you look at it, we come

out rather badly.
どう見ても、結果はあまりよくないよ。

Buy whichever one is cheaper.
安いほうを買って。

2 Use whichever you like.
(どっちでも)好きなほうを使ってください。

3 Whichever she chooses, she must choose wisely.
どれを選ぶにしろ、彼女は賢い選択をしなければならない。

whiff *n.* (act of inhaling) 一かぎ, (gust of air) 一吹き
v. (sniff) (...の)においをかぐ
take a whiff of ...のにおいをかぐ

while

1 *conj.* DURING THE TIME: ...間, ...中, (while a certain state/situation lasts) ...うちに

2 *conj.* IN CONTRAST TO WHICH: ...に対し(て), 一方

3 *conj.* ALTHOUGH: ...けれども, ...としても

4 *n.* PERIOD: (**a while**) 時間, 間, (**for a while**) しばらく, 当分, (**a while longer**) もう少し

5 *v.* PASS TIME: (**while away**) のんびり過ごす

1 Laura stayed with us while her mother was in the hospital.
お母さんが入院している間、ローラは私たちの所に泊まっていました。

While I was in Japan, my son attended university in England.
私が日本に滞在している間、息子はイギリスの大学に行っていました。

What did you do while you were in the Bahamas?
バハマにいる間、何をしていたの？

While I was on the phone, someone knocked at the door.
電話に出ている最中に、誰かがドアをノックした。

Let's go for another swim while there is still daylight.
まだ日のあるうちに、もう一泳ぎしに行こう。

2 Rob studied hard, while Jane just wasted the entire semester.
ロブが一生懸命勉強したのに対し、ジェーンは1学期を丸々むだにしただけだった。

3 While I won't rule out the possibility, I'm not convinced it's the best solution.
その可能性はあるとしても、それが最善の策だと確信しているわけではない。

4 We talked for a while about the old days.
私たちはしばらくの間、昔話をした。

Let him sleep a while longer.
もう少し彼を寝かせてあげよう。

5 We whiled away the time listening to our favorite CDs.
お気に入りのＣＤを聞いて、のんびり時間を過ごした。

once in a while たまに [→ ONCE]

quite a while かなりの時間, ずいぶん

It took quite a while to get here.
ここに着くのにかなり時間がかかった。

I saw that movie quite a while ago.
その映画はずいぶん前に見た。

whilst *conj.* → WHILE

whim *n.* 気まぐれ

whimper *v.* (cry) しくしく泣く
n. しくしく泣く声

whimsical *adj.* 気まぐれな

whine *v.* (of dog) クーンと鼻を鳴らす, (complain) 泣き言を言う

whinny *v.* (of horse) いななく

whip *n.* むち

v. (strike with a whip) むちで打つ; (beat: cream etc.) 泡立てる, ホイップする

♦ **whipping** *n.* (lashing) むちで打つこと

whip up *v.* (enthusiasm, support) かき立てる, 集める

whiplash *n.* (injury) むち打ち症

whipping cream *n.* ホイップクリーム

whir *v.* (make a buzzing sound) ブーンという音がする

whirl *v.* (spin around) ぐるぐる回る, (of head) くらくらする

n. (of smoke) 渦

whirlpool *n.* (in ocean) 渦, 渦巻き; (in home/hotel: bathtub) 渦巻きぶろ

whirlwind *n.* つむじ風, 旋風

whisk *v.* (eggs etc.) 泡立てる

n. (kitchen utensil) 泡立て器 [→ picture of COOKING UTENSILS]

whisker *n.* (of cat) ひげ, (**whiskers**: of person) ほおひげ

whiskey *n.* ウイスキー

whisper *v.* (say softly) ささやく, (so as not to be heard by others) ひそひそ話をする; (of wind) サラサラ音を立てる

n. (person's whisper) ささやき, (rumor) うわさ, (of wind) サラサラ(いう音)

What were you two whispering about? 二人で何をひそひそ話していたの？

The wind whispered among the reeds. 風がアシの間を、サラサラと音を立てて吹き抜けた。

whistle *n.* (sound) 口笛, (referee's whistle) ホイッスル, (train whistle) 汽笛

v. (make sounds/melody through pursed lips) 口笛を吹く

blow a whistle ホイッスルを鳴らす

♦ **whistle-blower** *n.* 内部告発者

white

1 *adj.* OF COLOR: 白い, 白みがかった, (**white hair**) 白髪, しらが, (of face: pale) 青白い, (of Caucasian) 白人の

2 *n.* COLOR: 白

3 *n.* COLORLESS PART: (of egg) 白身, ((*formal*)) 卵白, (of eye) 白目

4 *n.* LAUNDRY: (**whites**) 白い服, 白い物

5 *n.* PERSON: 白人

1 Her hair turned white as she grew older. 年をとるにつれて、彼女のしらがは増えていった。

You look white. Are you feeling all right? 顔色がよくないね。気分でも悪いの？

white wine 白ワイン

2 There's too much white in this room. この部屋は白が多すぎる。

You look good in white. 白が似合いますね。

3 Meringue is made from egg whites. メレンゲは卵の白身で作られています。

The whites of your eyes are bloodshot. 白目が充血しているよ。

4 Make sure to separate the whites from the darks. 白い物と黒い物は必ず別々にしてね。

♦ **whiteness** *n.* 白さ, 純白

white paper *n.* (government report) 白書

whiteboard *n.* 白板

white-collar *adj.* 事務労働の, ホワイトカラーの

white elephant *n.* 無用の長物

white flag *n.* 白旗

White House *n.* ホワイトハウス

whiten *v.* (make/become white) 白くする/なる

whitewash *v.* (apply whitewash to) (…に) しっくいを塗る; (deceptively conceal) ごまかす

n. (substance for walls) しっくい; (act of deceit) ごまかし

whiz *v.* (of bullet) ピューッと飛ぶ, (of car) 猛スピードで走る

n. (sound) ピューッ(という音)

who

1 *interrogative pron.* 誰, ((*polite*)) どなた

2 *interrogative pron.* INTRODUCING A WHO-CLAUSE: 誰…か, ((*polite*)) どなた…か

3 *relative pron.* See examples below [NOTE: No equivalent in Japanese.]

1 Who is that? あの人は誰ですか？

Who are you? あなた、誰？

"You know Brad, don't you?"
"Brad who?"
「ブラッドって知ってるだろ？」
「ブラッド何？」

(*in response to a knock on the door*) "Who is it?"「どなたですか？」

2 She didn't remember who I was.
彼女は私が誰だか覚えていなかった。

Did you ask who is coming?
誰が来るのか確かめましたか？

3 You're the only person who cares for me.
私のことを心配してくれるのは、あなただけよ。

If you're not prepared to do it, we'll find someone who is.
やる気がないのなら、別の人にやってもらうよ。

Those who failed can try again.
失敗した人は、もう一度挑戦できます。

My son, who has been in New Zealand for three years, is coming home next month.
息子が、3年間ニュージーランドにいたんですが、来月帰って来ます。

whoever

1 *relative pron.* THE PERSON WHO: …人は(誰でも)

2 *pron.* NO MATTER WHO: 誰が/を…ても/でも, 誰を…と, 誰が/を…にしろ

3 *interrogative pron.* WHO: ((*emphatic*)) 一体誰

1 Whoever did it is in big trouble.
やった人は誰でも、大変な目にあう。

2 "Whoever you are, don't call me again." (slams down the phone)
「誰だか知りませんが、二度とかけてこないでください」

Whoever you choose, just make sure it's someone trustworthy.
誰を選ぶにしろ、必ず信頼できる人にしなさい。

whole

1 *adj.* ENTIRE: すべての, 全部の, 全体の

2 *adj.* IN ONE PIECE: (undamaged) 無傷で, (not sliced up) まるごと

3 *n.* ENTIRE THING/ENTITY: (**the whole**) 全体

1 Look, let's forget the whole thing.
((*masculine*)) いいかい、もうすべて忘れよう。

The whole family went.

家族全員が行きました。

My dog's the best in the whole world.
うちの犬は世界中で一番だ。

Never in my whole life have I seen such a beautiful sight.
今までの人生で、こんなに美しい光景を目にしたことはない。

2 Fortunately, the vase arrived whole and unbroken.
幸い、花びんは割れずに無傷で届いた。

You're supposed to swallow the pill whole.
錠剤はまるごと飲み込むものなんですよ。

3 Imagine, that's only one small part of the whole.
考えてみて、それは全体のほんの一部にすぎないんだよ。

the whole of Russia ロシア全土

the whole of August 8月まるまる

as a whole 全体として

on the whole 全体的に見て, おおむね

On the whole, I thought the meeting was a success.
おおむね、会議は成功だと思いました。

wholehearted *adj.* 心からの

You have our wholehearted support.
心から支持しています。

wholesale *n., adj.* 卸売り(の)

the wholesale price 卸売価格

♦ **wholesaler** *n.* 卸売業者

wholesale store *n.* 卸問屋

wholesome *adj.* (morally/mentally good) 健全な, (healthy) 体にいい

wholly *adv.* (exclusively, solely) もっぱら, (completely) 完全に, 全く

whom *interrogative pron.* 誰を/に

relative pron. See examples below [NOTE: No equivalent in Japanese.]

The people about whom you're speaking happen to be my friends.
今話題にしている人たちは、私の友達なんです。

The man with the cane whom you met yesterday was a friend of your father's.
(あなたが)昨日会った、つえをついていた男性は、あなたのお父さんの友人だったんですよ。

whomever → WHOEVER 2

whoop *v.* (shout out of joy/excitement) 大声で叫ぶ, 歓声を上げる

n. 叫び声, 歓声

whooping cough *n.* 百日ぜき

whore *n.* (prostitute) 売春婦, (woman who sleeps around) ((*informal/rude*)) 尻軽女

whose

1 *interrogative pron.* 誰の, ((*polite*)) どなたの

2 *relative pron.* See examples below [NOTE: No equivalent in Japanese.]

1 Whose umbrella is this?
これはどなたの傘ですか？

This bag is mine, but whose is that?
このかばんは私のだけど、あれは誰のでしょう？

And whose fault is that?
で、それは誰の責任ですか？

2 The culprit, whose name I will not mention, is among us.
名前は伏せておくが、犯人は私たちの中にいる。

There are three suspects whose whereabouts are unaccounted for.

所在のわからない容疑者が3名いる。

why

1 ***interrogative adv.*** **FOR WHAT REASON:** どうして, なぜ, どういう訳で, ((*informal*)) なんで

2 ***interrogative adv.*** **INTRODUCING A WHY-CLAUSE:** どうして…か, なぜ…か, ((*informal*)) なんで…か

3 ***relative adv.*** **THE REASON WHY:** …理由, …のは, (**that's why**) そういう訳で, だから

4 ***interrogative adv.*** **MAKING A SUGGESTION:** (**why not…?**) …したら(どうですか)?, (**why don't we…?**) …しない?

5 ***interj.*** **SHOWING SURPRISE:** えーっ, おや, ((*feminine*)) あら

1 Why are you doing this?
どうしてこんなことをしているんですか?

"I had to refuse."
"Why?"
"It was a difficult decision."
"Why's that?"
「断らなければならなかった」
「どうして?」
「難しい決断だったんだよ」
「それはなぜ?」

Why all the fuss?
なんでそんなに騒ぐの?

Why are there so few people here?
どういう訳で、ここはこんなに人が少ないんだろう?

2 I know why he did it.
彼がなぜやったのか知っている。

I can't remember why I was so upset.
どうしてそんなに動揺したのか思い出せない。

He's not allowed to come, though I can't see why not.
なぜ(だめなの)かわからないけど、彼は来ちゃいけないらしい。

3 There are a number of good reasons why I don't wish to see him.
彼に会いたくない、きちんとした理由がいくつかあります。

The reason why religion is important to people is that it provides spiritual comfort.
宗教が人々にとって大切なのは、精神的な安らぎを与えているからです。

The door is warped. That's why it won't open.
ドアがゆがんでいるんです。だからあかないんです。

4 Why not do it now? 今やったら?

Why not get away for a few days and forget it all?
何日かここを離れて、すべて忘れたらどう?

Why don't we all go together?
みんなでいっしょに行かない?

5 Why, if it isn't Henry himself.
おや、ヘンリーじゃないか。

why not (accepting an offer, suggestion) もちろん, いいね, ぜひ

"How about going to a movie tonight?"
"Sure, why not."
「今夜、映画でも見に行こうよ」
「ああ、いいね」

"Would you like a cup of tea?"
"Why not."
「お茶はいかがですか?」
「ええ、いただきます」

wick ***n.*** (candle wick) しん

wicked ***adj.*** (evil) 邪悪な

♦ **wickedness** ***n.*** 邪悪

wicket ***n.*** (small entrance) 小門, くぐり戸

wide ***adj.*** (broad) 広い, 幅の広い, (giving measurement) 幅…, (of gap, difference) 大きい, (**a wide range/variety of**) 幅広い, 広範囲の, 多岐にわたる

adv. 広く, 大きく

a wide road 広い道路

It's a pity the passage isn't wider.
通路がもっと広かったらいいのに。

a river ten meters wide
幅10メートルの川

Put it in a wider context and it doesn't seem as important.
もっと広い視野からとらえれば、それは大した問題ではないような気がする。

The gap between technology and our understanding of it is very wide.
テクノロジーと、それについての我々の理解度との隔たりは大きい。

His interests are wide.
彼の興味は幅広い。

The party is gaining wide support.
その政党は幅広い支持を得ている。

The window was left wide open.
窓は、あけっぱなしになっていた。

He opened the door wide.
彼はドアを大きくあけた。

wide awake (not at all sleepy) すっかり目が覚めて, (alert) 頭がさえて

I feel wide awake. すっかり目が覚めた。

widely ***adv.*** 広く, 大きく, 幅広く

a widely accepted notion
広く受け入れられている考え

widen ***v.*** (make wide) 広げる, 広くする, (become wide) 広くなる, (of eyes: widen in surprise) 目を丸くする

wide-ranging ***adj.*** (of discussion) 広範囲にわたる

widespread ***adj.*** (of belief) 広く行き渡っている, (of panic, rumor) 広がる

widow ***n.*** 未亡人

♦ **widowed** ***adj.*** (of woman) 未亡人の, (of man) 男やもめの

widower ***n.*** 男やもめ

width ***n.*** 幅, 横幅, (…in width) 横…

have width 幅がある

The width of this table is one meter.
このテーブルの幅は1メートルです。

What's the width of this window?
この窓の幅は、どのくらいありますか？

wield ***v.*** (weapon) 振り回す, (power) ふるう, 行使する

wield a gun 銃を振り回す

wife ***n.*** (one's own) 妻, 女房, 家内, ((*informal*)) かみさん, (sb else's) 奥さん, ((*polite*)) 奥様, ((*formal*)) 夫人

Look, here's a photo of my wife.
ほら、これが女房の写真だよ。

Please give my regards to your wife.
奥様によろしくお伝えください。

wig ***n.*** かつら

wear a wig かつらをかぶる [着ける]

wiggle ***v.*** (foot, toes) 小刻みに動かす

wild ***adj.*** (of animal) 野生の, (of land) 未開の, 荒れ果てた, (stormy) 荒れた; (of child) 乱暴な, 手に負えない, (of party) 大騒ぎの, (of idea) とっぴな, (**wild guess**) 当てずっぽう

n. (**the wild**) 野生, (**the wilds**: an uninhabited area) 荒野, 未開の地

a wild duck 野生のカモ

Most of these plants are wild.
この植物のほとんどは野生です。

It was a cold, wild winter night.
寒くて荒れた冬の夜でした。

That was a wild guess, wasn't it?
あれは当てずっぽうだったんでしょう?

It's difficult to return animals to the wild once they've gotten used to people.
人になれた動物を野生に戻すのは難しい。

go wild (with excitement) 熱狂する, (with joy) 狂喜する, (with anger) 怒り狂う

The audience went wild.
観客は熱狂した。

If my old man hears about this, he'll go wild.
親父がこのことを聞いたら、怒り狂うだろうな。

wilderness *n.* 荒野, 荒れ地

wild-goose chase *n.* むだな追求, むだ足

wildlife *n.* 野生動物

will[1] *aux.*

1 SPEAKING OF FUTURE EVENTS/CONDITIONS: See examples below [NOTE: Usually expressed by the non-past tense.]

2 CONJECTURING: ((*polite*)) …でしょう, ((*masculine/informal*)) …だろう

3 EXPRESSING INTENTION: …するつもりだ, …する予定だ

4 INVITING/REQUESTING: (**will you**) …しませんか, (asking sb to do sth for you) ((*polite*)) …していただけませんか, …してくれませんか, ((*informal*)) …してくれる?

5 EXPRESSING THE FUTURE PERFECT TENSE: (**will have done**) …しているはずだ, …してしまっている

6 STATING RULE: …することになっている

1 I'll be back in a minute.
すぐに戻ります。

New Year's Eve will fall on a Tuesday next year.
来年の大みそかは火曜日です。

The road will be opened tomorrow.
道路は明日、開通します。

"It'll be good to get home and rest." "Yes, it will."
「家に帰って休みたいね」
「そうですね」

2 It'll rain tomorrow.
明日は雨になるでしょう。

Accidents will happen.
事故というのは起こるだろう。

Any bank will cash it for you.
どの銀行でも、現金にしてくれますよ。

3 But if you move, where will you live?
でも引っ越したら、どこに住むつもり?

We'll be visiting Paris the same time next year.
来年の同じ時期に、パリに行く予定です。

Will you be at the meeting tonight?
今夜の会議に出席しますか?

4 Will you stay and have dinner?
夕食を召し上がっていきませんか?

Will you do me a favor and tell Ms. Fukuda I won't be there on Friday?
お願いがあるんですが、福田さんに金曜日は行かないと伝えていただけませんか?

Will you lend me your calculator for a moment?

ちょっと電卓を貸してくれませんか？

Pass me the pepper, will you.

コショウを取ってくれる？

5 Mr. Morita will have arrived in New York this time next week.

来週の今ごろは、森田さんはニューヨークに着いているはずです。

By the time you get this letter, I will have left.

この手紙を受け取るころには、私はもういません。

6 Employees will be on time for work.

従業員は定刻に仕事に就くことになっています。

will² *n.*

1 MENTAL FACULTY: 意志, (determination) 意欲, 決意, (self-discipline) 精神力, 志

2 DOCUMENT: 遺言書, 遺言状

3 DESIRE: 意向, 望み

1 She has a strong [weak] will.

彼女は意志が強い [弱い]。

Where there's a will, there's a way.

意志ある所に道は開ける。

the will to live 生きる意欲

2 He failed to write a will.

彼は遺言状を書かなかった。

3 the nation's will 国民の意向

against one's will いやいやながら, 心ならずも, (by force) 無理やり

of one's own free will 自らの意志で, 自発的に

willful *adj.* (headstrong) わがままな, (deliberate) 故意の, 意図的な

willing *adj.* (**be willing to do**) …するのをいとわない, …してもかまわない

be willing to admit (that)

…に異存はない

be willing to die for

…のためなら死んでもかまわない

be willing to take risks

リスクを負うことをいとわない

be willing to listen (to) 聞く気はある

be willing to consider

検討する用意はある

Are you willing to do this for me?

私のために、これをしてもらえますか？

♦ **willingly** *adv.* (happily) 喜んで, (voluntarily) 進んで

willingness *n.* 乗り気, 意欲

willow *n.* ヤナギ, 柳

willpower *n.* 精神力, 気力, 意志の強さ

wilt *v.* (of plant) しおれる

win *v.* (…に) 勝つ, (finish first) 優勝する, (prize, contract) 獲得する, 勝ち取る, (support, respect) 得る, (sb's heart) 捕らえる, つかむ

n. 勝利, -勝

Which side is winning?

どっちが勝ってるの？

Aren't you interested in who's winning?

誰が勝つか興味はないの？

I won and you lost.

勝ったのは私で、あなたは負けたんだ。

Which party won the election?

どの政党が選挙に勝ったんですか？

That team hasn't won a game in ages.

あのチームはもう長い間、試合に勝っていない。

She won the tournament.

彼女がトーナメントに優勝した。

He won second prize.
彼は2等賞を獲得した。

His honesty has won him a lot of respect.
彼はその誠実さで、多くの人から尊敬を得ています。

How many wins is that?
今ので何勝ですか？

♦ **win over** *v.* (gain the support of) (…の) 支持/理解を得る

We must try to win over young voters.
若い有権者の支持を得るよう、努力しなければならない。

KANJI BRIDGE

勝 ON: しょう KUN: か(つ), まさ(る) | WIN, VICTORY

as one pleases/selfishly	勝手に
champion	優勝者
championship	優勝
decision (in contest)	決勝
finals	決勝戦
finish line	決勝線
series of victories	連勝
victor, winner	勝者
victory	勝利
victory or defeat	勝敗

wince *v.* (due to pain) 顔がゆがむ

winch *n.* (tool) ウィンチ, 巻き上げ機
v. ウィンチで巻き上げる

wind[1]

1 *n.* AIR BLOWING: 風
2 *n.* BREATH: (for exercise) 息, 呼吸
3 *v.* CAUSE TO LOSE BREATH: (**be winded**) 息切れする
4 *n.* INSTRUMENTS: (**winds**) 吹奏楽器

1 The wind's strong today.
今日は風が強い。

Look at the corn blowing in the wind.
見て、トウモロコシが風になびいているよ。

The wind's picking up [dropping].
風が強まっている [弱まっている]。

2 You'd better stop and get your wind before doing any more exercise.
次の運動をする前に、ちょっと休んで息を整えたほうがいい。

3 I was completely winded by that run.
あの一っ走りで完全に息切れしていた。

break wind (fart) おならをする

wind[2]

1 *v.* CAUSE TO BECOME WRAPPED AROUND: 巻く
2 *v.* TURN: (crank) 回す, (clock) 巻く
3 *v.* OF RIVER/ROAD: 曲がりくねる
4 *n.* SINGLE TURNING MOTION: 一回し, 一巻き

1 The snake wound itself around the branch.
蛇が枝に巻き付いていた。

2 "How do I get this toy to work?"
"You have to wind it up."
「このおもちゃは、どうやったら動くの？」
「ねじを巻くんだよ」

3 The road winds through the mountains.
道は山の中を曲がりくねっている。

The river twists and winds back on itself for several kilometers.
川は数キロにわたって蛇行している。

4 Give it another wind. もう一巻きして。

wind down *v.* (car window) あける; (relax) くつろぐ, 緊張がほぐれる, (of activity: draw to a close) しだいに収束する

Weekends are about the only time I can

W

wind down.
くつろげるのは週末ぐらいだ。

wind up *v.* (car window) 閉める; (bring to a close) 終える, (**wind up doing**) 結局…する
They wound up getting married.
結局、彼らは結婚した。

---

windbreaker *n.* ウインドブレーカー

windfall *n.* (unexpected luck) 意外な授かり物, ((*informal*)) 棚ぼた

winding *adj.* (of river, road) 曲がりくねった, (of staircase) らせんの
a winding staircase らせん階段

windmill *n.* 風車

window *n.* 窓 [→ picture of HOUSE]
open [close] the window
窓をあける [閉める]
a window overlooking the park
公園を見下ろす窓
a window with a view 眺めのいい窓
window of opportunity いい機会, チャンス

windowpane *n.* 窓ガラス

window-shopping *n.* ウインドーショッピング

windshield *n.* フロントガラス [→ picture of CAR]
♦ **windshield wiper** *n.* ワイパー [→ picture of CAR]

windsurfing *n.* ウインドサーフィン
♦ **windsurf** *v.* ウインドサーフィンをする

windy *adj.* (having strong winds) 風の強い

wine *n.* ワイン, ブドウ酒
red [white] wine 赤 [白] ワイン
a bottle of wine ワイン一びん [1本]
♦ **wine bar** *n.* ワインバー
wine cellar *n.* (room) ワイン貯蔵室, (appliance) ワインセラー
wineglass *n.* ワイングラス
wine list *n.* ワインリスト

wing *n.* (of bird, insect) 羽, (of airplane) 翼; (position on a team) ウイング
♦ **winged** *adj.* 翼のある

wink *v.* ウインクする

winner *n.* (person/team) 勝った人/チーム, 勝者, (champion) 優勝者, (recipient of a prize) 受賞者, 入賞者

winning *adj.* (of team) 勝利の, 勝った, (of shot or other action in a game) 決勝の
n. (**winnings**) 賞金
winning point/goal 決勝点

winter *n.* 冬
the Winter Olympics 冬季オリンピック
♦ **winter sports** *n.* ウインタースポーツ
wintertime *n.* 冬, ((*formal*)) 冬期
wintry *adj.* 冬の, 冬らしい

wipe *v.* (rub with a cloth) ふく, (wipe A off B) (BからAを/BのAを) ふき取る, (tears, sweat) ぬぐう
n. ふくこと, ぬぐうこと, 一ふき
I'll wipe the dishes.
お皿をふきましょう。
Don't wipe your filthy hands on that clean towel.
そのきれいなタオルで、汚い手をふかないでちょうだい。
Wipe the metal part dry to keep it from rusting.

さびないように、金属部分をふいておきなさい。

Let's wipe the dust off these shelves.
この棚のほこりを、ふき取ろう。

She wiped the tears from her eyes.
彼女は涙をぬぐった。

I'll give the tables a wipe and then you can start setting them.
テーブルをさっとふくから、そしたら並べ始めていいよ。

♦ **wipe out** *v.* (eliminate: crime, poverty etc.) 一掃する, (**be wiped out**: become extinct) 絶滅する; (on surfboard) ひっくり返る

wiper *n.* (windshield wiper) ワイパー [→ picture of CAR]

wire *n.* 針金, ワイヤー, (electric wire) 電線, (telegram) 電報
v. (money) 電信(為替)で送金する

♦ **wireless** *adj.* 無線の

wiring *n.* 配線

wiry *adj.* (of body) 筋張った

wisdom *n.* 知恵

wisdom tooth *n.* 親知らず

wise *adj.* 賢い, 賢明な, 聡明な

a wise man 賢人

It'd be wiser to wait and see.
様子を見るのが賢明でしょう。

wish

1 *n.* DESIRE: 願い, 願いごと, 望み, 希望, 願望

2 *v.* EXPRESSING DESIRE: (**I wish that...**) …したらいいのに, …したらなあ, (**wish for**) 望む, 願う, (**I wish to do**) …したい, (**he/she wishes to do**) …したがる

3 *v.* EXPRESSING HOPE FOR SB'S HAPPINESS: (wish sb luck) (…の幸運を) 祈る, (wish sb a happy birthday) (…にお誕生日おめでとうを) 言う

1 He told me of his wish to meet his true father.
本当の父親に会いたいという願いを、彼は話してくれました。

His last wish was to have his ashes scattered over the land he loved.
彼の最後の希望は、愛した土地に遺灰をまいてもらうことでした。

Let's make a wish. 願いごとをしよう。

If you could have three wishes, what would they be?
三つの望みがかなうとしたら、何をお願いする?

2 I wish you were here.
あなたがここにいてくれたらいいのに。

I wish they would give us an answer.
先方が返事をくれたらなあ。

We were all wishing for the best.
我々は皆、いい結果を望んでいました。

Everyone wished he would just quit the company.
彼が会社を辞めてくれればと、みんな願っていた。

Had he wished, he could have become managing director.
望めば、彼は常務取締役になれた。

I don't wish to upset anyone, but...
誰も動揺させたくはないけど…

They all wish to attend.
彼らはみんな出席したがっている。

3 I wished them the best of luck.
彼らの幸運を祈った。

Wish Miyuki a happy birthday for me,

will you?
美幸さんに、お誕生日おめでとうと伝えてくれる？

best wishes ((*written*)) ご成功をお祈りします, ご多幸をお祈りします

have no wish to do …するつもりはさらさらない, …する気は全くない, …したくない

We have no wish to repeat the same mistake again.
二度と同じあやまちを繰り返したくありません。

wishbone *n.* (鶏の) 鎖骨

wishful thinking *n.* 希望的観測

wishy-washy *adj.* はっきりしない, 生ぬるい

wisteria *n.* フジ, 藤

wistful *adj.* (of look) 物欲しそうな

♦ **wistfully** *adv.* 物欲しそうに, (sadly) 悲しげに

wit *n.* ウイット, 機知

be at one's wits' end 途方に暮れる

have the wits to do …する才覚がある

have one's wits about one 抜かりない, 油断しない

witch *n.* 魔女

♦ **witch hunt** *n.* 魔女狩り

witchcraft *n.* 魔術

with *prep.*

1 IN THE COMPANY/POSSESSION OF: (in the company of) …と (いっしょに), ((*formal*)) …と共に, (in the possession of) …に

2 HAVING/FEATURING: …のある, …付きの, (of movie: featuring) …主演の

3 INDICATING MEANS/METHOD: …で, (by using) …を使って

4 INDICATING MANNER OF ACTION: …で

5 INDICATING SOUND: …と

6 COVERED/FILLED/LINED WITH: …で, …に

7 BECAUSE OF: …のために, …で, …だから

8 INDICATING RELATIONSHIP: (**have to do with**) …と関係がある

9 KIND/CAREFUL/ANGRY/ROUGH WITH: …に

10 FIGHT/ARGUE WITH: …と

11 IN THE SAME DIRECTION AS: …と同じ方向に, …にまかせて

12 IN PROPORTION TO: …につれて

13 IN SUPPORT OF: (**be with**) …に賛成だ

14 COMPREHENDING: (**be with**) …の言っていることがわかっている

15 INDICATING DETAIL: See examples below

16 IN SPITE OF: (**with all…**) …にもかかわらず, …のに

1 I was with him at the time.
その時、彼といっしょにいました。

Until what time did you stay with her?
何時まで彼女といたの？

Did you go with him?
彼といっしょに行ったの？

He still lives with his mother.
彼は今でも母親と暮らしている。

Meetings were held with the managers.
支配人たちとの会議が行われました。

Get in the back seat with Sandy, and I'll sit up front with Ben.
サンディと後ろに座って、私はベンと前に座るから。

Put the knives with the rest of the silverware.
ナイフはフォークやスプーンといっしょにしておいてください。

W

I'll be with you in a minute.
少々お待ちください。

I'll walk home with you.
家まで送って行くよ。

We must learn to live with nature.
自然と共に生きることを学ばなければいけません。

The check is with the letter.
小切手は手紙に同封してあります。

All the information you need is with the personnel division.
ご入り用の情報はすべて人事課にあります。

2 a house with a large yard
大きな庭のある家

a room with a kitchen
キッチン付きの部屋

a man with a big nose 鼻の大きな男

a woman with a cane つえをついた女性

a young man with no previous experience
未経験の若い男性

a desk with no drawers 引き出しのない机

Terminator with Arnold Schwarzenegger
アーノルド・シュワルツェネッガー主演の『ターミネーター』

3 He poked it with a stick.
彼は棒でつついた。

Try gluing it together with superglue.
強力接着剤でくっつけてみたらどう?

Get it off with a knife.
ナイフを使ってはがして。

4 Mr. Ishida welcomed us with a handshake.
石田さんは私たちを握手で迎えてくれた。

With a shrug, he turned and left.
肩をすくめると、彼は背を向けて立ち去った。

The old man walked with difficulty.
老人は苦しそうに歩いた。

5 He stormed out of the room, slamming the door behind him with a bang.
彼はバーンとドアを閉めて、部屋から飛び出した。

The cork came out of the bottle with a pop.
コルクはポンとびんから抜けた。

The two cars collided with a loud crash.
2台の車は大きな音を立てて衝突した。

6 The room was filled with people.
部屋は人でいっぱいだった。

The car was covered with snow.
車は雪に埋もれていた。

The street is lined with willow trees.
道に沿って柳の木が植えられている。

7 My mother is in bed with the flu.
母はインフルエンザで寝ています。

With his knowledge of computers, he should be able to get a job easily.
あれだけのコンピューターの知識があるんだから、すぐに就職できるよ。

8 It's all to do with money.
すべてお金に関係のあることだ。

They (=those two matters) don't have much to do with one another.
その2つの件はお互いに、あまり関係がないです。

9 I got angry with her. 彼女に怒った。

Be careful with that glass—it's very fragile.
そのグラスに気をつけて—すごく割れやすいから。

10 That man got in a fight with somebody

at a bar.
その男はバーで誰かとけんかした。

11 Paddling with the current is much easier than paddling against it.
流れと同じ方向にこぐのは、流れに逆らってこぐよりずっと簡単です。

12 You'll get better at it with time.
時がたつにつれてうまくなりますよ。

13 Are you with me or against me?
私に賛成ですか、反対ですか？

14 Are you with me?
私の言ってることがわかりますか？

His class wasn't quite with him.
その先生のクラスは、あまり授業についていってなかった。

15 I'd like a salad with vinegar on the side.
ビネガーを別にして、サラダを下さい。

Dad was sleeping with his mouth open.
お父さんは口をあけて寝ていた。

16 With all this paperwork, it's a wonder anyone ever gets any work done.
こんなに事務手続きがあるのに、みんな仕事を順調にこなしているのが不思議だ。

withdraw *v.*
1 MONEY: 引き出す, おろす
2 PULL OUT: (from unfavorable situation) (…から) 手を引く, 引き下がる, (from course) 中退する, (from competition) (…への) 出場を取りやめる, おりる, (troops) 撤退させる
3 DRAW BACK: (hand) 引っ込める

1 I withdrew most of the money from my account.
私は預金口座から、ほとんどのお金を引き出した。

I need to withdraw some cash.
いくらか現金をおろさなきゃいけない。

2 He withdrew from the race.
彼はレースへの出場を取りやめた。

Orders were given for the army to withdraw its troops.
部隊を撤退させよとの命令が、軍に出された。

3 The lady withdrew her hand.
女性は手を引っ込めた。

withdraw into one's shell 自分の殻に閉じこもる

withdrawal *n.* (from alcohol/drug) (…の) 使用中止; (of money) 引き出し; (of troops) 撤退

♦ **withdrawal symptoms** *n.* 禁断症状

withdrawn *adj.* 内気な, 引っ込み思案の

wither *v.* 枯れる, しぼむ

♦ **withered** *adj.* 枯れた

withhold *v.* 差し控える, 与えない

within *prep.* …以内で/に, …内で/に, …の範囲内で/に

I want it done within the hour.
1時間以内でやってもらいたい。

Within a few weeks, she was out of the hospital.
数週間で、彼女は退院した。

We have to keep our spending within our budget.
支出は予算内に抑えなければならない。

I'm afraid it's not within our power to do anything.
残念ながら、我々の権限では何もできません。

The shops are within a short walking distance.

商店は歩いてすぐのところにあります。

Our team was within sight of victory.
僕らのチームは、勝利に手の届くところにいた。

without *prep.* …のない, …なしで/に, (**without doing**) …しないで, …せずに

a room without windows 窓のない部屋

They put people in prison without trial.
当局は裁判なしで人々を投獄した。

I went out without putting on a coat.
コートを着ないで出かけた。

He refused our request without giving any reason.
彼は理由も言わずに、私たちの要求を拒絶した。

withstand *v.* (endure) (…に) 耐える, (resist) (…に) 抵抗する

witness *n.* 目撃者, (testifier in court) 証人, (person who signs for another) 連署人

v. (see) 見る, 目撃する

There were several witnesses to the crime.
その犯行の目撃者は数名いた。

He witnessed the murder and gave evidence at the trial for the prosecution.
彼は殺人を目撃し、裁判で検察側の証人として証言した。

witticism *n.* しゃれ

witty *adj.* しゃれのうまい, 機知に富んだ

wizard *n.* 魔法使い

wobble *v.* (shake) がたがた揺れる, (of table) ぐらぐらする, (of person) ふらつく

wobbly *adj.* ぐらぐらする, ふらつく, 不安定な

woe *n.* 悲哀, (**woes**: problems, troubles) 問題, 悩み

♦ **woeful** *adj.* 悲惨な, 情けない

wok *n.* 中華なべ

wolf *n.* オオカミ, 狼

woman *n.* 女, 女性, 女の人, (older woman) 婦人

Do you know that woman?
あの女性をご存じですか?

There were about the same number of men and women there.
そこには同じくらいの人数の男女がいました。

That's Joe's woman.
あれがジョーの女だ。

the exploitation of women 女性搾取

be one's own woman → MAN

womanizer *n.* 女たらし

womanly *adj.* 女らしい, 女性らしい

womb *n.* 子宮

women → WOMAN

♦ **women's liberation** *n.* ウーマンリブ

women's room *n.* トイレ

won *n.* (Korean currency) ウォン

wonder

1 *v.* EXPRESSING CURIOSITY: (**I wonder…**) …かな, ((*feminine*)) …かしら

2 *v.* CONSIDER: 考える

3 *n.* EMOTION: 感激, 感嘆

4 *n.* MIRACLE: 奇跡, 不思議

5 *n.* MARVEL: 驚異

1 I wonder what sort of person the new manager is.
新しいマネージャーはどんな人なのかな。

When is the division chief going to get here, I wonder.
部長はいつ来るのかな。

I was wondering if you might have some

time this evening.
今晩お時間があればと思っていました。

2 Look, just stop wondering what everyone else might think.
いいね、ほかの人がどう思うかなんて考えるのは、もうやめなさい。

3 We were filled with wonder.
私たちは感激でいっぱいだった。

4 It's a wonder we didn't run out of gas.
ガス欠にならなかったのが不思議だ。

5 the wonders of nature 自然の驚異

(it is) no wonder 不思議ではない, 当然だ, 無理もない

No wonder she left you.
彼女が君を捨てたのも無理はない。

wonderful ***adj.*** すばらしい, いい

What a wonderful day!
なんてすばらしい日だ!

It was a wonderful experience.
いい経験になりました。

wood ***n.*** 木, (also **woods**: area covered with growing trees) 森, 林, (timber) 木材, 材木, (firewood) まき

a piece of wood 木片

We used to play in those woods when we were children.
子供のころ、あの森でよく遊んだものです。

Has the wood been seasoned?
その材木は乾燥させてありますか?

We need some wood for the fire.
火にくべるまきが必要だ。

knock on wood この調子でいきますように

I haven't caught a cold for over a year. Knock on wood.
1年以上もかぜをひいてない。この調子でいきますように。

wooden ***adj.*** 木でできた, 木の, 木製の, (of house) 木造の

woodland ***n.*** (**woodlands**) 森林地帯

woodpecker ***n.*** キツツキ

woodwind ***n.*** 木管楽器

woodwork ***n.*** 木工品

wool ***n.*** (sheep's hair) 羊毛, (thread) 毛糸, (fabric) ウール

a hat made from pure wool
純毛でできた帽子

♦**woolen** ***adj.*** ウールの

word ***n.***

1 UNIT OF LANGUAGE: 単語, 言葉

2 REMARK: (**a word**) 一言, (=a conversation, a talk) 話

3 NEWS: ニュース, 知らせ, (information) 情報, (rumor) うわさ

4 PROMISE: 約束

5 COMMUNICATION: 連絡, (letter) 便り, (message) 伝言

1 How many words are there in this dictionary?
この辞書には、単語が何語入っていますか?

I don't know what this word means.
この単語の意味がわかりません。

How can I put these feelings into words?
この気持ちを言葉でどう言い表したらいいんだろう?

There are no words to describe her grief.
彼女の悲しみは言葉では言い表せない。

2 He didn't say a word.
彼は一言もしゃべらなかった。

The president (=CEO) would like to have a word with you.

W

社長がちょっと話があるそうです。

3 If word of this gets out, we're in trouble.
この情報が漏れたら、大変なことになる。

Word has it that the two companies are talking about a merger.
その2社が合併するといううわさがある。

4 You have my word. 約束します。

5 Any word from Masako?
雅子から何か連絡あった？

by word of mouth 口コミで, 口伝えで

in a word 要するに, 一言で言えば

in other words 言い換えると, つまり

put words into sb's mouth (...が)言ってもいないことを言ったことにする

You're putting words into his mouth.
彼が言ってもいないことを、言ったことにしているんだね。

wording *n.* 言い回し, 言葉づかい

word processor *n.* ワープロ

wordy *adj.* くどい

work

1 *v.* BE EMPLOYED: 働く, 仕事をする, 勤める

2 *n.* EMPLOYMENT: 職, 仕事(の口), 勤め口

3 *v.* DO DUTY: 働く, 仕事をする

4 *n.* DUTIES: 仕事, やること

5 *n.* PLACE OF WORK: 職場, (the office/company) 会社, (work site) 仕事場

6 *n.* LABOR/EFFORT: 労働, 作業, (effort) 努力, (research) 研究

7 *n.* THING PRODUCED: (work of art/literature) 作品

8 *v.* MACHINE: (function) 動く, 作動する, (control) 動かす, 操作する

1 He works in a restaurant.
彼はレストランで働いています。

Where's Mr. Tamura working now?
田村さんは今どこに勤めてるの？

Ms. Koike used to work here, but she no longer does.
小池さんは以前ここで働いていましたが、今はもういません。

2 It's hard to get work these days.
最近は仕事に就くのも大変です。

My cousin found work in the city.
いとこは街で仕事の口を見つけた。

3 I work hard, but I enjoy what I do.
ばりばり働いていますが、楽しんでやっています。

I usually work till about 6 o'clock.
たいてい6時ごろまで仕事をします。

4 a day's work 1日の仕事

I've got loads of work to do.
やることがたくさんあります。

I'll finish this work by 5 o'clock.
この仕事は5時までに終えます。

5 I can't get to work until 9 o'clock.
9時にならないと会社に着けない。

Work is a drag. 会社はうんざりだ。

6 I don't want to do it—it's too much work.
それはやりたくないです——過剰労働です。

Mining for gold is dangerous work.
金の採掘は危険な作業です。

Hard work is good for you.
一生懸命努力することはいいことです。

7 Whose work is this?
これは誰の作品ですか？

This looks like one of Degas's works.
これはドガの作品のようですね。

8 How does this thing work?/How do you work this thing?

これはどうやって動くんですか/これはどうやって動かすんですか？

work out *v.*

1 SOLVE: (problem) 解く
2 MAKE/THINK UP: 練り上げる, 考え出す
3 EXERCISE: 体を鍛える, 運動する
4 BE SUCCESSFUL: うまくいく
5 ADD UP TO: (合計)…になる

1 I can't work out this (math) problem.
この問題を解けない。

2 The company is trying to work out an arrangement that'll please everyone.
会社は、全員が満足する取り決めを考え出そうとしています。

3 Andy works out at the gym every evening.
アンディは毎晩ジムで体を鍛えている。

4 Oh, don't worry. It'll all work out.
心配しないで。きっとうまくいくから。

5 Ten dollars an hour for five hours works out to fifty dollars.
1時間10ドルで5時間だと合計50ドルになる。

work up *v.* (**get worked up**) 興奮する

---

workable *adj.* (of plan) 現実的な, 実現可能な

workaholic *n.* ワーカホリック, 仕事中毒の人

worker *n.* 仕事をする人, 労働者, (white-collar worker: "salaryman") サラリーマン, (female office worker: "office lady") OL

workforce *n.* (in general) 労働力, (total part of a population available for work) 労働人口, (total number employed by a company) 全従業員

working *adj.* (of person) 働く, (of conditions, hours) 労働…, (of knowledge) 実用的な
a working mother 働く母親
working hours 労働 [勤務] 時間
a working knowledge of Japanese 日本語の実用的な知識

working class *n.* 労働者階級
adj. (**working-class**) 労働者階級の

workload *n.* 仕事量

work of art *n.* 芸術作品

workout *n.* (physical exercise) 運動

workplace *n.* 職場

workshop *n.* 作業所, (factory) 工場, (studio) 工房; (educational seminar) 研修会, 講習会, ワークショップ

workstation *n.* ワークステーション

world

1 *n.* ALL THE COUNTRIES: (**the world**) 世界, (=the earth) 地球
2 *n.* THE HUMAN RACE: (**the world**) 世界中の人々, 世界
3 *n.* SOCIETY: 社会, 世の中, 世間, (particular sphere of society) 世界, -界
4 *adj.* OF/CONCERNING THE WORLD: 世界の

1 He's traveled all over the world.
彼は世界中を旅しました。
Wouldn't we all like to travel around the world.
誰だって、世界一周旅行をしてみたいよね。

2 The whole world is waiting for the outcome.
全世界が結果を待ち望んでいる。

3 What is this world coming to?
この世の中はどうなってしまったんだ？

Soon you'll have to go out into the real world.
じきに君も、実社会に出なければならないよ。

the world of art アートの世界

the fashion world ファッション界

4 world peace 世界平和

world heritage 世界遺産

♦ **world-class** *adj.* 世界で一流の, 国際的な

world-famous *adj.* 世界的に有名な

world view *n.* 世界観

world war *n.* 世界大戦

World War I/II *n.* 第一次/第二次世界大戦

worldly *adj.* (of this world) この世の, 世間の, (material) 世俗的な

worldly desires 世俗的な願望

worldwide *adj.* 世界的な

adv. 世界中に, 世界的に

worm *n.* 虫, (earthworm) ミミズ, (inside the body) 寄生虫, (**worms**: illness caused by worms) 寄生虫病; (computer worm) コンピューターワーム

worn *adj.* (showing signs of wear) すり切れた, (tired) 疲れ切った

The carpet is badly worn in the middle.
カーペットの真ん中が、ひどくすり切れている。

worn-out *adj.* (exhausted) 疲れ切った

worry *v.* 心配する, 気をもむ, 気にする, 悩む, くよくよする

n. 心配, 悩み

Don't worry. I know you can do it.
心配しないで。あなたならできるよ。

I was worried that you might have had an accident.
事故にあったんじゃないかと心配してたんです。

She was worried by what you said.
あなたが言ったことで、彼女は悩んでいたよ。

Few people are free from financial worry.
経済的な心配のない人はほとんどいません。

Job insecurity is his main worry.
仕事の不安定さが彼の最大の悩みだ。

♦ **worrisome** *adj.* 厄介な, 面倒な

worrying *adj.* (of sign, development) 心配な, 気にかかる, 厄介な

worse *adj.* もっと悪い, さらに悪い

adv. もっと悪く, さらに悪く

I'm afraid the news is even worse than we imagined.
残念ながら、想像していたよりもっと悪い知らせです。

Which do you think is worse?
どっちのほうがひどいと思う?

The traffic is getting worse and worse in this town.
この町では渋滞がどんどんひどくなっている。

Your grades are worse than your brother's.
あなたの成績はお兄ちゃんより悪いよ。

be worse off 状況が悪くなる

I'm worse off now than I was before.
以前より状況は悪くなっている。

for the worse 悪いほうへ

Old people often think that things have changed for the worse.
年寄りは、しばしば物事が悪いほうへ変わったと考える。

get worse 悪化する, さらに悪くなる

If the situation gets worse, let me know.
状況が悪化したら、知らせてください。

go from bad to worse ますます悪化する

The political situation has gone from bad to worse.
政局はますます悪化している。

none the worse for …にもかかわらず何ともない

She seems none the worse for the accident.
彼女は事故にあったにもかかわらず、何ともないようだ。

to make matters/things worse さらに悪いことに(は)

And to make matters worse, he's now decided to quit his job.
さらに悪いことには、彼は今度は仕事を辞めると決めてしまった。

what is worse さらに悪いことに(は), その上

The tickets were expensive, and what was worse, the movie wasn't even good.
チケットは高いし、その上、映画もちっともよくなかった。

worsen *v.* もっと悪くなる, 悪化する

worship *v.* 崇拝する, あがめる, (love very much) 熱愛する, (admire) 賛美する
n. 崇拝

We worship the same god.
私たちは同じ神を崇拝している。

He worships her.
彼は彼女を熱愛している。

worst *adj.* 最悪の, 一番悪い, 最もひどい
adv. 一番悪く, 最もひどく

What's the worst thing that's ever happened to you?
今まで経験した中で、最悪のことは何ですか？

That's the worst grade we've ever had.
今までで一番悪い成績です。

The poor will be the worst hit by these new spending cuts.
この新たな支出削減政策によって、貧しい人々が最も打撃を受けるだろう。

Worst of all, we had to walk in heavy rain.
最悪なことに、どしゃ降りの中を歩かなければならなかった。

at worst 最悪の場合(には)

if worst comes to worst 最悪の場合(には)

worth

1 *adj.* DESERVING OF: (**be worth doing**) …する価値がある, …するに値する

2 *adj.* HAVING A VALUE OF: (be worth…) …相当の, …の値打ちがある, …に相当する価値がある, (=of person) …の財産がある

3 *n.* VALUE: (…worth) …分, …相当, (financial value) 価値, 値打ち

1 It's worth visiting.
行ってみるだけの価値はある。

It's a risk worth taking.
リスクを冒すだけの価値はある。

I didn't think it was worth my time.
時間を費やすほどの価値はないと思いました。

It'll be worth your while to stay there for at least a few days.
少なくとも数日は滞在する価値があります。

2 a house worth ¥70 million
7000万円相当の家

sales worth more than a million dollars

100万ドル<ruby>以上<rt>いじょう</rt></ruby>に<ruby>相当<rt>そうとう</rt></ruby>する<ruby>売<rt>う</rt></ruby>り<ruby>上<rt>あ</rt></ruby>げ

It's worth much more now.
<ruby>今<rt>いま</rt></ruby>ならもっと<ruby>値打<rt>ねう</rt></ruby>ちがあるよ。

This collection of paintings is worth a fortune.
この<ruby>絵<rt>え</rt></ruby>のコレクションは、<ruby>一財産<rt>ひとざいさん</rt></ruby>に<ruby>相当<rt>そうとう</rt></ruby>する<ruby>価値<rt>かち</rt></ruby>がある。

He's worth millions.
<ruby>彼<rt>かれ</rt></ruby>には<ruby>何百万<rt>なんびゃくまん</rt></ruby>という<ruby>財産<rt>ざいさん</rt></ruby>がある。

3 five dollars' worth 5ドル<ruby>分<rt>ぶん</rt></ruby>

ten days' worth of work 10<ruby>日分<rt>にちぶん</rt></ruby>の<ruby>仕事<rt>しごと</rt></ruby>

millions of yen worth of damage
<ruby>何百万円相当<rt>なんびゃくまんえんそうとう</rt></ruby>の<ruby>被害<rt>ひがい</rt></ruby>

The ring's worth is over ¥15 million.
<ruby>指輪<rt>ゆびわ</rt></ruby>は1500<ruby>万円以上<rt>まんえんいじょう</rt></ruby>の<ruby>値打<rt>ねう</rt></ruby>ちがある。

♦ **worthless** *adj.* (valueless) <ruby>価値<rt>かち</rt></ruby>のない, (useless) <ruby>役<rt>やく</rt></ruby>に<ruby>立<rt>た</rt></ruby>たない,

worthwhile *adj.* <ruby>価値<rt>かち</rt></ruby>のある

a worthwhile investment
<ruby>価値<rt>かち</rt></ruby>のある<ruby>投資<rt>とうし</rt></ruby>

worthy *adj.* (be worthy of) (...に) ふさわしい, <ruby>値<rt>あたい</rt></ruby>する; (admirable) <ruby>立派<rt>りっぱ</rt></ruby>な, <ruby>偉<rt>えら</rt></ruby>い

He's not worthy of your respect.
あの<ruby>人<rt>ひと</rt></ruby>は<ruby>尊敬<rt>そんけい</rt></ruby>に<ruby>値<rt>あたい</rt></ruby>しない<ruby>人<rt>ひと</rt></ruby>よ。

fight for a worthy cause
<ruby>正義<rt>せいぎ</rt></ruby>のために<ruby>戦<rt>たたか</rt></ruby>う

would *aux.*

1 SPEAKING OF THE FUTURE FROM A POINT OF VIEW IN THE PAST: See examples below [NOTE: No equivalent in Japanese.]

2 EXPRESSING PREFERENCE/DESIRE/INTENTION: (**I would like...**) (...が) <ruby>欲<rt>ほ</rt></ruby>しい, (**I would like to do**) ...したい, (in indirect speech) (**he/she would like...**) <ruby>欲<rt>ほ</rt></ruby>しがる, (**he/she would like to do**) ...したがる, (**I wouldn't mind doing**) ...したいなあ

3 OFFERING/REQUESTING: (**would you like ...?**) ...はいかがですか, (**would you like to...?**) ...しませんか, (**would you please ...?/would you mind...?**) ...していただけませんか, ...してもらえませんか, (shopping: **I'd like...**) <ruby>下<rt>くだ</rt></ruby>さい

4 EXPRESSING EXPECTATION: ...だろう, ...はずだ

5 EXPRESSING REFUSAL: (**wouldn't do**) ...しようとしなかった, どうしても...しなかった

6 USED WITH IF-CLAUSES: See examples below

7 SPEAKING OF HABITUAL BEHAVIOR IN THE PAST: (**would do**) (よく)...したものだ

1 I felt everything would turn out all right.
すべてがうまくいくような<ruby>気<rt>き</rt></ruby>がした。

I knew my friends would be there.
<ruby>友達<rt>ともだち</rt></ruby>がそこにいるとわかっていた。

In a few minutes the bus would arrive and I would be on my way.
<ruby>数分後<rt>すうふんご</rt></ruby>にはバスが<ruby>到着<rt>とうちゃく</rt></ruby>して、<ruby>目的地<rt>もくてきち</rt></ruby>に<ruby>向<rt>む</rt></ruby>かっていました。

2 He'd like another job, but he can't find one.
<ruby>彼<rt>かれ</rt></ruby>はほかの<ruby>仕事<rt>しごと</rt></ruby>をやりたいけど、<ruby>見<rt>み</rt></ruby>つからないんだ。

One day I'd like to go back to school and get a master's degree.
いつか<ruby>学校<rt>がっこう</rt></ruby>に<ruby>戻<rt>もど</rt></ruby>って<ruby>修士号<rt>しゅうしごう</rt></ruby>を<ruby>取<rt>と</rt></ruby>りたい。

I would love to visit Rome.
ローマに<ruby>行<rt>い</rt></ruby>ってみたいです。

"How about going out tonight?"
"I'd prefer to stay at home."
「<ruby>今夜<rt>こんや</rt></ruby>、<ruby>出<rt>で</rt></ruby>かけようか？」
「<ruby>家<rt>いえ</rt></ruby>にいるほうがいいよ」

I wouldn't teach at that school even if

they offered to triple my salary.
たとえ給料を3倍払うと言われても、あの学校では教えたくない。

The kids would like to see the movie.
子供たちはその映画を見たがっている。

I can't imagine why she'd want such information.
彼女がそんな情報を欲しがる理由が、さっぱりわからない。

I wouldn't mind living in an apartment like that.
あんなマンションに住んでみたいなあ。

3 Would you like some coffee or something?
コーヒーか何かいかがですか？

Would you like to come over to our place this weekend?
今週末、うちに遊びにいらっしゃいませんか？

Would you mind moving over a seat?
席を一つ詰めてもらえませんか？

I'd like five of those apples, please.
そのりんごを五つ下さい。

4 She'd never cheat on him.
彼女は絶対浮気をしないだろう。

It would look better if we polished it.
磨いたら見栄えがよくなるでしょう。

Wouldn't it be easier to go by train?
電車で行ったほうが簡単じゃない？

By Thursday they would have arrived in Tokyo.
木曜には、彼らは東京に到着していたはずです。

Anyway, the teacher wouldn't have noticed.
どっちみち先生は気づかなかっただろう。

Gosh, when was that? That would've been six or seven years ago, right?
うーん、いつだったかな？ 確か6、7年前だよね。

5 We told him to get lost, but he still wouldn't leave.
出て行けと言ったのに、彼はそれでも帰ろうとしなかった。

The car just wouldn't start.
どうしてもエンジンがかからなかった。

Despite all the complaints and scandals, he wouldn't resign.
あれだけの苦情とスキャンダルにもかかわらず、彼は辞めようとしなかった。

6 If I'd known what a bore the party would turn out to be, I wouldn't have gone.
あんなにつまらないパーティーになるとわかっていたら、行かなかっただろう。

I would've gotten a better grade if I had studied harder.
もっとしっかり勉強しておけば、もっといい成績が取れたのに。

7 We would often go there and listen to jazz.
よくそこへ行ってジャズを聴きました。

Dad would always say, "Are you sure you haven't forgotten anything?"
「本当に何も忘れてないか？」と父はいつも言ったものです。

would-be *adj.* …になるつもりの, …志望の

wound *n.* (physical) 傷, けが, (slight wound) 軽傷, (serious wound) 重傷, (mental) 傷, 痛手
v. 傷つける, ((*written*)) 負傷させる

wow *interj.* うわー, うおー

wrangle *v.* (argue) 言い争う, けんかする
n. 言い争い, 口論

wrap *v.* (gift) 包装する, (wrap A in B) (AをBで) 包む, くるむ, (wrap A around B) (AをBに) 巻く, (AをBで) くるむ

Let's wrap the presents.
プレゼントを包装しよう。

We wrapped the fish in newspaper.
魚を新聞紙で包んだ。

The package was wrapped in brown paper.
小包は茶色い紙に包まれていました。

She wrapped the blanket around herself.
彼女は毛布にくるまった。

be wrapped up in (be absorbed in) …に夢中になっている

♦**wrap up** *v.* (finish) 終える, 仕上げる

wrapper *n.* (plastic/paper covering for a product) 包むもの

wrapping *n.* (paper) 包装紙, 包み紙, (wrapping up of presents) ラッピング

wreak *v.* (havoc) もたらす [→ HAVOC]

wreath *n.* リース, 花輪

wreck

1 *n.* REMAINS OF A LARGE OBJECT: 残骸, (shipwreck) 難破船

2 *n.* ACCIDENT: (car crash) 交通事故

3 *n.* PERSON: しょうすいしている人, 参っている人

4 *v.* RUIN: 破壊する, ばらばらにする, 台なしにする

1 The wreck has not been found.
残骸は発見されなかった。

dive in a wreck 難破船に潜る

2 He got into a bad wreck.
彼はひどい交通事故にあった。

3 You look like a wreck.
しょうすいした顔してるね。

He's a mental wreck.
彼は精神的に参っている。

4 Don't wreck the puzzle.
パズルをばらばらにしないで。

wreckage *n.* 残骸

wrench *n.* レンチ, スパナ [→ picture of TOOL]

wrestle *v.* (…と) レスリングをする, (sumo wrestle) (…と) 相撲を取る; (wrestle with: a problem) (…に) 取り組む, (…と) 格闘する

wrestler *n.* (professional) プロレスラー, (amateur) レスラー, (sumo) 相撲取り, 力士

wrestling *n.* レスリング

wretched *adj.* (unhappy) 不幸な, みじめな, 情けない, (horrible) いやな, ひどい

wriggle *v.* 体をくねらせる, (**wriggle out of**) 体をくねらせて…から出る, (=responsibility, difficulty) うまく逃れる

wring *v.* 絞る, (**wring out**) 絞り取る, 絞り出す

wrinkle *n.* しわ

v. (…に) しわを寄せる

wrinkle one's brow 額にしわを寄せる

wrist *n.* 手首 [→ picture of HAND, BODY]

wristwatch *n.* 腕時計

writ *n.* 令状, -状

write *v.*

1 WORDS: 書く, (**write down**: for future reference) 書き留める, (fill in) 記入する

2 LETTER/E-MAIL: 書く, (**write back**: reply) 返事を書く, (write a letter to a newspaper) 投書する

3 BOOK/ARTICLE: 書く, ((*formal*)) 執筆する, (produce/publish a book) 出す

4 SONG/LYRICS: 書く, 作曲/作詞する

1 I can't write because I've hurt my hand.
手をけがしているので書くことができません。

This is well written.
これはよく書けている。

It's written in German.
ドイツ語で書かれています。

Did you learn to write Arabic?
アラビア語の書き方を習いましたか?

Write this down in your notebook.
ノートにこれを書き留めてください。

Please write your name here.
ここにお名前を記入してください。

2 Did you write that letter?
あなたがあの手紙を書いたの?

I've written to thank them.
彼らに礼状を書いた。

Do you think they'll write back?
あの人たち返事をくれると思う?

3 I have been asked to write a paper on literary translation.
文学作品の翻訳についての論文を書くように頼まれました。

He wrote a famous book on the Japanese language.
彼は日本語についての有名な本を執筆した人です。

Kirino Natsuo's written lots of mysteries.
桐野夏生さんはたくさんのミステリーを出しています。

4 Who wrote these lyrics?
この歌詞は誰が書いたの/この歌は誰が作詞したの?

writer ***n.*** (famous/professional writer) 作家, (author) 著者, 作者, (of article) 筆者, ライター, (person who has/will write sth) 書いた/書く人

the writer and critic Bernard Shaw
作家で批評家のバーナード・ショー

Who's the writer of this editorial?
この社説の筆者は誰ですか?

writhe ***v.*** (in agony/pain) もだえ苦しむ

writing ***n.*** (activity) 書くこと, ((*formal*)) 執筆, (written words) 文章, 書かれた物, (writing style) 書き方, (handwriting) 筆跡, (**writings**: works) 著作, 著書

♦ **writing desk** ***n.*** ライティングデスク, 机

writing paper ***n.*** 用紙, 便せん

written ***adj.*** (of exam) 筆記の, (of apology) 文書(で)の, 書面(で)の

a written exam 筆記試験

a written apology 文書での謝罪

a written agreement (=contract) 契約書

wrong

1 ***adj.*** **INCORRECT/MISTAKEN:** 間違った, 誤った, 違う, (off the mark) 外れる, 当たらない

2 ***adj.*** **NOT GOOD:** よくない, 悪い

3 ***adj.*** **UNSUITABLE:** ふさわしくない, 不適当な, 不適切な, (unjust) 不当な

4 ***adv.*** **INCORRECTLY:** (**get wrong**) 間違える

5 ***n.*** **INJUSTICE:** 悪いこと, 悪, 不正

6 ***v.*** **TREAT UNJUSTLY:** 不当に扱う

1 That's the wrong answer.
それは間違った答えです。

The newspapers were wrong.
新聞は間違っていた。

I might be wrong, but...
私が間違っているかもしれませんが...

We went to the wrong place.
違う場所に行ってしまいました。

The weather forecast was wrong.
天気予報が外れた。

2 I knew something was wrong when my husband didn't call.
夫が電話してこなかったので、何かよくないことが起こったのだとわかった。

The doctor said there's nothing wrong with me.
どこも悪くないとお医者さんは言った。

I asked what was wrong, but she continued to stare blankly.
どうしたのと聞いたけれど、彼女はぼんやりしているだけだった。

Is there something wrong with the car?
車にどこか調子の悪いところはある?

3 He's the wrong person for this job.
あの人はこの仕事にふさわしくない。

It seems wrong to me that all he got was a reprimand.
彼が叱責を受けただけだったのは、不当な気がする。

4 I'm afraid I'll get it wrong.
間違えそうな気がする。

I think I got his name wrong.
どうやら彼の名前を間違えたようだ。

5 We rely on prosecutors to right the wrongs in our society.
社会の不正を正すために、私たちは検察官を頼みにしています。

The poor child has no clear sense of right and wrong.
かわいそうに、その子は善悪の区別がはっきりつかない。

She knows she did no wrong.
彼女は何も悪いことはしていないと、自分でわかっています。

6 They wronged him by demoting him.
彼を降格して不当に扱った。

don't get me wrong 誤解しないでほしい

go wrong うまくいかない, 失敗する

Everything that could go wrong did.
失敗の可能性があったものがすべて、うまくいかなかった。

in the wrong place at the wrong time 悪い時に悪い所で

wrongdoing ***n.*** 悪事, 不正行為

wrongful ***adj.*** 不法な

wrongly ***adv.*** (unfairly) 不正に, (incorrectly) 間違って

wry ***adj.*** (of sense of humor) 皮肉たっぷりの

a wry smile 苦笑い

X, x

x *n.* (used in math: unknown factor) X（エックス）,
未知数（みちすう）, (mark) ばつ（印（じるし））, ばってん

Put an *X* here to mark the spot.
目印（めじるし）に、ここにばつ印（じるし）を付（つ）けてください。

xenophobia *n.* 外国人嫌（がいこくじんぎら）い

♦**xenophobe** *n.* 外国人嫌（がいこくじんぎら）いの人（ひと）

xenophobic *adj.* 外国人嫌（がいこくじんぎら）いの

xerox *n.* (photocopier) ゼロックス, (photocopy) コピー

v. (photocopy) コピーする

Xmas *n.* クリスマス [→ CHRISTMAS]

X-ray *n.* (photograph of the inside of the body) レントゲン写真（しゃしん）, X 線写真（エックスせんしゃしん）, (electromagnetic radiation) X 線（エックスせん）, 放射線（ほうしゃせん）

v. (...の) レントゲン（写真（しゃしん））を撮（と）る

have an X-ray
レントゲン写真（しゃしん）を撮（と）ってもらう

The doctor X-rayed my knee.
医者（いしゃ）は、私（わたし）のひざのレントゲンを撮（と）った。

xylophone *n.* シロホン, 木琴（もっきん）

Y, y

yacht ***n.*** ヨット

sail a yacht ヨットを走らせる

a yacht race ヨットレース

♦ **yachting** ***n.*** ヨット遊び

yakuza ***n.*** (gangster) やくざ

yam ***n.*** ヤマイモ, 山芋, (grated yam) とろろ

yank ***v.*** ぐいと引っ張る

yard[1] ***n.*** (unit of length) ヤード

A yard is 0.91 meters.
1ヤードは 0.91 メートルです。

yard[2] ***n.*** (front yard) 前庭, (backyard) 裏庭, (enclosed space of a building) 庭, 庭園 [→ picture of HOUSE], (railroad yard) 操車場

yardstick ***n.*** ((*figurative*)) 尺度, 基準

yarn ***n.*** 糸

yawn ***n., v.*** あくび(をする)

yeah ***interj.*** うん, ええ [→ YES]

year ***n.*** 年, -年, (one-year period) 年間, (financial year) 年度, (year in school) 学年, (counting age: ...**years old**) 年, -歳

this year 今年 [((*formal*)) 本年]

the year 2020 ２０２０年

the year of the dragon (according to the Chinese calendar) 辰年

last year 去年 [((*formal*)) 昨年]

next year 来年

the following year 翌年 [次の年]

the year after next 再来年

the year before last
おととし [((*formal*)) 一昨年]

every year 毎年

every other year 1年おきに

the first year
最初の年 [((*formal*)) 初年度]

the last year (of several)
最後の年 [((*formal*)) 最終年度]

many years ago 何年も前(に)

a year from tomorrow 1年後の明日

One year it snowed a whole meter.
ある年、たっぷり1メートルもの雪が降りました。

the school year 学校の年度

He looks old for his years.
あの人は年のわりに老けて見える。

She was nineteen years old when she got married.
結婚した時、彼女は 19 歳だった。

all year round 一年中

for years 何年も

from year to year 毎年毎年

year after year 年々

KANJI BRIDGE

年 ON: ねん KUN: とし | YEAR, AGE

annual income .... 年収
annual interest .... 年利
date of birth .... 生年月日
end of the year .... 年末
final years of one's life .... 晩年
new year .... 新年
New Year's card .... 年賀状
ordinary/typical year .... 例年
same age .... 同い年
start of the year .... 年始
within the year .... 年内に
youth .... 青年

yearbook ***n.*** 年鑑, 年報

yearly ***adj.*** (every year) 毎年の, 例年の, (once a year) 年に1度の, (for one year) 1年間の

adv. 年1回, 毎年

yearn ***v.*** (**yearn to do**) すごく…したい, (speaking about sb else) とても…したがっている, (**yearn for**) ((*written*)) 切望する

He yearns to return home to the farm.
彼は、田舎の農場にとても戻りたがっている。

yeast ***n.*** (for brewing) 酵母, イースト, (fungus) 酵母菌

♦**yeast extract** ***n.*** 酵母エキス

yell ***v.*** 大声を上げる, 叫ぶ, どなる [→ SCREAM, SHOUT]

yellow ***n.*** 黄色

adj. 黄色い, 黄色の

a yellow sweater 黄色のセーター

yellow light ***n.*** (traffic signal) 黄信号

yellowtail ***n.*** ブリ, 鰤

yen ***n.*** (Japanese currency) 円, ¥

The yen has appreciated [depreciated] recently.
最近、円が高騰 [下落]した。

a strong [weak] yen 円高 [円安]

I'd like to change these dollars into yen.
このドルを円に替えたいんですが。

yes ***adv.*** はい, ええ, ((*informal*)) うん [→ NO 5]

n. (affirmative answer) イエスという返事, 承諾の返事

"Are you coming tomorrow?"
"Yes, I am."
「明日、来る?」
「うん、行くよ」

"Would you like some coffee?"
"Yes, please."
「コーヒーを召し上がりますか?」
「はい、いただきます」

"Hello, is anyone home?"
"Yes, coming!"
「ごめんください。どなたかいらっしゃいますか?」
「はーい、今行きます!」

Was that a yes or a no?
イエスだったの、ノーだったの?

say yes はいと言う, (give permission) 承諾する

yesterday ***adv., n.*** 昨日, ((*formal*)) 昨日

What did you do yesterday?
昨日は、何をしたの?

I happened to bump into an old friend yesterday.
昨日偶然、古い友達にばったり出会った。

the day before yesterday
おととい [((*formal*)) 一昨日]

yesterday morning 昨日の朝

yesterday's newspaper 昨日の新聞

yesterday's dreams 過ぎし日の夢

yet

1 ***adv.*** BY NOW/THEN: (used in negative sentences) まだ

2 ***adv.*** ALREADY: (used in questions) もう, すでに

3 ***adv.*** SO FAR: (used with superlatives) 今までで, 今までのところ(では)

4 ***adv.*** STILL: まだ, (**yet another**) さらにもう一つ, (**yet more**) さらに, もっと

5 ***conj.*** BUT NEVERTHELESS: …が, …けれども, ((*informal*)) けど

1 I haven't finished eating yet.
まだ食べ終わっていません。

Aren't you ready yet?
まだ用意できてないの？

"Hasn't he arrived yet?"
"No, not yet."
「彼はまだ来ていないんですか？」
「ええ、まだです」

It's not dark yet.
まだ明るいよ/まだ暗くなってないよ。

We hadn't yet called to make a reservation.
まだ予約の電話をかけていなかった。

2 Has she left yet?
彼女、もう帰ったんですか？

Is it 9 o'clock yet?
もう9時なの？

3 It's the best car yet.
今までで最高の車です。

These are the most powerful computers yet.
これは今、最も高性能のコンピューターです。

4 There's hope for him yet.
彼にはまだ望みがある。

The court's decision may yet be overturned.
判決は、まだこれからくつがえされるかもしれません。

5 He complains, yet he does nothing.
あの人は文句は言うけど、自分では何にもしない。

as yet 今のところはまだ

As yet, no one seems to have presented a convincing argument.
今のところはまだ、誰も説得力のある意見を出していないようだ。

have yet to do まだ…していない

I've yet to meet Mr. Right.
私はまだ理想の男性に出会っていない。

KANJI BRIDGE

未 ON: み KUN: — | UN-, NOT YET

not yet arrived	未着
not yet officially recognized	未公認
not yet open to the public	未公開
not yet submitted	未提出
undecided	未定の
underage	未成年の
under, below, less than	未満の
unfinished	未完成の
unidentified	未確認の
unknown	未知の
unmarried	未婚の
unpaid	未納の
unripe	未熟な

Yiddish *n.* イディッシュ語

yield *v.* (crops) 産出する, (…が)できる, (interest) 生む; (yield to: give in to) (…に)負ける, 屈する

n. (harvested crops) 産出, (interest gained) 利益

yoga *n.* ヨガ

yogurt *n.* ヨーグルト

yolk *n.* (卵の) 黄身, ((*formal*)) 卵黄

you *pron.*

NOTE: Not usually translated into Japanese. Generally a person's name or occupational title is used instead.

1 SECOND PERSON: (singular) あなた [NOTE: Avoid using あなた in direct speech with social superiors.], (referring to a younger person or a person of the same age) ((*masculine*)) 君, ((*masculine/rude*)) おまえ, (plural) あなたたち, あなた方, ((*polite*)) そちら, (referring to younger people or people of the same age) ((*masculine*)) 君たち, ((*masculine/informal*)) 君ら, (used as the subject of a sentence) あなたは/が, (as direct object) あなたを, (as indirect object) あなたに

2 ANYONE: 人は [NOTE: Usually not translated into Japanese.]

1 What do you (=Mr. Tanaka) think?
(田中さんは) どう思います？

You went, didn't you?
行ったんですよね？

The teacher certainly praised you.
先生は、あなたのことをよくほめてたよ。

I remember I gave it back to you.
あなたに返したのを覚えています。

You! Stand up and answer the question.
君！ 立って質問に答えなさい。

You three can leave early.
君たち3人は早く帰っていいよ。

You all know why I'm here.
みなさんは、どうして私がここにいるか、ご存じのはずです。

2 Of course, you read all kinds of nonsense in the papers.
もちろん、新聞にはいろいろとくだらないことが書かれてますよ。

It's so embarrassing when you can't remember people's names.
人の名前を思い出せないときって、すごく気まずいよね。

young *adj.* 若い, (youthful) 若々しい, (of country) 新興の

n. (**the young**) 若い人(たち), ((*formal*)) 若者; (of animal) 子

He's still young and has a lot to learn.
彼はまだ若いし、学ぶべきことがたくさんある。

Just how young were you at that time?
その時、いくつだったの？

A young man delivered this letter.
若い男の人がこの手紙を持って来ました。

Who's the youngest?
((*polite*)) 一番若い方はどなたですか？

Tom's the younger brother.
トムは弟さんです。

You look young for your age.
年のわりには若く見えるよ。

How do you stay so young?
どうやったら、そんなに若々しいままでいられるの？

a young country 新興国家

The young will not understand.
若い人たちはわからないだろう。

youngster *n.* (young person) 若い人

your *adj.* (singular) あなたの, (plural) あなたたちの, あなた方の

your company あなたの会社, ((*honorific*)) 御社, 貴社

yours *pron.* (singular) あなたのもの, (plural) あなたたちのもの, あなた方のもの

yourself *pron.* 自分, (**you yourself**) あなた自身, 自分自身

Would you describe yourself as an eccentric?
ご自分で、変わり者だと思われますか？

I have three children. What about your-

self?
私は3人子供がいます。あなたは?

Don't put yourself out.
わざわざ苦労することはないよ。

Help yourselves to the food.
どうぞご自由にお召し上がりください。

Do it yourself!
自分でやりなさい。

Did you bake these cookies yourself?
このクッキー、自分で焼いたの?

by yourself 一人で [→ ONESELF]

yourselves ***pron.*** 自分たち, (**you yourselves**) あなたたち自身, 自分たち自ら

by yourselves あなたたちだけで, 自分たちで

youth ***n.*** (period of youth) 若いころ, 青春時代, ((*formal*)) 青年時代, (quality of being young) 若さ, (**the youth**: young people) 若い人(たち), ((*formal*)) 若者, 青年

During his youth, he was an active member of the student union.
若いころ、彼は学生自治会のメンバーとして積極的に活動していた。

The youth of today are not that different from how we were when we were young.
今の若者だって、我々の若いころとそれほど変わらないよ。

♦**youth culture** ***n.*** 若者文化

youthful ***adj.*** (of person) 若い時の, 若者らしい, (young-looking) 若々しい

youth hostel ***n.*** ユースホステル

yo-yo ***n.*** (toy) ヨーヨー

play with a yo-yo ヨーヨーで遊ぶ

yuan ***n.*** (Chinese currency) 元

yuck ***interj.*** ゲェー

yucky ***adj.*** いやな, (of food) まずい

yummy ***adj.*** おいしい

yuppie ***n.*** ヤッピー

Z, z

zany *adj.* (strange) 変わった, (funny) おかしな

zap *v.* (with laser) 撃つ, (in video game) やっつける; (cook in microwave) レンジにかける, ((*informal*)) チンする

zeal *n.* 熱意

zealot *n.* 狂信者

zealous *adj.* 熱心な

zebra *n.* シマウマ, ゼブラ

Zen *n.* 禅

Zen meditation 座禅

a Zen temple 禅寺

zenith *n.* (point in the sky) 天頂, (high point) 頂点, (of career) 絶頂

zero *n.* (number) ゼロ, 零, (degree of temperature) 零度, (score) 零点

five degrees below zero 零下5°

♦**zero in on** *v.* (focus on) ...に集中する; (aim at) ...にねらいを定める

zest *n.* (enthusiasm) 熱中, (joy) 大喜び, (element of excitement) 面白み; (of lemon) レモンの皮

zigzag *n.* ジグザグ

v. (form a zigzag) ジグザグになる, (move in a zigzag) ジグザグに進む

The road zigzagged up the mountain. 道は山をジグザグに上っていた。

zinc *n.* 亜鉛

zip *v.* (**zip up**) (...の) ジッパーを締める, ファスナーを上げる; (move fast) 飛ばす, 疾走する

n. → ZIPPER

The car zipped right past me. 車が疾走して行った。

zip code *n.* 郵便番号

Ziploc *n.* (bag) ジップロック

zipper *n.* (fastener) ジッパー, ファスナー, チャック

zit *n.* (pimple) にきび

zither *n.* チター

zodiac *n.* (zodiac sign) 星座, -座, (astrological diagram) 黄道12宮

"What's your zodiac sign?" "I'm a Scorpio." 「あなたの星座は？」「さそり座よ」

zombie *n.* ゾンビ

zone *n.* 地帯, 区域, 地区, -帯 [→ AREA]

a military zone 武装地帯

a no-smoking zone 禁煙区域

a no-fly zone 飛行禁止区域

a traffic-free zone 車両通行止め区間

the Temperate Zone 温帯

zoo *n.* 動物園

zookeeper *n.* 動物園の飼育係

zoologist *n.* 動物学者

zoology *n.* 動物学

zoom *v.* (**zoom in on**) クローズアップする; (move quickly) 突っ走る

n. (zoom lens) ズームレンズ, (telephoto lens) 望遠レンズ

zucchini *n.* ズッキーニ

NOTES ABOUT JAPANESE GRAMMAR

This appendix outlines some of the main grammatical differences between English and Japanese as an aid to understanding the example sentences in this dictionary.

WORD ORDER

The basic word order of English is subject-verb-object (SVO); in Japanese, it is subject-object-verb (SOV). This means that whereas in English one says, "I ate Mariko's chestnuts," the Japanese equivalent is, literally, "I Mariko's chestnuts ate." Furthermore, as with many SOV languages, even complex modifiers precede the elements they modify. Thus, whereas in English one says, "the delicious chestnuts" but "the chestnuts on the table" and "the chestnuts that I ate yesterday," the order in Japanese is (consistently) "delicious chestnuts," "on-the-table chestnuts," and "I-yesterday-ate chestnuts."

THE TOPIC

All languages distinguish between presupposed or given information and new or asserted information, though in various ways and with various grammatical devices. In both English and Japanese, topical (or thematic) information tends to occur at the beginning of a sentence.

> **Mrs. Tanaka's daughter** married a Ukrainian.
> **田中さんの娘さんは、**ウクライナ人と結婚した。

In English, however, intonation rather than word order is most often used to distinguish what is given from what is new. If the speaker assumes that the hearer already knows that someone married a Ukrainian but wishes to explain that it was Mrs. Tanaka's daughter, the word "daughter" will be given a higher pitch. In Japanese, on the other hand, such distinctions are typically marked syntactically rather than phonologically. In this case we can use a "cleft" construction, clearly separating the given from the new: ウクライナ人と結婚したのは、田中さんの娘さんです. (In English it is of course possible to say, "The one who married a Ukrainian is Mrs. Tanaka's daughter," but such is somewhat clumsy.)

In English, the subject (the element with which the verb agrees) tends to take grammatical precedence over topicality. Thus, to offer another example, there is no syntactic distinction between "Mariko ate *the chestnuts*" and "*Mariko* ate the chestnuts." In Japanese, on the other hand, Mariko in the first instance is marked with the topical/thematic marker は. In the second instance, one either says 栗を食べたのは真理子です (literally, "Ate-the-chestnuts one was Mariko") or 真理子が栗を食べました, where が is used as a subject marker either if the entire sentence is in itself an assertion or if the subject is the primary focus.

Topics are usually but not always what, from an English perspective, are nominal elements. They also typically belong to a shared register of discourse, e.g., proper names, generic terms, and the sort of words that are likely to be marked in English with "the."

> The library is closed.
> 図書館は閉まっている。

Note, however, that time words can also be topical, particularly when the sentence presents contrastive information:

> Until ten months ago (I) couldn't speak Italian at all, but now (I'm) already fluent.
> 10ヵ月前まではイタリア語が全然できなかったのに、今はもうぺらぺらです。

Mastering the distinction between は and が is, for native-English speakers, a matter of developing greater sensitivity to which elements in the sentence are being backgrounded and which are being asserted; and unfortunately it takes repeated exposure to natural Japanese discourse to develop this sensitivity. One difference between these particles that can be pointed out as an aid for learners is that while は is thematic, が is not and therefore tends to be used in sentences in which the verb describes a natural event or a condition rather than a (human) action.

地震があった。
There was an earthquake.

電気が消えた。
The lights went out.

床が汚れている。
The floor is dirty.

Of course, there are many more rules governing the use of は and が, but they are complex and beyond the scope of this dictionary.

PARTS OF SPEECH AND THEIR CHARACTERISTICS

Nouns

English countable nouns are marked according to a singular/plural distinction. Japanese speakers are, of course, perfectly capable of noting whether there are more or fewer than two of something—people, animals, or objects. Yet, unless they are counting, they manage to get by for the most part without grammatical markers. Thus, when a mother tells her children not to do something because they are being seen by others, she will simply say:

やめなさい。人が見てるから。
Cut it out. People are looking (at us).

A quasi-plural form through reduplication (人々) exists, but it is not used in such a context. Likewise, the suffix -達 is often fixed to human nouns to refer to a collective group. However, this too is not a true plural. Its real meaning is "and others," not "more than one of."

Like English nouns, Japanese nouns can be used attributively (to modify other words), in which case they are either followed by the particle の or joined with the word they modify to form a compound:

product development 商品の開発 *or* 商品開発
a factory worker 工場の労働者 *or* 工場労働者

In theory, any noun in Japanese can be followed by の and used as a modifier. Of more practical interest to the student of Japanese is whether の is required, and here the constraints on compounding are difficult or impossible to predict. One must simply learn that whereas one says 大学教授 (university professor), one does not say 大学先生 (university teacher), even though "university teacher" is perfectly acceptable English. Instead, one must say 大学の先生.

Pronouns

It might be said, albeit with some exaggeration, that Japanese lacks true personal pronouns. Instead there are quasi-nominal forms that are used in somewhat the same way that English personal pronouns are used, though with the following differences:

(1) Unlike English "I/me," "he/him" etc., the Japanese forms do not vary according to grammatical environment but are instead marked with postpositional particles (see "Particles" below).

(2) Whereas English requires pronouns as "placeholders" (as standing in the place of a noun, as the term implies), Japanese may simply leave a gap and count on the hearer or reader to "fill in the blank." In English, "[I] can't evaluate the movie because [I] haven't seen [it] yet" is ungrammatical without the bracketed pronominal forms. In Japanese, however, one can get by with no more than an initial 私は—and even that can be left out: 私はその映画をまだ見ていないので、評価はできません.

(3) English pronouns are more or less neutral in regard to social status. That is, unless one is addressing or referring to royal personages, second person "you" and third person "he/she" are consistently "safe." In Japanese, on the other hand, there are multiple terms for even the first person, ranging from humble to rough-and-tumble. The second person is particularly problematic, as there is no form that is more than tenuously neutral at best. The third-person pronouns 彼 (he) and 彼女 (she) turn up with some frequency in the translation of foreign fiction, but one must be careful when using them in real-life speech. One does not, for example, normally refer to one's parents, teachers, or

superiors as 彼 or 彼女. To make up for what may appear to be a "pronoun deficiency," the Japanese make use of third-person titles—or, again, simply expect their listeners and readers to supply subjects and objects that are left unsaid.

English and Japanese demonstrative pronouns likewise differ. Whereas English ones are limited to "this/these" (that which is close to the speaker) and "that/those" (that which is either close to the hearer or distant from both speaker and hearer), there is a three-way distinction in Japanese: これ (this/these), それ (that/those), and あれ (that/those over there). (These become この, その, and あの when they modify other words.) The wife of a man sees him wearing a new necktie and asks him how he has acquired it: そのネクタイは… (That necktie…). On the other hand, if the man asks his wife to identify a woman standing at the far end of the room, he will ask: あの女の人は… (That woman over there…). Once something has been introduced into the discourse, it tends to be marked with それ (or その).

Sometimes demonstrative pronouns are used to provide a collective (or quasi-plural) form to nouns that cannot themselves be inflected: この問題 (this problem) contrasts with これらの問題 (these [various] problems), for example.

All the English pronouns are included in this dictionary, together with glosses and speech labels that describe how they are used.

Particles

The term particle (Japanese 助詞) covers a range of heterogeneous function words. A small number are case particles, and of these some correspond to English prepositions, e.g., へ (to) and から (from); が and を, on the other hand, which mark subject and direct object respectively, are untranslatable. Other particles might be more appropriately labeled as conjunctions, e.g., けれど (but) and と (and). Particles come after nouns, not before them like English prepositions; and some particles come at the end of a sentence for emphasis. Table 1 outlines the basic usages of the most frequent particles.

TABLE 1: Particles and their usages

か	• Used at the end of a sentence or clause to turn the sentence or clause into a question. • Used at the end of a phrase or clause to present an option. "Or."
が	• Marks the noun that comes directly before it as the subject of the sentence or clause. • Used as a conjunction to introduce a new statement. "But," "however."
から	• Indicates a starting time/point. "From." • Marks what comes before it as the reason for a statement. "Because." • Used after a verb in the -て form, means "after," e.g., ...してから (after doing...).
けれども	• Used as a conjunction to introduce a new statement. "But," "however." Often shortened to けど or けれど.
し	• Signals a further point to be made. "And moreover."
で	• Marks the location where an action takes place. • Indicates a means by which sb/sth does sth. "By," "by means of." • Indicates the reason for an action. "Due to," "because of."
と	• Used to exhaustively list things/people. "And." • Indicates accompaniment. "With." • Marks the content of what sb has said. "Quote unquote." • Used as a conjunction. "When."
に	• Indicates the goal to which a subject goes. "To." • Indicates the place where sb/sth exists or is situated. "At," "in," "on." • Indicates the time of day ("at"), year ("in") or, used in the form ...ときに, a point in time ("when"). • Marks what comes directly before it as the indirect object. • Indicates the agent in a passive sentence. "By." • Indicates the secondary agent in a causative sentence.
ね	• Used as a tag question. "Isn't he/she/it?"
の	• Expresses possession or affiliation. "'s" (possessive). • Used after a noun/pronoun to modify another word. • Used after a verb in the dictionary form to turn the verb into a verbal noun (=gerund). • Used at the end of a sentence for emphasis or to pose a question.
ので	• Used to state the reason for a statement that follows. "Because," "since."
のに	• Expresses contrary condition, regret. "In spite of..."

	• "In order to..."
は	• Marks thematic information, sentence topics. • Used to express contrast between two things/people.
へ	• Indicates the direction in which a subject moves. "To," "toward."
まで	• Indicates a finishing time/point. "Until."
も	• "Also," "too," "even."
や	• Used to list things as samples. "And other such things."
よ	• Used at the end of a sentence for emphasis.
より	• Used to express a comparison. "Than." • Indicates a starting time/point. "From."
を	• Marks what comes directly before it as the direct object.

Verbs

Japanese verbs have polite and plain forms, and two basic tenses indicated by conjugation—non-past and past. The plain non-past form is also known as the "dictionary form" because it is the form that appears in most dictionaries. Table 2 shows the plain and polite forms of the verb 見(み)る (see).

TABLE 2: Plain/polite forms of the verb 見(み)る (see)

	affirmative		negative	
	non-past*	past	non-past*	past
plain	見(み)る	見(み)た	見(み)ない	見(み)なかった
polite	見(み)ます	見(み)ました	見(み)ません	見(み)ませんでした

* The non-past tense includes both the simple present ("see") and simple future ("will see"), and the past includes the simple past ("saw") as well as the present perfect ("have seen"). Tenses other than these are expressed not by conjugation but by the use of auxiliary verbs or other devices.

Japanese verbs fall into three conjugational categories: Regular I, Regular II, and Irregular. Regular I verbs (table 3) end in *-u* and include some verbs that end in *-ru*. Regular II verbs (table 4), on the other hand, always end in *-ru*, with the preceding vowel being either *i* or *e*. For irregular verbs (there are basically just two), see table 5.

TABLE 3: Regular I verbs

FORM \ TYPE	ends in う	ends in く		ends in ぐ	ends in す
plain (non-past)	思う (think)	書く (write)	行く (go)	泳ぐ (swim)	話す (talk)
polite (non-past)	思います	書きます	行きます	泳ぎます	話します
-ます stem	思い	書き	行き	泳ぎ	話し
-て form	思って	書いて	**行って***	泳いで	話して
past	思った	書いた	**行った***	泳いだ	話した
-たら conditional	思ったら	書いたら	**行ったら***	泳いだら	話したら
-たり form	思ったり	書いたり	**行ったり***	泳いだり	話したり
negative	思わない	書かない	行かない	泳がない	話さない
negative past	思わなかった	書かなかった	行かなかった	泳がなかった	話さなかった
passive	思われる	書かれる	行かれる	泳がれる	話される
causative	思わせる 思わす	書かせる 書かす	行かせる 行かす	泳がせる 泳がす	話させる
causative-passive	思わせられる 思わされる	書かせられる 書かされる	行かせられる 行かされる	泳がせられる 泳がされる	話させられる
imperative	思え	書け	行け	泳げ	話せ
-ば conditional	思えば	書けば	行けば	泳げば	話せば
potential	思える	書ける	行ける	泳げる	話せる
volitional	思おう	書こう	行こう	泳ごう	話そう

NOTE: Irregularities are in bold type.

* 行く is the only verb of the "ends in く" type that has this conjugation. All other Regular I verbs that end in く follow the pattern of 書く.

ends in つ	ends in ぬ	ends in ぶ	ends in む	ends in る	
待つ (wait)	死ぬ (die)	選ぶ (choose)	飲む (drink)	売る (sell)	ある (be)
待ちます	死にます	選びます	飲みます	売ります	あります
待ち	死に	選び	飲み	売り	あり
待って	死んで	選んで	飲んで	売って	あって
待った	死んだ	選んだ	飲んだ	売った	あった
待ったら	死んだら	選んだら	飲んだら	売ったら	あったら
待ったり	死んだり	選んだり	飲んだり	売ったり	あったり
待たない	死なない	選ばない	飲まない	売らない	**ない**
待たなかった	死ななかった	選ばなかった	飲まなかった	売らなかった	**なかった**
待たれる	死なれる	選ばれる	飲まれる	売られる	—
待たせる 待たす	死なせる 死なす	選ばせる 選ばす	飲ませる 飲ます	売らせる	—
待たせられる 待たされる	—	選ばせられる 選ばされる	飲ませられる 飲まされる	売らせられる 売らされる	—
待て	死ね	選べ	飲め	売れ	あれ
待てば	死ねば	選べば	飲めば	売れば	あれば
待てる	死ねる	選べる	飲める	売れる	—
待とう	死のう	選ぼう	飲もう	売ろう	あろう

TABLE 4: Regular II verbs

FORM \ TYPE	ends in **-eru**	ends in **-iru**
plain (non-past)	食べる (eat)	見る (see)
polite (non-past)	食べます	見ます
-ます stem	食べ	見
-て form	食べて	見て
past	食べた	見た
-たら conditional	食べたら	見たら
-たり form	食べたり	見たり
negative	食べない	見ない
negative past	食べなかった	見なかった
passive	食べられる	見られる
causative	食べさせる	見させる
causative-passive	食べさせられる	見させられる
imperative	食べろ	見ろ
-ば conditional	食べれば	見れば
potential	食べられる・食べれる*	見られる・見れる*
volitional	食べよう	見よう

NOTE: いる (exist) is a Regular II verb and follows the same pattern as 見る. Homophonous verbs such as 要る (need) and 射る (shoot [an arrow]), however, are Regular I verbs, as are 知る (know), 帰る (return) and a host of others. It should thus be borne in mind that just because a verb ends in *-iru* or *-eru* does not mean that it is necessarily a Regular II verb. To know for certain whether a verb is Regular I or Regular II requires knowing more than one of its forms; from this, one can deduce its classification.

* The shortened potential form (whereby the verbs are treated as though they belonged to the Regular I conjugation) is widespread but still regarded as substandard. Non-native speakers should use it with caution.

TABLE 5: Irregular verbs

FORM \ TYPE	"come"	"do"	KANJI + する†
plain (non-past)	くる［来(く)る］	する*	罰(ばっ)する（punish）
polite (non-past)	きます	します	罰(ばっ)します
-ます stem	き	し	罰(ばっ)し
-て form	きて	して	罰(ばっ)して
past	きた	した	罰(ばっ)した
-たら conditional	きたら	したら	罰(ばっ)したら
-たり form	きたり	したり	罰(ばっ)したり
negative	こない	しない	罰(ばっ)さない
negative past	こなかった	しなかった	罰(ばっ)さなかった
passive	こられる	される	罰(ばっ)される・罰(ばっ)せられる
causative	こさせる	させる	罰(ばっ)させる
causative-passive	こさせられる	させられる	罰(ばっ)させられる
imperative	こい	しろ・せよ	罰(ばっ)しろ・罰(ばっ)せよ
-ば conditional	くれば	すれば	罰(ばっ)すれば・罰(ばっ)せば
potential	こられる・これる	できる	罰(ばっ)せる
volitional	こよう	しよう	罰(ばっ)そう

* する is the all-purpose verb in Japanese, used after nominalized verb forms in native Japanese, after Sino-Japanese nouns, and even after many words borrowed from Western languages.

† The kanji is a single character.

One other very frequent verb that stands in a category of its own is the copula. The copula follows nouns and な-adjectives (see "Adjectives" below) when they appear as predicates. The copula has plain and polite forms, as shown in table 6.

TABLE 6: Plain/polite forms of the copula

	affirmative		negative	
	non-past	past	non-past	past
plain	だ	だった	ではない じゃない*	ではなかった じゃなかった*
polite	です	でした	ではありません じゃありません*	ではありませんでした じゃありませんでした*

* じゃ is a colloquial contraction of では.

As can be seen from the tables above, Japanese verbs have various forms. Table 7 summarizes these forms and explains their main usages.

TABLE 7: Japanese verb forms explained

FORM	USAGE
polite	• Used in everyday conversation among adults who are not intimates.
-ます stem	• Serves as a noun. Particles attach to it. The most common pattern is -ます stem + に + 行く/来る, e.g., 見に行く (go to see), 会いに来る (come to meet) etc. • In writing and formal speech, used as a conjunctive form, semi-interchangeably with -て (see below).
-て form	• Used as a conjunction. "And," "and then," "after ——ing." • Indicates that the action/event expressed by the verb is a reason for the action/event expressed in the predicate. "So." • Followed by a number of auxiliary verbs to express a variety of meanings.
-たら conditional	• Expresses a condition. "If." • Indicates that the action/event expressed by the verb in this form happens before the action/event expressed by the verb at the end of the sentence. "In the event that," "when," "after," "once." • Expresses a condition contrary to fact. "If … were …"
-たり form	• Typically occurs two or more times in a sentence, with the final occurrence followed by する. Expresses a variety of actions or occurrences. "(Doing) such things as …"

passive	• More than in English, the passive is used in Japanese to express an adverse experience on the part of the subject. Intransitive verbs are also more easily passivized than in English.
causative	• Used to express the idea of making or allowing sb to do sth.
causative-passive	• Same as the causative form but passive. “Be made to do sth.”
imperative	• Used to give orders.
-ば conditional	• Expresses a condition. “If.”
potential	• Expresses ability. “Can.”
volitional	• Used to make a suggestion or to invite sb to do sth. “Let's.” • Followed by と思う, means “I think I'll...” • Followed by とする, means “I'll try to...”

One final point about Japanese verbs is that there are transitive and intransitive types, just as there are in English. Transitive types take a direct object.

ラベルを付ける　　attach a label

Here ラベル (label) is the direct object of the transitive verb 付ける (attach). Intransitive verbs, on the other hand, do not take direct objects.

ラベルが付く　　the label attaches (itself)

However, they often take indirect objects.

スーツケースにラベルが付く
the label attaches to the suitcase

Here, スーツケース (suitcase) is the indirect object of the intransitive verb 付く.

Table 8 shows common transitive/intransitive verbs grouped according to their endings. Their endings follow a pattern.

TABLE 8: Transitive and intransitive verbs

-aru*/**-eru** type

meaning	intr.	trans.
decide	決(き)まる	決(き)める
end	終(お)わる	終(お)える
find	見(み)つかる	見(み)つける
gather	集(あつ)まる	集(あつ)める
harden	固(かた)まる	固(かた)める
heighten	高(たか)まる	高(たか)める
lower	下(さ)がる	下(さ)げる
mix	混(ま)ざる	混(ま)ぜる
rise/raise	上(あ)がる	上(あ)げる
take (time)	かかる	かける
tell	伝(つた)わる	伝(つた)える

-aru/**-u** type

meaning	intr.	trans.
put between	挟(はさ)まる	挟(はさ)む
stab	刺(さ)さる	刺(さ)す

-reru/**-su**† type

meaning	intr.	trans.
break	壊(こわ)れる	壊(こわ)す
dirty	汚(よご)れる	汚(よご)す
fall/push over	倒(たお)れる	倒(たお)す
flow/drain	流(なが)れる	流(なが)す

-reru/**-ru** type

meaning	intr.	trans.
break (bone)	折(お)れる	折(お)る
crack/split	割(わ)れる	割(わ)る
sell	売(う)れる	売(う)る

-ru/**-su**† type

meaning	intr.	trans.
fix	直(なお)る	直(なお)す
pass	通(とお)る	通(とお)す
return	帰(かえ)る	帰(かえ)す
turn	回(まわ)る	回(まわ)す

-eru/**-asu**† type

meaning	intr.	trans.
dissolve	溶(と)ける	溶(と)かす
escape	逃(に)げる	逃(に)がす
get/take out	出(で)る	出(だ)す

-u/**-asu**† type

meaning	intr.	trans.
fly	飛(と)ぶ	飛(と)ばす
move	動(うご)く	動(うご)かす

-iru/**-osu**† type

meaning	intr.	trans.
fall/drop	落(お)ちる	落(お)とす

-u/**-eru** type

meaning	intr.	trans.
open	あく	あける
stand	立(た)つ	立(た)てる

-eru/**-u** type

meaning	intr.	trans.
burn	焼(や)ける	焼(や)く
come/take off	脱(ぬ)げる	脱(ぬ)ぐ

irregular

meaning	intr.	trans.
ride	乗(の)る	乗(の)せる
see	見(み)える	見(み)る

NOTE: The English meanings above are intended only as a guide. In some cases they correspond to only one of the forms, transitive or intransitive.

* Most verbs that end in *-aru* are intransitive and can be turned into transitive verbs by changing the *a* to an *e* as in the examples here.

† All verbs ending in *-su* are transitive.

Adjectives

There are two kinds of adjectives in Japanese: the い-adjective and the な-adjective. The い-adjective has an inflectional ending; its dictionary form, as the term implies, ends in い. The な-adjective takes its name from the fact that な follows when such words appear directly before the elements they modify. (Japanese adjectives, like most English adjectives, can be used either attributively—that is, before a noun—or predicatively—that is, as part of a predicate.)

a) これは古(ふる)い建物(たてもの)です。
This is an old building.

b) この建物(たてもの)は古(ふる)い(です)。
This building is old.

c) これは(わ)きれいな花(はな)です。
This is a pretty flower.

d) この花(はな)はきれいです。
This flower is pretty.

Examples (*a*) and (*b*) for the い-adjectives and (*c*) and (*d*) for the な-adjectives illustrate, respectively, attributive and predicative forms. Note that while in English a predicate adjective must be preceded by the copula (This building *is* old), the copula is not used withい-adjectives, unless one wishes to add (polite) です. For な-adjectives, however, the copula, whether informal だ or polite です, is normally required.

な-adjectives are nominal forms that do not themselves inflect; it is the copula attached to them that does. い-adjectives, on the other hand, are verb-like in that they are inflected for tense and mood. Table 9 shows the inflections of い- and な-adjectives.

TABLE 9: Adjective inflections

FORM \ TYPE	い-adjective	な-adjective
attributive (before a noun)	うれしい (happy)	静かな (quiet)
plain (non-past) predicative	うれしい	静かだ
stem	うれし	静か
-て form	うれしくて	静かで
past	うれしかった	静かだった
-たら conditional	うれしかったら	静かだったら
-たり form	うれしかったり	静かだったり
negative	うれしくない	静かではない 静かじゃない
negative past	うれしくなかった	静かではなかった 静かじゃなかった
-ば conditional	うれしければ	静かであれば 静かなら(ば)

Also to note about Japanese adjectives is that all of them can be turned into adverbs and nouns. Tables 10 to 11 show how.

TABLE 10: Adverbial forms of adjectives

adjective	adverbial form	meaning	rule
おいしい (delicious)	おいしく	deliciously	い changes to く
穏やかな (calm)	穏やかに	calmly	な changes to に

TABLE 11: Nominal forms of adjectives

adjective	noun form	meaning	rule
おいしい (delicious)	おいしさ	deliciousness	い changes to さ
穏やかな (calm)	穏やかさ	calmness	な changes to さ

As in English, verb forms can be used adjectivally:

焦げたパン	burnt toast
年をとった人	an elderly person

Finally, as noted earlier, nouns can also take on an adjectival role, sometimes with the genitive/attributive particle の, sometimes without.

赤のペン	a red pen

Adverbs and Onomatopoeia

Japanese has an abundance of adverbs. Broadly speaking, there are three types: (1) adverbs that express manner or state of being, (2) adverbs that express degree, and (3) sentence adverbs. Here are some examples:

(1) **ゆっくり**歩きましょう。
Let's walk *slowly* (= leisurely).

(2) 今日は**かなり**暑いですね。
It's *rather* hot today, wouldn't you say?

(3) 彼は**たぶん**行かないでしょう。
He *probably* won't go.

Of these, the sentence adverbs deserve special attention. These adverbs work together with elements in the sentence's predicate to express conjecture, supposition, negation, and other meanings. In (3) above, the adverb たぶん is reinforced by でしょう to mean "probably." Here are more examples:

a) **もし**雨だったら中止しよう。
If it rains, let's call (it) off.

b) 私は**全然**興味がない。
I have *absolutely* no interest.

In (*a*) もし works with -たら to express supposition ("if"), and in (*b*) 全然 is used with the negative ない for emphatic negation.

Among the adverbs that express manner or state of being, onomatopoeic words—words that imitate sounds or actions—play a prominent role. Extremely frequent in both speech and writing, they add an indispensable flavor and nuance to the language. There are two types: (1) words that describe sounds, and (2) words that describe states. Here are some examples:

(1) 犬(いぬ)が**ワンワン**ほえた。
The dog *barked.*

猫(ねこ)が**ニャーニャー**鳴(な)いている。
The cat is *meowing.*

雨(あめ)が**ザーザー**降(ふ)った。
The rain *poured* down.

観客(かんきゃく)は**パチパチ**拍手(はくしゅ)した。
The audience *clapped.*

彼女(かのじょ)はドアを**バタン**と閉(し)めた。
She *slammed* the door shut.

誰(だれ)かがドアを**トントン**ノックした。
Someone *knocked* on the door.

(2) 彼(かれ)は**にこにこ**笑(わら)った。
He smiled *radiantly.*

少年(しょうねん)は**すらすら**答(こた)えた。
The boy answered *without hesitation.*

雨(あめ)で**びしょびしょ**になった。
I got *drenched* in the rain.

少女(しょうじょ)は母親(ははおや)に**べったり**くっついた。
The little girl *clung* to her mother.

きっぱり断(ことわ)りました。
I *flatly* refused.

留学(りゅうがく)して**みっちり**勉強(べんきょう)します。
I will study *hard* abroad.

赤(あか)ちゃんを起(お)こさないよう、**そっと**歩(ある)いて。
Walk *quietly* so as not to wake up the baby.

As the above examples demonstrate, not all onomatopoeic words translate into adverbs in English. Some are better conveyed by verbs.

Not given here, though examples can be found in the dictionary, are onomatopoeic words that take the particle と. With some words と is obligatory, while with others it is optional.

COUNTING

Up to the number 10, there are two systems of counting in Japanese, one native and the other borrowed from Chinese. Table 12 shows these two systems.

TABLE 12: Numbers 1 to 10

number	native Japanese	Sino-Japanese
1	一つ (ひと)	1 (いち)
2	二つ (ふた)	2 (に)
3	三つ (みっ)	3 (さん)
4	四つ (よっ)	4 (よん) [also read し]
5	五つ (いつ)	5 (ご)
6	六つ (むっ)	6 (ろく)
7	七つ (なな)	7 (なな) [also read しち]
8	八つ (やっ)	8 (はち)
9	九つ (ここの)	9 (きゅう) [also read く]
10	十 (とお)	10 (じゅう)

NOTE: In horizontal text, numerals are usually used in place of kanji, while in vertical text kanji are more frequently used.

After 10, except for sporadic residues, only the Sino-Japanese numerals are used. The numbers 11 to 20 and 30, 40, 50 and so on up to 100 are listed in this dictionary, as are 1,000, 10,000, and other large numbers. For their pronunciation, look them up.

Sino-Japanese numerals are used with "counters" to count different objects and concepts. Counters include words like 本(ほん), which is used for counting long, slender objects like pencils and poles, and 枚(まい), which is used for counting thin objects like sheets of paper and slices of bread. Table 13 is a list of the most common counters.

TABLE 13: Counters

accident/crime	-件(けん)	fruit (apple, orange)	-個(こ)	question	-題(だい), -問(もん)
age	-歳(さい)	haiku	-句(く)	rank/place	-位(い)
airplane	-機(き)	hour	-時間(じかん)	roll	-巻(ま)き
(big) animal	-頭(とう)	house	-軒(けん), -戸(こ)	room	-間(ま), -部屋(へや), -室(しつ)
(small) animal	-匹(ひき)	insect	-匹(ひき)	row (of seats)	-列(れつ)
bird	-羽(わ)	kanji stroke	-画(かく)	second	-秒(びょう)
boat	-そう	language	-ヵ国語(こくご)	ship	-隻(せき)
book/magazine	-冊(さつ)	lap/circuit	-周(しゅう)	slice of fish	-切(き)れ
bottle	-本(ほん)	lesson (in textbook)	-課(か)	song	-曲(きょく)
bowl of rice	-ぜん, -杯(はい)	letter/e-mail	-通(つう)	stay (overnight)	-泊(はく)
building	-棟(とう)	letter/kanji	-字(じ)	step	-歩(ほ)
bullet	-発(はつ)	line	-行(ぎょう)	step (on stairway)	-段(だん)
can	-個(こ)	loss/defeat	-敗(はい)	story (of building)	-階(かい)
car	-台(だい)	machine (TV, fridge)	-台(だい)	suit	-着(ちゃく)
car of train	-両(りょう)	meal	-食(しょく)	tablet/pill	-錠(じょう)
chair	-脚(きゃく)	minute	-分(ふん)	tanka	-首(しゅ)
chapter	-章(しょう)	month	-ヵ月(げつ)	tatami mat	-畳(じょう)
color	-色(しょく)	newspaper page	-面(めん)	time/frequency	-度(ど), -回(かい), -遍(へん)
court (for tennis etc.)	-面(めん)	o'clock	-時(じ)	(block of) tofu	-丁(ちょう)
cup, glass	-個(こ)	pair of chopsticks	-ぜん	university class	-こま
cup (of tea, coffee)	-杯(はい)	pair of scissors	-丁(ちょう)	vehicle (bicycle, bus)	-台(だい)
customer	-名様(めいさま)	people	-人(にん), -名(めい)	volume of a book	-巻(かん)
day	-日(にち)	place	-ヵ所(しょ)	week	-週(しゅう)
digit (of number)	-けた	plate	-枚(まい)	win/victory	-勝(しょう)
drop of liquid	-滴(てき)	platform (at station)	-番線(ばんせん)	word	-語(ご)
fish	-匹(ひき), -尾(び)	poem	-編(へん)	year	-年(ねん)
floor/story	-階(かい)	point/mark/score	-点(てん)	year (in school)	-年生(ねんせい)
footwear	-足(そく)	portion (of food)	-人前(にんまえ)		

RESPECT LANGUAGE

Japanese has a complex system of "respect language." Respect language includes *honorific language,* used to show respect for one's listener or another referent, *humble language* used to deprecate oneself or one's in-group (family, company, etc.), and *polite language.* The choice of which type of language to use—or whether to use it at all—depends on several factors: the speaker's age, rank, and social status vis-à-vis the other party; whether the speaker and listener are members of the same in-group or not; and the general level of intimacy between the two. In addition, respect language can also be used in reference to third persons. Here are some of the basics.

First, prefixes. The prefixes お and ご are used in honorific, humble, and polite language. Here are some examples of their uses:

お体(からだ)を大切(たいせつ)に。 (honorific)
Take care of yourself.

先生(せんせい)はお帰(かえ)りになりました。 (honorific)
The teacher went home.

お返事(へんじ)が遅(おく)れてしまい、申(もう)し訳(わけ)ありません。 (humble)
I am sorry (lit., "I have no excuse") for the late response.

ご意見(いけん)は？ (polite)
And what is your opinion?

私(わたし)がご案内(あんない)します。 (humble)
I'll escort you.

As a general rule, お is attached to words of native-Japanese origin, while ご is used before Sino-Japanese compounds.

Besides prefixes, respect language is expressed with verbs and auxiliary verbs as well as with honorific and humble forms of the copula. These elements are shown in tables 14 to 17.

TABLE 14: Honorific verbs

USAGE / VERB	honorific form of	meaning	example
下さる	与える	give	これは先生が下さったものです。 This is something my teacher gave me.
おっしゃる	言う	say	田辺さんのおっしゃるとおりです。 It is exactly as you (Mr. Tanabe) say.
	いる	be	お部屋にいらっしゃいます。 He's in the room.
いらっしゃる	来る	come	先生がここにいらっしゃいました。 The teacher came here.
	行く	go	お店にいらっしゃいましたか？ Did you go to the store?
召し上がる	食べる	eat	どうぞ召し上がってください。 Please help yourself (to the food).
ご存じ	知る	know	ご存じのように… As you know…
なさる	する	do	ゴルフをなさいますか？ Do you play golf?
ご覧になる	見る	see	これをご覧ください。 Look at this.

TABLE 15: Honorific expressions

FORM \ USAGE	honorific form of	meaning	example
～ていらっしゃる	～ている	is ——ing	先生がホワイトボードに概要を書いていらっしゃいます。 The teacher is writing an outline on the whiteboard.
～でいらっしゃる	copula	be	あの方はご多忙でいらっしゃる。 He is busy. お母さまは画家でいらっしゃいますね。 Your mother is a painter, isn't she?
～れる・～られる*	—	—	あの本は読まれましたか？ Did you read that book? お医者さんが戻られました。 The doctor has returned.
お～になる	—	—	お待ちになりましたか？ Have you been waiting (for me)?

* This has the same form as the passive, but its use is honorific and not passive.

TABLE 16: Humble verbs

VERB \ USAGE	honorific form of	meaning	example
お目にかかる	会う	meet	一度お目にかかりたいのですが。 I'd like to meet you, if I could.
差し上げる	与える	give	この本は差し上げます。 I'll give you this book.
申し上げる	言う	say	はい、それは申し上げました。 Yes, I said that.
いただく	食べる	eat	では、いただきましょう。 Well, let's eat.
	もらう	receive	すてきなものをいただいて、ありがとうございます。 Thank you for the nice gift.
参る	行く	go	そちらへ参ります。 I'll go there (where you are).
	来る	come	電車が参ります。* The train is coming.
存じる 存じ上げる	知る	know	その方は存じ上げています。 I know that person.
伺う	尋ねる	ask	一つ伺いたいのです。 There's something I'd like to ask.
	訪ねる	visit	京都のご自宅に伺いました。 I visited him (at his) home in Kyoto.
拝見する	見る	see	メールは拝見しました。 I saw the e-mail.

* Spoken, for example, by a conductor.

TABLE 17: Humble expressions

USAGE / FORM	honorific form of	meaning	example
～ていただく	～てもらう	receive sb's doing sth beneficial for you	先生に原稿を書いていただきました。 The professor wrote the manuscript for us.
～せていただく*	する	receive the kindness of being allowed to do	私が書かせていただきます。 I will take the liberty of writing it myself.

* The -て form of the causative form, followed by いただく.

Finally, a note is in order about the copula. です is the polite form, but in hyper-polite language, でございます is common. This form is used mainly in the service industry, when employees speak to customers.

ADDRESSING LETTERS IN JAPAN

A Japanese address includes a postal code (preceded by the symbol 〒), prefecture 県 (けん), and district (such as a city 市 (し) or county 郡 (ぐん)), and is ordered somewhat differently depending on whether it is (1) a Tokyo address, (2) a non-Tokyo, urban address, (3) a rural address, or (4) a company address. The following examples illustrate these minor differences.

(1) A Tokyo address: postal code, Tokyo-to (Tokyo Metropolitan District), Minato-ku (ward name), Azabudai (town name), 2 (postal district), –2 (subdistrict), –1 (house number), Tanaka Kazuo (family name followed by given name), -sama (form of address).

いちれいろく の ぜろぜろよんいち
〒１０６－００４１
とうきょうと みなと く あざ ぶ だい に の に のいち
東京都港区麻布台２－２－１
た なかかず お さま
田中一夫様

(2) A non-Tokyo, urban address: postal code, Osaka-fu (Osaka Prefecture), Toyonaka-shi (city name), Senrien (town name), 2–8–25–901, Hara Michiko-sama.

ごろくぜろ の ぜろぜろよんろく
〒５６０－００４６
おおさか ふ とよなか し せん り えん
大阪府豊中市千里園
に のはちのにじゅうごの きゅうまるいち
２－８－２５－９０１
はらみち こ さま
原道子様

Note that if the address is that of an apartment, a building number and room number follow the subdistrict number (25–901 in the above example).

(3) A rural address: postal code, Okayama-ken (Okayama Prefecture), Kume-gun (county name of district), Asahi-cho (town name), Koyama (town district), 471, Takada Yuriko-sensei (form of address of teachers).

ななぜろきゅう の さんよんいち に
〒７０９－３４１２
おかやまけん く め ぐんあさひちょう こ やま よんなないち
岡山県久米郡旭町小山４７１
たか だ ゆ り こ せんせい
高田百合子先生

(4) A company address: postal code, Kanagawa-ken (Kanagawa Prefecture), Yokohama-shi (city name), Midori-ku (ward name), Kirigaoka (town name), 1–33–5, Toyo Biru 605-go (building name followed by office number), Ato Koporeshon (company name), Imai Seiichi (name of person), -shacho (= president; occupational title), -dono (formal/written form of address).

に にろく の ぜろぜろいちろく
〒２２６－００１６
か な がわけんよこはまし みどり く きり おか
神奈川県横浜市緑区霧が丘
いち の さんじゅうさん の ご
１－３３－５
とうよう ろくまるごごう
東洋ビル６０５号
アートコーポレーション
いま い せいいちしゃちょうどの
今井清一社長殿

COMMON JAPANESE SURNAMES RANKED BY FREQUENCY

1	佐藤	さとう
2	鈴木	すずき
3	高橋	たかはし
4	田中	たなか
5	渡辺	わたなべ
6	伊藤	いとう
7	山本	やまもと
8	中村	なかむら
9	小林	こばやし
10	加藤	かとう
11	吉田	よしだ
12	山田	やまだ
13	佐々木	ささき
14	山口	やまぐち
15	松本	まつもと
16	井上	いのうえ
17	斎藤	さいとう
18	木村	きむら
19	林	はやし
20	清水	しみず
21	山崎	やまざき
22	森	もり
23	阿部	あべ
24	池田	いけだ
25	橋本	はしもと
26	山下	やました
27	石川	いしかわ
28	中島	なかじま
29	前田	まえだ
30	藤田	ふじた
31	小川	おがわ
32	岡田	おかだ
33	後藤	ごとう
34	長谷川	はせがわ
35	村上	むらかみ
36	近藤	こんどう
37	石井	いしい
38	坂本	さかもと
39	遠藤	えんどう
40	青木	あおき
41	藤井	ふじい
42	西村	にしむら
43	福田	ふくだ
44	太田	おおた
45	斉藤	さいとう
46	三浦	みうら
47	藤原	ふじわら
48	岡本	おかもと
49	松田	まつだ
50	中川	なかがわ
51	中野	なかの
52	原田	はらだ
53	小野	おの
54	田村	たむら
55	竹内	たけうち
56	金子	かねこ
57	和田	わだ
58	中山	なかやま
59	石田	いしだ
60	上田	うえだ
61	森田	もりた
62	原	はら
63	柴田	しばた
64	酒井	さかい
65	工藤	くどう
66	横山	よこやま
67	宮崎	みやざき
68	宮本	みやもと
69	内田	うちだ
70	高木	たかぎ
71	安藤	あんどう
72	谷口	たにぐち
73	大野	おおの
74	丸山	まるやま
75	今井	いまい
76	高田	たかだ
77	河野	こうの
78	藤本	ふじもと
79	小島	こじま
80	武田	たけだ
81	村田	むらた
82	上野	うえの
83	杉山	すぎやま
84	増田	ますだ
85	菅原	すがわら
86	平野	ひらの
87	小山	こやま
88	大塚	おおつか
89	千葉	ちば
90	久保	くぼ
91	松井	まつい
92	岩崎	いわさき
93	木下	きのした
94	野口	のぐち
95	松尾	まつお
96	野村	のむら
97	菊地	きくち
98	佐野	さの
99	渡部	わたなべ
100	大西	おおにし
101	杉本	すぎもと
102	新井	あらい
103	古川	ふるかわ
104	桜井	さくらい
105	市川	いちかわ
106	小松	こまつ
107	島田	しまだ
108	水野	みずの
109	高野	たかの
110	吉川	よしかわ
111	山内	やまうち
112	西田	にしだ
113	菊池	きくち
114	西川	にしかわ
115	北村	きたむら
116	五十嵐	いがらし
117	安田	やすだ
118	東 [or ひがし]	あずま
119	浜田	はまだ
120	中田	なかた
121	川口	かわぐち
122	平田	ひらた
123	川崎	かわさき
124	飯田	いいだ
125	本田	ほんだ
126	久保田	くぼた
127	辻	つじ
128	関	せき
129	吉村	よしむら
130	中西	なかにし
131	岩田	いわた
132	服部	はっとり
133	樋口	ひぐち
134	福島	ふくしま
135	川上	かわかみ
136	永井	ながい
137	松岡	まつおか
138	田口	たぐち
139	山中	やまなか
140	森本	もりもと
141	土屋	つちや
142	矢野	やの
143	秋山	あきやま
144	石原	いしはら
145	松下	まつした
146	馬場	ばば
147	大橋	おおはし
148	吉岡	よしおか
149	松浦	まつうら
150	小池	こいけ

JAPANESE ERA CONVERSION

Since 1872, Japan has used the Western calendar. The traditional practice of grouping years into eras that coincide with the reign of successive emperors has been retained, however. Thus, we have:

the Meiji period	明治時代	1868 (from Sep. 8)–1912
the Taisho period	大正時代	1912 (from Jul. 30)–1926
the Showa period	昭和時代	1926 (from Dec. 25)–1989
the Heisei period	平成時代	1989 (from Jan. 8)–

To convert the Japanese date into the Western year, remember the first year of the period, then add the number of the year of the period to it and subtract one. For example:

45th year of Showa →1926 + 45 – 1 = 1970
12th year of Heisei → 1989 + 12 – 1 = 2000

The Showa and Heisei years are as follows.

Showa		Showa		Showa		Showa		Heisei	
元年	1926	19	1944	37	1962	55	1980	元年	1989
2	1927	20	1945	38	1963	56	1981	2	1990
3	1928	21	1946	39	1964	57	1982	3	1991
4	1929	22	1947	40	1965	58	1983	4	1992
5	1930	23	1948	41	1966	59	1984	5	1993
6	1931	24	1949	42	1967	60	1985	6	1994
7	1932	25	1950	43	1968	61	1986	7	1995
8	1933	26	1951	44	1969	62	1987	8	1996
9	1934	27	1952	45	1970	63	1988	9	1997
10	1935	28	1953	46	1971	64	1989	10	1998
11	1936	29	1954	47	1972			11	1999
12	1937	30	1955	48	1973			12	2000
13	1938	31	1956	49	1974			13	2001
14	1939	32	1957	50	1975			14	2002
15	1940	33	1958	51	1976			15	2003
16	1941	34	1959	52	1977			16	2004
17	1942	35	1960	53	1978			17	2005
18	1943	36	1961	54	1979			18	2006

NATIONAL HOLIDAYS IN JAPAN

元日(がんじつ)	New Year's Day (Jan. 1)
成人(せいじん)の日(ひ)	Coming-of-Age Day (the second Monday of Jan.)
建国記念(けんこくきねん)の日(ひ)	National Foundation Day (Feb. 11)
春分(しゅんぶん)の日(ひ)	Vernal Equinox Day (around Mar. 21)
みどりの日(ひ)	Greenery Day (Apr. 29)
憲法記念日(けんぽうきねんび)	Constitution Day (May 3)
こどもの日(ひ)	Children's Day (May 5)
海(うみ)の日(ひ)	Marine Day (the third Monday of Jul.)
敬老(けいろう)の日(ひ)	Respect-for-the-Aged Day (the third Monday of Sep.)
秋分(しゅうぶん)の日(ひ)	Autumnal Equinox Day (around Sep. 23)
体育(たいいく)の日(ひ)	Health-Sports Day (the second Monday of Oct.)
文化(ぶんか)の日(ひ)	Culture Day (Nov. 3)
勤労感謝(きんろうかんしゃ)の日(ひ)	Labor Thanksgiving Day (Nov. 23)
天皇誕生日(てんのうたんじょうび)	Emperor's Birthday (Dec. 23)

JAPANESE GOVERNMENT MINISTRIES AND AGENCIES

- Cabinet Office 内閣府 (ないかくふ)
  - Imperial Household Agency 宮内庁 (くないちょう)
  - Fair Trade Commission 公正取引委員会 (こうせいとりひきいいんかい)
  - National Public Safety Commission 国家公安委員会 (こっかこうあんいいんかい)
  - Defense Agency 防衛庁 (ぼうえいちょう)
  - Financial Services Agency 金融庁 (きんゆうちょう)
- Ministry of Internal Affairs and Communications 総務省 (そうむしょう)
  - Fire and Disaster Management Agency 消防庁 (しょうぼうちょう)
- Ministry of Justice 法務省 (ほうむしょう)
  - Public Security Intelligence Agency 公安調査庁 (こうあんちょうさちょう)
- Ministry of Foreign Affairs 外務省 (がいむしょう)
- Ministry of Finance 財務省 (ざいむしょう)
  - National Tax Agency 国税庁 (こくぜいちょう)
- Ministry of Education, Culture, Sports, Science and Technology 文部科学省 (もんぶかがくしょう)
  - Agency for Cultural Affairs 文化庁 (ぶんかちょう)
- Ministry of Health, Labour and Welfare 厚生労働省 (こうせいろうどうしょう)
  - Social Insurance Agency 社会保険庁 (しゃかいほけんちょう)
- Ministry of Agriculture, Forestry and Fisheries 農林水産省 (のうりんすいさんしょう)
  - Forestry Agency 林野庁 (りんやちょう)
  - Fisheries Agency 水産庁 (すいさんちょう)
- Ministry of Economy, Trade and Industry 経済産業省 (けいざいさんぎょうしょう)
  - Agency for Natural Resources and Energy 資源エネルギー庁 (しげんエネルギーちょう)
  - Japan Patent Office 特許庁 (とっきょちょう)
  - Small and Medium Enterprise Agency 中小企業庁 (ちゅうしょうきぎょうちょう)
- Ministry of Land, Infrastructure and Transport 国土交通省 (こくどこうつうしょう)
  - Japan Meteorological Agency 気象庁 (きしょうちょう)
  - Japan Coast Guard 海上保安庁 (かいじょうほあんちょう)
  - Marine Accident Inquiry Agency 海難審判庁 (かいなんしんぱんちょう)
- Ministry of the Environment 環境省 (かんきょうしょう)